AMERICAN ENVIRONMENTAL STUDIES

Wilson's American Ornithology

ALEXANDER WILSON

ARNO &
THE NEW YORK TIMES

Collection Created and Selected
by CHARLES GREGG of Gregg Press

Reprint Edition 1970 by Arno Press Inc.

Reprinted from a copy in
The Rutgers University Library

LC# 78-125767
ISBN 0-405-02693-5

American Environmental Studies
ISBN for complete set: 0-405-02650-1

Manufactured in the United States of America

WILSON'S

AMERICAN ORNITHOLOGY,

WITH

NOTES BY JARDINE:

TO WHICH IS ADDED

A SYNOPSIS OF AMERICAN BIRDS,

INCLUDING THOSE DESCRIBED

BY

BONAPARTE, AUDUBON, NUTTALL, AND
RICHARDSON;

By T. M. BREWER.

BOSTON:
OTIS, BROADERS, AND COMPANY.

1840.

WILSON'S
AMERICAN ORNITHOLOGY

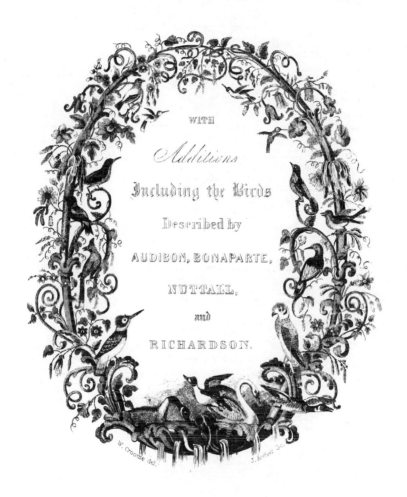

WITH

Additions

Including the Birds

Described by

AUDIBON, BONAPARTE,

NUTTALL,

and

RICHARDSON.

W. Croome del.   J. Archer Sc.

Boston.

OTIS, BROADERS AND COMPANY.

ADVERTISEMENT.

The want of an edition of WILSON'S ORNITHOLOGY, adapted to general circulation, has long been felt in the United States. While several popular editions have been published in Europe, there has been none here, except the original one, and another, with slight modifications; both of which, on account of their costliness, have been necessarily excluded from the hands of many who might desire to possess or peruse WILSON's work. The present work is designed to supply this want, and it is hoped it may serve at once to extend the fame of the author, to give a wider scope to the influence of his genius, and promote an interest in the study of American ornithology.

To accomplish these objects, the original work of WILSON has been followed, adding thereto the copious and valuable notes of JARDINE. In order, however, to present a complete view of the birds of North America, a Synopsis has been appended, including all the birds described by WILSON, NUTTALL, BONAPARTE, AUDUBON, and RICHARDSON. The Synopsis has been prepared solely with a view to supply, so far as could be done within such narrow limits, that which is wanting in the original text of WILSON. A brief explanation of the plan upon which it has been prepared, may not, therefore, be out of place.

It will be seen that the Synopsis comprises the names, both scientific and otherwise, of all the birds now known to exist in North America, arranged according to their natural affinities. Wherever birds have been fully described in the preceding pages, it has been deemed necessary to refer only to the works of American ornithologists, who have also given their history.

Where this has been imperfectly given, such additional facts relative to their manner of breeding, etc., as the space admitted, have been added; and where the bird was not known to WILSON, a brief scientific description has been appended.

I should be guilty of great injustice, were I to omit to add how much I have been assisted by the labors and writings of the illustrious AUDUBON. With his free and generous consent, I have been permitted to draw from the materials which his industry and perseverance had prepared to my hands, and without which I could have done but little. Whatever merits, therefore, may appear in my labors, will, I trust, be attributed to the source to which they are rightly due. It will also be seen that in the arrangement by genera and families, the present Synopsis owes a great deal to that of Mr. AUDUBON. It, however, differs in two material points. The latter has no division by *orders*. The omission is an important one, and it was deemed advisable to supply it. I have also judged it inexpedient to imitate the needless subdivisions into genera, which is the prevailing fault in modern ornithology. Without entering into a discussion of this controverted question, I have only to urge, in defence of my adhesion except in such instances as it appeared wrong to do so, to old genera — my conviction that the present mode of subdivision, instead of tending to simplify science, as its advocates assert, but adds to the difficulties of the beginner, and serves to discourage his efforts to master the subject.

In fine, I would venture to submit this brief catalogue of the birds of North America, with the assurance, which justice compels me to make, that its merits, if it has any, are due to others; its faults — and I am aware of its deficiencies — are partly mine, and partly those of my narrow limits.

T. M. B.

CONTENTS.

A *

CONTENTS.

1. *Blue Jay.* 2. *Yellow Bird or Goldfinch.* 3. *Baltimore Bird.* 4. *Wood Thrush.* 5. *Red-breasted Thrush or Robin.* 6. *White breasted Black-capped Nuthatch.* 7. *Red bellied black-capped Nuthatch.* 8. *Gold-winged Woodpecker.* 9. *Black-breasted Bunting.* 10. *Blue Bird.*

WILSON'S

AMERICAN ORNITHOLOGY.

BLUE JAY.—CORVUS CRISTATUS.—Fig. 1.

Linn. Syst. i. p. 157, 158. — Garrulus Canadensis cœruleus, *Briss.* ii. p. 54, 2. t. 4.
fig. 2. — Pica glandaria cristata, *Klein*, p. 61, 3. — Le geay bleu du Canada, *Buff.*
iii. p. 120. *Pl. enl.* 529. — Blue Jay, *Catesb. Car.* i. 15. — *Edw.* 239. — *Arct. Zool.*
ii. No. 38. — *Lath. Syn.* i. p. 386, 20. — *Bartram*, p. 290. — *Peale's Museum*,
No. 1290.

GARRULUS CRISTATUS.— Vieillot.

Garrulus cristatus, *Vieill. Gal. des Ois.* pl. 102. — *North. Zool.* ii. p. 293. — *Bonap.*
Synop. No. 63. — Pica cristata, *Wagl.* No. 8.

THIS elegant bird, which, as far as I can learn, is peculiar to North
America, is distinguished as a kind of beau among the feathered tenants of our woods, by the brilliancy of his dress ; and, like most other
coxcombs, makes himself still more conspicuous by his loquacity, and
the oddness of his tones and gestures. The Jay measures eleven inches
in length; the head is ornamented with a crest of light blue or purple
feathers, which he can elevate or depress at pleasure ; a narrow line of
black runs along the frontlet, rising on each side higher than the eye,
but not passing over it, as Catesby has represented, and as Pennant
and many others have described it; back and upper part of the neck
a fine light purple, in which the blue predominates ; a collar of black,
proceeding from the hind head, passes with a graceful curve down
each side of the neck to the upper part of the breast, where it forms
a crescent; chin, cheeks, throat, and belly, white, the three former
slightly tinged with blue ; greater wing-coverts, a rich blue ; exterior
sides of the primaries, light blue, those of the secondaries, a deep purple, except the three feathers next the body, which are of a splendid light
blue ; all these, except the primaries, are beautifully barred with
crescents of black, and tipped with white ; the interior sides of the
wing-feathers are dusky black ; tail long and cuneiform, composed
of twelve feathers of a glossy light blue, marked at half inches with
transverse curves of black, each feather being tipped with white,
except the two middle ones, which deepen into a dark purple at the
extremities ; breast and sides under the wings, a dirty white, faintly

1

stained with purple; inside of the mouth, the tongue, bill, legs, and claws, black; iris of the eye, hazel.

The Blue Jay is an almost universal inhabitant of the woods, frequenting the thickest settlements as well as the deepest recesses of the forest, where his squalling voice often alarms the deer, to the disappointment and mortification of the hunter; one of whom informed me, that he made it a point, in summer, to kill every Jay he could meet with. In the charming season of spring, when every thicket pours forth harmony, the part performed by the Jay always catches the ear. He appears to be among his fellow-musicians what the trumpeter is in a band, some of his notes having no distant resemblance to the tones of that instrument. These he has the faculty of changing through a great variety of modulations, according to the particular humor he happens to be in. When disposed for ridicule, there is scarce a bird whose peculiarities of song he cannot tune his notes to. When engaged in the blandishments of love, they resemble the soft chatterings of a Duck, and, while he nestles among the thick branches of the cedar, are scarce heard at a few paces' distance; but he no sooner discovers your approach than he sets up a sudden and vehement outcry, flying off, and screaming with all his might, as if he called the whole feathered tribes of the neighborhood to witness some outrageous usage he had received. When he hops undisturbed among the high branches of the oak and hickory, they become soft and musical; and his calls of the female a stranger would readily mistake for the repeated screakings of an ungreased wheelbarrow. All these he accompanies with various nods, jerks, and other gesticulations, for which the whole tribe of Jays are so remarkable, that, with some other peculiarities, they might have very well justified the great Swedish naturalist in forming them into a separate genus by themselves.*

* This has now been done; and modern ornithologists adopt the title *Garrulus* of Brisson, for this distinct and very well defined group, containing many species, which agree intimately in their general form and habits, and, are dispersed over every quarter of the world, New Holland excepted. The colors of their plumage are brown, gray, blue, and black; in some distributed with sober chastity, while, in others, the deep tints and decided markings rival the richest gems.

Proud of cerulean stains,
From Heaven's unsullied arch purloin'd, the Jay
Screams hoarse.   GISBORNE'S *Walks in a Forest.*

In geographical distribution, we find those of splendid plumage following the warmer climates, and associating there with our ideas of Eastern magnificence; while the more sober dressed, and, in our opinion, not the least pleasing, range through more temperate and northern regions, or those exalted tracts in tropical countries, where all the productions in some manner receive the impress of an alpine or northern station. This is no where better exemplified than in the specimens lately sent to this country from the lofty and extensive plains of the Himalaya, where we have already met with prototypes of the European Jay, Black and Green Woodpeckers, Greater Titmouse, and Nutcracker. They inhabit woody districts; in their dispositions are cunning, bold, noisy, active, and restless, but docile and easily tamed, when introduced to the care of man, and are capable of being taught tricks and various sounds. The following instance of the latter propensity is thus related by Bewick: — "We have heard one imitate the sound made by the action of a saw, so exactly, that, though it was on a Sunday, we could hardly be persuaded that the person who kept it, had not a carpenter at work in the house. Another, at the approach of cattle, had learned to hound a cur dog upon them, by whistling and calling

The Blue Jay builds a large nest, frequently in the cedar, sometimes on an apple-tree, lines it with dry, fibrous roots, and lays five eggs of a dull olive, spotted with brown. The male is particularly careful of not being heard near the place, making his visits as silently and secretly as possible. His favorite food is chestnuts, acorns, and Indian corn. He occasionally feeds on bugs and caterpillars, and sometimes pays a plundering visit to the orchard, cherry rows, and potato patch; and has been known, in times of scarcity, to venture into the barn, through openings between the weather boards. In these cases he is extremely active and silent, and, if surprised in the fact, makes his escape with precipitation, but without noise, as if conscious of his criminality.

Of all birds, he is the most bitter enemy to the Owl. No sooner has he discovered the retreat of one of these, than he summons the whole feathered fraternity to his assistance, who surround the glimmering *solitaire*, and attack him from all sides, raising such a shout as may be heard, in a still day, more than half a mile off. When, in my hunting excursions, I have passed near this scene of tumult, I have imagined to myself that I heard the insulting party venting their respective charges with all the virulency of a Billingsgate mob; the Owl, meanwhile, returning every compliment with a broad, goggling stare. The war becomes louder and louder, and the Owl at length, forced to betake himself to flight, is followed by his whole train of persecutors, until driven beyond the boundaries of their jurisdiction.

But the Blue Jay himself is not guiltless of similar depredations with the Owl, and becomes in his turn the very tyrant he detested, when he sneaks through the woods, as he frequently does, and among the thickets and hedge-rows, plundering every nest he can find of its eggs, tearing up the callow young by piecemeal, and spreading alarm and sorrow around him. The cries of the distressed parents soon bring together a number of interested spectators, (for birds in such circumstances seem truly to sympathize with each other,) and he is sometimes attacked with such spirit as to be under the necessity of making a speedy retreat.

upon him by his name. At last, during a severe frost, the dog was, by that means, excited to attack a cow big with calf, when the poor animal fell on the ice, and was much hurt: the Jay was complained of as a nuisance; and its owner was obliged to destroy it." They feed indiscriminately, and, according to circumstances, on either animal or vegetable substances; plundering nests of their eggs and young, and even, in the more exposed farm-yards, disappointing the hopes of the mistress, in the destruction of a favorite brood. They are also robbers of orchards and gardens of their finest fruits; but, when without the reach of these luxuries, they will be content to satisfy their hunger with Nature's own productions, the wild berries, or fruits and seeds of the forest and the field.

Several new species have been added to the North American list, some of which are described by the Prince of Musignano; and, in addition, we may mention one new species, published by Dr. Richardson and Mr. Swainson, in the *Arctic Zoology*. The only specimen brought home was killed on the roof of the dwelling-house at Fort Franklin, and was so similar to the Canada Jay, that it was not then recognized as a distinct species. The chief distinctions mentioned in the above work are the shorter bill, broader at the base, and narrower on the ridge; the plumage looser than in *G. Canadensis*; the secondaries proportionally longer, and all end in slender, but very distinct points, scarcely discernible in the Blue Jay, and not nearly so much developed in the Whisky-Jack. Tail is shorter than the latter; the tarsus is more robust. — ED.

He will sometimes assault small birds, with the intention of killing and devouring them; an instance of which I myself once witnessed, over a piece of woods near the borders of Schuylkill; where I saw him engaged for more than five minutes pursuing what I took to be a species of *Motacilla*, wheeling, darting, and doubling in the air, and, at last, to my great satisfaction, got disappointed, in the escape of his intended prey. In times of great extremity, when his hoard or magazine is frozen up, buried in snow, or perhaps exhausted, he becomes very voracious, and will make a meal of whatever carrion or other animal substance comes in the way, and has been found regaling himself on the bowels of a Robin in less than five minutes after it was shot.

There are, however, individual exceptions to this general character for plunder and outrage, a proneness for which is probably often occasioned by the wants and irritations of necessity. A Blue Jay, which I have kept for some time, and with whom I am on terms of familiarity, is in reality a very notable example of mildness of disposition and sociability of manners. An accident in the woods first put me in possession of this bird, while in full plumage, and in high health and spirits; I carried him home with me, and put him into a cage already occupied by a Golden-winged Woodpecker, where he was saluted with such rudeness, and received such a drubbing from the lord of the manor, for entering his premises, that, to save his life, I was obliged to take him out again. I then put him into another cage, where the only tenant was a female Orchard Oriole. She also put on airs of alarm, as if she considered herself endangered and insulted by the intrusion; the Jay, meanwhile, sat mute and motionless on the bottom of the cage, either dubious of his own situation, or willing to allow time for the fears of his neighbor to subside. Accordingly, in a few minutes, after displaying various threatening gestures, (like some of those Indians we read of in their first interviews with the whites,) she began to make her approaches, but with great circumspection, and readiness for retreat. Seeing, however, the Jay begin to pick up some crumbs of broken chestnuts, in a humble and peaceable way, she also descended, and began to do the same; but, at the slightest motion of her new guest, wheeled round, and put herself on the defensive. All this ceremonious jealousy vanished before evening; and they now roost together, feed, and play together, in perfect harmony and good humor. When the Jay goes to drink, his messmate very impudently jumps into the water to wash herself, throwing the water in showers over her companion, who bears it all patiently; venturing now and then to take a sip between every splash, without betraying the smallest token of irritation. On the contrary, he seems to take pleasure in his little fellow-prisoner, allowing her to pick (which she does very gently) about his whiskers, and to clean his claws from the minute fragments of chestnuts which happen to adhere to them. This attachment on the one part, and mild condescension on the other, may, perhaps, be partly the effect of mutual misfortunes, which are found not only to knit mankind, but many species of inferior animals, more closely together; and shows that the disposition of the Blue Jay may be humanized, and rendered susceptible of affectionate impressions, even for those birds which, in a state of nature, he would have no hesitation in making a meal of.

He is not only bold and vociferous, but possesses a considerable talent for mimicry, and seems to enjoy great satisfaction in mocking and teasing other birds, particularly the Little Hawk, (*F. sparverius,*) imitating his cry wherever he sees him, and squealing out as if caught: this soon brings a number of his own tribe around him, who all join in the frolic, darting about the Hawk, and feigning the cries of a bird sorely wounded, and already under the clutches of its devourer; while others lie concealed in bushes, ready to second their associates in the attack. But this ludicrous farce often terminates tragically. The Hawk, singling out one of the most insolent and provoking, sweeps upon him in an unguarded moment, and offers him up a sacrifice to his hunger and resentment. In an instant the tune is changed; all their buffoonery vanishes, and loud and incessant screams proclaim their disaster.

Wherever the Jay has had the advantage of education from man, he has not only shown himself an apt scholar, but his suavity of manners seems equalled only by his art and contrivances; though it must be confessed, that his itch for thieving keeps pace with all his other acquirements. Dr. Mease, on the authority of Colonel Postell, of South Carolina, informs me, that a Blue Jay, which was brought up in the family of the latter gentleman, had all the tricks and loquacity of a parrot; pilfered every thing he could conveniently carry off, and hid them in holes and crevices; answered to his name with great sociability, when called on; could articulate a number of words pretty distinctly; and, when he heard an uncommon noise, or loud talking, seemed impatient to contribute his share to the general festivity (as he probably thought it) by a display of all the oratorical powers he was possessed of.

Mr. Bartram relates an instance of the Jay's sagacity, worthy of remark. "Having caught a Jay in the winter season," says he, " I turned him loose in the greenhouse, and fed him with corn, (zea, maize,) the heart of which they are very fond of. This grain being ripe and hard, the bird at first found a difficulty in breaking it, as it would start from his bill when he struck it. After looking about, and, as if considering for a moment, he picked up his grain, carried and placed it close up in a corner on the shelf, between the wall and a plant box, where, being confined on three sides, he soon effected his purpose, and continued afterwards to make use of this same practical expedient. The Jay," continues this judicious observer, " is one of the most useful agents in the economy of nature, for disseminating forest-trees, and other cruciferous and hard-seeded vegetables on which they feed. Their chief employment, during the autumnal season, is foraging to supply their winter stores. In performing this necessary duty, they drop abundance of seed in their flight over fields, hedges, and by fences, where they alight to deposit them in the post holes, &c. It is remarkable what numbers of young trees rise up in fields and pastures after a wet winter and spring. These birds alone are capable, in a few years' time, to replant all the cleared lands." *

---

* Letter of Mr. William Bartram to the author.

1 *

The Blue Jays seldom associate in any considerable numbers, except in the months of September and October, when they hover about, in scattered parties of from forty to fifty, visiting the oaks, in search of their favorite acorns. At this season, they are less shy than usual, and keep chattering to each other in a variety of strange and querulous notes. I have counted fifty-three, but never more, at one time; and these generally following each other in straggling irregularity from one range of woods to another. Yet we are told by the learned Dr. Latham, — and his statement has been copied into many respectable European publications, — that the Blue Jays of North America "often unite into flocks of twenty thousand at least! which, alighting on a field of ten or twelve acres, soon lay waste the whole." * If this were really so, these birds would justly deserve the character he gives them, of being the most destructive species in America. But I will venture the assertion, that the tribe *Oriolus phœniceus*, or Red-winged Black-birds, in the environs of the River Delaware alone, devour and destroy more Indian corn than the whole Blue Jays of North America. As to their assembling in such immense multitudes, it may be sufficient to observe, that a flock of Blue Jays of twenty thousand would be as extraordinary an appearance in America, as the same number of Mag-pies or Cuckoos would be in Britain.

It has been frequently said, that numbers of birds are common to the United States and Europe; at present, however, I am not certain of many. Comparing the best descriptions and delineations of the European ones with those of our native birds, said to be of the same species, either the former are very erroneous, or the difference of plumage and habits in the latter justifies us in considering a great proportion of them to be really distinct species. Be this, however, as it may, the Blue Jay appears to belong exclusively to North America. I cannot find it mentioned by any writer or traveller among the birds of Guiana, Brazil, or any other part of South America. It is equally unknown in Africa. In Europe, and even in the eastern parts of Asia, it is never seen in its wild state. To ascertain the exact limits of its native regions, would be difficult. These, it is highly probable, will be found to be bounded by the extremities of the temperate zone. Dr. Latham has indeed asserted, that the Blue Jay of America is not found farther north than the town of Albany.† This, however, is a mistake. They are common in the Eastern States, and are mentioned by Dr. Bel-knap in his enumeration of the birds of New Hampshire.‡ They are also natives of Newfoundland. I myself have seen them in Upper Canada. Blue Jays and Yellow-Birds were found by Mr. M'Kenzie, when on his journey across the continent, at the head waters of the Unjigah, or Peace River, in N. lat. 54°, W. lon. 121°, on the west side of the great range of Stony Mountains.§ Steller, who, in 1741, accompanied Captain Behring in his expedition for the discovery of the north-west coast of America, and who wrote the journal of the voyage, relates, that he himself went on shore near Cape St. Elias, in N. lat. 58° 28',

---

* *Synopsis of Birds*, vol. i. p. 387. See also *Encyclopædia Britannica*, art. Corvus.

† *Synopsis*, vol. i. p. 387.

‡ *History of New Hampshire*, vol. iii. p. 163.

§ *Voyages from Montreal, &c.* p. 216, 4to., London, 1801.

W. lon. 141° 46', according to his estimation, where he observed several species of birds *not known in Siberia* ; and one, in particular, described by Catesby, under the name of the Blue Jay.* Mr. William Bartram informs me, that they are numerous in the peninsula of Florida, and that he also found them at Natchez, on the Mississippi. Captains Lewis and Clark, and their intrepid companions, in their memorable expedition across the continent of North America to the Pacific Ocean, continued to see Blue Jays for six hundred miles up the Missouri.† From these accounts it follows, that this species occupies, generally or partially, an extent of country stretching upwards of seventy degrees from east to west, and more than thirty degrees from north to south; though, from local circumstances, there may be intermediate tracts, in this immense range, which they seldom visit.

YELLOW-BIRD, OR GOLDFINCH. — FRINGILLA TRISTIS.
Fig. 2.

Linn. Syst. i. p. 320. — Carduelis Americana, *Briss.* iii. p. 6, 3. — Le Chardonnerat jaune, *Buff.* iv. p. 112. *Pl. enl.* 202, fo. 2. — American Goldfinch, *Arct. Zool.* ii. No. 242. — *Edw.* 274. — *Lath. Syn.* iii. p. 288, 57. *Id. Sup.* p. 166. — *Bartram*, p. 290. — *Peale's Museum*, No. 6344.

CARDUELIS AMERICANA. — Edwards.

New York Siskin, *Penn. Arct. Zool.* p. 372. (Male changing his plumage, and the male in his winter dress taken for female, auct. *Swains.*) — Fringilla tristis, *Bonap. Syn.* p. 111, No. 181. — Carduelis Americana, *North. Zool.* ii. p. 268.

This bird is four inches and a half in length, and eight inches in extent, of a rich lemon yellow, fading into white towards the rump and vent. The wings and tail are black, the former tipped and edged with white; the interior webs of the latter are also white; the fore part of the head is black, the bill and legs of a reddish cinnamon color. This is the summer dress of the male; but in the month of September the yellow gradually changes to a brown olive, and the male and female are then nearly alike. They build a very neat and delicately-formed little nest, which they fasten to the twigs of an apple-tree, or to the strong, branching stalks of hemp, covering it on the outside with pieces of lichen, which they find on the trees and fences; these they glue together with their saliva, and afterwards line the inside with the softest downy substances they can procure. The female lays five eggs, of a dull white, thickly marked at the greater end; and they generally raise two broods in a season. The males do not arrive at their perfect plumage until the succeeding spring; wanting, during that time, the black on the head, and the white on the wings being of a cream color. In the month of April, they begin to

* See Steller's *Journal*, apud *Pallas*.
† This fact I had from Captain Lewis.

change their winter dress, and, before the middle of May, appear in brilliant yellow: the whole plumage towards its roots is of a dusky bluish black.

The song of the Yellow-Bird resembles that of the Goldfinch of Britain; but is in general so weak as to appear to proceed from a considerable distance, when perhaps the bird is perched on the tree over your head. I have, however, heard some sing in cages with great energy and animation. On their first arrival in Pennsylvania, in February, and until early in April, they associate in flocks, frequently assembling in great numbers on the same tree to bask and dress themselves in the morning sun, singing in concert for half an hour together; the confused mingling of their notes forming a kind of harmony not at all unpleasant.*

About the last of November, and sometimes sooner, they generally leave Pennsylvania, and proceed to the south; some, however, are seen even in the midst of the severest winters. Their flight is not direct, but in alternate risings and sinkings; twittering as they fly, at each successive impulse of the wings.† During the latter part of summer they are almost constant visitants in our gardens, in search

---

* *Carduelis* of Brisson, having types in the common Goldfinch and Siskin of this country, is now generally used as the generic appellation for the group to which our present species belongs. It contains several American and European species. They are closely allied to the true Linnets; and the lesser Red-Poll (the *Fringilla linaria auctorum*) has even by some been ranked with them. They also much resemble the latter group in their manners, their haunts, their breeding, and feeding. Every one who has lived much in the country, must have often remarked the common European Gray Linnets, in the manner above described of the American Goldfinch, congregating towards the close of a fine winter's evening, perched on the summit of some bare tree, pluming themselves in the last rays of the sun, cheruping the commencement of their evening song, and then bursting simultaneously into one general chorus; again resuming their single strains, and again joining, as if happy, and rejoicing at the termination of their day's employment. Mr. Audubon has remarked the same trait in their manners, and confirms the resemblance of their notes: "So much does the song of our Goldfinch resemble that of the European species, that, whilst in France and England, I have frequently thought, and with pleasure thought, that they were the notes of our own bird which I heard." — ED.

† The flight of the American Goldfinch, and its manners during it, are described by Mr. Audubon with greater minuteness: it is exactly similar to the European bird of the same name, being performed in deep curved lines, alternately rising and falling, after each propelling motion of the wings. It scarcely ever describes one of those curves, without uttering two or three notes whilst ascending, such as its European relative uses on similar occasions. In this manner its flight is prolonged to considerable distances, and it frequently moves in a circling direction before alighting. Their migration is performed during the day. They seldom alight on the ground, unless to procure water, in which they wash with great liveliness and pleasure; after which they pick up some particles of gravel and sand. So fond of each other's company are they, that a party of them soaring on the wing will alter their course at the calling of a single one perched on a tree. This call is uttered with much emphasis: the bird prolongs its usual note, without much alteration; and, as the party approaches, erects its body, and moves to the right and left, as if turning on a pivot, apparently pleased at showing the beauty of its plumage and elegance of its manners.

This natural group has been long celebrated for their docility, and easy instruction, whether in music, or to perform a variety of tricks. They are, consequently, favorites with bird-fanciers, and often doomed to undergo a severe and cruel discipline. The Goldfinch, Canary, the various Linnets, the Siskin, and Chaffinch, are principally used for this purpose; and it is often astonishing, and almost incredible, with what correctness they will obey the voice or motions of their masters. Mr.

of seeds, which they dislodge from the husk with great address, while hanging, frequently head downwards, in the manner of the Titmouse. From these circumstances, as well as from their color, they are very generally known, and pass by various names expressive of their food, color, &c., such as Thistle-Bird, Lettuce-Bird, Salad-Bird, Yellow-Bird, &c. The gardeners, who supply the city of Philadelphia with vegetables, often take them in trap-cages, and expose them for sale in market. They are easily familiarized to confinement, and feed with seeming indifference a few hours after being taken.

The great resemblance which the Yellow-Bird bears to the Canary has made many persons attempt to pair individuals of the two species together. An ingenious French gentleman, who resides in Pottsgrove, Pennsylvania, assured me, that he had tried the male Yellow-Bird with the female Canary, and the female Yellow-Bird with the male Canary, but without effect, though he kept them for several years together, and supplied them with proper materials for building. Mr. Hassey of New York, however, who keeps a great number of native as well as foreign birds, informed me, that a Yellow-Bird paired with a Canary in his possession, and laid eggs, but did not hatch, which he attributed to the lateness of the season.

These birds were seen by Mr. M'Kenzie, in his route across the continent of North America, as far north as lat. 54°; they are numerous in all the Atlantic states north of the Carolinas; abound in Mexico, and are also found in great numbers in the savannahs of Guiana.

The seeds of the lettuce, thistle, hemp, &c., are their favorite food; and it is pleasant to observe a few of them at work in a calm day, detaching the thistle-down, in search of the seeds, making it fly in clouds around them.

The American Goldfinch has been figured and described by Mr Catesby,* who says, that the back part of the head is a dirty green, &c. This description must have been taken while the bird was

---

Syme, in his *History of British Song Birds*, when speaking of the Sieur Roman, who some years since exhibited Goldfinches, Linnets, and Canaries, wonderfully trained, relates, that " one appeared dead, and was held up by the tail or claw without exhibiting any signs of life; a second stood on its head with its claws in the air; a third imitated a Dutch milkmaid going to market with pails on its shoulders; a fourth mimicked a Venetian girl looking out at a window; a fifth appeared as a soldier, and mounted guard as a sentinel; and the sixth acted as a cannonier, with a cap on its head, a firelock on its shoulder, and a match in its claw, and discharged a small cannon. The same bird also acted as if it had been wounded. It was wheeled in a barrow, to convey it, as it were, to the hospital; after which it flew away before the company: the seventh turned a kind of windmill; and the last bird stood in the midst of some fireworks which were discharged all round it, and this without exhibiting the least symptom of fear." The American Goldfinch is no less docile than its congeners. Mr. Audubon relates, that they are often caught in trap-cages; and that he knew one, which had undergone severe training, draw water for its drink from a glass, by means of a little chain fastened to a soft, leathern belt round its body, and another, equally light, fastened to a little bucket, which was kept by its weight in the water: it was also obliged to supply 'tself with food, by being obliged to draw towards its bill a little chariot filled with seeds.

Female is represented in Bonaparte's continuation. — ED.
* *Nat. Hist. Car.* vol. i. p. 43.

changing its plumage. At the approach of fall, not only the rich yellow fades into a brown olive, but the spot of black on the crown and forehead becomes also of the same olive tint. Mr. Edwards has also erred in saying, that the young male bird has the spot of black on the forehead; this it does not receive until the succeeding spring.* The figure in Edwards is considerably too large; and that by Catesby has the wings and tail much longer than in nature, and the body too slender, — very different from the true form of the living bird. Mr. Pennant also tells us, that the legs of this species are black; they are, however, of a bright cinnamon color; but the worthy naturalist, no doubt, described them as he found them in the dried and stuffed skin, shrivelled up and blackened with decay; and thus too much of our natural history has been delineated.

BALTIMORE ORIOLE. — ORIOLUS BALTIMORE. — Fig. 3.

Linn. Syst. i. p. 162, 10. — Icterus Minor, *Briss.* ii. p. 109, 19, t. 12, fig. 1. — Le Baltimore, *Buff.* iii. p. 231. *Pl. enl.* 506, fig. 1. — Baltimore Bird, *Catesb. Car.* i. 48. — *Arct. Zool.* ii. p. 142. — *Lath. Syn.* ii. p. 432, 19. — *Bartram,* p. 290. — *Peale's Museum,* No. 1506.

ICTERUS BALTIMORE. — Daudin.

Yphantes Baltimore, *Vieill. Gal. des Ois.* pl. 87. — Icterus Baltimore, *Bonap. Syn.* p. 51. — *North. Zool.* ii. p. 234. — Baltimore Oriole, pl. 12, and *Orn. Biog.* p. 66.

This is a bird of passage, arriving in Pennsylvania, from the south, about the beginning of May, and departing towards the latter end of August, or beginning of September.† From the singularity of its colors, the construction of its nest, and its preferring the apple-trees, weeping willows, walnut and tulip-trees, adjoining the farm-house, to build on, it is generally known, and, as usual, honored with a variety

---

* These changes take place in the Common Siskin of this country : indeed changes, and, in many cases, similar to those alluded to, are common, according to season, ~~among all our *Fringillidæ*; the Common Chaffinch loses the pale gray of his fore-~~ head, which becomes deep bluish purple ; the head and back of the Brambling, or Mountain Finch, becomes a deep glossy black ; and the forehead and breasts of the different Linnets, from a russet brown, assume a rich and beautiful crimson. They are chiefly produced by the falling off of the ends of the plumules of each feather, which before concealed the richer tints of its lower parts ; at other times, by the entire change of color. The tint itself, however, is always much increased in beauty and gloss as the season for its display advances ; at its termination the general moult commences, when the feathers are replaced with their new elongated tips, of a more sombre hue, which, no doubt, adds to the heat of the winter clothing, and remain until warmer weather and desires promote their dispersion. — Ed.

† During migration, the flight of the Baltimore is high above all the trees, and is straight and continuous ; it is mostly performed during the day, as I have usually observed them alighting, always singly, about the setting of the sun, uttering a note or two, and darting into the lower branches to feed, and afterwards to rest. — Audubon. — Ed.

of names, such as Hang-Nest, Hanging-Bird, Golden Robin, Fire-Bird, (from the bright orange seen through the green leaves, resembling a flash of fire,) &c., but more generally the Baltimore Bird, so named, as Catesby informs us, from its colors, which are black and orange, being those of the arms or livery of Lord Baltimore, formerly proprietary of Maryland.

The Baltimore Oriole is seven inches in length; bill, almost straight, strong, tapering to a sharp point, black, and sometimes lead-colored, above, the lower mandible light blue towards the base. Head, throat, upper part of the back and wings, black; lower part of the back, rump, and whole under parts, a bright orange, deepening into vermilion on the breast; the black on the shoulders is also divided by a band of orange; exterior edges of the greater wing-coverts, as well as the edges of the secondaries, and part of those of the primaries, white; the tail-feathers under the coverts, orange; the two middle ones, from thence to the tips, are black; the next five, on each side, black near the coverts, and orange towards the extremities, so disposed that, when the tail is expanded, and the coverts removed, the black appears in the form of a pyramid, supported on an arch of orange. Tail, slightly forked, the exterior feather on each side, a quarter of an inch shorter than the others; legs and feet, light blue, or lead color; iris of the eye, hazel.

The female has the head, throat, upper part of the neck and back, of a dull black, each feather being skirted with olive yellow; lower part of the back, rump, upper tail-coverts, and whole lower parts, orange yellow, but much duller than that of the male; the whole wing-feathers are of a deep dirty brown, except the quills, which are exteriorly edged, and the greater wing-coverts, and next superior row, which are broadly tipped with a dull yellowish white; tail, olive yellow; in some specimens, the two middle feathers have been found partly black, in others wholly so; the black on the throat does not descend so far as in the male, is of a lighter tinge, and more irregular; bill, legs, and claws, light blue.*

Buffon and Latham have both described the male of the Bastard Baltimore (*Oriolus spurius*) as the female Baltimore. Mr. Pennant has committed the same mistake; and all the ornithologists of Europe, with whose works I am acquainted, who have undertaken to figure and describe these birds, have mistaken the proper males and females, and confounded the two species together in a very confused and extraordinary manner, for which, indeed, we ought to pardon them, on ac-

---

* The change of the plumage of this bird, according to age, is beautifully represented on one of Mr. Audubon's gigantic plates, together with its favorite tulip-tree, and curious pensile nest. According to that gentleman, the male does not receive his full plumage until the third spring. In the male of one year, the bill is dark brown above, pale blue beneath; the iris, brown; feet, light blue. The general color is dull brownish yellow, tinged with olive on the head and back; the wings, blackish brown; the quills and large coverts margined and tipped with white; the lesser coverts are olivaceous; the tail, destitute of black; and the under parts paler than in the adult, without any approach to the vivid orange tints displayed on it. In that of the second spring, the distribution of color has become the same as in the adult male, but the yellow is less vivid; the upper mandible is brownish black above, and the iris is light brown : in the third spring, they receive the rich and brilliant plumage described by our author. — Ed.

count of their distance from the native residence of these birds, and the strange alterations of color which the latter are subject to.

This obscurity I have endeavored to clear up in the present volume of this work, Figs. 11, 12, 13, 14, by exhibiting the male and female of the *Oriolus spurius* in their different changes of dress, as well as in their perfect plumage; and by introducing representations of the eggs of both, have, I hope, put the identity of these two species beyond all future dispute or ambiguity.

Almost the whole genus of Orioles belong to America, and, with a few exceptions, build pensile nests.* Few of them, however, equal the Baltimore in the construction of these receptacles for their young, and in giving them, in such a superior degree, convenience, warmth, and security. For these purposes he generally fixes on the high, bending extremities of the branches, fastening strong strings of hemp or flax round two forked twigs, corresponding to the intended width of the nest: with the same materials, mixed with quantities of loose tow, he interweaves or fabricates a strong, firm kind of cloth, not unlike the substance of a hat in its raw state, forming it into a pouch of six or seven inches in depth, lining it substantially with various soft substances, well interwoven with the outward netting, and, lastly, finishes with a layer of horse hair; the whole being shaded from the sun and rain by a natural pent-house, or canopy of leaves. As to a hole being left in the side for the young to be fed and void their excrements through, as Pennant and others relate, it is certainly an error: I have never met with any thing of the kind in the nest of the Baltimore.

Though birds of the same species have, generally speaking, a common form of building, yet, contrary to the usually received opinion, they do not build exactly in the same manner. As much difference will be found in the style, neatness, and finishing of the nests of the Baltimores, as in their voices. Some appear far superior workmen to

---

* The true Orioles, having the *Oriolus galbula* of Europe and Africa, with *O. melanocephalus* of India, as typical, are entirely excluded from the New World; nevertheless Wilson was perfectly correct, meaning the *Icteri* of Brisson, which are nearly confined to North and South America, represent the Orioles in that country, and have now been arranged into several genera. These contain many species remarkable as well for their elegant form and bright and beautiful plumage, as for the singular and often matchless workmanship of their nests. The materials of the latter are woven and entwined in such a way as would defy the skill of the most expert seamstress, and unite all the requisites of dryness, security, and warmth. They are mostly pendulous from the ends of branches, and form thus a security from snakes or other depredators, which could easily reach them if placed on a more solid foundation. They are formed of the different grasses, of dry roots, lichens, long and slender mosses, and in the present instances, mentioned by our author, of substances which could not occur in the early or really natural state of the country, but had been adopted either from necessity, or "*with the sagacity of a good architect,*" improving every circumstance to the best advantage. Among the different species, they vary in shape, from being round or resembling a compact ball, to nearly every bottle-shaped gradation of form, until they exceed three or four feet in length. Many species being gregarious, they breed numerously on the same tree, and their nests, suspended from the pensile branches, and waving in the wind, render the landscape and woods singular to an unaccustomed eye, and present appearances which those only who have had the good fortune to witness them in their native wilds can appreciate.

The female is given by Wilson, in fig. 212. — ED.

others; and probably age may improve them in this, as it does in their colors. I have a number of their nests now before me, all completed, and with eggs. One of these, the neatest, is in the form of a cylinder, of five inches' diameter, and seven inches in depth, rounded at bottom. The opening at top is narrowed, by a horizontal covering, to two inches and a half in diameter. The materials are flax, hemp, tow, hair, and wool, woven into a complete cloth; the whole tightly sewed through and through with long horse hairs, several of which measure two feet in length. The bottom is composed of thick tufts of cow hair, sewed also with strong horse hair. This nest was hung on the extremity of the horizontal branch of an apple-tree, fronting the southeast; was visible a hundred yards off, though shaded from the sun; and was the work of a very beautiful and perfect bird. The eggs are five, white, slightly tinged with flesh color, marked on the greater end with purple dots, and on the other parts with long hair-like lines, intersecting each other in a variety of directions. I am thus minute in these particulars, from a wish to point out the specific difference between the True and Bastard Baltimore, which Dr. Latham, and some others, suspect to be only the same bird in different stages of color.

So solicitous is the Baltimore to procure proper materials for his nest, that, in the season of building, the women in the country are under the necessity of narrowly watching their thread that may chance to be out bleaching, and the farmer to secure his young grafts; as the Baltimore, finding the former, and the strings which tie the latter, so well adapted for his purpose, frequently carries off both; or, should the one be too heavy, and the other too firmly tied, he will tug at them a considerable time before he gives up the attempt. Skains of silk and hanks of thread have been often found, after the leaves were fallen, hanging round the Baltimore's nest; but so woven up, and entangled, as to be entirely irreclaimable. Before the introduction of Europeans, no such material could have been obtained here; but, with the sagacity of a good architect, he has improved this circumstance to his advantage; and the strongest and best materials are uniformly found in those parts by which the whole is supported.

Their principal food consists of caterpillars, beetles, and bugs, particularly one of a brilliant glossy green, fragments of which I have almost always found in their stomach, and sometimes these only.

The song of the Baltimore is a clear, mellow whistle, repeated at short intervals, as he gleans among the branches. There is in it a certain wild plaintiveness and *naïveté* extremely interesting. It is not uttered with the rapidity of the Ferruginous Thrush, (*Turdus rufus*,) and some other eminent songsters; but with the pleasing tranquillity of a careless ploughboy, whistling merely for his own amusement. When alarmed by an approach to his nest, or any such circumstance, he makes a kind of rapid cheruping, very different from his usual note. This, however, is always succeeded by those mellow tones which seem so congenial to his nature.

High on yon poplar, clad in glossiest green,
The orange black-capped Baltimore is seen;
The broad extended boughs still please him best;
Beneath their bending skirts he hangs his nest;
2

There his sweet mate, secure from every harm,
Broods o'er her spotted store, and wraps them warm ;
Lists to the noontide hum of busy bees,
Her partner's mellow song, the brook, the breeze ;
These day by day the lonely hours deceive,
From dewy morn to slow descending eve.
Two weeks elapsed, behold ! a helpless crew
Claim all her care, and her affection too ;
On wings of love the assiduous nurses fly,
Flowers, leaves, and boughs, abundant food supply ;
Glad chants their guardian, as abroad he goes,
And waving breezes rock them to repose.

The Baltimore inhabits North America from Canada to Mexico, and is even found as far south as Brazil. Since the streets of our cities have been planted with that beautiful and stately tree, the Lombardy poplar, these birds are our constant visitors during the early part of summer; and, amid the noise and tumult of coaches, drays, wheelbarrows, and the din of the multitude, they are heard chanting "their native wood notes wild;" sometimes, too, within a few yards of an oysterman, who stands bellowing, with the lungs of a Stentor, under the shade of the same tree; so much will habit reconcile even birds to the roar of the city, and to sounds and noises, that, in other circumstances, would put a whole grove of them to flight.

These birds are several years in receiving their complete plumage. Sometimes the whole tail of a male individual in spring is yellow, sometimes only the two middle feathers are black, and frequently the black on the back is skirted with orange, and the tail tipped with the same color. Three years, I have reason to believe, are necessary to fix the full tint of the plumage, and then the male bird appears as already described.*

* The following interesting account has been furnished to the publisher of this edition.

"At your request I send you the following history of a Baltimore Oriole, that I had in my care between seven and eight years. This bird I took from the nest when very young, with three others; but, being unskilled in taking care of them, this only lived. I taught it to feed from my mouth, and it would often alight on my finger, and strike the end with its bill, until I raised it to my mouth, when it would insert its bill and open my lips, by using its upper and lower mandibles as levers, and then take out whatever I might have there for it.

"None, who have noted the Oriole, can have overlooked this peculiar power of its mandibles, bestowed by a wise and good Providence for gently opening the closed-up bud or leaf, and seizing the concealed insect. It sometimes takes peas in the same manner, leaving the open and empty pod on the vine.

"In winter, spring, and autumn, I kept a little cage lined with cotton batting for the bird to pass the night in, and, towards evening, it would leave its large cage, and fly to this. After entering, if I did not close up the aperture with cotton, it would do so itself by pulling the cotton from the sides of the cage, until it had shut up all openings for the cold to enter. I fed it with sponge cake ; and when this became dry and hard, and it wanted some softer, it would make its wants known to me by its look and note, and if I did not very soon attend to it, it would take up a piece of the hard cake, carry it to the saucer of water, and drop it in, and move it about, until it was sufficiently soft to be eaten.

"In very cold weather, the bird would leave its cage, fly to me, run under my cape, and place itself on my neck. Constantly, during the day, when it was at liberty, it would perch on my finger, and draw my needle and thread from me when I was sewing. At such times, if any child approached me and 'pulled my cape or dress a little, it would chase after the offender, with its wings and tail spread, and

WOOD THRUSH.— TURDUS MELODUS.— Fig. 4.

Bartram, p. 290. — Peale's Museum, No. 5264.

TURDUS MUSTELINUS. — Gmelin.

Turdus mustelinus, *Gm. Linn.* ii. 817, No. 57. — *Bonap. Synop.* p. 75. — *Penn. Arct. Zool.* ii. p. 337. — The Wood Trush, *Aud.* p. 372.

PARTICULAR attention has been paid to render the figure of this bird a faithful likeness of the original in Wilson's edition. It measures eight inches in length, and thirteen from tip to tip of the expanded wings; the bill is an inch long; the upper mandible, of a dusky brown, bent at the point, and slightly notched; the lower, a flesh color towards the base; the legs are long, and, as well as the claws, of a pale flesh color, or almost transparent. The whole upper parts are of a brown fulvous color, brightening into reddish on the head, and inclining to an olive on the rump and tail; chin, white; throat and breast, white, tinged with a light buff color, and beautifully marked

high resentment in its eye, which nothing would allay but a cessation of the offence.

"One afternoon, I left this bird in a cage with a recently-caught Red-Bird, on the piazza under my open chamber window, and on my return towards evening I found my Oriole in my chamber perched and peering out from under the collar of one of my dresses, (which was its usual custom when I left it at liberty during my absence,) and the Red-Bird gone.

"The next day, I put my Oriole out again in the same cage, and then learned how I lost my Red-Bird. The door, or entrance to the cage, was made of five or six round sticks that passed through some holes on one side of the opening, into some holes on the other side, very much, if not exactly, like a farmer's bars, which let down one after the other. About five o'clock, I observed my bird trying to draw my attention to its wants, which were to come into the room. As I did not immediately attend to it, I saw it go down to the "bars," and, while it held on to the side of the cage, it took the "bars" in its mouth and moved them, until it had got two or three down, thus making an opening large enough to allow it to come into the chamber.

"This bird made many journeys with me, and always appeared to be happy and contented could it be near me, although shut up in a cage six inches long, and eight or ten inches high and wide, with a green cloth covering, drawn together at top with tape, leaving an opening for it to look out and see me, and receive little crumbs, &c. It flew, at one time, from fright, out of the ladies' cabin in the steamboat, just before starting for Albany, up into the city of New York, and no one on board could tell which way the bird went. My husband, who knew how much the habits of the bird had been changed by domestication, thought it must have taken refuge in the first open dwelling; and so it proved, for it had flown up the street, and entered a new building, the windows of which were unglazed. At another time, in Portsmouth, N. H., it flew away, and none could say where it went; but we regained it by looking into the nearest open building, which was a livery stable, where we found the bird standing on the stall between two horses.

"In sickness, when I have been confined to the bed, my bird would visit my pillow many times during the day, often creeping under the bed-clothes to me. At such times it always appeared depressed and low spirited. When it wanted to bathe, it would approach me with a very expressive look, and shake its wings. On my return home from a call or visit, it would invariably show its pleasure by a peculiar sound.

P. A. MESSER.

"CONNECTICUT RIVER VALLEY,
       "July 10, 1839."

with pointed spots o. olack or dusky, running in chains from the sides
of the mouth, and intersecting each other all over the breast to the
belly, which, with the vent, is of a pure white; a narrow circle of
white surrounds the eye, which is large, full, the pupil black, and the
iris of a dark chocolate color; the inside of the mouth is yellow. The
male and female of this species, as, indeed, of almost the whole genus
of Thrushes, differ so little, as scarcely to be distinguished from each
other. It is called by some the Wood Robin, by others the Ground
Robin, and by some of our American ornithologists *Turdus minor*,
though, as will hereafter appear, improperly. The present name has
been adopted from Mr. William Bartram, who seems to have been the
first and almost only naturalist who has taken notice of the merits of
this bird.*

This sweet and solitary songster inhabits the whole of North America, from Hudson's Bay to the peninsula of Florida. He arrives in
Pennsylvania about the 20th of April, or soon after, and returns to the
south about the beginning of October. The lateness or earliness of
the season seems to make less difference in the times of arrival of our
birds of passage than is generally imagined. Early in April the woods
are often in considerable forwardness, and scarce a summer bird to
be seen. On the other hand, vegetation is sometimes no further
advanced on the 20th of April, at which time (*e. g.* this present year,
1807) numbers of Wood Thrushes are seen flitting through the moist,
woody hollows, and a variety of the *Motacilla* genus chattering from
almost every bush, with scarce an expanded leaf to conceal them.
But at whatever time the Wood Thrush may arrive, he soon announces
his presence in the woods. With the dawn of the succeeding morning,
mounting to the top of some tall tree that rises from a low, thick-shaded

* Almost every country has its peculiar and favorite songsters, and even among
the rudest nations the cries and songs of birds are listened to, and associated with
their general occupations, their superstitions, or religion. In America, the Wood
Thrush appears to hold a rank equal to the Nightingale and Song Thrush of Europe:
like the latter, he may be oftentimes seen perched on the summit of a topmost
branch, during a warm and balmy evening or morning, pouring forth in rich melody
his full voice, and will produce associations which a foreigner would assimilate
with the warblers of his own land.

"The song of the Wood Thrush," says Mr. Audubon, "although composed of but
few notes, is so powerful, distinct, clear, and mellow, that it is impossible for any
person to hear it without being struck with the effect it produces on the mind. I
do not know to what instrumental sounds I can compare these notes, for I really
know none so melodious and harmonical. They gradually rise in strength, and
then fall in gentle cadence, becoming at length so low as to be scarcely audible."
They are easily reared from the nest, and sing nearly as well in confinement as
when free.

Prince C. L. Bonaparte, in his *Nomenclature of Wilson's North American Ornithology*, remarks, that our author was the first to distinguish the three closely
allied species of North American Thrushes by decided characters, but that he has
nevertheless embroiled the nomenclature of this and his *T. mustelinus*: — "This
bird being evidently the *T. mustelinus* of Gmelin and Latham, Wilson's new name,
which is not modelled agreeably to any language, must be rejected."

The title for our present species, allowing Bonaparte to be correct, and of which
there appears little doubt, will therefore now stand, *Wood Thrush*, Wilson; *Turdus mustelinus*, Gmelin; and *T. melodus* will come in as a synonyme; while Wilson's *T. mustelinus*, being without a name, has been most deservedly dedicated to
the memory of the great American ornithologist himself. — ED.

part of the woods, he pipes his few, but clear and musical notes, in a kind of ecstasy; the prelude, or symphony to which, strongly resembles the double-tonguing of a German flute, and sometimes the tinkling of a small bell; the whole song consists of five or six parts, the last note of each of which is in such a tone as to leave the conclusion evidently suspended; the finalé is finely managed, and with such charming effect as to soothe and tranquillize the mind, and to seem sweeter and mellower at each successive repetition. Rival songsters, of the same species, challenge each other from different parts of the wood, seeming to vie for softer tones and more exquisite responses. During the burning heat of the day, they are comparatively mute; but in the evening the same melody is renewed, and continued long after sunset. Those who visit our woods, or ride out into the country at these hours, during the months of May and June, will be at no loss to recognize, from the above description, this pleasing musician. Even in dark, wet, and gloomy weather, when scarce a single chirp is heard from any other bird, the clear notes of the Wood Thrush thrill through the dropping woods, from morning to night; and it may truly be said that the sadder the day the sweeter is his song.

The favorite haunts of the Wood Thrush are low, thick-shaded hollows, through which a small brook or rill meanders, overhung with alder bushes, that are mantled with wild vines. Near such a scene he generally builds his nest, in a laurel or alder bush. Outwardly it is composed of withered beech leaves of the preceding year, laid at bottom in considerable quantities, no doubt to prevent damp and moisture from ascending through, being generally built in low, wet situations; above these are layers of knotty stalks of withered grass, mixed with mud, and smoothly plastered, above which is laid a slight lining of fine, black, fibrous roots of plants. The eggs are four, sometimes five, of a uniform light blue, without any spots.

The Wood Thrush appears always singly or in pairs, and is of a shy, retired, unobtrusive disposition. With the modesty of true merit, he charms you with his song, but is content, and even solicitous, to be concealed. He delights to trace the irregular windings of the brook, where, by the luxuriance of foliage, the sun is completely shut out, or only plays in a few interrupted beams on the glittering surface of the water. He is also fond of a particular species of lichen which grows in such situations, and which, towards the fall, I have uniformly found in their stomachs: berries, however, of various kinds, are his principal food, as well as beetles and caterpillars. The feathers on the hind head are longer than is usual with birds which have no crest; these he sometimes erects; but this particular cannot be observed but on a close examination.*

Those who have paid minute attention to the singing of birds, know well, that the voice, energy, and expression, in the same tribe, differ

---

* In addition to the above picture of the manners of this Thrush, Mr. Audubon remarks, that it performs its migrations during the day, gliding swiftly through the woods, without appearing in the open country; that, on alighting upon a branch, it gives its tail a few jets, uttering at each motion a low, chuckling note, peculiar to itself; it then stands still for a while, with the feathers of the hind part a little raised. It walks and hops along the branches with much ease, and bends down its head to peep at the objects around. — Ed.

2 *

as widely as the voices of different individuals of the human species, or as one singer does from another. The powers of song, in some individuals of the Wood Thrush, have often surprised and delighted me. Of these I remember one, many years ago, whose notes I could instantly recognize on entering the woods, and with whom I had been, as it were, acquainted from his first arrival. The top of a large white oak that overhung part of the glen, was usually the favorite pinnacle from whence he poured the sweetest melody ; to which I had frequently listened till night began to gather in the woods, and the fireflies to sparkle among the branches. But, alas! in the pathetic language of the poet —

> One morn I missed him on the accustomed hill,
> Along the vale, and on his favorite tree —
> Another came, nor yet beside the rill,
> Nor up the glen, nor in the wood was he.

A few days afterwards, passing along the edge of the rocks, I found fragments of the wings and broken feathers of a Wood Thrush killed by the Hawk, which I contemplated with unfeigned regret, and not without a determination to retaliate on the first of these murderers I could meet with.

That I may not seem singular in my estimation of this bird, I shall subjoin an extract of a letter from a distinguished American gentleman, to whom I had sent some drawings, and whose name, were I at liberty to give it, would do honor to my humble performance, and render any further observations on the subject from me unnecessary.

"As you are curious in birds, there is one well worthy your attention, to be found, or rather heard, in every part of America, and yet scarcely ever to be seen. It is in all the forests from spring to fall, and never but on the tops of the tallest trees, from which it perpetually serenades us with some of the sweetest notes, and as clear as those of the Nightingale. I have followed it for miles, without ever but once getting a good view of it. It is of the size and make of the Mocking Bird, lightly thrush-colored on the back, and a grayish white on the breast and belly. Mr. ——, my son-in-law, was in possession of one, which had been shot by a neighbor ; he pronounced it a *Muscicapa*, and I think it much resembles the *Mouche rolle de la Martinique*, 8 Buffon, 374, *Pl. enlum.* 568. As it abounds in all the neighborhood of Philadelphia, you may, perhaps, by patience and perseverance, (of which much will be requisite,) get a sight, if not a possession, of it. I have, for twenty years, interested the young sportsmen of my neighborhood to shoot me one, but, as yet, without success."

It may seem strange that neither Sloane,* Catesby, Edwards, nor Buffon, all of whom are said to have described this bird, should say any thing of its melody ; or rather, assert that it had only a single cry or scream. This I cannot account for in any other way than by supposing, what I think highly probable, that this bird has never been figured or described by any of the above authors.

Catesby has, indeed, represented a bird, which he calls *Turdus minimus*,† but it is difficult to discover, either from the figure or de-

---

* *Hist. Jam.* ii. 305.   † Catesby's *Nat. Hist. Car.* i. 31.

scription, what particular species is meant; or whether it be really intended for the Wood Thrush we are now describing. It resembles, he says, the English Thrush; but is less, never sings, has only a single note, and abides all the year in Carolina. It must be confessed that, except the first circumstance, there are few features of the Wood Thrush in this description. I have searched the woods of Carolina and Georgia, in winter, for this bird in vain, nor do I believe it ever winters in these states. If Mr. Catesby found his bird mute during spring and summer, it was not the Wood Thrush, otherwise he must have changed his very nature. But Mr. Edwards has also described and delineated the little Thrush,* and has referred to Catesby as having drawn and engraved it before. Now, this Thrush of Edwards I know to be really a different species; one not resident in Pennsylvania, but passing to the north in May, and returning the same way in October, and may be distinguished from the true Song Thrush (*Turdus melodus*) by the spots being much broader, brown, and not descending below the breast. It is also an inch shorter, with the cheeks of a bright tawny color. Mr. William Bartram, who transmitted this bird, more than fifty years ago, to Mr. Edwards, by whom it was drawn and engraved, examined the two species in my presence; and on comparing them with the one in Edwards, was satisfied that the bird there figured and described is not the Wood Thrush, (*Turdus melodus*,) but the tawny-cheeked species above mentioned. This I have never seen in Pennsylvania but in spring and fall. It is still more solitary than the former, and utters, at rare times, a single cry, similar to that of a chicken which has lost its mother. This very bird I found numerous in the myrtle swamps of Carolina in the depth of winter, and I have not a doubt of its being the same which is described by Edwards and Catesby.

As the Count de Buffon has drawn his description from those above mentioned, the same observations apply equally to what he has said on the subject; and the fanciful theory which this writer had formed to account for its want of song, vanishes into empty air; viz. that the Song Thrush of Europe (*Turdus musicus*) had, at some time after the creation, rambled round by the Northern Ocean, and made its way to America; that, advancing to the south, it had there (of consequence) become degenerated by change of food and climate, so that its cry is now harsh and unpleasant, "as are the cries of all birds that live in wild countries inhabited by savages." †

---

* EDWARDS, 296.
† BUFFON, vol. iii. 289. The figure in *Pl. enl.* 398 has little or no resemblance to the Wood Thrush, being of a deep green olive above, and spotted to the tail below with long streaks of brown.

ROBIN.—TURDUS MIGRATORIUS.—Fig. 5.

Linn. Syst. i. p. 292, 6. — Turdus Canadensis, *Briss.* ii. p. 225, 9. — La Litorne de Canada, *Buff.* iii. p. 307. — Grive de Canada, *Pl. enl.* 556, 1. — Fieldfare of Carolina, *Cat. Car.* i. 29. — Red-breasted Thrush, *Arct. Zool.* ii. No. 196. — *Lath. Syn.* ii. p. 26. — *Bartram,* p. 290. — *Peale's Museum,* No. 5278.

TURDUS MIGRATORIUS. * — Linnæus.

Turdus migratorius, *Bonap. Synop.* p. 75. — Merula migratoria.
North. Zool. ii. p. 177.

This well-known bird, being familiar to almost every body, will require but a short description. It measures nine inches and a half in
length; the bill is strong, an inch long, and of a full yellow, though

---

* In the beautifully wrought out arrangement of the *Merulidæ*, by Mr. Swainson,
in the second volume of the *Northern Zoology*, that family will form the second
among the *Dentirostres*, or the subtypical group; including, for its five principal
divisions, the families *Merulinæ, Myotherinæ, Brachypodinæ, Oriolinæ,* and *Cra-
teropodinæ;* among these, however, two, or at most three, only, come within the
range of the northern continent of America, — the first and third. The first, *Merulinæ,* or more properly the typical form, will now claim our attention.

In all the members taken collectively, and in adaptation to their general habits,
they show considerable perfection, though their form as a part of the *Dentirostres*
does not come up to the typical perfections of that group. The parts are adapted
for extensive locomotion, either in walking or perching, and in flight; many perform
very considerable migrations, and long and rapid flights are often taken in those
countries even where the climate does not seem to render this necessary. They
are nearly omnivorous. A great part of their sustenance is sought for upon the
ground, particularly during that season when insects are not indispensable for the
welfare of their broods; and their feet and tarsi are admirably formed for walking
and inspecting the various places where their food is then chiefly to be found. At
other times they live principally upon fruits and some vegetables, with the larvæ
of insects, and the abundant supply of large and succulent caterpillars; but during
winter, the harder grains, and more fleshy insects common to low meadows and
moist woods, such as the various snails, flies, and worms, are nearly their only
food; for after the first month of the inclement season has passed, most of the winter
wild fruits and berries have either fallen from their stocks, or have been already
consumed by these and many other tribes that subsist upon them. Very few are
quite solitary: during the breeding season they all separate, but after the broods
have been raised, they congregate either in very large flocks or in groups of five or six.
Those of smaller numbers generally either become more domestic, and approach
dwellings and cultivated districts on the approach of winter, or retire entirely to the
depths of solitary forests. Those that congregate in large flocks are always remarkably shy, suffer persons to approach with difficulty, and have a sentinel or watch
on the look-out, to warn them of danger. Their cry is harsh and sharp, or shrill
and monotonous, except during the season of incubation, when they all produce
strains of more interest. Some possess great melody, and in others the notes are
remarkably pensive and melancholy. On this account they are universal favorites;
and the early song of the *Mavis* is watched for, by those residing much in the country, as the harbinger of a new season and brighter days. The true Thrushes are all
inhabitants of woods, and only from the necessity of procuring food resort to the
open countries. In distribution, they range over the world, and the proportion
seems pretty equal; India and Southern Europe may, perhaps, have the most extensive list, and North America will rank in the least proportion. They are often
used as articles of food, and the immense havock made among the *Northern Robins*
of our author, will show the estimation in which they are held as luxuries for the

sometimes black, or dusky near the tip of the upper mandible; the head, back of the neck, and tail, is black; the back and rump, an ash color; the wings are black, edged with light ash; the inner tips of the two exterior tail-feathers, are white; three small spots of white border the eye; the throat and upper part of the breast is black, the former streaked with white; the whole of the rest of the breast, down as far as the thighs, is of a dark orange; belly and vent, white, slightly waved with dusky ash; legs, dark brown; claws, black and strong. The colors of the female are more of the light ash, less deepened with black; and the orange on the breast is much paler, and more broadly skirted with white. The name of this bird bespeaks him a bird of passage, as are all the different species of Thrushes we have; but the one we are now describing, being more unsettled, and continually roving about from one region to another, during fall and winter, seems particularly entitled to the appellation. Scarce a winter passes but innumerable thousands of them are seen in the lower parts of the whole Atlantic states, from New Hampshire to Carolina, particularly in the neighborhood of our towns; and, from the circumstance of their leaving, during that season, the country to the north-west of the great range of the Alleghany, from Maryland northward, it would appear that they not only migrate from north to south, but from west to east, to avoid the deep snows that generally prevail on these high regions for at least four months in the year.

The Robin builds a large nest, often on an apple-tree, plasters it in the inside with mud, and lines it with hay or fine grass. The female lays five eggs, of a beautiful sea-green. Their principal food is berries, worms, and caterpillars. Of the first he prefers those of the sour gum, (*Nyssa sylvatica.*) So fond are they of gum-berries, that, wherever there is one of these trees covered with fruit, and flocks of Robins in the neighborhood, the sportsman need only take his stand near it, load, take aim, and fire; one flock succeeding another, with little interruption, almost the whole day: by this method, prodigious

table; in Spain and Italy, great numbers are taken for the same purpose, with nets and various kinds of snares. With the severity of the season, however, and the difference of food, the flesh acquires a bitter flavor, which renders them unfit for culinary purposes, and affords a temporary respite from their merciless persecutions.

The title *Merula*, which Mr. Swainson and several of our modern ornithologists have adopted, was used by Ray only as a sub-genus among his "*Turdinum genus*," and contained that division to which the Blackbird and Ringousel would belong; *Turdus* being confined to those with spotted breasts. I do not consider the very trifling difference in form between the plain and spotted species to be of sufficient importance, and prefer retaining the generic name of *Turdus*, as one well known and long accepted.

Robin seems to be applied in America generally to several of the Thrushes; some expletive going before to designate the species by its habits, as "*Wood Robin*," "*Swamp Robin*," "*Ground Robin*," &c. Our present species is THE ROBIN; and, as the preceding was a favorite on account of its song, this is no less so from the unassuming and dependent familiarity of its manners: it was most probably this, joined with the color of the breast, which first suggested the name of our own homely bird to the earlier British settlers, and along with it part of the respect with which its namesake is treated in this country.

An African species, *Turdus olivaceus*, (*le Griveron*, Vieill.) is nearly allied in the distribution of the markings. I have another, I believe, from South America, which approaches both nearly. — Ed.

slaughter has been made among them with little fatigue. When berries fail, they disperse themselves over the fields, and along the fences, in search of worms and other insects. Sometimes they will disappear for a week or two, and return again in greater numbers than before; at which time the cities pour out their sportsmen by scores, and the markets are plentifully supplied with them at a cheap rate. In January, 1807, two young men, in one excursion after them, shot thirty dozen. In the midst of such devastation, which continued many weeks, and, by accounts, extended from Massachusetts to Maryland, some humane person took advantage of a circumstance common to these birds in winter, to stop the general slaughter. The fruit called poke-berries (*Phytolacca decandra*, Linn.) is a favorite repast with the Robin, after they are mellowed by the frost. The juice of the berries is of a beautiful crimson, and they are eaten in such quantities by these birds, that their whole stomachs are strongly tinged with the same red color. A paragraph appeared in the public papers, intimating, that, from the great quantities of these berries which the Robins had fed on, they had become unwholesome, and even dangerous food; and that several persons had suffered by eating of them. The strange appearance of the bowels of the birds seemed to corroborate this account. The demand for, and use of them, ceased almost instantly; and motives of self-preservation produced at once what all the pleadings of humanity could not effect.* When fat, they are in considerable esteem for the table, and probably not inferior to the *Turdi* of the ancients, which they bestowed so much pains on in feeding and fattening. The young birds are frequently and easily raised, bear the confinement of the cage, feed on bread, fruits, &c., sing well, readily learn to imitate parts of tunes, and are very pleasant and cheerful domestics. In these I have always observed that the orange on the breast is of a much deeper tint, often a dark mahogany or chestnut color, owing, no doubt, to their food and confinement.

The Robin is one of our earliest songsters; even in March, while snow yet dapples the fields, and flocks of them are dispersed about, some few will mount a post or stake of the fence, and make short and frequent attempts at their song.† Early in April, they are only to be

* Governor Drayton, in his *View of South Carolina*, p. 86, observes, that "the Robins in winter devour the berries of the bead-tree (*Melia azedarach*) in such large quantities, that, after eating of them, they are observed to fall down, and are readily taken. This is ascribed more to distention from abundant eating, than from any deleterious qualities of the plant." The fact, however, is, that they are literally choked, many of the berries being too large to be swallowed.

† "The male is one of the loudest and most assiduous of the songsters that frequent the fur countries, beginning his chant immediately on his arrival. Within the arctic circle, the woods are silent in the bright light of noon-day; but, towards midnight, when the sun travels near the horizon, and the shades of the forest are lengthened, the concert commences, and continues till six or seven in the morning." Thus speaks Dr. Richardson, in the *Northern Zoology*, regarding the song of this bird; and he further adds, regarding the breeding and geographical range, — "Its nests were observed, by the last Northern expedition, conducted by Captain Sir J. Franklin, as high as the 67th parallel of latitude. It arrives on the Missouri, in lat. 41½°, from the eastward, on the 11th of April; and, in the course of its northerly movement, reaches Severn River, in Hudson's Bay, about a fortnight later. Its first appearance at Carlton House, in the year 1827, in lat. 53°, was on the 22d April. In the same season, it reached Fort Chippewyan, in lat. 55¾°, on the 7th

seen in pairs, and deliver their notes with great earnestness, from the top of some tree detached from the woods. This song has some resemblance to, and indeed is no bad imitation of, the notes of the Thrush or Thrasher, (*Turdus rufus ;*) but, if deficient in point of execution, he possesses more simplicity, and makes up in zeal what he wants in talent; so that the notes of the Robin, in spring, are universally known, and as universally beloved. They are, as it were, the prelude to the grand general concert that is about to burst upon us from woods, fields, and thickets, whitened with blossoms, and breathing fragrance. By the usual association of ideas, we, therefore, listen with more pleasure to this cheerful bird, than to many others possessed of far superior powers, and much greater variety. Even his nest is held more sacred among schoolboys than that of some others ; and, while they will exult in plundering a Jay's or a Cat Bird's, a general sentiment of respect prevails on the discovery of a Robin's. Whether he owes not some little of this veneration to the well-known and long-established character of his namesake in Britain, by a like association of ideas, I will not pretend to determine. He possesses a good deal of his suavity of manners; and almost always seeks shelter for his young in summer, and subsistence for himself in the extremes of winter, near the habitations of man.

The Robin inhabits the whole of North America, from Hudson's Bay to Nootka Sound, and as far south as Georgia, though they rarely breed on this side the mountains farther south than Virginia. Mr. Forster says, that about the beginning of May they make their appearance in pairs at the settlements of Hudson's Bay, at Severn River; and adds a circumstance altogether unworthy of belief, viz. that, at Moose Fort, they build, lay, and hatch, in fourteen days! but that at the former place, four degrees more north, they are said to take twenty-six days.* They are also common in Newfoundland, quitting these northern parts in October. The young, during the first season, are spotted with white on the breast, and at that time have a good deal of resemblance to the Fieldfare of Europe.

Mr. Hearne informs us, that the red-breasted Thrushes are commonly called, at Hudson's Bay, the Red-Birds — by some, the Blackbirds, on

of May; and Fort Franklin, in lat. 65°, on the 20th of that month. Those that build their nests in the 54th parallel of latitude, begin to hatch in the end of May; but 11° farther to the north, that event is deferred till the 11th of June. The snow, even then, partially covers the ground; but there are, in those high latitudes, abundance of the berries of *Vaccinium uliginosum* and *Vitis idea, Arbutus alpina, Empetrum nigrum,* and of some other plants, which, after having been frozen up all winter, are exposed to the first melting of the snows, full of juice, and in high flavor: shortly after, the parents obtain abundance of grubs for their callow young."

We thus see the extreme regularity with which the migrations are performed, and cannot too much admire the power which enables them to perceive, and calculate so exactly, the time required for their journey to the climates best suited to their duties at that season. We also see another wonderful provision, both for the migratory species and those which subsist as they best can during the winter, in the preservation of the berries and fruits fresh and juicy under the snow. Were it not for this, the ground, on the melting of its covering, would present a more desolate appearance than in the extremest storms of winter, and all animal life would inevitably perish, for want of food, before the various and abundant plants could flower and perfect their fruits. — ED.

* *Phil. Trans.* lxii. 399.

account of their note — and by others, the American Fieldfares; that they make their appearance at Churchill River about the middle of May, and migrate to the south early in the fall. They are seldom seen there but in pairs; and are never killed for their flesh, except by the Indian boys.*

Several authors have asserted, that the red-breasted Thrush cannot brook the confinement of the cage, and never sings in that state. But, except the Mocking Bird, (*Turdus polyglottus,*) I know of no native bird which is so frequently domesticated, agrees better with confinement, or sings in that state more agreeably than the Robin. They generally suffer severely in moulting time, yet often live to a considerable age. A lady, who resides near Tarrytown, on the banks of the Hudson, informed me, that she raised and kept one of these birds for seventeen years; which sung as well, and looked as sprightly, at that age as ever; but was at last unfortunately destroyed by a cat. The morning is their favorite time for song. In passing through the streets of our large cities, on Sunday, in the months of April and May, a little after daybreak, the general silence which usually prevails without at that hour, will enable you to distinguish every house where one of these songsters resides, as he makes it then ring with his music.

Not only the plumage of the Robin, as of many other birds, is subject to slight periodical changes of color, but even the legs, feet, and bill; the latter, in the male, being frequently found tipped and ridged for half its length with black. In the depth of winter, their plumage is generally best; at which time the full-grown bird, in his most perfect dress, appears as exhibited in Fig. 5.

———◆———

WHITE-BREASTED, BLACK-CAPPED NUTHATCH. — SITTA CAROLINENSIS. — Fig. 6.

Catesb. i. 22, fig. 2. — *Lath.* i. 650, B. — *Briss.* iii. p. 596, 4. — Sitta Carolinensis, *Turton.* — Sitta Europea, Gray Black-capped Nuthatch, *Bartram*, p. 289. — *Peale's Museum*, No. 20, 36.

SITTA CAROLINENSIS.†

Sitta Carolinensis, *Bonap. Synop.* 96. — Sitta melanocephala, *Vieill. Gal. des Ois.* p. 280, pl. 174.

THE bill of this bird is black, the upper mandible straight, the lower one rounded upwards towards the point, and white near the base; the nostrils are covered with long, curving, black hairs; the

* *Journey to the Northern Ocean*, p. 418, quarto. Lond. 1795.
† The true Nuthatches, *Sittæ*, (for I would not admit *S. velata* of Horsfield, and some allied species, nor the *S. chrysoptera* from New Holland,) are all natives of Europe and South America. With this restriction of geographical distribution, the genus will contain only four species, three of which, *S. Carolinensis, Canadensis*, and *pusilla*, figured and described by our author, are confined to North America; and the fourth, *S. Europea*, has been only found in Europe. With regard to their

tongue is of a horny substance, and ending in several sharp points; the general color above is of a light blue or lead; the tail consists of twelve feathers, the two middle ones lead color, the next three are black, tipped with white for one tenth, one fourth, and half of an inch; the two next are also black, tipped half an inch or more with white, which runs nearly an inch up their exterior edges, and both have the white at the tips touched with black; the legs are of a purple or dirty flesh color; the hind claw is much the largest; the inside of the wing at the bend is black; below this is a white spot spreading over the roots of the first five primaries; the whole length is five inches and a half; extent, eleven.

Mr. Pennant considers this bird as a mere variety of the European Nuthatch; but if difference in size, color, and habits, be sufficient characteristics of a distinct species, this bird is certainly entitled to be considered as such. The head and back of the European species is of a uniform bluish gray; the upper parts of the head, neck, and shoulders of ours, are a deep black, glossed with green; the breast and belly of the former is a dull orange, with streaks of chestnut; those parts in

situation in our systems, I would prefer placing them near to *Certhia, Neops, Anabates, Dendrocolaptes,* and not far distant from the Titmice; with the former, they seem intimately connected, and there appears little in their structure in common with the Woodpeckers, except the act of running up the trunks of trees. In habit and general economy they resemble the Titmice, always actively employed in turning or twisting round the branches, or in running up or down the trunks, for they do both with equal facility, searching after the insects, or their eggs and larvæ, which lie concealed under the moss, or loose bark; but occasionally also, like them, feeding upon different grains, on the seeds of the pine cones, as mentioned by our author, in his description of the red-bellied species; or, according to Montagu, like the *S. Europea,* frequenting the orchards during the cider season, and picking the seeds from the refuse of the pressed apples. In a state of confinement, they will thrive well upon raw meat, or fat, and if taken at a proper age, become extremely familiar and amusing; if not, they will most likely destroy themselves in their endeavors to get free from confinement, as mentioned by the anonymous writer of an interesting account of this bird in Loudon's *Magazine of Natural History.* I had lately an opportunity of observing a nest of our native species, which had been taken young. They became remarkably tame; and, when released from their cage, would run over their owner in all directions, up or down his body and limbs, *poking* their bills into seams or holes, as if in search of food upon some old and rent tree, and uttering, during the time, a low and plaintive cry. When running up or down, they rest upon the back part of the whole tarsus, and make great use, as a support, of what may be called the real heel, and never use the tail. Their bills are comparatively strong, and the power they possess of using them great, equal apparently to that of a Woodpecker of like size. They breed in hollow trees, and produce a rather numerous brood. The male attends carefully during the time. According to Montagu, our British species chooses the deserted habitation of some Woodpecker. "The hole is first contracted by a plaster of clay, leaving only sufficient room for itself to pass out and in; the nest is made of dead leaves, chiefly those of the oak, which are heaped together without much order. If the barrier of plaster at the entrance is destroyed when they have eggs, it is speedily replaced, — a peculiar instinct to prevent their nest being destroyed by the Woodpecker, and other birds of superior size, which build in the same manner." Or, as Mr. Rennie, in his late edition of the same work, thinks probable, the wall may be to prevent the unfledged young from tumbling out of the nest, when they begin to stir about. It is probable that the Nuthatch does not look forward to any of these considerations; and although the effects above mentioned may be in reality the consequence, I should conceive the hole contracted as being really too large, and as increasing the heat and apparent comfort within. When roosting, they sleep with the head and back downwards, in the manner of several Titmice. — ED.

3

the latter are pure white. The European has a line of black passing through the eye, half way down the neck; the present species has nothing of the kind, but appears with the inner webs of the three shortest secondaries and the primaries of a jet black; the latter tipped with white, and the vent and lower parts of the thighs of a rust color: the European, therefore, and the present, are evidently two distinct and different species.*

This bird builds its nest early in April, in the hole of a tree, in a hollow rail in the fence, and sometimes in the wooden cornice under the eaves; and lays five eggs, of a dull white, spotted with brown at the greater end. The male is extremely attentive to the female while sitting; supplying her regularly with sustenance, stopping frequently at the mouth of the hole, calling and offering her what he has brought, in the most endearing manner. Sometimes he seems to stop merely to inquire how she is, and to lighten the tedious moments with his soothing chatter. He seldom rambles far from the spot; and when danger appears, regardless of his own safety, he flies instantly to alarm her. When both are feeding on the trunk of the same tree, or of adjoining ones, he is perpetually calling on her; and, from the momentary pause he makes, it is plain that he feels pleased to hear her reply.

The White-breasted Nuthatch is common almost every where in the woods of North America, and may be known, at a distance, by the notes, *quank, quank,* frequently repeated, as he moves, upward and down, in spiral circles, around the body and larger branches of the tree, probing behind the thin scaly bark of the white oak, and shelling off considerable pieces of it, in search after spiders, ants, insects, and their larvæ. He rests and roosts with his head downwards, and appears to possess a degree of curiosity not common to many birds; frequently descending, very silently, within a few feet of the root of the tree where you happen to stand, stopping, head downward, stretching out his neck in a horizontal position, as if to reconnoitre your appearance; and, after several minutes of silent observation, wheeling round, he again mounts, with fresh activity, piping his unisons as before. Strongly attached to his native forests, he seldom forsakes them; and, amidst the rigors of the severest winter weather, his note is still heard in the bleak and leafless woods, and among the howling branches. Sometimes the rain, freezing as it falls, encloses every twig, and even the trunk of the tree, in a hard, transparent coat or shell of ice. On these occasions I have observed his anxiety and dissatisfaction, at being, with difficulty, able to make his way along the smooth surface; at these times generally abandoning the trees, gleaning about the stables, around the house, mixing among the fowls, entering the barn, and examining the beams and rafters, and every place where he may pick up a subsistence.

The name Nuthatch has been bestowed on this family of birds, from their supposed practice of breaking nuts by repeated hatchings, or hammerings with their bills. Soft-shelled nuts, such as chestnuts,

---

* Wilson is perfectly correct in considering this species as distinct from that of Europe; he has marked out the distinctions well in the description. It is described by Vieillot as *Sitta melanocephala.* — ED.

chinkopins, and hazel-nuts, they may, probably, be able to demolish, though I have never yet seen them so engaged ; but it must be rather in search of maggots, that sometimes breed there, than for the kernel. It is, however, said, that they lay up a large store of nuts for winter ; but, as I have never either found any of their magazines, or seen them collecting them, I am inclined to doubt the fact. From the great numbers I have opened at all seasons of the year, I have every reason to believe that ants, bugs, small seeds, insects, and their larvæ, form their chief subsistence, such matters alone being uniformly found in their stomachs. Neither can I see what necessity they could have to circumambulate the trunks of trees with such indefatigable and restless diligence, while bushels of nuts lay scattered round their roots. As to the circumstance, mentioned by Dr. Plott, of the European Nuthatch "putting its bill into a crack in the bough of a tree, and making such a violent sound, as if it was rending asunder," this, if true, would be sufficient to distinguish it from the species we have been just describing, which possesses no such faculty.* The female differs little from the male in color, chiefly in the black being less deep on the head and wings.

RED-BELLIED, BLACK-CAPPED NUTHATCH — SITTA VARIA. — Fig. 7

Sitta varia, *Bart.* p. 289. — Sitta Canadensis. *Turton.* — Sma.. Nuuaawa *Latn*
1 65.

SITTA CANADENSIS. — Linnæu

Sitta Canadensis, *Bonap. Synop.* p. 96.

This bird is much smaller than the last, measuring only four inches and a half in length, and eight inches in extent. In the form of its bill, tongue, nostrils, and in the color of the back and tail-feathers, it exactly agrees with the former ; the secondaries are not relieved with the deep black of the other species ; and the legs, feet, and claws, are of a dusky greenish yellow ; the upper part of the head is black, bounded by a stripe of white passing round the frontlet ; a line of

---

* When the Nuthatch cracks or splits nuts, or stones of fruit, it is for the kernels alone ; it is seen, from our various accounts, to be both a seed and grain eater. The very curious manner in which our own Nuthatch splits nuts seems perfectly proved by several observers ; and it is no less curious, that the same place is often resorted to different times in succession, as if it were more fit than another, or required less labor than to seek a new situation. Montagu says, that the most favorite position for breaking a nut is with the head downwards ; and that in autumn it is no uncommon thing to find in the crevices of the bark of an old tree a great many broken nutshells, the work of this bird, who repeatedly returns to the same spot for this purpose : when it has fixed the nut firm in a chink, it turns on all sides to strike it with most advantage ; this, with the common hazel-nut, is a work of some labor ; but it breaks a filbert with ease. — Ed.

black passes through the eye to the shoulder; below this is another line of white; the chin is white; the other under parts a light rust color, the primaries and whole wings a dusky lead color. The breast and belly of the female are not of so deep a brown, and the top of the head is less intensely black.

This species is migratory, passing from the north, where they breed, to the Southern States in October, and returning in April. Its voice is sharper, and its motions much quicker than those of the other, being so rapid, restless, and small, as to make it a difficult point to shoot one of them. When the two species are in the woods together, they are easily distinguished by their voices, the note of the least being nearly an octave sharper than that of its companion, and repeated more hurriedly. In other respects, their notes are alike unmusical and monotonous. Approaching so near to each other in their colors and general habits, it is probable that their mode of building, &c., may be also similar.

Buffon's *Torchepot de la Canada* (Canada Nuthatch of other European writers) is either a young bird of the present species, in its imperfect plumage, or a different sort, that rarely visits the United States. If the figure (*Pl. enl.* 623) be correctly colored, it must be the latter, as the tail and head appear of the same bluish gray or lead color as the back. The young birds of this species, it may be observed, have also the crown of a lead color during the first season; but the tail-feathers are marked nearly as those of the old ones. Want of precision in the figures and descriptions of these authors makes it difficult to determine; but I think it very probable, that *Sitta Jamaicensis minor*, Briss., the Least Loggerhead of Brown, *Sitta Jamaicensis var. t. st.* Linn., and *Sitta Canadensis* of Linnæus, Gmelin, and Brisson, are names that have been originally applied to different individuals of the species we are now describing.

This bird is particularly fond of the seeds of pine-trees. You may traverse many thousand acres of oak, hickory, and chestnut woods, during winter, without meeting with a single individual; but no sooner do you enter among the pines than, if the air be still, you have only to listen for a few moments, and their note will direct you where to find them. They usually feed in pairs, climbing about in all directions, generally accompanied by the former species, as well as by the Titmouse, *Parus atricapillus,* and the Crested Titmouse, *Parus bicolor,* and not unfrequently by the Small-spotted Woodpecker, *Picus pubescens;* the whole company proceeding regularly from tree to tree through the woods like a corps of pioneers; while, in a calm day, the rattling of their bills, and the rapid motions of their bodies, thrown, like so many tumblers and rope-dancers, into numberless positions, together with the peculiar chatter of each, are altogether very amusing; conveying the idea of hungry diligence, bustle, and activity.* Both these little birds, from the great quantity of destruc-

---

* It is curious to remark the similarity, as it were, in the feeling and disposition of some species. In this country, during winter, when the different kinds have laid aside those ties which connected them by sexual intercourse, nothing is more common than to see a whole troop of the Blue, Marsh, Cole, and Long-tailed Titmice, accompanied with a host of Golden-crested Wrens, and perhaps a solitary Creeper, proceed in the manner here mentioned, and regularly follow each other, as if in

tive insects and larvæ they destroy, both under the bark and among the tender buds of our fruit and forest trees, are entitled to, and truly deserving of, our esteem and protection.

———◆———

GOLD-WINGED WOODPECKER. — PICUS AURATUS. — Fig. 8.

Le pic aux ailes dorees, *De Buffon*, vii. 39, *Pl. enl.* 693. — Picus auratus, *Linn. Syst.* 174. — Cuculus alis de auratis, *Klein*, p. 30. — *Catesby*, i. 18. — *Latham*, ii. 597. — *Bartram*, p. 289. — *Peale's Museum*, No. 1938.

COLAPTES AURATUS. — Swainson.*

Picus auratus, *Penn. Arct. Zool.* ii. p. 270. — *Wagler.* No. 84. — *Bonap. Synop.* p. 44. — Golden-winged Woodpecker, *Aud.* i. p. 191. — Colaptes auratus, *North. Zool.* ii. 314.

This elegant bird is well known to our farmers and junior sportsmen, who take every opportunity of destroying him ; the former, for the supposed trespasses he commits on their Indian corn, or the trifle

a laid-out path. An alarm may cause a temporary digression of some of the troop ; but these are soon perceived making up their way to the main body. The whole may be found out, and traced by their various and constantly reiterated cries. — Ed.

* This beautiful species is typical of one form among the *Picianæ*, and has been designated under the above title by Mr. Swainson. The form appears to range in North and South America, the West Indian Islands, and in Africa ; our present species is confined to North America alone. They are at once distinguished from the true Woodpeckers and the other groups, by the curved and compressed bill, the broad and strong shafts of the quills, which are also generally brightly colored, and appear very conspicuous during flight when the wings are expanded. In the typical species they are of a bright golden yellow, whence the common name ; and in one closely allied, the *C. Mexicanus*, Sw., of a bright reddish orange ; in a third, *C. Brasiliensis*, they are of a pale straw yellow. The upper parts of the plumage are, in general, barred, and the feathers on the hind head are of a uniform length, never crested. A difference in form will always produce a difference in habit ; and we accordingly find that these birds more frequently perch on the branches, and feed a great deal upon the ground ; they seem also to possess more of the activity of the Nuthatch and Titmice than the regular *climb* of the typical Woodpeckers. The Golden-winged Woodpecker is known to feed a great deal upon ants, seeking them about the hills, and, according to Mr. Audubon, also picks up grains and seed from the ground. In a Brazilian species, *Picus campestris* of Spix and Martius, we have analogous habits ; and, as the name implies, it is often seen upon the ground, frequenting the ordure of cattle, and turning it over in search of insects ; or in the neighborhood of ant hills, where they find an abundant and very favorite food. We find also the general development of form joined to habit, in the typical form of another group, the common Green and Gray-headed Woodpeckers of Europe, which feed much on ants, and of course seek them on the ground.

Mons. Lesson, in his *Manual d'Ornithologie*, has given it the title of *Cucupicus*, making the African species typical. He of course was not aware of its having been previously characterized ; and in that of America, all the forms are more clearly developed.

The *C. Mexicanus*, mentioned before, was met with in the last over-land expedition, and will form an addition to the North American species ; it was killed by Mr

3 *

he will bring in market; and the latter for the mere pleasure of destruction, and perhaps for the flavor of his flesh, which is in general esteem. In the state of Pennsylvania, he can scarcely be called a bird of passage, as, even in severe winters, they may be found within a few miles of the city of Philadelphia; and I have known them exposed for sale in market every week during the months of November, December, and January, and that, too, in more than commonly rigorous weather. They no doubt, however partially, migrate even here; being much more numerous in spring and fall, than in winter. Early in the month of April, they begin to prepare their nest, which is built in the hollow body or branch of a tree, sometimes, though not always, at a considerable height from the ground; for I have frequently known them fix on the trunk of an old apple-tree, at not more than six feet from the root. The sagacity of this bird in discovering, under a sound bark, a hollow limb or trunk of a tree, and its perseverance in perforating it for the purpose of incubation, are truly surprising; the male and female alternately relieving and encouraging each other, by mutual caresses, renewing their labors for several days, till the object is attained, and the place rendered sufficiently capacious, convenient, and secure. At this employment they are so extremely intent, that they may be heard till a very late hour in the evening, thumping like carpenters. I have seen an instance where they had dug first five inches straight forward, and then downward more than twice that distance, through a solid black oak. They carry in no materials for their nest, the soft chips and dust of the wood serving for this purpose. The female lays six white eggs, almost transparent, very thick at the greater end, and tapering suddenly to the other. The young early leave the nest, and, climbing to the higher branches, are there fed by their parents.

The food of this bird varies with the season. As the common cherries, bird cherries, and berries of the sour gum successively ripen, he regales plentifully on them, particularly on the latter; but the chief food of this species, or that which is most usually found in his stomach, is wood-lice, and the young and larvæ of ants, of which he is so immoderately fond, that I have frequently found his stomach distended with a mass of these, and these only, as large nearly as a plumb. For the procuring of these insects, nature has remarkably fitted him: the bills of Woodpeckers, in general, are straight, grooved or channelled, wedge-shaped, and compressed to a thin edge at the end, that they may the easier penetrate the hardest wood; that of the Gold-winged Woodpecker is long, slightly bent, ridged only on the top, and tapering almost to a point, yet still retaining a little of the wedge form there. Both, however, are admirably adapted for the peculiar manner each has of procuring its food; the former, like a powerful wedge, to penetrate the dead and decaying branches, after worms and insects; the latter, like a long and sharp pick-axe, to dig up the hillocks of pismires, that inhabit old stumps in prodigious multitudes. These beneficial services would entitle him to some

David Douglas to the westward of the Rocky Mountains. The more common country is Mexico, whence it extends along the shores of the Pacific, some distance northward of the Columbia River, and to New California. — ED.

regard from the husbandman, were he not accused, and perhaps not
without just cause, of being too partial to the Indian corn, when in
that state which is usually called *roasting-ears*. His visits are indeed
rather frequent about this time; and the farmer, suspecting what is
going on, steals through among the rows with his gun, bent on vengeance, and forgetful of the benevolent sentiment of the poet, that

> Just as wide of justice he must fall,
> Who thinks all made for one, not one for all.

But farmers, in general, are not much versed in poetry, and pretty
well acquainted with the value of corn, from the hard labor requisite
in raising it.

In rambling through the woods one day, I happened to shoot one of
these birds, and wounded him slightly in the wing. Finding him in
full feather, and seemingly but little hurt, I took him home, and put
him into a large cage, made of willows, intending to keep him in my
own room, that we might become better acquainted. As soon as he
found himself enclosed on all sides, he lost no time in idle fluttering,
but, throwing himself against the bars of the cage, began instantly to
demolish the willows, battering them with great vehemence, and uttering a loud, piteous kind of cackling, similar to that of a hen when
she is alarmed and takes to wing. Poor Baron Trenck never labored
with more eager diligence at the walls of his prison, than this son of
the forest in his exertions for liberty; and he exercised his powerful
bill with such force, digging into the sticks, seizing and shaking them
so from side to side, that he soon opened for himself a passage; and,
though I repeatedly repaired the breach, and barricadoed every opening, in the best manner I could, yet, on my return into the room, I
always found him at large, climbing up the chairs, or running about
the floor, where, from the dexterity of his motions, moving backward,
forward, and sidewise, with the same facility, it became difficult to get
hold of him again. Having placed him in a strong wire cage, he
seemed to give up all hopes of making his escape, and soon became
very tame; fed on young ears of Indian corn; refused apples, but ate
the berries of the sour gum greedily, small winter grapes, and several
other kinds of berries; exercised himself frequently in climbing, or
rather hopping perpendicularly along the sides of the cage; and, as
evening drew on, fixed himself in a high hanging, or perpendicular
position, and slept with his head in his wing. As soon as dawn
appeared, even before it was light enough to perceive him distinctly
across the room, he descended to the bottom of the cage, and began
his attack on the ears of Indian corn, rapping so loud, as to be heard
from every room in the house. After this, he would sometimes resume
his former position, and take another nap. He was beginning to
become very amusing, and even sociable, when, after a lapse of
several weeks, he became drooping, and died, as I conceived, from
the effects of his wound.*

---

* Mr. Audubon says they live well in confinement. "The Golden-winged
Woodpecker never suffers its naturally lively spirit to droop. It feeds well; and
by way of amusement will continue to destroy as much furniture in a day, as can
well be mended by a different kind of workman in a week." The same gentleman,

Some European naturalists (and, among the rest, Linnæus himself, in his tenth edition of *Systema Naturæ*) have classed this bird with the genus *Cuculus*, or Cuckoo, informing their readers, that it possesses many of the habits of the Cuckoo; that it is almost always on the ground; is never seen to climb trees like the other Woodpeckers, and that its bill is altogether unlike theirs; every one of which assertions, I must say, is incorrect, and could have only proceeded from an entire unacquaintance with the manners of the bird. Except in the article of the bill — and that, as has been before observed, is still a little wedge-formed at the point — it differs in no one characteristic from the rest of its genus. Its nostrils are covered with tufts of recumbent hairs, or small feathers; its tongue is round, worm-shaped, flattened towards the tip, pointed, and furnished with minute barbs; it is also long, missile, and can be instantaneously protruded to an uncommon distance. The os hyöides, or internal parts of the tongue, like

when speaking of their flight, again adds, that it is more "strong and prolonged, being performed in a straighter manner, than any other of our Woodpeckers. They propel themselves by numerous beats of the wings, with short intervals of sailing, during which they scarcely fall from the horizontal. When passing from one tree to another, they also fly in a straight line, until within a few yards of the spot on which they intend to alight, when they suddenly raise themselves a few feet, and fasten themselves to the bark of the trunk by their claws and tail. Their migrations, although partial, (as many remain even in the middle districts during the severest winters,) are performed under night, as is known by their note and the whistling of their wings, which are heard from the ground." Of its movement he also speaks : "It easily moves sidewise on a small branch, keeping itself as erect as other birds usually do; but with equal care does it climb by leaps along the trunks of trees or their branches, descend, and move sidewise or spirally, keeping at all times its head upwards, and its tail pressed against the bark, as a support."

I have thus at length transcribed Mr. Audubon's minuter details, as tending to show the differences of habit in this form, which will be still better observed when compared with those we have yet to describe.

There is another peculiarity in these birds, and some others of the genus, mentioned by Mr. Audubon, which does not seem to have been noticed before, though I am not sure that it is confined to the *Pici* only. In many of our Sandpipers — the Purre, for instance — the first plumage is that of the adult female in the nuptial dress ; and, in those which have black breasts, an occasional tinge of that color may be traced. A great portion of these also receive at least a part of the winter dress during the first year. What I have alluded to is as follows, and it may be well that it is attended to in the description of the different species of Woodpeckers ; Mr. Audubon, however, uses the word "*frequently*," as if it were not a constant appearance in the young :— "In this species, as in a few others, there is a singular arrangement in the coloring of the feathers of the upper part of the head, which I conceive it necessary for me to state, that it may enable persons better qualified than myself to decide as to the reasons of such arrangement. The young of this species frequently have the whole upper part of the head tinged with red, which, at the approach of winter, disappears, when merely a circular line of that color is to be observed on the hind part, becoming of a rich silky vermilion tint. The Hairy, Downy, and Red-cockaded Woodpeckers are subject to the same extraordinary changes, which, as far as I know, never reappear at any future period of their lives. I was at first of opinion, that this change appeared only on the head of the male birds; but, on dissection, I found it equally affecting both sexes. I am induced to believe, that, in consequence of this, many young Woodpeckers, of different species, have been described and figured as forming distinct species themselves. I have shot dozens of young Woodpeckers in this peculiar state of plumage, which, on being shown to other persons, were thought by them to be of different species from what the birds actually were. This occurrence is the more worthy of notice, as it is exhibited on all the species of this genus, on the heads of which, when in full plumage, a very narrow line exists." — ED.

those of its tribe, is a substance for strength and elasticity resembling whalebone, divided into two branches, each the thickness of a knitting needle, that pass, one on each side of the neck, to the hind head, where they unite, and run up along the skull in a groove, covered with a thin membrane, or sheath; descend into the upper mandible by the right side of the right nostril, and reach to within half an inch of the point of the bill, to which they are attached by another extremely elastic membrane, that yields when the tongue is thrown out, and contracts as it is retracted. In the other Woodpeckers we behold the same apparatus, differing a little in different species. In some, these cartilaginous substances reach only to the top of the cranium; in others, they reach to the nostril; and in one species they are wound round the bone of the right eye, which projects considerably more than the left for its accommodation.

The tongue of the Gold-winged Woodpecker, like the others, is also supplied with a viscid fluid, secreted by two glands that lie under the ear on each side, and are at least five times larger in this species than in any other of its size; with this the tongue is continually moistened, so that every small insect it touches instantly adheres to it. The tail, in its strength and pointedness, as well as the feet and claws, prove that the bird was designed for climbing; and in fact I have scarcely ever seen it on a tree five minutes at a time without climbing; hopping not only upward and downward, but spirally; pursuing and playing with its fellow in this manner round the body of the tree. I have also seen them a hundred times alight on the trunk of the tree, though they more frequently alight on the branches; but that they climb, construct like nests, lay the same number and the like-colored eggs, and have the manners and habits of the Woodpeckers, is notorious to every American naturalist; while neither in the form of their body, nor any other part, except in the bill being somewhat bent, and the toes placed two before and two behind, have they the smallest resemblance whatever to the Cuckoo.

It may not be improper, however, to observe, that there is another species of Woodpecker, called also Gold-winged,* which inhabits the country near the Cape of Good Hope, and resembles the present, it is said, almost exactly in the color and form of its bill, and in the tint and markings of its plumage, with this difference, that the mustaches are red, instead of black, and the lower side of the wings, as well as their shafts, are also red, where the other is golden yellow. It is also considerably less. With respect to the habits of this new species, we have no particular account; but there is little doubt that they will be found to correspond with the one we are now describing.

The abject and degraded character which the Count de Buffon, with equal eloquence and absurdity, has drawn of the whole tribe of Woodpeckers, belongs not to the elegant and sprightly bird now before us. How far it is applicable to any of them will be examined hereafter. He is not "constrained to drag out an insipid existence in boring the bark and hard fibres of trees to extract his prey," for he frequently finds in the loose, mouldering ruins of an old stump (the capital of a nation of pismires) more than is sufficient for the wants

* *Picus cafer*, Turton's Linn.

of a whole week. *He* cannot be said to "lead a mean and gloomy life, without an intermission of labor," who usually feasts by the first peep of dawn, and spends the early and sweetest hours of morning on the highest peaks of the tallest trees, calling on his mate or companions; or pursuing and gamboling with them round the larger limbs and body of the tree for hours together; for such are really his habits. Can it be said, that "necessity never grants an interval of sound repose" to that bird, who, while other tribes are exposed to all the peltings of the midnight storm, lodges dry and secure in a snug chamber of his own constructing? or that "the narrow circumference of a tree circumscribes *his* dull round of life," who, as seasons and inclination inspire, roams from the frigid to the torrid zone, feasting on the abundance of various regions? Or is it a proof that "his appetite is never softened by delicacy of taste," because he so often varies his bill of fare, occasionally preferring to animal food the rich milkiness of young Indian corn, and the wholesome and nourishing berries of the wild cherry, sour gum, and red cedar? Let the reader turn to the faithful representation of him given in Fig. 8, and say whether his looks be "sad and melancholy." It is truly ridiculous and astonishing that such absurdities should escape the lips or pen of one so able to do justice to the respective merits of every species; but Buffon had too often a favorite theory to prop up, that led him insensibly astray; and so, forsooth, the whole family of Woodpeckers must look sad, sour, and be miserable, to satisfy the caprice of a whimsical philosopher, who takes it into his head that they are, and ought to be so!

But the count is not the only European who has misrepresented and traduced this beautiful bird. One has given him brown legs;[*] another a yellow neck;[†] a third has declared him a Cuckoo;[‡] and, in an English translation of Linnæus's *System of Nature*, lately published, he is characterized as follows: "Body, striated with black and gray; cheeks, red; chin, black; never climbs on trees;"[§] which is just as correct as if, in describing the human species, we should say, — Skin, striped with black and green; cheeks, blue; chin, orange; never walks on foot, &c. The pages of natural history should resemble a faithful mirror, in which mankind may recognize the true images of the living originals; instead of which, we find this department of them too often like the hazy and rough medium of wretched window-glass, through whose crooked protuberances every thing appears so strangely distorted, that one scarcely knows their most intimate neighbors and acquaintances.

The Gold-winged Woodpecker has the back and wings above of a dark umber, transversely marked with equidistant streaks of black; upper part of the head, an iron gray; cheeks and parts surrounding the eyes, a fine cinnamon color; from the lower mandible a strip of black, an inch in length, passes down each side of the throat, and a lunated spot, of a vivid blood red, covers the hind head, its two points reaching within half an inch of each eye; the sides of the

---

[*] See *Encyc. Brit.* art. *Picus.*   [†] Latham.   [‡] Klein.
[§] P. griseo nigroque transversim striatus ——— truncos arborum non scandit. — *Ind. Orn.* vol. i. p. 242.

neck, below this, incline to a bluish gray; throat and chin, a very light cinnamon or fawn color; the breast is ornamented with a broad crescent of deep black; the belly and vent, white, tinged with yellow, and scattered with innumerable round spots of black, every feather having a distinct central spot, those on the thighs and vent being heart-shaped and largest; the lower or inner side of the wing and tail, shafts of all the larger feathers, and indeed of almost every feather, are of a beautiful golden yellow; that on the shafts of the primaries being very distinguishable, even when the wings are shut; the rump is white, and remarkably prominent; the tail-coverts white, and curiously serrated with black; upper side of the tail, and the tip below, black, edged with light, loose filaments of a cream color, the two exterior feathers serrated with whitish; shafts, black towards the tips, the two middle ones, nearly wholly so; bill, an inch and a half long, of a dusky horn color, somewhat bent, ridged only on the top, tapering, but not to a point, that being a little wedge-formed; legs and feet, light blue; iris of the eye, hazel; length, twelve inches; extent, twenty. The female differs from the male chiefly in the greater obscurity of the fine colors, and in wanting the black mustaches on each side of the throat. This description, as well as the drawing, was taken from a very beautiful and perfect specimen.

Though this species, generally speaking, is migratory, yet they often remain with us in Pennsylvania during the whole winter. They also inhabit the continent of North America, from Hudson's Bay to Georgia; and have been found by voyagers on the north-west coast of America. They arrive at Hudson's Bay in April, and leave it in September. Mr. Hearne, however, informs us, that "the Gold-winged Woodpecker is almost the only species of Woodpecker that winters near Hudson's Bay." The natives there call it *Ou-thee-quan-nor-ow*, from the golden color of the shafts and lower side of the wings. It has numerous provincial appellations in the different states of the Union, such as "High-hole," from the situation of its nest, and "Hittock," "Yucker," "Piut," "Flicker," by which last it is usually known in Pennsylvania. These names have probably originated from a fancied resemblance of its notes to the sound of the words; for one of its most common cries consists of two notes, or syllables, frequently repeated, which, by the help of the hearer's imagination, may easily be made to resemble any or all of them.

BLACK–THROATED BUNTING. — EMBERIZA AMERICANA. — Fig. 9.

Calandra pratensis, the May-bird, *Bartram.* p. 291. — *Peale's Museum*, No. 5952. — *Arct. Zool.* 228. — Emberiza Americana, *Ind. Orn.* p. 44.

EMBERIZA AMERICANA. — Linnæus.*

Fringilla Americana, *Bonap. Synop.* 107.

Of this bird I have but little to say. They arrive in Pennsylvania from the south about the middle of May; abound in the neighborhood of Philadelphia, and seem to prefer level fields covered with rye-grass, timothy, or clover, where they build their nest, fixing it in the ground, and forming it of fine, dried grass. The female lays five white eggs, sprinkled with specks and lines of black. Like most part of their genus, they are nowise celebrated for musical powers. Their whole song consists of five notes, or, more properly, of two notes; the first repeated twice, and slowly, the second thrice, and rapidly, resembling *chip, chip, che che ché.* Of this ditty, such as it is, they are by no means parsimonious, for, from their first arrival for the space of two or three months, every level field of grain or grass is perpetually serenaded with *chip, chip, che che ché.* In their shape and manners they very much resemble the Yellow-Hammer of Britain (*E. citrinella ;*) like them, they are fond of mounting to the top of some half-grown tree, and there cheruping for half an hour at a time. In travelling through different parts of New York and Pennsylvania in spring and summer, wherever I came to level fields of deep grass, I have constantly heard these birds around me. In August they become mute; and soon after, that is, towards the beginning of September, leave us altogether.

The Black-throated Bunting is six inches and a half in length; the upper part of the head is of a dusky greenish yellow; neck, dark ash; breast, inside shoulders of the wing, line over the eye, and at the lower angle of the bill, yellow; chin, and space between the bill and eye, white; throat, covered with a broad, oblong, somewhat heart-shaped patch of black, bordered on each side with white; back,

---

* America has no birds perfectly typical with the *Emberizæ* of Europe; the group appears to assume two forms, under modifications, that of *E. miliaria,* with the bill of considerable strength, and that of the weaker make, of *E. schœniculus.* To the former will be allied our present species; under the latter will rank the small *F. socialis, melodia,* and *palustris,* &c.; the form is further represented in North America by *Plectrophanes* and *Pipilo,* and may be said to run into the Finches by means of the latter, and Mr. Swainson's genus, *Zonotrichia.* The principal variations are the want, or smallness, of the palatial knob, and the wideness of the upper mandible, which exceeds that of the lower, while the reverse is the case in the true birds. Vieillot, I believe, proposed *Passerina* for some birds, but included many that were not so nearly allied, and Bonaparte has proposed *Spiza* to receive them, and to stand as a subgenus of *Fringilla.* We think the form, coloring, and markings, joined with their song and habit, associates them much closer to *Emberiza,* and as such have at present retained them. — Ed.

rump, and tail, ferruginous, the first streaked with black; wings, deep dusky, edged with a light clay color; lesser coverts and whole shoulder of the wing, bright bay; belly and vent, dull white; bill, light blue, dusky above, strong and powerful for breaking seeds; legs and feet, brown; iris of the eye, hazel. The female differs from the male in having little or no black on the breast, nor streak of yellow over the eye; beneath the eye she has a dusky streak, running in the direction of the jaw. In all those I opened, the stomach was filled with various seeds, gravel, eggs of insects, and sometimes a slimy kind of earth or clay.

This bird has been figured by Latham, Pennant, and several others. The former speaks of a bird which he thinks is either the same, or nearly resembling it, that resides in summer in the country about Hudson's Bay, and is often seen associating in flights with the Geese.* This habit, however, makes me suspect that it must be a different species; for, while with us here, the Black-throated Bunting is never gregarious, but is almost always seen singly, or in pairs, or, at most, the individuals of one family together.

BLUE–BIRD. — SYLVIA SIALIS. — Fig. 10.

Le rouge gorge bleu, *De Buffon*, v. 212. *Pl. enl.* 390. — Blue Warbler, *Lath.* ii. 446. — *Catesb.* i. 47. — Motacilla Sialis, *Linn. Syst.* 336. — *Bartram*, p. 291. — *Peale's Museum*, No. 7188.

SIALIA WILSONII. — Swainson.†

The Blue Redbreast. *Edw.* pl. 24. — Saxicola sialis, *Bonap. Synop.* p. 89. — Erythaca (Sialia) Wilsonii, *North. Zool.* ii. p. 210.

THE pleasing manners and sociable disposition of this little bird entitle him to particular notice. As one of the first messengers of spring, bringing the charming tidings to our very doors, he bears his

* Latham, *Synopsis, Supplement*, p. 158.

† This beautiful species, interesting both as regards its domestic economy and the intimate link which it fills up in the natural system, has been dedicated, by Mr. Swainson, to our author. It remained a solitary individual, until the discovery of a Mexican species by that gentleman, described under the title of *S. Mexicana;* and the return of the last over-land Arctic expedition brought forward a third, confirming the views that were before held regarding it. According to these, it will range among the *Saxicolinæ*, whence it had been previously removed from *Sylvia* by Vieillot and Bonaparte, and it will hold the place, in North and South America, of the Robin of Europe, and the Stonechats of that country and Africa; while, in New Holland, the *Muscicapa multicolor*, now bearing the generic title of *Petroica*, with some allied species, will represent it. The old species ranges extensively over North America and the northern parts of the south continent, extending also to some of the islands: the newly-discovered one appears confined to a more northern latitude. It has been described in the second volume of the *Northern Zoology*, under the name of *S. Arctica*, and I now add the information contained in that valuable work: —

"Color of the dorsal aspect, ultramarine blue; the webs of the tertiaries, and the

4

own recommendation always along with him, and meets with a hearty welcome from every body.

Though generally accounted a bird of passage, yet, so early as the middle of February, if the weather be open, he usually makes his appearance about his old haunts, the barn, orchard, and fence posts. Storms and deep snows sometimes succeeding, he disappears for a time; but about the middle of March is again seen, accompanied by his mate, visiting the box in the garden, or the hole in the old apple-tree, the cradle of some generations of his ancestors. " When he first begins his amours," says a curious and correct observer, " it is pleasing to behold his courtship, his solicitude to please and to secure the favor of his beloved female. He uses the tenderest expressions, sits close by her, caresses and sings to her his most endearing warblings. When seated together, if he espies an insect delicious to her taste, he takes it up, flies with it to her, spreads his wing over her, and puts it in her mouth." * If a rival makes his appearance, — for they are ardent in their loves, — he quits her in a moment, attacks and pursues the intruder as he shifts from place to place, in tones that bespeak the jealousy of his affection, conducts him, with many reproofs, beyond the extremities of his territory, and returns to warble out his transports of triumph beside his beloved mate. The preliminaries being thus settled, and the spot fixed on, they begin to clean out the old nest and the rubbish of the former year, and to prepare for the reception of their future offspring. Soon after this, another sociable little pilgrim (*Motacilla domestica* House Wren) also arrives from the south, and, finding such a snug birth preoccupied, shows his spite, by watching a convenient opportunity, and, in the absence of the owner, popping in and pulling out sticks, but takes special care to make off as fast as possible.

The female lays five, and sometimes six eggs, of a pale blue color; and raises two, and sometimes three broods in a season; the male taking the youngest under his particular care while the female is again sitting. Their principal food are insects, particularly large beetles, and others of the coleopterous kinds that lurk among old, dead, and decaying trees. Spiders are also a favorite repast with them. In the fall, they occasionally regale themselves on the berries of the sour gum; and, as winter approaches, on those of the red cedar, and on the fruit of a rough, hairy vine, that runs up and cleaves fast to the trunks of trees. Ripe persimmons is another of their favorite dishes, and many

---

tips of the inner margins of the quill and tail-feathers, dull umber brown; the base of the plumage, blackish gray. *Under surface* — the cheeks, throat, breast, and insides of the wings, greenish blue, bordering on the abdomen to grayish blue; vent-feathers, and under tail-coverts, white; tail beneath, and inside of the quill-feathers, olive brown, with a strong tinge of blue; bill and feet, pitch black; form, in general, that of *S. Wilsonii*, but the bill is considerably narrower at the base, and proportionably larger, straighter, and less notched, and bent at the tip of the upper mandible; its breadth is equal to its depth; wings, three quarters of an inch shorter than the tail; the second quill-feather is the longest; the first and third are equal, and about a line shorter; the tenth is an inch and a half shorter than the second; tail, forked, or deeply emarginated, the central feathers being more than half an inch shorter than the exterior ones; legs and feet, similarly formed with those of *S. Wilsonii*; length, seven inches nine lines." — ED.

* Letter from Mr. William Bartram to the author.

other fruits and seeds which I have found in their stomachs at that season, which, being no botanist, I am unable to particularize. They are frequently pestered with a species of tape worm, some of which I have taken from their intestines of an extraordinary size, and, in some cases, in great numbers. Most other birds are also plagued with those vermin; but the Blue-Bird seems more subject to them than any I know, except the Woodcock. An account of the different species of vermin, many of which, I doubt not, are nondescripts, that infest the plumage and intestines of our birds, would of itself form an interesting publication; but, as this belongs more properly to the entomologist, I shall only, in the course of this work, take notice of some of the most remarkable.

The usual spring and summer song of the Blue-Bird is a soft, agreeable, and oft-repeated warble, uttered with open, quivering wings, and is extremely pleasing. In his motions and general character, he has great resemblance to the Robin Redbreast of Britain; and, had he the brown olive of that bird, instead of his own blue, could scarcely be distinguished from him. Like him, he is known to almost every child; and shows as much confidence in man by associating with him in summer, as the other by his familiarity in winter. He is also of a mild and peaceful disposition, seldom fighting or quarreling with other birds. His society is courted by the inhabitants of the country, and few farmers neglect to provide for him, in some suitable place, a snug little summer-house, ready fitted and rent free. For this he more than sufficiently repays them by the cheerfulness of his song, and the multitude of injurious insects which he daily destroys. Towards fall, that is, in the month of October, his song changes to a single plaintive note, as he passes over the yellow many-colored woods; and its melancholy air recalls to our minds the approaching decay of the face of nature. Even after the trees are stripped of their leaves, he still lingers over his native fields, as if loath to leave them. About the middle or end of November, few or none of them are seen; but, with every return of mild and open weather, we hear his plaintive note amidst the fields, or in the air, seeming to deplore the devastations of winter. Indeed, he appears scarcely ever totally to forsake us; but to follow fair weather through all its journeyings till the return of spring.

Such are the mild and pleasing manners of the Blue-Bird, and so universally is he esteemed, that I have often regretted that no pastoral muse has yet arisen in this western, woody world, to do justice to his name, and endear him to us still more by the tenderness of verse, as has been done to his representative in Britain, the Robin Redbreast. A small acknowledgment of this kind I have to offer, which the reader, I hope, will excuse as a tribute to rural innocence.

When winter's cold tempests and snows are no more,
    Green meadows and brown furrow'd fields reappearing,
The fishermen hauling their shad to the shore,
    And cloud-cleaving Geese to the lakes are a-steering;
When first the lone butterfly flits on the wing,
    When red glow the maples, so fresh and so pleasing, —
O then comes the Blue-Bird, the herald of spring!
    And hails with his warblings the charms of the season.

Then loud-piping frogs make the marshes to ring;
   Then warm glows the sunshine, and fine is the weather;
The blue woodland flowers just beginning to spring,
   And spicewood and sassafras budding together :
O then to your gardens, ye housewives, repair,
   Your walks border up, sow and plant at your leisure;
The Blue-Bird will chant from his box such an air,
   That all your hard toils will seem truly a pleasure !

He flits through the orchard, he visits each tree,
   The red-flowering peach, and the apple's sweet blossoms;
He snaps up destroyers wherever they be,
   And seizes the caitiffs that lurk in their bosoms;
He drags the vile grub from the corn it devours,
   The worms from their webs, where they riot and welter;
His song and his services freely are ours,
   And all that he asks is — in summer a shelter.

The ploughman is pleased when he gleans in his train,
   Now searching the furrows, now mounting to cheer him;
The gardener delights in his sweet, simple strain,
   And leans on his spade to survey and to hear him
The slow, lingering schoolboys forget they'll be chid,
   While gazing intent as he warbles before them,
In mantle of sky-blue, and bosom so red,
   That each little loiterer seems to adore him.

When all the gay scenes of the summer are o'er,
   And autumn slow enters, so silent and sallow,
And millions of warblers, that charm'd us before,
   Have fled in the train of the sun-seeking Swallow,
The Blue-Bird, forsaken, yet true to his home,
   Still lingers, and looks for a milder to-morrow,
Till, forced by the horrors of winter to roam,
   He sings his adieu in a lone note of sorrow.

While spring's lovely season, serene, dewy, warm,
   The green face of earth, and the pure blue of heaven,
Or love's native music have influence to charm.
   Or sympathy's glow to our feelings are given,
Still dear to each bosom the Blue-Bird shall be;
   His voice, like the thrillings of hope, is a treasure;
For, through bleakest storms, if a calm he but see,
   He comes to remind us of sunshine and pleasure !

The Blue-Bird, in summer and fall, is fond of frequenting open pasture fields, and there perching on the stalks of the great mullein, to look out for passing insects. A whole family of them are often seen thus situated, as if receiving lessons of dexterity from their more expert parents, who can espy a beetle crawling among the grass, at a considerable distance; and, after feeding on it, instantly resume their former position.* But whoever informed Dr. Latham, that " this bird

* The very habits of our European *Saxicolæ* are here described; they invariably seek the summit of some elevation, a hillock, a stone, bush, or some of the taller wild plants, and if occasionally on a tree, the topmost branch is always preferred; there they perch, uttering their monotonous call, which increases in anxiety and frequency as we approach the nest, or the young before they are able to fly; or they alight at intervals, run for some distance, and again remount to a fresh station. When not annoyed, they retain the same elevated situations, looking out for food, taking the insects seldom on the wing, but generally by a sudden spring, or leap

is never seen on trees, though it makes its nest in the holes of them!" * might as well have said, that the Americans are never seen in the streets, though they build their houses by the sides of them. For what is there in the construction of the feet and claws of this bird to prevent it from perching? Or what sight more common to an inhabitant of this country than the Blue-Bird perched on the top of a peach or apple-tree; or among the branches of those reverend, broad-armed chestnut-trees, that stand alone in the middle of our fields, bleached by the rains and blasts of ages?

The Blue-Bird is six inches and three quarters in length, the wings remarkably full and broad; the whole upper parts are of a rich sky blue, with purple reflections; the bill and legs are black; inside of the mouth and soles of the feet, yellow, resembling the color of a ripe persimmon; the shafts of all the wing and tail-feathers are black; throat, neck, breast, and sides, partially under the wings, chestnut; wings, dusky black at the tips; belly and vent, white; sometimes the secondaries are exteriorly light brown, but the bird has in that case not arrived at his full color. The female is easily distinguished by the duller cast of the back, the plumage of which is skirted with light brown, and by the red on the breast being much fainter, and not descending nearly so low as in the male; the secondaries are also more dusky. This species is found over the whole United States; in the Bahama Islands, where many of them winter; as also in Mexico, Brazil, and Guiana.

Mr. Edwards mentions, that the specimen of this bird which he was favored with, was sent from the Bermudas; and, as these islands abound with the cedar, it is highly probable that many of those birds pass from our continent thence, at the commencement of winter, to enjoy the mildness of that climate as well as their favorite food.

As the Blue-Bird is so regularly seen in winter, after the continuance of a few days of mild and open weather, it has given rise to various conjectures as to the place of his retreat; some supposing it to be in close, sheltered thickets, lying to the sun; others, the neighborhood of the sea, where the air is supposed to be more temperate, and where the matters thrown up by the waves furnish him with a constant and plentiful supply of food. Others trace him to the dark recesses of hollow trees, and subterraneous caverns, where they suppose he dozes away the winter, making, like Robinson Crusoe, occasional reconnoitring excursions from his castle, whenever the weather happens to be favorable. But amidst the snows and severities of winter, I have sought for him in vain in the most favorable sheltered situations of the Middle States; and not only in the neighborhood of the sea, but on both sides of the mountains.† I have never, indeed, explored the depths of caverns in search of him, because I would as

down, and returning immediately with the prey in their bill, where it is retained for a few minutes, while they repeat their uniform note. The young, as soon as they are able to fly, have the same manners with their parents, and at the season when these are first on the wing, some extensive commons have appeared almost entirely in motion with our common species. — Ed.

* *Synopsis*, vol. ii. p. 446—40.

† I speak of the species here generally. Solitary individuals are found, particularly among our cedar-trees, sometimes in the very depth of winter.

soon expect to meet with tulips and butterflies there, as Blue-Birds;
but, among hundreds of woodmen, who have cut down trees of all
sorts, and at all seasons, I have never heard one instance of these
birds being found so immured in winter; while, in the whole of the
Middle and Eastern States, the same general observation seems to
prevail, that the Blue-Bird always makes his appearance in winter
after a few days of mild and open weather. On the other hand, I
have myself found them numerous in the woods of North and South
Carolina, in the depth of winter; and I have also been assured by
different gentlemen of respectability, who have resided in the islands
of Jamaica, Cuba, and the Bahamas and Bermudas, that this very
bird is common there in winter. We also find, from the works of
Hernandez, Piso, and others, that it is well known in Mexico, Guiana,
and Brazil; and, if so, the place of its winter retreat is easily ascertained, without having recourse to all the trumpery of holes and
caverns, torpidity, hybernation, and such ridiculous improbabilities.

Nothing is more common in Pennsylvania than to see large flocks
of these birds, in spring and fall, passing at considerable heights in
the air; from the south in the former, and from the north in the latter
season. I have seen, in the month of October, about an hour after
sunrise, ten or fifteen of them descend from a great height, and settle
on the top of a tall, detached tree, appearing, from their silence and
sedateness, to be strangers, and fatigued. After a pause of a few
minutes, they began to dress and arrange their plumage, and continued so employed for ten or fifteen minutes more; then, on a few
warning notes being given, perhaps by the leader of the party, the
whole remounted to a vast height, steering in a direct line for the
south-west. In passing along the chain of the Bahamas towards the
West Indies, no great difficulty can occur, from the frequency of
these islands; nor even to the Bermudas, which are said to be six
hundred miles from the nearest part of the continent. This may
seem an extraordinary flight for so small a bird; but it is, nevertheless, a fact that it is performed. If we suppose the Blue-Bird in this
case to fly only at the rate of a mile per minute, which is less than I
have actually ascertained him to do over land, ten or eleven hours
would be sufficient to accomplish the journey; besides the chances he
would have of resting-places by the way, from the number of vessels
that generally navigate those seas. In like manner, two days at most,
allowing for numerous stages for rest, would conduct him from the
remotest regions of Mexico to any part of the Atlantic States.
When the natural history of that part of the continent and its adjacent isles is better known, and the periods at which its birds of passage arrive and depart are truly ascertained, I have no doubt but
these suppositions will be fully corroborated.

11. Female Orchard Oriole. 12. Male of second year. 13. Male of third year. 14. Male in complete plumage. 15. Great American Shrike or Butcher Bird. 16. Pine Grosbeak. 17. Ruby-crowned Wren. 18. Shore Lark. 19. Maryland Yellow throat. 20. Yellow breasted Chat. 21. Prairie. 22. Summer Red Bird. 23. Indigo Bird. 24. American Redstart.

ORCHARD ORIOLE. — ORIOLUS MUTATUS. —
Figs. 11, 12, 13, 14.

Peale's Museum, No. 1508. — Bastard Baltimore, *Catesby*, i. 49. — Le Baltimore Batard, *De Buffon*, iii. 233. *Pl. enl.* 506. — Oriolus Spurius, *Gmelin, Syst.* i. p. 389. — *Lath. Syn.* ii. p. 433, 20, p. 437, 24. — *Bartram*, p. 290.

ICTERUS SPURIUS. — BONAPARTE.

Icterus Spurius, *Bonap. Synop.* p. 51. — The Orchard Oriole, *Aud.* i. 221, pl. xlii.

THERE are no circumstances, relating to birds, which tend so much to render their history obscure and perplexing, as the various changes of color which many of them undergo. These changes are in some cases periodical; in others progressive; and are frequently so extraordinary, that, unless the naturalist has resided for years in the country which the birds inhabit, and has examined them at almost every season, he is extremely liable to be mistaken and imposed on by their novel appearance. Numerous instances of this kind might be cited, from the pages of European writers, in which the same bird has been described two, three, and even four different times, by the same person, and each time as a different kind. The species we are now about to examine is a remarkable example of this; and as it has never, to my knowledge, been either accurately figured or described, I have devoted one plate to the elucidation of its history.

The Count de Buffon, in introducing what he supposed to be the male of this bird, but which appears evidently to have been the female of the Baltimore Oriole, makes the following observations, which I give in the words of his translator: — "This bird is so called, (Spurious Baltimore,) because the colors of its plumage are not so lively as in the preceding, (*Baltimore O.*) In fact, when we compare these birds, and find an exact correspondence in every thing except the colors, and not even in the distribution of these, but only in the different tints they assume, we cannot hesitate to infer that the Spurious Baltimore is a variety of a more generous race, degenerated by the influence of climate, or some other accidental cause."

How the influence of climate could affect one portion of a species and not the other, when both reside in the same climate, and feed nearly on the same food; or what accidental cause could produce a difference so striking, and also so regular, as exists between the two, are, I confess, matters beyond my comprehension. But if it be recollected that the bird which the Count was thus philosophizing upon, was nothing more than the female Baltimore Oriole, which exactly corresponds to the description of his male Bastard Baltimore, the difficulties at once vanish, and with them the whole superstructure of theory founded on this mistake. Dr. Latham, also, while he confesses the great confusion and uncertainty that prevail between the True and Bastard Baltimore, and their females, considers it highly probable that the whole will be found to belong to one and the same species, in their different changes of color. In this conjecture, however, the worthy naturalist has likewise been mistaken; and I shall endeavor to point out the fact, as well as the source of this mistake.

And here I cannot but take notice of the name which naturalists have bestowed on this bird, and which is certainly remarkable. Specific names, to be perfect, ought to express some peculiarity, common to no other of the genus; and should, at least, be consistent with truth; but, in the case now before us, the name has no one merit of the former, nor even that of the latter to recommend it, and ought henceforth to be rejected as highly improper, and calculated, like that of *Goatsucker*, and many others equally ridiculous, to perpetuate that error from which it originated. The word *bastard*, among men, has its determinate meaning; but when applied to a whole species of birds, perfectly distinct from any other, originally deriving their peculiarities of form, manners, color, &c., from the common source of all created beings, and perpetuating them, by the usual laws of generation, as unmixed and independent as any other, is, to call it by no worse name, a gross absurdity. Should the reader be displeased at this, I beg leave to remind him, that, as the faithful historian of our feathered tribes, I must be allowed the liberty of vindicating them from every misrepresentation whatever, whether originating in ignorance or prejudice, and of allotting to each respective species, as far as I can distinguish, that rank and place in the great order of nature to which it is entitled.

To convince the foreigner, (for Americans have no doubt on the subject,) that the present is a distinct species from the Baltimore, it might be sufficient to refer to the representation of the latter, in Fig. 3, and to Fig. 14, of this work. I will, however, add, that I conclude this bird to be specifically different from the Baltimore, from the following circumstances: its size — it is less, and more slender; its colors, which are different, and *very differently disposed*; the form of its bill, which is sharper pointed, and more bent; the form of its tail, which is not *even*, but *wedged*; its notes, which are neither so full nor so mellow, and uttered with much more rapidity; its mode of building, and the materials it uses, both of which are different; and, lastly, the shape and color of the eggs of each, (see Figs. *a* and *b*,*) which are evidently unlike. If all these circumstances — and I could enumerate a great many more — be not sufficient to designate this as a distinct species, by what criterion, I would ask, are we to discriminate between a *variety* and an *original* species, or to assure ourselves, that the Great Horned Owl is not, in fact, a *Bastard* Goose, or the Carrion Crow a mere *variety* of the Humming Bird?

These mistakes have been occasioned by several causes; principally by the changes of color to which the birds are subject, and the distance of Europeans from the country they inhabit. Catesby, it is true, while here, described and figured the Baltimore, and perhaps was the first who published figures of either species; but he entirely omitted saying any thing of the female, and, instead of the male and female of the present species, as he thought, he has only figured the male in two of his different dresses; and succeeding compilers have

---

* Referring to Wilson's original edition.

followed and repeated the same error. Another cause may be assigned, viz. the extreme shyness of the female Orchard Oriole, represented at Fig. 11. This bird has hitherto escaped the notice of European naturalists, or has been mistaken for another species, or perhaps for a young bird of the first season, which it almost exactly resembles. In none of the numerous works on ornithology has it ever before appeared in its proper character; though the male has been known to Europeans for more than a century, and has usually been figured in one of his dresses as male, and in another as female; these varying according to the fluctuating opinions of different writers. It is amusing to see how gentlemen have groped in the dark in pairing these two species of Orioles, of which the following examples may be given:

Buffon's and Latham's Baltimore Oriole.	*Male*. . . .	Male Baltimore.
	Female. . .	Male Orchard Oriole, Fig. 14.
Spurious Baltimore of ditto.	*Male*. . . .	Female Baltimore.
	Female. .	Male Orchard Oriole, Fig. 12.
Pennant's Baltimore Oriole.	*Male*. . . .	Male Baltimore.
	Female. .	Young male Baltimore.
Spurious Oriole of ditto.	*Male*. . . .	Male Orchard Oriole, Fig. 14.
	Female. .	Ditto ditto, Fig. 12.
Catesby's Baltimore Oriole.	*Male*. . . .	Male Baltimore.
	Female. .	Not mentioned.
Spurious Baltimore of ditto.	*Male*. . . .	Male Orchard Oriole, Fig. 12.
	Female. .	Ditto ditto, Fig. 14.

Among all these authors Catesby is doubtless the most inexcusable, having lived for several years in America, where he had an opportunity of being more correct: yet, when it is considered, that the female of this bird is so much shyer than the male; that it is seldom seen; and that, while the males are flying around and bewailing an approach to their nest, the females keep aloof, watching every movement of the enemy in restless but silent anxiety; it is less to be wondered at, I say, that two birds of the same kind, but different in plumage, making their appearance together at such times, should be taken for male and female of the same nest, without doubt or examination, as, from that strong sympathy for each other's distress which prevails so universally among them at this season, it is difficult sometimes to distinguish between the sufferer and the sympathizing neighbor.

The female of the Orchard Oriole, Fig. 11, is six inches and a half in length, and eleven inches in extent; the color above is a yellow olive, inclining to a brownish tint on the back; the wings are dusky brown, lesser wing-coverts tipped with yellowish white, greater coverts and secondaries exteriorly edged with the same, primaries slightly so; tail, rounded at the extremity, the two exterior feathers three quarters of an inch shorter than the middle ones; whole lower parts, yellow; bill and legs, light blue; the former bent a little, very sharp pointed, and black towards the extremity; iris of the eye, hazel; pupil, black. The young male of the first season corresponds nearly with the above description. But in the succeeding spring he makes his appearance with a large patch of black marking the front, lores, and throat, as represented in Fig. 12. In this stage, too, the black sometimes makes its appearance on the two middle feathers of the tail; and slight stains of reddish are seen commencing on the sides and belly. The rest of the plumage as in the female; this continuing nearly the same, on the same bird, during the remainder of the season. At the same time, other individuals are found, as represented by Fig. 13, which are at least birds of the third summer. These are mottled with black and olive on the upper parts of the back, and with reddish bay and yellow on the belly, sides, and vent, scattered in the most irregular manner, not alike in any two individuals; and, generally, the two middle feathers of the tail are black, and the others centred with the same color. This bird is now evidently approaching to its perfect plumage, as represented in Fig. 14, where the black spreads over the whole head, neck, upper part of the back, breast, wings, and tail; the reddish bay, or bright chestnut, occupying the lower part of the breast, the belly, vent, rump, tail-coverts, and three lower rows of the lesser wing-coverts. The black on the head is deep and velvety; that of the wings inclining to brown; the greater wing-coverts are tipped with white. In the same orchard, and at the same time, males in each of these states of plumage may be found, united to their respective plain-colored mates.

In all these, the manners, mode of building, food, and notes, are, generally speaking, the same, differing no more than those of any other individuals belonging to one common species. The female appears always nearly the same.

I have said that these birds construct their nests very differently from the Baltimores. They are so particularly fond of frequenting orchards, that scarcely one orchard in summer is without them. They usually suspend their nest from the twigs of the apple-tree; and often from the extremities of the outward branches. It is formed exteriorly of a particular species of long, tough, and flexible grass, knit, or sewed through and through in a thousand directions, as if actually done with a needle. An old lady of my acquaintance, to whom I was one day showing this curious fabrication, after admiring its texture for some time, asked me, in a tone between joke and earnest, whether I did not think it possible to learn these birds to darn stockings. This nest is hemispherical, three inches deep by four in breadth; the concavity scarcely two inches deep by two in diameter. I had the curiosity to detach one of the fibres, or stalks of dried grass, from the nest, and found it to measure thirteen inches in length, and in that distance was thirty-four times hooked through and returned, winding round and round the nest! The inside is usually composed of wool, or the light, downy appendages attached to the seeds of the *Platanus occidentalis*, or button-wood, which form a very soft and commodious bed. Here and there the outward work is extended to an adjoining twig, round which it is strongly twisted, to give more stability to the whole, and prevent it from being overset by the wind.

When they choose the long, pendent branches of the weeping willow to build in, as they frequently do, the nest, though formed of the same materials, is made much deeper, and of slighter texture. The circumference is marked out by a number of these pensile twigs that descend on each side like ribs, supporting the whole; their thick foliage, at the same time, completely concealing the nest from view. The depth in this case is increased to four or five inches, and the whole is made much slighter. These long, pendent branches, being sometimes twelve and even fifteen feet in length, have a large sweep in the wind, and render the first of these precautions necessary, to prevent the eggs or young from being thrown out; and the close shelter afforded by the remarkable thickness of the foliage is, no doubt, the cause of the latter. Two of these nests, such as I have here described, are now lying before me, and exhibit not only art in the construction, but judgment in adapting their fabrication so judiciously to their particular situations. If the actions of birds proceeded, as some would have us believe, from the mere impulses of that thing called *instinct*, individuals of the same species would uniformly build their nest in the same manner, wherever they might happen to fix it; but it is evident from those just mentioned, and a thousand such circumstances, that they reason *à priori*, from cause to consequence; providently managing with a constant eye to future necessity and convenience.

The eggs, one of which is represented on the same plate, (Fig. *a*,) are usually four, of a very pale bluish tint, with a few small specks of brown, and spots of dark purple. An egg of the Baltimore Oriole is exhibited beside it, (Fig. *b* ; *) both of these were minutely copied from nature, and are sufficient of themselves to determine, beyond all possibility of doubt, the identity of the two species. I may add, that Mr. Charles W. Peale, proprietor of the museum in Philadelphia, who, as a practical naturalist, stands deservedly first in the first rank of American connoisseurs, and who has done more for the promotion of that sublime science than all our speculative theorists together, has expressed to me his perfect conviction of the changes which these birds pass through; having himself examined them both in spring and towards the latter part of summer, and having at the present time in his possession thirty or forty individuals of this species, in almost every gradation of change.

The Orchard Oriole, though partly a dependant on the industry of the farmer, is no sneaking pilferer, but an open and truly beneficent friend. To all those countless multitudes of destructive bugs and caterpillars that infest the fruit trees in spring and summer, preying on the leaves, blossoms, and embryo of the fruit, he is a deadly enemy; devouring them wherever he can find them, and destroying, on an average, some hundreds of them every day, without offering the slightest injury to the fruit, however much it may stand in his way. I have witnessed instances where the entrance to his nest was more than half closed up by a cluster of apples, which he could have easily demolished in half a minute; but, as if holding the property of his patron sacred, or considering it as a natural bulwark to his own, he slid out and in with the greatest gentleness and caution. I am not sufficiently conversant in entomology to particularize the different species of insects on which he feeds, but I have good reason for believing that they are almost altogether such as commit the greatest depredations on the fruits of the orchard; and, as he visits us at a time when his services are of the greatest value, and, like a faithful guardian, takes up his station where the enemy is most to be expected,

* The references here are to Wilson's original edition.

he 'ought to be held in respectful esteem, and protected by every considerate husbandman. Nor is the gayety of his song one of his least recommendations. Being an exceedingly active, sprightly, and restless bird, he is on the ground — on the trees — flying and carolling in his hurried manner, in almost one and the same instant. His notes are shrill and lively, but uttered with such rapidity and seeming confusion, that the ear is unable to follow them distinctly. Between these, he has a single note, which is agreeable and interesting. Wherever he is protected, he shows his confidence and gratitude by his numbers and familiarity. In the botanic gardens of my worthy and scientific friends, the Messrs. Bartrams of Kingsess, which present an epitome of almost every thing that is rare, useful, and beautiful in the vegetable kingdom of this western continent, and where the murderous gun scarce ever intrudes, the Orchard Oriole revels without restraint through thickets of aromatic flowers and blossoms, and, heedless of the busy gardener that labors below, hangs his nest, in perfect security, on the branches over his head.

The female sits fourteen days; the young remain in the nest ten days afterwards, before they venture abroad, which is generally about the middle of June. Nests of this species, with eggs, are sometimes found so late as the 20th of July, which must either belong to birds that have lost their first nest, or, it is probable that many of them raise two broods in the same season, though I am not positive of the fact.

The Orchard Orioles arrive in Pennsylvania rather later than the Baltimores, commonly about the first week in May, and extend as far as the Province of Maine. They are also more numerous towards the mountains than the latter species. In traversing the country near the Blue Ridge, in the month of August, I have seen at least five of this species for one of the Baltimore. Early in September, they take their departure for the south; their term of residence here being little more than four months. Previous to their departure, the young birds become gregarious, and frequent the rich extensive meadows of the Schuylkill, below Philadelphia, in flocks of from thirty to forty, or upwards. They are easily raised from the nest, and soon become agreeable domestics. One which I reared and kept through the winter, whistled with great clearness and vivacity at two months old. It had an odd manner of moving its head and neck, slowly and regularly, and in various directions, when intent on observing any thing, without stirring its body. This motion was as slow and regular as that of a snake. When at night a candle was brought into the room, it became restless, and evidently dissatisfied, fluttering about the cage, as if seeking to get out; but, when the cage was placed on the same table with the candle, it seemed extremely well pleased, fed and drank, dressed, shook and arranged its plumage, sat as close to the light as possible, and sometimes chanted a few broken, irregular notes in that situation, as I sat writing or reading beside it. I also kept a young female of the same nest, during the greatest part of winter, but could not observe, in that time, any change in its plumage.*

---

* This bird is interesting, as showing the remarkable change of color which takes place in the group, and which, in many instances, has been the occasion of a mul-

GREAT AMERICAN SHRIKE, OR BUTCHER BIRD.
LANIUS EXCUBITOR.* — Fig. 15.

La pie grische-grise, *De Buffon*, i. 296. *Pl. enl.* 445. — *Peale's Museum*, No. 664. — White Whisky John, *Phil. Trans.* lxii. 386. — *Arct. Zool.* ii. No. 127.

LANIUS BOREALIS. — Vieillot.

Lanius borealis, *Vieill.* — *North. Zool.* ii. 3.

THE form and countenance of this bird bespeak him full of courage and energy; and his true character does not belie his appearance, for he possesses these qualities in a very eminent degree. He is represented on the plate rather less than his true size,† but in just proportion, and with a fidelity that will enable the European naturalist to determine, whether this be really the same with the great cinereous Shrike (*Lanius excubitor*, Linn.) of the eastern continent, or not; though the progressive variableness of the plumage, passing, according to age, and sometimes to climate, from ferruginous to pale ash, and even to a bluish white, renders it impossible that this should be an exact representation of every individual.

This species is by no means numerous in the lower parts of Pennsylvania; though most so during the months of November, December, and March. Soon after this, it retires to the north, and to the higher inland parts of the country to breed. It frequents the deepest forests; builds a large and compact nest in the upright fork of a small tree; composed outwardly of dry grass, and whitish moss, and warmly lined within with feathers. The female lays six eggs, of a pale cinereous color, thickly marked at the greater end with spots and streaks of rufous. She sits fifteen days. The young are produced early in June, sometimes towards the latter end of May; and during the greater part of the first season are of a brown ferruginous color on the back.

When we compare the beak of this species with his legs and claws,

tiplication of species. It will rank with the Baltimore Bird in the *Icterus* of Brisson, and they will form the only individuals belonging to the northern continent of America. According to Audubon, the flesh of the Orchard Oriole is esteemed by the Creoles of Louisiana, and at the season when the broods have collected, and feed most upon insects in the moist meadows, they are procured for the table in considerable abundance. — ED.

* Wilson has marked this species with a note of doubt, showing the accuracy of his observation where he had such slender means of making out species; a mistake also into which C. L. Bonaparte, with greater opportunities, has also fallen. Vieillot seems to have been the first to distinguish it, and Mr. Swainson has satisfactorily pointed out the differences, in the *Northern Zoology. Lanius excubitor* is not found at all in America, and this species seems to fill up its want; the chief differences are in the size, *Lanius borealis* being larger. The female is of a browner shade, with more gray underneath; the former a distribution of color in the females unknown among those bearing similar shades; in habits they in every way agree. — ED.

† In Wilson's original edition.

5

they appear to belong to two very different orders of birds; the former approaching, in its conformation, to that of the Accipitrine; the latter to those of the Pies; and, indeed, in his food and manners he is assimilated to both. For though man has arranged and subdivided this numerous class of animals into separate tribes and families, yet nature has united these to each other by such nice gradations, and so intimately, that it is hardly possible to determine where one tribe ends, or the succeeding commences. We therefore find several eminent naturalists classing this genus of birds with the Accipitrine, others with the Pies. Like the former, he preys occasionally on other birds; and, like the latter, on insects, particularly grasshoppers, which I believe to be his principal food; having at almost all times, even in winter, found them in his stomach. In the month of December, and while the country was deeply covered with snow, I shot one of these birds near the head waters of the Mohawk River, in the state of New York, the stomach of which was entirely filled with large black spiders. He was of a much purer white above, than any I have since met with; though evidently of the same species with the present; and I think it probable that the males become lighter colored as they advance in age, till the minute transverse lines of brown on the lower parts almost disappear.

In his manners he has more resemblance to the Pies than to birds of prey, particularly in the habit of carrying off his surplus food, as if to hoard it for future exigencies; with this difference, that Crows, Jays, Magpies, &c., conceal theirs at random, in holes and crevices, where, perhaps, it is forgotten, or never again found; while the Butcher Bird sticks his on thorns and bushes, where it shrivels in the sun, and soon becomes equally useless to the hoarder. Both retain the same habits in a state of confinement, whatever the food may be that is presented to them.

This habit of the Shrike, of seizing and impaling grasshoppers and other insects on thorns, has given rise to an opinion that he places their carcasses there by way of baits, to allure small birds to them, while he himself lies in ambush to surprise and destroy them. In this, however, they appear to allow him a greater portion of reason and contrivance than he seems entitled to, or than other circumstances will altogether warrant; for we find, that he not only serves grasshoppers in this manner, but even small birds themselves, as those have assured me who have kept them in cages in this country, and amused themselves with their manœuvres. If so, we might as well suppose the farmer to be inviting Crows to his corn when he hangs up their carcasses around it, as the Butcher Bird to be decoying small birds by a display of the dead bodies of their comrades!

In the *Transactions of the American Philosophical Society*, vol. iv. p. 124, the reader may find a long letter on this subject from Mr. John Heckewelder, of Bethlehem, to Dr. Barton; the substance of which is as follows:—That on the 17th of December, 1795, he (Mr. Heckewelder) went to visit a young orchard which had been planted a few weeks before, and was surprised to observe on every one of the trees one, and on some two and three grasshoppers, stuck down on the sharp, thorny branches; that, on inquiring of his tenant the reason of this, he informed him, that they were stuck there by a small bird of prey, called by the Germans, *Neuntoedter*, (Nine-killer,) which caught and stuck nine grasshoppers a day; and he supposed that, as the bird itself never fed on grasshoppers, it must do it for pleasure.   Mr. Heckewelder now recollected, that one of those Nine-killers had, many years before, taken a favorite bird of his out of his cage at the window; since which, he had paid particular attention to it; and being perfectly satisfied that it lived entirely on mice and small birds, and, moreover, observing the grasshoppers on the trees all fixed in natural positions, as if alive, he began to conjecture that this was done to decoy such small birds as feed on these insects to the spot, that he might have an opportunity of devouring them.   "If it were true," says he, "that this little hawk had stuck them up for himself, how long would he be in feeding on one or two hundred grasshoppers?   But if it be intended to seduce the smaller birds to feed on these insects, in order to have an opportunity of catching them, that number, or even one half, or less, may be a good bait all winter," &c.

This is, indeed, a very pretty, fanciful theory, and would entitle our bird to the epithet *fowler*, perhaps with more propriety than *lanius*, or *butcher*; but, notwithstanding the attention which Mr. Heckewelder professes to have paid to this bird, he appears not only to have been ignorant that grasshoppers were, in fact, the favorite food of this Nine-killer, but never once to have considered, that grasshoppers would be but a very insignificant and tasteless bait for our winter birds, which are chiefly those of the Finch kind, that feed almost exclusively on hard seeds and gravel; and among whom five hundred grasshoppers might be stuck up on trees and bushes, and remain there untouched by any of them forever.   Besides, where is his necessity of having recourse to such refined stratagems, when he can, at any time, seize upon small birds by mere force of flight?   I have seen him, in an open field, dart after one of our small Sparrows with the rapidity of an arrow, and kill it almost instantly.   Mr. William Bartram long ago informed me, that one of these Shrikes had the temerity to pursue a Snow Bird (*F. Hudsonia*) into an open cage, which stood in the garden; and, before they could arrive to its assistance, had already strangled and scalped it, though he lost his liberty by the exploit.   In short, I am of opinion, that his resolution and activity are amply sufficient to enable him to procure these small birds whenever he wants them, which, I believe, is never but when hard pressed by necessity, and a deficiency of his favorite insects; and that the Crow or the Blue Jay may, with the same probability, be supposed to be laying baits for mice and flying squirrels, when they are hoarding their Indian corn, as he for birds, while thus disposing of the exuberance of his favorite food.   Both the former and the latter retain the same habits in a state of confinement; the one filling every seam and chink of his cage with grain, crumbs of bread, &c., and the other sticking up, not only insects, but flesh, and the bodies of such birds as are thrown in to him, on nails or sharpened sticks fixed up for the purpose.   Nor, say others, is this practice of the Shrike difficult to be accounted for.   Nature has given to this bird a strong, sharp, and powerful beak, a broad head, and great strength in the muscles of his neck; but his legs, feet, and claws are by no means proportionably strong, and are unequal to the task of grasping and tearing his prey, like those of the Owl and Falcon kind. He, therefore, wisely avails himself of the powers of the former, both in strangling his prey, and in tearing it to pieces while feeding.

The character of the Butcher Bird is entitled to no common degree of respect. His activity is visible in all his motions; his courage and intrepidity beyond every other bird of his size, (one of his own tribe only excepted, *L. tyrannus,* or King Bird;) and in affection for his young, he is surpassed by no other. He associates with them in the latter part of summer, the whole family hunting in company. He attacks the largest Hawk or Eagle in their defence, with a resolution truly astonishing; so that all of them respect him, and, on every occasion, decline the contest. As the snows of winter approach, he descends from the mountainous forests, and from the regions of the north, to the more cultivated parts of the country, hovering about our hedge-rows, orchards, and meadows, and disappears again early in April.

The Great American Shrike is ten inches in length, and thirteen in extent; the upper part of the head, neck, and back, is pale cinereous; sides of the head, nearly white, crossed with a bar of black that passes from the nostril, through the eye, to the middle of the neck; the whole under parts, in some specimens, are nearly white, in others more dusky, and thickly marked with minute transverse curving lines of light brown; the wings are black, tipped with white, with a single spot of white on the primaries, just below their coverts; the scapulars, or long downy feathers that fall over the upper part of the wing, are pure white; the rump and tail-coverts, a very fine gray or light ash; the tail is cuneiform, consisting of twelve feathers, the two middle ones wholly black, the others tipped more and more with white to the exterior ones, which are nearly all white; the legs, feet, and claws are black; the beak straight, thick, of a light blue color; the upper mandible furnished with a sharp process, bending down greatly at the point, where it is black, and beset at the base with a number of long black hairs or bristles; the nostrils are also thickly covered with recumbent hairs; the iris of the eye is a light hazel; pupil, black. Fig. 15 will give a perfect idea of the bird. The female is easily distinguished by being ferruginous on the back and head, and having the band of black extending only behind the eye, and of a dirty brown or burnt color; the under parts are also something rufous, and the curving lines more strongly marked; she is rather less than the male, which is different from birds of prey in general, the females of which are usually the larger of the two.

In the *Arctic Zoology,* we are told that this species is frequent in Russia, but does not extend to Siberia; yet one was taken within Behring's Straits, on the Asiatic side, in lat. 66°; and the species probably extends over the whole continent of North America, from the Western Ocean. Mr. Bell, while on his travels through Russia, had one of these birds given him, which he kept in a room, having fixed up a sharpened stick for him in the wall; and on turning small birds loose in the room, the Butcher Bird instantly caught them by the throat in such a manner as soon to suffocate them; and then stuck them on the stick, pulling them on with bill and claws; and so served as many as were turned loose, one after another, on the same stick.*

PINE GROSBEAK. — LOXIA ENUCLEATOR. — Fig. 16.

Loxia enucleator, *Linn. Syst.* i. p. 299, 3. — Le dur bec, ou gros bec de Canada, *Buffon*, iii. p. 457. *Pl. enl.* 135, 1. — *Edw.* 123, 124. — *Lath. Syn.* iii. p. 111, 5. — *Peale's Museum*, No. 5652.

CORYTHUS ENUCLEATOR. — Cuvier.†

Loxia enucleator, *Penn. Arct. Zool.* ii. p. 348. — Corythus enucleator, *Cuv. Regn. Anim.* i. p. 391. — *Fleem. Br. Zool.* p. 76. — Bouvreuil dur bec, Pyrrhula enucleator, *Temm.* i. 333. — Pine Grosbeak, Pyrrhula enucleator, *Selby, Orn. Ill.* i. 256, pl. 53. — Pyrrhula enucleator, *Bonap. Syn.* 114.

THIS is perhaps one of the gayest plumaged land birds that frequent the inhospitable regions of the north, whence they are driven, as if with reluctance, by the rigors of winter, to visit Canada and some of the Northern and Middle States; returning to Hudson's Bay so early as April. The specimen from which our drawing was taken was shot on a cedar-tree, a few miles to the north of Philadelphia, in the month of December; and a faithful resemblance of the original, as it then appeared, is exhibited in Fig. 16. A few days afterwards, another bird of the same species was killed not far from Gray's Ferry,

---

* EDWARDS, vii. 231.

† This interesting species seems nowhere of common occurrence; it is very seldom seen in collections; and boxes of skins, either from different parts of Europe, or America, can seldom rank the Pine Grosbeak among their number; the testimony of all travellers in America, who have attended to nature, correspond in their accounts; and one of the latest, Mr. Audubon, has mentioned it to me as of extreme scarcity. In this country, they seem to be of equal rarity, though they are generally placed in our list of British birds without any remark. Pennant observes, (*Arct. Zool.* ii. 348,) that he has seen them in the forests of Invercauld; and Mr. Selby says, (*Br. Orn.* 257,) that, from the testimony of the gamekeepers, whom he had an opportunity of speaking with in the Highlands, they may be ranked only as occasional visitants. I am aware, however, of no instance of their being killed in this country. Pennant infers, from those which he saw in the month of August, that they breed here. "Such a conclusion," Mr. Selby justly remarks, "ought scarcely to be inferred from this fact, as a sufficient interval of time had elapsed for these individuals to have emigrated from Norway, or other northern countries, to Scotland, after incubation, as they are known to breed as early as May in their natural haunts." I have been unable to find any trace whatever of their ever breeding in this country; most of the migrating species breed very early, and those that change their station for the sake of finding a breeding place, commence the office of building, &c. immediately on their arrival, a necessary circumstance to enable the young to perform their migration before the change of season. Cuvier has formed his genus *Corythus* of this individual, which still remains the only one that has yet been placed in it; but I am of opinion, that the Crimson-necked Bullfinch (*Pyrrhula frontalis*, Say) should stand very near, or with it. Their alliance to the true Bullfinches is very great, and Mr. Swainson's genus, *Crithagra*, may form another near ally. — ED.

5 *

four miles south from Philadelphia, which proved to be a female. In this part of the state of Pennsylvania, they are rare birds, and seldom seen. As they do not, to my knowledge, breed in any part of this state, I am unable, from personal observation, to speak of their manners or musical talents. Mr. Pennant says, they sing on their first arrival in the country round Hudson's Bay, but soon become silent; make their nest on trees, at a small height from the ground, with sticks, and line it with feathers. The female lays four white eggs, which are hatched in June. Forster observes, that they visit Hudson's Bay only in May, on their way to the north; and are not observed to return in the autumn; and that their food consists of birchwillow buds, and others of the same nature.*

The Pine Grosbeak measures nine inches in length, and fourteen inches in extent; the head, neck, breast, and rump, are of a rich crimson, palest on the breast; the feathers on the middle of the back are centred with arrow-shaped spots of black, and skirted with crimson, which gives the plumage a considerable flush of red there; those on the shoulders are of a deep slate color, partially skirted with red, and light ash. The greater wing-coverts and next superior row are broadly tipped with white, and slightly tinged with reddish; wings and tail, black, edged with light brown; tail, considerably forked; lower part of the belly, ash color; vent-feathers, skirted with white, and streaked with black; legs, glossy black; bill, a brownish horn color, very thick, short, and hooked at the point; the upper mandible overhanging the lower considerably, approaching in its form to that of the Parrot; base of the bill, covered with recumbent hairs of a dark brown color. The whole plumage, near the roots, as in most other birds, is of a deep bluish ash color. The female was half an inch shorter, and answered nearly to the above description; only, those parts that in the male were crimson, were in her of a dirty yellowish color. The female, according to Forster, referred to above, has those parts which in the male are red, more of an orange tint; and he censures Edwards for having represented the female of too bright a red. It is possible, that my specimen of the female might have been a bird of the first season, not come to its full colors. Those figured by Mr. Edwards † were both brought from Hudson's Bay, and appear to be the same with the one now before us, though his coloring of the female differs materially from his description.

If this, as Mr. Pennant asserts, be the same species with that of the eastern continent, it would seem to inhabit almost the whole extent of the arctic regions. It is found in the north of Scotland, where Pennant suspects it breeds. It inhabits Europe as far north as Drontheim; is common in all the pine forests of Asia, in Siberia, and the north of Russia; is taken in autumn about Petersburg, and brought to market in great numbers. It returns to Lapland in spring; is found in Newfoundland, and on the western coast of North America.‡

Were I to reason from analogy, I would say, that, from the great resemblance of this bird to the Purple Finch, (*Fringilla purpurea*,) it does not attain its full plumage until the second summer; and is

* *Philosophical Transactions*, lxii. 402.   † EDW. iii. 124.   ‡ PENNANT.

subject to considerable change of color in moulting, which may have occasioned all the differences we find concerning it in different authors. But this is actually ascertained to be the case; for Mr. Edwards saw two of these birds alive in London, in cages; the person in whose custody they were, said they came from Norway; that they had moulted their feathers, and were not afterwards so beautiful as they were at first. One of them, he says, was colored very much like the Green Finch, (*L. chloris.*) The Purple Finch, though much smaller, has the rump, head, back, and breast, nearly of the same color as the Pine Grosbeak, feeds in the same manner, on the same food, and is also subject to like changes of color.

Since writing the above, I have kept one of these Pine Grosbeaks, a male, for more than half a year. In the month of August those parts of the plumage which were red became of a greenish yellow, and continue so still. In May and June its song, though not so loud as some birds of its size, was extremely clear, mellow, and sweet. It would warble out this for a whole morning together, and acquired several of the notes of a Red-Bird (*L. cardinalis*) that hung near it. It is exceedingly tame and familiar, and when it wants food or water, utters a continual melancholy and anxious note. It was caught in winter near the North River, thirty or forty miles above New York.

RUBY-CROWNED WREN. — SYLVIA CALENDULA. — Fig. 17.

Le Roitelet rubis, *De Buff.* v. 373. — *Edw.* 254. — *Lath. Syn.* ii. 511. — *Arct. Zool.* 320. — Regulus cristatus alter vertice rubini coloris, *Bartram,* p. 292. — *Peale's Museum,* No. 7244.

REGULUS CALENDULUS. — Stephens.[*]

Regulus calendulus, *Steph. Cont. Sh. Zool.* vol. x. p. 760. — *Bonap. Synop.* 91.

This little bird visits us early in the spring, from the south, and is generally first found among the maple blossoms, about the beginning of April. These failing, it has recourse to those of the peach, apple, and other fruit-trees, partly for the tops of the sweet and slender stamina of the flowers, and partly for the winged insects that hover among them. In the middle of summer, I have rarely met with these birds in Pennsylvania; and as they penetrate as far north as the country round Hudson's Bay, and also breed there, it accounts for their late arrival here, in fall. They then associate with the different species of Titmouse, and the Golden-crested Wren; and are particularly numerous in the month of October, and beginning of November, in orchards, among the decaying leaves of the apple-trees, that at

[*] See note to *Regulus cristatus.*

that season are infested with great numbers of small, black-winged insects, among which they make great havock. I have often regretted the painful necessity one is under of taking away the lives of such inoffensive, useful little creatures, merely to obtain a more perfect knowledge of the species; for they appear so busy, so active, and unsuspecting, as to continue searching about the same twig, even after their companions have been shot down beside them. They are more remarkably so in autumn, which may be owing to the great number of young and inexperienced birds which are then among them; and frequently, at this season, I have stood under the tree, motionless, to observe them, while they gleaned among the low branches sometimes within a foot or two of my head. They are extremely adroit in catching their prey; have only at times a feeble chirp; visit the tops of the tallest trees, as well as the lowest bushes; and continue generally for a considerable time among the branches of the same tree, darting about from place to place; appearing, when on the top of a high maple, no bigger than humble-bees.

The Ruby-crowned Wren is four inches long, and six in extent; the upper parts of the head, neck, and back, are of a fine greenish olive, with a considerable tinge of yellow; wings and tail, dusky purplish brown, exteriorly edged with yellow olive; secondaries, and first row of wing-coverts, edged and tipped with white, with a spot of deep purplish brown across the secondaries, just below their coverts; the hind head is ornamented with an oblong lateral spot of vermilion, usually almost hid by the other plumage; round the eye, a ring of yellowish white; whole under parts, of the same tint; legs, dark brown; feet and claws, yellow; bill, slender, straight, not notched, furnished with a few black hairs at the base; inside of the mouth, orange. The female differs very little in its plumage from the male, the colors being less lively, and the bird somewhat less. Notwithstanding my utmost endeavors, I have never been able to discover their nest; though, from the circumstance of having found them sometimes here in summer, I am persuaded that they occasionally breed in Pennsylvania; but I know several birds, no larger than this, that usually build on the extremities of the tallest trees in the woods; which I have discovered from their beginning before the leaves are out; many others, no doubt, choose similar situations; and should they delay building until the woods are thickened with leaves, it is no easy matter to discover them. In fall, they are so extremely fat, as almost to dissolve between the fingers as you open them; owing to the great abundance of their favorite insects at that time.

SHORE-LARK. — ALAUDA ALPESTRIS. — Fig. 18.

Alauda alpestris, *Linn. Syst.* 239. — *Lath. Synop.* ii. 385. — *Peale's Museum*, No. 5190. — Alauda campestris, gutture flavo, *Bartram*, p. 290. — L'Alouette de Virginia, *De Buff.* v. 55. — *Catesb.* i. 32.

ALAUDA ALPESTRIS. — Linnæus.

Alauda alpestris alouette à Hause col noir, *Temm.* i. 279. — *Bonap. Synop.* 102. — *Vieill. Gal. des Ois.* pl. 155, p. 256. — Alauda cornuta, *Swain. Synop.* — *Birds of Mexico, Phil. Mag. & Ann.* 1827, p. 434. — *North. Zool.* ii. p. 245.

This is the most beautiful of its genus, at least in this part of the world. It is one of our winter birds of passage, arriving from the north in the fall; usually staying with us the whole winter, frequenting sandy plains and open downs, and is numerous in the Southern States, as far as Georgia, during that season. They fly high, in loose, scattered flocks; and at these times have a single cry, almost exactly like the Sky-Lark of Britain. They are very numerous in many tracts of New Jersey, and are frequently brought to Philadelphia market. They are then generally very fat, and are considered excellent eating. Their food seems principally to consist of small, round, compressed, black seeds, buckwheat, oats, &c., with a large proportion of gravel. On the flat commons, within the boundaries of the city of Philadelphia, flocks of them are regularly seen during the whole winter. In the stomach of these I have found, in numerous instances, quantities of the eggs or larvæ of certain insects, mixed with a kind of slimy earth. About the middle of March they generally disappear, on their route to the north.[*] Forster informs us that they visit the environs of Albany Fort in the beginning of May, but go farther north to breed; that they feed on grass seeds and buds of the sprig birch, and run into small holes, keeping close to the ground, from whence the natives call them *Chi-chup-pi-sue.*[†] This same species appears also to be found in Poland, Russia, and Siberia, in winter, from whence they also retire farther north on the approach of spring; except in the north-east parts, and near the high mountains.[‡]

The length of this bird is seven inches, the extent twelve inches; the forehead, throat, sides of the neck, and line over the eye, are of a delicate straw, or Naples yellow, elegantly relieved by a bar of black,

---

[*] In winter, says Pennant, they retire to the southern provinces in great flights; but it is only by severe weather that they reach Virginia and Carolina. They frequent sand hills on the sea shore, and feed on the sea-side oats, or *Uniola paniculata.* They have a single note, like the Sky-Lark in winter. — Temminck mentions them as birds of passage in Germany, and that they breed also in Asia. One or two specimens have lately been killed in England, so that their geographic range is pretty considerable. The *Alauda calandra* of Linnæus is introduced into the *Northern Zoology*, as an inhabitant of the Fur countries, on the authority of a specimen in the British Museum, and will stand as the second Lark found in that country. — Ed.

[†] *Philosophical Transactions*, vol. lxii. p. 398.

[‡] *Arctic Zoology.*

that passes from the nostril to the eye, below which it falls, rounding, to the depth of three quarters of an inch; the yellow on the forehead and over the eye, is bounded within, for its whole length, with black, which covers part of the crown; the breast is ornamented with a broad, fan-shaped patch of black; this, as well as all the other spots of black, are marked with minute curves of yellow points; back of the neck, and towards the shoulders, a light drab, tinged with lake; lesser wing-coverts, bright cinnamon; greater wing-coverts, the same, interiorly dusky, and tipped with whitish; back and wings, drab colored, tinged with reddish, each feather of the former having a streak of dusky black down its centre; primaries, deep dusky, tipped and edged with whitish; exterior feathers, most so; secondaries, broadly edged with light drab, and scolloped at the tips; tail, forked, black; the two middle feathers, which by some have been mistaken for the coverts, are reddish drab, centred with brownish black; the two outer ones on each side, exteriorly edged with white; breast, of a dusky vinous tinge, and marked with spots or streaks of the same; the belly and vent, white; sides, streaked with bay; bill short, (Latham, in mistake, says seven inches,*) of a dusky blue color; tongue, truncate and bifid; legs and claws, black; hind heel, very long, and almost straight; iris of the eye, hazel. One glance at Fig. 18 will give a better idea than the whole of this minute description, which, however, has been rendered necessary by the errors of others. The female has little or no black on the crown; and the yellow on the front is narrow, and of a dirty tinge.

There is a singular appearance in this bird, which I have never seen taken notice of by former writers, viz., certain long, black feathers, which extend, by equal distances beyond each other, above the eye-brow; these are longer, more pointed, and of a different texture from the rest around them; and the bird possesses the power of erecting them, so as to appear as if horned, like some of the Owl tribe. Having kept one of these birds alive for some time, I was much amused at this odd appearance, and think it might furnish a very suitable specific appellation, viz. *Alauda cornuta*, or Horned Lark. These horns become scarcely perceivable after the bird is dead. The head is slightly crested.

Shore-Lark and Sky-Lark are names by which this species is usually known in different parts of the Union. They are said to sing well, mounting in the air, in the manner of the Song-Lark of Europe; but this is only in those countries where they breed. I have never heard of their nests being found within the territory of the United States.

* *Synopsis*, vol. ii. p. 385.

MARYLAND YELLOW-THROAT. — SYLVIA MARILANDICA. — Fig. 19.

Turdus trichas, *Linn. Syst.* i. 293. — *Edw.* 237. — Yellow-breasted Warbler, *Arct. Zool.* ii. No. 283. *Id.* 284. — Le Figuier aux joues noires, *De Buff.* v. 292. — La Fauvette à poitrine jaune de la Louisiane, *Buff.* v. 162. *Pl. enl.* 709, fig. 2. — *Lath. Syn.* iv. 433, 32. — *Peale's Museum,* No. 6902.

TRICHUS PERSONATUS. — Swainson.*

Trichas personatus, *Swain. Zool. Journ.* No. 10, p. 167. — The Yellow-breasted Warbler, or Maryland Yellow-Throat, *Aud.* i. pl. 23, p. 121.

THIS is one of the humble inhabitants of briers, brambles, alder bushes, and such shrubbery as grows most luxuriantly in low, watery situations; and might with propriety be denominated *Humility,* its business or ambition seldom leading it higher than the tops of the underwood. Insects and their larvæ are its usual food. It dives into the deepest of the thicket, rambles among the roots, searches round the stems, examines both sides of the leaf, raising itself on its legs, so as to peep into every crevice; amusing itself at times with a very simple, and not disagreeable, song or twitter, *whititilee, whititilee, whititilee;* pausing for half a minute or so, and then repeating its notes as before. It inhabits the whole United States from Maine to Florida, and also Louisiana; and is particularly numerous in the low, swampy thickets of Maryland, Pennsylvania, and New Jersey. It is by no means shy; but seems deliberate and unsuspicious, as if the places it frequented, or its own diminutiveness, were its sufficient security. It often visits the fields of growing rye, wheat, barley, &c., and no doubt performs the part of a friend to the farmer, in ridding the stalks of vermin, that might otherwise lay waste his fields. It seldom approaches the farm-house, or city; but lives in obscurity and peace, amidst its favorite

* Mr. Swainson has formed from this species his genus *Trichas,* and bestowed upon it the new and appropriate name of *personatus,* or *masked; Marilandica* of Brisson and Wilson could scarcely be retained, *Trochas* of Linnæus having the priority. The latter is now converted into a generic term; and as the species does not seem entirely confined to Maryland, another and more appropriate than either will perhaps make less confusion than the attempts to restore some old one. Mr. Swainson makes the following remarks upon the genus : — "This form is intimately connected with *Synalaxis,* and two or three other groups peculiar to Africa and Australia. Feebleness of flight and strength of foot separate these birds from the typical genera; while the strength and curvature of the hind claw forbid us to associate them with the true *Motacillæ.*"

The female is figured on No. 86, of this volume, where it is mentioned as one of the birds whose nest the Cow Bunting selects to deposit her eggs in. "The nest," according to Mr. Audubon, "is placed on the ground, and partly sunk in it : it is now and then covered over in the form of an oven, from which circumstance, children name this warbler the *Oven-bird.* It is composed externally of withered leaves and grass, and is lined with hair. The eggs are from four to six, of a white color, speckled with light brown, and are deposited about the middle of May. Sometimes two broods are reared in a season. I have never observed the egg of the Cow Bunting in the nests of the second brood."

The male birds do not attain their full plumage until the second spring. — ED.

thickets. It arrives in Pennsylvania about the middle, or last week, of April, and begins to build its nest about the middle of May: this is fixed on the ground, among the dried leaves, in the very depth of a thicket of briers, sometimes arched over, and a small hole left for entrance; the materials are dry leaves and fine grass, lined with coarse hair; the eggs are five, white, or semi-transparent, marked with specks of reddish brown. The young leave the nest about the 22d of June; and a second brood is often raised in the same season. Early in September they leave us, returning to the south.

This pretty little species is four inches and three quarters long, and six inches and a quarter in extent; back, wings, and tail, green olive, which also covers the upper part of the neck, but approaches to cinereous on the crown; the eyes are inserted in a band of black, which passes from the front, on both sides, reaching half way down the neck; this is bounded above by another band of white, deepening into light blue; throat, breast, and vent, brilliant yellow; belly, a fainter tinge of the same color; inside coverts of the wings, also yellow; tips and inner vanes of the wings, dusky brown; tail, cuneiform, dusky, edged with olive green; bill, black, straight, slender, of the true *Motacilla* form, though the bird itself was considered as a species of Thrush by Linnæus, but very properly removed to the genus *Motacilla* by Gmelin; legs, flesh colored; iris of the eye, dark hazel. The female wants the black band through the eye, has the bill brown, and the throat of a much paler yellow. This last, I have good reason to suspect, has been described by Europeans as a separate species; and that from Louisiana, referred to in the synonymes, appears evidently the same as the former, the chief difference, according to Buffon, being in its wedged tail, which is likewise the true form of our own species; so that this error corrected will abridge the European nomenclature of two species. Many more examples of this kind will occur in the course of our descriptions.

YELLOW-BREASTED CHAT.* — PIPRA POLYGLOTTA. —
Fig. 20.

Muscicapa viridis, *Gmel. Syst.* i. 936. — Le Merle vert de la Caroline, *Buffon,* iii. 396. — Chattering Flycatcher, *Arct. Zool.* ii. No. 266. — *Lath. Synop.* iii. 350, 48. — Garrulus australis, *Bartram,* 290. — *Peale's Museum,* No. 6661.

ICTERIA VIRIDIS. — Bonaparte.

Icteria dumicola, *Vieill. Gal. des Ois.* pl. 85, p. 119. — Icteria viridis, *Bonap. Synop.* p. 69.

THIS is a very singular bird. In its voice and manners, and the habit it has of keeping concealed, while shifting and vociferating around

* The Prince of Musignano remarks, when speaking of this bird, in his excellent *Observations on the Nomenclature of Wilson's Ornithology,* "It is not a little re-

you, it differs from most other birds with which I am acquainted, and has considerable claims to originality of character. It arrives in Pennsylvania about the first week in May, and returns to the south again as soon as its young are able for the journey, which is usually about the middle of August; its term of residence here being scarcely four months. The males generally arrive several days before the females—a circumstance common with many other of our birds of passage.

When he has once taken up his residence in a favorite situation, which is almost always in close thickets of hazel, brambles, vines, and thick underwood, he becomes very jealous of his possessions, and seems offended at the least intrusion; scolding every passenger as soon as they come within view, in a great variety of odd and uncouth monosyllables, which it is difficult to describe, but which may be readily imitated, so as to deceive the bird himself, and draw him after you for half a quarter of a mile at a time, as I have sometimes amused myself in doing, and frequently without once seeing him. On these occasions, his responses are constant and rapid, strongly expressive of anger and anxiety; and while the bird itself remains unseen, the voice shifts from place to place, among the bushes, as if it proceeded from a spirit. First is heard a repetition of short notes, resembling the whistling of the wings of a Duck or Teal, beginning loud and rapid, and falling lower and slower, till they end in detached notes; then a succession of others, something like the barking of young puppies, is followed by a variety of hollow, guttural sounds, each eight or ten times repeated, more like those proceeding from the throat of a quadruped than that of a bird; which are succeeded by others not unlike the mewing of a cat, but considerably hoarser. All these are uttered with great vehemence, in such different keys, and with such peculiar modulations of voice, as sometimes to seem at a considerable distance, and instantly as if just beside you; now on this hand, now on that; so that, from these manœuvres of ventriloquism, you are utterly at a loss to ascertain from what particular spot or quarter they proceed. If the weather be mild and serene, with clear moonlight, he continues gabbling in the same strange dialect, with very little intermission, during the whole night, as if disputing with his own echoes; but probably with a design of inviting the passing females to his retreat; for, when the season is further advanced, they are seldom heard during the night.

About the middle of May they begin to build. Their nest is usually fixed in the upper part of a bramble bush, in an almost impenetrable thicket; sometimes in a thick vine or small cedar; seldom more than four or five feet from the ground. It is composed out-

markable, that Wilson should have introduced this genus in his *Ornithology.* The bird he placed in it has certainly no relation to the Manakins, nor has any one of that genus been found within the United States. This bird has been placed by authors in half a dozen different genera. It was arranged in *Muscicapa,* by Gmelin, Latham, and Pennant; in *Turdus,* by Brisson and Buffon; in *Ampelis,* by Sparrman, and in *Tanagra,* by Desmarest. I was at first inclined to consider it as a *Vireo;* but, after having dwelt more upon the characters and habits of this remarkable species, I have concluded to adopt *Icteria* as an independent genus, agreeably to *Vieillot.*"—ED.

6

wardly of dry leaves; within these are laid thin strips of the bark of grape-vines, and the inside is lined with fibrous roots of plants, and fine, dry grass. The female lays four eggs, slightly flesh colored, and speckled all over with spots of brown or dull red. The young are hatched in twelve days, and make their first excursion from the nest about the second week in June. A friend of mine, an amateur in Canary Birds, placed one of the Chat's eggs under a hen Canary, who brought it out; but it died on the second day, though she was so solicitous to feed and preserve it, that her own eggs, which required two days more sitting, were lost through her attention to this.

While the female of the Chat is sitting, the cries of the male are still more loud and incessant. When once aware that you have seen him, he is less solicitous to conceal himself, and will sometimes mount up into the air, almost perpendicularly, to the height of thirty or forty feet, with his legs hanging; descending as he rose, by repeated jerks, as if highly irritated, or, as is vulgarly said, "dancing mad." All this noise and gesticulation we must attribute to his extreme affection for his mate and young; and when we consider the great distance which in all probability he comes, the few young produced at a time, and that seldom more than once in the season, we can see the wisdom of Providence very manifestly in the ardency of his passions.

Mr. Catesby seems to have first figured the Yellow-breasted Chat; and the singularity of its manners has not escaped him. After repeated attempts to shoot one of them, he found himself completely baffled, and was obliged, as he himself informs us, to employ an Indian for that purpose, who did not succeed without exercising all his ingenuity. Catesby also observed its dancing manœuvres, and supposed that it always flew with its legs extended; but it is only in these paroxysms of rage and anxiety that this is done, as I have particularly observed.

The food of these birds consists chiefly of large black beetles, and other coleopterous insects; I have also found whortleberries frequently in their stomach, in great quantities, as well as several other sorts of berries.* They are very numerous in the neighborhood of Philadelphia, particularly on the borders of rivulets, and other watery situations, in hedges, thickets, &c., but are seldom seen in the forest, even where there is underwood. Catesby indeed asserts, that they are only found on the banks of large rivers, two or three hundred miles from the sea; but, though this may be the case in South Carolina, yet in Maryland and New Jersey, and also in New York, I have met with these birds within two hours' walk of the sea, and in some places within less than a mile of the shore. I have not been able to trace him to any of the West India Islands; though they certainly retire to Mexico, Guiana, and Brazil, having myself seen skins of these birds in the possession of a French gentleman, which were brought from the two latter countries.

By recurring to the synonymes at the beginning of this article, it will be perceived how much European naturalists have differed in

* Vieillot mentions the fruit of the *Solanum Carolinense* as a particular favorite of this bird. — ED.

classing this bird. That the judicious Mr. Pennant, Gmelin, and even Dr. Latham, however, should have arranged it with the Flycatchers, is certainly very extraordinary; as neither in the particular structure of its bill, tongue, feet, nor in its food or manners, has it any affinity whatever to that genus. Some other ornithologists have removed it to the Tanagers; but the bill of the Chat, when compared with that of the Summer Red-Bird, (Fig. 21,) bespeaks it at once to be of a different tribe. Besides, the Tanagers seldom lay more than two or three eggs; the Chat usually four: the former build on trees; the latter in low thickets. In short, though this bird will not exactly correspond with any known genus, yet the form of its bill, its food, and many of its habits, would almost justify us in classing it with the genus *Pipra*, (Manakin,) to which family it seems most nearly related.

The Yellow-breasted Chat is seven inches long, and nine inches in extent; the whole upper parts are of a rich and deep olive green, except the tips of the wings and interior vanes of the wing and tail-feathers, which are dusky brown; the whole throat and breast is of a most brilliant yellow, which also lines the inside of the wings, and spreads on the sides immediately below; the belly and vent are white; the front, slate colored, or dull cinereous; lores, black; from the nostril, a line of white extends to the upper part of the eye, which it nearly encircles; another spot of white is placed at the base of the lower mandible; the bill is strong, slightly curved, sharply ridged on the top, compressed, overhanging a little at the tip, not notched, pointed, and altogether black; the tongue is tapering, more fleshy than those of the *Muscicapa* tribe, and a little lacerated at the tip; the nostril is oval, and half covered with an arching membrane; legs and feet, light blue, hind claw rather the strongest, the two exterior toes united to the second joint.

The female may be distinguished from the male by the black and white adjoining the eye being less intense or pure than in the male, and in having the inside of the mouth of a dirty flesh-color, which, in the male, is black; in other respects, their plumage is nearly alike.

SUMMER RED-BIRD.— TANAGRA ÆSTIVA.— Figs. 21, 22.

Tanagra Mississippensis, *Lath. Ind. Orn.* i. 421, 5. — Mexican Tanager, *Lath. Synop.* iii. 219, 5. B. — Tanagra variegata, *Ind. Orn.* i. 421, 6. — Tanagra æstiva, *Ind. Orn.* i. 422, 7. — Muscicapa rubra, *Linn. Syst.* i. 326, 8. — *Buff.* vi. 252, *Pl. enl.* 741. — *Catesby, Car.* i. 56. — Merula flammula, Sandhill Red-Bird, *Bartram,* 299. — *Peale's Museum,* No. 6134.

PYRANGA ÆSTIVA. — Vieillot.

Subgenus Pyranga,* Tanagra estiva, *Bonap. Synop.* p. 105.

THE change of color which this bird is subject to during the first year, and the imperfect figure first given of it by Catesby, have de-

---

* *Pyranga* has been used by Vieillot to designate a group among the *Tanagers*, having the bill of considerable strength, and furnished on the upper mandible with

ceived the European naturalists so much, that four different species have been formed out of this one, as appears by the above synonymes, all of which are referable to the present species, the Summer Red-Bird. As the female differs so much in color from the male, it has been thought proper to represent them both; the female having never, to my knowledge, appeared in any former publication; and all the figures of the other that I have seen being little better than carica-tures, from which a foreigner can form no just conception of the original.

The male of the Summer Red-Bird (Fig. 21) is wholly of a rich ver-milion color, most brilliant on the lower parts, except the inner vanes and tips of the wings, which are of a dusky brown; the bill is dispro-portionably large, and inflated, the upper mandible furnished with a process, and the whole bill of a yellowish horn color; the legs and feet are light blue, inclining to purple; the eye, large, the iris of a light hazel color; the length of the whole bird, seven inches and a quarter; and between the tips of the expanded wings, twelve inches. The female (Fig. 22) differs little in size from the male; but is, above, of a brownish yellow olive, lightest over the eye; throat, breast, and whole lower part of the body, of a dull orange yellow; tips and in-terior vanes of the wings, brown; bill, legs, and eye, as in the male. The nest is built in the woods, on the horizontal branch of a half-grown tree, often an evergreen, at the height of ten or twelve feet from the ground; composed, outwardly, of broken stalks of dry flax, and lined with fine grass; the female lays three light-blue eggs; the young are produced about the middle of June; and I suspect that the same pair raise no more than one brood in a season, for I have never found their nests but in May or June. Towards the middle of August, they take their departure for the south, their residence here being scarcely four months. The young are, at first, of a green olive above, nearly the same color as the female below, and do not acquire their full tints till the succeeding spring or summer.

The change, however, commences the first season before their de-parture. In the month of August, the young males are distinguished from the females by their motley garb; the yellow plumage below, as well as the olive green above, first becoming stained with spots of a buff color, which gradually brighten into red; these being irregularly scattered over the whole body, except the wings and tail, particularly the former, which I have often found to contain four or five green quills in the succeeding June. The first of these birds I ever shot was green winged; and conceiving it at that time to be a nondescript, I made a drawing of it with care; and on turning to it at this moment, I find the whole of the primaries, and two of the secondaries, yellowish green, the rest of the plumage a full red. This was about the middle

an obtuse tooth,—a structure which has been taken by Desmarest to denote his *Tanagras Coluriens*, or Shrike-like Tanagers. They are also the *Tanagras Car-dinal* of Cuvier. Bonaparte, again, retains Vieillot's group, but only as a subgenus to *Tanagra*.

It is composed of nine or ten species, three only being found in North America. They are generally of rich, sometimes gaudy, plumage, and require more than one year to arrive at maturity. They live in pairs, and feed on insects, berries, or soft seeds.—Ed.

of May. In the month of August, of the same year, being in the woods with the gun, I perceived a bird of very singular plumage, and having never before met with such an oddity, instantly gave chase to it. It appeared to me, at a small distance, to be sprinkled all over with red, green, and yellow. After a great deal of difficulty — for the bird had taken notice of my eagerness, and had become extremely shy — I succeeded in bringing it down ; and found it to be a young bird of the same species with the one I had killed in the preceding May, but less advanced to its fixed colors ; the wings entirely of a greenish yellow, and the rest of the plumage spotted, in the most irregular manner, with red, yellow, brown, and greenish. This is the *Variegated* Tanager, referred to in the synonymes prefixed to this article. Having, since that time, seen them in all their stages of color, during their residence here, I have the more satisfaction in assuring the reader that the whole four species mentioned by Dr. Latham are one and the same. The two figures in our plate represent the male and female in their complete plumage.

The food of these birds consists of various kinds of bugs, and large black beetles. In several instances, I have found the stomach entirely filled with the broken remains of humble-bees. During the season of whortleberries, they seem to subsist almost entirely on these berries ; but, in the early part of the season, on insects of the above description. In Pennsylvania, they are a rare species, having myself sometimes passed a whole summer without seeing one of them ; while in New Jersey, even within half a mile of the shore opposite the city of Philadelphia, they may generally be found during the season.

The note of the male is a strong and sonorous whistle, resembling a loose trill or shake on the notes of a fife, frequently repeated; that of the female is rather a kind of chattering, approaching nearly to the rapid pronunciation of *chicky-tucky-tuck, chicky-tucky-tuck*, when she sees any person approaching the neighborhood of her nest. She is, however, rarely seen, and usually mute, and scarcely to be distinguished from the color of the foliage at a distance ; while the loquacity and brilliant red of the male make him very conspicuous ; and when seen among the green leaves, particularly if the light falls strongly on his plumage, he has a most beautiful and elegant appearance. It is worthy of remark, that the females of almost all our splendid feathered birds are dressed in plain and often obscure colors, as if Providence meant to favor their personal concealment, and, consequently, that of their nest and young, from the depredations of birds of prey ; while, among the latter, such as Eagles, Owls, Hawks, &c., which are under no such apprehension, the females are uniformly covered with richer-colored plumage than the males.

The Summer Red-Bird delights in a flat, sandy country covered with wood, and interspersed with pine-trees, and is consequently more numerous towards the shores of the Atlantic than in the interior. In both Carolinas, and in Georgia and Florida, they are in great plenty. In Mexico some of them are probably resident, or, at least, winter there, as many other of our summer visitants are known to do. In the Northern States they are very rare ; and I do not know that they have been found either in Upper or Lower Canada. Du Pratz, in his *His-*

tory of Louisiana, has related some particulars of this bird, which have been repeated by almost every subsequent writer on the subject, viz., that " it inhabits the woods on the Mississippi, and collects against winter a vast magazine of maize, which it carefully conceals with dry leaves, leaving only a small hole for entrance; and is so jealous of it, as never to quit its neighborhood, except to drink." It is probable, though I cannot corroborate the fact, that individuals of this species may winter near the Mississippi; but that, in a climate so moderate, and where such an exuberance of fruits, seeds, and berries is to be found, even during winter, this, or any other bird, should take so much pains in hoarding a vast quantity of Indian corn, and attach itself so closely to it, is rather apocryphal. The same writer, vol. ii. p. 24, relates similar particulars of the Cardinal Grosbeak, (*Loxia cardinalis,*) which, though it winters in Pennsylvania, where the climate is much more severe, and where the length and rigors of that season would require a far larger magazine, and be a threefold greater stimulus to hoarding, yet has no such habit here. Besides, I have never found a single grain of Indian corn in the stomach of the Summer Red-Bird, though I have examined many individuals of both sexes. On the whole, I consider this account of Du Pratz's in much the same light with that of his countryman, Charlevoix, who gravely informs us, that the Owls of Canada lay up a store of live mice for winter; the legs of which they first break, to prevent them from running away, and then feed them carefully, and fatten them, till wanted for use.*

Its manners — though neither its bill nor tongue — partake very much of those of the Flycatcher; for I have frequently observed both male and female, a little before sunset, in parts of the forest clear of underwood, darting after winged insects, and continuing thus engaged till it was almost dusk.

INDIGO BIRD. — FRINGILLA CYANEA. — Fig. 23.

Tanagra cyanea, *Linn. Syst.* i. 315. — Le Ministre, *Buff.* iv. 86. — Indigo Bunting, *Arct. Zool.* ii. No. 235. — *Lath. Synop.* iii. 205, 63. — Blue Linnet, *Edw.* 273. — *Peale's Museum,* No. 6002. — Linaria cyanea, *Bart.* p. 290.

FRINGILLA CYANEA. — Wilson.

Fringilla cyanea, *Bonap. Synop.*† p. 107.

This is another of those rich plumaged tribes that visit us in spring from the regions of the south. It arrives in Pennsylvania on the second week in May, and disappears about the middle of September. It is numerous in all the settled parts of the Middle and Eastern States;

* *Travels in Canada,* vol. i. p. 239. Lond. 1761. 8vo.

† By a letter from my friend, Mr. Swainson, I am informed that the Prince of Musignano intends to form a genus of this bird; I have therefore provisionally added its present name, not wishing to interfere where I am acquainted with the intentions of another. It appears to range with the *Tanagrinæ.* — Ed.

in the Carolinas and Georgia it is also abundant. Though Catesby says that it is only found at a great distance from the sea, yet round the city of New York, and in many places along the shores of New Jersey, I have met with them in plenty. I may also add, on the authority of Mr. William Bartram, that "they inhabit the continent and sea-coast islands, from Mexico to Nova Scotia, from the sea-coast west beyond the Apalachian and Cherokee mountains." * They are also known in Mexico, where they probably winter. Its favorite haunts, while with us, are about gardens, fields of deep clover, the borders of woods, and road sides, where it is frequently seen perched on the fences. In its manners, it is extremely active and neat, and a vigorous and pretty good songster. It mounts to the highest tops of a large tree, and chants for half an hour at a time. Its song is not one continued strain, but a repetition of short notes, commencing loud and rapid, and falling, by almost imperceptible gradations, for six or eight seconds, till they seem hardly articulate, as if the little minstrel were quite exhausted; and, after a pause of half a minute, or less, commences again as before. Some of our birds sing only in spring, and then chiefly in the morning, being comparatively mute during the heat of noon; but the Indigo Bird chants with as much animation under the meridian sun, in the month of July, as in the month of May, and continues his song, occasionally, to the middle or end of August. His usual note, when alarmed by an approach to his nest, is a sharp *chip*, like that of striking two hard pebbles smartly together.

Notwithstanding the beauty of his plumage, the vivacity with which he sings, and the ease with which he can be reared and kept, the Indigo Bird is seldom seen domesticated. The few I have met with were taken in trap cages; and such of any species rarely sing equal to those which have been reared by hand from the nest. There is one singularity which, as it cannot be well represented in the figure, may be mentioned here, viz. that, in some certain lights, his plumage appears of a rich sky blue, and in others of a vivid verdigris green; so that the same bird, in passing from one place to another before your eyes, seems to undergo a total change of color. When the angle of incidence of the rays of light, reflected from his plumage, is acute, the color is green; when obtuse, blue. Such, I think, I have observed to be uniformly the case, without being optician enough to explain why it is so. From this, however, must be excepted the color of the head, which, being of a very deep blue, is not affected by a change of position.

The nest of this bird is usually built in a low bush, among rank grass, grain, or clover, suspended by two twigs, one passing up each side; and is composed outwardly of flax, and lined with fine dry grass. I have also known it to build in the hollow of an apple-tree. The eggs, generally five, are blue, with a blotch of purple at the great end.

The Indigo Bird is five inches long, and seven inches in extent; the whole body is of a rich sky blue, deepening on the head to an ultramarine, with a tinge of purple; the blue on the body, tail, and wings, varies in particular lights to a light green, or verdigris color, similar to that on the breast of a Peacock; wings, black, edged with

* *Travels,* p. 299.

light blue, and becoming brownish towards the tips; lesser coverts, light blue; greater, black, broadly skirted with the same blue; tail, black, exteriorly edged with blue; bill, black above, whitish below, somewhat larger in proportion than Finches of the same size usually are, but less than those of the genus *Emberiza*, with which Mr. Pennant has classed it, though, I think, improperly, as the bird has much more of the form and manners of the genus *Fringilla*, where I must be permitted to place it; legs and feet, blackish brown. The female is of a light flaxen color, with the wings dusky black, and the cheeks, breast, and whole lower parts, a clay color, with streaks of a darker color under the wings, and tinged in several places with bluish. Towards fall, the male, while moulting, becomes nearly of the color of the female, and in one which I kept through the winter, the rich plumage did not return for more than two months; though I doubt not, had the bird enjoyed his liberty and natural food under a warm sun, this brownness would have been of shorter duration. The usual food of this species is insects and various kinds of seeds.

AMERICAN REDSTART. — MUSCICAPA RUTICILLA. —
Fig. 24.

Muscicapa ruticilla, *Lynn. Syst.* i. 236, 10. — *Gmel. Syst.* i. 935. — Motacilla flavicauda, *Gmel. Syst.* i. 997, (female.) — Le gobe-mouche d'Amerique, *Briss. Orn.* ii. 383, 14. *Pl. enl.* 566, fig. 1, 2. — Small American Redstart, *Edw.* 80. *Id.* 257, (female.) Yellow-tailed Warbler, *Arct. Zool.* ii. No. 301. *Id.* ii. No. 282. — *Lath. Syn.* iv. 427, 18. — *Arct. Zool.* ii. No. 301, (female.) — *Peale's Museum,* No. 6658.

SETOPHAGA RUTICILLA. — Swainson.*

Muscicapa ruticilla, *Bonap. Synop.* p. 68. — Setophaga ruticilla, *North. Zool.* ii. 223. — Setophaga, *Swain. N. Groups, Zool. Journ.* Sept. 1827, p. 360.

THOUGH this bird has been classed by several of our most respectable ornithologists among the Warblers, yet in no species are the characteristics of the genus *Muscicapa* more decisively marked; and, in fact, it is one of the most expert fly-catchers of its tribe. It is almost perpetually in motion, and will pursue a retreating party of flies from the tops of the tallest trees, in an almost perpendicular, but zigzag direction, to the ground, while the clicking of its bill is distinctly heard; and I doubt not but it often secures ten or twelve of these in a descent of three or four seconds. It then alights on an adjoining branch, traverses it lengthwise for a few moments, flirting its expanded tail from side to side, and suddenly shoots off, in a direction quite unexpected, after fresh game, which it can discover at a great distance.

* This bird forms the type of *Setophaga*, Swainson; a genus formed of a few species belonging entirely to the New World, and intimately connected with the fan-tailed Flycatchers of Australia, the *Rhippiduræ* of Vigors and Horsfield.
The young bird is figured in No. 186. — ED.

Its notes, or twitter, though animated and sprightly, are not deserving the name of song; sometimes they are *weése, weése, weése*, repeated every quarter of a minute, as it skips among the branches; at other times this twitter varies to several other chants, which I can instantly distinguish in the woods, but cannot find words to imitate. The interior of the forest, the borders of swamps and meadows, deep glens covered with wood, and wherever flying insects abound, there this little bird is sure to be seen. It makes its appearance in Pennsylvania, from the south, late in April; and leaves us again about the beginning of September. It is very generally found over the whole United States, and has been taken at sea, in the fall, on its way to St. Domingo,* and other of the West India islands, where it winters, along with many more of our summer visitants. It is also found in Jamaica, where it remains all winter.†

The name Redstart, evidently derived from the German *rothsterts*, (red tail,) has been given this bird from its supposed resemblance to the Redstart of Europe, (*Motacilla phœnicurus ;*) but besides being decisively of a different genus, it is very different both in size and in the tints and disposition of the colors of its plumage. Buffon goes even so far as to question whether the differences between the two be more than what might be naturally expected from change of climate. This eternal reference of every animal of the New World to that of the Old, if adopted to the extent of this writer, with all the transmutations it is supposed to have produced, would leave us in doubt whether even the Ka-te-dids ‡ of America were not originally Nightingales of the Old World, degenerated by the inferiority of the food and climate of this upstart continent. We have in America many different species of birds that approach so near in resemblance to one another, as not to be distinguished but by the eye of a naturalist, and on a close comparison; these live in the same climate, feed on the same food, and are, I doubt not, the same now as they were five thousand years ago; and, ten thousand years hence, if the species then exist, will be found marked with the same nice discriminations as at present. It is therefore surprising, that two different species, placed in different quarters of the world, should have certain near resemblances to one another, without being bastards, or degenerated descendants, the one of the other, when the whole chain of created beings seems united to each other by such amazing gradations, that bespeak, not random chance and accidental degeneracy, but the magnificent design of an incomprehensibly wise and omnipotent Creator.

The American Redstart builds frequently in low bushes, in the fork of a small sapling, or on the drooping branches of the elm, within a few feet of the ground; outwardly it is formed of flax, well wound together, and moistened with its saliva, interspersed here and there with pieces of lichen, and lined with a very soft, downy substance. The female lays five white eggs, sprinkled with gray, and specks of blackish. The male is extremely anxious for its preservation; and,

* EDWARDS.
† SLOANE.
‡ A species of *Gryllus*, well known for its lively chatter during the evenings and nights of September and October.

on a person's approaching the place, will flirt about within a few feet, seeming greatly distressed.*

The length of this species is five inches; extent, six and a quarter; the general color above is black, which covers the whole head and neck, and spreads on the upper part of the breast in a rounding form, where, as well as on the head and neck, it is glossed with steel blue; sides of the breast below this, black; the inside of the wings, and upper half of the wing-quills, are of a fine aurora color; but the greater and lesser coverts of the wings, being black, conceal this; and the orange or aurora color appears only as a broad, transverse band across the wings; from thence to the tip, they are brownish; the four middle feathers of the tail are black, the other eight of the same aurora color, and black towards the tips; belly and vent, white, slightly streaked with pale orange; legs, black; bill, of the true *Muscicapa* form, triangular at the base, beset with long bristles, and notched near the point. The female has not the rich aurora band across the wing; her back and crown are cinereous, inclining to olive; the white below is not so pure; lateral feathers of the tail and sides of the breast, greenish yellow; middle tail-feathers, dusky brown. The young males of a year old are almost exactly like the female, differing in these particulars, that they have a yellow band across the wings which the female has not, and the back is more tinged with brown: the lateral tail-feathers are also yellow; middle ones, brownish black; inside of the wings, yellow. On the third season, they receive their complete colors; and, as males of the second year, in nearly the dress of the female, are often seen in the woods, having the same notes as the full-plumaged male, it has given occasion to some people to assert that the females sing as well as the males; and others have taken them for another species. The fact, however, is as I have stated it. This bird is too little known by people in general to have any provincial name.

CEDAR BIRD. — AMPELIS AMERICANA. — Fig. 25.

Ampelis garrulus, *Linn. Syst.* i. 297, 1, β. — Bombycilla Carolinensis, *Brisson*, ii. 337, 1. *Id.* 8vo. i. 251. — Chatterer of Carolina, *Catesb.* i. 46. — *Arct. Zool.* ii. No. 207. — *Lath. Syn.* iii. 93, 1, A. — *Edw.* 242. — *Cook's Last Voyage*, ii. 518. — *Ellis's Voyage*, ii. 13. — *Peale's Museum*, No. 5608.

BOMBYCILLA AMERICANA. — Swainson.

Le jaseur du cèdre, Bombycilla cedorum, *Vieill. Gal. des Ois.* pl. cxviii. p. 186. — Bombycilla Carolinensis, *Bonap. Synop.* p. 59. — Bombycilla Americana, *North. Zool.* ii. p. 239.

The figure of the Cedar Bird which accompanies this description was drawn from a very beautiful specimen; and exhibits the form of

---

* Mr. Audubon says, " The nest is slight, composed of lichens and dried fibres, of rank weeds, or grape vines, nicely lined with soft, cotton materials." — P. 203. — Ed.

its crest when erected, which gives it so gay and elegant an appearance. At pleasure it can lower and contract this so closely to its head and neck as not to be observed. The plumage of these birds is of an exquisitely fine and silky texture, lying extremely smooth and glossy. Notwithstanding the name *Chatterers* given to them, they are perhaps the most silent species we have ; making only a feeble, lisping sound, chiefly as they rise or alight. They fly in compact bodies, of from twenty to fifty ; and usually alight so close together on the same tree, that one half are frequently shot down at a time. In the months of July and August, they collect together in flocks, and retire to the hilly parts of the state, the Blue Mountains, and other collateral ridges of the Alleghany, to enjoy the fruit of the *Vaccinium uliginosum*, whortleberries, which grow there in great abundance ; whole mountains, for many miles, being almost entirely covered with them ; and where, in the month of August, I have myself found the Cedar Birds numerous. In October they descend to the lower, cultivated parts of the country, to feed on the berries of the sour gum and red cedar, of which last they are immoderately fond ; and thirty or forty may sometimes be seen fluttering among the branches of one small cedar-tree, plucking off the berries.* They are also found as far south as Mexico, as appears from the accounts of Fernandez, Seba,[†] and others. Fernandez saw them near Tetzeuco, and calls them *Coquantotl* ; says they delight to dwell in the mountainous parts of the country ; and that their flesh and song are both indifferent.[‡] Most of our epicures here are, however, of a different opinion, as to their palatableness ; for, in the fall and beginning of summer, when they become very fat, they are in considerable esteem for the table ; and great numbers are brought to the market of Philadelphia, where they are sold from twelve to twenty-five cents per dozen. During the whole winter and spring they are occasionally seen ; and, about the 25th of May, appear in numerous parties, making great havock among the early cherries, selecting the best and ripest of the fruit.

* They appear all to be berry-eaters, at least during winter. Those of Europe have generally been observed to feed on the fruit of the mountain ash, and one or two killed near Carlisle, which I had an opportunity of examining, were literally crammed with hollyberries. "The appetite of the Cedar Bird," Audubon remarks, "is of so extraordinary a nature as to prompt it to devour every fruit or berry that comes in its way. In this manner they gorge themselves to such excess as sometimes to be unable to fly, and suffer themselves to be taken by the hand ; and I have seen some, which, though wounded and confined to a cage, have eaten apples until suffocation deprived them of life."—P. 227. "But they are also excellent flycatchers, spending much of their time in the pursuit of winged insects : this is not, however, managed with the vivacity or suddenness of true Flycatchers, but with a kind of listlessness. They start from the branches, and give chase to the insects, ascending after them for a few yards, or move horizontally towards them, and as soon as the prey is secured, return to the spot, where they continue watching with slow motions of the head. This amusement is carried on during evening, and longer at the approach of autumn, when the berries become scarce. They become very fat during the season of fruits, and are then so tender and juicy as to be sought after by every epicure for the table,—a basketful of these birds is sometimes sent as a Christmas present."—P. 223.—Ed.

† The figure of this bird, in Seba's voluminous work, is too wretched for criticism ; it is there called "Oiseau Xomotl, d'Amerique, huppée." Seb. ii. p. 66, t. 65, fig. 5.

‡ *Hist. Av. Nov. Hisp.* 55.

Nor are they easily intimidated by the presence of Mr. Scarecrow; for I have seen a flock deliberately feasting on the fruit of a loaded cherry-tree, while on the same tree one of these *guardian angels,* and a very formidable one too, stretched his stiffened arms, and displayed his dangling legs, with all the pomposity of authority. At this time of the season most of our resident birds, and many of our summer visitants, are sitting, or have young; while, even on the 1st of June, the eggs in the ovary of the female Cedar Bird are no larger than mustard seed; and it is generally the 8th or 10th of that month before they begin to build. These last are curious circumstances, which it is difficult to account for, unless by supposing that incubation is retarded by a scarcity of suitable food in spring, berries and other fruit being their usual fare. In May, before the cherries are ripe, they are lean, and little else is found in their stomachs than a few shrivelled cedar berries, the refuse of the former season, and a few fragments of beetles and other insects, which do not appear to be their common food; but in June, while cherries and strawberries abound, they become extremely fat; and, about the 10th or 12th of that month, disperse over the country in pairs to breed; sometimes fixing on the cedar, but generally choosing the orchard for that purpose. The nest is large for the size of the bird, fixed in the forked or horizontal branch of an apple-tree, ten or twelve feet from the ground; outwardly, and at bottom, is laid a mass of coarse, dry stalks of grass, and the inside is lined wholly with very fine stalks of the same material. The eggs are three or four, of a dingy bluish white, thick at the great end, tapering suddenly, and becoming very narrow at the other; marked with small, roundish spots of black of various sizes and shades; and the great end is of a pale, dull, purple tinge, marked likewise with touches of various shades of purple and black. About the last week in June the young are hatched, and are at first fed on insects and their larvæ; but, as they advance in growth, on berries of various kinds. These facts I have myself been an eye-witness to. The female, if disturbed, darts from the nest in silence to a considerable distance; no notes of wailing or lamentation are heard from either parent, nor are they even seen, notwithstanding you are in the tree examining the nest and young. These nests are less frequently found than many others, owing, not only to the comparatively few numbers of the birds, but to the remarkable muteness of the species. The season of love, which makes almost every other small bird musical, has no such effect on them; for they continue, at that interesting period, as silent as before.

This species is also found in Canada, where it is called *Recollet,* probably, as Dr. Latham supposes, from the color and appearance of its crest resembling the hood of an order of friars of that denomination. It has also been met with by several of our voyagers on the north-west coast of America, and appears to have an extensive range.

Almost all the ornithologists of Europe persist in considering this bird as a variety of the European Chatterer, (*A. garrulus,*) with what justice or propriety a mere comparison of the two will determine.*

* The small American species, figured by our author, was by many considered as only the American variety of that which was thought to belong to Europe and

The European species is very nearly twice the cubic bulk of ours; has the whole lower parts of a uniform dark vinous bay; the tips of the wings streaked with lateral bars of yellow; the nostrils, covered with bristles;* the feathers on the chin, loose and tufted; the wings, black; and the markings of white and black on the sides of the head different from the American, which is as follows:—Length, seven inches, extent eleven inches; head, neck, breast, upper part of the back and wing-coverts, a dark fawn color, darkest on the back, and brightest on the front; head, ornamented with a high, pointed, almost upright, crest; line from the nostril over the eye to the hind head, velvety black, bordered above with a fine line of white, and another line of white passes from the lower mandible; chin, black, gradually brightening into fawn color, the feathers there lying extremely close; bill, black; upper mandible nearly triangular at the base, without bristles, short, rounding at the point, where it is deeply notched; the lower, scolloped at the tip, and turning up; tongue, as in the rest of the genus, broad, thin, cartilaginous, and lacerated at the end; belly, yellow; vent, white; wings, deep slate, except the two secondaries next the body, whose exterior vanes are of a fawn color, and interior ones, white; forming two whitish stripes there, which are very conspicuous; rump and tail-coverts, pale light blue; tail, the same, gradually deepening into black, and tipped for half an inch with rich yellow. Six or seven, and sometimes the whole nine, secondary feathers of the wings are ornamented at the tips with small, red, oblong appendages, resembling red sealing-wax; these appear to be a prolongation of the shafts, and to be intended for preserving the ends, and consequently the vanes, of the quills, from being broken and worn away by the almost continual fluttering of the bird among thick branches of the cedar. The feathers of those birds, which are without these appendages, are uniformly found ragged on the edges, but smooth and perfect in those on whom the marks are full and numerous. These singular marks have been usually considered as belonging to the male alone, from the circumstance, perhaps, of finding female birds without them. They are, however, common to both male and female. Six of the latter are now lying before me, each with large and numerous clusters of eggs, and having the waxen appendages in full perfection. The young birds do not receive them until the second fall, when, in moulting time, they may be seen fully formed, as the feather is developed from its sheath. I have once or twice found a solitary one on the extremity of one of the tail-feathers. The eye is of a dark blood color; the legs and claws, black; the inside of the mouth, orange;

Asia alone. The fallacy of this opinion was decided by the researches of several ornithologists, and latterly confirmed, by the discovery in America of the *B. garrulus* itself, the description of which will form a part of Vol. III. (of the London edition.)

The genus *Bombycilla* of Brisson is generally adopted for these two birds, and will now also contain a third very beautiful and nearly allied species, discovered in Japan by the enterprising, but unfortunate, naturalist Seibold, and figured in the *Planches Coloriées* of M. Temminck, under the name of *B. phœnicoptera*. It may be remarked, that the last wants the waxlike appendages to the wings and tail; at least so they are represented in M. Temminck's plate; but our own species sometimes wants them also. — Ed.

* TURTON.

gap, wide; and the gullet capable of such distention as often to contain twelve or fifteen cedar berries, and serving as a kind of craw to prepare them for digestion. No wonder, then, that this gluttonous bird, with such a mass of food almost continually in its throat, should want both the inclination and powers for vocal melody, which would seem to belong to those only of less gross and voracious habits. The chief difference in the plumage of the male and female consists in the dulness of the tints of the latter, the inferior appearance of the crest, and the narrowness of the yellow bar on the tip of the tail.

Though I do not flatter myself with being able to remove that prejudice from the minds of foreigners, which has made them look on this bird, also, as a degenerate and not a distinct species from their own, yet they must allow that the change has been very great, very uniform, and universal, all over North America, where I have never heard that the European species has been found; or, even if it were, this would only show more clearly the specific difference of the two, by proving that climate or food could never have produced these differences in either when both retain them, though confined to the same climate.

But it is not only in the color of their plumage that these two birds differ, but in several important particulars in their manners and habits. The breeding-place of the European species is absolutely unknown; supposed to be somewhere about the polar regions; from whence, in winter, they make different and very irregular excursions to various parts of Europe; seldom advancing farther south than the north of England, in lat. 54° N., and so irregularly, that many years sometimes elapse between their departure and reappearance; which, in more superstitious ages, has been supposed to portend some great national calamity. On the other hand, the American species inhabits the whole extensive range between Mexico and Canada, and perhaps much farther both northerly and southerly, building and rearing their young in all the intermediate regions, often in our gardens and orchards, within a few yards of our houses. Those of our fellow-citizens who have still any doubts, and wish to examine for themselves, may see beautiful specimens of both birds in the superb collection of Mr. Charles W. Peale of Philadelphia, whose magnificent museum is indeed a national blessing, and will be a lasting honor to his memory.

In some parts of the country they are called Crown Birds; in others Cherry Birds, from their fondness for that fruit. They also feed on ripe persimmons, small winter grapes, bird cherries, and a great variety of other fruits and berries. The action of the stomach on these seeds and berries does not seem to injure their vegetative powers, but rather to promote them, by imbedding them in a calcareous case; and they are thus transported to and planted in various and distant parts by these little birds. In other respects, however, their usefulness to the farmer may be questioned; and in the general chorus of the feathered songsters they can scarcely be said to take a part. We must, therefore, rank them far below many more homely and minute warblers, their neighbors, whom Providence seems to have formed, both as allies to protect the property of the husbandman from devouring insects, and as musicians to cheer him, while engaged in the labors of the field, with their innocent and delightful melody.

RED–BELLIED WOODPECKER. — PICUS CAROLINUS. —
Fig. 26.

Picus Carolinus, *Linn. Syst.* i. 174, 10. — Pic varié de la Jamaique, *Buffon*, vii. 72. *Pl enl.* 597. — Picus varius medius Jamaicensis, *Sloan. Jam.* 299, 15. — Jamaica Woodpecker, *Edw.* 244. — *Cates.* i. 19, fig. 2. *Arct. Zool.* ii. No. 161. — *Lath. Syn.* ii. 570, 17. *Id.* 571, 17, A. *Id.* β. — L'Epeiche rayé de la Louisiane, *Buff.* vii. 73. *Pl. enl.* 692. — *Peale's Museum*, No. 1944.

COLAPTES CAROLINUS. — Swainson.

Picus Carolinus, *Bonap. Synop.* p. 45. — Picus erythrauchen, *Wagl. Syst. Av* No. 38.

This species possesses all the restless and noisy habits so characteristic of its tribe. It is more shy and less domestic than the Red-headed one, (*P. erythrocephalus*,) or any of the other spotted Woodpeckers. It is also more solitary. It prefers the largest, high-timbered woods, and tallest decayed trees of the forest; seldom appearing near the ground, on the fences, or in orchards, or open fields; yet where the trees have been deadened, and stand pretty thick, in fields of Indian corn, as is common in new settlements, I have observed it to be very numerous, and have found its stomach sometimes completely filled with that grain.* Its voice is hoarser than any of the others; and its usual note, " chow," has often reminded me of the barking of a little lapdog. It is a most expert climber, possessing extraordinary strength in the muscles of its feet and claws, and moves about the body and horizontal limbs of the trees with equal facility in all directions. It rattles, like the rest of the tribe, on the dead limbs, and with such violence as to be heard, in still weather, more than half a mile off, and listens to hear the insects it has alarmed. In the lower side of some lofty branch that makes a considerable angle with the horizon, the male and female, in conjunction, dig out a circular cavity for their nest, sometimes out of the solid wood, but more generally into a hollow limb, twelve or fifteen inches above where it becomes solid. This is usually performed early in April. The female lays five eggs, of a pure white, or almost semi-transparent; and the young generally make their appearance towards the latter end of May, or beginning of

---

* This species will also range in the genus *Colaptes*, but will present a more aberrant form. In it we have the compressed and slightly bent shape of the bill, becoming stronger and more angular; we have the barred plumage of the upper parts, but that of the head is uniform and only slightly elongated behind; and in the wings and tail the shafts of the quills lose their strength and beautiful color. In Wilson's description of the habits, we also find them agreeing with the modifications of form. It prefers the more solitary recesses of lofty forests; and, though capable of turning and twisting, and possessing a great part of the activity of the Nuthatch and Titmice, it seldom appears about orchards or upon the ground; yet it occasionally visits the corn-fields, and feeds on the grain, and, as remarked above, is " capable of subsisting on coarser and more various fare." These modifications of habit we shall always find in unison with the structure; and we cannot too much admire the wisdom that has thus mutually adapted them to the various offices they are destined to fill. — Ed.

June, climbing up to the higher parts of the tree, being as yet unable to fly. In this situation they are fed for several days, and often become the prey of the Hawks. From seeing the old ones continuing their caresses after this period, I believe that they often, and perhaps always, produce two broods in a season. During the greatest part of the summer, the young have the ridge of the neck and head of a dull brownish ash; and a male of the third year has received his complete colors.

The Red-bellied Woodpecker is ten inches in length, and seventeen in extent; the bill is nearly an inch and a half in length, wedged at the point, but not quite so much grooved as some others, strong, and of a bluish black color; the nostrils are placed in one of these grooves, and covered with curving tufts of light brown hairs, ending in black points; the feathers on the front stand more erect than usual, and are of a dull yellowish red; from thence, along the whole upper part of the head and neck, down the back, and spreading round to the shoulders, is of the most brilliant, golden, glossy red; the whole cheeks, line over the eye, and under side of the neck, are a pale buff color, which, on the breast and belly, deepens into a yellowish ash, stained on the belly with a blood red; the vent and thigh feathers are dull white, marked down their centres with heart-formed and long arrow-pointed spots of black. The back is black, crossed with transverse curving lines of white; the wings are also black; the lesser wing-coverts circularly tipped, and the whole primaries and secondaries beautifully crossed with bars of white, and also tipped with the same; the rump is white, interspersed with touches of black; the tail-coverts, white near their extremities; the tail consists of ten feathers, the two middle ones black, their interior webs or vanes white, crossed with diagonal spots of black; these, when the edges of the two feathers just touch, coincide and form heart-shaped spots; a narrow sword-shaped line of white runs up the exterior side of the shafts of the same feathers; the next four feathers, on each side, are black; the outer edges of the exterior ones, barred with black and white, which, on the lower side, seems to cross the whole vane, as in the figure; the extremities of the whole tail, except the outer feather, are black, sometimes touched with yellowish or cream color; the legs and feet are of a bluish green, and the iris of the eye red. The tongue, or os hyoides, passes up over the hind head, and is attached, by a very elastic, retractile membrane, to the base of the right nostril; the extremity of the tongue is long, horny, very pointed, and thickly edged with barbs; the other part of the tongue is worm-shaped. In several specimens, I found the stomach nearly filled with pieces of a species of fungus that grows on decayed wood,[*] and, in all, with great numbers of insects, seeds, gravel, &c. The female differs from the male, in having the crown, for an inch, of a fine ash, and the black not so intense; the front is reddish, as in the male, and the whole hind head, down to the back, likewise of the same rich red as his. In the bird, from which this latter description was taken, I

---

[*] Most probably swallowed with the insects which infest and are nourished in the various *Boleti polypori*, &c., but forming no part of their real food. — ED.

found a large cluster of minute eggs, to the number of fifty, or upwards, in the beginning of the month of March.

This species inhabits a large extent of country, in all of which it seems to be resident, or nearly so. I found them abundant in Upper Canada, and in the northern parts of the state of New York, in the month of November; they also inhabit the whole Atlantic states as far as Georgia, and the southern extremity of Florida, as well as the interior parts of the United States, as far west as Chilicothe, in the state of Ohio, and, according to Buffon, Louisiana. They are said to be the only Woodpeckers found in Jamaica, though I question whether this be correct, and to be extremely fond of the capsicum, or Indian pepper.* They are certainly much hardier birds, and capable of subsisting on coarser and more various fare, and 'of sustaining a greater degree of cold, than several other of our Woodpeckers. They are active and vigorous; and, being almost continually in search of insects that injure our forest-trees, do not seem to deserve the injurious epithets that almost all writers have given them. It is true, they frequently perforate the timber, in pursuit of these vermin; but this is almost always in dead and decaying parts of the tree, which are the nests and nurseries of millions of destructive insects. Considering matters in this light, I do not think their services overpaid by all the ears of Indian corn they consume, and would protect them, within my own premises, as being more useful than injurious.

YELLOW-THROATED FLYCATCHER. MUSCICAPA SYLVICOLA. — Fig. 27.

Peale's Museum, No. 6327.

VIREO† FLAVIFRONS. — Vieillot.

Vireo flavifrons, *Bonap. Synop.* p. 70.

This summer species is found chiefly in the woods, hunting among the high branches; and has an indolent and plaintive note, which it repeats with some little variation, every ten or twelve seconds, like

* Sloane.

† *Vireo* is a genus originally formed by Vieillot to contain an American group of birds, since the formation of which several additions have been made by Bonaparte and Swainson of species which were not at first contemplated as belonging to it.

The group is peculiar to both continents of America, — they inhabit woods, feed on insects and berries, and in their manner have considerable alliance to the Warblers and Flycatchers. By Mr. Swainson they are placed among the *Ampelidæ,* or berry-eaters, but with a mark of uncertainty whether they should stand here or at the extremity of some other family. The arctic expedition has added a new species much allied to *V. olivaceus.* Mr. Swainson has dedicated it to the venerable naturalist Bartram, the intimate friend of Wilson, and mentions, that, on comparing seventeen species, *Vireo Bartramii* was much smaller, the colors rather

preeò, preeà, &c. It is often heard in company with the Red-eyed Flycatcher (*Muscicapa olivacea*) or Whip-tom-kelly of Jamaica; the loud, energetic notes of the latter, mingling with the soft, languid warble of the former, producing an agreeable effect, particularly during the burning heat of noon, when almost every other songster but these two is silent. Those who loiter through the shades of our magnificent forests at that hour, will easily recognize both species. It arrives from the south early in May; and returns again with its young about the middle of September. Its nest, which is sometimes fixed on the upper side of a limb, sometimes on a horizontal branch among the twigs, generally on a tree, is composed outwardly of thin strips of the bark of grape vines, moss, lichens, &c., and lined with fine fibres of such like substances; the eggs, usually four, are white, thinly dotted with black, chiefly near the great end. Winged insects are its principal food.

Whether this species has been described before or not, I must leave to the sagacity of the reader, who has the opportunity of examining European works of this kind, to discover.* I have met with no description in Pennant, Buffon, or Latham, that will properly apply to this bird, which may perhaps be owing to the imperfection of the account, rather than ignorance of the species, which is by no means rare.

The Yellow-throated Flycatcher is five inches and a half long, and nine inches from tip to tip of the expanded wings; the upper part of the head, sides of the neck, and the back, are of a fine yellow olive; throat, breast, and line over the eye, which it nearly encircles, a delicate lemon yellow, which, in a lighter tinge, lines the wings; belly and vent, pure silky white; lesser wing-coverts, lower part of the back, and rump, ash; wings, deep brown, almost black, crossed with two white bars; primaries, edged with light ash, secondaries, with white; tail, a little forked, of the same brownish black with the wings, the three exterior feathers edged on each vane with white; legs and claws, light blue; the two exterior toes united to the middle one, as far as the second joint; bill, broad at the base, with three or four slight bristles, the upper mandible overhanging the lower at the point, near which it is deeply notched; tongue, thin, broad, tapering near the end, and bifid; the eye is of a dark hazel; and the whole bill of a dusky light blue. The female differs very little in color from the male; the yellow on the breast, and round the eye, is duller, and the white on the wings less pure.

brighter, the wings considerably shorter and more rounded, and the first quill always shorter than the fifth, — that *V. olivaceus* is confined to North America, while *V. Bartramii* extends to Brazil. The species of the arctic expedition were procured by Mr. David Douglas on the banks of the Columbia. Mr. Swainson also met with the species in the Brazils; and, from specimens sent to us by that gentleman, I have no hesitation in considering them distinct, and of at once recognizing the differences he has pointed out.

Mr. Audubon has figured another species which will rank as an addition to this genus, and, if proved new, will stand as *Vireo Vigorsii;* he has only met with a single individual in Pennsylvania, and enters into no description of its history, or distinctions from other allied birds. — ED.

* See Orange-throated Warbler, LATHAM, *Syn.* ii. 481, 103.

PURPLE FINCH. — FRINGILLA PURPUREA. — Fig. 28.

Fringilla purpurea *Gmel. Syst.* i. 923. — Bouvreuil violet de la Caroline, *Buff.* iv.
395. — Purple Finch, *Arct. Zool.* ii. No. 258. — *Catesb.* i. 41. — *Lath. Synop.* iii.
275, 39. — Crimson-headed Finch, *Arct. Zool.* ii. No. 257. — *Lath. Synop.* iii.
275, 39. — *Gmel. Syst.* i. 864. — Fringilla rosea Pallas, iii. 699, 26. — Hemp
Bird, *Bartram*, 291. — Fringilla Purpurea, *Id.* 291. — *Peale's Museum*, No. 6504.

ERYTHROSPIZA PURPUREA. — Bonaparte.

Fringilla purpurea, *Bonap. Synop.* p. 114. — Purple Finch, *Aud.* i. p. 24. Pl. iv. —
Fringilla purpurea, Crested Purple Finch, *North. Zool.* ii. p. 264. — Erythrospiza
purpurea, *Osserv. di C. L. Bonap. Sulla Sec. Ed. del. Cuv. Reg. Anim.* p. 30.

THIS is a winter bird of passage, coming to us in large flocks from
the north, in September and October; great numbers remaining with
us in Pennsylvania during the whole winter, feeding on the seeds of
the poplar, button-wood, juniper, cedar, and on those of many rank
weeds that flourish in rich bottoms, and along the margin of creeks.
When the season is very severe, they proceed to the south, as far at
least as Georgia, returning north early in April. They now frequent
the elm-trees, feeding on the slender but sweet covering of the
flowers; and as soon as the cherries put out their blossoms, feed
almost exclusively on the stamina of the flowers; afterwards the
apple blossoms are attacked in the same manner; and their depredations on these continue till they disappear, which is usually about the
10th or middle of May. I have been told that they sometimes breed
in the northern parts of New York, but have never met with their
nests. About the middle of September, I found these birds numerous
on Long Island, and round Newark in New Jersey. They fly at a
considerable height in the air, and their note is a single *chink*, like
that of the Rice Bird. They possess great boldness and spirit, and,
when caught, bite violently, and hang by the bill from your hand,
striking with great fury; but they are soon reconciled to confinement, and in a day or two are quite at home. I have kept a pair of
these birds upwards of nine months to observe their manners. One
was caught in a trap, the other was winged with the gun; both are
now as familiar as if brought up from the nest by the hand, and
seem to prefer hemp seed and cherry blossoms to all other kinds
of food. Both male and female, though not crested, are almost
constantly in the habit of erecting the feathers of the crown; they
appear to be of a tyrannical and domineering disposition, for they
nearly killed an Indigo Bird, and two or three others, that were
occasionally placed with them, driving them into a corner of the cage,
standing on them, and tearing out their feathers, striking them on the
head, munching their wings, &c., till I was obliged to interfere; and,
even if called to, the aggressor would only turn up a malicious eye to
me for a moment, and renew his outrage as before. They are a hardy,
vigorous bird. In the month of October, about the time of their first
arrival, I shot a male, rich in plumage, and plump in flesh, but which
wanted one leg, that had been taken off a little above the knee; the

wound had healed so completely, and was covered with so thick a skin, that it seemed as though it had been so for years. Whether this mutilation was occasioned by a shot, or in party quarrels of its own, I could not determine; but our invalid seemed to have used his stump either in hopping or resting, for it had all the appearance of having been brought in frequent contact with bodies harder than itself.

This bird is a striking example of the truth of what I have frequently repeated in this work, that in many instances the same bird has been more than once described by the same person as a different species; for it is a fact which time will establish, that the Crimson-headed Finch of Pennant and Latham, the Purple Finch of the same and other naturalists, the Hemp Bird of Bartram, and the *Fringilla rosea* of Pallas, are one and the same, viz., the Purple Finch, the subject of the present article.*

The Purple Finch is six inches in length, and nine in extent; head, neck, back, breast, rump, and tail-coverts, dark crimson, deepest on the head and chin, and lightest on the lower part of the breast; the back is streaked with dusky; the wings and tail are also dusky black, edged with reddish, the latter a good deal forked; round the base of the bill, the recumbent feathers are of a light clay or cream color; belly and vent, white; sides under the wings, streaked with dull reddish; legs, a dirty purplish flesh color; bill, short, strong, conical, and of a dusky horn color; iris, dark hazel; the feathers covering the ears are more dusky red than the other parts of the head. This is the male when arrived at its full colors. The female is nearly of the same size, of a brown olive or flaxen color, streaked with dusky black; the head, seamed with lateral lines of whitish; above and below the hind part of the ear-feathers, are two streaks of white; the breast is whitish, streaked with a light flax color; tail and wings, as in the male, only both edged with dull brown, instead of red; belly and vent, white. This is also the color of the young during the first, and to at least the end of the

---

* The present figure is that of an adult male; and that sex in the winter state is again figured and described in the second volume. (London edition.) Bonaparte has shown that Wilson is wrong in making the *F. rosea* of Pallas, and the *Loxia erythrina* of Gmelin, the same with his bird. Mr. Swainson remarks, "We are almost persuaded that there are two distinct species of these Purple Finches, which not only Wilson, but all the modern ornithologists of America, have confounded under the same name." We may reasonably conclude, then, that another allied species may yet be discovered, and that perhaps Wilson was wrong regarding birds which he took for the *F. rosea*.

F. purpurea and *Pyrrhula frontalis* of Say and Bonaparte will rank as a subgenus in *Pyrrhula*, and, from the description of their habits, approach very near to both the Crossbills and Pine Grosbeaks.

By the attention of the Prince of Musignano, I have received his review of Cuvier's *Règne Animal*, and am now enabled to state from it the opinion of that ornithologist regarding the station of these birds. He agrees in the subordinate rank of the group, and its alliance to the Finches, Bullfinches, and *Coccothraustes* or Hawfinch, and proposes the subgeneric name of *Erythrospiza*, which I have provisionally adopted; having *Fringilla purpurea* of Wilson as typical, and containing *Pyrrhula frontalis*, Say and Bonap.; *P. githaginea*, Temm. Pl. Col.; *Loxia Siberica*, Falck.; *L. rosea*, Pall.; *L. erythrina*, Pall.; *P. synoica*, Temm. Pl. Col.; and *L. rubicilla*, Lath. According to the list of species which he has mentioned, and which we have no present opportunity of comparing with the true type, the group will have a very extensive distribution over America, Europe, Asia, and Africa. — ED.

second season, when the males begin to become lighter yellowish. which gradually brightens to crimson; the female always retains nearly the same appearance. The young male bird of the first year may be distinguished from the female by the tail of the former being edged with olive green, that of the latter with brown. A male of one of these birds, which I kept for some time, changed in the month of October from red to greenish yellow, but died before it recovered its former color.

BROWN CREEPER. — CERTHIA FAMILIARIS. — Fig. 29.

Little Brown Variegated Creeper, *Bartram*, 289. — *Peale's Museum*, No. 2434.

CERTHIA FAMILIARIS. — Linnæus.

Certhia familiaris, *Linn. Syst. Nat.* i. 469. *Bonap. Synop.* p. 95. — The Creeper, *Bewick, Brit. Birds*, i. p. 148. — Le Grimpereau, *Temm. Man.* i. p. 410. — Common Creeper, *Selby Ill.* plate 39, vol. i. p. 116.

This bird agrees so nearly with the Common European Creeper, (*Certhia familiaris*,) that I have little doubt of their being one and the same species.* I have examined, at different times, great numbers of these birds, and have endeavored to make a correct drawing of the male, that Europeans and others may judge for themselves; and the excellent artist to whom the plate was intrusted has done his part so well in the engraving, as to render the figure a perfect resemblance of the living original.

The Brown Creeper is an extremely active and restless little bird. In winter it associates with the small Spotted Woodpecker, Nuthatch, Titmouse, &c.; and often follows in their rear, gleaning up those

---

* I have compared numerous British specimens with skins from North America, and can find no differences that will entitle a separation of species. In this country they are very abundant, more so apparently in winter, so that we either receive a great accession from the more northern parts of Europe, or the colder season and diminished supply of food draws them from their woody solitudes nearer to the habitations of man. It is often said to be rare — an opinion no doubt arising from the difficulty of seeing it, and from its solitary and unassuming manners. A short quotation from a late author will best explain our meaning, and confirm the account of its manners, so correctly described above. "A retired inhabitant of the woods and groves, and not in any way conspicuous for voice or plumage, it passes its days with us, creating scarcely any notice or attention. Its small size, and the manner in which it procures its food, both tend to secrete him from sight. In these pursuits its actions are more like those of a mouse than of a bird, darting like a great moth from tree to tree, uttering a faint, trilling sound as it fixes on their boles, running round them in a spiral direction, when, with repeated wriggles, having gained the summit, it darts to the base of another, and commences again." The present species will form the type and only individual yet discovered of the genus *Certhia*. The other birds described by our author as *Certhiæ*, will all rank elsewhere; and the groups now known under the titles *Cinyris, Nectarinia*, &c., which were formerly included, making it of great extent, and certainly of very varied forms, will also with propriety hold their separate stations. The solitary type ranges in Europe, according to Pennant, as far north as Russia and Siberia, and Sandmore in Sweden. In North America, it will extend nearly over the whole continent. — Ed.

insects which their more powerful bills had alarmed and exposed; for its own slender, incurvated bill seems unequal to the task of penetrating into even the decayed wood; though it may into holes, and behind scales of the bark. Of the Titmouse, there are, generally, present the individuals of a whole family, and seldom more than one or two of the others. As the party advances through the woods from tree to tree, our little gleaner seems to observe a good deal of regularity in his proceedings; for I have almost always observed that he alights on the body near the root of the tree, and directs his course, with great nimbleness, upwards, to the higher branches, sometimes spirally, often in a direct line, moving rapidly and uniformly along, with his tail bent to the tree, and not in the hopping manner of the Woodpecker, whom he far surpasses in dexterity of climbing, running along the lower side of the horizontal branches with surprising ease. If any person be near when he alights, he is sure to keep the opposite side of the tree, moving round as he moves, so as to prevent him from getting more than a transient glimpse of him. The best method of outwitting him, if you are alone, is, as soon as he alights, and disappears behind the trunk, take your stand behind an adjoining one, and keep a sharp look-out twenty or thirty feet up the body of the tree he is upon, — for he generally mounts very regularly to a considerable height, examining the whole way as he advances. In a minute or two, hearing all still, he will make his appearance on one side or other of the tree, and give you an opportunity of observing him.

These birds are distributed over the whole United States, but are most numerous in the Western and Northern States, and particularly so in the depth of the forests, and in tracts of large timbered woods, where they usually breed, visiting the thicker settled parts of the country in fall and winter. They are more abundant in the flat woods of the lower district of New Jersey than in Pennsylvania, and are frequently found among the pines. Though their customary food appears to consist of those insects of the coleopterous class, yet I have frequently found in their stomachs the seeds of the pine-tree, and fragments of a species of fungus that vegetates in old wood, with generally a large proportion of gravel. There seems to be scarcely any difference between the colors and markings of the male and female. In the month of March, I opened eleven of these birds, among whom were several females, as appeared by the clusters of minute eggs with which their ovaries were filled, and also several well-marked males ; and, on the most careful comparison of their plumage, I could find little or no difference ; the colors, indeed, were rather more vivid and intense in some than in others : but sometimes this superiority belonged to a male, sometimes to a female, and appeared to be entirely owing to difference in age. I found, however, a remarkable and very striking difference in their sizes ; some were considerably larger, and had the bill, at least, one third longer and stronger than the others, and these I uniformly found to be males. I also received two of these birds from the country bordering on the Cayuga Lake, in New York state, from a person who killed them from the tree in which they had their nest. The male of this pair had the bill of the same extraordinary size with several others I had examined before ; the plumage in every respect the same. Other males, indeed, were found at the same time, of the usual size. Whether this be only an accidental variety, or whether the male, when full grown, be naturally so much larger than the female, (as is the case with many birds,) and takes several years in arriving at his full size, I cannot positively determine, though I think the latter most probable.

The Brown Creeper builds his nest in the hollow trunk or branch of a tree, where the tree has been shivered, or a limb broken off, or where Squirrels or Woodpeckers have wrought out an entrance; for nature has not provided him with the means of excavating one for himself. I have known the female begin to lay by the 17th of April. The eggs are usually seven, of a dull cinereous, marked with small dots of reddish yellow, and streaks of dark brown. The young come forth with great caution, creeping about long before they venture on wing. From the early season at which they begin to build, I have no doubts of their raising two broods during summer, as I have seen the old ones entering holes late in July.

The length of this bird is five inches, and nearly seven from the extremity of one wing to that of the other; the upper part of the head is of a deep brownish black; the back brown, and both streaked with white, the plumage of the latter being of a loose texture, with its filaments not adhering; the white is in the centre of every feather, and is skirted with brown; lower part of the back, rump, and tail-coverts, rusty brown, the last minutely tipped with whitish; the tail is as long as the body, of a light drab color, with the inner web dusky, and consists of twelve quills, each sloping off and tapering to a point in the manner of the Woodpeckers, but proportionably weaker in the shafts; in many specimens the tail was very slightly marked with transverse, undulating waves of dusky, scarce observable; the two middle feathers the longest, the others on each side shortening, by one sixth of an inch, to the outer one; the wing consists of nineteen feathers, the first an inch long, the fourth and fifth the longest, of a deep brownish black, and crossed about its middle with a curving band of rufous white, a quarter of an inch in breadth, marking ten of the quills; below this the quills are exteriorly edged, to within a little of their tips, with rufous white, and tipped with white; the three secondaries next the body are dusky white on their inner webs, tipped on the exterior margin with white, and above that, alternately streaked laterally with black and dull white; the greater and lesser wing-coverts are exteriorly tipped with white; the upper part of the exterior edges of the former, rufous white; the line over the eye, and whole lower parts, are white, a little brownish towards the vent, but, on the chin and throat, pure, silky, and glistening; the white curves inwards about the middle of the neck; the bill is half an inch long, slender, compressed sidewise, bending downwards, tapering to a point, dusky above, and white below; the nostrils are oblong, half covered with a convex membrane, and without hairs or small feathers; the inside of the mouth is reddish; the tongue tapering gradually to a point, and horny towards the tip; the eye is dark hazel; the legs and feet, a dirty clay color; the toes, placed three before and one behind, the two outer ones connected with the middle one to the first joint; the claws rather paler, large, almost semicircular, and extremely sharp pointed; the hind claw the largest.

GOLDEN-CRESTED WREN. — SYLVIA REGULUS. — Fig. 30.

Motacilla Regulus, *Linn. Syst.* i. 338, 48. — *Lath. Syn.* iv. 508, 145. — *Edw.* 254.
— *Peale's Museum*, No. 7246.

REGULUS REGULOIDES. — Jardine.

Regulus cristatus, *Bonap. Synop.* p. 91. — Female Golden-crowned Gold-Crest,
Cont. of N. A. Orn. i. pl. 2, p. 22. — Sylvia reguloides, *Sw.* MSS.

THIS diminutive species is a frequent associate of the one last
described, and seems to be almost a citizen of the world at large,
having been found not only in North and South America, the West
Indies, and Europe, but even in Africa and India. The specimen

---

* The Gold-Crests, the Common Wrens, with an immense and varied host of species, were associated together in the genus *Sylvia*, until ornithologists began to look,
not to the external characters in a limited view only, but in connection with the
habits and affinities which invariably connect species together. Then many divisions were formed, and among these subordinate groups, *Regulus* of Ray was proposed for this small but beautiful tribe. It was used by Stephens, the continuator
of Shaw's *Zoology*, and by Bonaparte in his *Synopsis of North American Birds*,
and the first volume of his elegant Continuation of Wilson. Mr. Swainson makes
this genus the typical form of the whole *Sylvianæ*, but designates it on that account
under the title *Sylvia*. I have retained the old name of *Regulus*, on account of its
former use by Ray, also from its having been adopted to this form by Stephens
and Bonaparte, and lastly, as liable to create less confusion than the bringing forward of an old name (though denoting the typical affinity of the typical group)
which has been applied to so many different forms in the same family.
    Wilson was in error regarding the species here figured and the Common Gold-
Crest of Europe being identical, and Bonaparte has fallen into the same mistake
when figuring the female. *Regulus cristatus* is exclusively European. *Regulus
reguloides* appears yet exclusively North American. Upon comparing the two
species minutely together, I find the following variations : — Length of *R. reguloides*, three inches seven eighths — of *R. cristatus*, from three inches and a half to
three inches six eighths. In *R. cristatus* the bill is longer and more dilated at the
base, and the under parts of the body are more tinged with olive, — in *R. reguloides* the orange part of the crest is much broader, and the black surrounding it,
with the bar in front, broader and more distinct ; the white streak above the eye is
also better marked, and the nape of the neck has a pale ash-gray tinge, nearly
wanting entirely in the British species.†
    This very hardy and active tribe, with one exception, inhabits the temperate and
northern climates, reaching even to the boundaries of the arctic circle. They are
migratory in the more northern countries ; and though some species are able to
brave our severest winters, others are no doubt obliged, by want of food and a lower
degree of cold, to quit the rigors of northern latitudes. The species of our author
performs migrations northward to breed ; and in Great Britain, at the commencement of winter, we have a regular accession to the numbers of our own Gold-Crest.
If we examine their size, strength, and powers of flight, we must view the extent
of their journeys with astonishment ; they are indeed often so much exhausted, on
their first arrival, as to be easily taken, and many sometimes even perish with the
fatigue. A remarkable instance of a large migration is related by Mr. Selby, as

---

† There is a curious structure in the covering of the nostrils in most birds ; where there
is any in addition to the horny substance, it is composed either of fine bristles or hairs, or
of narrow feathers closely spread together. In the Gold-Crests it consists of a single
plumelet on each side, the webs diverging widely.

from Europe, in Mr. Peale's collection, appears to be in nothing specifically different from the American; and the very accurate description given of this bird, by the Count de Buffon, agrees in every respect with ours. Here, as in Europe, it is a bird of passage, making its first appearance in Pennsylvania early in April, among the blossoms of the maple, often accompanied by the Ruby-crowned Wren, which, except in the markings of the head, it very much resembles. It is very frequent among evergreens, such as the pine, spruce, cedar, juniper, &c., and in the fall is generally found in company with the two species of Titmouse, Brown Creeper, and small Spotted Woodpecker. It is an active, unsuspicious, and diligent little creature, climbing and hanging, occasionally, among the branches, and sometimes even on the body of the tree, in search of the larvæ of insects attached to the leaves and stems, and various

occurring on the coast of Northumberland in 1822, when the sandhills and links were perfectly covered with them.

"On the 24th and 25th of October, 1822, after a very severe gale, with thick fog, from the north-east, (but veering, towards its conclusion, to the east and south of east,) thousands of these birds were seen to arrive upon the sea-shore and sandbanks of the Northumbrian coast; many of them so fatigued by the length of their flight, or perhaps by the unfavorable shift of wind, as to be unable to rise again from the ground, and great numbers were in consequence caught or destroyed. This flight must have been immense in quantity, as its extent was traced through the whole length of the coasts of Northumberland and Durham. There appears little doubt of this having been a migration from the more northern provinces of Europe, (probably furnished by the pine forests of Norway, Sweden, &c.,) from the circumstance of its arrival being simultaneous with that of large flights of the Woodcock, Fieldfare, and Redwing. Although I had never before witnessed the actual arrival of the Gold-crested Regulus, I had long felt convinced, from the great and sudden increase of the species during the autumnal and hyemal months, that our indigenous birds must be augmented by a body of strangers, making these shores their winter's resort.

"A more extraordinary circumstance in the economy of this bird took place during the same winter, (Memoirs of Wernerian Society, vol. v. p. 397,) viz., the total disappearance of the whole tribe, natives as well as strangers, throughout Scotland and the north of England. This happened towards the conclusion of the month of January, 1823, and a few days previous to the long-continued snow-storm so severely felt through the northern counties of England, and along the eastern parts of Scotland. The range and point of this migration are unascertained, but it must probably have been a distant one, from the fact of not a single pair having returned to breed, or pass the succeeding summer, in the situations they had been known always to frequent. Nor was one of the species to be seen till the following October, or about the usual time, as I have above stated, for our receiving an annual accession of strangers to our own indigenous birds."

They are chiefly, if not entirely, insectivorous, and very nimble and agile in search after their prey. They build their nests with great art, — that of this country has it usually suspended near the extremity of a branch, and the outside beautifully covered with different mosses, generally similar to those growing upon the tree on which they build. In colors and the distribution of them, they closely agree, and all possess the beautiful golden crown, the well-known and admired mark of their common name. Our own island possesses only one, and though strong hopes have lately been raised of finding the second European species, R. ignicapillus, our endeavors have hitherto been unsuccessful. But I do not yet despair; they are so closely allied that a very near inspection is necessary to determine the individuals.

Mr. Audubon has described and figured a bird under the name of R. Cuvierii, which may prove an addition to this genus. Only a single specimen was procured in Pennsylvania, and the species will rest on Mr. Audubon's plate alone, until some others are obtained. The centre of the crest is described and represented of a rich vermilion. — ED.

8

kinds of small flies, which it frequently seizes on wing. As it retires still farther north to breed, it is seldom seen in Pennsylvania from May to October; but is then numerous in orchards, feeding among the leaves of the apple-trees, which, at that season, are infested with vast numbers of small, black-winged insects. Its chirp is feeble, not much louder than that of a mouse; though, where it breeds, the male is said to have a variety of sprightly notes. It builds its nest frequently on the branches of an evergreen, covers it entirely round, leaving a small hole on one side for entrance, forming it outwardly of moss and lichens, and lining it warmly with down. The female lays six or eight eggs, pure white, with a few minute specks of dull red. Dr. Latham, on whose authority this is given, observes, "It seems to frequent the oak-trees in preference to all others. I have more than once seen a brood of these in a large oak, in the middle of a lawn, the whole little family of which, as soon as able, were in perpetual motion, and gave great pleasure to many who viewed them. The nest of one of these has also been made in a garden on a fir-tree; it was composed of moss, the opening on one side, in shape roundish; it was lined with a downy substance, fixed with small filaments. It is said to sing very melodiously, very like the Common Wren, but weaker."* In Pennsylvania, they continue with us from October to December, and sometimes to January.

The Golden-crested Wren is four inches long, and six inches and a half in extent; back, a fine yellow olive; hind head and sides of the neck, inclining to ash; a line of white passes round the frontlet, extending over and beyond the eye on each side; above this, another line or strip of deep black passes in the same manner, extending farther behind; between these two strips of black, lies a bed of glossy golden yellow, which, being parted a little, exposes another of a bright flame color, extending over the whole upper part of the head; when the little warbler flits among the branches, in pursuit of insects, he opens and shuts this golden ornament with great adroitness, which produces a striking and elegant effect; lores, marked with circular points of black; below the eye is a rounding spot of dull white; from the upper mandible to the bottom of the ear-feathers runs a line of black, accompanied by another of white, from the lower mandible; breast, light cream color; sides under the wings, and vent, the same; wings, dusky, edged exteriorly with yellow olive; greater wing-coverts, tipped with white, immediately below which, a spot of black extends over several of the secondaries; tail, pretty long, forked, dusky, exterior vanes broadly edged with yellow olive; legs, brown; feet and claws, yellow; bill, black, slender, straight, evidently of the *Muscicapa* form, the upper mandible being notched at the point, and furnished at the base with bristles, that reach half way to its point; but, what seems singular and peculiar to this little bird, the nostril on each side is covered by a single feather, that much resembles the antennæ of some butterflies, and is half the length of the bill. Buffon has taken notice of the same in the European. Inside of the mouth, a reddish orange; claws, extremely sharp, the hind one the longest. In the female, the tints and markings are nearly the same,

* *Synopsis,* ii. 509.

only the crown or crest is pale yellow. These birds are numerous in Pennsylvania, in the month of October, frequenting bushes that overhang streams of water, alders, briers, and particularly apple-trees, where they are eminently useful in destroying great numbers of insects, and are at that season extremely fat.

---◆---

HOUSE WREN.—SYLVIA DOMESTICA.—Fig. 31.

Motacilla domestica, (Regulus rufus,) *Bartram*, 291. — *Peale's Museum*, No. 7283.

TROGLODYTES ŒDON.—Vieillot.

Troglodytes œdon, *Bonap. Synop.* p. 93, and note p. 439.—*Northern Zool.* ii. p. 316.—The House Wren, *Aud.* pl. 83. *Orn. Biog.* i. 427.

This well-known and familiar bird arrives in Pennsylvania about the middle of April, and, about the 8th or 10th of May, begins to build its nest, sometimes in the wooden cornice under the eaves, or in a hollow cherry-tree; but most commonly in small boxes, fixed on the top of a pole, in or near the garden, to which he is extremely partial, for the great number of caterpillars and other larvæ with which it constantly supplies him. If all these conveniences are wanting, he will even put up with an old hat, nailed on the weather boards, with a small hole for entrance; and, if even this be denied him, he will find some hole, corner, or crevice about the house, barn, or stable, rather than abandon the dwellings of man. In the month of June, a mower hung up his coat under a shed, near a barn; two or three days elapsed before he had occasion to put it on again; thrusting his arm up the sleeve, he found it completely filled with some rubbish, as he expressed it, and, on extracting the whole mass, found it to be the nest of a wren completely finished, and lined with a large quantity of feathers. In his retreat, he was followed by the little forlorn proprietors, who scolded him with great vehemence for thus ruining the whole economy of their household affairs. The twigs with which the outward parts of the nest are constructed are short and crooked, that they may the better hook in with one another, and the hole or entrance is so much shut up, to prevent the intrusion of snakes or cats, that it appears almost impossible the body of the bird could be admitted; within this is a layer of fine dried stalks of grass, and lastly feathers. The eggs are six or seven, and sometimes nine, of a red purplish flesh color, innumerable fine grains of that tint being thickly sprinkled over the whole egg. They generally raise two broods in a season; the first about the beginning of June, the second in July.*

" The Wrens figured on this plate, and, indeed, all those of this northern continent, seem to be great favorites with the country people, to which distinction, their utility in gardens in destroying caterpillars and noxious insects, their sprightly, social manner, with their clean and neat appearance, fully entitle them. They

This little bird has a strong antipathy to cats; for, having frequent occasion to glean among the currant bushes, and other shrubbery in the garden, those lurking enemies of the feathered race often prove fatal to him. A box fitted up in the window of the room where I slept, was taken possession of by a pair of Wrens. Already the nest was built, and two eggs laid, when one day, the window being open, as well as the room door, the female Wren, venturing too far into the room to reconnoitre, was sprung upon by Grimalkin, who had planted herself there for the purpose, and, before relief could be given, was destroyed. Curious to see how the survivor would demean himself, I

form the genus *Troglodytes* of moderns, are limited in numbers, but distributed over Europe, America, and Africa; their habits are nearly alike, and the colors of the plumage are so similar, that some species are with difficulty distinguished from each other; and both those now figured have been confounded with that of this country, from which, however, the first differs, and the latter is still doubtful. The colors of the plumage are brown, with bars and crossings of darker shades, intermingled occasionally with spots, and irregular blotches of yellowish white. They make very commodious nests, with a single entrance; all those with which we are acquainted are very prolific, breed more than once in the year, and lay at a time from twelve to sixteen eggs; they are always to be met with, but never in such profusion as their numerous broods would lead us to infer if all arrived at maturity. That of this country, though not so tame as to make use of a *ready-made* convenient breeding-place, is extremely familiar, and will build close by a window, or above a door, where there is a constant thoroughfare. It roosts, during the night, in holes of banks, ricks, or in the eaves of thatched houses, and generally seven or eight individuals will occupy one hole, flitting about, and disputing, as it were, which should enter first. These are beautiful provisions for their welfare, and the proportion of animal heat possessed necessarily by so small a bulk. Another curious particular in the economy of these little birds, is the many useless nests which are built, or, as they are sometimes called by boys, *cock nests*. These are never built so carefully, or in such private and recluse situations, as those intended for incubation, and are even sometimes left in an unfinished, half-built state. I have never been able to satisfy myself whether they were the work of the male bird only, or of both conjointly; or to ascertain their use, whether really commenced with the view of breeding in them, or for roosting places. The generally-exposed situation in which they are placed, with the concealed spot chosen for those that have young, would argue against the former, and the latter would, perhaps, require a greater reasoning power than most people would be willing to grant to this animal. They may, perhaps, be the first instinctive efforts of the young. Notwithstanding their small bulk, and tender-looking frame, they are very hardy, and brave the severest winters of this country; driven nearer to our houses from the necessity of food, they seem to rejoice in a hard, clear frost, singing merrily on the top of some heap of brushwood, or sounding, in rapid succession, their note of alarm, when disturbed by any unwelcome visitor. A kitty hunt, in a snow storm, used to be a favorite amusement with boys; and many a tumble was got in the unseen ruggedness of the ground when in pursuit. At any time when annoyed, a hole, or thick heap of sticks, will form a refuge for this curious little bird, where it will either remain quiet until the danger is over, or, if there is any under way, will creep and run, escaping at another side; in like manner, it will duck and dive in the openings or hollows of the snow, and at the moment when capture seems inevitable, will escape at some distant opening, disappointing the hopes of the urchin who already anticipated possession.

We must here mention, in addition to the already-described North American species, one figured by Mr. Audubon, and dedicated to an artist, who will be long remembered by the British ornithologist, *Troglodytes Bewickii*. Mr. Audubon has killed three specimens of it in Louisiana, and observes, "In shape, form, color, and movements, it nearly resembles the great Carolina Wren, and forms a kind of link between that bird and the House Wren. It has not the quickness of motion, nor the liveliness of either of these birds." — Ed.

watched him carefully for several days. At first he sung with great vivacity for an hour or so, but, becoming uneasy, went off for half an hour; on his return, he chanted again as before, went to the top of the house, stable, and weeping-willow, that she might hear him; but, seeing no appearance of her, he returned once more, visited the nest, ventured cautiously into the window, gazed about with suspicious looks, his voice sinking to a low, melancholy note, as he stretched his little neck about in every direction. Returning to the box, he seemed for some minutes at a loss what to do, and soon after went off, as I thought, altogether, for I saw him no more that day. Towards the afternoon of the second day, he again made his appearance, accompanied with a new female, who seemed exceedingly timorous and shy, and who, after great hesitation, entered the box; at this moment the little widower or bridegroom seemed as if he would warble out his very life with ecstasy of joy. After remaining about half a minute in, they both flew off, but returned in a few minutes, and instantly began to carry out the eggs, feathers, and some of the sticks, supplying the place of the two latter with materials of the same sort, and ultimately succeeded in raising a brood of seven young, all of which escaped in safety.

The immense number of insects which this sociable little bird removes from the garden and fruit-trees, ought to endear him to every cultivator, even if he had nothing else to recommend him; but his notes, loud, sprightly, tremulous, and repeated every few seconds with great animation, are extremely agreeable. In the heat of summer, families in the country often dine under the piazza adjoining green canopies of mantling grape vines, gourds, &c., while overhead the trilling vivacity of the Wren, mingled with the warbling mimicry of the Mocking Bird, and the distant, softened sounds of numerous other songsters, that we shall hereafter introduce to the reader's acquaintance, form a soul-soothing and almost heavenly music, breathing peace, innocence, and rural repose. The European who judges of the song of this species by that of his own Wren, (*M. troglodytes*,) will do injustice to the former, as, in strength of tone and execution, it is far superior, as well as the bird is in size, figure, and elegance of markings, to the European one. Its manners are also different; its sociability greater. It is no underground inhabitant; its nest is differently constructed, the number of its eggs fewer; it is also migratory, and has the tail and bill much longer. Its food is insects and caterpillars, and, while supplying the wants of its young, it destroys, on a moderate calculation, many hundreds a day, and greatly circumscribes the ravages of these vermin. It is a bold and insolent bird against those of the Titmouse and Woodpecker kind that venture to build within its jurisdiction; attacking them without hesitation, though twice its size, and generally forcing them to decamp. I have known him drive a pair of Swallows from their newly-formed nest, and take immediate possession of the premises, in which his female also laid her eggs, and reared her young. Even the Blue-Bird, who claims an equal and sort of hereditary right to the box in the garden, when attacked by this little impertinent, soon relinquishes the contest, the mild placidness of his disposition not being a match

8 *

for the fiery impetuosity of his little antagonist. With those of his own species who settle and build near him, he has frequent squabbles; and when their respective females are sitting, each strains his whole powers of song to excel the other. When the young are hatched, the hurry and press of business leave no time for disputing, so true it is that idleness is the mother of mischief. These birds are not confined to the country; they are to be heard on the tops of the houses in the most central parts of our cities, singing with great energy. Scarce a house or cottage in the country is without at least a pair of them, and sometimes two; but unless where there is a large garden, orchard, and numerous outhouses, it is not often the case that more than one pair reside near the same spot, owing to their party disputes and jealousies. It has been said by a friend to this little bird, that "the esculent vegetables of a whole garden may, perhaps, be preserved from the depredations of different species of insects, by ten or fifteen pair of these small birds;" * and probably they might, were the combination practicable; but such a congregation of Wrens about one garden is a phenomenon not to be expected but from a total change in the very nature and disposition of the species.

Having seen no accurate description of this bird in any European publication, I have confined my references to Mr. Bartram and Mr. Peale; but though Europeans are not ignorant of the existence of this bird, they have considered it, as usual, merely as a slight variation from the original stock, (*M. troglodytes*,) their own Wren; in which they are, as usual, mistaken; the length and bent form of the bill, its notes, migratory habits, long tail, and red eggs, are sufficient specific differences.

The House Wren inhabits the whole of the United States, in all of which it is migratory. It leaves Pennsylvania in September; I have sometimes, though rarely, seen it in the beginning of October. It is four inches and a half long, and five and three quarters in extent, the whole upper parts of a deep brown, transversely crossed with black, except the head and neck, which is plain; throat, breast, and cheeks, light clay color; belly and vent, mottled with black, brown, and white; tail, long, cuneiform, crossed with black; legs and feet, light clay color, bill, black, long, slightly curved, sharp pointed, and resembling that of the genus *Certhia*, considerably; the whole plumage below the surface is bluish ash; that on the rump having large, round spots of white, not perceivable unless separated with the hand. The female differs very little in plumage from the male.

* BARTON's *Fragments*, part i. p. 22.

BLACK-CAPPED TITMOUSE. — PARUS ATRICAPILLUS. —
Fig. 32.

Parus atricapillus, *Linn. Syst.* i. 341, 6. — *Gmel. Syst.* i. 1008. — La Mésange à tête noire de Canada, *Buffon,* v. 408. — Canada Titmouse, *Arct. Zool.* ii. No. 323. — *Lath. Syn.* iv. 542, 9. — *Peale's Museum,* No. 7380.

PARUS ATRICAPILLUS. — LINNÆUS.*

Parus atricapillus, *Bonap. Synop.* p. 100. — *North. Zool.* p. 226.

THIS is one of our resident birds, active, noisy, and restless; hardy beyond any of his size, braving the severest cold of our continent as far north as the country round Hudson's Bay, and always appearing most lively in the coldest weather. The males have a variety of very sprightly notes, which cannot, indeed, be called a song, but rather a lively, frequently repeated, and often varied twitter. They are most usually seen during the fall and winter, when they leave the depths of the woods, and approach nearer to the scenes of cultivation. At such seasons, they abound among evergreens, feeding on the seeds of the pine-tree; they are also fond of sunflower seeds, and associate in parties of six, eight, or more, attended by the two species of Nuthatch already described, the Crested Titmouse, Brown Creeper, and small Spotted Woodpecker; the whole forming a very nimble and restless company, whose food, manners, and dispositions are pretty much alike. About the middle of April they begin to build, choosing the deserted hole of a Squirrel or Woodpecker, and sometimes, with incredible labor, digging out one for themselves. The female lays six white eggs, marked with minute specks of red; the first brood appear about the beginning of June, and the second towards the end of July; the whole of the family continue to associate together during winter. They traverse the woods in regular progression, from tree to tree, tumbling, chattering, and hanging from the extremities of the branches, examining about the roots of the leaves, buds, and crevices of the bark, for insects and their larvæ. They also frequently visit the orchards, particularly in fall, the sides of the barn and barn yard, in the same pursuit, trees in such situations being generally much infested with insects. We, therefore, with pleasure, rank this little bird among the farmer's friends, and trust our rural citizens will always recognize him as such.

This species has a very extensive range; it has been found on the western coast of America, as far north as lat. 62°; it is common at Hudson's Bay, and most plentiful there during winter, as it then approaches the settlements in quest of food. Protected by a remarkably thick covering of long, soft, downy plumage, it braves the severest cold of those northern regions.

* This is very closely allied to the *Parus palustris,* the Marsh Titmouse of Europe; but it is exclusively American, and ranges extensively to the north. The authors of the *Northern Zoology* mention them as one of the most common birds in the Fur countries; a family inhabits almost every thicket. — ED.

The Black-capped Titmouse is five inches and a half in length, and six and a half in extent; throat, and whole upper part of the head and ridge of the neck, black; between these lines a triangular patch of white, ending at the nostril; bill, black and short; tongue, truncate; rest of the upper parts, lead colored or cinereous, slightly tinged with brown; wings, edged with white; breast, belly, and vent, yellowish white; legs, light blue; eyes, dark hazel. The male and female are nearly alike. The Fig. 32, in the plate, renders any further description unnecessary.

The upper parts of the head of the young are for some time of a dirty brownish tinge; and in this state they agree so exactly with the *Parus Hudsonicus*,* described by Latham, as to afford good grounds for suspecting them to be the same.

These birds sometimes fight violently with each other, and are known to attack young and sickly birds, that are incapable of resistance, always directing their blows against the skull.† Being in the woods one day, I followed a bird for some time, the singularity of whose notes surprised me. Having shot him from off the top of a very tall tree, I found it to be the Black-headed Titmouse, with a long and deep indentation in the cranium, the skull having been evidently, at some former time, drove in and fractured, but was now perfectly healed. Whether or not the change of voice could be owing to this circumstance, I cannot pretend to decide.

CRESTED TITMOUSE. — PARUS BICOLOR. — Fig. 33.

Parus bicolor, *Linn. Syst.* i. 544, 1. — La Mésange huppée de la Caroline, *Buff.* v. 451. — Toupet Titmouse, *Arct. Zool.* i. No. 324. — *Lath. Syn.* iv. 544, 11. — *Peale's Museum,* No. 7364.

PARUS BICOLOR. — LINNÆUS.

Parus bicolor, *Bonap. Synop.* p. 100. — The Crested Titmouse, *Aud.* pl. 39. *Orn. Biog.* i. p. 198.

THIS is another associate of the preceding species, but more noisy, more musical, and more suspicious, though rather less active. It is, nevertheless, a sprightly bird, possessing a remarkable variety in the tones of its voice, at one time not much louder than the squeaking of a mouse, and a moment after whistling aloud, and clearly, as if calling a dog; and continuing this dog-call through the woods for half an hour at a time. Its high, pointed crest, or, as Pennant calls it, *toupet,*

---

* Hudson Bay Titmouse, *Synopsis,* ii. 557.

† I have frequently heard this stated regarding the British Titmice, particularly the Greater, but I have never been able to trace it to any authentic source; it is perhaps exaggerated. Feeding on carrion, which they have also been represented to do, must in a wild state be from necessity. Mr. Audubon asserts it as a fact, with regard to the *P. bicolor.* Mr. Selby has seen *P. major* eat young birds. — ED.

gives it a smart and not inelegant appearance. Its food corresponds with that of the foregoing; it possesses considerable strength in the muscles of its neck, and is almost perpetually digging into acorns, nuts, crevices, and rotten parts of the bark, after the larvæ of insects. It is also a constant resident here. When shot at and wounded, it fights with great spirit. When confined to a cage, it soon becomes familiar, and will subsist on hemp seed, cherry stones, apple seeds, and hickory nuts, broken and thrown into it. However, if the cage be made of willows, and the bird not much hurt, he will soon make his way through them. The great concavity of the lower side of the wings and tail of this genus of birds, is a strong characteristic, and well suited to their short, irregular flight.

This species is also found over the whole United States, but is most numerous towards the north. It extends also to Hudson's Bay, and, according to Latham, is found in Denmark, and in the southern parts of Greenland, where it is called *Avingarsak*. If so, it probably inhabits the continent of North America, from sea to sea.

The Crested Titmouse is six inches long, and seven inches and a half in extent. The whole upper parts, a dull cinereous or lead color, except the front, which is black, tinged with reddish; whole lower parts, dirty white, except the sides under the wings, which are reddish orange; legs and feet, light blue; bill, black, short, and pretty strong; wing-feathers, relieved with dusky on their inner vanes; eye, dark hazel; lores, white; the head, elegantly ornamented with a high, pointed, almost upright crest; tail, a little forked, considerably concave below, and of the same color above as the back; tips of the wings, dusky; tongue, very short, truncate, and ending in three or four sharp points. The female cannot be distinguished from the male by her plumage, unless in its being something duller, for both are equally marked with reddish orange on the sides under the wings, which some foreigners have made the distinguishing mark of the male alone.

The nest is built in a hollow tree, the cavity often dug by itself; the female begins to lay early in May; the eggs are usually six, pure white, with a few very small specks of red near the great end. The whole family, in the month of July, hunt together, the parents keeping up a continual chatter, as if haranguing and directing their inexperienced brood.*

---

* This beautiful and attractive race of birds, the genuine Titmice, have a geographical distribution over the whole world,—South America, New Holland, and the islands in the South Pacific Ocean, excepted. In the latter countries, they seem represented by the genus *Pardalotus*, yet, however, very limited in numbers. They are more numerous in temperate and even northern climates, than near the tropics; the greater numbers, both as to individuals and species, extend over Europe. In this country, when the want of foliage allows us to examine their manners, they form one of the most interesting of our winter visitants. I call them *visitants* only; for during summer they are occupied with the duties of incubation in retirement, amid the depths of the most solitary forests, and only at the commencement of winter, or during its rigors, become more domesticated, and flock in small parties, the amount of their broods, to our gardens, and the vicinity of our houses; several species together, and generally in company with the Gold-crested Wrens. The activity of their motions in search of food, or in dispute with one another; the variety of their cries, from something very shrill and timid, to loud and wild; their sometimes elegant, sometimes grotesque attitudes, contrasted by the difference of form; and the varied flights, from the short dart and jerk of the Marsh and Cole

WINTER WREN. — SYLVIA TROGLODYTES. — Fig. 34.

Motacilla troglodytes ? *Linn.* — *Peale's Museum.* No. 7284

TROGLODYTES HYEMALIS ? — Vieillot.

Troglodytes Europeus Leach, *Bonap. Synop.* p. 93. — Troglodytes hyemalis, *Vieill. Encyc. Méth.* ii. p. 470. — *North. Zool.* ii. p. 318.

This little stranger visits us from the north in the month of October, sometimes remaining with us all the winter, and is always observed, early in spring, on his route back to his breeding-place. In size, color, song, and manners, he approaches nearer to the European Wren

Titmouse, or Gold-crested Wren, to the stringy successive line of the Long-tailed one, — are objects which have, no doubt, called forth the notice of the ornithologist who has sometimes allowed himself to examine them in their natural abodes. The form of the different species is nearly alike ; thick-set, stout, and short, the legs comparatively strong, the whole formed for active motion, and uniting strength for the removal of loose bark, moss, or even rotten wood, in search of their favorite food, insects ; it, however, varies in two species of this country, (one of which will form a separate subdivision,) the Long-tailed and the Bearded Titmice, (*P. caudatus* and *biarmicus,*) in the weaker frame and more lengthened shape of the tail ; and it may be remarked, that both these make suspended nests, the one in woods, of a lengthened form and beautiful workmanship, generally hung near the extremity of a branch belonging to some thick silver, spruce, or Scotch fir ; the other balanced and waving among reeds, like some of the aquatic Warblers ; while all the other species, and indeed all those abroad with whole nidification I am acquainted, choose some hollow tree or rent wall, for their place of breeding. In a Brazilian species, figured by Temminck, the tail assumes a forked shape.

Insects are not their only food, though perhaps the most natural. When the season becomes too inclement for this supply, they become granivorous, and will plunder the farm yards, or eat grain and potatoes with the poultry and pigs. Some I have seen so domesticated, (the common Blue and Greater Titmice,) as to come regularly during the storm to the windows, for crumbs of bread. When confined, they become very docile, and will also eat pieces of flesh or fat. During winter, they roost in holes of trees or walls, eaves of thatched houses, or hay and corn ricks. When not in holes, they remain suspended, with the back downwards or outwards. A common Blue Tomtit (and, I have no doubt, the same individual) has roosted for three years in the same spot, under one of the projecting capitals of a pillar, by the side of my own front door. The colors of the group are chaste and pleasing, as might have been expected from their distribution. There are, however, one or two exceptions in those figured by M. Temminck, from Africa. The general shades are black, gray, white, blue, and different tints of olive, sometimes reddish brown ; and in these, when the brightest colors occur, the blue and yellow, they are so blended, as not to be hard or offensive. Most of the species have some decided marks or coloring about the head, and the plumage is thick and downy, and loose — a very necessary requisite to those which frequent the more northern latitudes.

Mr. Audubon says that this species sometimes forms a nest, by digging a hole for the purpose in the hardest wood with great industry and perseverance, although it is more frequently contented with the hole of the Downy Woodpecker, or some other small bird of that genus. We can hardly conceive that the Crested Titmouse, or indeed any of the race, had sufficient strength to dig its own nest. The bill, though very powerful, when compared with the individual's bulk, is not formed on the principle of those which excavate for themselves. I lately received the nest of this species, taken from some hollow tree. The inside lining was almost entirely composed of the scales and cast-off exuvia of snakes. — Ed.

(*M. troglodytes*) than any other species we have. During his residence
here, he frequents the projecting banks of creeks, old roots, decayed
logs, small bushes, and rushes near watery places; he even approaches
the farm-house, rambles about the wood pile, creeping among the interstices like a mouse. With tail erect, which is his constant habit,
mounted on some projecting point or pinnacle, he sings with great
animation. Even in the yards, gardens, and outhouses of the city,
he appears familiar and quite at home. In short, he possesses almost
all the habits of the European species. He is, however, migratory,
which may be owing to the superior coldness of our continent. Never
having met with the nest and eggs, I am unable to say how nearly
they approximate to those of the former.

I can find no precise description of this bird, as an American species,
in any European publication. Even some of our own naturalists seem
to have confounded it with another very different bird, the Marsh
Wren,* which arrives in Pennsylvania from the south in May, builds
a globular or pitcher-shaped nest, which it suspends among the rushes
and bushes by the river side, lays five or six eggs of a dark fawn
color, and departs again in September. But the colors and markings
of that bird are very unlike those of the Winter Wren, and its song
altogether different. The circumstance of the one arriving from the
north as the other returns to the south, and *vice versa*, with some general resemblance between the two, may have occasioned this mistake.
They, however, not only breed in different regions, but belong to
different genera, the Marsh Wren being decisively a species of *Certhia*, and the Winter Wren a true *Motacilla*. Indeed, we have no
less than five species of these birds in Pennsylvania, that, by a superficial observer, would be taken for one and the same, but between each
of which nature has drawn strong, discriminating, and indelible lines
of separation. These will be pointed out in their proper places.

If this bird, as some suppose, retires only to the upper regions of the
country and mountainous forests to breed, as is the case with some
others, it will account for his early and frequent residence along the
Atlantic coast during the severest winters; though I rather suspect
that he proceeds considerably to the northward; as the Snow Bird,
(*F. Hudsonia,*) which arrives about the same time with the Winter
Wren, does not even breed at Hudson's Bay, but passes that settlement in June, on his way to the northward; how much farther is unknown.

The length of the Winter Wren is three inches and a half, breadth,
five inches; the upper parts are of a general dark brown, crossed
with transverse touches of black, except the upper parts of the head
and neck, which are plain; the black spots on the back terminate in
minute points of dull white; the first row of wing-coverts is also
marked with specks of white at the extremities of the back, and
tipped minutely with black; the next row is tipped with points of
white; the primaries are crossed with alternate rows of black and
cream color; inner vanes of all the quills, dusky, except the three secondaries next the body; tips of the wings, dusky; throat, line over the

---

* See Professor Barton's observations on this subject, under the article *Motacilla
troglodytes? Fragments,* &c. p. 18; *Ibid.* p. 12.

eye, sides of the neck, ear-feathers and breast, dirty white, with minute, transverse touches of a drab or clay color; sides under the wings, speckled with dark brown, black, and dirty white; belly and vent, thickly mottled with sooty black, deep brown, and pure white, in transverse touches; tail, very short, consisting of twelve feathers, the exterior one on each side a quarter of an inch shorter, the rest lengthening gradually to the middle ones; legs and feet, a light clay color, and pretty stout; bill, straight, slender, half an inch long, and not notched at the point, of a dark brown or black above, and whitish below; nostril, oblong; eye, light hazel. The female wants the points of white on the wing-coverts. The food of this bird is derived from that great magazine of so many of the feathered race, insects and their larvæ, particularly such as inhabit watery places, roots of bushes, and piles of old timber.

It were much to be wished that the summer residence, nest, and eggs of this bird, were precisely ascertained, which would enable us to determine whether it be, what I strongly suspect it is, the same species as the common domestic Wren of Britain.*

RED–HEADED WOODPECKER. — PICUS ERYTHROCE-PHALUS. — Fig. 35.

Picus erythrocephalus, *Linn. Syst.* i. 174, 7. — *Gmel. Syst.* i. 429. — Pic noir à domino rouge, *Buffon,* vii. 55. *Pl. enl.* 117. — *Catesby,* i. 20. — *Arct. Zool.* ii. No. 160. — *Lath. Syn.* ii. 561. — *Peale's Museum,* No. 1922.

MELANERPES ERYTHROCEPHALUS. — Swainson.†

Picus erythrocephalus, *Bonap. Synop.* p. 45. — *Wagler Spec. Av. Picus,* No. 14. — The Red-headed Woodpecker, *Aud.* pl. 27; *Orn. Biog.* i. p. 141. — Melanerpes erythrocephalus, *North. Zool.* ii. p. 316.

THERE is perhaps no bird in North America more universally known than this. His tricolored plumage, red, white, and black, glossed with

---

* There is a very great alliance between the British and American specimens; and all authors who have described this bird and that of Europe, have done so with uncertainty. Wilson evidently had a doubt, both from what he says, and from marking the species and his synonymes with a query. Vieillot had doubts, and Bonaparte goes a good deal on his authority, but points out no difference between the birds. Mr. Swainson, in the *Northern Zoology,* has described a bird, as that of Vieillot's, killed on the shores of Lake Huron, and proves distinctly that the plumage, and some of the relative proportions, vary. It is likely that there are two American species concerned in this, — one northern, another extending to the south, and that one perhaps may be identical with that of Europe; one certainly seems distinct. I have retained *hyemalis* with a mark of doubt, it being impossible to determine those so closely allied, without an examination of numerous species. — Ed.

† This will point out another of Mr. Swainson's groups among the Woodpeckers, equally distinct with *Colaptes.* The form is long and swallow-like; the bill more rounded than angular, the culmen quite round; the wings nearly as long as the tail. In their manners, they are extremely familiar; and during summer,

steel blue, is so striking and characteristic, and his predatory habits
in the orchards and corn-fields, added to his numbers, and fondness for
hovering along the fences, so very notorious, that almost every child
is acquainted with the Red-headed Woodpecker. In the immediate
neighborhood of our large cities, where the old timber is chiefly cut
down, he is not so frequently found; and yet, at this present time,
(June, 1808,) I know of several of their nests within the boundaries
of the city of Philadelphia. Two of these are in buttonwood-trees
(*Platanus occidentalis*,) and another in the decayed limb of an elm.
The old ones, I observe, make their excursions regularly to the woods
beyond the Schuylkill, about a mile distant; preserving great silence
and circumspection in visiting their nests, — precautions not much
attended to by them in the depth of the woods, because there the
prying eye of man is less to be dreaded. Towards the mountains,
particularly in the vicinity of creeks and rivers, these birds are extremely abundant, especially in the latter end of summer. Wherever
you travel in the interior at that season, you hear them screaming
from the adjoining woods, rattling on the dead limbs of trees, or on
the fences, where they are perpetually seen flitting from stake to
stake, on the roadside, before you. Wherever there is a tree, or trees,
of the wild cherry, covered with ripe fruit, there you see them busy
among the branches; and, in passing orchards, you may easily know
where to find the earliest, sweetest apples, by observing those trees,
on or near which the Red-headed Woodpecker is skulking; for he is
so excellent a connoisseur in fruit, that wherever an apple or pear is
found broached by him, it is sure to be among the ripest and best
flavored: when alarmed, he seizes a capital one by striking his open
bill deep into it, and bears it off to the woods. When the Indian
corn is in its rich, succulent, milky state, he attacks it with great
eagerness, opening a passage through the numerous folds of the husk,
and feeding on it with voracity. The girdled, or deadened timber, so
common among corn-fields in the back settlements, are his favorite
retreats, whence he sallies out to make his depredations. He is fond
of the ripe berries of the sour gum, and pays pretty regular visits to
the cherry-trees, when loaded with fruit. Towards fall he often approaches the barn or farm-house, and raps on the shingles and weather
boards: he is of a gay and frolicsome disposition; and half a dozen
of the fraternity are frequently seen diving and vociferating around
the high, dead limbs of some large tree, pursuing and playing with
each other, and amusing the passenger with their gambols. Their
note, or cry, is shrill and lively, and so much resembles that of a
species of tree-frog which frequents the same tree, that it is sometimes difficult to distinguish the one from the other.

Such are the *vicious* traits, if I may so speak, in the character of
the Red-headed Woodpecker; and I doubt not but, from what has
been said on this subject, that some readers would consider it merito-
rious to exterminate the whole tribe as a nuisance; and, in fact, the
legislatures of some of our provinces, in former times, offered pre-

feed almost entirely on the rich fruits and ripe grains of the country. The chaste
and simple-colored *Picus bicolor*, from the *Minas Geraies*, I believe, will be another
representative of this form. — ED.
9

miums to the amount of twopence per head for their destruction.*
But let us not condemn the species unheard: they exist—they must
therefore be necessary.† If their merits and usefulness be found, on
examination, to preponderate against their vices, let us avail ourselves
of the former, while we guard as well as we can against the latter.

Though this bird occasionally regales himself on fruit, yet his
natural and most useful food is insects, particularly those numerous and
destructive species that penetrate the bark and body of the tree to
deposit their eggs and larvæ, the latter of which are well known to
make immense havock. That insects are his natural food is evident
from the construction of his wedge-formed bill, the length, elasticity,
and figure of his tongue, and the strength and position of his claws,
as well as from his usual habits. In fact, insects form at least two
thirds of his subsistence; and his stomach is scarcely ever found without them. He searches for them with a dexterity and intelligence, I
may safely say, more than human; he perceives, by the exterior appearance of the bark, where they lurk below; when he is dubious, he
rattles vehemently on the outside with his bill, and his acute ear distinguishes the terrified vermin shrinking within to their inmost retreats,
where his pointed and barbed tongue soon reaches them. The masses
of bugs, caterpillars, and other larvæ, which I have taken from the
stomachs of these birds, have often surprised me. These larvæ, it
should be remembered, feed not only on the buds, leaves, and blossoms,
but on the very vegetable life of the tree,—the alburnum, or newly-
forming bark and wood; the consequence is, that the whole branches
and whole trees decay under the silent ravages of these destructive
vermin; witness the late destruction of many hundred acres of pine-

---

* KALM.

† The abundance of this species must be very great, and from the depredations
they commit, must be more felt. Mr. Audubon says that a hundred have been shot,
in one day, from a single cherry-tree. In addition to their other bad habits, they
carry off apples by thrusting in their bill as a spike, and thus supporting them.
They also frequent pigeon-houses, and suck the eggs,—a habit not very common
among this tribe; and, for the same purpose, enter the boxes prepared for the Martins and Blue-Birds. Another method of adding to their destruction, in Kentucky
and the Southern States, is in the following manner related by Audubon :—

"As soon as the Red-heads have begun to visit a cherry or apple-tree, a pole is
placed along the trunk of the tree, passing up amongst the central branches, and
extending six or seven feet above the highest twigs. The Woodpeckers alight by
preference on the pole, and whilst their body is close to it, a man, standing at the
foot of the pole, gives it a twist below with the head of an axe, on the opposite side
to that on which the Woodpecker is, when, in consequence of the sudden vibration
produced in the upper part, the bird is thrown off dead."

According to the same gentleman, many of the *Red-heads* (a name by which
they are universally known) remain in the southern districts of the United States
during the whole winter. The greater number, however, pass to countries farther
south. Their migration takes place during night, is commenced in the middle of
September, and continues for a month or six weeks. They then fly high above the
trees, far apart, like a disbanded army, propelling themselves by reiterated flaps
of their wings at the end of each successive curve which they describe in their flight.
The note which they emit at this time is different from the usual one, sharp, and
easily heard from the ground, although the birds may be out of sight. At the dawn
of day, the whole alight on the tops of the dead trees about the plantations, and remain in search of food until the approach of sunset, when they again, one after
another, mount the air, and continue their journey. — ED.

trees, in the north-eastern parts of South Carolina,* and the thousands of peach-trees that yearly decay from the same cause. Will any one say, that taking half a dozen, or half a hundred, apples from a tree, is equally ruinous with cutting it down? or, that the services of a useful animal should not be rewarded with a small portion of that which it has contributed to preserve? We are told, in the benevolent language of the Scriptures, not to muzzle the mouth of the ox that treadeth out the corn; and why should not the same generous liberality be extended to this useful family of birds, which forms so powerful a phalanx against the inroads of many millions of destructive vermin?

The Red-headed Woodpecker is, properly speaking, a bird of passage; though, even in the Eastern States, individuals are found during moderate winters, as well as in the states of New York and Pennsylvania; in Carolina, they are somewhat more numerous during that season, but not one tenth of what are found in summer. They make their appearance in Pennsylvania about the 1st of May, and leave us about the middle of October. They inhabit from Canada to the Gulf of Mexico, and are also found on the western coast of North America. About the middle of May they begin to construct their nests, which, like the rest of the genus, they form in the body or large limbs of trees, taking in no materials, but smoothing it within to the proper shape and size. The female lays six eggs, of a pure white, and the young make their first appearance about the 20th of June. During the first season, the head and neck of the young birds are blackish gray, which has occasioned some European writers to mistake them for females; the white on the wing is also spotted with black; but in the succeeding spring they receive their perfect plumage, and the male and female then differ only in the latter being rather smaller, and its colors not quite so vivid, both have the head and neck deep scarlet; the bill light blue, black towards the extremity, and strong; back, primaries, wing-coverts, and tail, black, glossed with steel blue; rump, lower part of the back, secondaries, and whole under parts from the breast downward, white; legs and feet, bluish green; claws, light blue; round the eye, a dusky narrow skin, bare of feathers; iris, dark hazel; total length, nine inches and a half; extent, seventeen inches. The Fig. 35, on the plate, was drawn and colored from a very elegant living specimen.

Notwithstanding the care which this bird, in common with the rest of its genus, takes to place its young beyond the reach of enemies, within the hollows of trees, yet there is one deadly foe, against whose depredations neither the height of the tree, nor the depth of the cavity, is the least security. This is the black snake, (*Coluber constrictor*,) who frequently glides up the trunk of the tree, and, like a skulking savage, enters the Woodpecker's peaceful apartment, devours the eggs or helpless young, in spite of the cries and flutterings of the parents; and, if the place be large enough, coils himself up in the spot they occupied, where he will sometimes remain for several days. The eager schoolboy, after hazarding his neck to reach the Woodpecker's hole,

---

* In one place, on a tract of two thousand acres of pine land, on the Sampit River, near Georgetown, at least ninety trees in every hundred were destroyed by this pernicious insect,—a small, black-winged bug, resembling the weevil, but somewhat larger.

at the triumphant moment when he thinks the nestlings his own, and strips his arm, launching it down into the cavity, and grasping what he conceives to be the callow young, starts with horror at the sight of a hideous snake, and almost drops from his giddy pinnacle, retreating down the tree with terror and precipitation. Several adventures of this kind have come to my knowledge ; and one of them was attended with serious consequences, where both snake and boy fell to the ground ; and a broken thigh, and long confinement, cured the adventurer completely of his ambition for robbing Woodpeckers' nests.

YELLOW–BELLIED WOODPECKER.— PICUS VARIUS.—
Fig. 36.

Picus varius, *Linn. Syst.* i. 176, 20.— *Gmel. Syst.* i. 735.— Le pic varié de la Caroline, *Buff.* vii. 77. *Pl. enl.* 785.— Yellow-bellied Woodpecker, *Catesb.* i. 21. — *Arct. Zool.* ii. No. 166.— *Lath. Syn.* ii. 574, 20. *Id. Sup.* p. 109.— *Peale's Museum,* No. 2004.

DENDROCOPUS VARIUS.— Swainson.*

Picus varius, *Bonap. Synop.* p. 45.— *Wagl. Syst. Av. Picus,* No. 16.— Dendrocopus varius, *North. Zool.* ii. p. 309.

This beautiful species is one of our resident birds. It visits our orchards in the month of October in great numbers, is occasionally seen during the whole winter and spring, but seems to seek the depths of the forest, to rear its young in ; for, during summer, it is rarely seen among our settlements ; and even in the intermediate woods, I have seldom met with it in that season. According to Brisson, it inhabits the continent from Cayenne to Virginia ; and I may add, as far as to Hudson's Bay, where, according to Hutchins, they are called *Meksewe*

---

* In this species, and the two following, the little Woodpecker of this country, and many others, we have the types of a sub-genus (*Dendrocopus,* Koch) among the Woodpeckers, which I have no hesitation in adopting, as containing a very marked group of black and white spotted birds, allied to confusion with each other. The genus is made use of, for the first time, in a British publication, the *Northern Zoology,* by Mr. Swainson, as the third sub-genus of *Picus.* He thus remarks :—
"The third sub-genus comprehends all the smaller black and white spotted Woodpeckers of Europe and America. Some few occur in the mountainous parts of India ; but, with these exceptions, the group, which is very extensive, seems to belong more particularly to temperate latitudes."
"It was met with by the over-land expedition in flocks, on the banks of the Saskatchewon, in May. Its manners, at that period of the year, were strikingly contrasted with those of the resident Woodpeckers ; for, instead of flitting in a solitary way, from tree to tree, and assiduously boring for insects, it flew about in crowded flocks, in a restless manner, and kept up a continual chattering. Its geographical range is extensive, from the sixty-first parallel of latitude, to Mexico."
Mr. Swainson mentions having received a single specimen of a Woodpecker from Georgia, closely allied to this, which he suspects to be undescribed ; and, in the event of being correct, he proposes to dedicate it to Mr. Audubon,— *Dendrocopus Audubonii,* Sw.— Ed.

Paupastaow;* they are also common in the states of Kentucky and Ohio, and have been seen in the neighborhood of St. Louis. They are reckoned by Georgi among the birds that frequent the Lake Baikal, in Asia; † but their existence there has not been satisfactorily ascertained.

The habits of this species are similar to those of the Hairy and Downy Woodpeckers, with which it generally associates. The only nest of this bird which I have met with, was in the body of an old pear-tree, about ten or eleven feet from the ground. The hole was almost exactly circular, small for the size of the bird, so that it crept in and out with difficulty; but suddenly widened, descending by a small angle, and then running downward about fifteen inches. On the smooth, solid wood lay four white eggs. This was about the twenty-fifth of May. Having no opportunity of visiting it afterwards, I cannot say whether it added any more eggs to the number; I rather think it did not, as it appeared at that time to be sitting.

The Yellow-bellied Woodpecker is eight inches and a half long, and in extent fifteen inches; whole crown, a rich and deep scarlet, bordered with black on each side, and behind forming a slight crest, which it frequently erects; ‡ from the nostrils, which are thickly covered with recumbent hairs, a narrow strip of white runs downward, curving round the breast; mixing with the yellowish white on the lower part of the breast; throat, the same deep scarlet as the crown, bordered with black, proceeding from the lower mandible on each side, and spreading into a broad, rounding patch on the breast; this black, in birds of the first and second year, is dusky gray, the feathers being only crossed with circular touches of black; a line of white, and below it another of black, proceed, the first from the upper part of the eye, the other from the posterior half of the eye, and both lose themselves on the neck and back; back, dusky yellow, sprinkled and elegantly waved with black; wings, black, with a large, oblong spot of white; the primaries, tipped and spotted with white; the three secondaries next the body are also variegated with white; rump, white, bordered with black; belly, yellow; sides under the wings, more dusky yellow, marked with long arrow-heads of black; legs and feet, greenish blue; tail, black, consisting of ten feathers, the two outward feathers on each side tipped with white, the next totally black, the fourth edged on its inner vane half way down with white, the middle one white on its interior vane, and spotted with black; tongue, flat, horny for half an inch at the tip, pointed, and armed along its sides with reflected barbs; the other extremities of the tongue pass up behind the skull in a groove, and end near the right nostril; in birds of the first and second year they reach only to the crown; bill, an inch long, channeled, wedge-formed at the tip, and of a dusky horn color. The female is marked nearly as the male, but wants the scarlet on the throat, which is whitish; she is also darker under the wings and on the sides of the breast. The young of the first season, of both sexes, in October, have the crown sprinkled with black and deep scarlet; the scarlet on the throat may be also observed in the young males. The principal food of these birds is insects; and they seem particularly fond of frequent-

---

* Latham. † Ibid.
‡ This circumstance seems to have been overlooked by naturalists.

9 *

ing orchards, boring the trunks of the apple-trees in their eager search after them. On opening them, the liver appears very large, and of a dirty gamboge color; the stomach strongly muscular, and generally filled with fragments of beetles and gravel. In the morning, they are extremely active in the orchards, and rather shyer than the rest of their associates. Their cry is also different, but, though it is easily distinguishable in the woods, cannot be described by words.

HAIRY WOODPECKER. — PICUS VILLOSUS. — Fig. 37.

Picus villosus, *Linn. Syst.* i. 175, 16. — Pic chevelu de Virginie, *Buffon*, vii. 7. — Pic varié male de Virginie, *Pl. enl.* 754. — Hairy Woodpecker, *Catesb.* i. 19, Fig. 2. — *Arct. Zool.* ii. No. 164. — *Lath. Syn.* ii. 572, 18. *Id. Sup.* 108. — *Peale's Museum*, No. 1983.

DENDROCOPUS VILLOSUS. — Swainson.

Picus villosus, *Bonap. Synop.* p. 46. — *Wagl. Syst. Av. Picus*, 22. — Dendrocopus villosus, *North. Zool.* ii. p. 305.

This is another of our resident birds, and, like the former, a haunter of orchards, and borer of apple-trees, an eager hunter of insects, their eggs and larvæ, in old stumps and old rails, in rotten branches and crevices of the bark; having all the characters of the Woodpecker strongly marked. In the month of May he retires with his mate to the woods, and either seeks out a branch already hollow, or cuts out an opening for himself. In the former case I have known his nest more than five feet distant from the mouth of the hole; and in the latter he digs first horizontally, if in the body of the tree, six or eight inches, and then downward, obtusely, for twice that distance; carrying up the chips with his bill, and scraping them out with his feet. They also not unfrequently choose the orchard for breeding in, and even an old stake of the fence, which they excavate for this purpose. The female lays five white eggs, and hatches in June. This species is more numerous than the last in Pennsylvania, and more domestic; frequently approaching the farm-house and skirts of the town. In Philadelphia I have many times observed them examining old ragged trunks of the willow and poplar while people were passing immediately below. Their cry is strong, shrill, and tremulous; they have also a single note, or *chuck*, which they often repeat, in an eager manner, as they hop about, and dig into the crevices of the tree. They inhabit the continent from Hudson's Bay to Carolina and Georgia.

The Hairy Woodpecker is nine inches long, and fifteen in extent; crown, black; line over and under the eye, white; the eye is placed in a black line, that widens as it descends to the back; hind head, scarlet, sometimes intermixed with black; nostrils, hid under remarkably thick, bushy, recumbent hairs, or bristles; under the bill are certain long hairs thrown forward and upward, as represented in Fig. 37; bill, a bluish horn color, grooved, wedged at the end, straight, and about an inch and a quarter long; touches of black, proceeding from the lower mandible, end in a broad black strip that joins the black on the shoulder; back, black, divided by a broad, lateral strip of white, the feathers composing which are loose and unwebbed, resembling hairs, — whence its name; rump and shoulders of the wing, black; wings, black, tipped and spotted with white, three rows of spots being visible on the secondaries, and five on the primaries; greater wing-coverts, also spotted with white; tail, as in the others, cuneiform, consisting of ten strong-shafted and pointed feathers, the four middle ones black, the next partially white, the two exterior ones white, tinged at the tip with a brownish burnt color; tail-coverts, black; whole lower side, pure white; legs, feet, and claws, light blue, the latter remarkably large and strong; inside of the mouth, flesh colored; tongue, pointed, beset with barbs, and capable of being protruded more than an inch and a half; the os hyoides, in this species, passes on each side of the neck, ascends the skull, passes down towards the nostril, and is wound round the bone of the right eye, which projects considerably more than the left, for its accommodation. The great mass of hairs, that cover the nostril, appears to be designed as a protection to the front of the head, when the bird is engaged in digging holes into the wood. The membrane which encloses the brain in this, as in all the other species of Woodpeckers, is also of extraordinary strength, no doubt to prevent any bad effects from violent concussion while the bird is employed in digging for food. The female wants the red on the hind head; and the white below is tinged with brownish. The manner of flight of these birds has been already described under a former species, as consisting of alternate risings and sinkings. The Hairy Woodpeckers generally utter a loud, tremulous scream as they set off, and when they alight. They are hard to kill; and, like the Red-headed Woodpecker, hang by the claws, even of a single foot, as long as a spark of life remains, before they drop.

This species is common at Hudson's Bay, and has lately been found in England.* Dr. Latham examined a pair which were shot near Halifax, in Yorkshire; and, on comparing the male with one brought from North America, could perceive no difference, but in a slight interruption of the red that marked the hind head of the former; a circumstance which I have frequently observed in our own. The two females corresponded exactly.

---

* This, I believe, is a mistake; and although this bird is beginning to creep into our fauna in the rank of an occasional visitant, I can find no authentic trace of the Hairy Woodpecker being ever killed in Great Britain. It is a bird belonging to a northern climate; and although it closely resembles a native species, it can never be mistaken, with any ordinary examination or comparison. The Halifax in Yorkshire will turn out in reality the Halifax of the New World. — Ed.

DOWNY WOODPECKER. — PICUS PUBESCENS. — Fɪɢ. 38.

Picus pubescens, *Linn. Syst.* i. 175, 15. — *Gmel. Syst.* i. 435. — Petit pic varié de Virginie, *Buffon*, vii. 76. — Smallest Woodpecker, *Catesb.* i. 21. — *Arct. Zool.* ii. No. 963. — Little Woodpecker, *Lath. Synop.* ii. 573, 19. *Id. Sup.* 106. — *Pe ıle's Museum*, No. 1986.

DENDROCOPUS PUBESCENS. — Swainson.

Picus pubescens, *Bonap. Synop.* p. 46. — *Wagl. Syst. Av. Picus,* No. 23. — Dendrocopus pubescens, *North. Zool.* ii. p. 307.

Tʜɪs is the smallest of our Woodpeckers,* and so exactly resembles the former in its tints and markings, and in almost every thing except its diminutive size, that 1 wonder how it passed through the Count de Buffon's hands without being branded as a "spurious race, degenerated by the influence of food, climate, or some unknown cause." But, though it has escaped this infamy, charges of a much more heinous nature have been brought against it, not only by the writer above mentioned, but by the whole venerable body of zoologists in Europe, who have treated of its history, viz., that it is almost constantly boring and digging into apple-trees, and that it is the most destructive of its whole genus to the orchards. The first part of this charge I shall not pretend to deny ; how far the other is founded in truth will appear in the sequel. Like the two former species, it remains with us the whole year. About the middle of May, the male and female look out for a suitable place for the reception of their eggs and young. An apple, pear, or cherry-tree, often in the near neighborhood of the farm-house, is generally fixed upon for this purpose. The tree is minutely reconnoitred for several days previous to the operation, and the work is first begun by the male, who cuts out a hole in the solid wood as circular as if described with a pair of compasses. He is occasionally relieved by the female, both parties working with the most indefatigable diligence. The direction of the hole, if made in the body of the tree, is generally downwards, by an angle of thirty or forty degrees, for the distance of six or eight inches, and then straight down for ten or twelve more ; within, roomy, capacious, and as smooth as if polished by the cabinet-maker ; but the entrance is judiciously left just so large as

---

* This species, as Wilson observes, is the smallest of the American Woodpeckers, and it will fill the place in that country which is occupied in Europe and Great Britain by the *Picus minor*, or Least Woodpecker ; unlike the latter, however, it is both abundant, and is familiar in its manners.

Mr. Swainson, in a note to the *Northern Zoology*, thinks that several American species are confounded under this. " We have no doubt," he says, " that two, if not three, species of these little Woodpeckers, from different parts of North America, have been confounded under the common name of *pubescens*." He proposes to distinguish them by the names of *Dendrocopus medianus*, inhabiting the middle parts of North America, chiefly different from *D. pubescens* in the greater portion of red on the hind head, relative length of the quills, and shape of the tail-feathers ; and *Dendrocopus meridionalis*, inhabiting Georgia, less than *D. pubescens*, and with the under plumage hair brown. — Eᴅ.

to admit the bodies of the owners. During this labor, they regularly carry out the chips, often strowing them at a distance, to prevent suspicion. This operation sometimes occupies the chief part of a week. Before she begins to lay, the female often visits the place, passes out and in, examines every part, both of the exterior and interior, with great attention, as every prudent tenant of a new house ought to do, and at length takes complete possession. The eggs are generally six, pure white, and laid on the smooth bottom of the cavity. The male occasionally supplies the female with food while she is sitting; and about the last week in June the young are perceived making their way up the tree, climbing with considerable dexterity. All this goes on with great regularity where no interruption is met with; but the House Wren, who also builds in the hollow of a tree, but who is neither furnished with the necessary tools nor strength for excavating such an apartment for himself, allows the Woodpeckers to go on, till he thinks it will answer his purpose, then attacks them with violence, and generally succeeds in driving them off. I saw some weeks ago a striking example of this, where the Woodpeckers we are now describing, after commencing in a cherry-tree, within a few yards of the house, and having made considerable progress, were turned out by the Wren; the former began again on a pear-tree in the garden, fifteen or twenty yards off, whence, after digging out a most complete apartment, and one egg being laid, they were once more assaulted by the same impertinent intruder, and finally forced to abandon the place.

The principal characteristics of this little bird are diligence, familiarity, perseverance, and a strength and energy in the head and muscles of the neck, which are truly astonishing. Mounted on the infected branch of an old apple-tree, where insects have lodged their corroding and destructive brood in crevices between the bark and wood, he labors sometimes for half an hour incessantly at the same spot, before he has succeeded in dislodging and destroying them. At these times you may walk up pretty close to the tree, and even stand immediately below it, within five or six feet of the bird, without in the least embarrassing him; the strokes of his bill are distinctly heard several hundred yards off; and I have known him to be at work for two hours together on the same tree. Buffon calls this "incessant toil and slavery;" their attitude, "a painful posture;" and their life, "a dull and insipid existence;" expressions improper, because untrue; and absurd, because contradictory. The posture is that for which the whole organization of his frame is particularly adapted; and though, to a Wren or a Humming Bird, the labor would be both toil and slavery, yet to him it is, I am convinced, as pleasant and as amusing, as the sports of the chase to the hunter, or the sucking of flowers to the Humming Bird. The eagerness with which he traverses the upper and lower sides of the branches; the cheerfulness of his cry, and the liveliness of his motions while digging into the tree and dislodging the vermin, justify this belief. He has a single note, or *chink*, which, like the former species, he frequently repeats; and when he flies off, or alights on another tree, he utters a rather shriller cry, composed of nearly the same kind of note, quickly reiterated. In fall and winter, he associates with the Titmouse, Creeper, &c., both in their wood and orchard excursions, and usually leads the van. Of all our Woodpeckers, none rid the apple-trees of so many vermin as this, digging off the moss which the negligence of the proprietor had suffered to accumulate, and probing every crevice. In fact, the orchard is his favorite resort in all seasons; and his industry is unequalled, and almost incessant, which is more than can be said of any other species we have. In fall, he is particularly fond of boring the apple-trees for insects, digging a circular hole through the bark, just sufficient to admit his bill, after that a second, third, &c., in pretty regular, horizontal circles round the body of the tree; these parallel circles of holes are often not more than an inch or an inch and a half apart, and sometimes so close together, that I have covered eight or ten of them at once with a dollar. From nearly the surface of the ground up to the first fork, and sometimes far beyond it, the whole bark of many apple-trees is perforated in this manner, so as to appear as if made by successive discharges of buck-shot; and our little Woodpecker, the subject of the present account, is the principal perpetrator of this supposed mischief, — I say supposed, for so far from these perforations of the bark being ruinous, they are not only harmless, but, I have good reason to believe, really beneficial to the health and fertility of the tree. I leave it to the philosophical botanist to account for this; but the fact I am confident of. In more than fifty orchards which I have myself carefully examined, those trees which were marked by the Woodpecker (for some trees they never touch, perhaps because not penetrated by insects) were uniformly the most thriving, and seemingly the most productive; many of these were upwards of sixty years old, their trunks completely covered with holes, while the branches were broad, luxuriant, and loaded with fruit. Of decayed trees, more than three fourths were untouched by the Woodpecker. Several intelligent farmers, with whom I have conversed, candidly acknowledge the truth of these observations, and with justice look upon these birds as beneficial; but the most common opinion is, that they bore the trees to suck the sap, and so destroy its vegetation; though pine and other resinous trees, on the juices of which it is not pretended they feed, are often found equally perforated. Were the sap of the tree their object, the saccharine juice of the birch, the sugar maple, and several others, would be much more inviting, because more sweet and nourishing, than that of either the pear or apple-tree; but I have not observed one mark on the former, for ten thousand that may be seen on the latter. Besides, the early part of spring is the season when the sap flows most abundantly; whereas, it is only during the months of September, October, and November, that Woodpeckers are seen so indefatigably engaged in orchards, probing every crack and crevice, boring through the bark, and, what is worth remarking, chiefly on the south and south-west sides of the tree, for the eggs and larvæ deposited there by the countless swarms of summer insects. These, if suffered to remain, would prey upon the very vitals, if I may so express it, of the tree, and in the succeeding summer give birth to myriads more of their race, equally destructive.

Here, then, is a whole species, I may say, genus, of birds, which Providence seems to have formed for the protection of our fruit and forest-trees from the ravages of vermin which every day destroy millions of those noxious insects that would otherwise blast the hopes of

39 Mocking Bird. 40 & R. Male & Female Humming Bird. 42. Towhe Bunting. 43. Cardinal Grosbeak. 44. Female. 45. Red Tanager. 46.Female & egg. 47. Rice Bunting. 48. Female 49. Red spot Flycatcher. 50. Marsh Wren. 51. Great Carolina Wren. 52.Yellow throat Warbler.

the husbandman, and which even promote the fertility of the tree and, in return, are proscribed by those who ought to have been their protectors, and incitements and rewards held out for their destruction! Let us examine better into the operations of nature, and many of our mistaken opinions and groundless prejudices will be abandoned for more just, enlarged, and humane modes of thinking.

The length of the Downy Woodpecker is six inches and three quarters, and its extent twelve inches; crown, black; hind head, deep scarlet; stripe over the eye, white; nostrils, thickly covered with recumbent hairs, or small feathers, of a cream color; these, as in the preceding species, are thick and bushy, as if designed to preserve the forehead from injury during the violent action of digging; the back is black, and divided by a lateral strip of white, loose, downy, unwebbed feathers; wings, black, spotted with white; tail-coverts, rump, and four middle feathers of the tail, black; the other three on each side, white, crossed with touches of black; whole under parts, as well as the sides of the neck, white; the latter marked with a streak of black, proceeding from the lower mandible, exactly as in the Hairy Woodpecker; legs and feet, bluish green; claws, light blue, tipped with black; tongue formed like that of the preceding species, horny towards the tip, where, for one eighth of an inch, it is barbed; bill, of a bluish horn color, grooved, and wedge-formed, like most of the genus; eye, dark hazel. The female wants the red on the hind head, having that part white; and the breast and belly are of a dirty white.

This, and the two former species, are generally denominated *Sapsuckers*. They have also several other provincial appellations, equally absurd, which it may, perhaps, be more proper to suppress than to sanction by repeating.

MOCKING BIRD.— TURDUS POLYGLOTTUS.— Fig. 39.

Mimic Thrush, *Lath. Syn.* iii. p. 40, No. 42.— *Arct. Zool.* ii. No. 194.— Turdus polyglottus, *Lin. Syst.* i. p. 293, No. 10.— Le grand moqueur, *Briss. Orn.* n. p. 266, 29.— *Buff. Ois.* iii. p. 325, *Pl. enl.* 558, Fig. 1.— Singing Bird, Mocking Bird, or Nightingale, *Raii Syn.* p. 64, No. 5, p. 185, 31.— *Sloan. Jam.* ii. 306, No. 34.— The Mock Bird, *Catesb. Car.* i. pl. 27.— *Peale's Museum*, No. 5288.

ORPHEUS POLYGLOTTUS.— Swainson.

Turdus polyglottus, *Bonap. Synop.* p. 74.— The Mocking Bird, *Aud.* pl. xxi. *Orn. Biog.* 108.

THIS celebrated and very extraordinary bird, in extent and variety of vocal powers, stands unrivalled by the whole feathered songsters of this, or perhaps any other country, and shall receive from us, in this place, all that attention and respect which superior merit is justly entitled to.

Among the many novelties which the discovery of this part of the western continent first brought into notice, we may reckon that of the

Mocking Bird, which is not only peculiar to the New World, but inhabits a very considerable extent of both North and South America; having been traced from the states of New England to Brazil, and also among many of the adjacent islands. They are, however, much more numerous in those states south, than in those north, of the River Delaware; being generally migratory in the latter, and resident (at least many of them) in the former. A warm climate, and low country, not far from the sea, seems most congenial to their nature; accordingly, we find the species less numerous to the west than east of the great range of the Alleghany, in the same parallels of latitude. In the severe winter of 1808–9, I found these birds, occasionally, from Fredericksburg, in Virginia, to the southern parts of Georgia; becoming still more numerous the farther I advanced to the south. The berries of the red cedar, myrtle, holly, Cassine shrub, many species of smilax, together with gum berries, gall berries, and a profusion of others with which the luxuriant, swampy thickets of those regions abound, furnish them with a perpetual feast. Winged insects, also, of which they are very fond, and remarkably expert at catching, abound there even in winter, and are an additional inducement to residency. Though rather a shy bird in the Northern States, here he appeared almost half domesticated, feeding on the cedars, and among the thickets of smilax that lined the roads, while I passed within a few feet; playing around the planter's door, and hopping along the shingles. During the month of February, I sometimes heard a solitary one singing; but, on the 2d of March, in the neighborhood of Savannah, numbers of them were heard on every hand, vieing in song with each other, and with the Brown Thrush, making the whole woods vocal with their melody. Spring was at that time considerably advanced, and the thermometer ranging between 70 and 78 degrees. On arriving at New York, on the 22d of the same month, I found many parts of the country still covered with snow, and the streets piled with ice to the height of two feet; while neither the Brown Thrush nor Mocking Bird were observed, even in the lower parts of Pennsylvania, until the 20th of April.

The precise time at which the Mocking Bird begins to build his nest, varies according to the latitude in which he resides. In the lower parts of Georgia, he commences building early in April; but in Pennsylvania, rarely before the 10th of May; and in New York, and the states of New England, still later. There are particular situations to which he gives the preference. A solitary thorn bush; an almost impenetrable thicket; an orange-tree, cedar, or holly bush, are favorite spots, and frequently selected. It is no great objection with him that these happen, sometimes, to be near the farm, or mansion-house: always ready to defend, but never over-anxious to conceal, his nest, he very often builds within a small distance of the house; and not unfrequently in a pear or apple-tree; rarely at a greater height than six or seven feet from the ground. The nest varies a little with different individuals, according to the conveniency of collecting suitable materials. A very complete one is now lying before me, and is composed of the following substances: First, a quantity of dry twigs and sticks, then, withered tops of weeds, of the preceding year, intermixed with fine straws, hay, pieces of wool and tow; and, lastly, a thick layer of fine fibrous roots, of a light brown color, lines the whole. The eggs, one of which is represented on the plate, are four, sometimes five, of a cinereous blue, marked with large blotches of brown. The female sits fourteen days, and generally produces two broods in the season, unless robbed of her eggs, in which case she will even build and lay the third time. She is, however, extremely jealous of her nest, and very apt to forsake it if much disturbed. It is even asserted by some of our bird-dealers that the old ones will actually destroy the eggs, and poison the young, if either the one or the other have been handled. But I cannot give credit to this unnatural report. I know, from my own experience, at least, that it is not always their practice; neither have I ever witnessed a case of the kind above mentioned. During the period of incubation, neither cat, dog, animal, nor man, can approach the nest without being attacked. The cats, in particular, are persecuted whenever they make their appearance, till obliged to retreat. But his whole vengeance is most particularly directed against that mortal enemy of his eggs and young, the black snake. Whenever the insidious approaches of this reptile are discovered, the male darts upon it with the rapidity of an arrow, dexterously eluding its bite, and striking it violently and incessantly about the head, where it is very vulnerable. The snake soon becomes sensible of its danger, and seeks to escape; but the intrepid defender of his young redoubles his exertions, and, unless his antagonist be of great magnitude, often succeeds in destroying him. All its pretended powers of fascination avail it nothing against the vengeance of this noble bird. As the snake's strength begins to flag, the Mocking Bird seizes and lifts it up, partly, from the ground, beating it with his wings; and, when the business is completed, he returns to the repository of his young, mounts the summit of the bush, and pours out a torrent of song in token of victory.

As it is of some consequence to be able to distinguish a young male bird from a female, the following marks may be attended to; by which some pretend to be able to distinguish them in less than a week after they are hatched. These are, the breadth and purity of the white on the wings, for that on the tail is not so much to be depended on. This white, in a full-grown male bird, spreads over the whole nine primaries, down to, and considerably below, their coverts, which are also white, sometimes slightly tipped with brown. The white of the primaries also extends equally far on both vanes of the feathers. In the female, the white is less pure, spreads over only seven or eight of the primaries, does not descend so far, and extends considerably farther down on the broad, than on the narrow, side of the feathers. The black is also more of a brownish cast.

The young birds, if intended for the cage, ought not to be left till they are nearly ready to fly, but should be taken rather young than otherwise; and may be fed, every half hour, with milk, thickened with Indian meal; mixing occasionally with it a little fresh meat, cut or minced very fine. After they begin to eat of their own accord, they ought still to be fed by hand, though at longer intervals, and a few cherries, strawberries, &c., now and then thrown in to them. The same sort of food, adding grasshoppers and fruit, particularly the various kinds of berries in which they delight, and plenty of clear, fine

10

gravel, is found very proper for them after they are grown up. Should the bird at any time appear sick or dejected, a few spiders thrown in to him will generally remove these symptoms of disease.

If the young bird is designed to be taught by an old one, the best singer should be selected for this office, and no other allowed to be beside him. Or, if by the bird organ, or mouth-whistling, it should be begun early, and continued, pretty constantly, by the same person, until the scholar, who is seldom inattentive, has completely acquired his lesson. The best singing birds, however, in my own opinion, are those that have been reared in the country, and educated under the tuition of the feathered choristers of the surrounding fields, groves, woods, and meadows.

The plumage of the Mocking Bird, though none of the homeliest, has nothing gaudy or brilliant in it; and, had he nothing else to recommend him, would scarcely entitle him to notice; but his figure is well proportioned, and even handsome. The ease, elegance, and rapidity of his movements, the animation of his eye, and the intelligence he displays in listening and laying up lessons from almost every species of the feathered creation within his hearing, are really surprising, and mark the peculiarity of his genius. To these qualities we may add that of a voice full, strong, and musical, and capable of almost every modulation, from the clear, mellow tones of the Wood Thrush, to the savage scream of the Bald Eagle. In measure and accent, he faithfully follows his originals. In force and sweetness of expression, he greatly improves upon them. In his native groves, mounted on the top of a tall bush, or half-grown tree, in the dawn of dewy morning, while the woods are already vocal with a multitude of warblers, his admirable song rises preëminent over every competitor. The ear can listen to *his* music alone, to which that of all the others seems a mere accompaniment. Neither is this strain altogether imitative. His own native notes, which are easily distinguishable by such as are well acquainted with those of our various song birds, are bold and full, and varied seemingly beyond all limits. They consist of short expressions of two, three, or, at the most, five or six syllables; generally interspersed with imitations, and all of them uttered with great emphasis and rapidity; and continued, with undiminished ardor, for half an hour, or an hour, at a time. His expanded wings and tail, glistening with white, and the buoyant gayety of his action, arresting the eye, as his song most irresistibly does the ear, he sweeps round with enthusiastic ecstasy—he mounts and descends as his song swells or dies away ; and, as my friend Mr. Bartram has beautifully expressed it, " He bounds aloft with the celerity of an arrow, as if to recover or recall his very soul, expired in the last elevated strain." *
While thus exerting himself, a bystander, destitute of sight, would suppose that the whole feathered tribes had assembled together, on a trial of skill, each striving to produce his utmost effect; so perfect are his imitations. He many times deceives the sportsman, and sends him in search of birds that perhaps are not within miles of him, but whose notes he exactly imitates : even birds themselves are frequently imposed on by this admirable mimic, and are decoyed, by the fancied

* *Travels*, p. 32. Introd.

calls of their mates, or dive, with precipitation, into the depth of
thickets, at the scream of what they suppose to be the Sparrow Hawk.
The Mocking Bird loses little of the power and energy of his song
by confinement. In his domesticated state, when he commences his
career of song, it is impossible to stand by uninterested. He whistles
for the dog, — Cæsar starts up, wags his tail, and runs to meet his
master. He squeaks out, like a hurt Chicken, — and the Hen hurries
about with hanging wings, and bristled feathers, clucking to protect
its injured brood. The barking of the dog, the mewing of the cat,
the creaking of a passing wheelbarrow, follow, with great truth and
rapidity. He repeats the tune taught him by his master, though of
considerable length, fully and faithfully. He runs over the quiverings
of the Canary, and the clear whistlings of the Virginia Nightingale,
or Red-Bird, with such superior execution and effect, that the mortified songsters feel their own inferiority, and become altogether silent;
while he seems to triumph in their defeat by redoubling his exertions.

This excessive fondness for variety, however, in the opinion of
some, injures his song. His elevated imitations of the Brown Thrush
are frequently interrupted by the crowing of Cocks; and the warblings
of the Blue-Bird, which he exquisitely manages, are mingled with the
screaming of Swallows, or the cackling of Hens; amidst the simple
melody of the Robin, we are suddenly surprised by the shrill reiterations of the Whip-poor-will; while the notes of the Killdeer, Blue
Jay, Martin, Baltimore, and twenty others, succeed, with such impos-
ing reality, that we look round for the originals, and discover, with
astonishment, that the sole performer in this singular concert is the
admirable bird now before us. During this exhibition of his powers,
he spreads his wings, expands his tail, and throws himself around the
cage in all the ecstasy of enthusiasm, seeming not only to sing, but
to dance, keeping time to the measure of his own music. Both in his
native and domesticated state, during the solemn stillness of night,
as soon as the moon rises in silent majesty, he begins his delightful
solo, and serenades us the livelong night with a full display of his
vocal powers, making the whole neighborhood ring with his inimitable
medley.*

Were it not to seem invidious in the eyes of foreigners, I might, in
this place, make a comparative statement between the powers of the
Mocking Bird, and the only bird, I believe, in the world, worthy of
being compared with him, — the European Nightingale. This, however, I am unable to do from my own observation, having never
myself heard the song of the latter; and, even if I had, perhaps

* The hunters in the Southern States, when setting out upon an excursion by
night, as soon as they hear the Mocking Bird begin to sing, know that the moon is
rising.
A certain anonymous author, speaking of the Mocking Birds in the island of
Jamaica, and their practice of singing by moonlight, thus gravely philosophizes, and
attempts to account for the habit. "It is not certain," says he, "whether they are
kept so wakeful by the clearness of the light, or by any extraordinary attention and
vigilance, at such times, for the protection of their nursery from the piratical as-
saults of the Owl and the Night Hawk. It is possible that fear may operate upon
them, much in the same manner as it has been observed to affect some cowardly
persons, who whistle stoutly in a lonesome place, while their mind is agitated with
the terror of thieves or hobgoblins." — History of Jamaica, vol. iii. p. 894, quarto.

something might be laid to the score of partiality, which, as a faithful biographer, I am anxious to avoid. I shall, therefore, present the reader with the opinion of a distinguished English naturalist and curious observer, on this subject, the Honorable Daines Barrington, who, at the time he made the communication, was vice-president of the Royal Society, to which it was addressed.*

"It may not be improper here," says this gentleman, "to consider whether the Nightingale may not have a very formidable competitor in the American Mocking Bird, though almost all travellers agree, that the concert in the European woods is superior to that of the other parts of the globe." "I have happened, however, to hear the American Mocking Bird, in great perfection, at Messrs. Vogels and Scotts, in Love Lane, Eastcheap. This bird is believed to be still living, and hath been in England these six years. During the space of a minute, he imitated the Woodlark, Chaffinch, Blackbird, Thrush, and Sparrow; I was told also that he would bark like a dog; so that the bird seems to have no choice in his imitations, though his pipe comes nearest to our Nightingale of any bird I have yet met with. With regard to the original notes, however, of this bird, we are still at a loss, as this can only be known by those who are accurately acquainted with the song of the other American birds. Kalm indeed informs us, that the natural song is excellent;† but this traveller seems not to have been long enough in America to have distinguished what were the genuine notes: with us, mimics do not often succeed but in imitations. I have little doubt, however, but that this bird would be fully equal to the song of the Nightingale in its whole compass; but then, from the attention which the Mocker pays to any other sort of disagreeable noise, these capital notes would be always debased by a bad mixture."

On this extract I shall make a few remarks. If, as is here conceded, the Mocking Bird be fully equal to the song of the Nightingale, and, as I can with confidence add, not only to that, but to the song of almost every other bird, besides being capable of exactly imitating various other sounds and voices of animals, — his vocal powers are unquestionably superior to those of the Nightingale, which possesses its own native notes alone. Further, if we consider, as is asserted by Mr. Barrington, that "one reason of the Nightingale's being more attended to than others is, that it sings in the night;" and if we believe, with Shakspeare, that

> The Nightingale, if she should sing by day,
> When every Goose is cackling, would be thought
> No better a musician than a Wren,

what must we think of that bird, who, in the glare of day, when a multitude of songsters are straining their throats in melody, overpowers all competition, and, by the superiority of his voice, expression, and action, not only attracts every ear, but frequently strikes dumb his mortified rivals; when the silence of night, as well as the bustle of day, bear witness to his melody; and when, even in captivity, in a

* *Philosophical Transactions*, vol. lxii. part ii. p. 284.
† *Travels*, vol. i. p. 219.

foreign country, he is declared, by the best judges in that country, to be fully equal to the song of their sweetest bird *in its whole compass?* The supposed degradation of his song by the introduction of extraneous sounds and unexpected imitations, is, in fact, one of the chief excellences of this bird; as these changes give a perpetual novelty to his strain, keep attention constantly awake, and impress every hearer with a deeper interest in what is to follow. In short, if we believe in the truth of that mathematical axiom, that the whole is greater than a part, all that is excellent or delightful, amusing or striking, in the music of birds, must belong to that admirable songster, whose vocal powers are equal to the whole compass of their whole strains.

The native notes of the Mocking Bird have a considerable resemblance to those of the Brown Thrush, but may easily be distinguished by their greater rapidity, sweetness, energy of expression, and variety. Both, however, have, in many parts of the United States, particularly in those to the south, obtained the name of Mocking Bird; the first, or Brown Thrush, from its inferiority of song, being called the French, and the other the English Mocking Bird, — a mode of expression probably originating in the prejudices of our forefathers, with whom every thing French was inferior to every thing English.*

The Mocking Bird is frequently taken in trap-cages, and, by proper management, may be made sufficiently tame to sing. The upper parts of the cage (which ought to be of wood) should be kept covered, until the bird becomes a little more reconciled to confinement. If placed in a wire cage, uncovered, he will soon destroy himself in attempting to get out. These birds, however, by proper treatment, may be brought to sing perhaps superior to those raised by hand, and cost less trouble. The opinion which the naturalists of Europe entertain of the great difficulty of raising the Mocking Bird, and that not one in ten survives, is very incorrect. A person called on me a few days ago, with twenty-nine of these birds, old and young, which he had carried about the fields with him for several days, for the convenience of feeding them while engaged in trapping others. He had carried them thirty miles, and intended carrying them ninety-six miles farther, viz., to New York, and told me that he did not expect to lose one out of ten of them. Cleanliness, and regularity in feeding, are the two principal things to be attended to; and these rarely fail to succeed.

The eagerness with which the nest of the Mocking Bird is sought after in the neighborhood of Philadelphia, has rendered this bird extremely scarce for an extent of several miles round the city. In the country round Wilmington and Newcastle, they are very numerous, from whence they are frequently brought here for sale. The usual price of a singing bird is from seven to fifteen, and even twenty dollars. I have known fifty dollars paid for a remarkably fine singer, and one instance where one hundred dollars were refused for a still more extraordinary one.

---

* The observations of Mr. Barrington, in the paper above referred to, make this supposition still more probable. "Some Nightingales," says he, "are so vastly inferior, that the bird-catchers will not keep them, branding them with the name of Frenchmen." P. 283.

10 *

Attempts have been made to induce these charming birds to pair, and rear their young, in a state of confinement, and the result has been such as to prove it, by proper management, perfectly practicable. In the spring of 1808, a Mr. Klein, living in North Seventh Street, Philadelphia, partitioned off about twelve feet square in the third story of his house. This was lighted by a pretty large wire-grated window. In the centre of this small room he planted a cedar bush, five or six feet high, in a box of earth, and scattered about a sufficient quantity of materials suitable for building. Into this place a male and female Mocking Bird were put, and soon began to build. The female laid five eggs, all of which she hatched, and fed the young with great affection until they were nearly able to fly. Business calling the proprietor from home for two weeks, he left the birds to the care of his domestics, and, on his return, found, to his great regret, that they had been neglected in food. The young ones were all dead, and the parents themselves nearly famished. The same pair have again commenced building this season, in the same place, and have at this time, July 4, 1809, three young, likely to do well. The place might be fitted up with various kinds of shrubbery, so as to resemble their native thickets, and ought to be as remote from noise and interruption of company as possible, and strangers rarely allowed to disturb, or even approach them.

The Mocking Bird is nine and a half inches long, and thirteen in breadth. Some individuals are, however, larger, and some smaller, those of the first hatch being uniformly the biggest and stoutest.* The upper parts of the head, neck, and back, are a dark, brownish ash, and when new moulted, a fine light gray; the wings and tail are nearly black, the first and second rows of coverts tipped with white; the primary coverts, in some males, are wholly white, in others, tinged with brown. The three first primaries are white from their roots as far as their coverts; the white on the next six extends from an inch to one and three fourths farther down, descending equally on both sides of the feather; the tail is cuneiform, the two exterior feathers wholly white, the rest, except the middle ones, tipped with white; the chin is white; sides of the neck, breast, belly, and vent, a brownish white, much purer in wild birds than in those that have been domesticated; iris of the eye, yellowish cream colored, inclining to golden; bill, black, the base of the lower mandible, whitish; legs and feet, black, and strong. The female very much resembles the male; what difference there is, has been already pointed out in a preceding part of this account. The breast of the young bird is spotted like that of the Thrush.†

* Many people are of opinion that there are two sorts, the large and the small Mocking Bird; but, after examining great numbers of these birds in various regions of the United States, I am satisfied that this variation of size is merely accidental, or owing to the circumstance above mentioned.

† A bird is described in the *Northern Zoology* as the Varied Thrush of Pennant, the *Turdus nævius* of Latham, which will rank as an addition to the North American species of this genus, and has been named by Mr. Swainson *O. meruloides,* Thrushlike Mocking Bird. Mr. Swainson has changed the name of Latham, to give it one expressive of its form; as he considers the structure intermediate between *Orpheus* and *Turdus,* though leaning most to the former. According to Dr. Rich-

Mr. William Bartram observes of the Mocking Bird, that " formerly, say thirty or forty years ago, they were numerous, and often staid all winter with us, or the year through, feeding on the berries of ivy, smilax, grapes, persimmons, and other berries. The ivy (*Hedera helix*) they were particularly fond of, though a native of Europe. We have an ancient plant adhering to the wall of the house, covering many yards of surface; this vine is very fruitful, and here many would feed and lodge during the winter, and, in very severe cold weather, sit on the top of the chimney to warm themselves." He also adds, " I have observed that the Mocking Bird ejects from his stomach through his mouth the hard kernels of berries, such as smilax, grapes, &c., retaining the pulpy part." *

HUMMING BIRD.† —TROCHILUS COLUBRIS. — Figs. 40, 41.

Trochilus colubris, *Linn. Syst.* i. p. 191, No. 12. — L'Oiseau mouche à gorge rouge de la Caroline, *Briss. Orn.* iii. p. 716, No. 13, t. 36, Fig. 6. — Le Rubis, *Buff. Ois.* vi. p. 13. — Humming Bird, *Catesb. Car.* i. 65. — Red-throated Humming Bird, *Edw.* i. 38, male and female. — *Lath. Syn.* ii. 769, No. 35. — *Peale's Museum*, No. 2520.

TROCHILUS COLUBRIS. — Linnæus.

Trochilus colubris, *Bonap. Synop.* p. 98. — The Ruby-throated Humming Bird, *Aud.* pl. xlvii. *Orn. Biog.* i. 248. — Trochilus colubris, Northern Humming Bird, *North. Zool.* ii. p. 323.

NATURE, in every department of her work, seems to delight in variety; and the present subject of our history is almost as singular for its minuteness, beauty, want of song, and manner of feeding, as the preceding is for unrivalled excellence of notes, and plainness of plu-

---

ardson, it was discovered by Captain Cook at Nootka Sound, and described by Latham from these specimens. — ED.

* Letter from Mr. Bartram to the author.

† The " Fairy Humming Birds," " The Jewels of Ornithology,"

" Least of the winged vagrants of the sky,"

though amply dispersed over the southern continent of the New World, from their delicate and slender structure, being unable to bear the severities of a hardier climate, are, with two exceptions, withdrawn from its northern parts; and it is with wonder that we see creatures of such tiny dimensions occasionally daring to brave even the snows and frosts of a northern latitude. The present species, though sometimes exceeding its appointed time, is obliged to seek warmer abodes during winter; and it is another subject for astonishment and reflection, how they are enabled to perform a lengthened migration, where the slightest gale would waft them far from their proper course. Mr. Audubon is of opinion, that they migrate during the night, passing through the air in long undulations, raising themselves for some distance at an angle of about 40°, and then falling in a curve; but he adds, that the smallness of their size precludes the possibility of following them farther than fifty or sixty yards, even with a good glass.

The Humming Birds, or what are generally known by the genus *Trochilus* of Linnæus, have been, through the researches of late travellers and naturalists, vastly

mage. Though this interesting and beautiful genus of birds comprehends upwards of seventy species, all of which, with a very few exceptions, are natives of America and its adjacent islands, it is yet singular that the species now before us should be the only one of its tribe that ever visits the territory of the United States.

According to the observations of my friend Mr. Abbot, of Savannah, in Georgia, who has been engaged these thirty years in collecting and drawing subjects of natural history in that part of the country, the Humming Bird makes its first appearance there, from the south, about the 23d of March, two weeks earlier than it does in the county of Burke, sixty miles higher up the country towards the interior, and at least five weeks sooner than it reaches this part of Pennsylvania. As it passes on to the northward, as far as the interior of Canada, where it is seen in great numbers,* the wonder is excited how so feebly constructed and delicate a little creature can make its way over such extensive regions of lakes and forests, among so many enemies, all its superiors in strength and magnitude. But its very minuteness, the rapidity of its flight, which almost eludes the eye, and that admirable instinct, reason, or whatever else it may be called, and daring courage, which Heaven has implanted in its bosom, are its guides and protectors. In these we may also perceive the reason why an all-wise Providence has made this little hero an exception to a rule which prevails almost universally through nature, viz., that the smallest species of a tribe are the most prolific. The Eagle lays one, sometimes two, eggs ; the Crow, five ; the Titmouse, seven or eight ; the small European Wren, fifteen ; the Humming Bird *two* : and yet this latter is abundantly more numerous in America than the Wren is in Europe.

About the 25th of April, the Humming Bird usually arrives in Pennsylvania, and, about the 10th of May, begins to build its nest. This is generally fixed on the upper side of a horizontal branch, not among the twigs, but on the body of the branch itself. Yet I have known instances where it was attached by the side to an old moss-grown trunk ; and others where it was fastened on a strong rank stalk, or weed, in the garden ; but these cases are rare. In the woods, it very often chooses a white oak sapling to build on ; and in the orchard or garden, selects a pear-tree for that purpose. The branch is sel-

increased in their numbers ; they form a large and closely-connected group, but show a considerable variety of form and character, and have been divided into different genera. They may be said to be strictly confined to the New World, with her islands ; and although other countries possess many splendid and closely-allied forms, " with gemmed frontlets and necks of verdant gold," which have been by some included, none we consider can properly range with any of those found in this division of the world. In India and the Asiatic continent, they may be represented by *Cœreba*, &c. ; in Africa, by *Nectarinia* and *Cyniris ;* and in Australia and in the Southern Pacific, by *Meliphaga, Myrzomela,* &c. Europe possesses no direct prototype.

The second northern species alluded to was discovered by Captain Cook in Nootka Sound, and first described by Dr. Latham, as the Ruffed-necked Humming Bird. Mr. Swainson introduces it in the *Northern Zoology*, under his genus *Selasphorus*. It ranges southwards to Real del Monte, on the table-land of Mexico. — ED.

* Mr. M'Kenzie speaks of seeing a " beautiful Humming Bird " near the head of the Unjigah, or Peace River, in lat. 54 deg., but has not particularized the species.

dom more than ten feet from the ground. The nest is about an inch in diameter, and as much in depth. A very complete one is now lying before me, and the materials of which it is composed are as follows: — The outward coat is formed of small pieces of a species of bluish gray lichen that vegetates on old trees and fences, thickly glued on with the saliva of the bird, giving firmness and consistency to the whole, as well as keeping out moisture. Within this are thick, matted layers of the fine wings of certain flying seeds, closely laid together; and, lastly, the downy substance from the great mullein, and from the stalks of the common fern, lines the whole. The base of the nest is continued round the stem of the branch, to which it closely adheres; and, when viewed from below, appears a mere mossy knot or accidental protuberance. The eggs are two, pure white, and of equal thickness at both ends. The nest and eggs in the plate were copied with great precision, and by actual measurement, from one just taken in from the woods. On a person's approaching their nest, the little proprietors dart around with a humming sound, passing frequently within a few inches of one's head; and, should the young be newly hatched, the female will resume her place on the nest even while you stand within a yard or two of the spot. The precise period of incubation I am unable to give; but the young are in the habit, a short time before they leave the nest, of thrusting their bills into the mouths of their parents, and sucking what they have brought them. I never could perceive that they carried them any animal food; though, from circumstances that will presently be mentioned, I think it highly probable they do. As I have found their nests with eggs so late as the 12th of July, I do not doubt but that they frequently, and perhaps usually, raise two broods in the same season.

The Humming Bird is extremely fond of tubular flowers, and I have often stopped, with pleasure, to observe his manœuvres among the blossoms of the trumpet flower. When arrived before a thicket of these, that are full blown, he poises, or suspends, himself on wing, for the space of two or three seconds, so steadily, that his wings become invisible, or only like a mist; and you can plainly distinguish the pupil of his eye looking round with great quickness and circumspection; the glossy, golden green of his back, and the fire of his throat, dazzling in the sun, form altogether a most interesting appearance. The position into which his body is usually thrown while in the act of thrusting his slender tubular tongue into the flower, to extract its sweets, is exhibited in the figure on the plate. When he alights, which is frequently, he always prefers the small, dead twigs of a tree or bush, where he dresses and arranges his plumage with great dexterity. His only note is a single chirp, not louder than that of a small cricket or grasshopper, generally uttered while passing from flower to flower, or when engaged in fight with his fellows; for, when two males meet at the same bush or flower, a battle instantly takes place; and the combatants ascend in the air, chirping, darting and circling around each other, till the eye is no longer able to follow them. The conqueror, however, generally returns to the place to reap the fruits of his victory. I have seen him attack, and for a few moments tease the King Bird; and have also seen him, in his turn, assaulted by a humble-bee, which he soon put to flight. He is one of those few birds that are universally beloved; and amidst the sweet, dewy serenity of a summer's morning, his appearance among the arbors of honeysuckles, and beds of flowers, is truly interesting.

> When the morning dawns, and the blest sun again
> Lifts his red glories from the eastern main,
> Then through our woodbines, wet with glittering dews,
> The flower-fed Humming Bird his round pursues;
> Sips, with inserted tube, the honey'd blooms,
> And chirps his gratitude as round he roams;
> While richest roses, though in crimson drest,
> Shrink from the splendor of his gorgeous breast.
> What heavenly tints in mingling radiance fly!
> Each rapid movement gives a different dye;
> Like scales of burnish'd gold they dazzling show,
> Now sink to shade — now like a furnace glow!

The singularity of this little bird has induced many persons to attempt to raise them from the nest, and accustom them to the cage. Mr. Coffer, of Fairfax county, Virginia, a gentleman who has paid great attention to the manners and peculiarities of our native birds, told me that he raised and kept two, for some months, in a cage; supplying them with honey dissolved in water, on which they readily fed. As the sweetness of the liquid frequently brought small flies and gnats about the cage and cup, the birds amused themselves by snapping at them on wing, and swallowing them with eagerness, so that these insects formed no inconsiderable part of their food. Mr. Charles Wilson Peale, proprietor of the museum, tells me that he had two young Humming Birds, which he raised from the nest. They used to fly about the room, and would frequently perch on Mrs. Peale's shoulder to be fed. When the sun shone strongly in the chamber, he has observed them darting after the motes that floated in the light, as Flycatchers would after flies. In the summer of 1803, a nest of young Humming Birds was brought me, that were nearly fit to fly. One of them actually flew out by the window the same evening, and, falling against a wall, was killed. The other refused food, and the next morning I could but just perceive that it had life. A lady in the house undertook to be its nurse, placed it in her bosom, and, as it began to revive, dissolved a little sugar in her mouth, into which she thrust its bill, and it sucked with great avidity. In this manner it was brought up until fit for the cage. I kept it upwards of three months, supplied it with loaf sugar dissolved in water, which it preferred to honey and water, gave it fresh flowers every morning sprinkled with the liquid, and surrounded the space in which I kept it with gauze, that it might not injure itself. It appeared gay, active, and full of spirit, hovering from flower to flower, as if in its native wilds, and always expressed, by its motions and chirping, great pleasure at seeing fresh flowers introduced to its cage. Numbers of people visited it from motives of curiosity; and I took every precaution to preserve it, if possible, through the winter. Unfortunately, however, by some means it got at large, and, flying about the room, so injured itself that it soon after died.

This little bird is extremely susceptible of cold, and, if long deprived of the animating influence of the sunbeams, droops, and soon dies. A very beautiful male was brought me this season, [1809,] which I put into a wire cage, and placed in a retired, shaded part of the room. After fluttering about for some time, the weather being uncommonly cool, it clung by the wires, and hung in a seemingly torpid state for a whole forenoon. No motion whatever of the lungs could be perceived, on the closest inspection, though, at other times, this is remarkably observable; the eyes were shut; and, when touched by the finger, it gave no signs of life or motion. I carried it out to the open air, and placed it directly in the rays of the sun, in a sheltered situation. In a few seconds, respiration became very apparent; the bird breathed faster and faster, opened its eyes, and began to look about, with as much seeming vivacity as ever. After it had completely recovered, I restored it to liberty; and it flew off to the withered top of a pear-tree, where it sat for some time dressing its disordered plumage, and then shot off like a meteor.

The flight of the Humming Bird, from flower to flower, greatly resembles that of a bee, but is so much more rapid, that the latter appears a mere loiterer to him. He poises himself on wing, while he thrusts his long, slender, tubular tongue into the flowers in search of food. He sometimes enters a room by the window, examines the bouquets of flowers, and passes out by the opposite door or window. He has been known to take refuge in a hot-house during the cool nights of autumn, to go regularly out in the morning, and to return as regularly in the evening, for several days together.

The Humming Bird has, hitherto, been supposed to subsist altogether on the honey, or liquid sweets, which it extracts from flowers. One or two curious observers have, indeed, remarked, that they have found evident fragments of insects in the stomach of this species; but these have been generally believed to have been taken in by accident. The few opportunities which Europeans have to determine this point by observations made on the living bird, or by dissection of the newly-killed one, have rendered this mistaken opinion almost general in Europe. For myself, I can speak decisively on this subject: I have seen the Humming Bird, for half an hour at a time, darting at those little groups of insects that dance in the air in a fine summer evening, retiring to an adjoining twig to rest, and renewing the attack with a dexterity that sets all our other Flycatchers at defiance. I have opened, from time to time, great numbers of these birds; have examined the contents of the stomach with suitable glasses, and, in three cases out of four, have found these to consist of broken fragments of insects. In many subjects, entire insects of the coleopterous class, but very small, were found unbroken. The observations of Mr. Coffer, as detailed above, and the remarks of my worthy friend Mr. Peale, are corroborative of these facts. It is well known that the Humming Bird is particularly fond of tubular flowers, where numerous small insects of this kind resort to feed on the farina, &c.; and there is every reason for believing that he is as often in search of these insects as of honey, and that the former compose at least as great a portion of his usual sustenance as the latter. If this food be so necessary for the parents, there is no doubt but the young also occasionally partake of it.

To enumerate all the flowers of which this little bird is fond, would be to repeat the names of half our American Flora. From the blossoms of the towering poplar or tulip-tree, through a thousand intermediate flowers, to those of the humble larkspur, he ranges at will, and almost incessantly. Every period of the season produces a fresh multitude of new favorites. Towards the month of September, there is a yellow flower which grows in great luxuriance along the sides of creeks and rivers, and in low, moist situations; it grows to the height of two or three feet, and the flower, which is about the size of a thimble, hangs in the shape of a cap of liberty above a luxuriant growth of green leaves. It is the *Balsamina noli me tangere* of botanists, and is the greatest favorite with the Humming Bird of all our other flowers. In some places, where these plants abound, you may see, at one time, ten or twelve Humming Birds darting about, and fighting with and pursuing each other. About the 20th of September they generally retire to the south. I have, indeed, sometimes seen a solitary individual on the 28th and 30th of that month, and sometimes even in October; but these cases are rare. About the beginning of November, they pass the southern boundary of the United States into Florida.

The Humming Bird is three inches and a half in length, and four and a quarter in extent; the whole back, upper part of the neck, sides under the wings, tail-coverts, and two middle feathers of the tail, are of a rich, golden green; the tail is forked, and, as well as the wings, of a deep brownish purple; the bill and eyes are black; the legs and feet, both of which are extremely small, are also black; the bill is straight, very slender, a little inflated at the tip, and very incompetent to the exploit of penetrating the tough, sinewy side of a Crow, and precipitating it from the clouds to the earth, as Charlevoix would persuade his readers to believe.* The nostrils are two small, oblong slits, situated at the base of the upper mandible, scarcely perceivable when the bird is dead, though very distinguishable and prominent when living; the sides of the belly, and belly itself, dusky white, mixed with green; but what constitutes the chief ornament of this little bird is the splendor of the feathers of his throat, which, when placed in a proper position, glow with all the brilliancy of the ruby. These feathers are of singular strength and texture, lying close together like scales, and vary, when moved before the eye, from a deep black to a fiery crimson and burning orange. The female is destitute of this ornament, but differs little in other appearance from the male; her tail is tipped with white, and the whole lower parts are of the same tint. The young birds of the first season, both male and female, have the tail tipped with white, and the whole lower parts nearly white; in the month of September, the ornamental feathers on the throat of the young males begin to appear.

On dissection, the heart was found to be remarkably large, nearly as big as the cranium; and the stomach, though distended with food, uncommonly small, not exceeding the globe of the eye, and scarcely more than one sixth part as large as the heart; the fibres of the last were also exceedingly strong. The brain was in large quantity, and very thin; the tongue, from the tip to an extent equal with the length of the bill, was perforated, forming two closely-attached parallel and cylindrical tubes; the other extremities of the tongue corresponded

---

* *Histoire de la Nouvelle France*, iii. p. 185.

exactly to those of the Woodpecker, passing up the hind head, and reaching to the base of the upper mandible. These observations were verified in five different subjects, all of whose stomachs contained fragments of insects, and some of them whole ones.

TOWHE BUNTING. — EMBERIZA ERYTHROPTHALMA. —
Fig. 42.

Fringilla erythropthalma, *Linn. Syst.* p. 318, 6. — Le Pinson de la Caroline, *Briss. Orn.* iii. p. 169, 44. — *Buff. Ois.* iv. p. 141. — *Lath.* ii. p. 199, No. 43. — *Catesb. Czr.* i. plate 34. — *Peale's Museum*, No. 5970.

PIPILO ERYTHROPTHALMA. — Vieillot.

Pipilo erythropthalma, *Vieill. Gal. des Ois.* plate 80. — Fringilla erythropthalma, *Bonap. Synop.* p. 112. — The Towhe Bunting, *Aud.* plate 29, male and female; *Orn. Biog.* i. p. 150.

THIS is a very common, but humble and inoffensive species, frequenting close-sheltered thickets, where it spends most of its time in scratching up the leaves for worms, and for the larvæ and eggs of insects. It is far from being shy, frequently suffering a person to walk round the bush or thicket, where it is at work, without betraying any marks of alarm, and when disturbed, uttering the notes *tow-he* repeatedly. At times the male mounts to the top of a small tree, and chants his few, simple notes for an hour at a time. These are loud, not unmusical, something resembling those of the Yellow Hammer of Britain, but more mellow and more varied. He is fond of thickets with a southern exposure, near streams of water, and where there is plenty of dry leaves; and is found, generally, over the whole United States. He is not gregarious, and you seldom see more than two together. About the middle or 20th of April, they arrive in Pennsylvania, and begin building about the first week in May. The nest is fixed on the ground among the dry leaves, near, and sometimes under, a thicket of briers, and is large and substantial. The outside is formed of leaves and dry pieces of grape-vine bark, and the inside, of fine stalks of dried grass, the cavity completely sunk beneath the surface of the ground, and sometimes half covered above with dry grass or hay. The eggs are usually five, of a pale flesh color, thickly marked with specks of rufous, most numerous near the great end. The young are produced about the beginning of June, and a second brood commonly succeeds in the same season. This bird rarely winters north of the state of Maryland, retiring from Pennsylvania to the south about the 12th of October. Yet in the middle districts of Virginia, and thence south to Florida, I found it abundant during the months of January, February, and March. Its usual food is obtained by scratching up the leaves; it also feeds, like the rest of its tribe, on various hard seeds and gravel, but rarely commits any depredations on the harvest of the husbandman, gener-

11

ally preferring the woods, and traversing the bottom of fences sheltered with briers. He is generally very plump and fat; and, when confined in a cage, soon becomes familiar. In Virginia, he is called the Bullfinch; in many places, the Towhe Bird; in Pennsylvania, the Chewink, and by others, the Swamp Robin. He contributes a little to the harmony of our woods in spring and summer; and is remarkable for the cunning with which he conceals his nest. He shows great affection for his young, and the deepest marks of distress on the appearance of their mortal enemy, the black snake.

The specific name which Linnæus has bestowed on this bird, is deduced from the color of the iris of its eye, which, in those that visit Pennsylvania, is dark red. But I am suspicious that this color is not permanent, but subject to a periodical change. I examined a great number of these birds in the month of March, in Georgia, every one of which had the iris of the eye white. Mr. Abbot, of Savannah, assured me that, at this season, every one of these birds he shot had the iris white, while at other times it was red; and Mr. Elliot, of Beaufort, a judicious naturalist, informed me, that in the month of February he killed a Towhe Bunting with one eye red and the other white! It should be observed that the iris of the young bird's eye is of a chocolate color during its residence in Pennsylvania: perhaps this may brighten into a white during winter, and these may have been all birds of the preceding year, which had not yet received the full color of the eye.

The Towhe Bunting is eight inches and a half long, and eleven broad; above, black, which also descends, rounding on the breast, the sides of which are bright bay, spreading along under the wings; the belly is white; the vent, pale rufous; a spot of white marks the wing just below the coverts, and another a little below that extends obliquely across the primaries; the tail is long, nearly even at the end; the three exterior feathers, white for an inch or so from the tips, the outer one wholly white, the middle ones black; the bill is black; the legs and feet, a dirty flesh color, and strong, for scratching up the ground. The female differs in being of a light reddish brown in those parts where the male is black, and in having the bill more of a light horn color.*

---

* Mr. Swainson makes *Pipilo* a sub-genus among the Sparrows. Six species have been described, and the above-mentioned gentleman has lately received two in addition. They are confined to both continents of America, and the species of our author was considered as the only one belonging to the northern parts; the *Northern Zoology* will give to the public a second under the title *Pipilo arctica*, which was only met with on the plains of the Saskatchewan, where it was supposed to breed, from a specimen being killed late in July. It frequents shady and moist clumps of wood, and is generally seen on the ground. It feeds on grubs; is a solitary and retired, but not distrustful bird. It approaches nearest to the Mexican *Pipilo maculata,* Sw.

Mr. Audubon says, "The haunts of the Towhe Bunting are dry, barren tracts, but not, as others have said, low and swampy grounds, at least during the season of incubation." The name of *Swamp Robin* would indicate something the reverse of this, and provincial names are generally pretty correct in their application; different habits may perhaps be sought at different seasons. In "the Barrens of Kentucky they are found in the greatest abundance. They rest upon the ground at night. Their migrations are performed by day, from bush to bush; and they

CARDINAL GROSBEAK. — LOXIA CARDINALIS. —
FIGS. 43, 44.

Linn Syst i p. 300, No. 5. *Le Gros-bec de Virginie, Briss. Orn.* III. p. 255. No. 17. — *Buff.* iii. p. 458, pl. 28. *Pl. enl.* 37. — *Lath. Syn.* ii. p. 118, No. 13. — Cardinal, *Brown's Jam.* p. 647. — *Peale's Museum,* No. 5668.

GUARICA CARDINALIS. — SWAINSON.

Fringilla cardinalis, *Bonap. Synop.* p. 113.

THIS is one of our most common cage birds; and is very generally known, not only in North America, but even in Europe, numbers of them having been carried over both to France and England, in which last country they are usually called Virginia Nightingales. To this name, Dr. Latham observes, "they are fully entitled," from the clearness and variety of their notes, which, both in a wild and domestic state, are very various and musical: many of them resemble the high notes of a fife, and are nearly as loud. They are in song from March to September, beginning at the first appearance of dawn, and repeating a favorite stanza, or passage, twenty or thirty times successively; sometimes, with little intermission, for a whole morning together, which, like a good story too often repeated, becomes at length tiresome and insipid. But the sprightly figure and gaudy plumage of the Red-Bird, his vivacity, strength of voice, and actual variety of note, and the little expense with which he is kept, will always make him a favorite.

This species, like the Mocking Bird, is more numerous to the east of the great range of the Alleghany Mountains, and inhabits from New England to Carthagena. Michaux the younger, son to the celebrated botanist, informed me, that he found this bird numerous in the Bermudas. In Pennsylvania and the Northern States, it is rather a scarce species; but through the whole lower parts of the Southern States, in the neighborhood of settlements, I found them much more numerous; their clear and lively notes, in the months of January and February, being, at that time, almost the only music of the season. Along the road sides and fences I found them hovering in half dozens together, associated with Snow Birds, and various kinds of Sparrows. In the Northern States, they are migratory; but in the lower parts of Pennsylvania, they reside during the whole year, frequenting the borders of creeks and rivulets, in sheltered hollows, covered with holly, laurel, and other evergreens. They love also to reside in the vicinity of fields of Indian corn, a grain that constitutes their chief and favorite food. The seeds of apples, cherries, and of many other sorts of fruit, are also eaten by them; and they are accused of destroying bees.

seem to be much at a loss when a large extent of forest is to be traversed by them. They perform these journeys almost singly. The females set out before the males in autumn, the males before the females in spring; the latter not appearing in the middle districts until the end of April, a fortnight after the males had arrived." — ED.

In the months of March and April, the males have many violent engagements for their favorite females. Early in May, in Pennsylvania, they begin to prepare their nest, which is very often fixed in a holly, cedar, or laurel bush. Outwardly, it is constructed of small twigs, tops of dry weeds, and slips of vine bark, and lined with stalks of fine grass. The female lays four eggs, thickly marked all over with touches of brownish olive, on a dull white ground, as represented in the figure; and they usually raise two broods in the season. These birds are rarely raised from the nest for singing, being so easily taken in trap-cages, and soon domesticated. By long confinement, and perhaps unnatural food, they are found to fade in color, becoming of a pale whitish red. If well taken care of, however, they will live to a considerable age. There is at present in Mr. Peale's museum, the stuffed skin of one of these birds, which is there said to have lived in a cage upwards of twenty-one years.

The opinion which so generally prevails in England, that the music of the groves and woods of America is far inferior to that of Europe, I, who have a thousand times listened to both, cannot admit to be correct. We cannot with fairness draw a comparison between the depth of the forest in America, and the cultivated fields of England; because it is a well-known fact, that singing birds seldom frequent the former in any country. But let the latter places be compared with the like situations in the United States, and the superiority of song, I am fully persuaded, would justly belong to the western continent. The few of our song birds that have visited Europe extort admiration from the best judges. "The notes of the Cardinal Grosbeak," says Latham, "are almost equal to those of the Nightingale." Yet these notes, clear and excellent as they are, are far inferior to those of the Wood Thrush, and even to those of the Brown Thrush, or Thrasher. Our inimitable Mocking Bird is also acknowledged, by themselves, to be fully equal to the song of the Nightingale, "in its whole compass." Yet these are not one tenth of the number of our singing birds. Could these people be transported to the borders of our woods and settlements, in the month of May, about half an hour before sunrise, such a ravishing concert would greet their ear as they have no conception of.

The males of the Cardinal Grosbeak, when confined together in a cage, fight violently. On placing a looking-glass before the cage, the gesticulations of the tenant are truly laughable; yet with this he soon becomes so well acquainted, that, in a short time, he takes no notice whatever of it; a pretty good proof that he has discovered the true cause of the appearance to proceed from himself. They are hardy birds, easily kept, sing six or eight months in the year, and are most lively in wet weather. They are generally known by the names, Red-Bird, Virginia Red-Bird, Virginia Nightingale, and Crested Red-Bird, to distinguish them from another beautiful species, the Scarlet Tanager, Figs. 45 and 46.

I do not know that any successful attempts have been made to induce these birds to pair and breed in confinement; but I have no doubt of its practicability, by proper management. Some months ago, I placed a young, unfledged Cow-Bird, (the *Fringilla pecoris* of Turton,) whose mother, like the Cuckoo of Europe, abandons her eggs and progeny to the mercy and management of other smaller birds, in the same cage with a Red-Bird, which fed and reared it with great tenderness. They both continue to inhabit the same cage, and I have hopes that the Red-Bird will finish his pupil's education by teaching him his song.

I must here remark, for the information of foreigners, that the story told by Le Page du Pratz, in his *History of Louisiana*, and which has been so often repeated by other writers, that the Cardinal Grosbeak " collects together great hoards of maize and buck-wheat, often as much as a bushel, which it artfully covers with leaves and small twigs, leaving only a small hole for entrance into the magazine," is entirely fabulous.

This species is eight inches long, and eleven in extent; the whole upper parts are a dull, dusky red, except the sides of the neck and head, which, as well as the whole lower parts, are bright vermilion; chin, front, and lores, black; the head is ornamented with a high, pointed crest, which it frequently erects in an almost perpendicular position, and can also flatten at pleasure, so as to be scarcely perceptible; the tail extends three inches beyond the wings, and is nearly even at the end; the bill is of a brilliant coralline color, very thick and powerful, for breaking hard grain and seeds; the legs and feet, a light clay color, (not blood red, as Buffon describes them;) iris of the eye, dark hazel. The female (Fig. 44) is less than the male, has the upper parts of a brownish olive, or drab color, the tail, wings, and tip of the crest excepted, which are nearly as red as those of the male; the lores, front, and chin, are light ash; breast, and lower parts, a reddish drab; bill, legs, and eyes, as those of the male; the crest is shorter, and less frequently raised.

One peculiarity in the female of this species is, that she often sings nearly as well as the male. I do not know whether it be owing to some little jealousy on this score or not, that the male, when both occupy the same cage, very often destroys the female.

SCARLET TANAGER. — TANAGRA RUBRA. — Figs. 45, 46.

Tanagra rubra, *Lynn. Syst.* i. p. 314, 3. — Cardinal de Canada, *Briss. Orn.* iii. p. 43, pl. 2, fig. 5. — *Lath.* ii. p. 217, No. 3. — Scarlet Sparrow, *Edw.* pl. 343. — Canada Tanager, and Olivo Tanager, *Arct. Zool.* p. 369, No. 237, 238. — *Peale's Museum*, No. 6128.

PYRANGA* RUBRA. — Swainson.

Pyranga erythropis, *Vieill. Enc. Method.* p. 793. — Tanagra rubra, *Bonap. Synop.* p. 105. — Pyranga rubra, *North. Zool.* ii. p. 273.

This is one of the gaudy foreigners (and perhaps the most showy) that regularly visit us from the torrid regions of the south. He is

* *Pyranga* has been established for the reception of this bird as the type, and a few others, all natives of the New World, and more particularly inhabiting the

11 *

dressed in the richest scarlet, set off with the most jetty black, and comes, over extensive countries, to sojourn for a time among us. While we consider him entitled to all the rights of hospitality, we may be permitted to examine a little into his character, and endeavor to discover whether he has any thing else to recommend him, besides that of having a fine coat, and being a great traveller.

On or about the first of May, this bird makes his appearance in Pennsylvania. He spreads over the United States, and is found even in Canada. He rarely approaches the habitations of man, unless, perhaps, to the orchard, where he sometimes builds, or to the cherry-trees, in search of fruit. The depth of the woods is his favorite abode. There, among the thick foliage of the tallest trees, his simple and almost monotonous notes, *chip, churr*, repeated at short intervals, in a pensive tone, may be occasionally heard, which appear to proceed from a considerable distance, though the bird be immediately above you, — a faculty bestowed on him by the beneficent Author of Nature, no doubt, for his protection, to compensate, in a degree, for the danger to which his glowing color would often expose him. Besides this usual note, he has, at times, a more musical chant, something resembling in mellowness that of the Baltimore Oriole. His food consists of large-winged insects, such as wasps, hornets, and humble-bees, and also of fruit, particularly those of that species of *Vaccinium* usually called huckle-berries, which, in their season, form almost his whole fare. His nest is built, about the middle of May, on the horizontal branch of a tree, sometimes an apple-tree, and is but slightly put together; stalks of broken flax and dry grass, so thinly woven together, that the light is easily perceivable through it, form the repository of his young. The eggs are three, of a dull blue, spotted with brown or purple. They rarely raise more than one brood in a season, and leave us for the south about the last week in August.

Among all the birds that inhabit our woods, there is none that strikes the eye of a stranger, or even a native, with so much brilliancy as this. Seen among the green leaves, with the light falling strongly on his plumage, he really appears beautiful. If he has little of melody in his notes to charm us, he has nothing in them to disgust. His manners are modest, easy, and inoffensive. He commits no depredations on the property of the husbandman, but rather benefits him by the daily destruction, in spring, of many noxious insects; and, when winter approaches, he is no plundering dependent, but seeks, in a distant country, for that sustenance which the severity of the season denies to his industry in this. He is a striking ornament to our rural scenery, and none of the meanest of our rural songsters. Such being the true traits of his character, we shall always with pleasure welcome this beautiful, inoffensive stranger to our orchards, groves, and forests.

warmer parts of it. The present species is, indeed, the only one which is common to the north and south continents; and, in the former, it ranks only as a summer visitant. They are all of very bright colors, and distinct markings. They are distinguished from the true Tanagers, by their stout and rounded bill, slightly notched, bent at the tip, and having a jutting-out, blunt tooth about the middle of the upper mandible. They are placed by Desmarest among his *Tanagras colluriens*, or Shrike-like Tanagers; and by Lesson among the *Tanagras cardinales*. The latter writer enumerates only three species belonging to his division. — ED.

The male of this species, (Fig. 45,) when arrived at his full size and colors, is six inches and a half in length, and ten and a half broad. The whole plumage is of a most brilliant scarlet, except the wings and tail, which are of a deep black; the latter, handsomely forked, sometimes minutely tipped with white, and the interior edges of the wing-feathers nearly white; the bill is strong, considerably inflated, like those of his tribe, the edge of the upper mandible, somewhat irregular, as if toothed, and the whole of a dirty gamboge, or yellowish horn color; this, however, like that of most other birds, varies according to the season. About the 1st of August he begins to moult; the young feathers coming out, of a greenish yellow color, until he appears nearly all dappled with spots of scarlet and greenish yellow. In this state of plumage he leaves us. How long it is before he recovers his scarlet dress, or whether he continues of this greenish color all winter, I am unable to say. The iris of the eye is of a cream color; the legs and feet, light blue. The female, Fig. 46, (now, I believe, for the first time figured,) is green above, and yellow below; the wings and tail, brownish black, edged with green. The young birds, during their residence here the first season, continue nearly of the same color with the female. In this circumstance we again recognize the wise provision of the Deity, in thus clothing the female and the inexperienced young in a garb so favorable for concealment among the foliage; as the weakness of the one, and the frequent visits of the other to her nest, would greatly endanger the safety of all. That the young males do not receive their red plumage until the early part of the succeeding spring, I think highly probable, from the circumstance of frequently finding their red feathers, at that season, intermixed with green ones, and the wings also broadly edged with green. These facts render it also probable that the old males regularly change their color, and have a summer and winter dress; but this further observations must determine.

There is in the Brazils a bird of the same genus with this, and very much resembling it, so much so as to have been frequently confounded with it by European writers. It is the *Tanagra Brazilia* of Turton; and, though so like, is yet a very distinct species from the present, as I have myself had the opportunity of ascertaining, by examining two very perfect specimens from Brazil, now in the possession of Mr. Peale, and comparing them with this. The principal differences are these: The plumage of the Brazilian is almost black at bottom, very deep scarlet at the surface, and of an orange tint between; ours is ash colored at bottom, white in the middle, and bright scarlet at top. The tail of ours is forked, that of the other cuneiform, or rounded. The bill of our species is more inflated, and of a greenish yellow color; the other's is black above, and whitish below, towards the base. The whole plumage of the southern species is of a coarser, stiffer quality, particularly on the head. The wings and tail, in both, are black.

In the account which Buffon gives of the Scarlet Tanager and Cardinal Grosbeak, there appears to be very great confusion, and many mistakes; to explain which, it is necessary to observe that Mr. Edwards, in his figure of the Scarlet Tanager, or Scarlet Sparrow, as he calls it, has given it a hanging crest, owing, no doubt, to the loose, disordered state of the plumage of the stuffed or dried skin from which he made his drawing. Buffon has afterwards confounded the two together, by applying many stories, originally related of the Cardinal Grosbeak, to the Scarlet Tanager, and the following he gravely gives as his reason for so doing: "We may presume," says he, "that when travellers talk of the warble of the Cardinal, they mean the Scarlet Cardinal, for the other Cardinal is of the genus of the Grosbeaks, consequently a silent bird." * This silent bird, however, has been declared by an eminent English naturalist to be almost equal to their own Nightingale! The count also quotes the following passage from Charlevoix to prove the same point, which, if his translator has done him justice, evidently proves the reverse. "It is scarcely more than a hundred leagues," says this traveller, "south of Canada that the Cardinal begins to be seen. Their song is sweet, their plumage beautiful, and their head wears a crest." But the Scarlet Tanager is found even in Canada, as well as a hundred leagues to the south, while the Cardinal Grosbeak is not found in any great numbers north of Maryland. The latter, therefore, it is highly probable, was the bird meant by Charlevoix, and not the Scarlet Tanager. Buffon also quotes an extract of a letter from Cuba, which, if the circumstance it relates be true, is a singular proof of the estimation in which the Spaniards hold the Cardinal Grosbeak. "On Wednesday arrived at the port of Havannah, a bark from Florida, loaded with Cardinal birds, skins, and fruit. The Spaniards bought the Cardinal birds at so high a price as ten dollars apiece; and, notwithstanding the public distress, spent on them the sum of 18,000 dollars!" *

With a few facts more I shall conclude the history of the Scarlet Tanager: When you approach the nest, the male keeps cautiously at a distance, as if fearful of being seen; while the female hovers around in the greatest agitation and distress. When the young leave the nest, the male parent takes a most active part in feeding and attending them, and is then altogether indifferent of concealment.

Passing through an orchard one morning, I caught one of these young birds, that had but lately left the nest. I carried it with me about half a mile, to show it to my friend, Mr. William Bartram; and, having procured a cage, hung it up on one of the large pine-trees in the botanic garden, within a few feet of the nest of an Orchard Oriole, which also contained young; hopeful that the charity or tenderness of the Orioles would induce them to supply the cravings of the stranger. But charity with them, as with too many of the human race, began and ended at home. The poor orphan was altogether neglected, notwithstanding its plaintive cries; and, as it refused to be fed by me, I was about to return it back to the place where I found it, when, towards the afternoon, a Scarlet Tanager, no doubt its own parent, was seen fluttering round the cage, endeavoring to get in. Finding this impracticable, he flew off, and soon returned with food in his bill, and continued to feed it till after sunset, taking up his lodgings on the higher branches of the same tree. In the morning, almost as soon as day broke, he was again seen most actively engaged in the same affectionate manner; and, notwithstanding the insolence of the Orioles, continued his benevolent offices the whole day, roosting at night as before. On the

* BUFFON, vol. iv. p. 209.   † GMELLI CARERI.

third or fourth day, he appeared extremely solicitous for the liberation of his charge, using every expression of distressful anxiety, and every call and invitation that nature had put in his power, for him to come out. This was too much for the feelings of my venerable friend; he procured a ladder, and, mounting to the spot where the bird was suspended, opened the cage, took out the prisoner, and restored him to liberty and to his parent, who, with notes of great exultation, accompanied his flight to the woods. The happiness of my good friend was scarcely less complete, and showed itself in his benevolent countenance; and I could not refrain saying to myself, — If such sweet sensations can be derived from a single circumstance of this kind, how exquisite — how unspeakably rapturous — must the delight of those individuals have been, who have rescued their fellow-beings from death, chains, and imprisonment, and restored them to the arms of their friends and relations! Surely, in such godlike actions, virtue is its own most abundant reward.

RICE BUNTING.— EMBERIZA ORYZIVORA.—Figs. 47, 48.

Emberiza oryzivora, *Linn. Syst.* p. 311, 16. — Le Ortolan da la Caroline, *Briss. Orn.* iii. p. 282, 8, pl. 15, fig. 3. *Pl. enl.* 388. fig. 1. — L'Agripenne ou l'Ortolan de Riz, *Buff. Ois.* iv. p. 337. — Rice Bird, *Catesb. Car.* i. pl. 14. — *Edw.* pl. 2. — *Latham*, ii. p. 188, No. 25. — *Peale's Museum,* No. 6026.

DOLYCHONYX ORYZIVORUS. — Swainson.

Icterus agripennis, *Bonap. Synop.* p. 53. — Dolychonyx oryzivorus, *Sw. Synop. Birds of Mexico,* 435. — *North. Zool.* ii. p. 278. — *Aud.* pl. 54. *Orn. Biog.* i. p. 283.

This is the *Boblink* of the Eastern and Northern States, and the *Rice* and *Reed Bird* of Pennsylvania and the Southern States. Though small in size, he is not so in consequence; his coming is hailed by the sportsman with pleasure; while the careful planter looks upon him as a devouring scourge, and worse than a plague of locusts. Three good qualities, however, entitle him to our notice, particularly as these three are rarely found in the same individual, — his plumage is beautiful, his song highly musical, and his flesh excellent. I might also add, that the immense range of his migrations, and the havock he commits, are not the least interesting parts of his history.*

* To Wilson's interesting account of the habits of this curious bird, Mr. Audubon adds the following particulars: — In Louisiana they pass under the name of *Meadow Birds*, and they arrive there in small flocks of males and females about the middle of March or beginning of April. Their song in spring is extremely interesting, and, emitted with a volubility bordering on the burlesque, is heard from a whole party at the same time, and it becomes amusing to hear thirty or forty of them beginning one after another, as if ordered to follow in quick succession, after the first notes are given by a leader, and producing such a medley as it is impossible to describe, although it is extremely pleasant to hear. While you are listening, the whole flock simultaneously ceases, which appears equally extraordinary. This curious exhibition takes place every time the flock has alighted on a tree.

Another curious fact mentioned by this gentleman is, that during their spring

The winter residence of this species I suppose to be from Mexico to the mouth of the Amazon, from whence, in hosts innumerable, they regularly issue every spring; perhaps to both hemispheres, extending their migrations northerly as far as the banks of the Illinois and the shores of the St. Lawrence. Could the fact be ascertained, which has been asserted by some writers, that the emigration of these birds was altogether unknown in this part of the continent, previous to the introduction of rice plantations, it would certainly be interesting. Yet, why should these migrations reach at least a thousand miles beyond those places where rice is now planted; and this, not in occasional excursions, but regularly to breed, and rear their young, where rice never was, and probably never will be, cultivated? Their so recent arrival on this part of the continent, I believe to be altogether imaginary, because, though there were not a single grain of rice cultivated within the United States, the country produces an exuberance of food of which they are no less fond. Insects of various kinds, grubs, May-flies, and caterpillars, the young ears of Indian corn, and the seed of the wild oats, or, as it is called in Pennsylvania, reeds, (the *Zizania aquatica* of Linnæus,) which grows in prodigious abundance along the marshy shores of our large rivers, furnish, not only them, but millions of Rail, with a delicious subsistence for several weeks. I do not doubt, however, that the introduction of rice, but more particularly the progress of agriculture, in this part of America, has greatly increased their numbers, by multiplying their sources of subsistence fifty fold within the same extent of country.

In the month of April, or very early in May, the Rice Bunting, male and female, in the dresses in which they appear in Figs. 47 and 48, arrive within the southern boundaries of the United States, and are seen around the town of Savannah in Georgia, about the 4th of May, sometimes in separate parties of males and females, but more generally promiscuously. They remain there but a short time; and, about the 12th of May, make their appearance in the lower parts of Pennsylvania, as they did at Savannah. While here, the males are extremely gay and full of song; frequenting meadows, newly-ploughed fields, sides of creeks, rivers, and watery places, feeding on May-flies and caterpillars, of which they destroy great quantities. In their passage, however, through Virginia, at this season, they do great damage to the early wheat and barley, while in its milky state. About the 20th of May, they disappear, on their way to the north. Nearly at the same time, they arrive in the state of New York, spread over the whole New England States, as far as the River St. Lawrence, from Lake Ontario to the sea; in all of which places, north of Pennsylvania, they remain during the summer, building, and rearing their young. The nest is fixed in the ground, generally in a field of grass; the outside is composed of dry leaves and coarse grass, the inside is lined with fine stalks of the same, laid in considerable quantity. The female lays five eggs, of a bluish white, marked with numerous, irregular spots of blackish brown. The song of the male, while the female is sitting, is singular, and very agreeable. Mounting and hovering on wing, at a

migrations eastward, they fly mostly at night; whereas, in autumn, when they are returning southward, their flight is diurnal. — Ed.

small height above the field, he chants out such a jingling medley of short, variable notes, uttered with such seeming confusion and rapidity, and continued for a considerable time, that it appears as if half a dozen birds of different kinds were all singing together. Some idea may be formed of this song by striking the high keys of a piano-forte at random, singly and quickly, making as many sudden contrasts of high and low notes as possible. Many of the tones are, in them-selves, charming ; but they succeed each other so rapidly, that the ear can hardly separate them. Nevertheless, the general effect is good; and, when ten or twelve are all singing on the same tree, the concert is singularly pleasing. I kept one of these birds for a long time, to observe its change of color. During the whole of April, May, and June, it sang almost continually. In the month of June, the color of the male begins to change, gradually assimilating to that of the female, and before the beginning of August it is difficult to distinguish the one from the other, both being then in the dress of Fig. 48. At this time, also, the young birds are so much like the female, or rather like both parents, and the males so different in appearance from what they were in spring, that thousands of people in Pennsylvania, to this day, persist in believing them to be a different species altogether; while others allow them, indeed, to be the same, but confidently assert that they are all females—none but females, according to them, returning in the fall ; what becomes of the males they are totally at a loss to conceive. Even Mr. Mark Catesby, who resided for years in the coun-try they inhabit, and who, as he himself informs us, examined by dis-section great numbers of them in the fall, and repeated his experi-ment the succeeding year, lest he should have been mistaken, declares that he uniformly found them to be females. These assertions must appear odd to the inhabitants of the Eastern States, to whom the change of plumage in these birds is familiar, as it passes immediately under their eye ; and also to those who, like myself, have kept them in cages, and witnessed their gradual change of color.* That accu-rate observer, Mr. William Bartram, appears, from the following extract, to have taken notice of, or at least suspected, this change of color in these birds, more than forty years ago. "Being in Charles-ton," says he, "in the month of June, I observed a cage full of Rice Birds, that is, of the yellow, or female color, who were very merry and vociferous, having the same variable music with the pied, or male bird, which I thought extraordinary, and, observing it to the gentle-man, he assured me that they were all of the male kind, taken the pre-ceding spring, but had changed their color, and would be next spring of the color of the pied, thus changing color with the seasons of the year. If this is really the case, it appears they are both of the same species intermixed, spring and fall." Without, however, implicating the veracity of Catesby, who, I have no doubt, believed as he wrote, a few words will easily explain why he was deceived: The internal

* The beautiful plumage of the male represented on the plate, is that during the breeding season, and is lost as soon as the duties incumbent thereon are completed. In this we have a striking analogy with some nearly allied African *Fringillidæ.*

The genus *Dolyconyx* has been made by Mr. Swainson to contain this curious and interesting form : by that gentleman it is placed in the aberrant families of the *Sturnidæ.* — ED.

organization of undomesticated birds, of all kinds, undergoes a re-markable change every spring and summer; and those who wish to ascertain this point by dissection will do well to remember, that in this bird those parts that characterize the male are, in autumn, no larger than the smallest pin's head, and in young birds of the first year can scarcely be discovered; though in spring their magnitude in each is at least one hundred times greater.   To an unacquaintance with this extraordinary circumstance, I am persuaded, has been owing the mis-take of Mr. Catesby, that the females only return in the fall; for the same opinion I long entertained myself, till a more particular examina-tion showed me the source of my mistake.   Since that, I have opened and examined many hundreds of these birds, in the months of Sep-tember and October, and, on the whole, have found about as many males as females among them.   The latter may be distinguished from the former by being of a rather more shining yellow on the breast and belly: it is the same with the young birds of the first season.

During the breeding season, they are dispersed over the country; but, as soon as the young are able to fly, they collect together in great multitudes, and pour down on the oat-fields of New England like a torrent, depriving the proprietors of a good tithe of their harvest; but, in return, often supply his table with a very delicious dish.   From all parts of the north and western regions, they direct their course towards the south; and, about the middle of August, revisit Pennsylvania, on their route to winter quarters.   For several days, they seem to confine themselves to the fields and uplands; but, as soon as the seeds of the reed are ripe, they resort to the shores of the Delaware and Schuylkill in multitudes; and these places, during the remainder of their stay, appear to be their grand rendezvous.   The reeds, or wild oats, furnish them with such abundance of nutritious food, that in a short time they become extremely fat, and are supposed, by some of our epicures, to be equal to the famous Ortolans of Europe.   Their note at this season is a single *chink*, and is heard overhead, with little intermission, from morning to night.   These are halcyon days for our gunners of all descriptions, and many a lame and rusty gun-barrel is put in requisi-tion for the sport.   The report of musketry along the reedy shores of the Schuylkill and Delaware is almost incessant, resembling a running fire.   The markets of Philadelphia, at this season, exhibit proofs of the prodigious havock made among these birds; for almost every stall is ornamented with strings of Reed Birds.   This sport, however, is considered inferior to that of Rail shooting, which is carried on at the same season and places, with equal slaughter.   Of this, as well as of the Rail itself, we shall give a particular account in its proper place.

Whatever apology the people of the Eastern and Southern States may have for the devastation they spread among the Rice and Reed Birds, the Pennsylvanians — at least those living in this part of it — have little to plead in justification but the pleasure of destruction, or the savory dish they furnish their tables with; for the oat harvest is gen-erally secured before the great body of these birds arrive, the Indian corn too ripe and hard, and the reeds seem to engross all their atten-tion.   But in the states south of Maryland, the harvest of early wheat and barley in spring, and the numerous plantations of rice in fall, suffer severely.   Early in October, or as soon as the nights begin to act in cold, they disappear from Pennsylvania, directing their course to the south. At this time they swarm among the rice fields; and appear in the island of Cuba in immense numbers, in search of the same delicious grain. About the middle of October, they visit the island of Jamaica in equal numbers, where they are called Butter Birds. They feed on the seed of the Guinea grass, and are also in high esteem there for the table.*

Thus it appears that the regions north of the fortieth degree of latitude, are the breeding places of these birds; that their migrations northerly are performed from March to May, and their return southerly from August to November; their precise winter quarters, or farthest retreat southerly, are not exactly known.

The Rice Bunting is seven inches and a half long, and eleven and a half in extent. His spring dress is as follows: — Upper part of the head, wings, tail, and sides of the neck, and whole lower parts, black; the feathers frequently skirted with brownish yellow, as he passes into the colors of the female; back of the head, a cream color; back, black, seamed with brownish yellow; scapulars, pure white; rump and tail-coverts the same; lower part of the back, bluish white; tail, formed like those of the Woodpecker genus, and often used in the same manner, being thrown in to support it while ascending the stalks of the reed; this habit of throwing in the tail it retains even in the cage; legs, a brownish flesh color; hind heel, very long; bill, a bluish horn color; eye, hazel; see Fig. 47. In the month of June this plumage gradually changes to a brownish yellow, like that of the female, (Fig. 48,) which has the back streaked with brownish black; whole lower parts, dull yellow; bill, reddish flesh color; legs and eyes as in the male. The young birds retain the dress of the female until the early part of the succeeding spring; the plumage of the female undergoes no material change of color.

RED-EYED FLYCATCHER. — MUSCICAPA OLVIACEA. —
Fig. 49.

Linn. Syst. i. p. 327, 14. — Gobe mouche de la Caroline et de la Jamaique, *Buff.* iv. p. 539. *Edw.* t. 253. — *Catesb.* t. 54. — *Lath. Syn.* iii. p. 351, No. 52. — Muscicapa sylvicola, *Bartram*, p. 290.— *Peale's Museum*, No. 6675.

VIREO OLIVACEUS. — BONAPARTE.

Vireo olivaceus, *Bonap. Synop.* p. 71. — Vireo olivaceus, Red-eyed Greenlet, *North. Zool.* ii. p. 233.

THIS is a numerous species, though confined chiefly to the woods and forests, and, like all the rest of its tribe that visit Pennsylvania, is a bird of passage. It arrives here late in April; has a loud, lively,

* RENNEL'S *Hist. Jam.*

and energetic song, which it continues, as it hunts among the thick foliage, sometimes for an hour with little intermission. In the months of May, June, and to the middle of July, it is the most distinguishable of all the other warblers of the forest; and even in August, long after the rest have almost all become mute, the notes of the Red-eyed Flycatcher are frequently heard with unabated spirit. These notes are in short, emphatical bars, of two, three, or four syllables. In Jamaica, where this bird winters, and is probably also resident, it is called, as Sloane informs us, Whip-tom-kelly, from an imagined resemblance of its notes to these words. And, indeed, on attentively listening for some time to this bird in his full ardor of song, it requires but little of imagination to fancy that you hear it pronounce these words, "Tom-kelly, whip-tom-kelly!" very distinctly. It inhabits from Georgia to the River St. Lawrence, leaving Pennsylvania about the middle of September.

This bird builds, in the month of May, a small, neat, pensile nest, generally suspended between two twigs of a young dog-wood or other small sapling. It is hung by the two upper edges, seldom at a greater height than four or five feet from the ground. It is formed of pieces of hornets' nests, some flax, fragments of withered leaves, slips of vine bark, bits of paper, all glued together with the saliva of the bird, and the silk of caterpillars, so as to be very compact; the inside is lined with fine slips of grape-vine bark, fibrous grass, and sometimes hair. These nests are so durable, that I have often known them to resist the action of the weather for a year; and, in one instance, I have found the nest of the Yellow-Bird built in the cavity of one of those of the preceding year. The mice very often take possession of them after they are abandoned by the owners. The eggs are four, sometimes five, pure white, except near the great end, where they are marked with a few small dots of dark brown or reddish. They generally raise two broods in the season.

The Red-eyed Flycatcher is one of the adopted nurses of the Cow Bird, and a very favorite one, showing all the symptoms of affection for the foundling, and as much solicitude for its safety, as if it were its own. The figure of that singular bird, accompanied by a particular account of its history, is given in Fig. 83.

Before I take leave of this bird, it may not be amiss to observe that there is another, and a rather less species of Flycatcher, somewhat resembling the Red-eyed, which is frequently found in its company. Its eyes are hazel; its back more cinereous than the other, and it has a single light streak over the eye. The notes of this bird are low, somewhat plaintive, but warbled out with great sweetness, and form a striking contrast with those of the Red-eyed Flycatcher. I think it probable that Dr. Barton had reference to this bird when he made the following remarks, (see his *Fragments of the Natural History of Pennsylvania*, page 19:) — "*Muscicapa olivacea.* — I do not think with Mr. Pennant that this is the same bird as the Whip-tom-kelly of the West Indies. Our bird has no such note, but a great variety of soft, tender, and agreeable notes. It inhabits forests, and does not, like the West India bird, build a pendulous nest." Had the learned professor, however, examined into this matter with his usual accuracy, he would have found that the *Muscicapa olivacea*, and the soft and tender songster he mentions, are two very distinct species; and that both the one and the other actually build very curious, pendulous nests.

This species is five inches and a half long, and seven inches in extent; crown, ash, slightly tinged with olive, bordered on each side with a line of black, below which is a line of white passing from the nostril over and a little beyond the eye; the bill is longer than usual with birds of its tribe, the upper mandible overhanging the lower considerably, and notched, dusky above, and light blue below; all the rest of the plumage above is of a yellow olive, relieved on the tail, and at the tips of the wings, with brown; chin, throat, breast, and belly, pure white; inside of the wings and vent-feathers, greenish yellow; the tail is very slightly forked; legs and feet, light blue; iris of the eye, red. The female is marked nearly in the same manner, and is distinguishable only by the greater obscurity of the colors.

MARSH WREN. — CERTHIA PALUSTRIS. — Fig. 50.

Lath. Syn. Suopl. p. 244. — Motacilla palustris, (regulus minor,) *Bartram,* p. 291. — *Peale's Museum,* No. 7282.

TROGLODYTES PALUSTRIS. — Bonaparte.

Troglodytes pálustris, *Bonap. Synop.* p. 93. — The Marsh Wren, *Aud.* pl. 100. *Orn. Biog.* i. p. 500. — *North. Zool.* ii. p. 319.

This obscure but spirited little species has been almost overlooked by the naturalists of Europe, as well as by those of its own country, The singular attitude in which it is represented will be recognized, by those acquainted with its manners, as one of its most common and favorite ones, while skipping through among the reeds and rushes. The Marsh Wren arrives in Pennsylvania about the middle of May, or as soon as the reeds and a species of nymphea, usually called splatterdocks, which grow in great luxuriance along the tide water of our rivers, are sufficiently high to shelter it. To such places it almost wholly limits its excursions, seldom venturing far from the river. Its food consists of flying insects, and their larvæ, and a species of green grasshoppers that inhabit the reeds. As to its notes, it would be mere burlesque to call them by the name of song. Standing on the reedy borders of the Schuylkill or Delaware, in the month of June, you hear a low, crackling sound, something similar to that produced by air bubbles forcing their way through mud or boggy ground when trod upon; this is the song of the Marsh Wren. But as, among the human race, it is not given to one man to excel in every thing, and yet each, perhaps, has something peculiarly his own, so, among birds, we find a like distribution of talents and peculiarities. The little bird now before us, if deficient and contemptible in singing, excels in the art of design, and constructs a nest, which, in durability, warmth, and convenience, is scarcely inferior to one, and far superior to many, of its more musical brethren. This is formed outwardly of wet rushes mixed with mud, well intertwisted, and fashioned into the form of a cocoa nut. A small hole is left two thirds up, for entrance, the upper edge of which projects like a pent-house over the lower, to prevent the admission of rain. The inside is lined with fine, soft grass, and sometimes feathers; and the outside, when hardened by the sun, resists every kind of weather. This nest is generally suspended among the reeds, above the reach of the highest tides, and is tied so fast in every part to the surrounding reeds, as to bid defiance to the winds and the waves. The eggs are usually six, of a dark fawn color, and very small. The young leave the nest about the 20th of June, and they generally have a second brood in the same season.

The size, general color, and habit of this bird of erecting its tail, give it, to a superficial observer, something of the appearance of the Common House Wren, represented in Fig. 31; and still more that of the Winter Wren, Fig. 34; but with the former of these it never associates; and the latter has left us some time before the Marsh Wren makes his appearance. About the middle of August, they begin to go off: and, on the 1st of September, very few of them are to be seen. How far north the migrations of this species extend, I am unable to say; none of them, to my knowledge, winter in Georgia, or any of the Southern States.

The Marsh Wren is five inches long, and six in extent; the whole upper parts are dark brown, except the upper part of the head, back of the neck, and middle of the back, which are black, the two last streaked with white; the tail is short, rounded, and barred with black; wings, slightly barred; a broad strip of white passes over the eye half way down the neck; the sides of the neck are also mottled with touches of a light clay color on a whitish ground; whole under parts, pure silvery white, except the vent, which is tinged with brown; the legs are light brown; the hind claw, large, semicircular, and very sharp; bill, slender, slightly bent; nostrils, prominent; tongue, narrow, very tapering, sharp pointed, and horny at the extremity; eye, hazel. The female almost exactly resembles the male in plumage.

From the above description, and a view of Fig. 50, the naturalist will perceive that this species is truly a *Certhia*, or Creeper; and indeed its habits confirm this, as it is continually climbing along the stalks of reeds, and other aquatic plants, in search of insects.

GREAT CAROLINA WREN. — CERTHIA CAROLINIANA. —

FIG. 51.

Le Roitelet de la Louisiana, *Pl. enl.* 730, fig. 1. — *Lath. Syn.* vii. p. 507, var. D. — Le Troglodytes de la Louisiana, *Buff. Ois.* v. p. 361. — Motacilla Caroliniana, (regulus magnus,) *Bartram*, p. 291. — *Peale's Museum*, No. 7248.

TROGLODYTES LUDOVICIANUS. — BONAPARTE.

Troglodytes Ludovicianus, *Bonap. Synop.* p. 93. — The Great Carolina Wren, *Aud.* pl. 78, male and female. *Orn. Biog.* i. p. 399.

THIS is another of those equivocal species that so often occur to puzzle the naturalist. The general appearance of this bird is such, that the most illiterate would at first sight call it a Wren; but the Common Wren of Europe, and the Winter Wren of the United States, are both Warblers, judging them according to the simple principle of Linnæus. The present species, however, and the preceding, (the Marsh Wren,) though possessing great family likeness to those above mentioned, are decisively Creepers, if the bill, the tongue, nostrils, and claws, are to be the criteria by which we are to class them.

The color of the plumage of birds is but an uncertain and inconstant guide; and though in some cases it serves to furnish a trivial or specific appellation, yet can never lead us to the generic one. I have, therefore, notwithstanding the general appearance of these birds, and the practice of former ornithologists, removed them to the genus *Certhia*, from that of *Motacilla*, where they have hitherto been placed.*

This bird is frequently seen, early in May, along the shores of the Delaware, and other streams that fall into it on both sides, thirty or forty miles below Philadelphia; but is rather rare in Pennsylvania. This circumstance is a little extraordinary; since, from its size and stout make, it would seem more capable of braving the rigors of a northern climate than any of the others. It can, however, scarcely be called migratory. In the depth of winter I found it numerous in Virginia, along the shores and banks of the James River, and its tributary streams, and thence as far south as Savannah. I also observed it on

---

* Of this bird, and some others, Vieillot formed his genus *Tryothorus*, containing the larger Wrens, with long, and somewhat curved bills, and possessing, if possible, more of the habits of the Creepers. This has, with almost universal consent, been laid aside even as a sub-genus, and they are all included in *Troglodytes*. Read the descriptions of our author, or of Audubon, and the habits of the *Wren* will be at once perceived. "Its tail," says the latter ornithologist, " is almost constantly erect; and before it starts to make the least flight, it uses a quick motion, which brings its body almost in contact with the object on which it stands. The quickness of the motions of this little bird is fully equal to that of a mouse: it appears, and is out of sight in a moment; peeps into a crevice, passes rapidly through it, and shows itself at a different place the next instant. These Wrens often sing from the roof of an abandoned flat-boat. When the song is finished, they creep from one board to another, thrust themselves through an auger hole, entering the boat's side at one place, and peeping out at another." In them we have exactly portrayed the manners of our British Wren, when engaged about a heap of rubbish, old stones, or barrels in a farm yard. — ED.

12 *

the banks of the Ogechee. It seemed to be particularly attached to the borders of cypress swamps, deep hollows, among piles of old, decaying timber, and by rivers and small creeks. It has all the restless, jerking manners of the Wrens, skipping about with great nimbleness, hopping into caves, and disappearing into holes and crevices, like a rat, for several minutes, and then reappearing in another quarter. It occasionally utters a loud, strong, and singular twitter, resembling the word *chirr-rup*, dwelling long and strongly on the first syllable; and so loud, that I at first mistook it for the Red-Bird, (*L. cardinalis.*) It has also another chant, rather more musical, like " *Sweet William Sweet William,*" much softer than the former. Though I cannot positively say, from my own observations, that it builds in Pennsylvania, and have never yet been so fortunate as to find its nest, yet, from the circumstance of having several times observed it within a quarter of a mile of the Schuylkill, in the month of August, I have no doubt that some few breed here, and think it highly probable that Pennsylvania and New York may be the northern boundaries of their visits, having sought for it in vain among the states of New England. Its food appears to consist of those insects, and their larvæ, that frequent low, damp caves, piles of dead timber, old roots, projecting banks of creeks, &c. It certainly possesses the faculty of seeing in the dark better than day birds usually do; for I have observed it exploring the recesses of caves, where a good acute eye must have been necessary to enable it to distinguish its prey.

In the Southern States, as well as in Louisiana, this species is generally resident; though in summer they are more numerous, and are found rather farther north than in winter. In this last season their chirrupping is frequently heard in gardens soon after daybreak, and along the borders of the great rivers of the Southern States, not far from the sea-coast.

The Great Wren of Carolina is five inches and a quarter long, and seven broad; the whole upper parts are reddish brown, the wings and tail being barred with black; a streak of yellowish white runs from the nostril over the eye, down the side of the neck, nearly to the back; below that, a streak of reddish brown extends from the posterior part of the eye to the shoulder; the chin is yellowish white; the breast, sides, and belly, a light rust color, or reddish buff; vent-feathers, white, neatly barred with black; in the female, plain; wing-coverts, minutely tipped with white; legs and feet, flesh-colored, and very strong; bill, three quarters of an inch long, strong, a little bent, grooved, and pointed; the upper mandible, bluish black; lower, light blue; nostrils, oval, partly covered with a prominent, convex membrane; tongue, pointed and slender; eyes, hazel; tail, cuneiform, the two exterior feathers on each side three quarters of an inch shorter, whitish on their exterior edges, and touched with deeper black; the same may be said of the three outer primaries. The female wants the white on the wing-coverts, but differs little in color from the male.

In this species I have observed a circumstance common to the House and Winter Wren, but which is not found in the Marsh Wren — the feathers of the lower part of the back, when parted by the hand, or breath, appear spotted with white, being at bottom deep ash, reddish brown at the surface, and each feather with a spot of white between these two colors. This, however, cannot be perceived without parting the feathers.

YELLOW-THROAT WARBLER. — SYLVIA FLAVICOLLIS. —
Fig. 52.

Yellow-throat Warbler,* *Arct. Zool.* p. 400. No. 286. — *Catesb.* i. 62. — *Lath.* ii. 437. — La Mesange grise à gorge jaune, *Buff.* v. 454. — La gorge jaune de St. Domingue, *Pl. enl.* 686, fig. 1.

SYLVICOLA FLAVICOLLIS. — Swainson.

Sylvia pensilis, *Bonap. Synop.* p. 79. — S. pensilis, *Lath.*

The habits of this beautiful species, like those of the preceding, are not consistent with the shape and construction of its bill; the former would rank it with the Titmouse, or with the Creepers; the latter is decisively that of the Warbler. The first opportunity I had of examining a living specimen of this bird, was in the southern parts of Georgia, in the month of February. Its notes, which were pretty

---

* As with many others, there has been some confusion in the synonymes of this species, and it has been described under different names by the same authors. That of *flavicollis*, adopted by our author, is characteristic of the markings; whereas *pensilis*, of Latham and Vieillot, is applicable to the whole group; and perhaps restoring Wilson's name will create less confusion than taking one less known. The genus *Sylvicola*, with the sub-genus *Verminora*, have been used by Mr. Swainson to designate almost all those birds in North America, which will represent the European *Sylvianæ*, or Warblers. They are generally of a stronger make; the bill, though slender, is more conical, and the wings have the first and second quills of nearly equal length. The general dress is chaste and unobtrusive; but, at the same time, we have exceptions, showing great brilliancy and beauty of coloring. Their habits are precisely the same with our Warblers. They frequent woods and thickets. They are in constant motion, creeping and clinging about the branches, and inspecting the crevices in the bark, or under sides of the leaves, in search of insects. When their duties of incubation are over, they become less retired, and, with their broods, assemble in the gardens and cultivated grounds, where they find sustenance in the various fruits and berries. The notes of all are sprightly and pleasant; and a few possess a melody hardly inferior to the best songsters of Europe.

Mr. Audubon has figured the following birds, which appear to rank under this genus, as hitherto undescribed: — *Sylvia Rathbonia*, Aud., male and female, plate lxv. He met with this species only once; it is entirely of a bright yellow color, about four and a half inches in length. The bill appears more bent than in the typical species. *Sylvia Roscoe*, Aud. plate xxiv. male; looking more like a *Trichas*, shot on the Mississippi, the only one seen. The colors of the upper parts are dark olive, a slender white streak over each eye, and a broad black band from the eye downwards; the under parts, yellow. *Sylvia Childrenii*, Aud. plate xxxv.; killed in the state of Louisiana; only two specimens were met with. General color of the plumage, yellowish green; length, about four inches and three quarters.

We cannot but regret the want of specimens of these interesting and rare species. Their authority will rest upon Mr. Audubon's plates. It is impossible, from them alone, to say, with precision, that they belong to this genus; and they are placed in it provisionally, with the view of making the list as complete as possible, and to point them out to others who may have the opportunity of examining them. — Ed.

loud and spirited, very much resembled those of the Indigo Bird. It continued a considerable time on the same pine-tree, creeping around the branches, and among the twigs, in the manner of the Titmouse, uttering its song every three or four minutes. On flying to another tree, it frequently alighted on the body, and ran nimbly up or down, spirally and perpendicularly, in search of insects. I had afterwards many opportunities of seeing others of the same species, and found them all to correspond in these particulars. This was about the 24th of February, and the first of their appearance there that spring, for they leave the United States about three months during winter, and, consequently, go to no great distance. I had been previously informed that they also pass the summer in Virginia, and in the southern parts of Maryland ; but they very rarely proceed as far north as Pennsylvania.

This species is five inches and a half in length, and eight and a half broad ; the whole back, hind head, and rump, are a fine light slate color ; the tail is somewhat forked, black, and edged with light slate ; the wings are also black, the three shortest secondaries, broadly edged with light blue ; all the wing-quills are slightly edged with the same ; the first row of wing-coverts is tipped and edged with white, the second, wholly white, or nearly so ; the frontlet, ear-feathers, lores, and above the temple, are black ; the line between the eye and nostril, whole throat, and middle of the breast, brilliant golden yellow ; the lower eyelid, line over the eye, and spot behind the ear-feathers, as well as the whole lower parts, are pure white ; the yellow on the throat is bordered with touches of black, which also extend along the sides, under the wings ; the bill is black, and faithfully represented in the figure ; the legs and feet, yellowish brown ; the claws, extremely fine pointed ; the tongue, rather cartilaginous, and lacerated at the end. The female has the wings of a dingy brown, and the whole colors, particularly the yellow on the throat, much duller ; the young birds of the first season are without the yellow.

TYRANT FLYCATCHER, OR KING BIRD. — MUSCICAPA TYRANNUS.* — Fig. 53.

Lanius tyrannus, *Lin. Syst.* 136. — *Lath. Syn.* i. 186. — *Catesb.* i. 55. — Le Tyran de la Caroline, *Buff.* iv. 577. *Pl. enl.* 676. — *Arct. Zool.* p. 384. No. 263. — *Peale's Museum,* No. 578.

TYRANNUS INTREPIDUS, Vieillot.

Muscicapa tyrannus, *Bonap. Synop.* p. 66. — Tyrannus intrepidus, *Vieill. Gal. des Ois.* pl. 133. — *North. Zool.* ii. 137. — The Tyrant Flycatcher, *Aud.* pl. 79, male and female. *Orn. Biog.* i. 403.

This is the Field Martin of Maryland and some of the Southern States, and the King Bird of Pennsylvania and several of the

* Among the family of the *Lanaidæ*, North America possesses only two of the sub-families ; the typical one, *Lanianæ*, represented by Lanius, and an aberrant

55. Tyrant Flycatcher. 54. Great Crested F. 55. Small Green Crested F. 56. Pe-we F. 57. Wood Pe-we F. 58. Brown Thrush. 59. Golden crowned Th. 60. Cat Bird. 61. Log breasted Warbler. 65. Brown sided W. 65. Mourning W. 64. Red Cockaded Woodpecker. 65. Brown headed Nuthatch. 66. Pigeon Hawk. 67. Blue winged Yellow Warbler. 68. Golden winged W. 68. Blue eyed Yellow W. 70. Black-breasted Blue W.

northern districts. The epithet *Tyrant*, which is generally applied to him by naturalists, I am not altogether so well satisfied with; some, however, may think the two terms pretty nearly synonymous.

form, *Tyranninæ*, represented by Tyrannus. Of the former, we have already seen an example at page 49. These are comparatively few; the great bulk of that form being confined to Africa and the warmer parts of Asia and India; and, with the latter, we enter into the great mass of American Flycatchers, ranging over both the continents, particularly the southern.

"Tropical America," Mr. Swainson remarks, "swarms with the *Tyranninæ*, so much so, that several individuals, of three or four species, may be seen in the surrounding trees at the same moment, watching for passing insects; each, however, looks out for its own particular prey, and does not interfere with such as appear destined by Nature for its stronger and less feeble associates. It is only towards the termination of the rainy season, when myriads of the *Termites* and *Formicæ* emerge from the earth in their winged state, that the whole family of Tyrants, of all sizes and species, commence a regular and simultaneous attack upon the thousands which then spring from the ground."

From their long-accepted name we have some idea of their manners. They possess extensive powers of locomotion, to enable them to secure a prey at once active and vigilant; and their long and sharp wings are beautifully formed for quick and rapid flight.[*] The tail, next in importance as a locomotive organ, is also generally of a form joining the greatest advantages, — that of a forked shape; in some with the anterior feathers extending to a considerable length, while, in others, certainly only slightly divaricating, or nearly square; but never, as among the *Thamnophilinæ*, or Bush Shrikes, of a graduated or rounded form, where the individuals seek their prey by stealth and prowling, and require no great extent of flight; on the other hand, those organs of less utility for securing the means of sustenance, are of much inferior strength and power. The accessory members for seizing their insect prey are, in like manner, adapted to their other powers; the bill, though of considerable strength, is flattened; the rictus being ample, and furnished with bristles. The genus *Tyrannus*, however, does not entirely feed on insects when on wing, like the smaller *Tyrannulæ*, but, as shown by Mr. Swainson, will also feed on small fish and aquatic insects; and, if this fact be united with the weak formation of the tarsi, and, in several species, having the toes united at the base, there will be an evident connection between this group and the *Fissirostres*. That gentleman, in the second volume of the *Northern Zoology*, relates a fact from his journal when resident in Brazil, most beautifully illustrative of this affinity, and shows the value of attending to all circumstances relative to the habits of individuals, which, though, like the present, of no importance alone, will, when taken in connection with other views, be of the *very utmost consequence.* "April 7, 1817. Sitting in the house this morning, I suddenly heard a splash in the lake close to the window; on looking out, I saw a common Gray-breasted Tyrant (*Tyrannus crudelis*) perched upon a dead branch hanging over the water, plunging and drying itself. Intent upon watching this bird, I saw it, within a quarter of an hour, dive into the lake two successive times, after some small fish or aquatic insects, precisely like a Kingfisher; this action was done with amazing celerity, and it then took its former station to plume and dry its feathers." Here we have exactly the habits of the Kingfisher; and I believe a contrariety of manner, equally worthy of remark, is observed among some of the *Dacelones*, frequenting woods, and darting by surprise on the larger insects. Both tribes have another similarity in their economy, and delight to sit motionless, either watching their prey, or pluming and resting on the extremity or top of some dead branch, pale, or peaked rock. With regard to the Tyrant's being not only carnivorous, but preying also on the weaker reptiles, we have the authority of Azara, who mentions the common *Tyrannus sulphuratus*, or Bentivo of Brazil, as "S'approchent des animaux morts pour l'emporter des debris et des petits morceaux de chair que laissent les Caracaras." And Mr. Swainson (*North. Zool.* ii. 133) has himself taken from the stomach of this species

---

[*] In many species the quills become suddenly emarginated at the tips. This also occurs in the sub-genera *Milvulus* and *Negeta*, both much allied, and possessing great powers of flight.

The trivial name *King*, as well as *Tyrant*, has been bestowed on this bird for its extraordinary behavior, and the authority it assumes over all others during the time of breeding. At that season his extreme affection for his mate, and for his nest and young, makes him suspicious of every bird that happens to pass near his residence, so that he attacks, without discrimination, every intruder. In the months of May, June, and part of July, his life is one continued scene of broils and battles; in which, however, he generally comes off conqueror. Hawks and Crows, the Bald Eagle, and the Great Black Eagle, all equally dread a rencounter with this dauntless little champion, who, as soon as he perceives one of these last approaching, launches into the air to meet him, mounts to a considerable height above him, and darts down on his back, sometimes fixing there to the great annoyance of his sovereign, who, if no convenient retreat or resting-place be near, endeavors by various evolutions to rid himself of his merciless adversary. But the King Bird is not so easily dismounted. He teases the Eagle incessantly, sweeps upon him from right to left, remounts, that he may descend on his back with the greater violence; all the while keeping up a shrill and rapid twittering; and continuing the attack sometimes for more than a mile, till he is relieved by some other of his tribe equally eager for the contest.

There is one bird, however, which, by its superior rapidity of flight, is sometimes more than a match for him; and I have several times witnessed his precipitate retreat before this active antagonist. This is the Purple Martin, one whose food and disposition are pretty similar to his own, but who has greatly the advantage of him on wing, in eluding all his attacks, and teasing him as he pleases. I have also seen the Red-headed Woodpecker, while clinging on a rail of the fence, amuse himself with the violence of the King Bird, and play *bo-peep* with him round the rail, while the latter, highly irritated, made every attempt, as he swept from side to side, to strike him — but in vain. All this turbulence, however, vanishes as soon as his young are able to

lizards, in an entire state, sufficiently large to excite surprise how they possibly could have been swallowed by the bird; it is also here that we have the habits, and, in some respects, the form of the *Laniance*, serving at the other extremity as a connecting link. The North American species, coming under the definition which we would wish to adopt for this group, are comparatively few. A new and more northern species is added by the authors of the *Northern Zoology*,[*] — the *Tyrannus borealis*, Sw.

Only one specimen of this species, which Mr. Swainson considers undescribed, was procured. It was shot on the banks of the Saskatchewan River. Like the King Bird, it is found in the Fur countries only in summer. It is considerably smaller than the *Tyrannus intrepidus*, and may at once be distinguished from it by the forked tail not tipped with white, and much shorter tarsi, as well as by very evident differences in the colors of the plumage. Its bill is rather more depressed at the base, and its lower mandible is dissimilar to the upper one; the relative length of the tail-feathers in the two species are also different; the first of *T. borealis*, *shorter* than the third, the fourth being farther apart from the latter than in *T. intrepidus*. — ED.

[*] They are also baccivorous, as shown by our author in the description of this species and *T. crinitus*.

shift for themselves; and he is then as mild and peaceable as any other bird.

But he has a worse habit than all these,—one much more obnoxious to the husbandman, and often fatal to himself. He loves, not the honey, but the *bees;* and, it must be confessed, is frequently on the look-out for these little industrious insects. He plants himself on a post of the fence, or on a small tree in the garden, not far from the hives, and from thence sallies on them as they pass and repass, making great havock among their numbers. His shrill twitter, so near to the house, gives intimation to the farmer of what is going on, and the gun soon closes his career forever. Man arrogates to himself, in this case, the exclusive privilege of murder; and, after putting thousands of these same little insects to death, seizes on the fruits of their labor.

The King Birds arrive in Pennsylvania about the 20th of April, sometimes in small bodies of five and six together, and are at first very silent, until they begin to pair, and build their nest. This generally takes place about the first week in May. The nest is very often built in the orchard, on the horizontal branch of an apple-tree; frequently also, at Catesby observes, on a sassafras-tree, at no great height from the ground. The outside consists of small slender twigs, tops of withered flowers of the plant yarrow, and others, well wove together with tow and wool; and is made large, and remarkably firm and compact. It is usually lined with fine, dry, fibrous grass, and horse hair. The eggs are five, of a very pale cream color, or dull white, marked with a few, large spots of deep purple, and other smaller ones of light brown, chiefly, though not altogether, towards the great end. They generally build twice in the season.

The King Bird is altogether destitute of song, having only the shrill twitter above mentioned. His usual mode of flight is singular. The vibrations of his broad wings, as he moves slowly over the fields, resemble those of a Hawk hovering and settling in the air to reconnoitre the ground below; and the object of the King Bird is no doubt something similar, viz., to look out for passing insects, either in the air, or among the flowers and blossoms below him. In fields of pasture he often takes his stand on the tops of the mullein, and other rank weeds, near the cattle, and makes occasional sweeps after passing insects, particularly the large, black gadfly, so terrifying to horses and cattle. His eye moves restlessly around him, traces the flight of an insect for a moment or two, then that of a second, and even a third, until he perceives one to his liking, when, with a shrill sweep, he pursues, seizes it, and returns to the same spot again, to look out for more. This habit is so conspicuous when he is watching the bee-hive, that several intelligent farmers of my acquaintance are of opinion that he picks out only the drones, and never injures the working bees. Be this as it may, he certainly gives a preference to one bee, and one species of insect, over another. He hovers over the river, sometimes for a considerable time, darting after insects that frequent such places, snatching them from the surface of the water, and diving about in the air like a Swallow; for he possesses at will great powers of wing. Numbers of them are frequently seen thus engaged, for hours together, over the Rivers Delaware and Schuylkill, in a calm day, particularly towards evening. He bathes himself by diving repeatedly into the water from the overhanging branches of some tree, where he sits to dry and dress his plumage.

Whatever antipathy may prevail against him for depredations on the drones, or, if you will, on the bees, I can assure the cultivator that this bird is greatly his friend, in destroying multitudes of insects, whose larvæ prey on the harvests of his fields, particularly his corn, fruit-trees, cucumbers, and pumpkins. These noxious insects are the daily food of this bird; and he destroys, upon a very moderate average, some hundreds of them daily. The death of every King Bird is therefore an actual loss to the farmer, by multiplying the numbers of destructive insects, and encouraging the depredations of Crows, Hawks, and Eagles, who avoid as much as possible his immediate vicinity. For myself, I must say that the King Bird possesses no common share of my regard. I honor this little bird for his extreme affection for his young; for his contempt of danger, and unexampled intrepidity; for his meekness of behavior when there are no calls on his courage, a quality which, even in the human race, is justly considered so noble:

> In peace there's nothing so becomes a man
> As modest stillness and humility;
> But when the blast of war, &c.;

but, above all, I honor and esteem this bird for the millions of ruinous vermin which he rids us of; whose depredations, in *one* season, but for the services of this and other friendly birds, would far overbalance all the produce of the bee-hives in fifty.

As a friend to this persecuted bird, and an enemy to prejudices of every description, will the reader allow me to set this matter in a somewhat clearer and stronger light, by presenting him with a short poetical epitome of the King Bird's history?

> Far in the south, where vast Maragnon flows,
> And boundless forests unknown wilds enclose;
> Vine-tangled shores, and suffocating woods,
> Parched up with heat or drowned with pouring floods;
> Where each extreme alternately prevails,
> And Nature sad their ravages bewails;
> Lo! high in air, above those trackless wastes,
> With spring's return the King Bird hither hastes;
> Coasts the famed Gulf,* and, from his height, explores
> Its thousand streams, its long-indented shores,
> Its plains immense, wide opening on the day,
> Its lakes and isles, where feathered millions play:
> All tempt not him; till, gazing from on high,
> COLUMBIA's regions wide below him lie;
> There end his wanderings and his wish to roam,
> There lie his native woods, his fields, his *home;*
> Down, circling, he descends, from azure heights,
> And on a full-blown sassafras alights.
> Fatigued and silent, for a while he views
> His old frequented haunts, and shades recluse;
> Sees brothers, comrades, every hour arrive —
> Hears, humming round, the tenants of the hive:
> Love fires his breast; he wooes, and soon is blest;
> And in the blooming orchard builds his nest.

* Of Mexico.

Come now, ye cowards! ye whom Heaven disdains,
Who boast the happiest home — the richest plains ;
On whom, perchance, a wife, an infant's eye
Hang as their hope, and on your arm rely ;
Yet, when the hour of danger and dismay
Comes on your country, sneak in holes away,
Shrink from the perils ye were bound to face,
And leave those babes and country to disgrace ;
Come here, (if such we have,) ye dastard herd !
And kneel in dust before this noble bird.
    When the specked eggs within his nest appear,
Then glows affection, ardent and sincere ;
No discord sours him when his mate he meets ;
But each warm heart with mutual kindness beats.
For her repast he bears along the lea
The bloated gadfly, and the balmy bee ;
For her repose scours o'er th' adjacent farm,
Whence Hawks might dart, or lurking foes alarm ;
For now abroad a band of ruffians prey,
The Crow, the Cuckoo, and th' insidious Jay ;
These, in the owner's absence, all destroy,
And murder every hope and every joy.
    Soft sits his brooding mate, her guardian he,
Perched on the top of some tall, neighboring tree ;
Thence, from the thicket to the concave skies,
His watchful eye around unceasing flies.
Wrens, Thrushes, Warblers, startled at his note,
Fly in affright the consecrated spot.
He drives the plundering *Jay*, with honest scorn,
Back to his woods ; the *Mocker*, to his thorn ;
Sweeps round the *Cuckoo*, as the thief retreats ;
Attacks the *Crow ;* the diving *Hawk* defeats ;
Darts on the *Eagle* downwards from afar,
And, 'midst the clouds, prolongs the whirling war,
All danger o'er, he hastens back elate,
To guard his post, and feed his faithful mate.
    Behold him now, his little family flown,
Meek, unassuming, silent, and alone ;
Lured by the well-known hum of favorite bees,
As slow he hovers o'er the garden trees ;
(For all have failings, passions, whims that lead,
Some favorite wish, some appetite to feed ;)
Straight he alights, and, from the pear-tree, spies
The circling stream of humming insects rise ;
Selects his prey ; darts on the busy brood,
And shrilly twitters o'er his savory food.
    Ah ! ill-timed triumph ! direful note to thee,
That guides thy murderer to the fatal tree ;
See where he skulks ! and takes his gloomy stand,
The deep-charged musket hanging in his hand ;
And, gaunt for blood, he leans it on a rest,
Prepared, and pointed at thy snow-white breast.
Ah, friend ! good friend ! forbear that barbarous deed ;
Against it valor, goodness, pity, plead ;
If e'er a family's griefs, a widow's woe,
Have reached thy soul, in mercy let him go !
Yet, should the tear of pity nought avail,
Let *interest* speak, let *gratitude* prevail ;
Kill not thy friend, who thy whole harvest shields,
And sweeps ten thousand vermin from thy fields ;
Think how this dauntless bird, thy poultry's guard,
Drove every Hawk and Eagle from thy yard ;

13

Watched round thy cattle as they fed, and slew
The hungry, blackening swarms that round them flew;
Some small return — some little right resign,
And spare *his* life whose services are thine!
—— I plead in vain! Amid the bursting roar,
The poor, lost King Bird welters in his gore!

This species is eight inches long, and fourteen in extent; the general color above is a dark slaty ash; the head and tail are nearly black; the latter *even* at the end, and tipped with white; the wings are more of a brownish cast; the quills and wing-coverts are also edged with dull white; the upper part of the breast is tinged with ash; the throat, and all the rest of the lower parts, are pure white; the plumage on the crown, though not forming a crest, is frequently erected, as represented in the plate, and discovers a rich bed of brilliant orange, or flame color, called by the country people his crown: when the feathers lie close, this is altogether concealed. The bill is very broad at the base, overhanging at the point, and notched, of a glossy black color, and furnished with bristles at the base; the legs and feet are black, seamed with gray; the eye, hazel. The female differs in being more brownish on the upper parts, has a smaller streak of paler orange on the crown, and a narrower border of duller white on the tail. The young birds do not receive the orange on the head during their residence here the first season.

This bird is very generally known from the Lakes to Florida. Besides insects, they feed, like every other species of their tribe with which I am acquainted, on various sorts of berries, particularly blackberries, of which they are extremely fond. Early in September they leave Pennsylvania, on their way to the south.

A few days ago, I shot one of these birds, the whole plumage of which was nearly white, or a little inclining to a cream color; it was a bird of the present year, and could not be more than a month old. This appeared also to have been its original color, as it issued from the egg. The skin was yellowish white; the eye, much lighter than usual; the legs and bill, blue. It was plump, and seemingly in good order. I presented it to Mr. Peale. Whatever may be the cause of this loss of color, if I may so call it, in birds, it is by no means uncommon among the various tribes that inhabit the United States. The Sparrow Hawk, Sparrow, Robin, Red-winged Blackbird, and many others, are occasionally found in white plumage; and I believe that such birds do not become so by climate, age, or disease, but that they are universally hatched so. The same phenomena are observable not only among various sorts of animals, but even among the human race; and a white negro is no less common, in proportion to their numbers, than a white Blackbird; though the precise cause of this in either is but little understood.

GREAT CRESTED FLYCATCHER. — MUSCICAPA
CRINITA. — Fig. 54.

Linn. Syst. 325. — *Lath.* ii. 357. — *Arct. Zool.* p. 386, No. 267. — Le Mouche-rolle de Virginie à huppe verte, *Buff.* iv. 565. *Pl. enl.* 569. — *Peale's Museum,* No. 6645.

TYRANNUS CRINITUS. — Swainson.

Tyrannus crinitus, *Swain. Monog. Journ. of Science,* vol. xx. p. 271. — Muscicapa crinita, *Bonap. Synop.* p. 67.

By glancing at the physiognomy of this bird, and the rest of the figures of the same genus, it will readily be observed that they all be-long to one particular family of the same genus. They possess strong traits of their particular *caste,* and are all remarkably dexterous at their profession of fly-catching. The one now before us is less generally known than the preceding, being chiefly confined to the woods. There his harsh *squeak* — for he has no song — is occasionally heard above most others. He also visits the orchard; is equally fond of bees, but wants the courage and magnanimity of the King Bird. He arrives in Pennsylvania early in May, and builds his nest in a hollow tree, deserted by the Blue-Bird or Woodpecker. The materials of which this is formed are scanty, and rather novel. One of these nests, now before me, is formed of a little loose hay, feathers of the Guinea fowl, hogs' bristles, pieces of cast snake skins, and dogs' hair. Snake skins with this bird appear to be an indispensable article, for I have never yet found one of his nests without this material forming a part of it.* Whether he surrounds his nest with this by way of *terrorem,* to prevent other birds or animals from entering, or whether it be that he finds its silky softness suitable for his young, is uncertain; the fact, however, is notorious. The female lays four eggs, of a dull cream color, thickly scratched with purple lines of various tints as if done with a pen.

This species is eight inches and a half long, and thirteen inches in extent; the upper parts are of a dull greenish olive; the feathers on the head are pointed, centred with dark brown, ragged at the sides, and form a kind of blowzy crest; the throat, and upper parts of the breast, delicate ash; rest of the lower parts, a sulphur yellow; the wing-coverts are pale drab, crossed with two bars of dull white; the primaries are of a bright ferruginous, or sorrel color; the tail is slightly forked, its interior vanes of the same bright ferruginous as the primaries; the bill is blackish, very much like that of the King Bird, furnished also with bristles; the eye is hazel; legs and feet, bluish black. The female can scarcely be distinguished, by its colors, from the male.

---

* As I have mentioned at page 94, this forms the lining to the nests of other birds also; and, as the number of snakes is considerable in those uncultivated and woody countries, their castings may form a more frequent substitute than is gener-ally supposed. — Ed.

. This bird also feeds on berries towards the end of summer, particularly on huckle-berries, which, during the time they last, seem to form the chief sustenance of the young birds. I have observed this species here as late as the 10th of September; rarely later. They do not, to my knowledge, winter in any of the Southern States.

SMALL GREEN-CRESTED FLYCATCHER.* — MUSCICAPA QUERULA. — Fig. 55.

Muscicapa subviridis, *Bartram,* p. 289. — *Arct. Zool.* p. 386, No. 268. — *Peale's Museum,* No. 6825.

TYRANNULA ACADICA. — Swainson.

Muscicapa acadica, *Bonap. Synop.* p. 68.

This bird is but little known. It inhabits the deepest, thick-shaded, solitary parts of the woods, sits generally on the lower branches, utters, every half minute or so, a sudden, sharp squeak, which is heard

---

* This species, with the two following of our author, have been separated from the Tyrants, and placed in a sub-genus, *Tyrannula.* They are, however, in reality, *little Tyrants,* and agree in their habits, as far as their smaller size and weaker powers enable them. Their food is nearly the same, more confined, however, to insects, sufficient power being wanting to overcome any stronger prey. *Tyrannula* will contain a great many species most closely allied to each other in form, size, and color ; so much so, that it is nearly impossible to distinguish them, without a comparison of many together. When they are carefully analyzed, they seem distinct, and, the characters being constant, are also of sufficient specific importance. They are natives of both North and South America, and the adjacent islands ; the North American known species are, — those described by our author, which will be found in another part of this volume, one or two figured by Bonaparte, with two new species discovered in the course of the last over-land arctic expedition, and described by Mr. Swainson in the second volume of the *Northern Zoology.* South America, however, possesses the great host of species, where we may yet expect many novelties. The extent and the closely-allied features of the group render them most difficult of distinction.*

Both this form and the Tyrants are confined to the New World, and the latter may be said to represent the great mass of our Flycatchers.

The new species described by Mr. Swainson are, *Tyrannula pusilla,* Sw., very closely allied to *Muscicapa querula* of Wilson, but satisfactorily proved distinct ; the wings are much shorter, somewhat rounded, and the comparative proportion of the quills differ ; the colors, however, nearly agree : the species brought home by the expedition was killed at Carlton House in 53° N. lat., and it extends southward to Mexico. — *T. Richardsonii,* closely resembling *T. fusca ;* it differs in the form of the bill, and size of the feet ; the crest is thick and lengthened ; the upper plumage is more olive, while the under has an olive whitish tint ; the tail is more forked : it was found in the neighborhood of Cumberland House, frequenting moist, shady woods by the banks of rivers and lakes.

Mr. Audubon also figures a species as new, and dedicates it to Dr. Trail, of Liverpool ; but, as I have remarked before, it is impossible to decide from a plate,

* It may be here remarked that the Prince of Musignano, in his *Synopsis,* evidently recognizes this form as a sub-genus, though he has not characterized it. — Ed.

a considerable way through the woods; and, as it flies from one tree to another, has a low, querulous note, something like the twitterings of Chickens nestling under the wings of the Hen. On alighting, this sound ceases, and it utters its note as before. It arrives from the south about the middle of May; builds on the upper side of a limb, in a low, swampy part of the woods, and lays five white eggs. It leaves us about the beginning of September. It is a rare and very solitary bird, always haunting the most gloomy, moist, and unfrequented parts of the forest. It feeds on flying insects, devours bees, and, in the season of huckle-berries, they form the chief part of its food. Its northern migrations extend as far as Newfoundland.

The length of this species is five inches and a half; breadth, nine inches; the upper parts are of a green olive color, the lower, pale greenish yellow, darkest on the breast; the wings are deep brown, crossed with two bars of yellowish white, and a ring of the same surrounds the eye, which is hazel. The tail is rounded at the end; the bill is remarkably flat and broad, dark brown above, and flesh color below; legs and feet, pale ash. The female differs little from the male in color.

PEWIT FLYCATCHER. — MUSCICAPA NUNCIOLA. — Fig. 56.

Bartram, p. 289. — Blackcap Flycatcher, *Lath. Syn.* ii. 353. — Phœbe Flycatcher, *Id. Sup.* p. 173. — Le Gobe mouche noirâtre de la Caroline, *Buff.* iv. 541. — *Arct. Zool.* p. 387, No. 269. — *Peale's Museum*, No. 6618.

TYRANNULA FUSCA. — JARDINE.

Muscicapa fusca, *Bonap. Synop.* p. 68.

THIS well-known bird is one of our earliest spring visitants, arriving in Pennsylvania about the first week in March, and continuing with us until October. I have seen them here as late as the 12th of November. In the month of February, I overtook these birds lingering in the low, swampy woods of North and South Carolina. They were feeding on smilax berries, and chanting, occasionally, their simple notes. The favorite resort of this bird is by streams of water, under or near bridges, in caves, &c. Near such places he sits on a projecting twig, calling out, *pe-wée, pe-wittitee pe-wée*, for a whole morning; darting after insects, and returning to the same twig; frequently flirting his tail, like the Wagtail, though not so rapidly. He begins to build about the 20th or 25th of March, on some projecting part under a bridge, in a cave, in an open well, five or six feet down among the interstices of the side walls, often under a shed, in the low eaves of a

---

however accurate. *Tyrannula Trailii* will come nearest to the Wood Pewee, but differs as well in some parts of the plumage as in the habits. It is found in the woods which skirt the prairie lands of the Arkansas River. — ED.

13 *

cottage, and such like places.* The outside is composed of mud, mixed with moss, is generally large and solid, and lined with flax and horse hair. The eggs are five, pure white, with two or three dots of red near the great end. I have known them rear three broods in one season.

In a particular part of Mr. Bartram's woods, with which I am acquainted, by the side of a small stream, in a cave, five or six feet high, formed by the undermining of the water below, and the projection of two large rocks above, —

> There down smooth, glistening rocks the rivulet pours,
>   Till in a pool its silent waters sleep,
> A dark-browed cliff, o'ertopped with fern and flowers,
>   Hangs, grimly lowering, o'er the glassy deep ;
> Above through every chink the woodbines creep,
>   And smooth-barked beeches spread their arms around,
> Whose roots cling twisted round the rocky steep ;
>   A more sequestered scene is no where found,
> For contemplation deep, and silent thought profound ; —

in this cave I knew the Pewit to build for several years. The place was solitary, and he was seldom disturbed. In the month of April, one fatal Saturday, a party of boys from the city, armed with guns, dealing indiscriminate destruction among the feathered tribes around them, directed their murderous course this way, and, within my hearing, destroyed both parents of this old and peaceful settlement. For two successive years, and, I believe, to this day, there has been no Pewee seen about this place. This circumstance almost convinces me that birds, in many instances, return to the same spots to breed ; and who knows, but, like the savage nations of Indians, they may usurp a kind of exclusive right of tenure to particular districts, where they themselves have been reared?

The notes of the Pewee, like those of the Blue-Bird, are pleasing, not for any melody they contain, but from the ideas of spring and returning verdure, with all the sweets of this lovely season, which are associated with his simple but lively ditty. Towards the middle of June, he becomes nearly silent ; and late in the fall gives us a few farewell and melancholy repetitions, that recall past imagery, and make the decayed and withered face of nature appear still more melancholy.

The Pewit is six inches and a half in length, and nine and a half broad ; the upper parts are of a dark dusky olive ; the plumage of the

* The general manners of this species, and indeed of the greater part of the smaller *Tyrannulæ*, bear a considerable resemblance to those of the Common Spotted Flycatcher of this country, which the dilatation at the base of the bill and the color of the plumage render still greater. The peculiar droop of the tail, and occasional rise and depression of the feathers on the crown, which are somewhat elongated — the motionless perch on some bare branch — the impatient call — the motion of the tail — and the sudden dart after some insect, and return to the same spot — are all close resemblances to the manners delineated by our author ; and the resort by streams, bridges, or caves, with the manner and place of building — even the color of the eggs — are not to be mistaken. In one instance our Flycatcher and the *Tyrannulæ* disagree ; the former possess no pleasing notes ; its only cries are a single, rather harsh and monotonous *click* and a shrill *peep*. The song of the *Tyrannulæ* is " simple," but " lively." — ED.

head, like that of the two preceding, is loose, subcrested, and of a deep brownish black ; wings and tail, deep dusky ; the former edged, on every feather, with yellowish white, the latter forked, and widening remarkably towards the end ; bill, formed exactly like that of the King Bird ; whole lower parts, a pale, delicate yellow ; legs and bill, wholly black ; iris, hazel. The female is almost exactly like the male, except in having the crest somewhat more brown. This species inhabits from Canada to Florida ; great numbers of them usually wintering in the two Carolinas and Georgia. In New York they are called the Phœby Bird, and are accused of destroying bees. With many people in the country, the arrival of the Pewee serves as a sort of almanac, reminding them that now it is time such and such work should be done. "Whenever the Pewit appears," says Mr. Bartram, "we may plant peas and beans in the open grounds, French beans, sow radishes, onions, and almost every kind of esculent garden seeds, without fear or danger from frosts ; for, although we have sometimes frosts after their first appearance for a night or two, yet not so severe as to injure the young plants." *

WOOD PEWEE FLYCATCHER. — MUSCICAPA RAPAX. —
Fig. 57.

Muscicapa virens, *Linn. Syst.* 327. — *Lath. Syn* ii. 350.   *Id. Sup.* p. 174, No. 82. — *Catesb.* i. 54, fig. 1. — Le Gobe-mouche brun de la Caroline, *Buff.* iv. 543. — Muscicapa acadica, *Gmel. Syst.* i. p. 947. — *Arct. Zool.* 387, No. 270. — *Peale's Museum*, No. 6660.

TYRANNULA VIRENS. — Jardine.

Muscicapa virens, *Linn. Syst.* — *Bonap. Synop.* p. 68.

I have given the name Wood Pewee to this species, to discriminate it from the preceding, which it resembles so much in form and plumage as scarcely to be distinguished from it, but by an accurate examination of both. Yet in manners, mode of building, period of migration, and notes, the two species differ greatly. The Pewee is among the first birds that visit us in spring, frequenting creeks, building in caves, and under arches of bridges ; the Wood Pewee, the subject of our present account, is among the latest of our summer birds, seldom arriving before the 12th or 15th of May ; frequenting the shadiest high-timbered woods, where there is little underwood, and abundance of dead twigs and branches shooting across the gloom ; generally in low situations ; builds its nest on the upper side of a limb or branch, forming it outwardly of moss, but using no mud, and lining it with various soft materials. The female lays five white eggs ; and the first brood leave the nest about the middle of June.

This species is an exceeding expert fly-catcher. It loves to sit on

* *Travels*, p. 288.

the high dead branches, amid the gloom of the woods, calling out in a feeble, plaintive tone, *peto way, peto way, pee way;* occasionally darting after insects; sometimes making a circular sweep of thirty or forty yards, snapping up numbers in its way with great adroitness; and returning to its position and chant as before. In the latter part of August, its notes are almost the only ones to be heard in the woods; about which time, also, it even approaches the city, where I have frequently observed it busily engaged under trees, in solitary courts, gardens, &c., feeding and training its young to their profession. About the middle of September, it retires to the south, a full month before the other.

Length, six inches; breadth, ten; back, dusky olive, inclining to greenish; head, subcrested, and brownish black; tail, forked, and widening towards the tips; lower parts, pale yellowish white. The only discriminating marks between this and the preceding are, the size and the color of the lower mandible, which in this is yellow, in the Pewèe black. The female is difficult to be distinguished from the male.

This species is far more numerous than the preceding, and, probably, winters much farther south. The Pewèe was numerous in North and South Carolina in February; but the Wood Pewèe had not made its appearance in the lower parts of Georgia, even so late as the 16th of March.

FERRUGINOUS THRUSH.* — TURDUS RUFUS. — Fig. 58.

Fox-colored Thrush, *Catesb.* i. 28. — Turdus rufus, *Linn. Syst.* 293. — *Lath.* iii. 39. — La Grive de la Caroline, *Briss.* ii. 223. — Le Moquer François, *De Buff.* iii. 323. *Pl. enl.* 645. — *Arct. Zool.* p. 335, No. 195. — *Peale's Museum,* No. 5285.

ORPHÆUS RUFUS. — Swainson.

Turdus rufus, *Bonap. Synop.* p. 75. — Orphæus rufus, Fox-colored Mock Bird, *North. Zool.* ii. p. 190.

This is the Brown Thrush, or Thrasher, of the Middle and Eastern States, and the French Mocking Bird of Maryland, Virginia, and the

* This species, with *O. polyglottos*, is the typical form of Mr. Swainson's genus *Orphæus*, differing from *Turdus* in its longer form, chiefly apparent from the greater length of its tail, its rounded and shorter wings, its long and bending, and in proportion more slender bill. The form is confined to the New World, and will be represented in Africa by *Crateropus* and *Donocobius.* Swain.; and in Asia and Australia by *Pomatorhinus*, Horsf. They appear to live nearer the ground than the true Thrushes, frequenting the lower brushwood; and it is only during the spring and breeding season that they mount aloft, to serenade their mates. The cries or notes are generally loud; some possess considerable melody, which, however, is only exercised as above mentioned; but many of the aberrant species possess only harsh and grating notes, incessantly kept up; in which respect they resemble the more typical African form and many of the aquatic Warblers.

In the account given by our author of the manners of *O. rufus*, we perceive a very close resemblance to our Common Blackbird. The Blackbird is seldom seen

Carolinas.*   It is the largest of all our Thrushes, and is a well-known
and very distinguished songster.   About the middle or 20th of April,
or generally about the time the cherry-trees begin to blossom, he
arrives in Pennsylvania, and, from the tops of our hedge-rows, sassafras, apple or cherry-trees, he salutes the opening morning with his
charming song, which is loud, emphatical, and full of variety.   At that
serene hour, you may plainly distinguish his voice fully half a mile
off.   These notes are not imitative, as his name would import, and as
some people believe, but seem solely his own; and have considerable
resemblance to the notes of the Song Thrush (*Turdus musicus*) of
Britain.   Early in May he builds his nest, choosing a thorn bush, low
cedar, thicket of briers, dogwood sapling, or cluster of vines, for its
situation, generally within a few feet of the ground.   Outwardly, it is
constructed of small sticks; then layers of dry leaves, and, lastly,
lined with fine, fibrous roots, but without any plaster.   The eggs are
five, thickly sprinkled with ferruginous grains, on a very pale bluish
ground.   They generally have two broods in a season.   Like all birds
that build near the ground, he shows great anxiety for the safety
of his nest and young, and often attacks the black snake in their
defence; generally, too, with success, his strength being greater, and
his bill stronger and more powerful, than any other of his tribe within
the United States.   His food consists of worms, which he scratches
from the ground, caterpillars, and many kinds of berries.   Beetles,
and the whole race of coleopterous insects, wherever he can meet
with them, are sure to suffer.   He is accused, by some people, of
scratching up the hills of Indian corn, in planting time; this may be
partly true; but, for every grain of maize he pilfers, I am persuaded he
destroys five hundred insects; particularly a large dirty-colored grub,
with a black head, which is more pernicious to the corn, and other
grain and vegetables, than nine tenths of the whole feathered race.
He is an active, vigorous bird, flies generally low, from one thicket to
another, with his long, broad tail spread like a fan; is often seen about
brier and bramble bushes, along fences; and has a single note or
chuck, when you approach his nest.   In Pennsylvania, they are
numerous, but never fly in flocks.   About the middle of September,
or as soon as they have well recovered from moulting, in which
they suffer severely, they disappear for the season.   In passing through
the southern parts of Virginia, and south as far as Georgia, in the
depth of winter, I found them lingering in sheltered situations, particularly on the border of swamps and rivers.   On the first of March,

on lofty trees, except during the season of incubation, or occasionally in search of
a roosting place; its true habitat is brushwood or shrubbery, and, unless at one
season, its only note is that of alarm, shrill and rapid, or a kind of chuck.   The
manner of flight, when raised from cover, along a hedge, or among bushes, with the
tail expanded, is also similar; we have thus two types of very nearly allied genera,
varying decidedly in form, but agreeing almost entirely in habit.   The gregarious
Thrushes, again, possess much more activity, enjoy lofty forests, or the open
country, and protect themselves by vigilance, not by stealth and concealment.
  This species was met by Dr. Richardson at Carlton House. . It extends from
Pennsylvania to the Saskatchewan; but Dr. Richardson thinks it probable that it
does not extend its range beyond the 54th parallel of latitude.   It quits the Fur
countries, with the other migratory birds, early in September. — ED.
  * See p. 113, for the supposed origin of this name.

they were in full song round the commons at Savannah, as if straining to outstrip the Mocking Bird, that prince of feathered musicians.

The Thrasher is a welcome visitant in spring, to every lover of rural scenery and rural song. In the months of April and May, when our woods, hedge-rows, orchards, and cherry-trees, are one profusion of blossoms, when every object around conveys the sweet sensations of joy, and Heaven's abundance is, as it were, showering around us, the grateful heart beats in unison with the varying, elevated strains of this excellent bird; we listen to its notes with a kind of devotional ecstasy, as a morning hymn to the great and most adorable Creator of all. The human being who, amidst such scenes, and in such seasons of rural serenity and delight, can pass them with cold indifference, and even contempt, I sincerely pity; for abject must that heart be, and callous those feelings, and depraved that taste, which neither the charms of nature, nor the melody of innocence, nor the voice of gratitude or devotion, can reach.

This bird inhabits North America, from Canada to the point of Florida. They are easily reared, and become very familiar when kept in cages; and though this is rarely done, yet I have known a few instances where they sang in confinement with as much energy as in their native woods. They ought frequently to have earth and gravel thrown in to them, and have plenty of water to bathe in.

The Ferruginous Thrush is eleven inches and a half long, and thirteen in extent; the whole upper parts are of a bright reddish brown; wings, crossed with two bars of white, relieved with black; tips and inner vanes of the wings, dusky; tail, very long, rounded at the end, broad, and of the same reddish brown as the back; whole lower parts, yellowish white; the breast, and sides under the wings, beautifully marked with long, pointed spots of black, running in chains; chin, white; bill, very long and stout, not notched, the upper mandible overhanging the lower a little, and beset with strong bristles at the base, black above, and whitish below, near the base; legs, remarkably strong, and of a dusky clay color; iris of the eye, brilliant yellow. The female may be distinguished from the male by the white on the wing being much narrower, and the spots on the breast less. In other respects, their plumage is nearly alike.

Concerning the sagacity and reasoning faculty of this bird, my venerable friend Mr. Bartram writes me as follows:—"I remember to have reared one of these birds from the nest, which, when full grown, became very tame and docile. I frequently let him out of his cage to give him a taste of liberty. After fluttering and dusting himself in dry sand and earth, and bathing, washing, and dressing himself, he would proceed to hunt insects, such as beetles, crickets, and other shelly tribes; but, being very fond of wasps, after catching them, and knocking them about to break their wings, he would lay them down, then examine if they had a sting, and, with his bill, squeeze the abdomen to clear it of the reservoir of poison before he would swallow his prey. When in his cage, being very fond of dry crusts of bread, if, upon trial, the corners of the crumbs were too hard and sharp for his throat, he would throw them up, carry, and put them in his water dish to soften; then take them out and swallow them. Many other remarkable circumstances might be mentioned that would fully demonstrate faculties of *mind;* not only innate, but acquired ideas, (derived from necessity in a state of domestication,) which we call understanding and knowledge. We see that this bird could associate those ideas, arrange and apply them in a rational manner, according to circumstances. For instance, if he knew that it was the hard, sharp corners of the crumb of bread that hurt his gullet, and prevented him from swallowing it, and that water would soften and render it easy to be swallowed, this knowledge must be acquired by observation and experience; or some other bird taught him. Here the bird perceived, by the effect, the cause, and then took the quickest, the most effectual, and agreeable method to remove that cause. What could the wisest man have done better? Call it reason, or instinct, it is the same that a sensible man would have done in this case.

"After the same manner this bird reasoned with respect to the wasps. He found, by experience and observation, that the first he attempted to swallow hurt his throat, and gave him extreme pain; and, upon examination, observed that the extremity of the abdomen was armed with a poisonous sting; and, after this discovery, never attempted to swallow a wasp until he first pinched his abdomen to the extremity, forcing out the sting, with the receptacle of poison."

It is certainly a circumstance highly honorable to the character of birds, and corroborative of the foregoing sentiments, that those who have paid the most minute attention to their manners, are uniformly their advocates and admirers. "He must," said a gentleman to me the other day, when speaking of another person, "he must be a good man; for those who have long known him, and are most intimate with him, respect him greatly, and always speak well of him."

GOLDEN-CROWNED THRUSH.* — TURDUS AUROCAPILLUS. — Fig. 59.

Edw. 252. — *Lath.* iii. 21. — La Figuier à tête d'or, *Briss.* iii. 504. — La Grivelette de St. Domingue, *Buff.* iii. 317. *Pl. enl.* 390. — *Arct. Zool.* p. 339, No. 203. — Turdus minimus, vertice aureo, The Least Golden-crown Thrush, *Bartram*, p. 290. — *Peale's Museum,* No. 7122.

SEIURUS AUROCAPILLUS. — Swainson,

Sylvia aurocapilla, *Bonap. Synop.* p. 77. — Seiurus aurocapillus, *North. Zool.* ii. 227.

THOUGH the epithet *Golden-crowned* is not very suitable for this bird, that part of the head being rather of a brownish orange, yet, to avoid confusion, I have retained it.

---

* This curious species, with the *S. aquaticus,* No. 109, and some others, differs materially in economy from the Thrushes, notwithstanding their general form and colors; and, to judge from the account of the manners of our present species given by Wilson, it will approach very closely to *Anthus,* and our *A. arboreus,* and in form and structure to some of the Warblers. The manners of *S. aquaticus,* again, resemble more those of the Wagtails; but it has somewhat of

This is also a migratory species, arriving in Pennsylvania late in April, and leaving us again late in September. It is altogether an inhabitant of the woods, runs along the ground like a lark, and even along the horizontal branches, frequently moving its tail in the manner of the Wagtails. It has no song, but a shrill, energetic twitter, formed by the rapid reiteration of two notes, *peche, peche, peche,* for a quarter of a minute at a time. It builds a snug, somewhat singular nest, on the ground, in the woods, generally on a declivity facing the south. This is formed of leaves and dry grass, and lined with hair. Though sunk below the surface, it is arched over, and only a small hole left for entrance: the eggs are four, sometimes five, white, irregularly spotted with reddish brown, chiefly near the great end. When alarmed, it escapes from the nest with great silence and rapidity, running along the ground like a mouse, as if afraid to tread too heavily on the leaves; if you stop to examine its nest, it also stops, droops its wings, flutters, and tumbles along, as if hardly able to crawl, looking back now and then to see whether you are taking notice of it. If you slowly follow, it leads you fifty or sixty yards off, in a direct line from its nest, seeming at every advance to be gaining fresh strength; and when it thinks it has decoyed you to a sufficient distance, it suddenly wheels off and disappears. This kind of deception is practised by many other species of birds that build on the ground; and is sometimes so adroitly performed, as actually to have the desired effect of securing the safety of its nest and young.

This is one of those birds frequently selected by the Cow-Pen Bunting to be the foster parent of its young. Into the nest of this bird the Cow Bird deposits its egg, and leaves the result to the mercy and management of the Thrush, who generally performs the part of a faithful and affectionate nurse to the foundling.

The Golden-crowned Thrush is six inches long, and nine in extent; the whole upper parts, except the crown and hind head, are a rich yellow olive; the tips of the wings, and inner vanes of the quills, are dusky brown; from the nostrils, a black strip passes to the hind head on each side, between which lies a bed of brownish orange; the sides of the neck are whitish; the whole lower parts, white, except the breast, which is handsomely marked with pointed spots of black, or deep brown, as in the figure; round the eye is a narrow ring of yellowish white; legs, pale flesh color; bill, dusky above, whitish below. The female has the orange on the crown considerably paler.

This bird might with propriety be ranged with the Wagtails, its notes, manners, and habit of building on the ground being similar to these. It usually hatches twice in the season; feeds on small bugs and the larvæ of insects, which it chiefly gathers from the ground. It is very generally diffused over the United States, and winters in Jamaica, Hispaniola, and other islands of the West Indies.

the true Thrush in perching high, and in possessing a sweet and pensive song. We have, therefore, in shape, color, and some of the habits, an alliance to the Thrushes, while the colors and their distribution agree both with *Merula* and *Anthus,* and in their principal economy a combination of the *Sylvianæ* and *Motacillanæ,* — altogether a most interesting form; while, in the structure of their nest, and the color of the eggs, they agree with the Wrens. Mr. Swainson has made from it his genus *Seiurus.* — ED.

CAT BIRD.* — TURDUS LIVIDUS. — Fig. 60.

Muscicapa Carolinensis, *Linn. Syst.* 300. — Le Gobe-mouche brun de Virginie, *Briss.* ii. 365. — Cat Bird, *Catesb.* i. 66. — *Latham,* ii. 353. — Le Moucherolle de Virginie, *Buff.* iv. 562. — Lucar lividus, apice nigra, The Cat Bird, or Chicken Bird, *Bartram,* p. 290. — *Peale's Museum,* No. 6770.

ORPHÆUS FELIVOX. — Swainson.

Turdus felivox, *Bonap. Synop.* p. 75.

WE have here before us a very common and very numerous species, in this part of the United States ; and one as well known to all classes of people, as his favorite briers, or blackberry bushes. In spring or summer, on approaching thickets of brambles, the first salutation you receive is from the Cat Bird ; and a stranger, unacquainted with its note, would instantly conclude that some vagrant, orphan kitten had got bewildered among the briers, and wanted assistance ; so exactly does the call of the bird resemble the voice of that animal. Unsuspicious, and extremely familiar, he seems less apprehensive of man than almost any other of our summer visitants ; for whether in the woods, or in the garden, where he frequently builds his nest, he seldom allows you to pass without approaching to pay his respects, in his usual way. This humble familiarity and deference, from a stranger, too, who comes to rear his young, and spend the summer with us, ought to entitle him to a full share of our hospitality. Sorry I am, however, to say, that this, in too many instances, is cruelly the reverse. Of this I will speak more particularly in the sequel.

About the 28th of February, the Cat Bird first arrives in the lower parts of Georgia from the south, consequently winters not far distant, probably in Florida. On the second week in April, he usually reaches this part of Pennsylvania, and, about the beginning of May, has already succeeded in building his nest. The place chosen for this purpose is generally a thicket of briers or brambles, a thorn bush, thick vine, or the fork of a small sapling ; no great solicitude is shown for concealment, though few birds appear more interested for the safety of their nest and young. The materials are dry leaves and weeds, small twigs, and fine, dry grass ; the inside is lined with the fine, black, fibrous roots of some plant. The female lays four, sometimes five eggs, of a uniform greenish blue color, without any spots. They generally raise two, and sometimes three broods in a season.

In passing through the woods in summer, I have sometimes amused

---

* At first sight, this species, singular both in habits and structure, appears to range with *Brachypus ;* but a more minute inspection shows that it will rather stand as an aberrant form with *Orphœus.* The structure of the bill, feet, and tail, are all of the latter ; while the colors, and their distribution, agree with *Brachypus,* particularly the rufous vent ; that part is a nearly constant mark among the *Brachipi,* being of a different and brighter color, and very generally red or yellow. The true *Brachipi* do not seem to extend to North America ; they are chiefly confined to Africa, and the warmer countries of India.

14

myself with imitating the violent chirping or squeaking of young birds, in order to observe what different species were around me ; for such sounds, at such a season, in the woods, are no less alarming to the feathered tenants of the bushes, than the cry of fire or murder in the streets is to the inhabitants of a large and populous city. On such occasions of alarm and consternation, the Cat Bird is the first to make his appearance, not singly, but sometimes half a dozen at a time, flying from different quarters to the spot. At this time, those who are disposed to play with his feelings may almost throw him into fits, his emotion and agitation are so great, at the distressful cries of what he supposes to be his suffering young. Other birds are variously affected ; but none show symptoms of such extreme suffering. He hurries backwards and forwards, with hanging wings and open mouth, calling out louder and faster, and actually screaming with distress, till he appears hoarse with his exertions. He attempts no offensive means ; but he bewails — he implores — in the most pathetic terms with which nature has supplied him, and with an agony of feeling which is truly affecting. Every feathered neighbor within hearing hastens to the place, to learn the cause of the alarm, peeping about with looks of consternation and sympathy. But their own powerful parental duties and domestic concerns soon oblige each to withdraw. At any other season, the most perfect imitations have no effect whatever on him.

The Cat Bird will not easily desert its nest. I took two eggs from one which was sitting, and in their place put two of the Brown Thrush, or Thrasher, and took my stand at a convenient distance, to see how she would behave. In a minute or two, the male made his approaches, stooped down, and looked earnestly at the strange eggs, then flew off to his mate, who was not far distant, with whom he seemed to have some conversation, and instantly returning, with the greatest gentleness took out both the Thrasher's eggs, first one and then the other, carried them singly about thirty yards, and dropped them among the bushes. I then returned the two eggs I had taken, and, soon after, the female resumed her place on the nest as before.

From the nest of another Cat Bird I took two half-fledged young, and placed them in that of another, which was sitting on five eggs. She soon turned them both out. The place where the nest was not being far from the ground, they were little injured, and the male, observing their helpless situation, began to feed them with great assiduity and tenderness.

I removed the nest of a Cat Bird, which contained four eggs, nearly hatched, from a fox grape vine, and fixed it firmly and carefully in a thicket of briers close by, without injuring its contents. In less than half an hour I returned, and found it again occupied by the female.

The Cat Bird is one of our earliest morning songsters, beginning generally before break of day, and hovering from bush to bush, with great sprightliness, when there is scarce light sufficient to distinguish him. His notes are more remarkable for singularity than for melody. They consist of short imitations of other birds, and other sounds ; but, his pipe being rather deficient in clearness and strength of tone, his imitations fail where these are requisite. Yet he is not easily discouraged, but seems to study certain passages with great perseverance ; uttering them at first low, and, as he succeeds, higher and more free, nowise embarrassed by the presence of a spectator even within a few yards of him. On attentively listening for some time to him, one can perceive considerable variety in his performance, in which he seems to introduce all the odd sounds and quaint passages he has been able to collect. Upon the whole, though we cannot arrange him with the grand leaders of our vernal choristers, he well merits a place among the most agreeable *general* performers.

This bird, as has been before observed, is very numerous, in summer, in the Middle States. Scarcely a thicket in the country is without its Cat Birds; and were they to fly in flocks, like many other birds, they would darken the air with their numbers. But their migrations are seldom observed, owing to their gradual progress and recession, in spring and autumn, to and from their breeding places. They enter Georgia late in February, and reach New England about the beginning of May. In their migrations, they keep pace with the progress of agriculture; and the first settlers in many parts of the Gennesee country, have told me, that it was several years after they removed there, before the Cat Bird made his appearance among them. With all these amiable qualities to recommend him, few people in the country respect the Cat Bird; on the contrary, it is generally the object of dislike; and the boys of the United States entertain the same prejudice and contempt for this bird, its nest and young, as those of Britain do for the Yellow Hammer, and its nest, eggs, and young. I am at a loss to account for this cruel prejudice. Even those by whom it is entertained, can scarcely tell you why; only they "hate Cat Birds;" as some persons tell you they hate Frenchmen, they hate Dutchmen, &c., — expressions that bespeak their own narrowness of understanding, and want of liberality. Yet, after ruminating over in my own mind all the probable causes, I think I have at last hit on some of them; the principal of which seems to me to be a certain similarity of taste, and clashing of interest, between the Cat Bird and the farmer. The Cat Bird is fond of large, ripe garden strawberries; so is the farmer, for the good price they bring in market: the Cat Bird loves the best and richest early cherries; so does the farmer, for they are sometimes the most profitable of his early fruit: the Cat Bird has a particular partiality for the finest, ripe, mellow pears; and these are also particular favorites with the farmer. But the Cat Bird has frequently the advantage of the farmer, by snatching off the first fruits of these delicious productions; and the farmer takes revenge, by shooting him down with his gun, as he finds old hats, windmills, and scarecrows, are no impediments in his way to these forbidden fruits; and nothing but this resource — the ultimatum of farmers as well as kings — can restrain his visits. The boys are now set to watch the cherry-trees with the gun: and thus commences a train of prejudices and antipathies, that commonly continue through life. Perhaps, too, the common note of the Cat Bird, so like the mewing of the animal whose name it bears, and who itself sustains no small share of prejudice, the homeliness of his plumage, and even his familiarity, so proverbially known to beget contempt, may also contribute to this mean, illiberal, and persecuting prejudice; but, with the generous and the good, the lovers of nature and of rural charms, the confidence which this familiar bird places in man by building in his garden, under his eye, the music of his song, and the interesting playfulness of his manners, will always be more than a recompense for all the little stolen morsels he snatches.

The Cat Bird measures nine inches in length; at a small distance he appears nearly black; but, on a closer examination, is of a deep slate color above, lightest on the edges of the primaries, and of a considerably lighter slate color below, except the under tail-coverts, which are very dark red; the tail, which is rounded, and upper part of the head, as well as the legs and bill, are black, The female differs little in color from the male. Latham takes notice of a bird, exactly resembling this, being found at Kamtschatka, only it wanted the red under the tail. Probably it might have been a young bird, in which the red is scarcely observable.

This bird has been very improperly classed among the Flycatchers. As he never seizes his prey on wing, has none of their manners, feeds principally on fruit, and seems to differ so little from the Thrushes, I think he more properly belongs to the latter tribe, than to any other genus we have. His bill, legs, and feet, place and mode of building, the color of the eggs, his imitative notes, food, and general manners, all justify me in removing him to this genus.

The Cat Bird is one of those unfortunate victims, and indeed the principal, against which credulity and ignorance have so often directed the fascinating quality of the black snake. A multitude of marvellous stories have been told me by people who have themselves seen the poor Cat Birds drawn, or sucked, as they sometimes express it, from the tops of the trees, (which, by the by, the Cat Bird rarely visits,) one by one into the yawning mouth of the immovable snake. It has so happened with me that, in all the adventures of this kind that I have personally witnessed, the Cat Bird was actually the assailant, and always the successful one. These rencounters never take place but during the breeding time of birds; for whose eggs and young the snake has a particular partiality. It is no wonder that those species, whose nests are usually built near the ground, should be the greatest sufferers, and the most solicitous for their safety: hence the cause why the Cat Bird makes such a distinguished figure in most of these marvellous narrations. That a poisonous snake will strike a bird or mouse, and allow it to remain till nearly expiring before he begins to devour it, our observations on the living rattle-snake, at present [1811] kept by Mr. Peale, satisfy us is a fact; but that the same snake, with eyes, breath, or any other known quality he possesses, should be capable of drawing a bird, reluctantly, from the tree tops to its mouth, is an absurdity too great for me to swallow.

I am led to these observations by a note which I received this morning from my worthy friend Mr. Bartram: "Yesterday," says this gentleman, " I observed a conflict, or contest, between a Cat Bird and a snake. It took place in a gravel walk in the garden, near a dry wall of stone. I was within a few yards of the combatants. The bird pounced or darted upon the snake, snapping his bill; the snake would then draw himself quickly into a coil, ready for a blow; but the bird would cautiously circumvent him at a little distance, now and then running up to, and snapping at him; but keeping at a sufficient distance to avoid a blow. After some minutes, it became a running fight, the snake retreating; and, at last, he took shelter in the wall. The Cat Bird had young ones in the bushes near the field of battle.

"This may show the possibility of poisonous snakes biting birds; the operation of the poison causing them to become, as it were, fascinated."

BAY-BREASTED WARBLER. — SYLVIA CASTANEA. — Fig. 61.

Parus peregrinus, The Little Chocolate-breasted Titmouse, *Bartram*, p. 292. — *Peale's Museum*, No. 7311.

SYLVICOLA CASTANEA. — Swainson.

Sylvia castanea, *Bonap. Synop.* p. 81. *

This very rare species passes through Pennsylvania about the beginning of May, and soon disappears. It has many of the habits of the Titmouse, and all its activity; hanging among the extremities of the twigs, and darting about from place to place, with restless diligence, in search of various kinds of the larvæ of insects. It is never seen here in summer, and very rarely on its return, owing, no doubt, to the greater abundance of foliage at that time, and to the silence and real scarcity of the species. Of its nest and eggs we are altogether uninformed.

The length of this bird is five inches, breadth eleven; throat, breast, and sides under the wings, pale chestnut, or bay; forehead, cheeks, line over and strip through the eye, black; crown, deep chestnut; lower parts, dull yellowish white; hind head and back, streaked with black, on a grayish buff ground; wings, brownish black, crossed with two bars of white; tail, forked, brownish black, edged with ash, the three exterior feathers marked with a spot of white on the inner edges; behind the eye is a broad, oblong spot of yellowish white. The female has much less of the bay color on the breast; the black on the forehead is also less, and of a brownish tint. The legs and feet, in both, are dark ash, the claws extremely sharp for climbing and hanging; the bill is black; irides, hazel.

The ornithologists of Europe take no notice of this species, and have probably never met with it. Indeed, it is so seldom seen in this part of Pennsylvania, that few even of our own writers have mentioned it.

I lately received a very neat drawing of this bird, done by a young lady in Middletown, Connecticut, where it seems also to be a rare species.

* According to Bonaparte, discovered and first described by Wilson. — Ed.

14 *

CHESTNUT–SIDED WARBLER. — SYLVIA PENNSYLVANICA. — Fig. 62.

Linn. Syst. 333. — Red-throated Flycatcher, *Edw.* 301. — Bloody-side Warbler, *Turton, Syst.* i. p. 596. — Le figuier à poitrine rouge, *Buff.* v. 308 — *Briss. Add.* 105. — *Lath.* ii. 489. — *Arct. Zool.* p. 405, No. 298. — *Peale's Museum,* No. 7006.

SYLVICOLA ICTEROCEPHALA. — Swainson.

Sylvia icterocephala, *Bonap. Synop.* p. 80. — The Chestnut-sided Warbler, *Aud.* pl. 59. *Orn. Biog.* p. 306.

Of this bird I can give but little account. It is one of those transient visitors that pass through Pennsylvania, in April and May, on their way farther north to breed. During its stay here, which seldom exceeds a week or ten days, it appears actively engaged among the opening buds and young leaves, in search of insects; has no song but a feeble chirp, or twitter, and is not numerous. As it leaves us early in May, it probably breeds in Canada, or, perhaps, some parts of New England; though I have no certain knowledge of the fact. In a whole day's excursion, it is rare to meet with more than one or two of these birds; though a thousand individuals of some species may be seen in the same time. Perhaps they may be more numerous on some other part of the continent.

The length of this species is five inches; the extent, seven and three quarters. The front, line over the eye, and ear-feathers, are pure white; upper part of the head, brilliant yellow; the lores and space immediately below are marked with a triangular patch of black; the back and hind head are streaked with gray, dusky black, and dull yellow; wings, black; primaries, edged with pale blue, the first and second row of coverts, broadly tipped with pale yellow; secondaries, broadly edged with the same; tail, black, handsomely forked, exteriorly edged with ash; the inner webs of the three exterior feathers with each a spot of white; from the extremity of the black at the lower mandible, on each side, a streak of deep reddish chestnut descends along the sides of the neck, and under the wings, to the root of the tail; the rest of the lower parts are pure white; legs and feet, ash; bill, black; irides, hazel. The female has the hind head much lighter, and the chestnut on the sides is considerably narrower, and not of so deep a tint.

Turton, and some other writers, have bestowed on this little bird the singular epithet of "bloody-sided," for which I was at a loss to know the reason, the color of that part being a plain chestnut; till, on examining Mr. Edwards's colored figure of this bird in the public library of Philadelphia, I found its side tinged with a brilliant blood color. Hence, I suppose, originated the name!

MOURNING WARBLER. — SYLVIA PHILADELPHIA. — Fig. 63.

TRICHAS? PHILADELPHIA. — Jardine.

Sylvia Philadelphia, *Bonap. Synop.* p. 85.

I HAVE now the honor of introducing to the notice of naturalists and others a very modest and neat little species, which has hitherto eluded their research. I must also add, with regret, that it is the only one of its kind I have yet met with. The bird from which the figure in the plate was taken, was shot in the early part of June, on the border of a marsh, within a few miles of Philadelphia. It was flitting from one low bush to another, very busy in search of insects ; and had a sprightly and pleasant warbling song, the novelty of which first attracted my attention. I have traversed the same and many such places, every spring and summer since, in expectation of again meeting with some individual of the species, but without success. I have, however, the satisfaction to say, that the drawing was done with the greatest attention to peculiarity of form, markings, and tint of plumage ; and the figure on the plate is a good resemblance of the original. I have yet hopes of meeting, in some of my excursions, with the female, and, should I be so fortunate, shall represent her in some future volume of the present work, with such further remarks on their manners, &c., as I may then be enabled to make.

There are two species mentioned by Turton, to which the present has some resemblance, viz., *Motacilla mitrata,* or Mitred Warbler, and *M. cucullata,* or Hooded Warbler ; both birds of the United States, or, more properly, a single bird ; for they are the same species twice described, namely, the Hooded Warbler. The difference, however, between that and the present is so striking, as to determine this at once to be a very distinct species. The singular appearance of the head, neck, and breast, suggested the name.

The Mourning Warbler is five inches long, and seven in extent ; the whole back, wings, and tail, are of a deep greenish olive, the tips of the wings, and the centre of the tail-feathers, excepted, which are brownish ; the whole head is of a dull slate color ; the breast is ornamented with a singular crescent of alternate, transverse lines of pure glossy white, and very deep black ; all the rest of the lower parts are of a brilliant yellow ; the tail is rounded at the end ; legs and feet, a pale flesh color ; bill, deep brownish black above, lighter below ; eye, hazel.*

* Wilson saw this bird only once, and I have met with no one who has since seen it. From the general appearance of the representation, it seems to approach nearest to the generic appellation we have given, but which must rest yet undecided. Bonaparte observes, " The excessive rarity might lead us to suppose it an accidental variety of some other, — *perhaps S. trichas.*" — Ed.

RED–COCKADED WOODPECKER. — PICUS QUERULUS. —
Fig. 64.

Peale's Museum, No. 2027.

DENDROCOPUS QUERULUS. — Koch.

Picus querulus, *Bonap. Synop.* p. 46.

This new species I first discovered in the pine woods of North Carolina. The singularity of its voice, which greatly resembles the chirping of young nestlings, and the red streak on the side of its head, suggested the specific name I have given it. It also extends through South Carolina and Georgia, at least as far as the Altamaha River. Observing the first specimen I found to be so slightly marked with red, I suspected it to be a young bird, or imperfect in its plumage; but the great numbers I afterwards shot, satisfied me that this is a peculiarity of the species. It appeared exceedingly restless, active, and clamorous; and every where I found its manners the same.

This bird seems to be an intermediate link between the Red-bellied and the Hairy Woodpecker, represented in Nos. 26 and 37. It has the back of the former, and the white belly and spotted neck of the latter; but wants the breadth of red in both, and is less than either. A preserved specimen has been deposited in the Museum of Philadelphia.

This Woodpecker is seven inches and a half long, and thirteen broad; the upper part of the head is black; the back barred with twelve white transversely semicircular lines, and as many of black, alternately; the cheeks and sides of the neck are white; whole lower parts, the same; from the lower mandible, a list of black passes towards the shoulder of the wing, where it is lost in small black spots on each side of the breast; the wings are black, spotted with white; the four middle tail-feathers, black; the rest white, spotted with black; rump, black, variegated with white; the vent, white, spotted with black; the hairs that cover the nostrils are of a pale cream color; the bill, deep slate. But what forms the most distinguishing peculiarity of this bird, is a fine line of vermilion on each side of the head, seldom occupying more than the edge of a single feather. The female is destitute of this ornament; but, in the rest of her plumage, differs in nothing from the male. The iris of the eye, in both, was hazel.

The stomachs of all those I opened were filled with small black insects and fragments of large beetles. The posterior extremities of the tongue reached nearly to the base of the upper mandible.

BROWN-HEADED NUTHATCH. — SITTA PUSILLA. — Fig. 65.

Small Nuthatch, *Catesby*, *Car*. i. 22, upper figure. — La petite sitelle à tête brune, *Buff.* v. 474. — *Peale's Museum*, No. 2010. — *Briss.* iii. 958. — *Lath.* i. 651, C.

SITTA PUSILLA. — Latham.

Sitta pusilla, *Bonap. Synop.* p. 97.

This bird is chiefly an inhabitant of Virginia and the Southern States, and seems particularly fond of pine-trees. I have never yet discovered it either in Pennsylvania or any of the regions north of this. Its manners are very similar to those of the Red-bellied Nuthatch, represented in No. 7; but its notes are more shrill and chirping. In the countries it inhabits it is a constant resident; and in winter associates with parties, of eight or ten, of its own species, who hunt busily from tree to tree, keeping up a perpetual creeping. It is a frequent companion of the Woodpecker figured beside it; and you rarely find the one in the woods without observing or hearing the other not far off. It climbs equally in every direction, on the smaller branches as well as on the body of the tree, in search of its favorite food, small insects and their larvæ. It also feeds on the seeds of the pine-tree. I have never met with its nest.

This species is four inches and a quarter long, and eight broad; the whole upper part of the head and neck, from the bill to the back, and as far down as the eyes, is light brown, or pale ferruginous, shaded with darker touches, with the exception of a spot of white near the back; from the nostril through the eyes, the brown is deepest, making a very observable line there; the chin, and sides of the neck under the eyes, are white; the wings, dusky; the coverts and three secondaries next the body, a slate or lead color, which is also the color of the rest of the upper parts; the tail is nearly even at the end, the two middle feathers slate color, the others black, tipped with slate, and crossed diagonally with a streak of white; legs and feet, dull blue; upper mandible, black; lower, blue at the base; iris, hazel. The female differs in having the brown on the head rather darker, and the line through the eye less conspicuous.

This diminutive bird is little noticed in history, and what little has been said of it by Europeans is not much to its credit. It is characterized as "a very stupid bird," which may easily be knocked down, from the sides of the tree, with one's cane. I confess I found it a very dexterous climber, and so rapid and restless in its motions as to be shot with difficulty. Almost all very small birds seem less suspicious of man than large ones; but that activity and restless diligence should constitute stupidity, is rather a new doctrine. Upon the whole, I am of opinion, that a person who should undertake the destruction of these birds, at even a dollar a head for all he knocked down with his cane, would run a fair chance of starving by his profession.*

* In our note at page 24, we mentioned that the American Nuthatches and that of Europe were the only species known. M. Vigors has since described, in the

PIGEON HAWK.—FALCO COLUMBARIUS.—Fig. 66.—Male.

Linn. Syst. p. 128, No. 21.—*Lath. Syn.* i. p. 101, No. 86.—L'Epervier de la Caroline, *Briss. Orn.* i. p. 238.—*Catesb.* i. p. 3, t. 3.—*Bartram,* p. 290.—*Turton, Syst.* i. p. 162.—*Peale's Museum,* No. 352.

FALCO COLUMBARIUS.—Linnæus.

Pigeon Hawk, *Penn. Arct. Zool.* ii. 222.—Falco Columbarius, *Bonap. Synop.* p. 28.—*North. Zool.* ii. p. 35.

This small Hawk possesses great spirit and rapidity of flight. He is generally migratory in the Middle and Northern States, arriving in Pennsylvania early in spring, and extending his migrations as far north as Hudson's Bay. After building, and rearing his young, he retires to the south early in November. Small birds and mice are his principal food. When the Reed Birds, Grakles, and Red-winged Blackbirds congregate in large flights, he is often observed hovering in their rear, or on their flanks, picking up the weak, the wounded, or stragglers, and frequently making a sudden and fatal sweep into the very midst of their multitudes. The flocks of Robins and Pigeons are honored with the same attentions from this marauder, whose daily excursions are entirely regulated by the movements of the great body on whose unfortunate members he fattens. The individual from which the drawing on the plate was taken, was shot in the meadows below Philadelphia in the month of August. He was carrying off a Blackbird (*Oriolus phœniceus*) from the flock, and, though mortally wounded and dying, held his prey fast till his last expiring breath, having struck his claws into its very heart. This was found to be a male. Sometimes when shot at, and not hurt, he will fly in circles over the sportsman's head, shrieking out with great violence, as if highly irritated. He frequently flies low, skimming a little above the field. I have never seen his nest.*

The Pigeon Hawk is eleven inches long, and twenty-three broad; the whole upper parts are of a deep dark brown, except the tail, which is crossed with bars of white; the inner vanes of the quill-feathers are marked with round spots of reddish brown; the bill is short, strongly toothed, of a light blue color, and tipped with black; the skin surrounding the eye, greenish; cere, the same; temples and line over the eye,

proceedings of the Committee of Science of the Zoological Society, one under the name of *Sitta castaneoventris,* from India, which, if true to the type, may prove an addition. In the same place, that gentleman also describes a second species of *Certhia,* (*C. spilonota,*) but adds, " the tail of this bird is soft and flexible." We have noticed, in a former note, the *C. familiaris* as the only known species, and we doubt if that now mentioned can rank with it.—Ed.

* Mr. Hutchins, in his notes on the Hudson's Bay birds, informs us that this species makes its nest in hollow rocks and trees, of sticks and grass, lined with feathers, laying from two to four white eggs, thinly marked with red spots.

This species has the form of the Falcons, with the bill strongly toothed, but somewhat of the plumage of the Sparrow Hawks. The color of the eggs is also that of the latter.—Ed.

lighter brown; the lower parts, brownish white, streaked laterally with dark brown; legs, yellow; claws, black. The female is an inch and a half longer, of a still deeper color, though marked nearly in the same manner, with the exception of some white on the hind head The femoral, or thigh feathers, in both are of a remarkable length, reaching nearly to the feet, and are also streaked longitudinally with dark brown. The irides of the eyes of this bird have been hitherto described as being of a brilliant yellow; but every specimen I have yet met with had the iris of a deep hazel. I must therefore follow nature, in opposition to very numerous and respectable authorities.

I cannot, in imitation of European naturalists, embellish the history of this species with anecdotes of its exploits in falconry. This science, if it may be so called, is among the few that have never yet travelled across the Atlantic; neither does it appear that the idea of training our Hawks or Eagles to the chase, ever suggested itself to any of the Indian nations of North America. The Tartars, however, from whom, according to certain writers, many of these nations originated, have long excelled in the practice of this sport, which is indeed better suited to an open country than to one covered with forest. Though once so honorable and so universal, it is now much disused in Europe, and in Britain is nearly extinct. Yet I cannot but consider it as a much more noble and princely amusement than horse-racing and cock-fighting, cultivated in certain states with so much care; or even than pugilism, which is still so highly patronized is some of those enlightened countries.

BLUE–WINGED YELLOW WARBLER. — SYLVIA SOLITARIA. — Fig. 67.

Parus aureus alis cœruleis, *Bartram*, p. 292. — *Edw.* pl. 277, upper figure. — Pine Warbler, *Arct. Zool.* p. 412, No. 318. — *Peale's Museum*, No. 7307.

VERMIVORA SOLITARIA. — Swainson.

Sylvia solitaria, *Bonap. Synop.* p. 87. — The Blue-winged Yellow Warbler, *Aud.* pl. 20, *Orn. Biog.* i. 102.

This bird has been mistaken for the Pine Creeper of Catesby. It is a very different species. It comes to us early in May from the south; haunts thickets and shrubberies, searching the branches for insects; is fond of visiting gardens, orchards, and willow-trees, of gleaning among blossoms and currant bushes; and is frequently found in very sequestered woods, where it generally builds its nest. This is fixed in a thick bunch or tussock of long grass, sometimes sheltered by a brier bush. It is built in the form of an inverted cone, or funnel, the bottom thickly bedded with dry beech leaves, the sides formed of the dry bark of strong weeds, lined within with fine, dry grass. These materials are not placed in the usual manner, circularly, but shelving downwards on all sides from the top; the mouth being wide, the bottom very narrow, filled with leaves, and the eggs or young occupying the middle. The female lays five eggs, pure white, with a few very faint dots of reddish near the great end; the young appear the first week in June. I am not certain whether they raise a second brood in the same season.

I have met with several of these nests, always in a retired, though open, part of the woods, and very similar to each other.

The first specimen of this bird taken notice of by European writers was transmitted, with many others, by Mr. William Bartram to Mr. Edwards, by whom it was drawn and etched in the 277th plate of his *Ornithology.* In his remarks on this bird, he seems at a loss to determine whether it is not the Pine Creeper of Catesby;* a difficulty occasioned by the very imperfect coloring and figure of Catesby's bird. The Pine Creeper, however, is a much larger bird; is of a dark yellow olive above, and orange yellow below; has all the habits of a Creeper, alighting on the trunks of the pine-trees, running nimbly round them, and, according to Mr. Abbot, builds a pensile nest. I observed thousands of them in the pine woods of Carolina and Georgia, where they are resident, but have never met with them in any part of Pennsylvania.

This species is five inches and a half long, and seven and a half broad; hind head, and whole back, a rich green olive; crown and front, orange yellow; whole lower parts, yellow, except the vent-feathers, which are white; bill, black above, lighter below; lores, black; the form of the bill approximates a little to that of the Finch; wings and tail, deep brown, broadly edged with pale slate, which makes them appear wholly of that tint, except at the tips; first and second row of coverts, tipped with white slightly stained with yellow; the three exterior tail-feathers have their inner vanes nearly all white; legs, pale bluish; feet, dirty yellow; the two middle tail-feathers are pale slate. The female differs very little in color from the male.

This species very much resembles the Prothonotary Warbler of Pennant and Buffon; the only difference I can perceive, on comparing specimens of each, is, that the yellow of the Prothonotary is more of an orange tint, and the bird somewhat larger.

* CATESBY, *Car.* vol. i. pl. 61.

BLUE-EYED YELLOW WARBLER. — SYLVIA CITRINELLA. — Fig. 68.

Yellow-Poll Warbler, *Lath. Syn.* vol. ii. No. 148. — *Arct. Zool.* p. 402, No. 292. — Le Figuier tacheté, *Buff. Ois.* v. p. 285. — Motacilla æstiva, *Turton's Syst.* p. 615. — Parus luteus, Summer Yellow-Bird, *Bartram,* p. 292. — *Peale's Museum,* No. 7266.

SYLVICOLA ÆSTIVA. — Swainson.

Sylvia æstiva, *Bonap. Synop.* p. 83. — Sylvicola æstiva, *North. Zool.* ii. p. 212.

This is a very common summer species, and appears almost always actively employed among the leaves and blossoms of the willows, snow-ball shrub, and poplars, searching after small green caterpillars, which are its principal food. It has a few shrill notes, uttered with emphasis, but not deserving the name of song. It arrives in Pennsylvania about the beginning of May, and departs again for the south about the middle of September. According to Latham, it is numerous in Guiana, and is also found in Canada. It is a very sprightly, unsuspicious, and familiar little bird; is often seen in and about gardens, among the blossoms of fruit-trees and shrubberies; and, on account of its color, is very noticeable. Its nest is built with great neatness, generally in the triangular fork of a small shrub, near or among brier bushes. Outwardly it is composed of flax or tow, in thick, circular layers, strongly twisted round the twigs that rise through its sides, and lined within with hair and the soft downy substance from the stalks of fern. The eggs are four or five, of a dull white, thickly sprinkled near the great end with specks of pale brown. They raise two broods in the season. This little bird, like many others, will feign lameness to draw you away from its nest, stretching out his neck, spreading and bending down his tail, until it trails along the branch, and fluttering feebly along, to draw you after him; sometimes looking back, to see if you are following him, and returning back to repeat the same manœuvres, in order to attract your attention. The male is most remarkable for this practice.

The Blue-eyed Warbler is five inches long, and seven broad; hind head and back, greenish yellow; crown, front, and whole lower parts, rich golden yellow; breast and sides, streaked laterally with dark red; wings and tail, deep brown, except the edges of the former, and the inner vanes of the latter, which are yellow; the tail is also slightly forked; legs, a pale clay color; bill and eyelids, light blue. The female is of a less brilliant yellow, and the streaks of red on the breast are fewer and more obscure. Buffon is mistaken in supposing No. 1. of Pl. enl. plate lviii. to be the female of this species.

15

GOLDEN-WINGED WARBLER. — SYLVIA CHRYSOPTERA. — Fig. 69.

Edw. 299. — Le Figuier aux ailes dorées, *Buff.* v. 311. — *Lath.* ii. 492. — *Arct. Zool.* 403, No. 295. *Ib.* No. 296. — Motacilla chrysoptera, *Turt. Syst.* i. 597. — Mot. flavifrons, Yellow-fronted Warbler, *Id.* 601. — Parus alis aureis, *Bartram,* v. 292. — *Peale's Museum,* No. 7010.

VERMIVORA CHRYSOPTERA. — Swainson.

Sylvia chrysoptera, *Bonap. Synop.* p. 87.

This is another spring passenger through the United States to the north. This bird, as well as Fig. 67, from the particular form of its bill, ought rather to be separated from the Warblers; or, along with several others of the same kind, might be arranged as a sub-genera, or particular family of that tribe, which might with propriety be called Worm-eaters, the *Motacilla vermivora* of Turton having the bill exactly of this form. The habits of these birds partake a good deal of those of the Titmouse; and, in their language and action, they very much resemble them. All that can be said of this species is, that it appears in Pennsylvania for a few days, about the last of April or beginning of May, darting actively among the young leaves and opening buds, and is rather a scarce species.

The Golden-winged Warbler is five inches long, and seven broad; the crown, golden yellow; the first and second row of wing-coverts, of the same rich yellow; the rest of the upper parts, a deep ash, or dark slate color; tail, slightly forked, and, as well as the wings, edged with whitish; a black band passes through the eye, and is separated from the yellow of the crown, by a fine line of white; chin and throat, black, between which and that passing through the eye runs a strip of white, as in the figure; belly and vent, white; bill, black, gradually tapering to a sharp point; legs, dark ash; irides, hazel.

Pennant has described this species twice, first, as the Golden-winged Warbler, and, immediately after, as the Yellow-fronted Warbler. See the synonymes at the beginning of this article.

BLACK-THROATED BLUE WARBLER. — SYLVIA CANADENSIS. — Fig. 70.

Motacilla Canadensis, *Linn. Syst.* 336. — Le Figuier bleu, *Buff.* v. 304. *Pl. enl* 685, fig. 2. — *Lath. Syn.* ii. p. 487, No. 113. — *Edw.* 252. — *Arct. Zool.* p. 399, No. 285. — *Peale's Museum,* No. 7222.

SYLVICOLA CANADENSIS. — Swainson.

Sylvia Canadensis, *Bonap. Synop.* p. 84.

I know little of this bird. It is one of those transient visitors that, in the month of April, pass through Pennsylvania, on its way to the

72. *American Sparrow-Hawk.* 73. *Field Sparrow.* 73. *Tree Sp.* 74. *Song Sp.* 75. *Chipping Sp.* 76. *Snow Bird.* 77. *American Siskin.* 78. *Rose-breasted Grosbeak.* 79. *Green Black-throat ed Warbler.* 80. *Yellow-rump W.* 81. *Cerulean W.* 82. *Solitary Flycatcher.* 83. *Cow Bunting.* 85. *Young.* 84. *Female.* 85. *Maryland Yellow-throat.* 87. *Blue-grey Flycatcher.* 88. *White-eyed F.*

north, to breed. It has much of the Flycatcher in its manners, though the form of its bill is decisively that of the Warbler. These birds are occasionally seen for about a week or ten days, viz., from the 25th of April to the end of the first week in May. I sought for them in the Southern States in winter, but in vain. It is highly probable that they breed in Canada; but the summer residents among the feathered race on that part of the continent are little known or attended to. The habits of the bear, the deer, and beaver, are much more interesting to those people, and for a good, substantial reason too, because more lucrative; and unless there should arrive an order from England for a cargo of skins of Warblers and Flycatchers, sufficient to make them an object worth speculation, we are likely to know as little of them hereafter as at present.

This species is five inches long, and seven and a half broad, and is wholly of a fine, light slate color above; the throat, cheeks, front and upper part of the breast, are black; wings and tail, dusky black, the primaries marked with a spot of white immediately below their coverts; tail, edged with blue; belly and vent, white; legs and feet, dirty yellow; bill, black, and beset with bristles at the base. The female is more of a dusky ash on the breast, and, in some specimens, nearly white.

They, no doubt, pass this way on their return in autumn, for I have myself shot several in that season; but as the woods are then still thick with leaves, they are much more difficult to be seen, and make a shorter stay than they do in spring.

AMERICAN SPARROW HAWK.—FALCO SPARVERIUS—
Fig. 71.—Female.

Emerillon de St. Domingue, *Buff.* i. 291. *Pl. enl.* 465.—*Arct. Zool.* 212.—Little Falcon, *Lath. Syn.* i. p. 110, No. 94. *Ib.* 95.—*Peale's Museum*, No. 389.

FALCO SPARVERIUS.—Linnæus.

Falco sparverius, *Bonap. Synop.* p. 27.—Falco sparverius, Little Rusty-crowned Falcon, *North. Zool.* ii. p. 31.

In no department of ornithology has there been greater confusion, or more mistakes made, than among this class of birds of prey. The great difference of size between the male and female, the progressive variation of plumage to which, for several years, they are subject, and the difficulty of procuring a sufficient number of specimens for examination,—all these causes conspire to lead the naturalist into almost unavoidable mistakes. For these reasons, and in order, if possible, to ascertain each species of this genus distinctly, I have determined, where any doubt or ambiguity prevails, to represent both male and female, as fair and perfect specimens of each may come into my possession. According to fashionable etiquette, the honor of precedence, in the present instance, is given to the *female* of this species ; both because she is the most courageous, the largest and handsomest of the two, best ascertained, and less subject to change of color than the male, who will require some further examination, and more observation, before we can venture to introduce him.

This bird is a constant resident in almost every part of the United States, particularly in the states north of Maryland. In the Southern States there is a smaller species found, which is destitute of the black spots on the head ; the legs are long and very slender, and the wings light blue. This has been supposed, by some, to be the male of the present species ; but this is an error. The eye of the present species is dusky ; that of the smaller species a brilliant orange ; the former has the tail *rounded* at the end, the latter slightly *forked*. Such essential differences never take place between two individuals of the same species. It ought, however, to be remarked, that in all the figures and descriptions I have hitherto met with of the bird now before us, the iris is represented of a bright golden color; but, in all the specimens I have shot, I uniformly found the eye very dark, almost black, resembling a globe of black glass. No doubt the golden color of the iris would give the figure of the bird a more striking appearance ; but, in works of natural history, to sacrifice truth to mere picturesque effect is detestable, though, I fear, but too often put in practice.

The nest of this species is usually built in a hollow tree ; generally pretty high up, where the top, or a large limb, has been broken off. I have never seen its eggs ; but have been told that the female generally lays four or five, which are of a light brownish yellow color, spotted with a darker tint; the young are fed on grasshoppers, mice, and small birds, the usual food of the parents.

The habits and manners of this bird are well known. It flies rather irregularly, occasionally suspending itself in the air, hovering over a particular spot for a minute or two, and then shooting off in another direction. It perches on the top of a dead tree or pole, in the middle of a field or meadow, and, as it alights, shuts its long wings so suddenly, that they seem instantly to disappear ; it sits here in an almost perpendicular position, sometimes for an hour at a time, frequently jerking its tail, and reconnoitring the ground below, in every direction, for mice, lizards, &c. It approaches the farm-house, particularly in the morning, skulking about the barn-yard for mice or young chickens. It frequently plunges into a thicket after small birds, as if by random, but always with a particular, and generally a fatal, aim. One day I observed a bird of this species perched on the highest top of a large poplar, on the skirts of the wood, and was in the act of raising the gun to my eye, when he swept down, with the rapidity of an arrow, into a thicket of briers, about thirty yards off, where I shot him dead, and, on coming up, found the small Field Sparrow (Fig. 72) quivering in his grasp. Both our aims had been taken in the same instant, and, unfortunately for him, both were fatal. It is particularly fond of watching along hedge-rows, and in orchards, where those small birds represented in the same plate usually resort. When grasshoppers are plenty, they form a considerable part of its food.

Though small snakes, mice, lizards, &c., be favorite morsels with this active bird, yet we are not to suppose it altogether destitute of delicacy in feeding. It will seldom or never eat of any thing that it has not itself killed, and even that, if not (as epicures would term it) *in good eating order*, is sometimes rejected. A very respectable friend, through the medium of Mr. Bartram, informs me, that one morning he observed one of these Hawks dart down on the ground, and seize a mouse, which he carried to a fence post, where, after examining it for some time, he left it, and, a little while after, pounced upon another mouse, which he instantly carried off to his nest, in the hollow of a tree hard by. The gentleman, anxious to know why the Hawk had rejected the first mouse, went up to it, and found it to be almost covered with lice, and greatly emaciated! Here was not only delicacy of taste, but sound and prudent reasoning:—If I carry this to my nest, thought he, it will fill it with vermin, and hardly be worth eating.

The Blue Jays have a particular antipathy to this bird, and frequently insult it by following and imitating its notes so exactly, as to deceive even those well acquainted with both. In return for all this abuse, the Hawk contents himself with, now and then, feasting on the plumpest of his persecutors, who are, therefore, in perpetual dread of him; and yet, through some strange infatuation, or from fear that, if they lose sight of him, he may attack them unawares, the Sparrow Hawk no sooner appears than the alarm is given, and the whole posse of Jays follow.

The female of this species, which is here faithfully represented from a very beautiful living specimen, furnished by a particular friend, is eleven inches long, and twenty-three from tip to tip of the expanded wings. The cere and legs are yellow ; bill, blue, tipped with black ; space round the eye, greenish blue ; iris, deep dusky ; head, bluish ash ; crown, rufous ; seven spots of black on a white ground surround the head, in the manner represented in the figure ; whole upper parts reddish bay, transversely streaked with black ; primary and secondary quills, black, spotted on their inner vanes with brownish white ; whole lower parts, yellowish white, marked with longitudinal streaks of brown, except the chin, vent, and femoral feathers, which are white ; claws, black.

The male of this species (which is an inch and a half shorter, has the shoulder of the wings blue, and also the black marks on the head, but is, in other respects, very differently marked from the female) will appear in an early part of the present work, with such other particulars as may be thought worthy of communicating.*

* See description of male, and note, in a subsequent part of this work.

15 *

FIELD SPARROW.* — FRINGILLA PUSILLA. — Fig. 72.

Passer agrestis, *Bartram*, p. 291. — *Peale's Museum*, No. 6560.

EMBERIZA PUSILLA. — Jardine, Sw. MSS.

Fringilla pusilla, *Bonap. Synop.* p. 110.

This is the smallest of all our Sparrows, and, in Pennsylvania, is generally migratory. It arrives early in April, frequents dry fields covered with long grass, builds a small nest on the ground, generally at the foot of a brier; lines it with horse hair; lays six eggs, so thickly sprinkled with ferruginous, as to appear altogether of that tint; and raises two, and often three, broods in a season. It is more frequently found in the middle of fields and orchards than any of the other species, which usually lurk along hedge-rows. It has no song, but a kind of cheruping, not much different from the chirpings of a cricket. Towards fall they assemble in loose flocks, in orchards and corn-fields, in search of the seeds of various rank weeds; and are then very numerous. As the weather becomes severe, with deep snow, they disappear. In the lower parts of North and South Carolina, I found this species in multitudes in the months of January and February. When disturbed, they take to the bushes, clustering so close together, that a dozen may easily be shot at a time. I continued to see them equally numerous through the whole lower parts of Georgia; from whence, according to Mr. Abbot, they all disappear early in the spring.

None of our birds have been more imperfectly described than that family of the Finch tribe usually called Sparrows. They have been considered as too insignificant for particular notice, yet they possess distinct characters, and some of them peculiarities well worthy of notice. They are innocent in their habits, subsisting chiefly on the small seeds of wild plants, and seldom injuring the property of the farmer. In the dreary season of winter, some of them enliven the prospect by hopping familiarly about our doors, humble pensioners on the sweepings of the threshold.

The present species has never before, to my knowledge, been figured. It is five inches and a quarter long, and eight inches broad; bill and legs, a reddish cinnamon color; upper part of the head, deep chestnut, divided by a slight streak of drab, widening as it goes back; cheeks, line over the eye, breast, and sides under the wings, a brownish clay color, lightest on the chin, and darkest on the ear-feathers; a

---

* The American *Bunting Finches* are most puzzling, the forms being constantly intermediate, and never assuming the true type. Mr. Swainson has also felt this, and has been obliged to form a new genus, to contain one portion nearly inadmissible to any of the others. The present species will rank as allied nearest to the Reed Bunting of Europe, *E. schœniculus.* Another, mentioned neither by Wilson nor Bonaparte, has been added by the over-land expedition, — *Emberiza pallida,* Clay-colored Bunting, Sw. and Richard. *North. Zool.* It approaches nearest to *E. socialis,* but differs in wanting the bright rufous crown, and having the ear-feathers brown, margined above and below with a dark edge. — Ed.

small streak of brown at the lower angle of the bill; back, streaked with black, drab, and bright bay, the latter being generally centred with the former; rump, dark drab, or cinereous; wings, dusky black, the primaries edged with whitish, the secondaries bordered with bright bay; greater wing-coverts, black, edged and broadly tipped with brownish white; tail, dusky black, edged with clay color: male and female nearly alike in plumage; the chestnut on the crown of the male rather brighter.

TREE SPARROW. — FRINGILLA ARBOREA. — Fig. 73.

Le Soulciet, *Buff*. iii. 500. — Moineau de Canada, *Briss*. iii. 10ŕ. *Pl. enl.* 223. — *Lath.* ii. 252. — *Edw.* 269. — *Arct. Zool.* p. 373, No. 246. — *Peale's Museum*, No. 6575.

EMBERIZA CANADENSIS. — Swainson.

Fringilla Canadensis, *Bonap. Synop.* p. 109. — Emberiza Canadensis, *North. Zool.* ii. p. 252.

This Sparrow is a native of the north, who takes up his winter quarters in Pennsylvania, and most of the Northern States, as well as several of the Southern ones. He arrives here about the beginning of November, and leaves us again early in April; associates in flocks with the Snow Birds; frequents sheltered hollows, thickets, and hedge-rows, near springs of water; and has a low, warbling note, scarcely audible at the distance of twenty or thirty yards. If disturbed, he takes to trees, like the White-throated Sparrow, but contrary to the habit of most of the others, who are inclined rather to dive into thickets. Mr. Edwards has erroneously represented this as the female of the Mountain Sparrow; but that judicious and excellent naturalist, Mr. Pennant, has given a more correct account of it, and informs us that it inhabits the country bordering on Hudson's Bay during summer; comes to Severn settlement in May; advances farther north to breed; and returns in autumn on its way southward. It also visits Newfoundland.*

By some of our own naturalists, this species has been confounded with the Chipping Sparrow, (Fig. 75,) which it very much resembles, but is larger and handsomer, and is never found with us in summer. The former departs for the south about the same time that the latter arrives from the north; and, from this circumstance, and their general resemblance, has arisen the mistake.

The Tree Sparrow is six inches and a half long, and nine and a half in extent; the whole upper part of the head is of a bright reddish chestnut, sometimes slightly skirted with gray; from the nostrils, over the eye, passes a white strip, fading into pale ash, as it extends back; sides of the neck, chin, and breast, very pale ash; the centre of the breast marked with an obscure spot of dark brown; from the lower

* *Arctic Zoology,* vol. ii. p. 373.

angle of the bill proceeds a slight streak of chestnut; sides, under the wings, pale brown; back, handsomely streaked with pale drab, bright bay, and black; lower part of the back and rump, brownish drab; lesser wing-coverts, black, edged with pale ash; wings, black, broadly edged with bright bay; the first and second row of coverts, tipped with pure white; tail, black, forked, and exteriorly edged with dull white; belly and vent, brownish white; bill, black above, yellow below; legs, a brownish clay color; feet, black. The female is about half an inch shorter; the chestnut or bright bay on the wings, back, and crown, is less brilliant; and the white on the coverts narrower, and not so pure. These are all the differences I can perceive.*

SONG SPARROW. — FRINGILLA MELODIA. — Fig. 74.

Fasciated Finch ? *Arct. Zool.* p. 375, No. 252. — *Peale's Museum*, No. 6573.

EMBERIZA? † *MELODIA.* — Jardine.

Bonap. Synop. p. 108. — The Song Sparrow, *Aud.* pl. 25, *Orn. Biog.* i. p. 126.

So nearly do many species of our Sparrows approximate to each other in plumage, and so imperfectly have they been taken notice of, that it is absolutely impossible to say, with certainty, whether the present species has ever been described or not. And yet, of all our Sparrows, this is the most numerous, the most generally diffused over the United States, and by far the earliest, sweetest, and most lasting songster. It may be said to be partially migratory, many passing to the south in the month of November; and many of them still remaining with us, in low, close, sheltered meadows and swamps, during the whole of winter. It is the first singing bird in spring, taking precedence even of the Pewee and Blue-Bird. Its song continues occasionally during the whole summer and fall, and is sometimes heard even in the depth of winter. The notes, or chant, are short, but very sweet, resembling the beginning of the Canary's song, and frequently repeated, generally from the branches of a bush or small tree, where it sits chanting for an hour together. It is fond of frequenting the borders of rivers, meadows, swamps, and such like watery places; and, if wounded, and unable to fly, will readily take to the water, and swim with considerable rapidity. In the great cypress swamps of the Southern States, in the depth of winter, I observed multitudes of these birds mixed with several other species; for these places appear to be the grand winter rendezvous of almost all our Sparrows. I have found

---

* Peculiar to America, and we should say, going more off from the group than *F. socialis*, Wils., as mentioned by Swainson in the *Northern Zoology.* — ED.

† I have been puzzled where to place this bird — in *Emberiza*, or as a sub-genus of it. There seems much difference in the form of the bill, though it has "a rudiment of the knob." I have been unable to obtain a specimen for comparison. Mr. Swainson thinks it connects the American Bunting with his *Zonotrichia.* — ED.

this bird in every district of the United States, from Canada to the southern boundaries of Georgia; but Mr. Abbot informs me that he knows of only one or two species that remain in that part of Georgia during the summer.

The Song Sparrow builds in the ground, under a tuft of grass; the nest is formed of fine, dry grass, and lined with horse hair; the eggs are four or five, thickly marked with spots of reddish brown, on a white, sometimes bluish white, ground; if not interrupted, raises three broods in the season. I have found his nest with young as early as the 26th of April, and as late as the 12th of August. What is singular, the same bird often fixes his nest in a cedar-tree, five or six feet from the ground. Supposing this to have been a variety, or different species, I have examined the bird, nest, and eggs, with particular care, several times, but found no difference. I have observed the same accidental habit in the Red-winged Blackbird, which sometimes builds among the grass, as well as on alder bushes.

This species is six inches and a half long, and eight and a half in extent; upper part of the head, dark chestnut, divided laterally by a line of pale dirty white; spot at each nostril, yellow ochre; line over the eye, inclining to ash; chin, white; streak from the lower mandible, slit of the mouth, and posterior angle of the eye, dark chestnut; breast, and sides under the wings, thickly marked with long-pointed spots of dark chestnut, centred with black, and running in chains; belly, white; vent, yellow ochre, streaked with brown; back, streaked with black, bay, and pale ochre; tail, brown, rounded at the end, the two middle feathers streaked down their centres with black; legs, flesh colored; wing-coverts, black, broadly edged with bay, and tipped with yellowish white; wings, dark brown. The female is scarcely distinguishable by its plumage from the male. The bill in both, horn colored.

CHIPPING SPARROW. — FRINGILLA SOCIALIS. — Fig. 75.

Passer domesticus, The Little House Sparrow, or Chipping Bird, *Bartram*, p. 291.
— *Peale's Museum*, No. 6571.

EMBERIZA SOCIALIS. — Swainson.

Fringilla socialis, Bonap. Synop. p. 109.

This species, though destitute of the musical talents of the former, is, perhaps, more generally known, because more familiar, and even domestic. He inhabits, during summer, the city, in common with man, building in the branches of the trees with which our streets and gardens are ornamented; and gleaning up crumbs from our yards, and even our doors, to feed his more advanced young with. I have known one of these birds attend regularly every day, during a whole summer, while the family were at dinner, under a piazza, fronting the garden, and pick up the crumbs that were thrown to him. This sociable habit, which continues chiefly during the summer, is a singular characteristic. Towards the end of summer he takes to the fields and hedges, until the weather becomes severe, with snow, when he departs for the south.

The Chipping Bird builds his nest most commonly in a cedar bush, and lines it thickly with cow hair. The female lays four or five eggs, of a light blue color, with a few dots of purplish black near the great end.

This species may easily be distinguished from the four preceding ones by his black bill and frontlet, and by his familiarity in summer; yet, in the months of August and September, when they moult their feathers, the black on the front, and partially on the bill, disappears. The young are also without the black during the first season.

The Chipping Sparrow is five inches and a quarter long, and eight inches in extent; frontlet, black; chin, and line over the eye, whitish; crown, chestnut; breast and sides of the neck, pale ash; bill, in winter, black; in summer, the lower mandible flesh colored; rump, dark ash; belly and vent, white; back, variegated with black and bright bay; wings, black, broadly edged with bright chestnut; tail, dusky, forked, and slightly edged with pale ochre; legs and feet, a pale flesh color. The female differs in having less black on the frontlet, and the bay duller. Both lose the black front in moulting.

----------◆----------

SNOW BIRD.— FRINGILLA HUDSONIA.* — Fig. 76.

Fringilla Hudsonia, *Turton, Syst.* i. 568. — Emberiza hyemalis, *Id.* 531. — *Lath.* i. 66. — *Catesb.* i. 36. — *Arct. Zool.* p. 359, No. 223. — Passer nivalis, *Bartram,* p. 291. — *Peale's Museum,* No. 6532.

FRINGILLA HYEMALIS. — Linnæus.

Fringilla hyemalis, *Bonap. Synop.* p. 109. — *North. Zool.* ii. p. 259. — The Snow Bird, *Aud.* pl. 13, *Orn. Biog.* i. p. 72.

This well-known species, small and insignificant as it may appear, is by far the most numerous, as well as the most extensively disseminated, of all the feathered tribes that visit us from the frozen regions of the north, — their migrations extending from the arctic circle, and, probably, beyond it, to the shores of the Gulf of Mexico, spreading over the whole breadth of the United States, from the Atlantic Ocean to Louisiana; how much farther westward, I am unable to say. About the 20th of October, they make their first appearance in those parts of Pennsylvania east of the Alleghany Mountains. At first they are most generally seen on the borders of woods among the falling and decayed leaves, in loose flocks of thirty or forty together, always taking to the trees when disturbed. As the weather sets in colder,

* *Nivalis* of first edition.

they approach nearer the farm-house and villages; and on the appearance of, what is usually called, falling weather, assemble in larger flocks, and seem doubly diligent in searching for food. This increased activity is generally a sure prognostic of a storm. When deep snows cover the ground, they become almost half domesticated. They collect about the barn, stables, and other out-houses, spread over the yard, and even round the steps of the door; not only in the country and villages, but in the heart of our large cities; crowding around the threshold early in the morning, gleaning up the crumbs; appearing very lively and familiar. They have also recourse, at this severe season, when the face of the earth is shut up from them, to the seeds of many kinds of weeds that still rise above the snow, in corners of fields, and low, sheltered situations, along the borders of creeks and fences, where they associate with several species of Sparrows, particularly those represented in Nos. 72, 73, and 74. They are, at this time, easily caught with almost any kind of trap; are generally fat, and, it is said, are excellent eating.

I cannot but consider this bird as the most numerous of its tribe of any within the United States. From the northern parts of the District * of Maine to the Ogeechee River in Georgia, — a distance, by the circuitous route in which I travelled, of more than 1800 miles, — I never passed a day, and scarcely a mile, without seeing numbers of these birds, and frequently large flocks of several thousands. Other travellers with whom I conversed, who had come from Lexington, in Kentucky, through Virginia, also declared that they found these birds numerous along the whole road. It should be observed that the road-sides are their favorite haunts, where many rank weeds, that grow along the fences, furnish them with food, and the road with gravel. In the vicinity of places where they were most numerous, I observed the Small Hawk, represented in No. 71, and several others of his tribe, watching their opportunity, or hovering cautiously around, making an occasional sweep among them, and retiring to the bare branches of an old cypress to feed on their victims. In the month of April, when the weather begins to be warm, they are observed to retreat to the woods, and to prefer the shaded sides of hills and thickets; at which time the males warble out a few very low, sweet notes, and are almost perpetually pursuing and fighting with each other. About the 20th of April, they take their leave of our humble regions, and retire to the north and to the high ranges of the Alleghany, to build their nests, and rear their young. In some of those ranges, in the interior of Virginia, and northward, about the waters of the west branch of the Susquehanna, they breed in great numbers. The nest is fixed in the ground, or among the grass, sometimes several being within a small distance of each other. According to the observations of the gentlemen residing at Hudson Bay Factory, they arrive there about the beginning of June, stay a week or two, and proceed farther north to breed. They return to that settlement in the autumn, on their way to the south.

In some parts of New England, I found the opinion pretty general that the Snow Bird, in summer, is transformed into the Small Chipping

Now State of Maine.

Sparrow, which we find so common in that season, and which is represented in No. 75. I had convinced a gentleman of New York of his mistake in this matter, by taking him to the house of a Mr. Gautier there, who amuses himself by keeping a great number of native, as well as foreign, birds. This was in the month of July, and the Snow Bird appeared there in the same colored plumage he usually has. Several individuals of the Chipping Sparrow were also in the same apartment. The evidence was, therefore, irresistible; but, as I had not the same proofs to offer to the eye in New England, I had not the same success.

There must be something in the temperature of the blood or constitution of this bird, which unfits it for residing, during summer, in the lower parts of the United States, as the country here abounds with a great variety of food, of which, during its stay, it appears to be remarkably fond. Or, perhaps, its habit of associating in such numbers to breed, and building its nest with so little precaution, may, to insure its safety, require a solitary region, far from the intruding footsteps of man.

The Snow Bird is six inches long, and nine in extent; the head, neck, and upper parts of the breast, body, and wings, are of a deep slate color; the plumage sometimes skirted with brown, which is the color of the young birds; the lower parts of the breast, the whole belly, and vent, are pure white; the three secondary quill-feathers next the body are edged with brown, the primaries with white; the tail is dusky slate, a little forked, the two exterior feathers wholly white, which are flirted out as it flies, and appear then very prominent; the bill and legs are of a reddish flesh color; the eye, bluish black. The female differs from the male in being considerably more brown. In the depth of winter, the slate color of the male becomes more deep, and much purer, the brown disappearing nearly altogether.

PINE FINCH. — FRINGILLA PINUS. — Fig. 77.

Peale's Museum, No. 6577.

CARDUELIS PINUS. — Swainson.

Fringilla pinus, (sub-genus Carduelis,) *Bonap. Synop.* p. 111.

This little northern stranger visits us in the month of November, and seeks the seeds of the black alder on the borders of swamps, creeks, and rivulets. As the weather becomes more severe, and the seeds of the *Pinus Canadensis* are fully ripe, these birds collect in larger flocks, and take up their residence almost exclusively among these trees. In the gardens of Bush Hill, in the neighborhood of Philadelphia, a flock of two or three hundred of these birds have regularly wintered many years; where a noble avenue of pine-trees, and walks covered with fine, white gravel, furnish them with abundance through the winter. Early in March, they disappear, either to the north or to the pine woods that cover many lesser ranges of the Alleghany. While here, they are often so tame as to allow you to walk within a few yards of the spot where a whole flock of them are sitting. They flutter among the branches, frequently hanging by the cones, and uttering a note almost exactly like that of the Goldfinch, (*F. tristis*.) I have not a doubt but this bird appears in a richer dress in summer in those places where he breeds, as he has so very great a resemblance to the bird above mentioned, with whose changes we are well acquainted.

The length of this species is four inches; breadth, eight inches; upper part of the head, the neck, and back, a dark flaxen color, streaked with black; wings black, marked with two rows of dull white or cream color; whole wing-quills, under the coverts, rich yellow, appearing even when the wings are shut; rump and tail-coverts, yellowish, streaked with dark brown; tail-feathers, rich yellow from the roots half way to the tips, except the two middle ones, which are blackish brown, slightly edged with yellow; sides, under the wings, of a cream color, with long streaks of black; breast, a light flaxen color, with small streaks or pointed spots of black; legs, purplish brown; bill, a dull horn color; eyes, hazel. The female was scarcely distinguishable by its plumage from the male. The New York Siskin of Pennant * appears to be only the Yellow-Bird (*Fringilla tristis*) in his winter dress.

This bird has a still greater resemblance to the Siskin of Europe, (*F. spinus*,) and may, perhaps, be the species described by Turton † as the Black Mexican Siskin, which he says is varied above with black and yellowish, and is white beneath, and which is also said to sing finely. This change from flaxen to yellow is observable in the Goldfinch; and no other two birds of our country resemble each other more than these do in their winter dresses. Should these surmises be found correct, a figure of this bird, in his summer dress, shall appear in some future part of our work. ‡

---

* *Arctic Zoology*, p. 372, No. 243.   † TURTON, vol. i. p. 560.

‡ This is a true Siskin; and we have a very accurate description of the general manners of the group in those of the individual now described by Wilson. Little seems to be known of their summer haunts; and, indeed, the more northern species remain in the same obscurity. They generally all migrate, go north to breed, and winter in southern latitudes. The species of Great Britain and Europe performs a like migration, assembling in very large flocks during winter, feeding upon seeds, &c., and retiring north to breed. A few pairs, not performing the migration to its utmost northern extent, breed in the larger pine woods in the Highlands of Scotland. In 1829, they were met with in June, in a large fir wood at Killin, evidently breeding; last year, they were known to breed in an extensive wood at New Abbey, in Galloway. In their winter migrations, they are not regular, particular districts being visited by them at uncertain periods. In Annandale, Dumfriesshire, they were always accounted rare, and the first pair I ever saw there was shot in 1827. Early in October, as the winter advanced, very large flocks arrived, and fed chiefly upon the rag-weed, and under some large beech-trees, turning over the fallen mast, and eating part of the kernels, as well as any seeds they could find among them. In 1828, they again appeared; but in 1829, not one was seen; and the present winter, (1830,) they are equally wanting. The plate of our author is that of the bird in its winter dress. As he justly observes, the plumage becomes much richer during the season of incubation. The black parts become brighter and deeper, and the olive of a yellower green. — ED.

16

ROSE-BREASTED GROSBEAK.* — LOXIA ROSEA. — Fig. 78.

Loxia Ludoviciana, *Turton's Syst.* — Red-breasted Grosbeak, *Arct. Zool.* p. 350, No. 212. — Red-breasted Finch, *Id.* 372, No. 245. — Le rose gorge, *Buff.* iii. 460. — Gros-bec de la Louisiane, *Pl. enl.* 153, fig. 2. — *Lath.* ii. 126. — *Peale's Museum,* No. 5806, male; 5807, female; 5806, A, male of one year old.

GUIRACA LUDOVICIANA. — Swainson.

Fringilla (sub-genus Coccothraustes) Ludoviciana, *Bonap. Synop.* p. 113. — Coccothraustes (Guiraca) Ludoviciana, *North. Zool.* i. p. 271.

THIS elegant species is rarely found in the lower parts of Pennsylvania; in the state of New York, and those of New England, it is more frequently observed, particularly in fall, when the berries of the sour gum are ripe, on the kernels of which it eagerly feeds. Some of its trivial names would import that it is also an inhabitant of Louisiana; but I have not heard of its being seen in any of the Southern States. A gentleman of Middletown, Connecticut, informed me that he kept one of these birds for some considerable time in a cage, and observed that it frequently sang at night, and all night; that its notes were extremely clear and mellow, and the sweetest of any bird with which he is acquainted.

The bird from which the figure on the plate was taken, was shot, late in April, on the borders of a swamp, a few miles from Philadelphia. Another male of the same species was killed at the same time, considerably different in its markings; a proof that they do not acquire their full colors until at least the second spring or summer.

The Rose-breasted Grosbeak is eight inches and a half long, and thirteen inches in extent; the whole upper parts are black, except the second row of wing-coverts, which are broadly tipped with white; a spot of the same extends over the primaries, immediately below their coverts; chin, neck, and upper part of the breast, black; lower part of the breast, middle of the belly, and lining of the wings, a fine light carmine, or rose color; tail, forked, black, the three exterior feathers, on each side, white on their inner vanes for an inch or more from the tips; bill, like those of its tribe, very thick and strong, and pure white; legs and feet, light blue; eyes, hazel. The young male of the first spring has the plumage of the back variegated with light brown, white

* This species seems to have been described, under various specific names, by various authors. Wilson, in the body of his work, calls it *L. rosea;* but he corrects that name afterwards in the index, and restores that by which it must now stand. The generic appellation has also been various, and the necessity of some decided one cannot be better shown, than in the different opinions expressed by naturalists, who have placed it in three or four of the known genera, without being very well satisfied with any of its situations. Gmelin and Latham have even placed the young and old in different genera, *Loxia* and *Fringilla;* by Brisson, it is a *Coccothraustes;* and by Sabine, a *Phyrrhula.* It appears a form exclusively American, supplanting the *Coccothraustes* of Asia and the Indian continent, and *Guiraca* has been appropriated to it by Mr. Swainson, in which will also range the Cardinal and Blue Grosbeaks of our author. — ED.

and black; a line of white extends over the eye; the rose color also reaches to the base of the bill, where it is speckled with black and white. The female is of a light yellowish, flaxen color, streaked with dark olive, and whitish; the breast is streaked with olive, pale flaxen, and white; the lining of the wings is pale yellow; the bill, more dusky than in the male, and the white on the wing less.

BLACK-THROATED GREEN WARBLER. — SYLVIA VIRENS. —
Fig. 79.

Motacilla virens, *Gmel. Syst.* i. p. 985. — Le Figuier à cravate noire, *Buff.* v. p. 298. — Black-throated Green Flycatcher, *Edw.* t. 300. — Green Warbler, *Arct. Zool.* ii. No. 297. — *Lath. Syn.* iv. p. 434, 108. — *Turton, Syst.* p. 607 — Parus viridis gutture nigro, The Green Black-throated Flycatcher, *Bartram*, p. 292.

SYLVICOLA VIRENS. — Swainson.

Sylvia virens, *Bonap. Synop.* p. 80.

This is one of those transient visitors that pass through Pennsylvania, in the latter part of April and beginning of May, on their way to the north to breed. It generally frequents the high branches and tops of trees, in the woods, in search of the *larvæ* of insects that prey on the opening buds. It has a few singular cheruping notes; and is very lively and active. About the 10th of May it disappears. It is rarely observed on its return in the fall, which may probably be owing to the scarcity of its proper food at that season obliging it to pass with greater haste; or to the foliage, which prevents it and other passengers from being so easily observed. Some few of these birds, however, remain all summer in Pennsylvania, having myself shot three this season, (1809,) in the month of June; but I have never yet seen their nest.

This species is four inches and three quarters long, and seven broad; the whole back, crown, and hind head, is of a rich yellowish green; front, cheek, sides of the breast, and line over the eye, yellow; chin and throat, black; sides, under the wings, spotted with black; belly and vent, white; wings, dusky black, marked with two white bars; bill, black; legs and feet, brownish yellow; tail, dusky, edged with light ash; the three exterior feathers spotted on their inner webs with white. The female is distinguished by having no black on the throat.

YELLOW–RUMPED WARBLER. — SYLVIA CORONATA. —
Fig. 80.

Motacilla maculosa, *Gmel. Syst.* i. p. 984. — Motacilla coronata, *Linn. Syst.* i. p.
332, No. 31. — Le Figuier à tête cendrée, *Buff.* v. p. 291. — Le Figuier couronné
d'or, *Id.* v. p. 312. — Yellow-Rump Flycatcher, *Edw.* t. 255. — Golden-crowned
Flycatcher, *Id.* t. 298. — Yellow-Rump Warbler, *Arct. Zool.* ii. No. 288. — Golden-
crowned Warbler, *Id.* ii. No. 294. — *Lath. Syn.* iv. p. 481, No. 104. *Id. Supp.* p.
182. *Id. Syn.* iv. p. 486, No. 11. — *Turton*, p. 599, *Id.* 606. — Parus cedrus uro-
pygio flavo. — The Yellow Rump. *Bartram*, p. 292. — Parus aurio vertice. —
The Golden-Crown Flycatcher, *Id.* 292. — *Peale's Museum*, No. 7134.

SYLVICOLA CORONATA. — Swainson.

Sylvia coronata, *Bonap. Synop.* p. 77, (summer plumage.*) — Sylvicola coronata,
North. Zool. ii. p. 216.

In this beautiful little species we have another instance of the mistakes occasioned by the change of color to which many of our birds
are subject. In the present case this change is both progressive and
periodical. The young birds of the first season are of a brown olive
above, which continues until the month of February and March;
about which time it gradually changes into a fine slate color, as in Fig.
80. About the middle of April this change is completed. I have
shot them in all their gradations of change. While in their brown
olive dress, the yellow on the sides of the breast and crown is scarcely
observable, unless the feathers be parted with the hand; but that on
the rump is still vivid; the spots of black on the cheek are then also
obscured. The difference of appearance, however, is so great, that
we need scarcely wonder that foreigners, who have no opportunity of
examining the progress of these variations, should have concluded
them to be two distinct species, and designated them as in the above
synonymes.

This bird is also a passenger through Pennsylvania. Early in October he arrives from the north, in his olive dress, and frequents the
cedar-trees, devouring the berries with great avidity. He remains
with us three or four weeks, and is very numerous wherever there are
trees of the red cedar covered with berries. He leaves us for the
south, and spends the winter season among the myrtle swamps of Virginia, the Carolinas, and Georgia. The berries of the *Myrica cerifera*,
both the large and dwarf kind, are his particular favorites. On those
of the latter I found them feeding, in great numbers, near the sea-
shore, in the District of Maine, in October; and through the whole of
the lower parts of the Carolinas, wherever the myrtles grew, these
birds were numerous, skipping about, with hanging wings, among the
bushes. In those parts of the country, they are generally known by
the name of Myrtle Birds. Round Savannah, and beyond it as far as
the Altamaha, I found him equally numerous, as late as the middle of
March, when his change of color had considerably progressed to the
slate hue. Mr. Abbot, who is well acquainted with this change, assured
me, that they attain this rich slate color fully before their departure

* Winter plumage, Fig. 187.

from thence, which is about the last of March, and to the 10th of April. About the middle or 20th of the same month, they appear in Pennsylvania, in full dress, as represented in Fig. 80; and after continuing to be seen, for a week or ten days, skipping among the high branches and tops of the trees, after those larvæ that feed on the opening buds, they disappear until the next October. Whether they retire to the north, or to the high ranges of our mountains to breed, like many other of our passengers, is yet uncertain. They are a very numerous species, and always associate together in considerable numbers, both in spring, winter, and fall.

This species is five inches and a half long, and eight inches broad; whole back, tail-coverts, and hind head, a fine slate color, streaked with black; crown, sides of the breast, and rump, rich yellow; wings and tail, black; the former crossed with two bars of white, the three exterior feathers of the latter, spotted with white; cheeks and front, black; chin, line over and under the eye, white; breast, light slate, streaked with black, extending under the wings; belly and vent, white, the latter spotted with black; bill and legs, black. This is the spring and summer dress of the male; that of the female of the same season differs but little, chiefly in the colors being less vivid, and not so strongly marked with a tincture of brownish on the back.

In the month of October the slate color has changed to a brownish olive; the streaks of black are also considerably brown, and the white is stained with the same color; the tail-coverts, however, still retain their slaty hue; the yellow on the crown and sides of the breast becomes nearly obliterated. Their only note is a kind of chip, occasionally repeated; their motions are quick, and one can scarcely ever observe them at rest.

Though the form of the bill of this bird obliges me to arrange him with the Warblers, yet, in his food and all his motions, he is decidedly a Flycatcher.

On again recurring to the descriptions in Pennant of the " Yellow-Rump Warbler," * " Golden-crowned Warbler,"† and " Belted Warble.,"‡ I am persuaded that the whole three have been drawn from the present species.

CERULEAN WARBLER. — SYLVIA CŒRULEA. — Fig. 81.

Peale's Museum, No. 7309.

SYLVICOLA CŒRULEA. — Swainson. — Male.

Sylvia azurea, *Bonap. Synop.* p. 85. — Sylvia azurea, Azure Warbler, *Steph. Sh. Zool.* x. p. 653. — Sylvia cœrulea, Cerulean Warbler, *Steph. Sh. Zool.* x. p. 652. — Sylvia bifasciata, *Say, Journ. to Rocky Mount.* i. p. 170. — The Azure Warbler, Sylvia azurea, *Aud.* pl. 48, male and female, *Orn. Biog.* i. p. 255.

This delicate little species is now, for the first time, introduced to public notice. Except my friend, Mr. Peale, I know of no other natu-

* *Arctic Zoology*, p. 400, No. 188.   † *Ibid.* No. 294.   ‡ *Ibid.* No. 306.
16 *

ralist who seems to have hitherto known of its existence. At what time it arrives from the south I cannot positively say, as I never met with it in spring, but have several times found it during summer. On the borders of streams and marshes, among the branches of the poplar, it is sometimes to be found. It has many of the habits of the Flycatcher; though, like the preceding, from the formation of its bill, we must arrange it with the Warblers. It is one of our scarce birds in Pennsylvania, and its nest has hitherto eluded my search. I have never observed it after the 20th of August, and therefore suppose it retires early to the south.

This bird is four inches and a half long, and seven and a half broad; the front and upper part of the head is of a fine verditer blue; the hind head and back, of the same color, but not quite so brilliant; a few lateral streaks of black mark the upper part of the back; wings and tail, black, edged with sky blue; the three secondaries next the body, edged with white, and the first and second row of coverts also tipped with white; tail-coverts, large, black, and broadly tipped with blue; lesser wing-coverts, black, also broadly tipped with blue, so as to appear nearly wholly of that tint; sides of the breast, spotted or streaked with blue; belly, chin, and throat, pure white; the tail is forked, the five lateral feathers on each side with each a spot of white; the two middle more slightly marked with the same; from the eye backwards extends a line of dusky blue; before and behind the eye, a line of white; bill, dusky above, light blue below; legs and feet, light blue.

SOLITARY FLYCATCHER. — MUSCICAPA SOLITARIA. —
Fig. 82.

VIREO SOLITARIUS. — Vieillot.

Vireo solitarius, *Bonap. Synop.* p. 70.

This rare species I can find nowhere described. I have myself never seen more than three of them, all of whom corresponded in their markings; and, on dissection, were found to be males. It is a silent, solitary bird. It is also occasionally found in the state of Georgia, where I saw a drawing of it in the possession of Mr. Abbot, who considered it a very scarce species. He could give me no information of the female. The one from which Fig. 82 was taken, was shot in Mr. Bartram's woods, near Philadelphia, among the branches of dogwood, in the month of October. It appears to belong to a particular family, or subdivision of the *Muscicapa* genus, among which are the White-eyed, the Yellow-throated, and several others already described in the present work. Why one species should be so rare, while another, much resembling it, is so numerous, at least a thousand for one, is a question I am unable to answer, unless by supposing the few we meet with here to be accidental stragglers from the great body which may have their residence in some other parts of our extensive continent.

The Solitary Flycatcher is five inches long, and eight inches in breadth; cheeks, and upper part of the head and neck, a fine bluish gray; breast, pale cinereous; flanks and sides of the breast, yellow; whole back and tail-coverts, green olive; wings, nearly black; the first and second row of coverts, tipped with white; the three secondaries next the body, edged with pale yellowish white; the rest of the quills, bordered with light green; tail, slightly forked, of the same tint as the wings, and edged with light green; from the nostrils a line of white proceeds to and encircles the eye; lores, black; belly and vent, white; upper mandible, black; lower, light blue; legs and feet, light blue; eyes, hazel.

COW BUNTING.* — EMBERIZA PECORIS. — Figs. 83, 84, 85.

Le Brunet, *Buff.* iv. 138. — Le Pinçon do Virginie, *Briss.* iii. 165. — Cow-Pen Bird, *Catesb.* i. 34. — *Lath.* ii. 269. — *Arct. Zool.* p. 371, No. 241. — Sturnus stercorarius, *Bartram*, p. 291. — *Peale's Museum*, No. 6378, male; 6379, female.

MOLOTHRUS PECORIS. — Swainson.

Fringilla pecoris, *Sab. Frank. Journ.* p. 676. — Sturnus junceti, *Lath. Ind. Orn.* — Emberiza pecoris, *Bonap. Nomencl.* No. 89. — Icterus pecoris, *Bonap. Synop.* p. 53. — Aglaius pecoris, *Sw. Synop. Birds of Mex. Phil. Mag.* June, 1827, p. 436. — The Cow-Pen Bird, *Aud.* pl. 99, *Orn. Biog.* i. p. 493. — Molothrus pecoris, *North. Zool.* ii. p. 277.

There is one striking peculiarity in the works of the great Creator, which becomes more amazing the more we reflect on it; namely, that he has formed no species of animals so minute, or obscure, that are not invested with certain powers and peculiarities, both of outward conformation and internal faculties, exactly suited to their pursuits, sufficient to distinguish them from all others; and forming for them a character solely and exclusively their own. This is particularly so among the feathered race. If there be any case where these characteristic features are not evident, it is owing to our want of observation; to our little intercourse with that particular tribe; or to that contempt for inferior animals, and all their habitudes, which is but too general, and which bespeaks a morose, unfeeling, and unreflecting mind. These peculiarities are often surprising, always instructive where understood, and (as in the subject of our present chapter) at least amusing, and worthy of being further investigated.†

* The American Cuckoo (*Cuculus Carolinensis*) is by many people called the Cow Bird, from the sound of its notes resembling the words *Cow, cow.* This bird builds its own nest very artlessly in a cedar or an apple-tree, and lays four greenish blue eggs, which it hatches, and rears its young with great tenderness.

† In this curious species, we have another instance of those wonderful provisions of Nature, which have hitherto baffled the knowledge and perseverance of man to discover for what uses they were intended. The only authenticated instance of a like circumstance that we are aware of, is in the economy of the Common Cuckoo of Europe. Some foreign species, which rank as true *Cuculi*, are said to deposit their eggs in the nests of other birds; but I am not sure that the fact is confirmed. With regard to the birds in question, there is little common between them, except

The most remarkable trait in the character of this species is, the unaccountable practice it has of dropping its eggs into the nests of other birds, instead of building and hatching for itself; and thus entirely abandoning its progeny to the care and mercy of strangers. More than two thousand years ago, it was well known, in those countries where the bird inhabits, that the Cuckoo of Europe (*Cuculus canorus*) never built herself a nest, but dropped her eggs in the nests of other birds; but, among the thousands of different species that spread over that and other parts of the globe, no other instance of the same uniform habit has been found to exist, until discovered in the bird now before us. Of the reality of the former there is no doubt; it is known to every school-boy in Britain; of the truth of the latter I can myself speak with confidence, from personal observation, and from the testimony of gentlemen, unknown to each other, residing in different and distant parts of the United States. The circumstances by which I became first acquainted with this peculiar habit of the bird are as follows: —

I had, in numerous instances, found, in the nests of three or four particular species of birds, one egg, much larger, and differently marked from those beside it; I had remarked, that these odd-looking eggs were all of the same color, and marked nearly in the same manner, in whatever nest they lay, though frequently the eggs beside them were of a quite different tint; and I had also been told, in a vague way, that the Cow Bird laid in other birds' nests. At length I detected the female of this very bird in the nest of the Red-eyed Flycatcher, which nest is very small, and very singularly constructed. Suspecting her purpose, I cautiously withdrew without disturbing her; and had the satisfaction to find, on my return, that the egg which she had just dropped corresponded as nearly as eggs of the same species usually do, in its size, tint, and markings, to those formerly taken notice of. Since that time, I have found the young Cow Bunting, in many instances, in the nests of one or other of these small birds; I have seen these last followed by the young Cow Bird calling out clamorously for food, and often engaged in feeding it; and I have now, in a cage before me, a very fine one, which, six months ago, I took from the nest of the Maryland Yellow-Throat, and from which the figures of the young bird and male Cow Bird in the plate were taken: the figure in the act of feeding it, is the female Maryland Yellow-Throat, in whose nest it was found. I claim, however, no merit for a discovery not originally my own, these singular habits having long

that both are migratory, and both deposit their eggs in the nest of an alien. The Cow Bunting is polygamous; and I strongly suspect that our Cuckoo is the same. In the deposition of the egg, the mode of procedure is nearly similar; great uneasiness, and a sort of fretting, previously, with a calm of quiet satisfaction afterwards. In both species we have beautiful provisions to insure the non-disturbance of the intruder by its foster-progeny: in the one, by a greater strength, easily overcoming and driving out the natural but more tender young; in all love of the natural offspring being destroyed in the parents, and succeeded by a powerful desire to preserve and rear to maturity the usurper of their rights: in the other, where the young would, in some instances, be of a like size and strength, and where a combat might prove fatal in an opposite direction to the intentions of Providence, all necessity of contest is at once avoided by the eggs of the Cow Bunting requiring a shorter period to hatch than any of the birds chosen as foster-parents. — ED.

been known to people of observation resident in the country, whose information, in this case, has preceded that of all our school philosophers and closet naturalists, to whom the matter has, till now, been totally unknown.

About the 25th of March, or early in April, the Cow-Pen Bird makes his first appearance in Pennsylvania from the south, sometimes in company with the Red-winged Blackbird, more frequently in detached parties, resting early in the morning, an hour at a time, on the tops of trees near streams of water, appearing solitary, silent, and fatigued. They continue to be occasionally seen, in small, solitary parties, particularly along creeks and banks of rivers, so late as the middle of June; after which, we see no more of them until about the beginning or middle of October, when they reappear in much larger flocks, generally accompanied by numbers of the Redwings; between whom and the present species there is a considerable similarity of manners, dialect, and personal resemblance. In these aerial voyages, like other experienced navigators, they take advantage of the direction of the wind, and always set out with a favorable gale. My venerable and observing friend, Mr. Bartram, writes me, on the 13th of October, as follows:—"The day before yesterday, at the height of the north-east storm, prodigious numbers of the Cow-Pen Birds came by us, in several flights of some thousands in a flock; many of them settled on trees in the garden to rest themselves, and then resumed their voyage southwards. There were a few of their *cousins*, the Redwings, with them. We shot three, a male and two females."

From the early period at which these birds pass in the spring, it is highly probable that their migrations extend very far north. Those which pass in the months of March and April can have no opportunity of depositing their eggs here, there being not more than one or two of our small birds which build so early. Those that pass in May and June are frequently observed loitering singly about solitary thickets, reconnoitring, no doubt, for proper nurses, to whose care they may commit the hatching of their eggs, and the rearing of their helpless orphans. Among the birds selected for this duty are the following, all of which are figured and described in this volume:—The Blue-Bird, which builds in a hollow tree; the Chipping Sparrow, in a cedar bush; the Golden-crowned Thrush, on the ground, in the shape of an oven; the Red-eyed Flycatcher, a neat, pensile nest, hung by the two upper edges on a small sapling, or drooping branch; the Yellow-Bird, in the fork of an alder; the Maryland Yellow-Throat, on the ground, at the roots of brier bushes; the White-eyed Flycatcher, a pensile nest on the bending of a smilax vine; and the small Blue-gray Flycatcher, also a pensile nest, fastened to the slender twigs of a tree, sometimes at the height of fifty or sixty feet from the ground. The three last-mentioned nurses are represented on the same plate with the bird now under consideration. There are, no doubt, others to whom the same charge is committed; but all these I have myself met with acting in that capacity.

Among these, the Yellow-Throat and the Red-eyed Flycatcher appear to be particular favorites; and the kindness and affectionate attention which these two little birds seem to pay to their nurslings, fully justify the partiality of the parents.

It is well known to those who have paid attention to the manners of birds, that, after their nest is fully finished, a day or two generally elapses before the female begins to lay. This delay is in most cases necessary to give firmness to the yet damp materials, and allow them time to dry. In this state it is sometimes met with, and laid in by the Cow Bunting; the result of which I have invariably found to be the desertion of the nest by its rightful owner, and the consequent loss of the egg thus dropped in it by the intruder. But when the owner herself has begun to lay, and there are one or more eggs in the nest before the Cow Bunting deposits hers, the attachment of the proprietor is secured, and remains unshaken until incubation is fully performed, and the little stranger is able to provide for itself.

The well-known practice of the young Cuckoo of Europe in turning out all the eggs and young which it feels around it, almost as soon as it is hatched, has been detailed in a very satisfactory and amusing manner by the amiable Dr. Jenner,* who has since risen to immortal celebrity in a much nobler pursuit; and to whose genius and humanity the whole human race are under everlasting obligations. In our Cow Bunting, though no such habit has been observed, yet still there is something mysterious in the disappearance of the nurse's own eggs soon after the foundling is hatched, which happens regularly before all the rest. From twelve to fourteen days is the usual time of incubation with our small birds; but although I cannot exactly fix the precise period requisite for the egg of the Cow Bunting, I think I can say almost positively, that it is a day or two less than the shortest of the above-mentioned spaces! In this singular circumstance, we see a striking provision of the Deity; for did this egg require a day or two more, instead of so much less, than those among which it has been dropped, the young it contained would in every instance most inevitably perish; and thus, in a few years, the whole species must become extinct. On the first appearance of the young Cow Bunting, the parent being frequently obliged to leave the nest to provide sustenance for the foundling, the business of incubation is thus necessarily interrupted; the disposition to continue it abates; nature has now given a new direction to the zeal of the parent; and the remaining eggs, within a day or two at most, generally disappear. In some instances, indeed, they have been found on the ground near, or below, the nest; but this is rarely the case.

I have never known more than one egg of the Cow Bunting dropped in the same nest. This egg is somewhat larger than that of the Blue-Bird, thickly sprinkled with grains of pale brown on a dirty white ground. It is of a size proportionable to that of the bird.

So extraordinary and unaccountable is this habit, that I have sometimes thought it might not be general among the whole of this species in every situation; that the extreme heat of our summers, though suitable enough for their young, might be too much for the comfortable residence of the parents; that, therefore, in their way to the north, through our climate, they were induced to secure suitable places for their progeny; and that in the regions where they more generally pass the summer, they might perhaps build nests for themselves, and

* See *Philosophical Transactions* for 1788, part ii.

rear their own young, like every other species around them. On the other hand, when I consider that many of them tarry here so late as the middle of June, dropping their eggs, from time to time, into every convenient receptacle — that in the states of Virginia, Maryland, Delaware, New Jersey, and Pennsylvania, they uniformly retain the same habits — and, in short, that in all these places I have never yet seen or heard of their nest, — reasoning from these facts, I think I may safely conclude that they never build one ; and that in those remote northern regions their manners are the same as we find them here.

What reason Nature may have for this extraordinary deviation from her general practice is, I confess, altogether beyond my comprehension. There is nothing singular to be observed in the anatomical structure of the bird that would seem to prevent or render it incapable of incubation. The extreme heat of our climate is probably one reason why, in the months of July and August, they are rarely to be seen here. Yet we have many other migratory birds that regularly pass through Pennsylvania to the north, leaving a few residents behind them, who, without exception, build their own nests and rear their own young. This part of the country also abounds with suitable food, such as they usually subsist on. Many conjectures indeed might be formed as to the probable cause ; but all of them that have occurred to me are unsatisfactory and inconsistent. Future and more numerous observations, made with care, particularly in those countries where they most usually pass the summer, may throw more light on this matter ; till then, we can only rest satisfied with the reality of the fact.

This species winters regularly in the lower parts of North and South Carolina and Georgia ; I have also met with them near Williamsburg, and in several other parts of Virginia. In January, 1809, I observed strings of them for sale in the market of Charleston, South Carolina. They often frequent corn and rice fields, in company with their cousins, as Mr. Bartram calls them, the Red-winged Blackbirds ; but are more commonly found accompanying the cattle, feeding on the seeds, worms, &c., which they pick up amongst the fodder, and from the excrements of the cattle, which they scratch up for this purpose. Hence they have pretty generally obtained the name of *Cow-Pen Birds, Cow Birds,* or *Cow Blackbirds.* By the naturalists of Europe they have hitherto been classed with the Finches, though improperly, as they have no family resemblance to that tribe, sufficient to justify that arrangement. If we are to be directed by the conformation of their bill, nostrils, tongue, and claws, we cannot hesitate a moment in classing them with the Red-winged Blackbirds, *Oriolus phœniceus ;* not, however, as Orioles, but as Buntings, or some new intermediate genus ; the notes or dialect of the Cow Bunting and those of the Redwings, as well as some other peculiarities of voice and gesticulation, being strikingly similar.

Respecting this extraordinary bird, I have received communications from various quarters, all corroborative of the foregoing particulars. Among these is a letter from Dr. Potter, of Baltimore, which, as it contains some new and interesting facts, and several amusing incidents, illustrative of the character of the bird, I shall with pleasure lay before the reader, apologizing to the obliging writer for a few unimportant omissions which have been anticipated in the preceding pages.

"I regret exceedingly that professional avocations have put it out of my power to have replied earlier to your favor of the 19th of September; and although I shall not now reflect all the light you desire, a faithful transcript from memoranda, noted at the moment of observation, may not be altogether uninteresting.

"The *Fringilla pecoris* is generally known in Maryland by the name of the Cow Blackbird; and none but the naturalist view it as a distinct species. It appears about the last of March, or first week in April, though sometimes a little earlier, when the spring is unusually forward. It is less punctual in its appearance than many other of our migratory birds.

"It commonly remains with us till about the last of October, though unusually cold weather sometimes banishes it much earlier. It, however, sometimes happens that a few of them remain with us all winter, and are seen hovering about our barns and farm-yards when straitened for sustenance by snow or hard frost. It is remarkable that in some years I have not been able to discover one of them during the months of July and August; when they have suddenly appeared in September in great numbers. I have noticed this fact always immediately after a series of very hot weather, and then only. The general opinion is, that they then retire to the deep recesses of the shady forest; but, if this had been the fact, I should probably have discovered them in my rambles in every part of the woods. I think it more likely that they migrate farther north, till they find a temperature more congenial to their feelings, or find a richer repast in following the cattle in a better pasture.*

"In autumn, we often find them congregated with the Marsh Blackbirds, committing their common depredations upon the ears of the Indian corn; and at other seasons, the similarity of their pursuits in feeding introduces them into the same company. I could never observe that they would keep the company of any other bird.

"The Cow-Pen Finch differs, moreover, in another respect, from all the birds with which I am acquainted. After an observance of many years, I could never discover any thing like *pairing*, or a mutual attachment between the sexes. Even in the season of love, when other birds are separated into pairs, and occupied in the endearing office of providing a receptacle for their offspring, the *Fringillæ* are seen feeding in odd as well as even numbers, from one to twenty, and discovering no more disposition towards perpetuating their species than birds

---

* "It may not be improper to remark here, that the appearance of this bird in spring is sometimes looked for with anxiety by the farmers. If the horned cattle happen to be diseased in spring, they ascribe it to worms, and consider the pursuit of the birds as an unerring indication of the necessity of medicine. Although this hypothesis of the worms infesting the cattle so as to produce much disease, is problematical, their superabundance at this season cannot be denied. The larvæ of several species are deposited in the vegetables when green, and the cattle are fed on them as fodder in winter. This furnishes the principal inducement for the bird to follow the cattle in spring, when the aperient effects of the green grasses evacuate great numbers of worms. At this season the *Pecoris* often stuffs its crop with them till it can contain no more. There are several species, but the most numerous is a small white one similar to, if not the same as, the *Ascaris* of the human species."

of any other species at other seasons, excepting a promiscuous concubinage, which pervades the whole tribe. When the female separates from the company, her departure is not noticed; no gallant partner accompanies her, nor manifests any solicitude in her absence; nor is her return greeted by that gratulatory tenderness that so eminently characterizes the males of other birds. The male proffers the same civilities to any female, indiscriminately, and they are reciprocated accordingly, without exciting either resentment or jealousy in any of the party. This want of sexual attachment is not inconsistent with the general economy of this singular bird; for, as they are neither their own architect, nor nurse of their own young, the degree of attachment that governs others would be superfluous.

"That the *Fringilla* never builds a nest for itself, you may assert without the hazard of a refutation. I once offered a premium for the nest, and the negroes in the neighborhood brought me a variety of nests; but they were always traced to some other bird. The time of depositing their eggs is from the middle of April to the last of May, or nearly so; corresponding with the season of laying observed by the small birds on whose property it encroaches. It never deposits but one egg in the same nest, and this is generally after the rightful tenant begins to deposit hers, but never, I believe, after she has commenced the process of incubation. It is impossible to say how many they lay in a season, unless they could be watched when confined in an aviary.

"By a minute attention to a number of these birds when they feed in a particular field, in the laying season, the deportment of the female, when the time of laying draws near, becomes particularly interesting. She deserts her associates, assumes a drooping, sickly aspect, and perches upon some eminence where she can reconnoitre the operations of other birds in the process of nidification. If a discovery suitable to her purpose cannot be made from her stand, she becomes more restless, and is seen flitting from tree to tree, till a place of deposit can be found. I once had an opportunity of witnessing a scene of this sort, which I cannot forbear to relate. Seeing a female prying into a bunch of bushes in search of a nest, I determined to see the result, if practicable; and, knowing how easily they are disconcerted by the near approach of man, I mounted my horse, and proceeded slowly, sometimes seeing and sometimes losing sight of her, till I had travelled nearly two miles along the margin of a creek. She entered every thick place, prying with the strictest scrutiny into places where the small birds usually build, and at last darted suddenly into a thick copse of alders and briers, where she remained five or six minutes, when she returned, soaring above the underwood, and returned to the company she had left feeding in the field. Upon entering the covert, I found the nest of a Yellow-Throat, with an egg of each. Knowing the precise time of deposit, I noted the spot and date, with a view of determining a question of importance — the time required to hatch the egg of the Cow Bird, which I supposed to commence from the time of the Yellow-Throat's laying the last egg. A few days after, the nest was removed, I knew not how, and I was disappointed. In the progress of the Cow Bird along the creek's side, she entered the thick boughs of a small cedar, and returned several

17

times before she could prevail on herself to quit the place; and, upon examination, I found a Sparrow sitting on its nest, on which she, no doubt, would have stolen in the absence of the owner. It is, I believe, certain that the Cow-Pen Finch never makes a forcible entry upon the premises by attacking other birds, and ejecting them from their rightful tenements, although they are all, perhaps, inferior in strength, except the Blue-Bird, which, although of a mild as well as affectionate disposition, makes a vigorous resistance when assaulted. Like most other tyrants and thieves, they are cowardly, and accomplish by stealth what they cannot obtain by force.

" The deportment of the Yellow-Throat, on this occasion, is not to be omitted. She returned while I waited near the spot, and darted into her nest, but returned immediately, and perched upon a bough near the place; remained a minute or two, and entered it again; returned, and disappeared. In ten minutes, she returned with the male. They chattered with great agitation for half an hour, seeming to participate in the affront, and then left the place. I believe all the birds thus intruded on manifest more or less concern at finding the egg of a stranger in their own nests. Among these, the Sparrow is particularly punctilious; for she sometimes chirps her complaints for a day or two, and often deserts the premises altogether, even after she has deposited one or more eggs. The following anecdote will show, not only that the Cow-Pen Finch insinuates herself slyly into the nests of other birds, but that even the most pacific of them will resent the insult. A Blue-Bird had built, for three successive seasons, in the cavity of a mulberry-tree near my dwelling. One day, when the nest was nearly finished, I discovered a female Cow Bird perched upon a fence-stake near it, with her eyes apparently fixed upon the spot, while the builder was busy in adjusting her nest. The moment she left it, the intruder darted into it, and in five minutes returned, and sailed off to her companions with seeming delight, which she expressed by her gestures and notes. The Blue-Bird soon returned, and entered the nest, but instantaneously fluttered back, with much apparent hesitation, and perched upon the highest branch of the tree, uttering a rapidly-repeated note of complaint and resentment, which soon brought the male, who reciprocated her feelings by every demonstration of the most vindictive resentment. They entered the nest together, and returned several times, uttering their uninterrupted complaints for ten or fifteen minutes. The male then darted away to the neighboring trees, as if in quest of the offender, and fell upon a Cat Bird, which he chastised severely, and then turned to an innocent Sparrow that was chanting its ditty in a peach-tree. Notwithstanding the affront was so passionately resented, I found the Blue-Bird had laid an egg the next day. Perhaps a tenant less attached to a favorite spot would have acted more fastidiously, by deserting the premises altogether. In this instance, also, I determined to watch the occurrences that were to follow; but, on one of my morning visits, I found the common enemy of the eggs and young of all the small birds had despoiled the nest, — a Coluber was found coiled in the hollow, and the eggs sucked.

" Agreeably to my observation, all the young birds destined to cherish the young Cow Bird are of a mild and affectionate disposition; and it is not less remarkable that they are all smaller than the intruder; the Blue-Bird is the only one nearly as large. This is a good-natured, mild creature, although it makes a vigorous defence when assaulted. The Yellow-Throat, the Sparrow, the Goldfinch, the Indigo Bird, and the Blue-Bird, are the only birds in whose nests I have found the eggs or the young of the Cow-Pen Finch, though, doubtless, there are some others.

" What becomes of the eggs or young of the proprietor? This is the most interesting question that appertains to this subject. There must be some special law of nature which determines that the young of the proprietors are never to be found tenants in common with the young Cow Bird. I shall offer the result of my own experience on this point, and leave it to you and others better versed in the mysteries of nature than I am, to draw your own conclusions. Whatever theory may be adopted, the facts must remain the same. Having discovered a Sparrow's nest with five eggs, four and one, and the Sparrow sitting, I watched the nest daily. The egg of the Cow Bird occupied the centre, and those of the Sparrow were pushed a little up the sides of the nest. Five days after the discovery, I perceived the shell of the Finch's egg broken, and the next, the bird was hatched. The Sparrow returned, while I was near the nest, with her mouth full of food, with which she fed the young Cow Bird, with every possible mark of affection, and discovered the usual concern at my approach. On the succeeding day, only two of the Sparrow's eggs remained, and the next day there were none. I sought in vain for them on the ground, and in every direction.

" Having found the eggs of the Cow Bird in the nest of a Yellow-Throat, I repeated my observations. The process of incubation had commenced, and on the seventh day from the discovery, I found a young Cow Bird that had been hatched during my absence of twenty-four hours, all the eggs of the proprietor remaining. I had not an opportunity of visiting the nest for three days, and, on my return, there was only one egg remaining, and that rotten. The Yellow-Throat attended the young interloper with the same apparent care and affection as if it had been its own offspring.

" The next year, my first discovery was in a Blue-Bird's nest built in a hollow stump. The nest contained six eggs, and the process of incubation was going on. Three or four days after my first visit, I found a young Cow Bird, and three eggs remaining. I took the eggs out; two contained young birds, apparently come to their full time, and the other was rotten. I found one of the other eggs on the ground at the foot of the stump, differing in no respect from those in the nest, no signs of life being discoverable in either.

" Soon after this, I found a Goldfinch's nest, with one egg of each only, and I attended it carefully till the usual complement of the owner were laid. Being obliged to leave home, I could not ascertain precisely when the process of incubation commenced; but, from my reckoning, I think the egg of the Cow Bird must have been hatched in nine or ten days from the commencement of incubation. On my return, I found the young Cow Bird occupying nearly the whole nest, and the foster-mother as attentive to it as she could have been to her own. I ought to acknowledge here, that in none of these instances could

I ascertain exactly the time required to hatch the Cow Bird's eggs, and that, of course, none of them are decisive; but is it not strange that the egg of the intruder should be so uniformly the first hatched? The idea of the egg being larger, and therefore, from its own gravity, finding the centre of the nest, is not sufficient to explain the phenomenon; for in this situation the other eggs would be proportionably elevated at the sides, and therefore receive as much or more warmth from the body of the incumbent than the other.* This principle would scarcely apply to the eggs of the Blue-Bird, for they are nearly of the same size; if there be any difference, it would be in favor of the eggs of the builder of the nest. How do the eggs get out of the nest? Is it by the size and nestling of the young Cow Bird? This cannot always be the case; because, in the instance of the Blue-Bird's nest in the hollow stump, the cavity was a foot deep, the nest at the bottom, and the ascent perpendicular; nevertheless, the eggs were removed, although filled with young ones. Moreover, a young Cow-Pen Finch is as helpless as any other young bird, and so far from having the power of ejecting others from the nest, or even the eggs, that they are sometimes found on the ground under the nest, especially when the nest happens to be very small. I will not assert that the eggs of the builder of the nest are never hatched; but I can assert that I have never been able to find one instance to prove the affirmative. If all the eggs of both birds were to be hatched, in some cases the nest would not hold half of them; for instance, those of the Sparrow or Yellow-Bird. I will not assert that the supposititious egg is brought to perfection in less time than those of the bird to which the nest belongs; but, from the facts stated, I am inclined to adopt such an opinion. How are the eggs removed, after the accouchement of the spurious occupant? By the proprietor of the nest, unquestionably; for this is consistent with the rest of her economy. After the power of hatching them is taken away by her attention to the young stranger, the eggs would be only an encumbrance, and therefore instinct prompts her to remove them. I might add that I have sometimes found the eggs of the Sparrow, in which were unmatured young ones, lying near the nest containing a Cow Bird, and therefore I cannot resist this conclusion. Would the foster-parent feed two species of young at the same time? I believe not. I have never seen an instance of any bird feeding the young of another, unless immediately after losing her own. I should think the sooty-looking stranger would scarcely interest a mother, while the cries of her own offspring, always intelligible, were to be heard. Should such a competition ever take place, I judge the stranger would be the sufferer, and probably the species soon become extinct. Why the *lex naturæ conservatrix* should decide in favor of the surreptitious progeny, is not for me to determine.

"As to the vocal powers of this bird, I believe its pretensions are very humble, none of its notes deserving the epithet musical. The sort of simple, cackling complaint it utters at being disturbed, consti-

---

* The ingenious writer seems not to be aware that almost all birds are in the habit, while sitting, of changing the eggs from the centre to the circumference, and *vice versa,* that all of them may receive an equal share of warmth.

tutes also the expression of its pleasure at finding its companions, varying only in a more rapidly repeated monotony. The deportment of the male, during his promiscuous intercourse with the other sex, resembles much that of a pigeon in the same situation. He uses nearly the same gestures ; and, by attentively listening, you will hear a low, guttural sort of muttering, which is the most agreeable of his notes, and not unlike the cooing of a pigeon.

"This, sir, is the amount of my information on this subject, and is no more than a transcript from my notes made several years ago. For ten years past, since I have lived in this city, many of the impressions of nature have been effaced, and artificial ideas have occupied their places. The pleasure I formerly received in viewing and examining the objects of nature are, however, not entirely forgotten ; and those which remain, if they can interest you, are entirely at your service. With the sincerest wishes for the success of your useful and arduous undertaking, I am, dear sir, yours very respectfully,   NATHANIEL POTTER."

To the above very interesting detail I shall add the following recent fact which fell under my own observation, and conclude my account of this singular species.

In the month of July last, I took from the nest of the Maryland Yellow-Throat, which was built among the dry leaves at the root of a brier bush, a young male Cow Bunting, which filled and occupied the whole nest. I had previously watched the motions of the foster-parents for more than an hour, in order to ascertain whether any more of their young were lurking about or not ; and was fully satisfied that there were none. They had, in all probability, perished in the manner before mentioned. I took this bird home with me, and placed it in the same cage with a Red-Bird, (*Loxia cardinalis*,) who, at first, and for several minutes after, examined it closely, and seemingly with great curiosity. It soon became clamorous for food, and from that moment the Red-Bird seemed to adopt it as his own, feeding it with all the assiduity and tenderness of the most affectionate nurse. When he found that the grasshopper which he had brought it was too large for it to swallow, he took the insect from it, broke it in small portions, chewed them a little to soften them, and, with all the gentleness and delicacy imaginable, put them separately into its mouth. He often spent several minutes in looking at and examining it all over, and in picking off any particles of dirt that he observed on its plumage. In teaching and encouraging it to learn to eat of itself, he often reminded me of the lines of Goldsmith, —

> He tried each art, reproved each dull delay,
> Allured to "*favorite food*," and led the way.

This Cow Bird is now six months old ; is in complete plumage ; and repays the affectionate services of his foster-parent with a frequent display of all the musical talents with which nature has gifted him. These, it must be confessed, are far from being ravishing ; yet, for their singularity, are worthy of notice. He spreads his wings, swells his body into a globular form, bristling every feather in the

17 *

manner of a Turkey cock, and, with great seeming difficulty, utters a few low, spluttering notes, as if proceeding from his belly; always, on these occasions, strutting in front of the spectator with great consequential affectation.

To see the Red-Bird, who is himself so excellent a performer, silently listening to all this guttural splutter, reminds me of the great Handel contemplating a wretched catgut scraper. Perhaps, however, these may be meant for the notes of *love* and *gratitude*, which are sweeter to the ear, and dearer to the heart, than all the artificial solos or concertos on this side heaven.

The length of this species is seven inches, breadth eleven inches; the head and neck are of a very deep silky drab; the upper part of the breast, a dark changeable violet; the rest of the bird is black, with a considerable gloss of green when exposed to a good light; the form of the bill is faithfully represented in the plate — it is evidently that of an *Emberiza*; the tail is slightly forked; legs and claws, glossy black, strong and muscular; iris of the eye, dark hazel. Catesby says of this bird, "It is all over of a brown color, and something lighter below;" a description that applies only to the female, and has been repeated, in nearly the same words, by almost all succeeding ornithologists. The young male birds are at first altogether brown, and for a month, or more, are naked of feathers round the eye and mouth; the breast is also spotted like that of a Thrush, with light drab and darker streaks. In about two months after they leave the nest, the black commences at the shoulders of the wings, and gradually increases along each side, as the young feathers come out, until the bird appears mottled on the back and breast with deep black and light drab. At three months, the colors of the plumage are complete, and, except in moulting, are subject to no periodical change.

MARYLAND YELLOW-THROAT — SYLVIA MARILANDICA.
— Fig. 86. — Female.

TRICHAS PERSONATUS. — Swainson. — Female.

The male of this species having already been represented,[*] accompanied by a particular detail of its manners, I have little further to add here relative to this bird. I found several of them round Wilmington, North Carolina, in the month of January, along the margin of the river, and by the Cypress Swamp, on the opposite side. The individual from which the figure in the plate was taken, was the actual nurse of the young Cow-Pen Bunting, which it is represented in the act of feeding.

It is five inches long, and seven in extent; the whole upper parts, green olive; something brownish on the neck, tips of the wings, and head; the lower parts, yellow, brightest on the throat and vent; legs,

* See Fig. 19.

flesh colored. The chief difference between this and the male, in the markings of their plumage, is, that the female is destitute of the black bar through the eyes, and the bordering one of pale bluish white.

———◆———

SMALL BLUE–GRAY FLYCATCHER. — MUSCICAPA CŒRULEA. — Fig. 87.

Motacilla cœrulea, *Turton, Syst.* i. p. 612. — Blue Flycatcher, *Edw.* pl. 302. — Regulus griseus, the Little Bluish-gray Wren, *Bartram,* p. 291. — Le figuier gris de fer, *Buff.* v. p. 309. — Cerulean Warbler, *Arct. Zool.* ii. No. 299. — *Lath. Syn.* iv. p. 490, No. 127. — *Peale's Museum,* No. 6829.

CULICIVORA CŒRULEA. — Swainson.*

Culicivora, *Sw. New Groups in Orn. Zool. Journ.* No. 11, p. 359. — Sylvia cœrulea, *Bonap. Synop.* p. 85. — The Blue Gray Flycatcher, *Aud.* pl. 84, male and female; *Orn. Biog.* i. p. 431.

This diminutive species, but for the length of the tail, would rank next to our Humming Bird in magnitude. It is a very dexterous flycatcher, and has also something of the manners of the Titmouse, with whom, in early spring, and fall, it frequently associates. It arrives in Pennsylvania, from the south, about the middle of April; and, about the beginning of May, builds its nest, which it generally fixes among the twigs of a tree, sometimes at the height of ten feet from the ground, sometimes fifty feet high, on the extremities of the tops of a high tree in the woods. This nest is formed of very slight and perishable materials, — the husks of buds, stems of old leaves, withered blossoms of weeds, down from the stalks of fern, coated on the outside with gray lichen, and lined with a few horse hairs. Yet in this frail receptacle, which one would think scarcely sufficient to admit the body of the owner, and sustain even its weight, does the female Cow Bird venture to deposit her egg; and to the management of these pygmy nurses leaves the fate of her helpless young. The motions of this little bird are quick; he seems always on the look-out for insects; darts about from one part of the tree to another, with hanging wings and erected tail, making a feeble chirping, *tsee, tsee,* no louder than a mouse. Though so small in itself, it is ambitious of hunting on the highest branches, and is seldom seen among the humbler thickets. It remains with us until the 20th or 28th of September; after which we see no more of it until the succeeding spring. I observed this bird near Savannah, in Georgia, early in March; but it does not winter even in the southern parts of that state.

The length of this species is four inches and a half; extent, six and a half; front, and line over the eye, black; bill, black, very slender,

* This species will represent another lately-formed genus, of which the *Muscicapa stenura* of Temminck's *Pl. coloriees* forms the type. It is a curious group, connecting *Tyrannula, Setophaga,* the Flycatchers, and the *Sylviadœ.* — Ed.

overhanging at the tip, notched, broad, and furnished with bristles at
the base; the color of the plumage above is a light bluish gray,
bluest on the head, below bluish white; tail, longer than the body, a
little rounded, and black, except the exterior feathers, which are almost all white, and the next two also tipped with white; tail-coverts,
black; wings, brownish black, some of the secondaries next the body
edged with white; legs, extremely slender, about three fourths of an
inch long, and of a bluish black color. The female is distinguished
by wanting the black line round the front.

The food of this bird is small winged insects, and their larvæ, but
particularly the former, which it seems almost always in pursuit of.

WHITE-EYED FLYCATCHER. — MUSCICAPA CANTATRIX.—
Fig. 88.

Muscicapa Noveboracensis, *Gmel. Syst.* i. p. 947. — Hanging Flycatcher, *Lath.
Syn. Supp.* p. 174. — *Arct. Zool.* p. 389, No. 274. — Muscicapa cantatrix, the
Little Domestic Flycatcher, or Green Wren, *Bartram,* p. 290. — *Peale's Mu-
seum,* No. 6778.

VIREO NOVEBORACENSIS. — Bonaparte.

Vireo Noveboracensis, *Bonap. Synop.* p. 70. — The White-Eyed Flycatcher, or
Vireo, *Aud.* pl. 63, male; *Orn. Biog.* i. p. 328.

This is another of the Cow Bird's adopted nurses; a lively, active,
and sociable little bird, possessing a strong voice for its size, and a
great variety of notes; and singing with little intermission, from its
first arrival, about the middle of April, till a little before its departure
in September. On the 27th of February, I heard this bird in the
southern parts of the state of Georgia, in considerable numbers, singing with great vivacity. They had only arrived a few days before.
Its arrival in Pennsylvania, after an interval of seven weeks, is a proof
that our birds of passage, particularly the smaller species, do not migrate at once from south to north; but progress daily, keeping company, as it were, with the advances of spring. It has been observed
in the neighborhood of Savannah so late as the middle of November; and probably winters in Mexico and the West Indies.

This bird builds a very neat little nest, often in the figure of an inverted cone; it is suspended, by the upper edge of the two sides, on
the circular bend of a prickly vine, — a species of smilax that generally grows in low thickets. Outwardly, it is constructed of various light materials, bits of rotten wood, fibres of dry stalks of weeds,
pieces of paper, commonly newspapers, an article almost always found
about its nest, so that some of my friends have given it the name of
the *Politician;* all these substances are interwoven with the silk of
caterpillars, and the inside is lined with fine, dry grass and hair. The
female lays five eggs, pure white, marked near the great end with a
very few small dots of deep black or purple. They generally raise
two broods in a season. They seem particularly attached to thickets

90. Meadow Owl. 91. Meadow Lark. 92. Black and white Creeper. 93. Pine creeping Warbler. 95. Louisiana Tanager. 94. Clarks Crow. 95. Lewis Woodpecker. 96. Canada Jay. 97. Snow Bunting. 98. Rusty Grakle. 99. Purple Grakle.

of this species of smilax, and make a great ado when any one comes near their nest; approaching within a few feet, looking down, and scolding with great vehemence. In Pennsylvania they are a numerous species.

The White-eyed Flycatcher is five inches and a quarter long, and seven in extent; the upper parts are a fine yellow olive, those below, white, except the sides of the breast, and under the wings, which are yellow; line round the eye, and spot near the nostril, also rich yellow; wings, deep dusky black, edged with olive green, and crossed with two bars of pale yellow; tail, forked, brownish black, edged with green olive; bill, legs, and feet, light blue; the sides of the neck incline to a grayish ash. The female and young of the first season are scarcely distinguishable in plumage from the male.

MOTTLED OWL.—STRIX NÆVIA.—Fig. 89.

Arct. Zool. 231, No. 118.— *Lath.* i. 126.— *Turton,* i. 167.—*Peale's Museum,* No. 444.

STRIX ASIO.—Linnæus.*

Strix asio, *Bonap. Synop.* p. 36.— Hibou asio, *Temm. Pl. col.* pl. 80.— The Little Screech Owl, *Aud.* pl. 97, adult and young; *Orn. Biog.* i. p. 486.

On contemplating the grave and antiquated figure of this *night wanderer*, so destitute of every thing like gracefulness of shape, I can scarcely refrain from smiling at the conceit of the ludicrous appearance this bird must have made, had Nature bestowed on it the powers of song, and given it the faculty of warbling out sprightly airs, while robed in such a solemn exterior. But the great God of Nature hath,

* The difference in the plumage of the young and old has caused Wilson to fall into a mistake, and multiply species, by introducing the different states under distinct specific appellations. In Fig. 174, is represented the young plumage of the bird, under the name which must be adopted for it, as the original one of Linnæus. The Tawny Owls of this country present similar changes, and were long held as distinct, until accurate observers proved their difference. C. L. Bonaparte appears to have been the first who made public mention of the confusion which existed; and Mr. Audubon has illustrated the sexes and young in one of his best plates. The species appears peculiar to America. They are scarce in the southern districts; but above the Falls of the Ohio they increase in number, and are plentiful in Virginia, Maryland, and all the eastern districts. Its range to the northward perhaps is not very extensive; it does not appear to have been met with in the last over-land expedition, no mention being made of it in the *Northern Zoology.* The flight of this Owl, like its congeners, is smooth and noiseless. By Audubon, it is said sometimes to rise above the top branches of the highest forest-trees, while in pursuit of large beetles, and at other times to sail low and swiftly over the fields or through the woods, in search of small birds, field mice, moles, or wood rats, from which it chiefly derives its subsistence. According to some gentlemen, the nest is placed at the bottom of the hollow trunk of a tree, often not at a greater height than six or seven feet from the ground, at other times so high, as from thirty to forty. It is composed of a few grasses and feathers. The eggs are four or five, of a nearly globular form, and pure white color.— Ed.

in His wisdom, assigned to this class of birds a more unsocial, and less noble, though, perhaps, not less useful, disposition, by assimilating them, not only in form of countenance, but in voice, manners, and appetite, to some particular beasts of prey; secluding them from the enjoyment of the gay sunshine of day, and giving them little more than the few solitary hours of morning and evening twilight, to procure their food and pursue their amours; while all the tuneful tribes, a few excepted, are wrapt in silence and repose. That their true character, however, should not be concealed from those weaker animals on whom they feed, (for Heaven abhors deceit and hypocrisy,) He has stamped their countenance with strong traits of their murderer, the cat; and birds in this respect are, perhaps, better physiognomists than men.

The Owl now before us is chiefly a native of the northern regions, arriving here, with several others, about the commencement of cold weather; frequenting the uplands and mountainous districts, in preference to the lower parts of the country; and feeding on mice, small birds, beetles, and crickets. It is rather a scarce species in Pennsylvania; flies usually in the early part of night and morning; and is sometimes observed sitting on the fences during day, when it is easily caught, its vision at that time being very imperfect.

The bird represented in Fig. 89 was taken in this situation, and presented to me by a friend. I kept it in the room beside me for some time, during which its usual position was such as I have given it. Its eyelids were either half shut, or slowly and alternately opening and shutting, as if suffering from the glare of day; but no sooner was the sun set than its whole appearance became lively and animated; its full and globular eyes shone like those of a cat; and it often lowered its head, in the manner of a cock when preparing to fight, moving it from side to side, and also vertically, as if reconnoitring you with great sharpness. In flying through the room, it shifted from place to place with the silence of a spirit, (if I may be allowed the expression,) the plumage of its wings being so extremely fine and soft as to occasion little or no friction with the air,—a wise provision of Nature, bestowed on the whole genus, to enable them, without giving alarm, to seize their prey in the night. For an hour or two in the evening, and about break of day, it flew about with great activity. When angry, it snapped its bill repeatedly with violence, and so loud as to be heard in the adjoining room, swelling out its eyes to their full dimensions, and lowering its head as before described. It swallowed its food hastily, in large mouthfuls; and never was observed to drink. Of the eggs and nest of this species, I am unable to speak.

The Mottled Owl is ten inches long, and twenty-two in extent; the upper part of the head, the back, ears, and lesser wing-coverts, are dark brown, streaked and variegated with black, pale brown, and ash; wings, lighter, the greater coverts and primaries spotted with white; tail, short, even, and mottled with black, pale brown, and whitish, on a dark brown ground; its lower side, gray; horns, (as they are usually called,) very prominent, each composed of ten feathers, increasing in length from the front backwards, and lightest on the inside; face, whitish, marked with small touches of dusky, and bounded on each side with a circlet of black; breast and belly, white, beautifully variegated with ragged streaks of black, and small transverse touches of brown; legs, feathered nearly to the claws, with a kind of hairy down, of a pale brown color; vent and under tail-coverts white, the latter slightly marked with brown; iris of the eye, a brilliant golden yellow; bill and claws, bluish horn color.

This was a female. The male is considerably less in size; the general colors darker; and the white on the wing-coverts not so observable.

Hollow trees, either in the woods or orchard, or close evergreens in retired situations, are the usual roosting-places of this and most of our other species. These retreats, however, are frequently discovered by the Nuthatch, Titmouse, or Blue Jay, who instantly raise the alarm; a promiscuous group of feathered neighbors soon collect round the spot, like crowds in the streets of a large city, when a thief or murderer is detected; and, by their insults and vociferation, oblige the recluse to seek for another lodging elsewhere. This may account for the circumstance of sometimes finding them abroad during the day, on fences and other exposed situations.

MEADOW LARK. — ALAUDA MAGNA. — Fig. 90.

Linn. Syst. 289 — Crescent Stare, *Arct. Zool.* 330, No. 192, *Lath.* iii. 6, *var. A.* — Le fer-à-cheval, ou Merle a Collier d'Amerique, *Buff.* iii. p. 371. — *Catesb. Car.* i. pl. 33. — *Bartram*, p. 290. — *Peale's Museum*, No. 5212.

STURNELLA LUDOVICIANA. — Swainson.*

Sturnus Ludovicianus, (sub-genus Sturnella,) *Bonap. Synop.* p. 49. — Sturnella collaris, *Vieill. Gal. des Ois.* pl. 80. — Sturnella Ludoviciana, *North. Zool.* ii. p. 282.

Though this well-known species cannot boast of the powers of song which distinguish that "harbinger of day," the Sky Lark of Europe, yet in richness of plumage, as well as in sweetness of voice,

---

* In changing the specific name of this species, C. L. Bonaparte thinks that Wilson must have been misled by some European author, as he was acquainted with the works wherein it was previously described. It ought to remain under the appellation bestowed on it by Linnæus, Brisson, &c. With regard to the generic term, this curious form has been chosen by Vieillot, as the type of his genus *Sturnella*, containing yet only two species, — that of Wilson, and another from the southern continent. The form is peculiar to the New World, and seems to have been a subject of uncertainty to most ornithologists, as we find it placed in the genera *Turdus, Sturnus, Alauda*, and *Cassicus*, to all of which it is somewhat allied, but to none can it rank as a congener. In the bill, head, and wings, with some modification, we have the forms of the two first and last; in the colors of the plumage, the elongation of the scapularies and tail-coverts, in the legs, feet, and hinder claw, that of the *Alauda*. The tarsi and feet are decidedly ambulatorial, as is confirmed by the habits of the species, though the tail indicates that of a scansorial bird; but as far as we yet know, it is the only indication of this power. In the structure of the nest, we have the weaving of the *Icteri*, the situation of many of the Warblers, and the form of the true Wrens. — Ed.

(as far as his few notes extend,) he stands eminently its superior. He differs from the greater part of his tribe in wanting the long straight hind claw, which is probably the reason why he has been classed, by some late naturalists, with the Starlings. But in the particular form of his bill, in his manners, plumage, mode and place of building his nest, Nature has clearly pointed out his proper family.

This species has a very extensive range, having myself found them in Upper Canada, and in each of the states, from New Hampshire to New Orleans. Mr. Bartram also informs me, that they are equally abundant in East Florida. Their favorite places of retreat are pasture fields and meadows, particularly the latter, which have conferred on them their specific name; and no doubt supplies them abundantly with the particular seeds and insects on which they feed. They are rarely or never seen in the depth of the woods; unless where, instead of underwood, the ground is covered with rich grass, as in the Chactaw and Chickasaw countries, where I met with them in considerable numbers in the months of May and June. The extensive and luxuriant prairies between Vincennes and St. Louis also abound with them.

It is probable that, in the more rigorous regions of the north, they may be birds of passage, as they are partially so here; though I have seen them among the meadows of New Jersey, and those that border the Rivers Delaware and Schuylkill, in all seasons; even when the ground was deeply covered with snow. There is scarcely a market day in Philadelphia, from September to March, but they may be found exposed to sale. They are generally considered, for size and delicacy, little inferior to the Quail, or what is here usually called the Partridge, and valued accordingly. I once met with a few of these birds in the month of February, during a deep snow, among the heights of the Alleghany, between Shippensburgh and Somerset, gleaning on the road, in company with the small Snow Birds. In the state of South Carolina and Georgia, at the same season of the year, they swarm among the rice plantations, running about the yards and out-houses, accompanied by the Killdeers, with little appearance of fear, as if quite domesticated.

These birds, after the building season is over, collect in flocks, but seldom fly in a close, compact body; their flight is something in the manner of the Grouse and Partridge, laborious and steady, sailing, and renewing the rapid action of the wings alternately. When they alight on trees or bushes, it is generally on the tops of the highest branches, whence they send forth a long, clear, and somewhat melancholy note, that, in sweetness and tenderness of expression, is not surpassed by any of our numerous Warblers. This is sometimes followed by a kind of low, rapid chattering, the particular call of the female; and again the clear and plaintive strain is repeated as before. They afford tolerably good amusement to the sportsman, being most easily shot while on wing; as they frequently squat among the long grass, and spring within gunshot. The nest of this species is built generally in, or below, a thick tuft, or tussock, of grass; it is composed of dry grass, and fine bent, laid at the bottom, and wound all around, leaving an arched entrance level with the ground; the inside is lined with fine stalks of the same materials, disposed with great regularity. The eggs are four, sometimes five, white, marked with specks, and several large blotches of reddish brown, chiefly at the thick end. Their food consists of caterpillars, grub worms, beetles, and grass seeds, with a considerable proportion of gravel. Their general name is the Meadow Lark; among the Virginians, they are usually called the Old Field Lark.

The length of this bird is ten inches and a half; extent, sixteen and a half; throat, breast, belly, and line from the eye to the nostrils, rich yellow; inside lining and edge of the wing, the same; an oblong crescent of deep velvety black ornaments the lower part of the throat; lesser wing-coverts, black, broadly bordered with pale ash; rest of the wing-feathers, light brown, handsomely serrated with black; a line of yellowish white divides the crown, bounded on each side by a stripe of black, intermixed with bay, and another line of yellowish white passes over each eye, backwards; cheeks, bluish white; back, and rest of the upper parts, beautifully variegated with black, bright bay, and pale ochre; tail, wedged, the feathers neatly pointed, the four outer ones on each side, nearly all white; sides, thighs, and vent, pale yellow ochre, streaked with black; upper mandible, brown; lower, bluish white; eyelids, furnished with strong, black hairs; legs and feet, very large, and of a pale flesh color.

The female has the black crescent more skirted with gray, and not of so deep a black. In the rest of her markings, the plumage differs little from that of the male. I must here take notice of a mistake committed by Mr. Edwards in his *History of Birds*, vol. vi. p. 123, where, on the authority of a bird-dealer of London, he describes the Calandre Lark, (a native of Italy and Russia,) as belonging also to North America, and having been brought from Carolina. I can say with confidence, that, in all my excursions through that and the rest of the Southern States, I never met such a bird, nor any person who had over seen it. I have no hesitation in believing, that the Calandre is not a native of the United States.

BLACK AND WHITE CREEPER. — CERTHIA MACULATA. — Fig. 91.

Edw. pl. 300. — White Poll Warbler, *Arct. Zool.* 402, No. 293. — Le figuier varié, *Buff.* v. 305. — *Lath.* ii. 488. — *Turton,* i. p. 603. — *Peale's Museum,* No. 7092.

SYLVICOLA VARIA. — Jardine. *

Sylvia varia, *Bonap. Synop.* p. 81. — Le Mniotilla varié, Mniotilla varia, *Vieill. Gall. des Ois.* pl. 169.

This nimble and expert little species seldom perches on the small twigs; but circumambulates the trunk and larger branches, in quest of

* This forms the type of Vieillot's *Mniotilla*, and will, perhaps, show the scansorial form in *Sylvicola.* — Ed.

18

ants and other insects, with admirable dexterity. It arrives in Pennsylvania, from the south, about the 20th of April; the young begin to fly early in July; and the whole tribe abandon the country about the beginning of October. Sloane describes this bird as an inhabitant of the West India Islands, where it probably winters. It was first figured by Edwards from a dried skin sent him by Mr. William Bartram, who gave it its present name. Succeeding naturalists have classed it with the Warblers, — a mistake which I have endeavored to rectify.

The genus of Creepers comprehends about thirty different species, many of which are richly adorned with gorgeous plumage; but, like their congenial tribe, the Woodpeckers, few of them excel in song; their tongues seem better calculated for extracting noxious insects from the bark of trees, than for trilling out sprightly airs; as the hardened hands of the husbandman are better suited for clearing the forest, or guiding the plough, than dancing among the keys of a fortepiano. Which of the two is the more honorable and useful employment, is not difficult to determine. Let the farmer, therefore, respect this little bird for its useful qualities in clearing his fruit and forest-trees from destructive insects, though it cannot serenade him with its song.

The length of this species is five inches and a half; extent, seven and a half; crown, white, bordered on each side with a band of black, which is again bounded by a line of white passing over each eye; below this is a large spot of black covering the ear-feathers; chin and throat, black; wings, the same, crossed transversely by two bars of white; breast and back, streaked with black and white; tail, upper, and also under coverts, black, edged, and bordered with white; belly, white; legs and feet, dirty yellow; hind claw the longest, and all very sharp pointed; bill, a little compressed sidewise, slightly curved, black above, paler below; tongue, long, fine-pointed, and horny at the extremity. These last circumstances, joined to its manners, characterize it, decisively, as a Creeper.

The female, and young birds of the first year, want the black on the throat, having that part of a grayish white.

------◆------

PINE–CREEPING WARBLER. — SYLVIA PINUS. — Fig. 92.

Pine Creeper, *Catesb.* i. 61. — *Peale's Museum*, No. 7312.

SYLVICOLA PINUS. — Jardine.

Sylvia pinus, *Bonap. Synop.* p. 81.

This species inhabits the pine woods of the Southern States, where it is resident, and where I first observed it, running along the bark of the pines; sometimes alighting, and feeding on the ground, and almost always, when disturbed, flying up, and clinging to the trunks of the trees. As I advanced towards the south, it became more numerous.

Its note is a simple, reiterated cherup, continued for four or five seconds.

Catesby first figured and described this bird; but so imperfectly, as to produce among succeeding writers great confusion, and many mistakes as to what particular bird was intended. Edwards has supposed it to be the Blue-winged Yellow Warbler! Latham has supposed another species to be meant; and the worthy Mr. Pennant has been led into the same mistakes; describing the male of one species, and the female of another, as the male and female Pine Creeper. Having shot and examined great numbers of these birds, I am enabled to clear up these difficulties by the following descriptions, which will be found to be correct:

The Pine-creeping Warbler is five and a half inches long, and nine inches in extent; the whole upper parts are of a rich green olive, with a considerable tinge of yellow; throat, sides, and breast, yellow; wings and tail, brown, with a slight cast of bluish, the former marked with two bars of white, slightly tinged with yellow; tail, forked, and edged with ash; the three exterior feathers, marked near the tip with a broad spot of white; middle of the belly and vent-feathers, white. The female is brown, tinged with olive green on the back; breast, dirty white, or slightly yellowish. The bill in both is truly that of a Warbler; and the tongue, slender, as in the *Motacilla* genus, notwithstanding the habits of the bird.

The food of these birds is the seeds of the pitch pine, and various kinds of bugs. The nest, according to Mr. Abbot, is suspended from the horizontal fork of a branch, and formed outwardly of slips of grapevine bark, rotten wood, and caterpillars' webs, with sometimes pieces of hornets' nests interwoven; and is lined with dry pine leaves, and fine roots of plants. The eggs are four, white, with a few dark brown spots at the great end.

These birds, associating in flocks of twenty or thirty individuals, are found in the depth of the pine barrens; and are easily known by their manner of rising from the ground, and alighting on the body of the tree. They also often glean among the topmost boughs of the pine-tree, hanging, head downwards, like the Titmouse.

LOUISIANA TANAGER.—TANAGRA COLUMBIANUS.—Fig. 93.

Peale's Museum, No. 6236

PYRANGA? LUDOVICIANA.—Jardine.*

Tanagra Ludoviciana, *Bonap. Synop.* p. 105.—Pyranga erythropis, *Vieill.* auct. *Bonap.*

This bird, and the two others that occupy the same plate, were discovered in the remote regions of Louisiana, by an exploring party

---

* It is impossible to decide the generic station of this bird. It appears very rare; and it is probable that the British collections do not possess any specimen.—Ed.

under the command of Captain George Merriwether Lewis, and Lieutenant, now General, William Clark, in their memorable expedition across the Continent to the Pacific Ocean. They are entitled to a distinguished place in the pages of AMERICAN ORNITHOLOGY, both as being, till now, altogether unknown to naturalists, and as natives of what *is*, or at least *will be,* and that at no distant period, part of the western territory of the United States.

The frail remains of the bird now under consideration, as well as of the other two, have been set up by Mr. Peale, in his museum, with as much neatness as the state of the skins would permit. Of three of these, which were put into my hands for examination, the most perfect was selected for the drawing. Its size and markings were as follows : — Length, six inches and a half; back, tail, and wings, black ; the greater wing-coverts, tipped with yellow ; the next superior row, wholly yellow ; neck, rump, tail-coverts, and whole lower parts, greenish yellow ; forepart of the head, to and beyond the eyes, light scarlet ; bill, yellowish horn color ; edges of the upper mandible, ragged, as in the rest of its tribe ; legs, light blue ; tail, slightly forked, and edged with dull whitish : the whole figure about the size, and much resembling in shape, the Scarlet Tanager, (Figs. 45 and 46 ;) but evidently a different species, from the black back and yellow coverts. Some of the feathers on the upper part of the back were also skirted with yellow. A skin of what I supposed to be the female, or a young bird, differed in having the wings and back brownish, and in being rather less.

The family, or genus, to which this bird belongs, is particularly subject to changes of color, both progressively, during the first and second seasons, and also periodically, afterwards. Some of those that inhabit Pennsylvania, change from an olive green to a greenish yellow, and, lastly, to a brilliant scarlet ; and, I confess, when the preserved specimen of the present species was first shown me, I suspected it to have been passing through a similar change at the time it was taken. But, having examined two more skins of the same species, and finding them all marked very nearly alike, which is seldom the case with those birds that change while moulting, I began to think that this might be its most permanent, or, at least, its summer or winter dress.

The little information I have been able to procure of the species generally, or at what particular season these were shot, prevents me from being able to determine this matter to my wish.

I can only learn that they inhabit the extensive plains or prairies of the Missouri, between the Osage and Mandan nations, building their nests in low bushes, and often among the grass. With us, the Tanagers usually build on the branches of a hickory, or white-oak sapling. These birds delight in various kinds of berries, with which those rich prairies are said to abound.

CLARK'S CROW. — CORVUS COLUMBIANUS. — Fig. 94.

Peale's Museum, No. 1371.

CORVUS COLUMBIANUS. — Wilson.

Corvus Columbianus, *Bonap. Synop.* p. 56.

This species resembles, a little, the Jackdaw of Europe, (*Corvus monedula*,) but is remarkable for its formidable claws, which approach to those of the *Falco* genus, and would seem to intimate that its food consists of living animals, for whose destruction these weapons must be necessary. In conversation with different individuals of the party, I understood that this bird inhabits the shores of the Columbia, and the adjacent country, in great numbers, frequenting the rivers and sea-shore, probably feeding on fish; and that it has all the gregarious and noisy habits of the European species, several of the party supposing it to be the same. Fig. 94 was drawn with particular care, after a minute examination and measurement of the only preserved skin that was saved, and which is now deposited in Mr. Peale's museum.

This bird measures thirteen inches in length; the wings, the two middle tail-feathers, and the interior vanes of the next, (except at the tip,) are black, glossed with steel-blue; all the secondaries, except the three next the body, are white for an inch at their extremities, forming a large spot of white on that part when the wing is shut; the tail is rounded, yet the two middle feathers are somewhat shorter than those adjoining; all the rest are pure white, except as already described; the general color of the head, neck, and body, above and below, is a light, silky drab, darkening almost to a dove color on the breast and belly; vent, white; claws, black, large, and hooked, particularly the middle and hind claw; legs, also black; bill, a dark horn color; iris of the eye, unknown.

In the state of Georgia, and several parts of West Florida, I discovered a Crow, not hitherto taken notice of by naturalists, rather larger than the present species, but much resembling it in the form and length of its wings, in its tail, and particularly its claws. This bird is a constant attendant along the borders of streams and stagnating ponds, feeding on small fish and lizards, which I have many times seen him seize as he swept along the surface. A well-preserved specimen of this bird was presented to Mr. Peale, and is now in his museum. It is highly probable that, with these external resemblances, the habits of both may be nearly alike.

18 *

LEWIS'S WOODPECKER.—PICUS TORQUATUS.—Fig. 95.

Peale's Museum, No. 2020.

MELANERPES? TORQUATUS.—Jardine.*

Picus torquatus, *Bonap. Synop.* p. 46.

Of this very beautiful and singularly-marked species, I am unable to give any further account than as relates to its external appearance. Several skins of this species were preserved, all of which I examined with care, and found little or no difference among them, either in the tints or disposition of the colors.

The length of this was eleven inches and a half; the back, wings, and tail were black, with a strong gloss of green; upper part of the head, the same; front, chin, and cheeks beyond the eyes, a dark, rich red; round the neck passes a broad collar of white, which spreads over the breast, and looks as if the fibres of the feathers had been silvered: these feathers are also of a particular structure, the fibres being separate, and of a hair-like texture; belly, deep vermilion, and of the same strong, hair-like feathers, intermixed with silvery ones; vent, black; legs and feet, dusky, inclining to greenish blue; bill, dark horn color.

For a more particular, and doubtless a more correct account of this and the two preceding species, the reader is referred to General Clark's History of the Expedition. The three birds I have here introduced are but a small part of the valuable collection of new subjects in natural history discovered and preserved, amidst a thousand dangers and difficulties, by those two enterprising travellers, whose intrepidity was only equalled by their discretion, and by their active and laborious pursuit of whatever might tend to render their journey useful to science and to their country. It was the request and particular wish of Captain Lewis, made to me in person, that I should make drawings of such of the feathered tribes as had been preserved, and were new. That brave soldier, that amiable and excellent man, over whose solitary grave in the wilderness I have since shed tears of affliction, having been cut off in the prime of his life, I hope I shall be pardoned for consecrating this humble note to his memory, until a more able pen shall do better justice to the subject.

* Having no authority from the founder of the genus, and not having seen the bird, I place it with the Red-headed Woodpecker provisionally. The lengthened wings, proportion of toes, and distribution of the colors, seem, however, to warrant it.

The female is said by Bonaparte, on the authority of Mr. Peale, who shot them breeding on the Rocky Mountains, to resemble the male closely.—Ed.

CANADA JAY. — CORVUS CANADENSIS. — Fig. 96.

Linn. Syst. 158. — Cinereous Crow, *Arct. Zool.* p. 248, No. 137. — *Lath.* i, 389 — Le Geay brun de Canada, *Brise,* ii. 54 — *Buff.* iii. 117.

GARRULUS CANADENSIS. — Swainson.

Corvus Canadensis, *Bonap. Synop.* p. 58. — Garrulus Canadensis, *North. Zool.* ii. p. 295.

WERE I to adopt the theoretical reasoning of a celebrated French naturalist, I might pronounce this bird to be a debased descendant from the Common Blue Jay of the United States, degenerated by the influence of the bleak and chilling regions of Canada, or perhaps a *spurious* production between the Blue Jay and the Cat Bird; or, what would be more congenial to the count's ideas, trace its degradation to the circumstance of migrating, some thousand years ago, from the genial shores of Europe, — where nothing like degeneracy or degradation ever takes place among any of God's creatures. I shall, however, on the present occasion, content myself with stating a few particulars better supported by facts, and more consonant to the plain homespun of common sense.

This species inhabits the country extending from Hudson's Bay, and probably farther north, to the River St. Lawrence; also, in winter, the inland parts of the District of Maine and northern tracts of the States of Vermont and New York. When the season is very severe, with deep snow, they sometimes advance farther south, but generally return northward as the weather becomes more mild.

The character given of this bird by the people of those parts of the country where it inhabits, is, that it feeds on black moss, worms, and even flesh; when near habitations or tents, pilfers every thing it can come at; is bold, and comes even into the tent to eat meat out of the dishes; watches the hunters while baiting their traps for martens, and devours the bait as soon as their backs are turned; that they breed early in spring, building their nests on pine-trees, forming them of sticks and grass, and lay blue eggs; that they have two, rarely three, young at a time, which are at first quite black, and continue so for some time; that they fly in pairs; lay up hoards of berries in hollow trees; are seldom seen in January, unless near houses; are a kind of Mock Bird; and, when caught, pine away, though their appetite never fails them; notwithstanding all which ingenuity and good qualities, they are, as we are informed, detested by the natives.[*]

The only individuals of this species that I ever met with in the United States were on the shores of the Mohawk, a short way above the Little Falls. It was about the last of November, when the ground was deeply covered with snow. There were three or four in company, or within a small distance of each other, flitting leisurely along the road-side, keeping up a kind of low chattering with one another, and

[*] HEARNE'S *Journey,* p. 405.

seemed nowise apprehensive at my approach. I soon secured the whole; from the best of which the drawing in the plate was carefully made. On dissection, I found their stomachs occupied by a few spiders and the aureliæ of some insects. I could perceive no difference between the plumage of the male and female.

The Canada Jay is eleven inches long, and fifteen in extent; back, wings, and tail, a dull, leaden gray, the latter long, cuneiform, and tipped with dirty white; interior vanes of the wings, brown, and also partly tipped with white; plumage of the head, loose and prominent; the forehead, and feathers covering the nostril, as well as the whole lower parts, a dirty brownish white, which also passes round the bottom of the neck like a collar; part of the crown and hind head, black; bill and legs, also black; eye, dark hazel. The whole plumage on the back is long, loose, unwebbed, and in great abundance, as if to protect it from the rigors of the regions it inhabits.

A gentleman of observation, who resided for many years near the North River, not far from Hudson, in the state of New York, informs me that he has particularly observed this bird to arrive there at the commencement of cold weather. He has often remarked its solitary habits. It seemed to seek the most unfrequented, shaded retreats, keeping almost constantly on the ground, yet would sometimes, towards evening, mount to the top of a small tree, and repeat its notes (which a little resemble those of the Baltimore) for a quarter of an hour together; and this it generally did immediately before snow or falling weather.

SNOW BUNTING. — EMBERIZA NIVALIS. — FIG. 97.

Linn. Syst. 308. — *Arct. Zool.* p. 355, No. 222. — Tawny Bunting, *Br. Zool.* No. 121. — L'Ortolan de Neige, *Buff.* iv. 329. *Pl. enl.* 497. — *Peale's Museum,* No. 5900.

PLECTROPHANES NIVALIS. — MEYER.*

Emberiza nivalis, *Flem. Br. Anim.* p. 79. — Snow Bunting, *Mont. Orn. Dict.* i. *Bew. Br. Birds,* i. p. 143. — *Selb. Ill. Orn.* i. 247. pl. 52. — Tawny Bunting, *Mont. Orn. Dict. Bew. Br. Birds,* i. 150. — Bruent de neize, *Temm. Man. d'Orn.* i. p. 319. — Emberiza nivalis, *Bonap. Synop.* p. 103. — Emberiza (plectrophanes) nivalis, *North. Zool.* ii. p. 246.

THIS being one of those birds common to both continents, its migrations extending almost from the very pole to a distance of forty or fifty degrees around; and its manners and peculiarities having been

---

* This species, from its various changes of plumage, has been multiplied into several; and in form being allied to many genera, it has been variously placed by different ornithologists. Meyer was the first to institute a place for itself, and, with a second, the *Fringilla Lapponica,* it will constitute his genus *Plectrophanes,* which is generally adopted into our modern systems. The discrepancies of form were also seen by Vieillot, who, without attending to his predecessor, made the genus *Passerina* of the Lapland Finch. They are both natives of America; the latter has been added by the Prince of Musignano, and figured in Vol. III. It has

long familiarly known to the naturalists of Europe, I shall in this place avail myself of the most interesting parts of their accounts, subjoining such particulars as have fallen under my own observation.

"These birds," says Mr. Pennant, "inhabit not only Greenland,[*] but even the dreadful climate of Spitzbergen, where vegetation is nearly extinct, and scarcely any but *cryptogamous* plants are found. It therefore excites wonder, how birds, which are graminivorous in every other than those frost-bound regions, subsist; yet are there found in great flocks, both on the land and ice of Spitzbergen.[†] They annually pass to this country by way of Norway; for, in the spring, flocks innumerable appear, especially on the Norwegian isles, continue only three weeks, and then at once disappear.[‡] As they do not breed in Hudson's Bay, it is certain that many retreat to this last of lands, and totally uninhabited, to perform, in full security, the duties of love, incubation, and nutrition. That they breed in Spitzbergen, is very probable; but we are assured that they do so in Greenland. They arrive there in April, and make their nests in the fissures of the rocks on the mountains, in May; the outside of their nest is grass, the middle of feathers, and the lining the down of the arctic fox. They lay five eggs, white, spotted with brown: they sing finely near their nest.

also been lately discovered to be an occasional visitant in this country, being taken by the bird-catchers about London. The following very proper observations occur in Mr. Selby's account of the Lapland Finch:—

"The appropriate station for this genus, I conceive to be intermediate between *Alauda* and *Emberiza*, forming, as it were, the medium of connection or passage from one genus to the other. In *Alauda*, it is met with that section of the genus which, in the increasing thickness and form of the bill, shows a deviation from the more typical species, and a nearer approach to the thick-billed *Fringillidæ*; to this section *Alauda calandra* and *brachydactyla* belong. Its affinity to the Larks is also shown, by the form of the feet, and production of the hinder claw; this, in *Lapponica*, is nearly straight, and longer than the toe, resembling, in every respect, that of many of the true Larks. The habits and manners of the two known species also bear a much greater resemblance to those of the Larks than the Buntings. Like the members of the first genus, they live entirely upon the ground, and never perch. Their mode of progression is also the same, being by successive steps, and not the hopping motion used by all the true *Emberizæ*. A power of flight, superior to that possessed by the true Buntings, is also indicated by the greater length of the wings and form of the tail-feathers. In *Plectrophanes*, the first and second quills are nearly equal in length, and the longest in the wing; in *Emberiza*, on the contrary, the second and third are equal, and longer than the first. The affinity of our genus to *Emberiza*, is shown in the form of the bill, which, with the exception of being shorter and more rounded on the back, possesses the characteristic distinctions of that genus."

During the spring and breeding season, the plumage assumes a pure white on the under parts, and deep black on all the brown markings of the upper. The feathers are at first edged with brown, which gradually drop off as the summer advances. A third species is figured in the *Northern Zoology*, (*Plectrophanes picta*, Sw.) Only one specimen was obtained, associating with the Lapland Buntings, on the banks of the Saskatchewan. The description of the bird in the summer plumage is nearly thus given:—"Head and sides, velvet black; three distinct spots of pure white on the sides of the head, one bordering the chin, another on the ear, a third above the eye, a less distinct spot in the middle of the nape; the neck above, wood brown, the dorsal plumage and lowest rows of wing-coverts, blackish brown; the under plumage, entirely of a color intermediate between wood brown and buff orange."—ED.

* CRANTZ, i. 77.
† LORD MULGRAVE's *Voyage*, 108; MARTIN's *Voyage*, 73.
‡ LEEMS, 256.

"They are caught by the boys in autumn, when they collect near the shores in great flocks, in order to migrate; and are eaten dried.*

"In Europe, they inhabit, during summer, the most naked Lapland alps, and descend in rigorous seasons into Sweden, and fill the roads and fields; on which account the Dalecarlians call them *illwarsfogel*, or bad-weather birds — the Uplanders, *hardwarsfogel*, expressive of the same. The Laplanders style them *alaipg*. Leems† remarks, I know not with what foundation, that they fatten on the flowing of the tides in Finmark, and grow lean on the ebb. The Laplanders take them in great numbers in hair springs, for the tables, their flesh being very delicate.

"They seem to make the countries within the whole arctic circle their summer residence, from whence they overflow the more southern countries in amazing multitudes, at the setting in of winter in the frigid zone. In the winter of 1778-9, they came in such multitudes into Birsa, one of the Orkney Islands, as to cover the whole barony; yet of all the numbers, hardly two agreed in colors.

"Lapland, and perhaps Iceland, furnishes the north of Britain with the swarms that frequent these parts during winter, as low as the Cheviot Hills, in lat. 52° 32'. Their resting-places, the Feroe Isles, Shetland, and the Orkneys. The Highlands of Scotland, in particular, abound with them. Their flights are immense, and they mingle so closely together in form of a ball, that the fowlers make great havock among them. They arrive lean, soon become very fat, and are delicious food. They either arrive in the Highlands very early, or a few breed there, for I had one shot for me at Invercauld, the 4th of August. But there is a certainty of their migration; for multitudes of them fall, wearied with their passage, on the vessels that are sailing through the Pentland Firth.‡

"In their summer dress, they are sometimes seen in the south of England,§ the climate not having severity sufficient to affect the colors; yet now and then a milk-white one appears, which is usually mistaken for a white Lark.

"Russia and Siberia receive them in their severe seasons annually, in amazing flocks, overflowing almost all Russia. They frequent the villages, and yield a most luxurious repast. They vary there infinitely in their winter colors, are pure white, speckled, and even quite brown.|| This seems to be the influence of difference of age, more than of season. Germany has also its share of them. In Austria, they are caught and fed with millet, and afford the epicure a treat equal to that of the Ortolan."¶

These birds appear in the northern districts of the United States early in December, or with the first heavy snow, particularly if drifted by high winds. They are usually called the *white* Snow Bird, to distinguish them from the small dark bluish Snow Bird already described. Their numbers increase with the increasing severity of weather, and depth of snow. Flocks of them sometimes reach as far south as the borders of Maryland; and the whiteness of their plumage is observed to be greatest towards the depth of winter. They spread over the

* *Faun. Greenl.* 118.   † *Finmark*, 255.
‡ BISHOP POCOCK'S *Journal*, MS.   § MORTON'S *Northamp.* p. 427.
|| BELL'S *Travels*, i. 198.   ¶ KRAMER, *Anim. Austr.* 372.

Gennesee country, and the interior of the District of Maine, flying in close, compact bodies, driving about most in a high wind; sometimes alighting near the doors, but seldom sitting long, being a roving, restless bird. In these plentiful regions, where more valuable game is abundant, they hold out no temptation to the sportsman or hunter; and, except the few caught by boys in snares, no other attention is paid to them. They are, however, universally considered as the harbingers of severe cold weather. How far westward they extend I am unable to say. One of the most intelligent and expert hunters who accompanied Captains Lewis and Clark on their expedition to the Pacific Ocean, informs me that he has no recollection of seeing these birds in any part of their tour, not even among the bleak and snowy regions of the Stony Mountains; though the little blue one was in abundance.

The Snow Bunting derives a considerable part of its food from the seeds of certain aquatic plants, which may be one reason for its preferring these remote northern countries, so generally intersected with streams, ponds, lakes, and shallow arms of the sea, that probably abound with such plants. In passing down the Seneca River towards Lake Ontario, late in the month of October, I was surprised by the appearance of a large flock of these birds feeding on the surface of the water, supported on the tops of a growth of weeds that rose from the bottom, growing so close together that our boat could with great difficulty make its way through them. They were running about with great activity; and those I shot and examined, were filled, not only with the seeds of this plant, but with a minute kind of shell fish that adheres to the leaves. In these kind of aquatic excursions they are doubtless greatly assisted by the length of their hind heel and claws. I also observed a few on Table Rock, above the Falls of Niagara, seemingly in search of the same kind of food.

According to the statements of those traders who have resided near Hudson's Bay, the Snow Buntings are the earliest of their migratory birds, appearing there about the 11th of April, staying about a month or five weeks, and proceeding farther north to breed. They return again in September, stay till November, when the severe frosts drive them southward.*

The summer dress of the Snow Bunting is a tawny brown, interspersed with white, covering the head, neck, and lower parts; the back is black, each feather being skirted with brown; wings and tail, also black, marked in the following manner:— The three secondaries next the body are bordered with bay, the next with white, and all the rest of the secondaries, as well as their coverts, and shoulder of the wing, pure white; the first six primaries are black from their coverts downwards to their extremities; tail, forked, the three exterior feathers on each side white, marked on the outer edge near the tip with black, the rest nearly all black; tail-coverts, reddish brown, fading into white; bill, pale brown; legs and feet, black; hind claw, long, like that of the lark, though more curved. In winter, they become white on the head, neck, and whole under-side, as well as great part of the wings and rump; the back continues black, skirted with brown. Some are even found pure white. Indeed, so much does their plumage vary according to age and season, that no two are found at any time alike.

* *London Philosophical Transactions,* lxii. 403.

RUSTY GRAKLE. — GRACULA FERRUGINEA. — Fig. 98.

Black Oriole, *Arct. Zool.* p. 259, No. 144. — Rusty Oriole, *Ibid.* p. 260, No. 146. — New York Thrush, *Ibid.* p. 339, No. 205. — Hudsonian Thrush, *Ibid.* No. 234, female. — Labrador Thrush, *Ibid.* p. 340, No. 206. — *Peale's Museum*, No. 5514.

SCOLEPHAGUS FERRUGINEUS. — Swainson.

Quiscalus ferrugineus, *Bonap. Synop.* p. 55. — Scolephagus ferrugineus, *North. Zool.* ii. p. 286.

Here is a single species described by one of the most judicious naturalists of Great Britain no less than five different times! — The greater part of these descriptions is copied by succeeding naturalists, whose synonymes it is unnecessary to repeat: so great is the uncertainty in judging, from a mere examination of their dried or stuffed skins, of the particular tribes of birds, many of which, for several years, are constantly varying in the colors of their plumage, and, at different seasons, or different ages, assuming new and very different appearances. Even the size is by no means a safe criterion, the difference in this respect between the male and female of the same species (as in the one now before us) being sometimes very considerable.

This bird arrives in Pennsylvania, from the north, early in October; associates with the Redwings and Cow-Pen Buntings, frequents corn-fields and places where grasshoppers are plenty; but Indian corn, at that season, seems to be its principal food. It is a very silent bird, having only now and then a single note, or *chuck.* We see them occasionally until about the middle of November, when they move off to the south. On the 12th of January, I overtook great numbers of these birds in the woods near Petersburgh, Virginia, and continued to see occasional parties of them almost every day as I advanced southerly, particularly in South Carolina, around the rice plantations, where they were numerous, feeding about the hog pens, and wherever Indian corn was to be procured. They also extend to a considerable distance westward. On the 5th of March, being on the banks of the Ohio, a few miles below the mouth of the Kentucky River, in the midst of a heavy snow storm, a flock of these birds alighted near the door of the cabin where I had taken shelter, several of which I shot, and found their stomachs, as usual, crammed with Indian corn. Early in April they pass hastily through Pennsylvania, on their return to the north to breed.

From the accounts of persons who have resided near Hudson's Bay, it appears that these birds arrive there in the beginning of June, as soon as the ground is thawed sufficiently for them to procure their food, which is said to be worms and maggots; sing with a fine note till the time of incubation, when they have only a chucking noise, till the young take their flight; at which time they resume their song. They build their nests in trees, about eight feet from the ground, forming them with moss and grass, and lay five eggs of a dark color, spotted with black. It is added, they gather in great flocks, and retire southerly in September.[*]

* *Arctic Zoology*, p. 259.

The male of this species, when in perfect plumage, is nine inches in length, and fourteen in extent; at a small distance appears wholly black; but, on a near examination, is of a glossy dark green; the irides of the eye are silvery, as in those of the Purple Grakle; the bill is black, nearly of the same form with that of the last-mentioned species; the lower mandible a little rounded, with the edges turned inward, and the upper one furnished with a sharp, bony process on the inside, exactly like that of the purple species. The tongue is slender, and lacerated at the tip; legs and feet, black and strong, the hind claw the largest; the tail is slightly rounded. This is the color of the male when of full age; but three fourths of these birds which we meet with, have the whole plumage of the breast, head, neck, and back, tinctured with brown, every feather being skirted with ferruginous; over the eye is a light line of pale brown, below that one of black passing through the eye. This brownness gradually goes off towards spring, for almost all those I shot in the Southern States were but slightly marked with ferruginous. The female is nearly an inch shorter; head, neck, and breast, almost wholly brown; a light line over the eye; lores, black; belly and rump, ash; upper and under tail-coverts, skirted with brown; wings, black, edged with rust color; tail, black, glossed with green; legs, feet, and bill, as in the male.

These birds might easily be domesticated. Several that I had winged and kept for some time, became, in a few days, quite familiar, seeming to be very easily reconciled to confinement.

PURPLE GRAKLE. — GRACULA QUISCALA. — Fig. 99.

Linn. Syst. 165. — La pie de la Jamaique, *Briss.* ii. 41. — *Buff.* iii. 97, *Pl. enl.* 538. *Arct. Zool.* p. 263, No. 153. — Gracula purpurea, the Lesser Purple Jackdaw, or Crow Blackbird, *Bartram*, p. 289. — *Peale's Museum*, No. 1582.

QUISCALUS VERSICOLOR. — Vieillot.*

Quiscalus versicolor, *Vieill. Gall. des Ois.* pl. 108. — *Bonap. Synop.* p. 54. — Purple Grakle, or Common Crow Blackbird, *Aud.* pl. 7; *Orn. Biog.* i. p. 35. — Quiscalus versicolor, Common Purple Boat-Tail, *North. Zool.* ii. p. 285.

This noted depredator is well known to every careful farmer of the Northern and Middle States. About the 20th of March, the Purple Grakles visit Pennsylvania from the south, fly in loose flocks, frequent swamps and meadows, and follow in the furrows after the plough; their food at this season consisting of worms, grubs, and caterpillars,

---

* *Gracula* will be given exclusively to a form inhabiting India, of which, though one species only is described, I have every reason to believe that at least two are confounded under it. *Quiscalus* has been, on this account, taken, by Vieillot, for our present bird, and some others confined to America. There has been considerable confusion among the species, which has been satisfactorily cleared up by Bonaparte, and will be seen in the sequel of the work. The female is figured Plate V. of the Continuation by the Prince of Musignano. — Ed.

of which they destroy prodigious numbers, as if to recompense the
husbandman beforehand for the havock they intend to make among
his crops of Indian corn.   Towards evening, they retire to the nearest cedars and pine-trees to roost, making a continual chattering as
they fly along.   On the tallest of these trees they generally build their
nests in company, about the beginning or middle of April; sometimes
ten or fifteen nests being on the same tree.   One of these nests, taken
from a high pine-tree, is now before me.   It measures full five inches
in diameter within, and four in depth; is composed outwardly of mud,
mixed with long stalks and roots of a knotty kind of grass, and lined
with fine bent and horse hair.   The eggs are five, of a bluish olive
color, marked with large spots and straggling streaks of black and
dark brown, also with others of a fainter tinge.   They rarely produce
more than one brood in a season.*

The trees where these birds build are often at no great distance
from the farm-house, and overlook the plantations.   From thence they
issue, in all directions, and with as much confidence, to make their
daily depredations among the surrounding fields, as if the whole were
intended for their use alone.   Their chief attention, however, is directed to the Indian corn in all its progressive stages.   As soon as the
infant blade of this grain begins to make its appearance above ground,
the Grakles hail the welcome signal with screams of peculiar satisfaction, and, without waiting for a formal invitation from the proprietor,
descend on the fields, and begin to pull up and regale themselves on
the seed, scattering the green blades around.   While thus eagerly
employed, the vengeance of the gun sometimes overtakes them; but
these disasters are soon forgotten, and those

———— who live to get away,
Return to steal, another day.

About the beginning of August, when the young ears are in their
milky state, they are attacked with redoubled eagerness by the Grakles
and Redwings, in formidable and combined bodies.   They descend

* Audubon's account of their manner of building is at considerable variance
with that given above by our author.   "The lofty dead trees left standing in our
newly-cultivated fields, have many holes and cavities, some of which have been
bored by Woodpeckers, and others caused by insects or decay.   These are visited
and examined in succession, until, a choice being made, and a few dry weeds and
feathers collected, the female deposits her eggs, which are from four to six in number,
blotched and streaked with brown and black."   Such is the manner of building in
Louisiana; but, in the Northern States, their nests are differently constructed, and,
as mentioned by our author, it is a singular circumstance that a comparatively short
distance should so vary this formation.   "In the Northern States, their nests are
constructed in a more perfect manner.   A pine-tree, whenever it occurs in a convenient place, is selected by preference.   There the Grakle forms a nest, which, from
the ground, might easily be mistaken for that of our Robin, were it less bulky.
But it is much larger, and is associated with others, often to the number of a dozen
or more, on the horizontal branches of the pine, forming tier above tier, from the
lowest to the highest branches.   It is composed of grass, slender roots and mud,
lined with hair and finer grasses."   Mr. Audubon has also once or twice observed
them build in the fissures of rocks.   " The flesh is little better than that of a Crow,
being dry and ill-flavored; notwithstanding it is often used, with the addition of
one or two Golden-winged Woodpeckers, or Redwings, to make what is called
pot-pie.   The eggs, on the contrary, are very delicate." — ED.

like a blackening, sweeping tempest on the corn, dig off the external
covering of twelve or fifteen coats of leaves, as dexterously as if done
by the hand of man, and, having laid bare the ear, leave little behind
to the farmer but the cobs, and shrivelled skins, that contained their
favorite fare. I have seen fields of corn of many acres, where more
than one half was thus ruined. Indeed the farmers, in the immediate
vicinity of the Rivers Delaware and Schuylkill, generally allow one
fourth of this crop to the Blackbirds, among whom our Grakle comes
in for his full share. During these depredations, the gun is making
great havock among their numbers, which has no other effect on the
survivors than to send them to another field, or to another part of the
same field. This system of plunder and retaliation continues until
November, when, towards the middle of that month, they begin to
sheer off towards the south. The lower parts of Virginia, North and
South Carolina, and Georgia, are the winter residences of these flocks.
Here numerous bodies, collecting together from all quarters of the
interior and northern districts, and darkening the air with their numbers,
sometimes form one congregated multitude of many hundred thousands.
A few miles from the banks of the Roanoke, on the 20th of January,
I met with one of those prodigious armies of Grakles. They rose
from the surrounding fields with a noise like thunder, and, descending
on the length of road before me, covered it and the fences completely
with black; and when they again rose, and, after a few evolutions,
descended on the skirts of the high-timbered woods, at that time
destitute of leaves, they produced a most singular and striking effect;
the whole trees for a considerable extent, from the top to the lowest
branches, seemed as if hung in mourning; their notes and screaming
the mean while resembling the distant sound of a great cataract, but in
more musical cadence, swelling and dying away on the ear, according
to the fluctuation of the breeze. In Kentucky, and all along the Mississippi, from its juncture with the Ohio to the Balize, I found numbers
of these birds, so that the Purple Grakle may be considered as a very
general inhabitant of the territory of the United States.

Every industrious farmer complains of the mischief committed on
his corn by the *Crow Blackbirds*, as they are usually called; though,
were the same means used, as with Pigeons, to take them in clap nets,
multitudes of them might thus be destroyed, and the products of them
in market, in some measure, indemnify him for their depredations.
But they are most numerous and most destructive at a time when the
various harvests of the husbandman demand all his attention, and all
his hands, to cut, cure, and take in; and so they escape with a few
sweeps made among them by some of the younger boys with the gun,
and by the gunners from the neighboring towns and villages; and return
from their winter quarters, sometimes early in March, to renew the
like scenes over again. As some consolation, however, to the industrious cultivator, I can assure him, that were I placed in his situation,
I should hesitate whether to consider these birds most as friends or
enemies, as they are particularly destructive to almost all the noxious
worms, grubs and caterpillars, that infest his fields, which, were they
allowed to multiply unmolested, would soon consume nine tenths of
all the production of his labor, and desolate the country with the
miseries of famine! Is not this another striking proof that the Deity

has created nothing in vain? and that it is the duty of man, the lord of the creation, to avail himself of their usefulness, and guard against their bad effects as securely as possible, without indulging in the barbarous and even impious wish for their utter extermination?

The Purple Grakle is twelve inches long, and eighteen in extent; on a slight view, seems wholly black, but placed near, in a good light, the whole head, neck, and breast, appear of a rich glossy steel blue, dark violet, and silky green; the violet prevails most on the head and breast, and the green on the hind part of the neck. The back, rump, and whole lower parts, the breast excepted, reflect a strong coppery gloss; wing-coverts, secondaries, and coverts of the tail, rich light violet, in which the red prevails; the rest of the wings, and rounded tail, are black, glossed with steel blue. All the above colors are extremely shining, varying as differently exposed to the light; iris of the eye, silvery; bill, more than an inch long, strong, and furnished on the inside of the upper mandible with a sharp process, like the stump of the broken blade of a penknife, intended to assist the bird in macerating its food; tongue, thin, bifid at the end, and lacerated along the sides.

The female is rather less, has the upper part of the head, neck, and the back, of a dark sooty brown; chin, breast, and belly, dull pale brown, lightest on the former; wings, tail, lower parts of the back and vent, black, with a few reflections of dark green; legs, feet, bill, and eyes, as in the male.

The Purple Grakle is easily tamed, and sings in confinement. They have also, in several instances, been taught to articulate some few words pretty distinctly.

A singular attachment frequently takes place between this bird and the Fish Hawk. The nest of this latter is of very large dimensions, often from three to four feet in breadth, and from four to five feet high; composed, externally, of large sticks, or fagots, among the interstices of which sometimes three or four pairs of Crow Blackbirds will construct their nests, while the Hawk is sitting or hatching above. Here each pursues the duties of incubation and of rearing their young; living in the greatest harmony, and mutually watching and protecting each other's property from depredators.

SWAMP SPARROW. — FRINGILLA PALUSTRIS. — Fig. 100.

Passer palustris, *Bartram*, p. 291. — *Peale's Museum*, No. 6569.

ZONOTRICHIA PALUSTRIS — Jardine.*

Fringilla palustris, *Bonap. Synop.* p. 111. — The Swamp Sparrow, *Aud.* pl. 64, male; *Orn. Biog.* i. p. 331.

THE history of this obscure and humble species is short and uninteresting. Unknown or overlooked by the naturalists of Europe, it is

* The four species figured in Nos. 100, 101, 102, and 103, will point out the form which Mr. Swainson has designated as above. Of these, the present and

100. Swamp Sparrow. 101. White throated Sp. 102. Savannah Sp. 103. Fox-coloured Sp. 104. Loggerhead Strike. 105. Pelted Kingfisher; 106. Black and Yellow Warbler; 107. Black-
kurian Warbler. 108. Jaurawah W. 109. Water Thrush. 110. Painted Bunting. 111. Female. 112. Featherwing; Warbler. 113. Wormeating W. 114. Yellow winged Sparrow. 115. Rice-crested.

now, for the first time, introduced to the notice of the world. It is one of our summer visitants, arriving in Pennsylvania early in April, frequenting low grounds and river courses; rearing two, and sometimes three, broods in a season; and returning to the south as the cold weather commences. The immense cypress swamps and extensive grassy flats of the Southern States, that border their numerous rivers, and the rich rice plantations, abounding with their favorite seeds and sustenance, appear to be the general winter resort, and grand annual rendezvous, of this and all the other species of Sparrow that remain with us during summer. From the River Trent in North Carolina, to that of Savannah, and still farther south, I found this species very numerous; not flying in flocks, but skulking among the canes, reeds, and grass, seeming shy and timorous, and more attached to the water than any other of their tribe. In the month of April, numbers pass through Pennsylvania to the northward, which I conjecture from the circumstance of finding them at that season in particular parts of the woods, where, during the rest of the year, they are not to be seen. The few that remain frequent the swamps and reedy borders of our creeks and rivers. They form their nest in the ground, sometimes in a tussock of rank grass, surrounded by water, and lay four eggs, of a dirty white, spotted with rufous. So late as the 15th of August, I have seen them feeding their young that were scarcely able to fly. Their principal food is grass seeds, wild oats, and insects. They have no song; are distinguished by a single *chip* or *cheep*, uttered in a rather hoarser tone than that of the Song Sparrow; flirt the tail as they fly; seldom or never take to the trees, but skulk from one low bush or swampy thicket to another.

The Swamp Sparrow is five inches and a half long, and seven inches and a half in extent; the back of the neck and front are black; crown, bright bay, bordered with black; a spot of yellowish white between the eye and nostril; sides of the neck and whole breast, dark ash; chin, white; a streak of black proceeds from the lower mandible, and another from the posterior angle of the eye; back, black, slightly skirted with bay; greater coverts also black, edged with bay; wings and tail, plain brown; belly and vent, brownish white; bill, dusky above, bluish below; eyes, hazle; legs, brown; claws, strong and sharp, for climbing the reeds. The female wants the bay on the crown, or has it indistinctly; over the eye is a line of dull white.

the last will recede from the type, the one in the more slender, the other in the stronger bill, and its even, cutting margins. They in every respect show a strong assimilation with the Bunting, Sparrow, and Lark family, though they cannot properly rank with these. According to the characters now laid down, and I believe properly so, they are a most interesting form when taken in comparison with their representatives in other countries. They appear confined to America. — ED.

19 *

WHITE-THROATED SPARROW.—FRINGILLA ALBICOL-LIS.—Fig. 101.

Fringilla fusca, *Bartram*, p. 291.— *Lath.* ii. 272.— *Edwards*, 304.— *Arct. Zool.* p. 373, No. 248.— *Peale's Museum*, No. 6486.

ZONOTRICHIA PENNSYLVANICA.— Swainson.

Fringilla Pennsylvanica, *Lath. Ind. Orn.* i. p. 445.— *Bonap. Synop.* p. 108.— The White-Throated Sparrow, *Aud.* pl. 8, male and female; *Orn. Biog.* i. p. 42.— *North. Zool.* ii. p. 256.

This is the largest as well as handsomest of all our Sparrows. It winters with the preceding species and several others in most of the states south of New England. From Connecticut to Savannah I found these birds numerous, particularly in the neighborhood of the Roanoke River, and among the rice plantations. In summer they retire to the higher inland parts of the country, and also farther north, to breed. According to Pennant, they are also found at that season in Newfoundland. During their residence here in winter, they collect together in flocks, always preferring the borders of swampy thickets, creeks, and mill-ponds, skirted with alder bushes and long, rank weeds, the seeds of which form their principal food. Early in spring, a little before they leave us, they have a few remarkably sweet and clear notes, generally in the morning a little after sunrise. About the 20th of April they disappear, and we see no more of them till the beginning or second week of October, when they again return; part to pass the winter with us, and part on their route farther south.

The length of the White-throated Sparrow is six inches and a half, breadth, nine inches; the upper part of the back and the lesser wing-coverts are beautifully variegated with black, bay, ash, and light brown; a stripe of white passes from the base of the upper mandible to the hind head; this is bordered on each side with a stripe of black; below this again is another of white passing over each eye, and deepening into orange yellow between that and the nostril; this is again bordered by a stripe of black proceeding from the hind part of the eye; breast, ash; chin, belly, and vent, white; tail, somewhat wedged; legs, flesh colored; bill, a bluish horn color; eye, hazel. In the female, the white stripe on the crown is a light drab; the breast not so dark; the chin less pure; and the line of yellow before the eye scarcely half as long as in the male. All the parts that are white in the male are in the female of a light drab color.

FOX-COLORED SPARROW. — FRINGILLA RUFA. — Fig. 103.

Rusty Bunting, *Arct. Zool.* p. 364, No. 231. *Ibid.* 233. — Ferruginous Finch,
   Ibid. 375, No. 251. — Fringilla rufa, *Bartram*, p. 291. — *Peale's Museum*, No.
   6092.

ZONOTRICHIA ILIACA. — SWAINSON.

Fringilla iliaca, *Bonap. Synop.* p. 112. — Fringilla (zonotrichia) iliaca, *North.
   Zool.* ii. p. 257.

THIS plump and pretty species arrives in Pennsylvania from the
north about the 20th of October; frequents low, sheltered thickets;
associates in little flocks of ten or twelve; and is almost continually
scraping the ground, and rustling among the fallen leaves. I found
this bird numerous in November, among the rich, cultivated flats that
border the River Connecticut; and was informed that it leaves those
places in spring. I also found it in the northern parts of the state of
Vermont. Along the borders of the great reed and cypress swamps
of Virginia and North and South Carolina, as well as around the rice
plantations, I observed this bird very frequently. They also inhabit
Newfoundland.* They are rather of a solitary nature, seldom feeding in the open fields, but generally under thickets, or among tall, rank
weeds on the edges of fields. They sometimes associate with the
Snow Bird, but more generally keep by themselves. Their manners
very much resemble those of the Red-eyed Bunting; they are silent,
tame, and unsuspicious. They have generally no other note while
here than a *shep, shep;* yet I suspect they have some song in the
places where they breed; for I once heard a single one, a little before
the time they leave us, warble out a few very sweet, low notes.
   The Fox-colored Sparrow is six inches long, and nine and a quarter
broad; the upper part of the head and neck is cinereous, edged with
rust color; back, handsomely mottled with reddish brown, and cinereous; wings and tail, bright ferruginous; the primaries, dusky
within and at the tips, the first and second row of coverts, tipped
with white; breast and belly, white; the former, as well as the ear-
feathers, marked with large blotches of bright bay, or reddish brown,
and the beginning of the belly with little arrow-shaped spots of
black; the tail-coverts and tail are a bright fox-color; the legs and
feet, a dirty brownish white, or clay color, and very strong; the bill is
strong, dusky above and yellow below; iris of the eye, hazel. The
chief difference in the female is, that the wings are not of so bright a
bay, inclining more to a drab; yet this is scarcely observable, unless
by a comparison of the two together. They are generally very fat,
live on grass seeds, eggs of insects, and gravel.

* PENNANT.

SAVANNAH SPARROW.—FRINGILLA SAVANNA.—Fig. 102.—
FEMALE.*

Peale's Museum, No. 6584.

ZONOTRICHIA SAVANNA.—Jardine.

Fringilla Savanna, *Bonap. Synop.* p. 108.

THIS new species is an inhabitant of the low countries on the
Atlantic coast, from Savannah, where I first discovered it, to the state
of New York, and is generally resident in these places, though rarely
found inland, or far from the sea-shore. The drawing of this bird
was in the hands of the engraver before I was aware that the male (a
figure of which will appear hereafter) was so much its superior in
beauty of markings and in general colors. With a representation of
the male will also be given particulars of their nest, eggs, and manners, which, from the season, and the few specimens I had the opportunity of procuring, I was at that time unable to collect. I have since
found these birds numerous on the sea-shore, in the state of New
Jersey, particularly near Great Egg Harbor. A pair of these I presented to Mr. Peale of this city, in whose noble collection they now
occupy a place.

The female of the Savannah Sparrow is five inches and a half long,
and eight and a half in extent; the plumage of the back is mottled
with black, bright bay, and whitish; chin, white; breast, marked with
pointed spots of black, edged with bay, running in chains from each
base of the lower mandible; sides, touched with long streaks of the
same; temples, marked with a spot of delicate yellow; ear-feathers,
slightly tinged with the same; belly, white, and a little streaked;
inside of the shoulders, and lining of the wing, pale yellowish; first
and second rows of wing-coverts, tipped with whitish; secondaries
next the body, pointed and very black, edged also with bay; tail,
slightly forked, and without any white feathers; legs, pale flesh color;
hind claw, pretty long.

The very slight distinctions of color which Nature has drawn
between many distinct species of this family of Finches, render these
minute and tedious descriptions absolutely necessary, that the particular species may be precisely discriminated.

* The Male is figured, No. 153.

LOGGERHEAD SHRIKE.—LANIUS CAROLINENSIS.—Fig. 104.

Peale's Museum, No. 557.

LANIUS LUDOVICIANUS.—Bonaparte.

Lanius Ludovicianus, *Bonap. Synop.* p. 72. — The Loggerhead Shrike, *Aud.* pl. 57, male and female ; *Orn. Biog.* i. p. 300.

This species has a considerable resemblance to the Great American Shrike.* It differs, however, from that bird in size, being a full inch shorter; and in color, being much darker on the upper parts ; and in having the frontlet black. It also inhabits the warmer parts of the United States; while the Great American Shrike is chiefly confined to the northern regions, and seldom extends to the south of Virginia.

This species inhabits the rice plantations of Carolina and Georgia, where it is protected for its usefulness in destroying mice. It sits, for hours together, on the fence, beside the stacks of rice, watching like a cat ; and as soon as it perceives a mouse, darts on it like a Hawk. It also feeds on crickets and grasshoppers. Its note, in March, resembled the clear creaking of a sign-board in windy weather. It builds its nest, as I was informed, generally in a detached bush, much like that of the Mocking Bird; but, as the spring was not then sufficiently advanced, I had no opportunity of seeing its eggs. It is generally known by the name of the *Loggerhead.* †

* See Fig. 15.

† In the remarks on the *Tyranninæ*, I observed that only two of the sub-families of the greater division *Laniadæ* existed in North America, — that now alluded to, and the *Lanianæ*, of which our present species, with the *L. borealis* of a former plate, and that of Europe, will form typical examples. Ornithologists have always been at variance with regard to the position of these birds, and have placed them alike with the rapacious Falcons and timid Thrushes. They are, however, the " Falcons of the insect world;" and among the *Insessores* will be the representatives of that group.

America was seen to be the great country of the *Tyranninæ ;* in like manner may the Shrikes claim Africa for their great birth-place. They there wage incessant war on the numerous insect hosts, the larger species occasionally exercising their greater strength on some of the weaker individuals of the feathered race ; and by some gamekeepers, that of this country is killed as a bird of prey, being found to destroy young birds, and even to drag the weak young pheasants through the bars of the breeding coops. Small animals and reptiles also form a part of their prey. They decrease in numbers as the colder and more temperate countries are approached; and the vast extent of North America appears only to contain five species. New Holland alone is without any true *Lanius*, but is supplied by another genus, *Falcunculus*, allied in form, and now containing two species, which also unite somewhat of their habits, and feed on insects, though the mode of taking their prey shows something scansorial.

Among the Tyrants, the powers of flight are developed to a great extent, as suitable to the capture of the particular prey upon which they feed. In the Shrikes, the form is considerably modified ; the wings become more rounded, and the tail graduated ; and the general prey is the larger insects of the orders *Coleoptera* and *Hemiptera*, to capture which does not require so great an exercise of very quick or active powers, and which are often patiently watched for and pounced upon by surprise, in a similar manner to that described of the North American Loggerhead. They have all the character of being cruel and tyrannous, arising from the pecu-

This species is nine inches long, and thirteen in extent; the color above is cinereous, or dark ash; scapulars and line over the eye,

liar manner of impaling their prey upon thorns, or fastening it in the clefts of branches, often in a wanton manner, as if for the sake of murder only, thus fixing up all it can seize upon. One species is particularly remarkable for the regular exhibition of this propensity, and has become proverbial for its cruelty, — *Lanius collaris* of Southern Africa. Its habits are thus described by Le Vaillant : — " When it sees a locust, a mantis, or a small bird, it springs upon it, and immediately carries it off, in order to impale it on a thorn, which it does with great dexterity, always passing the thorn through the head of its victim. Every animal which it seizes is subjected to the same fate ; and it thus continues all day long its murderous career, apparently instigated rather by the love of mischief than the desire of food. Its throne of tyranny is usually a dry and elevated branch of a tree, from which it pounces on all intruders, driving off the stronger and more troublesome, and impaling the inexperienced alive ; when hungry, it visits its shambles, and helps itself to a savory meal." The Hottentots assured Le Vaillant that it does not love fresh food, and therefore leaves its prey on the gibbet till it becomes putrescent ; but beneath the scorching sun of Africa, the process of decomposition sometimes does not take place, from the rapid exhalation of the animal fluids in a warm and arid atmosphere, and, consequently, whatever spiny shrub may have been chosen by the Butcher Bird as the place of execution, is frequently found covered, not with sweet-smelling and many-colored blossoms, but with the dried carcasses of singing birds, and the bodies of locusts, and other insects of the larger size. The species of Great Britain, also, exercises this propensity ; but, according to Mr. Selby, it invariably kills its prey by strangulation before transfixing it. That gentleman mentions once having the gratification of witnessing this operation of the Shrike upon a Hedge Accentor, which it had just killed. " In this instance, after killing the bird, it hovered, with its prey in its bill, for a short time over the hedge, apparently occupied in selecting a thorn fit for its purpose. Upon disturbing it, and advancing to the spot, I found the Accentor firmly fixed by the tendons of the wing at the selected twig." When in confinement, this peculiarity is also displayed, in placing the food against or between the wires of the cage. They frequent woody countries, with occasional shrubs and hedges, among which they also breed ; the notes, as might be expected, are hoarse and grating, and during the season of incubation become very garrulous, particularly when alarmed ; they are very attentive to their young, and continue long to feed and attend them after they are able to shift for themselves. It may be here remarked that the *Falconidæ*, which our present knowledge leads us to think is represented by this group, always take their prey to some eminence before commencing to devour it — a bare hillock or rock in an open country, the top of some old mound or dike, or, if in a wood, some decayed stump ; and I have known one spot of frequent recurrence by the same individuals ; thus showing some analogy to each other.

The following seem to be the species which are known to belong to North America : —

1. *L. borealis*, Vieill. — *L. excubitor*, Wils. Vol. i. p. 74, *L. borealis*, Bonap. Synop. App.*

2. *L. ludovicianus*, Bonap. — *L. Carolinensis*, Wils. Vol. iii. p. 57 ; found only in the warmer and more southern states, the Carolinas and Georgia.

3. *Lanius excubitroides*, Sw. *Nov. spec.* — American Gray Shrike, *North. Zool.* Vol. ii. p. 115.

Specimens were brought to this country by the last over-land arctic expedition. According to Dr. Richardson, it is a more northern bird than *L. borealis*, and does not advance farther north in summer than the 54° of latitude, and it attains that parallel only in the meridian of the warm and sandy plains of the Saskatchewan, which enjoy an earlier spring, and longer summer, than the densely-wooded country betwixt them and Hudson's Bay. Its manners are precisely similar to those of *L. borealis*, feeding chiefly on grasshoppers, which are exceedingly

---

* When writing the note at page 49, I was not aware that Bonaparte had taken notice of the mistake mentioned there in his Appendix to the Synopsis of North American Birds. — ED.

whitish; wings, black, with a small spot of white at the base of the primaries, and tipped with white; a stripe of black passes along the front, through each eye, half way down the side of the neck; eye, dark hazel, sunk below the eyebrow; tail, cuneiform, the four middle feathers wholly black; the four exterior ones, on each side, tipped, more and more with white to the outer one, which is nearly all white; whole lower parts, white; and in some specimens, both of males and females, marked with transverse lines of very pale brown; bill and legs, black.

The female is considerably darker both above and below, but the black does not reach so high on the front; it is also rather less in size.

BELTED KINGSFISHER. — ALCEDO ALCYON. — Fig. 105. —
Female.

Bartram, p. 289. — *Turton*, p. 278. — *Peale's Museum*, No. 2145.

ALCEDO ALCYON. — Linnæus.*

Alcedo alcyon, *Bonap. Synop.* p. 49. — The Belted Kingsfisher, *Aud.* pl. 77; *Orn. Biog.* i. p. 394.

This is a general inhabitant of the banks and shores of all our fresh water rivers, from Hudson's Bay to Mexico; and is the only species of its tribe found within the United States. This last circum-

numerous. Its nest was found in a bush of willows, built of twigs of *Artemesiæ* and dried grass, and lined with feathers; the eggs, six in number, were very pale yellowish gray, with many irregular and confluent spots of oil green, interspersed with a few of smoke gray.

The merit of unravelling this species from several very closely allied to it in its native country, and from that to which it approaches nearest, the *L. excubitor* of Europe, is due to Mr. Swainson; the chief distinctive characters given by that naturalist are the small proportions of the bill, the frontal feathers crossed by a narrow band of deep black, the black stripe on the side of the head encircling the upper margin of the eyelid, lateral scales of the tarsus being divided in several pieces, the shorter length of the wing when closed, and in the tail being more graduated; the total length is nine inches, six lines.

4. *Lanius elegans*, Sw. — White-crowned Shrike.
Described by Mr. Swainson, from a specimen in the British Museum, to which it was presented from the Fur countries by the Hudson's Bay Company. It may at once be distinguished from the other American Shrikes, by the much greater quantity of white on the wings and tail; its narrower tail-feathers, longer tarsi, and less curved claws; the length is about nine inches.

5. *Lanius* (?) *natka*, Penn. — Natka Shrike.
This species, the Nootka Shrike of Dr. Latham, from Nootka Sound, on the north-west coast of North America, seems to be of such dubious authority, that little can be said regarding it. — Ed.

* The description of Wilson, and that of Audubon, which has been added in a note from the *Ornithological Biography*, give a very correct detail of the general manners of the true Kingsfishers, or those resembling that of this country; there is throughout the family, however, a very considerable difference in form, and, as a matter of course, a corresponding difference in habit; this has occasioned a di-

stance, and its characteristic appearance, make it as universally known here as its elegant little brother, the Common Kingsfisher of Europe, is in Britain. Like the lovelorn swains, of whom poets tell us, he delights in murmuring streams and falling waters; not, however,

vision of them into various groups, by almost all ornithologists; that to which our present species belongs, and of which it is the largest, contains all those of smaller size with four toes and sharp angular and lengthened bills; they feed entirely on fish and aquatic insects, and live on the banks of rivers, lakes, and creeks, and occasionally on the sea-shore. They are distributed over the world, but the warmer parts of India, Africa, and South America, possess the greatest share, North America and Europe possessing only one each. The colors of the plumage, with a few exceptions, particularly the upper parts, are very bright and shining, the webs of the feathers unconnected and loose; the under parts generally white, with shades of reddish brown and orange; the division nearest to this, containing but a few species of very small size, but similar in form and coloring, has been separated on account of having three toes, and, I believe, is exclusively Indian. Another and a well-marked group is the Halcyon of Mr. Swainson; it differs materially in the form and manners of living, and ranges every where, except in North America and Europe. The birds are all above the middle size, with a stouter and more robust form; the colors sometimes very gaudy, in others of rich and pleasing shades of brown. The bill, a chief organ of distinction, is large, much dilated at the base, and, in one or two instances, very strong. They inhabit moist woods and shady streams or creeks, where they watch on a motionless perch for the larger insects, as the common European species does for fish, and they dart upon them when passing, or when seen on the ground, and return again to the same branch or rock; they also chase their prey in the manner of the Flycatchers. Notwithstanding these are their common food, fish, water insects, in a few instances crabs, are resorted to, and in all cases the vicinity of water seems requisite for their healthy support. There is an individual (*Alcedo dea*) which has been separated from this under the name of *Tanysiptera;* the only distinction, now, (for it has four toes,) is the elongation of two tail-feathers, which exceed the length of the body considerably; it was originally discovered in the Isle of Ternate, and, according to Lesson, is abundant in New Guinea, where it is killed by the natives for ornaments, and those coming to this country, being impaled on reeds, are consequently much mutilated. Another division will comprise the very large New Holland species, under the title of *Dacelo;* [*] this contains yet only two species, commonly known by the name of "Laughing Jackasses;" by the natives they are called Cuck'unda; they are nearly as large as a Common Pigeon, and have all the members very powerful; the bill is much dilated, and bent at the tip; according to Lesson, their chief food is large insects, which they seize on the ground; that ornithologist extends the genus to several of the larger-billed small species; we would now restrict it as bearing better marks to those of New Holland only, *D. gigantea* and *Leachii.* Another division has been formed among these curious birds, also by M. Lesson, of the *Alcedo rufipes* of Cuvier, under the name of *Syma,* and, as a specific appellation, that of *Torotora,* by which it is known to the Papous, in its native country, New Guinea. It frequents rivers and the sea-shores, and feeds on fish; the principal distinction for which it has been separated is a serrature of the mandibles of the bill. M. Lesson, however, did not perceive any thing different from its congeners to which this structure could be applied. From the above remarks it will be seen that the old genus *Alcedo* has been separated into no less than nine divisions. Four of these will, perhaps, only be necessary, and are as follows:—
1. *Alcedo;* having the form of *Alcedo ispida;* feeding principally on fish; the geographical distribution, the known world, except very northern latitudes; the number of species and individuals increasing from the extremes. 2. *Halcyon;* the form of *Sanctus, cinamomeus, omnicolor,* &c.; containing Lesson's *Todyrampus;* also, perhaps, his *Syma,* and the *Tanysiptera* of Vigors; the two latter groups, as

---

[*] M. Lesson proposes a genus (*Todyrampus*) for all the smaller New Holland species, taking *A. sacra* as the type, on account, principally, of the more dilated bill. The same gentleman proposes the titles *Melidora* and *Choucalcyon,* to designate forms among the Kingsfishers which I have not ascertained.

merely that they may soothe his ear, but for a gratification somewhat
more substantial. Amidst the roar of the cataract, or over the foam of
a torrent, he sits perched upon an overhanging bough, glancing his
piercing eye in every direction below for his scaly prey, which, with
a sudden, circular plunge, he sweeps from their native element, and
swallows in an instant. His voice, which is not unlike the twirling
of a watchman's rattle, is naturally loud, harsh, and sudden; but is
softened by the sound of the brawling streams and cascades among
which he generally rambles. He courses along the windings of the
brook or river, at a small height above the surface, sometimes suspending himself by the rapid action of his wings, like certain species of
Hawks, ready to pounce on the fry below ; now and then settling on
an old, dead, overhanging limb to reconnoitre.* Mill-dams are particularly visited by this feathered fisher ; and the sound of his pipe is as
well known to the miller as the rattling of his own hopper. Rapid
streams, with high, perpendicular banks, particularly if they be of a
hard clayey or sandy nature, are also favorite places of resort for this
bird ; not only because in such places the small fish are more exposed
to view, but because those steep and dry banks are the chosen situations for his nest. Into these he digs with bill and claws horizontally,
sometimes to the extent of four or five feet, at the distance of a foot or
two from the surface. The few materials he takes in are not always
placed at the extremity of the hole, that he and his mate may have
room to turn with convenience. The eggs are five, pure white, and
the first brood usually comes out about the beginning of June, and
sometimes sooner, according to the part of the country where they
reside. On the shores of Kentucky River, near the town of Frankfort,
I found the female sitting early in April. They are very tenacious of
their haunts, breeding for several successive years in the same hole,
and do not readily forsake it, even though it be visited. An intelligent
young gentleman informed me, that having found where a Kingsfisher
built, he took away its eggs from time to time, leaving always one
behind, until he had taken no less than eighteen from the same nest.
At some of these visits, the female, being within, retired to the extremity of the hole, while he withdrew the egg, and next day, when
he returned, he found she had laid again as usual.

The fabulous stories related by the ancients of the nest, manner of

species, would be at once distinguished by the peculiarities of form, which are perhaps not sufficient to indicate a genus without more of like characters ; the geographical distribution, South America, New Holland, Africa, and India. 3. *Dacelo;* the form, *D. gigantea;* geographical distribution, New Holland. And,
4. *Ceyx;* containing the Three-toed Kingsfisher, *C. tridactyla;* geographical distribution, India. — ED.

* Mr. Audubon mentions, that this species sometimes also visits the salt water
creeks, diving after fish ; when crossing from one lake to another, which it frequently does, it passes over forests in a direct line, not unfrequently by a course of
twenty or thirty miles, towards the interior of the country. Its motions at this time
consist of a series of slops, about five or six in number, followed by a direct glide,
without any apparent undulation

They dig the holes for their nest with great despatch. As an instance of their
working with celerity, the same gentleman mentions, that he hung a small net in
front of one of their holes to entrap the bird ; but, ere morning, it
had scratched its way out. On the following evening, he stopped up the hole for
upwards of a foot with a stick, but the same thing again took place. — ED.

hatching, &c., of the Kingsfisher, are too trifling to be repeated here. Over the winds and the waves the humble Kingsfishers of our days — at least, the species now before us — have no control. Its nest is neither constructed of glue nor fish-bones, but of loose grass and a few feathers; it is not thrown on the surface of the water to float about, with its proprietor, at random, but snugly secured from the winds and the weather in the recesses of the earth. Neither is its head or its feathers believed, even by the most illiterate of our clowns or seamen, to be a charm for love, a protection against witchcraft, or a security for fair weather. It is neither venerated, like those of the Society Isles, nor dreaded, like those of some other countries; but is considered merely as a bird that feeds on fish; is generally fat; relished by *some* as good eating; and is now and then seen exposed for sale in our markets.

Though the Kingsfisher generally remains with us, in Pennsylvania, until the commencement of cold weather, it is seldom seen here in winter; but returns to us early in April. In North and South Carolina, I observed numbers of these birds in the months of February and March. I also frequently noticed them on the shores of the Ohio, in February, as high up as the mouth of the Muskingum.

I suspect this bird to be a native of the Bahama Islands, as well as of our continent. In passing between these isles and the Florida shore, in the month of July, a Kingsfisher flew several times round our ship, and afterwards shot off to the south.

The length of this species is twelve inches and a half; extent, twenty; back and whole upper parts, a light bluish slate color; round the neck is a collar of pure white, which reaches before to the chin; head, large, crested; the feathers, long and narrow, black in the centre, and generally erect; the shafts of all the feathers, except the white plumage, are black; belly and vent, white; sides under the wings, variegated with blue; round the upper part of the breast passes a band of blue, interspersed with some light brown feathers; before the eye is a small spot of white, and another immediately below it; the bill is three inches long from the point to the slit of the mouth, strong, sharp-pointed, and black, except near the base of the lower mandible, and at the tip, where it is of a horn color; primaries and interior webs of the secondaries, black, spotted with white; the interior vanes of the tail-feathers, elegantly spotted with white on a jet-black ground; lower side, light colored; exterior vanes, blue; wing-coverts and secondaries, marked with small specks of white; legs, extremely short; when the bird perches, it generally rests on the lower side of the second joint, which is thereby thick and callous; claws, stout and black; whole leg, of a dirty yellowish color; above the knee, bare of feathers for half an inch; the two exterior toes united together for nearly their whole length.

The female is sprinkled all over with specks of white; the band of blue around the upper part of the breast is nearly half reddish brown; and a little below this passes a band of bright reddish bay, spreading on each side under the wings. The blue and rufous feathers on the breast are strong, like scales. The head is also of a much darker blue than the back, and the white feathers on the chin and throat of an exquisite fine, glossy texture, like the most beautiful satin.

BLACK AND YELLOW WARBLER. — SYLVIA MAGNOLIA. —
Fig. 106.

Peale's Museum, No. 7783.

SYLVICOLA MACULOSA. — Swainson.

Sylvia maculosa, *Lath. Ind. Orn.* ii. p. 536. — *Bonap. Synop.* p. 78. — Yellow-Rump Warbler, *Penn. Arct. Zool.* ii. p. 400. — The Black and Yellow Warbler, (the young is figured only,) *Aud.* pl. 50; *Orn. Biog.* i. p. 260. — Sylvicola maculosa, *North. Zool.* ii. p. 212.

THIS bird I first met with on the banks of the Little Miami, near its junction with the Ohio. I afterwards found it among the magnolias, not far from Fort Adams, on the Mississippi. These two, both of which happened to be males, are all the individuals I have ever shot of this species; from which I am justified in concluding it to be a very scarce bird in the United States. Mr. Peale, however, has the merit of having been the first to discover this elegant species, which, he informs me, he found, several years ago, not many miles from Philadelphia. No notice has ever been taken of this bird by any European naturalist whose works I have examined. Its notes, or rather chirpings, struck me as very peculiar and characteristic, but have no claim to the title of song. It kept constantly among the higher branches, and was very active and restless.

Length, five inches; extent, seven inches and a half; front, ores, and behind the ear, black; over the eye, a fine line of white, and another small touch of the same immediately under; back, nearly all black; shoulders, thinly streaked with olive; rump, yellow; tail-coverts, jet black; inner vanes of the lateral tail-feathers, white to within half an inch of the tip, where they are black; two middle ones, wholly black; whole lower parts, rich yellow, spotted from the throat downwards with black streaks; vent, white; tail, slightly forked; wings, black, crossed with two broad, transverse bars of white; crown, fine ash; legs, brown; bill, black. Markings of the female not known.

BLACKBURNIAN WARBLER. — SYLVIA BLACKBURNIÆ. —
Fig. 107.

Lath. ii. p. 461, No. 67. — *Peale's Museum*, No. 7060.

SYLVICOLA BLACKBURNIÆ. — Jardine.

Sylvia Blackburniæ, *Bonap. Synop.* p. 80.

THIS is another scarce species in Pennsylvania, making its appearance here about the beginning of May, and again in September, on its return, but is seldom seen here during the middle of summer. It is an active, silent bird; inhabits also the state of New York, from whence it was first sent to Europe. Mr. Latham has numbered this as a variety of the Yellow-fronted Warbler, a very different species. The specimen sent to Europe, and first described by Pennant, appears also to have been a female, as the breast is said to be yellow, instead of the brilliant orange with which it is ornamented. Of the nest and habits of this bird I can give no account, as there is not more than one or two of these birds to be found here in a season, even with the most diligent search.

The Blackburnian Warbler is four inches and a half long, and seven in extent; crown, black, divided by a line of orange; the black again bounded on the outside by a stripe of rich orange passing over the eye; under the eye, a small touch of orange yellow; whole throat and breast, rich, fiery orange, bounded by spots and streaks of black; belly, dull yellow, also streaked with black; vent, white; back, black, skirted with ash; wings, the same, marked with a large lateral spot of white; tail, slightly forked; the interior vanes of the three exterior feathers, white; cheeks, black; bill and legs, brown. The female is yellow where the male is orange; the black streaks are also more obscure and less numerous.

AUTUMNAL WARBLER. — SYLVIA AUTUMNALIS. — Fig. 108.

SYLVICOLA? AUTUMNALIS. — Jardine.

Sylvicola autumnalis, *Bonap. Synop.* p. 84. — The Autumnal Warbler, *Aud.* plate 88; *Orn. Biog.* i. p. 447.

This plain, little species regularly visits Pennsylvania from the north, in the month of October, gleaning among the willow leaves; but, what is singular, is rarely seen in spring. From the 1st to the 15th of October, they may be seen in considerable numbers, almost every day, in gardens, particularly among the branches of the weeping-willow, and seem exceedingly industrious. They have some resemblance, in color, to the Pine-creeping Warbler; but do not run along the trunk like that bird, neither do they give a preference to the pines. They are also less. After the first of November, they are no longer to be found, unless the season be uncommonly mild. These birds, doubtless, pass through Pennsylvania in spring, on their way to the north; but either make a very hasty journey, or frequent the tops of the tallest trees; for I have never yet met with one of them in that season, though in October I have seen more than a hundred in an afternoon's excursion.

Length, four inches and three quarters; breadth, eight inches; whole upper parts, olive green, streaked on the back with dusky stripes; tail-coverts, ash, tipped with olive; tail, black, edged with dull white; the three exterior feathers, marked near the tip with white; wings, deep dusky, edged with olive, and crossed with two bars of white; primaries, also tipped, and three secondaries next the body, edged with white; upper mandible, dusky brown; lower, as well as the chin and breast, dull yellow; belly and vent, white; legs, dusky brown; feet and claws, yellow; a pale, yellow ring surrounds the eye. The males of these birds often warble out some low but very sweet notes, while searching among the leaves in autumn.

WATER THRUSH. — TURDUS AQUATICUS. — Fig. 109.

Peale's Museum, No. 6896.

SEIURUS AQUATICUS. — Swainson.

New York Warbler, *Penn. Arct. Zool.* ii. p. 303. — Sylvia Noveboracensis, *Bonap. Synop.* p. 77. — Seiurus aquaticus, Aquatic Accentor, *North. Zool.* ii. p. 229.

This bird is remarkable for its partiality to brooks, rivers, shores, ponds, and streams of water; wading in the shallows in search of aquatic insects, wagging the tail almost continually, chattering as it flies; and, in short, possesses many strong traits and habits of the Water Wagtail. It is also exceedingly shy, darting away on the least attempt to approach it, and uttering a sharp *chip* repeatedly, as if greatly alarmed. Among the mountain streams in the state of Tennessee, I found a variety of this bird pretty numerous, with legs of a bright yellow color; in other respects, it differed not from the rest. About the beginning of May, it passes through Pennsylvania to the north; is seen along the channels of our solitary streams for ten or twelve days; afterwards disappears until August. It is probable that it breeds in the higher mountainous districts even of this state, as do many other of our spring visitants that regularly pass a week or two with us in the lower parts, and then retire to the mountains and inland forests to breed.

But Pennsylvania is not the favorite resort of this species. The cane brakes, swamps, river shores, and deep, watery solitudes of Louisiana, Tennessee, and the Mississippi Territory, possess them in abundance; there they are eminently distinguished by the loudness, sweetness, and expressive vivacity of their notes, which begin very high and clear, falling with an almost imperceptible gradation till they are scarcely articulated. At these times the musician is perched on the middle branches of a tree over the brook or river bank, pouring out his charming melody, that may be distinctly heard for nearly half a mile. The voice of this little bird appeared to me so exquisitely sweet and expressive, that I was never tired of listening to it, while traversing the deep-shaded hollows of those cane brakes where it usually resorts. I have never yet met with its nest.

The Water Thrush is six inches long, and nine and a half in extent; the whole upper parts are of a uniform and very dark olive, with a line of white extending over the eye, and along the sides of the neck; the lower parts are white, tinged with yellow ochre; the whole breast and sides are marked with pointed spots or streaks of black or deep brown; bill, dusky brown; legs, flesh colored; tail, nearly even; bill, formed almost exactly like the Golden-crowned Thrush, above described, (Fig. 59;) and, except in frequenting the water, much resembling it in manners. Male and female nearly alike.

20 *

PAINTED BUNTING. — EMBERIZA CIRIS. — Fig. 110, Male;
Fig. 111, Female.

Linn. Syst. 313. — Painted Finch, *Catesb.* i. 44. — *Edw.* 130, 173. — *Arct. Zool.*
p. 362, No. 226. — Le Verdier de la Louisiane, dit vulgairement le Pape, *Briss.*
iii. 200, *App.* 74. — *Buff.* iv. 76, *Pl. enl.* 159. — *Lath.* ii. 206. — Linaria ciris,
The Painted Finch, or Nonpareil, *Bartram*, p. 291. — *Peale's Museum*, No. 6062
and 6063.

SPIZA CIRIS. — Bonaparte.*

Fringilla (sub-genus Spiza) ciris, *Bonap. Synop.* p. 107. — La pesserine nonpareil
ou le papa, Passerina ciris, *Vieill. Gall. des Ois.* pl. 66. — The Painted Finch,
Aud. pl. 53, male and female; *Orn. Biog.* i. 279.

This is one of the most numerous of the little summer birds of
Lower Louisiana, where it is universally known among the French inhabitants, and called by them *Le Pape*, and by the Americans *The
Nonpareil.* Its gay dress and docility of manners have procured it
many admirers; for these qualities are strongly attractive, and carry
their own recommendations always along with them. The low countries of the Southern States, in the vicinity of the sea, and along the
borders of our large rivers, particularly among the rice plantations, are
the favorite haunts of this elegant little bird. A few are seen in North
Carolina; in South Carolina they are more numerous, and still more
so in the lower parts of Georgia. To the westward, I first met them
at Natchez, on the Mississippi, where they seemed rather scarce.
Below Baton Rouge, along the Levee, or embankment of the river, they
appeared in great numbers; and continued to become more common
as I approached New Orleans, where they were warbling from almost
every fence, and crossing the road before me every few minutes.
Their notes very much resemble those of the Indigo Bird, (Fig. 23,)
but want the strength and energy of the latter, being more feeble and
more concise.

* From the general request of this species as a pet, it is requisite that considerable
numbers should be taken, and the method used is thus described by Audubon. I
may remark, in the taking of various birds alive, "call birds," or tame ones,
trained for the purpose of decoy, are commonly used in all countries, and in some
instances, a stuffed specimen, or even a representation made of Paris plaster, is
used with success.

"A male bird, in full plumage, is shot, and stuffed in a defensive attitude, and
perched among some grass seed, rice, or other food, on the same platform as the
trap-cage. This is taken to the fields, or near the orangeries, and placed in so open
a situation, that it would be difficult for a living bird of any species to fly over it
without observing it. The trap is set. A male Painted Finch passes, perceives it,
and dives towards the stuffed bird, brings down the trap, and is made prisoner.
In this manner, thousands of these birds are caught every spring; and so pertina-
cious are they in their attacks, that, even when the trap has closed upon them, they
continue pecking at the feathers of the supposed rival."

They feed immediately, and some have been kept in confinement for ten years.
They cost about sixpence in New Orleans; but, in London, three guineas are
sometimes asked.

The various generic nomenclature to which this bird has been subjected, shows
that ornithologists are at variance in opinion. It forms part of the first section of
Bonaparte's sub-genus *Spiza*, to which should also be referred the *Fringilla Cyanea*, (Fig. 23.) — Ed.

I found these birds very commonly domesticated in the houses of the French inhabitants of New Orleans, appearing to be the most common cage bird they have. The negroes often bring them to market, from the neighboring plantations, for sale; either in cages, taken in traps, or in the nest. A wealthy French planter, who lives on the banks of the Mississippi, a few miles below Bayou Fourche, took me into his garden, which is spacious and magnificent, to show me his aviary; where, among many of our common birds, I observed several Nonpareils, two of which had nests, and were then hatching.

Were the same attention bestowed on these birds as on the Canary, I have no doubt but they would breed with equal facility, and become equally numerous and familiar, while the richness of their plumage might compensate for their inferiority of song. Many of them have been transported to Europe; and I think I have somewhere read, that in Holland attempts have been made to breed them, and with success. When the employments of the people of the United States become more sedentary, like those of Europe, the innocent and agreeable amusement of keeping and rearing birds in this manner, will become more general than it is at present, and their manners better known. And I cannot but think, that an intercourse with these little innocent warblers is favorable to delicacy of feeling and sentiments of humanity; for I have observed the rudest and most savage softened into benevolence while contemplating the interesting manners of these inoffensive little creatures.

Six of these birds, which I brought with me from New Orleans by sea, soon became reconciled to the cage. In good weather, the males sang with great sprightliness, though they had been caught only a few days before my departure. They were greedily fond of flies, which accompanied us in great numbers during the whole voyage; and many of the passengers amused themselves with catching these, and giving them to the Nonpareils; till, at length, the birds became so well acquainted with this amusement, that as soon as they perceived any of the people attempting to catch flies, they assembled at the front of the cage, stretching out their heads through the wires with eager expectation, evidently much interested in the issue of their efforts.

These birds arrive in Louisiana, from the south, about the middle of April, and begin to build early in May. In Savannah, according to Mr. Abbot, they arrive about the 20th of April. Their nests are usually fixed in orange hedges, or on the lower branches of the orange-tree; I have also found them in a common bramble or blackberry bush. They are formed exteriorly of dry grass, intermingled with the silk of caterpillars, lined with hair, and, lastly, with some extremely fine roots of plants. The eggs are four or five, white, or rather pearl colored, marked with purplish brown specks. As some of these nests had eggs so late as the 25th of June, I think it probable that they sometimes raise two broods in the same season. The young birds of both sexes, during the first season, are of a fine green olive above, and dull yellow below. The females undergo little or no change, but that of becoming of a more brownish cast. The males, on the contrary, are long and slow in arriving at their full variety of colors. In the second season, the blue on the head begins to make its appearance, intermixed with the olive green; the next year, the yellow shows itself on the back and rump, and also the red, in detached spots, on the throat and lower parts. All these colors are completed in the fourth season, except, sometimes, that the green still continues on the tail. On the fourth and fifth season, the bird has attained his complete colors, and appears then as represented in the plate, (Fig. 110.) No dependence, however, can be placed on the regularity of this change in birds confined in a cage, as the want of proper food, sunshine, and variety of climate, all conspire against the regular operations of nature.

The Nonpareil is five inches and three quarters long, and eight inches and three quarters in extent; head, neck above, and sides of the same, a rich purplish blue; eyelid, chin, and whole lower parts, vermilion; back and scapulars, glossy yellow, stained with rich green, and in old birds with red; lesser wing-coverts, purple; larger, green; wings, dusky red, sometimes edged with green; lower part of the back, rump, and tail-coverts, deep glossy red, inclining to carmine; tail, slightly forked, purplish brown, (generally green;) legs and feet, leaden gray; bill, black above, pale blue below; iris of the eye, hazel.

The female (Fig. 111) is five and a half inches long, and eight inches in extent; upper parts, green olive, brightest on the rump; lower parts, a dusky Naples yellow, brightest on the belly, and tinged considerably on the breast with dull green, or olive; cheeks, or ear-feathers, marked with lighter touches; bill, wholly a pale lead color, lightest below; legs and feet, the same.

The food of these birds consists of rice, insects, and various kinds of seeds that grow luxuriantly in their native haunts. I also observed them eating the seeds or internal grains of ripe figs. They frequent gardens, building within a few paces of the house; are particularly attached to orangeries; and chant occasionally during the whole summer. Early in October they retire to more southern climates, being extremely susceptible of cold.

PROTHONOTARY WARBLER. — SYLVIA PROTONOTARIUS.
— Fig. 112.

Arct. Zool. p. 410. — *Buff.* v. 316. — *Lath.* ii. 494. *Pl. enl.* 704. — *Peale's Museum*, No. 7020.

VERMIVORA? PROTONOTARIUS. — Jardine.

Sylvia (sub-genus Dacnis, *Cuv.*) protonotarius, *Bonap. Synop.* p. 86. — The Prothonotary Warbler, *Aud.* pl. 3, male and female; *Orn. Biog.* i. p. 22.

This is an inhabitant of the same country as the preceding species, and also a passenger from the south, with this difference, that the bird now before us seldom approaches the house or garden, but keeps among the retired, deep, and dark, swampy woods, through which it flits nimbly in search of small caterpillars, uttering every now and then a few screaking notes, scarcely worthy of notice. They are abundant in the Mississippi and New Orleans Territories, near the river, but are rarely found on the high ridges inland.

From the peculiar form of its bill, being roundish and remarkably pointed, this bird might, with propriety, be classed as a sub-genera, or separate family, including several others, viz., the Blue-winged Yellow Warbler, the Gold-crowned Warbler, and Golden-winged Warbler, represented in No. 68, and the Worm-eating Warbler, No. 113, and a few more. The bills of all these correspond nearly in form and pointedness, being generally longer, thicker at the base, and more round than those of the genus *Sylvia*, generally. The first-mentioned species, in particular, greatly resembles this in its general appearance; but the bill of the Prothonotary is rather stouter, and the yellow much deeper, extending farther on the back; its manners, and the country it inhabits, are also different.

This species is five inches and a half long, and eight and a half in extent; the head, neck, and whole lower parts, (except the vent,) are of a remarkably rich and brilliant yellow, slightly inclining to orange; vent, white; back, scapulars, and lesser wing-coverts, yellow olive; wings, rump, and tail-coverts, a lead blue; interior vanes of the former, black; tail, nearly even, and black, broadly edged with blue; all the feathers, except the two middle ones, are marked on their inner vanes, near the tip, with a spot of white; bill, long, stout, sharp-pointed, and wholly black; eyes, dark hazel; legs and feet, a leaden gray. The female differs in having the yellow and blue rather of a duller tint; the inferiority, however, is scarcely noticeable.

WORM-EATING WARBLER. — SYLVIA VERMIVORA. —
Fig. 113.

Arct. Zool. p. 406, No. 300. — *Edw.* 305. — *Lath.* ii. 499. — Le demi-fin mangeur de vers, *Buff.* v. 325. — *Peale's Museum*, No. 6848.

VERMIVORA PENNSYLVANICA. — Swainson.*

Ficedula Pennsylvanica, *Briss.* i. 457. — Sylvia (sub-genus Dacnis, *Cuv.*) Pennsylvanica, *Bonap. Synop.* p. 86. — The Worm-eating Warbler, *Aud.* pl. 34, male and female; *Orn. Biog.* i. p. 177.

THIS is one of the nimblest species of its whole family, inhabiting the same country with the preceding, but extending its migrations much farther north. It arrives in Pennsylvania about the middle of May, and leaves us in September. I have never yet met with its nest, but have seen them feeding their young about the 25th of June. This bird is remarkably fond of spiders, darting about wherever there is a probability of finding these insects. If there be a branch broken, and the leaves withered, it shoots among them in preference to every other

---

* This species is the type of Mr. Swainson's genus *Vermivora*. The specific title is therefore lost, and I see none better than the restoration of Brisson's old one. — ED.

part of the tree, making a great rustling, in search of its prey. I have often watched its manœuvres while thus engaged, and flying from tree to tree in search of such places. On dissection, I have uniformly found their stomachs filled with spiders or caterpillars, or both. Its note is a feeble chirp, rarely uttered.

The Worm-Eater is five inches and a quarter in length, and eight inches in extent; back, tail, and wings, a fine clear olive; tips and inner vanes of the wing-quills, a dusky brown; tail, slightly forked, yet the exterior feathers are somewhat shorter than the middle ones; head and whole lower parts, a dirty buff; the former marked with four streaks of black, one passing from each nostril, broadening as it descends the hind head; and one from the posterior angle of each eye; the bill is stout, straight, pretty thick at the base, roundish, and tapering to a fine point; no bristles at the side of the mouth; tongue, thin, and lacerated at the tip; the breast is most strongly tinged with the orange buff; vent, waved with dusky olive; bill, blackish above, flesh-colored below; legs and feet, a pale clay color; eye, dark hazel. The female differs very little in color from the male.

On this species Mr. Pennant makes the following remarks : — " Does not appear in Pennsylvania till July, in its passage northward. Does not return the same way, but is supposed to go beyond the mountains which lie to the west. This seems to be the case with all the transient vernal visitants of Pennsylvania." * That a small bird should permit the whole spring, and half of the summer, to pass away before it thought of "passing to the north to breed," is a circumstance, one should think, would have excited the suspicion of so discerning a naturalist as the author of *Arctic Zoology*, as to its truth. I do not know that this bird breeds to the northward of the United States. As to their returning home by "the country beyond the mountains," this must, doubtless, be for the purpose of finishing the education of their striplings here, as is done in Europe, by making the grand tour. This, by the by, would be a much more convenient retrograde route for the Ducks and Geese; as, like the Kentuckians, they could take advantage of the current of the Ohio and Mississippi, to float down to the southward. Unfortunately, however, for this pretty theory, all our vernal visitants, with which I am acquainted, are contented to plod home by the same regions through which they advanced, not even excepting the Geese.

* *Arctic Zoology*, p. 406.

YELLOW-WINGED SPARROW.—FRINGILLA PASSERINA.—
Fig. 114.

Peale's Museum, No. 6585

EMBERIZA? PASSERINA.—JARDINE.*

Fringilla (sub-genus Spiza) passerina, *Bonap. Synop.* p. 109.

THIS small species is now for the first time introduced to the notice of the public. I can, however, say little towards illustrating its history, which, like that of many individuals of the human race, would be but a dull detail of humble obscurity. It inhabits the lower parts of New York and Pennsylvania; is very numerous on Staten Island, where I first observed it; and occurs also along the sea-coast of New Jersey. But, though it breeds in each of these places, it does not remain in any of them during the winter. It has a short, weak, interrupted cherup, which it occasionally utters from the fences and tops of low bushes. Its nest is fixed on the ground among the grass; is formed of loose, dry grass, and lined with hair and fibrous roots of plants. The eggs are five, of a grayish white, sprinkled with brown. On the first of August I found the female sitting.

I cannot say what extent of range this species has, having never met with it in the Southern States; though I have no doubt that it winters there, with many others of its tribe. It is the scarcest of all our summer Sparrows. Its food consists principally of grass seeds, and the larvæ of insects, which it is almost continually in search of among the loose soil and on the surface; consequently it is more useful to the farmer than otherwise.

The length of this species is five inches; extent, eight inches; upper part of the head, blackish, divided by a slight line of white; hind head and neck above, marked with short lateral touches of black and white; a line of yellow extends from above the eye to the nostril; cheeks, plain brownish white; back, streaked with black, brown, and pale ash; shoulders of the wings, above and below, and lesser coverts, olive yellow; greater wing-coverts, black, edged with pale ash; primaries, light drab; tail, the same, the feathers rather pointed at the ends, the outer ones white; breast, plain yellowish white, or pale ochre, which distinguishes it from the Savannah Sparrow, (Fig. 102;) belly and vent, white; three or four slight touches of dusky at the sides of the breast; legs, flesh color; bill, dusky above, pale bluish white below. The male and female are nearly alike in color.

* " A few of these birds," the Prince of Musignano remarks, " can never be separated in any natural arrangement." What are now placed under the name *Emberiza*, will require a sub-genus for themselves, perhaps the analogous form of that genus in the New World. In this species we have the palatial knob, and converging edges of the mandibles; and, by Bonaparte, it is placed among the Finches, in the second section of his sub-genus *Spiza*, as forming the passage to the Buntings.—ED.

BLUE GROSBEAK.—LOXIA CŒRULEA.—Fig. 115.

Linn. Syst. 304.—*Lath.* iii. 116.—*Arct. Zool.* p. 351, No. 217.—*Catesb.* i. 39.— *Buff.* iii. 454. *Pl. enl.* 154.—*Peale's Museum,* No. 5826.

GUIRACA CŒRULEA.—Swainson.*

Fringilla cœrulea, *Bonap. Synop.* p. 114.

This solitary and retired species inhabits the warmer parts of America, from Guiana, and probably farther south,† to Virginia. Mr. Bartram also saw it during a summer's residence near Lancaster, Pennsylvania. In the United States, however, it is a scarce species; and having but few notes, is more rarely observed. Their most common note is a loud *chuck;* they have also at times a few low, sweet-toned notes. They are sometimes kept in cages, in Carolina; but seldom sing in confinement. The individual represented in Fig. 115, was a very elegant specimen, in excellent order, though just arrived from Charleston, South Carolina. During its stay with me, I fed it on Indian corn, which it seemed to prefer, easily breaking with its powerful bill the hardest grains. They also feed on hemp seed, millet, and the kernels of several kinds of berries. They are timid birds, watchful, silent, and active, and generally neat in their plumage. Having never yet met with their nest, I am unable at present to describe it.

The Blue Grosbeak is six inches long, and ten inches in extent; lores and frontlet, black; whole upper parts, a rich purplish blue, more dull on the back, where it is streaked with dusky; greater wing-coverts, black, edged at the tip with bay; next superior row, wholly chestnut; rest of the wing, black, skirted with blue; tail, forked, black, slightly edged with bluish, and sometimes minutely tipped with white; legs and feet, lead color; bill, a dusky bluish horn color; eye, large, full, and black.

The female is of a dark drab color, tinged with blue, and considerably lightest below. I suspect the males are subject to a change of color during winter. The young, as usual with many other species, do not receive the blue color until the ensuing spring, and, till then, very much resemble the female.

Latham makes two varieties of this species; the first, wholly blue, except a black spot between the bill and eye; this bird inhabits Brazil, and is figured by Brisson, *Ornithology,* iii. 321, No. 6, pl. 17, Fig. 2. The other is also generally of a fine deep blue, except the quills, tail, and legs, which are black; this is Edwards's " Blue Grosbeak, from Angola," pl. 125; which Dr. Latham suspects to have been brought from some of the Brazilian settlements, and considers both as mere varieties of the first. I am sorry I cannot at present clear up this matter, but shall take some further notice of it hereafter.

* Loxia cœrulea is not figured in the *Pl. enl.* That bird is a *Pitylus.*
† Latham, ii. p. 116.

MISSISSIPPI KITE — FALCO MISSISSIPPIENSIS. — Fig. 116. —
Male.

Peale's Museum, No. 403.

ICTINIA PLUMBEA. — Vieillot.*

L'Ictinie ophiophaga, Ictinia ophiophaga, *Vieill. Gall. des Ois.* pl. 17. — Faucon
ophiophaga, 2d edit. *du Nouv. Dict. d'Hist. Nat.* ii. p. 103, female, (auct.
Vieill.) — Falco plumbeus, *Bonap. Synop.* p. 30.

This new species I first observed in the Mississippi Territory, a few
miles below Natchez, on the plantation of William Dunbar, Esq.,
where the bird represented in the plate was obtained, after being
slightly wounded; and the drawing made with great care from the
living bird. To the hospitality of the gentleman above mentioned,
and his amiable family, I am indebted for the opportunity afforded me
of procuring this and one or two more new species. This excellent
man, whose life has been devoted to science, though at that time confined to bed by a severe and dangerous indisposition, and personally
unacquainted with me, no sooner heard of my arrival at the town of
Natchez, than he sent a servant and horses, with an invitation and
request to come and make his house my home and head-quarters,
while engaged in exploring that part of the country. The few happy
days I spent there I shall never forget.

In my perambulations I frequently remarked this Hawk sailing
about in easy circles, and at a considerable height in the air, generally in company with the Turkey Buzzards, whose manner of flight it
so exactly imitates as to seem the same species, only in miniature, or
seen at a more immense height. Why these two birds, whose food
and manners, in other respects, are so different, should so frequently
associate together in air, I am at a loss to comprehend. We cannot
for a moment suppose them mutually deceived by the similarity of
each other's flight: the keenness of their vision forbids all suspicion
of this kind. They may perhaps be engaged, at such times, in mere
amusement, as they are observed to soar to great heights previous to
a storm, or, what is more probable, they may both be in pursuit of
their respective food; — one, that he may reconnoitre a vast extent of
surface below, and trace the tainted atmosphere to his favorite carrion; the other in search of those large beetles, or coleopterous
insects, that are known often to wing the higher regions of the air;

* This, from every authority, appears to be the *Falco plumbeus* of Latham.
Vieillot has described it in his *Gallerie des Oiseaux*, under the title of *Ictinia
ophiophaga*, descriptive of its manner of feeding; but has since restored the
specific name to what it should be by the right of priority entitled. The genus,
however, is retained, and appears yet confined to America, inhabiting the Southern
States of the northern continent, South America, and Mexico. It will be characterized by a short bill; short, slender, scutellated, and partly feathered tarsi, and
with the outer toe connected by a membrane; the claws, short; wings, very long,
reaching beyond the tail; the tail, even. Bonaparte thinks that it should stand
intermediate between *Falco* and *Milsus*, somewhat allied to *Buteo.* — Ed.

21

and which, in the three individuals of this species of Hawk which I examined by dissection, were the only substances found in their stomachs. For several miles, as I passed near Bayou Manchak, the trees were swarming with a kind of *Cicada*, or locust, that made a deafening noise; and here I observed numbers of the Hawk now before us sweeping about among the trees like Swallows, evidently in pursuit of these locusts; so that insects, it would appear, are the principal food of this species. Yet when we contemplate the beak and talons of this bird, both so sharp and powerful, it is difficult to believe that they were not intended by nature for some more formidable prey than beetles, locusts, or grasshoppers; and I doubt not but mice, lizards, snakes, and small birds, furnish him with an occasional repast.

This Hawk, though wounded and precipitated from a vast height, exhibited, in his distress, symptoms of great strength and an almost unconquerable spirit. I no sooner approached to pick him up than he instantly gave battle, striking rapidly with his claws, wheeling round and round as he lay partly on his rump, and defending himself with great vigilance and dexterity; while his dark, red eye sparkled with rage. Notwithstanding all my caution in seizing him to carry him home, he struck his hind claw into my hand with such force as to penetrate into the bone. Anxious to preserve his life, I endeavored gently to disengage it; but this made him only contract it the more powerfully, causing such pain that I had no other alternative but that of cutting the sinew of his heel with my penknife. The whole time he lived with me, he seemed to watch every movement I made; erecting the feathers of his hind head, and eyeing me with savage fierceness; considering me, no doubt, as the greater savage of the two. What effect education might have had on this species under the tutorship of some of the old European professors of falconry, I know not; but if extent of wing, and energy of character, and ease and rapidity of flight, would have been any recommendations to royal patronage, this species possesses all these in a very eminent degree.

The long-pointed wings and forked tail point out the affinity of this bird to that family or subdivision of the *Falco* genus, distinguished by the name of Kites, which sail without flapping the wings, and eat from their talons as they glide along.

The Mississippi Kite measures fourteen inches in length, and thirty-six inches, or three feet in extent! The head, neck, and exterior webs of the secondaries, are of a hoary white; the lower parts, a whitish ash; bill, cere, lores, and narrow line round the eye, black; back, rump, scapulars, and wing-coverts, dark blackish ash; wings, very long and pointed, the third quill the longest; the primaries are black, marked down each side of the shaft with reddish sorel; primary coverts also slightly touched with the same; all the upper plumage at the roots is white; the scapulars are also spotted with white — but this cannot be perceived unless the feathers be blown aside; tail, slightly forked, and, as well as the rump, jet black; legs, vermilion, tinged with orange, and becoming blackish towards the toes; claws, black; iris of the eye, dark red; pupil, black.

This was a male. With the female, which is expected soon from that country, I shall, in a future volume, communicate such further information relative to their manners and incubation as I may be able to collect.

TENNESSEE WARBLER. — SYLVIA PEREGRINA — Fɪɢ. 117.

Peale's Museum, No. 7787.

VERMIVORA PEREGRINA. — Sᴡᴀɪɴsᴏɴ.

Sylvia peregrina, *Bonap. Synop.* p. 87. — Sylvicola (Vermivora) peregrina, *North. Zool.* ii. p. 185.

Tʜɪs plain, little bird has hitherto remained unknown. I first found it on the banks of Cumberland River, in the state of Tennessee, and suppose it to be rare, having since met with only two individuals of the same species. It was hunting nimbly among the young leaves, and, like all the rest of the family of worm-eaters, to which, by its bill, it evidently belongs, seemed to partake a good deal of the habits of the Titmouse. Its notes were few and weak; and its stomach, on dissection, contained small green caterpillars, and a few winged insects.

As this species is so very rare in the United States, it is most probably a native of a more southerly climate, where it may be equally numerous with any of the rest of its genus. The small Cerulean Warbler, (Fig. 81,) which, in Pennsylvania, and almost all over the Atlantic states, is extremely rare, I found the most numerous of its tribe in Tennessee and West Florida; and the Carolina Wren, (Fig. 51,) which is also scarce to the northward of Maryland, is abundant through the whole extent of country from Pittsburgh to New Orleans.

Particular species of birds, like different nations of men, have their congenial climes and favorite countries; but wanderers are common to both; some in search of better fare, some of adventures, others led by curiosity, and many driven by storms and accident.

The Tennessee Warbler is four inches and three quarters long, and eight inches in extent; the back, rump, and tail-coverts are of a rich yellow olive; lesser wing-coverts, the same; wings, deep dusky, edged broadly with yellow olive; tail, forked, olive, relieved with dusky; cheeks and upper part of the head, inclining to light bluish, and tinged with olive; line from the nostrils over the eye, pale yellow, fading into white; throat and breast, pale cream color; belly and vent, white; legs, purplish brown; bill, pointed, and thicker at the base than those of the *Sylvia* genus generally are; upper mandible, dark dusky; lower, somewhat paler; eye, hazel.

The female differs little, in the color of her plumage, from the male; the yellow line over the eye is more obscure, and the olive not of so rich a tint.

KENTUCKY WARBLER. — SYLVIA FORMOSA. — Fig. 118.

Peale's Museum, No. 7786.

SYLVICOLA? FORMOSA. — Jardine.

Sylvia formosa, *Bonap. Synop.* p. 84. — The Kentucky Warbler, *Aud.* pl. 38, male and female ; *Orn. Biog.* i. p. 196.

This new and beautiful species inhabits the country whose name it bears. It is also found generally in all the intermediate tracts between Nashville and New Orleans, and below that as far as the Balize, or mouths of the Mississippi ; where I heard it several times twittering among the high, rank grass and low bushes of those solitary and desolate looking morasses. In Kentucky and Tennessee it is particularly numerous, frequenting low, damp woods, and builds its nest in the middle of a thick tuft of rank grass, sometimes in the fork of a low bush, and sometimes on the ground ; in all of which situations I have found it. The materials are loose, dry grass, mixed with the light pith of weeds, and lined with hair. The female lays four, and sometimes six eggs, pure white, sprinkled with specks of reddish. I observed her sitting early in May. This species is seldom seen among the high branches ; but loves to frequent low bushes and cane swamps, and is an active, sprightly bird. Its notes are loud, and in threes, resembling *tweedle, tweedle, tweedle.* It appears in Kentucky from the south about the middle of April, and leaves the territory of New Orleans on the approach of cold weather ; at least I was assured that it does not remain there during the winter. It appeared to me to be a restless, fighting species ; almost always engaged in pursuing some of its fellows ; though this might have been occasioned by its numbers, and the particular season of spring, when love and jealousy rage with violence in the breasts of the feathered tenants of the grove ; who experience all the ardency of those passions no less than their lord and sovereign, man.

The Kentucky Warbler is five inches and a half long, and eight inches in extent ; the upper parts are an olive green ; line over the eye, and partly under it, and whole lower parts, rich brilliant yellow ; head, slightly crested, the crown, deep black, towards the hind part spotted with light ash ; lores, and spot curving down the neck, also black ; tail, nearly *even* at the end, and of a rich olive green ; interior vanes of that and the wings, dusky ; legs, an almost transparent, pale flesh color.

The female wants the black under the eye, and the greater part of that on the crown, having those parts yellowish. This bird is very abundant in the moist woods along the Tennessee and Cumberland Rivers.

PRAIRIE WARBLER. — SYLVIA MINUTA. — Fig. 119.

Peale's Museum, No. 7784.

SYLVICOLA? DISCOLOR. — Jardine.*

Sylvia discolor, *Vieill.* pl. 98, (auct. *Bonap.*) — *Bonap. Synop.* p. 82.

This pretty little species I first discovered in that singular tract of country in Kentucky, commonly called the Barrens. I shot several afterwards in the open woods of the Chactaw nation, where they were more numerous. They seem to prefer these open plains and thinly-wooded tracts; and have this singularity in their manners, that they are not easily alarmed; and search among the leaves the most leisurely of any of the tribe I have yet met with; seeming to examine every blade of grass and every leaf; uttering at short intervals a feeble *chirr*. I have observed one of these birds to sit on the lower branch of a tree for half an hour at a time, and allow me to come up nearly to the foot of the tree, without seeming to be in the least disturbed, or to discontinue the regularity of its occasional note. In activity it is the reverse of the preceding species; and is rather a scarce bird in the countries where I found it. Its food consists principally of small caterpillars and winged insects.

The Prairie Warbler is four inches and a half long, and six inches and a half in extent; the upper parts are olive, spotted on the back with reddish chestnut; from the nostril over and under the eye, yellow; lores, black; a broad streak of black also passes beneath the yellow under the eye; small pointed spots of black reach from a little below that along the side of the neck and under the wings; throat, breast, and belly, rich yellow; vent, cream colored, tinged with yellow, wings, dark dusky olive; primaries and greater coverts, edged and tipped with pale yellow; second row of coverts, wholly yellow; lesser, olive; tail, deep brownish black, ligher on the edges; the three exterior feathers, broadly spotted with white.

The female is destitute of the black mark under the eye; has a few slight touches of blackish along the sides of the neck; and some faint shades of brownish red on the back.

The nest of this species is of very neat and delicate workmanship, being pensile, and generally hung on the fork of a low bush or thicket; it is formed outwardly of green moss, intermixed with rotten bits of wood and caterpillar's silk; the inside is lined with extremely fine fibres of grape-vine bark; and the whole would scarcely weigh a quarter of an ounce. The eggs are white, with a few brown spots at the great end. These birds are migratory, departing for the south in October.

* Bonaparte is of opinion that this is the same with Vieillot's *Sylvia discolor.* I have not had an opportunity of examining it. — Ed.

CAROLINA PARROT. — PSITTACUS CAROLINENSIS. —
Fig. 120.

Linn. Syst. 141. — *Catesb.* i. 11. — *Lath.* i. 227. — *Arct. Zool.* 242, No. 132. *Ibid.*
133. — *Peale's Museum,* No. 762.

CONURUS CAROLINENSIS. — Kuhl.*

Conurus Carolinensis, *Kuhl. consp. psitt. Nov. act. Ceas. Leop.* tom. x. p. 4. 23. —
Psittacus Carolinensis, *Bonap. Synop.* p. 41.

Of one hundred and sixty-eight kinds of Parrots enumerated by
European writers as inhabiting the various regions of the globe, this
is the only species found native within the territory of the United
States. The vast and luxuriant tracts lying within the torrid zone
seem to be the favorite residence of those noisy, numerous, and richly-
plumaged tribes. The Count de Buffon has, indeed, circumscribed
the whole genus of Parrots to a space not extending more than twenty-
three degrees on each side of the equator; but later discoveries have
shown this statement to be incorrect, as these birds have been found
on our continent as far south as the Straits of Magellan, and even on
the remote shores of Van Diemen's Land, in Terra Australasia. The
species now under consideration is also known to inhabit the interior
of Louisiana, and the shores of the Mississippi and Ohio, and their
tributary waters, even beyond the Illinois River, to the neighborhood
of Lake Michigan, in lat. 42 deg. north; and, contrary to the generally received opinion, is chiefly *resident* in all these places. Eastward, however, of the great range of the Alleghany, it is seldom seen
farther north than the state of Maryland, though straggling parties
have been occasionally observed among the valleys of the Juniata;

---

* In all countries Parrots have been favorites, arising from their playful and docile manners in domestication, the beauty of their plumage, and the nearly solitary
example of imitating with comparative accuracy the voice and articulation of man.
In ancient times, the extravagance with which these birds were sought after, either
as objects of amusement and recreation, or as luxuries for the table, surpasses, if
possible, the many fashionable maniæ of latter days. We find frequent allusions
to these birds both in the prose and poetical writers, railing against the expenses
of price and maintenance, or celebrating their docility, or their love and gratitude
to their mistress; and at the height and splendor of the then Mistress of the World,
they were brought forward to the less honorable avocation of conveying praise
and flattery to the great. At the present period they are much sought after, and a
" good Parrot" will still bring a high price.
Intertropical countries are the natural abodes of the *Psittacidæ,* where they are
gregarious, and present most conspicuous and noisy attraction, revelling in free or
grotesque attitudes, among the forest and mountain glades, which, without these,
and many other brilliant tenants, would present only a solitude of luxuriant vegetation. It is impossible for any one who has only seen these birds in a cage or
small enclosure, to conceive what must be the gorgeous appearance of a flock,
either in full flight, and performing their various evolutions, under a vertical sun, or
sporting among the superb foliage of a tropical forest :

> In gaudy robes of many-colored patches,
> The Parrots swung like blossoms from the trees,
> While their harsh voices undeceived the ear.   Ed.

and, according to some, even twenty-five miles to the north-west of Albany, in the state of New York.* But such accidental visits furnish no certain criterion by which to judge of their usual extent of range,—those aerial voyagers, as well as others who navigate the deep, being subject to be cast away, by the violence of the elements, on distant shores and unknown countries.

From these circumstances of the northern residence of this species, we might be justified in concluding it to be a very hardy bird, more capable of sustaining cold than nine tenths of its tribe; and so I believe it is,—having myself seen them, in the month of February, along the banks of the Ohio, in a snow storm, flying about like Pigeons, and in full cry.

The preference, however, which this bird gives to the western countries, lying in the same parallel of latitude with those eastward of the Alleghany Mountains, which it rarely or never visits, is worthy of remark; and has been adduced, by different writers, as a proof of the superior mildness of climate in the former to that of the latter. But there are other reasons for this partiality equally powerful, though hitherto overlooked; namely, certain peculiar features of country to which these birds are particularly and strongly attached; these are, low, rich, alluvial bottoms, along the borders of creeks, covered with a gigantic growth of sycamore-trees, or button wood; deep, and almost impenetrable swamps, where the vast and towering cypress lifts its still more majestic head; and those singular salines, or, as they are usually called, *licks*, so generally interspersed over that country, and which are regularly and eagerly visited by the Paroquets. A still greater inducement is the superior abundance of their favorite fruits. That food which the Paroquet prefers to all others, is the seeds of the cockle bur, a plant rarely found in the lower parts of Pennsylvania or New York; but which unfortunately grows in too great abundance along the shores of the Ohio and Mississippi; so much so as to render the wool of those sheep that pasture where it most abounds, scarcely worth the cleaning, covering them with one solid mass of burs, wrought up and embedded into the fleece, to the great annoyance of this valuable animal. The seeds of the cypress-tree and hackberry, as well as beech nuts, are also great favorites with these birds; the two former of which are not commonly found in Pennsylvania, and the latter by no means so general or so productive. Here, then, are several powerful reasons, more dependent on soil than climate, for the preference given by these birds to the luxuriant regions of the west. Pennsylvania, indeed, and also Maryland, abound with excellent apple orchards, on the ripe fruit of which the Paroquets occasionally feed. But I have my doubts whether their depredations in the orchard be not as much the result of wanton play and mischief, as regard for the seeds of the fruit, which they are supposed to be in pursuit of. I have known a flock of these birds alight on an apple-tree, and have myself seen them twist off the fruit, one by one, strowing it in every direction around the tree, without observing that any of the depredators descended to pick them up. To a Paroquet, which I wounded and kept for some considerable time, I very often offered apples, which

* BARTON's *Fragments, &c.* p. 6. Introduction.

it uniformly rejected; but burs or beech nuts, never. To another very beautiful one, which I brought from New Orleans, and which is now sitting in the room beside me, I have frequently offered this fruit, and also the seeds separately, which I never knew it to taste. Their local attachments, also, prove that food, more than climate, determines their choice of country. For even in the states of Ohio, Kentucky, and the Mississippi Territory, unless in the neighborhood of such places as have been described, it is rare to see them. The inhabitants of Lexington, as many of them assured me, scarcely ever observe them in that quarter. In passing from that place to Nashville, a distance of two hundred miles, I neither heard nor saw any, but at a place called Madison's Lick. In passing on, I next met with them on the banks and rich flats of the Tennessee River: after this, I saw no more till I reached Bayou St. Pierre, a distance of several hundred miles; from all which circumstances, I think we cannot, from the residences of these birds, establish with propriety any correct standard by which to judge of the comparative temperatures of different climates.

In descending the River Ohio, by myself, in the month of February, I met with the first flock of Paroquets at the mouth of the Little Scioto. I had been informed, by an old and respectable inhabitant of Marietta, that they were sometimes, though rarely, seen there. I observed flocks of them, afterwards, at the mouth of the Great and Little Miami, and in the neighborhood of numerous creeks that discharge themselves into the Ohio. At Big Bone Lick, thirty miles above the mouth of Kentucky River, I saw them in great numbers. They came screaming through the woods in the morning, about an hour after sunrise, to drink the salt water, of which they, as well as the Pigeons, are remarkably fond. When they alighted on the ground, it appeared at a distance as if covered with a carpet of the richest green, orange, and yellow: they afterwards settled, in one body, on a neighboring tree, which stood detached from any other, covering almost every twig of it, and the sun, shining strongly on their gay and glossy plumage, produced a very beautiful and splendid appearance. Here I had an opportunity of observing some very particular traits of their character: Having shot down a number, some of which were only wounded, the whole flock swept repeatedly around their prostrate companions, and again settled on a low tree, within twenty yards of the spot where I stood. At each successive discharge, though showers of them fell, yet the affection of the survivors seemed rather to increase; for, after a few circuits around the place, they again alighted near me, looking down on their slaughtered companions with such manifest symptoms of sympathy and concern, as entirely disarmed me. I could not but take notice of the remarkable contrast between their elegant manner of flight, and their lame and crawling gait among the branches. They fly very much like the Wild Pigeon, in close, compact bodies, and with great rapidity, making a loud and outrageous screaming, not unlike that of the Red-headed Woodpecker. Their flight is sometimes in a direct line; but most usually circuitous, making a great variety of elegant and easy serpentine meanders, as if for pleasure. They are particularly attached to the large sycamores, in the hollow of the trunks and branches of which they generally roost, thirty or forty, and sometimes more, entering at the same hole. Here they cling close to the sides of the tree, holding fast by the claws and also by the bills. They appear to be fond of sleep, and often retire to their holes during the day, probably to take their regular *siesta*. They are extremely sociable, and fond of each other, often scratching each other's heads and necks, and always, at night, nestling as close as possible to each other, preferring, at that time, a perpendicular position, supported by their bill and claws. In the fall, when their favorite cockle burs are ripe, they swarm along the coast or high grounds of the Mississippi, above New Orleans, for a great extent. At such times, they are killed and eaten by many of the inhabitants; though, I confess, I think their flesh very indifferent. I have several times dined on it from necessity, in the woods; but found it merely passable, with all the sauce of a keen appetite to recommend it.

A very general opinion prevails that the brains and intestines of the Carolina Paroquet are a sure and fatal poison to cats. I had determined, when at Big Bone, to put this to the test of experiment; and for that purpose collected the brains and bowels of more than a dozen of them. But after close search, Mistress Puss was not to be found, being engaged, perhaps, on more agreeable business. I left the medicine with Mr. Colquhoun's agent, to administer it at the first opportunity, and write me the result; but I have never yet heard from him. A respectable lady near the town of Natchez, and on whose word I can rely, assured me, that she herself had made the experiment, and that, whatever might be the cause, the cat had actually died either on that or the succeeding day. A French planter near Bayou Fourche pretended to account to me for this effect by positively asserting that the seeds of the cockle burs, on which the Paroquets so eagerly feed, were deleterious to cats; and thus their death was produced by eating the intestines of the bird. These matters might easily have been ascertained on the spot, which, however, a combination of trifling circumstances prevented me from doing. I several times carried a dose of the first description in my pocket till it became insufferable, without meeting with a suitable *patient* on whom, like other professional gentlemen, I might conveniently make a fair experiment.

I was equally unsuccessful in my endeavors to discover the time of incubation or manner of building among these birds. All agreed that they breed in hollow trees; and several affirmed to me that they had seen their nests. Some said they carried in no materials; others, that they did. Some made the eggs white; others, speckled. One man assured me that he cut down a large beech-tree, which was hollow, and in which he found the broken fragments of upwards of twenty Paroquets' eggs, which were of a greenish yellow color. The nests, though destroyed in their texture by the falling of the tree, appeared, he said, to be formed of small twigs glued to each other, and to the side of the tree, in the manner of the Chimney Swallow. He added, that if it were the proper season, he could point out to me the weed from which they procured the gluey matter. From all these contradictory accounts nothing certain can be deduced, except that they build in companies, in hollow trees. That they commence incubation late in summer, or very early in spring, I think highly probable, from the numerous dissections I made in the months of March, April, May, and June; and the great variety which I found in the color of the plumage of the head and neck of both sexes, during the two former of these months, convinces me that the young birds do not receive their full colors until the early part of the succeeding summer.*

While Parrots and Paroquets, from foreign countries, abound in almost every street of our large cities, and become such great favorites, no attention seems to have been paid to our own, which, in elegance of figure, and beauty of plumage, is certainly superior to many of them. It wants, indeed, that disposition for perpetual screaming and chattering that renders some of the former pests, not only to their keepers, but to the whole neighborhood in which they reside. It is alike docile and sociable; soon becomes perfectly familiar; and, until equal pains be taken in its instruction, it is unfair to conclude it incapable of equal improvement in the language of man.

As so little has hitherto been known of the disposition and manners of this species, the reader will not, I hope, be displeased at my detailing some of these, in the history of a particular favorite, my sole companion in many a lonesome day's march, and of which the figure in the plate is a faithful resemblance.

Anxious to try the effects of education on one of those which I procured at Big Bone Lick, and which was but slightly wounded in the wing, I fixed up a place for it in the stern of my boat, and presented it with some cockle burs, which it freely fed on in less than an hour after being on board. The intermediate time between eating and sleeping was occupied in gnawing the sticks that formed its place of confinement, in order to make a practicable breach; which it repeatedly effected. When I abandoned the river, and travelled by land, I wrapped it up closely in a silk handkerchief, tying it tightly around, and carried it in my pocket. When I stopped for refreshment, I unbound my prisoner, and gave it its allowance, which it generally despatched with great dexterity, unhusking the seeds from the bur in a twinkling; in doing which, it always employed its left foot to hold the bur, as did several others that I kept for some time. I began to think that this might be peculiar to the whole tribe, and that the whole were, if I may use the expression, left-footed; but, by shooting a number afterwards while engaged in eating mulberries, I found sometimes the left, sometimes the right, foot stained with the fruit, the other always clean; from which, and the constant practice of those I kept, it appears, that, like the human species in the use of their hands, they do not prefer one or the other indiscriminately, but are either left or right-footed. But to return to my prisoner: In recommitting it

* Mr. Audubon's information on their manner of breeding is as follows:—
" Their nest, or the place in which they deposit their eggs, is simply the bottom of such cavities in trees as those to which they usually retire at night. Many females deposit their eggs together. I am of opinion that the number of eggs which each individual lays is two, although I have not been able absolutely to assure myself of this. They are nearly round, of a rich greenish white. The young are at first covered with soft down, such as is seen on young Owls."

It may be remarked that most of the Parrots, whose nidification we are acquainted with, build in hollow trees, or holed banks. Few make a nest for themselves, but lay the eggs on the bare wood or earth; and when the nest is built outward, as by other birds, it is of a slight and loose structure. The eggs are always white. — ED.

to "durance vile," we generally had a quarrel; during which it frequently paid me in kind for the wound I had inflicted, and for depriving it of liberty, by cutting and almost disabling several of my fingers with its sharp and powerful bill. The path through the wilderness between Nashville and Natchez is in some places bad beyond description. There are dangerous creeks to swim, miles of morass to struggle through, rendered almost as gloomy as night by a prodigious growth of timber, and an underwood of canes and other evergreens; while the descent into these sluggish streams is often ten or fifteen feet perpendicular, into a bed of deep clay. In some of the worst of these places, where I had, as it were, to fight my way through, the Paroquet frequently escaped from my pocket, obliging me to dismount and pursue it through the worst of the morass before I could regain it. On these occasions, I was several times tempted to abandon it; but I persisted in bringing it along. When at night I encamped in the woods, I placed it on the baggage beside me, where it usually sat with great composure, dozing and gazing at the fire till morning. In this manner I carried it upwards of a thousand miles, in my pocket, where it was exposed all day to the jolting of the horse, but regularly liberated at meal times and in the evening, at which it always expressed great satisfaction. In passing through the Chickasaw and Chactaw nations, the Indians, wherever I stopped to feed, collected around me, men, women, and children, laughing, and seeming wonderfully amused with the novelty of my companion. The Chickasaws called it in their language "*Kelinky ;*" but when they heard me call it Poll, they soon repeated the name; and, wherever I chanced to stop among these people, we soon became familiar with each other through the medium of Poll. On arriving at Mr. Dunbar's, below Natchez, I procured a cage, and placed it under the piazza, where, by its call, it soon attracted the passing flocks; such is the attachment they have for each other. Numerous parties frequently alighted on the trees immediately above, keeping up a constant conversation with the prisoner. One of these I wounded slightly in the wing, and the pleasure Poll expressed on meeting with this new companion was really amusing. She crept close up to it as it hung on the side of the cage; chattered to it in a low tone of voice, as if sympathizing in its misfortune; scratched about its head and neck with her bill; and both at night nestled as close as possible to each other, sometimes Poll's head being thrust among the plumage of the other. On the death of this companion, she appeared restless and inconsolable for several days. On reaching New Orleans, I placed a looking-glass beside the place where she usually sat, and the instant she perceived her image, all her former fondness seemed to return, so that she could scarcely absent herself from it a moment. It was evident that she was completely deceived. Always when evening drew on, and often during the day, she laid her head close to that of the image in the glass, and began to doze with great composure and satisfaction. In this short space she had learned to know her name; to answer, and come when called on; to climb up my clothes, sit on my shoulder, and eat from my mouth. I took her with me to sea, determined to persevere in her education; but, destined to another fate, poor Poll, having one morning, about day break, wrought her way through the cage, while I was asleep, instantly flew overboard, and perished in the Gulf of Mexico.

The Carolina or Illinois Parrot (for it has been described under both these appellations) is thirteen inches long, and twenty-one in extent; forehead and cheeks, orange red; beyond this, for an inch and a half, down and round the neck, a rich and pure yellow; shoulder and bend of the wing, also edged with rich orange red. The general color of the rest of the plumage is a bright yellowish, silky green, with light blue reflections, lightest and most diluted with yellow below; greater wing-coverts and roots of the primaries, yellow, slightly tinged with green; interior webs of the primaries, deep dusky purple, almost black; exterior ones, bluish green; tail, long, cuneiform, consisting of twelve feathers, the exterior one only half the length, the others increasing to the middle ones, which are streaked along the middle with light blue; shafts of all the larger feathers, and of most part of the green plumage, black; knees and vent, orange yellow; feet, a pale, whitish flesh color; claws, black; bill, white, or slightly tinged with pale cream; iris of the eye, hazel; round the eye is a small space without feathers, covered with a whitish skin; nostrils placed in an elevated membrane at the base of the bill, and covered with feathers; chin, wholly bare of feathers, but concealed by those descending on each side; from each side of the palate hangs a lobe or skin of a blackish color; tongue, thick and fleshy; inside of the upper mandible near the point, grooved exactly like a file, that it may hold with more security.

The female differs very little in her colors and markings from the male. After examining numerous specimens, the following appear to be the principal differences: — The yellow on the neck of the female does not descend quite so far; the interior vanes of the primaries are brownish, instead of black, and the orange red on the bend and edges of the wing is considerably narrower; in other respects, the colors and markings are nearly the same.

The young birds of the preceding year, of both sexes, are generally destitute of the yellow on the head and neck, until about the beginning or middle of March, having those parts wholly green, except the front and cheeks, which are orange red in them, as in the full-grown birds. Towards the middle of March, the yellow begins to appear, in detached feathers, interspersed among the green, varying in different individuals. In some which I killed about the last of that month, only a few green feathers remained among the yellow, and these were fast assuming the yellow tint; for the color changes without change of plumage. A number of these birds, in all their grades of progressive change from green to yellow, have been deposited in Mr. Peale's museum.

What is called by Europeans the Illinois Parrot, (*Psittacus pertinax*,) is evidently the young bird in its imperfect colors. Whether the present species be found as far south as Brazil, as these writers pretend, I am unable to say; but, from the great extent of country in which I have myself killed and examined these birds, I am satisfied that the present species, now described, is the only one inhabiting the United States.

Since the foregoing was written, I have had an opportunity, by the

death of a tame Carolina Paroquet, to ascertain the fact of the poisonous effects of their head and intestines on cats. Having shut up a cat
and her two kittens, the latter only a few days old, in a room with the
head, neck, and whole intestines of the Paroquet, I found, on the next
morning, the whole eaten, except a small part of the bill. The cat
exhibited no symptom of sickness; and, at this moment, three days
after the experiment has been made, she and her kittens are in their
usual health. Still, however, the effect might have been different, had
the daily food of the bird been cockle burs, instead of Indian corn.

CANADA FLYCATCHER. — MUSCICAPA CANADENSIS. —
Fig. 121.

Lynn. Syst. 324. — *Arct. Zool.* p. 338, No. 273. — *Lath.* ii. 354. —
Peale's Museum, No. 6969.

SETOPHAGA CANADENSIS. — Swainson.*

Sylvia pardalina, *Bonap. Synop.* p. 79.

THIS is a solitary, and, in the lower parts of Pennsylvania, rather a
rare species; being more numerous in the interior, particularly near
the mountains, where the only two I ever met with were shot. They
are silent birds, as far as I could observe, and were busily darting
among the branches after insects. From the specific name given
them, it is probable that they are more plenty in Canada than in the
United States; where it is doubtful whether they be not mere passengers in spring and autumn.

This species is four inches and a half long, and eight in extent;
front, black; crown, dappled with small streaks of gray and spots of
black; line from the nostril to and around the eye, yellow; below the
eye, a streak or spot of black, descending along the sides of the throat,
which, as well as the breast and belly, is brilliant yellow, the breast

---

* Mr. Swainson, in a note to the *Northern Zoology*, has hinted his suspicion that
this bird and *Muscicapa Bonapartii* of Audubon are the same. As far as we can
judge from the two plates, there does not seem any resemblance. Mr. Swainson
adds, " As regards the generic name (of *Setophaga Bonapartii*,) we consider the
whole structure of the bird as obviously intermediate between the *Sylvicolæ* and
the typical *Setophagæ*, but more closely allied to the latter than the former." For
the present, we shall place the two following species in *Setophaga*, but suspect that
this intermediate form will hereafter rank in the value of a sub-genus.* To this,
also, may be referred the *Muscicapa Selbii* of Audubon, which seems to approach
nearer *Setophaga* in the more flattened representation of the bill and stronger bristles. Mr. Audubon has only met with it three times in Louisiana. The upper parts
are of a dark olive color; the whole under parts, with a streak over each eye, rich
yellow. The length is about five inches and a half. It was very active in pursuit
of flies, and the snapping of the bill, when seizing them, was distinctly heard at
some distance. — ED.

* They are all furnished with rictorial bristles, but the bill is not so much depressed.
The habits are those of *Setophaga*.

22

being marked with a broad, rounding band of black, composed of large, irregular streaks; back, wings, and tail, cinereous brown; vent, white; upper mandible, dusky; lower, flesh colored; legs and feet, the same; eye, hazel.

Never having met with the female of this bird, I am unable, at present, to say in what its colors differ from those of the male.

HOODED FLYCATCHER. — MUSCICAPA CUCULLATA. —
Fig. 122.

Le gobe-mouche citrin, *Buff.* iv. 538, *Pl. enl.* 666. — Hooded Warbler, *Arct. Zool.* p. 400, No. 287. — *Lath.* ii. 462. — *Catesb.* i. 60. — Mitred Warbler, *Turton,* i. 601. — Hooded Warbler, *ibid.* — *Peale's Museum,* No. 7062.

SETOPHAGA MITRATA. — Swainson.

Sylvia mitrata, *Bonap. Synop.* p. 79.

Why those two judicious naturalists, Pennant and Latham, should have arranged this bird with the Warblers, is to me unaccountable, as few of the *Muscicapæ* are more distinctly marked than the species now before us. The bill is broad at the base, where it is beset with bristles; the upper mandible, notched, and slightly overhanging at the tip; and the manners of the bird, in every respect, those of a Flycatcher. This species is seldom seen in Pennsylvania and the Northern States, but through the whole extent of country south of Maryland, from the Atlantic to the Mississippi, is very abundant. It is, however, most partial to low situations, where there is plenty of thick underwood; abounds among the canes in the state of Tennessee, and in the Mississippi Territory; and seems perpetually in pursuit of winged insects; now and then uttering three loud, not unmusical, and very lively notes, resembling *twee, twee, twitchie,* while engaged in the chase. Like almost all its tribe, it is full of spirit, and exceedingly active. It builds a very neat and compact nest, generally in the fork of a small bush; forms it outwardly of moss and flax, or broken hemp, and lines it with hair, and sometimes feathers; the eggs are five, of a grayish white, with red spots towards the great end. In all parts of the United States where it inhabits, it is a bird of passage. At Savannah, I met with it about the 20th of March; so that it probably retires to the West India Islands, and perhaps Mexico, during winter. I also heard this bird, among the rank reeds and rushes, within a few miles of the mouth of the Mississippi. It has been sometimes seen in the neighborhood of Philadelphia, but rarely; and, on such occasions, has all the mute timidity of a stranger at a distance from home.

This species is five inches and a half long, and eight in extent; forehead, cheeks, and chin, yellow, surrounded with a hood of black that covers the crown, hind head, and part of the neck, and descends, rounding, over the breast; all the rest of the lower parts are rich yellow; upper parts of the wings, the tail, and back, yellow olive; interior vanes, and tips of the wing and tail, dusky; bill, black; legs, flesh colored; inner webs of the three exterior tail-feathers, white for half their length from the tips; the next, slightly touched with white; the tail, slightly forked, and exteriorly edged with rich, yellow olive.

The female has the throat and breast yellow, slightly tinged with blackish; the black does not reach so far down the upper part of the neck, and is not of so deep a tint. In the other parts of her plumage, she exactly resembles the male. I have found some females that had little or no black on the head or neck above, but these I took to be young birds, not yet arrived at their full tints.

GREEN BLACK–CAPPED FLYCATCHER. — MUSCICAPA PUSILLA. — Fig. 123.

Peale's Museum, No. 7785.

SETOPHAGA ? WILSONII. — Jardine.*

Sylvia Wilsonii, *Bonap. Synop.* p. 86. — *Nomenclature*, No. 127.

This neat and active little species I have never met with in the works of any European naturalist. It is an inhabitant of the swamps of the Southern States, and has been several times seen in the lower parts of the states of New Jersey and Delaware. Amidst almost unapproachable thickets of deep morasses it commonly spends its time during summer, and has a sharp, squeaking note, no wise musical. It leaves the Southern States early in October.

This species is four inches and a half long, and six and a half in extent; front line over the eye, and whole lower parts, yellow, brightest over the eye, and dullest on the checks, belly, and vent, where it is tinged with olive; upper parts, olive green; wings and tail, dusky brown, the former very short; legs and bill, flesh colored; crown, covered with a patch of deep black; iris of the eye, hazel.

The female is without the black crown, having that part of a dull yellow olive, and is frequently mistaken for a distinct species. From her great resemblance, however, in other respects, to the male, now first figured, she cannot hereafter be mistaken.

* The Prince of Musignano has never seen this species, but was of opinion that it would prove a *Sylvia;* and the specific name being preoccupied, he chose that of its discoverer. I have retained his specific name, though the reason of the change will not now be available. The services of Wilson, however, can scarcely be overpaid, and the reputation of no one is here implicated. — Ed.

PINNATED GROUSE. — TETRAO CUPIDO. — Fig. 124.

Linn. Syst. i. p. 274–5. — *Lath.* ii. p. 740. — *Arct. Zool.* — La Gelinote huppèe d'Amérique, *Briss. Orn.* i. p. 212, 10. — Urogalus minor, fuscus cervice, plumis alas imitantibus donatâ, *Catesb. Car. App.* pl. 1. — Tetrao lagopus, the Mountain Cock, or Grouse, *Bartram*, p. 290. — Heath-Hen, Prairie Hen, Barren Hen. — *Peale's Museum*, No. 4700, male ; 4701, female.

TETRAO CUPIDO. — Linnæus.

Attagan Americana, *Brisson*, i. p. 59. — Pinnated Heathcock, Bonasa cupido, *Steph. Sh. Cont.* xi. p. 299. — Tetrao cupido, *Bonap. Synop.* p. 126.

BEFORE I enter on a detail of the observations which I have myself personally made on this singular species, I shall lay before the reader a comprehensive and very circumstantial memoir on the subject, communicated to me by the writer, Dr. Samuel L. Mitchill, of New York, whose exertions, both in his public and private capacity, in behalf of science, and in elucidating the natural history of his country, are well known, and highly honorable to his distinguished situation and abilities. That peculiar tract, generally known by the name of the Brushy Plains of Long Island, having been, for time immemorial, the resort of the bird now before us, some account of this particular range of country seemed necessarily connected with the subject, and has, accordingly, been obligingly attended to by the learned professor.

"New York, Sept. 19, 1810.

" DEAR SIR, — It gives me much pleasure to reply to your letter of the 12th instant, asking of me information concerning the Grouse of Long Island.

" The birds which are known there emphatically by the name of Grouse, inhabit chiefly the forest range. This district of the island may be estimated as being between forty and fifty miles in length, extending from Bethphage, in Queen's County, to the neighborhood of the Court-House, in Suffolk. Its breadth is not more than six or seven. For, although the island is bounded by the Sound, separating it from Connecticut on the north, and by the Atlantic Ocean on the south, there is a margin of several miles, on each side, in the actual possession of human beings.

" The region in which these birds reside, lies mostly within the towns of Oysterbay, Huntington, Islip, Smithtown, and Brookhaven ; though it would be incorrect to say that they were not to be met with sometimes in Riverhead and Southampton. Their territory has been defined by some sportsmen, as situated between Hampstead Plain on the West, and Shinnecock Plain on the east.

" The more popular name for them is Heath-Hens. By this they are designated in the act of our Legislature for the preservation of them and of other game. I well remember the passing of this law. The bill was introduced by Cornelius J. Bogert, Esq., a member of the Assembly from the city of New York. It was in the month of February, 1791, the year when, as a representative from my native county of Queens, I sat for the first time in a legislature.

"The statute declares, among other things, that the person who shall kill any Heath-Hen within the counties of Suffolk or Queens, between the 1st day of April and the 5th day of October, shall, for every such offence, forfeit and pay the sum of two dollars and a half, to be recovered, with costs of suit, by any person who shall prosecute for the same, before any justice of the peace, in either of the said counties ; the one half to be paid to the plaintiff, and the other half to the overseers of the poor ; and if any Heath-Hen, so killed, shall be found in the possession of any person, he shall be deemed guilty of the offence, and suffer the penalty. But it is provided that no defendant shall be convicted, unless the action shall be brought within three months after the violation of the law.*

"The country selected by these exquisite birds requires a more particular description. You already understand it to be the midland and interior district of the island. The soil of this island is, generally speaking, a sandy or gravelly loam. In the parts less adapted to tillage, it is more of an unmixed sand. This is so much the case, that the shore of the beaches beaten by the ocean affords a material from which glass has been prepared. Siliceous grains and particles predominate in the region chosen by the Heath-Hens or Grouse. Here there are no rocks, and very few stones of any kind. This sandy tract appears to be a dereliction of the ocean, but is, nevertheless, not doomed to total sterility. Many thousand acres have been reclaimed from the wild state, and rendered very productive to man ; and within the towns frequented by these birds, there are numerous inhabitants, and among them, some of our most wealthy farmers.

"But within the same limits, there are also tracts of great extent where men have no settlements, and others where the population is spare and scanty. These are, however, by no means naked deserts ; they are, on the contrary, covered with trees, shrubs, and smaller plants. The trees are mostly pitch-pines of inferior size, and white oaks of a small growth. They are of a quality very fit for burning. Thousands of cords of both sorts of fire-wood are annually exported from these barrens. Vast quantities are occasionally destroyed by the fires which, through carelessness or accident, spread far and wide through the woods. The city of New York will probably, for ages, derive fuel from the Grouse grounds. The land, after having been cleared, yields to the cultivator poor crops. Unless, therefore, he can help it by manure, the best disposition is to let it grow up to forest again. Experience has proved, that, in a term of forty or fifty years, the new growth of timber will be fit for the axe. Hence it may be perceived, that the reproduction of trees, and the protection they afford to Heath-

---

* The doctor has probably forgotten a circumstance of rather a ludicrous kind, that occurred at the passing of this law, and which was, not long ago, related to me by my friend Mr. Gardiner, of Gardiner's Island, Long Island. The bill was entitled, "An Act for the preservation of Heath-Hen, and other game." The honest Chairman of the Assembly — no sportsman, I suppose — read the title, "An Act for the preservation of *Heathen*, and other game !" which seemed to astonish the northern members, who could not see the propriety of preserving *Indians*, or any other heathen.

22 *

Hens, would be perpetual, or, in other words, not circumscribed by any calculable time, provided the persecutors of the latter would be quiet.

" Beneath these trees grow more dwarfish oaks, overspreading the surface, sometimes with here and there a shrub, and sometimes a thicket. These latter are from about two to ten feet in height. Where they are the principal product, they are called, in common conversation, *brush*, as the flats on which they grow are termed *brushy plains*. Among this hardy shrubbery may frequently be seen the creeping vegetable named the partridgeberry, covering the sand with its lasting verdure. In many spots, the plant which produces hurtleberries sprouts up among the other natives of the soil. These are the more important; though I ought to inform you, that the hills reaching from east to west, and forming the spine of the island, support kalmias, hickories, and many other species; that I have seen azalias and andromedas, as I passed through the wilderness; and that, where there is water, cranberries, alders, beeches, maples, and other lovers of moisture, take their stations.

" This region, situated thus between the more thickly inhabited strips, or belts, on the north and south sides of the island, is much travelled by wagons, and intersected, accordingly, by a great number of paths.

" As to the birds themselves, the information I possess scarcely amounts to an entire history. You, who know the difficulty of collecting facts, will be the most ready to excuse my deficiencies. The information I give you is such as I rely on. For the purpose of gathering the materials, I have repeatedly visited their haunts. I have likewise conversed with several men who were brought up at the precincts of the Grouse ground, who had been witnesses of their habits and manners, who were accustomed to shoot them for the market, and who have acted as guides to gentlemen who go there for sport.

" *Bulk.* — An adult Grouse, when fat, weighs as much as a barn-door fowl of moderate size, or about three pounds avoirdupois. But the eagerness of the sportsman is so great, that a large proportion of those they kill are but a few months old, and have not attained their complete growth. Notwithstanding the protection of the law, it is very common to disregard it. The retired nature of the situation favors this. It is well understood that an arrangement can be made which will blind and silence informers, and that the gun is fired with impunity for weeks before the time prescribed in the act. To prevent this unfair and unlawful practice, an association was formed a few years ago, under the title of the *Brush Club*, with the express and avowed intention of enforcing the game law. Little benefit, however, has resulted from its laudable exertions; and under a conviction that it was impossible to keep the poachers away, the society declined. At present, the statute may be considered as operating very little towards their preservation. Grouse, especially full-grown ones, are becoming less frequent. Their numbers are gradually diminishing, and, assailed as they are on all sides, almost without cessation, their scarcity may be viewed as foreboding their eventual extermination.

" *Price.* — Twenty years ago, a brace of Grouse could be bought for a dollar. They now cost from three to five dollars. A handsome

pair seldom sells in the New York market now-a-days for less than
thirty shillings, [three dollars, seventy-five cents,] nor for more than
forty, [five dollars.]   These prices indicate, indeed, the depreciation
of money and the luxury of eating.   They prove, at the same time,
that Grouse are become rare; and this fact is admitted by every man
who seeks them, whether for pleasure or for profit.

"*Amours.* — The season for pairing is in March, and the breeding
time is continued through April and May.   Then the male Grouse
distinguishes himself by a peculiar sound.   When he utters it, the
parts about the throat are sensibly inflated and swelled.   It may be
heard on a still morning for three or more miles; some say they have
perceived it as far as five or six.   This noise is a sort of ventriloquism.
It does not strike the ear of a bystander with much force, but impresses
him with the idea, though produced within a few rods of him, of
a voice a mile or two distant.   This note is highly characteristic.
Though very peculiar, it is termed *tooting*, from its resemblance to the
blowing of a conch or horn from a remote quarter.   The female makes
her nest on the ground, in recesses very rarely discovered by men.   She
usually lays from ten to twelve eggs.   Their color is of a brownish,
much resembling those of a Guinea Hen.   When hatched, the brood
is protected by her alone.   Surrounded by her young, the mother bird
exceedingly resembles a domestic Hen and Chickens.   She frequently
leads them to feed in the roads crossing the woods, on the remains of
maize and oats contained in the dung dropped by the travelling horses.
In that employment they are often surprised by the passengers.   On
such occasions the dam utters a cry of alarm.   The little ones immediately scamper to the brush; and while they are skulking into places
of safety, their anxious parent beguiles the spectator by drooping and
fluttering her wings, limping along the path, rolling over in the dirt,
and other pretences of inability to walk or fly.

"*Food.*   A favorite article of their diet is the *heath hen plum*, or
partridgeberry before mentioned.   They are fond of hurtleberries
and cranberries.   Worms and insects of several kinds are occasionally found in their crops.   But, in the winter, they subsist chiefly on
acorns, and the buds of trees which have shed their leaves.   In their
stomachs have been sometimes observed the leaves of a plant supposed to be a winter green; and it is said, when they are much
pinched, they betake themselves to the buds of the pine.   In convenient
places, they have been known to enter cleared fields, and regale themselves on the leaves of clover; and old gunners have reported that
they have been known to trespass upon patches of buckwheat, and
pick up the grains.

"*Migration.* — They are stationary, and never known to quit their
abode.   There are no facts showing in them any disposition to migration.   On frosty mornings, and during snows, they perch on the upper
branches of pine-trees.   They avoid wet and swampy places, and are
remarkably attached to dry ground.   The low and open brush is preferred to high shrubbery and thickets.   Into these latter places they
fly for refuge when closely pressed by the hunters; and here, under a
stiff and impenetrable cover, they escape the pursuit of dogs and men.
Water is so seldom met with on the true Grouse ground, that it is
necessary to carry it along for the pointers to drink.   The flights of

Grouse are short, but sudden, rapid, and whirring. I have not heard of any success in taming them. They seem to resist all attempts at domestication. In this, as well as in many other respects, they resemble the Quail of New York, or the Partridge of Pennsylvania.

"*Manners.* — During the period of mating, and while the females are occupied in incubation, the males have a practice of assembling, principally by themselves. To some select and central spot, where there is very little underwood, they repair from the adjoining district. From the exercises performed there, this is called a *scratching-place*. The time of meeting is the break of day. As soon as the light appears, the company assembles from every side, sometimes to the number of forty or fifty. When the dawn is past, the ceremony begins by a low tooting from one of the cocks. This is answered by another. They then come forth one by one from the bushes, and strut about with all the pride and ostentation they can display. Their necks are incurvated; the feathers on them are erected into a sort of ruff; the plumes of their tails are expanded like fans; they strut about in a style resembling, as nearly as small may be illustrated by great, the pomp of the Turkey cock. They seem to vie with each other in stateliness; and, as they pass each other, frequently cast looks of insult, and utter notes of defiance. These are the signals for battles. They engage with wonderful spirit and fierceness. During these contests, they leap a foot or two from the ground, and utter a cackling, screaming, and discordant cry.

"They have been found in these places of resort even earlier than the appearance of light in the east. This fact has led to the belief that a part of them assemble over night. The rest join them in the morning. This leads to the further belief that they roost on the ground. And the opinion is confirmed by the discovery of little rings of dung, apparently deposited by a flock which had passed the night together. After the appearance of the sun they disperse.

"These places of exhibition have been often discovered by the hunters; and a fatal discovery it has been for the poor Grouse. Their destroyers construct for themselves lurking holes made of pine branches, called *bough houses*, within a few yards of the parade. Hither they repair with their fowling-pieces, in the latter part of the night, and wait the appearance of the birds. Watching the moment when two are proudly eyeing each other, or engaged in battle, or when a greater number can be seen in a range, they pour on them a destructive charge of shot. This annoyance has been given in so many places, and to such extent, that the Grouse, after having been repeatedly disturbed, are afraid to assemble. On approaching the spot to which their instinct prompts them, they perch on the neighboring trees, instead of alighting at the scratching-place. And it remains to be observed how far the restless and tormenting spirit of the marksmen may alter the native habits of the Grouse, and oblige them to betake themselves to new ways of life.

"They commonly keep together in coveys, or packs, as the phrase is, until the pairing season. A full pack consists, of course, of ten or a dozen. Two packs have been known to associate. I lately heard of one whose number amounted to twenty-two. They are so unapt to be startled, that a hunter, assisted by a dog, has been able to shoot almost a whole pack, without making any of them take wing. In like manner, the men lying in concealment near the scratching-places have been known to discharge several guns before either the report of the explosion, or the sight of their wounded and dead fellows, would rouse them to flight. It has further been remarked that when a company of sportsmen have surrounded a pack of Grouse, the birds seldom or never rise upon their pinions while they are encircled; but each runs along until it passes the person that is nearest, and then flutters off with the utmost expedition.

" As you have made no inquiry of me concerning the ornithological character of these birds, I have not mentioned it, presuming that you are already perfectly acquainted with their classification and description. In a short memoir written in 1803, and printed in the eighth volume of the *Medical Repository*, I ventured an opinion as to the genus and species. Whether I was correct is a technical matter, which I leave you to adjust. I am well aware that European accounts of our productions are often erroneous, and require revision and amendment. This you must perform. For me it remains to repeat my joy at the opportunity your invitation has afforded me to contribute somewhat to your elegant work, and at the same time to assure you of my earnest hope that you may be favored with ample means to complete it.
"SAMUEL L. MITCHILL."

Duly sensible of the honor of the foregoing communication, and grateful for the good wishes with which it is concluded, I shall now, in further elucidation of the subject, subjoin a few particulars properly belonging to my own department.

It is somewhat extraordinary that the European naturalists, in their various accounts of our different species of Grouse, should have said little or nothing of the one now before us, which, in its voice, manners, and peculiarity of plumage, is the most singular, and, in its flesh, the most excellent of all those of its tribe that inhabit the territory of the United States. It seems to have escaped Catesby during his residence and different tours through this country, and it was not till more than twenty years after his return to England, viz., in 1743, that he first saw some of these birds, as he informs us, at Cheswick, the seat of the Earl of Wilmington. His lordship said they came from America; but from what particular part, could not tell.* Buffon has confounded it with the Ruffed Grouse, the Common Partridge of New England, or Pheasant of Pennsylvania, (*Tetrao umbellus;*) Edwards and Pennant have, however, discovered that it is a different species, but have said little of its note, of its flesh, or peculiarities; for, alas! there was neither voice, nor action, nor delicacy of flavor in the shrunk and decayed skin from which the former took his figure, and the latter his description; and to this circumstance must be attributed the barrenness and defects of both.

That the curious may have an opportunity of examining to more advantage this singular bird, a figure of the male is here given, as large as life, drawn with great care from the most perfect of several elegant specimens shot in the Barrens of Kentucky. He is represented in the act of *strutting*, as it is called, while with inflated throat

* CATESBY, *Car.* p. 101. App.

he produces that extraordinary sound so familiar to every one who resides in his vicinity, and which has been described in the foregoing account. So very novel and characteristic did the action of these birds appear to me at first sight, that, instead of shooting them down, I sketched their attitude hastily on the spot, while concealed among a brush-heap, with seven or eight of them within a short distance. Three of these I afterwards carried home with me.

This rare bird, though an inhabitant of different and very distant districts of North America, is extremely particular in selecting his place of residence ; pitching only upon those tracts whose features and productions correspond with his modes of life, and avoiding immense, intermediate regions that he never visits. Open, dry plains, thinly interspersed with trees, or partially overgrown with shrub oak, are his favorite haunts. Accordingly we find these birds on the Grouse plains of New Jersey, in Burlington county, as well as on the brushy plains of Long Island ; among the pines and shrub oaks of Pocano, in Northampton county, Pennsylvania ; over the whole extent of the Barrens of Kentucky ; on the luxuriant plains and prairies of the Indiana Territory, and Upper Louisiana ; and, according to the information of the late Governor Lewis, on the vast and remote plains of the Columbia River; in all these places preserving the same singular habits.

Their predilection for such situations will be best accounted for by considering the following facts and circumstances : — First, their mode of flight is generally direct, and laborious, and ill calculated for the labyrinth of a high and thick forest, crowded and intersected with trunks and arms of trees, that require continual angular evolution of wing, or sudden turnings, to which they are by no means accustomed. I have always observed them to avoid the high-timbered groves that occur here and there in the Barrens. Connected with this fact, is a circumstance related to me by a very respectable inhabitant of that country, viz., that one forenoon a cock Grouse struck the stone chimney of his house with such force as instantly to fall dead to the ground.

Secondly, their known dislike of ponds, marshes, or watery places, which they avoid on all occasions, drinking but seldom, and, it is believed, never from such places. Even in confinement this peculiarity has been taken notice of. While I was in the state of Tennessee, a person living within a few miles of Nashville had caught an old hen Grouse in a trap ; and, being obliged to keep her in a large cage, as she struck and abused the rest of the poultry, he remarked that she never drank, and that she even avoided that quarter of the cage where the cup containing the water was placed. Happening, one day, to let some water fall on the cage, it trickled down in drops along the bars, which the bird no sooner observed, than she eagerly picked them off, drop by drop, with a dexterity that showed she had been habituated to this mode of quenching her thirst; and, probably, to this mode only, in those dry and barren tracts, where, except the drops of dew and drops of rain, water is very rarely to be met with. For the space of a week he watched her closely, to discover whether she still refused to drink ; but, though she was constantly fed on Indian Corn, the cup and water still remained untouched and untasted. Yet no sooner did he again sprinkle water on the bars of the cage, than she eagerly and rapidly picked them off as before.

The last, and, probably, the strongest inducement to their preferring these plains, is the small acorn of the shrub oak, the strawberries, huckleberries, and partridgeberries, with which they abound, and which constitute the principal part of the food of these birds. These brushy thickets also afford them excellent shelter, being almost impenetrable to dogs or birds of prey.

In all these places where they inhabit, they are, in the strictest sense of the word, resident; having their particular haunts and places of rendezvous, (as described in the preceding account,) to which they are strongly attached. Yet they have been known to abandon an entire tract of such country, when, from whatever cause it might proceed, it became again covered with forest. A few miles south of the town of York, in Pennsylvania, commences an extent of country, formerly of the character described, now chiefly covered with wood, but still retaining the name of Barrens. In the recollection of an old man born in that part of the country, this tract abounded with Grouse. The timber growing up, in progress of years, these birds totally disappeared; and, for a long period of time, he had seen none of them, until, migrating with his family to Kentucky, on entering the Barrens, he, one morning, recognized the well known music of his old acquaintance, the Grouse; which, he assures me, are the very same with those he had known in Pennsylvania.

But what appears to me the most remarkable circumstance relative to this bird, is, that not one of all those writers who have attempted its history, have taken the least notice of those two extraordinary bags of yellow skin which mark the neck of the male, and which constitute so striking a peculiarity. These appear to be formed by an expansion of the gullet, as well as of the exterior skin of the neck, which when the bird is at rest, hangs in loose, pendulous, wrinkled folds, along the side of the neck, the supplemental wings, at the same time, as well as when the bird is flying, lying along the neck, in the manner represented in one of the distant figures on the plate. But when these bags are inflated with air, in breeding time, they are equal in size, and very much resemble in color, a middle-sized, fully ripe orange. By means of this curious apparatus, which is very observable several hundred yards off, he is enabled to produce the extraordinary sound mentioned above, which, though it may easily be imitated, is yet difficult to describe by words. It consists of three notes, of the same tone, resembling those produced by the Night Hawks in their rapid descent; each strongly accented, the last being twice as long as the others. When several are thus engaged, the ear is unable to distinguish the regularity of these triple notes, there being, at such times, one continued humming, which is disagreeable and perplexing, from the impossibility of ascertaining from what distance, or even quarter, it proceeds. While uttering this, the bird exhibits all the ostentatious gesticulations of a Turkey cock; erecting and fluttering his neck wings, wheeling and passing before the female, and close before his fellows, as in defiance. Now and then are heard some rapid, cackling notes, not unlike that of a person tickled to excessive laughter; and, in short, one can scarcely listen to them without feeling disposed to laugh from sympathy. These are uttered by the males while engaged in fight, on which occasion they leap up against each other, exactly in the manner of Turkeys, seemingly with more malice than effect. This bumming continues from a little before daybreak to eight or nine o'clock in the morning, when the parties separate to seek for food.

Fresh ploughed fields, in the vicinity of their resorts, are sure to be visited by these birds every morning, and frequently also in the evening. On one of these I counted, at one time, seventeen males, most of whom were in the attitude represented in the plate ; making such a continued sound, as, I am persuaded, might have been heard for more than a mile off. The people of the Barrens informed me, that, when the weather becomes severe, with snow, they approach the barn and farm-house, are sometimes seen sitting on the fences in dozens, mix with the poultry, and glean up the scattered grains of Indian corn, seeming almost half domesticated. At such times, great numbers are taken in traps. No pains, however, or regular plan, has ever been persisted in, as far as I was informed, to domesticate these delicious birds. A Mr. Reed, who lives between the Pilot Knobs and Bairdstown, told me, that, a few years ago, one of his sons found a Grouse's nest with fifteen eggs, which he brought home, and immediately placed below a Hen then sitting, taking away her own. The nest of the Grouse was on the ground, under a tussock of long grass, formed with very little art, and few materials ; the eggs were brownish white, and about the size of a pullet's. In three or four days, the whole were hatched. Instead of following the Hen, they compelled her to run after them, distracting her with the extent and diversity of their wanderings ; and it was a day or two before they seemed to understand her language, or consent to be guided by her. They were let out to the fields, where they paid little regard to their nurse ; and, in a few days, only three of them remained. These became extremely tame and familiar ; were most expert flycatchers ; but, soon after, they also disappeared.

The Pinnated Grouse is nineteen inches long, twenty-seven inches in extent, and, when in good order, weighs about three pounds and a half ; the neck is furnished with supplemental wings, each composed of eighteen feathers, five of which are black, and about three inches long ; the rest shorter, also black, streaked laterally with brown, and of unequal lengths ; the head is slightly crested ; over the eye is an elegant, semicircular comb of rich orange, which the bird has the power of raising or relaxing ; under the neck wings are two loose, pendulous, and wrinkled skins, extending along the side of the neck for two thirds of its length ; each of which, when inflated with air, resembles, in bulk, color, and surface, a middle-sized orange ; chin, cream colored ; under the eye runs a dark streak of brown ; whole upper parts, mottled transversely with black, reddish brown, and white ; tail short, very much rounded, and of a plain brownish soot color ; throat, elegantly marked with touches of reddish brown, white, and black ; lower part of the breast and belly, pale brown, marked transversely with white ; legs, covered to the toes with hairy down of a dirty drab color ; feet, dull yellow ; toes, pectinated ; vent, whitish ; bill, brownish horn color ; eye, reddish hazel. The female is considerably less ; of a lighter color, destitute of the neck wings, the naked, yellow skin on the neck, and the semicircular comb of yellow over the eye.

On dissecting these birds, the gizzard was found extremely muscular, having almost the hardness of a stone; the heart remarkably large; the crop was filled with brier knots, containing the larvæ of some insect, quantities of a species of green lichen, small, hard seeds, and some grains of Indian corn.

BLUE-GREEN WARBLER.—SYLVIA RARA.—Fig. 125.

Peale's Museum, No. 7783.

VERMIVORA? RARA.—Jardine.*

Sylvia rara, *Bonap. Synop.* p. 82.—*Aud.* pl. 49, male; *Orn. Biog.* i. p. 258.

THIS new species, the only one of its sort I have yet met with, was shot on the banks of Cumberland River, about the beginning of April, and the drawing made with care immediately after. Whether male or female, I am uncertain. It is one of those birds that usually glean among the high branches of the tallest trees, which renders it difficult to be procured. It was darting about with great nimbleness among the leaves, and appeared to have many of the habits of the Flycatcher. After several ineffectual excursions in search of another of the same kind, with which I might compare the present, I am obliged to introduce it with this brief account.

The specimen has been deposited in Mr. Peale's museum.

The Blue-green Warbler is four inches and a half long, and seven and a half in extent; the upper parts are verditer, tinged with pale green, brightest on the front and forehead; lores, line over the eye, throat, and whole lower parts, very pale cream; cheeks, slightly tinged with greenish; bill and legs, bright light blue, except the upper mandible, which is dusky; tail, forked, and, as well as the wings, brownish black; the former marked on the three exterior vanes with white, and edged with greenish; the latter having the first and second row of coverts tipped with white. Note, a feeble chirp.

* This species was discovered by Wilson, and does not seem to have been again met with by any ornithologist except Mr. Audubon, who has figured it, and added somewhat to our knowledge of its manners.

"It is rare in the middle districts, and is only found in the dark recesses of the pine swamp. On its passage through the states, it appears in Louisiana, in April. They are met with in Kentucky, in Ohio, upon the Missouri, and along Lake Erie." Mr. Audubon has never seen the nest. In spring the song is soft and mellow, and not heard beyond the distance of a few paces; it is performed at intervals, between the times at which the bird secures an insect, which it does with great expertness, either on the wing, or among the leaves of the trees and bushes. While catching it on the wing, it produces a slight, clicking sound with its bill, like *Vireo*. It also, like them, eats small berries, particularly towards autumn, when insects begin to fail. There seems little difference between the sexes. Such is the most important information given by Mr. Audubon.—ED.

23

NASHVILLE WARBLER. — SYLVIA RUFICAPILLA. — Fig. 126.

Peale's Museum, No. 7789.

VERMIVORA RUBRICAPILLA. — Swainson.*

Sylvia rubricapilla, *Wils. Catal.* — *Bonap. Synop.* p. 87. — Sylvicola (Vermivora) rubricapilla, *North. Zool.* ii. p. 220. — The Nashville Warbler, *Aud.* pl. 89 ; *Orn. Biog.* i. p. 450.

The very uncommon notes of this little bird were familiar to me for several days before I succeeded in obtaining it. These notes very much resembled the breaking of small dry twigs, or the striking of small pebbles of different sizes smartly against each other for six or seven times, and loud enough to be heard at the distance of thirty or forty yards. It was some time before I could ascertain whether the sound proceeded from a bird or an insect. At length I discovered the bird, and was not a little gratified at finding it an entire new and hitherto undescribed species. I was also fortunate enough to meet afterwards with two others exactly corresponding with the first, all of them being males. These were shot in the state of Tennessee, not far from Nashville. It had all the agility and active habits of its family, the Worm-eaters.

The length of this species is four inches and a half, breadth, seven inches ; the upper parts of the head and neck, light ash, a little inclining to olive ; crown, spotted with deep chestnut in small touches ; a pale yellowish ring round the eye ; whole lower parts, vivid yellow, except the middle of the belly, which is white ; back, yellow olive, slightly skirted with ash ; rump and tail-coverts, rich yellow olive ; wings, nearly black, broadly edged with olive ; tail, slightly forked, and very dark olive ; legs, ash ; feet, dirty yellow ; bill, tapering to a fine point, and dusky ash ; no white on wings or tail ; eye, hazel.

---

* Wilson discovered this species, and afterwards, in his Catalogue of Birds in the United States, changed the specific name as above. Like the last, it seems very rare ; Wilson saw only three ; Audubon, three or four ; and a single individual was shot by the over-land arctic expedition. " The latter was killed hopping about the branches of a tree, and emitting a creaking noise something like the whetting of a saw." The nest does not yet seem to be known. — Ed.

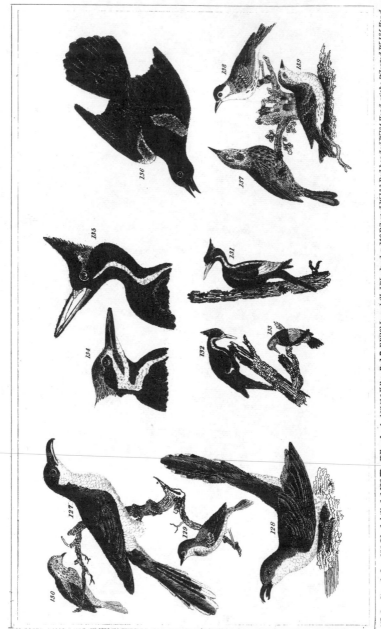

127 Carolina Cuckoo. 128 Black billed C. 129 Blue Yellow backed W. 130 Yellow Red Poll. 131 Ivory billed Woodpecker. 132 Pileated W. 133 Red headed W. 134 Head o' the Pileated W. 135 Head o' the Ivory billed W. 136 Red winged Starling. 137 Female. 138 Black Poll Warbler. 139 Lesser Red Poll.

YELLOW-BILLED CUCKOO.—CUCULUS CAROLINENSIS.—
Fig. 127.

Cuculus Americanus, *Linn. Syst.* 170. — *Catesb.* i. 9. — *Lath.* i. 537. — Le Coucou
de la Caroline, *Briss.* iv. 112. — *Arct. Zool.* 265, No. 155. — *Peale's Museum*,
No. 1778.

COCCYZUS AMERICANUS. — Bonaparte.*

Coccyzus Americanus, *Bonap. Synop.* p. 42. — The Yellow-billed Cuckoo,
Aud. pl. 2; *Orn. Biog.* i. p. 18.

A STRANGER who visits the United States, for the purpose of
examining their natural productions, and passes through our woods in
the month of May or June, will sometimes hear, as he traverses the
borders of deep, retired, high-timbered hollows, an uncouth, guttural
sound or note, resembling the syllables *kowe, kowe, kowe kowe kowe*, beginning slowly, but ending so rapidly, that the notes seem to run into
each other ; and *vice versa :* he will hear this frequently, without being
able to discover the bird or animal from which it proceeds, as it is both
shy and solitary, seeking always the thickest foliage for concealment.
This is the Yellow-billed Cuckoo, the subject of the present account.
From the imitative sound of its note, it is known in many parts by the

---

* Bonaparte has preferred restoring the specific name of Linnæus to that given
by Catesby and Brisson, and by this it should stand in our systems.
    This form will represent in America the true Cuckoos, which otherwise range
over the world ; it was first separated by Vaillant under the French name Conec,
and the same division was adopted by Vieillot, under the name of *Coccyzus*, which
is now retained. They differ from the Cuckoos chiefly in habit, — building a regular nest, and rearing their young. North America possesses only two species, our
present and the following, which are both migratory. Some beautiful species are
met with in different parts of the southern continent.
    Mr. Audubon has added little to their history further than confirming the accounts
of Wilson. In their migrations northward, they move singly ; but when removing
again to a warmer latitude, they appear to be gregarious, flying high in the air, and
in loose flocks.
    They appear to delight more in deep, woody solitudes than the true Cuckoos, or
those which approach nearest to the form of the European species. They, again,
though often found near woods, and in richly-clothed countries, are fond of open
and extensive heaths or commons, studded or fringed with brush and forest : here
they may expect an abundant supply of the foster-parent to their young. The
gliding and turning motion when flying in a thicket, however, is similar to that of
the American *Coccyzus*. Like them, also, they are seldom on the ground ; but,
when obliged to be near it, alight on some hillock or twig, where they will continue
for a considerable time, swinging round their body in a rather ludicrous manner,
with lowered wings and expanded tail, and uttering a rather low, monotonous
sound, resembling the *kowe* of our American bird, —

Turning round and round with *cutty-coo.*

When suddenly surprised or disturbed from their roost at night, they utter a short,
tremulous whistle, three or four times repeated ; it is only on their first arrival, during the early part of incubation, when in search of a mate, that their well-known
and welcome note is heard ; by the first of July all is silent. The idea that the
Common Cuckoo destroys eggs and young birds, like the American *Coccyzus*, is
also entertained ; I have never seen them do so, but the fact is affirmed by most
country persons, and many gamekeepers destroy them on this account. — ED.

name of the *Cow Bird*; it is also called in Virginia the *Rain Crow*, being observed to be most clamorous immediately before rain.

This species arrives in Pennsylvania, from the south, about the twenty-second of April, and spreads over the country, as far at least as Lake Ontario; is numerous in the Chickasaw and Chactaw nations; and also breeds in the upper parts of Georgia; preferring, in all these places, the borders of solitary swamps and apple orchards. It leaves us, on its return southward, about the middle of September.

The singular — I will not say unnatural — conduct of the European Cuckoo, (*Cuculus canorus*,) which never constructs a nest for itself, but drops its eggs in those of other birds, and abandons them to their mercy and management, is so universally known, and so proverbial, that the whole tribe of Cuckoos have, by some inconsiderate people, been stigmatized as destitute of all parental care and affection. Without attempting to account for this remarkable habit of the European species, far less to consider as an error what the wisdom of Heaven has imposed as a duty on the species, I will only remark, that the bird now before us builds its own nest, hatches its own eggs, and rears its own young; and, in conjugal and parental affection, seems nowise behind any of its neighbors of the grove.

Early in May, they begin to pair, when obstinate battles take place among the males. About the tenth of that month, they commence building. The nest is usually fixed among the horizontal branches of an apple-tree; sometimes in a solitary thorn, crab, or cedar, in some retired part of the woods. It is constructed, with little art, and scarcely any concavity, of small sticks and twigs, intermixed with green weeds, and blossoms of the common maple. On this almost flat bed, the eggs, usually three or four in number, are placed; these are of a uniform greenish blue color, and of a size proportionable to that of the bird. While the female is sitting, the male is generally not far distant, and gives the alarm, by his notes, when any person is approaching. The female sits so close, that you may almost reach her with your hand, and then precipitates herself to the ground, feigning lameness, to draw you away from the spot, fluttering, trailing her wings, and tumbling over, in the manner of the Partridge, Woodcock, and many other species. Both parents unite in providing food for the young. This consists, for the most part, of caterpillars, particularly such as infest apple-trees. The same insects constitute the chief part of their own sustenance. They are accused, and with some justice, of sucking the eggs of other birds, like the Crow, the Blue Jay, and other pillagers. They also occasionally eat various kinds of berries. But, from the circumstance of destroying such numbers of very noxious larvæ, they prove themselves the friends of the farmer, and are highly deserving of his protection.

The Yellow-billed Cuckoo is thirteen inches long, and sixteen inches in extent; the whole upper parts are of a dark glossy drab, or what is usually called a Quaker color, with greenish silky reflections; from this must, however, be excepted the inner vanes of the wings, which are bright reddish cinnamon; the tail is long, composed of ten feathers, the two middle ones being of the same color as the back; the others, which gradually shorten to the exterior ones, are black, largely tipped with white; the two outer ones are scarcely half the length of the middle ones. The whole lower parts are pure white; the feathers covering the thighs being large, like those of the Hawk tribe; the legs and feet are light blue, the toes placed two before and two behind, as in the rest of the genus. The bill is long, a little bent, very broad at the base, dusky black above, and yellow below; the eye hazel, feathered close to the eyelid, which is yellow. The female differs little from the male; the four middle tail-feathers in her are of the same uniform drab; and the white, with which the others are tipped, not so pure as in the male.

In examining this bird by dissection, the inner membrane of the gizzard, which in many other species is so hard and muscular, in this is extremely lax and soft, capable of great distention; and, what is remarkable, is covered with a growth of fine down, or hair, of a light fawn color. It is difficult to ascertain the particular purpose which nature intends by this excrescence; perhaps it may serve to shield the tender parts from the irritating effects produced by the hairs of certain caterpillars, some of which are said to be almost equal to the sting of a nettle.

BLACK-BILLED CUCKOO. — CUCULUS ERYTHROPTHALMA. — Fig. 128.

Peale's Museum, No. 1854.

COCCYZUS ERYTHROPTHALMUS. — Bonaparte. [*]

Coccyzus erythrophthalmus, *Bonap. Synop.* p. 42. — The Black-billed Cuckoo, *Aud.* pl. 32, male and female; *Orn. Biog.* i. p. 170.

This Cuckoo is nearly as numerous as the former, but has hitherto escaped the notice of European naturalists; or, from its general resemblance, has been confounded with the preceding. Its particular markings, however, and some of its habits, sufficiently characterize it as a distinct species. Its general color above is nearly that of the former, inclining more to a pale ash on the cheeks and front; it is about an inch less in length; the tail is of a uniform dark silky drab, except at the tip, where each feather is marked with a spot of white, bordered above with a slight touch of dull black; the bill is wholly black, and much smaller than that of the preceding; and it wants the bright cinnamon on the wings. But what constitutes its most distinguishing trait is, a bare, wrinkled skin, of a deep red color, that surrounds the eye. The female differs little in external appearance from the male.

The Black-billed Cuckoo is particularly fond of the sides of creeks,

---

[*] Wilson, I believe, deserves the credit of distinguishing this species. It is closely allied to, but differs widely, both in its habits and feeding, from its congeners and the true Cuckoos. In addition to shells and water insects, Audubon mentions having found in their stomachs a small black frog, which appears after a summer shower. — Ed.

23 *

feeding on small shell-fish, snails, &c. I have also often found broken pieces of oyster shells in its gizzard, which, like that of the other, is covered with fine downy hair.

The nest of this bird is most commonly built in a cedar, much in the same manner, and of nearly the same materials, as that of the other; but the eggs are smaller, usually four or five in number, and of a rather deeper greenish blue.

This bird is likewise found in the state of Georgia, and has not escaped the notice of Mr. Abbot, who is satisfied of its being a distinct species from the preceding.

BLUE YELLOW-BACK WARBLER. — SYLVIA PUSILLA. —
Fig. 129.

Parus Americanus, *Linn. Syst.* 341. — Finch Creeper, *Catesb.* i. 64. — *Lath.* ii. 558. — Creeping Titmouse, *Arct. Zool.* 423, No. 326. — Parus varius, Various-colored Little Finch Creeper, *Bart.* p. 292. — *Peale's Museum*, No. 6910.

SYLVICOLA AMERICANA. — Swainson.*

Sylvia Americana, *Lath. Ind. Orn.* ii. p. 520. — *Bonap. Synop.* p. 83. — Sylvicola pusilla, *Sw. Synop. Birds of Mex. Ann. of Phil.* p. 433. — *Zool. Journ.* No. 10, p. 169. — The Blue Yellow-backed Warbler, *Aud.* pl. 15, male and female; *Orn. Biog.* i. p. 78.

Notwithstanding the respectability of the above authorities, I must continue to consider this bird as a species of Warbler. Its habits, indeed, partake something of the Titmouse; but the form of its bill is decidedly that of the *Sylvia* genus. It is remarkable for frequenting the tops of the tallest trees, where it feeds on the small winged insects and caterpillars that infest the young leaves and blossoms. It has a few, feeble, cheruping notes, scarcely loud enough to be heard at the foot of the tree. It visits Pennsylvania from the south, early in May; is very abundant in the woods of Kentucky; and is also found in the northern parts of the state of New York. Its nest I have never yet met with. †

This little species is four inches and a half long, and six inches and a half in breadth; the front, and between the bill and eyes, is black; the upper part of the head and neck, a fine Prussian blue; upper part of the back, brownish yellow; lower, and rump, pale blue; wings and

---

* There is nothing more annoying than the unravelling of names. That of *Americana*, without doubt, seems to have been the specific appellation first applied; and if we are to adhere to any given rule in nomenclature, that should be now adopted. The present species has also been made typical of the group which is confined to the New World. — Ed.

† According to Audubon, the nest is small, formed of lichens, beautifully arranged on the outside, and lined with the cotton substances found on the edges of different mosses; it is placed in the fork of a small twig, near the extremity of the branch. The eggs are pure white, with a few reddish dots at the longer end. Mr. Audubon thinks two broods are raised in the year. — Ed.

tail, black; the former crossed with two bars of white, and edged with blue; the latter marked on the inner webs of the three exterior feathers with white, a circumstance common to a great number of the genus; immediately above and below the eye is a small touch of white; the upper mandible is black; the lower, as well as the whole throat and breast, rich yellow, deepening about its middle to orange red, and marked on the throat with a small crescent of black; on the edge of the breast is a slight touch of rufous; belly and vent, white; legs, dark brown; feet, dirty yellow. The female wants both the black and orange on the throat and breast; the blue on the upper parts is also of a duller tint.

YELLOW RED-POLL WARBLER. — SYLVIA PETECHIA. —
Fig. 130.

Red-headed Warbler, *Turton*, i. 605. — *Peale's Museum*, No. 7124.

SYLVICOLA PETECHIA. — Swainson.

Lath. Ind. Orn. ii. p. 535. — Sylvia petechia, *Bonap. Synop.* p. 83. — Red-headed Warbler, *Penn. Arct. Zool.* ii. p. 401. — Sylvicola petechia, *North. Zool.* ii. p. 215.

This delicate little bird arrives in Pennsylvania early in April, while the maples are yet in blossom, among the branches of which it may generally be found at that season, feeding on the stamina of the flowers, and on small winged insects. Low, swampy thickets are its favorite places of resort. It is not numerous, and its notes are undeserving the name of song. It remains with us all summer, but its nest has hitherto escaped me. It leaves us late in September. Some of them probably winter in Georgia, having myself shot several, late in February, on the borders of the Savannah River.

Length of the Yellow Red-Poll, five inches; extent, eight; line over the eye, and whole lower parts, rich yellow; breast, streaked with dull red; upper part of the head, reddish chestnut, which it loses in winter; back, yellow olive, streaked with dusky; rump, and tail-coverts, greenish yellow; wings, deep blackish brown, exteriorly edged with olive; tail, slightly forked, and of the same color as the wings.

The female wants the red cap, and the yellow of the lower part is less brilliant; the streaks of red on the breast are also fewer and less distinct.

IVORY-BILLED WOODPECKER.—PICUS PRINCIPALIS.—
Fig. 131.

Picus principalis, *Lynn. Syst.* i. p. 173, 2.— *Gmel. Syst.* i. p. 425.— Picus Niger
Carolinensis, *Briss.* iv. p. 26, 9 ; *Id.* 8vo. ii. p. 49.— Pic noir à bec blanc, *Buff.*
vii. p. 46. *Pl. enl.* 690.— King of the Woodpeckers, *Kalm,* ii. p. 85.— White-
billed Woodpecker, *Catesb. Car.* i. 6, 16.— *Arct. Zool.* ii. No. 156.— *Lath. Syst.*
ii. p. 553.— *Bartram,* p. 289.— *Peale's Museum,* No. 1384.

PICUS PRINCIPALIS. — Linnæus.*

Picus principalis, *Bonap. Synop.* p. 44.— *Wagl. Syst. Av. Picus,* No. 1.— The
Ivory-billed Woodpecker, *Aud.* pl. 66, male and female ; *Orn. Biog.* i. p. 341.

THIS majestic and formidable species, in strength and magnitude,
stands at the head of the whole class of Woodpeckers hitherto discovered. He may be called the king or chief of his tribe ; and Nature

* The genus *Picus,* or Woodpeckers, with the exception of the Parrots, forms
the most extensive group among the *Scansores,* and perhaps one of the most natural among the numerous divisions now assigned to the feathered race. In a former
note, we mentioned the difference of form, and corresponding modification of habit,
that nevertheless existed among them. Most ornithologists have divided them into
three groups only, taking the common form of Woodpeckers for the type, making
another of the Golden-winged, and including in a third the very minute species
which form Temminck's genus *Picumnus,* but which, I believe, will be found to
rank in a family somewhat different. Mr. Swainson, again, in following out the
views which he holds regarding the affinities of living beings, has formed five
groups, — taking our present form as typical, under the title *Picus ;* that of the
Green Woodpecker, under *Chrysoptilus ;* that of the Red-headed Woodpecker, as
Melanerpes ; the Golden-Wings, as *Colaptes ;* and *Malacolophus,* as the Soft-
crested Brazilian and Indian species. Of these forms, the northern parts of America will contain only three : two we have had occasion already to remark upon ;
and the third forms the subject of our author's present description — the most powerful of the whole tribe, and showing all the forms and peculiarities of the true Woodpecker developed to the utmost.
    The *Pici* are very numerous, and are distributed over the whole world, New
Holland excepted ; America, however, including both continents, may be termed
the land of Woodpeckers. Her vast and solitary forests afford abundance to satisfy their various wants, and furnish a secluded retirement from the inroads of cultivation. Next in number, I believe, India and her islands are best stored ; then,
Africa ; and lastly, Europe. The numbers, however, are always greatest between
the tropics, and generally diminish as we recede from and approach temperate or
cold regions. They are mostly insectivorous ; a few species only feed occasionally
on different fruits and berries. The various *Coleoptera,* that form their abodes in
dead and decaying timber, and beneath their bark and moss, with their eggs and
large larvæ, form an essential part of their subsistence. For securing this prey,
digging it out from their burrows in the wood, and the peculiar mode of life incident
to such pursuits, they are most admirably adapted. The bill is strong and wedge-
shaped ; the neck possesses great muscularity. The tongue, — fitted by the curious construction of its muscles and the *os hyoides,* and lubricated with a viscous
saliva, either gently to secure and draw in the weaker prey, or with great force
and rapidity to dart out, and, it is said, to transfix the larger and more nimble insects, — joined to the short legs and hooked, scansorial claws, with the stiff, bent
tail, are all provisions beautifully arranged for their wants.
    All the species are solitary ; live in pairs only during the season of incubation ; or
are met with in small flocks, the amount of the year's brood, in the end of autumn,
before they have separated. This solitary habit, and their haunts being generally

seems to have designed him a distinguished characteristic in the superb carmine crest and bill of polished ivory with which she has ornamented him. His eye is brilliant and daring; and his whole frame so admirably adapted for his mode of life and method of procuring subsistence, as to impress on the mind of the examiner the most reverential ideas of the Creator. His manners have also a dignity in them superior to the common herd of Woodpeckers. Trees, shrubbery, orchards, rails, fence-posts, and old, prostrate logs, are alike interesting to those, in their humble and indefatigable search for prey; but the royal hunter now before us scorns the humility of such situations, and seeks the most towering trees of the forests; seeming particularly attached to those prodigious cypress swamps, whose crowded giant sons stretch their bare and blasted or moss-hung arms midway to the skies. In these almost inaccessible recesses, amid ruinous piles of impending timber, his trumpet-like note and loud strokes resound through the solitary, savage wilds, of which he seems the sole lord and inhabitant. Wherever he frequents, he leaves numerous monuments of his industry behind him. We there see enormous pine-trees, with cartloads of bark lying around their roots, and chips of the trunk itself, in such quantities as to suggest the idea that half a dozen of axe-men had been at work there for the whole morning. The body of the tree is also disfigured with such numerous and so large excavations, that one can hardly conceive it possible for the whole to be the work of a Woodpecker. With such strength, and an apparatus so powerful, what havock might he not commit, if numerous, on the most useful of our forest-trees! And yet, with all these appearances, and much of

gloomy and retired, has given rise to the opinion, entertained by many, that the life of the Woodpecker was hard and laborious, dragged on in the same unvaried tract for one purpose, — the supply of food. It has been painted in vivid and imaginary coloring, and its existence has been described to be painful and burdensome in the extreme; its cries have been converted into complaints, and its search for food into exertions of no use. We cannot agree to this. The cry of the Woodpecker is wild, and no doubt the incessant hewing of holes, without an adequate object, would be sufficiently miserable. These, however, are the pleasures of the bird. The knowledge to search after food is implanted in it, and organs most admirably formed to prevent exhaustion and insure success, have been granted to it. Its cries, though melancholy to us, are so from association with the dark forests and the stillness which surrounds their haunts, but perhaps, at the time when we judge, are expressive of the greatest enjoyment. An answer of kindness in reply to a mate, the calling together of the newly-fledged brood, or exultation over the discovery of some favorite hoard of food, are what are set down as painful and discontented.

Mr. Audubon's remarks on this splendid species, "the King of the Woodpeckers," I have transcribed at some length, as indicating the particular manner of the typical family of this great group : —

"The Ivory-billed Woodpecker confines its rambles to a comparatively very small portion of the United States, it never having been observed in the Middle States within the memory of any person now living there. In fact, in no portion of these districts does the nature of the woods appear suitable to its remarkable habits.

"Descending the Ohio, we meet with this splendid bird for the first time near the confluence of that beautiful river and the Mississippi; after which, following the windings of the latter, either downwards toward the sea, or upwards in the direction of the Missouri, we frequently observe it. On the Atlantic coast, North Carolina may be taken as the limit of its distribution, although now and then an individual of the spe-

vulgar prejudice against him, it may fairly be questioned whether he is at all injurious; or, at least, whether his exertions do not contribute most powerfully to the protection of our timber. Examine closely the tree where he has been at work, and you will soon perceive that it is neither from motives of mischief nor amusement that he slices off the bark, or digs his way into the trunk; for the sound and healthy tree is the least object of his attention. The diseased, infested with insects, and hastening to putrefaction, are *his* favorites; there the deadly, crawling enemy have formed a lodgment between the bark and tender wood, to drink up the very vital part of the tree. It is the ravages of these vermin, which the intelligent proprietor of the forest deplores as the sole perpetrators of the destruction of his timber. Would it be believed that the larvæ of an insect, or fly, no larger than a grain of rice, should silently, and in one season, destroy some thousand acres of pine-trees, many of them from two to three feet in diameter, and a hundred and fifty feet high? Yet whoever passes along the high road from Georgetown to Charleston, in South Carolina, about twenty miles from the former place, can have striking and melancholy proofs of this fact. In some places, the whole woods, as far as you can see around you, are dead, stripped of the bark, their wintry-looking arms and bare trunks bleaching in the sun, and tumbling in ruins before every blast, presenting a frightful picture of desolation. And yet ignorance and prejudice stubbornly persist in directing their indignation against the bird now before us, the constant and mortal enemy of these very vermin; as if the hand that probed the wound to extract its cause, should be equally detested with that which inflicted it; or as if the thief-

cies may be accidentally seen in Maryland. To the westward of the Mississippi, it is found in all the dense forests bordering the streams which empty their waters into that majestic river, from the very declivities of the Rocky Mountains. The lower parts of the Carolinas, Georgia, Alabama, Louisiana, and Mississippi, are, however, the most favorite resorts of this bird, and in those states it constantly resides, breeds, and passes a life of peaceful enjoyment, finding a profusion of food in all the deep, dark, and gloomy swamps dispersed throughout them.

"The flight of this bird is graceful in the extreme, although seldom prolonged to more than a few hundred yards at a time, unless when it has to cross a large river, which it does in deep undulations, opening its wings at first to their full extent, and nearly closing them to renew the propelling impulse. The transit from one tree to another, even should the distance be as much as a hundred yards, is performed by a single sweep, and the bird appears as if merely swinging itself from the top of the one tree to that of the other, forming an elegantly curved line. At this moment, all the beauty of the plumage is exhibited, and strikes the beholder with pleasure. It never utters any sound whilst on wing, unless during the love season; but, at all other times, no sooner has this bird alighted than its remarkable voice is heard, at almost every leap which it makes, whilst ascending against the upper parts of the trunk of a tree or its highest branches. Its notes are clear, loud, and yet very plaintive; they are heard at a considerable distance, perhaps half a mile, and resemble the false high note of a clarionet. They are usually repeated three times in succession, and may be represented by the monosyllable *pait, pait, pait.* These are heard so frequently as to induce me to say that the bird spends few minutes of the day without uttering them; and this circumstance leads to its destruction, which is aimed at, not because (as is supposed by some) this species is a destroyer of trees, but more because it is a beautiful bird, and its rich scalp attached to the upper mandible forms an ornament for the war-dress of most of our Indians, or for the shot-pouch of our squatters and hunters, by all of whom the bird is shot merely for that purpose." — ED.

catcher should be confounded with the thief. Until some effectual preventive, or more complete mode of destruction, can be devised against these insects and their larvæ, I would humbly suggest the propriety of protecting, and receiving, with proper feelings of gratitude, the services of this and the whole tribe of Woodpeckers, letting the odium of guilt fall upon its proper owners.

In looking over the accounts given of the Ivory-billed Woodpecker by the naturalists of Europe, I find it asserted that it inhabits from New Jersey to Mexico. I believe, however, that few of them are ever seen to the north of Virginia, and very few of them even in that state. The first place I observed this bird at, when on my way to the south, was about twelve miles north of Wilmington in North Carolina. There I found the bird from which the drawing of Fig. 131 was taken. This bird was only wounded slightly in the wing, and, on being caught, uttered a loudly reiterated and most piteous note, exactly resembling the violent crying of a young child; which terrified my horse so, as nearly to have cost me my life. It was distressing to hear it. I carried it with me in the chair, under cover, to Wilmington. In passing through the streets, its affecting cries surprised every one within hearing, particularly the females, who hurried to the doors and windows with looks of alarm and anxiety. I drove on, and, on arriving at the piazza of the hotel, where I intended to put up, the landlord came forward, and a number of other persons who happened to be there, all equally alarmed at what they heard; this was greatly increased by my asking, whether he could furnish me with accommodations for myself and my baby. The man looked blank and foolish, while the others stared with still greater astonishment. After diverting myself for a minute or two at their expense, I drew my Woodpecker from under the cover, and a general laugh took place. I took him up stairs, and locked him up in my room, while I went to see my horse taken care of. In less than an hour, I returned, and, on opening the door, he set up the same distressing shout, which now appeared to proceed from grief that he had been discovered in his attempts at escape. He had mounted along the side of the window, nearly as high as the ceiling, a little below which he had begun to break through. The bed was covered with large pieces of plaster; the lath was exposed for at least fifteen inches square, and a hole, large enough to admit the fist, opened to the weather-boards; so that, in less than another hour, he would certainly have succeeded in making his way through. I now tied a string round his leg, and, fastening it to the table, again left him. I wished to preserve his life, and had gone off in search of suitable food for him. As I reascended the stairs, I heard him again hard at work, and on entering had the mortification to perceive that he had almost entirely ruined the mahogany table to which he was fastened, and on which he had wreaked his whole vengeance. While engaged in taking the drawing, he cut me severely in several places, and, on the whole, displayed such a noble and unconquerable spirit, that I was frequently tempted to restore him to his native woods. He lived with me nearly three days, but refused all sustenance, and I witnessed his death with regret.

The head and bill of this bird is in great esteem among the southern Indians, who wear them by way of amulet or charm, as well as ornament; and, it is said, dispose of them to the northern tribes at considerable prices. An Indian believes that the head, skin, or even feathers of certain birds, confer on the wearer all the virtues or excellences of those birds. Thus I have seen a coat made of the skins, heads, and claws of the Raven; caps stuck round with heads of Butcher Birds, Hawks, and Eagles; and as the disposition and courage of the Ivory-billed Woodpecker are well known to the savages, no wonder they should attach great value to it, having both beauty, and, in their estimation, distinguished merit to recommend it.

This bird is not migratory, but resident in the countries where it inhabits. In the low countries of the Carolinas, it usually prefers the large-timbered cypress swamps for breeding in. In the trunk of one of these trees, at a considerable height, the male and female alternately, and in conjunction, dig out a large and capacious cavity for their eggs and young. Trees thus dug out have frequently been cut down, with sometimes the eggs and young in them. This hole, according to information, — for I have never seen one myself, — is generally a little winding, the better to keep out the weather, and from two to five feet deep. The eggs are said to be generally four, sometimes five, as large as a Pullet's, pure white, and equally thick at both ends — a description that, except in size, very nearly agrees with all the rest of our Woodpeckers. The young begin to be seen abroad about the middle of June. Whether they breed more than once in the same season is uncertain.*

---

* The description of the nestling, &c., is thus also given by Audubon. Wilson observes that he had no opportunity of ever seeing their holes, and the following will tend to render his account more complete : —

"The Ivory-billed Woodpecker nestles earlier in spring than any other species of its tribe. I have observed it boring a hole for that purpose in the beginning of March. The hole is, I believe, always made in the trunk of a live tree, generally an ash or a hagberry, and is at a great height. The birds pay great regard to the particular situation of the tree and the inclination of its trunk; first, because they prefer retirement, and again, because they are anxious to secure the aperture against the access of water during beating rains. To prevent such a calamity, the hole is generally dug immediately under the junction of a large branch with the trunk. It is first bored horizontally for a few inches, then directly downwards, and not in a spiral manner, as some people have imagined. According to circumstances, this cavity is more or less deep, being sometimes not more than ten inches, whilst at other times it reaches nearly three feet downwards into the core of the tree. I have been led to think that these differences result from the more or less immediate necessity under which the female may be of depositing her eggs, and again have thought that the older the Woodpecker is, the deeper does it make its hole. The average diameter of the different nests which I have examined, was about seven inches within, although the entrance, which is perfectly round, is only just large enough to admit the bird.

"Both birds work most assiduously at this excavation, one waiting outside to encourage the other, whilst it is engaged in digging, and when the latter is fatigued, taking its place. I have approached trees whilst these Woodpeckers were thus busily employed in forming their nest, and by resting my head against the bark, could easily distinguish every blow given by the bird. I observed that in two instances, when the Woodpecker saw me thus at the foot of the tree in which they were digging their nest, they abandoned it forever. For the first brood there are generally six eggs. They are deposited on a few chips at the bottom of the hole, and are of a pure white color. The young are seen creeping out of the hole about a fortnight before they venture to fly to any other tree. The second brood makes its appearance about the 15th of August.

So little attention do the people of the countries where these birds inhabit pay to the minutiæ of natural history, that, generally speaking, they make no distinction between the Ivory-billed and Pileated Woodpecker, represented in the same plate ; and it was not till I showed them the two birds together, that they knew of any difference. The more intelligent and observing part of the natives, however, distinguish them by the name of the Large and Lesser *Logcocks.* They seldom examine them but at a distance, gunpowder being considered too precious to be thrown away on Woodpeckers ; nothing less than a Turkey being thought worth the value of a load.

"In Kentucky and Indiana, the Ivory-Bills seldom raise more than one brood in the season. The young are at first of the color of the female, only that they want the crest, which, however, grows rapidly, and towards autumn — particularly in birds of the first breed — is nearly equal to that of the mother. The males have then a slight line of red on the head, and do not attain their richness of plumage until spring, or their full size until the second year. Indeed, even then, a difference is easily observed between them and individuals which are much older.

"The food of this species consists principally of beetles, larvæ, and large grubs. No sooner, however, are the grapes of our forests ripe than they are eaten by the Ivory-billed Woodpecker with great avidity. I have seen this bird hang by its claws to the vines, in the position so often assumed by a Titmouse, and, reaching downwards, help itself to a bunch of grapes with much apparent pleasure. Persimmons are also sought for by them, as soon as the fruit becomes quite mellow, as are hagberries.

"The Ivory-Bill is never seen attacking the corn, or the fruit of the orchard, although it is sometimes observed working upon and chipping off the bark from the belted trees of the newly-cleared plantations. It seldom comes near the ground, but prefers at all times the tops of the tallest trees. Should it, however, discover the half-standing broken shaft of a large dead and rotten tree, it attacks it in such a manner as nearly to demolish it in the course of a few days. I have seen the remains of some of these ancient monarchs of our forests so excavated, and that so singularly, that the tottering fragments of the trunk appeared to be merely supported by the great pile of chips by which its base was surrounded. The strength of this Woodpecker is such, that I have seen it detach pieces of bark seven or eight inches in length at a single blow of its powerful bill, and by beginning at the top branch of a dead tree, tear off the bark, to an extent of twenty or thirty feet, in the course of a few hours, leaping downwards, with its body in an upward position, tossing its head to the right and left, or leaning it against the bark to ascertain the precise spot where the grubs were concealed, and immediately after renewing its blows with fresh vigor, all the while sounding its loud notes, as if highly delighted.

"This species generally moves in pairs, after the young have left their parents. The female is always the most clamorous and the least shy. Their mutual attachment is, I believe, continued through life. Excepting when digging a hole for the reception of their eggs, these birds seldom, if ever, attack living trees, for any other purpose than that of procuring food, in doing which they destroy the insects that would otherwise prove injurious to the trees.

"I have frequently observed the male and female retire to rest for the night, into the same hole in which they had long before reared their young. This generally happens a short time after sunset.

"When wounded and brought to the ground, the Ivory-Bill immediately makes for the nearest tree, and ascends it with great rapidity and perseverance until it reaches the top branches, when it squats and hides, generally with great effect. Whilst ascending, it moves spirally round the tree, utters its loud *pait, pait, pait,* at almost every hop, but becomes silent the moment it reaches a place where it conceives itself secure. They sometimes cling to the bark with their claws so firmly as to remain cramped to the spot for several hours after death. When taken by the hand, which is rather a hazardous undertaking. they strike with great violence, and inflict very severe wounds with their bill as well as claws, which are extremely sharp and strong. On such occasions, this bird utters a mournful and very piteous cry." — ED.

21

The food of this bird consists, 1 believe, entirely of insects and their larvæ.* The Pileated Woodpecker is suspected of sometimes tasting the Indian corn; the Ivory-billed never. His common note, repeated every three or four seconds, very much resembles the tone of a trumpet, or the high note of a clarionet, and can plainly be distinguished at the distance of more than half a mile; seeming to be immediately at hand, though perhaps more than one hundred yards off. This it utters while mounting along the trunk or digging into it. At these times it has a stately and novel appearance; and the note instantly attracts the notice of a stranger. Along the borders of the Savannah River, between Savannah and Augusta, I found them very frequently; but my horse no sooner heard their trumpet-like note, than, remembering his former alarm, he became almost ungovernable.

The Ivory-billed Woodpecker is twenty inches long, and thirty inches in extent; the general color is black, with a considerable gloss of green when exposed to a good light; iris of the eye, vivid yellow; nostrils, covered with recumbent white hairs; fore part of the head, black; rest of the crest, of a most splendid red, spotted at the bottom with white, which is only seen when the crest is erected, as represented in Fig. 135; this long red plumage being ash-colored at its base, above that white, and ending in brilliant red; a stripe of white proceeds from a point, about half an inch below each eye, passes down each side of the neck, and along the back, where they are about an inch apart, nearly to the rump; the first five primaries are wholly black; on the next five the white spreads from the tip, higher and higher, to the secondaries, which are wholly white from their coverts downward. These markings, when the wings are shut, make the bird appear as if his back were white; hence he has been called by some of our naturalists the large White-backed Woodpecker. The neck is long; the beak an inch broad at the base, of the color and consistence of ivory, prodigiously strong and elegantly fluted. The tail is black, tapering from the two exterior feathers, which are three inches shorter than the middle ones, and each feather has the singularity of being greatly concave below; the wing is lined with yellowish white; the legs are about an inch and a quarter long, the exterior toe about the same length, the claws exactly semicircular and remarkably powerful, — the whole of a light blue or lead color. The female is about half an inch shorter, the bill rather less, and the whole plumage of the head black, glossed with green; in the other parts of the plumage, she exactly resembles the male. In the stomachs of three which I opened, I found large quantities of a species of worm called borers, two or three inches long, of a dirty cream color, with a black head; the stomach was an oblong pouch, not muscular, like the gizzards of some

* Mr. Audubon says, that though the greater part of their food consists of insects and their larvæ, no sooner are the grapes of our forests ripe, than they are eaten with the greatest avidity. I have seen this bird hang by its claws to the vines, in the position so often assumed by the Titmouse, and, reaching down, help itself to a bunch of grapes. Persimmons are also sought by them, as soon as the fruit becomes quite mellow, and hagberries. — ED.

others. The tongue was worm-shaped, and for half an inch at the tip as hard as horn, flat, pointed, of the same white color as the bill, and thickly barbed on each side.*

PILEATED WOODPECKER. — PICUS PILEATUS. — Fig. 132.

Picus niger, crista rubra, *Lath. Ind. Orn.* i. p. 225, 4. — Picus pileatus, *Linn. Syst.*
i. p. 173, 3. — *Gmel. Syst.* i. p. 425. — Picus Virginianus pileatus, *Briss.* iv. p.
29, 10. — *Id.* 8vo. ii. p. 50. — Pic noir à huppé rouge, *Buff.* vii. p. 48. — Pic noir
huppé de la Louisiana, *Pl. enl.* 718. — Larger Crested Woodpecker, *Catesb. Car.*
i. 6, 17. — Pileated Woodpecker, *Arct. Zool.* ii. No. 157. — *Lath. Syn.* ii. p. 554,
3. — *Id. Supp.* p. 105. — *Bartram,* p. 289. — *Peale's Museum,* No. 1836.

PICUS PILEATUS. — Linnæus.†

Picus pileatus, *Bonap. Synop.* p. 44. — *Wagl. Syst. Av.* No. 2. — Picus (dryotomus) pileatus, *North. Zool.* ii. p. 304.

This American species is the second in size among his tribe, and may be styled the great northern chief of the Woodpeckers, though, in fact, his range extends over the whole of the United States from the interior of Canada to the Gulf of Mexico. He is very numerous in the Genesee country, and in all the tracts of high-timbered forests, particularly in the neighborhood of our large rivers, where he is noted for making a loud and almost incessant cackling before wet weather, flying at such times in a restless, uneasy manner from tree to tree, making the woods echo to his outcry. In Pennsylvania and the North-ern States, he is called the Black Woodcock; in the Southern States, the Logcock. Almost every old trunk in the forest where he resides bears the marks of his chisel. Wherever he perceives a tree beginning to decay, he examines it round and round with great skill and dexterity, strips off the bark in sheets of five or six feet in length, to get at the hidden cause of the disease, and labors with a gayety and activity really surprising. I have seen him separate the greatest part of the bark from a large, dead pine tree, for twenty or thirty feet, in less than a quarter of an hour. Whether engaged in flying from tree to tree, in digging, climbing, or barking, he seems perpetually in a hurry. He is extremely hard to kill, clinging close to the tree even after he has received his mortal wound; nor yielding up his hold but with his ex-piring breath. If slightly wounded in the wing, and dropped while

---

* Wilson seems to have been in some uncertainty regarding the nidification of this species, and probably never saw the nest. The account of Mr. Audubon will fill up what is here wanting. — Ed.
† As we remarked in our last note, Mr. Swainson, according to the views he en-tertains, has divided the large family *Picianæ* into five great divisions, and the different forms in these again into groups of lesser value. For the type of one of them, he has chosen the *Picus pileatus,* under the title of *Dryotomus,* differing from *Picus* in the *exterior* outer toe being shorter than the *anterior* external one, exactly the reverse of the proportions of *Picus.* — Ed.

flying, he instantly makes for the nearest tree, and strikes with great bitterness at the hand stretched out to seize him; and can rarely be reconciled to confinement. He is sometimes observed among the hills of Indian corn, and it is said by some that he frequently feeds on it. Complaints of this kind are, however, not general; many farmers doubting the fact, and conceiving that at these times he is in search of insects which lie concealed in the husk. I will not be positive that they never occasionally taste maize; yet I have opened and examined great numbers of these birds, killed in various parts of the United States, from Lake Ontario to the Alatamaha River, but never found a grain of Indian corn in their stomachs.

The Pileated Woodpecker is not migratory, but braves the extremes of both the arctic and torrid regions. Neither is he gregarious, for it is rare to see more than one or two, or at the most three, in company. Formerly they were numerous in the neighborhood of Philadelphia; but gradually, as the old timber fell, and the country became better cleared, they retreated to the forest. At present few of those birds are to be found within ten or fifteen miles of the city.

Their nest is built, or rather the eggs are deposited, in the hole of a tree, dug out by themselves, no other materials being used but the soft chips of rotten wood. The female lays six large eggs, of a snowy whiteness; and, it is said, they generally raise two broods in the same season.

This species is eighteen inches long, and twenty-eight in extent; the general color is a dusky brownish black; the head is ornamented with a conical cap of bright scarlet; two scarlet mustaches proceed from the lower mandible; the chin is white; the nostrils are covered with brownish white, hair-like feathers, and this stripe of white passes from thence down the side of the neck to the sides, spreading under the wings; the upper half of the wings is white, but concealed by the black coverts; the lower extremities of the wings are black, so that the white on the wing is not seen but when the bird is flying, at which time it is very prominent; the tail is tapering, the feathers being very convex above, and strong; the legs are of a leaden gray color, very short, scarcely half an inch; the toes very long; claws, strong and semicircular, and of a pale blue; the bill is fluted, sharply ridged, very broad at the base, bluish black above, below and at the point bluish white; the eye is of a bright golden color, the pupil black; the tongue, like those of its tribe, is worm-shaped, except near the tip, where for one eighth of an inch it is horny, pointed, and beset with barbs.

The female has the forehead, and nearly to the crown, of a light brown color, and the mustaches are dusky, instead of red. In both, a fine line of white separates the red crest from the dusky line that passes over the eye.

RED-WINGED STARLING.—STURNUS PREDATORIUS.—
Fig. 136, Male; Fig. 137, Female.

Bartram, 291.—Oriolus phœniceus, *Linn. Syst.* 161.—Red-winged Oriole, *Arct. Zool.* 255, No. 140.—Le Troupiale à aisles rouges, *Briss.* ii. 97.—Le comman-deur, *Buff.* iii. 214, *Pl. enl.* 402.— *Lath.* i. 428.—Acolchichi, *Fernand. Nov. Hisp.* p. 14.— *Peale's Museum,* No. 1466, 1467.

AGLAIUS PHŒNICEUS. — Vieillot.*

Aglaius Phœniceus, *Vieill. Gall. des Ois.— North. Zool.* ii. p. 280.—Icterus Phœ-niceus, *Bonap. Synop.* p. 52.—The Red-winged Starling, or Marsh Blackbird. *Aud.* pl. 67. male in different states, female, and young; *Orn. Biog.* i. p. 348.

This notorious and celebrated corn thief, the long-reputed plunderer and pest of our honest and laborious farmers, now presents himself before us, with his copartner in iniquity, to receive the character due for their very active and distinguished services. In investigating the nature of these, I shall endeavor to render strict historical justice to this noted pair; adhering to the honest injunctions of the poet—

> Nothing extenuate,
> Nor set down aught in malice.

Let the reader divest himself equally of prejudice, and we shall be at no loss to ascertain accurately their true character.

---

* This bird, I believe, will rank under the *Icteri* of Brisson, but seems first men-tioned by Daudin under that title. Like the others of this intricate family, it has been described under a multitude of names; but the above seems the preferable one to be adopted. Wilson also changed the specific name to *Predatorius,* taken from its plundering habits, whereas, without doubt, he should have retained its ori-ginal designation. North America possesses another beautiful species, figured in the Continuation of the *Ornithology* by Bonaparte. Wilson is somewhat puzzled in what genus to place this bird, and is only recon-ciled to join it with our Common Starling, which it much resembles in its congrega-ted flights. In this country, we cannot expect to see a flight of such numbers as Wilson mentions; still they are sometimes very numerous, and one might almost conceive the appearance of the one, from their recollections of the other. In the low meadows of Holland, again, some relative proportion may be found. I have seen an extent of flat surface, as far as the eye could reach around, covered with flocks of Starlings, associated with Lapwings and Golden Plovers; and the flocks that rose on the approach of night were sometimes immense. In the islands of Sardinia, and those adjacent, and where they may be augmented by the presence of another species, the *St. unicolor* of Temminck, I am told that the assemblage of birds is innumerable in the lower valleys, and among the lakes and reedy marshes which cover so much of the lower parts of these countries. In their evo-lutions before retiring to rest among reeds or bushes, the two birds also resemble each other. That of Europe is thus described by an observing naturalist:—" There is something singularly curious and mysterious in the conduct of these birds, pre-vious to their nightly retirement, by the variety and intricacy of the evolutions they execute at that time. They will form themselves, perhaps, into a triangle, then shoot into a long, pear-shaped figure, expand like a sheet, wheel into a ball, as Pliny observes, each individual striving to get into the centre, &c., with a prompti-tude more like parade movements, than the action of birds." I have known them watched for, when coming to roost, and shot in considerable numbers. Their wings afford favorite feathers for fishers.— Ed.

24 *

The Red-winged Starlings, though generally migratory in the states north of Maryland, are found during winter in immense flocks, sometimes associated with the Purple Grakles, and often by themselves, along the whole lower parts of Virginia, both Carolinas, Georgia, and Louisiana, particularly near the sea-coast, and in the vicinity of large rice and corn fields. In the months of January and February, while passing through the former of these countries, I was frequently entertained with the aerial evolutions of these great bodies of Starlings. Sometimes they appeared driving about like an enormous black cloud carried before the wind, varying its shape every moment; sometimes suddenly rising from the fields around me with a noise like thunder; while the glittering of innumerable wings of the brightest vermilion amid the black cloud they formed, produced on these occasions a very striking and splendid effect. Then, descending like a torrent, and covering the branches of some detached grove, or clump of trees, the whole congregated multitude commenced one general concert or chorus, that I have plainly distinguished at the distance of more than two miles, and, when listened to at the intermediate space of about a quarter of a mile, with a slight breeze of wind to swell and soften the flow of its cadences, was to me grand, and even sublime. The whole season of winter, that, with most birds, is passed in struggling to sustain life in silent melancholy, is, with the Red-Wings, one continued carnival. The profuse gleanings of the old rice, corn, and buckwheat fields, supply them with abundant food, at once ready and nutritious; and the intermediate time is spent either in aerial manœuvres, or in grand vocal performances, as if solicitous to supply the absence of all the tuneful summer tribes, and to cheer the dejected face of nature with their whole combined powers of harmony.

About the 20th of March, or earlier, if the season be open, they begin to enter Pennsylvania in numerous, though small parties. These migrating flocks are usually observed from daybreak to eight or nine in the morning, passing to the north, chattering to each other as they fly along; and, in spite of all our antipathy, their well-known notes and appearance, after the long and dreary solitude of winter, inspire cheerful and pleasing ideas of returning spring, warmth, and verdure. Selecting their old haunts, every meadow is soon enlivened by their presence. They continue in small parties to frequent the low borders of creeks, swamps, and ponds, till about the middle of April, when they separate in pairs to breed; and, about the last week in April, or first in May, begin to construct their nest. The place chosen for this is generally within the precincts of a marsh or swamp, meadow, or other like watery situation, — the spot, usually a thicket of alder bushes, at the height of six or seven feet from the ground; sometimes in a detached bush, in a meadow of high grass; often in a tussock of rushes, or coarse, rank grass; and not unfrequently on the ground; in all of which situations I have repeatedly found them. When in a bush, they are generally composed outwardly of wet rushes, picked from the swamp, and long, tough grass, in large quantity, and well lined with very fine bent. The rushes, forming the exterior, are generally extended to several of the adjoining twigs, round which they are repeatedly and securely twisted — a precaution absolutely necessary for its preservation, on account of the flexible nature of the bushes in which

it is placed.   The same caution is observed when a tussock is chosen,
by fastening the tops together, and intertwining the materials of which
the nest is formed with the stalks of rushes around.   When placed on
the ground, less care and fewer materials being necessary, the nest is
much simpler and slighter than before.   The female lays five eggs, of
a very pale light blue, marked with faint tinges of light purple, and
long, straggling lines and dashes of black.   It is not uncommon to find
several nests in the same thicket, within a few feet of each other.

During the time the female is sitting, and still more particularly
after the young are hatched, the male, like most other birds that build
in low situations, exhibits the most violent symptoms of apprehension
and alarm on the approach of any person to its near neighborhood.
Like the Lapwing of Europe, he flies to meet the intruder, hovers at a
short height overhead, uttering loud notes of distress ; and, while in
this situation, displays to great advantage the rich, glowing scarlet of
his wings, heightened by the jetty black of his general plumage.   As
the danger increases, his cries become more shrill and incessant, and
his motions rapid and restless ; the whole meadow is alarmed, and a
collected crowd of his fellows hover around, and mingle their notes of
alarm and agitation with his.   When the young are taken away, or
destroyed, he continues for several days near the place, restless and
dejected, and generally recommences building soon after, in the same
meadow.   Towards the beginning or middle of August, the young
birds begin to fly in flocks, and at that age nearly resemble the female,
with the exception of some reddish or orange, that marks the shoulders
of the males, and which increases in space and brilliancy as winter
approaches.   It has been frequently remarked, that, at this time, the
young birds chiefly associate by themselves, there being sometimes
not more than two or three old males observed in a flock of many
thousands.   These, from the superior blackness and rich red of their
plumage, are very conspicuous.

Before the beginning of September, these flocks have become numerous and formidable ; and the young ears of maize, or Indian corn,
being then in their soft, succulent, milky state, present a temptation
that cannot be resisted.   Reënforced by numerous and daily flocks
from all parts of the interior, they pour down on the low countries in
prodigious multitudes.   Here they are seen, like vast clouds, wheeling
and driving over the meadows and devoted corn-fields, darkening the
air with their numbers.   Then commences the work of destruction on
the corn, the husks of which, though composed of numerous envelop-
ments of closely-wrapped leaves, are soon completely or partially torn
off ; while from all quarters myriads continue to pour down like a
tempest, blackening half an acre at a time ; and, if not disturbed, repeat their depredations, till little remains but the cob and the shrivelled
skins of the grain ; what little is left of the tender ear, being exposed
to the rains and weather, is generally much injured.   All the attacks
and havock made at this time among them with the gun, and by the
Hawks, — several species of which are their constant attendants, —
has little effect on the remainder.   When the Hawks make a sweep
among them, they suddenly open on all sides, but rarely in time to
disappoint them of their victims ; and, though repeatedly fired at, with
mortal effect, they only remove from one field to an adjoining one, or

to another quarter of the same enclosure. From dawn to nearly sunset, this open and daring devastation is carried on, under the eye of the proprietor ; and a farmer, who has any considerable extent of corn, would require half-a-dozen men at least, with guns, to guard it ; and even then, all their vigilance and activity would not prevent a good tithe of it from becoming the prey of the Blackbirds. The Indians, who usually plant their corn in one general field, keep the whole young boys of the village all day patrolling round and among it ; and each being furnished with bow and arrows, with which they are very expert, they generally contrive to destroy great numbers of them.

It must, however, be observed, that this scene of pillage is principally carried on in the low countries, not far from the sea-coast, or near the extensive flats that border our large rivers ; and is also chiefly confined to the months of August and September. After this period, the corn having acquired its hard, shelly coat, and the seeds of the reeds or wild oats, with a profusion of other plants, that abound along the river shores, being now ripe, and in great abundance, they present a new and more extensive field for these marauding multitudes. The reeds also supply them with convenient roosting places, being often in almost unapproachable morasses ; and thither they repair every evening, from all quarters of the country. In some places, however, when the reeds become dry, advantage is taken of this circumstance, to destroy these birds, by a party secretly approaching the place, under cover of a dark night, setting fire to the reeds in several places at once, which being soon enveloped in one general flame, the uproar among the Blackbirds becomes universal ; and, by the light of the conflagration, they are shot down in vast numbers, while hovering and screaming over the place. Sometimes straw is used for the same purpose, being previously strewed near the reeds and alder bushes, where they are known to roost, which being instantly set on fire, the consternation and havock are prodigious ; and the party return by day to pick up the slaughtered game. About the first of November, they begin to move off towards the south ; though, near the sea-coast, in the states of New Jersey and Delaware, they continue long after that period.

Such are the general manners and character of the Red-winged Starling ; but there remain some facts to be mentioned, no less authentic, and well deserving the consideration of its enemies, more especially of those whose detestation of this species would stop at nothing short of total extirpation.

It has been already stated, that they arrive in Pennsylvania late in March. Their general food at this season, as well as during the early part of summer, (for the Crows and Purple Grakles are the principal pests in planting time,) consists of grub-worms, caterpillars, and various other larvæ, the silent, but deadly enemies of all vegetation, and whose secret and insidious attacks are more to be dreaded by the husbandman than the combined forces of the whole feathered tribes together. For these vermin, the Starlings search with great diligence, in the ground, at the roots of plants, in orchards, and meadows, as well as among buds, leaves, and blossoms ; and, from their known voracity, the multitudes of these insects which they destroy must be immense. Let me illustrate this by a short computation : If we suppose each bird, on an average, to devour fifty of these larvæ in a day, (a very moderate allowance,) a single pair, in four months, the usual time such food is sought after, will consume upwards of twelve thousand. It is believed that not less than a million pair of these birds are distributed over the whole extent of the United States in summer, whose food, being nearly the same, would swell the amount of vermin destroyed to twelve thousand millions. But the number of young birds may be fairly estimated at double that of their parents; and, as these are constantly fed on larvæ for at least three weeks, making only the same allowance for them as for the old ones, their share would amount to four thousand two hundred millions; making a grand total of sixteen thousand two hundred millions of noxious insects destroyed in the space of four months by this single species! The combined ravages of such a hideous host of vermin would be sufficient to spread famine and desolation over a wide extent of the richest and best-cultivated country on earth. All this, it may be said, is mere supposition. It is, however, supposition founded on known and acknowledged facts. I have never dissected any of these birds in spring without receiving the most striking and satisfactory proofs of those facts; and though, in a matter of this kind, it is impossible to ascertain precisely the amount of the benefits derived by agriculture from this, and many other species of our birds, yet, in the present case, I cannot resist the belief, that the services of this species, in spring, are far more important and beneficial than the value of all that portion of corn which a careful and active farmer permits himself to lose by it.

The great range of country frequented by this bird extends from Mexico, on the south, to Labrador. Our late enterprising travellers across the continent to the Pacific Ocean, observed it numerous in several of the valleys at a great distance up the Missouri. When taken alive, or reared from the nest, it soon becomes familiar, sings frequently, bristling out its feathers, something in the manner of the Cow Bunting. These notes, though not remarkably various, are very peculiar. The most common one resembles the syllables *conk-quer-rée*; others, the shrill sounds produced by filing a saw; some are more guttural; and others remarkably clear. The usual note of both male and female is a single *chuck*. Instances have been produced where they have been taught to articulate several words distinctly; and, contrary to what is observed of many birds, the male loses little of the brilliancy of his plumage by confinement.

A very remarkable trait of this bird is, the great difference of size between the male and female; the former being nearly two inches longer than the latter, and of proportionate magnitude. They are known by various names in the different states of the Union; such as the *Swamp Blackbird, Marsh Blackbird, Red-winged Blackbird, Corn* or *Maize Thief, Starling,* &c. Many of them have been carried from this to different parts of Europe; and Edwards relates, that one of them, which had, no doubt, escaped from a cage, was shot in the neighborhood of London; and, on being opened, its stomach was found to be filled with grub-worms, caterpillars, and beetles; which Buffon seems to wonder at, as, "in their own country," he observes, "they feed exclusively on grain and maize."

Hitherto this species has been generally classed by naturalists with the Orioles. By a careful comparison, however, of its bill with those of that tribe, the similarity is by no means sufficient to justify this arrangement; and its manners are altogether different. I can find no genus to which it makes so near an approach, both in the structure of the bill, and in food, flight, and manners, as those of the Stare ; with which, following my judicious friend Mr. Bartram, I have accordingly placed it. To the European, the perusal of the foregoing pages will be sufficient to satisfy him of their similarity of manners. For the satisfaction of those who are unacquainted with the Common Starling of Europe, I shall select a few sketches of its character, from the latest and most accurate publication I have seen from that quarter.* Speaking of the Stare, or Starling, this writer observes, — "In the winter season, these birds fly in vast flocks, and may be known at a great distance by their whirling mode of flight, which Buffon compares to a sort of vortex, in which the collective body performs a uniform circular revolution, and, at the same time, continues to make a progressive advance. The evening is the time when the Stares assemble in the greatest numbers, and betake themselves to the fens and marshes, where they roost among the reeds : they chatter much in the evening and morning, both when they assemble and disperse. So attached are they to society, that they not only join those of their own species, but also birds of a different kind ; and are frequently seen in company with Red-Wings, (a species of Thrush,) Fieldfares, and even with Crows, Jackdaws, and Pigeons. Their principal food consists of worms, snails, and caterpillars ; they likewise eat various kinds of grain, seeds, and berries." He adds, that, "in a confined state, they are very docile, and may easily be taught to repeat short phrases, or whistle tunes with great exactness."

The Red-winged Starling (Fig. 136) is nine inches long, and fourteen inches in extent ; the general color is a glossy black, with the exception of the whole lesser wing-coverts, the first or lower row of which is of a reddish cream color, the rest a rich and splendid scarlet ; legs and bill, glossy brownish black ; irides, hazel ; bill, cylindrical above, compressed at the sides, straight, running considerably up the forehead, where it is prominent, rounding and flattish towards the tip, though sharp-pointed ; tongue, nearly as long as the bill, tapering, and lacerated at the end ; tail, rounded, the two middle feathers also somewhat shorter than those immediately adjoining.

The female (Fig. 137) is seven inches and a quarter in length, and twelve inches in extent ; chin, a pale reddish cream ; from the nostril over the eye, and from the lower mandible, run two stripes of the same, speckled with black ; from the posterior angle of the eye backwards, a streak of brownish black covers the auriculars ; throat, and whole lower parts, thickly streaked with black and white, the latter inclining to cream on the breast ; whole plumage above, black, each feather bordered with pale brown, white, or bay, giving the bird a very mottled appearance ; lesser coverts, the same ; bill and legs as in the male.

The young birds at first greatly resemble the female ; but have the plumage more broadly skirted with brown. The red early shows

---

* Bewick's *British Birds*, part i. p. 119. Newcastle, 1809.

itself on the lesser wing-coverts of the males, at first pale, inclining to orange, and partially disposed. The brown continues to skirt the black plumage for a year or two, so that it is rare to find an old male altogether destitute of some remains of it; but the red is generally complete in breadth and brilliancy by the succeeding spring. The females are entirely destitute of that ornament.

The flesh of these birds is but little esteemed, being, in general, black, dry, and tough. Strings of them are, however, frequently seen exposed for sale in our markets.

BLACK-POLL WARBLER. — SYLVIA STRIATA. — Fig. 138.

Lath. ii. 460. — *Arct. Zool.* 401. — *Turton*, 600. — *Peale's Museum*, No. 7054.

SYLVICOLA STRIATA. * — Swainson.

Sylvia striata, *Bonap. Synop.* p. 81. — Sylvicola striata, *North. Zool.* ii. p. 218.

This species has considerable affinity to the Flycatchers in its habits. It is chiefly confined to the woods, and even there, to the tops of the tallest trees, where it is descried skipping from branch to branch, in pursuit of winged insects. Its note is a single screep, scarcely audible from below. It arrives in Pennsylvania about the 20th of April, and is first seen on the tops of the highest maples, darting about among the blossoms. As the woods thicken with leaves, it may be found pretty generally, being none of the least numerous of our summer birds. It is, however, most partial to woods in the immediate neighborhood of creeks, swamps, or morasses, probably from the greater number of its favorite insects frequenting such places. It is also pretty generally diffused over the United States, having myself met with it in most quarters of the Union; though its nest has hitherto defied all my researches.

This bird may be considered as occupying an intermediate station between the Flycatchers and the Warblers, having the manners of the former, and the bill, partially, of the latter. The nice gradations by which nature passes from one species to another, even in this department of the great chain of beings, will forever baffle all the artificial rules and systems of man. And this truth every fresh discovery must impress more forcibly on the mind of the observing naturalist. These birds leave us early in September.

The Black-Poll Warbler is five and a half inches long, and eight and a half in extent; crown and hind head, black; cheeks, pure white; from each lower mandible runs a streak of small black spots, those on the side, larger; the rest of the lower parts, white; primaries, black, edged with yellow; rest of the wing, black, edged with ash; the first and second row of coverts, broadly tipped with white; back,

* This is an aberrant *Sylvicola*, approaching *Setophaga* in the form and bristling of the bill, and also in the manners of the Flycatchers. — Ed.

ash, tinged with yellow ochre, and streaked laterally with black; tail, black, edged with ash, the three exterior feathers marked on the inner webs with white; bill, black above, whitish below, furnished with bristles at the base; iris, hazel; legs and feet, reddish yellow.

The female differs very little in plumage from the male.

LESSER REDPOLL. — FRINGILLA LINARIA. — Fig. 139.

Lath. ii. 305. — *Arct. Zool.* 379. — Le Sizeren, *Buff.* iv. 216. *Pl. enl.* 151, 2. — *Peale's Museum*, No. 6579.

LINARIA MINOR. — Willoughby.

Fringilla linaria, *Bonap. Synop.* p. 112.

This bird corresponds so exactly in size, figure, and color of plumage, with that of Europe of the same name, as to place their identity beyond a doubt. They inhabit, during summer, the most northern parts of Canada, and still more remote northern countries, from whence they migrate at the commencement of winter. They appear in the Genesee country with the first deep snow, and on that account are usually called by the title of Snow Birds. As the female is destitute of the crimson on the breast and forehead, and the young birds do not receive that ornament till the succeeding spring, such a small proportion of the individuals that form these flocks are marked with red, as to induce a general belief among the inhabitants of those parts that they are two different kinds associated together. Flocks of these birds have been occasionally seen in severe winters in the neighborhood of Philadelphia. They seem particularly fond of the seeds of the common alder, and hang, head downwards, while feeding, in the manner of the Yellow-Bird. They seem extremely unsuspicious at such times, and will allow a very near approach without betraying any symptoms of alarm.

The specimen represented in Fig. 139 was shot, with several others of both sexes, in Seneca county, between the Seneca and Cayuga lakes. Some individuals were occasionally heard to chant a few interrupted notes, but no satisfactory account can be given of their powers of song.

This species extends throughout the whole northern parts of Europe, is likewise found in the remote wilds of Russia, was seen by Steller in Kamtschatka, and probably inhabits corresponding climates round the whole habitable parts of the northern hemisphere. In the Highlands of Scotland they are common, building often on the tops of the heath, sometimes in a low furze bush, like the Common Linnet, and sometimes on the ground. The nest is formed of light stalks of dried grass, intermixed with tufts of wool, and warmly lined with feathers. The eggs are usually four, white, sprinkled with specks of reddish.*

---

* I have not been able to procure American specimens of this bird; but, comparing the description of Wilson and of Ord, there seems little doubt of their

[Mr. Ord has added to the description of Wilson as follows:—
"Contrary to the usual practice of Mr. Wilson, he omitted to furnish
a *particular* description of this species. But this supplementary notice would not have been considered necessary, if our author had not
fallen into a mistake respecting the markings of the female and the
young male; the former of which he describes as 'destitute of the
crimson on the forehead,' and the latter 'not receiving that ornament
till the succeeding spring.' When Mr. Wilson procured his specimens, it was in the autumn, previously to their receiving their perfect
winter dress; and he was never afterwards aware of his error, owing

identity. Wilson is certainly confounding the Mountain Linnet (*L. montium,*)
when he says, "In the Highlands of Scotland they are common, building often on
the tops of the heath, sometimes in a low furze bush, like the Common Linnet, and
sometimes on the ground." This is exactly the habit of the Mountain Linnet, and
Mr. Ord is wrong in saying the young possess the crimson head; I have many in
my possession without it, and have shot them at all seasons; they receive that
mark at the commencement of the first breeding season, when the adult birds also
receive an addition of plumage and lustre. They seem very fond of the beech, as
well as of the birch and alder, and appear to find insects in the husks of the old mast,
which they are constantly picking and looking into. I have found their nests also
pretty frequently in a young fir plantation: it was in a low situation, but they were
invariably lined with the wool of willow catkins. I shall here add Mr. Selby's correct description of the manners of this species, which is in every way confirmed by
my own observations. "It is only known in the southern parts of Britain as a winter
visitant, and is at that period gregarious, and frequently taken in company with the
other species by the bird-catchers, by whom it is called the Stone Redpoll. In the
northern counties of England, and in Scotland and its isles, it is resident through
the year. It retires, during the summer, to the underwood that covers the bases of
many of our mountains and hills, and that often fringes the banks of their precipitous streams, in which sequestered situations it breeds. The nest is built in a
bush or low tree, (such as willow, alder, or hazel,) of moss and the stalks of dry
grass, intermixed with down from the catkin of the willow, which also forms the
lining, and renders it a particularly soft and warm receptacle for the eggs and
young. From this substance being a constant material of the nest, it follows, that
the young are produced late in the season, and are seldom able to fly before the
end of June, or the beginning of July. The eggs are four or five in number; their
color, pale bluish green, spotted with orange brown, principally towards the larger
end. In winter, the Lesser Redpoll descends to the lower grounds, in considerable
flocks, frequenting woods and plantations, more especially such as abound in birch
or alder-trees, the catkins of which yield it a plentiful supply of food. When feeding, its motion affords both interest and amusement; since, in order to reach the
catkins, which generally grow near the extremities of the smaller branches, it is
obliged, like the Titmouse, to hang with its back downwards, and assume a variety
of constrained attitudes; and, when thus engaged, it is so intent upon its work, as
frequently to allow itself to be taken by a long stick smeared with bird-lime, in
which way I have occasionally captured it when in want of specimens for examination. It also eats the buds of trees, and (when in flocks) proves in this way seri-
ously injurious to young plantations. Its call note is very frequently repeated
when on wing, and by this it may be always distinguished from the other species.
The notes it produces during the pairing season, although few, and not delivered
in continuous song, are sweet and pleasing."

"This bird is widely diffused through all the northern parts of Europe; inhabits
Northern Asia as far as Siberia and Kamtschatka; and is also abundant in North
America."

The authors of the *Northern Zoology* describe another bird allied to the Linnets,
of which one individual only was obtained in the last northern expedition. It is
said to be new, and is described as *Linaria* (*Leocosticte*) *Teprocotis,* Sw. Gray-
crowned Linnet. It is an aberrant form of *Linaria,* which Mr. Swainson proposes
to designate under the above sub-generic title. — ED.

to the circumstance of these birds seldom appearing in the neighborhood of Philadelphia. Considerable flocks of them, however, have visited us this winter, (1813–14;) and we have been enabled to procure several fine specimens of both sexes, from the most perfect of which we have taken the following description. We will add, that having had the good fortune to observe a flock, consisting of nearly a hundred, within a few feet of them, as they were busily engaged in picking the seeds of the wild orache,* we can, with confidence, assert, that they *all* had the red patch on the crown; but there were very few which had the red rump and breast: the young males, it is probable, are not thus marked until the spring, and the females are destitute of that ornament altogether.

" The Lesser Redpoll is five inches and a quarter in length, and eight inches and a half in breadth; the bill is pale yellow, ridged above and below with dark horn color, the upper mandible projecting somewhat over the lower at the tip; irides, dark hazel; the nostrils are covered with recumbent, hair-like feathers, of drab color; a line of brown extends from the eyes, and encircles the base of the bill, forming, in some specimens, a patch below the chin; the crown is ornamented with a pretty large spot of deep, shining crimson; the throat, breast, and rump, stained with the same, but of a more delicate red; the belly is of a very pale ash, or dull white; the sides are streaked with dusky; the whole upper parts are brown or dusky; the plumage, edged with yellowish white and pale ash, the latter most predominant near the rump; wings and tail, dusky; the latter is forked, and consists of twelve feathers edged with white; the primaries are very slightly tipped and edged with white, the secondaries more so; the greater and lesser coverts are also tipped with white, forming the bars across the wings; thighs, cinereous; legs and feet, black; hind claw, considerably hooked, and longer than the rest. The female is less bright in her plumage above; and her under parts incline more to an ash color; the spot on her crown is of a golden crimson, or reddish saffron color. One male specimen was considerably larger than the rest; it measured five inches and three quarters in length, and nine inches and a quarter in extent; the breast and rump were tawny; its claws were uncommonly long; the hind one measured nearly three eighths of an inch; and the spot on the crown was of a darker hue than that of the rest.

" The call of this bird exactly resembles that of the *Fringilla tristis*, or Common Yellow-Bird of Pennsylvania. The Redpolls linger in the neighborhood of Philadelphia until about the middle of April; but whither they retire for the business of incubation, we cannot determine. In common with almost all our Finches, the Redpolls become very fat, and are then accounted delicious eating. During the last winter, many hundreds of them were exposed to sale in the Philadelphia market, and were readily purchased by those epicures, whose love of variety permits no delicacy to escape them."]

* *Atriplex hastata*, Linn.

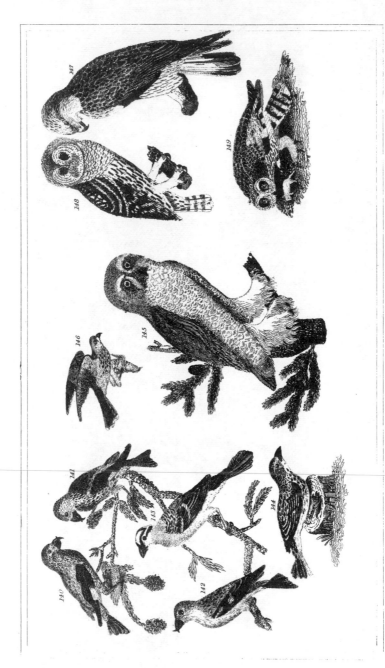

140 American Crossbill. 141 Female H 2 White winged Crossbill. 143 White crowned Bunting. 144 Bay winged B. 145 Snow Owl. 146 Male Sparrow Hawk. 147 Rough legged Falcon. 148 Barred Owl. 149 Short eared Owl.

AMERICAN CROSSBILL.—CURVIROSTRA AMERICANA.—

FIG. 140, MALE; FIG. 141, FEMALE.

Peale's Museum, No. 5640.

LOXIA CURVIROSTRA?—BONAPARTE.*

Loxia curvirostra, *Bonap. Synop.* p. 117.

ON first glancing at the bill of this extraordinary bird, one is apt to pronounce it deformed and monstrous; but on attentively observing the use to which it is applied by the owner, and the dexterity with which he detaches the seeds of the pine-tree from the cone, and from

---

* Brisson first limited the Crossbills to a genus, and proposed for them the title *Loxia*, which has been adopted by most ornithologists. *Crucirostra* and *Curvirostra* have also been formed for it from the shape of the bill; but ought to be rejected, from the priority of the former. They are a very limited group, being composed of at most four species, provided that of America be proved distinct, or one differing from those of Europe be found in the former continent. Their distribution appears to extend pretty generally over the north of Europe, decreasing in numbers to the south, and over North America. In form, all the members are similar. They are endowed with considerable power of flight; are of a thick, stout make, and in addition to the curiously-formed bill, possess scansorial habits, using their bills and feet to disengage the seeds from the fir cones, when in confinement, holding their food like a Parrot in the latter member, and by the same means climbing about the wires of the cage.

Regarding the identity of our author's species with that of this country, I am uncertain, not having a specimen of the bird from America. Wilson thinks it distinct, and I have been told the same thing by Audubon. On the other hand, we have the authority of Bonaparte, who thus writes in his *Observations on Wilson's Nomenclature:*—" I think Wilson is in error when he considered this bird a new species, and stated that it differs considerably from the European. He probably compared it with the *L. pytiopsittacus*, and not with the *curvirostra*, with which latter it is identical. Wilson's new names must therefore be rejected, and the name of *Loxia curvirostra* must be restored to this bird." Our author was also incorrect in remarking, that "the young males, as is usual with most other birds, very much resemble the female." The fact is, that the young of all the Crossbills, as well as that of *Pyrrhula enucleator*, contrary to the habit of the generality of birds, lose their red color as they advance in age, instead of gaining an additional brilliancy of plumage. The figure (140) which our author gives as that of an adult male, represents a young bird of about one year, and his supposed female (Fig. 141) is a remarkably fine adult male.

The species of this group, then, are,—*L. pytiopsittacus*, or Parrot-billed Crossbill of Europe, and which Bonaparte also hints the possibility of finding in America, a circumstance I should think very likely,—the *L. leucoptera*, and the *L. curvirostra;* but I fear we must remain uncertain whether the last constitutes one or two, until the examination of numerous specimens from both countries decide the point. The haunts of our common species in Europe are the immense northern pine forests, where their chief food is the seeds of the fir cones; from thence, after breeding, they appear to migrate to various parts southward, in comparatively small flocks, at uncertain intervals. This is the case with those which visit Britain. They must hatch very early, arriving in this country by the middle of June; the females at that time bear all the marks of incubation, but have never yet been authentically proved to breed in this country, as supposed by Mr. Knap, from the bareness of the breast. They descend, at the same season, to the orchards, where they do considerable damage, by splitting the apples for the pips, thus leaving the fruit useless, and incapable of further growth; and, at the same time, giving us a

the husks that enclose them, we are obliged to confess, on this, as on many other occasions, where we have judged too hastily of the operations of Nature, that no other conformation could have been so excellently adapted to the purpose; and that its deviation from the common form, instead of being a defect or monstrosity, as the celebrated French naturalist insinuates, is a striking proof of the wisdom and kind, superintending care of the great Creator.

This species is a regular inhabitant of almost all our pine forests situated north of 40°, from the beginning of September to the middle of April. It is not improbable that some of them remain during summer within the territory of the United States to breed. Their numbers must, however, be comparatively few, as I have never yet met with any of them in summer; though lately I took a journey to the Great Pine Swamp beyond Pocano Mountain, in Northampton county, Pennsylvania, in the month of May, expressly for that purpose; and ransacked, for six or seven days, the gloomy recesses of that extensive and desolate morass, without being able to discover a single Crossbill. In fall, however, as well as in winter and spring, this tract appears to be their favorite rendezvous; particularly about the head waters of the Lehigh, the banks of the Tobyhanna, Tunkhannock, and Bear Creek, where I have myself killed them at these seasons. They then appear in large flocks, feeding on the seeds of the hemlock and white pine, have a loud, sharp, and not unmusical note; chatter as they fly; alight, during the prevalence of deep snows, before the door of the hunter, and around the house, picking off the clay with which the logs are plastered, and searching in corners where urine, or any substance of a saline quality, had been thrown. At such times they are so tame as only to settle on the roof of the cabin when disturbed, and a moment after descend to feed as before. They are then easily caught in traps; and will frequently permit one to approach so near as to knock them down with a stick. Those killed and opened at such

good instance of the power of their bills. Some old writers accuse them of visiting Worcester and Herefordshire, "in great flocks, for the sake of the seeds of the apple. Repeated persecution on this account perhaps lessened their numbers, and their depredations at the present day are unnoticed or unknown:" their visitations, at least, are less frequent; for a later writer in Loudon's *Magazine* observes, that, in 1821, and the commencement of 1822, (the same season of their great appearance mentioned by Mr. Selby,) a large flock of Crossbills frequented some fir groves at Cothoridge, near Worcester, where they used to visit the same spot pretty regularly twice a day, delighting chiefly on the Weymouth pines. When feeding, they seem in this country, as well as with our author, to be remarkably tame, or so much engrossed with their food, as to be unmindful of danger. Montague relates, that a bird-catcher at Bath had taken a hundred pairs in the month of June and July, 1791; and so intent were these birds when picking out the seeds of a cone, that they would suffer themselves to be caught with a hair noose at the end of a long fishing-rod. In 1821, this country was visited with large flocks; they appeared in June, and gradually moved northward, as they were observed by Mr. Selby in September among the fir tracts of Scotland, after they had disappeared to the southward of the River Tweed. In 1828, a pretty large flock visited the vicinity of Ambleside, Westmoreland. Their favorite haunt was a plantation of young larches, where they might be seen disporting almost every day, particularly between the hours of eleven and one.

I have quoted no synonymes which belong to our British species. The American birds appear to me much smaller; that is, to judge from our author's plate, and the usually correct drawings of Mr. Audubon. — ED.

times are generally found to have the stomach filled with a soft, greasy kind of earth or clay. When kept in a cage, they have many of the habits of the Parrot; often climbing along the wires; and using their feet to grasp the cones in, while taking out the seeds.

This same species is found in Nova Scotia, and as far north as Hudson's Bay, arriving at Severn River about the latter end of May; and, according to accounts, proceeding farther north to breed. It is added by Pennant, that "they return at the first setting in of frost."

Hitherto this bird has, as usual, been considered a mere variety of the European species; though differing from it in several respects, and being nearly one third less, and although the singular conformation of the bill of these birds, and their peculiarity of manners, are strikingly different from those of the Grosbeaks, yet many, disregarding these plain and obvious discriminations, still continue to consider them as belonging to the genus *Loxia*; as if the particular structure of the bill should, in all cases but this, be the criterion by which to judge of a species; or perhaps, conceiving themselves the wiser of the two, they have thought proper to associate together what Nature has, in the most pointed manner, placed apart.

In separating these birds, therefore, from the Grosbeaks, and classing them as a family by themselves, substituting the specific for the generic appellation, I have only followed the steps and dictates of that great Original, whose arrangements ought never to be disregarded by any who would faithfully copy her.

The Crossbills are subject to considerable changes of color; the young males of the present species being, during the first season, olive yellow, mixed with ash; then bright greenish yellow, intermixed with spots of dusky olive, all of which yellow plumage becomes, in the second year, of a light red, having the edges of the tail inclining to yellow. When confined in a cage, they usually lose the red color at the first moulting, that tint changing to a brownish yellow, which remains permanent. The same circumstance happens to the Purple Finch and Pine Grosbeak, both of which, when in confinement, exchange their brilliant crimson for a motley garb of light brownish yellow; as I have had frequent opportunities of observing.

The male of this species, when in perfect plumage, is five inches and three quarters long, and nine inches in extent; the bill is a brown horn color, sharp, and single-edged towards the extremity, where the mandibles cross each other; the general color of the plumage is a red-lead color, brightest on the rump, generally intermixed on the other parts with touches of olive; wings and tail, brown black, the latter forked, and edged with yellow; legs and feet, brown; claws, large, much curved, and very sharp; vent, white, streaked with dark ash; base of the bill, covered with recumbent down, of a pale brown color; eye, hazel.

The female is rather less than the male; the bill of a paler horn color; rump, tail-coverts, and edges of the tail, golden yellow; wings and tail, dull brownish black; the rest of the plumage, olive yellow mixed with ash; legs and feet, as in the male. The young males, during the first season, as is usual with most other birds, very much resemble the female. In moulting, the males exchange their red for brownish yellow, which gradually brightens into red. Hence, at different seasons, they differ greatly in color.

25 *

WHITE-WINGED CROSSBILL. — CURVIROSTRA LEUCOPTERA. — Fig. 142.

Turton, Syst. i. p. 515.

LOXIA LEUCOPTERA. — Gmelin.*

Loxia leucoptera, *Bonap. Synop.* p. 117.

This is a much rarer species than the preceding; though found frequenting the same places, and at the same seasons; differing, however, from the former in the deep black wings and tail, the large bed of white on the wing, the dark crimson of the plumage; and a less and more slender conformation of body. The bird represented in Fig. 142 was shot in the neighborhood of the Great Pine Swamp, in the month of September, by my friend Mr. Ainsley, a German naturalist, collector in this country for the emperor of Austria. The individual of this species mentioned by Turton and Latham, had evidently been shot in moulting time. The present specimen was a male in full and perfect plumage.

The White-winged Crossbill is five inches and a quarter long, and eight inches and a quarter in extent; wings and tail, deep black, the former crossed with two broad bars of white; general color of the plumage, dark crimson, partially spotted with dusky; lores and frontlet, pale brown; vent, white, streaked with black; bill, a brown horn color, the mandibles crossing each other as in the preceding species, the lower sometimes bending to the right, sometimes to the left, usually to the left in the male, and to the right in the female, of the American Crossbill. The female of the present species will be introduced as soon as a good specimen can be obtained, with such additional facts relative to their manners as may then be ascertained.

---

* Bonaparte has fulfilled Wilson's promise, and figured the female of this species, with some valuable remarks regarding its first discovery and habits. From these it appears to be very like its congeners, performing its migrations at uncertain periods and in various abundance, enjoying the pine forests, though not further known by any destructive propensities among orchards. It may be looked upon yet as exclusively North American. The only record of its being found in another country is in extracts from the minute-book of the Linnæan Society for 1803. "Mr. Templeton, A. L. S., of Orangegrove, near Belfast, in a letter to Mr. Dawson Turner, F. L. S., mentions, that the White-winged Crossbill, *Loxia falcirostra* of Latham, was shot within two miles of Belfast, in the month of January, 1802. It was a female, and perfectly resembled the figure in Dixon's *Voyage to the Northwest Coast of America.*" Such is the only record we have of this bird as a British visitor. When Ireland becomes more settled, and her naturalists more devoted to actual observation, we may hear more of *L. leucoptera, Cypselus melba,* &c. Bonaparte, in his description of the female, has entered fully into the reasons for adopting the specific name of *leucoptera.* — Ed.

WHITE-CROWNED BUNTING. — EMBERIZA LEUCOPHRYS. — Fig. 143.

Turton, Syst. p. 536. — *Peale's Museum,* No. 6587.

ZONOTRICHIA LEUCOPHRYS. — Swainson.

Fringilla leucophrys, *Bonap. Synop.* p. 107. — Fringilla (Zonotrichia) leucophrys, *North. Zool.* ii. p. 255.

THIS beautifully-marked species is one of the rarest of its tribe in the United States, being chiefly confined to the northern districts, or higher interior parts of the country, except in severe winters, when some few wanderers appear in the lower parts of the state of Pennsylvania. Of three specimens of this bird, the only ones I have yet met with, the first was caught in a trap near the city of New York, and lived with me several months. It had no song, and, as I afterwards discovered, was a female. Another, a male, was presented to me by Mr. Michael of Lancaster, Pennsylvania. The third, a male, and in complete plumage, was shot in the Great Pine Swamp, in the month of May, and is faithfully represented in Fig. 143. It appeared to me to be unsuspicious, silent, and solitary; flitting in short flights among the underwood and piles of prostrate trees, torn up by a tornado, that some years ago passed through the swamp. All my endeavors to discover the female or nest were unsuccessful.

From the great scarcity of this species, our acquaintance with its manners is but very limited. Those persons who have resided near Hudson's Bay, where it is common, inform us, that it makes its nest in June, at the bottom of willows, and lays four chocolate-colored eggs. Its flight is said to be short and silent; but, when it perches, it sings very melodiously.*

The White-crowned Bunting is seven inches long, and ten inches in extent; the bill, a cinnamon brown; crown, from the front to the hind head, pure white, bounded on each side by a stripe of black proceeding from each nostril; and these again are bordered by a stripe of pure white passing over each eye to the hind head, where they meet; below this, another narrow stripe of black passes from the posterior angle of the eye, widening as it descends to the hind head; chin, white; breast, sides of the neck, and upper parts of the same, very pale ash; back, streaked laterally with dark rusty brown and pale bluish white; wings, dusky, edged broadly with brown; the greater and lesser coverts tipped broadly with white, forming two handsome bands across the wing; tertials, black, edged with brown and white; rump and tail-coverts, drab, tipped with a lighter tint; tail, long, rounded, dusky, and edged broadly with drab; belly, white; vent, pale yellow ochre; legs and feet, reddish brown; eye, reddish hazel; lower eyelid, white.

The female may easily be distinguished from the male, by the white

* *Arctic Zoology.*

on the head being less pure, the black also less in extent, and the ash on the breast darker; she is also smaller in size.

There is a considerable resemblance between this species and the White-throated Sparrow, already described in this work. Yet they rarely associate together; the latter remaining in the lower parts of Pennsylvania in great numbers, until the beginning of May, when they retire to the north and to the high inland regions to breed; the former inhabiting much more northern countries, and, though said to be common in Canada, rarely visiting this part of the United States.

BAY-WINGED BUNTING—EMBERIZA GRAMINEA.—
Fig. 144.

Grass Finch, *Arct. Zool.* No. 253.— *Lath.* iii. 273.— *Turton, Syst.* i. p. 565.

ZONOTRICHIA GRAMINEA. —SWAINSON.

Fringilla graminea, *Bonap. Synop.* p. 108.— Fringilla (Zonotrichia) graminea, *North. Zool.* ii. p. 254.

THE manners of this bird bear great affinity to those of the Common Bunting of Britain. It delights in frequenting grass and clover fields, perches on the tops of the fences, singing, from the middle of April to the beginning of July, with a clear and pleasant note, in which particular it far excels its European relation. It is partially a bird of passage here, some leaving us, and others remaining with us during the winter. In the month of March I observed them numerous in the lower parts of Georgia, where, according to Mr. Abbot, they are only winter visitants. They frequent the middle of fields more than hedges or thickets; run along the ground like a Lark, which they also resemble in the great breadth of their wings. They are timid birds, and rarely approach the farm-house.

Their nest is built on the ground, in a grass or clover field, and formed of old withered, leaves and dry grass, and lined with hair. The female lays four or five eggs, of a grayish white. On the first week in May, I found one of their nests with four young, from which circumstance I think it probable that they raise two or more broods in the same season.

This bird measures five inches and three quarters in length, and ten inches and a half in extent; the upper parts are cinereous brown, mottled with deep brown or black; lesser wing-coverts, bright bay; greater, black, edged with very pale brown; wings, dusky, edged with brown; the exterior primary, edged with white; tail, sub-cuneiform, the outer feather white on the exterior edge, and tipped with white; the next, tipped and edged for half an inch with the same; the rest, dusky, edged with pale brown; bill, dark brown above, paler below; round the eye is a narrow circle of white; upper part of the breast, yellowish white, thickly streaked with pointed spots of black that pass along the sides; belly and vent, white; legs and feet, flesh colored; third wing-feather from the body, nearly as long as the tip of the wing when shut.

I can perceive little or no difference between the colors and markings of the male and female.

SNOW OWL.— STRIX NYCTEA.— Fig. 145.— Male.

Lath. i. 132. No. 17.— *Buff.* i. 387.— Great White Owl, *Edw.* 61.— Snowy Owl, *Arct. Zool.* 233, No. 121.— *Peale's Museum,* No. 458.

SURNIA NYCTEA.— Dumeril.

Snowy Owl, *Mont. Orn. Dict. Supp.*— *Bewick's Brit. Birds, Supp.*— Snowy Owl, Strix nyctea, *Selby's Brit. Orn.* p. 58, pl. 23.— Strix nyctea, *Temm. Man.* i. p. 82.— *Flem. Br. Anim.* p. 58.— *Bonap. Synop.* p. 36.— *North. Zool.* ii. p. 88.

This great northern hunter inhabits the coldest and most dreary regions of the northern hemisphere on both continents. The forlorn mountains of Greenland, covered with eternal ice and snows, where, for nearly half the year, the silence of death and desolation might almost be expected to reign, furnish food and shelter to this hardy adventurer; whence he is only driven by the extreme severity of weather towards the sea-shore. He is found in Lapland, Norway, and the country near Hudson's Bay, during the whole year; is said to be common in Siberia, and numerous in Kamtschatka. He is often seen in Canada and the northern districts of the United States; and sometimes extends his visits to the borders of Florida. Nature, ever provident, has so effectually secured this bird from the attacks of cold, that not even a point is left exposed. The bill is almost completely hid among a mass of feathers that cover the face; the legs are clothed with such an exuberance of long, thick, hair-like plumage, as to appear nearly as large as those of a middle-sized dog, nothing being visible but the claws, which are large, black, much hooked, and extremely sharp. The whole plumage below the surface is of the most exquisitely-soft, warm, and elastic kind, and so closely matted together as to make it a difficult matter to penetrate to the skin.

The usual food of this species is said to be hares, grouse, rabbits, ducks, mice, and even carrion. Unlike most of his tribe, he hunts by day as well as by twilight, and is particularly fond of frequenting the shores and banks of shallow rivers, over the surface of which he slowly sails, or sits on a rock a little raised above the water, watching for fish. These he seizes with a sudden and instantaneous stroke of the foot, seldom missing his aim. In the more southern and thickly-settled parts, he is seldom seen; and when he appears, his size, color, and singular aspect, attract general notice.*

---

* The following observations by Mr. Bree, of Allesly, taken from *Loudon's Magazine of Natural History,* will show that other Owls also fish for their prey:—

In the month of October, I met with this bird on Oswego River, New York state, a little below the Falls, vigilantly watching for fish. At Pittsburg, in the month of February, I saw another, which had been shot in the wing some time before. At a place on the Ohio called Long Reach, I examined another, which was the first ever recollected to have been seen there. In the town of Cincinnati, state of Ohio, two of these birds alighted on the roof of the court-house, and alarmed the whole town. A people more disposed to superstition would have deduced some dire or fortunate prognostication from their selecting such a place; but the only solicitude was how to get possession of them, which, after several volleys, was at length effected. One of these, a female, I afterwards examined, when on my way through that place to New Orleans. Near Bairdstown, in Kentucky, I met with a large and very beautiful one, which appeared to be altogether unknown to the inhabitants of that quarter, and excited general surprise. A person living on the eastern shore of Maryland shot one of these birds, a few months ago, a female; and, having stuffed the skin, brought it to Philadelphia, to Mr. Peale, in expectation, no doubt, of a great reward. I have examined eleven of these birds, within these fifteen months last past, in different and very distant parts of the country, all of which were shot either during winter, late in the fall, or early in spring; so that it does not appear certain whether any remain during summer within the territory of the United States; though I think it highly probable that a few do, in some of the more northern inland parts, where they are most numerous during winter.

The color of this bird is well suited for concealment, while roaming over the general waste of snows; and its flight strong and swift, very similar to that of some of our large Hawks. Its hearing must be exquisite, if we judge from the largeness of these organs in it; and its voice is so dismal that, as Pennant observes, it adds horror even to the regions of Greenland by its hideous cries, resembling those of a man in deep distress.

The male of this species measures twenty-two inches and a half in length, and four feet six inches in breadth; head and neck, nearly white, with a few small dots of dull brown interspersed; eyes, deep sunk under projecting eyebrows, the plumage at their internal angles fluted or pressed in, to admit direct vision; below this, it bristles up, covering nearly the whole bill; the irides are of the most brilliant golden yellow, and the countenance, from the proportionate smallness of the head, projection of the eyebrow, and concavity of the plumage at the angle of the eye, very different from that of any other of the genus; general color of the body, white, marked with lunated spots of

"Probably it may not be generally known to naturalists that the Common Brown Owl (*Strix stridula*) is in the habit, occasionally, at least, of feeding its young with live fish—a fact which I have ascertained beyond doubt. Some years since, several young Owls were taken from the nest, and placed in a yew-tree, in the rectory garden here. In this situation, the parent birds repeatedly brought them live fish, bull-heads, (*Cottus gobbius*,) and loach, (*Cobitis barbatula*,) which had doubtless been procured from a neighboring brook, in which these species abound. Since the above period, I have, upon more than one occasion, found the same fish, either whole or in fragments, lying under the trees on which I have observed the young Owls to perch after they have left the nest, and where the old birds were accustomed to feed them."—ED.

pale brown above, and with semicircular dashes below; femoral feathers, long, and legs covered, even over the claws, with long, shaggy, hair-like down, of a dirty white; the claws, when exposed, appear large, much hooked, of a black color, and extremely sharp pointed; back, white; tail, rounded at the end, white, slightly dotted with pale brown near the tips; wings, when closed, reach near the extremity of the tail; vent-feathers, large, strong-shafted, and extending also to the point of the tail; upper part of the breast and belly, plain white; body, very broad and flat.

The female, which measures two feet in length, and five feet two inches in extent, is covered more thickly with spots of a much darker color than those on the male; the chin, throat, face, belly, and vent, are white; femoral feathers, white, long, and shaggy, marked with a few heart-shaped spots of brown; legs, also covered to the claws with long, white, hairy down; rest of the plumage, white, every feather spotted or barred with dark brown, largest on the wing-quills, where they are about two inches apart; fore part of the crown, thickly marked with roundish, black spots; tail, crossed with bands of broad, brownish spots; shafts of all the plumage, white; bill and claws, as in the male, black; third and fourth wing-quill, the longest; span of the foot, four inches.

From the various individuals of these birds which I have examined, I have reason to believe that the male alone approaches nearly to white in his plumage, the female rarely or never. The bird from which Fig. 145 was drawn was killed at Egg Harbor, New Jersey, in the month of December. The conformation of the eye of this bird forms a curious and interesting subject to the young anatomist. The globe of the eye is immovably fixed in its socket by a strong, elastic, hard, cartilaginous case, in form of a truncated cone; this case, being closely covered with a skin, appears, at first, to be of one continued piece; but, on removing the exterior membrane, it is found to be formed of fifteen pieces, placed like the staves of a cask, overlapping a little at the base, or narrow end, and seem as if capable of being enlarged or contracted, perhaps by the muscular membrane with which they are encased. In five other different species of Owls, which I have since examined, I found nearly the same conformation of this organ, and exactly the same number of staves. The eye being thus fixed, these birds, as they view different objects, are always obliged to turn the head; and Nature has so excellently adapted their neck to this purpose, that they can, with ease, turn it round, without moving the body, in almost a complete circle.*

* In prefixing the generic appellations to this curious family, I must at once confess my inability to do it in a manner satisfactory to myself. They have been yet comparatively unstudied; and the organs of greatest importance have been seemingly most neglected. Neither my own collection, nor those accessible in Britain, contain sufficient materials to decide upon. I will, therefore, consider any attempt now to divide them, in the words of Mr. Swainson, "as somewhat speculative, and certainly not warranted by any evidence that has yet been brought forward on the subject." The names are applied, then, on the authority of ornithologists of high standing.

This Owl, and some others, will form the genus *Noctua* of Savigny and Cuvier, and are closely allied to the *Surnia* of Dumeril. In fact, the characters of the latter appear to me to agree better than those of *Noctua;* and Lesson says, "Les

AMERICAN SPARROW HAWK.— FALCO SPARVERIUS.—
Fig. 146.— Male.

Little Hawk, *Arct. Zool.* 211, No. 110.— Emerillon de Cayenne, *Buff.* i. 291.
Pl. enl. No. 444.— *Lath.* i. 110.— *Peale's Museum*, No. 340.

FALCO SPARVERIUS.— Linnæus.

Falco sparverius, *Bonap. Synop.* p. 27.— Falco sparverius, Little Rusty-crowned
Falcon, *North. Zool.* ii. p. 31.

The female of this species has been already figured and described
at page 171 of this work. As they differ considerably in the markings of their plumage, the male is introduced here, (Fig. 146.)

The male Sparrow Hawk measures about ten inches in length, and
twenty-one in extent; the whole upper parts of the head are of a fine
slate blue, the shafts of the plumage being black, the crown excepted,
which is marked with a spot of bright rufous; the slate tapers to a
point on each side of the neck; seven black spots surround the head,
as in the female, on a reddish white ground, which also borders each
sloping side of the blue; front, lores, line over and under the eye,

cheveches ne se font pas reconnaître très nettement des chouettes." The Snowy
Owl feeds by day, as well as by night, and is much more active than the night-
feeding birds; it approaches nearer to the Hawk Owls. The head is less; the tail
and wings, elongated; and the plumage is more compact and rigid. It appears to
extend as far north in America as any inhabited country, and is found in the coldest
districts of Europe. It is also mentioned by Pennant to reach beyond the Asiatic
frontier to the hot latitude of Astracan, (*a contrast, if it should turn out the same
species,*) and was discovered to breed in Orkney and Shetland by Mr. Bullock,
who procured several specimens. Its visits to the mainland of Britain are, again,
more rare; indeed, I believe one of the only instances on record is that of a male
and female killed near Rothbury, in Northumberland, in January, 1823,— a winter
remarkable for a severe snow-storm. They were killed on an open moor, in a
wild and rocky part of the country, and were generally seen perched upon the
snow, or upon some large stone projecting from it. Both now form beautiful specimens in the collection of Mr. Selby.

They become very familiar in winter, approaching close to the dwellings of the
Indians. In Lapland, they are shot with ball when hunting after moles and lem-
mings; and in that country, like many other Owls, they are looked upon with superstition. They utter a sound at night, when perched, like the grunting of pigs,
which, by the common and uninformed people, is thought to be some apparition or
spectre. By Hearne the Snow Owl is said to be known to watch the Grouse
shooters a whole day, for the purpose of sharing in the spoil. On such occasions,
it perches on a high tree, and when a bird is shot, skims down, and carries it off
before the sportsman can get near it. We have the following remarks by Dr.
Richardson, in the *Northern Zoology :* — "Frequents most of the arctic lands that
have been visited, but retires with the Ptarmigan, on which it preys, to more sheltered districts in winter; hunts by day. When I have seen it on the barren
grounds, it was generally squatting on the earth; and if put up, it alighted again
after a short flight, but was always so wary as to be approached with difficulty.
In woody districts, it shows less caution. I have seen it pursue the American
hare on the wing, making repeated strokes at the animal with its feet. In winter,
when this Owl is fat, the Indians and white residents in the Fur Countries esteem
it to be good eating. Its flesh is delicately white." By the Cree Indians it is
called Wapow-keethoo, or Wapahoo; by the Esquimaux, Oookpēēguak; by the
Norwegians, Lemensgrūs and Gysfugl; by the Swedes, Harfang.— Ed.

chin, and throat, white; femoral and vent-feathers, yellowish white; the rest of the lower parts, of the same tint, each feather being streaked down the centre with a long black drop; those on the breast, slender, on the sides, larger; upper part of the back and scapulars, deep reddish bay, marked with ten or twelve transverse waves of black; whole wing-coverts and ends of the secondaries, bright slate, spotted with black; primaries and upper half of the secondaries, black, tipped with white, and spotted on their inner vanes with the same; lower part of the back, the rump, and tail-coverts, plain bright bay; tail rounded, the two exterior feathers white, their inner vanes beautifully spotted with black; the next, bright bay, with a broad band of black near its end, and tipped for half an inch with yellowish white; part of its lower exterior edge, white, spotted with black, and its opposite interior edge, touched with white; the whole of the others are very deep red bay, with a single, broad band of black near the end, and tipped with yellowish white; cere and legs, yellow; orbits, the same; bill, light blue; iris of the eye, dark, almost black; claws, blue black.

The character of this corresponds with that of the female, given at large in page 171. I have reason, however, to believe, that these birds vary considerably in the color and markings of their plumage during the first and second years; having met with specimens every way corresponding with the above, except in the breast, which was a plain rufous white, without spots; the markings on the tail also differing a little in different specimens. These I uniformly found, on dissection, to be males; from the stomach of one of which I took a considerable part of the carcass of a Robin, (*Turdus migratorius*,) including the unbroken feet and claws; though the Robin actually measures within half an inch as long as the Sparrow Hawk.*

---

* Bonaparte has separated the small American Falcons from the larger kinds, characterizing the group as having the wings shorter than the tail, tarsi scutellated; and Mr. Swainson says, that the group seems natural, differing somewhat in their manners from the larger Falcons, and having analogies in their habits to the Shrikes.

With both these we agree. It is long since we thought the general form and habits of our Common Kestrel — analogous to Wilson's bird in Europe — differed from those of the true Falcons, as much, certainly. as *Astur* does from *Accipiter*, and both should be only by subordinate divisions. The manner of suspending itself in the air is exactly similar to that of our Windhover; and I am not aware that this peculiar manner of hunting is made use of by any other of the *Falconidæ*, with the exception of the Kestrels, that is, those of Europe or Africa, *F. rupicola, tinunculoides*, &c. The true Falcons survey the ground by extensive sweeps, or a rapid flight, and stoop at once on their prey with the velocity and force of lightning; the others quietly watch their quarry when suspended or perched on a bare eminence or tree in the manner described, and take it by surprise. Insects, reptiles, and small animals form part of their food; and to the old falconists they were known by the name of "Ignoble." The whole of the Kestrels are very familiar, easily tamed, and when in confinement become even playful. Their great breeding place is steep rocks, clothed with ivy, and fringed with the various wild plants incident to the different climes; in the chinks and hearts of these they nestle, often in security from any clamberer that has not the assistance of a rope; though the appearance of a stranger immediately calls forth peculiarly shrill and timid notes of alarm. When the young are hatched, and partly advanced, they may be seen stretching out from their hole; and, on the appearance of their parent, mutual greetings are heard, and in a tone at once different from those before mentioned. Our native species, in addition to rocks, delights in ruined buildings as a breeding place; and it is re-

ROUGH-LEGGED FALCON. — FALCO LAGOPUS. — Fig. 147.

Arct. Zool. p. 200, No. 92. — *Lath.* i. 75. — *Peale's Museum,* No. 116.

BUTEO LAGOPUS. — Bechstein?

Rough-legged Falcon, *Mont. Ornith. Dict. Supp.* — *Bew. Br. Birds, Supp.* — Rough-legged Buzzard, *Selby's Illust. Br. Ornith.* i. p. 20, pl. 7. — Falco lagopus, *Temm. Man.* i. p. 65. — *Bonap. Synop.* p. 32. — Buteo lagopus, *Flem. Br. Anim.* p. 54. — *North. Zool.* ii. p. 52.

This handsome species, notwithstanding its formidable size and appearance, spends the chief part of the winter among our low swamps and meadows, watching for mice, frogs, lame ducks, and other inglorious game. Twenty or thirty individuals of this family have regularly taken up their winter quarters, for several years past, and probably long anterior to that date, in the meadows below this city, between the Rivers Delaware and Schuylkill, where they spend their time watching along the dry banks like cats; or sailing low and slowly over the surface of the ditches. Though rendered shy from the many attempts made to shoot them, they seldom fly far, usually from one tree to another at no great distance, making a loud squealing as they arise, something resembling the neighing of a young colt, though in a more shrill and savage tone.

The bird represented in Fig. 147 was one of this fraternity; and several others of the same association have been obtained and examined during the present winter. On comparing these with Pennant's description, referred to above, they correspond so exactly, that no doubts remain of their being the same species. Towards the beginning of

markable, that perhaps more Kestrels build and bring to maturity their young in *London,* than in any space of the same dimensions : the breeding-places there are the belfries of the different churches, where neither the bustle beneath, nor the *jingle* of the bells, seems to have any effect upon them.

We have the following characteristic observations on this species in the *Northern Zoology :* —

"In the vicinity of Carlton House, where the plains are beautifully ornamented by numerous small clumps of aspens, that give a rich, picturesque effect to the landscape, which I have never seen equalled in an English park, this small Falcon was frequently discovered, perched upon the most lofty tree in the clump, sitting with his eye apparently closed, but, nevertheless, sufficiently awake to what was going on, as it would occasionally evince, by suddenly pouncing upon any small bird that happened to come within its reach. It is the least shy of any of the American Hawks; and, when on its perch, will suffer the fowler to advance to the foot of the tree, provided he has the precaution to make a slow and devious approach. He is not, however, unnoticed; for the bird shows, by the motion of its head, that he is carefully watching his manœuvres, though, unless he walks directly towards it, it is not readily alarmed. When at rest, the wings are closely applied to the sides, with their tips lying over the tail, about one third from its end; and the tail itself, being closely shut up, looks long and narrow. If its suspicion be excited, it raises and depresses its head quickly two or three times, and spreads its tail, but does not open its wings until the instant it takes its flight. The individuals shot at Carlton House, had mice and small birds in their stomachs. They were not observed by the expedition beyond the 54th degree of latitude." — Ed.

April, these birds abandon this part of the country, and retire to the north to breed.

They are common, during winter, in the lower parts of Maryland, and numerous in the extensive meadows below Newark, New Jersey; are frequent along the Connecticut River; and, according to Pennant, inhabit England, Norway, and Lapmark. Their flight is slow and heavy. They are often seen coursing over the surface of the meadows, long after sunset, many times in pairs. They generally roost on the tall detached trees that rise from these low grounds; and take their stations at day-break, near a ditch, bank, or hay-stack, for hours together, watching, with patient vigilance, for the first unlucky frog, mouse, or lizard, to make its appearance. The instant one of these is descried, the Hawk, sliding into the air, and taking a circuitous course along the surface, sweeps over the spot, and in an instant has his prey grappled and sprawling in the air.

The Rough-legged Hawk measures twenty-two inches in length, and four feet two inches in extent; cere, sides of the mouth, and feet, rich yellow; legs, feathered to the toes, with brownish yellow plumage, streaked with brown; femorals, the same; toes, comparatively short; claws and bill, blue black; iris of the eye, bright amber; upper part of the head, pale ochre, streaked with brown; back and wings, chocolate, each feather edged with bright ferruginous; first four primaries, nearly black about the tips, edged externally with silvery in some lights; rest of the quills, dark chocolate; lower side, and interior vanes, white; tail-coverts, white; tail, rounded, white, with a broad band of dark brown near the end, and tipped with white; body below, and breast, light yellow ochre, blotched and streaked with chocolate. What constitutes a characteristic mark of this bird, is a belt or girdle, of very dark brown, passing round the belly just below the breast, and reaching under the wings to the rump; head, very broad, and bill uncommonly small, suited to the humility of its prey.

The female is much darker, both above and below, particularly in the belt, or girdle, which is nearly black; the tail-coverts are also spotted with chocolate; she is also something larger. *

* From their different form, *Buteo* has been now adopted for the Buzzards. They will also rank in two divisions; those with clothed, and those with bare tarsi. The American species belonging to the first, will be our present one, Wilson's *Falco niger*, and Audubon's *F. Harlanii*;† to the second, Wilson's *B. borealis, hyemalis,* and the common European Buzzard, which was met with in the last overland arctic expedition. The Buzzards are sluggish and inactive in their habits; their bills, feet, and claws, comparatively weak; the form heavy, and the plumage more soft and downy, as if a smooth flight was to supply in part their want of activity. Their general flight is in sweeping circles, after mounting from their resting-place. They watch their prey either from the air, or on some tree or eminence, and sometimes pounce upon it when sailing near the ground. When satiated, they again return to their perch, and if undisturbed, will remain in one situation until hunger again calls them forth. Our present species is one of the more active, and is common also to the European continent. In Britain, it is an occasional visitant. They seem to appear at uncertain intervals, in more abundance; thus, in 1823, I received two beautiful specimens from East Lothian; and, in the same year, two or three more were killed on that coast. Mr. Selby mentions, that in the year 1815, Northumberland was visited by them, and several specimens were obtained. He re-

† See description of *F. Niger.*

BARRED OWL. — STRIX NEBULOSA. — Fig. 148.

Turton, Syst. 169. — *Arct. Zool.* p. 234, No. 122. — *Lath.* 133. — Strix acclamator, The Whooting Owl, *Bartram,* 289. — *Peale's Museum,* No. 464.

STRIX NEBULOSA. — Forster.*

La chouette du Canada, (Ulula,) *Cuv. Regn. Anim.* i. p. 328. — Strix nebulosa, (sub-gen. Ulula, *Cuv.) Bonap. Synop.* p. 38. — Chouette nébuleuse, *Temm. Man.* i. p. 86. — Strix nebulosa, *North. Zool.* ii. p. 81.

This is one of our most common Owls. In winter particularly, it is numerous in the lower parts of Pennsylvania, among the woods that border the extensive meadows of Schuylkill and Delaware. It is

marks, "Two of these birds, from having attached themselves to a neighboring marsh, passed under my frequent observation. Their flight was smooth but slow, and not unlike that of the common Buzzard; and they seldom continued for any length of time on the wing. They preyed upon wild ducks and other birds, frogs and mice, which they mostly pounced upon on the ground." They appear to prefer trees for their breeding-place, whereas rocks, and the sides of deep ravines, are more frequently selected by the common Buzzard. No instance has occurred of their breeding in this country. In plumage, they vary as much as the common species, the color of the upper parts being of lighter or darker shades ; the breast sometimes largely patched with deep brown, and sometimes entirely of that color ; and the white bar at the base of the tail, though always present, is of various dimensions. Dr. Richardson says it arrives in the Fur Countries in April and May ; and having reared its young, retires southward early in October. They were so shy, that only one specimen could be got by the expedition. — Ed.

* Cuvier places this bird in his genus *Ulula.* It may be called nocturnal, though it does show a greater facility of conducting itself during the day than the really night-living species, and will approach nearer to the Tawny Owl of this country than any other ; indeed, it almost seems the American representative of that species. The Tawny Owl, though not so abundant, has the very same manners ; and when raised from its dormitory in a spruce or silver fir, or holly, or oak that still carries its leaves, it will flit before one for half a day, moving its station whenever it thinks the aggressor too near. It does not utter any cry during flight. It is common to both continents, visiting, however, only the more northern parts of the European, and does not extend so generally as many of those which inhabit both.

According to Mr. Audubon, this Owl was a most abundant visitor to his various solitary encampments, often a most amusing one ; and, by less accustomed travellers, might easily have been converted into some supposed inhabitant of another world.

"How often," says this distinguished ornithologist, "when snugly settled under the boughs of my temporary encampment, and preparing to roast a venison steak, or the body of a squirrel, on a wooden spit, have I been saluted with the exulting bursts of this nightly disturber of the peace, that, had it not been for him, would have prevailed around me, as well as in my lonely retreat ! How often have I seen this nocturnal marauder alight within a few yards of me, exposing his whole body to the glare of my fire, and eye me in such a curious manner, that, had it been reasonable to do so, I would gladly have invited him to walk in and join me in my repast, that I might have enjoyed the pleasure of forming a better acquaintance with him. The liveliness of his motions, joined to their oddness, have often made me think that his society would be at least as agreeable as that of many of the buffoons we meet with in the world. But as such opportunities of forming acquaintance have not existed, be content, kind reader, with the imperfect information which I can give you of the habits of this Sancho Pança of our woods.

very frequently observed flying during day, and certainly sees more distinctly at that time than many of its genus. In one spring, at different times, I met with more than forty of them, generally flying or

"Such persons as conclude, when looking upon Owls in the glare of day, that they are, as they then appear, extremely dull, are greatly mistaken. Were they to state, like Buffon, that Woodpeckers are miserable beings, they would be talking as incorrectly; and, to one who might have lived long in the woods, they would seem to have lived only in their libraries.

"The Barred Owl is found in all those parts of the United States which I have visited, and is a constant resident. In Louisiana, it seems to be more abundant than in any other state. It is almost impossible to travel eight or ten miles in any of the retired woods there, without seeing several of them even in broad day; and, at the approach of night, their cries are heard proceeding from every part of the forest around the plantations. Should the weather be lowering, and indicative of the approach of rain, their cries are so multiplied during the day, and especially in the evening, and they respond to each other in tones so strange, that one might imagine some extraordinary fête about to take place among them. On approaching one of them, its gesticulations are seen to be of a very extraordinary nature. The position of the bird, which is generally erect, is immediately changed. It lowers its head and inclines its body, to watch the motions of the person beneath; throws forward the lateral feathers of its head, which thus has the appearance of being surrounded by a broad ruff; looks towards him as if half blind, and moves its head to and fro in so extraordinary a manner, as almost to induce a person to fancy that part dislocated from the body. It follows all the motions of the intruder with its eyes; and should it suspect any treacherous intentions, flies off to a short distance, alighting with its back to the person, and immediately turning about with a single jump, to recommence its scrutiny. In this manner, the Barred Owl may be followed to a considerable distance, if not shot at; for to halloo after it does not seem to frighten it much. But if shot at and missed, it removes to a considerable distance, after which, its *whah-whah-whah* is uttered with considerable pomposity. This Owl will answer the imitation of its own sounds, and is frequently decoyed by this means.

"The flight of the Barred Owl is smooth, light, noiseless, and capable of being greatly protracted. I have seen them take their departure from a detached grove in a prairie, and pursue a direct course towards the skirts of the main forest, distant more than two miles, in broad daylight. I have thus followed them with the eye until they were lost in the distance, and have reason to suppose that they continued their flight until they reached the woods. Once, whilst descending the Ohio, not far from the well-known *Cave-in-rock*, about two hours before sunset, in the month of November, I saw a Barred Owl teased by several Crows, and chased from the tree in which it was. On leaving the tree, it gradually rose in the air, in the manner of a Hawk, and at length attained so great a height, that our party lost sight of it. It acted, I thought, as if it had lost itself, now and then describing small circles, and flapping its wings quickly, then flying in zigzag lines. This being so uncommon an occurrence, I noted it down at the time. I felt anxious to see the bird return towards the earth, but it did not make its appearance again. So very lightly do they fly, that I have frequently discovered one passing over me, and only a few yards distant, by first seeing its shadow on the ground, during clear moonlight nights, when not the faintest rustling of its wings could be heard.

"Their power of sight during the day seems to be rather of an equivocal character, as I once saw one alight on the back of a cow, which it left so suddenly afterwards, when the cow moved, as to prove to me that it had mistaken the object on which it had perched for something else. At other times, I have observed that the approach of the gray squirrel intimidated them, if one of these animals accidentally jumped on a branch close to them, although the Owl destroys a number of them during the twilight."

Audubon has heard it said, in addition to small animals and birds, and a peculiar sort of frog, common in the woods of Louisiana, that the Barred Owl catches fish. He never saw this performed, though it may be as natural for it as those species which have been ascertained to feed on them. It is often exposed for sale in the New Orleans market, and the Creoles make *gumbo* of it, and pronounce it palatable.

26 *

sitting exposed. I also once met with one of their nests, containing three young, in the crotch of a white oak, among thick foliage. The nest was rudely put together, composed outwardly of sticks, intermixed with some dry grass and leaves, and lined with smaller twigs. At another time, in passing through the woods, I perceived something white, on the high shaded branch of a tree, close to the trunk, that, as I thought, looked like a cat asleep. Unable to satisfy myself, I was induced to fire, when, to my surprise and regret, four young Owls, of this same species, nearly full grown, came down headlong, and, fluttering for a few moments, died at my feet. Their nest was probably not far distant. I have also seen the eggs of this species, which are nearly as large as those of a young Pullet, but much more globular, and perfectly white.

These birds sometimes seize on fowls, partridges, and young rabbits; mice and small game are, however, their most usual food. The difference in size between the male and female of this Owl is extraordinary, amounting sometimes to nearly eight inches in the length. Both scream during day, like a Hawk.

The male Barred Owl measures sixteen inches and a half in length, and thirty-eight inches in extent; upper parts a pale brown, marked with transverse spots of white; wings, barred with alternate bands of pale brown, and darker; head, smooth, very large, mottled with transverse touches of dark brown, pale brown, and white; eyes, large, deep blue, the pupil not perceivable; face, or radiated circle of the eyes, gray, surrounded by an outline of brown and white dots; bill, yellow, tinged with green; breast, barred transversely with rows of brown and white; belly, streaked longitudinally with long stripes of brown, on a yellowish ground; vent, plain yellowish white; thighs and feathered legs, the same, slightly pointed with brown; toes, nearly covered with plumage; claws, dark horn color, very sharp; tail, rounded, and

In this place may be introduced another species, mentioned by Bonaparte as inhabiting Arctic America, and met with by Dr. Richardson during the last northern expedition. It is the largest of the American Owls, exceeding even the size of the Virginian Horned Owl, and seems to have been first noticed and described by Dr. Latham, from Hudson's Bay specimens. Dr. Richardson has more lately given the following sketch of its manners : — "It is by no means a rare bird in the Fur Countries, being an inhabitant of all the woody districts lying between Lake Superior and latitudes 67° or 68°, and between Hudson's Bay and the Pacific. It is common on the borders of Great Bear Lake; and there and in the higher parallels of latitude it must pursue its prey, during the summer months, by daylight. It keeps, however, within the woods, and does not frequent the barren grounds, like the Snowy Owl, nor is it so often met with in broad daylight as the Hawk Owl, but hunts principally when the sun is low; indeed, it is only at such times, when the recesses of the woods are deeply shadowed, that the American Hare and the marine animals, on which this Owl chiefly preys, come forth to feed. On the 23d of May, I discovered a nest of this Owl, built, on the top of a lofty balsam poplar, of sticks, and lined with feathers. It contained three young, which were covered with a whitish down. We could get at the nest only by felling the tree, which was remarkably thick; and whilst this operation was going on, the two parent birds flew in circles round the objects of their care, keeping, however, so high in the air as to be out of gunshot : they did not appear to be dazzled by the light. The young ones were kept alive for two months, when they made their escape. They had the habit common also to other Owls, of throwing themselves back, and making a loud snapping noise with their bills, when any one entered the room in which they were kept." — ED.

remarkably concave below, barred with six broad bars of brown, and
as many narrow ones of white ; the back and shoulders have a cast of
chestnut; at each internal angle of the eye, is a broad spot of black;
the plumage of the radiated circle round the eye ends in long black
hairs; and the bill is encompassed by others of a longer and more
bristly kind. These probably serve to guard the eye when any danger
approaches it in sweeping hastily through the woods ; and those usually
found on flycatchers may have the same intention to fulfil; for, on the
slightest touch of the point of any of these hairs, the nictitant membrane was instantly thrown over the eye.

The female is twenty-two inches long, and four feet in extent; the
chief difference of color consists in her wings being broadly spotted
with white ; the shoulder being a plain chocolate brown; the tail extends considerably beyond the tips of the wings; the bill is much
larger, and of a more golden yellow; iris of the eye, the same as that
of the male.

The different character of the feathers of this, and, I believe, of
most Owls, is really surprising. Those that surround the bill differ
little from bristles; those that surround the region of the eyes are
exceedingly open, and unwebbed; these are bounded by another set,
generally proceeding from the external edge of the ear, of a most peculiar small, narrow, velvety kind, whose fibres are so exquisitely fine,
as to be invisible to the naked eye ; above, the plumage has one general character at the surface, calculated to repel rain and moisture;
but, towards the roots, it is of the most soft, loose, and downy substance
in nature — so much so, that it may be touched without being felt;
the webs of the wing-quills are also of a delicate softness, covered
with an almost imperceptible hair, and edged with a loose silky down,
so that the owner passes through the air without interrupting the most
profound silence. Who cannot perceive the hand of God in all these
things ?

SHORT-EARED OWL. — STRIX BRACHYOTOS. — Fig. 149.

Turton, Syst. p. 167. — *Arct. Zool.* p. 229, No. 116. — *Lath.* i. 124. — La chouette,
ou la grand chevêche, *Buff.* i. *Pl. enl.* 438. — *Peale's Museum,* No. 440.

OTUS BRACHYOTOS. — Cuvier.*

Short-eared Owl, *Bew. Br. Birds,* i. p. 48, 50. — *Selby, Illust. Br. Orn.* i. p. 54.
pl. 21. — Hibou brachyote, *Temm. Man.* i. p. 99. — La Chouette, ou le moyen
duc, à Huppes courtes, *Cuv. Regn. Anim.* i. p. 328. — Otus brachyotus, *Flem.
Br. Anim.* p. 56. — Strix brachyotos, *Bonap. Synop.* p. 37. — Strix brachyota,
North. Zool. p. 75.

THIS is another species common to both continents, being found in
Britain as far north as the Orkney Isles, where it also breeds, building

---

This Owl, as Wilson observes, is also common to both continents, but the
British history of it is comparatively unknown. The following observations may
perhaps advance some parts of it : —

its nest upon the ground, amidst the heath; arrives and disappears in the south parts of England with the Woodcock, that is, in October and April; consequently does not breed there. It is called at Hudson's Bay, the Mouse Hawk; and is described as not flying, like other Owls, in search of prey, but sitting quiet, on a stump of a tree, watching for mice. It is said to be found in plenty in the woods near Chatteau Bay, on the coast of Labrador. In the United States, it is also a bird of passage, coming to us from the north in November, and departing in April. The bird represented in fig. 149, was shot in New Jersey, a few miles below Philadelphia, in a thicket of pines. It has the stern

In England it bears the name of Woodcock Owl, from its appearance nearly about the same time with that bird, and its reappearance again in the spring. Very few, if any, remain during the whole season, and they are only met with in their migrations to and from the north, their breeding-places, similar to the appearance, for a few days, of the Ringousels and Dotterels; in spring, singly or in pairs; and in the fall, in small groups, the amount of their broods when again retiring. They do not appear to be otherwise gregarious; and it is only in this way that we can account for the flock of twenty-eight in a turnip field, quoted by our author, and the instances of five or six of these birds frequently found roosting together, as mentioned by Mr. Selby. They appear at the same seasons, (according to Temminck,) and are plentiful in Holland. It is only in the north of England, and over Scotland, that they will rank as summer visitants. Hoy, and the other Hebrides, where they were first discovered to breed, were considered the southern limit of their incubation. It extends, however, much farther; and may be, perhaps, stated as the extensive muirland ranges of Cumberland, Westmoreland, and Northumberland. Over all the Scottish muirs, it occurs in considerable abundance; there are few sportsmen who are unacquainted with it; many are killed during the Grouse season, and those individuals which Mr. Selby mentions as found on upland moors, I have no doubt bred there. On the extensive moors at the Head of Dryfe, (a small rivulet in Dumfries-shire,) I have, for many years past, met with one or two pairs of these birds, and the accidental discovery of their young first turned my attention to the range of their breeding; for, previous to this, I also held the opinion, that they had commenced their migration southward. The young was discovered by one of my dogs pointing it; and, on the following year, by searching at the proper season, two nests were found with five eggs. They were formed upon the ground among the heath; the bottom of the nest scraped until the fresh earth appeared, on which the eggs were placed, without any lining or other accessory covering. When approaching the nest or young, the old birds fly and hover round, uttering a shrill cry, and snapping with their bills. They will then alight at a short distance, survey the aggressor, and again resume their flight and cries. The young are barely able to fly by the 12th of August, and appear to leave the nest some time before they are able to rise from the ground. I have taken them, on that great day to sportsmen, squatted on the heath like young black game, at no great distance from each other, and always attended by the parent birds. Last year (1831) I found them in their old haunts, to which they appear to return very regularly; and the female, with a young bird, was procured; the young could only fly for sixty or seventy yards.*

In form, this species will bear the same analogy to those furnished with horns, which the Snowy Owl bears to the earless birds. The name of *Hawk Owl* implies more activity and boldness, and a different make; and we find the head small, the body more slender, the wings and tail powerful. They hunt regularly by day, and will sometimes soar to a great height. They feed on small birds, and destroy young game, as well as mice and moles.

It seems to have a pretty extensive geographical range. Pennant mentions it as inhabiting the Falkland Isles. It extends to Siberia; and I have received it from the neighborhood of Canton, in China. — ED.

* A specimen was shot in December, (1831,) on the same ground, and one was seen when drawing a whin covert for a fox, on 31st January, 1832. I believe some reside during the whole year. -- ED.

aspect of a keen, vigorous, and active bird; and is reputed to be an excellent mouser. It flies frequently by day, and, particularly in dark cloudy weather, takes short flights; and, when sitting and looking sharply around, erects the two slight feathers that constitute its horns, which are at such times very noticeable; but, otherwise, not perceivable. No person on slightly examining this bird after being shot, would suspect it to be furnished with horns; nor are they discovered but by careful search, or previous observation on the living bird. Bewick, in his *History of British Birds*, remarks, that this species is sometimes seen in companies, — twenty-eight of them having been once counted in a turnip field in November.

Length, fifteen inches; extent, three feet four inches; general color above, dark brown, the feathers broadly skirted with pale yellowish brown; bill, large, black; irides, rich golden yellow, placed in a bed of deep black, which radiates outwards all around, except towards the bill, where the plumage is whitish; ears, bordered with a semicircular line of black and tawny yellow dots; tail, rounded, longer than usual with Owls, crossed with five bands of dark brown, and as many of yellow ochre, some of the latter have central spots of dark brown, the whole tipped with white quills also banded with dark brown and yellow ochre; breast and belly streaked with dark brown, on a ground of yellowish; legs, thighs, and vent, plain dull yellow; tips of the three first quill-feathers, black; legs, clothed to the claws, which are black, curved to about the quarter of a circle, and exceedingly sharp.

The female I have never seen; but she is said to be somewhat larger, and much darker, and the spots on the breast larger, and more numerous.*

LITTLE OWL. — STRIX PASSERINA. — Fig. 150.

Arct. Zool. 236, No. 126. — *Turton, Syst.* 172. — *Peale's Museum*, No. 522.

STRIX ACADICA. — Gmelin.†

Chouette chevêchette, *Temm. Man.* i. p. 96. — Strix acadica, *Bonap. Synop.* p. 33. — Monog. sinot strigi mauric. osserv. sulla, 2d edit. *del Reg. Anim. Cuv.* p. 52. — Strix acadica, American Sparrow Owl, *North. Zool.* p. 97.

This is one of the least of its whole genus; but, like many other little folks, makes up, in neatness of general form and appearance, for

---

* The female is nearly of the same size with the male; the colors are all of a browned tinge, the markings more clouded and indistinct; the white of the lower parts, and under the wings, is less pure, and the belly and vent are more thickly dashed with black streaks; the ears are nearly of the same length with the other feathers, but can be easily distinguished. She is always foremost to attack any intruder on her nest or young. — Ed.

† There is so much alliance between many of the Small Owls, that it is a matter of surprise more species have not been confounded. Wilson appears to have been mistaken, or to have confounded the name at least of the Little Owl; and, on the authority of Temminck and Bonaparte, we have given it as above, that of *acadica*. It is a native of both Continents, but does not yet appear to have reached the British shores. According to Temminck, it is found in the deep, German forests,

deficiency of size, and is, perhaps, the most shapely of all our Owls. Nor are the colors and markings of its plumage inferior in simplicity and effect to most others. It also possesses an eye fully equal in spirit and brilliancy to the best of them.

This species is a general and constant inhabitant of the middle and northern states; but is found most numerous in the neighborhood of the sea-shore, and among woods and swamps of pine trees. It rarely rambles much during day; but, if disturbed, flies a short way, and again takes shelter from the light; at the approach of twilight it is all life and activity, being a noted and dexterous mouse-catcher. It is found as far north as Nova Scotia, and even Hudson's Bay; is frequent in Russia; builds its nest generally in pines, half way up the tree, and lays two eggs, which, like those of the rest of its genus, are white. The melancholy and gloomy umbrage of those solitary evergreens forms its favorite haunts, where it sits dozing and slumbering all day, lulled by the roar of the neighboring ocean.

The Little Owl is seven inches and a half long, and eighteen inches in extent; the upper parts are a plain brown olive, the scapulars and some of the greater and lesser coverts being spotted with white; the first five primaries are crossed obliquely with five bars of white; tail, rounded, rather darker than the body, crossed with two rows of white spots, and tipped with white; whole interior vanes of the wings, spotted with the same; auriculars, yellowish brown; crown, upper part of the neck, and circle surrounding the ears, beautifully marked with numerous points of white on an olive brown ground; front, pure white, ending in long blackish hairs; at the internal angle of the eyes, a broad spot of black radiating outwards; irides, pale yellow; bill, a blackish horn color; lower parts, streaked with yellow ochre and reddish bay; thighs, and feathered legs, pale buff; toes, covered to the claws, which are black, large, and sharp-pointed.

The bird, from which figure 150 was taken, was shot on the sea-shore, near Great Egg Harbor, in New Jersey, in the month of November, and, on dissection, was found to be a female. Turton describes a species called the White-fronted Owl, (*S. albifrons*,) which, in every thing except the size, agrees with this bird, and has, very probably,

---

though rarely, but is plentiful in Livonia. Bonaparte hints at the probability of the *St. passerina* being yet discovered in America, which seems very likely, considering the similarity of its European haunts. The last overland arctic expedition met with this and another allied species, *St. Tengmalmi*, which will rank as an addition to the ornithology of that continent. Dr. Richardson has the following observations regarding the latter: "When it accidentally wanders abroad in the day, it is so much dazzled by the light of the sun as to become stupid, and it may be easily caught by the hand. Its cry in the night is a single melancholy note, repeated at intervals of a minute or two, and it is one of the superstitious practices of the natives to whistle when they hear it. If the bird is silent when thus challenged, the speedy death of the inquirer is thus augured; hence its Cree appellation of *Death Bird*.

On the banks of the Sascatchewan it is so common, that its voice is heard almost every night by the traveller, wherever he selects his bivouack.

Both the latter species extend over the north of Europe, and are found occasionally in Britain. The specimens which I have seen in confinement seem to sleep or doze away the morning and forenoon, but are remarkably active when roused, and move about with great agility. Both are often exposed for sale, with other birds, in the Dutch and Belgian markets. — ED.

been taken from a young male, which is sometimes found considerably less than the female.

SEA-SIDE FINCH.—FRINGILLA MARITIMA.—Fig. 151.

AMMODRAMUS MARITIMUS.— Swainson.*

Ammodramus, *Swain. Zool. Journ.* No. 11, p. 348.—Fringilla maritima, *Bonap. Synop.* p. 110.—The Sea-side Finch, *Aud. Orn. Biog.* i. p. 470, pl. 93, male and female.

Of this bird I can find no description. It inhabits the low, rush-covered sea islands along our Atlantic coast, where I first found it; keeping almost continually within the boundaries of tide water, except when long and violent east or northeasterly storms, with high tides, compel it to seek the shore. On these occasions it courses along the margin, and among the holes and interstices of the weeds and sea-wrack, with a rapidity equalled only by the nimblest of our Sand-pipers, and very much in their manner. At these times also it roosts on the ground, and runs about after dusk.

This species derives its whole subsistence from the sea. I examined a great number of individuals by dissection, and found their stomachs universally filled with fragments of shrimps, minute shell-fish, and broken limbs of small sea-crabs. Its flesh, also, as was to be expected, tasted of fish, or what is usually termed sedgy. Amidst the recesses of these wet sea-marshes, it seeks the rankest growth of grass and sea-weed, and climbs along the stalks of the rushes with as much dexterity as it runs along the ground, which is rather a singular circumstance, most of our climbers being rather awkward at running.

The Sea-side Finch is six inches and a quarter long, and eight and a quarter in extent; chin, pure white, bordered on each side by a stripe of dark ash, proceeding from each base of the lower mandible; above that is another slight streak of white; from the nostril over the eye extends another streak, which immediately over the lores is rich

---

* The Sea-side and Short-tailed Finches constitute the genus *Ammodramus* of Swainson. The former was discovered by Wilson; the latter is the Sharp-tailed Oriole of Latham. They are both peculiar to North America, and are nearly confined to the salt marshes on the coast. They are very curious in their structure, combining, as remarked by our author, properties for either running or climbing. The tail is truly scansorial; the feet partly so; the hallux formed for running, having the claw elongated, and of a flat bend, as among the Larks.
Mr. Audubon has figured this bird with the nest. He says it is placed so near the ground, that one might suppose it sunk into it, although this is not actually the case. It is composed externally of coarse grass, and is lined with finer kinds, but exhibits little regularity. The eggs are from four to six, elongated, grayish white, freckled with brown all over. They build in elevated, shrubby places, where many nests may be found in the space of an acre. When the young are grown, they betake themselves to the ditches and sluices which intersect the salt marshes, and find abundant food. They enter the larger holes of crabs, and every crack and crevice of the drying mud. In this they much resemble the Wrens, who enjoy entering and prying into every chink or opening of their own haunts. Mr. Audubon had some dressed in a pie, but found them quite unpalatable. — Ed.

yellow, bordered above with white and ending in yellow olive ; crown, brownish olive, divided laterally by a stripe of slate blue, or fine, light ash ; breast, ash, streaked with buff ; belly, white ; vent, buff colored, and streaked with black ; upper parts of the back, wings, and tail, a yellowish brown olive, intermixed with very pale blue ; greater and lesser coverts, tipped with dull white ; edge of the bend of the wing, rich yellow ; primaries, edged with the same immediately below their coverts ; tail, cuneiform, olive brown, centered with black ; bill, dusky above, pale blue below, longer than is usual with Finches ; legs and feet, a pale bluish white ; irides, hazel. Male and female nearly alike in color.

SHARP-TAILED FINCH. — FRINGILLA CAUDACUTA. —
Fig. 152.

Sharp-tailed Oriole, *Lath. Gen. Synop.* ii. p. 448, pl. 17. — *Peale's Museum,* No. 6442.

AMMODRAMUS CAUDACUTUS. — Swainson.*

Ammodramus, *Swain. Zool. Journ.* No. ii. p. 348. — Fringilla caudacuta, *Bonap. Synop.* p. 110.

A bird of this denomination is described by Turton, Syst. p. 562, but which by no means agrees with the present. This, however, may be the fault of the describer, as it is said to be a bird of Georgia. Unwilling, therefore, to multiply names unnecessarily, I have adopted his appellation. In some future part of the work, I shall settle this matter with more precision.

This new (as I apprehend it) and beautiful species is an associate of the former ; inhabits the same places ; lives on the same food ; and resembles it so much in manners, that, but for their dissimilarity in some essential particulars, I would be disposed to consider them as the same in a different state of plumage. They are much less numerous than the preceding, and do not run with equal celerity.

The Sharp-tailed Finch is five inches and a quarter long, and seven inches and a quarter in extent ; bill, dusky ; auriculars, ash ; from the bill over the eye, and also below it, run two broad stripes of brownish orange ; chin, whitish ; breast, pale buff, marked with small, pointed spots of black ; belly, white ; vent, reddish buff ; from the base of the upper mandible a broad stripe of pale ash runs along the crown and hind head, bordered on each side by one of blackish brown ; back, a yellowish brown olive, some of the feathers curiously edged with semi-

---

* Mr. Audubon has figured a bird, very closely allied in plumage, under the title of *Ammodramus Henslowii,* and, in the letter-press, has described it as Henslow's Bunting, *Emberiza Henslowii.* It will evidently come under the first genus, and, if new and distinct, will form a third North American species. It is named after Professor Henslow, of Cambridge, and was obtained near Cincinnati. There is no account of its history and habits. — Ed.

circles of white; sides under the wings, buff, spotted with black; wing-coverts and tertials, black, broadly edged with light reddish buff; tail, cuneiform, short; all the feathers, sharp-pointed; legs, a yellow clay color; irides, hazel.

I examined many of these birds, and found but little difference in the color and markings of their plumage.

SAVANNAH FINCH. — FRINGILLA SAVANNA. — Fig. 153. — MALE.*

Peale's Museum, No. 6583.

ZONOTRICHIA ? SAVANNA. — Jardine.

Fringilla Savanna, *Bonap. Synop.* p. 108.

This delicately-marked Sparrow has been already taken notice of, in a preceding part of this work, where a figure of the female is introduced. Fig. 153 was drawn from a very beautiful male, and is a faithful representation of the original.

The length is five and a half inches; extent, eight and a half; bill, pale brown; eyebrows, Naples yellow; breast and whole lower parts, pure white, the former marked with small, pointed spots of brown; upper parts, a pale whitish drab, mottled with reddish brown; wing-coverts, edged and tipped with white; tertials, black, edged with white and bay; legs, pale clay; ear-feathers, tinged with Naples yellow. The female and young males are less, and much darker.

This is, probably, the most timid of all our Sparrows. In winter, it frequents the sea-shores; but, as spring approaches, migrates to the interior, as I have lately discovered, building its nest in the grass, nearly in the same form, though with fewer materials, as that of the Bay-winged Bunting. On the 23d of May, I found one of these at the root of a clump of rushes in a grass field, with three young, nearly ready to fly. The female counterfeited lameness, spreading her wings and tail, and using many affectionate stratagems to allure me from the place. The eggs I have never seen.

* The female is described at p. 224.

27

WINTER FALCON. — FALCO HYEMALIS. — Fig. 154.

Turton, Syst. p. 156. — *Arct. Zool.* p. 209, No. 107. — *Peale's Museum*, No. 272, and 273.

ASTUR ? HYEMALIS. — Jardine.*

The Winter Hawk, *Aud.* pl. 71 ; *Orn. Biog.* p. 164.

This elegant and spirited Hawk is represented in Fig. 154. He visits us from the north early in November, and leaves us late in March.

This is a dexterous frog-catcher ; who, that he may pursue his profession with full effect, takes up his winter residence almost entirely among our meadows and marshes. He sometimes stuffs himself so enormously with these reptiles, that the prominency of his craw makes a large bunch, and he appears to fly with difficulty. I have taken the broken fragments and whole carcasses of ten frogs, of different dimensions, from the crop of a single individual. Of his genius, and other exploits, I am unable to say much. He appears to be a fearless and active bird, silent, and not very shy. One which I kept for some time, and which was slightly wounded, disdained all attempts made to rec-

---

* This species, with the *Falco lineatus* of our author, have been the subject of dispute as to their identity. The Prince of Musignano thinks they are the same, but in different states of plumage, according to age. Audubon says they are decidedly distinct, and has given plates of each, with an account of the differences he observed in their habits. I have transcribed his observations at some length, that these distinctions may be seen and judged of individually. I am inclined to consider them distinct, and cannot reconcile the great difference of habit to birds of one species, particularly in the same country. With regard to their station, again, they present a most interesting form. They are intermediate, as it were, between *Buteo, Astur,* and *Circus.* The colors are those of *Buteo* and *Circus ;* while the form and active habits of the one is that of *Astur ;* those of the Winter Hawk more of *Circus ;* the wings are short for a true Buzzard, and possess the proportional length of the feathers of the Goshawks. The feet of both are decidedly *Astur,* running, perhaps, into the more slender form of *Circus ;* and from the preponderance of their form to the Goshawks, I have chosen that as their present appellation, but certainly with a query.

I have transcribed the habits of both species as given by Audubon, that the comparison may be the more easy, and, at the description of *F. lineatus,* have referred to this page : —

" The Winter Hawk is not a constant resident in the United States, but merely visits them, making its first appearance there at the approach of winter. The flight is smooth and light, although greatly protracted, when necessity requires it to be so. It sails, at times, at a considerable elevation ; and, notwithstanding the comparative shortness of its wings, performs this kind of motion with grace, and in circles of more than ordinary diameter. It is a remarkably silent bird, often spending the greater part of the day without uttering its notes more than once or twice, which it does just before it alights to watch. with great patience and perseverance, for the appearance of its prey. Its haunts are the extensive meadows and marshes which occur along our rivers. There it pounces, with a rapid motion, on the frogs, which it either devours on the spot, or carries to the perch, or the top of the hay-stack, on which it previously stood. It generally rests at night on the ground, among the tall sedges of the marshes. I have never seen this Hawk in pursuit of any other birds than those of its own species, each individual chasing the others

oncile him to confinement; and would not suffer a person to approach without being highly irritated, throwing himself backward, and striking with expanded talons, with great fury. Though shorter winged than some of his tribe, yet I have no doubt but, with proper care, he might be trained to strike nobler game in a bold style, and with great effect. But the education of Hawks, in this country, may well be postponed for a time, until fewer improvements remain to be made in that of the human subject.

Length of the Winter Hawk, twenty inches; extent, forty-one inches, or nearly three feet six inches; cere and legs, yellow, the latter long, and feathered for an inch below the knee; bill, bluish black, small, furnished with a tooth in the upper mandible; eye, bright amber; cartilage over the eye, very prominent, and of a dull green; head, sides of the neck, and throat, dark brown, streaked with white; lesser coverts, with a strong glow of ferruginous; secondaries, pale brown, indistinctly barred with darker; primaries, brownish orange, spotted with black, wholly black at the tips; tail, long, slightly rounded, barred alternately with dark and pale brown; inner vanes, white; exterior feathers, brownish orange; wings, when closed, reach rather beyond the middle of the tail; tail-coverts, white, marked with heart-shaped spots of brown; breast and belly, white, with numerous long drops of brown, the shafts blackish; femoral feathers, large, pale yellow ochre, marked with numerous minute streaks of pale brown; claws, black. The legs of this bird are represented by differ-

---

from the district which it had selected for itself. The cry of the Winter Hawk is clear and prolonged, and resembles the syllables *kay-o*."

" The Red-shouldered Hawk, or, as I would prefer calling it, the Red-breasted Hawk, although dispersed over the greater part of the United States, is rarely observed in the middle districts; where, on the contrary, the Winter Falcon usually makes its appearance from the north at the approach of every autumn, and is of more common occurrence. This bird is one of the most noisy of its genus, during spring especially, when it would be difficult to approach the skirts of woods bordering a large plantation, without hearing its discordant, shrill notes, *ka-hee, ka-hee*, as it is seen sailing, in rapid circles, at a very great elevation. Its ordinary flight is even and protracted. It is a more general inhabitant of the woods than most of our other species, particularly during the summer.

" The interior of woods seems, as I have said, the fittest haunts for the Red-shouldered Hawk. He sails through them, a few yards above the ground, and suddenly alights on the low branch of a tree, or the top of a dead stump, from which he silently watches, in an erect posture, for the appearance of squirrels, upon which he pounces directly, and kills them in an instant, afterwards devouring them on the ground.

" At the approach of spring, this species begins to pair; and its flight is accompanied with many circlings and zigzag motions, during which it emits its shrill cries. The top of a tall tree seems to be preferred, as I have found its nest most commonly placed there, not far from the edges of woods bordering plantations; it is seated in the forks of a large branch, towards its extremity, and is as bulky as that of the common Crow; it is formed externally of dry sticks and Spanish moss, and is lined with withered grass and fibrous roots of different sorts, arranged in a circular manner. The eggs are generally four, sometimes five, of a broad, oval form, granulated all over, pale blue, faintly blotched with brownish red at the smaller end."

From the above account, it is seen that the Red-shouldered Hawk has much more the habits of an *Astur* than the other, which seems to lean towards the *Circi*; the breeding-places of the latter are, however, not mentioned by any writer. The different states of plumage in these birds are deserving of further research. — ED.

ent authors as slender; but I saw no appearance of this in those I examined.

The female is considerably darker than the male, and about two inches longer.

———◆———

MAGPIE. — CORVUS PICA. — Fig. 155.

Arct. Zool. No. 136.—*Lath.* i. 392. — *Buff.* iii. 85. — *Peale's Museum,* No. 1333.

PICA CAUDATA. — Ray.*

This bird is much better known in Europe than in this country, where it has not been long discovered; although it is now found to inhabit a wide extent of territory, and in great numbers. The drawing was taken from a very beautiful specimen, sent from the Mandan nation, on the Missouri, to Mr. Jefferson, and by that gentleman presented to Mr. Peale of this city, in whose Museum it lived for several months, and where I had an opportunity of examining it. On carefully comparing it with the European Magpie in the same collection, no material

---

* The common Magpie of Europe is typical of that section among the *Corvidæ,* to which the name of *Pica* has been given. They retain the form of the bill as in *Corvus;* their whole members are weaker; the feathers on the rump are more lax and puffy, and the tail is always very lengthened.

The Appendix to Captain Franklin's Narrative, by Mr. Sabine, first gave rise to the suspicion, that two very nearly allied species of Magpie were found in the northern parts of America; and that gentleman has accordingly described the specimens killed at Cumberland House, during the first arctic expedition, under the name of *Corvus Hudsonicus* — of which the following are the principal distinctions — and he seems to consider that bird more particularly confined to the more northern parts of the continent, while the other was met with in the United States and the Missouri country:

"The Hudson's Bay Magpie is of less size in all its parts than the common Magpie, except in its tail, which exceeds that of its congener in length; but the most remarkable and obvious difference is, in a loose tuft of grayish and white feathers on the back. Length of the body, exclusive of the tail, seven inches, that of the tail from eleven to twelve inches, that of the common being from nine to ten."

In the Northern Zoology, *Corvus Hudsonicus* is quoted as a synonym. The authors remark, "This bird, so common in Europe, is equally plentiful in the interior prairie lands of America; but it is singular, that, though it abounds on the shores of Sweden, and other maritime parts of the Old World, it is very rare on the Atlantic, eastward of the Mississippi, or Lake Winipeg." "The manners of the American bird are precisely what we have been accustomed to observe in the English one. On comparing its eggs with those of the European bird, they were found to be longer and narrower; and though the colors are the same, the blotches are larger and more diffused."

The distinctions mentioned by Mr. Sabine seem very trivial; indeed they may be confined entirely to a less size. The grayish tuft of feathers on the rump is the same in the common Magpie of Britain. I have had an opportunity of examining only one North American specimen, which is certainly smaller, but in no other respect different. The authors of the *Northern Zoology* mention their having compared arctic specimens with one from the interior of China, and they found no difference. The geographical distribution may therefore extend to a greater range than was supposed, — Europe, China, and America. — Ed.

difference could be perceived. The figure on the plate is reduced to exactly half the size of life.

This bird unites in its character, courage and cunning, turbulency and rapacity. Not inelegantly formed, and distinguished by gay as well as splendid plumage, he has long been noted in those countries where he commonly resides, and his habits and manners are there familiarly known. He is particularly pernicious to plantations of young oaks, tearing up the acorns; and also to birds, destroying great numbers of their eggs and young, even young chickens, partridges, grouse, and pheasants. It is perhaps on this last account that the whole vengeance of the game laws has lately been let loose upon him in some parts of Britain, as appears by accounts from that quarter, where premiums, it is said, are offered for his head, as an arch poacher; and penalties inflicted on all those who permit him to breed on their premises. Under the lash of such rigorous persecution, a few years will probably exterminate the whole tribe from the island. He is also destructive to gardens and orchards; is noisy and restless, almost constantly flying from place to place; alights on the backs of the cattle, to rid them of the larvæ that fester in the skin; is content with carrion when nothing better offers; eats various kinds of vegetables, and devours greedily grain, worms, and insects of almost every description. When domesticated, he is easily taught to imitate the human voice, and to articulate words pretty distinctly; has all the pilfering habits of his tribe, filling every chink, nook, and crevice, with whatever he can carry off; is subject to the epilepsy, or some similar disorder; and is, on the whole, a crafty, restless, and noisy bird.

He generally selects a tall tree, adjoining the farm house, for his nest, which is placed among the highest branches; this is large, composed outwardly of sticks, roots, turf, and dry weeds, and well lined with wool, cow hair, and feathers; the whole is surrounded, roofed, and barricaded with thorns, leaving only a narrow entrance. The eggs are usually five, of a greenish color, marked with numerous black or dusky spots. In the northern parts of Europe, he migrates at the commencement of winter.

In this country, the Magpie was first taken notice of at the factories, or trading houses on Hudson's Bay, where the Indians used sometimes to bring it in, and gave it the name of Heart-bird, — for what reason is uncertain. It appears, however, to be rather rare in that quarter. These circumstances are taken notice of by Mr. Pennant and other British naturalists.

In 1804, an exploring party under the command of Captains Lewis and Clark, on their route to the Pacific Ocean across the continent, first met with the Magpie somewhere near the great bend of the Missouri, and found that the number of these birds increased as they advanced. Here also the Blue Jay disappeared; as if the territorial boundaries and jurisdiction of these two noisy and voracious families of the same tribe had been mutually agreed on, and distinctly settled. But the Magpie was found to be far more daring than the Jay, dashing into their very tents, and carrying off the meat from the dishes. One of the hunters who accompanied the expedition informed me, that they frequently attended him while he was engaged in skinning and cleaning the carcass of the deer, bear, or buffalo he had killed, often

27 *

seizing the meat that hung within a foot or two of his head.   On the shores of the Koos-koos-ke river, on the west side of the great range of Rocky Mountains, they were found to be equally numerous.

It is highly probable that those vast plains, or prairies, abounding with game and cattle, frequently killed for the mere hides, tallow, or even marrow-bones, may be one great inducement for the residency of these birds, so fond of flesh and carrion.   Even the rigorous severity of winter in the high regions along the head waters of Rio du Nord, the Arkansaw, and Red River, seems insufficient to force them from those favorite haunts ; though it appears to increase their natural voracity to a very uncommon degree.   Colonel Pike relates, that in the month of December, in the neighborhood of the North Mountain, N. lat. 41° W. long. 34°, Reaumur's thermometer standing at 17° below 0, these birds were seen in great numbers.   " Our horses," says he, " were obliged to scrape the snow away to obtain their miserable pittance ; and, to increase their misfortunes, the poor animals were attacked by the Magpies, who, attracted by the scent of their sore backs, alighted on them, and, in defiance of their wincing and kicking, picked many places quite raw ; the difficulty of procuring food rendering those birds so bold, as to alight on our men's arms, and eat meat out of their hands." *

The Magpie is eighteen inches in length ; the head, neck, upper part of the breast and back, are a deep velvety black ; primaries, brownish black, streaked along their inner vanes with white ; secondaries, rich purplish blue ;   greater coverts, green blue ; scapulars, lower part of the breast and belly, white ; thighs and vent, black ; tail, long ; the two exterior feathers scarcely half the length of the longest, the others increasing to the two middle ones, which taper towards their extremities.   The color of this part of the plumage is very splendid, being glossy green, dashed with blue and bright purple ; this last color bounds the green ; nostrils, covered with a thick tuft of recumbent hairs, as are also the sides of the mouth ; bill, legs, and feet, glossy black.   The female differs only in the less brilliancy of her plumage.

CROW. — CORVUS CORONE.† — Fig. 156.

Peale's Museum, No. 1246.

CORVUS CORONE? — Linnæus.

This is perhaps the most generally known, and least beloved, of all our land birds ; having neither melody of song, nor beauty of plumage, nor excellence of flesh, nor civility of manners to recommend him ; on

---

* Pike's *Journal,* p. 170.
† " The voice of this bird is so remarkably different from that of the *Corone* of Europe, that I was at first led to believe it a distinct species ; but the most scrupu-

the contrary, he is branded as a thief and a plunderer — a kind of black-coated vagabond, who hovers over the fields of the industrious, fattening on their labors, and, by his voracity, often blasting their expectations. Hated as he is by the farmer, watched and persecuted by almost every bearer of a gun, who all triumph in his destruction, had not Heaven bestowed on him intelligence and sagacity far beyond common, there is reason to believe that the whole tribe (in these parts at least) would long ago have ceased to exist.

The Crow is a constant attendant on agriculture, and a general inhabitant of the cultivated parts of North America. In the interior of the forest he is more rare, unless during the season of breeding. He is particularly attached to low flat corn countries, lying in the neighborhood of the sea, or of large rivers; and more numerous in the northern than southern states, where Vultures abound, with whom the Crows are unable to contend. A strong antipathy, it is also said, prevails between the Crow and the Raven, insomuch, that where the latter is numerous, the former rarely resides. Many of the first settlers of the Genesee country have informed me, that, for a long time, Ravens were numerous with them, but no Crows; and even now the latter are seldom observed in that country. In travelling from Nashville to Natchez, a distance of four hundred and seventy miles, I saw few or no Crows, but Ravens frequently, and Vultures in great numbers.

The usual breeding time of the Crow, in Pennsylvania, is in March, April, and May, during which season they are dispersed over the woods in pairs, and roost in the neighborhood of the tree they have selected for their nest. About the middle of March they begin to build, generally choosing a high tree; though I have also known them prefer a middle-sized cedar. One of their nests, now before me, is formed externally of sticks, wet moss, thin bark, mixed with mossy earth, and lined with large quantities of horse hair, to the amount of more than half a pound, some cow hair, and some wool, forming a very soft and elastic bed. The eggs are four, of a pale green color, marked with numerous specks and blotches of olive.

During this interesting season, the male is extremely watchful, mak-

---

lous examination and comparison of European and American specimens proved them to be the same," are the words of Bonaparte in his Nomenclature to Wilson; and *Corvus corone* is quoted as the name and synonym to this species in the *Northern Zoology*, from a male killed on the plains of the Saskatchewan.

This is one of the birds I have yet been unable to obtain for comparison with European specimens, and it may seem presumption to differ from the above authorities, without ever having seen the bird in question. I cannot, nevertheless, reconcile Wilson's account of the difference of habits and cry to those of Britain and Europe. It seems a species more intermediate between the Common Rook, *C. frugilegus*, and the *C. corone*; their gregarious habits, and feeding so much on grain, are quite at variance with the Carrion Crow; Wilson's account of the Crow roost on the Delaware is so different, that, as far as habit is concerned, it is impossible to refer them to one; and though some allowance might be made for the diversity of habit in the two countries, I do not see in what manner the cry of the bird should be so distinctly affected as to be remarked by nearly all authors who have mentioned them.

Burns's line in the Cottar's Saturday Night alludes certainly to the Common Rook; and he, I am sure, knew the difference between a Crow and a Corbie. — ED.

ing frequent excursions of half a mile or so in circuit, to reconnoitre; and the instant he observes a person approaching, he gives the alarm, when both male and female retire to a distance till the intruder has gone past. He also regularly carries food to his mate, while she is sitting; occasionally relieves her; and, when she returns, again resigns up his post. At this time, also, as well as until the young are able to fly, they preserve uncommon silence, that their retreat may not be suspected.

It is in the month of May, and until the middle of June, that the Crow is most destructive to the corn-fields, digging up the newly planted grains of maize, pulling up by the roots those that have begun to vegetate, and thus frequently obliging the farmer to replant, or lose the benefit of the soil; and this sometimes twice, and even three times, occasioning a considerable additional expense, and inequality of harvest. No mercy is now shown him. The myriads of worms, moles, mice, caterpillars, grubs, and beetles, which he has destroyed, are altogether overlooked on these occasions. Detected in robbing the hens' nests, pulling up the corn, and killing the young chickens, he is considered as an outlaw, and sentenced to destruction. But the great difficulty is, how to put this sentence in execution. In vain the gunner skulks along the hedges and fences; his faithful sentinels, planted on some commanding point, raise the alarm, and disappoint vengeance of its object. The coast again clear, he returns once more in silence, to finish the repast he had begun. Sometimes he approaches the farmhouse by stealth, in search of young Chickens, which he is in the habit of snatching off, when he can elude the vigilance of the mother hen, who often proves too formidable for him. A few days ago, a Crow was observed eagerly attempting to seize some young Chickens in an orchard, near the room where I write; but these clustering close round the Hen, she resolutely defended them, drove the Crow into an apple-tree, whither she instantly pursued him with such spirit and intrepidity, that he was glad to make a speedy retreat, and abandon his design.

The Crow himself sometimes falls a prey to the superior strength and rapacity of the great Owl, whose weapons of offence are by far the more formidable of the two.*

* " A few years ago," says an obliging correspondent, " I resided on the banks of the Hudson, about seven miles from the city of New York. Not far from the place of my residence was a pretty thick wood or swamp, in which great numbers of Crows, who used to cross the river from the opposite shore, were accustomed to roost. Returning homeward one afternoon, from a shooting excursion, I had occasion to pass through this swamp. It was near sunset, and troops of Crows were flying in all directions over my head. While engaged in observing their flight, and endeavoring to select from among them an object to shoot at, my ears were suddenly assailed by the distressful cries of a Crow, who was evidently struggling under the talons of a merciless and rapacious enemy. I hastened to the spot whence the sounds proceeded, and, to my great surprise, found a Crow lying on the ground, just expiring, and, seated upon the body of the yet warm and bleeding quarry, *a large brown Owl*, who was beginning to make a meal of the unfortunate robber of corn-fields. Perceiving my approach, he forsook his prey with evident reluctance, and flew into a tree at a little distance, where he sat watching all my movements, alternately regarding, with longing eyes, the victim he had been forced to leave, and darting at me no very friendly looks, that seemed to reproach me for having deprived him of his expected regale. I confess that the scene before me was altogether novel and surprising. I am but little conversant with natural his-

Towards the close of summer, the parent Crows, with their new families, forsaking their solitary lodgings, collect together, as if by previous agreement, when evening approaches. About an hour before sunset, they are first observed, flying, somewhat in Indian file, in one direction, at a short height above the tops of the trees, silent and steady, keeping the general curvature of the ground, continuing to pass sometimes till after sunset, so that the whole line of march would extend for many miles. This circumstance, so familiar and picturesque, has not been overlooked by the poets, in their descriptions of a rural evening. Burns, in a single line, has finely sketched it: —

> The blackening trains of Crows to their repose.

The most noted Crow roost with which I am acquainted is near Newcastle, on an island in the Delaware. It is there known by the name of the Pea Patch, and is a low, flat, alluvial spot, of a few acres, elevated but a little above high water mark, and covered with a thick growth of reeds. This appears to be the grand rendezvous, or headquarters, of the greater part of the Crows within forty or fifty miles of the spot. It is entirely destitute of trees, the Crows alighting and nestling among the reeds, which by these means are broken down and matted together. The noise created by those multitudes, both in their evening assembly and reascension in the morning, and the depredations they commit in the immediate neighborhood of this great resort, are almost incredible. Whole fields of corn are sometimes laid waste by thousands alighting on it at once, with appetites whetted by the fast of the preceding night; and the utmost vigilance is unavailing to prevent, at least, a partial destruction of this their favorite grain. Like the stragglers of an immense, undisciplined, and rapacious army, they spread themselves over the fields, to plunder and destroy wherever they alight. It is here that the character of the Crow is universally execrated; and to say to the man who has lost his crop of corn by these birds, that Crows are exceedingly useful for destroying vermin, would be as consolatory as to tell him who had just lost his house and furniture by the flames, that fires are excellent for destroying bugs.

tory; but I had always understood, that the depredations of the Owl were confined to the smaller birds, and animals of the lesser kind, such as mice, young rabbits, &c. and that he obtained his prey rather by fraud and stratagem, than by open rapacity and violence. I was the more confirmed in this belief, from the recollection of a passage in Macbeth, which now forcibly recurred to my memory. — The courtiers of King Duncan are recounting to each other the various prodigies that preceded his death, and one of them relates to his wondering auditors, that

> An Eagle, towering in his pride of place,
> Was by a *mousing Owl*, hawked at and killed.

But to resume my relation: That the Owl was the murderer of the unfortunate Crow, there could be no doubt. No other bird of prey was in sight; I had not fired my gun since I entered the wood; nor heard any one else shoot: besides, the unequivocal situation in which I found the parties, would have been sufficient before any ' twelve good men and true,' or a jury of Crows, to have convicted him of his guilt. It is proper to add, that I avenged the death of the hapless Crow, by a well-aimed shot at the felonious robber, that extended him breathless on the ground."

The strong attachment of the Crows to this spot may be illustrated by the following circumstance: Some years ago, a sudden and violent north-east storm came on during the night, and the tide, rising to an uncommon height, inundated the whole island. The darkness of the night, the suddenness and violence of the storm, and the incessant torrents of rain that fell, it is supposed, so intimidated the Crows, that they did not attempt to escape, and almost all perished. Thousands of them were next day seen floating in the river; and the wind, shifting to the northwest, drove their dead bodies to the Jersey side, where for miles they blackened the whole shore.

This disaster, however, seems long ago to have been repaired; for they now congregate on the Pea Patch in as immense multitudes as ever.*

So universal is the hatred to Crows, that few states, either here or in Europe, have neglected to offer rewards for their destruction. In the United States, they have been repeatedly ranked in our laws with the wolves, the panthers, foxes, and squirrels, and a proportionable premium offered for their heads, to be paid by any justice of the peace to whom they are delivered. On all these accounts, various modes have been invented for capturing them. They have been taken in clap nets, commonly used for taking pigeons; two or three live Crows being previously procured as decoys, or, as they are called, *Stool-Crows*. Corn has been steeped in a strong decoction of hellebore, which, when eaten by them, produces giddiness, and finally, it is said, death. Pieces of paper formed into the shape of a hollow cone, besmeared within with birdlime, and a grain or two of corn dropped on the bottom, have also been adopted. Numbers of these being placed on the ground, where corn has been planted, the Crows attempting to reach the grains, are instantly hoodwinked, fly directly upwards to a great height; but generally descend near the spot whence they rose, and are easily taken. The reeds of their roosting places are sometimes set on fire during a dark night, and the gunners having previously posted themselves around, the Crows rise in great uproar, and, amidst the general consternation, by the light of the burnings, hundreds of them are shot down.

Crows have been employed to catch Crows, by the following stratagem: A live Crow is pinned by the wings down to the ground on his back, by means of two sharp, forked sticks. Thus situated, his cries are loud and incessant, particularly if any other Crows are within view. These, sweeping down about him, are instantly grappled by the

---

* The following is extracted from a late number of a newspaper printed in that neighborhood: —
"The farmers of Red Lion Hundred held a meeting at the village of St. George's, in the state of Delaware, on Monday, the 6th inst., to receive proposals of John Deputy, on a plan for banishing or destroying the Crows. Mr. Deputy's plan being heard and considered, was approved, and a committee appointed to contract with him, and to procure the necessary funds to carry the same into effect. Mr. Deputy proposes, that for five hundred dollars he will engage to kill or banish the Crows from their roost on the Pea Patch, and give security to return the money on failure.
"The sum of five hundred dollars being thus required, the committee beg leave to address the farmers and others of Newcastle county and elsewhere on the subject."

prostrate prisoner, by the same instinctive impulse that urges a drowning person to grasp at every thing within his reach. Having disengaged the game from his clutches, the trap is again ready for another experiment; and by pinning down each captive, successively, as soon as taken, in a short time you will probably have a large flock screaming above you, in concert with the outrageous prisoners below. Many farmers, however, are content with hanging up the skins, or dead carcasses, of Crows in their corn-fields, *in terrorem;* others depend altogether on the gun, keeping one of their people supplied with ammunition, and constantly on the look out. In hard winters the Crows suffer severely; so that they have been observed to fall down in the fields, and on the roads, exhausted with cold and hunger. In one of these winters, and during a long-continued, deep snow, more than six hundred Crows were shot on the carcass of a dead horse, which was placed at a proper distance from the stable, from a hole of which the discharges were made. The premiums awarded for these, with the price paid for the quills, produced nearly as much as the original value of the horse, besides, as the man himself assured me, saving feathers sufficient for filling a bed.

The Crow is easily raised and domesticated; and it is only when thus rendered unsuspicious of, and placed on terms of familiarity with man, that the true traits of his genius and native disposition fully develope themselves. In this state he soon learns to distinguish all the members of the family; flies towards the gate, screaming, at the approach of a stranger; learns to open the door by alighting on the latch; attends regularly at the stated hours of dinner and breakfast, which he appears punctually to recollect; is extremely noisy and loquacious; imitates the sounds of various words pretty distinctly; is a great thief and hoarder of curiosities, hiding in holes, corners, and crevices, every loose article he can carry off, particularly small pieces of metal, corn, bread, and food of all kinds; is fond of the society of his master, and will know him even after a long absence, of which the following is a remarkable instance, and may be relied on as a fact: — A very worthy gentleman, now [1811] living in the Genesee country, but who, at the time alluded to, resided on the Delaware, a few miles below Easton, had raised a Crow, with whose tricks and society he used frequently to amuse himself. This Crow lived long in the family; but at length disappeared, having, as was then supposed, been shot by some vagrant gunner, or destroyed by accident. About eleven months after this, as the gentleman, one morning, in company with several others, was standing on the river shore, a number of Crows happening to pass by, one of them left the flock, and flying directly towards the company, alighted on the gentleman's shoulder, and began to gabble away with great volubility, as one long absent friend naturally enough does on meeting with another. On recovering from his surprise, the gentleman instantly recognized his old acquaintance, and endeavored, by several civil but sly manœuvres, to lay hold of him; but the Crow, not altogether relishing quite so much familiarity, having now had a taste of the sweets of liberty, cautiously eluded all his attempts; and suddenly glancing his eye on his distant companions, mounted in the air after them, soon overtook and mingled with them, and was never afterwards seen to return.

The habits of the Crow in his native state are so generally known as to require little further illustration. His watchfulness, and jealous sagacity in distinguishing a person with a gun, are notorious to every one. In spring, when he makes his appearance among the groves and low thickets, the whole feathered songsters are instantly alarmed, well knowing the depredations and murders he commits on their nests, eggs, and young. Few of them, however, have the courage to attack him, except the King Bird, who, on these occasions, teases and pursues him from place to place, diving on his back while high in air, and harassing him for a great distance. A single pair of these noble-spirited birds, whose nest was built near, have been known to protect a whole field of corn from the depredations of the Crows, not permitting one to approach it.

The Crow is eighteen inches and a half long, and three feet two inches in extent; the general color is a shining glossy blue black, with purplish reflections; the throat and lower parts are less glossy; the bill and legs, a shining black, the former two inches and a quarter long, very strong, and covered at the base with thick tufts of recumbent feathers; the wings, when shut, reach within an inch and a quarter of the tip of the tail, which is rounded; fourth primary, the longest; secondaries scolloped at the ends, and minutely pointed, by the prolongation of the shaft; iris, dark hazel.

The above description agrees so nearly with the European species, as to satisfy me that they are the same; though the voice of ours is said to be less harsh, not unlike the barking of a small spaniel: the pointedness of the ends of the tail-feathers, mentioned by European naturalists, and occasioned by the extension of the shafts, is rarely observed in the present species; though always very observable in the secondaries.

The female differs from the male in being more dull colored, and rather deficient in the glossy and purplish tints and reflections. The difference, however, is not great.

Besides grain, insects, and carrion, they feed on frogs, tadpoles, small fish, lizards, and shell fish; with the latter they frequently mount to a great height, dropping them on the rocks below, and descending after them to pick up the contents. The same habit is observable in the Gull, the Raven, and Sea-side Crow. Many other aquatic insects, as well as marine plants, furnish them with food; which accounts for their being so generally found, and so numerous, on the sea shore, and along the banks of our large rivers.

WHITE-HEADED, OR BALD EAGLE.*—FALCO LEUCOCE-PHALUS.—Fig. 157.

Linn. Syst. 124.— *Lath.* i. 29.— Le pygargue à tête blanche, *Buff.* i. 99, *Pl. enl.* 411.— *Arct. Zool.* 196, No. 89.— Bald Eagle, *Catesby*, i. 1.—*Peale's Museum*, No. 78.

HALIÆETUS LEUCOCEPHALUS.—Savigny.†

Aigle à tête blanche, *Cuv. Regn. Anim.* i. p. 315.— *Temm. Man.* i. p. 52. — Falco leucocephalus, (sub-gen. Haliæetus,) *Bonap. Synop.* p. 26. — The White-headed Eagle, *Aud. Orn. Biog.* i. p. 160, pl. 31, male. — Aquila (Haliæetus) leucocephala, *North. Zool.* ii. p. 15.

This distinguished bird, as he is the most beautiful of his tribe in this part of the world, and the adopted emblem of our country, is entitled to particular notice. He was drawn from one of the largest and most perfect specimens I have yet met with. In the back ground is seen a distant view of the celebrated Cataract of Niagara, a noted place of resort for these birds, as well on account of the fish procured

---

* The epithet *bald* applied to this species, whose head is thickly covered with feathers, is equally improper and absurd with the titles Goatsucker, Kingsfisher, &c. bestowed on others ; and seems to have been occasioned by the white appearance of the head, when contrasted with the dark color of the rest of the plumage. The appellation, however, being now almost universal, is retained in the following pages.

† This species and the Sea Eagle of Europe, have been thought to be the same by many ornithologists ; some of a latter date appear still to confound them, and to be unable to satisfy themselves regarding the distinction. The subject has even been left in doubt in a work which has been recommended as a text-book to the British student. They are decidedly distinct, the one being the representing form of the other in their respective countries. The common Sea Eagle, *Haliæetus albicilla*, is, I believe, exclusively European ; the *H. leucocephalus*, according to Temminck, is common to the northern hemispheres of both the Old and New World, though much more abundant in the latter. The adult birds may be at once distinguished, and the confusion can only have arisen from the similarity of the young : when closely compared, they will also be found to possess considerable distinctions.

In habit, too, there is a difference. I have had both species alive in my possession for several years ; that of America, more active and restless in disposition, is constantly in motion, and incessantly utters its shrill barking cry. Both species are difficult to be tamed, but the stranger will hardly allow his cage to be cleaned out. Though four years old, the head and tail have not attained their pure whiteness, being still marked with some patches of brown ; but I have found this to be invariably the case with birds in confinement, from three to five years being then required to complete their perfect change,‡ whereas three years is the generally supposed time in a wild state. Fish is preferred to any other food by both, but nothing appears to come amiss to them.

Savigny established his genus for this form, or for the large Bare-legged Fishing Eagles. They are not so powerfully formed, or so much adapted for rapid flight as the Falcons and Eagles. The tarsi are weaker — the tail more graduated — the whole form more inelegant ; and when at rest, the secondaries hang in a drooping and sluggish manner over their wings ; their habits, unless when in search of prey, or in the breeding season, much less daring and active. Such may be said to be the general characters of the group ; our present species, however, seems to have a disposition more akin to the very fiercest : we have seen him to be very

‡ Mr. Audubon mentions having known it six, and says, in a wild state they breed the second year in full plumage.

28

there, as for the numerous carcasses of squirrels, deer, bears, and various other animals, that, in their attempts to cross the river above the Falls, have been dragged into the current, and precipitated down that tremendous gulf, where, among the rocks that bound the Rapids below, they furnish a rich repast for the Vulture, the Raven, and the Bald Eagle, the subject of the present account. This bird has been long known to naturalists, being common to both continents, and occa-

savage in his cage; in his native wilds he seems little less so. Fish is the favorite food, though they do not seem able to take them by plunging, but content themselves with either seizing from the Ospreys what they have caught, or, where the water is so shallow as to allow them, clutch the fish without diving. Audubon says it only now and then procures fish for itself. He has seen them several times attempting to take red-fins by wading briskly through the water, and striking at them with their bill. When fish are not to be had, they appear hardly contented with the smaller animals or birds; pigs and sheep are a common fare, and our author has even mentioned one instance of a child being attacked. The male and female hunt in concert, and it must be when attacking some large-winged game, or water-fowl, which have had recourse to the lake or river for safety, that their energies will be best observed. Audubon thus describes a Swan hunt: —

"The next moment, however, the wild trumpet-like sound of a yet distant but approaching Swan is heard: a shriek from the female Eagle comes across the stream; for she is fully as alert as her mate. The snow-white bird is now in sight: her long neck is stretched forward; her eye is on the watch, vigilant as that of her enemy; her large wings seem with difficulty to support the weight of her body, although they flap incessantly. So irksome do her exertions seem, that her very legs are spread beneath her tail, to aid her in her flight. She approaches; the Eagle has marked her for his prey. As the Swan is passing the dreaded pair, starts from his perch, in full preparation for the chase, the male bird, with an awful scream.

"Now is the moment to witness a display of the Eagle's powers. He glides through the air like a falling star, and, like a flash of lightning, comes upon the timorous quarry, which now, in agony and despair, seeks, by various manœuvres, to elude the grasp of his cruel talons. It mounts, doubles, and willingly would plunge into the stream, were it not prevented by the Eagle, which, long possessed of the knowledge that, by such a stratagem, the Swan might escape him, forces it to remain in the air, by attempting to strike it with his talons from beneath. The hope of escape is soon given up by the Swan. It has already become much weakened, and its strength fails at the sight of the courage and swiftness of its antagonist. Its last gasp is about to escape, when the ferocious Eagle strikes with his talons the under side of its wing, and, with unresisted power, forces the bird to fall in a slanting direction upon the nearest shore."

And, again, when hunting in concert after some bird which has alighted on the water: —

"At other times, when these Eagles, sailing in search of prey, discover a Goose, a Duck, or a Swan, that has alighted on the water, they accomplish its destruction in a manner that is worthy of our attention. Well aware that water-fowl have it in their power to dive at their approach, and thereby elude their attempts upon them, they ascend in the air, in opposite directions, over the lake or river on which the object which they are desirous of possessing has been observed. Both reach a certain height, immediately after which, one of them glides with great swiftness towards the prey; the latter, meantime, aware of the Eagle's intention, dives the moment before he reaches the spot. The pursuer then rises in the air, and is met by its mate, which glides toward the water-bird, that has just emerged to breathe, and forces it to plunge again beneath the surface, to escape the talons of this second assailant. The first Eagle is now poising itself in the place where its mate formerly was, and rushes anew, to force the quarry to make another plunge. By thus alternately gliding, in rapid and often-repeated rushes, over the ill-fated bird, they soon fatigue it, when it stretches out its neck, swims deeply, and makes for the shore in the hope of concealing itself among the rank weeds. But this is of no avail; for the Eagles follow it in all its motions; and the moment it approaches the margin, one of them darts upon it."

sionally met with from a very high northern latitude, to the borders of the torrid zone, but chiefly in the vicinity of the sea, and along the shores and cliffs of our lakes and large rivers. Formed by nature for braving the severest cold; feeding equally on the produce of the sea and of the land; possessing powers of flight capable of outstripping even the tempests themselves; unawed by any thing but man; and, from the ethereal heights to which he soars, looking abroad, at one

The Bald Eagle was met with in the overland arctic expedition, but, towards the north, was only a summer visitant: in the Fur Countries, it is one of the earliest, arriving in the month of March, which has thence received the name of *Meekeeshew*, or *Eepeeshim*, or Eagle month. It appears also migratory every where to the north; it was not met with to the north of the Great Slave Lake, lat. 62° N., although it is common in the summer in the country lying between that and Lake Superior, and its breeding-places in the district are numerous. In the month of October, when the rivers are frozen over, it entirely quits Hudson's Bay lands; and it is only on the sea coasts that individuals can be then met with.

In this place we must introduce another splendid Fishing Eagle, which, if ultimately proved to be an undescribed species, will stand as the *Haliæetus Washingtonii* of Audubon. It has been first beautifully figured and described by that gentleman, and a specimen of it exists in the Academy of Philadelphia. Its immense size, and some other differences, seem to keep it distinct from any species we are acquainted with, and it is most probably before this time proved to be new. We strongly suspect, however, that the state in which it is figured is not that of the adult plumage, and that this is yet to be found: we can only wish that its discoverer may be successful in his present arduous journey. It must be of very rare occurrence, three or four being all that Mr. Audubon has ever found of it. We have transcribed the more essential parts of his description. From it there will be seen a difference in their habits from the White-headed bird, building and roosting on rocks; and in their mode of fishing, which is performed like the Osprey.

It was in February, 1814, that Mr. Audubon first saw this bird, while on a trading voyage on the Upper Mississippi. He was assured that it was rare; and, from the accounts he received, being convinced that it was unknown to naturalists, he felt anxious to learn its habits, and to discover in what particulars it differed from the rest of its genus. Mr. Audubon did not again meet with it for some years, and his next meeting was partly accidental: he was engaged in collecting Crayfish, and perceived, on the steep and rocky banks of the Ohio, the marks of the breeding-place of some bird of prey. His inquiries among the people in the neighborhood led him to suppose that it was an Eagle, different from any of those known in America. He resolved to watch the nest; and the following is the result:—

"In high expectation I seated myself about a hundred yards from the foot of the rock. Never did time pass more slowly. I could not help betraying the most impatient curiosity, for my hopes whispered it was a Sea Eagle's nest. Two long hours had elapsed before the old bird made his appearance, which was announced to us by the loud hissings of the two young ones, which crawled to the extremity of the hole to receive a fine fish. I had a perfect view of this noble bird, as he held himself to the edging rock, hanging like the Barn, Bank, or Social Swallow, his tail spread, and his wings partly so. I trembled lest a word should escape my companions. The slightest murmur had been treason from them. They entered into my feelings, and, though little interested, joined with me. In a few minutes the other parent joined her mate. She glanced her quick and piercing eye around, and instantly perceived that her abode had been discovered. She dropped her prey, with a loud shriek, communicated the alarm to the male, and, hovering with him over our heads, kept up a growling cry." It was not till two years after that Mr. Audubon had the good fortune to shoot this Eagle; and the following description was then taken:—

" Bill, bluish black, the edges pale; the soft margin towards the commissure, and the base of the under mandible, yellow; cere, yellowish brown; lore, light greenish blue; iris, chestnut brown; feet, deep yellow; claws, bluish black; upper part of the head, hind neck, back scapulars, rump, tail-coverts, and posterior tibial feathers, blackish brown, glossed with a coppery tint; throat, fore neck, breast, and belly,

glance, on an immeasurable expanse of forests, fields, lakes, and ocean, deep below him, he appears indifferent to the little localities of change of seasons; as, in a few minutes, he can pass from summer to winter, from the lower to the higher regions of the atmosphere, the abode of eternal cold, and thence descend, at will, to the torrid, or the arctic regions of the earth. He is, therefore, found, at all seasons, in the countries he inhabits; but prefers such places as have been mentioned above, from the great partiality he has for fish.

In procuring these, he displays, in a very singular manner, the genius and energy of his character, which is fierce, contemplative, daring, and tyrannical, — attributes not exerted but on particular occasions, but, when put forth, overpowering all opposition. Elevated on the high dead limb of some gigantic tree that commands a wide view of the neighboring shore and ocean, he seems calmly to contemplate the motions of the various feathered tribes that pursue their busy avocations below, — the snow-white Gulls slowly winnowing the air; the busy *Tringæ* coursing along the sands; trains of Ducks streaming over the surface; silent and watchful Cranes, intent and wading; clamorous Crows; and all the winged multitudes that subsist by the bounty of this vast liquid magazine of nature. High over all these hovers one, whose action instantly arrests his whole attention. By his wide curvature of wing, and sudden suspension in air, he knows him to be the Fish Hawk, settling over some devoted victim of the deep. His eye kindles at the sight, and, balancing himself, with half opened wings, on the branch, he watches the result. Down, rapid as an arrow from heaven, descends the distant object of his attention, the roar of its wings reaching the ear as it disappears in the deep, making the surges foam around. At this moment, the eager looks of the Eagle are all ardor; and, levelling his neck for flight, he sees the Fish Hawk once more emerge, struggling with his prey, and mounting in the air with screams of exultation. These are the signal for our hero, who, launching into the air, instantly gives chase, and soon gains on the Fish Hawk; each exerts his utmost to mount above the other, displaying in these rencontres the most elegant and sublime aërial evolutions. The unencumbered Eagle rapidly advances, and is just on the point of reaching his opponent, when, with a sudden scream, probably of despair and honest execration, the latter drops his fish; the Eagle, poising himself for a moment, as if to take a more certain aim, descends like a whirlwind, snatches it in his grasp ere it

---

light brownish yellow, each feather marked along the centre with blackish brown; wing-coverts, light grayish brown, those next the body becoming darker, and approaching the color of the back; primary quills, dark brown, deeper on their inner webs; secondaries, lighter, and on their outer webs, of nearly the same light tint as their coverts; tail, uniform dark brown; anterior tibial feathers, grayish brown.

" Length, three feet seven inches; extent of wings, ten feet two inches; bill, three and a quarter inches along the back; along the gap, which commences directly under the eye, to the tip of the lower mandible, three and one-third, and one and three-quarters deep; length of wing when folded, thirty-two inches; length of tail, fifteen inches; tarsus, four and a half; middle, four and three quarters; hind claw, two and a half.

" The two stomachs, large and baggy; their contents in the individual described were fish, fishes' scales, and entrails of various kinds; intestines, large, but thin and transparent." — ED.

reaches the water, and bears his ill-gotten booty silently away to the woods.

These predatory attacks, and defensive manœuvres of the Eagle and the Fish Hawk, are matters of daily observation along the whole of our seaboard, from Georgia to New England, and frequently excite great interest in the spectators. Sympathy, however, on this, as on most other occasions, generally sides with the honest and laborious sufferer, in opposition to the attacks of power, injustice, and rapacity — qualities for which our hero is so generally notorious, and which, in his superior, *man*, are certainly detestable. As for the feelings of the poor fish, they seem altogether out of the question.

When driven, as he sometimes is, by the combined courage and perseverance of the Fish Hawks, from their neighborhood, and forced to hunt for himself, he retires more inland, in search of young pigs, of which he destroys great numbers. In the lower parts of Virginia and North Carolina, where the inhabitants raise vast herds of those animals, complaints of this kind are very general against him. He also destroys young lambs in the early part of spring; and will sometimes attack old sickly sheep, aiming furiously at their eyes.

In corroboration of the remarks I have myself made on the manners of the Bald Eagle, many accounts have reached me from various persons of respectability, living on or near our sea coast; the substance of all these I shall endeavor to incorporate with the present account.

Mr. John L. Gardiner, who resides on an island of three thousand acres, about three miles from the eastern point of Long Island, from which it is separated by Gardiner's Bay, and who has, consequently, many opportunities of observing the habits of these birds, has favored me with a number of interesting particulars on this subject; for which I beg leave thus publicly to return my grateful acknowledgment.

"The Bald Eagles," says this gentleman, "remain on this island during the whole winter. They can be most easily discovered on evenings, by their loud snoring while asleep on high oak trees; and, when awake, their hearing seems to be nearly as good as their sight. I think I mentioned to you, that I had myself seen one flying with a lamb ten days old, and which it dropped on the ground from about ten or twelve feet high. The struggling of the lamb, more than its weight, prevented its carrying it away. My running, hallooing, and being very near, might prevent its completing its design. It had broke the back in the act of seizing it; and I was under the necessity of killing it outright to prevent its misery. The lamb's dam seemed astonished to see its innocent offspring borne off into the air by a bird.

"I was lately told," continues Mr. Gardiner, "by a man of truth, that he saw an Eagle rob a Hawk of its fish, and the Hawk seemed so enraged as to fly down at the Eagle, while the Eagle very deliberately, in the air, threw himself partly over on his back, and, while he grasped with one foot the fish, extended the other to threaten or seize the Hawk. I have known several Hawks unite to attack the Eagle; but never knew a single one to do it. The Eagle seems to regard the Hawks as the Hawks do the King Birds — only as teasing, troublesome fellows."

From the same intelligent and obliging friend, I lately received a

28 *

well preserved skin of the Bald Eagle, which, from its appearance, and the note that accompanied it, seems to have belonged to a very formidable individual. "It was shot," says Mr. Gardiner, "last winter, on this island, and weighed thirteen pounds; measured three feet in length, and seven from tip to tip of the expanded wings; was extremely fierce looking; though wounded, would turn his back to no one; fastened his claws into the head of a dog, and was with difficulty disengaged. I have ridden on horseback within five or six rods of one, who, by his bold demeanor, raising his feathers, &c. seemed willing to dispute the ground with its owner. The crop of the present was full of mutton, from my part blood Merinos; and his intestines contained feathers, which he probably devoured with a Duck, or Winter Gull, as I observed an entire foot and leg of some water fowl. I had two killed previous to this, which weighed ten pounds avoirdupois each."

The intrepidity of character, mentioned above, may be further illustrated by the following fact, which occurred a few years ago, near Great Egg Harbor, New Jersey: — A woman, who happened to be weeding in the garden, had set her child down near, to amuse itself while she was at work; when a sudden and extraordinary rushing sound, and a scream from her child, alarmed her, and, starting up, she beheld the infant thrown down, and dragged some few feet, and a large Bald Eagle bearing off a fragment of its frock, which being the only part seized, and giving way, providentially saved the life of the infant.

The appetite of the Bald Eagle, though habituated to long fasting, is of the most voracious, and often the most indelicate kind. Fish, when he can obtain them, are preferred to all other fare. Young lambs and pigs are dainty morsels, and made free with on all favorable occasions. Ducks, Geese, Gulls, and other sea fowl, are also seized with avidity. The most putrid carrion, when nothing better can be had, is acceptable; and the collected groups of gormandizing Vultures, on the approach of this dignified personage, instantly disperse, and make way for their master, waiting his departure in sullen silence, and at a respectful distance, on the adjacent trees.

In one of those partial migrations of tree squirrels that sometimes take place in our western forests, many thousands of them were drowned in attempting to cross the Ohio; and at a certain place, not far from Wheeling, a prodigious number of their dead bodies were floated to the shore by an eddy. Here the Vultures assembled in great force, and had regaled themselves for some time, when a Bald Eagle made his appearance, and took sole possession of the premises, keeping the whole Vultures at their proper distance for several days. He has also been seen navigating the same river on a floating carrion, though scarcely raised above the surface of the water, and tugging at the carcass, regardless of snags, sawyers, planters, or shallows. He sometimes carries his tyranny to great extremes against the Vultures. In hard times, when food happens to be scarce, should he accidentally meet with one of these who has its craw crammed with carrion, he attacks it fiercely in the air; the cowardly Vulture instantly disgorges, and the delicious contents are snatched up by the Eagle before they reach the ground.

The nest of this species is generally fixed on a very large and lofty tree, often in a swamp or morass, and difficult to be ascended. On some noted tree of this description, often a pine or cypress, the Bald Eagle builds, year after year, for a long series of years. When both male and female have been shot from the nest, another pair has soon after taken possession. The nest is large, being added to and repaired every season, until it becomes a black, prominent mass, observable at a considerable distance. It is formed of large sticks, sods, earthy rubbish, hay, moss, &c. Many have stated to me that the female lays first a single egg, and that, after having sat on it for some time, she lays another; when the first is hatched, the warmth of that, it is pretended, hatches the other. Whether this be correct or not, I cannot determine; but a very respectable gentleman of Virginia assured me, that he saw a large tree cut down, containing the nest of a Bald Eagle, in which were two young, one of which appeared nearly three times as large as the other. As a proof of their attachment to their young, a person near Norfolk informed me, that, in clearing a piece of wood on his place, they met with a large dead pine tree, on which was a Bald Eagle's nest and young. The tree being on fire more than half way up, and the flames rapidly ascending, the parent Eagle darted around and among the flames, until her plumage was so much injured that it was with difficulty she could make her escape, and even then, she several times attempted to return to relieve her offspring.

No bird provides more abundantly for its young than the Bald Eagle. Fish are daily carried thither in numbers, so that they sometimes lie scattered round the tree, and the putrid smell of the nest may be distinguished at the distance of several hundred yards. The young are at first covered with a thick whitish or cream colored cottony down; they gradually become of a gray color as their plumage develops itself; continue of the brown gray until the third year, when the white begins to make its appearance on the head, neck, tail-coverts, and tail; these, by the end of the fourth year, are completely white, or very slightly tinged with cream; the eye also is at first hazel, but gradually brightens into a brilliant straw color, with the white plumage of the head. Such at least was the gradual progress of this change, witnessed by myself, on a very fine specimen brought up by a gentleman, a friend of mine, who, for a considerable time, believed it to be what is usually called the Gray Eagle, and was much surprised at the gradual metamorphosis. This will account for the circumstance, so frequently observed, of the Gray and White-headed Eagle, being seen together, both being, in fact, the same species, in different stages of color, according to their difference of age.

The flight of the Bald Eagle, when taken into consideration with the ardor and energy of his character, is noble and interesting. Sometimes the human eye can just discern him, like a minute speck, moving in slow curvatures along the face of the heavens, as if reconnoitring the earth at that immense distance. Sometimes he glides along in a direct horizontal line, at a vast height, with expanded and unmoving wings, till he gradually disappears in the distant blue ether. Seen gliding in easy circles over the high shores and mountainous cliffs that tower above the Hudson and Susquehanna, he attracts the

eye of the intelligent voyager, and adds great interest to the scenery.
At the great Cataract of Niagara, already mentioned, there rises from
the gulf into which the Fall of the Horse-Shoe descends, a stupendous
column of smoke, or spray, reaching to the heavens, and moving off in
large, black clouds, according to the direction of the wind, forming a
very striking and majestic appearance. The Eagles are here seen
sailing about, sometimes losing themselves in this thick column, and
again reappearing in another place, with such ease and elegance of
motion, as renders the whole truly sublime.

> High o'er the watery uproar, silent seen,
> Sailing sedate in majesty serene,
> Now midst the pillared spray sublimely lost,
> And now, emerging, down the Rapids tossed,
> Glides the Bald Eagle, gazing, calm and slow,
> O'er all the horrors of the scene below;
> Intent alone to sate himself with blood,
> From the torn victims of the raging flood.

The White-headed Eagle is three feet long, and seven feet in
extent; the bill is of a rich yellow; cere, the same, slightly tinged
with green; mouth, flesh-colored; tip of the tongue, bluish black;
the head, chief part of the neck, vent, tail-coverts, and tail, are white
in the perfect, or old birds of both sexes, — in those under three years
of age these parts are of a gray brown; the rest of the plumage is
deep dark brown, each feather tipped with pale brown, lightest on the
shoulder of the wing, and darkest towards its extremities. The conformation of the wing is admirably adapted for the support of so large
a bird; it measures two feet in breadth on the greater quills, and sixteen inches on the lesser; the longest primaries are twenty inches in
length, and upwards of one inch in circumference where they enter
the skin; the broadest secondaries are three inches in breadth across
the vane; the scapulars are very large and broad, spreading from the
back to the wing, to prevent the air from passing through; another
range of broad flat feathers, from three to ten inches in length, also
extends from the lower part of the breast to the wing below, for the
same purpose; between these lies a deep triangular cavity; the thighs
are remarkably thick, strong, and muscular, covered with long feathers
pointing backwards, usually called the femoral feathers; the legs,
which are covered half way below the knee, before, with dark brown
downy feathers, are of a rich yellow, the color of ripe Indian corn;
feet, the same; claws, blue black, very large and strong, particularly
the inner one, which is considerably the largest; soles, very rough
and warty; the eye is sunk under a bony, or cartilaginous projection,
of a pale yellow color, and is turned considerably forwards, not
standing parallel with the cheeks; the iris is of a bright straw color,
pupil black.

The male is generally two or three inches shorter than the female;
the white on the head, neck, and tail being more tinged with yellowish, and its whole appearance less formidable; the brown plumage
is also lighter, and the bird itself less daring than the female, — a
circumstance common to almost all birds of prey.

The bird from which this description, and Fig. 157, were taken, was shot near Great Egg Harbor, in the month of January. It was in excellent order, and weighed about eleven pounds. Dr. Samuel B. Smith, of this city, obliged me with a minute and careful dissection of it; from whose copious and very interesting notes on the subject, I shall extract such remarks as are suited to the general reader.

" The Eagle you sent me for dissection was a beautiful female. It had two expansions of. the gullet. The first principally composed of longitudinal bundles of fibre, in which (as the bird is ravenous and without teeth) large portions of unmasticated meats are suffered to dissolve before they pass to the lower or proper stomach, which is membranous. I did not receive the bird time enough to ascertain whether any chilification was effected by the juices from the vessels of this enlargement of the œsophagus. I think it probable, that it also has a regurgitating, or vomiting power, as the bird constantly swallows large quantities of indigestible substances, such as quills, hairs, &c. In this sac of the Eagle, I found the quill-feathers of the small White Gull; and in the true stomach, the tail and some of the breast-feathers of the same bird, and the dorsal vertebræ of a large fish. This excited some surprise, until you made me acquainted with the fact of its watching the Fish Hawks, and robbing them of their prey. Thus we see, throughout the whole empire of animal life, power is almost always in a state of hostility to justice; and of the Deity only can it truly be said, that *justice* is commensurate with *power!*

" The Eagle has the several auxiliaries to digestion and assimilation in common with man. The liver was unusually large in your specimen. It secretes bile, which stimulates the intestines, prepares the chyle for blood, and by this very secretion of bile, (as it is a deeply respiring animal,) separates or removes some obnoxious principles from the blood. (See Dr. Rush's admirable lecture on this important viscus in the human subject.) The intestines were also large, long, convolute, and supplied with numerous lacteal vessels, which differ little from those of men, except in color, which was transparent. The kidneys were large, and seated on each side the vertebræ, near the anus. They are also destined to secrete some offensive principles from the blood.

" The eggs were small and numerous; and, after a careful examination, I concluded that no sensible increase takes place in them till the *particular* season. This may account for the unusual excitement which prevails in these birds in the sexual intercourse. Why there are so many eggs, is a mystery. It is, perhaps, consistent with natural law, that every thing should be abundant.; but, from this bird, it is said, no more than two young are hatched in a season, consequently, no more eggs are wanted than a sufficiency to produce that effect. Are the eggs numbered originally, and is there no increase of number, but a gradual loss, till all are deposited? If so, the number may correspond to the long life and vigorous health of this noble bird. Why there are but two young in a season, is easily explained. Nature has been studiously parsimonious of her physical strength, from whence the tribes of animals incapable to resist, derive security and confidence."

The Eagle is said to live to a great age, — sixty, eighty, and, as some assert, one hundred years. This circumstance is remarkable, when we consider the seeming intemperate habits of the bird. Sometimes fasting, through necessity, for several days, and at other times gorging itself with animal food till its craw swells out the plumage of that part, forming a large protuberance on the breast. This, however, is its natural food, and for these habits its whole organization is particularly adapted. It has not, like men, invented rich wines, ardent spirits, and a thousand artificial poisons, in the form of soups, sauces, and sweetmeats. Its food is simple, it indulges freely, uses great exercise, breathes the purest air, is healthy, vigorous, and long lived. The lords of the creation themselves might derive some useful hints from these facts, were they not already, in general, too wise, or too proud, to learn from their *inferiors*, the fowls of the air and beasts of the field.

FISH HAWK, OR OSPREY. — FALCO HALIÆTUS. — Fig. 158.

Carolina Osprey, *Lath. Syn.* i. p. 46. — 26. A. — Falco piscator, *Briss.* i. p. 361. 14. 362. 15. — Faucon Pêcheur de la Caroline, *Buff.* i. p. 142. — Fishing Hawk, *Catesby, Car.* i. p. 2. — *Turt. Syst.* i. 149. — *Peale's Museum*, No. 144.

PANDION HALIÆETUS. — Savigny.*

Le Balbuzard, *Cuv. Regn. Anim.* i. p. 316. — Aigle Balbuzard, *Temm. Man.* i. p. 47. — Balbusardus haliætus, *Flem. Br. Anim.* p. 51. — Osprey, Falco haliætus, *Selby, Illust. Br. Ornith.* i. p. 12, pl. 4. — Falco haliætus, (sub-gen. *Pandion*,) *Bonap. Synop.* p. 26. — The Fish Hawk, or Osprey, *Aud.* pl. 81, male; *Orn. Biog.* i. 415. — Aquila (*Pandion*) haliæta, *North. Zool.* ii. p. 20.

This formidable, vigorous-winged, and well-known bird, subsists altogether on the finny tribes that swarm in our bays, creeks, and rivers; procuring his prey by his own active skill and industry; and

---

* This is the type of another aquatic group, and a real fisher. It does not, like the White-Headed Eagle, though fond of fish, subsist only upon the plunder of others, but labors for itself in the most dexterous manner; and for this, the beautiful adaptation of its form renders every assistance. The body is very strongly built, but is rather of a narrow and elongated shape; the head is less than the ordinary proportional dimensions; and the wings are expansive, powerful, and sharp-pointed. The manner of seizing their prey is by soaring above the surface of the sea, or lake, and, when in sight of a fish, closing the wings, and darting, as it were, by the weight of the body, which, in the descent, may be perceived to be directed by the motion of the tail. For this purpose, those parts which we have mentioned are finely framed, and for the remainder of the operation, the legs and feet are no less beautifully modelled. The thighs, instead of being clothed with finely lengthened plumes, as in most of the other Falcons, and which, when wet, would prove a great encumbrance, are covered with a thick downy plumage; the tarsi are short and very strong; the toes have the same advantages; and underneath, at the junction of each joint, have a large protuberance, covered, as are the other parts of the sole, with a thick and strong array of hard jagged scales, which are sufficient, by the roughness, to prevent any escape of their slippery prey when it is once fairly clutched; the claws are also very strong, and hooked, and are round as a cylinder, both above and beneath, which will ensure an easy piercing, or quick retraction from any body at which they may be struck. The outer toe is also capable of being turned either way, — a most essential assistance in grasping. In striking their prey they do not appear to dive deep; indeed, their feet, by which alone it is taken, could

seeming no farther dependent on the land than as a mere resting-place, or, in the usual season, a spot of deposit for its nest, eggs, and young. The figure (158) is reduced to one third the size of life.

The Fish Hawk is migratory, arriving on the coasts of New York and New Jersey about the twenty-first of March, and retiring to the south about the twenty-second of September. Heavy equinoctial storms may vary these periods of arrival and departure a few days; but long observation has ascertained that they are kept with remarkable regularity. On the arrival of these birds in the northern parts of the United States, in March, they sometimes find the bays and ponds frozen, and experience a difficulty in procuring fish for many days. Yet there is no instance on record of their attacking birds, or inferior land animals, with intent to feed on them; though their great strength of flight, as well as of feet and claws, would seem to render this no difficult matter. But they no sooner arrive, than they wage war on the Bald Eagles, as against a horde of robbers and banditti; sometimes succeeding, by force of numbers and perseverance, in driving them from their haunts, but seldom or never attacking them in single combat.

The first appearance of the Fish Hawk in spring, is welcomed by the fishermen, as the happy signal of the approach of those vast shoals of herring, shad, &c., that regularly arrive on our coasts, and enter

not then be brought into action, but they are often concealed in the spray occasioned by their rapid descent.

The size of a fish they are able to bear away is very great, and sometimes exceeds their own weight. That of the female is little more than five pounds, and Mr. Audubon has figured his specimen with a *weak fish* more than that weight; while our author mentions a shad that, when partly eaten, weighed more than six pounds. These authenticated accounts lead us almost to credit the more marvellous stories of that amusing sporting writer, Mr. Loyd.

That gentleman relates, that in Sweden the Eagle sometimes strikes so large a pike, that not being able to disengage his talons, he is carried under water and drowned. Dr. Mullenborg vouched for this, by the fact of having himself seen an enormous pike, with an Eagle fastened to his back, lying dead on a piece of ground which had been overflowed, but from whence the water had retreated.

He mentions also an account of a struggle between an Eagle and a pike, witnessed by a gentleman, on the Gotha river, at no great distance from Wenersborg. In this instance, when the Eagle first seized the pike, he was enabled to lift him a short distance into the air, but the weight of the fish, together with its struggles, soon carried them back again to the water, under which for a while they both disappeared. Presently, however, the Eagle again came to the surface, uttering the most piercing cries, and making apparently every endeavor to extricate his talons, but all in vain; and, after struggling, he was carried under water.

Savigny formed his well-marked genus *Pandion* from this species, which we now adopt. The Osprey is common to both continents, and I possess one from New Holland in no way different. It is met with in England occasionally, but, according to Montague, is particularly plentiful in Devonshire. In Scotland, a pair or two may be found about most of the Highland lochs, where they fish, and, during the breeding season, build on the ruined towers so common on the edges or insulated rocks of these wild waters. The nest is an immense fabric of rotten sticks —

Itself a burden for the tallest tree,

and is generally placed, if such exists, on the top of a chimney, and if this be wanting, on the highest summit of the building. An aged tree may sometimes be chosen, but ruins are always preferred, if near. They have the same propensity of returning to an old station with those of America; and if one is shot, a mate is soon found, and brought to the ancient abode. Loch Lomond, Loch Awe, and Killchurn Castle, and Loch Menteith, have been long breeding places. — ED.

our rivers in such prodigious multitudes. Two of a trade, it is said, seldom agree; the adage, however, will not hold good in the present case, for such is the respect paid the Fish Hawk, not only by this class of men, but, generally, by the whole neighborhood where it resides, that a person who should attempt to shoot one of them, would stand a fair chance of being insulted. This prepossession in favor of the Fish Hawk is honorable to their feelings. They associate, with its first appearance, ideas of plenty, and all the gaiety of business; they see it active and industrious like themselves; inoffensive to the productions of their farms; building with confidence, and without the least disposition to concealment, in the middle of their fields, and along their fences; and returning, year after year, regularly to its former abode.

The nest of the Fish Hawk is usually built on the top of a dead or decaying tree, sometimes not more than fifteen, often upwards of fifty feet, from the ground. It has been remarked by the people of the seacoasts, that the most thriving tree will die in a few years after being taken possession of by the Fish Hawk. This is attributed to the fish oil, and to the excrements of the bird; but is more probably occasioned by the large heap of wet salt materials of which the nest is usually composed. In my late excursions to the sea shore, I ascended to several of these nests that had been built in from year to year, and found them constructed as follows: Externally, large sticks, from half an inch to an inch and a half in diameter, and two or three feet in length, piled to the height of four or five feet, and from two to three feet in breadth; these were intermixed with corn-stalks, sea-weed, pieces of wet turf, in large quantities, mullein-stalks, and lined with dry sea-grass; the whole forming a mass very observable at half a mile's distance, and large enough to fill a cart, and be no inconsiderable load for a horse. These materials are so well put together, as often to adhere, in large fragments, after being blown down by the wind. My learned and obliging correspondent of New York, Dr. Samuel L. Mitchill, observes, that "A sort of superstition is entertained in regard to the Fish Hawk. It has been considered a fortunate incident to have a nest, and a pair of these birds, on one's farm. They have, therefore, been generally respected; and neither the axe nor the gun has been lifted against them. Their nest continues from year to year. The same couple, or another, as the case may be, occupies it, season after season. Repairs are duly made, or, when demolished by storms, it is industriously rebuilt. There was one of these nests, formerly, upon the leafless summit of a venerable chestnut-tree on our farm, directly in front of the house, at the distance of less than half a mile. The withered trunk and boughs, surmounted by the coarse wrought and capacious nest, was a more picturesque object than an obelisk: and the flights of the Hawks, as they went forth to hunt — returned with their game — exercised themselves in wheeling round and round, and circling about it — were amusing to the beholder, almost from morning to night. The family of these Hawks, old and young, was killed by the Hessian *Jagers.* A succeeding pair took possession of the nest; but, in the course of time, the prongs of the trunk so rotted away, that the nest could no longer be supported. The Hawks have been obliged to seek new quarters. We have lost this part of our prospect; and our trees have not afforded a convenient site for one of their habitations since."

About the first of May, the female Fish Hawk begins to lay her eggs, which are commonly three in number, sometimes only two, and rarely four. They are somewhat larger than those of the common Hen, and nearly of the same shape. The ground color varies, in different eggs, from a reddish cream, to nearly a white, splashed and daubed all over with dark Spanish brown, as if done by art.* During the time the female is sitting, the male frequently supplies her with fish; though she occasionally takes a short circuit to sea herself, but quickly returns again. The attention of the male, on such occasions, is regulated by the circumstances of the case. A pair of these birds, on the south side of Great Egg Harbor River, and near its mouth, was noted for several years. The female, having but one leg, was regularly furnished, while sitting, with fish in such abundance, that she seldom left the nest, and never to seek for food. This kindness was continued both before and after incubation. Some animals, who claim the name and rationality of man, might blush at the recital of this fact.

On the appearance of the young, which is usually about the last of June, the zeal and watchfulness of the parents are extreme. They stand guard, and go off to fish, alternately; one parent being always within a short distance of the nest. On the near approach of any person, the Hawk utters a plaintive whistling note, which becomes shriller as she takes to wing, and sails around, sometimes making a rapid descent, as if aiming directly for you; but checking her course, and sweeping past, at a short distance over head, her wings making a loud whizzing in the air. My worthy friend Mr. Gardiner informs me, that they have even been known to fix their claws in a negro's head, who was attempting to climb to their nest; and I had lately a proof of their daring spirit in this way, through the kindness of a friend, resident, for a few weeks, at Great Egg Harbor. I had requested of him the favor to transmit me, if possible, a live Fish Hawk, for the purpose of making a drawing of it, which commission he very faithfully executed; and I think I cannot better illustrate this part of the bird's character, than by quoting his letter at large: —

"*Beasley's, Great Egg Harbor, 30th June,* 1811.

"Sir, — Mr. Beasley and I went to reconnoitre a Fish Hawk's nest on Thursday afternoon. When I was at the nest, I was struck with so great violence on the crown of the hat, that I thought a hole was made in it. I had ascended fearlessly, and never dreamt of being

* Of the palatableness of these eggs I cannot speak from personal experience; but the following incident will show that the experiment has actually been made : — A country fellow, near Cape May, on his way to a neighboring tavern, passing a tree, on which was a Fish Hawk's nest, immediately mounted, and robbed it of the only egg it contained, which he carried with him to the tavern, and desired the landlord to make it into egg-nogg. The tavern keeper, after a few wry faces, complied with his request, and the fellow swallowed the cordial. Whether from its effects on the olfactory nerves, (for he said it smelt abominably,) on the imagination, or on the stomach alone, is uncertain, but it operated as a most outrageous emetic, and cured the man, for that time at least, of his thirst for egg-nogg. What is rather extraordinary, the landlord (Mr. Beasley) assured me, that, to all appearance, the egg was perfectly fresh.

29

attacked. I came down quickly. There were in the nest three young
ones, about the size of Pullets, which though full feathered, were unable
to fly. On Friday morning, I went again to the nest to get a young one,
which I thought I could nurse to a considerable growth, sufficient to
answer your purpose, if I should fail to procure an old one, which
was represented to me as almost impossible, on account of his shyness, and the danger from his dreadful claws. On taking a young
one, I intended to lay a couple of snares in the nest, for which purpose
I had a strong cord in my pocket. The old birds were on the tree
when Captain H. and I approached it. As a defence, profiting by the
experience of yesterday, I took a walking stick with me. When I
was about half up the tree, the bird I send you struck at me repeatedly with violence ; he flew round, in a small circle, darting at me
at every circuit, and I striking at him. Observing that he always
described a circle in the air, before he came at me, I kept a *hawk's
eye* upon him, and the moment he passed me, I availed myself of the
opportunity to ascend. When immediately under the nest, I hesitated
at the formidable opposition I met, as his rage appeared to increase
with my presumption in invading his premises. But I mounted to the
nest. At that moment he darted directly at me with all his force,
whizzing through the air, his choler apparently redoubled. Fortunately for me, I struck him on the extreme joint of the right wing
with my stick, which brought him to the ground. During this contest,
the female was flying round and round at a respectful distance.
Captain H. held him till I tied my handkerchief about his legs : the
captain felt the effect of his claws. I brought away a young one to
keep the old one in a good humor. I put them in a very large coop ;
the young one ate some fish, when broken and put into its throat ; but
the old one would not eat for two days. He continued sullen and
obstinate, hardly changing his position. He walks about now and is
approached without danger. He takes very little notice of the young
one. A Joseph Smith, working in the field where this nest is, had the
curiosity to go up and look at the eggs : the bird clawed his face in
a shocking manner ; his eye had a narrow escape. I am told that it
has never been considered dangerous to approach a Hawk's nest. If
this be so, this bird's character is peculiar ; his affection for his young,
and his valiant opposition to an invasion of his nest, entitle him to
conspicuous notice. He is the *prince* of Fish Hawks ; his character
and his portrait seem worthy of being handed to the historic muse.
A Hawk more worthy of the honor which awaits him could not have
been found. I hope no accident will happen to him, and that he
may fully answer your purpose. — Yours,

" THOMAS SMITH."

" This morning the female was flying to and fro, making a mournful
noise."

The young of the Fish Hawk are remarkable for remaining long in
the nest before they attempt to fly. Mr. Smith's letter is dated June
30th, at which time, he observes, they were as large as Pullets, and full
feathered. Seventeen days after, I myself ascended to this same
Hawk's nest, where I found the two remaining young ones seemingly
full grown. They made no attempts to fly, though they both placed

themselves in a stern posture of defence as I examined them at my leisure. The female had procured a *second* helpmate; but he did not seem to inherit the spirit of his predecessor, for, like a true stepfather, he left the nest at my approach, and sailed about at a safe distance with his mate, who showed great anxiety and distress during the whole of my visit. It is universally asserted, by the people of the neighborhood where these birds breed, that the young remain so long before they fly, that the parents are obliged at last to compel them to shift for themselves, beating them with their wings, and driving them from the nest. But that they continue to assist them even after this, I know to be a fact, from my own observation, as I have seen the young bird meet its parent in the air, and receive from him the fish he carried in his claws.

The flight of the Fish Hawk, his manœuvres while in search of fish, and his manner of seizing his prey, are deserving of particular notice. In leaving the nest, he usually flies direct till he comes to the sea, then sails around, in easy curving lines, turning sometimes in the air as on a pivot, apparently without the least exertion, rarely moving the wings, his legs extended in a straight line behind, and his remarkable length, and curvature, or bend of wing, distinguishing him from all other Hawks. The height at which he thus elegantly glides is various, from one hundred to one hundred and fifty, and two hundred feet, sometimes much higher, all the while calmly reconnoitering the face of the deep below. Suddenly he is seen to check his course, as if struck by a particular object, which he seems to survey for a few moments with such steadiness, that he appears fixed in air, flapping his wings. This object, however he abandons, or rather the fish he had in his eye has disappeared, and he is again seen sailing around as before. Now his attention is again arrested, and he descends with great rapidity; but ere he reaches the surface, shoots off on another course, as if ashamed that a second victim had escaped him. He now sails at a short height above the surface, and by a zigzag descent, and without seeming to dip his feet in the water, seizes a fish, which, after carrying a short distance, he probably drops, or yields up to the Bald Eagle, and again ascends, by easy spiral circles, to the higher regions of the air, where he glides about in all the ease and majesty of his species. At once, from this sublime aërial height, he descends like a perpendicular torrent, plunging into the sea with a loud rushing sound, and with the certainty of a rifle. In a few moments he emerges, bearing in his claws his struggling prey, which he always carries head foremost, and, having risen a few feet above the surface, shakes himself as a water spaniel would do, and directs his heavy and laborious course directly for the land. If the wind blow hard, and his nest lie in the quarter from whence it comes, it is amusing to observe with what judgment and exertion he beats to windward, not in a direct line, that is, *in the wind's eye,* but making several successive tacks to gain his purpose. This will appear the more striking, when we consider the size of the fish which he sometimes bears along. A shad was taken from a Fish Hawk near Great Egg Harbor, on which he had begun to regale himself, and had already ate a considerable portion of it; the remainder weighed six pounds. Another Fish Hawk was passing Mr. Beasley's, at the same place, with a large flounder in his grasp, which struggled and shook him so, that he dropped it on the shore. The flounder was picked up, and served the whole family for dinner. It is singular that the Hawk never descends to pick up a fish which he happens to drop, either on the land or on the water. There is a kind of abstemious dignity in this habit of the Hawk, superior to the gluttonous voracity displayed by most other birds of prey, particularly by the Bald Eagle, whose piratical robberies committed on the present species have been already fully detailed in treating of his history. The Hawk, however, in his fishing pursuits, sometimes mistakes his mark, or overrates his strength, by striking fish too large and powerful for him to manage, by whom he is suddenly dragged under; and, though he sometimes succeeds in extricating himself, after being taken three or four times down, yet oftener both parties perish. The bodies of sturgeon, and several other large fish, with that of a Fish Hawk fast grappled in them, have at different times, been found dead on the shore, cast up by the waves.

The Fish Hawk is doubtless the most numerous of all its genus within the United States. It penetrates far into the interior of the country up our large rivers, and their head waters. It may be said to line the sea-coast from Georgia to Canada. In some parts I have counted, at one view, more than twenty of their nests within half a mile. Mr. Gardiner informs me, that on the small island on which he resides, there are at least "three hundred nests of Fish Hawks that have young, which, on an average, consume probably not less than six hundred fish daily." Before they depart in the autumn, they regularly repair their nests, carrying up sticks, sods, &c., fortifying them against the violence of the winter storms, which, from this circumstance, they would seem to foresee and expect. But, notwithstanding all their precautions, they frequently, on their return in spring, find them lying in ruins around the roots of the tree; and sometimes the tree itself has shared the same fate. When a number of Hawks, to the amount of twenty or upwards, collect together on one tree, making a loud squealing noise, there is generally a nest built soon after on the same tree. Probably this congressional assembly were settling the right of the new pair to the premises; or it might be a kind of wedding, or joyous festive meeting on the occasion. They are naturally of a mild and peaceable disposition, living together in great peace and harmony; for, though with them, as in the best regulated communities, instances of attack and robbery occur among themselves, yet these instances are extremely rare. Mr. Gardiner observes, that they are sometimes seen high in the air, sailing and cutting strange gambols, with loud vociferations, darting down several hundred feet perpendicular, frequently with part of a fish in one claw, which they seem proud of, and to claim *high hook*, as the fishermen call *him* who takes the greatest number. On these occasions, they serve as a barometer to foretell the changes of the atmosphere; for, when the Fish Hawks are seen thus sailing high in air, in circles, it is universally believed to prognosticate a change of weather, often a thunder storm, in a few hours. On the faith of the certainty of these signs, the experienced coaster wisely prepares for the expected storm, and is rarely mistaken.

There is one singular trait in the character of this bird, which is mentioned in treating of the Purple Grakle, and which I have since had many opportunities of witnessing. The Grakles, or Crow Black-birds, are permitted by the Fish Hawk to build their nests among the interstices of the sticks of which his own is constructed, — several pairs of Grakles taking up their abode there, like humble vassals around the castle of their chief, laying, hatching their young, and living together in mutual harmony. I have found no less than four of these nests clustered around the sides of the former, and a fifth fixed on the nearest branch of the adjoining tree; as if the proprie-tor of this last, unable to find an unoccupied corner on the premises, had been anxious to share, as much as possible, the company and pro-tection of this generous bird.

The Fish Hawk is twenty-two inches in length, and five feet three inches in extent; the bill is deep black, the upper as well as lower cere, (for the base of the lower mandible has a loose moveable skin,) and also the sides of the mouth, from the nostrils backwards, are light blue; crown and hind head pure white, front streaked with brown; through the eye, a bar of dark blackish brown passed to the neck behind, which, as well as the whole upper parts, is deep brown, the edges of the feathers lighter; shafts of the wing-quills, brownish white; tail slightly rounded, of rather a paler brown than the body, crossed with eight bars of very dark brown; the wings, when shut, extend about an inch beyond the tail, and are nearly black towards the tips; the inner vanes of both quill and tail-feathers are whitish, barred with brown; whole lower parts, pure white, except the thighs, which are covered with short plumage, and streaked down the fore part with pale brown; the legs and feet are a very pale light blue, prodig-iously strong and disproportionably large; they are covered with flat scales of remarkable strength and thickness, resembling, when dry, the teeth of a large rasp, particularly on the soles, intended, no doubt, to enable the bird to seize with more security his slippery prey; the thighs are long, the legs short, feathered a little below the knee, and, as well as the feet and claws, large; the latter hooked into semi-circles, black, and very sharp-pointed; the iris of the eye, a fiery yellow orange.

The female is full two inches longer; the upper part of the head of a less pure white, and the brown streaks on the front spreading more over the crown; the throat and upper part of the breast are also dashed with large blotches of a pale brown, and the bar passing through the eye, not of so dark a brown. The toes of both are ex-ceedingly strong and warty, and the hind claw a full inch and a quar-ter in diameter. The feathers on the neck and hind head are long and narrow, and generally erected when the bird is irritated, resem-bling those of the Eagle. The eye is destitute of the projecting bone common to most of the Falcon tribe; the nostril, large, and of a curv-ing, triangular shape. On dissection, the two glands on the rump, which supply the bird with oil for lubricating its feathers to protect them from the wet, were found to be remarkably large, capable, when opened, of admitting the end of the finger, and contained a large quantity of white, greasy matter, and some pure yellow oil; the gall was in small quantity. The numerous convolutions and length of the intestines surprised me; when carefully extended, they measured within an inch or two of nine feet, and were no thicker than those of

29 *

a Robin! The crop, or craw, was middle sized, and contained a nearly-dissolved fish; the stomach was a large, oblong pouch, capable of considerable distension, and was also filled with half-digested fish: no appearance of a muscular gizzard.

By the descriptions of European naturalists, it would appear that this bird, or one near akin to it, is a native of the eastern continent, in summer, as far north as Siberia; the Bald Buzzard of Turton almost exactly agreeing with the present species in size, color, and manners, with the exception of its breeding or making its nest among the reeds, instead of on trees. Mr. Bewick, who has figured and described the female of this bird under the appellation of the Osprey, says that "it builds on the ground, among reeds, and lays three or four eggs, of an elliptical form, rather less than those of a Hen." This difference of habit may be owing to particular local circumstances, such deviations being usual among many of our native birds. The Italians are said to compare its descent upon the water to a piece of lead falling upon that element; and distinguish it by the name of *Aquila plumbina*, or the Leaden Eagle. In the United States, it is every where denominated the Fish Hawk, or Fishing Hawk — a name truly expressive of its habits.

The regular arrival of this noted bird at the vernal equinox, when the busy season of fishing commences, adds peculiar interest to its first appearance, and procures it many a benediction from the fisherman. With the following lines, illustrative of these circumstances, I shall conclude its history:—

Soon as the sun, great ruler of the year,
Bends to our northern climes his bright career,
And from the caves of Ocean calls from sleep
The finny shoals and myriads of the deep;
When freezing tempests back to Greenland ride,
And day and night the equal hours divide;
True to the season, o'er our sea-beat shore,
The sailing Osprey high is seen to soar
With broad, unmoving wing; and, circling slow,
Marks each loose straggler in the deep below;
Sweeps down like lightning! plunges with a roar!
And bears his struggling victim to the shore.

The long-housed fisherman beholds, with joy,
The well-known signals of his rough employ;
And, as he bears his nets and oars along,
Thus hails the welcome season with a song:—

THE FISHERMAN'S HYMN.

The Osprey sails above the sound;
  The Geese are gone, the Gulls are flying;
The herring shoals swarm thick around;
  The nets are launched, the boats are plying.
Yo, ho, my hearts! let 's seek the deep,
  Raise high the song, and cheerly wish her,
Still as the bending net we sweep,
  "God bless the Fish Hawk and the fisher!"

She brings us fish — she brings us spring,
  Good times, fair weather, warmth, and plenty ;
Fine store of shad, trout, herring, ling,
  Sheepshead and drum, and old-wives dainty.
    Yo, ho, my hearts ! let 's seek the deep,
    Ply every oar, and cheerly wish her,
    Still as the bending net we sweep,
      " God bless the Fish Hawk and the fisher ! "

She rears her young on yonder tree ;
  She leaves her faithful mate to mind 'em ;
Like us, for fish, she sails to sea,
  And, plunging, shows us where to find 'em.
    Yo, ho, my hearts ! let 's seek the deep,
    Ply every oar, and cheerly wish her,
    While the slow-bending net we sweep,
      " God bless the Fish Hawk and the fisher ! "

FISH CROW. — CORVUS OSSIFRAGUS. — Fig. 159.

Peale's Museum, No. 1369.

CORVUS OSSIFRAGUS. — Wilson.*

Corvus ossifragus, *Bonap. Synop.* p. 57.

THIS is another roving inhabitant of our sea-coasts, ponds, and river-shores, though a much less distinguished one than the preceding ; this being the first time, as far as I can learn, that he has ever been introduced to the notice of the world.

I first met with this species on the sea-coast of Georgia, and observed that they regularly retired to the interior as evening approached, and came down to the shores of the River Savannah by the first appearance of day. Their voice first attracted my notice, being very different from that of the Common Crow, more hoarse and guttural, uttered as if something stuck in their throat, and varied into several modulations as they flew along. Their manner of flying was also unlike the others, as they frequently sailed about, without flapping the wings, something in the manner of the Raven ; and I soon perceived that their food, and their mode of procuring it, were also both differ-

---

* This is a very curious bird, first named and described by our author. It is one of the predacious species, with the nostrils clothed with feathers, and seems to feed nearly alone on fish or reptiles, doing almost no harm to the husbandman. In the latter circumstance, it resembles also our Carrion Crow, which often kills the common frog ; and, last summer, I observed one flying with an adder in his bill. He had caught it on a detached piece of muir, and, on my approach, rose, taking the prey along with him, most probably before it was sufficiently despatched, as the writhings of the reptile caused him to alight several times, at short distances, before being perfectly at ease. Being on horseback, I could not follow to see the end of the engagement. The species seems peculiar to the coast of North America, and does not extend very far northward. — ED.

ent; their favorite haunts being about the banks of the river, along which they usually sailed, dexterously snatching up with their claws dead fish, or other garbage, that floated on the surface. At the country seat of Stephen Elliot, Esq., near the Ogechee River, I took notice of these Crows frequently perching on the backs of the cattle, like the Magpie and Jackdaw of Britain; but never mingling with the Common Crows, and differing from them in this particular, that the latter generally retire to the shore, the reeds, and marshes, to roost, while the Fish Crow always, a little before sunset, seeks the interior high woods to repose in.

On my journey through the Mississippi Territory, last year, I resided for some time at the seat of my hospitable friend, Dr. Samuel Brown, a few miles from Fort Adams, on the Mississippi. In my various excursions there, among the lofty, fragrance-breathing magnolia woods, and magnificent scenery, that adorn the luxuriant face of nature in those southern regions, this species of Crow frequently made its appearance, distinguished by the same voice and habits it had in Georgia. There is, in many of the ponds there, a singular kind of lizard, that swims about, with its head above the surface, making a loud sound, not unlike the harsh jarring of a door. These the Crow now before us would frequently seize with his claws, as he flew along the surface, and retire to the summit of a dead tree to enjoy his repast. Here I also observed him a pretty constant attendant at the pens where the cows were usually milked, and much less shy, less suspicious, and more solitary than the Common Crow. In the county of Cape May, New Jersey, I again met with these Crows, particularly along Egg Harbor River; and, latterly, on the Schuylkill and Delaware, near Philadelphia, during the season of shad and herring fishing, viz. from the middle of March till the beginning of June. A small party of these Crows, during this period, regularly passed Mr. Bartram's gardens to the high woods to roost, every evening, a little before sunset, and as regularly returned, at or before sunrise, every morning, directing their course towards the river. The fishermen along these rivers also inform me that they have particularly remarked this Crow, by his croaking voice, and his fondness for fish; almost always hovering about their fishing places to glean up the refuse. Of their manner of breeding I can only say, that they separate into pairs, and build in tall trees near the sea or river shore; one of their nests having been built, this season, in a piece of tall woods near Mr. Beasley's, at Great Egg Harbor. The male of this nest furnished me with Fig. 159. From the circumstance of six or seven being usually seen here together in the month of July, it is probable that they have at least four or five young at a time.

I can find no description of this species by any former writer. Mr. Bartram mentions a bird of this tribe, which he calls the *Great Seaside Crow;* but the present species is considerably inferior in size to the Common Crow; and, having myself seen and examined it in so many and remotely-situated parts of the country, and found it in all these places alike, I have no hesitation in pronouncing it to be a new, and hitherto undescribed species.

The Fish Crow is sixteen inches long, and thirty-three in extent; black all over, with reflections of steel-blue and purple; the chin is bare of feathers around the base of the lower mandible; upper mandible, notched near the tip, the edges of both turned inwards about the middle; eye, very small, placed near the corner of the mouth, and of a dark hazel color; recumbent hairs or bristles, large and long; ear-feathers, prominent; first primary, little more than half the length, fourth the longest; wings, when shut, reach within two inches of the tip of the tail; tail, rounded, and seven inches long from its insertion; thighs, very long; legs, stout; claws, sharp, long, and hooked, hind one the largest, all jet black. Male and female much alike.

I would beg leave to recommend to the watchful farmers of the United States, that, in their honest indignation against the Common Crow, they would spare the present species, and not shower destruction indiscriminately on their black friends and enemies; at least, on those who *sometimes* plunder them, and those who never molest or injure their property.

RINGED PLOVER.— CHARADRIUS HIATICULA.— Fig. 160.

Lath. Syn. v. p. 201. 8.— *Arct. Zool.* ii. No. 401. — Petit pluvier, à Collier, *Buff.* viii. p. 90. 6. *Pl. enl.* 921. — Pluvialis torquato minor, *Briss.* v. p. 63. 8. t. 5. f. 2. — *Turt. Syst.* p. 411. 2. — *Peale's Museum*, No. 4150.

CHARADRIUS MELODUS. — Ord.*

Charadrius melodus, *Bonap. Synop.* p. 296. — Charadrius Okenii? *Wagl. Syst. Av.* No. 24.

It was not altogether consistent with my original plan, to introduce any of the Grallæ, or Waders, until I had advanced nearer to a close with the Land Birds; but as the scenery here seemed somewhat appropriate, I have taken the liberty of placing in it two birds, (Figs. 160 and 161,) reduced to one-third of their natural size, both being *varieties* of their respective species, each of which will appear in their proper places, in some future part of this work, in full size, and in their complete plumage.

The Ringed Plover is very abundant on the low sandy shores of our whole sea-coast during summer. They run, or rather seem to

* This little Plover has proved to be one of those very closely allied species so difficult of distinction, without a comparison with its congeners. The present figure (No. 160) is in the adult spring dress. The synonyms of Wilson are, of course, erroneous. Those also of Temminck, quoted in his Manual, and the observations on Wilson's plate and description, must share a similar fate. The observations in the Nomenclature of Wilson, by the Prince of Musignano, will best explain how this species ought to stand. "C. hiaticula was at first given by Wilson as a variety, of which he intended to describe the type in a future volume; but when he did so in his seventh volume, he clearly and positively pointed out the difference in markings, habits, migration, voice, &c. between the two, which he then considered as distinct species, but without applying a new name; and we have no doubt that, if he had made out the index himself, he would then have supplied the deficiency, as he had before done in respect to some land birds. Mr. Ord supplied this void, by calling it C. melodus." — Ed.

glide, rapidly along the surface of the flat sands, frequently spreading out their wings and tail like a fan, and fluttering along, to draw or entice one away from their nests. These are formed with little art, being merely shallow concavities dug in the sand, in which the eggs are laid, and, during the day at least, left to the influence of the sun to hatch them. The parents, however, always remain near the spot to protect them from injury, and probably, in cold, rainy, or stormy weather, to shelter them with their bodies. The eggs are three, sometimes four, large for the bird, of a dun clay color, and marked with numerous small spots of reddish purple.

The voice of these little birds, as they move along the sand, is soft and musical, consisting of a single plaintive note occasionally repeated. As you approach near their nests, they seem to court your attention, and, the moment they think you observe them, they spread out their wings and tail, dragging themselves along, and imitating the squeaking of young birds; if you turn from them, they immediately resume their proper posture, until they have again caught your eye, when they display the same attempts at deception as before. A flat, dry, sandy beach, just beyond the reach of the summer tides, is their favorite place for breeding.

This species is subject to great variety of change in its plumage. In the month of July, I found most of those that were breeding on Summers's Beach, at the mouth of Great Egg Harbor, such as I have here figured; but, about the beginning or middle of October, they had become much darker above, and their plumage otherwise varied. They were then collected in flocks; their former theatrical and deceptive manœuvres seemed all forgotten. They appeared more active than before, as well as more silent, alighting within a short distance of one, and feeding about without the least appearance of suspicion. At the commencement of winter, they all go off towards the south.

This variety of the Ringed Plover is seven inches long, and fourteen in extent; the bill is reddish yellow for half its length, and black at the extremity; the front and whole lower parts, pure white, except the side of the breast, which is marked with a curving streak of black, another spot of black bounding the front above; back and upper parts, very pale brown, inclining to ashy white, and intermixed with white; wings, pale brown; greater coverts, broadly tipped with white; interior edges of the secondaries, and outer edges of the primaries, white, and tipped with brown; tail, nearly even, the lower half white, brown towards the extremity, the outer feather pure white, the next white, with a single spot of black; eye, black and full, surrounded by a narrow ring of yellow; legs, reddish yellow; claws, black; lower side of the wings, pure white.

LITTLE SANDPIPER.—TRINGA PUSILLA.— Fig. 161.

Lath. Syn. v. p. 184. 32.— *Arct. Zool.* ii. No. 397.— Cinclus dominicensis minor, *Briss.* v. p. 222. 13. t. 25. f. 2.— *Turt. Syst.* p. 410.— *Peale's Museum,* No. 4138.

TRINGA MINUTILLA? —Vieillot.*

Tringa pusilla, *Bonap. Synop.* p. 319.

THIS is the least of its tribe in this part of the world, and in its mode of flight has much more resemblance to the Snipe than to the Sandpiper. It is migratory, departing early in October for the South. It resides chiefly among the sea marshes, and feeds among the mud at low water; springs with a zigzag irregular flight, and a feeble twit. It is not altogether confined to the neighborhood of the sea, for I have found several of them on the shores of the Schuylkill, in the month of August. In October, immediately before they go away, they are usually very fat. Their nests or particular breeding-places I have not been able to discover.

This minute species is found in Europe, and also at Nootka Sound, on the western coast of America. Length, five inches and a half; extent, eleven inches; bill and legs, brownish black; upper part of the breast, gray brown, mixed with white; back and upper parts, black; the whole plumage above, broadly edged with bright bay and yellow ochre, primaries, black; greater coverts, the same, tipped with white; eye, small, dark hazel; tail, rounded, the four exterior feathers on each side, dull white, the rest, dark brown; tertials, as long as the primaries; head above, dark brown, with paler edges; over the eye, a streak of whitish; belly and vent, white; the bill is thick at the base, and very slender towards the point; the hind toe, small. In some specimens, the legs were of a dirty yellowish color. Sides of the rump, white; just below the greater coverts, the primaries are crossed with white.

Very little difference could be perceived between the plumage of the males and females. The bay on the edges of the back and scapulars was rather brighter in the male, and the brown deeper.

* The Prince of Musignano considers this species peculiar to America; that it is different from the *T. minuta* and *Temminckii* of Europe, and that it is not the Linnæan *T. pusilla.* If the latter opinion be correct, *pusilla* cannot be retained, and I have added with a query the name given to it by Vieilliot. — ED.

BARN SWALLOW.—HIRUNDO AMERICANA.—Fig. 162, Male;
Fig. 163, Female.

Peale's Museum, No. 7609.

HIRUNDO AMERICANA?—Wilson.*

Hirundo rufa, *Bonap. Synop.* p. 64.—Hirundo Americana, *North. Zool.* ii. p. 329.

There are but few persons in the United States unacquainted with this gay, innocent, and active little bird. Indeed the whole tribe are so distinguished from the rest of small birds by their sweeping rapidity

* Wilson at once perceived the difference between the present species, and as it is commonly called the " Chimney Swallow" of Europe, though many of his contemporaries considered them only as varieties. The Prince of Musignano has, however, considered it as previously described by Latham under the title of *H. rufa,* and again figured as the same by Vieillot.

The authors of the *Northern Zoology* have again appended the following note to their notice of the bird ; and in the uncertainty, we have chosen to retain Wilson's original name, until the species is really determined from authentic specimens.

" It appears to us very doubtful whether the *Hirondelle à ventre roux de Cayenne* of Buffon, (*Ed. Sonn.* xix. p. 35,) of which methodists have made their *Hirundo rufa,* is really the same as the *H. Americana* of Wilson. From the evidence we at present have, we are disposed to consider them distinct. The only authentic account of the Cayenne species is that given by Buffon, which all the compilers have since copied. From this, it appears to be only *five inches and a half long,* (French measure ?) ours is fully seven. The front is whitish, (*le front blanchâtre,*) ours is very deep rufous. But the most remarkable difference between the birds is in the construction of their nests,—the Cayenne bird building one *without* mud, and so long as sometimes to measure a foot and a half, with an opening *near the bottom ;* the *Americana* of Wilson, on the contrary, using a good deal of mud ; the length is only seven inches, and the opening *at top,* with an external rim, for the parents occasionally to sit upon. Until this matter is investigated, we cannot suppose that individuals of the *same species* would, in different countries, build their nests in such very dissimilar ways."

It appears to be exclusively American, and migrates from north to south, and the reverse. There is a great resemblance between the two species ; but they may be at once distinguished by the pure white, and the rich chestnut which clothes the under parts of each, and they would seem to be another of those representing forms which are so frequent, and run so closely in color and habits through both continents.

Wilson, when mentioning the distinctions of this species, includes a difference in habit, from our species building in chimneys, and not in barns, like the American. Chimneys are by no means the common building place of the British Swallow, although those in the neighborhood of towns may use that resort for want of another, in the same way that those in a mining country use the neglected shafts. In the country, barns, shades of thrashing-mills, or any outhouse with an open door or window, under the portico of a front door, are their constant building place ; and although houses in the country have chimneys as well as those in town, they are very seldom, if ever, resorted to. Their nests are also of the same structure and materials, built with clay mingled with straw. and lined with feathers, placed against a rafter, beam, or wall, and open at top.† The eggs also very similar.

Bewick mentions a curious instance of variation, which may be also taken as a

† According to Professor Rennie, it is called, in Sweden, *Ladu Swala,* Barn Swallow ; while, in the south of Europe, where chimneys are rare, it builds in gateways, porches, and **galleries.**

of flight, their peculiar aërial evolutions of wing over our fields and rivers, and through our very streets, from morning to night, that the light of heaven itself, the sky, the trees, or any other common objects

strong proof of the annual return of birds to the same building places. " At Cameston Hall, near Bath, a pair of Swallows built their nests on the upper part of the frame of an old picture over the chimney — coming in through a broken pane in the window of the room. They came three years successively, and, in all probability, would have continued to do so, if the room had not been put into repair, which prevented their access to it."

Swallows have been divided into various genera, as might be supposed from their being commonly indicated Swallows, Swifts, or Martins. Some form among these are found in almost every country, except as we approach the poles; and in North America, where the whole *Hirundinidæ* will be comprised in six individuals, we have two real Swallows, two Martins, the very strongly formed Purple Swallow, and the representative of the Swifts in *Chætura pelasgica.* These will come under observation as we proceed. The present, with the Republican, or Cliff Swallow, figured by Bonaparte in his continuation, with that of Europe, are true forms of *Hirundo,* one which possesses great activity though not so much strength in flight as the Swifts, but which will show the more exact relative proportion of power between the members. They are very generally distributed, have the wings long, and the tail forked; the only form where these members are more extended, is in the genus *Macropterix,* lately formed by Mr. Swainson from an Indian group, which will perhaps show the farthest developement of the wings and tail, but which bear the same disproportion as in the broad-shaped and sickle-winged Humming Birds. In all their various flights, the motions are conducted with great celerity and elegance, and are directed by the rapid motion of the tail.

The subject of their migrations, which I believe takes place with all species, and in all countries, has occupied much speculation; of the fact, there can now be no doubt, and the collection of vast crowds together before departure, seems more confined to this form than to any of the others; so far, at least, as my own observation has extended The American species congregate; so do the Republican Swallows; and towards the end of August, our own may be seen daily in flocks, on the house tops or cornices, on railings, or on a bare tree, where the later broods are still fed and exercised by the parents, and the southern journey of the whole mass, as it were delayed until all had acquired sufficient strength.

At times, these congregations are much greater than at others, or like some great assemblage from the neighboring country. One of these took place in 1815, near Rotherham, and has been made the subject of an anonymous pamphlet, by a clergyman in that neighborhood. The assemblage and departure is thus described in it: — " Early in the month of September, 1815, the Swallows, that beautiful and social tribe of the feathered race, began to assemble in the neighborhood of Rotherham, at the willow ground, on the banks of the Canal, preparatory to their migration to a warmer climate ; and their numbers were daily augmented, until they became a vast flock, which no man could easily number. Thousands upon thousands — tens of thousands — and myriads ; so great indeed, that the spectator would almost have concluded, the whole swallow race were there collected in one huge host.

" It was their manner, while there, to rise from the willows in the morning, a little before six o'clock, when their thick columns literally darkened the sky. Their divisions were then into four, five, and sometimes into six grand wings, each of these filing and taking a different route, — one east, another west, another south ; as if not only to be equally dispersed throughout the country, to provide food for their numerous troops, but also to collect with them whatever of their fellows, or straggling parties, might still be left behind.

" In the evening, about five o'clock, they began to return to their station, and continued coming in from all quarters, until nearly dark. It was here that you might see them go through their various aërial evolutions, in many a sportive ring and airy gambol, strengthening their pinions in these playful feats, for their long ethereal journey, as they cut the air and frolicked in the last beams' of the setting sun, or lightly skimmed the surface of the glassy pool.

" The verdant enamel of summer had given place to the warm and mellow tints
30

of Nature, are not better known than the Swallows. We welcome
their first appearance with delight, as the faithful harbingers and companions of flowery spring and ruddy summer; and when, after a long,
frost-bound, and boisterous winter, we hear it announced, that "the
Swallows are come," what a train of charming ideas are associated
with the simple tidings!

The wonderful activity displayed by these birds forms a striking
contrast to the slow habits of most other animals. It may be fairly
questioned, whether, among the whole feathered tribes which Heaven
has formed to adorn this part of creation, there be any that, in the same
space of time, pass over an equal extent of surface with the Swallow.
Let a person take his stand, on a fine summer evening, by a new-mown
field, meadow, or river shore, for a short time, and, among the numerous individuals of this tribe that flit before him, fix his eye on a particular one, and follow, for a while, all its circuitous labyrinths — its
extensive sweeps — its sudden, rapidly-reiterated zigzag excursions,
little inferior to the lightning itself, — and then attempt, by the powers
of mathematics, to calculate the length of the various lines it describes.
Alas! even his omnipotent fluxions would avail him little here, and
he would soon abandon the task in despair. Yet, that some defi-
nite conception may be formed of this extent, let us suppose that this
little bird flies, in his usual way, at the rate of one mile in a minute,
which, from the many experiments I have made, I believe to be within
the truth; and that he is so engaged for ten hours every day; and farther, that this active life is extended to ten years, (many of our small
birds being known to live much longer, even in a state of domestication,) the amount of all these, allowing three hundred and sixty-five
days to a year, would give us two million one hundred and ninety
thousand miles; upwards of eighty-seven times the circumference of
the globe! Yet this little winged seraph, if I may so speak, who, in a
few days, and at will, can pass from the borders of the arctic regions
to the torrid zone, is forced, when winter approaches, to descend to
the bottoms of lakes, rivers, and mill-ponds, to bury itself in the mud
with eels and snapping turtles; or to creep ingloriously into a cavern,
a rat-hole, or a hollow tree, there to doze, with snakes, toads, and
other reptiles, until the return of spring! Is not this true, ye wise
men of Europe and America, who have published so many *credible*
narratives on this subject? The Geese, the Ducks, the Cat-Bird, and
even the Wren, which creeps about our outhouses in summer like a
mouse, are all acknowledged to be migratory, and to pass to southern
regions at the approach of winter; the Swallow alone, on whom
Heaven has conferred superior powers of wing, must sink in torpidity
at the bottom of our rivers, or doze all winter in the caverns of the
earth. I am myself something of a traveller, and foreign countries

of autumn. The leaves were now fast falling from their branches, while the naked
tops of many of the trees appeared. The golden sheaves were safely lodged in
the barns, and the reapers had shouted their harvest-home. Frosty and misty
mornings succeeded, the certain presages of the approach of winter. They were
omens understood by the Swallows, as signals for their march; and on the morning
of the 7th of October, their mighty army broke up their encampment, debouched
from their retreat, rising, covered the heavens with their legions, and, directed by
an unerring guide, took their trackless way." — ED.

afford many novel sights: should I assert, that in some of my peregrinations I had met with a nation of Indians, all of whom, old and young, at the commencement of cold weather, descend to the bottom of their lakes and rivers, and there remain until the breaking up of frost; nay, should I affirm, that thousands of people, in the neighborhood of this city, regularly undergo the same semi-annual submersion — that I myself had fished up a whole family of these from the bottom of the Schuylkill, where they had lain *torpid* all winter, carried them home, and brought them all comfortably to themselves again; should I even publish this in the learned pages of the *Transactions* of our Philosophical Society, — who would believe me? Is, then, the organization of a Swallow less delicate than that of a man? Can a bird, whose vital functions are destroyed by a short privation of pure air and its usual food, sustain, for six months, a situation where the most robust man would perish in a few hours, or minutes? Away with such absurdities! they are unworthy of a serious refutation. I should be pleased to meet with a man who has been personally more conversant with birds than myself, who has followed them in their wide and devious routes — studied their various manners — mingled with and marked their peculiarities more than I have done; yet the miracle of a resuscitated Swallow, in the depth of winter, from the bottom of a millpond, is, I confess, a phenomenon in ornithology that I have never met with.

What better evidence have we that these fleet-winged tribes, instead of following the natural and acknowledged migrations of many other birds, lie torpid all winter in hollow trees, caves, and other subterraneous recesses? That the Chimney Swallow, in the early part of summer, may have been found in a hollow tree, and in great numbers too, is not denied; such being, in some places of the country, (as will be shown in the history of that species,) their actual places of rendezvous, on their first arrival, and their common roosting place long after: or, that the Bank Swallows, also, soon after their arrival, in the early part of spring, may be chilled by the cold mornings which we frequently experience at that season, and be found in this state in their holes, I would as little dispute; but that either the one or the other has ever been found, *in the midst of winter,* in a state of *torpidity,* I do not — cannot believe. Millions of trees, of all dimensions, are cut down every fall and winter of this country, where, in their proper season, Swallows swarm around us. Is it, therefore, in the least probable that we should, only once or twice in an age, have no other evidence than one or two solitary and very suspicious reports of a Mr. Somebody having made a discovery of this kind? If caves were their places of winter retreat, perhaps no country on earth could supply them with a greater choice. I have myself explored many of these, in various parts of the United States, both in winter and in spring, particularly in that singular tract of country in Kentucky, called the Barrens, where some of these subterraneous caverns are several miles in length, lofty and capacious, and pass under a large and deep river — have conversed with the saltpetre workers by whom they are tenanted: but never heard or met with one instance of a Swallow having been found there in winter. These people treated such reports with ridicule.

It is to be regretted that a greater number of experiments have not been made, by keeping live Swallows through the winter, to convince these believers in the torpidity of birds of their mistake. That class of cold-blooded animals which are *known* to become torpid during winter, and of which hundreds and thousands are found every season, are subject to the same when kept in a suitable room for experiment. How is it with the Swallows in this respect? Much powerful testimony might be produced on this point: the following experiments, recently made by Mr. James Pearson of London, and communicated by Sir John Trevelyn, Bart., to Mr. Bewick, the celebrated engraver in wood, will be sufficient for our present purpose, and throw great light on this part of the subject.*

"Five or six of these birds were taken about the latter end of August, 1784, in a bat fowling-net at night. They were put separately into small cages, and fed with Nightingale's food: in about a week or ten days, they took food of themselves; they were then put all together into a deep cage, four feet long, with gravel at the bottom; a broad shallow pan, with water, was placed in it, in which they sometimes washed themselves, and seemed much strengthened by it. One day Mr. Pearson observed that they went into the water with unusual eagerness, hurrying in and out again repeatedly with such swiftness as if they had been suddenly seized with a frenzy. Being anxious to see the result, he left them to themselves about half an hour, and, going to the cage again, found them all huddled together in a corner, apparently dead; the cage was then placed at a proper distance from the fire, when only two of them recovered, and were as healthy as before: the rest died. The two remaining ones were allowed to wash themselves occasionally for a short time only; but their feet soon after became swelled and inflamed, which Mr. Pearson attributed to their perching, and they died about Christmas. Thus the first year's experiment was in some measure lost. Not discouraged by the failure of this, Mr. Pearson determined to make a second trial the succeeding year, from a strong desire of being convinced of the truth of their going into a state of torpidity. Accordingly, the next season, having taken some more birds, he put them into the cage, and in every respect pursued the same methods as with the last; but, to guard their feet from the bad effects of the damp and cold, he covered the perches with flannel, and had the pleasure to observe, that the birds throve extremely well; they sang their song during the winter, and, soon after Christmas, began to moult, which they got through without any difficulty, and lived three or four years, regularly moulting every year at the usual time. On the renewal of their feathers, it appeared that their tails were forked exactly the same as in those birds which return hither in the spring, and in every respect their appearance was the same. These birds, says Mr. Pearson, were exhibited to the Society for promoting Natural History, on the 14th day of February, 1786, at the time they were in a deep moult, during a severe frost, when the snow was on the ground. Minutes of this circumstance were entered in the books of the Society. These birds died at last from neglect, during a long illness which Mr. Pearson

* See Bewick's *British Birds,* vol. i. p. 254.

had: they died in the summer. Mr. Pearson concludes his very interesting account in these words: — 20th January, 1797, — I have now in my house, No. 21, Great Newport Street, Long Acre, four Swallows in moult, in as perfect health as any birds ever appeared to be when moulting."

The Barn Swallow of the United States has hitherto been considered by many writers as the same with the common Chimney Swallow of Europe. They differ, however, considerably in color, as well as in habits; the European species having the belly and vent white, the American species those parts of a bright chestnut; the former building in the corners of chimneys, near the top; the latter never in such places, but usually in barns, sheds, and other outhouses, on beams, braces, rafters, &c. It is difficult to reconcile these constant differences of manners and markings in one and the same bird; I shall therefore take the liberty of considering the present as a separate and distinct species.

The Barn Swallow arrives in this part of Pennsylvania from the south on the last week in March, or the first week in April, and passes on to the north, as far, at least, as the river St. Lawrence. On the east side of the great range of the Alleghany, they are dispersed very generally over the country, wherever there are habitations, even to the summit of high mountains; but, on account of the greater coldness of such situations, are usually a week or two later in making their appearance there. On the 16th of May, being on a shooting expedition on the top of Pocano mountain, Northampton, when the ice on that and on several successive mornings was more than a quarter of an inch thick, I observed, with surprise, a pair of these Swallows which had taken up their abode on a miserable cabin there. It was then about sunrise, the ground white with hoar frost, and the male was twittering on the roof by the side of his mate with great sprightliness. The man of the house told me that a single pair came regularly there every season, and built their nest on a projecting beam under the eaves, about six or seven feet from the ground. At the bottom of the mountain, in a large barn belonging to the tavern there, I counted upwards of twenty nests, all seemingly occupied. In the woods they are never met with; but, as you approach a farm, they soon catch the eye, cutting their gambols in the air. Scarcely a barn, to which these birds can find access, is without them; and, as public feeling is universally in their favor, they are seldom or never disturbed. The proprietor of the barn last mentioned, a German, assured me, that if a man permitted the Swallows to be shot, his cows would give bloody milk, and also that no barn where Swallows frequented would ever be struck with lightning; and I nodded assent. When the tenets of superstition "lean to the side of humanity," one can readily respect them. On the west side of the Alleghany these birds become more rare. In travelling through the states of Kentucky and Tennessee, from Lexington to the Tennessee River, in the months of April and May, I did not see a single individual of this species; though the Purple Martin, and, in some places, the Bank Swallow, was numerous.

Early in May they begin to build. From the size and structure of the nest, it is nearly a week before it is completely finished. One of

30 *

these nests, taken on the 21st of June from the rafter to which it was closely attached, is now lying before me. It is in the form of an inverted cone, with a perpendicular section cut off on that side by which it adhered to the wood. At the top it has an extension of the edge, or offset, for the male or female to sit on occasionally, as appeared by the dung; the upper diameter was about six inches by five, the height externally seven inches. This shell is formed of mud, mixed with fine hay, as plasterers do their mortar with hair, to make it adhere the better; the mud seems to have been placed in regular strata, or layers, from side to side; the hollow of this cone (the shell of which is about an inch in thickness) is filled with fine hay, well stuffed in; above that is laid a handful of very large downy Geese feathers. The eggs are five, white, specked, and spotted all over with reddish brown. Owing to the semi-transparency of the shell, the eggs have a slight tinge of flesh color. The whole weighs about two pounds.

They have generally two broods in the season. The first make their appearance about the second week in June; and the last brood leave the nest about the 10th of August. Though it is not uncommon for twenty, and even thirty, pair to build in the same barn, yet every thing seems to be conducted with great order and affection; all seems harmony among them, as if the interest of each were that of all. Several nests are often within a few inches of each other; yet no appearance of discord or quarrelling takes place in this peaceful and affectionate community.

When the young are fit to leave the nest, the old ones entice them out by fluttering backwards and forwards, twittering and calling to them every time they pass; and the young exercise themselves, for several days, in short essays of this kind within doors, before they first venture abroad. As soon as they leave the barn, they are conducted by their parents to the trees, or bushes, by the pond, creek, or river shore, or other suitable situation, where their proper food is most abundant, and where they can be fed with the greatest convenience to both parties. Now and then they take a short excursion themselves, and are also frequently fed while on wing by an almost instantaneous motion of both parties, rising perpendicularly in air, and meeting each other. About the middle of August they seem to begin to prepare for their departure. They assemble on the roof in great numbers, dressing and arranging their plumage, and making occasional essays, twittering with great cheerfulness. Their song is a kind of sprightly warble, sometimes continued for a considerable time. From this period to the 8th of September, they are seen near the Schuylkill and Delaware, every afternoon, for two or three hours before sunset, passing along to the south in great numbers, feeding as they skim along. I have counted several hundreds pass within sight in less than a quarter of an hour, all directing their course towards the south. The reeds are now their regular roosting places; and, about the middle of September, there is scarcely an individual of them to be seen. How far south they continue their route is uncertain; none of them remain in the United States. Mr. Bartram informs me, that, during his residence in Florida, he often saw vast flocks of this and our other Swallows, passing from the peninsula towards the south in September and

October; and also on their return to the north about the middle of March. It is highly probable, that, were the countries to the south of the Gulf of Mexico, and as far south as the great River Maranon, visited and explored by a competent naturalist, these regions would be found to be the winter rendezvous of the very birds now before us, and most of our other migratory tribes.

In a small volume which I have lately met with, entitled *An Account of the British Settlement of Honduras,* by Captain George Henderson, of the 5th West India regiment, published in London in 1809, the writer, in treating of that part of its natural history which relates to birds, gives the following particulars : — " Myriads of Swallows," says he, " are also the occasional inhabitants of Honduras. The time of their residence is generally confined to the period of the rains, [that is, from October to February,] after which, they totally disappear. There is something remarkably curious and deserving of notice in the ascent of these birds. As soon as the dawn appears, they quit their place of rest, which is usually chosen amid the rushes of some watery savannah, and invariably rise to a certain height, in a compact spiral form, and which at a distance often occasions them to be taken for an immense column of smoke. This attained, they are then seen separately to disperse in search of food, the occupation of their day. To those who may have had the opportunity of observing the phenomenon of a waterspout, the similarity of evolution, in the ascent of these birds, will be thought surprisingly striking. The descent, which regularly takes place at sunset, is conducted much in the same way, but with inconceivable rapidity. And the noise which accompanies this can only be compared to the falling of an immense torrent, or the rushing of a violent gust of wind. Indeed, to an observer, it seems wonderful, that thousands of these birds are not destroyed, in being thus propelled to the earth with such irresistible force." [*]

How devoutly it is to be wished that the natural history of those regions were more precisely known, so absolutely necessary as it is to the perfect understanding of this department of our own!

The Barn Swallow is seven inches long, and thirteen inches in extent; bill, black; upper part of the head, neck, back, rump, and tail-coverts, steel blue, which descends rounding on the breast; front and chin, deep chestnut; belly, vent, and lining of the wing, light chestnut; wings and tail, brown black, slightly glossed with reflections of green; tail, greatly forked, the exterior feather on each side an inch and a half longer than the next, and tapering towards the extremity, each feather, except the two middle ones, marked on its inner vane with an oblong spot of white; lores, black; eye, dark hazel; sides of the mouth, yellow; legs, dark purple.

The female differs from the male in having the belly and vent rufous white, instead of light chestnut : these parts are also slightly clouded with rufous; and the exterior tail feathers are shorter.

These birds are easily tamed, and soon become exceedingly gentle and familiar. I have frequently kept them in my room for several days at a time, where they employed themselves in catching flies, picking them from my clothes, hair, &c., calling out occasionally, as they observed some of their old companions passing the windows.

[*] HENDERSON'S *Honduras,* p. 119.

GREEN–BLUE, OR WHITE–BELLIED SWALLOW.
HIRUNDO VIRIDIS. — Fig. 164.

Peale's Museum, No. 7707.

HIRUNDO BICOLOR. — Vieillot.*

Hirundo viridis, *Aud. Ann. Lyc. of New York,* i. p. 166. — The White-bellied
Swallow, *Aud. Orn. Biog.* i. p. 491, pl. 98. — Hirundo bicolor, *Bonap. Synop.*
p. 65. — *North. Zool.* ii. p. 328.

This is the species hitherto supposed by Europeans to be the same
with their common Martin, *Hirundo urbica,* a bird no where to be
found within the United States. The English Martin is blue black
above, the present species greenish blue; the former has the whole
rump white, and the legs and feet are covered with short, white, downy
feathers, the latter has nothing of either. That ridiculous propensity
in foreign writers, to consider most of our birds as varieties of their
own, has led them into many mistakes, which it shall be the business

---

* This beautiful and highly curious little bird has, like the last, been confused
with a European species, *H. urbica.* Gmelin and Latham esteem it only a variety,
while other writers make it identical. From the European Martin it may always at
once be distinguished by wanting the purely white rump, so conspicuous during the
flight of the former. The priority of the name will be in favor of Vieillot, and it
should stand as *H. bicolor* of that naturalist.

The Martins possess a greater preponderance of power in the wings over the tail
than the Swallows; and their flight, as our author remarks, is consequently more
like sailing than flying. All their turns are round and free, and performed most
frequently in large sweeps, without any motion of the wings. In their other forms,
they hardly differ, though almost any one will say this is a Martin, that a Swallow.
I am inclined to keep them as a subordinate group, and there also would be placed
the Water Martins, which have already been made into a genus by Boje. They
are all nearly of the same form, are gregarious, and build and feed in large companies.

The White-bellied Swallow bears more analogy to the Water Martins, than that
of Europe, or those which frequent inland districts. According to Audubon, they
sit and roost on the sedges and tall water plants, as well as upon the bushes; and
they sometimes, in the beginning of autumn, as mentioned by our author, collect on
the shores or sandbanks of rivers, in considerable numbers. About the end of July,
in the present year, I had an opportunity of seeing the latter incident take place
with our Common Sand Martin, (*H. riparia,*) one very hot evening, when residing
on the shores of the Solway Frith, where the beach is unusually flat and sandy.
Several hundreds of these were collected upon a space not exceeding two acres;
most of them were upon the ground, a few occasionally rising and making a short
circuit. At this part, a small stream entered the sea, and they seemed partly resting and washing, and partly feeding on a small fly that had apparently come newly
to existence, and covered the sands in immense profusion. None of our other
species mingled, though they were abundant in the neighborhood.

The American Bird is also remarkable as being a berry eater, an occurrence
nearly unknown among the *Hirundinidæ.* Neither is their breeding in holes of
trees frequent among them. The nly instance of a similar propensity, is one related of the Common Swift, in *Loudon's Magazine of Natural History,* which,
however, is a species more likely to suit itself to circumstances of the kind, as it
appears to have done in this instance, where it formed its breeding place in the
deserted holes of Woodpeckers. Audubon has traced their migrations through the
year, and has proved that they winter in Louisiana. I believe they belong exclusively to the New World. — Ed.

of the author of the present work to point out, decisively, wherever he may meet with them.

The White-bellied Swallow arrives in Pennsylvania a few days later than the preceding species. It often takes possession of an apartment in the boxes appropriated to the Purple Martin; and also frequently builds and hatches in a hollow tree. The nest consists of fine, loose, dry grass, lined with large, downy feathers, rising above its surface, and so placed as to curl inwards, and completely conceal the eggs. These last are usually four or five in number, and pure white. They also have two broods in the season.

The voice of this species is low and guttural; they are more disposed to quarrel than the Barn Swallows, frequently fighting in the air for a quarter of an hour at a time, particularly in spring, all the while keeping up a low, rapid chatter. They also sail more in flying; but, during the breeding season, frequent the same situations in quest of similar food. They inhabit the northern Atlantic States as far as the District of Maine, where I have myself seen them; and my friend Mr. Gardiner informs me, that they are found on the coast of Long Island and its neighborhood. About the middle of July, I observed many hundreds of these birds sitting on the flat sandy beach near the entrance of Great Egg Harbor. They were also very numerous among the myrtles of these low islands, completely covering some of the bushes. One man told me, that he saw one hundred and two shot at a single discharge. For some time before their departure, they subsist principally on the myrtle berries, (*Myrica cerifera*,) and become extremely fat. They leave us early in September.

This species appears to have remained hitherto undescribed, owing to the misapprehension before mentioned. It is not, perhaps, quite so numerous as the preceding, and rarely associates with it to breed, never using mud of any kind in the construction of its nest.

The White-bellied Swallow is five inches and three quarters long, and twelve inches in extent; bill and eye, black; upper parts, a light, glossy, greenish blue; wings, brown black, with slight reflections of green; tail, forked, the two exterior feathers being about a quarter of an inch longer than the middle ones, and all of a uniform brown black; lores, black; whole lower parts, pure white; wings, when shut, extend about a quarter of an inch beyond the tail; legs, naked, short, and strong, and, as well as the feet, of a dark, purplish, flesh color; claws, stout.

The female has much less of the greenish gloss than the male, the colors being less brilliant; otherwise alike.

BANK-SWALLOW, OR SAND MARTIN. — HIRUNDO RIPARIA. — Fig. 165.

Lath. Syn. iv. p. 568, 10. — *Arct. Zool.* ii. No. 332. — L'Hirondelle de rivage, *Buff.* vi. 632. *Pl. enl.* 543, f. 2. — *Turt. Syst.* 629. — *Peale's Museum*, No. 7637.

HIRUNDO? RIPARIA? — Linnæus.*

Hirundo riparia, *Bonap. Synop.* p. 65. — Cotile riparia, *Boje.*

This appears to be the most sociable with its kind, and the least intimate with man, of all our Swallows; living together in large communities of sometimes three or four hundred. On the high sandy bank of a river, quarry, or gravel-pit, at a foot or two from the surface, they commonly scratch out holes for their nests, running them in a horizontal direction to the depth of two and sometimes three feet. Several of these holes are often within a few inches of each other, and extend in various strata along the front of the precipice, sometimes for eighty or one hundred yards. At the extremity of this hole, a little fine, dry grass, with a few large, downy feathers, form the bed on which their eggs, generally five in number, and pure white, are deposited. The young are hatched late in May; and here I have taken notice of the Common Crow, in parties of four or five, watching at the entrance of these holes, to seize the first straggling young that should make its appearance. From the clouds of Swallows that usually play round these breeding-places, they remind one at a distance of a swarm of bees.

The Bank Swallow arrives here earlier than either of the preceding; begins to build in April, and has commonly two broods in the season. Their voice is a low mutter. They are particularly fond of the shores of rivers, and, in several places along the Ohio, they congregate in immense multitudes. We have sometimes several days of cold rain and severe weather after their arrival in spring, from which they take refuge in their holes, clustering together for warmth, and have been frequently found at such times in almost a lifeless state with the cold; which circumstance has contributed to the belief that they lie torpid

---

* I have been unable to compare specimens of these birds from both countries, but, from the best authorities, I am induced to consider them identical. A doubt has been expressed by Vieillot, who considered the American bird as possessing a greater length of tarsus, and having that part also clothed with short plumes. Bonaparte has, again, from actual comparison, said they were entirely similar.

As in America, they are the first Swallow which appears in this country, arriving soon after the commencement of March. Their breeding-places are in the same situations, but often pierced into the banks for a much greater length. If the bank is sandy and easily scratched, seven or eight feet will scarcely reach the extremity — a wonderful length, if we consider the powers of the worker.

They are abundant over every part of North America, and were met by Dr. Richardson in the 68th parallel. "We observed," says that naturalist, "thousands of these Sand Martins fluttering at the entrance of their burrows, near the mouth of the Mackenzie, in the 68th parallel, on the 4th of July. They are equally numerous in every district of the Fur Countries, wherein banks suitable for burrowing exist; but it is not likely that they ever rear more than one brood north of the Lake Superior." — Ed.

all winter in these recesses. I have searched hundreds of these holes in the months of December and January, but never found a single Swallow, dead, living, or torpid. I met with this bird in considerable numbers on the shores of the Kentucky river, between Lexington and Danville. They likewise visit the sea-shore, in great numbers, previous to their departure, which continues from the last of September to the middle of October.

The Bank Swallow is five inches long, and ten inches in extent; upper parts, mouse colored, lower, white, with a band of dusky brownish across the upper part of the breast; tail, forked, the exterior feather slightly edged with whitish; lores and bill, black; legs, with a few tufts of downy feathers behind; claws, fine-pointed, and very sharp; over the eye, a streak of whitish; lower side of the shafts, white; wings and tail, darker than the body. The female differs very little from the male.

This bird appears to be in nothing different from the European species; from which circumstance, and its early arrival here, I would conjecture that it passes to a high northern latitude on both continents.

CHIMNEY SWALLOW. — HIRUNDO PELASGIA. — Fig. 166.

Lath. Syn. v. p. 583, 32. — *Catesb. Car. App.* t. 8. — Hirondelle de la Caroline, *Buff.* vi. p. 700. — Hirundo Carolinensis, *Briss.* ii. p. 501, 9. — Aculeated Swallow, *Arct. Zool.* ii. No. 335, 18. — *Turt. Syst.* p. 630. *Peale's Museum,* No. 7663.

CHÆTURA PELASGIA. — Stephens.[*]

Chætura pelasgia, *Steph. Cont. Sh. Zool. Sup.* p. 76. — Cypselus pelasgius, *Bonap. Synop.* p. 63.

This species is peculiarly our own, and strongly distinguished from all the rest of our Swallows by its figure, flight, and manners. Of the first of these, the representation in Fig. 166 will give a correct idea; its other peculiarities shall be detailed as fully as the nature of the subject requires.

[*] This species has been taken as the type of Mr. Stephens's genus *Chætura*. In form they resemble the Swifts, and the first observed distinction will be the structure of the tail, where the quills of the feathers are elongated, and run to a sharp or subulated point. The bill is more compressed laterally; the legs and feet possess very great muscularity; the toes alone are scaled, and the tarsi are covered with a naked skin, through which the form of the muscles is plainly visible; the claws are much hooked. All these provisions are necessary to their mode of life. Without some strong support, they could not cling for a great length of time in the hollows of trees, or in chimneys; and their tails are used, in the manner of a Woodpecker, to assist the power of the strong feet. They present, in a beautiful manner, the scansorial form among the *Fissirostres;* one species, the *Ch. senex,* (*Cypselus senex,* Temm.,) even feeds in the manner of the true Climbers, running up the steep rocks, assisted by its tail, in search of food.

The group will contain a considerable number. We have them from India, North and South America, and New Holland; but I am not aware that Africa has yet produced any species. — Ed.

This Swallow, like all the rest of its tribe in the United States, is migratory, arriving in Pennsylvania late in April or early in May, and dispersing themselves over the whole country wherever there are vacant chimneys in summer sufficiently high and convenient for their accommodation. In no other situation with us are they observed at present to build. This circumstance naturally suggests the query, Where did these birds construct their nests before the arrival of Europeans in this country, when there were no such places for their accommodation? I would answer, Probably in the same situations in which they still continue to build in the remote regions of our western forests, where European improvements of this kind are scarcely to be found, namely, in the hollow of a tree, which in some cases has the nearest resemblance to their present choice, of any other. One of the first settlers in the state of Kentucky informed me, that he cut down a large, hollow, beech tree, which contained forty or fifty nests of the Chimney Swallow, most of which, by the fall of the tree, or by the weather, were lying at the bottom of the hollow; but sufficient fragments remained, adhering to the sides of the tree, to enable him to number them. They appeared, he said, to be of many years' standing. The present site which they have chosen must, however, hold out many more advantages than the former, since we see that, in the whole thickly settled parts of the United States, these birds have uniformly adopted this new convenience, not a single pair being observed to prefer the woods. Security from birds of prey and other animals — from storms that frequently overthrow the timber, and the numerous ready conveniences which these new situations afford, are doubtless some of the advantages. The choice they have made certainly bespeaks something more than mere unreasoning instinct, and does honor to their discernment.

The nest of this bird is of a singular construction, being formed of very small twigs, fastened together with a strong, adhesive glue or gum, which is secreted by two glands, one on each side of the hind head, and mixes with the saliva. With this glue, which becomes hard as the twigs themselves, the whole nest is thickly besmeared. The nest itself is small and shallow, and attached by one side or edge to the wall, and is totally destitute of the soft lining with which the others are so plentifully supplied. The eggs are generally four, and white. This Swallow has two broods in the season. The young are fed at intervals during the greater part of the night, — a fact which I have had frequent opportunities of remarking, both here and in the Mississippi Territory. The noise which the old ones make, in passing up and down the funnel, has some resemblance to distant thunder. When heavy and long-continued rains occur, the nest, losing its hold, is precipitated to the bottom. This disaster frequently happens. The eggs are destroyed; but the young, though blind, (which they are for a considerable time,) sometimes scramble up along the vent, to which they cling like squirrels, the muscularity of their feet, and the sharpness of their claws, at this tender age, being remarkable. In this situation, they continue to be fed for perhaps a week or more. Nay, it is not uncommon for them voluntarily to leave the nest long before they are able to fly, and to fix themselves on the wall, where they are fed until able to hunt for themselves.

When these birds first arrive in spring, and for a considerable time after, they associate together every evening in one general rendezvous; those of a whole district roosting together. This place of repose, in the more unsettled parts of the country, is usually a large, hollow tree, open at top; trees of that kind, or *Swallow trees*, as they are usually called, having been noticed in various parts of the country, and generally believed to be the winter-quarters of these birds, where, heaps upon heaps, they dozed away the winter in a state of torpidity. Here they have been seen on their resurrection in spring, and here they have again been remarked descending to their deathlike sleep in autumn.

Among the various accounts of these trees that might be quoted, the following are selected, as bearing the marks of authenticity : —

"At Middlebury, in this state," says Mr. Williams, (*History of Vermont*, p. 16,) "there was a large, hollow elm, called by the people in the vicinity the Swallow tree. From a man who, for several years, lived within twenty rods of it, I procured this information. He always thought the Swallows tarried in the tree through the winter, and avoided cutting it down on that account. About the first of May, the Swallows came out of it in large numbers, about the middle of the day, and soon returned. As the weather grew warmer, they came out in the morning, with a loud noise, or roar, and were soon dispersed. About half an hour before sundown, they returned in millions, circulating two or three times round the tree, and then descending like a stream into a hole about sixty feet from the ground. It was customary for persons in the vicinity to visit this tree, to observe the motions of these birds : and when any person disturbed their operations, by striking violently against the tree with their axes, the Swallows would rush out in millions, and with a great noise. In November, 1791, the top of this tree was blown down twenty feet below where the Swallows entered : there has been no appearance of the Swallows since. Upon cutting down the remainder, an immense quantity of excrements, quills, and feathers, were found, but no appearance or relics of any nests.

"Another of these Swallow trees was at Bridport. The man who lived the nearest to it gave this account: The Swallows were first observed to come out of the tree in the spring, about the time that the leaves first began to appear on the trees ; from that season they came out in the morning about half an hour after sunrise. They rushed out like a stream, as big as the hole in the tree would admit, and ascended in a perpendicular line, until they were above the height of the adjacent trees ; then assumed a circular motion, performing their evolutions two or three times, but always in a larger circle, and then dispersed in every direction. A little before sundown, they returned in immense numbers, forming several circular motions, and then descended like a stream into the hole, from whence they came out in the morning. About the middle of September, they were seen entering the tree for the last time. These birds were all of the species called the House, or Chimney Swallow. The tree was a large, hollow elm; the hole at which they entered was about forty feet above the ground, and about nine inches in diameter. The Swallows made their first appearance in the spring, and their last appearance in the fall, in the vicinity of this tree; and the neighboring inhabitants had no doubt

31

but that the Swallows continued in it during the winter. A few years ago, a hole was cut at the bottom of the tree: from that time the Swallows have been gradually forsaking the tree, and have now almost deserted it."

Though Mr. Williams himself, as he informs us, is led to believe, from these and some other particulars which he details, "that the House Swallow, in this part of America, generally resides during the winter in the hollow of trees; and the Ground Swallows (Bank Swallows) find security in the mud at the bottom of lakes, rivers, and ponds;" yet I cannot, in the cases just cited, see any sufficient cause for such a belief. The birds were seen to pass out on the first of May, or in the spring, when the leaves began to appear on the trees, and, about the middle of September, they were seen entering the tree for the last time; but there is no information here of their being seen at any time during winter, either within or around the tree. This most important part of the matter is taken for granted, without the least examination, and, as will be presently shown, without foundation. I shall, I think, also prove that, if these trees had been cut down in the depth of winter, not a single Swallow would have been found, either in a living or torpid state! And that this was merely a place of rendezvous for *active, living birds*, is evident from the "immense quantity of excrements" found within it, which birds in a state of *torpidity* are not supposed to produce. The total absence of the relics of nests is a proof that it was not a breeding place, and that the whole was nothing more than one of those places to which this singular bird resorts immediately on its arrival in May, in which, also, many of the males continue to roost during the whole summer, and from which they regularly depart about the middle of September. From other circumstances, it appears probable that some of these trees have been for ages the summer rendezvous, or general roosting place of the whole Chimney Swallows of an extensive district. Of this sort I conceive the following to be one, which is thus described by a late traveller to the westward:—

Speaking of the curiosities of the state of Ohio, the writer observes — "In connection with this, I may mention a large collection of feathers found within a hollow tree, which I examined, with the Rev. Mr. Story, May 18th, 1803. It is in the upper part of Waterford, about two miles distant from the Muskingum. A very large sycamore, which, through age, had decayed and fallen down, contained in its hollow trunk, five and a half feet in diameter, and for nearly fifteen feet upwards, a mass of decayed feathers, with a small admixture of brownish dust, and the exuviæ of various insects. The feathers were so rotten, that it was impossible to determine to what kinds of birds they belonged. They were less than those of the Pigeon; and the largest of them were like the pinion and tail-feathers of the Swallow. I examined carefully this astonishing collection, in the hope of finding the bones and bills, but could not distinguish any. The tree, with some remains of its ancient companions lying around, was of a growth preceding that of the neighboring forest. Near it, and even out of its mouldering ruins, grow thrifty trees, of a size which indicate two or three hundred years of age." *

* HARRIS's *Journal*, p. 180.

Such are the usual roosting places of the Chimney Swallow in the more thinly settled parts of the country. In towns, however, they are differently situated; and it is matter of curiosity to observe that they frequently select the court-house chimney for their general place of rendezvous, as being usually more central, and less liable to interruption during the night. I might enumerate many places where this is their practice. Being in the town of Reading, Pennsylvania, in the month of August, I took notice of sixty or eighty of these birds, a little before evening, amusing themselves by ascending and descending the chimney of the court-house. I was told that, in the early part of summer, they were far more numerous at that particular spot. On the 20th of May, in returning from an excursion to the Great Pine Swamp, I spent part of the day in the town of Easton, where I was informed by my respected friend, Mordecai Churchman, cashier of the bank there, and one of the people called Quakers, that the Chimney Swallows of Easton had selected the like situation; and that, from the windows of his house, which stands nearly opposite to the court-house, I might, in an hour or two, witness their whole manœuvres.

I accepted the invitation with pleasure. Accordingly, a short time after sunset, the Chimney Swallows, which were generally dispersed about town, began to collect around the court-house, their numbers every moment increasing, till, like motes in the sunbeams, the air seemed full of them. These, while they mingled amongst each other seemingly in every direction, uttering their peculiar note with great sprightliness, kept a regular, circuitous sweep around the top of the court-house, and about fourteen or fifteen feet above it, revolving with great rapidity for the space of at least ten minutes. There could not be less than four or five hundred of them. They now gradually varied their line of motion, until one part of its circumference passed immediately over the chimney, and about five or six feet above it. Some, as they passed, made a slight feint of entering, which was repeated by those immediately after, and by the whole circling multitude in succession: in this feint, they approached nearer and nearer at every revolution, dropping perpendicularly, but still passing over; the circle meantime becoming more and more contracted, and the rapidity of its revolution greater, as the dusk of evening increased, until, at length, one, and then another, dropped in, another and another followed, the circle still revolving until the whole multitude had descended, except one or two. These flew off, as if to collect the stragglers, and, in a few seconds, returned, with six or eight more, which, after one or two rounds, dropped in, one by one, and all was silence for the night. It seemed to me hardly possible that the internal surface of the vent could accommodate them all, without clustering on one another, which I am informed they never do; and I was very desirous of observing their ascension in the morning, but, having to set off before day, I had not that gratification. Mr. Churchman, however, to whom I have since transmitted a few queries, has been so obliging as to inform me that, towards the beginning of June, the number of those that regularly retired to the court-house to roost was not more than one-fourth of the former; that, on the morning of the 23d of June, he particularly observed their reascension, which took place at a quarter past four, or twenty minutes before sunrise, and that they passed out in less than

three minutes ; that, at my request, the chimney had been examined
from above ; but that, as far down, at least, as nine feet, it contained
no nests ; though, at a former period, it is certain that their nests
were very numerous there, so that the chimney was almost choked,
and a sweep could with difficulty get up it. But then it was observed
that their place of nocturnal retirement was in another quarter of the
town. " On the whole," continues Mr. Churchman, " I am of opinion
that those who continue to roost at the court-house are male birds, or
such as are not engaged in the business of incubation, as that operation is going on in almost every unoccupied chimney in town. It is
reasonable to suppose, if they made use of that at the court-house for
this purpose, at least some of their nests would appear towards the
top, as we find such is the case where but few nests are in a place."

In a subsequent letter Mr. Churchman writes as follows : — " After
the young brood produced in the different chimneys in Easton had
taken wing, and a week or ten days previous to their total disappearance, they entirely forsook the court-house chimney, and rendezvoused,
in accumulated numbers, in the southernmost chimney of John Ross's
mansion, situated perhaps one hundred feet north-eastward of the
court-house. In this last retreat I several times counted more than
two hundred go in of an evening, when I could not perceive a single
bird enter the court-house chimney. I was much diverted one evening on seeing a cat, which came upon the roof of the house, and
placed herself near the chimney, where she strove to arrest the birds
as they entered, without success : she at length ascended to the chimney top and took her station, and the birds descended in gyrations
without seeming to regard grimalkin, who made frequent attempts to
grab them. I was pleased to see that they all escaped her fangs.
About the first week in the ninth month, [September,] the birds quite
disappeared ; since which I have not observed a single individual.
Though I was not so fortunate as to be present at their general assembly and council, when they concluded to take their departure, nor did
I see them commence their flight, yet I am fully persuaded that none
of them remain in any of our chimneys here. I have had access to
Ross's chimney, where they last resorted, and could see the lights out
from bottom to top, without the least vestige or appearance of any
birds. Mary Ross also informed me, that they have had their chimneys swept previous to their making fires, and, though late in autumn,
no birds have been found there. Chimneys, also, which have not been
used, have been ascended by sweeps in the winter without discovering
any. Indeed, all of them are swept every fall and winter, and I have
never heard of the Swallows being found, in either a dead, living, or
torpid state. As to the court-house, it has been occupied as a place
of worship two or three times a-week for several weeks past, and at
those times there has been fire in the stoves, the pipes of them going
into the chimney, which is shut up at bottom by brick work ; and, as
the birds had forsaken that place, it remains pretty certain that they
did not return there ; and, if they did, the smoke, I think, would be
deleterious to their existence, especially as I never knew them to
resort to kitchen chimneys where fire was kept in the summer. I
think I have noticed them enter such chimneys for the purpose of
exploring ; but I have also noticed that they immediately ascended,
and went off, on finding fire and smoke."

The Chimney Swallow is easily distinguished in air from the rest of its tribe here, by its long wings, its short body, the quick and slight vibrations of its wings, and its wide unexpected diving rapidity of flight; shooting swiftly in various directions without any apparent motion of the wings, and uttering the sounds *tsip tsip tsip tsee tsee* in a hurried manner. In roosting, the thorny extremities of its tail are thrown in for its support. It is never seen to alight but in hollow trees or chimneys; is always most gay and active in wet and gloomy weather; and is the earliest abroad in the morning, and latest out in evening, of all our Swallows. About the first or second week in September, they move off to the south, being often observed on their route, accompanied by the Purple Martins.

When we compare the manners of these birds, while here, with the account given by Captain Henderson of those that winter in such multitudes at Honduras, it is impossible not to be struck with the resemblance, or to suppress our strong suspicions that they may probably be the very same.

This species is four inches and a half in length, and twelve inches in extent; altogether of a deep sooty brown, except the chin and line over the eye, which are of a dull white; the lores, as in all the rest, are black; bill extremely short, hard, and black; nostrils, placed in a slightly elevated membrane; legs, covered with a loose purplish skin; thighs, naked and of the same tint; feet, extremely muscular; the three fore toes, nearly of a length; claws, very sharp; the wing, when closed, extends an inch and a half beyond the tip of the tail, which is rounded, and consists of *ten* feathers, scarcely longer than their coverts; their shafts extend beyond the vanes, are sharp-pointed, strong, and very elastic, and of a deep black color; the shafts of the wing quills are also remarkably strong; eye, black, surrounded by a bare blackish skin, or orbit.

The female can scarcely be distinguished from the male by her plumage.

PURPLE MARTIN. — HIRUNDO PURPUREA. — Fig. 167, Male;
Fig. 168, Female.

Lath. Syn. iv. p. 574, 21.   *Ibid.* iv. p. 575, 25.—*Catesb. Car.* i. 51.— *Arct. Zool.* ii. No. 333. — Hirondelle blue de la Caroline, *Buff.* vi. p. 674.   *Pl. enl.* 722.— Le Martinet couleur de pourpre, *Buff.* vi. p. 676. — *Turt. Syst.* 629. — *Edw.* 120. — Hirundo subis, *Lath.* iv. p. 575, 24. — *Peale's Museum,* Nos. 7645, 7646.

HIRUNDO PURPUREA. — Linnæus.*

Hirundo purpurea, *Bonap. Synop.* p. 64. — *North. Zool.* ii. p. 335. — The Purple
Martin, *Aud. Orn. Biog.* i. p. 114, pl. 22, male and female.

This well-known bird is a general inhabitant of the United States, and a particular favorite wherever he takes up his abode. I never met

---

* This bird, at first sight, almost, presents a different appearance from a Swallow; but, upon examination, all the members are truly that of *Hirundo,* developed, par-

31*

with more than one man who disliked the Martins, and would not permit them to settle about his house. This was a penurious, close-fisted German, who hated them, because, as he said, "they eat his *peas*." I told him he must certainly be mistaken, as I never knew an instance of Martins eating *peas*; but he replied with coolness, that he had many times seen them himself "blaying near the hife, and going *schnip, schnap,*" by which I understood that it was his *bees* that had been the sufferers; and the charge could not be denied.

This sociable and half-domesticated bird arrives in the southern frontiers of the United States late in February, or early in March: reaches Pennsylvania about the 1st of April, and extends his migrations as far north as the country round Hudson's Bay, where he is first seen in May, and disappears in August; so, according to the doctrine of torpidity, has, consequently, a pretty long annual nap, in those frozen regions, of eight or nine months under the ice! We, however, choose to consider him as advancing northerly with the gradual approach of spring, and retiring with his young family, on the first decline of summer, to a more congenial climate.

The summer residence of this agreeable bird is universally among the habitations of man; who, having no interest in his destruction, and deriving considerable advantage, as well as amusement, from his company, is generally his friend and protector. Wherever he comes, he finds some hospitable retreat fitted up for his accommodation, and that of his young, either in the projecting wooden cornice, on the top of the roof, or sign-post, in the box appropriated to the Blue Bird; or, if all these be wanting, in the Dove-house among the Pigeons. In this last case, he sometimes takes possession of one quarter, or tier, of the premises, in which not a Pigeon dare for a moment set its foot. Some people have large conveniences formed for the Martins, with many apartments, which are usually full tenanted, and occupied regularly every spring; and, in such places, particular individuals have been

---

ticularly the bill, to an extraordinary extent. The bill is very nearly that of a *Procnias*, or *Ptiliogonys*, but the economy of the bird presents no affinity to the berry-eaters; and the only difference in its feeding seems the preference to larger beetles, wasps, or bees, which its strength enables it to despatch without any danger to itself.

This bird exclusively belongs to the New World, and its migrations have a very extensive range. It makes its first appearance at Great Bear Lake on the 17th May, at which time the snow still partially covers the ground, and the rivers and lakes are fast bound in ice. In the middle of August, it retires again with its young brood from the Fur Countries. In a southern direction, Mr. Swainson observed numbers round Pernambuco, $8\frac{1}{2}$ degrees south of the line. They migrate in flocks, and at a very slow rate. The account of Mr. Audubon, who witnessed them, will show the possibility of much less powerful birds performing an immense distance, especially where every mile brings them an additional supply of food, and a more genial climate. I give his own words:— "I have had several opportunities, at the period of their arrival, of seeing prodigious flocks moving over that city (New Orleans) or its vicinity, at a considerable height, each bird performing circular sweeps as it proceeded, for the purpose of procuring food. These flocks were loose, and moved either westward, or towards the north-west, at a rate not exceeding four miles in the hour, as I walked under one of them, with ease, for upwards of two miles, at that rate, on the 4th of February, 1821, on the bank of the river below the city, constantly looking up at the birds, to the great astonishment of many passengers, who were bent on far different pursuits. My Fahrenheit's thermometer stood at 68°, the weather being calm and drizzly. This flock extended about a mile and a half in length, by a quarter of a mile in breadth." — Ed.

noted to return to the same box for several successive years. Even the solitary Indian seems to have a particular respect for this bird. The Chactaws and Chickasaws cut off all the top branches from a sapling near their cabins, leaving the prongs a foot or two in length, on each of which they hang a gourd, or calabash, properly hollowed out for their convenience. On the banks of the Mississippi, the negroes stick up long canes, with the same species of apartment fixed to their tops, in which the Martins regularly breed. Wherever I have travelled in this country, I have seen with pleasure the hospitality of the inhabitants to this favorite bird.

As superseding the necessity of many of my own observations on this species, I beg leave to introduce in this place an extract of a letter from the late learned and venerable John Joseph Henry, Esq. judge of the supreme court of Pennsylvania, a man of most amiable manners, which was written to me but a few months before his death, and with which I am happy to honor my performance : — "The history of the Purple Martin of America," says he, "which is indigenous in Pennsylvania, and countries very far north of our latitude, will, under your control, become extremely interesting. We know its manners, habitudes, and useful qualities here ; but we are not generally acquainted with some traits in its character, which, in my mind, rank it in the class of the most remarkable birds of passage. Somewhere (I cannot now refer to book and page) in Anson's *Voyage*, or in Dampier, or some other southern voyager, I recollect that the Martin is named as an inhabitant of the regions of southern America, particularly of Chili ; and, in consequence, from the knowledge we have of its immense emigration northward in our own country, we may fairly presume that its flight extends to the south as far as Terra del Fuego. If the conjecture be well founded, we may, with some certainty, place this useful and delightful companion and friend of the human race as the first in order of birds of passage. Nature has furnished it with a long, strong, and nervous pinion ; its legs are short, too, so as not to impede its passage ; the head and body are flattish ; in short, it has every indication from bodily formation, that Providence intended it as a bird of the longest flight. Belknap speaks of it as a visitant of New Hampshire. I have seen it in great numbers at Quebec. Hearne speaks of it in lat. 60 degrees north. To ascertain the times of the coming of the Martin to New Orleans, and its migration to and from Mexico, Quito, and Chili, are desirable data in the history of this bird ; but it is probable that the state of science in those countries renders this wish hopeless.

" Relative to the domestic history, if it may be so called, of the Blue Bird (of which you have given so correct and charming a description) and the Martin, permit me to give you an anecdote : — In 1800 I removed from Lancaster to a farm a few miles above Harrisburgh. Knowing the benefit derivable to a farmer from the neighborhood of the Martin, in preventing the depredations of the Bald Eagle, the Hawks, and even the Crows, my carpenter was employed to form a large box, with a number of apartments for the Martin. The box was put up in the autumn. Near and around the house were a number of well-grown apple-trees and much shrubbery, — a very fit haunt for the feathered race. About the middle of February, the Blue Birds came; in a short time they were very familiar, and took possession of the box; these consisted of two or three pairs. By the 15th of May, the Blue Birds had eggs, if not young. Now the Martins arrived in numbers, visited the box, and a severe conflict ensued. The Blue Birds, seemingly animated by their right of possession, or for the protection of their young, were victorious. The Martins regularly arrived about the middle of May, for the eight following years, examined the apartments of the box, in the absence of the Blue Birds, but were uniformly compelled to fly upon the return of the latter.

"The trouble caused you by reading this note you will be pleased to charge to the Martin. A box replete with that beautiful traveller, is not very distant from my bed-head. Their notes seem discordant because of their numbers; yet to me they are pleasing. The industrious farmer and mechanic would do well to have a box fixed near the apartments of their drowsy laborers. Just as the dawn approaches, the Martin begins its notes, which last half a minute or more; and then subside until the twilight is fairly broken. An animated and incessant musical chattering now ensues, sufficient to arouse the most sleepy person. Perhaps chanticleer is not their superior in this beneficial qualification; and he is far beneath the Martin in his powers of annoying birds of prey."

I shall add a few particulars to this faithful and interesting sketch by my deceased friend: — About the middle, or 20th, of April, the Martins first begin to prepare their nest. The last of these which I examined, was formed of dry leaves of the weeping willow, slender straws, hay, and feathers in considerable quantity. The eggs were four, very small for the size of the bird, and pure white, without any spots. The first brood appears in May, the second late in July. During the period in which the female is laying, and before she commences incubation, they are both from home the greater part of the day. When the female is sitting, she is frequently visited by the male, who also occupies her place while she takes a short recreation abroad. He also often passes a quarter of an hour in the apartment beside her, and has become quite domesticated since her confinement. He sits on the outside, dressing and arranging his plumage, occasionally passing to the door of the apartment as if to inquire how she does. His notes, at this time, seemed to have assumed a peculiar softness, and his gratulations are expressive of much tenderness. Conjugal fidelity, even where there is a number together, seems to be faithfully preserved by these birds. On the 25th of May, a male and female Martin took possession of a box in Mr. Bartram's garden. A day or two after, a second female made her appearance, and staid for several days; but, from the cold reception she met with, being frequently beat off by the male, she finally abandoned the place, and set off, no doubt, to seek for a more sociable companion.

The Purple Martin, like his half-cousin the King Bird, is the terror of Crows, Hawks, and Eagles. These he attacks whenever they make their appearance, and with such vigor and rapidity, that they instantly have recourse to flight. So well known is this to the lesser birds, and to the domestic poultry, that, as soon as they hear the Martin's voice engaged in fight, all is alarm and consternation. To observe with what spirit and audacity this bird dives and sweeps upon and around the

Hawk or the Eagle, is astonishing. He also bestows an occasional bastinading on the King Bird when he finds him too near his premises; though he will, at any time, instantly co-operate with him in attacking the common enemy.

The Martin differs from all the rest of our Swallows in the particu- lar prey which he selects. Wasps, bees, large beetles, particularly those called by the boys *goldsmiths*, seem his favorite game. I have taken four of these large beetles from the stomach of a Purple Martin, each of which seemed entire, and even unbruised.

The flight of the Purple Martin unites in it all the swiftness, ease, rapidity of turning, and gracefulness of motion of its tribe. Like the Swift of Europe, he sails much with little action of the wings. He passes through the most crowded parts of our streets, eluding the pas- sengers with the quickness of thought; or plays among the clouds, gliding about at a vast height, like an aërial being. His usual note, *peuo, peuo, peuo*, is loud and musical; but is frequently succeeded by others more low and guttural. Soon after the 20th of August, he leaves Pennsylvania for the south.

This bird has been described, three or four different times, by Eu- ropean writers, as so many different species, — the Canadian Swallow of Turton, and the Great American Martin of Edwards, being evi- dently the female of the present species. The Violet Swallow of the former author, said to inhabit Louisiana, differs in no respect from the present. Deceived by the appearance of the flight of this bird, and its similarity to that of the Swift of Europe, strangers from that country have also asserted that the Swift is common to North America and the United States. No such bird, however, inhabits any part of this continent that I have as yet visited.

The Purple Martin is eight inches in length, and sixteen inches in extent; except the lores, which are black, and the wings and tail, which are of a brownish black, he is of a rich and deep purplish blue, with strong violet reflections; the bill is strong, the gap very large; the legs also short, stout, and of a dark, dirty purple; the tail consists of twelve feathers, is considerably forked, and edged with purple blue; the eye full and dark.

The female measures nearly as large as the male; the upper parts are blackish brown, with blue and violet reflections thinly scattered; chin and breast, grayish brown; sides under the wings, darker; belly and vent, whitish, not pure, with stains of dusky and yellow ochre; wings and tail, blackish brown.

CONNECTICUT WARBLER. — SYLVIA AGILIS. — Fig. 169.

SYLVICOLA AGILIS. — Jardine.*

Sylvia agilis, *Bonap. Synop.* p. 84; *Nomenclature,* p. 163.

This is a new species, first discovered in the state of Connecticut, and twice since met with in the neighborhood of Philadelphia. As to its notes or nest, I am altogether unacquainted with them. The different specimens I have shot corresponded very nearly in their markings; two of these were males, and the other undetermined, but conjectured also to be a male. It was found in every case among low thickets, but seemed more than commonly active, not remaining for a moment in the same position. In some of my future rambles I may learn more of this solitary species.

Length, five inches and three quarters; extent, eight inches; whole upper parts, a rich yellow olive; wings, dusky brown, edged with olive; throat, dirty white, or pale ash; upper part of the breast, dull greenish yellow; rest of the lower parts, a pure rich yellow; legs, long, slender, and of a pale flesh color; round the eye, a narrow ring of yellowish white; upper mandible, pale brown; lower, whitish; eye, dark hazel.

Since writing the above, I have shot two specimens of a bird, which in every particular agrees with the above, except in having the throat of a dull buff color, instead of pale ash; both of these were females; and I have little doubt but they are of the same species with the present, as their peculiar activity seemed exactly similar to the males above described.

These birds do not breed in the lower parts of Pennsylvania, though they probably may be found in summer in the Alpine swamps and northern regions, in company with a numerous class of the same tribe that breed in these unfrequented solitudes.

* According to Bonaparte, this is a new species discovered by Wilson. Comparatively little is known regarding it. — Ed.

170. Night Hawk.171 Female.172 Whip poor will.173 Female.174 Red Owl.175 Warbling Flycatcher.176 Purple Finch.177 Brown Lark.

NIGHT HAWK. — CAPRIMULGUS AMERICANUS. — Fig. 170, MALE; Fig. 171, FEMALE.

Long-winged Goatsucker, *Arct. Zool.* No. 337. — *Peale's Museum*, No. 7723, male; 7724, female.

CAPRIMULGUS AMERICANUS? — WILSON.*

Caprimulgus Virginianus, *Bonap. Synop.* p. 62. — Chordeiles Virgimorus, *Sw. North. Zool.* ii. p. 337.

THIS bird, in Virginia and some of the southern districts, is called a Bat; the name Night Hawk is usually given it in the Middle and Northern States, probably on account of its appearance when on wing

---

* North America appears to contain three species of this curious genus, — the present one, with the following, and *C. Carolinensis*, afterwards described. The whole are nearly of like size, and, from the general similarity of marking which runs through the group, will somewhat resemble each other. Wilson may, therefore, claim the first merit of clearly distinguishing them, although he remained in uncertainty regarding the descriptions and synonyms of other authors. Vieillot appears to have described this species under the name of *C. popetue;* but, notwithstanding, I cannot help preferring that given by Wilson, particularly as it seems confined to the New World.

Bonaparte remarks, that the Night Hawks are among the Swallows what the Owls are among the *Falconidæ;* and, if we may be allowed the expression, the *C. Americanus* has more of the hirundine look than the others. The whole plumage is harder, the ends of the quills are more pointed, the tail is forked, and the rictus wants the strong array of bristles which we consider one of the essentials in the most perfect form of *Caprimulgus.* We may here remark, (although we know that there are exceptions,) that we have generally observed, in those having the tail forked, and, consequently, with a greater power of quick flight and rapid turnings, that the plumage is more rigid, and the flight occasionally diurnal. This is borne out, also, in our present species, which play " about in the air, over the breeding-place, even during the day;" and, in their migrations, "may be seen almost everywhere, from five o'clock until after sunset, passing along the Schuylkill and the adjacent shores."

The truly night-feeding species have the plumage loose and downy, as in the nocturnal Owls; the wings more blunted, and the plumules coming to a slender point, and unconnected; the tail rounded, and the rictus armed, in some instances, with very powerful bristles. Their organs of sight are also fitted only for a more gloomy light. They appear only at twilight, reposing during the day among furze or brake, or sitting, in their own peculiar manner, on a branch; but if inactive amidst the clearer light, they are all energy and action when their own day has arrived. To these last will belong the Common Night Hawk of Europe; and a detail, in comparison of its manners with those of our author, may assist in giving some idea of the truly nocturnal species, which are similar, so far as variation of country and circumstances will allow. They are thus, in a few lines, accurately described by a poet whom Wilson would have admired: —

> Hark! from yon quivering branch your direst foe,
> Insects of night, its whirring note prolongs,
> Loud as the sound of busy maiden's wheel:
> Then, with expanded beak, and throat enlarged
> Even to its utmost stretch, its 'customed food
> Pursues voracious.

It frequents extensive moors and commons, perhaps more abundantly if they are either interspersed or bordered with brush or wood. At the commencement of twi-

very much resembling some of our small Hawks, and from its habit of flying chiefly in the evening. Though it is a bird universally known in the United States, and inhabits North America, in summer, from

light, when they are first roused from their daily slumber, they perch on some bare elevation of the ground, an old wall or fence, or heap of stones, in a moss county on a *peat stack*, and commence their monotonous *drum*, or *whirr*, closely resembling the dull sound produced by a spinning-wheel, and possessing the same variation of apparent distance in the sound, a modification of ventriloquism, which is perceived in the croak of the Land Rail, or the cry of the Coot and Water Rail, or croaking of frogs; at one time, it is so near as to cause an alarm that you will disturb the utterer; at another, as if the bird had removed to the extreme limit of the listener's organs, while it remained unseen at a distance of perhaps not more than forty or fifty yards. At the commencement, this drumming sound seems to be continued for about ten or fifteen minutes, and occasionally during the night in the intervals of relaxation; it is only, however, when perched that it is uttered, and never for so great a length of time as at the first. Their flight is never high, and is performed without any regularity; sometimes straight forward and in gliding circles, with a slow, steady clap of the wings, in the middle of which they will abruptly start into the air for thirty or forty feet, resuming their former line by a gradual fall; at other times it will be performed in sudden jerks upwards, in the fall keeping the wings steady and closed over the back, skimming in the intervals near the ground, and still retaining the wings like some Gulls or Terns, or a Swallow dipping in the water, until they are again required to give the stroke upwards; all the while the tail is much expanded, and is a conspicuous object in the male, from the white spots on the outer feathers. When in woods, or hawking near trees, the flight is made in glides among the branches, or it flutters close to the summits, and seizes the various *Phalœnœ* which play around them. I once observed three or four of these birds hawking in this manner, on the confines of a spruce fir plantation, and after various evolutions, they balanced themselves for a few seconds on the very summit of the leading shoots. This was frequently repeated while I looked on. During the whole of their flight, a short snap of the bill is heard, and a sort of *click, click*, with the distinct sound of the monosyllable *whip*, or, to convey the idea better, the sound of a whip suddenly lashed without cracking. The female, when disturbed from her nest, flits or skims along the surface for a short distance; but I have never seen the young or eggs removed in the manner related of the American species, even after frequent annoyance. When the young are approached at night, before they are perfectly fledged, the old birds fly in circles round, approach very near, utter incessantly their clicking cry, and make frequent dashes at the intruder, like a Lapwing.

Among the Night Hawks, taking the form as understood to rank under *Caprimulgus* of Linnæus, we have a close resemblance of general form and characters, though there are one or two modifications which fully entitle the species to separation, and which work beautifully in the system of affinities or gradual development of form.* From these circumstances, Mr. Swainson has formed a new genus from our present species.

In color, the whole of *Caprimulgus* is very closely allied; "drest, but with nature's tenderest pencil touched," in various shades of brown, white, and russet; the delicate blending of the markings produce an effect always pleasing—often more so than in those which can boast of a more gorgeous apparel.

There is another structure in this bird, which has given rise to much conjecture among naturalists, particularly those whose opportunities of observation have been comparatively limited, and has been looked upon as a peculiarity existing in this genus only,—I allude to the serrature of the centre claw. This structure we also

---

* In some the mouth is furnished with very strong bristles, and in others it is entirely destitute of them, as may be seen in the species of North America. Again, the tail is square, round, or forked, sometimes to an extraordinary extent, as in the *C. psalurus*, of Azara, and in *C. acutus* the shafts of the feathers project beyond the webs, and remind us of the genus *Chœtura*. In some the tarsus is extremely short and weak, and covered with plumes to the very toes, in others long and naked. The wings are rounded or sharp-pointed; and in the Sierra Goatsucker we have the shaft of one of the secondaries running out to the length of twenty inches, with the web much expanded at the extremity, and presenting, no doubt, during flight, a most unique appearance. — ED.

Florida to Hudson's Bay, yet its history has been involved in considerable obscurity by foreign writers, as well as by some of our own country. Of this I shall endeavor to divest it in the present account.

Three species only, of this genus, are found within the United States, — the Chuck-will's-widow, the Whip-poor will, and the Night Hawk. The first of these is confined to those States lying south of Maryland; the other two are found generally over the Union, but are frequently confounded one with the other, and by some supposed to be one and the same bird. A comparison of Figs. 170 and 171 with Figs. 172 and 173, of the Whip-poor-will, will satisfy those who still have their doubts on this subject; and the great difference of manners which distinguishes each will render this still more striking and satisfactory.

On the last week in April, the Night Hawk commonly makes its first appearance in this part of Pennsylvania. At what particular period they enter Georgia, I am unable to say; but I find, by my notes, that, in passing to New Orleans by land, I first observed this bird in Kentucky on the 21st of April. They soon after disperse generally over the country, from the sea-shore to the mountains, even to the heights of the Alleghany; and are seen, towards evening, in pairs, playing about, high in air, pursuing their prey, wasps, flies, beetles, and various other winged insects of the larger sort. About the middle of May, the female begins to lay. No previous preparation or construction of a nest is made; though doubtless the particular spot has been reconnoitered and determined on. This is sometimes in an open space in the woods, frequently in a ploughed field, or in the corner of a cornfield. The eggs are placed on the bare ground, in all cases on a dry situation, where the color of the leaves, ground, stones, or other circumjacent parts of the surface, may resemble the general tint of the eggs, and thereby render them less easy to be discovered. The eggs are most commonly two, rather oblong, equally thick at both ends, of a dirty bluish white, and marked with innumerable touches of dark olive brown. To the immediate neighborhood of this spot the male and female confine themselves, roosting on the high trees adjoining during the greater part of the day, seldom, however, together, and almost always on separate trees. They also sit lengthwise on the branch, fence, or limb, on which they roost, and never across, like most other birds: this seems occasioned by the shortness and slender form of their legs and feet, which are not at all calculated to grasp the branch with sufficient firmness to balance their bodies.

find in many other genera, totally different from the present in almost every particular, and where the uses of combing its bristles or freeing itself from the vermin that persons have been willing to afflict this species with in more than ordinary proportions, could not be in any way applied. We find it among the *Ardeadæ, Platalea, Ibis, Phalacracorax,* and *Cursorius.* all widely differing in habit: the only assimilating form among them is the generally loose plumage. I have no hesitation in saying that the use of this structure has not yet been ascertained, and that, when found out, it will be different from any that has been yet suggested. The very variety of forms among which we find it, will bear this out; and the presence of it in *Caprimulgus* will more likely turn out the extreme limit of the structure, than that from which we should draw our conclusions. It is much more prevalent among the *Grallatores,* and our present form is the only one in any other division where it is at all found. — ED.

32

As soon as incubation commences, the male keeps a most vigilant watch around. He is then more frequently seen playing about in the air over the place, even during the day, mounting by several quick vibrations of the wings, then a few slower, uttering all the while a sharp, harsh squeak, till, having gained the highest point, he suddenly precipitates himself, head foremost, and with great rapidity, down sixty or eighty feet, wheeling up again as suddenly; at which instant is heard a loud booming sound, very much resembling that produced by blowing strongly into the bunghole of an empty hogshead; and which is doubtless produced by the sudden expansion of his capacious mouth, while he passes through the air, as exhibited in the figure on the plate. He again mounts by alternate quick and leisurely motions of the wings, playing about as he ascends, uttering his usual hoarse squeak, till, in a few minutes, he again dives with the same impetuosity and violent sound as before. Some are of opinion that this is done to intimidate man or beast from approaching his nest; and he is particularly observed to repeat these divings most frequently around those who come near the spot, sweeping down past them, sometimes so near, and so suddenly, as to startle and alarm them. The same individual is, however, often seen performing these manœuvres over the river, the hill, the meadow, and the marsh, in the space of a quarter of an hour, and also towards the fall, when he has no nest. This singular habit belongs peculiarly to the male. The female has, indeed, the common hoarse note, and much the same mode of flight; but never precipitates herself in the manner of the male. During the time she is sitting, she will suffer you to approach within a foot or two before she attempts to stir, and, when she does, it is in such a fluttering, tumbling manner, and with such appearance of a lame and wounded bird, as nine times in ten to deceive the person, and induce him to pursue her. This " pious fraud," as the poet Thomson calls it, is kept up until the person is sufficiently removed from the nest, when she immediately mounts and disappears. When the young are first hatched, it is difficult to distinguish them from the surface of the ground, their down being of a pale brownish color, and they are altogether destitute of the common shape of birds, sitting so fixed and so squat as to be easily mistaken for a slight prominent mouldiness lying on the ground. I cannot say whether they have two broods in the season; I rather conjecture that they have generally but one.

The Night Hawk is a bird of strong and vigorous flight, and of large volume of wing. It often visits the city, darting and squeaking over the streets at a great height, diving perpendicularly with the same hollow sound as before described. I have also seen them sitting on chimney-tops in some of the most busy parts of the city, occasionally uttering their common note.

When the weather happens to be wet and gloomy, the Night Hawks are seen abroad at all times of the day, generally at a considerable height; their favorite time, however, is from two hours before sunset until dusk. At such times they seem all vivacity, darting about in the air in every direction, making frequent short sudden turnings, as if busily engaged in catching insects. Even in the hottest, clearest weather, they are occasionally seen abroad, squeaking at short intervals. They are also often found sitting along the fences, basking themselves in the sun. Near the sea-shore, in the vicinity of extensive salt marshes, they are likewise very numerous, skimming over the meadows, in the manner of Swallows, until it is so dark that the eye can no longer follow them.

When wounded and taken, they attempt to intimidate you by opening their mouth to its utmost stretch, throwing the head forward, and uttering a kind of guttural whizzing sound, striking also violently with their wings, which seem to be their only offensive weapons; for they never attempt to strike with the bill or claws.

About the middle of August, they begin to move off towards the south; at which season they may be seen almost every evening, from five o'clock until after sunset, passing along the Schuylkill and the adjacent shores, in widely-scattered multitudes, all steering towards the south. I have counted several hundreds within sight at the same time, dispersed through the air, and darting after insects as they advanced. These occasional processions continue for two or three weeks; none are seen travelling in the opposite direction. Sometimes they are accompanied by at least twice as many Barn Swallows, some Chimney Swallows and Purple Martins. They are also most numerous immediately preceding a northeast storm. At this time also they abound in the extensive meadows on the Schuylkill and Delaware, where I have counted fifteen skimming over a single field in an evening. On shooting some of these, on the 14th of August, their stomachs were almost exclusively filled with crickets. From one of them I took nearly a common snuff-box full of these insects, all seemingly fresh swallowed.

By the middle or 20th of September, very few of these birds are to be seen in Pennsylvania: how far south they go, or at what particular time they pass the southern boundaries of the United States, I am unable to say. None of them winter in Georgia.

The ridiculous name Goatsucker, — which was first bestowed on the European species, from a foolish notion that it sucked the teats of the goats, because, probably, it inhabited the solitary heights where they fed, which nickname has been since applied to the whole genus, — I have thought proper to omit. There is something worse than absurd in continuing to brand a whole family of birds with a knavish name, after they are universally known to be innocent of the charge. It is not only unjust, but tends to encourage the belief in an idle fable that is totally destitute of all foundation.

The Night Hawk is nine inches and a half in length, and twenty-three inches in extent; the upper parts are of a very deep blackish brown, unmixed on the primaries, but thickly sprinkled or powdered on the back scapulars and head with innumerable minute spots and streaks of a pale cream color, interspersed with specks of reddish; the scapulars are barred with the same, also the tail-coverts and tail, the inner edges of which are barred with white and deep brownish black for an inch and a half from the tip, where they are crossed broadly with a band of white, the two middle ones excepted, which are plain deep brown, barred and sprinkled with light clay; a spot of pure white extends over the five first primaries, the outer edge of the exterior feather excepted, and about the middle of the wing; a triangular spot of white also marks the throat, bending up on each side of the neck; the bill is exceedingly small, scarcely one-eighth of an inch in length, and of a black color; the nostrils circular, and surrounded with a prominent rim; eye, large and full, of a deep bluish black; the legs are short, feathered a little below the knees, and, as well as the toes, of a purplish flesh color, seamed with white; the middle claw is pectinated on its inner edge, to serve as a comb to clear the bird of vermin; the whole lower parts of the body are marked with transverse lines of dusky and yellowish. The tail is somewhat shorter than the wings when shut, is handsomely forked, and consists of ten broad feathers; the mouth is extremely large, and of a reddish flesh color within; there are no bristles about the bill; the tongue is very small, and attached to the inner surface of the mouth.

The female measures about nine inches in length, and twenty-two in breadth; differs in having no white band on the tail, but has the spot of white on the wing, wants the triangular spot of white on the throat, instead of which there is a dully-defined mark of a reddish cream color; the wings are nearly black, all the quills being slightly tipped with white; the tail is as in the male, and minutely tipped with white; all the scapulars, and whole upper parts, are powdered with a much lighter gray.

There is no description of the present species in Turton's translation of Linnæus. The characters of the genus given in the same work are also in this case incorrect, viz. "mouth furnished with a series of bristles; tail not forked,"—the Night Hawk having nothing of the former, and its tail being largely forked.

WHIP-POOR-WILL. — CAPRIMULGUS VOCIFERUS. — Fig. 172, Male; Fig. 173, Female.

Peale's Museum, No. 7721, male; 7722, female.

CAPRIMULGUS VOCIFERUS. — Wilson.

Caprimulgus vociferus, *Bonap. Synop.* p. 61. — *North. Zool.* ii. p. 336. — Whip-poor-will, *Aud. Orn. Biog.* i. p. 422, pl. 32.

This is a singular and very celebrated species, universally noted over the greater part of the United States for the loud reiterations of his favorite call in spring; and yet personally he is but little known, most people being unable to distinguish this from the preceding species, when both are placed before them; and some insisting that they are the same. This being the case, it becomes the duty of his historian to give a full and faithful delineation of his character and peculiarity of manners, that his existence as a distinct and independent species may no longer be doubted, nor his story mingled confusedly with that of another. I trust that those best acquainted with him will bear witness to the fidelity of the portrait.

On or about the 25th of April, if the season be not uncommonly cold, the Whip-poor-will is first heard in this part of Pennsylvania, in the evening, as the dusk of twilight commences, or in the morning as soon as dawn has broke. In the state of Kentucky I first heard this bird on the 14th of April, near the town of Danville. The notes of this solitary bird, from the ideas which are naturally associated with them, seem like the voice of an old friend, and are listened to by almost all with great interest. At first they issue from some retired part of the woods, the glen, or mountain; in a few evenings, perhaps, we hear them from the adjoining coppice, the garden fence, the road before the door, and even from the roof of the dwelling-house, long after the family have retired to rest. Some of the more ignorant and superstitious consider this near approach as foreboding no good to the family, — nothing less than sickness, misfortune, or death, to some of its members. These visits, however, so often occur without any bad consequences, that this superstitious dread seems on the decline.

He is now a regular acquaintance. Every morning and evening his shrill and rapid repetitions are heard from the adjoining woods, and when two or more are calling out at the same time, as is often the case in the pairing season, and at no great distance from each other, the noise, mingling with the echoes from the mountains, is really surprising. Strangers, in parts of the country where these birds are numerous, find it almost impossible for some time to sleep; while to those long acquainted with them, the sound often serves as a lullaby to assist their repose.

These notes seem pretty plainly to articulate the words which have been generally applied to them, *whip-poor-will*, the first and last syllables being uttered with great emphasis, and the whole in about a second to each repetition; but when two or more males meet, their whip-poor-will altercations become much more rapid and incessant, as if each were straining to overpower or silence the other. When near, you often hear an introductory cluck between the notes. At these times, as well as at almost all others, they fly low, not more than a few feet from the surface, skimming about the house and before the door, alighting on the wood-pile, or settling on the roof. Towards midnight they generally become silent, unless in clear moonlight, when they are heard with little intermission till morning. If there be a creek near, with high precipitous bushy banks, they are sure to be found in such situations. During the day they sit in the most retired, solitary, and deep-shaded parts of the woods, generally on high ground, where they repose in silence. When disturbed, they rise within a few feet, sail low and slowly through the woods for thirty or forty yards, and generally settle on a low branch or on the ground. Their sight appears deficient during the day, as, like Owls, they seem then to want that vivacity for which they are distinguished in the morning and evening twilight. They are rarely shot at or molested; and from being thus transiently seen in the obscurity of dusk, or in the deep umbrage of the woods, no wonder their particular markings of plumage should be so little known, or that they should be confounded with the Night Hawk, whom in general appearance they so much resemble. The female begins to lay about the second week in May, selecting for this purpose the most unfrequented part of the wood, often where some brush, old logs, heaps of leaves, &c. had been

32 *

lying, and always on a dry situation. The eggs are deposited on the ground, or on the leaves, not the slightest appearance of a nest being visible. These are usually two in number, in shape much resembling those of the Night Hawk, but having the ground color much darker, and more thickly marbled with dark olive. The precise period of incubation, I am unable to say.

In traversing the woods one day in the early part of June, along the brow of a rocky declivity, a Whip-poor-will rose from my feet, and fluttered along, sometimes prostrating herself, and beating the ground with her wings, as if just expiring. Aware of her purpose, I stood still, and began to examine the space immediately around me for the eggs or young, one or other of which I was certain must be near. After a long search, to my mortification, I could find neither; and was just going to abandon the spot, when I perceived somewhat like a slight mouldiness among the withered leaves, and, on stooping down, discovered it to be a young Whip-poor-will, seemingly asleep, as its eyelids were nearly closed; or perhaps this might only be to protect its tender eyes from the glare of day. I sat down by it on the leaves, and drew it as it then appeared. It was probably not a week old. All the while I was thus engaged, it neither moved its body, nor opened its eyes more than half; and I left it as I found it. After I had walked about a quarter of a mile from the spot, recollecting that I had left a pencil behind, I returned and found my pencil, but the young bird was gone.

Early in June, as soon as the young appear, the notes of the male usually cease, or are heard but rarely. Towards the latter part of summer, a short time before these birds leave us, they are again occasionally heard; but their call is then not so loud — much less emphatical, and more interrupted than in spring. Early in September they move off towards the south.

The favorite places of resort for these birds are on high, dry situations; in low, marshy tracts of country, they are seldom heard. It is probably on this account that they are scarce on the sea-coast and its immediate neighborhood; while towards the mountains they are very numerous. The Night Hawks, on the contrary, delight in these extensive sea marshes; and are much more numerous there than in the interior and higher parts of the country. But no where in the United States have I found the Whip-poor-will in such numbers as in that tract of country in the state of Kentucky called the Barrens. This appears to be their most congenial climate and place of residence. There, from the middle of April to the 1st of June, as soon as the evening twilight draws on, the shrill and confused clamors of these birds are incessant, and very surprising to a stranger. They soon, however, become extremely agreeable; the inhabitants lie down at night lulled by their whistlings; and the first approach of dawn is announced by a general and lively chorus of the same music; while the full-toned *tooting*, as it is called, of the Pinnated Grouse, forms a very pleasing bass to the whole.

I shall not, in the manner of some, attempt to amuse the reader with a repetition of the unintelligible names given to this bird by the Indians, or the superstitious notions generally entertained of it by the same people. These seem as various as the tribes, or even families, with which you converse; scarcely two of them will tell you the same story. It is easy, however, to observe, that this, like the Owl, and other nocturnal birds, is held by them in a kind of suspicious awe, as a bird with which they wish to have as little to do as possible. The superstition of the Indian differs very little from that of an illiterate German, or Scots Highlander, or the less informed of any other nation. It suggests ten thousand fantastic notions to each, and these, instead of being recorded with all the punctilio of the most important truths, seem only fit to be forgotten. Whatever, among either of these people, is strange and not comprehended, is usually attributed to supernatural agency; and an unexpected sight, or uncommon incident, is often ominous of good, but more generally of bad, fortune to the parties. Night, to minds of this complexion, brings with it its kindred horrors, its apparitions, strange sounds, and awful sights; and this solitary and inoffensive bird, being a frequent wanderer in these hours of ghosts and hobgoblins, is considered by the Indians as being, by habit and repute, little better than one of them. All these people, however, are not so credulous: 1 have conversed with Indians who treated these silly notions with contempt.

The Whip-poor-will is never seen during the day, unless in circumstances such as have been described. Their food appears to be large moths, grasshoppers, pismires, and such insects as frequent the bark of old rotten and decaying timber. They are also expert in darting after winged insects. They will sometimes skim in the dusk, within a few feet of a person, uttering a kind of low chatter as they pass. In their migrations north, and on their return, they probably stop a day or two at some of their former stages, and do not advance in one continued flight. The Whip-poor-will was first heard this season [1811] on the 2d day of May, in a corner of Mr. Bartram's woods, not far from the house, and for two or three mornings after in the same place, where I also saw it From this time until the beginning of September, there were none of these birds to be found within at least one mile of the place; though I frequently made search for them. On the 4th of September, the Whip-poor-will was again heard for two evenings, successively, in the same part of the woods. I also heard several of them passing, within the same week, between dusk and nine o'clock at night, it being then clear moonlight. These repeated their notes three or four times, and were heard no more. It is highly probable that they migrate during the evening and night.

The Whip-poor-will is nine inches and a half long, and nineteen inches in extent; the bill is blackish, a full quarter of an inch long, much stronger than that of the Night Hawk, and bent a little at the point, the under mandible arched a little upwards, following the curvature of the upper; the nostrils are prominent and tubular, their openings directed forward; the mouth is extravagantly large, of a pale flesh color within, and beset along the sides with a number of long, thick, elastic bristles, the longest of which extends more than half an inch beyond the point of the bill, end in fine hair, and curve inwards; these seem to serve as feelers, and prevent the escape of winged insects; the eyes are very large, full, and bluish black; the plumage above is so variegated with black, pale cream, brown, and rust color, sprinkled and powdered in such minute streaks and spots, as to defy description; the upper part of the head is of a light brownish gray, marked with a longitudinal streak of black, with others radiating from it; the back is darker, finely streaked with a less deep black; the scapulars are very light whitish ochre, beautifully variegated with two or three oblique streaks of very deep black; the tail is rounded, consisting of ten feathers, the exterior one an inch and a quarter shorter than the middle ones, the three outer feathers on each side are blackish brown for half their length, thence pure white to the tips; the exterior one is edged with deep brown nearly to the tip; the deep brown of these feathers is regularly studded with light brown spots; the four middle ones are without the white at the ends, but beautifully marked with herring-bone figures of black and light ochre finely powdered; cheeks and sides of the head, of a brown orange or burnt color; the wings, when shut, reach scarcely to the middle of the tail, and are elegantly spotted with very light and dark brown, but are entirely without the large spot of white which distinguishes those of the Night Hawk; chin, black, streaked with brown; a narrow semi-circle of white passes across the throat; breast and belly, irregularly mottled and streaked with black and yellow ochre; the legs and feet are of a light purplish flesh color, seamed with white; the former feathered before, nearly to the feet; the two exterior toes are joined to the middle one, as far as the first joint, by a broad membrane; the inner edge of the middle claw is pectinated, and, from the circumstance of its being frequently found with small portions of down adhering to the teeth, is probably employed as a comb to rid the plumage of its head of vermin; this being the principal and almost only part so infested in all birds.

The female is about an inch less in length and in extent; the bill, mustaches, nostrils, &c., as in the male. She differs in being much lighter on the upper parts, seeming as if powdered with grains of meal; and, instead of the white on the three lateral tail-feathers, has them tipped for about three quarters of an inch with a cream color; the bar across the throat is also of a brownish ochre; the cheeks and region of the eyes are brighter brownish orange, which passes also to the neck, and is sprinkled with black and specks of white; the streak over the eye is also lighter.

The young was altogether covered with fine down, of a pale brown color; the shafts, or rather sheaths, of the quills, bluish; the point of the bill, just perceptible.

Twenty species of this singular genus are now known to naturalists; of these one only belongs to Europe, one to Africa, one to New Holland, two to India, and fifteen to America.

The present species, though it approaches nearer in its plumage to that of Europe than any other of the tribe, differs from it in being entirely without the large spot of white on the wing, and in being considerably less. Its voice, and particular call, are also entirely different.

Further to illustrate the history of this bird, the following notes are added, made at the time of dissection: — Body, when stripped of the skin, less than that of the Wood Thrush; breast-bone, one inch in length; second stomach, strongly muscular, filled with fragments of pismires and grasshoppers; skin of the bird, loose, wrinkly, and scarcely attached to the flesh; flesh, also loose, extremely tender; bones, thin and slender; sinews and muscles of the wing, feeble; distance between the tips of both mandibles, when expanded, full two inches, length of the opening, one inch and a half; breadth, one inch and a quarter; tongue, very short, attached to the skin of the mouth, its internal parts, or *os hyoïdes*, pass up the hind head, and reach to the front, like those of the Woodpecker; which enable the bird to revert the lower part of the mouth in the act of seizing insects, and in calling; skull, extremely light and thin, being semi-transparent, its cavity nearly half occupied by the eyes; aperture for the brain, very small, the quantity not exceeding that of a Sparrow; an Owl of the same extent of wing has at least ten times as much.

Though this noted bird has been so frequently mentioned by name, and its manners taken notice of by almost every naturalist who has written on our birds, yet personally it has never been described by any writer with whose works I am acquainted. Extraordinary as this may seem, it is nevertheless true; and in proof I offer the following facts : —

Three species only of this genus are found within the United States — the Chuck-will's-widow, the Night Hawk, and the Whip-poor-will. Catesby, in the eighth plate of his *Natural History of Carolina*, has figured the first, and, in the sixteenth of his *Appendix*, the second; to this he has added particulars of the Whip-poor-will, believing it to be that bird, and has ornamented his figure of the Night Hawk with a large bearded appendage, of which in nature it is entirely destitute. After him, Mr. Edwards, in his sixty-third plate, has in like manner figured the Night Hawk, also adding the bristles, and calling his figure the Whip-poor-will, accompanying it with particulars of the notes, &c., of that bird, chiefly copied from Catesby. The next writer of eminence who has spoken of the Whip-poor-will, is Mr. Pennant, justly considered as one of the most judicious and discriminating of English naturalists; but, deceived by "the lights he had," he has, in his account of the Short-winged Goatsucker,[*] (*Arct. Zool.*, p. 434,) given the size, markings of plumage, &c., of the Chuck-will's-widow; and, in the succeeding account of his Long-winged Goatsucker, describes pretty accurately the Night Hawk. Both of these birds he considers to be the Whip-poor-will, and as having the same notes and manners.

After such authorities, it was less to be wondered at, that many of our own citizens, and some of our naturalists and writers, should fall into the like mistake; as copies of the works of those English naturalists are to be found in several of our colleges, and in some of our public as well as private libraries. The means which the author of *American Ornithology* took to satisfy his own mind and those of his friends, on this subject, were detailed at large, in a paper published about two years ago, in a periodical work of this city,[†] with which extract I shall close my account of the present species : —

" On the question, Is the Whip-poor-will and the Night Hawk one

[*] The figure is, by mistake, called the *Long-winged* Goatsucker. See *Arctic Zoology*, vol. ii. pl. 18.
[†] *The Portfolio.*

and the same bird, or are they really two distinct species? there has long been an opposition of sentiment, and many fruitless disputes. Numbers of sensible and observing people, whose intelligence and long residence in the country entitle their opinion to respect, positively assert that the Night Hawk and the Whip-poor-will are very different birds, and do not even associate together. The naturalists of Europe, however, have generally considered the two names as applicable to one and the same species; and this opinion has also been adopted by two of our most distinguished naturalists, Mr. William Bartram, of Kingsessing,* and Professor Barton, of Philadelphia.† The writer of this, being determined to ascertain the truth by examining for himself, took the following effectual mode of settling this disputed point, the particulars of which he now submits to those interested in the question:—

"Thirteen of those birds usually called Night Hawks, which dart about in the air like Swallows, and sometimes descend with rapidity from a great height, making a hollow sounding noise like that produced by blowing into the bunghole of an empty hogshead, were shot at different times and in different places, and accurately examined, both outwardly and by dissection. Nine of these were found to be males, and four females. The former all corresponded in the markings and tints of their plumage; the latter also agreed in their marks, differing slightly from the males, though evidently of the same species. Two others were shot as they rose from the nests, or rather from the eggs, which, in both cases, were two in number, lying on the open ground. These also agreed in the markings of their plumage with the four preceding; and, on dissection, were found to be females. The eggs were also secured. A Whip-poor-will was shot in the evening, while in the act of repeating his usual and well-known notes. This bird was found to be a male, differing in many remarkable particulars from all the former. Three others were shot at different times during the day, in solitary and dark-shaded parts of the wood. Two of these were found to be females, one of which had been sitting on two eggs. The two females resembled each other almost exactly; the male also corresponded in its markings with the one first found; and all four were evidently of one species. The eggs differed from the former, both in color and markings.

"The differences between these two birds were as follows:—The sides of the mouth, in both sexes of the Whip-poor-will, were beset with ranges of long and very strong bristles, extending more than half an inch beyond the point of the bill; both sexes of the Night Hawk were entirely destitute of bristles. The bill of the Whip-poor-will was also more than twice the length of that of the Night Hawk. The long wing-quills, of both sexes of the Night Hawk, were of a deep brownish black, with a large spot of white nearly in their middle, and, when shut, the tips of the wings extended a little *beyond* the tail. The wing-quills of the Whip-poor-will, of both sexes, were beautifully

---

* *Caprimulgus Americanus*, Night Hawk, or Whip-poor-will. *Travels*, p. 292.
† *Caprimulgus Virginianus*, Whip-poor-will, or Night Hawk. *Fragments of the Natural History of Pennsylvania*, p. 3. See also *American Phil. Trans.*, vol. iv. pp. 208, 209, note.

spotted with light brown — had no spot of white on them — and, when shut, the tips of the wings did not reach to the tip of the tail by at least *two inches*. The tail of the Night Hawk was handsomely *forked*, the exterior feathers being the longest, shortening gradually to the middle ones; the tail of the Whip-poor-will was *rounded*, the exterior feathers being the shortest, lengthening gradually to the middle ones.

"After a careful examination of these and several other remarkable differences, it was impossible to withstand the conviction, that these birds belonged to two distinct species of the same genus, differing in size, color, and conformation of parts.

"A statement of the principal of these facts having been laid before Mr. Bartram, together with a male and female of each of the abovementioned species, and also a male of the Great Virginian Bat, or Chuck-will's-widow, after a particular examination, that venerable naturalist was pleased to declare himself fully satisfied: adding, that he had now no doubt of the Night Hawk and the Whip-poor-will being two very distinct species of *Caprimulgus*.

"It is not the intention of the writer of this to enter at present into a description of either the plumage, manners, migrations, or economy of these birds, the range of country they inhabit, or the superstitious notions entertained of them; his only object at present is the correction of an error, which, from the respectability of those by whom it was unwarily adopted, has been but too extensively disseminated, and received by too many as a truth."

RED OWL. — STRIX ASIO. — Fig. 174. — Female.

Little Owl, *Catesb.* i. 7. — *Lath.* i. 123. — *Linn. Syst.* 132. — *Arct. Zool.* ii. No. 117. — *Turton. Syst.* i. p. 166. — *Peale's Museum*, No. 428.

STRIX ASIO. — Linnæus. — Young.*

Strix Asio, *Bonap. Synop.* p. 36.

THIS is another of our nocturnal wanderers, well known by its common name, the *Little Screech Owl*; and noted for its melancholy quivering kind of wailing in the evenings, particularly towards the latter part of summer and autumn, near the farm-house. On clear moonlight nights, they answer each other from various parts of the fields or orchard; roost during the day in thick evergreens, such as cedar, pine, or juniper trees, and are rarely seen abroad in sunshine. In May, they construct their nest in the hollow of a tree, often in the orchard in an old apple tree; the nest is composed of some hay and a few feathers; the eggs are four, pure white, and nearly round. The young are at first covered with a whitish down.

* See p. 201 for description of the adult of this species, and note.

The bird represented in Fig. 174 I kept for several weeks in the room beside me. It was caught in a barn, where it had taken up its lodging, probably for the greater convenience of mousing; and, being unhurt, I had an opportunity of remarking its manners. At first, it struck itself so forcibly against the window as frequently to deprive it, seemingly, of all sensation for several minutes: this was done so repeatedly that I began to fear that either the glass or the Owl's skull must give way. In a few days, however, it either began to comprehend something of the matter, or to take disgust at the glass, for it never repeated its attempts; and soon became quite tame and familiar. Those who have seen this bird only in the day can form but an imperfect idea of its activity, and even sprightliness, in its proper season of exercise. Throughout the day, it was all stillness and gravity, — its eyelids half shut, its neck contracted, and its head shrunk, seemingly, into its body; but scarcely was the sun set, and twilight began to approach, when its eyes became full and sparkling, like two living globes of fire; it crouched on its perch, reconnoitred every object around with looks of eager fierceness; alighted and fed; stood on the meat with clenched talons, while it tore it in morsels with its bill; flew round the room with the silence of thought, and perching, moaned out its melancholy notes, with many lively gesticulations, not at all accordant with the pitiful tone of its ditty, which reminded one of the shivering moanings of a half-frozen puppy.

This species is found generally over the United States, and is not migratory.

The Red Owl is eight inches and a half long, and twenty-one inches in extent; general color of the plumage above, a bright nut brown, or tawny red; the shafts, black; exterior edges of the outer row of scapulars, white; bastard wing, the five first primaries, and three or four of the first greater coverts, also spotted with white; whole wing-quills, spotted with dusky on their exterior webs; tail, rounded, transversely barred with dusky and pale brown; chin, breast, and sides, bright reddish brown, streaked laterally with black, intermixed with white; belly and vent, white, spotted with bright brown; legs, covered to the claws with pale brown hairy down; extremities of the toes and claws, pale bluish, ending in black; bill, a pale bluish horn color; eyes, vivid yellow; inner angles of the eyes, eyebrows, and space surrounding the bill, whitish; rest of the face, nut brown; head, horned or eared, each horn consisting of nine or ten feathers of a tawny red, shafted with black.

WARBLING FLYCATCHER. — MUSCICAPA MELODIA. —
Fig. 175.

VIREO GILVUS, — Bonaparte.

Muscicapa gilva, *Vieill.* pl. 34. (auct. *Bonap.*) — Vireo gilvus, *Bonap. Synop.* p.
70. *Nomen.* sp. 123.

This sweet little Warbler is for the first time figured and described
in Fig. 175. In its general appearance it resembles the Red-eyed
Flycatcher; but, on a close comparison, differs from that bird in many
particulars. It arrives in Pennsylvania about the middle of April, and
inhabits the thick foliage of orchards and high trees; its voice is soft,
tender, and soothing, and its notes flow in an easy, continued strain,
that is extremely pleasing. It is often heard among the weeping willows and Lombardy poplars of this city; is rarely observed in the
woods; but seems particularly attached to the society of man. It
gleans among the leaves, occasionally darting after winged insects,
and searching for caterpillars; and seems by its manners to partake
considerably of the nature of the genus *Sylvia.* It is late in departing,
and I have frequently heard its notes among the fading leaves of the
poplar in October.

This little bird may be distinguished from all the rest of our songsters by the soft, tender, easy flow of its notes, while hid among the
foliage. In these there is nothing harsh, sudden, or emphatical; they
glide along in a kind of meandering strain, that is peculiarly its own.
In May and June it may be generally heard in the orchards, the borders
of the city, and around the farm-house.

This species is five inches and a half long, and eight inches and a
half in extent; bill, dull lead color above, and notched near the point,
lower, a pale flesh color; eye, dark hazel; line over the eye, and whole
lower parts, white, the latter tinged with very pale greenish yellow
near the breast; upper parts, a pale green olive; wings, brown, broadly
edged with pale olive green; tail, slightly forked, edged with olive;
the legs and feet, pale lead; the head inclines a little to ash; no white
on the wings or tail. Male and female nearly alike.

33

PURPLE FINCH. — FRINGILLA PURPUREA. — Fig. 176.

ERYTHROSPIZA PURPUREA. — Bonaparte.*

This bird is represented as he appears previous to receiving his crimson plumage, and also when moulting. By recurring to Fig. 28 of this work, which exhibits him in his full dress, the great difference of color will be observed to which this species is annually subject.

It is matter of doubt with me whether this species ought not to be classed with the *Loxia;* the great thickness of the bill, and similarity that prevails between this and the Pine Grosbeak, almost induced me to adopt it into that class. But respect for other authorities has prevented me from making this alteration.

When these birds are taken in their crimson dress, and kept in a cage till they moult their feathers, they uniformly change to their present appearance, and sometimes never after receive their red color. They are also subject, if well fed, to become so fat as literally to die of corpulency, of which I have seen several instances; being at these times subject to something resembling apoplexy, from which they sometimes recover in a few minutes, but oftener expire in the same space of time.

The female is entirely without the red, and differs from the present only in having less yellow about her.

These birds regularly arrive from the north, where they breed, in September; and visit us from the south again early in April, feeding on the cherry blossoms as soon as they appear. Of the particulars relative to this species, the reader is referred to the account already mentioned.

The individual represented in Fig. 176, measured six inches and a quarter in length, and ten inches in extent; the bill was horn colored; upper parts of the plumage, brown olive, strongly tinged with yellow, particularly on the rump, where it was brownish yellow; from above the eye, backwards, passed a streak of white, and another more irregular one from the lower mandible; feathers of the crown, narrow, rather long, and generally erected, but not so as to form a crest; nostrils, and base of the bill, covered with reflected brownish hairs; eye, dark hazel; wings and tail, dark blackish brown, edged with olive; first and second row of coverts, tipt with pale yellow; chin, white; breast pale cream, marked with pointed spots of deep olive brown; belly and vent, white; legs, brown. This bird, with several others marked nearly in the same manner, was shot 25th April, while engaged in eating the buds from the beech tree.

* See description of adult male, Note and Synonyms, p. 79.

BROWN LARK. — ALAUDA RUFA. — Fig. 177.

Red Lark, *Edw.* 297. — *Arct. Zool.* No. 279. — *Lath.* ii. 376. — L'Alouette aux joues brunes de Pennsylvanie, *Buff.* v. 58. — *Peale's Museum,* No. 5138.

ANTHUS LUDOVICIANUS. — Bonaparte.*

Synonyms of Anthus Ludovicianus, *Bonap.* (*from his Nomenclature,*) — "Alauda rubra, *Gmel. Lath.* — Alauda Ludoviciana, *Gmel. Lath.* — Alauda Pennsylvanica, *Briss.* — Farlouzanne, *Buff. Ois.* — Alouette aux joues brunes de Pennsylvanie, *Buff. Ois.* — Lark from Pennsylvania, *Ed. Glean.* p. 297. — Red Lark, *Penn. Brit. and Arct. Zool. Lath. Syn.* — Louisiana Lark, *Lath. Syn.*" — Anthus spinoletta, *Bonap. Synop.* p. 90.

In what particular district of the northern regions this bird breeds, I am unable to say. In Pennsylvania, it first arrives from the north about the middle of October; flies in loose scattered flocks; is strongly attached to flat, newly-ploughed fields, commons, and such like situations; has a feeble note, characteristic of its tribe; runs rapidly along the ground; and, when the flock takes to wing, they fly high, and generally to a considerable distance before they alight. Many of them continue in the neighborhood of Philadelphia all winter, if the season be moderate. In the Southern States, particularly in the lower parts of North and South Carolina, I found these Larks in great abundance in the middle of February. Loose flocks of many hundreds were driving about from one corn-field to another; and, in the low rice grounds, they were in great abundance. On opening numbers of these, they appeared to have been feeding on various small seeds, with a large quantity of gravel. On the 8th of April, I shot several of these birds in the neighborhood of Lexington, Kentucky. In Pennsylvania, they generally disappear, on their way to the north, about the beginning of May, or earlier. At Portland, in the District of Maine, I met with a flock of these birds in October. I do not know that they breed within the United States. Of their song, nest, eggs, &c. we have no account.

* *Anthus* is a genus of Bechstein's, formed to contain birds which have been generally called *Larks,* but which have a nearer resemblance to the *Motacillæ,* or Wagtails, and the Accentors. They are also allied to the *Seiurus* of Swainson.

The Prince of Musignano made this identical with the European Rock Lark, *Anthus aquaticus,* Bechst. *Alauda spinoletta,* Linn.; but in his observations on Wilson's nomenclature, saw reason to change his opinion, and it will now stand as *A. Ludovicianus* of that gentleman. Audubon has, on the other hand, placed it in his *Biography* as the European bird, but, I fear, with too slender comparison; and the same name is mentioned in the *Northern Zoology,* without comparing the arctic specimens with those of Britain or Europe. On these accounts, I rather trust to the observations of Bonaparte, which have been made from actual comparison. It must also be recollected, that the summer and winter dress of the *Anthi* differ very considerably in their shades.

Audubon has introduced in his *Biography* another *Anthus,* which he considers new, under the title of *pipiens.* It was only met with once, in the extensive prairies of the Northwestern States, where two were killed; and though allied to the common Brown Titlark, were distinguished by the difference of their notes. If these specimens were not preserved, the species must rest on the authority of Mr. Audubon's plate, and, of course, admitted with doubt. — Ed.

The Brown Lark is six inches long, and ten inches and a half in extent; the upper parts, brown olive, touched with dusky; greater coverts and next superior row, lighter; bill, black, slender; nostril, prominent; chin and line over the eye, pale rufous; breast and belly, brownish ochre, the former spotted with black; tertials, black, the secondaries brown, edged with lighter; tail, slightly forked, black; the two exterior feathers, marked largely with white; legs, dark purplish brown; hind heel, long, and nearly straight; eye, dark hazel. Male and female nearly alike. Mr. Pennant says that one of these birds was shot near London.

CAROLINA PIGEON, OR TURTLE DOVE. — COLUMBA CAROLINENSIS. — Fig. 178.

Linn. Syst. 286. — *Catesb. Car.* i. 24. — *Buff.* ii. 557, *Pl. enl.* 175. — La tourterelle de la Caroline, *Brisson*, i. 110. — *Peale's Museum*, No. 5088. — *Turton*, 479. — *Arct. Zool.* ii. No. 188.

ECTOPISTES CAROLINENSIS. — Swainson.

Genus Ectopistes, *Swain. N. Groups. Zool. Journ.* No. xi. p. 362. — Columba Carolinensis, *Bonap. Synop.* p. 119. — The Carolina Turtle-Dove, *Aud. Orn. Biog.* i. 91, pl. 17, male and female.

This is a favorite bird with all those who love to wander among our woods in spring, and listen to their varied harmony. They will there hear many a singular and sprightly performer, but none so mournful as this. The hopeless wo of settled sorrow, swelling the heart of female innocence itself, could not assume tones more sad, more tender and affecting. Its notes are four; the first is somewhat the highest, and preparatory, seeming to be uttered with an inspiration of the breath, as if the afflicted creature were just recovering its voice from the last convulsive sobs of distress; this is followed by three long, deep, and mournful moanings, that no person of sensibility can listen to without sympathy. A pause of a few minutes ensues, and again the solemn voice of sorrow is renewed as before. This is generally heard in the deepest shaded parts of the woods, frequently about noon and towards the evening.

There is, however, nothing of real distress in all this; quite the reverse. The bird who utters it wantons by the side of his beloved partner, or invites her by his call to some favorite retired and shady retreat. It is the voice of love, of faithful connubial affection, for which the whole family of Doves are so celebrated; and, among them all, none more deservingly so than the species now before us.

The Turtle Dove is a general inhabitant, in summer, of the United States, from Canada to Florida, and from the sea-coast to the Mississippi, and far to the westward. They are, however, partially migratory in the northern and middle states; and collect together in North and South Carolina, and their corresponding parallels, in great numbers,

178.Turtle Dove. 179.Hermit Thrush. 180.Tawney Thrush. 181.Pine Swamp Warbler. 182.Passenger Pigeon. 183.Blue Mountain Warbler.184.Hemlock W.185.Sharp Shinned Hawk.
186.Red Start.187.Yellow Rump.

during the winter. On the 2d of February, in the neighborhood of
Newbern, North Carolina, I saw a flock of Turtle Doves of many
hundreds; in other places, as I advanced farther south, particularly
near the Savannah River, in Georgia, the woods were swarming with
them, and the whistling of their wings was heard in every direction.

On their return to the north in March, and early in April, they disperse so generally over the country, that there are rarely more than
three or four seen together—most frequently only two. Here they
commonly fly in pairs, resort constantly to the public roads to dust
themselves and procure gravel; are often seen in the farmer's yard
before the door, the stable, barn, and other outhouses, in search of
food, seeming little inferior in familiarity, at such times, to the domestic Pigeon. They often mix with the poultry while they are fed
in the morning, visit the yard and adjoining road many times a-day,
and the pump, creek, horse trough, and rills for water.

Their flight is quick, vigorous, and always accompanied by a peculiar whistling of the wings, by which they can easily be distinguished
from the Wild Pigeon. They fly with great swiftness, alight on trees,
fences, or on the ground indiscriminately; are exceedingly fond of
buckwheat, hempseed, and Indian corn; feed on the berries of the
holly, the dogwood, and poke, huckleberries, partridgeberries, and the
small acorns of the live oak and shrub oak. They devour large quantities of gravel, and sometimes pay a visit to the kitchen garden for
peas, for which they have a particular regard.

In this part of Pennsylvania, they commence building about the
beginning of May. The nest is very rudely constructed, generally in
an evergreen, among the thick foliage of the vine, in an orchard, on
the horizontal branches of an apple tree, and, in some cases, on the
ground. It is composed of a handful of small twigs, laid with little
art, on which are scattered dry, fibrous roots of plants; and in this
almost flat bed are deposited two eggs of a snowy whiteness. The
male and female unite in feeding the young, and they have rarely
more than two broods in the same season.

The flesh of this bird is considered much superior to that of the
Wild Pigeon; but its seeming confidence in man, the tenderness of
its notes, and the innocency attached to its character, are, with many,
its security and protection; with others, however, the tenderness of its
flesh, and the sport of shooting, overcome all other considerations.
About the commencement of frost, they begin to move off to the south;
numbers, however, remain in Pennsylvania during the whole winter.

The Turtle Dove is twelve inches long, and seventeen inches in
extent; bill, black; eye, of a glossy blackness, surrounded with a pale
greenish blue skin; crown, upper part of the neck and wings, a fine
silky slate blue; back, scapulars, and lesser wing-coverts, ashy brown;
tertials spotted with black; primaries, edged and tipped with white;
forehead, sides of the neck, and breast, a pale brown vinous orange;
under the ear-feathers, a spot or drop of deep black; immediately
below which the plumage reflects the most vivid tints of green, gold,
and crimson; chin, pale yellow ochre; belly and vent, whitish; legs
and feet, coral red, seamed with white; the tail is long and cuneiform,
consisting of fourteen feathers; the four exterior ones, on each side,
are marked with black, about an inch from the tips, and white thence
33 *

to the extremity; the next has less of the white at the tip; these gradually lengthen to the four middle ones, which are wholly dark slate; all of them taper towards the points, the two middle ones most so.

The female is an inch shorter, and is otherwise only distinguished by the less brilliancy of her color; she also wants the rich silky blue on the crown, and much of the splendor of the neck; the tail is also somewhat shorter, and the white, with which it is marked, less pure.*

HERMIT THRUSH. — TURDUS SOLITARIUS. — Fig. 179.

Little Thrush, *Catesby*, i. 31. — *Edwards*, 296. — Brown Thrush, *Arct. Zool.* 337. No. 199. — *Peale's Museum*, No. 3542.

TURDUS SOLITARIUS. — Wilson.†

Turdus minor, *Bonap. Synop.* p. 75. — The Hermit Thrush, *Aud. Orn. Biog.* i. p. 303, pl. 58, male and female.

THE dark solitary cane and myrtle swamps of the southern states are the favorite native haunts of this silent and recluse species; and the more deep and gloomy these are, the more certain we are to meet with this bird flitting among them. This is the species mentioned in a former part of this work, while treating of the Wood Thrush, as having been figured and described, more than fifty years ago, by Edwards, from a dried specimen sent him by my friend Mr. William Bartram, under the supposition that it was the Wood Thrush, (*Turdus melodus.*) It is, however, considerably less, very differently marked, and altogether destitute of the clear voice and musical powers of that charming minstrel. It also differs, in remaining in the southern states during the whole year; whereas the Wood Thrush does not winter even in Georgia; nor arrives within the southern boundary of that state until some time in April.

The Hermit Thrush is rarely seen in Pennsylvania, unless for a few weeks in spring, and late in the fall, long after the Wood Thrush has left us, and when scarcely a summer bird remains in the woods. In both seasons it is mute, having only, in spring, an occasional squeak,

---

* In addition to their history by Wilson, Audubon mentions, that though regularly migrating in numbers, they are never in such vast extent as the Passenger Pigeon, from two hundred and fifty to three hundred being considered a large flock. He also mentions them differing in another more important particular — the manner of roosting. They prefer sitting among the long grass of abandoned fields, at the foot of the dry stalks of maize, and only occasionally resort to the dead foliage of trees, or the different species of evergreens. They do not sit near each other, but are dispersed over the field, whereas the Passenger Pigeon roosts in compact masses, on limbs of trees. In every respect, they run more into the Ground Doves, or Bronze-winged Pigeons, which similarity some parts of the plumage will strengthen. — ED.

† Bonaparte has wished to restore Gmelin's old name of *minor* to this bird, which Wilson had thought in some manner erroneous, on account of *solitarius* being preoccupied by another species. That, however, will rank in the genus *Petrocincla;* and Mr. Swainson has since described a small species under the name of *minor.* — ED.

like that of a young, stray chicken. Along the Atlantic coast, in New Jersey, they remain longer and later, as I have observed them there late in November. In the cane swamps of the Chactaw nation, they were frequent in the month of May, on the 12th of which I examined one of their nests on a horizontal branch, immediately over the path. The female was sitting, and left it with great reluctance, so that I had nearly laid my hand on her before she flew. The nest was fixed on the upper part of the body of the branch, and constructed with great neatness; but without mud or plaster, contrary to the custom of the Wood Thrush. The outside was composed of a considerable quantity of coarse, rooty grass, intermixed with horse-hair, and lined with a fine, green colored, thread-like grass, perfectly dry, laid circularly, with particular neatness. The eggs were four, of a pale, greenish blue, marked with specks and blotches of olive, particularly at the great end. I also observed this bird on the banks of the Cumberland River, in April. Its food consists chiefly of berries, of which these low swamps furnish a perpetual abundance, such as those of the holly, myrtle, gall bush, (a species of *vaccinium*,) yapon shrub, and many others.

A superficial observer would instantly pronounce this to be only a variety of the Wood Thrush; but, taking into consideration its difference of size, color, manners, want of song, secluded habits, differently-formed nest, and spotted eggs, all unlike those of the former, with which it never associates, it is impossible not to conclude it to be a distinct and separate species, however near it may approach to that of the former. Its food, and the country it inhabits, for half the year, being the same, neither could have produced those differences; and we must believe it to be now, what it ever has been, and ever will be, a distinct connecting link in the great chain of this part of animated nature; all the sublime reasoning of certain theoretical closet philosophers to the contrary notwithstanding.

Length of the Hermit Thrush, seven inches; extent, ten inches and a half; upper parts, plain deep olive brown; lower, dull white; upper part of the breast and throat, dull cream color, deepest where the plumage falls over the shoulders of the wing, and marked with large dark brown pointed spots; ear-feathers, and line over the eye, cream, the former mottled with olive; edges of the wings, lighter; tips, dusky; tail-coverts and tail, inclining to a reddish fox color. In the Wood Thrush, these parts incline to greenish olive. Tail, slightly forked; legs, dusky; bill, black above and at the tip, whitish below; iris, black, and very full; chin, whitish.

The female differs very little, — chiefly in being generally darker in the tints, and having the spots on the breast larger and more dusky.

TAWNY THRUSH. — TURDUS MUSTELINUS. — Fig. 180.

Peale's Museum, No. 5570.

TURDUS WILSONII. — Bonaparte.*

Turdus Wilsonii, *Bonap. Synop.* p. 76. — Merula Wilsonii, *North. Zool.* ii. p. 183.

This species makes its appearance in Pennsylvania from the south regularly about the beginning of May, stays with us a week or two, and passes on to the north and to the high mountainous districts to breed. It has no song, but a sharp chuck. About the 20th of May I met with numbers of them in the Great Pine Swamp, near Pocano; and on the 25th of September, in the same year, I shot several of them in the neighborhood of Mr. Bartram's place. I have examined many of these birds in spring, and also on their return in fall, and found very little difference among them between the male and female. In some specimens the wing-coverts were brownish yellow; these appeared to be young birds. I have no doubt but they breed in the northern high districts of the United States; but I have not yet been able to discover their nests.

The Tawny Thrush is ten inches long, and twelve inches in extent; the whole upper parts are a uniform tawny brown; the lower parts, white; sides of the breast, and under the wings, slightly tinged with ash; chin, white; throat, and upper parts of the breast, cream colored, and marked with pointed spots of brown; lores, pale ash, or bluish white; cheeks, dusky brown; tail, nearly even at the end, the shafts of all, as well as those of the wing-quills, continued a little beyond their webs; bill, black above and at the point, below at the base, flesh colored; corners of the mouth, yellow; eye, large and dark, surrounded with a white ring; legs, long, slender, and pale brown.

Though I have given this bird the same name that Mr. Pennant has applied to one of our Thrushes, it must not be considered as the same; the bird which he has denominated the Tawny Thrush being evidently, from its size, markings, &c. the Wood Thrush, already described.

No description of this bird has, to my knowledge, appeared in any former publication.

* The Wood Thrush, the Hermit Thrush, and our present species, have so much similarity to each other, that they have been confused together, and their synonyms often misquoted by different authors. From these circumstances, the name of *mustelinus*, given by Wilson to this species, is incorrect; and Bonaparte has deservedly dedicated it to its first describer, a name which ought now to be used in our systems. Another bird has been also lost sight of, in the alliance which exists among those, and which will now rank as an addition to the Northern Fauna, the *Turdus parvus* of Edwards, and confounded by Bonaparte with the *T. solitaria.* From the observations of Dr. Richardson and Mr. Swainson, in the second volume of the *Northern Zoology*, there can be little doubt of its being distinct from any of the others just mentioned, and will be distinguished by the more rufous tinge of the upper parts. It was met by the Overland Expedition on the banks of the Saskatchewan, where it is migratory in summer, and appears as nearly allied to the others in its habits, as it is in its external appearance. It spreads, no doubt, over the other parts of North America, getting more abundant, perhaps, towards the south. Mr. Swainson has received it from Georgia, and remarks that the rufous tinge of the plumage is much clearer and more intense in the southern specimens. — Ed.

PINE-SWAMP WARBLER.—SYLVIA PUSILLA.—Fig. 181.

VIREO SPHAGNOSA. — Jardine.*

Sylvia sphagnosa, *Bonap. Synop.* p. 85.

This little bird is, for the first time, figured or described. Its favorite haunts are in the deepest and gloomiest pine and hemlock swamps of our mountainous regions, where every tree, trunk, and fallen log, is covered with a luxuriant coat of moss, that even mantles over the surface of the ground, and prevents the sportsman from avoiding a thousand holes, springs, and swamps, into which he is insensibly plunged. Of the nest of this bird I am unable to speak. I found it associated with the Blackburnian Warbler, the Golden-crested Wren, Ruby-crowned Wren, Yellow-Rump, and others of that description, in such places as I have described, about the middle of May. It seemed as active in flycatching as in searching for other insects, darting nimbly about among the branches, and flirting its wings; but I could not perceive that it had either note or song. I shot three, one male and two females. I have no doubt that they breed in those solitary swamps, as well as many other of their associates.

The Pine-Swamp Warbler is four inches and a quarter long, and seven inches and a quarter in extent; bill, black, not notched, but furnished with bristles; upper parts, a deep green olive, with slight bluish reflections, particularly on the edges of the tail and on the head; wings, dusky, but so broadly edged with olive green as to appear wholly of that tint; immediately below the primary coverts, there is a single triangular spot of yellowish white; no other part of the wings is white; the three exterior tail-feathers, with a spot of white on their inner vanes; the tail is slightly forked; from the nostrils over the eye, extends a fine line of white, and the lower eyelid is touched with the same tint; lores, blackish; sides of the neck and auriculars, green olive; whole lower parts, pale yellow ochre, with a tinge of greenish; duskiest on the throat; legs, long and flesh coloured.

The plumage of the female differs in nothing from that of the male.

---

* This species seems evidently a *Vireo.* Bonaparte thus observes, in his Nomenclature, and we have used his name:— "A new species, called by a preoccupied name, but altered in the Index to that of *leucoptera,* which is used for one of Vieillot's species, and was, therefore, changed to that of *palustris,* by Stephens; but as this also is preoccupied, I propose for it the name of *S. sphagnosa.*"—Ed.

PASSENGER PIGEON. — COLUMBA MIGRATORIA. — Fig. 182.

Catesby, i. 23. — *Linn. Syst.* 285. — *Turton,* 479. — *Arct. Zool.* p. 322, No.
187. — *Briss.* i. 100. — *Buff.* ii. 527. — *Peale's Museum,* No. 5084.

ECTOPISTES MIGRATORIA. — Swainson.*

Ectopistes, *Swain. N. Groups, Zool. Journ.* No. xi. p. 362. — Columba migratoria
Bonap. Synop. p. 120. — The Passenger Pigeon, *Aud. Orn. Biog.* i. p. 319, male
and female. — Columba (Ectopistes) migratoria, *North. Zool.* ii. p. 363.

THIS remarkable bird merits a distinguished place in the annals of
our feathered tribes, — a claim to which I shall endeavor to do justice ;
and, though it would be impossible, in the bounds allotted to this

* In all the large natural groups which have already come under our notice, we
have seen a great variation of form, though the essential parts of it were always
beautifully kept up. In the present immense family, Mr. Swainson has characterized the Passenger Pigeons under the name of *Ectopistes,* at once distinguished
by their graceful and lengthened make, and well represented by the common *Columba migratoria* and the Carolina Pigeon of our author. The nicer distinctions
will be found in the slender bill, and the relative proportions of the feet and wings.
As far as our knowledge extends, the group is confined to both the continents of
America. A single individual of this species was shot, while perched on a wall, in
the neighborhood of a pigeon-house at Westhall, in the parish of Monymeal, Fifeshire,
in December, 1825. It came into the possession of Dr. Fleming, of Flisk, who has
recorded its occurrence in his *British Zoology.* He remarks, that the feathers were
quite fresh and entire, like a wild bird; but we can only rank it as a very rare
straggler.
    Mr. Audubon mentions having brought over 350 of these birds, when he last vis-
ited this country, and distributed them among different country gentlemen. Lord
Stanley received fifty of them, which he intended to turn out in his park, in the
neighborhood of Liverpool.
    We have the following additional account from Audubon, of their flights, roost-
ing, and destruction, in every thing corroborating the history of Wilson, but too
interesting to pass by : —
    "Their great power of flight enables them to survey and pass over an astonish-
ing extent of country in a very short time. Thus, Pigeons have been killed in the
neighborhood of New York, with their crops full of rice, which they must have
collected in the fields of Georgia and Carolina, these districts being the nearest in
which they could possibly have procured a supply of food. As their power of digestion is so great, that they will decompose food entirely in twelve hours, they
must, in this case, have travelled between three and four hundred miles in six hours,
which shows their speed to be, at an average, about one mile in a minute. A velocity such as this, would enable one of these birds, were it so inclined, to visit the
European continent in less than three days.
    "In the autumn of 1813, I left my house at Henderson, on the banks of the
Ohio, on my way to Louisville. In passing over the Barrens, a few miles beyond
Hardensburgh, I observed the Pigeons flying from northeast to southwest, in greater
numbers than I thought I had ever seen them before. I travelled on, and still met
more, the farther I proceeded. The air was literally filled with Pigeons. The light
of the noon day was obscured as by an eclipse. The dung fell in spots not unlike
melting flakes of snow ; and the continued buzz of wings had a tendency to lull
my senses to repose.
    "Before sunset I reached Louisville, distant from Hardensburgh fifty-five miles.
The Pigeons were still passing in undiminished numbers, and continued to do so for
three days in succession. The people were all in arms. The banks of the Ohio
were crowded with men and boys, incessantly shooting at the pilgrims, which there

account, to relate all I have seen and heard of this species, yet no circumstance shall be omitted with which I am acquainted, (however extraordinary some of these may appear,) that may tend to illustrate its history.

flew lower as they passed the river. Multitudes were thus destroyed. For a week or more, the population fed on no other flesh than that of Pigeons. The atmosphere, during this time, was strongly impregnated with the peculiar odor which emanates from the species." In estimating the number of these mighty flocks, and the food consumed by them daily, he adds, — "Let us take a column of one mile in breadth, which is far below the average size, and suppose it passing over us, at the rate of one mile per minute. This will give us a parallelogram of 180 miles by 1, covering 180 square miles; and, allowing two Pigeons to the square yard, we have one billion one hundred and fifteen millions one hundred and thirty-six thousand Pigeons in one flock; and, as every Pigeon consumes fully half a pint per day, the quantity required to feed such a flock, must be eight millions seven hundred and twelve thousand bushels per day."

The accounts of their roosting places are as remarkable: —

"Let us now, kind reader, inspect their place of nightly rendezvous: — It was, as is always the case, in a portion of the forest where the trees were of great magnitude, and where there was little underwood. I rode through it upwards of forty miles, and, crossing it at different parts, found its average breadth to be rather more than three miles. Few Pigeons were to be seen before sunset; but a great number of persons, with horses and wagons, guns and ammunition, had already established encampments on the borders. Two farmers from the vicinity of Russelsville, distant more than a hundred miles, had driven upwards of three hundred hogs, to be fattened on the Pigeons which were to be slaughtered. Here and there, the people employed in plucking and salting what had already been procured, were seen sitting in the midst of large piles of these birds. The dung lay several inches deep, covering the whole extent of the roosting place, like a bed of snow. Many trees, two feet in diameter, I observed, were broken off at no great distance from the ground; and the branches of many of the largest and tallest had given way, as if the forest had been swept by a tornado. Every thing proved to me, that the number of birds resorting to this part of the forest, must be immense beyond conception. As the period of their arrival approached, their foes anxiously prepared to seize them. Some were furnished with iron pots, containing sulphur, others with torches of pine knots, many with poles, and the rest with guns. The sun was lost to our view; yet not a Pigeon had arrived. Every thing was ready, and all eyes were gazing on the clear sky, which appeared in glimpses amidst the tall trees. Suddenly, there burst forth a general cry of 'Here they come!' The noise which they made, though yet distant, reminded me of a hard gale at sea, passing through the rigging of a close-reefed vessel. As the birds arrived, and passed over me, I felt a current of air that surprised me. Thousands were soon knocked down by the polemen. The current of birds, however, still kept increasing. The fires were lighted, and a most magnificent, as well as a wonderful and terrifying sight, presented itself. The Pigeons, coming in by thousands, alighted everywhere, one above another, until solid masses, as large as hogsheads, were formed on every tree, in all directions. Here and there the perches gave way under the weight with a crash, and, falling to the ground, destroyed hundreds of the birds beneath, forcing down the dense groups with which every stick was loaded. It was a scene of uproar and confusion. I found it quite useless to speak, or even to shout, to those persons who were nearest me. The reports, even, of the nearest guns, were seldom heard; and I knew of the firing, only by seeing the shooters reloading. No one dared venture within the line of devastation; the hogs had been penned up in due time, the picking up of the dead and wounded being left for the next morning's employment. The Pigeons were constantly coming; and it was past midnight before I perceived a decrease in the number of those that arrived. The uproar continued, however, the whole night; and, as I was anxious to know to what distance the sound reached, I sent off a man, accustomed to perambulate the forest, who, returning two hours afterwards, informed me he had heard it distinctly when three miles from the spot. Towards the approach of day, the noise rather subsided; but, long ere objects were at all distinguishable, the Pigeons began to move off, in a direction quite

The Wild Pigeon of the United States inhabits a wide and extensive region of North America, on this side of the great Stony Mountains, beyond which, to the westward, I have not heard of their being seen. According to Mr. Hutchins, they abound in the country round Hudson's Bay, where they usually remain as late as December, feeding, when the ground is covered with snow, on the buds of juniper. They spread over the whole of Canada; were seen by Captain Lewis and his party near the Great Falls of the Missouri, upwards of 2500 miles from its mouth, reckoning the meanderings of the river; were also met with in the interior of Louisiana by Colonel Pike; and extend their range as far south as the Gulf of Mexico; occasionally visiting or breeding in almost every quarter of the United States.

But the most remarkable characteristic of these birds is their associating together, both in their migrations, and also during the period of incubation, in such prodigious numbers, as almost to surpass belief; and which has no parallel among any other of the feathered tribes on the face of the earth, with which naturalists are acquainted.

These migrations appear to be undertaken rather in quest of food, than merely to avoid the cold of the climate; since we find them lingering in the northern regions, around Hudson's Bay, so late as December; and, since their appearance is so casual and irregular, sometimes not visiting certain districts for several years in any considerable numbers, while at other times they are innumerable. I have witnessed these migrations in the Genesee country, often in Pennsylvania, and also in various parts of Virginia, with amazement; but all that I had then seen of them were mere straggling parties, when compared with the congregated millions which I have since beheld in our western forests, in the states of Ohio, Kentucky, and the Indiana territory. These fertile and extensive regions abound with the nutritious beech nut, which constitutes the chief food of the Wild Pigeon. In seasons when these nuts are abundant, corresponding multitudes of Pigeons may be confidently expected. It sometimes happens that, having consumed the whole produce of the beech trees, in an extensive district, they discover another, at the distance perhaps of sixty or eighty miles, to which they regularly repair every morning, and return as regularly in the course of the day, or in the evening, to their place of general rendezvous, or, as it is usually called, the roosting place. These roosting places are always in the woods, and sometimes occupy a large extent of forest. When they have frequented one of these places for some time, the appearance it exhibits is surprising. The ground is covered to the depth of several inches with their dung; all the tender grass and underwood destroyed; the surface strewed with large limbs of trees, broken down by the weight of the birds clustering one above

different from that in which they had arrived the evening before; and, at sunrise, all that were able to fly had disappeared. The howlings of the wolves now reached our ears; and the foxes, lynxes, cougars, bears, raccoons, opossums, and pole-cats, were seen sneaking off from the spot, whilst Eagles and Hawks, of different species, accompanied by a crowd of Vultures, came to supplant them, and enjoy their share of the spoil. It was then that the authors of all this devastation began their entry amongst the dead, the dying, and the mangled. The Pigeons were picked up and piled in heaps, until each had as many as he could possibly dispose of, when the hogs were let loose to feed on the remainder." — Ed.

another; and the trees themselves, for thousands of acres, killed as completely as if girdled with an axe. The marks of this desolation remain for many years on the spot; and numerous places could be pointed out, where, for several years after, scarcely a single vegetable made its appearance.

When these roosts are first discovered, the inhabitants, from considerable distances, visit them in the night, with guns, clubs, long poles, pots of sulphur, and various other engines of destruction. In a few hours, they fill many sacks, and load their horses with them. By the Indians, a Pigeon roost, or breeding place, is considered an important source of national profit and dependence for that season; and all their active ingenuity is exercised on the occasion. The breeding place differs from the former in its greater extent. In the western countries above mentioned, these are generally in beech woods, and often extend, in nearly a straight line, across the country for a great way. Not far from Shelbyville, in the state of Kentucky, about five years ago, there was one of these breeding places, which stretched through the woods in nearly a north and south direction; was several miles in breadth, and was said to be upwards of forty miles in extent! In this tract, almost every tree was furnished with nests, wherever the branches could accommodate them. The Pigeons made their first appearance there about the 10th of April, and left it altogether, with their young, before the 25th of May.

As soon as the young were fully grown, and before they left the nests, numerous parties of the inhabitants, from all parts of the adjacent country, came with wagons, axes, beds, cooking utensils, many of them accompanied by the greater part of their families, and encamped for several days at this immense nursery. Several of them informed me, that the noise in the woods was so great as to terrify their horses, and that it was difficult for one person to hear another speak, without bawling in his ear. The ground was strewed with broken limbs of trees, eggs, and young Squab Pigeons, which had been precipitated from above, and on which herds of hogs were fattening. Hawks, Buzzards, and Eagles, were sailing about in great numbers, and seizing the Squabs from their nests at pleasure; while, from twenty feet upwards to the tops of the trees, the view through the woods presented a perpetual tumult of crowding and fluttering multitudes of Pigeons, their wings roaring like thunder, mingled with the frequent crash of falling timber; for now the axe-men were at work, cutting down those trees that seemed to be most crowded with nests, and contrived to fell them in such a manner, that, in their descent, they might bring down several others; by which means the falling of one large tree sometimes produced two hundred Squabs, little inferior in size to the old ones, and almost one mass of fat. On some single trees, upwards of one hundred nests were found, each containing *one* young only; a circumstance, in the history of this bird, not generally known to naturalists. It was dangerous to walk under these flying and fluttering millions, from the frequent fall of large branches, broken down by the weight of the multitudes above, and which, in their descent, often destroyed numbers of the birds themselves; while the clothes of those engaged in traversing the woods were completely covered with the excrements of the Pigeons.

34

These circumstances were related to me by many of the most respectable part of the community in that quarter, and were confirmed, in part, by what I myself witnessed. I passed for several miles through this same breeding place, where every tree was spotted with nests, the remains of those above described. In many instances, I counted upwards of ninety nests on a single tree; but the Pigeons had abandoned this place for another, sixty or eighty miles off, towards Green River, where they were said at that time to be equally numerous. From the great numbers that were constantly passing over head to or from that quarter, I had no doubt of the truth of this statement. The mast had been chiefly consumed in Kentucky, and the Pigeons, every morning, a little before sunrise, set out for the Indiana territory, the nearest part of which was about sixty miles distant. Many of these returned before ten o'clock, and the great body generally appeared, on their return, a little after noon.

I had left the public road to visit the remains of the breeding place near Shelbyville, and was traversing the woods with my gun, on my way to Frankfort, when, about one o'clock, the Pigeons, which I had observed flying the greater part of the morning northerly, began to return, in such immense numbers as I never before had witnessed. Coming to an opening, by the side of a creek called the Benson, where I had a more uninterrupted view, I was astonished at their appearance. They were flying, with great steadiness and rapidity, at a height beyond gunshot, in several strata deep, and so close together, that, could shot have reached them, one discharge could not have failed of bringing down several individuals. From right to left, far as the eye could reach, the breadth of this vast procession extended, seeming every where equally crowded. Curious to determine how long this appearance would continue, I took out my watch to note the time, and sat down to observe them. It was then half past one. I sat for more than an hour, but instead of a diminution of this prodigious procession, it seemed rather to increase both in numbers and rapidity; and, anxious to reach Frankfort before night, I rose and went on. About four o'clock in the afternoon I crossed the Kentucky River, at the town of Frankfort, at which time the living torrent above my head seemed as numerous and as extensive as ever. Long after this I observed them, in large bodies, that continued to pass for six or eight minutes, and these again were followed by other detached bodies, all moving in the same south-east direction, till after six in the evening. The great breadth of front which this mighty multitude preserved would seem to intimate a corresponding breadth of their breeding place, which, by several gentlemen, who had lately passed through part of it, was stated to me at several miles. It was said to be in Green county, and that the young began to fly about the middle of March. On the 17th of April, forty-nine miles beyond Danville, and not far from Green River, I crossed this same breeding place, where the nests, for more than three miles, spotted every tree: the leaves not being yet out, I had a fair prospect of them, and was really astonished at their numbers. A few bodies of Pigeons lingered yet in different parts of the woods, the roaring of whose wings was heard in various quarters around me.

All accounts agree in stating, that each nest contains only one young Squab. These are so extremely fat, that the Indians, and many

of the whites, are accustomed to melt down the fat for domestic purposes, as a substitute for butter and lard. At the time they leave the
nest, they are nearly as heavy as the old ones ; but become much
leaner after they are turned out to shift for themselves.

It is universally asserted, in the western countries, that the Pigeons,
though they have only one young at a time, breed thrice, and sometimes four times, in the same season : the circumstances already mentioned render this highly probable. It is also worthy of observation,
that this takes place during that period when acorns, beech nuts, &c.
are scattered about in the greatest abundance, and mellowed by the
frost. But they are not confined to these alone, — buckwheat, hempseed, Indian corn, hollyberries, hackberries, huckleberries, and many
others, furnish them with abundance at almost all seasons. The
acorns of the live oak are also eagerly sought after by these birds,
and rice has been frequently found in individuals killed many hundred
miles to the northward of the nearest rice plantation. The vast quantity of mast which these multitudes consume is a serious loss to the
bears, pigs, squirrels, and other dependents on the fruits of the forest.
I have taken, from the crop of a single Wild Pigeon, a good handful
of the kernels of beech nuts, intermixed with acorns and chestnuts.
To form a rough estimate of the daily consumption of one of these
immense flocks, let us first attempt to calculate the numbers of that
above mentioned, as seen in passing between Frankfort and the Indiana territory : If we suppose this column to have been one mile in
breadth, (and I believe it to have been much more,) and that it moved
at the rate of one mile in a minute, four hours, the time it continued
passing, would make its whole length two hundred and forty miles.
Again, supposing that each square yard of this moving body comprehended three Pigeons, the square yards in the whole space, multiplied
by three, would give two thousand two hundred and thirty millions,
two hundred and seventy-two thousand Pigeons! — an almost inconceivable multitude, and yet probably far below the actual amount.
Computing each of these to consume half a pint of mast daily, the
whole quantity at this rate would equal seventeen millions, four hundred and twenty-four thousand bushels per day! Heaven has wisely
and graciously given to these birds rapidity of flight and a disposition
to range over vast uncultivated tracts of the earth, otherwise they
must have perished in the districts where they resided, or devoured up
the whole productions of agriculture, as well as those of the forests.

A few observations on the mode of flight of these birds must not be
omitted : the appearance of large detached bodies of them in the air,
and the various evolutions they display, are strikingly picturesque and
interesting. In descending the Ohio by myself, in the month of February, I often rested on my oars to contemplate their aerial manœuvres. A column, eight or ten miles in length, would appear from Kentucky, high in air, steering across to Indiana. The leaders of this
great body would sometimes gradually vary their course, until it
formed a large bend, of more than a mile in diameter, those behind
tracing the exact route of their predecessors. This would continue
sometimes long after both extremities were beyond the reach of sight ;
so that the whole, with its glittery undulations, marked a space on the
face of the heavens resembling the windings of a vast and majestic

river. When this bend became very great, the birds, as if sensible of the unnecessary circuitous course they were taking, suddenly changed their direction, so that what was in column before became an immense front, straightening all its indentures, until it swept the heavens in one vast and infinitely extended line. Other lesser bodies also united with each other as they happened to approach, with such ease and elegance of evolution, forming new figures, and varying these as they united or separated, that I never was tired of contemplating them. Sometimes a Hawk would make a sweep on a particular part of the column, from a great height, when, almost as quick as lightning, that part shot downwards out of the common track; but, soon rising again, continued advancing at the same height as before. This inflection was continued by those behind, who, on arriving at this point, dived down, almost perpendicularly, to a great depth, and rising, followed the exact path of those that went before. As these vast bodies passed over the river near me, the surface of the water, which was before smooth as glass, appeared marked with innumerable dimples, occasioned by the dropping of their dung, resembling the commencement of a shower of large drops of rain or hail.

Happening to go ashore, one charming afternoon, to purchase some milk at a house that stood near the river, and while talking with the people within doors, I was suddenly struck with astonishment at a loud rushing roar, succeeded by instant darkness, which, on the first moment, I took for a tornado, about to overwhelm the house and every thing around in destruction. The people, observing my surprise, coolly said, "It is only the Pigeons;" and, on running out, I beheld a flock, thirty or forty yards in width, sweeping along very low, between the house and the mountain, or height, that formed the second bank of the river. These continued passing for more than a quarter of an hour, and at length varied their bearing so as to pass over the mountain, behind which they disappeared before the rear came up.

In the Atlantic States, though they never appear in such unparalleled multitudes, they are sometimes very numerous; and great havoc is then made amongst them with the gun, the clap net, and various other implements of destruction. As soon as it is ascertained in a town that the Pigeons are flying numerously in the neighborhood, the gunners rise en masse; the clap nets are spread out on suitable situations, commonly on an open height in an old buckwheat field; four or five live Pigeons, with their eyelids sewed up, are fastened on a moveable stick — a small hut of branches is fitted up for the fowler, at the distance of forty or fifty yards — by the pulling of a string, the stick on which the Pigeons rest, is alternately elevated and depressed, which produces a fluttering of their wings similar to that of birds just alighting; this being perceived by the passing flocks, they descend with great rapidity, and, finding corn, buckwheat, &c., strewed about, begin to feed, and are instantly, by the pulling of a cord, covered by the net. In this manner, ten, twenty, and even thirty dozen, have been caught at one sweep. Meantime, the air is darkened with large bodies of them, moving in various directions; the woods also swarm with them in search of acorns; and the thundering of musketry is perpetual on all sides, from morning to night. Wagon loads of them are poured into market, where they sell from fifty to twenty-five, and even twelve cents, per dozen; and Pigeons become the order of the day at dinner, breakfast, and supper, until the very name becomes sickening. When they have been kept alive, and fed for some time on corn and buckwheat, their flesh acquires great superiority; but, in their common state, they are dry and blackish, and far inferior to the full grown young ones, or Squabs.

The nest of the Wild Pigeon is formed of a few dry slender twigs, carelessly put together, and with so little concavity, that the young one, when half grown, can easily be seen from below. The eggs are pure white. Great numbers of Hawks, and sometimes the Bald Eagle himself, hover about those breeding places, and seize the old or the young from the nest, amidst the rising multitudes, and with the most daring effrontery. The young, when beginning to fly, confine themselves to the under part of the tall woods, where there is no brush, and where nuts and acorns are abundant, searching among the leaves for mast, and appear like a prodigious torrent rolling along through the woods, every one striving to be in the front. Vast numbers of them are shot while in this situation. A person told me, that he once rode furiously into one of these rolling multitudes, and picked up thirteen Pigeons, which had been trampled to death by his horse's feet. In a few minutes they will beat the whole nuts from a tree with their wings, while all is a scramble, both above and below, for the same. They have the same cooing notes common to domestic Pigeons, but much less of their gesticulations. In some flocks you will find nothing but young ones, which are easily distinguishable by their motley dress. In others, they will be mostly females; and again, great multitudes of males, with few or no females. I cannot account for this in any other way than that, during the time of incubation, the males are exclusively engaged in procuring food, both for themselves and their mates; and the young, being unable yet to undertake these extensive excursions, associate together accordingly. But, even in winter, I know of several species of birds who separate in this manner, particularly the Red-winged Starling, among whom thousands of old males may be found, with few or no young or females along with them.

Stragglers from these immense armies settle in almost every part of the country, particularly among the beech woods, and in the pine and hemlock woods of the eastern and northern parts of the continent. Mr. Pennant informs us, that they breed near Moose Fort, at Hudson's Bay, in N. lat. 51°, and I myself have seen the remains of a large breeding place as far south as the country of the Chactaws, in lat. 32°. In the former of these places they are said to remain until December; from which circumstance, it is evident that they are not regular in their migrations, like many other species, but rove about, as scarcity of food urges them. Every spring, however, as well as fall, more or less of them are seen in the neighborhood of Philadelphia: but it is only once in several years that they appear in such formidable bodies; and this commonly when the snows are heavy to the north, the winter here more than usually mild, and acorns, &c., abundant.

The Passenger Pigeon is sixteen inches long, and twenty-four inches in extent; bill, black; nostril, covered by a high rounding protuberance; eye, brilliant fiery orange; orbit or space surrounding it,

34 *

purplish flesh colored skin; head, upper part of the neck, and chin, a fine slate blue, lightest on the chin; throat, breast, and sides, as far as the thighs, a reddish hazel; lower part of the neck, and sides of the same, resplendent changeable gold, green, and purplish crimson, the latter most predominant; the ground color, slate; the plumage of this part is of a peculiar structure, ragged at the ends; belly and vent, white; lower part of the breast, fading into a pale vinaceous red; thighs, the same; legs and feet, lake, seamed with white; back, rump, and tail-coverts, dark slate, spotted on the shoulders with a few scattered marks of black; the scapulars tinged with brown; greater coverts, light slate; primaries and secondaries, dull black, the former tipped and edged with brownish white; tail, long, and greatly cuneiform, all the feathers tapering towards the point, the two middle ones plain deep black, the other five, on each side, hoary white, lightest near the tips, deepening into bluish near the bases, where each is crossed on the inner vane with a broad spot of black, and nearer the root with another of ferruginous; primaries, edged with white; bastard wing, black.

The female is about half an inch shorter, and an inch less in extent; breast, cinereous brown; upper part of the neck, inclining to ash; the spot of changeable gold, green, and carmine, much less, and not so brilliant; tail-coverts, brownish slate; naked orbits, slate colored; in all other respects like the male in color, but less vivid, and more tinged with brown; the eye not so brilliant an orange. In both, the tail has only twelve feathers.

BLUE MOUNTAIN WARBLER. — SYLVIA MONTANA. —
Fig. 183.

SYLVICOLA MONTANA. — Jardine.*

Sylvia tigrina, *Bonap. Synop.* p. 82.

This new species was first discovered near that celebrated ridge, or range of mountains, with whose name I have honored it. Several of these solitary Warblers remain yet to be gleaned up from the airy heights of our alpine scenery, as well as from the recesses of our swamps and morasses, whither it is my design to pursue them by every opportunity. Some of these, I believe, rarely or never visit the lower cultivated parts of the country; but seem only at home among the glooms and silence of those dreary solitudes. The present species seems of that family, or subdivision, of the Warblers, that approach the Flycatcher, darting after flies wherever they see them, and also searching with great activity among the leaves. Its song was a feeble screep, three or four times repeated.

* Bonaparte is inclined to think that this is the *Sylvia tigrina* of Latham. He acknowledges, however, not having seen the bird, and, as we have no means at present of deciding the question, have retained Wilson's name. Both this and the following will range in *Sylvicola.* — Ed.

This species is four inches and three quarters in length; the upper parts, a rich, yellow olive; front, cheeks, and chin, yellow, also the sides of the neck; breast and belly, pale yellow, streaked with black or dusky; vent, plain pale yellow; wings, black; first and second row of coverts, broadly tipped with pale yellowish white; tertials, the same; the root of the quills, edged with whitish; tail, black, handsomely rounded, edged with pale olive; the two exterior feathers, on each side, white on the inner vanes from the middle to the tips, and edged on the outer side with white; bill, dark brown; legs and feet, purple brown; soles, yellow; eye, dark hazel.

This was a male. The female I have never seen.

HEMLOCK WARBLER. — SYLVIA PARUS. — Fig. 184.

SYLVICOLA PARUS. — Jardine.

Sylvia parus, *Bonap. Synop.* p. 82.

This is another nondescript, first met with in the Great Pine Swamp, Pennsylvania. From observing it almost always among the branches of the hemlock trees, I have designated it by that appellation, the markings of its plumage not affording me a peculiarity sufficient for a specific name. It is a most lively and active little bird, climbing among the twigs, and hanging like a Titmouse on the branches; but possessing all the external characters of the Warblers. It has a few low and very sweet notes, at which times it stops and repeats them for a short time, then darts about as before. It shoots after flies to a considerable distance; often begins at the lower branches, and hunts with great regularity and admirable dexterity, upwards to the top, then flies off to the next tree, at the lower branches of which it commences hunting upwards as before.

This species is five inches and a half long, and eight inches in extent; bill, black above, pale below; upper parts of the plumage, black, thinly streaked with yellow olive; head above, yellow, dotted with black; line from the nostril over the eye, sides of the neck, and whole breast, rich yellow; belly, paler, streaked with dusky; round the breast, some small streaks of blackish; wing, black, the greater coverts, and next superior row, broadly tipped with white, forming two broad bars across the wing; primaries, edged with olive, tertials, with white; tail-coverts, black, tipped with olive; tail, slightly forked, black, and edged with olive: the three exterior feathers altogether white on their inner vanes; legs and feet, dirty yellow; eye, dark hazel; a few bristles at the mouth; bill, not notched.

Fig. 184 was a male. Of the female I can at present give no account.

SHARP-SHINNED HAWK.—FALCO VELOX.—Fig. 185.

ACCIPITER PENNSYLVANICUS.—Swainson.—young female.

Autour à bec sineuse, *Temm. Pl. Col.* 67.

This is a bold and daring species, hitherto unknown to naturalists. The only Hawk we have which approaches near it in color is the Pigeon Hawk, already figured in this work. But there are such striking differences in the present, not only in color, but in other respects, as to point out decisively its claims to rank as a distinct species. Its long and slender legs and toes—its red fiery eye, feathered to the eyelids—its triangular grooved nostril, and length of tail,—are all different from the Pigeon Hawk, whose legs are short, its eyes dark hazel, surrounded with a broad bare yellow skin, and its nostrils small and circular, centered with a slender point that rises in it like the pistil of a flower. There is no Hawk mentioned by Mr. Pennant, either as inhabiting Europe or America, agreeing with this. I may, therefore, with confidence, pronounce it a nondescript; and have chosen a very singular peculiarity which it possesses for its specific appellation.

This Hawk was shot on the banks of the Schuylkill, near Mr. Bartram's. Its singularity of flight surprised me long before I succeeded in procuring it. It seemed to. throw itself from one quarter of the heavens to the other, with prodigious velocity, inclining to the earth, swept suddenly down into a thicket, and instantly reappeared with a small bird in its talons. This feat I saw it twice perform, so that it was not merely an accidental manœuvre. The rapidity and seeming violence of these zigzag excursions were really remarkable, and appeared to me to be for the purpose of seizing his prey by sudden surprise and main force of flight. I kept this Hawk alive for several days, and was hopeful I might be able to cure him; but he died of his wound.

On the 15th of September, two young men whom I had despatched on a shooting expedition, met with this species on one of the ranges of the Alleghany. It was driving around in the same furious headlong manner, and had made a sweep at a red squirrel, which eluded its grasp, and itself became the victim. These are the only individuals of this bird I have been able to procure, and fortunately they were male and female.

The female of this species (represented in Fig. 185) is thirteen inches long, and twenty-five inches in extent; the bill is black towards the point on both mandibles, but light blue at its base; cere, a fine pea green; sides of the mouth, the same; lores, pale whitish blue, beset with hairs; crown and whole upper parts, very dark brown, every feather narrowly skirted with a bright rust color; over the eye a stripe of yellowish white, streaked with deep brown; primaries, spotted on their inner vanes with black; secondaries, crossed on both vanes with three bars of dusky, below the coverts; inner vanes of both primaries and secondaries, brownish white; all the scapulars marked with large round spots of white, not seen unless the plumage be parted with the hand; tail long, nearly even, crossed with four bars of black and as many of brown ash, and tipt with white; throat and whole lower parts, pale yellowish white; the former marked with fine long-pointed spots of dark brown, the latter with large oblong spots of reddish brown; femorals, thickly marked with spade-formed spots on a pale rufous ground; legs, long, and feathered a little below the knee, of a greenish yellow color, most yellow at the joints; edges of the inside of the shins, below the knee, projecting like the edge of a knife, hard and sharp, as if intended to enable the bird to hold its prey with more security between them; eye, brilliant yellow, sunk below a projecting cartilage.

The male was nearly two inches shorter; the upper parts, dark brown; the feathers, skirted with pale reddish, the front streaked with the same; cere, greenish yellow; lores, bluish; bill, black, as in the female; streak over the eye, lighter than in the former; chin, white; breast the same, streaked with brown; bars on the tail, rather narrower, but in tint and number the same; belly and vent, white; feet and shins, exactly as in the female; the toes have the same pendulous lobes which mark those of the female, and of which the representation in the plate will give a correct idea; the wings barred with black, very noticeable on the lower side.

Since writing the above, I have shot another specimen of this Hawk, corresponding in almost every particular with the male last mentioned; and which, on dissection, also proves to be a male. This last had within the grasp of his sharp talons a small lizard, just killed, on which he was about to feed. How he contrived to get possession of it appeared to me matter of surprise, as lightning itself seems scarcely more fleet than this little reptile. So rapid are its motions, that, in passing from one place to another, it vanishes, and actually eludes the eye in running a distance of twelve or fifteen feet. It is frequently seen on fences that are covered with gray moss and lichen, which in color it very much resembles; it seeks shelter in hollow trees, and also in the ground about their decayed roots. They are most numerous in hilly parts of the country, particularly on the declivities of the Blue Mountain, among the crevices of rocks and stones. When they are disposed to run, it is almost impossible to shoot them, as they disappear at the first touch of the trigger. For the satisfaction of the curious, I have introduced a full-sized figure of this lizard, which is known in many parts of the country by the name of the Swift.

REDSTART. — MUSCICAPA RUTICILLA. — Fig. 186.

Edw. 257. — Yellow Tail, *Arct. Zool.* ii. p. 466, No. 301.

SETOPHAGA RUTICILLA. — Swainson.

By recurring to Fig. 24, the male of this species may be seen in his perfect dress. Fig. 186 represents the young bird as he appears for the first two seasons; the female differs very little from this, chiefly in the green olive being more inclined to ash.

This is one of our summer birds, and, from the circumstance of being found off Hispaniola in November, is supposed to winter in the islands. They leave Pennsylvania about the 20th of September; are dexterous flycatchers, though ranked by European naturalists among the Warblers, having the bill notched and beset with long bristles.

In its present dress the Redstart makes its appearance in Pennsylvania about the middle or 20th of April; and, from being heard chanting its few sprightly notes, has been supposed by some of our own naturalists to be a different species. I have, however, found both parents of the same nest in the same dress nearly; the female, eggs and nest, as well as the notes of the male, agreeing exactly with those of the Redstart, — evidence sufficiently satisfactory to me.

Head above, dull slate; throat, pale buff; sides of the breast and four exterior tail feathers, fine yellow, tipt with dark brown; wings and back, greenish olive; tail-coverts, blackish, tipt with ash; belly, dull white; no white or yellow on the wings; legs, dirty purplish brown; bill, black.

The Redstart extends very generally over the United States, having myself seen it on the borders of Canada, and also on the Mississippi territory.

This species has the constant habit of flirting its expanded tail from side to side, as it runs along the branches, with its head levelled almost in a line with its body; occasionally shooting off after winged insects, in a downward zigzag direction, and, with admirable dexterity, snapping its bill as it descends. Its notes are few and feeble, repeated at short intervals, as it darts among the foliage; having at some times a resemblance to the sounds, *sic, sic, sàic;* at others, *weesy, weesy, weesy;* which last seems to be its call for the female, while the former appears to be its most common note.

YELLOW-RUMP WARBLER. — SYLVIA CORONATA. — Fig. 187.

Edw. 255. — *Arct. Zool.* ii. p. 400, No. 288.

SYLVICOLA CORONATA. — Swainson. — winter plumage.

Sylvia coronata, *Bonap. Synop.* p. 78. — Sylvicola coronata, *North. Zool.* ii. p. 210.

I MUST again refer the reader to Fig. 80 for this bird in his perfect colors; Fig. 187 exhibits him in his winter dress, as he arrives to us, from the north, early in September; the former shows him in his spring and summer dress, as he visits us, from the south, about the 20th of March. These birds remain with us, in Pennsylvania, from September, until the season becomes severely cold, feeding on the berries of the red cedar; and, as December's snows come on, they retreat to the lower countries of the Southern States, where, in February, I found them in great numbers, among the myrtles, feeding on the berries of

that shrub ; from which circumst?
quarter, Myrtle Birds. Their b
northern districts, among the sw?
having myself shot them in t?
of May.

They range along our who?
ticularly fond of the red ced?
numerous, in October, on ?
Jersey, in the same pursuit
can see them, generally s?

Length, five inches an?
and sides of the neck, ?
back with dusky black ;
marked with faint streaks o? ?
yellow ; at each side of the breas?
fainter yellow ; this last not observable, ?
bill, legs, and wings, black ; lesser coverts,
tail-coverts, slate ; the three exterior tail-feathers ?
vanes with white ; a touch of the same on the upper ?
Male and female at this season nearly alike. They begin
about the middle of February ; and, in four or five weeks, are ?
slate-colored dress, as represented in the figure referred to.

SLATE-COLORED HAWK. — FALCO PENNSYLVANICUS. —
Fig. 188.

ACCIPITER PENNSYLVANICUS. — Swainson.*

Falco velox, *Bonap. Synop.* p. 29. — Autour a bec sineuse, *Temm. Pl. Col.* 67.
(young.) — Accipiter Pennsylvanicus, *North. Zool.* ii. p. 44.

THIS elegant and spirited little Hawk is a native of Pennsylvania,
and of the Atlantic states generally ; and is now for the first time introduced to the notice of the public. It frequents the more settled
parts of the country, chiefly in winter ; is at all times a scarce species ;
flies wide, very irregular, and swiftly ; preys on lizards, mice, and small
birds, and is an active and daring little hunter. It is drawn of full size,
from a very beautiful specimen shot in the neighborhood of Philadelphia. The bird within his grasp is the *Tanagra rubra*, or Black-winged

* It is now satisfactorily ascertained that this, and the *Falco velox* of Fig. 185 are
the same species, the latter representing the plumage of the young female. The
changes and differences are the same with those of the common European Sparrow
Hawk, *Accipiter nisus*.

This bird most probably extends to the intertropical parts of South America. Its
occurrence far to the northward is not so common. It was not met with by Dr.
Richardson ; and the authority of its existence in the Fur Countries rests on a specimen in the Hudson's Bay Company Museum, killed at Moose Factory. It very
nearly resembles two small species from Mexico, the *A. fringilloides* of Mr. Vigors,
and one newly characterized by Mr. Swainson as *A. Mexicanus.* — ED.

Red-Bird, in its green or first year's dress. In the spring of the succeeding year the green and yellow plumage of this bird becomes of a most splendid scarlet, and the wings and tail deepen into a glossy black. For a particular account of this Tanager, see page 125 of the present work.

The great difficulty of accurately discriminating between different species of the Hawk tribe, on account of the various appearances they assume at different periods of their long lives, at first excited a suspicion that this might be one of those with which I was already acquainted, in a different dress, namely, the Sharp-shinned Hawk, just described ; for such are the changes of color to which many individuals of this genus are subject, that, unless the naturalist has recourse to those parts that are subject to little or no alteration in the full-grown bird, viz. the particular conformation of the legs, nostril, tail, and the relative length of the latter to that of the wings, also the peculiar character of the countenance, he will frequently be deceived. By comparing these, the same species may often be detected under a very different garb. Were all these changes accurately known, there is no doubt but the number of species of this tribe, at present enumerated, would be greatly diminished, the same bird having been described by certain writers, three, four, and even five different times, as so many distinct species. Testing, however, the present Hawk by the rules above mentioned, I have no hesitation in considering it as a species different from any hitherto described ; and I have classed it accordingly.

The Slate-colored Hawk is eleven inches long, and twenty-one inches in extent ; bill, blue black ; cere and sides of the mouth, dull green ; eyelid, yellow ; eye, deep sunk under the projecting eyebrow, and of a fiery orange color ; upper parts of a fine slate ; primaries, brown black, and, as well as the secondaries, barred with dusky ; scapulars, spotted with white and brown, which is not seen, unless the plumage be separated by the hand ; all the feathers above are shafted with black ; tail, very slightly forked, of an ash color, faintly tinged with brown, crossed with four broad bands of black, and tipt with white ; tail, three inches longer than the wings ; over the eye extends a streak of dull white ; chin, white, mixed with fine black hairs ; breast and belly, beautifully variegated with ferruginous and transverse spots of white ; femorals, the same ; vent, pure white ; legs, long, very slender, and of a rich orange yellow ; claws, black, large, and remarkably sharp ; lining of the wing, thickly marked with heart-shaped spots of black. This bird, on dissection, was found to be a male. In the month of February, I shot another individual of this species, near Hampton, in Virginia, which agreed almost exactly with the present.

188. Kite Coloured Hawk. 189 Ground Dove. 190. Female. 191. Snipe 192. Quail or Partridge. 193. Rail. 194 Woodcock.

GROUND DOVE.—COLUMBA PASSERINA.—Fig. 189, Male ; Fig. 190, Female.

Lynn. Syst. 285.— *Sloan. Jam.* ii. 305.— Le Cocotzin, *Fernandez,* 24.— *Buff.* ii. 559.   *Pl. enl.* 243.— *Turt. Syst.* 478.— Columba minuta, *Ibid.* p. 479.— *Arct. Zool.* p. 328, No. 191.— *Catesb.* i. 26.— La petite tourterelle d'Amerique, *Briss.* i. 113.

CHÆMEPELLA PASSERINA. — Swainson.

Chæmepelia, *Swain. N. Groups. Zool. Journ.* No. XI. p. 361. — Columba passeri-na, (sub-genus Goura,) *Bonap. Synop.* p. 120.

THIS is one of the least of the Pigeon tribe, whose timid and inno-cent appearance forms a very striking contrast to the ferocity of the preceding bird.   Such as they are in nature, such 1 have endeavored faithfully to represent them.   I have been the more particular with this minute species, as no correct figure of it exists in any former work with which I am acquainted.

The Ground Dove is a native of North and South Carolina, Georgia, the new state of Louisiana, Florida, and the islands of the West In-dies.   In the latter, it is frequently kept in cages ; is esteemed excel-lent for the table, and honored by the French planters with the name of Ortolan.   They are numerous in the sea islands on the coast of Carolina and Georgia ; fly in flocks, or coveys, of fifteen or twenty ; seldom visit the woods, preferring open fields and plantations ; are almost constantly on the ground, and, when disturbed, fly to a short distance, and again alight.   They have a frequent jetting motion with the tail ; feed on rice, various seeds and berries, particularly those of the toothach tree,* under or near which, in the proper season, they are almost sure to be found.   Of their nest, or manner of breeding, I am unable at present to give any account.

These birds seem to be confined to the districts lying south of Vir-ginia.   They are plenty on the upper parts of Cape Fear River, and in the interior of Carolina and Georgia ; but I never have met with them either in Maryland, Delaware, or Pennsylvania.   They never congre-gate in such multitudes as the Common Wild Pigeon ; or even as the Carolina Pigeon, or Turtle Dove ; but, like the Partridge, or Quail, frequent the open fields in small coveys.   They are easily tamed ; have a low, tender, cooing note, accompanied with the usual gesticu-tions of their tribe.

The Ground Dove is a bird of passage, retiring to the islands, and to the more southerly parts of the continent, on the approach of win-ter, and returning to its former haunts early in April.   It is of a more slender and delicate form, and less liable to bear the rigors of cold, than either of the other two species common in the United States, both of which are found in the northern regions of Canada, as well as in the genial climate of Florida.

* *Xanthoxylum Clava Herculis.*

35

The Dove, generally speaking, has long been considered as the favorite emblem of peace and innocence, probably from the respectful manner in which its name is mentioned in various parts of Scripture; its being selected from among all the birds, by Noah, to ascertain the state of the deluge, and returning to the ark, bearing the olive leaf, as a messenger of peace and good tidings; the Holy Ghost, it is also said, was seen to descend like a Dove from heaven, &c. In addition to these, there is in the Dove an appearance of meekness and innocency very interesting, and well calculated to secure our partiality in its favor. These remarks are applicable to the whole genus; but are more particularly so to the species now before us, as being among the least, the most delicate, and inoffensive of the whole.

The Ground Dove is six inches and a quarter long; bill, yellow, black at the point; nostril, covered with a prominent membrane, as is usual with the genus; iris of the eye, orange red; front, throat, breast, and sides of the neck, pale vinaceous purple; the feathers, strongly defined by semicircular outlines, those on the throat, centered with dusky blue; crown and hind head, a fine pale blue, intermixed with purple, the plumage, like that on the throat, strongly defined; back, cinereous brown, the scapulars deeply tinged with pale purple, and marked with detached drops of glossy blue, reflecting tints of purple; belly, pale vinaceous brown, becoming dark cinereous towards the. vent, where the feathers are bordered with white; wing-quills, dusky outwardly, and at the tips; lower sides, and whole interior vanes, a fine red chestnut, which shows itself a little below their coverts; tail, rounded, consisting of twelve feathers, the two middle ones cinereous brown, the rest black, tipped and edged with white; legs and feet, yellow.

The female has the back and tail-coverts of a mouse color, with little or none of the vinaceous tint on the breast and throat, nor any of the light blue on the hind head; the throat is speckled with dull white, pale clay color, and dusky; sides of the neck, the same, the plumage strongly defined; breast, cinereous brown, slightly tinctured with purple; scapulars, marked with large drops of a dark purplish blood color, reflecting tints of blue; rest of the plumage, nearly the same as that of the male.

SNIPE. — SCOLOPAX GALLINAGO? — Fig. 191.

La Beccassine, *Briss.* v. 298, pl. 26, fig. 1. — *Lath. Syn.* iii. 134.

SCOLOPAX WILSONII. — Temminck.*

Scolopax Wilsonii, *Temm. Pl. Col.* Note to description of S. Gigantea. — *Bonap. Synop.* p. 330. — Monog. del Gen. Scolopax Osserv. Sulla, 2d edit. *Del. Reg. Anim.* p. 120. — Scolopax Brehmii, *Bonap. Observ. on Nomencl.*

This bird is well known to our sportsmen; and, if not the same, has a very near resemblance to the Common Snipe of Europe. It is usually known by the name of the English Snipe, to distinguish it from the Woodcock, and from several others of the same genus. It arrives

* Five or six species of Snipes are so much allied in the colors and general marking of the plumage, that a very narrow examination is often necessary for their determination; from this reason, the birds from America, Asia, and the Indian continent, were considered as identical, and a much wider geographical range allotted to the European Snipe than it was generally entitled to. Wilson had some doubts of this bird being the same with the European Snipe, as he marks his name with a query, and observed the difference in the number of tail-feathers. Bonaparte observed the difference as soon as his attention was turned to the ornithology of America; and, about the same time, a new Snipe was described by Mr. Kaup, in the Isis, as found occasionally, in cold winters, in the north of Germany. The Prince of Musignano, on comparing this description with the American species, from their very close alliance, judged them identical; while, in the mean time, Temminck, comparing both together, perceived distinctions, and dedicated that of America to her own ornithologist — an opinion which Bonaparte afterwards confirmed, and adopted in his monograph of that genus.

Mr. Swainson has introduced a Snipe, which he thinks is distinct, killed on the Rocky Mountains, and named by him *S. Drummondii;* and another, killed on the Columbia, which he calls *S. Douglasii.* The first " is common in the Fur Countries up to lat. 65°, and is also found in the recesses of the Rocky Mountains. It is intermediate in size between the *S. major* and *gallinago;* it has a much longer bill than the latter, and two more tail-feathers. Its head is divided by a pale central stripe, as in *S. gallinula* and *major;* its dorsal plumage more distinctly striped than that of the latter; and the outer tail-feather is a quarter of an inch shorter than that of *S. Douglasii."* The latter, in Mr. Swainson's collection, has the tail of sixteen feathers, not narrowed, all banded with ferruginous, except the outer pair, which are paler; total length, eleven and a half inches.

Most of the Snipes partially migrate in their native countries, and some perform a regular distant migration. Such is the case with the *S. gallinula* of Europe. The American species is a winter visitant in the Northern States, and will most probably breed farther to the south, without leaving the country. In India, the Snipes move according to the supply of water in the tanks, and, at the season when they are comparatively dry, leave that district entirely. In this country, although many breed in the mosses, we have a large accession of numbers about the middle of September, both from the wilder high grounds, and from the continent of Europe · and these, according to the weather, change their stations during the whole winter. Their movements are commenced generally about twilight, when they fly high, surveying the country as they pass, and, one day, may be found in abundance on the highest moorland ranges, while, the next, they have removed to some low and sheltered glade or marsh. In this we have a curious instance of that instinctive knowledge which causes so simultaneous a change of station in a single night. By close observation, during the winter months, it may be regularly perceived, sometimes even daily, and some change certainly takes place before and after any sudden variation of weather. — Ed.

in Pennsylvania about the 10th of March, and remains in the low grounds for several weeks; the greater part then move off to the north, and to the higher inland districts, to breed. A few are occasionally found, and consequently breed, in our low marshes, during the summer. When they first arrive, they are usually lean; but, when in good order, are accounted excellent eating. They are perhaps the most difficult to shoot of all our birds, as they fly in sudden zigzag lines, and very rapidly. Great numbers of these birds winter on the rice grounds of the Southern States, where, in the month of February, they appeared to be much tamer than they are usually here, as I frequently observed them running about among the springs and watery thickets. I was told by the inhabitants that they generally disappeared early in the spring. On the 20th of March, I found these birds extremely numerous on the borders of the ponds near Louisville, Kentucky, and also in the neighborhood of Lexington, in the same state, as late as the 10th of April. I was told by several people that they are abundant in the Illinois country, up as far as Lake Michigan. They are but seldom seen in Pennsylvania during the summer, but are occasionally met with in considerable numbers on their return in autumn, along the whole eastern side of the Alleghany, from the sea to the mountains. They have the same soaring, irregular flight in the air, in gloomy weather, as the Snipe of Europe; the same bleating note and occasional rapid descent; spring from the marshes with the like feeble *squeak*; and in every respect resemble the Common Snipe of Britain, except in being about an inch less, and in having sixteen feathers in the tail, instead of fourteen, — the number said by Bewick to be in that of Europe. From these circumstances, we must either conclude this to be a different species, or partially changed by difference of climate; the former appears to me the most probable opinion of the two.

These birds abound in the meadows and low grounds along our large rivers, particularly those that border the Schuylkill and Delaware, from the 10th of March to the middle of April, and sometimes later, and are eagerly sought after by many of our gunners. The nature of the grounds, however, which these birds frequent, the coldness of the season, and peculiar shyness and agility of the game, render this amusement attractive only to the most dexterous, active, and eager of our sportsmen.

The Snipe is eleven inches long, and seventeen inches in extent; the bill is more than two inches and a half long, fluted lengthwise, of a brown color, and black towards the tip, where it is very smooth while the bird is alive, but, soon after it is killed, becomes dimpled, like the end of a thimble; crown, black, divided by an irregular line of pale brown; another broader one of the same tint passes over each eye; from the bill to the eye, there is a narrow, dusky line; neck and upper part of the breast, pale brown, variegated with touches of white and dusky; chin, pale; back and scapulars, deep velvety black, the latter elegantly marbled with waving lines of ferruginous, and broadly edged exteriorly with white; wings, plain dusky, all the feathers, as well as those of the coverts, tipped with white; shoulder of the wing, deep dusky brown, exterior quill, edged with white; tail-coverts long, reaching within three quarters of an inch of the tip, and of a pale rust

color, spotted with black; tail, rounded, deep black, ending in a bar
of bright ferruginous, crossed with a narrow, waving line of black, and
tipped with whitish; belly, pure white; sides, barred with dusky; legs
and feet, a very pale ashy green; sometimes the whole thighs and sides
of the vent are barred with dusky and white.

The female differs in being more obscure in her colors; the white
on the back being less pure, and the black not so deep.

QUAIL, OR PARTRIDGE. — PERDIX VIRGINIANUS. —
FIG. 192.

Arct. Zool. 318, No. 185. — *Catesb. App.* p. 12. — Virginian Quail, *Turt. Syst.*
p. 460. — Maryland Quail, *Ibid.* — La perdrix d'Amerique, *Briss.* i. 231. — *Buff.*
ii. 447.

ORTYX VIRGINIANUS. — BONAPARTE.*

Perdix Virginiana, *Lath. Ind. Orn.* ii. p. 650. — Colin Colgnicui, *Temm. Pig. et
Gall.* iii. p. 436. — Perdix Borealis, *Temm. Pig. et Gall. Ind.* p. 735. — Ortyx
Borealis, *Steph. Cont. Shaw's Zool.* xi. p. 377. — Perdix (Ortyx) Virginiana,
Bonap. Synop. p. 124. — The Virginian Partridge, *Aud.* i. p. 388, pl. 76.

THIS well-known bird is a general inhabitant of North America,
from the northern parts of Canada and Nova Scotia, in which latter
place it is said to be migratory, to the extremity of the peninsula of
Florida; and was seen in the neighborhood of the Great Usage Village, in the interior of Louisiana. They are numerous in Kentucky

---

* The genus *Ortyx* was formed by Mr. Stephens, the continuator of Shaw's
Zoology, for the reception of the thick and strong-billed Partridges, peculiar to
both continents of the New World, and holding the place there with the Partridges,
Francolins, and Quails of other countries. They live on the borders of woods,
among brushwood, or on the thick grassy plains, and, since the cultivation of the
country, frequent cultivated fields. During the night, they roost on trees, and occasionally perch during the day; when alarmed, or chased by dogs, they fly to the
middle branches; and Mr. Audubon remarks, "they walk with ease on the
branches." In all these habits, they show their alliance to the perching *Gallinæ*,
and a variation from the true Partridge. The same naturalist also remarks, that
they occasionally perform partial migrations, from northwest to southeast, in the
beginning of October, and that, for a few weeks, the northwestern shores of the
Ohio are covered with Partridges.

Their general form is robust; the bill very strong, and apparently fitted for a mode
of feeding requiring considerable exertion, such as the digging up of bulbous and
tuberous roots. The head is crested in all the known species, the feathers sometimes of a peculiar structure, the shafts bare, and the extremity of the webs folding
on each other. The tail also exhibits different forms; in the more typical species
short, as in the Partridges, and in others becoming broad and long, as seen in the
Indian genus *Crax*, or the more extensively distributed genus *Penelope*. Considerable additions to the number of species have been lately made. Those belonging
to the northern continent, and consequently coming under our notice, are two, discovered by Mr. Douglas, — *Ortyx picta*, described in the last volume of the *Linnæan
Transactions*, and *O. Douglasii*, so named by Mr. Vigors, in honor of its discoverer, and also described with the former. To these may be added the lovely *O. Californica*, which, previous to this expedition and the voyage of Captain Beechy to
the coast of California, was held in the light of a dubious species. I have added

and Ohio. Mr. Pennant remarks, that they have been lately introduced into the island of Jamaica, where they appear to thrive greatly, breeding in that warm climate twice in the year. Captain Henderson mentions them as being plenty near the Balize, at the Bay of Honduras. They

the descriptions of these new species from 'Mr. Douglas's account in the *Transactions of the Linnæan Society:* —

Ortyx picta. — Douglas.

Male. — Bill, small, black; crown of the head, and breast, lead color; crest, three linear black feathers, two inches long; irides, bright hazel red; throat, purple red, bounded by a narrow, white line, forming a gorget above the breast, and extending round the eye and root of the beak; back, scapulars, and outer coverts of the wings, fuscous brown; belly, bright tawny, or rusty color, waved with black; the points of the feathers, white; quills, thirteen feathers, the fourth the longest; under coverts, light brown, mixed with a rusty color; tail, twelve feathers, of unequal length, rounded, lead color, but less bright than the breast or crown of the head; tarsi, one inch and a quarter long, reddish; toes, webbed nearly to the first joint.

Female. — Head and breast, light fuscous brown; the middle of the feathers, black; crest, half an inch long; throat, whitish, or light gray; belly, light gray, waved with black, less bright than the male; under coverts of the tail, foxy red; length, ten inches; girth, sixteen inches; weight, about twelve ounces; flesh, brown, well-flavored.

From October until March, these birds congregate in vast flocks, and seem to live in a state of almost perpetual warfare; dreadful conflicts ensue between the males, which not unfrequently end in the destruction of one or both combatants, if we may judge from the number of dead birds daily seen plucked, mutilated, and covered with blood. When feeding, they move in compact bodies, each individual endeavoring to outdo his neighbor in obtaining the prize. The voice is *quick-quick-quick*, pronounced slowly, with a gentle suspension between each syllable. At such times, or when surprised, the crest is usually thrown forward over the back; and the reverse when retreating, being brought backwards, and laid quite close. Their favorite haunts are dry upland, or undulating, gravelly, or sandy soils, in open woods, or coppice thickets of the interior; but, during the severity of winter, when the ground is covered with snow, they migrate, in large flocks, to the more temperate places in the immediate vicinity of the ocean. Seeds of *Bromus altissimus, Madia sativa,* and a tribe of plants allied to *Wadelia,* catkins of *Corylus,* leaves of *Fragaria,* and various insects, are their common food. Nest on the ground, in thickets of *Pteris, Aspidium, Rubus, Rhamnus,* and *Ceanothus;* neatly built with grass and dry leaves; secreted with so much caution, that, without the help of a dog, they can hardly be found. Eggs, eleven to fifteen, yellowish white, with minute brown spots; large in proportion to the bird. Pair in March. Common in the interior of California; and, during the summer months, extending as far northward as 45° north latitude, that is, within a few miles of the Columbian Valley.

Ortyx Douglasii. — Vigors.

Male. — Bill, brown; crest, linear, black, one inch long; irides, hazel red; body, fuscous brown, with a mixture of lead color, and rusty or yellow streaks; throat, whitish, with brown spots; belly, foxy red or tawny, white spotted; scapulars and outer coverts, bright brown; under coverts, light reddish brown; tail, twelve unequal, rounded feathers; legs, reddish; length, nine inches; girth, twelve inches; weight, ten ounces; flesh, pleasant, dark colored.

Female. — Crest, scarcely perceptible, dark.

This species appears to be an inhabitant of a more temperate climate than the preceding one, as it is never seen higher than 42° north latitude, and even that very sparingly in comparison to *O. picta* and *Californica.* The species do not associate together. In manner they are similar, at least as far as the opportunity I had of observing them went. I have never seen them but in winter dress, and know nothing of their nesting. — Ed.

rarely frequent the forest, and are most numerous in the vicinity of well-cultivated plantations, where grain is in plenty. They, however, occasionally seek shelter in the woods, perching on the branches, or secreting themselves among the brushwood; but are found most usually in open fields, or along fences sheltered by thickets of briers. Where they are not too much persecuted by the sportsmen, they become almost half domesticated; approach the barn, particularly in winter, and sometimes, in that severe season, mix with the poultry to glean up a subsistence. They remain with us the whole year, and often suffer extremely by long, hard winters and deep snows. At such times, the arts of man combine with the inclemency of the season for their destruction. To the ravages of the gun are added others of a more insidious kind; traps are placed on almost every plantation, in such places as they are known to frequent. These are formed of lath, or thinly-split sticks, somewhat in the shape of an obtuse cone, laced together with cord, having a small hole at top, with a sliding lid, to take out the game by. This is supported by the common figure 4 trigger; and grain is scattered below and leading to the place. By this contrivance, ten or fifteen have sometimes been taken at a time.* These are sometimes brought alive to market, and occasionally bought up by sportsmen, who, if the season be very severe, sometimes preserve and feed them till spring, when they are humanely turned out to their native fields again, to be put to death at some future time *secundem artem*. Between the months of August and March, great numbers of these birds are brought to the market of Philadelphia, where they are sold at from twelve to eighteen cents a piece.

The Quail begins to build early in May. The nest is made on the ground, usually at the bottom of a thick tuft of grass, that shelters and conceals it. The materials are leaves and fine dry grass in considerable quantity. It is well covered above, and an opening left on

---

* In addition to the common traps now described, Mr. Audubon mentions that they are also netted, or *driven*, as it is called. He thus describes the method of driving : —

"A number of persons on horseback, provided with a net, set out in search of Partridges, riding along the fences or brier thickets which the birds are known to frequent. One or two of the party whistle in imitation of the call note, and, as Partridges are plentiful, the call is soon answered by a covey, when the sportsmen immediately proceed to ascertain their position and number, seldom considering it worth while to set the net when there are only a few birds. They approach in a careless manner, talking and laughing as if merely passing by. When the birds are discovered, one of the party gallops off in a circuitous manner, gets in advance of the rest by a hundred yards or more, according to the situation of the birds and their disposition to run, while the rest of the sportsmen move about on their horses, talking to each other, but at the same time watching every motion of the Partridges. The person in advance, being provided with the net, dismounts, and at once falls to placing it, so that his companions can easily drive the Partridges into it. No sooner is the machine ready, than the net-bearer remounts, and rejoins the party. The sportsmen separate to a short distance, and follow the Partridges, talking, whistling, clapping their hands, or knocking the fence-rails. The birds move with great gentleness, following each other, and are kept in the right direction by the sportsmen. The leading bird approaches and enters the mouth of the net; the others follow in succession, when the net-bearer leaps from his horse, runs up and secures the entrance, and soon despatches the birds. In this manner, fifteen or twenty Partridges are caught at one driving, and sometimes many hundreds in the course of the day."
—ED.

one side for entrance. The female lays from fifteen to twenty-four eggs, of a pure white, without any spots. The time of incubation has been stated to me, by various persons, at four weeks, when the eggs were placed under the domestic Hen. The young leave the nest as soon as they are freed from the shell, and are conducted about in search of food by the female; are guided by her voice, which at that time resembles the twittering of young Chickens, and sheltered by her wings, in the same manner as those of the domestic fowl; but with all that secrecy and precaution for their safety, which their helplessness and greater danger require. In this situation, should the little timid family be unexpectedly surprised, the utmost alarm and consternation instantly prevail. The mother throws herself in the path, fluttering along, and beating the ground with her wings, as if sorely wounded; using every artifice she is master of to entice the passenger in pursuit of herself, uttering at the same time certain peculiar notes of alarm, well understood by the young, who dive separately amongst the grass, and secrete themselves till the danger is over; and the parent, having decoyed the pursuer to a safe distance, returns, by a circuitous route, to collect and lead them off. This well-known manœuvre, which nine times in ten is successful, is honorable to the feelings and judgment of the bird, but a severe satire on man. The affectionate mother, as if sensible of the avaricious cruelty of his nature, tempts him with a larger prize, to save her more helpless offspring; and pays him, as avarice and cruelty ought always to be paid, with mortification and disappointment.

The eggs of the Quail have been frequently placed under the domestic Hen, and hatched and reared with equal success as her own; though, generally speaking, the young Partridges, being more restless and vagrant, often lose themselves, and disappear. The Hen ought to be a particular good nurse, not at all disposed to ramble, in which case they are very easily raised. Those that survive, acquire all the familiarity of common Chickens; and there is little doubt that, if proper measures were taken, and persevered in for a few years, they might be completely domesticated. They have been often kept during the first season, and through the whole of the winter, but have uniformly deserted in the spring. Two young Partridges that were brought up by a Hen, when abandoned by her, associated with the cows, which they regularly followed to the fields, returned with them when they came home in the evening, stood by them while they were milked, and again accompanied them to the pasture. These remained during the winter, lodging in the stable, but, as soon as spring came, they disappeared. Of this fact, I was informed by a very respectable lady, by whom they were particularly observed.

It has been frequently asserted to me, that the Quails lay occasionally in each other's nests. Though I have never myself seen a case of this kind, I do not think it altogether improbable, from the fact, that they have often been known to drop their eggs in the nest of the common Hen, when that happened to be in the fields, or at a small distance from the house. The two Partridges above mentioned were raised in this manner; and it was particularly remarked by the lady who gave me the information, that the Hen sat for several days after her own eggs were hatched, until the young Quails made their appearance.

The Partridge, on her part, has sometimes been employed to hatch the eggs of the common domestic Hen. A friend of mine, who himself made the experiment, informs me, that, of several Hen's eggs which he substituted in place of those of the Partridge, she brought out the whole; and that, for several weeks, he occasionally surprised her in various parts of the plantation, with her brood of Chickens; on which occasions she exhibited all that distressful alarm, and practised her usual manœuvres for their preservation. Even after they were considerably grown, and larger than the Partridge herself, she continued to lead them about; but, though their notes or call were those of common Chickens, their manners had all the shyness, timidity, and alarm of young Partridges; running with great rapidity, and squatting in the grass exactly in the manner of the Partridge. Soon after this, they disappeared, having probably been destroyed by dogs, by the gun, or by birds of prey. Whether the domestic fowl might not by this method be very soon brought back to its original savage state, and thereby supply another additional subject for the amusement of the sportsman, will scarcely admit of a doubt. But the experiment, in order to secure its success, would require to be made in a quarter of the country less exposed than ours to the ravages of guns, traps, dogs, and the deep snows of winter, that the new tribe might have full time to become completely naturalized, and well fixed in all their native habits.

About the beginning of September, the Quails being now nearly full grown, and associated in flocks, or coveys, of from four or five to thirty, afford considerable sport to the gunner. At this time the notes of the male are most frequent, clear, and loud. His common call consists of two notes, with sometimes an introductory one, and is similar to the sound produced by pronouncing the words "Bob White." This call may be easily imitated by whistling, so as to deceive the bird itself, and bring it near. While uttering this, he is usually perched on a rail of the fence, or on a low limb of an apple tree, where he will sometimes sit, repeating, at short intervals, "Bob White," for half an hour at a time. When a covey are assembled in a thicket, or corner of a field, and about to take wing, they make a low twittering sound, not unlike that of young Chickens; and, when the covey is dispersed, they are called together again by a loud and frequently-repeated note, peculiarly expressive of tenderness and anxiety.

The food of the Partridge consists of grain, seeds, insects, and berries of various kinds. Buckwheat and Indian corn are particular favorites. In September and October the buckwheat fields afford them an abundant supply, as well as a secure shelter. They usually roost at night in the middle of a field on high ground; and from the circumstance of their dung being often found in such places in one round heap, it is generally conjectured that they roost in a circle, with their heads outwards, each individual in this position forming a kind of guard to prevent surprise. They also continue to lodge for several nights in the same spot.

The Partridge, like all the rest of the gallinaceous order, flies with a loud whirring sound, occasioned by the shortness, concavity, and rapid motion of its wings, and the comparative weight of its body.

The steadiness of its horizontal flight, however, renders it no difficult mark to the sportsman, particularly when assisted by his sagacious pointer. The flesh of this bird is peculiarly white, tender, and delicate, unequalled, in these qualities, by that of any other of its genus in the United States.

The Quail, as it is called in New England, or the Partridge, as in Pennsylvania, is nine inches long, and fourteen inches in extent; the bill is black; line over the eye, down the neck, and whole chin, pure white, bounded by a band of black, which descends and spreads broadly over the throat; the eye is dark hazel; crown, neck, and upper part of the breast, red brown; sides of the neck, spotted with white and black on a reddish brown ground; back, scapulars, and lesser coverts, red brown, intermixed with ash, and sprinkled with black; tertials, edged with yellowish white; wings, plain dusky; lower part of the breast and belly, pale yellowish white, beautifully marked with numerous curving spots, or arrowheads of black; tail, ash, sprinkled with reddish brown; legs, very pale ash.

The female differs in having the chin and sides of the head yellowish brown, in which dress it has been described as a different kind. There is, however, only one species of Quail at present known within the United States.

RAIL. — RALLUS CAROLINUS. — FIG. 193.

Soree, *Catesb.* i. 70. — *Arct. Zool.* p. 491, No. 409. — Little American Water-hen. *Edw.* 144. — Le Râle de Virginie, *Buff.* viii. 165.

CREX CAROLINUS. — BONAPARTE.*

Rallus (Crex) Carolinus, *Bonap. Synop.* 335.

OF all our land or water fowl, perhaps none afford the sportsmen more agreeable amusement, or a more delicious repast, than the little bird now before us. This amusement is indeed temporary, lasting only two or three hours in the day, for four or five weeks in each

---

* Almost every ornithologist has been at variance with regard to the propriety and limitation of the genera *Rallus*, *Crex*, and *Gallinula*. They appear to be sufficiently distinct, and not to run more into each other than many other groups, and, in the present state of ornithology, their separation is indispensable. *Crex* may be characterized by the bill shorter than the head; strong at the base, and tapering; the forehead feathered; the Common Land Rail, or Corncrake of Europe, and our present species, may be taken as very good typical examples. In *Gallinula*, the forehead is defended with a flat cartilaginous shield, and the habits are more open. In *Rallus*, the bill is longer than the head, and comparatively slender.

In habit they nearly agree; timid, and fond of concealment during the day, they frequent low meadows or marshy grounds, and run swiftly: the Common Land Rail will beat a good runner for a short way, as I have sometimes experienced. They run with the body near the ground, and make their turns with astonishing celerity. When raised or surprised during the day, they fly clumsily; but in the evening, and when that faculty is exerted with their will, it is much more actively

year; but, as it occurs in the most agreeable and temperate of our seasons, is attended with little or no fatigue to the gunner, and is frequently successful, it attracts numerous followers, and is pursued, in such places as the birds frequent, with great eagerness and enthusiasm.

The natural history of the Rail, or, as it is called in Virginia, the Sora, and in South Carolina, the Coot, is, to the most of our sportsmen, involved in profound and inexplicable mystery. It comes, they know not whence; and goes, they know not where. No one can detect their first moment of arrival; yet all at once the reedy shores and grassy marshes of our large rivers swarm with them, thousands being sometimes found within the space of a few acres. These, when they do venture on wing, seem to fly so feebly, and in such short fluttering flights among the reeds, as to render it highly improbable to most people that they could possibly make their way over an extensive tract of country. Yet, on the first smart frost that occurs, the whole suddenly disappear, as if they had never been.

To account for these extraordinary phenomena, it has been supposed by some that they bury themselves in the mud; but as this is every year dug into by ditchers, and people employed in repairing the banks, without any of those sleepers being found, where but a few weeks before these birds were innumerable, this theory has been generally abandoned. And here their researches into this mysterious matter generally end in the common exclamation of "What can become of them!" Some profound inquirers, however, not discouraged with these difficulties, have prosecuted their researches with more success; and one of those, living a few years ago near the mouth of James River, in Virginia, where the Rail, or Sora, are extremely numerous, has (as I was informed on the spot) lately discovered that they change into frogs! having himself found in his meadows an animal of an extraordinary kind, that appeared to be neither a Sora nor a frog, but, as he expressed it, "something between the two." He carried it to his negroes, and afterwards took it home, where it lived three days;

performed; their time for exertion is evening and morning, often during the night; then they feed, and, during breeding season, utter the incessant and unharmonious cry which almost all possess. The cry is remarkable in all that I have heard, appearing to be uttered sometimes within a few yards, and, in a second or two, as if at an opposite part of the ground. The Land Rail possesses this ventriloquism to a great extent, and, knowing their swift running powers, I at first thought that the bird was actually traversing the field; and it was not until I had observed one perched upon a stone utter its cry for some time, and give full evidence of its powers, that I became convinced of the contrary. The Corncrake, and, indeed, I rather think most of the others, and also the Rails, seem to remain stationary when uttering the cry. A stone, clod of earth, or old sod wall, is the common calling place of our own bird; and they may be easily watched, in the beginning of summer, if approached with caution, before the herbage begins to thicken. They seem to feed on larger prey than what are assigned to them: large water insects, and the smaller reptiles, may assist in sustaining the aquatic species; while slugs and larger snails will furnish subsistence to the others. I have found the common short-tailed field mouse in the stomach of our Land Rail.

Their flesh is generally delicate, some as much esteemed as the American bird, and the young, before commencing their migrations, become extremely fat.

Crex Carolinus is the only species of the genus yet discovered in North America, and is peculiar to that continent. — ED.

and, in his own and his negroes' opinion, it looked like nothing in this world but a real Sora changing into a frog! What farther confirms this grand discovery is the well-known circumstance of the frogs ceasing to hollow as soon as the Sora comes in the fall.

This sagacious discoverer, however, like many others renowned in history, has found but few supporters, and, except his own negroes, has not, as far as I can learn, made a single convert to his opinion. Matters being so circumstanced, and some explanation necessary, I shall endeavor to throw a little more light on the subject by a simple detail of facts, leaving the reader to form his own theory as he pleases.

The Rail, or Sora, belongs to a genus of birds of which about thirty different species are enumerated by naturalists; and those are distributed over almost every region of the habitable parts of the earth. The general character of these is every where the same. They run swiftly, fly slowly, and usually with the legs hanging down; become extremely fat; are fond of concealment; and, wherever it is practicable, prefer running to flying. Most of them are migratory, and abound, during the summer, in certain countries, the inhabitants of which have very rarely an opportunity of seeing them. Of this last the Land Rail of Britain is a striking example. This bird, which during the summer months may be heard in almost every grass and clover field in the kingdom, uttering its common note *crek, crek,* from sunset to a late hour in the night, is yet unknown by sight to more than nine-tenths of the inhabitants. "Its well-known cry," says Bewick, " is first heard as soon as the grass becomes long enough to shelter it, and continues till the grass is cut; but the bird is seldom seen, for it constantly skulks among the thickest part of the herbage, and runs so nimbly through it, winding and doubling in every direction, that it is difficult to come near it; when hard pushed by the dog, it sometimes stops short, and squats down, by which means its too eager pursuer overshoots the spot, and loses the trace. It seldom springs but when driven to extremity, and generally flies with its legs hanging down, but never to a great distance; as soon as it alights, it runs off, and, before the fowler has reached the spot, the bird is at a considerable distance." * The Water Crake, or Spotted Rail, of the same country, which in its plumage approaches nearer to our Rail, is another notable example of the same general habit of the genus. " Its common abode," says the same writer, " is in low, swampy grounds, in which are pools or streamlets overgrown with willows, reeds, and rushes, where it lurks and hides itself with great circumspection; it is wild, solitary, and shy, and will swim, dive, or skulk under any cover, and sometimes suffer itself to be knocked on the head, rather than rise before the sportsman and his dog." The Water Rail of the same country is equally noted for the like habits. In short, the whole genus possess this strong family character in a very remarkable degree.

These three species are well known to migrate into Britain early in spring, and to leave it for the more southern parts of Europe in autumn. Yet they are rarely or never seen on their passage to or from the countries where they are regularly found at different seasons of the year; and this for the very same reasons that they are so rarely seen even in the places where they inhabit.

* BEWICK's *British Birds,* vol. i. p. 308.

It is not, therefore, at all surprising, that the regular migrations of the American Rail, or Sora, should in like manner have escaped notice in a country like this, whose population bears so small a proportion to its extent, and where the study of natural history is so little attended to. But that these migrations do actually take place, from north to south, and *vice versa*, may be fairly inferred from the common practice of thousands of other species of birds less solicitous of concealment, and also from the following facts:

On the 22d day of February, I killed two of these birds in the neighborhood of Savannah, in Georgia, where they have never been observed during the summer. On the 2d of the May following, I shot another in a watery thicket below Philadelphia, between the rivers Schuylkill and Delaware, in what is usually called the Neck. This last was a male, in full plumage. We are also informed, that they arrive at Hudson's Bay early in June, and again leave that settlement for the south early in autumn. That many of them also remain here to breed is proven by the testimony of persons of credit and intelligence with whom I have conversed, both here and on James River, in Virginia, who have seen their nests, eggs, and young. In the extensive meadows that border the Schuylkill and Delaware, it was formerly common, before the country was so thickly settled there, to find young Rail, in the first mowing time, among the grass. Mr. James Bartram, brother to the botanist, a venerable and still active man of eighty-three, and well acquainted with this bird, says, that he has often seen and caught young Rail in his own meadows in the month of June; he has also seen their nest, which he says is usually in a tussock of grass, is formed of a little dry grass, and has four or five eggs, of a dirty whitish color, with brown or blackish spots; the young run off as soon as they break the shell, are then quite black, and run about among the grass like mice. The old ones he has very rarely observed at that time, but the young often. Almost every old settler along these meadows, with whom I have conversed, has occasionally seen young Rail in mowing time; and all agree in describing them as covered with blackish down. There can, therefore, be no reasonable doubt as to the residence of many of these birds, both here and to the northward, during the summer. That there can be as little doubt relative to their winter retreat, will appear more particularly towards the sequel of the present account. During their residence here, in summer, their manners exactly correspond with those of the Water Crake of Britain, already quoted, so that, though actually a different species, their particular habits, common places of resort, and eagerness for concealment, are as nearly the same as the nature of the climates will admit.

Early in August, when the reeds along the shores of the Delaware have attained their full growth, the Rail resort to them in great numbers, to feed on the seeds of this plant, of which they, as well as the Rice Birds, and several others, are immoderately fond. These reeds, which appear to be the *Zizania panicula effusa* of Linnæus, and the *Zizania clavulosa* of Willdenow, grow up from the soft muddy shores of the tide water, which are alternately dry, and covered with four or five feet of water. They rise with an erect, tapering stem, to the height of eight or ten feet, being nearly as thick below as a man's wrist, and cover tracts along the river of many acres. The cattle feed on their long green leaves with avidity, and wade in after them as far as they dare safely venture. They grow up so close together, that, except at or near high water, a boat can with difficulty make its way through among them. The seeds are produced at the top of the plant, the blossoms, or male parts, occupying the lower branches of the panicle, and the seeds the higher. These seeds are nearly as long as a common-sized pin, somewhat more slender, white, sweet to the taste, and very nutritive, as appears by their effects on the various birds that at this season feed on them.

When the reeds are in this state, and even while in blossom, the Rail are found to have taken possession of them in great numbers. These are generally numerous in proportion to the full and promising crop of the former. As you walk along the embankment of the river at this season, you hear them squeaking in every direction like young puppies. If a stone be thrown among the reeds, there is a general outcry, and a reiterated *kuk, kuk, kuk*, something like that of a Guinea-fowl. Any sudden noise, or the discharge of a gun, produces the same effect. In the mean time none are to be seen, unless it be at or near high water; for, when the tide is low, they universally secrete themselves among the interstices of the reeds, and you may walk past, and even over them, where there are hundreds, without seeing a single individual. On their first arrival, they are generally lean, and unfit for the table; but, as the reeds ripen, they rapidly fatten, and, from the 20th of September to the middle of October, are excellent, and eagerly sought after. The usual method of shooting them, in this quarter of the country, is as follows: — The sportsman furnishes himself with a light batteau, and a stout, experienced boatman, with a pole of twelve or fifteen feet long, thickened at the lower end to prevent it from sinking too deep into the mud. About two hours or so before high water, they enter the reeds, and each takes his post, the sportsman standing in the bow ready for action, the boatman, on the stern seat, pushing her steadily through the reeds. The Rail generally spring singly, as the boat advances, and at a short distance ahead, are instantly shot down, while the boatman, keeping his eye on the spot where the bird fell, directs the boat forward, and picks it up as the gunner is loading. It is also the boatman's business to keep a sharp look-out, and give the word "Mark!" when a Rail springs on either side without being observed by the sportsman, and to note the exact spot where it falls until he has picked it up; for this, once lost sight of, owing to the sameness in the appearance of the reeds, is seldom found again. In this manner the boat moves steadily through and over the reeds, the birds flushing and falling, the gunner loading and firing, while the boatman is pushing and picking up. The sport continues till an hour or two after high water, when the shallowness of the water, and the strength and weight of the floating reeds, as also the backwardness of the game to spring as the tide decreases, oblige them to return. Several boats are sometimes within a short distance of each other, and a perpetual cracking of musketry prevails along the whole reedy shores of the river. In these excursions it is not uncommon for an active and expert marksman to kill ten or twelve dozen in a tide. They are usually shot singly, though I have known five killed at one discharge of a double-barrelled piece. These instances, however, are rare.

The flight of these birds among the reeds is usually low; and, shelter being abundant, is rarely extended to more than fifty or one hundred yards. When winged, and uninjured in their legs, they swim and dive with great rapidity, and are seldom seen to rise again. I have several times, on such occasions, discovered them clinging with their feet to the reeds under the water, and at other times skulking under the floating reeds, with their bill just above the surface. Sometimes, when wounded, they dive, and, rising under the gunwale of the boat, secrete themselves there, moving round as the boat moves, until they have an opportunity of escaping unnoticed. They are feeble and delicate in every thing but the legs, which seem to possess great vigor and energy; and their bodies being so remarkably thin, or compressed, as to be less than an inch and a quarter through transversely, they are enabled to pass between the reeds like rats. When seen, they are almost constantly jetting up the tail. Yet, though their flight among the reeds seems feeble and fluttering, every sportsman who is acquainted with them here must have seen them occasionally rising to a considerable height, stretching out their legs behind them, and flying rapidly across the river where it is more than a mile in width.

Such is the mode of Rail shooting in the neighborhood of Philadelphia. In Virginia, particularly along the shores of James River, within the tide water, where the Rail, or Sora, are in prodigious numbers, they are also shot on the wing, but more usually taken at night in the following manner:— A kind of iron grate is fixed on the top of a stout pole, which is placed like a mast, in a light canoe, and filled with fire. The darker the night the more successful is the sport. The person who manages the canoe is provided with a light paddle ton or twelve feet in length, and, about an hour before high water, proceeds through among the reeds, which lie broken and floating on the surface. The whole space, for a considerable way round the canoe, is completely enlightened; the birds stare with astonishment, and, as they appear, are knocked on the head with a paddle, and thrown into the canoe. In this manner, from twenty to eighty dozen have been killed by three negroes in the short space of three hours!

At the same season, or a little earlier, they are very numerous in the lagoons near Detroit, on our northern frontiers, where another species of reed (of which they are equally fond) grows in shallows in great abundance. Gentlemen who have shot them there, and on whose judgment I can rely, assure me, that they differ in nothing from those they have usually killed on the shores of the Delaware and Schuylkill; they are equally fat, and exquisite eating. On the seacoast of New Jersey, where these reeds are not to be found, this bird is altogether unknown; though along the marshes of Maurice River, and other tributary streams of the Delaware, and wherever the reeds abound, the Rail are sure to be found also. Most of them leave Pennsylvania before the end of October, and the southern states early in November, though numbers linger in the warm southern marshes the whole winter. A very worthy gentleman, Mr. Harrison, who lives in Kittiwan, near a creek of that name, on the borders of James River, informed me, that, in burning his meadows early in March, they generally raise and destroy several of these birds. That the great body of these Rail winter in countries beyond the United States, is rendered highly probable from their being so frequently met with at sea, between our shores and the West India islands. A Captain Douglas informed me, that, on his voyage from St. Domingo to Philadelphia, and more than a hundred miles from the capes of the Delaware, one night the man at the helm was alarmed by a sudden crash on deck, that broke the glass in the binnacle, and put out the light. On examining into the cause, three Rail were found on deck, two of which were killed on the spot, and the other died soon after. The late Bishop Madison, president of William and Mary College, Virginia, assured me, that a Mr. Skipwith, for some time our consul in Europe, on his return to the United States, when upwards of three hundred miles from the capes of the Chesapeake, several Rail, or Soras, I think five or six, came on board, and were caught by the people.. Mr. Skipwith, being well acquainted with the bird, assured him that they were the very same with those usually killed on James River. I have received like assurances from several other gentlemen and captains of vessels who have met with these birds between the mainland and the islands, so as to leave no doubt on my mind of the fact. For why should it be considered incredible that a bird which can both swim and dive well, and at pleasure fly with great rapidity, as I have myself frequently witnessed, should be incapable of migrating, like so many others, over extensive tracts of land or sea? Inhabiting as they do, the remote regions of Hudson's Bay, where it is impossible they could subsist during the rigors of their winter, they must either emigrate from thence or perish; and as the same places in Pennsylvania which abound with them in October, are often laid under ice and snow during the winter, it is as impossible that they could exist here in that inclement season: Heaven has, therefore, given them, in common with many others, certain prescience of these circumstances, and judgment, as well as strength of flight, sufficient to seek more genial climates abounding with their suitable food.

The Rail is nine inches long, and fourteen inches in extent; bill, yellow, blackish towards the point; lores, front, crown, chin, and stripe down the throat, black; line over the eye, cheeks, and breast, fine light ash; sides of the crown, neck, and upper parts generally, olive brown, streaked with black, and also with long lines of pure white, the feathers being centred with black on a brown olive ground, and edged with white; these touches of white are shorter near the shoulder of the wing, lengthening as they descend; wing, plain olive brown; tertials, streaked with black, and long lines of white; tail, pointed, dusky olive brown, centred with black; the four middle feathers bordered for half their length with lines of white; lower part of the breast marked with semicircular lines of white, on a light ash ground; belly, white; sides under the wings, deep olive, barred with black, white, and reddish buff; vent, brownish buff; legs, feet, and naked part of the thighs, yellowish green; exterior edge of the wing, white; eyes, reddish hazel.

The females, and young of the first season, have the throat white, the breast pale brown, and little or no black on the head. The males may always be distinguished by their ashy blue breasts and black throats.

During the greater part of the months of September and October, the market of Philadelphia is abundantly supplied with Rail, which are sold from half a dollar to a dollar a dozen. Soon after the 20th of October, at which time our first smart frosts generally take place, these birds move off to the south. In Virginia, they usually remain until the first week in November.

Since the above was written, I have received from Mr. George Ord, of Philadelphia, some curious particulars relative to this bird, which, as they are new, and come from a gentleman of respectability, are worthy of being recorded, and merit further investigation.

" My personal experience," says Mr. Ord, "has made me acquainted with a fact in the history of the Rail, which perhaps is not generally known, and I shall, as briefly as possible, communicate it to you. Some time in the autumn of the year 1809, as I was walking in a yard, after a severe shower of rain, I perceived the feet of a bird projecting from a spout. I pulled it out, and discovered it to be a Rail, very vigorous, and in perfect health. The bird was placed in a small room, on a gin-case, and I was amusing myself with it, when, in the act of pointing my finger at it, it suddenly sprang forward, apparently much irritated, fell to the floor, and, stretching out its feet, and bending its neck until the head nearly touched the back, became to all appearance lifeless. Thinking the fall had killed the bird, I took it up, and began to lament my rashness in provoking it. In a few minutes it again breathed, and it was some time before it perfectly recovered from the fit, into which, it now appeared evident, it had fallen. I placed the Rail in a room, wherein Canary Birds were confined, and resolved that, on the succeeding day, I would endeavor to discover whether or not the passion of anger had produced the fit. I entered the room at the appointed time, and approached the bird, which had retired, on beholding me, in a sullen humor, to a corner. On pointing my finger at it, its feathers were immediately ruffled, and in an instant it sprang forward, as in the first instance, and fell into a similar fit. The following day, the experiment was repeated with the like effect. In the fall of 1811, as I was shooting amongst the reeds, I perceived a Rail rise but a few feet before my batteau. The bird had risen about a yard when it became entangled in the tops of a small bunch of reeds, and immediately fell. Its feet and neck were extended, as in the instances above mentioned, and, before it had time to recover, I killed it. Some few days afterwards, as a friend and I were shooting in the same place, he killed a Rail, and, as we approached the spot to pick it up, another was perceived, not a foot off, in a fit. I took up the latter, and placed it in the crown of my hat. In a few moments it revived, and was as vigorous as ever. These facts go to prove, that the Rail is subject to gusts of passion, which operate to so violent a degree as to produce a disease, similar in its effects to epilepsy. I leave the explication of the phenomenon to those pathologists who are competent and willing to investigate it. It may be worthy of remark, that the birds affected as described, were all females of the *Gallinula Carolina*, or Common Rail.

" The Rail, though generally reputed a simple bird, will sometimes manifest symptoms of considerable intelligence. To those acquainted with Rail shooting, it is hardly necessary to mention, that the tide, in
36 *

its flux, is considered an almost indispensable auxiliary ; for, when the water·is off the marsh, the lubricity of the mud, the height and compactness of the reed, and the swiftness of foot of the game, tend to weary the sportsman and to frustrate his endeavors. Even should he succeed in a tolerable degree, the reward is not commensurate to the labor. I have entered the marsh in a batteau at a common tide, and in a well-known haunt have beheld but few birds. The next better tide, on resorting to the same spot, I have perceived abundance of game. The fact is, the Rail dive and conceal themselves beneath the fallen reed, merely projecting their heads above the surface of the water for air, and remain in that situation until the sportsman has passed them ; and it is well known, that it is a common practice with wounded Rail to dive to the bottom, and, holding upon some vegetable substance, support themselves in that situation until exhausted. During such times, the bird, in escaping from one enemy, has often to encounter another not less formidable. Eels and cat-fish swarm in every direction prowling for prey, and it is ten to one if a wounded Rail escapes them. I myself have beheld a large eel make off with a bird that I had shot, before I had time to pick it up; and one of my boys, in bobbing for eels, caught one with a whole Rail in its belly.

"I have heard it observed, that on the increase of the moon·the Rail improves in fatness, and decreases in a considerable degree with that planet. Sometimes I have conceited that the remark was just. If it be a fact, I think it may be explained on the supposition that the bird is enabled to feed at night, as well as by day, while it has the benefit of the moon, and with less interruption than at other periods."

I have had my doubts as to the propriety of classing this bird under the genus *Rallus*. Both Latham and Pennant call it a Gallinule ; and when one considers the length and formation of its bill, the propriety of its nomenclature is obvious. As the article was commenced by our printers before I could make up my mind on the subject, the reader is requested to consider this species the *Gallinula Carolina* of Dr. Latham.

WOODCOCK.— SCOLOPAX MINOR.— Fig. 194.

Arct. Zool. p. 463, No. 365. — *Turt. Syst.* 396. — *Lath. Syn.* iii. 131.

RUSTICOLA MINOR. — Vieillot.*

Rusticola minor, *Vieill. Gal. des Ois.* 242. — Great Red Woodcock, Scolopax Americana rufa, *Bart. Trav.* 292. — Scolopax Rusticola minor, *Bonap. Synop.* p. 331. — *Monog. del Gen. Scolopax Osser. sulla, 2d ed. del Reg. Anim. Cuv.*

THIS bird, like the preceding, is universally known to our sportsmen. It arrives in Pennsylvania early in March, sometimes sooner; and I doubt not but in mild winters some few remain with us the whole of that season. During the day, they keep to the woods and

---

* Among many natural groups, such as *Scolopax* of Linnæus, there are gradations of form which have not been thought of sufficient importance to constitute a

thickets, and, at the approach of evening, seek the springs and open watery places to feed in. They soon disperse themselves over the country to breed. About the beginning of July, particularly in long-continued hot weather, they descend to the marshy shores of our large rivers, their favorite springs and watery recesses inland being chiefly dried up. To the former of these retreats they are pursued by the merciless sportsman, flushed by dogs, and shot down in great numbers. This species of amusement, when eagerly followed, is still more laborious and fatiguing than that of Snipe shooting; and from the nature of the ground, or cripple, as it is usually called, viz., deep mire intersected with old logs, which are covered and hid from sight by high reeds, weeds, and alder bushes, the best dogs are soon tired out; and it is customary with sportsmen who regularly pursue this diversion, to have two sets of dogs, to relieve each other alternately.

The Woodcock usually begins to lay in April. The nest is placed on the ground, in a retired part of the woods, frequently at the root of an old stump. It is formed of a few withered leaves and stalks of grass laid with very little art. The female lays four, sometimes five eggs, about an inch and a half long, and an inch or rather more in diameter, tapering suddenly to the small end. These are of a dun clay color, thickly marked with spots of brown, particularly at the great end, and interspersed with others of a very pale purple. The nest of the Woodcock has, in several instances that have come to my knowledge, been found with eggs in February; but its usual time of beginning to lay is early in April. In July, August, and September, they are considered in good order for shooting.

The Woodcock is properly a nocturnal bird, feeding chiefly at night, and seldom stirring about till after sunset. At such times, as well as in the early part of the morning, particularly in spring, he rises, by a kind of spiral course, to a considerable height in the air, uttering at

genus, but have been mentioned as divisions only. Such is the case with the present, which is generally classed under those with the tibiæ feathered and the tibiæ bare. Vieillot, following this division, proposed *Rusticola* for the Woodcocks, or those with plumed tibiæ; and, as far as artificial systems are concerned, and facility of reference, we should prefer keeping them as a sub-genus.

The Woodcocks, in addition to the plumed tibiæ, differ in other respects; and an individual, technically unacquainted with ornithology, would at once pick them out from the Snipes, from a something in their *tourneur*, as Mr. Audubon would call it. The tarsi are much shorter, and show that the bird is not intended to wade, or to frequent very marshy situations, like the Snipes. They are all inhabitants of woods, and it is only during severe storms that they are constantly found near a rill or streamlet. Their food is as much found by searching under the fallen leaves and decayed grasses, as in wet places; and, in this country, where Woodcocks are abundant, they may be traced through a wood by the newly scratched up leaves. There is a marked difference, also, in the plumage; it is invariably of a more sombre shade; sometimes the under parts are closely barred with a darker color, while, in the Snipes, the latter part is oftener pure white. We have a beautiful connection between the divisions in the *Scolopax Sabina* of Vigors,[*] which, though of the lesser size of the Snipes, has the entire plumage of the Woodcock, and also the thighs feathered to a greater length downwards.

The species are few in number, amounting only to three or four. America, Europe, and India, seem as yet their only countries. The habits of most agree, and all partially migrate from north to south to breed. — Ed.

* Is this the *Scolopax Sakhalina* of Vieillot, *Nouv. Dict.*? — Ed.

times a sudden *quack*, till, having gained his utmost height, he hovers around in a wild, irregular manner, making a sort of murmuring sound; then descends with rapidity as he rose. When uttering his common note on the ground, he seems to do it with difficulty, throwing his head towards the earth, and frequently jetting up his tail. These notes and manœuvres are most usual in spring, and are the call of the male to his favorite female. Their food consists of various larvæ, and other aquatic worms, for which, during the evening, they are almost continually turning over the leaves with their bill, or searching in the bogs. Their flesh is reckoned delicious, and prized highly. They remain with us till late in autumn, and, on the falling of the first snows, descend from the ranges of the Alleghany to the lower parts of the country in great numbers; soon after which, viz., in November, they move off to the south.

This bird, in its general figure and manners, greatly resembles the Woodcock of Europe, but is considerably less, and very differently marked below, being an entirely distinct species. A few traits will clearly point out their differences. The lower parts of the European Woodcock are thickly barred with dusky waved lines, on a yellowish white ground. The present species has those parts of a bright ferruginous. The male of the American species weighs from five to six ounces, the female, eight; the European, twelve. The European Woodcock makes its first appearance in Britain in October and November, that country being in fact only its winter quarters; for, early in March, they move off to the northern parts of the Continent to breed. The American species, on the contrary, winters in countries south of the United States, arrives here early in March, extends its migrations as far, at least, as the River St. Lawrence, breeds in all the intermediate places, and retires again to the south on the approach of winter. The one migrates from the torrid to the temperate regions, the other, from the temperate to the arctic. The two birds, therefore, notwithstanding their names are the same, differ not only in size and markings, but also in native climate. Hence the absurdity of those who would persuade us, that the Woodcock of America crosses the Atlantic to Europe, and *vice versa*. These observations have been thought necessary, from the respectability of some of our own writers, who seem to have adopted this opinion.

How far to the north our Woodcock is found, I am unable to say. It is not mentioned as a bird of Hudson's Bay, and, being altogether unknown in the northern parts of Europe, it is very probable that its migrations do not extend to a very high latitude; for it may be laid down as a general rule, that those birds which migrate to the arctic regions, in either continent, are very often common to both. The head of the Woodcock is of singular conformation, large, somewhat triangular, and the eye fixed at a remarkable distance from the bill, and high in the head. This construction was necessary to give a greater range of vision, and to secure the eye from injury, while the owner is searching in the mire. The flight of the Woodcock is slow. When flushed at any time in the woods, he rises to the height of the bushes or underwood, and almost instantly drops behind them again at a short distance, generally running off for several yards as soon as he touches the ground. The notion that there are two species of

Woodcock in this country, probably originated from the great difference of size between the male and female, the latter being considerably the larger.

The male Woodcock is ten inches and a half long, and sixteen inches in extent; bill, a brownish flesh color, black towards the tip, the upper mandible ending in a slight knob, that projects about one tenth of an inch beyond the lower,* each grooved, and, in length, somewhat more than two inches and a half; forehead, line over the eye, and whole lower parts, reddish tawny; sides of the neck, inclining to ash; between the eye and bill, a slight streak of dark brown; crown, from the forepart of the eye backwards, black, crossed by three narrow bands of brownish white; cheeks, marked with a bar of black, variegated with light brown; edges of the back, and of the scapulars, pale bluish white; back and scapulars, deep black, each feather tipped or marbled with light brown and bright ferruginous, with numerous fine zigzag lines of black crossing the lighter parts; quills, plain dusky brown; tail, black, each feather marked along the outer edge with small spots of pale brown, and ending in narrow tips, of a pale drab color above, and silvery white below; lining of the wing, bright rust; legs and feet, a pale reddish flesh color; eye, very full and black, seated high and very far back in the head; weight, five ounces and a half, sometimes six.

The female is twelve inches long, and eighteen in extent; weighs eight ounces; and differs also in having the bill very near three inches in length: the black on the back is not quite so intense; and the sides under the wings are slightly barred with dusky.

The young Woodcocks of a week or ten days old are covered with down of a brownish white color, and are marked from the bill along the crown to the hind head, with a broad stripe of deep brown; another line of the same passes through the eyes to the hind head, curving under the eye; from the back to the rudiments of the tail, runs another of the same tint, and also on the sides under the wings; the throat and breast are considerably tinged with rufous; and the quills at this age are just bursting from their light blue sheaths, and appear marbled, as in the old birds; the legs and bill are of a pale purplish ash color, the latter about an inch long. When taken, they utter a long, clear, but feeble *peep*, not louder than that of a mouse. They are far inferior to young Partridges in running and skulking; and, should the female unfortunately be killed, may easily be taken on the spot.

* Mr. Pennant, (*Arctic Zoology*, p. 463,) in describing the American Woodcock, says, that the lower mandible is much shorter than the upper. From the appearance of his figure, it is evident that the specimen from which that and his description were taken, had lost nearly half an inch from the lower mandible, probably broken off by accident. Turton and others have repeated the mistake.

RUFFED GROUSE.— TETRAO UMBELLUS.— Fɪɢ. 195.

Arct. Zool. p. 301, No. 179. — Ruffed Heathcock, or Grouse, *Edw.* 248. —La gelinote huppée de Pennsylvanie, *Briss.* i. 214.   *Pl. enl.* 104. — *Buff.* ii. 281. —
Phil. Trans. 62, 393. — *Turt. Syst.* 454. — *Peale's Museum,* No. 4702

BONASIA UMBELLUS. — Bᴏɴᴀᴘᴀʀᴛᴇ.*

Tetrao umbellus, *Temm. Pig. et Gall. Ind.* p. 704. — Tétrao hurpecal, *Temm. Pig.
et Gall.* iii. p. 161. — Bonasia umbellus, *Steph. Cont. Sh. Zool.* xi. p. 300. — Bonasia umbellus, *Bonap. Synop.* p. 126. — The Ruffed Grouse, *Aud. Orn. Biog.*
i. p. 211, pl. 41, male and female.

Tʜɪs is the Partridge of the Eastern States, and the Pheasant of
Pennsylvania and the southern districts. It is represented in Fig.
195, of its full size, and was faithfully copied from a perfect and very
beautiful specimen.

This elegant species is well known in almost every quarter of the
United States, and appears to inhabit a very extensive range of country. It is common at Moose Fort, on Hudson's Bay, in lat. 51°; is
frequent in the upper parts of Georgia; very abundant in Kentucky
and the Indiana Territory; and was found by Capt. Lewis and Clark
in crossing the great range of mountains that divide the waters of
the Columbia and Missouri, more than three thousand miles, by their
measurement, from the mouth of the latter. Its favorite places of resort are high mountains, covered with the balsam pine, hemlock, and
such like evergreens. Unlike the Pinnated Grouse, it always prefers
the woods; is seldom or never found in open plains; but loves the
pine-sheltered declivities of mountains near streams of water. This
great difference of disposition in two species, whose food seems to be
nearly the same, is very extraordinary. In those open plains called
the Barrens of Kentucky, the Pinnated Grouse was seen in great
numbers, but none of the Ruffed; while, in the high groves with which
that singular tract of country is interspersed, the latter, or Pheasant,
was frequently met with; but not a single individual of the former.

The native haunts of the Pheasant being a cold, high, mountainous,
and woody country, it is natural to expect that, as we descend from
thence to the sea-shores, and the low, flat, and warm climate of the
Southern States, these birds should become more rare; and such indeed is the case. In the lower parts of Carolina, Georgia, and Florida, they are very seldom observed; but, as we advance inland to the
mountains, they again make their appearance. In the lower parts of
New Jersey, we indeed occasionally meet with them; but this is
owing to the more northerly situation of the country; for even here
they are far less numerous than among the mountains.

Dr. Turton, and several other English writers, have spoken of a
Long-tailed Grouse, said to inhabit the back parts of Virginia, which
can be no other than the present species, there being, as far as I am

* *Bonasia* is a sub-genus, formed by the Prince of Musignano, for the reception
of this bird. The distinctions are, the unplumed tarsi and toes, contrasted with
Tetrao, where the former are thickly clothed. — Eᴅ.

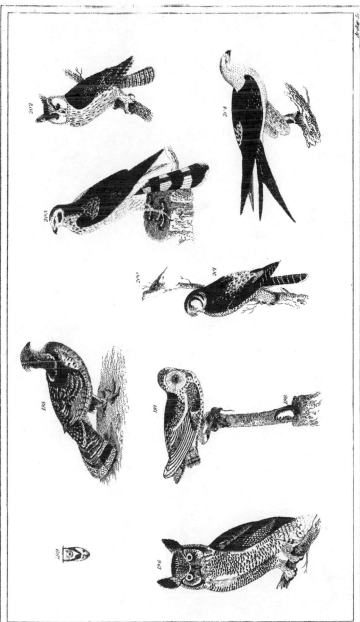

195 Barred Owl. 196 Great Horned Owl. 197 Barn O. 198 Meadow Mouse. 199 Red Bat. 200 Small Headed Flycatcher. 201 Hawk Owl. 202 Long eared Owl. 203 Hawk Owl. 204 Swallow tailed Hawk. 204½ Marsh Hawk.

acquainted, only these two, the Ruffed and Pinnated Grouse, found native within the United States.

The manners of the Pheasant are solitary; they are seldom found in coveys of more than four or five together, and more usually in pairs, or singly. They leave their sequestered haunts in the woods early in the morning, and seek the path or road, to pick up gravel, and glean among the droppings of the horses. In travelling among the mountains that bound the Susquehanna, I was always able to furnish myself with an abundant supply of these birds every morning without leaving the path. If the weather be foggy, or lowering, they are sure to be seen in such situations. They generally move along with great stateliness, their broad, fan-like tail spread out in the manner exhibited in the drawing. The drumming, as it is usually called, of the Pheasant, is another singularity of this species. This is performed by the male alone. In walking through solitary woods, frequented by these birds, a stranger is surprised by suddenly hearing a kind of thumping, very similar to that produced by striking two full-blown ox-bladders together, but much louder; the strokes at first are slow and distinct; but gradually increase in rapidity, till they run into each other, resembling the rumbling sound of very distant thunder, dying away gradually on the ear. After a few minutes' pause, this is again repeated, and, in a calm day, may be heard nearly half a mile off. This drumming is most common in spring, and is the call of the cock to his favorite female. It is produced in the following manner: The bird, standing on an old, prostrate log, generally in a retired and sheltered situation, lowers his wings, erects his expanded tail, contracts his throat, elevates the two tufts of feathers on the neck, and inflates his whole body, something in the manner of the Turkey Cock, strutting and wheeling about with great stateliness. After a few manœuvres of this kind, he begins to strike with his stiffened wings in short and quick strokes, which become more and more rapid until they run into each other, as has been already described. This is most common in the morning and evening, though I have heard them drumming at all hours of the day. By means of this, the gunner is led to the place of his retreat; though, to those unacquainted with the sound, there is great deception in the supposed distance, it generally appearing to be much nearer than it really is.*

The Pheasant begins to pair in April, and builds its nest early in May. This is placed on the ground, at the root of a bush, old log, or

---

* Mr. Audubon confirms the correctness of Wilson's comparison of the drumming noise produced by this bird. He mentions having often called them within shot by imitating the sound, which he accomplished "by beating a large, inflated bullock's bladder with a stick, keeping up as much as possible the same *time* as that in which the bird beats. At the sound produced by the bladder and the stick, the male Grouse, inflamed with jealousy, has flown directly towards me, when, being prepared, I have easily shot it. An equally successful stratagem is employed to decoy the males of our Little Partridge, by imitating the call-note of the female during spring and summer; but in no instance, after repeated trials, have I been able to entice the Pinnated Grouse to come towards me, whilst imitating the *booming* sounds of that bird."

Most game are very easily called by those expert at imitating sounds. Grouse are often called by poachers, and Partridges may be brought near by a quill and horse-hair. Many of the *Tringæ* and *Totani* are easily whistled. — ED.

other sheltered and solitary situation, well surrounded with withered leaves. Unlike that of the Quail, it is open above, and is usually composed of dry leaves and grass. The eggs are from nine to fifteen in number, of a brownish white, without any spots, and nearly as large as those of a Pullet. The young leave the nest as soon as hatched, and are directed by the cluck of the mother, very much in the manner of the Common Hen. On being surprised, she exhibits all the distress and affectionate manœuvres of the Quail, and of most other birds, to lead you away from the spot. 1 once started a hen Pheasant with a single young one, seemingly only a few days old: there might have been more, but I observed only this one. The mother fluttered before me for a moment; but, suddenly darting towards the young one, seized it in her bill, and flew off along the surface through the woods, with great steadiness and rapidity, till she was beyond my sight, leaving me in great surprise at the incident. I made a very close and active search around the spot for the rest, but without success. Here was a striking instance of something more than what is termed blind instinct, in this remarkable deviation from her usual manœuvres when she has a numerous brood. It would have been impossible for me to have injured this affectionate mother, who had exhibited such an example of presence of mind, reason, and sound judgment, as must have convinced the most bigoted advocates of mere instinct. To carry off a whole brood in this manner at once would have been impossible, and to attempt to save one at the expense of the rest would be unnatural. She therefore usually takes the only possible mode of saving them in that case, by decoying the person in pursuit of herself, by such a natural imitation of lameness as to impose on most people. But here, in the case of a single solitary young one, she instantly altered her plan, and adopted the most simple and effectual means for its preservation.

The Pheasant generally springs within a few yards, with a loud, whirring noise,* and flies with great vigor through the woods, beyond

---

* Mr. Audubon has the following observations on the flight and whirring noise produced during it:— " When this bird rises from the ground at a time when pursued by an enemy, or tracked by a dog, it produces a loud, whirring sound, resembling that of the whole tribe, excepting the Black Cock of Europe, which has less of it than any other species. This whirring sound is never heard when the Grouse rises of its own accord, for the purpose of removing from one place to another; nor, in similar circumstances, is it commonly produced by our Little Partridge. In fact, I do not believe that it is emitted by any species of Grouse, unless when surprised and forced to rise. I have often been lying on the ground in the woods or the fields for hours at a time, for the express purpose of observing the movements and habits of different birds, and have frequently seen a Partridge or a Grouse rise on wing from within a few yards of the spot in which I lay, unobserved by them, as gently and softly as any other bird, and without producing any whirring sound. Nor even when this Grouse ascends to the top of a tree, does it make any greater noise than other birds of the same size would do."

The structure of the wings among all the *Tetraonidœ* and *Phasianidœ* is such as to preclude the possibility of an entirely noiseless flight, when the members are actively used; but I have no doubt that it can be, and is sometimes, increased. When any kind of game is suddenly sprung, or alarmed, the wings are made use of with more violence than when the flight is fairly commenced, or a rise to the branch of a tree is only contemplated. I have heard it produced by all our British game to a certain extent, when flying over me, perfectly unalarmed. The noise is certainly produced by the rapid action of the wings, and I believe the birds cannot

reach of view, before it alights. With a good dog, however, they are easily found ; and at some times exhibit a singular degree of infatuation, by looking down from the branches where they sit, on the dog be low, who, the more noise he keeps up, seems the more to confuse and stupefy them, so that they may be shot down, one by one, till the whole are killed, without attempting to fly off. In such cases, those on the lower limbs must be taken first ; for, should the upper ones be first killed, in their fall they alarm those below, who immediately fly off. In deep snows they are usually taken in traps, commonly dead traps, supported by a figure 4 trigger. At this season, when suddenly alarmed, they frequently dive into the snow, particularly when it has newly fallen, and, coming out at a considerable distance, again take wing. They are pretty hard to kill, and will often carry off a large load to the distance of two hundred yards, and drop down dead. Sometimes, in the depth of winter, they approach the farm-house, and lurk near the barn, or about the garden. They have also been often taken young, and tamed, so as to associate with the fowls ; and their eggs have frequently been hatched under the Common Hen ; but these rarely survive until full grown. They are exceedingly fond of the seeds of grapes ; occasionally eat ants, chestnuts, blackberries, and various vegetables. Formerly they were numerous in the immediate vicinity of Philadelphia ; but, as the woods were cleared and population increased, they retreated to the interior. At present there are very few to be found within several miles of the city, and those only singly, in the most solitary and retired woody recesses.

The Pheasant is in best order for the table in September and October. At this season they feed chiefly on whortleberries, and the little, red, aromatic partridgeberries ; the last of which give their flesh a peculiar, delicate flavor. With the former our mountains are literally covered from August to November ; and these constitute, at that season, the greater part of their food. During the deep snows of winter, they

exert that with a totally noiseless flight. Sounds at variance from that occasioned by ordinary flight, are produced by many birds ; particularly during the breeding season, when different motions are employed, and it appears to me to be rather a consequence depending on the peculiar flight, than the flight employed to produce the sound as a love or other call. Such is the booming noise produced by Snipes in spring, always accompanied by the almost imperceptible motion of the wings in the very rapid descent of the bird. A somewhat similar sound is produced by the Lapwing, when flying near her nest or young, and is always heard during a rapid flight performed diagonally downwards. The cock Pheasant produces a loud *whir* by a violent motion of his wings after calling. A very peculiar rustling is heard when the Peacock raises his train, and the cause, a rapid, trembling motion of the feathers, is easily perceived ; and the strut of the Turkey Cock is produced apparently by the rapid exertion of the muscles acting on the roots of the quills.

Under this species may be mentioned the *T. Sabinii* of Douglas. It is so very closely allied, that Dr. Richardson remarks, "After a careful comparison of Mr. Douglas's *T. Sabinii,* deposited in the Edinburgh Museum, they appeared to me to differ in no respect from the young of *T. umbellus."*

The characters of *T. Sabinii,* given by Mr. Douglas, are, — Rufus, nigro notatus ; dorso maculis cordiformibus, nucha aliaque lineis ferrugineo-flovis ; abdomine albo brunneo fasciato ; rectricibus fasciatis, fascia subapicali lata nigra.

Mr. Douglas thinks that there is some difference between the specimens of *T. umbellus,* killed on the Rocky Mountains, and more northern parts, from those in the states of New York and Pennsylvania, and proposes, if they should be hereafter found distinct, that it should stand as *T. umbelloides.* — ED.

have recourse to the buds of alder, and the tender buds of the laurel. I have frequently found their crops distended with a large handful of these latter alone; and it has been confidently asserted, that, after having fed for some time on the laurel buds, their flesh becomes highly dangerous to eat of, partaking of the poisonous qualities of the plant. The same has been asserted of the flesh of the deer, when, in severe weather and deep snows, they subsist on the leaves and bark of the laurel. Though I have myself ate freely of the flesh of the Pheasant, after emptying it of large quantities of laurel buds, without experiencing any bad consequences, yet, from the respectability of those, some of them eminent physicians, who have particularized cases in which it has proved deleterious, and even fatal, I am inclined to believe, that, in certain cases, where this kind of food has been long continued, and the birds allowed to remain undrawn for several days, until the contents of the crop and stomach have had time to diffuse themselves through the flesh, as is too often the case, it may be unwholesome, and even dangerous. Great numbers of these birds are brought to our markets, at all times, during fall and winter; some of which are brought from a distance of more than a hundred miles, and have been probably dead a week or two, unpicked and undrawn, before they are purchased for the table. Regulations, prohibiting them from being brought to market, unless picked and drawn, would, very probably, be a sufficient security from all danger. At these inclement seasons, however, they are generally lean and dry; and, indeed, at all times their flesh is far inferior to that of the Pinnated Grouse. They are usually sold, in Philadelphia market, at from three quarters of a dollar to a dollar and a quarter a pair, and sometimes higher.

The Pheasant, or Partridge, of New England, is eighteen inches long, and twenty-three inches in extent; bill, a horn color, paler below; eye, reddish hazel, immediately above which is a small spot of bare skin, of a scarlet color; crested; head and neck, variegated with black, red brown, white, and pale brown; sides of the neck, furnished with a tuft of large black feathers, twenty-nine or thirty in number, which it occasionally raises; this tuft covers a large space of the neck destitute of feathers; body above, a bright rust color, marked with oval spots of yellowish white, and sprinkled with black; wings, plain olive brown, exteriorly edged with white, spotted with olive; the tail is rounding, extends five inches beyond the tips of the wings, is of a bright reddish brown, beautifully marked with numerous, waving, transverse bars of black, is also crossed by a broad band of black, within half an inch of the tip, which is bluish white, thickly sprinkled and specked with black; body below, white, marked with large blotches of pale brown; the legs are covered half way to the feet with hairy down of a brownish white color; legs and feet, pale ash; toes, pectinated along the sides; the two exterior ones joined at the base, as far as the first joint, by a membrane; vent, yellowish rust color.

The female, and young birds, differ in having the ruff or tufts of feathers on the neck of a dark brown color; as well as the bar of black on the tail inclining much to the same tint.

GREAT HORNED OWL.— STRIX VIRGINIANA.— Fig. 196.

Arct. Zool. p. 228, No. 114.— *Edw.* 60.— *Lath.* i. 119.— *Turt. Syst.* p. 166.—
Peale's Museum, No. 410.

BUBO VIRGINIANA.— Cuvier.*

Le grand Hibou d'Amerique, *Cuv. Reg. Anim.* i. p. 329.— Strix Virginia, *Bonap.
Synop.* p. 37.— The Great Horned Owl, *Aud. Orn. Biog.* i. p. 313, pl. 61, male
and female.— Strix (Bubo) Virginiana, *North. Zool.* ii. p. 82.

THIS noted and formidable Owl is found in almost every quarter of
the United States. His favorite residence, however, is in the dark

* Cuvier uses the title *Bubo* to distinguish those species, which, as in the genus
Otus, have the tarsi feathered, and are furnished with egrets, but have the disk surrounding the face less distinctly marked, and have a small external conch. He assumes, as the type, the Eagle Owl of Europe, but places the Virginian species, in
his genus *Otus*, with the small Long-eared Owl of Britain ; the latter has the disk
very distinct, and the ears large, the characters of *Otus ;* but the American bird is
in every way a true *Bubo*, as defined by the great French naturalist. It is a genus
of very extensive geographical distribution ; individuals exist in almost every latitude, and in the four quarters of the world. Their abodes are the deep and interminable forests, their habits nocturnal, though they are not so much annoyed or stupefied
if disturbed in the day, and much more difficult to approach, earnestly watching
their pursuer.

An Eagle Owl, in my possession, remains quiet during the day, unless he is shown
some prey, when he becomes eager to possess it, and, when it is put within his reach,
at once clutches it, and retires to a corner to devour at leisure. During night he is
extremely active, and sometimes keeps up an incessant bark. It is so similar to that
of a cur, or terrier, as to annoy a large Labrador house dog, who expressed his dissatisfaction by replying to him, and disturbing the inmates nightly. I at first mistook the cry also for that of a dog, and, without any recollection of the Owl, sallied
forth to destroy this disturber of our repose ; and it was not until tracing the sound
to the cage, that I became satisfied of the author of the annoyance. I have remarked, that he barks more incessantly during a clear winter night than at any other
time, and the thin air at that season makes the cry very distinctly heard to a considerable distance. This bird also shows a great antipathy to dogs, and will perceive
one at a considerable distance, nor is it possible to distract his attention so long as
the animal remains in sight. When first perceived, the feathers are raised, and the
wings lowered, as when feeding, and the head moved round, following the object
while in sight ; if food is thrown, it will be struck with the foot, and held, but no
further attention paid to it.

The Virginian Owl seems to be very extensively distributed over America, is
tolerably common over every part of the continent, and Mr. Swainson has seen
specimens from the table-land of Mexico. The southern specimens present only a
brighter coloring in the rufous parts of the plumage.

According to all authorities, Owls have been regarded as objects of superstition ;
and this has sometimes been taken advantage of by the well informed, for purposes
far from what ought to be the duty of a better education to inculcate. None are
more accessible to such superstitions than the primitive natives of Ireland, and the
north of Scotland. Dr. Richardson thus relates an instance, which came to his own
knowledge, of the consequences arising from a visit of this nocturnal wanderer.

" A party of Scottish Highlanders, in the service of the Hudson's Bay Company,
happened, in a winter journey, to encamp after nightfall in a dense clump of trees,
whose dark tops and lofty stems, the growth of more than one century, gave a
solemnity to the scene that strongly tended to excite the superstitious feelings of the
Highlanders. The effect was heightened by the discovery of a tomb, which, with a
natural taste often exhibited by the Indians, had been placed in this secluded spot.

solitudes of deep swamps, covered with a growth of gigantic timber ;
and here, as soon as evening draws on, and mankind retire to rest, he
sends forth such sounds as seem scarcely to belong to this world,
startling the solitary pilgrim as he slumbers by his forest fire,

Making night hideous.

Along the mountainous shores of the Ohio, and amidst the deep
forests of Indiana, alone, and reposing in the woods, this ghostly watchman has frequently warned me of the approach of morning, and

Our travellers, having finished their supper, were trimming their fire preparatory to
retiring to rest, when the slow and dismal notes of the Horned Owl fell on the ear
with a startling nearness. None of them being acquainted with the sound, they at
once concluded, that so unearthly a voice must be the moaning of the spirit of the
departed, whose repose they supposed they had disturbed, by inadvertently making
a fire of some of the wood of which his tomb had been constructed. They passed
a tedious night of fear, and, with the first dawn of day, hastily quitted the ill-omened
spot."

In India there is a large Owl, known by the native name of *Googoo*, or *Ooloo*,
which, according to some interesting notices, accompanying a large box of birds
sent to Mr. Selby from the vicinity of Hydrabad, is held as an object of both fear
and veneration. "If an *Ooloo* should alight on the house of a Hindoo, he would
leave it immediately, take the thatch off, and put fresh on. The eyes and brain are
considered an infallible cure for fits in children, and both are often given to women
in labor. The flesh, bones, &c., boiled down to a jelly, are used to cure spasms or
rheumatism. Some of the fat, given to a child newly born, averts misfortune from
him for life." Independent of these, says our correspondent, "there are innumerable superstitions regarding this bird, and a native will always kill one when he
has an opportunity."

We must mention here a very beautiful species, which is certainly *first accurately*
described in the second volume of the *Northern Zoology*, though Wilson appears to
have had some information regarding a large white Owl ; and Dr. Richardson is of
opinion, that the *Strix Scandiaca* of Linnæus, if not actually the species, at least
resembles it. It is characterized and figured by the northern travellers under the
name of *Bubo arctica*, Arctic, or White-horned Owl ; and we add the greater part
of their description.

"This very beautiful Owl appears to be rare, only one specimen having been
seen by the members of the expedition. It was observed flying at mid-day, in the
immediate vicinity of Carlton House, and was brought down with an arrow by an
Indian boy. I obtained no information respecting its habits.

"The facial disk is very imperfect; the ears, small, and without an operculum,
as in *Strix Virginiana;* the ear-feathers, ample; but the disk even smaller than
in the last-mentioned bird, and the tarsi somewhat longer. The toes are similarly
connected. The tail is of moderate length, and considerably rounded. The bill
is strong and rather short.

"*Description.* — Color of the bill and claws, bluish black. Irides, yellow.
The face is white, bounded posteriorly by blackish brown, succeeded by white,
which two latter colors are continued in a mixed band across the throat. Egrets,
colored at the base, like the adjoining plumage; the longer feathers tipped with
blackish brown, their inner webs, white, varied with wood brown. The whole dorsal aspect is marked with undulated lines, or fine bars, of umber brown, alternating
with white ; the markings bearing some resemblance to those of the Virginian Owl,
but being much more lively and handsome. On the greater wing-coverts, on the
inner half of the scapularies, and also partially on the neck and lesser wing-coverts,
the white is tinged, or replaced by pale wood brown. The primaries and secondaries are wood brown, with a considerable portion of white along the margins of
their inner webs. They are crossed by from five to six distant umber brown bars
on both webs, the intervening spaces being finely speckled with the same. Near the
tips of the primaries, the fine sprinkling of the dark color nearly obscures the wood
brown. On the tertiaries, the wood brown is mostly replaced by white. The tail-
feathers are white, deeply tinged on their inner webs by wood brown, and crossed

amused me with his singular exclamations, sometimes sweeping down and around my fire, uttering a loud and sudden *Waugh O! Waugh O!* sufficient to have alarmed a whole garrison. He has other nocturnal solos, no less melodious, one of which very strikingly resembles the half-suppressed screams of a person suffocating, or throttled, and cannot fail of being exceedingly entertaining to a lonely, benighted traveller, in the midst of an Indian wilderness!

This species inhabits the country round Hudson's Bay; and according to Pennant, who considers it a mere variety of the Eagle Owl (*Strix bubo*) of Europe, is found in Kamtschatka; extends even to the

by six bars of umber brown, about half as broad as the intervening spaces; their tips are white.

"*Under surface.*—Chin, white. Throat, crossed by the band above mentioned, behind which there is a large space of pure snow white, that is bounded on the breast by blotches of liver brown, situated on the tips of the feathers. The belly and long plumage of the flanks are white, crossed by narrow, regular bars of dark brown. The vent-feathers, under tail-coverts, thighs, and feet, are pure white. The linings of the wings are also white, with the exception of a brown spot on the tips of the greater interior coverts."

Audubon has the following remarks on their incubation, which are somewhat at variance with Wilson. It would also appear that this bird makes love during the day.

"Early in February, the Great Horned Owls are seen to pair. The curious evolutions of the male in the air, or his motions when he has alighted near his beloved, it is impossible to describe. His bowings, and the snappings of his bill, are extremely ludicrous; and no sooner is the female assured that the attentions paid her by the beau are the result of a sincere affection, than she joins in the motions of her future mate.

"The nest, which is very bulky, is usually fixed on a large, horizontal branch, not far from the trunk of the tree. It is composed externally of crooked sticks, and is lined with coarse grasses and some feathers. The whole measures nearly three feet in diameter. The eggs, which are from three to six, are almost globular in form, and of a dull white color. The male assists the female in sitting on the eggs. Only one brood is raised in the season. The young remain in the nest until fully fledged, and afterwards follow the parents for a considerable time, uttering a mournful sound, to induce them to supply them with food. They acquire the full plumage of the old birds in the first spring, and until then are considerably lighter, with more dull buff in their tints. I have found nests belonging to this species in large hollows of decayed trees, and twice in the fissures of rocks. In all these cases, little preparation had been made previous to the laying of the eggs, as I found only a few grasses and feathers placed under them.

"The Great Horned Owl lives retired, and it is seldom that more than one is found in the neighborhood of a farm, after the breeding season; but as almost every detached farm is visited by one of these dangerous and powerful marauders, it may be said to be abundant. The havock which it commits is very great. I have known a plantation almost stripped of the whole of the poultry raised upon it during spring, by one of these daring foes of the feathered race, in the course of the ensuing winter.

"This species is very powerful, and equally spirited. It attacks wild Turkeys when half grown, and often masters them. Mallards, Guinea-Fowls, and common barn-fowls, prove an easy prey; and on seizing them, it carries them off in its talons from the farm-yards to the interior of the woods. When wounded it exhibits a revengeful tenacity of spirit, scarcely surpassed by any of the noblest of the Eagle tribe, disdaining to scramble away like the Barred Owl, but facing its enemy with undaunted courage, protruding its powerful talons, and snapping its bill, as long as he continues in its presence. On these occasions, its large goggle eyes are seen to open and close in quick succession, and the feathers of its body, being raised, swell out its apparent bulk to nearly double the natural size."—Ed.

37 *

Arctic Regions, where it is often found white; and occurs as low as Astrakan. It has also been seen white in the United States; but this has doubtless been owing to disease or natural defect, and not to climate. It preys on young rabbits, squirrels, rats, mice, partridges, and small birds of various kinds. It has been often known to prowl about the farm-house, and carry off Chickens from roost. A very large one, wing-broken while on a foraging excursion of this kind, was kept about the house for several days, and at length disappeared, no one knew how. Almost every day after this, Hens and Chickens also disappeared, one by one, in an unaccountable manner, till, in eight or ten days, very few were left remaining. The fox, the minx, and weasel, were alternately the reputed authors of this mischief, until one morning, the old lady herself, rising before day to bake, in passing towards the oven, surprised her late prisoner, the Owl, regaling himself on the body of a newly-killed Hen! The thief instantly made for his hole under the house, from whence the enraged matron soon dislodged him with the brush handle, and without mercy despatched him. In this snug retreat were found the greater part of the feathers, and many large fragments, of her whole family of Chickens.

There is something in the character of the Owl so recluse, solitary, and mysterious, something so discordant in the tones of its voice, heard only amid the silence and gloom of night, and in the most lonely and sequestered situations, as to have strongly impressed the minds of mankind in general with sensations of awe and abhorrence of the whole tribe. The poets have indulged freely in this general prejudice; and in their descriptions and delineations of midnight storms, and gloomy scenes of nature, the Owl is generally introduced to heighten the horror of the picture. Ignorance and superstition, in all ages, and in all countries, listen to the voice of the Owl, and even contemplate its physiognomy with feelings of disgust, and a kind of fearful awe. The priests, or conjurers, among some of our Indian nations, have taken advantage of the reverential horror for this bird, and have adopted the *Great Horned Owl*, the subject of the present account, as the symbol or emblem of their office. "Among the Creeks," says Mr. Bartram, in his *Travels*, p. 504, "the junior priests, or students, constantly wear a white mantle, and have a Great Owl skin cased and stuffed very ingeniously, so well executed as almost to appear like the living bird, having large, sparkling, glass beads, or buttons, fixed in the head for eyes. This insignia of wisdom and divination they wear sometimes as a crest on the top of the head; at other times the image sits on the arm, or is borne on the hand. These bachelors are also distinguished from the other people by their taciturnity, grave and solemn countenance, dignified step, and singing to themselves songs or hymns in a low, sweet voice, as they stroll about the town."

Nothing is a more effectual cure for superstition than a knowledge of the general laws and productions of nature; nor more forcibly leads our reflections to the first, great, self-existent CAUSE of all, to whom our reverential awe is then humbly devoted, and not to any of his dependent creatures. With all the gloomy habits and ungracious tones of the Owl, there is nothing in this bird supernatural or mysterious, or more than that of a simple bird of prey, formed for feeding by night, like many other animals, and of reposing by day. The harshness of its voice, occasioned by the width and capacity of its throat, may be intended by Heaven as an alarm and warning to the birds and animals on which it preys, to secure themselves from danger. The voices of all carnivorous birds and animals are also observed to be harsh and hideous, probably for this very purpose.

The Great Horned Owl is not migratory, but remains with us the whole year. During the day he slumbers in the thick evergreens of deep swamps, or seeks shelter in large hollow trees. He is very rarely seen abroad by day, and never but when disturbed. In the month of May they usually begin to build. The nest is generally placed in the fork of a tall tree, and is constructed of sticks piled in considerable quantities, lined with dry leaves and a few feathers. Sometimes they choose a hollow tree; and, in that case, carry in but few materials. The female lays four eggs, nearly as large as those of a Hen, almost globular, and of a pure white. In one of these nests, after the young had flown, were found the heads and bones of two Chickens, the legs and head of the Golden-winged Woodpecker, and part of the wings and feathers of several other birds. It is generally conjectured that they hatch but once in the season.

The length of the male of this species is twenty inches; the bill is large, black, and strong, covered at the base with a cere; the eyes, golden yellow; the horns are three inches in length, and very broad, consisting of twelve or fourteen feathers, their webs black, broadly edged with bright tawny; face, rusty, bounded on each side by a band of black; space between the eyes and bill, whitish; whole lower parts elegantly marked with numerous transverse bars of dusky on a bright tawny ground, thinly interspersed with white; vent, pale yellow ochre, barred with narrow lines of brown; legs and feet large, and covered with feathers or hairy down of a pale brown color; claws, very large blue black; tail, rounded, extending about an inch beyond the tips of the wings, crossed with six or seven narrow bars of brown, and variegated or marbled with brown and tawny; whole upper parts finely pencilled with dusky, on a tawny and whitish ground; chin, pure white, under that a band of brown, succeeded by another narrow one of white; eyes, very large.

The female is full two feet in length, and has not the white on the throat so pure. She has also less of the bright ferruginous or tawny tint below; but is principally distinguished by her superior magnitude.

WHITE, OR BARN OWL.—STRIX FLAMMEA.—Fig. 197.

Lath. i. 138. — *Arct. Zool.* p. 235, No. 124. — *Phil. Trans.* iii. 138. — L'Effraie,
ou la Fresaie, *Buff.* i. 366, pl. 26, *Pl. enl.* 440. — *Bewick's Brit. Birds,* i. p. 89.
— Common Owl, *Turt. Syst.* p. 170. — *Peale's Museum,* No. 486.

ULULA FLAMMEA. — Cuvier.*

Strix flammea, *Bonap. Synop.* p. 38.

THIS Owl, though so common in Europe, is much rarer in this part of the United States than the preceding, and is only found here during very severe winters. This may possibly be owing to the want of those favorite recesses in this part of the world, which it so much affects in the eastern continent. The multitudes of old, ruined castles, towers, monasteries, and cathedrals, that every where rise to view in those countries, are the chosen haunts of this well-known species. Its savage cries at night give, with vulgar minds, a cast of supernatural horror to those venerable, mouldering piles of antiquity. This species, being common to both continents, doubtless extends to the Arctic Regions. It also inhabits Tartary, where, according to Pennant, " the Monguls and natives almost pay it divine honors, because they attribute to this species the preservation of the founder of their empire, Ginghis Khan. That prince, with his small army, happened to be surprised and put to flight by his enemies, and forced to conceal himself in a little coppice ; an owl settled on the bush under which he was hid, and induced his pursuers not to search there, as they thought it impossible that any man could be concealed in a place where that

---

* From the authority of most writers, this Owl is common to both continents. Temminck says those from America are *exactly* the same. I have not personally had an opportunity of comparing them.

In all true night-feeding birds, or those that require to steal upon their prey unobserved, the general plumage is formed for a light, smooth, and noiseless flight; but the members are not adapted for great swiftness, or for seizing their prey by quick and sudden evolutions. The form is comparatively light, as far as the necessary requisites for sufficient strength can be combined with it ; and the plumage, being ample and loose, assists by its buoyancy, and does not offer the same resistance to the air as one of a stiff and rigid texture. The wings, the great organs of locomotion, and which, in flight, produce the most noise, are rounded, having the webs of the feathers very broad, calculated for a powerful and *sustaining* flight ; and the mechanism of the feathers at once bespeaks an intention to destroy the sound produced by motion. In all those birds which perform very swift and rapid flights — the Falcons, for instance, Swifts, or Swallows, many of the sea fowl, the Fregate Bird — the wings are very pointed, (a contrariety of form to the *Strigidæ*,) with the plumules very closely united, and locked together, so as to form almost a thin or solid slip. These produce more resistance, and act as a strong propelling medium, when vigorously used. In the Owls the wings present a larger surface, but are not so capable of swift motion ; and, to prevent the noise which would necessarily be produced by the violent percussion of so great an expanse, the webs are entirely detached at the tips, and the plumules of the inner ones being drawn to a fine point, thus offer a free passage to the air, and a gradual diminution of resistance. As a further proof that this structure is so intended, we find it to a much less extent in those species that feed occasionally during the day, and we have also the narrowing and acumination of the wings, denoting superior flight ; while, in some, there is a still greater digression in the elongated tail. — ED.

bird would perch. From thenceforth they held it to be sacred, and every one wore a plume of the feathers of this species on his head. To this day the Kalmucs continue the custom on all great festivals; and some tribes have an idol in form of an owl, to which they fasten the real legs of one." *

This species is rarely found in Pennsylvania in summer. Of its place and manner of building, I am unable, from my own observation, to speak. The bird itself has been several times found in the hollow of a tree, and was once caught in a barn in my neighborhood. European writers inform us that it makes no nest, but deposits its eggs in the holes of walls, and lays five or six, of a whitish color; it is said to feed on mice and small birds, which, like the most of its tribe, it swallows whole, and afterwards emits the bones, feathers, and other indigestible parts, at its mouth, in the form of small round cakes, which are often found in the empty buildings it frequents. During its repose it is said to make a blowing noise resembling the snoring of a man.†

It is distinguished in England by various names, the Barn Owl, the Church Owl, Gillihowlet, and Screech Owl. In the lowlands of Scotland it is universally called the Hoolet.

The White or Barn Owl is fourteen inches long, and upwards of three feet six inches in extent; bill, a whitish horn color, longer than is usual among its tribe; space surrounding each eye, remarkably concave, the radiating feathers meeting in a high, projecting ridge, arching from the bill upwards; between these lies a thick tuft of bright tawny feathers, that are scarcely seen, unless the ridges be separated; face, white, surrounded by a border of narrow, thickset, velvety feathers, of a reddish cream color at the tip, pure silvery white below, and finely shafted with black; whole upper parts, a bright tawny yellow, thickly sprinkled with whitish and pale purple, and beautifully interspersed with larger drops of white, each feather of the back and wing-coverts ending in an oblong spot of white, bounded by black; head, large, tumid; sides of the neck, pale yellow ochre, thinly sprinkled with small touches of dusky; primaries and secondaries, the same, thinly barred, and thickly sprinkled with dull purplish brown; tail, two inches shorter than the tips of the wings, even, or very slightly forked, pale yellowish, crossed with five bars of brown, and thickly dotted with the same; whole lower parts, pure white, thinly interspersed with small round spots of blackish; thighs, the same; legs, long, thinly covered with short white down nearly to the feet, which are of a dirty white, and thickly warted; toes, thinly clad with white hairs; legs and feet, large and clumsy; the ridge, or shoulder of the wing, is tinged with bright orange brown. The aged bird is more white; in some, the spots of black on the breast are wanting, and the color below, a pale yellow; in others, a pure white.

The female measures fifteen inches and a half in length, and three feet eight inches in extent; is much darker above; the lower parts tinged with tawny, and marked also with round spots of black. One of these was lately sent me, which was shot on the border of the

* *Arctic Zoology*, p. 235.   † BEWICK, i. p. 90.

meadows below Philadelphia. Its stomach contained the mangled carcasses of four large meadow mice, hair, bones, and all. The common practice of most Owls is, after breaking the bones, to swallow the mouse entire; the bones, hair, and other indigestible parts, are afterwards discharged from the mouth in large, roundish, dry balls, that are frequently met with in such places as these birds usually haunt.

As the meadow mouse is so eagerly sought after by those birds, and also by great numbers of Hawks, which regularly, at the commencement of winter, resort to the meadows below Philadelphia, and to the marshes along the sea-shore, for the purpose of feeding on these little animals, some account of them may not be improper in this place. Fig. 198 represents the meadow mouse, reduced to one half its natural dimensions. This species appears not to have been taken notice of by Turton in the latest edition of his translation of Linnæus. From the nose to the insertion of the tail, it measures four inches; the tail is between three quarters and an inch long, hairy, and usually curves upwards; the fore feet are short, five-toed, the inner toe very short, but furnished with a claw; hind feet also five-toed; the ears are shorter than the fur, through which, though large, they are scarcely noticeable; the nose is blunt; the color of the back is dark brown, that of the belly, hoary; the fur is long, and extremely fine; the hind feet are placed very far back, and are also short; the eyes exceeding small. This mischievous creature is a great pest to the meadows, burrowing in them in every direction; but is particularly injurious to the embankments raised along the river, perforating them in numerous directions, and admitting the water, which afterwards effects dangerous breaches, inundating large extents of these low grounds, — and thus they become the instruments of their own destruction. In their general figure they bear great resemblance to the common musk rat, and like them swim and dive well. They feed on the bulbous roots of plants, and also on garlic, of which they are remarkably fond.

Another favorite prey of most of our Owls is the Bat, one species of which is represented Fig. 199, as it hung during the day in the woods where I found it. This also appears to be a nondescript. The length of this Bat, from the nose to the tip of the tail, is four inches; the tail itself is as long as the body, but generally curls up inwards; the general color is a bright iron gray, the fur being of a reddish cream at bottom, then strongly tinged with lake, and minutely tipped with white; the ears are scarcely half an inch long, with two slight valves; the nostrils are somewhat tubular; fore teeth, in the upper jaw none, in the lower four, not reckoning the tusks; the eyes are very small black points; the chin, upper part of the breast, and head, are of a pale reddish cream color; the wings have a single hook or claw each, and are so constructed, that the animal may hang either with its head or tail downward. I have several times found two hanging fast locked together behind a leaf, the hook of one fixed in the mouth of the other; the hind feet are furnished with five toes, sharp clawed; the membrane of the wings is dusky; shafts, light brown; extent, twelve inches. In a cave, not far from Carlisle, in Pennsylvania, I found a number of these Bats in the depth of winter, in very severe weather: they were lying on the projecting shelves of the rocks, and when the brand of fire was held near them, wrinkled up their mouths, showing their teeth; when held in the hand for a short time, they became active, and, after being carried into a stove room, flew about as lively as ever.

SMALL-HEADED FLYCATCHER. — MUSCICAPA MINUTA. —
Fig. 200.

SYLVICOLA? MINUTA. — Jardine.

Sylvia minuta, Bonap. Synop. p. 86.

THIS very rare bird, represented in Fig. 200, is the only one I have met with. It was shot on the 24th of April, in an orchard, and was remarkably active, running, climbing, and darting about among the opening buds and blossoms with extraordinary agility. From what quarter of the United States or of North America it is a wanderer, I am unable to determine, having never before met with an individual of the species. Its notes and manner of breeding are also alike unknown to me. This was a male: it measured five inches long, and eight and a quarter in extent; the upper parts were dull yellow olive; the wings, dusky brown, edged with lighter; the greater and lesser coverts, tipped with white; the lower parts, dirty white, stained with dull yellow, particularly on the upper parts of the breast; the tail, dusky brown, the two exterior feathers marked, like those of many others, with a spot of white on the inner vanes; head, remarkably small; bill, broad at the base, furnished with bristles, and notched near the tip; legs, dark brown; feet, yellowish; eye, dark hazel.

Since writing the above, I have shot several individuals of this species in various quarters of New Jersey, particularly in swamps. They all appear to be nearly alike in plumage. Having found them there in June, there is no doubt of their breeding in that state, and, probably, in such situations far to the southward; for many of the southern summer birds that rarely visit Pennsylvania, are yet common to the swamps and pine woods of New Jersey. Similarity of soil and situation, of plants and trees, and, consequently, of fruits, seeds, and insects, &c., are, doubtless, their inducements. The Summer Red-Bird, Great Carolina Wren, Pine-creeping Warbler, and many others, are rarely seen in Pennsylvania, or to the northward, though they are common in many parts of West Jersey.

HAWK OWL. — STRIX HUDSONIA. — Fig. 201.

Little Hawk Owl, *Edw.* 62. — *Lath.* i. 142, No. 29. — *Phil. Trans.* 61, 385. — Le Chat-huant de Canada, *Briss.* ı. 518. — *Buff.* i. 391. — Chouette à longue queue de Siberie, *Pl. enl.* 463. — *Arct. Zool.* p. 234, No. 123. — *Peale's Museum*, No. 500.

SURNIA FUNEREA. — Dumeril.*

Strix (sub-gen. Surnia) funerea, *Bonap. Synop.* p. 35. — Strix funerea, *Temm. Man.* i. p. 86. — *North. Zool.* ii. p. 92.

This is another inhabitant of both continents, a kind of equivocal species, or rather a connecting link between the Hawk and Owl tribes, resembling the latter in the feet, and in the radiating feathers round the eye and bill; but approaching nearer to the former in the smallness of its head, narrowness of its face, and in its length of tail. In short, it seems just such a figure as one would expect to see generated between a Hawk and an Owl of the same size, were it possible for them to produce; and yet is as distinct, independent, and original a species as any other. It has also another strong trait of the Hawk tribe, — in flying and preying by day, contrary to the general habit of Owls. It is characterized as a bold and active species, following the fowler, and carrying off his game as soon as it is shot. It is said to prey on Partridges and other birds; and is very common at Hudson's Bay, where it is called by the Indians *Coparacoch.*† We are also informed that this same species inhabits Denmark and Sweden, is frequent in all Siberia, and on the west side of the Uralian chain as far as Casan and the Volga; but not in Russia.‡ It was also seen by the navigators near Sandwich Sound, in lat. 61 degrees north.

This species is very rare in Pennsylvania, and the more southern parts of the United States. Its favorite range seems to be along the borders of the Arctic Regions, making occasional excursions southwardly when compelled by severity of weather, and consequent scarcity of food. I some time ago received a drawing of this bird, from the district of Maine, where it was considered rare: that, and the specimen from which the drawing in Fig. 201 was taken, which was shot in the neighborhood of Philadelphia, are the only two that have come under my notice. These having luckily happened to be male and female, have enabled me to give a description of both. Of their nest, or manner of breeding, we have no account.

The male of this species is fifteen inches long; the bill, orange

* In this we have the true form of a diurnal Owl. The head is comparatively small; facial disk, imperfect; the ears hardly larger than in birds of prey, and not operculated; the wings and tail more Hawk like, the former, as Wilson observes, with the webs scarcely divided at the tips. Flies by day, and, according to Dr. Richardson, preys during winter on Ptarmigan, which it constantly attends in their spring migrations northward, and is even so bold, on a bird being killed by the hunters, as to pounce down upon it, though it may be unable, from its size, to carry it off. — Ed.

† Edwards.   ‡ Pennant.

yellow, and almost hid among the feathers; plumage of the chin, curving up over the under mandible; eyes, bright orange; head, small; face, narrow, and with very little concavity; cheeks, white; crown and hind head, dusky black, thickly marked with round spots of white; sides of the neck, marked with a large, curving streak of brown black, with another, a little behind it, of a triangular form; back, scapulars, rump, and tail-coverts, brown olive, thickly speckled with broad spots of white; the tail extends three inches beyond the tips of the wings, is of a brown olive color, and crossed with six or seven narrow bars of white, rounded at the end, and also tipped with white; the breast and chin are marked with a large spot of brown olive; upper part of the breast, light; lower, and all the parts below, elegantly barred with dark brown and white; legs and feet, covered to and beyond the claws with long, whitish plumage, slightly yellow, and barred with fine lines of olive; claws, horn color. The weight of this bird was twelve ounces.

The female is much darker above; the quills are nearly black; and the upper part of the breast is blotched with deep blackish brown.

It is worthy of remark, that, in all Owls that fly by night, the exterior edges and sides of the wing-quills are slightly recurved, and end in fine hairs or points; by which means the bird is enabled to pass through the air with the greatest silence — a provision necessary for enabling it the better to surprise its prey. In the Hawk Owl now before us, which flies by day, and to whom this contrivance would be of no consequence, it is accordingly omitted, or at least is scarcely observable. So judicious, so wise, and perfectly applicable, are all the dispositions of the Creator!

MARSH HAWK.—FALCO ULIGINOSUS.—Fig. 203.

Edw. iv. 291.— *Lath.* i. 90.— *Arct. Zool.* p. 208, No. 105.— *Bartram*, p. 290.— *Peale's Museum*, No. 318.

CIRCUS CYANEUS. —Bechstein.

Falco (sub-gen. Circus,) *Bonap. Synop.* p. 33.—Buteo (Circus) cyaneus? var. Americanus, *North. Zool.* ii. p. 55.

A DRAWING of this Hawk was transmitted to Mr. Edwards, more than fifty years ago, by Mr. William Bartram, and engraved in Plate 291 of *Edwards's Ornithology*. At that time, and I believe till now, it has been considered as a species peculiar to this country.

I have examined various individuals of this Hawk, both in summer and in the depth of winter, and find them to correspond so nearly with the Ring-tail of Europe, that I have no doubt of their being the same species.

This Hawk is most numerous where there are extensive meadows and salt marshes, over which it sails very low, making frequent circuitous sweeps over the same ground, in search of a species of mouse, and very abundant in such situations. It occasionally flaps the wings, but is most commonly seen sailing about within a few feet of the surface. They are usually known by the name of the Mouse Hawk along the sea-coast of New Jersey, where they are very common. Several were also brought me last winter from the meadows below Philadelphia. Having never seen its nest, I am unable to describe it from my own observation. It is said, by European writers, to build on the ground, or on low limbs of trees. Mr. Pennant observes, that it sometimes changes to a rust colored variety, except on the rump and tail. It is found, as was to be expected, at Hudson's Bay, being native in both this latitude and that of Britain. We are also informed that it is common in the open and temperate parts of Russia and Siberia; and extends as far as Lake Baikal, though it is said not to be found in the north of Europe.*

The Marsh Hawk is twenty-one inches long, and three feet eleven inches in extent; cere and legs, yellow, the former tinged with green, the latter long and slender; nostril, large, triangular; this and the base of the bill, thickly covered with strong, curving hairs, that rise from the space between the eye and bill, arching over the base of the bill and cere; this is a particular characteristic; bill, blue, black at the end; eye, dark hazel; cartilage overhanging the eye, and also the eyelid, bluish green; spot under the eye, and line from the front over it, brownish white; head above and back, dark glossy chocolate brown, the former slightly seamed with bright ferruginous; scapulars, spotted with the same *under the surface;* lesser coverts and band of the wing, here and there edged with the same; greater coverts and primaries, tipped with whitish; quills, deep brown at the extreme half, some of the outer ones hoary on the exterior edge; all the primaries, yellowish white on the inner vanes and upper half, also barred on the inner vanes with black; tail, long, extending three inches beyond the wings, rounded at the end, and of a pale sorel color, crossed by four broad bars of very dark brown, the two middle feathers excepted, which are barred with deep and lighter shades of chocolate brown; chin, pale ferruginous; round the neck, a collar of bright rust color; breast, belly, and vent, pale rust, shafted with brown; femorals, long, tapering, and of the same pale rust tint; legs, feathered near an inch below the knee. This was a female. The male differs chiefly in being rather lighter, and somewhat less.

This Hawk is particularly serviceable to the rice-fields of the Southern States, by the havock it makes among the clouds of Rice Buntings that spread such devastation among that grain, in its early stage. As it sails low and swiftly over the surface of the field, it keeps the flocks in perpetual fluctuation, and greatly interrupts their depredations. The planters consider one Marsh Hawk to be equal to several negroes for alarming the Rice Birds. Formerly the Marsh Hawk used to be numerous along the Schuylkill and Delaware, during the time the reeds were ripening, and the Reed Birds abundant; but they have of late years become less numerous here.

Mr. Pennant considers the "*strong, thick, and short legs*" of this species, as specific distinctions from the Ring-tailed Hawk; the legs, however, are *long* and *slender;* and a Marsh Hawk such as he has described, with strong, thick, and short legs, is nowhere to be found in the United States.

* PALLAS, as quoted by PENNANT.

SWALLOW-TAILED HAWK. — FALCO FURCATUS. —
FIG. 204.

Linn. Syst. 129. — *Lath.* i. 60. — Hirundo maxima Peruviana avis prædatoris cal-
caribus instructa, *Feuillee, Voy. Peru,* tom. ii. 33. — *Catesb.* i. 4. — Le Milan de
la Caroline, *Briss.* i. 418. — *Buff.* i. 221. — *Turt. Syst.* 149. — *Arct. Zool.* p. 210,
No. 103. — *Peale's Museum,* No. 142.

ELANUS FURCATUS. — SAVIGNY.*

Le Milan de Caroline, *Cuv. Regn. Anim.* i. p. 322. — Elanus furcatus, *Bonap. Synop.* p. 31. — Nauclerus furcatus, *Vig. Zool. Journ.* No. VII. p. 337. — *Less.
Man. d'Ornith.* i. p. 101. — The Swallow-tailed Hawk, *Aud.* pl. 72; *Orn. Biog.*
i. p. 368.

THIS very elegant species inhabits the southern districts of the
United States in summer; is seldom seen as far north as Pennsylvania, but is very abundant in South Carolina and Georgia, and still
more so in West Florida, and the extensive prairies of Ohio and the
Indiana Territory. I met with these birds, in the early part of May,
at a place called Duck Creek, in Tennessee; and found them sailing

---

* The characters of the birds composing this genus are, — general form, of less
strength than most of the *Falconidæ;* bill, rather weak; tooth, little seen; the tarsi,
short, thick, reticulated, and partly feathered in front; wings, greatly elongated;
timorous, and, like the Kites, excel in flight, circling in the air. Mr. Vigors has
formed a genus, *Nauclerus,* of this and a small African species, dividing them from
Elanus, where they were placed by most prior ornithologists. In these two birds,
the tail is forked to a great extent; while, in the others, it only commences to assume that form, and, in one, is altogether square. The claws also are not circular
underneath, as in the others, to which Mr. Vigors would restrict *Elanus.* The
wings of the two birds, however, show considerable difference; the quills, in the
American, being abruptly emarginated, the third longest; in the African, the second is longest, and only a slight emargination on the two first. Altogether, we are
not quite satisfied with the distinctions. I have for the present retained *Elanus,*
notwithstanding the differences that do exist between some of its members.
According to Audubon, they feed chiefly on the wing; and having pounced on
any prey upon the ground, rise with it, and devour it while flying. " In calm and
warm weather," he remarks, " they soar to an immense height, pursuing the large
insects called *Musquito Hawks,* and performing the most singular evolutions that
can be conceived, using their tail with an elegance peculiar to themselves." They
thus show a manner of feeding entirely different from most birds of prey, which generally retire to some distance, and devour in quiet on the ground. There are some
partly insectivorous Hawks, — *Penis,* for instance, — which seize and devour the
insect during flight; but larger prey is treated at leisure. I am aware of none that
feed so decidedly on the wing as that now described; in every thing, it will appear
more like a large Swallow than an accipitrine bird.
Mr. Audubon remarks another curious circumstance, at variance with the wary
manners of the *Falconidæ.* " When one is killed, and falls to the ground, the
whole flock comes over the dead bird, as if intent upon carrying it off. I have
killed several of these Hawks in this manner, firing as fast as I could load my
gun."
This bird occurred to the late Dr. Walker, at Ballachulish, in Argyleshire, in
1792. Another specimen was taken near Howes, in Wensleydale, Yorkshire, by
W. Fotheringill, Esq., and communicated to the London Society, November,
1823. — ED.

about in great numbers near Bayou Manchac, on the Mississippi, twenty or thirty being within view at the same time. At that season, a species of cicada, or locust, swarmed among the woods, making a deafening noise, and I could perceive these Hawks frequently snatching them from the trees. A species of lizard, which is very numerous in that quarter of the country, and has the faculty of changing its color at will, also furnishes the Swallow-tailed Hawk with a favorite morsel. These lizards are sometimes of the most brilliant light green; in a few minutes change to a dirty clay color; and again become nearly black. The Swallow-tailed Hawk, and Mississippi Kite, feed eagerly on this lizard; and, it is said, on a small, green snake also, which is the mortal enemy of the lizard, and frequently pursues it to the very extremity of the branches, where both become the prey of the Hawk.*

The Swallow-tailed Hawk retires to the south in October, at which season, Mr. Bartram informs me, they are seen in Florida, at a vast height in the air, sailing about with great steadiness; and continue to be seen thus, passing to their winter quarters, for several days. They usually feed from their claws as they fly along. Their flight is easy and graceful, with sometimes occasional sweeps among the trees, the long feathers of their tail spread out, and each extremity of it used alternately to lower, elevate, or otherwise direct their course. I have never yet met with their nests.

These birds are particularly attached to the extensive prairies of the western countries, where their favorite snakes, lizards, grasshoppers, and locusts, are in abundance. They are sometimes, though rarely, seen in Pennsylvania and New Jersey, and that only in warm and very long summers. A specimen, now in the Museum of Philadelphia, was shot within a few miles of that city. We are informed that one was taken in the South Sea, off the coast which lies between Ylo and Arica, in about lat. 23 deg. south, on the 11th of September, by the Reverend the Father Louis Feuillee.† They are also common in Mexico, and extend their migrations as far as Peru.

The Swallow-tailed Hawk measures full two feet in length, and upwards of four feet six inches in extent; the bill is black; cere, yellow, covered at the base with bristles; iris of the eye, silvery cream, surrounded with a blood-red ring; whole head and neck, pure white, the shafts, fine black hairs; the whole lower parts, also pure white; the throat and breast, shafted in the same manner; upper parts, or back, black, glossed with green and purple; whole lesser coverts, very dark purple; wings, long, reaching within two inches of the tip of the tail, and black; tail, also very long, and remarkably forked, consisting of twelve feathers, all black, glossed with green and purple; several of the tertials, white, or edged with white, but generally covered by the scapulars; inner vanes of the secondaries, white on their upper half, black towards their points; lining of the wings, white; legs, yellow, short, and thick, and feathered before half way below the knee; claws, much curved, whitish; outer claw, very small. The greater

---

* This animal, if I mistake not, is the *Lacerta bullaris*, or *Bladder Lizard*, of Turton, vol. i. p. 666. The facility with which it changes color is surprising, and not generally known to naturalists.

† *Jour. des Obs.* tom. ii. 33.

part of the plumage is white at the base; and, when the scapulars are a little displaced, they appear spotted with white.

Fig. 204 was a male in perfect plumage. The color and markings of the male and female are nearly alike.

LONG-EARED OWL. — STRIX OTUS. — Fig. 202.

Turt. Syst. p. 167. — *Bewick,* i. p. 84. — *Peale's Museum,* No. 434.

OTUS VULGARIS. — Fleming.*

Strix otus, *Bonap. Synop.* p. 37. — *North. Zool.* ii. p. 72.

This Owl is common to both continents, and is much more numerous in Pennsylvania than the White, or Barn Owl: six or seven were found in a single tree, about fifteen miles from Philadelphia. There is little doubt but this species is found inhabiting America to a high latitude; though we have no certain accounts of the fact. Except in size, this species has more resemblance to the Great Horned Owl than any other of its tribe. It resembles it also in breeding among the branches of tall trees; lays four eggs, of nearly a round form, and pure white.† The young are grayish white until nearly full grown, and roost during the day close together on a limb, among the thickest of the foliage. This Owl is frequently seen abroad during the day, but is not remarkable for its voice or habits.

The Long-eared Owl is fourteen inches and a half long, and three feet two inches in extent; ears, large, composed of six feathers, gradually lengthening from the front one backwards, black, edged with rusty yellow; irides, vivid yellow; inside of the circle of the face, white, outside or cheeks, rusty; at the internal angle of the eye, a streak of black; bill, blackish horn color; forehead and crown, deep brown, speckled with minute points of white and pale rusty; outside

---

* Upon the authority of the Prince of Musignano, and the examinations of the various writers who have mentioned this bird, it appears very near indeed, if not identical with, the *O. vulgaris* of Europe; and I have ventured to retain it as such, until I can decide from personal observation. The opinions of Vieillot, &c., have been confused by the existence of a second species in the United States, which will appear in the fifth volume of the elegant Continuation of Wilson, now in progress by Bonaparte, under the title of *Otus Mexicanus.*

In the second volume of the *Northern Zoology,* we have the Long-eared Owl referred to this species, and no mention is made of any difference arising even from climate. The habits described by Wilson and Dr. Richardson are precisely similar to those exhibited by our European bird.

Otus has been formed by Cuvier for the reception of those species with aigrettes, where the facial disk is conspicuous, and the head proportionally small, as in *Bubo;* and where the ear-conch is large, extending, as in this species, from the posterior part of the orbit to behind the limb of the lower jaw. The plumage is loose and downy, the habits nocturnal. — Ed.

† Buffon remarks that it rarely constructs a nest of its own; but not unfrequently occupies that of others, particularly the Magpie.

38 *

circle of the face, black, finely marked with small, curving spots of white; back and wings, dark brown, sprinkled and spotted with white, pale ferruginous, and dusky; primaries, barred with brownish yellow and dusky, darkening towards the tips; secondaries, more finely barred and powdered with white and dusky; tail, rounded at the end, of the same length with the wings, beautifully barred and marbled with dull white and pale rusty, on a dark brown ground; throat and breast, clouded with rusty, cream, black and white; belly, beautifully streaked with large arrow-heads of black; legs and thighs, plain pale rusty, feathered to the claws, which are blue black, large, and sharp; inside of the wing, brownish yellow, with a large spot of black at the root of the primaries. Fig. 202 was a female. Of the male I cannot speak precisely; though, from the number of these birds which I have examined in the fall, when it is difficult to ascertain their sex, I conjecture that they differ very little in color.

About six or seven miles below Philadelphia, and not far from the Delaware, is a low swamp, thickly covered with trees, and inundated during great part of the year. This place is the resort of great numbers of the Qua-Bird, or Night Raven, (*Ardea nycticorax,*) where they build in large companies. On the 25th of April, while wading among the dark recesses of this place, observing the habits of these birds, I discovered a *Long-eared Owl*, which had taken possession of one of their nests, and was sitting. On mounting to the nest, I found it contained four eggs; and, breaking one of these, the young appeared almost ready to leave the shell. There were numbers of the Qua-Birds' nests on the adjoining trees all around, and one of them actually on the same tree. Thus we see how unvarying are the manners of this species, however remote and different the countries may be where it has taken up its residence.

RED-TAILED HAWK. — FALCO BOREALIS. — Fig. 205.

Arct. Zool. p. 205, No. 100. — American Buzzard, *Lath.* i. 50. — *Turt. Syst.* p. 151. — F. aquilinus cauda ferruga, Great Eagle Hawk, *Bartram,* p. 290. — *Peale's Museum,* No. 182.

BUTEO BOREALIS. — Swainson.*

Falco (sub-genus *Buteo*) borealis, *Bonap. Synop.* p. 32. — The Red-tailed Hawk, *Aud.* pl. 51, male and female; *Orn. Biog.* i. p. 265. — Buteo borealis, *North. Zool.* ii. p. 50.

The figure of this bird, (No. 205,) and those of Nos. 206 and 207, are offered to the public with a confidence in their fidelity; but *these*, I am sorry to say, are almost all I have to give towards elucidating

---

* The Red-tailed Buzzard is a species peculiar to America, and, in its adult state, seems perfectly known to ornithologists. The figure on the same plate, and next described by our author, has been subject to more discussion, and has been

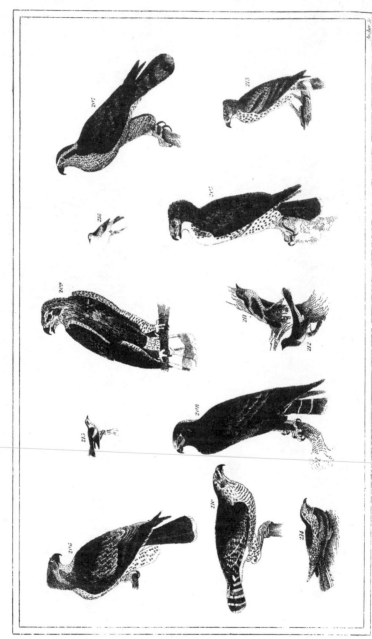

205. Red tailed Hawk. 206. American Buzzard. 207. Ash coloured Hawk. 208. Black Hawk. 209. Varied-ride. 210. Red shouldered H. 211. Female Baltimore Oide. 212. Female Towhee Bunting. 213. Broad winged Hawk. 214. Duck with widow. 215. cape May Warbler. 216. French. Black-cap W.

their history. Birds, naturally thinly dispersed over a vast extent of country; retiring during summer to the depth of the forests to breed; approaching the habitations of man, like other thieves and plunderers, with shy and cautious jealousy; seldom permitting a near advance; subject to great changes of plumage; and, since the decline of falconry, seldom or never domesticated, — offer to those who wish eagerly to investigate their history, and to delineate their particular character and manners, great and insurmountable difficulties. Little more can be done in such cases than to identify the species, and trace it through the various quarters of the world where it has been certainly met with.

The Red-tailed Hawk is most frequently seen in the lower parts of Pennsylvania during the severity of winter. Among the extensive meadows that border the Schuylkill and Delaware, below Philadelphia, where flocks of Larks, (*Alauda magna,*) and where mice and moles are in great abundance, many individuals of this Hawk spend the greater part of the winter. Others prowl around the plantations, looking out for vagrant Chickens; their method of seizing which is, by sweeping swiftly over the spot, and, grappling them with their talons, bear them away to the woods. The bird from which Fig. 205 was drawn, was surprised in the act of feeding on a Hen he had just killed, and which he was compelled to abandon. The remains of the Chicken were immediately baited to a steel trap, and early the next morning the unfortunate Red-Tail was found a prisoner, securely fastened by the leg. The same Hen which the day before he had massacred, was, the very next, made the means of decoying him to his destruction, — in the eye of the farmer, a system of fair and just retribution.

This species inhabits the whole United States, and, I believe, is not migratory, as I found it, in the month of May, as far south as Fort Adams, in the Mississippi Territory. The young were, at that time, nearly as large as their parents, and were very clamorous, making an incessant squealing noise. One, which I shot, contained in his stomach mingled fragments of frogs and lizards.

The Red-tailed Hawk is twenty inches long, and three feet nine inches in extent; bill, blue black; cere, and sides of the mouth, yellow, tinged with green; lores, and spot on the under eyelid, white, the former marked with fine, radiating hairs; eyebrow, or cartilage, a dull eel-skin color, prominent, projecting over the eye; a broad streak of dark brown extends from the sides of the mouth backwards; crown and hind head, dark brown, seamed with white, and ferruginous; sides of the neck, dull ferruginous, streaked with brown; eye, large; iris, pale amber; back and shoulders, deep brown; wings, dusky, barred with blackish; ends of the five first primaries, nearly black; scapulars, barred broadly with white and brown; sides of the tail-coverts, white, barred with ferruginous, middle ones dark, edged with rust;

variously named. From the testimonies of Bonaparte and Audubon, is may, however, be certainly considered as the young or immature bird — an idea which Wilson himself entertained, and showed by his mark of interrogation to the young, and the quotation of its synonymes. The figure at Fig. 2 is the young in immature plumage, where the red tail has not yet appeared, and which is known to authors under the name of *F. Leverianus.* — Ed.

tail, rounded, extending two inches beyond the wings, and of a bright red brown, with a single band of black near the end, and tipped with brownish white; on some of the lateral feathers are slight indications of the remains of other narrow bars; lower parts, brownish white; the breast, ferruginous, streaked with dark brown; across the belly, a band of interrupted spots of brown; chin, white; femorals and vent, pale brownish white, the former marked with a few minute heart-shaped spots of brown; legs, yellow, feathered half way below the knees.

This was a male. Another specimen, shot within a few days after, agreed, in almost every particular of its color and markings, with the present; and, on dissection, was found to be a female.

AMERICAN BUZZARD, OR WHITE-BREASTED HAWK.— FALCO LEVERIANUS? — FIG. 206.

Lath. Syn. Sup. p. 31.— *Ind. Orn.* i. p. 18, No. 31.— *Peale's Museum,* No. 400.

BUTEO BOREALIS. — YOUNG OF THE YEAR. — BONAPARTE.

Falco (sub-genus *Buteo*) borealis, *Bonap. Synop.* p. 32.

IT is with some doubt and hesitation that I introduce the present as a distinct species from the preceding. In their size and general aspect they resemble each other considerably; yet I have found both males and females among each; and in the present species I have sometimes found the ground color of the tail strongly tinged with ferruginous, and the bars of dusky but slight; while in the preceding the tail is sometimes wholly red brown, the single bar of black near the tip excepted; in other specimens evident remains of numerous other bars are visible. In the mean time, both are figured, and future observations may throw more light on the matter.

This bird is more numerous than the last; but frequents the same situations in winter. One, which was shot on the wing, lived with me several weeks; but refused to eat. It amused itself by frequently hopping from one end of the room to the other; and sitting for hours at the window, looking down on the passengers below. At first, when approached by any person, he generally put himself in the position in which he is represented; but after some time he became quite familiar, permitting himself to be handled, and shutting his eyes, as if quite passive. Though he lived so long without food, he was found on dissection to be exceedingly fat, his stomach being enveloped in a mass of solid fat of nearly an inch in thickness.

The White-breasted Hawk is twenty-two inches long, and four feet in extent; cere, pale green; bill, pale blue, black at the point; eye, bright straw color; eyebrow, projecting greatly; head, broad, flat, and large; upper part of the head, sides of the neck and back, brown, streaked and seamed with white and some pale rust; scapulars and wing-coverts, spotted with white; wing-quills, much resembling the preceding species; tail-coverts, white, handsomely barred with brown; tail, slightly rounded, of a pale brown color, varying in some to a sorrel, crossed by nine or ten bars of black, and tipped for half an inch with white; wings, brown, barred with dusky; inner vanes nearly all white; chin, throat, and breast, pure white, with the exception of some slight touches of brown that enclose the chin; femorals, yellowish white, thinly marked with minute touches of rust; legs, bright yellow, feathered half way down; belly, broadly spotted with black or very deep brown; the tips of the wings reach to the middle of the tail.

My reason for inclining to consider this a distinct species from the last, is the circumstance of having uniformly found the present two or three inches larger than the former, though this may possibly be owing to their greater age.

ASH-COLORED, OR BLACK-CAP HAWK.—FALCO ATRICAPILLUS.—Fig. 207.

Ash-colored Buzzard? *Lath. Syn.* i. p. 55, No. 35.— *Peale's Museum*, No! 406.

ASTUR ATRICAPILLUS.—Bonaparte.*

Falco palumbarius, *Bonap. Synop.* p. 28.— Autour royal, Falco regalis, *Temm. Pl. Col.* tab. 495.— Accipiter (*Astur*) atricapillus, *North. Zool.* ii. p. 39.— Astur atricapillus, *Jard. and Selb. Illust. Orn.* pl. 121.

Of this beautiful species I can find no precise description. The Ash-colored Buzzard of Edwards differs so much from this, particularly in wanting the fine zigzag lines below, and the black cap, that I

---

* The *Falco atricapillus* of Wilson has been confounded by all writers, except the Prince of Musignano, in his review of Cuvier, and the authors of the *Northern Zoology*, with the Goshawk of Europe. Wilson expresses his doubt, from being unable to compare it with actual specimens. Sabine makes out the Arctic specimens to be identical. Audubon is of opinion, also, that they were identical; but from what I recollect of that gentleman's drawing, it must have been made from this bird. While Temminck makes a new species altogether in his *Autour royal*, without noticing Wilson.

The greatest difference between the two birds is the marking of the breast and under parts, and it is so distinct as to be at once perceived. In the American species, the under parts are of a uniform pale grayish white, having the tail and centre of each feather black, forming a dark streak. This extends to those in the centre of the belly, after which it is hardly visible; every feather in addition is clouded transversely with irregular bars of gray. In the European bird, the markings are in the shape of two decided transverse bars on each feather, with the shaft dark, but not exceeding its own breadth,— each, as a whole, having a very different appearance. The upper parts of the American bird are also of a blue shade, and the markings of the head and auriculars are darker and more decided. Wilson's figure is a most correct representation.

The genus *Astur*, of Bechstein, has now been used for this form, and is generally synonymous with *Les autours* of the French. Mr. Swainson, however, is inclined to make it rather a sub-genus of *Accipiter*, in which the Sparrow Hawks,

cannot for a moment suppose them to be the same. The individual from which the drawing was made, is faithfully represented in Fig. 207, reduced to one half its natural dimensions. This bird was shot within a few miles of Philadelphia, and is now preserved, in good order, in Mr. Peale's Museum.

Its general make and aspect denotes great strength and spirit; its legs are strong, and its claws of more than proportionate size. Should any other specimen or variety of this Hawk, differing from the present, occur during the publication of this work, it will enable me more accurately to designate the species.

The Black-Cap Hawk is twenty-one inches in length; the bill and cere are blue; eye, reddish amber; crown, black, bordered on each side by a line of white finely specked with black; these lines of white meet on the hind head; whole upper parts, slate, tinged with brown, slightest on the quills; legs, feathered half way down, and, with the feet, of a yellow color; whole lower parts and femorals, white, most elegantly speckled with fine, transverse, pencilled, zigzag lines of dusky, all the shafts being a long, black line; vent, pure white.

If this be not the celebrated *Goshawk*, formerly so much esteemed in falconry, it is very closely allied to it. I have never myself seen a specimen of that bird in Europe, and the descriptions of their best naturalists vary considerably; but, from a careful examination of the figure and account of the Goshawk, given by the ingenious Mr. Bewick, (*Brit. Birds*, vol. i. p. 65,) I have very little doubt that the present will be found to be the same.

The Goshawk inhabits France and Germany; is not very common in South Britain, but more frequent in the northern parts of the island, and is found in Russia and Siberia. Buffon, who reared two young birds of this kind, a male and female, observes, that "the Gos-

---

and lesser species, have been placed. There is some difference in the construction of the tarsi, but the habits and general form are nearly similar. In the Ornithology of America, the *Astur Pennsylvanicus* will show an example of the one; the bird now in question that of the other.

In general form, the birds of this group are strong, but do not show the firm and compact structure of the true Falcon. The wings are short and rounded, and present a considerable under surface, favorable to a smooth and sailing flight, which power is rendered more perfect by the lengthened and expanded tail. The tarsi and feet bear a relative proportion of strength to their bodies, and the claws are more than usually hooked and sharp; that of the inner toe always equal to the hallux. Their favorite abodes are woods, or well-clothed countries, where they build and rear their young, hunting for prey about the skirts. They are extremely active and bold; their flight is sailing in circles, or, when in search of prey, skimming near to the ground, about fences and brush, and darting at any thing, either on the ground or on wing, with great celerity. I have seen some of our native species pick up a bird, when flying near the ground, so rapidly, that the motion of stooping and clutching was hardly perceptible, and the flight continued, as if nothing had happened. During their higher flights, or when threading through a thick wood, which they do with great dexterity, the motions of the tail are perceived directing their movements, and, in the latter case, is most conspicuously necessary. When perched at rest the position is unusually erect; so much, that the line of the back and tail is almost perpendicular. The plumage in the adults is often of a dark leaden color above, with bars and crosses on the under parts; in the young, the upper surface assumes different shades of brown, while the markings beneath are longitudinal. — ED.

hawk, before it has shed its feathers, that is, in its first year, is marked on the breast and belly with longitudinal brown spots; but after it has had two moultings, they disappear, and their place is occupied by transverse, waving bars, which continue during the rest of its life;" he also takes notice, that though the male was much smaller than the female, it was fiercer and more vicious.

Mr. Pennant informs us, that the Goshawk is used by the Emperor of China in his sporting excursions, when he is usually attended by his grand falconer, and a thousand of inferior rank. Every bird has a silver plate fastened to its foot, with the name of the falconer who has charge of it, that, in case it should be lost, it may be restored to the proper person; but, if he should not be found, the bird is delivered to another officer, called "the guardian of lost birds," who, to make his situation known, erects his standard in a conspicuous place among the army of hunters. The same writer informs us, that he examined, in the Leverian Museum, a specimen of the Goshawk which came from America, and which was superior in size to the European. He adds, " They are the best of all Hawks for falconry." *

BLACK HAWK.—FALCO SANCTI JOHANNIS?—Fig. 208.

Lath. Ind. Orn. p. 34, No. 74. — Chocolate-colored Falcon, *Penn. Arct. Zool.* No. 94.

BUTEO SANCTI JOHANNIS?—Bonaparte.

Falco (sub-genus *Buteo*) Sancti Johannis, *Bonap. Synop.* p. 32.

This is a remarkably shy and wary bird, found most frequently along the marshy shores of our large rivers; feeds on mice, frogs, and moles; sails much, and sometimes at a great height; has been seen to kill a Duck on wing; sits, by the side of the marshes, on a stake, for an hour at a time, in an almost perpendicular position, as if dozing; flies with great ease, and occasionally with great swiftness, seldom flapping the wings; seems particularly fond of river shores, swamps, and marshes; is most numerous with us in winter, and but rarely seen in summer; is remarkable for the great size of its eye, length of its wings, and shortness of its toes. The breadth of its head is likewise uncommon.

The Black Hawk is twenty-one inches long, and four feet two inches in extent; bill, bluish black; cere, and sides of the mouth, orange yellow; feet, the same; eye, very large; iris, bright hazel; cartilage overhanging the eye, prominent, of a dull greenish color; general color above, brown black, slightly dashed with dirty white; nape of the neck, pure white under the surface; front, white; whole lower parts, black, with slight tinges of brown; and a few circular touches of the same on the femorals; legs, feathered to the toes, and black, touched with brownish; the wings reach rather beyond the tip of the tail; the five

* *Arctic Zoology,* p. 204.

first primaries are white on their inner vanes; tail, rounded at the end, deep black, crossed with five narrow bands of pure white, and broadly tipped with dull white; vent, black, spotted with white; inside vanes of the primaries, snowy; claws, black, strong, and sharp; toes, remarkably short.

I strongly suspect this bird to be of the very same species with the next, though both were found to be males. Although differing greatly in plumage, yet, in all their characteristic features, they strikingly resemble each other. The Chocolate-colored Hawk of Pennant, and St. John's Falcon of the same author, (*Arct. Zool.* No. 93 and 94,) are doubtless varieties of this; and, very probably, his Rough-legged Falcon also. His figures, however, are bad, and ill calculated to exhibit the true form and appearance of the bird.

This species is a native of North America alone. We have no account of its ever having been seen in any part of Europe; nor have we any account of its place or manner of breeding.

BLACK HAWK. Young.—Fig. 209.

Peale's Museum, No. 405.

BUTEO SANCTI JOHANNIS. Young. — Bonaparte.

Falco (sub-genus *Buteo*) Sancti Johannis, young, *Bonap. Synop.* p. 32.

This is probably a younger bird of the preceding species, being, though a male, somewhat less than its companion. Both were killed in the same meadow, at the same place and time. In form, features, and habitudes, it exactly agreed with the former.

This bird measures twenty inches in length, and in extent four feet; the eyes, bill, cere, toes, and claws, were as in the preceding; head above, white, streaked with black and light brown; along the eyebrows, a black line; cheeks, streaked like the head; neck, streaked with black and reddish brown, on a pale yellowish white ground; whole upper parts, brown black, dashed with brownish white and pale ferruginous; tail, white for half its length, ending in brown, marked with one or two bars of dusky and a larger bar of black, and tipped with dull white; wings, as in the preceding, their lining variegated with black, white, and ferruginous; throat and breast, brownish yellow, dashed with black; belly, beautifully variegated with spots of white, black, and pale ferruginous; femorals and feathered legs, the same, but rather darker; vent, plain brownish white.

The original color of these birds in their young state may probably be pale brown, as the present individual seemed to be changing to a darker color on the neck and sides of the head. This change, from pale brown to black, is not greater than some of the genus are actually known to undergo. One great advantage of examining living or newly-killed specimens is, that whatever may be the difference of color between any two, the eye, countenance, and form of the head, instantly betray the common family to which they belong; for this family likeness is never lost in the living bird, though in stuffed skins and preserved specimens it is frequently entirely obliterated. I have no hesitation, therefore, in giving it as my opinion, that the present and preceding birds are of the same species, differing only in age, both being males. Of the female I am unable at present to speak.

Pennant, in his account of the Chocolate-colored Hawk, which is, very probably, the same with the present and preceding species, observes that it preys much on Ducks, sitting on a rock, and watching their rising, when it instantly strikes them.

While traversing our sea-coast and salt marshes, between Cape May and Egg Harbor, I was every where told of a *Duck Hawk*, noted for striking down Ducks on wing, though flying with their usual rapidity. Many extravagances were mingled with these accounts, particularly, that it always struck the Ducks with its breast bone, which was universally said to project several inches, and to be strong and sharp. From the best verbal descriptions I could obtain of this Hawk, I have strong suspicions that it is no other than the *Black Hawk*, as its wings were said to be long and very pointed, the color very dark, the size nearly alike, and several other traits given, that seemed particularly to belong to this species. As I have been promised specimens of this celebrated Hawk next winter, a short time will enable me to determine the matter more satisfactorily. Few gunners in that quarter are unacquainted with the *Duck Hawk*, as it often robs them of their wounded birds before they are able to reach them.

Since writing the above, I have ascertained that the *Duck Hawk* is not this species, but the celebrated Peregrine Falcon, a figure and description of which will be given hereafter.

RED-SHOULDERED HAWK. — FALCO LINEATUS. — Fig. 210.

Arct. Zool. p. 206, No. 102. — *Lath.* i. 56, No. 36. — *Turt. Syst.* p. 153. — *Peale's Museum,* No. 205.

BUTEO? *LINEATUS.* — Jardine.*

Falco (sub-genus *Circus*) hyemalis, *Bonap. Synop.* p. 33. — Red-shouldered Hawk, *Aud.* pl. 56, male and female; *Orn. Biog.* i. p. 296.

This species is more rarely met with than either of the former. Its haunts are in the neighborhood of the sea. It preys on Larks, Sandpipers, and the Small Ringed Plover, and frequently on Ducks.

* This bird is certainly distinct from the *F. hyemalis* of this volume; and, independent of the distinctions of plumage, the very different habits of both, pointed out by Mr. Audubon, can hardly be reconciled. All the characters and habits of the bird lean much more to the Goshawks; it delights in woody countries, builds on trees, and is much more active. The plumage generally is that of the Buzzards and *Circi;* but the under parts present a combination of the transverse barring of *Astur.* In addition to the description of Wilson, Audubon observes, that this bird

It flies high and irregularly, and not in the sailing manner of the Long-winged Hawks. I have occasionally observed this bird near Egg Harbor, in New Jersey, and once in the meadows below this city. This Hawk was first transmitted to Great Britain by Mr. Blackburne, from Long Island, in the state of New York. With its manner of building, eggs, &c., we are altogether unacquainted.

The Red-shouldered Hawk is nineteen inches in length; the head and back are brown, seamed and edged with rusty; bill, blue black; cere and legs, yellow; greater wing-coverts and secondaries, pale olive brown, thickly spotted on both vanes with white and pale rusty; primaries, very dark, nearly black, and barred or spotted with white; tail, rounded, reaching about an inch and a half beyond the wings, black, crossed by five bands of white, and broadly tipped with the same; whole breast and belly, bright rusty, speckled and spotted with trans-verse rows of white, the shafts black; chin and cheeks, pale brown-ish, streaked also with black; iris, reddish hazel; vent, pale ochre, tipped with rusty; legs, feathered a little below the knees, long; these and the feet, a fine yellow; claws black; femorals, pale rusty, faintly barred with a darker tint.

In the month of April I shot a female of this species, and the only one I have yet met with, in a swamp, seven or eight miles below Philadelphia. The eggs were, some of them, nearly as large as peas; from which circumstance, I think it probable they breed in such solitary parts even in this state. In color, size, and markings, it differed very little from the male described above. The tail was scarcely quite so black, and the white bars not so pure; it was also something larger.

FEMALE BALTIMORE ORIOLE. — ORIOLUS BALTIMORUS. —
Fig. 211

Amer. Orn. vol. i. p. 23.

ICTERUS BALTIMORE. — Daudin.

THE history of this beautiful species has been particularly detailed in a former part of the present work; to this representation of the female, drawn of half the size of nature, a few particulars may be

is rarely observed in the middle districts, where, on the contrary, the Winter Fal-con usually makes its appearance from the north at the approach of autumn. "It is one of the most noisy of its genus, during spring especially, when it would be difficult to walk the skirts of woods bordering a large plantation, without hearing its discordant shrill notes, *ka-hee, ka-hee*, as it sails in rapid circles at a very great elevation. The interior of the woods seems the fittest haunts for the Red-shoulder-ed Hawk, where they also breed. The nest is seated near the extremity of a large branch, and is as bulky as that of a Common Crow. It is formed externally of dry sticks and Spanish moss, and is lined with withered grass and fibrous roots. The female lays four eggs, sometimes five; they are of a broad, oval form, granulated all over, pale blue, faintly blotched with brownish red at the smaller end." — ED.

added. The males generally arrive several days before the females, saunter about their wonted places of residence, and seem lonely, and less sprightly, than after the arrival of their mates. In the spring and summer of 1811, a Baltimore took up its abode in Mr. Bartram's garden, whose notes were so singular as particularly to attract my attention; they were as well known to me as the voice of my most intimate friend. On the 30th of April, 1812, I was again surprised and pleased at hearing this same Baltimore in the garden, whistling his identical old chant; and I observed, that he particularly frequented that quarter of the garden where the tree stood, on the pendent branches of which he had formed his nest the preceding year. This nest had been taken possession of by the House Wren, a few days after the Baltimore's brood had abandoned it; and, curious to know how the little intruder had furnished it within, I had taken it down early in the fall, after the Wren herself had also raised a brood of six young in it, and which was her second that season. I found it stripped of its original lining, floored with sticks or small twigs, above which were laid feathers; so that the usual complete nest of the Wren occupied the interior of that of the Baltimore.

The chief difference between the male and female Baltimore Oriole, is the superior brightness of the orange color of the former to that of the latter. The black on the head, upper part of the back and throat of the female is intermixed with dull orange; whereas, in the male, those parts are of a deep shining black; the tail of the female also wants the greater part of the black, and the whole lower parts are of a much duskier orange.

I have observed, that these birds are rarely seen in pine woods, or where these trees generally prevail. On the ridges of our high mountains they are seldom to be met with. In orchards, and on well-cultivated farms, they are most numerous, generally preferring such places to build in, rather than the woods or forest.

FEMALE TOWHE BUNTING. — EMBERIZA ERYTHROPTHALMA. — Fig. 212.

Amer. Orn. vol. ii. p. 35. — *Turt. Syst.* p. 534. — *Peale's Museum*, No. 5970.

PIPILO ERYTHROPTHALMA. — Vieillot.

This bird differs considerably from the male in color; and has, if I mistake not, been described as a distinct species by European naturalists, under the appellation of the "*Rusty Bunting*." The males of this species, like those of the preceding, arrive several days sooner than the females. In one afternoon's walk through the woods, on the 23d of April, I counted more than fifty of the former, and did not observe any of the latter, though I made a very close search for them. This species frequents in great numbers the barrens covered with shrub oaks; and inhabits even to the tops of our mountains. They are almost perpetually scratching among the fallen leaves, and feed chiefly on worms, beetles, and gravel. They fly low, flirting out their broad, white-streaked tail, and uttering their common note *Tow-heé*. They build always on the ground, and raise two broods in the season. For a particular account of the manners of this species, see our history of the male, p. 121.

The female Towhe is eight inches long, and ten inches in extent; iris of the eye, a deep blood color; bill, black; plumage above and on the breast, a dark reddish drab, reddest on the head and breast; sides under the wings, light chestnut; belly, white; vent, yellow ochre; exterior vanes of the tertials, white; a small spot of white marks the primaries immediately below their coverts, and another slighter streak crosses them in a slanting direction; the three exterior tail-feathers are tipped with white; the legs and feet, flesh-colored.

This species seems to have a peculiar dislike to the sea-coast, as in the most favorable situations, in other respects, within several miles of the sea, it is scarcely ever to be met with. Scarcity of its particular kinds of favorite food in such places may probably be the reason; as it is well known that many kinds of insects, on the larvæ of which it usually feeds, carefully avoid the neighborhood of the sea.

BROAD-WINGED HAWK. — FALCO PENNSYLVANICUS. —
Fig. 213.

Peale's Museum, No. 407.

ASTUR? LATISSIMUS. — Jardine.*

Falco latissimus, Ord's *reprint of Wilson.* — Falco (sub-genus Astur) Pennsylvanicus, *Bonap. Synop.* p. 29. — The Broad-winged Hawk, *Aud.* pl. 91, male and female; *Orn. Biog.* i. p. 461.

The Hawk, Fig. 213, was shot on the 6th of May, in Mr. Bartram's woods, near the Schuylkill, and was afterwards presented to Mr. Peale, in whose collection it now remains. It was perched on the dead limb of a high tree, feeding on something, which was afterwards found to be the meadow mouse. On my approach, it uttered a whining kind of whistle, and flew off to another tree, where I followed and shot it.

* Mr. Ord's name of *latissimus* is the most proper for this Hawk. Wilson seems inadvertently to have given the name of *Pennsylvanicus* to two species, and the latter being applied to the adult plumage, and *velox* to the young, the former has been retained by Temminck and the authors of the *Northern Zoology*, while Ord seems to have the merit of discriminating the large species, and giving it the title above adopted. I have taken *Astur*, on the authority of Bonaparte, for its generic appellation; though the habits and kind of food ally it more to the Buzzards, it is one of those birds with dubious and combined characters. Mr. Audubon describes it as of a quiet and sluggish disposition, allowing itself to be tormented by the Little Sparrow Hawk, and Tyrant Flycatcher. It feeds on animals and birds, and also on frogs and snakes; breeds on trees; the nest is placed near the stem or trunk, and is composed of dry thistles, and lined with numerous small roots and large feathers; the eggs are four or five, of a dull grayish white, blotched with dark brown. — Ed.

Its great breadth of wing, or width of the secondaries, and also of its head and body, when compared with its length, struck me as peculiarities. It seemed a remarkably strong-built bird, handsomely marked, and was altogether unknown to me. Mr. Bartram, who examined it very attentively, declared he had never before seen such a Hawk. On the afternoon of the next day, I observed another, probably its mate or companion, and certainly one of the same species, sailing about over the same woods. Its motions were in wide circles, with unmoving wings, the exterior outline of which seemed a complete semicircle. I was extremely anxious to procure this also, if possible; but it was attacked and driven away by a King-Bird before I could effect my purpose; and I have never since been fortunate enough to meet with another. On dissection, the one which I had shot proved to be a male.

In size this Hawk agrees, nearly, with the *Buzzardet* (*Falco albidus*) of Turton, described also by Pennant; * but either the descriptions of these authors are very inaccurate, the change of color which that bird undergoes very great, or the present is altogether a different species. Until, however, some other specimens of this Hawk come under my observation, I can only add to the figure here given, and which is a good likeness of the original, the following particulars of its size and plumage: —

Length, fourteen inches; extent, thirty-three inches; bill, black, blue near the base, slightly toothed; cere and corners of the mouth, yellow; irides, bright amber; frontlet and lores, white; from the mouth backwards runs a streak of blackish brown; upper parts, dark brown, the plumage tipped, and the head streaked with whitish; almost all the feathers above are spotted or barred with white, but this is not seen unless they be separated by the hand; head, large, broad, and flat; cere, very broad; the nostril, also large; tail, short, the exterior and interior feathers somewhat the shortest, the others rather longer, of a full black, and crossed with two bars of white, tipped also slightly with whitish; tail-coverts, spotted with white; wings, dusky brown, indistinctly barred with black; greater part of the inner vanes, snowy; lesser coverts, and upper part of the back, tipped and streaked with bright ferruginous; the bars of black are very distinct on the lower side of the wing; lining of the wing, brownish white, beautifully marked with small arrow-heads of brown; chin, white, surrounded by streaks of black; breast and sides, elegantly spotted with large arrowheads of brown, centred with pale brown; belly and vent, like the breast, white, but more thinly marked with pointed spots of brown; femorals, brownish white, thickly marked with small touches of brown and white; vent, white; legs, very stout; feet, coarsely scaled, both of a dirty orange yellow; claws, semicircular, strong, and very sharp, hind one considerably the largest.

While examining the plumage of this bird, a short time after it was shot, one of those winged ticks with which many of our birds are infested, appeared on the surface of the feathers, moving about as they usually do, backwards or sideways like a crab, among the plumage, with great facility. The Fish Hawk, in particular, is greatly pestered with these vermin, which occasionally leave him, as suits their con-

* *Arctic Zoology,* No. 109.

39 *

venience. A gentleman, who made the experiment, assured me, that, on plunging a live Fish Hawk under water, several of these winged ticks remained hovering over the spot, and, the instant the Hawk rose above the surface, darted again among his plumage. The experiment was several times made, with the like result. As soon, however, as these parasites perceive the dead body of their patron beginning to become cold, they abandon it; and, if the person who holds it have his head uncovered, dive instantly among his hair, as I have myself frequently experienced; and, though driven from thence, repeatedly return, till they are caught and destroyed. There are various kinds of these ticks; the one found on the present Hawk is figured beside him. The head and thorax were light brown; the legs, six in number, of a bright green, their joints moving almost horizontally, and thus enabling the creature to pass with the greatest ease between the laminæ of feathers; the wings were single, of a dark amber color, and twice as long as the body, which widened towards the extremity, where it was slightly indented; feet, two clawed.

This insect lived for several days between the crystal and dial-plate of a watch, carried in the pocket; but, being placed for a few minutes in the sun, fell into convulsions and died.

CHUCK–WILL'S–WIDOW. — CAPRIMULGUS CAROLINENSIS. — Fig. 214.

Peale's Museum, No. 7723.

CAPRIMULGUS CAROLINENSIS. — Brisson.*

Caprimulgus Carolinensis, *Lath. Gen. Hist.* — Caprimulgus rufus, *Vieill.* (auct. *Bonap.) Bonap. Synop.* p. 61. — Chuck-will's-widow, *Aud.* pl. 52, male and female; *Orn. Biog.* i. p. 273.

This solitary bird is rarely found to the north of James River, in Virginia, on the seaboard, or of Nashville, in the state of Tennessee, in the interior; and no instance has come to my knowledge of its having been seen either in New Jersey, Pennsylvania, or Maryland.

* According to Mr. Audubon, this species, when disturbed or annoyed about the nest, removes its eggs or young to a distance. This circumstance seems known to the Negroes and American farmers, who give various accounts of the mode in which it is performed. Mr. Audubon could not satisfy himself as to the truth of these accounts, and resolved to watch and judge for himself. What follows is the result of his observation : —

"When the Chuck-will's-widow, either male or female, (for each sits alternately,) has discovered that the eggs have been touched, it ruffles its feathers, and appears extremely dejected for a minute or two, after which it emits a low, murmuring cry, scarcely audible to me, as I lay concealed at a distance not more than eighteen or twenty yards. At this time, I have seen the other parent reach the spot, flying so low over the ground, that I thought its little feet must have touched it, as it skimmed along, and after a few low notes and some gesticulations, all indicative of great distress, take an egg in its large mouth, the other bird doing the same, when they would fly off together, skimming closely over the ground, until they disappeared among the branches and trees." — Ed.

On my journey south, I first met with it between Richmond and Petersburg, in Virginia, and also on the banks of the Cumberland in Tennessee.

Mr. Pennant has described this bird under the appellation of the "Short-winged Goatsucker," (*Arct. Zool.* No. 336,) from a specimen which he received from Dr. Garden, of Charleston, South Carolina; but, in speaking of its manners, he confounds it with the Whip-poor-will, though the latter is little more than half the cubic bulk of the former, and its notes altogether different. "In South Carolina," says this writer, speaking of the present species, "it is called, from one of its notes, *chuck, Chuck-will's-widow*; and, in the northern provinces, *Whip-poor-will*, from the resemblance which another of its notes bears to those words." (*Arct. Zool.* p. 434.) He then proceeds to detail the manners of the Common Whip-poor-will, by extracts from Dr. Garden and Mr. Kalm, which clearly prove that all of them were personally unacquainted with that bird; and had never seen or examined any other than two of our species, the Short-winged or Chuck-will's-widow, and the Long-winged, or Night Hawk, to both of which they indiscriminately attribute the notes and habits of the Whip-poor-will.

The Chuck-will's-widow, so called from its notes, which seem exactly to articulate those words, arrives on the sea-coast of Georgia about the middle of March, and in Virginia early in April. It commences its singular call generally in the evening, soon after sunset, and continues it, with short, occasional interruptions, for several hours. Towards morning these repetitions are renewed, and continue until dawn has fairly appeared. During the day it is altogether silent. This note, or call, instantly attracts the attention of a stranger, and is strikingly different from that of the Whip-poor-will. In sound and articulation it seems plainly to express the words which have been applied to it, (*Chuck-will's-widow*,) pronouncing each syllable leisurely and distinctly, putting the principal emphasis on the last word. In a still evening it may be heard at the distance of nearly a mile, the tones of its voice being stronger and more full than those of the Whip-poor-will, who utters his with much greater rapidity. In the Chickasaw country, and throughout the whole Mississippi Territory, I found the present species very numerous in the months of April and May, keeping up a continual noise during the whole evening, and, in moonlight, throughout the whole of the night.

The flight of this bird is low, skimming about at a few feet above the surface of the ground, frequently settling on old logs, or on the fences, and from thence sweeping around, in pursuit of various winged insects that fly in the night. Like the Whip-poor-will, it prefers the declivities of glens and other deeply-shaded places, making the surrounding mountains ring with echoes the whole evening. I several times called the attention of the Chickasaws to the notes of this bird, on which occasions they always assumed a grave and thoughtful aspect; but it appeared to me that they made no distinction between the two species; so that whatever superstitious notions they may entertain of the one, are probably applied to the other.

This singular genus of birds, formed to subsist on the superabundance of nocturnal insects, are exactly and surprisingly fitted for their peculiar mode of life. Their flight is low, to accommodate itself to their prey; silent, that they may be the better concealed, and sweep upon it unawares; their sight, most acute in the dusk, when such insects are abroad; their evolutions, something like those of the Bat, quick and sudden; their mouths, capable of prodigious expansion, to seize with more certainty, and furnished with long, branching hairs, or bristles, serving as palisadoes to secure what comes between them. Reposing so much during the heats of day, they are much infested with vermin, particularly about the head, and are provided with a comb on the inner edge of the middle claw, with which they are often employed in ridding themselves of these pests, at least when in a state of captivity. Having no weapons of defence, except their wings, their chief security is in the solitude of night, and in their color and close retreats by day; the former so much resembling that of dead leaves of various hues, as not to be readily distinguished from them even when close at hand.

The Chuck-will's-widow lays its eggs, two in number, on the ground generally, and, I believe, always in the woods; it makes no nest; the eggs are of a dull olive color, sprinkled with darker specks, are about as large as those of a Pigeon, and exactly oval. Early in September they retire from the United States.

This species is twelve inches long, and twenty-six in extent; bill, yellowish, tipped with black; the sides of the mouth are armed with numerous long bristles, strong, tapering, and furnished with finer hairs branching from each; cheeks and chin, rust color, specked with black; over the eye extends a line of small whitish spots; head and back, very deep brown, powdered with cream, rust, and bright ferruginous, and marked with long, ragged streaks of black; scapulars, broadly spotted with deep black, bordered with cream, and interspersed with whitish; the plumage of that part of the neck which falls over the back, is long, something like that of a cock, and streaked with yellowish brown; wing quills, barred with black and bright rust; tail, rounded, extending about an inch beyond the tips of the wings; it consists of ten feathers; the four middle ones are powdered with various tints of ferruginous, and elegantly marked with fine zigzag lines, and large herring-bone figures of black; exterior edges of the three outer feathers, barred like the wings; their interior vanes, for two thirds of their length, are pure snowy white, marbled with black, and ferruginous at the base; this white spreads over the greater part of the three outer feathers near their tips; across the throat is a slight band or mark of whitish; breast, black, powdered with rust; belly and vent, lighter; legs, feathered before nearly to the feet, which are of a dirty purplish flesh color; inner side of the middle claw, deeply pectinated.

The female differs chiefly in wanting the pure white on the three exterior tail-feathers, these being more of a brownish cast.

CAPE MAY WARBLER.—SYLVIA MARITIMA.—Fig. 215.

SYLVICOLA MARITIMA. — Jardine.*

Sylvia maritima, *Bonap. Synop.* p. 79. — The Carbonated Warbler? *Aud.* pl. 60,
male; *Orn. Biog.* i. p. 308.

This new and beautiful little species was discovered in a maple
swamp, in Cape May county, not far from the coast, by Mr. George Ord
of Philadelphia, who accompanied me on a shooting excursion to that
quarter in the month of May last, [1811.] Through the zeal and
activity of this gentleman, I succeeded in procuring many rare and
elegant birds among the sea islands and extensive salt marshes that
border that part of the Atlantic; and much interesting information
relative to their nests, eggs, and particular habits. I have also at
various times been favored with specimens of other birds from the
same friend, for all which I return my grateful acknowledgments.

The same swamp that furnished us with this elegant little stranger,
(Fig. 215,) and indeed several miles around it, were ransacked by us
both for another specimen of the same; but without success. Fortunately it proved to be a male, and being in excellent plumage, enabled
me to preserve a faithful portrait of the original.

Whether this be a summer resident in the lower parts of New Jersey, or merely a transient passenger to a more northern climate, I
cannot with certainty determine. The spring had been remarkably
cold, with long and violent north-east storms, and many winter birds,
as well as passengers from the south, still lingered in the woods as
late as the 20th of May, gleaning, in small companies, among the
opening buds and infant leaves, and skipping nimbly from twig to
twig, which was the case with the bird now before us when it was first
observed. Of its notes, or particular history, I am equally uninformed.

The length of this species is five inches and a half, extent, eight
and a half; bill and legs, black; whole upper part of the head, deep
black; line from the nostril over the eye, chin, and sides of the neck,
rich yellow; ear-feathers, orange, which also tints the back part of the
yellow line over the eye; at the anterior and posterior angle of the
eye is a small touch of black; hind head and whole back, rump, and
tail-coverts, yellow olive, thickly streaked with black; the upper
exterior edges of several of the greater wing-coverts are pure white,
forming a broad bar on the wing, the next superior row being also
broadly tipped with white; rest of the wing, dusky, finely edged with
dark olive yellow; throat and whole breast, rich yellow, spreading also
along the sides under the wings, handsomely marked with spots of
black running in chains; belly and vent, yellowish white; tail, forked,
dusky black, edged with yellow olive, the three exterior feathers on

---

* The Prince of Musignano first directed my attention to the identity of this bird
of Wilson and Audubon's Carbonated Warbler. I cannot perceive any essential
difference, that is, judging from the two plates and descriptions. Mr. Audubon
procured his species in the state of Kentucky. — Ed.

each side marked on their inner vanes with a spot of white. The yellow on the throat and sides of the neck reaches nearly round it, and is very bright.

FEMALE BLACK-POLL WARBLER. — SYLVIA STRIATA. —
Fig. 216.

Amer. Orn. vol. iv. p. 40.

SYLVICOLA STRIATA. — Swainson.

This bird was shot in the same excursion with the preceding, and is introduced here for the purpose of preventing future collectors, into whose hands specimens of it may chance to fall, from considering it as another and a distinct species. Its history, as far as was then known, has been detailed in a preceding part of this work. Of its nest and eggs I am still ignorant. It doubtless breeds both here and in New Jersey, having myself found it in both places during the summer. From its habit of keeping on the highest branches of trees, it probably builds in such situations, and its nest may long remain unknown to us.

Pennant, who describes this species, says that it inhabits, during summer, Newfoundland and New York, and is called in the last *Sailor.* This name, for which, however, no reason is given, must be very local, as the bird itself is one of those silent, shy, and solitary individuals, that seek the deep retreats of the forest, and are known to few or none but the naturalist.

Length of the female Black-Cap, five inches and a quarter, extent, eight and a quarter; bill, brownish black; crown, yellow olive, streaked with black; back, the same, mixed with some pale slate; wings, dusky brown, edged with olive; first and second wing-coverts, tipped with white; tertials, edged with yellowish white; tail-coverts, pale gray; tail, dusky, forked, the two exterior feathers marked on their inner vanes with a spot of white; round the eye is a whitish ring; cheeks and sides of the breast, tinged with yellow, and slightly spotted with black; chin, white, as are also the belly and vent; legs and feet, dirty orange.

The young bird of the first season, and the female, as is usually the case, are very much alike in plumage. On their arrival early in April, the black feathers on the crown are frequently seen coming out, intermixed with the former ash-colored ones.

This species has all the agility and many of the habits of the Flycatcher.

[Parts VII. and VIII. of Wilson's work, commencing with the next description, (Ring-tailed Eagle,) seem to have been finished more hur-

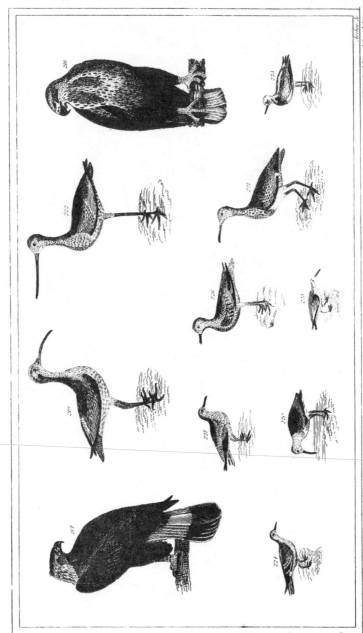

217. Ring-tail Eagle. 218. Sea Eagle. 219. Esquimaux Curlew. 220. Red backed Snipe. 221. Semipalmated S. 222. Marbled Godwit. 223. Turnstone. 224. Ash Colowed Sandpiper. 225. The Purre. 226. Black bellied Plover. 227. Red breasted Sandpiper.

riedly, and contain greater mistakes in the nomenclature than any of the preceding ones; the descriptions, however, are alike vivid and well drawn. In 1824, Mr. Ord, the personal friend of Wilson, undertook, at the request of the publisher, to improve these two parts; and they were accordingly re-published with that gentleman's additions. We have thought it better to print from the original edition, as showing the true opinions of its author but have occasionally inserted, at the conclusion of the descriptions, the observations of Mr. Ord, taken from his reprint. — ED.]

RING-TAILED EAGLE.—FALCO FULVUS.—Fig. 217.

Linn. Syst. 125. — Black Eagle, *Arct. Zool.* p. 195, No. 87. — *Lath.* i. 32, No. 6. — White-tailed Eagle, *Edw.* i. 1. — L'Aigle commun, *Buff.* i. 86. *Pl. enl.* 409. — *Bewick*, i. p. 49. — *Turt. Syst.* p. 145. — *Peale's Museum*, No. 84.

AQUILA CHRYSAETOS. — WILLOUGHBY.*

Ayle royal, *Temm. Man. d'Orn.* i. p. 38. — Aquila chrysaëtos, *Flem.* 138. — *Zool.* p. 52. — Golden Eagle, *Selby, Illust. Br. Orn.* pl. 1 and 2, the young and adult, part i. p. 4. — Aquila chrysaëtos ? *North. Zool.* ii. p. 12. — *Bonap. Synop.* p. 24.

THE reader is now presented with a portrait of this celebrated Eagle, drawn from a fine specimen shot in the county of Montgomery, Pennsylvania. Fig. 217, here given, is strongly characteristic of its original. With respect to the habits of the species, such particulars only shall be selected as are well authenticated, rejecting whatever seems vague, or savors two much of the marvellous.

* Wilson, like many other ornithologists, imagined that the Ring-tailed and Golden Eagles constituted two species. Temminck, I believe, first asserted the fact of their being identical, and the attention of naturalists in this country was attracted to the circumstance, by the different opinions entertained by Mr. James Wilson and Mr. Selby. The latter gentleman has long since satisfactorily proved their identity, from observation, and the numerous specimens kept alive in various parts of Britain, have set the question completely at rest. The Ring-Tail is the young of the first year, and as such is correctly figured by our author. In a wild state, three years are required to complete the clouded barring, the principal mark of the adults, and which, even after that period, increase in darkness of color. When kept in confinement, the change is generally longer in taking place; and I have seen it incomplete at six years. It commences by an extension of the bar at the end of the tail, and by additional cloudings on the white parts, which increase yearly until perfected. This bird does not seem very common in any part of America, and is even more rarely met with in the adult plumage. It was found on the borders of the Rocky Mountains by the overland arctic expedition, and is known also on the plains of the Saskatchewan.
The noble bearing and aspect of the Eagles and Falcons have always associated them, among rude nations, and in poetical comparisons, with the true courage of the warrior, and the magnanimity of the prince or chief. The young Indian warrior glories in his Eagle's plume, as the most honorable ornament with which he can adorn himself; the dress of a Highland Chieftain is incomplete without this badge of high degree. The feathers of the War Eagle are also used at the propitiatory sacrifices, and so highly are they prized, that a valuable horse is sometimes exchanged for the tail of a single Eagle. — ED

This noble bird, in strength, spirit, and activity, ranks among the first of its tribe. It is found, though sparingly dispersed, over the whole temperate and arctic regions, particularly the latter; breeding on high, precipitous rocks, always preferring a mountainous country. In its general appearance, it has great resemblance to the Golden Eagle, from which, however, it differs in being rather less, as also in the colors and markings of the tail, and, as it is said, in being less noisy. When young, the color of the body is considerably lighter, but deepens into a blackish brown as it advances in age.

The tail-feathers of this bird are highly valued by the various tribes of American Indians, for ornamenting their calumets, or pipes of peace. Several of these pipes, which were brought from the remote regions of Louisiana, by Captain Lewis, are now deposited in Mr. Peale's museum, each of which has a number of the tail-feathers of this bird attached to it. The northern as well as southern Indians seem to follow the like practice, as appears by the numerous calumets, formerly belonging to different tribes, to be seen in the same magnificent collection.

Mr. Pennant informs us, that the independent Tartars train this Eagle for the chase of hares, foxes, wolves, antelopes, &c., and that they esteem the feathers of the tail the best for pluming their arrows. The Ring-Tail Eagle is characterized by all as a generous, spirited, and docile bird; and various extraordinary incidents are related of it by different writers, not, however, sufficiently authenticated to deserve repetition. The truth is, the solitary habits of the Eagle now before us, the vast, inaccessible cliffs to which it usually retires, united with the scarcity of the species in those regions inhabited by man, all combine to render a particular knowledge of its manners very difficult to be obtained. The author has, once or twice, observed this bird sailing along the alpine declivities of the White Mountains of New Hampshire, early in October, and again, over the Highlands of Hudson's River, not far from West Point. Its flight was easy, in high, circuitous sweeps; its broad, white tail, tipped with brown, expanded like a fan. Near the settlements on Hudson's Bay, it is more common, and is said to prey on hares, and the various species of Grouse which abound there. Buffon observes, that, though other Eagles also prey upon hares, this species is a more fatal enemy to those timid animals, which are the constant object of their search, and the prey which they prefer. The Latins, after Pliny, termed the Eagle *Valeria quasi valens viribus,* because of its strength, which appears greater than that of the other Eagles in proportion to its size.

The Ring-Tail Eagle measures nearly three feet in length; the bill is of a brownish horn color; the cere, sides of the mouth, and feet, yellow; iris of the eye, reddish hazel, the eye turned considerably forwards; eyebrow, remarkably prominent, projecting over the eye, and giving a peculiar sternness to the aspect of the bird; the crown is flat; the plumage of the head, throat, and neck, long and pointed; that on the upper part of the head and neck, very pale ferruginous; fore part of the crown, black; all the pointed feathers are shafted with black; whole upper parts, dark blackish brown; wings, black; tail, rounded, long, of a white, or pale cream color, minutely sprinkled with specks of ash, and dusky, and ending in a broad band of deep dark brown, of nearly one third its length; chin, cheeks, and throat, black; whole lower parts, a deep dark brown, except the vent and inside of the thighs, which are white, stained with brown; legs, thickly covered to the feet with brownish white down, or feathers; claws, black, very large, sharp, and formidable, the hind one full two inches long.

The Ring-Tail Eagle is found in Russia, Switzerland, Germany, France, Scotland, and the northern parts of America. As Marco Polo, in his description of the customs of the Tartars, seems to allude to this species, it may be said to inhabit the whole circuit of the arctic regions of the globe. The Golden Eagle, on the contrary, is said to be found only in the more warm and temperate countries of the ancient continent.* Later discoveries, however, have ascertained it to be also an inhabitant of the United States.

SEA EAGLE. — FALCO OSSIFRAGUS. — Fig. 218.

Arct. Zool. p. 194, No. 86. — *Linn. Syst.* 124. — *Lath.* i. 30. — L'Orfraie, *Buff.* i. 112, pl. 3. *Pl. enl.* 12, 415. — *Br. Zool.* i. No. 44. — *Bewick*, i. 53. — *Turt. Syst.* p. 144. — *Peale's Museum*, No. 80.

HALIÆETUS LEUCOCEPHALUS. — Savigny. †

Bald Eagle, Falco leucocephalus, young, *Ord's reprint.*

This Eagle inhabits the same countries, frequents the same situations, and lives on the same kind of food, as the Bald Eagle, with whom it is often seen in company. It resembles this last so much in figure, size, form of the bill, legs, and claws, and is so often seen associating with it, both along the Atlantic coast and in the vicinity of our lakes and large rivers, that I have strong suspicions, notwithstanding ancient and very respectable authorities to the contrary, of its being the same species, only in a different stage of color.

That several years elapse before the young of the Bald Eagle receive the white head, neck, and tail, and that, during the intermediate period, their plumage strongly resembles that of the Sea Eagle, I am satisfied from my own observation on three several birds, kept by persons of Philadelphia. One of these, belonging to the late Mr. Enslen, collector of natural subjects for the Emperor of Austria, was confidently believed by him to be the Black, or Sea Eagle, until the fourth year, when the plumage on the head, tail, and tail-coverts, began gradually to become white; the bill also exchanged its dusky hue for that of yellow; and, before its death, this bird, which I frequently examined, assumed the perfect dress of the full-plumaged Bald Eagle. Another circumstance, corroborating these suspicions, is the variety that occurs in the colors of the Sea Eagle. Scarcely two of these are found to be alike, their plumage being more or less diluted with white. In some, the chin, breast, and tail-coverts are of a deep brown; in others nearly white; and in all evidently unfixed, and varying to a pure white.

* Buffon, vol. i. p. 56. *Trans.*
† See note to the adult, p. 325, for synonymes, &c.

Their place and manner of building, on high trees, in the neighborhood of lakes, large rivers, or the ocean, exactly similar to the Bald Eagle, also strengthens the belief. At the celebrated Cataract of Niagara, great numbers of these birds, called there Gray Eagles, are continually seen sailing high and majestically over the watery tumult, in company with the Bald Eagles, eagerly watching for the mangled carcasses of those animals that have been hurried over the precipice, and cast up on the rocks below, by the violence of the rapids. These are some of the circumstances on which my suspicions of the identity of those two birds are founded. In some future part of the work, I hope to be able to speak with more certainty on this subject.

Were we disposed, after the manner of some, to substitute, for plain matters of fact, all the narratives, conjectures, and fanciful theories of travellers, voyagers, compilers, &c., relative to the history of the Eagle, the volumes of these writers, from Aristotle down to his admirer, the Count de Buffon, would furnish abundant materials for this purpose. But the author of the present work feels no ambition to excite surprise and astonishment at the expense of truth, or to attempt to elevate and embellish his subject beyond the plain realities of nature. On this account, he cannot assent to the assertion, however eloquently made, in the celebrated parallel drawn by the French naturalist, between the Lion and the Eagle, viz. that the Eagle, like the Lion, " disdains the possession of that property which is not the fruit of his own industry, and rejects with contempt the prey which is not procured by his own exertions ; " since the very reverse of this is the case, in the conduct of the Bald and the Sea Eagle, who, during the summer months, are the constant robbers and plunderers of the Osprey, or Fish Hawk, by whose industry alone both are usually fed. Nor that, " *though famished for want of prey, he disdains to feed on carrion,*" since we have ourselves seen the Bald Eagle, while seated on the dead carcass of a horse, keep a whole flock of Vultures at a respectful distance, until he had fully sated his own appetite. The Count has also taken great pains to expose the ridiculous opinion of Pliny, who conceived that the Ospreys formed no separate race, and that they proceeded from the intermixture of different species of Eagles, the young of which were not Ospreys, only Sea Eagles; "*which Sea Eagles,*" says he, "*breed small Vultures, which engender great Vultures, that have not the power of propagation.*" * But, while laboring to confute these absurdities, the Count himself, in his belief of an occasional intercourse between the Osprey and the Sea Eagle, contradicts all actual observation, and one of the most common and fixed laws of nature; for it may be safely asserted, that there is no habit more universal among the feathered race, in their natural state, than that chastity of attachment, which confines the amours of individuals to those of their own species only. That perversion of nature, produced by domestication, is nothing to the purpose. In no instance have I ever observed the slightest appearance of a contrary conduct. Even in those birds which never build a nest for themselves, nor hatch their young, nor even pair, but live in a state of general concubinage, — such as the Cuckoo of the old, and the Cow Bunting of the new continent, — there is no instance

* *Hist. Nat.* lib. x. c. 3.

of a deviation from this striking habit. I cannot, therefore, avoid considering the opinion above alluded to, that "the male Osprey, by coupling with the female Sea Eagle, produces Sea Eagles; and that the female Osprey, by pairing with the male Sea Eagle, gives birth to Ospreys,"* or Fish Hawks, as altogether unsupported by facts, and contradicted by the constant and universal habits of the whole feathered race, in their state of nature.

The Sea Eagle is said, by Salerne, to build on the loftiest oaks a very broad nest, into which it drops two large eggs, that are quite round, exceedingly heavy, and of a dirty white color. Of the precise time of building, we have no account; but something may be deduced from the following circumstance : — In the month of May, while on a shooting excursion along the sea-coast, not far from Great Egg Harbor, accompanied by my friend Mr. Ord, we were conducted about a mile into the woods to see an Eagle's nest. On approaching within a short distance of the place, the bird was perceived slowly retreating from the nest, which, we found, occupied the centre of the top of a very large yellow pine. The woods were cut down, and cleared off, for several rods around the spot, which, from this circumstance, and the stately, erect trunk, and large, crooked, wriggling branches of the tree, surmounted by a black mass of sticks and brush, had a very singular and picturesque effect. Our conductor had brought an axe with him, to cut down the tree; but my companion, anxious to save the eggs, or young, insisted on ascending to the nest, which he fearlessly performed, while we stationed ourselves below, ready to defend him, in case of an attack from the old Eagles. No opposition, however, was offered : and, on reaching the nest, it was found, to our disappointment, empty. It was built of large sticks, some of them several feet in length; within which lay sods of earth, sedge, grass, dry reeds, &c., piled to the height of five or six feet, by more than four in breadth. It was well lined with fresh pine tops, and had little or no concavity. Under this lining lay the recent exuviæ of the young of the present year, such as scales of the quill-feathers, down, &c. Our guide had passed this place late in February, at which time both male and female were making a great noise about the nest; and, from what we afterwards learnt, it is highly probable it contained young, even at that early time of the season. †

* Buffon, vol. i. p. 80. *Trans.*

† Mr. Ord adds the following : — "The succeeding year, on the first day of March, a friend of ours took from the same nest three eggs, the largest of which measured three inches and a quarter in length, two and a quarter in diameter, upwards of seven in circumference, and weighed four ounces five drams apothecaries weight; the color, a dirty yellowish white; one was of a very pale bluish white; the young were perfectly formed. Such was the solicitude of the female to preserve her eggs, that she did not abandon the nest until several blows, with an axe, had been given the tree."

In the History of Lewis and Clark's Expedition, we find the following account of an Eagle's nest, which must have added not a little to the picturesque effect of the magnificent scenery at the Falls of the Missouri : —

"Just below the upper pitch is a little island in the middle of the river, well covered with timber. Here, on a cottonwood-tree, an Eagle had fixed its nest, and seemed the undisputed mistress of a spot, to contest whose dominion neither man nor beast would venture across the gulfs that surrounded it, and which is further secured by the mist rising from the falls." — *Hist. of the Expedition*, vol. i. p. 264.

A few miles from this is another Eagle's nest, built also on a pine-tree, which, from the information received from the proprietor of the woods, had been long the residence of this family of Eagles. The tree on which the nest was originally built, had been, for time immemorial, or at least ever since he remembered, inhabited by these Eagles. Some of his sons cut down this tree to procure the young, which were two in number; and the Eagles, soon after, commenced building another nest, on the very next adjoining tree, thus exhibiting a very particular attachment to the spot. The Eagles, he says, make it a kind of *home* and *lodging place*, in all seasons. This man asserts that the Gray, or Sea Eagles, are the young of the Bald Eagle, and that they are several years old before they begin to breed. It does not drive its young from the nest, like the Osprey, or Fish Hawk, but continues to feed them long after they leave it.

The bird from which Fig. 218 was drawn measured three feet in length, and upwards of seven feet in extent. The bill was formed exactly like that of the Bald Eagle, but of a dusky brown color; cere and legs, bright yellow; the latter, as in the Bald Eagle, feathered a little below the knee; irides, a bright straw color; head above, neck, and back, streaked with light brown, deep brown, and white, the plumage being white, tipped and centred with brown; scapulars, brown; lesser wing-coverts, very pale, intermixed with white; primaries, black, their shafts brownish white; rump, pale brownish white; tail, rounded, somewhat longer than the wings, when shut, brown on the exterior vanes, the inner ones white, sprinkled with dirty brown; throat, breast, and belly, white, dashed and streaked with different tints of brown and pale yellow; vent, brown, tipped with white; femorals, dark brown, tipped with lighter; auriculars, brown, forming a bar from below the eye backwards; plumage of the neck, long, narrow, and pointed, as is usual with Eagles, and of a brownish color, tipped with white.

The Sea Eagle is said, by various authors, to hunt at night, as well as during the day, and that, besides fish, it feeds on chickens, birds, hares, and other animals. It is also said to catch fish during the night; and that the noise of its plunging into the water is heard at a great distance. But, in the descriptions of these writers, this bird has been so frequently confounded with the Osprey, as to leave little doubt that the habits and manners of the one have been often attributed to both, and others added that are common to neither.

ESQUIMAUX CURLEW. — SCOLOPAX BOREALIS. — Fig. 219.

Arct. Zool. p. 461, No. 364. — *Lath.* iii. — *Turt. Syst.* p. 392. — *Peale's Museum,*
No. 4003.

NUMENIUS BOREALIS. — Latham.*

Numenius borealis, *Lath. Ind. Orn.* ii. p. 712. — *Bonap. Synop.* No. 244. — *North.
Zool.* ii. p. 378, pl. 55.

IN prosecuting our researches among the feathered tribes of this
extensive country, we are at length led to the shores of the ocean,
where a numerous and varied multitude, subsisting on the gleanings
of that vast watery magazine of nature, invite our attention ; and, from
their singularities and numbers, promise both amusement and instruction. These we shall, as usual, introduce in the order we chance to
meet with them in their native haunts. Individuals of various tribes
thus promiscuously grouped together, the peculiarities of each will appear more conspicuous and striking, and the detail of their histories
less formal, as well as more interesting.

The Esquimaux Curlew, or, as it is called by our gunners on the
sea-coast, the Short-billed Curlew, is peculiar to the new continent.
Mr. Pennant, indeed, conceives it to be a mere variety of the English
Whimbrel, (*S. phæopus ;*) but, among the great numbers of these birds
which I have myself shot and examined, I have never yet met with one
corresponding to the descriptions given of the Whimbrel, the colors
and markings being different, the bill much more bent, and nearly an
inch and a half longer ; and the manners, in certain particulars, very
different : these reasons have determined its claim to that of an independent species.

The Short-billed Curlew arrives in large flocks on the sea-coast of
New Jersey early in May, from the south, frequents the salt marshes,
muddy shores and inlets, feeding on small worms and minute shell-
fish. They are most commonly seen on mud flats at low water, in
company with various other Waders ; and at high water roam along
the marshes. They fly high, and with great rapidity. A few are seen
in June, and as late as the beginning of July, when they generally
move off towards the north. Their appearance, on these occasions, is
very interesting : they collect together from the marshes, as if by pre-
meditated design, rise to a great height in the air, usually about an
hour before sunset, and, forming in one vast line, keep up a constant
whistling on their way to the north, as if conversing with one another

---

* This species has been by some supposed to be identical with the *N. phæopus*
of Europe, but I believe later investigations have proved that it is entirely distinct,
the Whimbrel having not yet been found to inhabit any part of America. The
Northern Zoology mentions it as inhabiting the barren lands within the arctic circle
in summer, where it feeds on insects and the berries of *Empetrum nigrum*. The
Copper Indians believe that this bird, and some others, betray the approach of an
enemy. Their nests and habits, while breeding, resemble those of the Common
Curlew. — Ed.

to render the journey more agreeable. Their flight is then more slow and regular, that the feeblest may keep up with the line of march; while the glittering of their beautifully-speckled wings, sparkling in the sun, produces altogether a very pleasing spectacle.

In the month of June, while the dew-berries are ripe, these birds sometimes frequent the fields, in company with the Long-billed Curlews, where brambles abound; soon get very fat, and are at that time excellent eating. Those who wish to shoot them fix up a shelter of brushwood in the middle of the field, and by that means kill great numbers. In the early part of spring, and, indeed, during the whole time that they frequent the marshes, feeding on shell-fish, they are much less esteemed for the table.

Pennant informs us that the Esquimaux Curlews "were seen in flocks innumerable on the hills about Chatteaux Bay, on the Labrador coast, from August the 9th to September 6th, when they all disappeared, being on their way from their northern breeding place." He adds, "They kept on the open grounds, fed on the *Empetrum nigrum,* and were very fat and delicious. They arrive at Hudson's Bay in April, or early in May; pair and breed to the north of Albany Fort among the woods; return in August to the marshes, and all disappear in September." * About this time, they return in accumulated numbers to the shores of New Jersey, whence they finally depart for the south early in November.

The Esquimaux Curlew is eighteen inches long, and thirty-two inches in extent; the bill, which is four inches and a half long, is black towards the point, and a pale purplish flesh color near the base; upper part of the head, dark brown, divided by a narrow stripe of brownish white; over each eye extends a broad line of pale drab; iris, dark colored; hind part of the neck, streaked with dark brown; fore part and whole breast, very pale brown; upper part of the body, pale drab, centred and barred with dark brown, and edged with spots of white on the exterior vanes; three first primaries, black, with white shafts; rump and tail-coverts, barred with dark brown; belly, white; vent, the same, marked with zigzag lines of brown; whole lining of the wing, beautifully barred with brown, on a dark cream ground; legs and naked thighs, a pale lead color.

* *Arct. Zool.* vol. ii. p. 163. *Phil. Trans.* lxii. 411.

RED-BACKED SANDPIPER. — TRINGA ALPINA. — Fig. 220.

Arct. Zool. p. 476, No. 391. — *Bewick*, ii. p. 113. — La Brunette, *Buff.* vii. 493. — *Peale's Museum*, No. 4094.

TRINGA ALPINA. — Pennant.*

Dunlin, *Mont. Orn. Dict.* — The Dunlin, *Bewick's Brit. Birds*, ii. p. 113. — Purre, *Id.* ii. p. 115. — Bécasseau brunette ou variable, *Temm.* ii. 612. — Tringa alpina, *Flem. Br. Zool.* p. 108. — *Bonap. Synop.* p. 25. — Tringa alpina, The American Dunlin, *North. Zool.* ii. p. 383.

This bird inhabits both the old and new continents, being known in England by the name of the Dunlin, and in the United States, along the shores of New Jersey, by that of the Red-Back. Its residence

---

* This species is again represented (Fig. 225) in the plumage of the winter, and the decided change undergone, at the different ages and seasons, has caused great multiplication and confusion among the synonymes. Wilson's two figures show very well the distinctions between the nuptial dress and that of winter; and, in the bird of the first year, the plumage assumes a ruddy tinge on the upper parts, but wants the greater part of the black, so conspicuous during the love season.

On the coasts of Great Britain, the Purre is the most common of the whole race, and may generally be met with, no matter what is the character of the shore. Before they have been much driven about and annoyed, they are also one of the most familiar. During winter, the flocks are sometimes immense, and will allow a person to approach very near, looking, and running a few steps, or stretching their wings in preparation for flight, listlessly, and indicative of little alarm; a few shots, however, render them as timorous and wary as they were before careless. In spring, they separate into pairs, when some perform a migration to a considerable extent northward, while others retire to the nearer marshes and sea merses, a few to the shores of inland lakes, and still fewer to the higher inland muirs. Having there performed the duties of incubation, they return again in autumn to the shore, where they may be found in small parties, the amount of the broods, and which gradually congregate as the season advances, and more distant travellers arrive, until many hundreds are thus joined. Their nests are formed beneath or at the side of any small bush or tuft of grass, rather neatly scraped, and with a few straws of grass round the sides. The male is generally in attendance, perched on some near elevation, and, on any danger approaching, runs round, uttering, at quick intervals, his shrill, monotonous whistle. The female, when raised from the nest, flutters off for a few yards, and then assumes the same manners with the male. The young sit and squat among the grass or reeds, and, at that time, the parents will come within two yards of the person in search of them. The Purre seems extensively distributed over both the European and American continents. I have not, however, received it from the Asiatic side, or any part of India, where so many of this tribe are commonly found.

The genus *Pelinda* has been instituted and adopted, by several naturalists, for the Purre, the Little Sandpiper, and a few others, with the exclusion of the Pygmy Curlew and Knots. Though an advocate, generally, for subdivisions, wherever any character can be seized upon, I cannot reconcile that of these birds. I can fix upon no character which is not equally applicable; and the habits, the changes of plumage, and the form, are so similar, that, with the exception of modifications essential to every group, they compose one whole. The differences in form will be noticed under the respective species; and, for the present, I prefer retaining these birds under the generic name of *Tringa*.

The following species, not noticed by Wilson, have been added to the American list by different ornithologists : —

T. Schinzii, Breh. On the authority of Bonaparte, identical with the *Pelinda cinclus*, var. of Say's expedition to the Rocky Mountains, and met with by the

here is but transient, chiefly in April and May, while passing to the arctic regions to breed ; and in September and October, when on its return southward to winter quarters. During their stay, they seldom collect in separate flocks by themselves, but mix with various other species of strand birds, among whom they are rendered conspicuous by the red color of the upper part of their plumage. They frequent the muddy flats and shores of the salt marshes at low water, feeding on small worms, and other insects, which generally abound in such places. In the month of May, they are extremely fat.

This bird is said to inhabit Greenland, Iceland, Scandinavia, the Alps of Siberia, and, in its migrations, the coasts of the Caspian Sea.* It has not, till now, been recognized by naturalists as inhabiting this part of North America. Wherever its breeding place may be, it probably begins to lay at a late period of the season, as, in numbers of females which I examined on the 1st of June, the eggs were no larger than grains of mustard seed.

Length of the Red-Back, eight inches and a half; extent, fifteen inches ; bill, black, longer than the head, (which would seem to rank it with the Snipes,) slightly bent, grooved on the upper mandible, and wrinkled at the base ; crown, back, and scapulars, bright reddish rust, spotted with black; wing-coverts, pale olive ; quills, darker ; the first tipped, the latter crossed with white; front, cheeks, hind head, and

arctic expedition on the borders of the lakes which skirt the Saskatchewan plains. So nearly allied to *T. alpina,* as to be confounded with it ; differs in size, and the distribution of markings.

Tringa pectoralis, Bonap. *Pelinda pectoralis* of Say. This seems to have been first noticed in the valuable notes to Major Laing's expedition to the Rocky Mountains. The following description is there given by Say : —

P. pectoralis, Say. Bill, black, reddish yellow at base ; upper mandible, with a few indented punctures near the tip ; head above, black, plumage margined with ferruginous, a distinct brown line from the eye to the upper mandible ; cheeks, and neck beneath, cinereous, very slightly tinged with rufous, and lineate with blackish ; orbits, and line over the eye, white ; chin, white ; neck above, dusky, plumage margined with cinereous ; scapulars, interscapulars, and wing-coverts, black, margined with ferruginous, and, near the exterior tips, with whitish ; primaries, dusky, slightly edged with whitish ; outer quill-shaft, white ; back, (beneath the interscapulars,) rump, and tail-coverts, black, immaculate ; tail-feathers, dusky, margined with white at tip, two intermediate ones longest, acute, attaining the tip of the wings, black, edged with ferruginous ; breast, venter, vent, and inferior tail-coverts, white, plumage, blackish at base ; sides, white, the plumage towards the tail slightly lineate with dusky ; feet, greenish yellow ; toes, divided to the base ; length, nearly nine inches ; bill, 11–8.

T. Douglasii, Swainson. Described in the *Northern Zoology,* from a specimen killed on the Saskatchewan, and is not uncommon in the Fur Countries, up to the 60th parallel. The authors express a kind of doubt regarding this species, having been unable to compare it with a specimen of Bonaparte's *T. himantopus ;* but mention the tail as even with the central feathers alone, longest, and not barred with ferruginous ; with chestnut-colored ear-feathers, and somewhat smaller in size.

To these nearly undescribed species, the Prince of Musignano mentions, in his catalogue, *T. Temminckii,* Leisler ; *T. minuta,* Leisler ; *Numenius pygmœus,* Latham ; the *Tringa platyrhyncha,* Temminck, and Pygmy Curlew of our shores ; and the *T. maritima,* Brunnich, our Purple Sandpiper. The latter has been met with by most of the late arctic expeditions, and breeds abundantly on Melville Island and the shores of Hudson's Bay ; and *T. subarquata, Becasseau corcoli,* Temm. ; and we may add the *T. rufescens* of Vieillot, lately taken in this country. — Ed.

* Pennant.

sides of the neck, quite round ; also the breast, grayish white, marked with small specks of black ; belly, white, marked with a broad crescent of black ; tail, pale olive, the two middle feathers centred with black ; legs and feet, ashy black ; toes, divided to their origin, and bordered with a slightly scalloped membrane ; irides, very dark.

The males and females are nearly alike in one respect, both differing greatly in color, even at the same season, probably owing to difference of age ; some being of a much brighter red than others, and the plumage dotted with white. In the month of September many are found destitute of the black crescent on the belly ; these have been conjectured to be young birds.

SEMI-PALMATED SNIPE. — SCOLOPAX SEMIPALMATA. — Fig. 221.

Arct. Zool. p. 469, No. 380. — *Peale's Museum*, No. 3942.

TOTANUS SEMIPALMATUS. — Temminck.*

Chevalier semi-palmé, Totanus semipalmatus, *Temm. Man. d'Orn.* ii. p. 637. — Totanus crassirostris, *Vieill.* winter plumage, *auct. Bonap.* — *Bonap. Cat.* p. 26.

This is one of the most noisy and noted birds that inhabit our salt marshes in summer. Its common name is the Willet, by which appellation it is universally known along the shores of New York, New Jersey, Delaware, and Maryland, — in all of which places it breeds in great numbers.

The Willet is peculiar to America. It arrives from the south on the shores of the Middle States about the 20th of April, or beginning of May ; and from that time to the last of July, its loud and shrill reiterations of *pill-will-willet, pill-will-willet,* resound, almost incessantly, along the marshes, and may be distinctly heard at the distance of more than half a mile. About the 20th of May, the Willets generally begin to lay.† Their nests are built on the ground, among the grass of the salt marshes, pretty well towards the land, or cultivated fields, and are composed of wet rushes and coarse grass, forming a slight hollow or cavity in a tussock. This nest is gradually increased, during the period of laying and sitting, to the height of five or six inches. The eggs are usually four in number, very thick at the great end, and tapering to a narrower point at the other than those of the common Hen ; they measure two inches and one eighth in length, by one and a half in their greatest breadth, and are of a dark dingy olive, largely blotched with blackish brown, particularly at the great end. In some, the ground color has a tinge of green ; in others, of bluish. They

---

* Wilson has figured the winter dress of this curious species, and the Prince of Musignano has signified his intention of representing its other states. It is admitted as an accidental straggler among the species of Europe by Temminck. — Ed.

† From some unknown cause, the height of laying of these birds is said to be full two weeks later than it was twenty years ago.

are excellent eating, as I have often experienced when obliged to dine on them in my hunting excursions through the salt marshes. The young are covered with a gray-colored down; run off soon after they leave the shell; and are led and assisted in their search of food by the mother, while the male keeps a continual watch around for their safety.

The anxiety and affection manifested by these birds for their eggs and young, are truly interesting. A person no sooner enters the marshes, than he is beset by the Willets, flying around and skimming over his head, vociferating with great violence their common cry of *pill-will-willet*; and uttering at times a loud, clicking note, as he approaches nearer to their nest. As they occasionally alight, and slowly shut their long white wings speckled with black, they have a mournful note, expressive of great tenderness. During the term of incubation, the female often resorts to the sea-shore, where, standing up to the belly in water, she washes and dresses her plumage, seeming to enjoy great satisfaction from these frequent immersions. She is also at other times seen to wade more in the water than most of her tribe; and, when wounded in the wing, will take to the water without hesitation, and swims tolerably well.

The eggs of the Willet, in every instance which has come under my observation, are placed, during incubation, in an almost upright position, with the large end uppermost; and this appears to be the constant practice of several other species of birds that breed in these marshes. During the laying season, the Crows are seen roaming over the marshes in search of eggs, and, wherever they come, spread consternation and alarm among the Willets, who, in united numbers, attack and pursue them with loud clamors. It is worthy of remark, that, among the various birds that breed in these marshes, a mutual respect is paid to each other's eggs; and it is only from intruders from the land side, such as crows, jays, weasels, foxes, minx, and man himself, that these affectionate tribes have most to dread.

The Willet subsists chiefly on small shell-fish, marine worms, and other aquatic insects; in search of which it regularly resorts to the muddy shores and flats at low water, its general rendezvous being the marshes.

This bird has a summer and also a winter dress, its colors differing so much in these seasons as scarcely to appear to be the same species. Fig. 221 exhibits it in its spring and summer plumage, which in a good specimen is as follows: —

Length, fifteen inches; extent, thirty inches; upper parts, dark olive brown; the feathers, streaked down the centre, and crossed with waving lines of black; wing coverts, light olive ash, and the whole upper parts sprinkled with touches of dull yellowish white; primaries, black, white at the root half; secondaries, white, bordered with brown; rump, dark brown; tail, rounded, twelve feathers, pale olive, waved with bars of black; tail-coverts, white, barred with olive; bill, pale lead color, becoming black towards the tip; eye, very black; chin, white; breast, beautifully mottled with transverse spots of olive on a cream ground; belly and vent, white, the last barred with olive; legs and feet, pale lead color; toes, half webbed.

Towards the fall, when these birds associate in large flocks, they become of a pale dun color above, the plumage being shafted with dark brown, and the tail white, or nearly so. At this season they are extremely fat, and esteemed excellent eating. Experienced gunners always select the lightest colored ones from a flock, as being uniformly the fattest.

The female of this species is generally larger than the male. In the months of October and November, they gradually disappear.

GREAT MARBLED GODWIT. — SCOLOPAX FEDOA. —
Fig. 222. — Female.

Arct. Zool. p. 465, No. 371. — La barge rousse de Baie d'Hudson, *Buff.* vii. 507. — *Peale's Museum*, No. 4019.

LIMOSA FEDOA. — Vieillot.

Limosa fedoa, *Ord's edit. of Wils.* — *Bonap. Synop.* p. 328.

This is another transient visitant of our sea-coasts in spring and autumn, to and from its breeding place in the north. Our gunners call it the *Straight-billed Curlew*, and sometimes the *Red Curlew*. It is a shy, cautious, and watchful bird; yet so strongly are they attached to each other, that, on wounding one in a flock, the rest are immediately arrested in their flight, making so many circuits over the spot where it lies fluttering and screaming, that the sportsman often makes great destruction among them. Like the Curlew, they may also be enticed within shot, by imitating their call, or whistle; but can seldom be approached without some such manœuvre. They are much less numerous than the Short-billed Curlews, with whom, however, they not unfrequently associate. They are found among the salt marshes in May, and for some time in June, and also on their return in October and November; at which last season they are usually fat, and in high esteem for the table.

The female of this bird having been described by several writers as a distinct species from the male, it has been thought proper to represent the former, (Fig. 222;) the chief difference consists in the undulating bars of black with which the breast of the male is marked, and which are wanting in the female.

The male of the Great Marbled Godwit is nineteen inches long, and thirty-four inches in extent; the bill is nearly six inches in length, a little turned up towards the extremity, where it is black, the base is of a pale purplish flesh color; chin and upper part of the throat, whitish; head and neck, mottled with dusky brown and black on a ferruginous ground; breast, barred with wavy lines of black; back and scapulars, black, marbled with pale brown; rump and tail-coverts, of a very light brown, barred with dark brown; tail, even, except the two middle feathers, which are a little the longest; wings, pale ferruginous, elegantly marbled with dark brown, the four first primaries black on the outer edge; whole lining and lower parts of the wings, bright ferruginous; belly and vent, light rust color, with a tinge of lake.

The female differs in wanting the bars of black on the breast. The bill does not acquire its full length before the third year.

About fifty different species of the Scolopax genus are enumerated by naturalists. These are again by some separated into three classes or sub-genera; viz., the straight-billed, or Snipes; those with bills bent downwards, or the Curlews; and those whose bills are slightly turned upwards, or Godwits. The whole are a shy, timid, and solitary tribe, frequenting those vast marshes, swamps, and morasses, that frequently prevail in the vicinity of the ocean, and on the borders of large rivers. They are also generally migratory, on account of the periodical freezing of those places in the northern regions where they procure their food. The Godwits are particularly fond of salt marshes, and are rarely found in countries remote from the sea.

TURNSTONE. — TRINGA INTERPRES. — Fig. 223.

Hebridal Sandpiper, *Arct. Zool.* p. 472, No. 382. — Le Tourne-pierre, *Buff.* vii. 130. *Pl. enl.* 130. — *Bewick*, ii. p. 119, 121. — *Catesby*, i. 72. — *Peale's Museum*, No. 4044.

STREPSILAS INTERPRES. — Illiger.*

Tourne-pierre à collier, (Strepsilas collaris,) *Temm. Man. d'Orn.* ii. p. 553. — Strepsilas interpres, *Flem. Br. Zool.* p. 110. — *North. Zool.* ii. p. 371. — Strepsilas collaris, *Bonap. Synop.*

This beautifully-variegated species is common to both Europe and America; consequently extends its migrations far to the north. It arrives from the south on the shores of New Jersey in April; leaves them early in June; is seen on its return to the south in October; and continues to be occasionally seen until the commencement of cold weather, when it disappears for the season. It is rather a scarce species in this part of the world, and of a solitary disposition, seldom mingling among the large flocks of other Sandpipers, but either coursing the sands alone, or in company with two or three of its own species. On the coast of Cape May and Egg Harbor, this bird is well known by the name of the Horse-Foot Snipe, from its living, during the months of May and June, almost wholly on the eggs, or

---

* This is the only species of Turnstone known, and it is apparently distributed over the whole world. Its breeding places, according to the *Northern Zoology*, are the shores of Hudson's Bay and the Arctic Sea, probably in the most northern districts. On the Scotch and English coasts they arrive in small flocks about the beginning of August, and, as the season advances, congregate into larger assemblies; the greater proportion of these are still in their young dress, and it is not until the ensuing spring that this is completely changed; in this state they have been frequently described as a second species. Early in spring, a few straggling birds, in perfect breeding plumage, may be observed on most of our shores, which have either been left at the general migration, or remain during the year in a state of barrenness. It is then that the finest specimens for stuffing are obtained. — Ed.

spawn, of the great king crab, called here by the common people the horse-foot. This animal is the *Monoculus polyphemus* of entomologists. Its usual size is from twelve to fifteen inches in breadth, by two feet in length; though sometimes it is found much larger. The head, or forepart, is semicircular, and convex above, covered with a thin, elastic, shelly case. The lower side is concave, where it is furnished with feet and claws resembling those of a crab. The posterior extremity consists of a long, hard, pointed, dagger-like tail, by means of which, when overset by the waves, the animal turns itself on its belly again. The male may be distinguished from the female by his two large claws having only a single hook each, instead of the forceps of the female. In the Bay of Delaware, below Egg Island, and in what is usually called Maurice River Cove, these creatures seem to have formed one of their principal settlements. The bottom of this cove is generally a soft mud, extremely well suited to their accommodation. Here they are resident, burying themselves in the mud during the winter; but, early in the month of May, they approach the shore in multitudes to obey the great law of nature, in depositing their eggs within the influence of the sun, and are then very troublesome to the fishermen, who can scarcely draw a scine for them, they are so numerous. Being of slow motion, and easily overset by the surf, their dead bodies cover the shore in heaps, and in such numbers, that for ten miles one might walk on them without touching the ground.

The hogs from the neighboring country are regularly driven down, every spring, to feed on them, which they do with great avidity; though by this kind of food their flesh acquires a strong, disagreeable, fishy taste. Even the small turtles, or terrapins, so eagerly sought after by our epicures, contract so rank a taste by feeding on the spawn of the king crab, as to be at such times altogether unpalatable. This spawn may sometimes be seen lying in hollows and eddies, in bushels, while the Snipes and Sandpipers, particularly the Turnstone, are hovering about, feasting on the delicious fare. The dead bodies of the animals themselves are hauled up in wagons for manure, and when placed at the hills of corn, in planting time, are said to enrich the soil, and add greatly to the increase of the crop.

The Turnstone derives its name from another singularity it possesses, of turning over with its bill small stones and pebbles, in search of various marine worms and insects. At this sort of work it is exceedingly dexterous; and, even when taken and domesticated, is said to retain the same habit.* Its bill seems particularly well constructed for this purpose, differing from all the rest of its tribe, and very much resembling in shape that of the Common Nuthatch. We learn from Mr. Pennant that these birds inhabit Hudson's Bay, Greenland, and the arctic flats of Siberia, where they breed, wandering southerly in autumn. It is said to build on the ground, and to lay four eggs, of an olive color, spotted with black, and to inhabit the isles of the Baltic during summer.

The Turnstone flies with a loud, twittering note, and runs with its wings lowered; but not with the rapidity of others of its tribe. It examines more completely the same spot of ground, and, like some of

* CATESBY.

41

the Woodpeckers, will remain searching in the same place, tossing the stones and pebbles from side to side for a considerable time.

These birds vary greatly in color; scarcely two individuals are to be found alike in markings. These varieties are most numerous in autumn, when the young birds are about, and are less frequently met with in spring. The most perfect specimens I have examined are as follows:—

Length, eight inches and a half; extent, seventeen inches; bill, blackish horn; frontlet, space passing through the eyes, and thence dropping down and joining the under mandible, black, enclosing a spot of white. Crown, white, streaked with black; breast, black, from whence it turns up half across the neck; behind the eye, a spot of black; upper part of the neck, white, running down and skirting the black breast as far as the shoulder; upper part of the back, black, divided by a strip of bright ferruginous; scapulars, black, glossed with greenish, and interspersed with rusty red; whole back below this, pure white, but hid by the scapulars; rump, black; tail-coverts, white; tail, rounded, white at the base half, thence black to the extremity; belly and vent, white; wings, dark dusky, crossed by two bands of white; lower half of the lesser coverts, ferruginous; legs and feet, a bright vermilion, or red lead; hind toe standing inwards, and all of them edged with a thick, warty membrane. The male and female are alike variable; and, when in perfect plumage, nearly resemble each other.

Bewick, in his *History of British Birds*, has figured and described what he considers to be two species of Turnstone; one of which, he says, is chiefly confined to the southern, and the other to the northern parts of Great Britain. The difference, however, between these two appears to be no greater than commonly occurs among individuals of the same flock, and evidently of the same species, in this country. As several years probably elapse before these birds arrive at their complete state of plumage, many varieties must necessarily appear, according to the different ages of the individuals.

ASH-COLORED SANDPIPER.—TRINGA CINEREA.—Fig. 224.

Arct. Zool. p. 474, No. 386.—*Bewick*, ii. p. 102.—*Peale's Museum*, No. 4060.

TRINGA CANUTUS. — Linnæus.— plumage of the young.*

Synonymes of young; Tringa calidris, *Linn.* i. 252.—Tringa nævia, *Lath. Ind. Orn.* ii. 732.—Maubeche tachete, *Buff.*—Freckled Sandpiper, *Arct. Zool.* ii. p. 480.

THE regularly-disposed concentric semicircles of white and dark brown that mark the upper parts of the plumage of this species, dis-

---

* This beautiful Sandpiper has also, from its changes, been described under various names, and our author has well represented the states of the young and summer plumage, in his Ash-colored and Red-breasted Sandpipers. In the winter plumage of the adult, the upper parts are of a uniform gray, and want the black and light edges, represented in Fig. 225.

America and Europe seem the only countries of the Knot. I have never seen it

tinguish it from all others, and give it a very neat appearance. In activity it is superior to the preceding; and traces the flowing and recession of the waves along the sandy beach with great nimbleness, wading and searching among the loosened particles for its favorite food, which is a small, thin, oval, bivalve shell-fish, of a white or pearl color, and not larger than the seed of an apple. These usually lie at a short depth below the surface; but in some places are seen at low water in heaps, like masses of wet grain, in quantities of more than a bushel together. During the latter part of summer and autumn, these minute shell-fish constitute the food of almost all those busy flocks that run with such activity along the sands, among the flowing and retreating waves. They are universally swallowed whole; but the action of the bird's stomach, assisted by the shells themselves, soon reduces them to a pulp. If we may judge from their effects, they must be extremely nutritious, for almost all those tribes that feed on them are at this season mere lumps of fat. Digging for these in the hard sand would be a work of considerable labor, whereas, when the particles are loosened by the flowing of the sea, the birds collect them with great ease and dexterity. It is amusing to observe with what adroitness they follow and elude the tumbling surf, while at the same time they seem wholly intent on collecting their food.

The Ash-colored Sandpiper, the subject of our present account, inhabits both Europe and America. It has been seen in great numbers on the Seal Islands, near Chatteaux Bay; is said to continue the whole summer in Hudson's Bay, and breeds there. Mr. Pennant suspects that it also breeds in Denmark; and says, that they appear in vast flocks on the Flintshire shore during the winter season.[*] With us they are also migratory, being only seen in spring and autumn. They are plump birds; and, by those accustomed to the sedgy taste of this tribe, are esteemed excellent eating.

The length of this species is ten inches, extent twenty; bill, black,

from India, but have a single specimen of a Knot from New Holland, very similar, and which I considered identical, until a closer examination has led me to have doubts on the subject. Like the other migratory species, they only appear on our coasts in autumn, on their return with their broods, or more sparingly in spring, when on their way north. The young possess a good deal of the rufous color on the under parts, which leaves them as the winter approaches. I once met a large flock on the east side of Holy Island, in the month of September, which were so tame as to allow me to kill as many as I wanted with stones from the beach: it may have been on their first arrival, when they were fatigued. I have a specimen, in full plumage, killed by a boy on Portobello sands by the same means. In general they are rather shy, and it is only in their wheeling round that a good shot can be obtained. Before the severity of the winter sets in, they are fat, and are sought after by persons who *know them*, for the table.

There is a peculiarity in the gregarious *Tringæ*, and most of the *Charadriadæ*, which is very nearly confined to these tribes, — the simultaneous flight, and the acting as it were by concert in their wheels and evolutions. Among none is it more conspicuous than in this species; and every one who has been on the shore during winter, on a day gleaming and cloudy, may have seen the masses of these birds at a distance, when the whole were only visible, appear like a dark and swiftly moving cloud, suddenly vanish, but in a second appear at some distance, glowing with a silvery light almost too intense to gaze upon, the consequences of the simultaneous motions of the flock, at once changing their position, and showing the dark gray of their backs, or the pure white of their under parts. — ED.

[*] *Arctic Zoology*, p. 474.

straight, fluted to nearly its tip, and about an inch and a half long; upper parts, brownish ash, each feather marked near the tip with a narrow semicircle of dark brown, bounded by another of white; tail-coverts, white, marbled with olive; wing-quills, dusky, shafts, white; greater coverts, black, tipped with white; some of the primaries edged also with white; tail, plain pale ash, finely edged and tipped with white; crown and hind head, streaked with black, ash, and white; stripe over the eye, cheeks, and chin, white, the former marked with pale streaks of dusky, the latter pure; breast, white, thinly specked with blackish; belly and vent, pure white; legs, a dirty yellowish clay color; toes, bordered with a narrow, thick, warty membrane; hind toe, directed inwards, as in the Turnstone; claws and eye, black.

These birds vary a little in color, some being considerably darker above, others entirely white below; but, in all, the concentric semicircles on the back, scapulars, and wing-coverts, are conspicuous.

I think it probable that these birds become much lighter colored during the summer, from the circumstance of having shot one late in the month of June, at Cape May, which was of a pale drab or dun color. It was very thin and emaciated; and on examination appeared to have been formerly wounded, which no doubt occasioned its remaining behind its companions.

Early in December I examined the same coast every day for nearly two weeks, without meeting with more than one solitary individual of this species, although in October they were abundant. How far to the southward they extend their migrations, we have no facts that will enable us to ascertain, though it is probable that the shores of the West India islands afford them shelter and resources during our winter.

THE PURRE. — TRINGA CINCLUS. — Fig. 225.

Lynn. Syst. 251. — *Arct. Zool.* p. 475, No. 390. — *Bewick*, ii. p. 115. — L'Alouette de mer, *Buff.* vii. 548. — *Peale's Museum*, No. 4126.

TRINGA ALPINA. — Pennant.

This is one of the most numerous of our strand birds, as they are usually called, that frequent the sandy beach on the frontiers of the ocean. In its habits it differs so little from the preceding, that except in being still more active and expert in running and searching among the sand, on the reflux of the waves, as it nimbly darts about for food, what has been said of the former will apply equally to both, they being pretty constant associates on these occasions.

The Purre continues longer with us, both in spring and autumn, than either of the two preceding; many of them remain during the very severest of the winter, though the greater part retire to the more genial regions of the south, where I have seen them at such seasons, particularly on the sea-coasts of both Carolinas, during the month of February, in great numbers.

These birds, in conjunction with several others, sometimes collect together in such flocks, as to seem, at a distance, a large cloud of thick smoke, varying in form and appearance every instant, while it performs its evolutions in air. As this cloud descends and courses along the shores of the ocean, with great rapidity, in a kind of waving, serpentine flight, alternately throwing its dark and white plumage to the eye, it forms a very grand and interesting appearance. At such times the gunners make prodigious slaughter among them; while, as the showers of their companions fall, the whole body often alight, or descend to the surface with them, till the sportsman is completely satiated with destruction. On some of those occasions, while crowds of these victims are fluttering along the sand, the Small Pigeon Hawk, constrained by necessity, ventures to make a sweep among the dead in presence of the proprietor, but as suddenly pays for his temerity with his life. Such a tyrant is man, when vested with power, and unrestrained by the dread of responsibility!

The Purre is eight inches in length, and fifteen inches in extent; the bill is black, straight, or slightly bent downwards, about an inch and a half long, very thick at the base, and tapering to a slender, blunt point at the extremity; eye, very small; iris, dark hazel; cheeks, gray; line over the eye, belly, and vent, white; back and scapulars, of an ashy brown, marked here and there with spots of black, bordered with bright ferruginous; sides of the rump, white; tail-coverts, olive, centred with black; chin, white; neck below, gray; breast and sides, thinly marked with pale spots of dusky, in some pure white; wings, black, edged and tipped with white; two middle tail-feathers, dusky, the rest, brown ash, edged with white; legs and feet, black; toes, bordered with a very narrow scalloped membrane. The usual broad band of white crossing the wing, forms a distinguishing characteristic of almost the whole genus.

On examining more than a hundred of these birds, they varied considerably in the black and ferruginous spots on the back and scapulars; some were altogether plain, while others were thickly marked, particularly on the scapulars, with a red rust color, centred with black. The females were uniformly more plain than the males; but many of the latter, probably young birds, were destitute of the ferruginous spots. On the 24th of May, the eggs in the females were about the size of partridge shot. In what particular regions of the north these birds breed is altogether unknown.

41 *

BLACK-BELLIED PLOVER. — CHARADRIUS APRICARIUS. —
Fig. 226.

Alwagrim Plover, *Arct. Zool.* p. 483, No. 398. — Le pluvier doré à gorge noire *Buff.* viii. 85. — *Peale's Museum*, No. 4196.

SQUATAROLA CINEREA. — Fleming.*

Pluvialis cinerea, *Will. Orn.* 229. — Gray Squatarol, Squatarola grisea, *Steph. Cont. Sh. Zool.* vol. xi. p. 505. — Le vanneau gris, *Cuv. Reg. Anim.* vol. i. p. 467. — Squatarola cinerea, *Flem. Br. Zool.* p. 3. — Vanellus melanogaster, *North. Zool.* ii. p. 370.

THIS bird is known in some parts of the country by the name of the Large Whistling Field Plover. It generally makes its first appearance in Pennsylvania late in April; frequents the countries towards the mountains; seems particularly attached to newly-ploughed fields, where it forms its nest of a few slight materials, as slightly put together. The female lays four eggs, large for the size of the bird, of a light olive color, dashed with black; and has frequently two broods in the same season. It is an extremely shy and watchful bird, though clamorous during breeding time. The young are without the black color on the breast and belly until the second year, and the colors of the plumage above are likewise imperfect till then. They feed on worms, grubs, winged insects, and various kinds of berries, particularly those usually called dew-berries, and are at such times considered exquisite eating. About the beginning of September, they descend with their young to the sea-coast, and associate with the numerous multitudes then returning from their breeding-places in the north. At this season they abound on the plains of Long Island. They have a loud, whistling note; often fly at a great height; and are called by many gunners along the coast the Black-bellied Kildeer. The young

---

* This species, with some others, forms the division *Vanneau pluviers*, the genus *Squatarola* of Cuvier, and, according to modern ornithologists, has been separated from the *Charadrii*, on account of the presence of a hinder toe.

In the arrangement of this group, as in many others, I fear the characteristic marks have been taken in a manner too arbitrary. Those birds known by the name of *Plovers* form a small but apparently distinct group; they contain the *C. pluvialis*, *Virginianus*, &c., and, but for the rudimentary toe, the Gray Plover would also enter it; they agree in their manners, their incubation, and changes of plumage. We, again, have another well-defined group, which is called the *Dotterels*, agreeing in similar common habitudes; but, in one species, bearing according to arrangement the name of *Squatarola*, we have all the marks and form of plumage, but the hinder toe much developed. It therefore becomes a question, whether the presence or want of this appendage should be brought into the generic character, (as it always has been,) or should be looked upon as one of the connections of forms. In the latter way the Plovers should form the genus *Squatarola*, the Dotterels *Charadrius*, and the two birds in question be placed opposite in their respective circles.

Vanellus, or the *Lapwings*, again, form another group, as well marked in their different habits, and intimately connected with *Pluvianus*; neither of these, however, have any representative in North America.

Many Gray Plovers breed in the English fens, and, like the migratory Sandpipers, flocks appear on the shores, at the commencement of winter, where they mingle with the other species. The plate is that of the summer or breeding plumage. — ED.

of the first year have considerable resemblance to those of the Golden
Plover; but may be easily distinguished from this last by the largeness
of their head and bill, and in being at least two inches more in length.
The greater number of those which I have examined have the rudiments of a hind toe; but the character and manners of the Plover are
so conspicuous in the bird, as to determine, at the first glance, the tribe
it belongs to. They continue about the sea-coast until early in November, when they move off to the south.

This same bird, Mr. Pennant informs us, inhabits all the north of
Europe, Iceland, Greenland, and Hudson's Bay, and all the arctic part
of Siberia. It is said, that at Hudson's Bay it is called the Hawk's-
Eye, on account of its brilliancy. It appears, says the same author, in
Greenland, in the spring, about the southern lakes, and feeds on worms
and berries of the heath.

This species is twelve inches long, and twenty-four inches in extent; the bill is thick, deeply grooved on the upper mandible, an inch
and a quarter in length, and of a black color; the head and globe of
the eye are both remarkably large, the latter deep bluish black; forehead, white; crown and hind head, black, spotted with golden yellow;
back and scapulars, dusky, sprinkled with the same golden or orange
colored spots, mixed with others of white; breast, belly, and vent,
black; sides of the breast, whitish; wing-quills, black; middle of the
shafts, white; greater coverts, black, tipped with white; lining of the
wing, black; tail, regularly barred with blackish and pure white; tail-
coverts, pure white; legs and feet, a dusky lead color; the exterior
toe joined to the middle by a broad membrane; hind toe, very small.

From the length of time which these birds take to acquire their full
colors, they are found in very various stages of plumage. The breast
and belly are at first white, gradually appear mottled with black, and
finally become totally black. The spots of orange, or golden, on the
crown, hind head, and back, are at first white, and sometimes even the
breast itself is marked with these spots, mingled among the black. In
every stage, the seemingly disproportionate size of the head, and
thickness of the bill, will distinguish this species.

RED-BREASTED SANDPIPER. — TRINGA RUFA. — Fig. 227.

Peale's Museum, No. 4050.

TRINGA CANUTUS. — Linnæus.

Tringa Islandica, *Linn.* and *Lath.* — Red Sandpiper, *Mont. Orn. Dict. Supp.* —
Aberdeen Sandpiper, *Penn. Brit. Zool.* ii. No. 203.

Of this prettily marked species I can find no description. The
Tringa Icelandica, or Aberdeen Sandpiper of Pennant and others, is
the only species that has any resemblance to it; the descriptions of
that bird, however, will not apply to the present.

The common name of this species on our sea-coast is the Gray-
Back, and among the gunners it is a particular favorite, being gener-

ally a plump, tender, and excellent bird for the table; and, consequently, brings a good price in market.

The Gray-Backs do not breed on the shores of the Middle States. Their first appearance is early in May. They remain a few weeks, and again disappear until October. They usually keep in small flocks, alight in a close body together on the sand flats, where they search for the small bivalve shells already described. On the approach of the sportsman, they frequently stand fixed and silent for some time; do not appear to be easily alarmed, neither do they run about in the water as much as some others, or with the same rapidity, but appear more tranquil and deliberate. In the month of November, they retire to the south.

This species is ten inches long, and twenty in extent; the bill is black, and about an inch and a half long; the chin, eyebrows, and whole breast, are a pale brownish orange color; crown, hind head from the upper mandible backwards, and neck, dull white, streaked with black; back, a pale slaty olive, the feathers tipped with white, barred and spotted with black and pale ferruginous; tail-coverts, white, elegantly barred with black; wings, plain dusky, black towards the extremity; the greater coverts, tipped with white; shafts of the primaries, white; tail, pale ashy olive, finely edged with white, the two middle feathers somewhat the longest; belly and vent, white, the latter marked with small arrow-heads of black; legs and feet, black; toes, bordered with a narrow membrane; eye, small and black.

In some specimens, both of males and females, the red on the breast was much paler; in others it descended as far as the thighs. Both sexes seemed nearly alike.

RED–BREASTED SNIPE. — SCOLOPAX NOVEBORACENSIS. —
Fig. 228.

Arct. Zool. p. 464, No. 368. — *Peale's Museum,* No. 3932.

MACRORHAMPUS GRISEUS. — Leach.*

Macrorhampus griseus, *Steph. Cont. Shaw's Zool.* vol. xii. p. 61. — Scolopax grisea, *Flem. Br. Zool.* p. 106. — *Bonap. Cat.* p. 27. — Le becassine grise, Scolopax leucophœa, *Vieill. Gal. des Ois.* pl. 241. — Limosa scolopacea, *Say's Exped. to Rocky Mount.* i. p. 170, 171, note. — Brown Snipe, *Mont. Orn. Dict.* — Becassine ponctuée, *Temm. Man.* ii. p. 679. — Brown Snipe, *Selby's Illust. Br. Orn.* pl. 24, fig. 2.

This bird has a considerable resemblance to the Common Snipe, not only in its general form, size, and colors, but likewise in the excellence of its flesh, which is in high estimation. It differs, however,

* This bird will stand in the rank of a sub-genus. It was first indicated by Leach, in the *Catalogue to the British Museum,* under the above title. It is one of those beautifully connecting forms, which it is impossible to place without giving a situation to themselves, and intimately connects the Snipes with *Totanus* and *Limosa.* The bill is truly that of *Scolopax,* while the plumage and changes ally it to the

greatly from the Common Snipe in its manners, and in many other peculiarities, a few of which, as far as I have myself observed, may be sketched as follows : —

The Red-breasted Snipe arrives on the sea-coast of New Jersey early in April; is seldom or never seen inland : early in May, it proceeds to the north to breed, and returns by the latter part of July, or beginning of August. During its stay here, it flies in flocks, sometimes very high, and has then a loud and shrill whistle, making many evolutions over the marshes; forming, dividing, and re-uniting. They sometimes settle in such numbers, and so close together, that eighty-five have been shot at one discharge of a musket. They spring from the marshes with a loud, twirling whistle, generally rising high, and making several circuitous manœuvres in air before they descend. They frequent the sand bars and mud flats at low water, in search of food; and, being less suspicious of a boat than of a person on shore, are easily approached by this medium, and shot down in great numbers. They usually keep by themselves, being very numerous; are in excellent order for the table in September; and, on the approach of winter, retire to the south.

I have frequently amused myself with the various action of these birds. They fly very rapidly, sometimes wheeling, coursing, and doubling along the surface of the marshes; then shooting high in air, there separating and forming in various bodies, uttering a kind of quivering whistle. Among many which I opened in May, were several females that had very little rufous below, and the backs were also much lighter, and less marbled with ferruginous. The eggs contained in their ovaries were some of them as large as garden peas. Their stomachs contained masses of those small snail shells that lie in millions on the salt marshes; the wrinkles at the base of the bill, and the red breast, are strong characters of this species, as also the membrane which unites the outer and middle toes together.

other genera; from these blending characters it had been termed *Limosa scolopacea*, by Say, who gave the characters of the form without applying the name. He has the following observations in the work above quoted : —

"Several specimens were shot in a pond near the Bowyer Creek. Corresponds with the genus *Scolopax*, Cuvier, in having the dorsal grooves at the tip of the upper mandible, and in having this part dilated and rugose; but the eye is not large, nor is it placed far back upon the head; which two latter characters, combined with its more elevated and slender figure, and the circumstance of the thighs being denudated of feathers high above the knee, and the exterior toe being united to the middle toe by a membrane which extends as far as the first joint, and the toes being also margined, combine to distinguish this species from those of the genus to which the form and characters of its bill would refer it, and approach it more closely to *Limosa*. In one specimen, the two exterior primaries on each wing were light brown, but the quills were white. It may, perhaps, with propriety, be considered as the type of a new genus; and, under the following characters, be placed between the genera *Scolopax* and *Limosa*. Bill, longer than the head, dilated, and rugose at tip, slightly curved downwards, and with a dorsal groove; nasal groove, elongated; feet, long, an extensive naked space above the knee; toes, slightly margined, a membrane connecting the joints of the exterior toes; first of the primaries, rather longest."

It is of rare occurrence in Europe, a few specimens only being mentioned, and a solitary instance of its appearance on the coast of Britain is recorded by Montagu. — Ed.

The Red-breasted Snipe is ten inches and a half long, and eighteen inches in extent; the bill is about two inches and a quarter in length, straight, grooved, black towards the point, and of a dirty eel-skin color at the base, where it is tumid and wrinkled; lores, dusky; cheeks and eyebrows, pale yellowish white, mottled with specks of black; throat and breast, a reddish buff' color; sides, white, barred with black; belly and vent, white, the latter barred with dusky; crown, neck above, back, scapulars, and tertials, black, edged, mottled, and marbled with yellowish white, pale and bright ferruginous, much in the same manner as the Common Snipe; wings, plain olive, the secondaries, centred and bordered with white; shaft of the first quill, very white; rump, tail-coverts, and tail, (which consists of twelve feathers,) white, thickly spotted with black; legs and feet, dull yellowish green; outer toe united to the middle one by a small membrane; eye, very dark. The female, which is paler on the back, and less ruddy on the breast, has been described by Mr. Pennant as a separate species.*

These birds, doubtless, breed not far to the northward of the United States, if we may judge from the lateness of the season when they leave us in spring, the largeness of the eggs in the ovaries of the females before they depart, and the short period of time they are absent. Of all our sea-side Snipes, it is the most numerous, and the most delicious for the table. From these circumstances, and the crowded manner in which it flies and settles, it is the most eagerly sought after by our gunners, who send them to market in great numbers.

LONG–LEGGED AVOSET. — RECURVIROSTRA HIMANTO-PUS. — Fig. 229.

Long-legged Plover, *Arct. Zool.* p. 487, No. 405. — *Turton*, p. 416. — *Bewick*, ii. 21. — L'Echasse, *Buff.* viii. 114, *Pl. enl.* 878. — *Peale's Museum*, No. 4210.

HIMANTOPUS NIGRICOLLIS. — Vieillot. †

Himantopus Mexicanus, *Ord's Edit. of Wils.* — Himantopus nigricollis, *Bonap. Synop.* p. 322.

Naturalists have most unaccountably classed this bird with the genus *Charadrius*, or Plover, and yet affect to make the particular conformation of the bill, legs, and feet, the rule of their arrangement. In the present subject, however, excepting the trivial circumstance of the want of a hind toe, there is no resemblance whatever of those parts to

---

* See his Brown Snipe, *Arct. Zool.* No. 369.

† Wilson confounded this species with the Long-legged Plover of Europe, and ranged it with the Avosets. Mr. Ord, in his reprint, placed it in the genus *Himantopus*, properly established for these birds, but under the name *Mexicanus*. The Prince of Musignano is of opinion, that it cannot range under this, being much smaller, and refers it to the *H. nigricollis* of Vieillot. The genus contains only a few species, all so closely allied, that near examination is necessary to distinguish them. They are all remarkable for the great disproportion of their legs. — Ed.

the bill, legs, or feet, of the Plover; on the contrary, they are so entirely different, as to create no small surprise at the adoption and general acceptation of a classification, evidently so absurd and unnatural. This appears the more reprehensible, when we consider the striking affinity there is between this bird and the Common Avoset, not only in the particular form of the bill, nostrils, tongue, legs, feet, wings, and tail, but extending to the voice, manners, food, place of breeding, form of the nest, and even the very color of the eggs of both, all of which are strikingly alike, and point out, at once, to the actual observer of Nature, the true relationship of these remarkable birds.

Strongly impressed with these facts, from an intimate acquaintance with the living subjects, in their native wilds, I have presumed to remove the present species to the true and proper place assigned it by Nature, and shall now proceed to detail some particulars of its history.

This species arrives on the sea-coast of New Jersey about the 25th of April, in small, detached flocks, of twenty or thirty together. These sometimes again subdivide into lesser parties; but it rarely happens that a pair is found solitary, as, during the breeding season, they usually associate in small companies. On their first arrival, and, indeed, during the whole of their residence, they inhabit those particular parts of the salt marshes pretty high up towards the land, that are broken into numerous shallow pools, but are not usually overflowed by the tides during the summer. These pools, or ponds, are generally so shallow, that, with their long legs, the Avosets can easily wade them in every direction; and, as they abound with minute shell-fish, and multitudes of aquatic insects and their larvæ, besides the eggs and spawn of others deposited in the soft mud below, these birds find here an abundant supply of food, and are almost continually seen wading about in such places, often up to the breast in water.

In the vicinity of these *bald places*, as they are called by the country people, and at the distance of forty or fifty yards off, among the thick tufts of grass, one of these small associations, consisting perhaps of six or eight pair, takes up its residence during the breeding season. About the first week in May they begin to construct their nests, which are at first slightly formed of a small quantity of old grass, scarcely sufficient to keep the eggs from the wet marsh. As they lay and sit, however, either dreading the rise of the tides, or for some other purpose, the nest is increased in height, with dry twigs of a shrub very common in the marshes, roots of the salt grass, sea-weed, and various other substances, the whole weighing between two and three pounds. This habit of adding materials to the nest after the female begins sitting, is common to almost all other birds that breed in the marshes. The eggs are four in number, of a dark yellowish clay color, thickly marked with large blotches of black. These nests are often placed within fifteen or twenty yards of each other; but the greatest harmony seems to prevail among the proprietors.

While the females are sitting, the males are either wading through the ponds, or roaming over the adjoining marshes; but should a person make his appearance, the whole collect together in the air, flying with their long legs extended behind them, keeping up a continual yelping note of *click, click, click*. Their flight is steady, and not in short, sudden jerks, like that of the Plover. As they frequently alight on the bare marsh, they drop their wings, stand with their legs half bent, and trembling, as if unable to sustain the burden of their bodies. In this ridiculous posture they will sometimes stand for several minutes, uttering a curring sound, while, from the corresponding quiverings of their wings and long legs, they seem to balance themselves with great difficulty. This singular manœuvre is, no doubt, intended to induce a belief that they may be easily caught, and so turn the attention of the person, from the pursuit of their nests and young, to themselves. The Red-necked Avoset, whom we have introduced in the present volume, practises the very same deception, in the same ludicrous manner, and both alight indiscriminately on the ground or in the water. Both will also occasionally swim for a few feet, when they chance, in wading, to lose their depth, as I have had several times an opportunity of observing.

The name by which this bird is known on the sea-coast is the Stilt, or Tilt, or Long-Shanks. They are but sparingly dispersed over the marshes, having, as has been already observed, their particular favorite spots, while in large, intermediate tracts there are few or none to be found. They occasionally visit the shore, wading about in the water and, in the mud, in search of food, which they scoop up very dexterously with their delicately-formed bills. On being wounded while in the water, they attempt to escape by diving, at which they are by no means expert. In autumn, their flesh is tender and well tasted. They seldom raise more than one brood in the season, and depart for the south early in September. As they are well known in Jamaica, it is probable some of them may winter in that and other of the West India islands.

Mr. Pennant observes, that this bird is not a native of northern Europe; and there have been but few instances where it has been seen in Great Britain. It is common, says Latham, in Egypt, being found there in the marshes in October. It is likewise plentiful about the salt lakes, and is often seen on the shores of the Caspian Sea, as well as by the rivers which empty themselves into it, and in the southern deserts of Independent Tartary. The same author adds, on the authority of Ray, that it is known at Madras, in the East Indies.

All the figures and descriptions which I have seen of this curious bird, represent the bill as straight, and of almost an equal thickness throughout, but I have never found it so in any of the numerous specimens I have myself shot and examined. Many of these accounts, as well as figures, have been taken from dried and stuffed skins, which give but an imperfect and often erroneous idea of the true outlines of nature. The dimensions, colors, and markings, of a very beautiful specimen, newly shot, were as follows: —

Length, from the point of the bill to the end of the tail, fourteen inches, to the tips of the wings, sixteen; extent, twenty-eight inches; bill, three inches long, slightly curved upwards, tapering to a fine point, the upper mandible rounded above, the whole of a deep black color; nostrils, an oblong slit, pervious; tongue, short, pointed; forehead, spot behind the eye, lower eyelid, sides of the neck, and whole lower parts, pure white; back, rump, and tail-coverts, also white, but so concealed by the scapulars as to appear black; tail, even, or very slightly forked, and of a dingy white; the vent-feathers reach to the tip of the tail below; line before the eye, auriculars, back part of the neck, scapulars, and whole wings, deep black, richly glossed with green; legs and naked thighs, a fine pale carmine; the latter measures three, the former four inches and a half in length, exceedingly thin, and so flexible that they may be bent considerably without danger of breaking. This thinness of the leg enables the bird to wade with expedition, and without fatigue. Feet, three-toed, the outer toe connected to the middle one by a broad membrane; wings, long, extending two inches beyond the tail, and sharp pointed; irides, a bright, rich scarlet; pupil, black. In some, the white from the breast extends quite round the neck, separating the black of the hind neck from that of the body; claws, blackish horn.

The female is about half an inch shorter, and differs in having the plumage of the upper back and scapulars, and also the tertials, of a deep brown color. The stomach, or gizzard, was extremely muscular, and contained fragments of small snail shells, winged bugs, and a slimy matter, supposed to be the remains of some aquatic worms. In one of these females I counted upwards of one hundred and fifty eggs, some of them as large as buck-shot. The singular form of the legs and feet, with the exception of the hind toe and one membrane of the foot, is exactly like those of the Avoset. The upper curvature of the bill, though not quite so great, is also the same as in the other, being rounded above, and tapering to a delicate point in the same manner. In short, a slight comparison of the two is sufficient to satisfy the most scrupulous observer that Nature has classed these two birds together; and so believing, we shall not separate them.

SOLITARY SANDPIPER.—TRINGA SOLITARIA.—Fig. 230.

Peale's Museum, No. 7763.

TOTANUS CHLOROPIGIUS.—Vieillot.[*]

Totanus glareolus, *Ord's reprint,* p. 57.—Totanus chloropigius, *Vieill.*—*Bonap. Cat.* p. 26.—*Synop.* p. 325.

This new species inhabits the watery solitudes of our highest mountains during the summer, from Kentucky to New York; but is no where numerous, seldom more than one or two being seen together. It takes short, low flights; runs nimbly about among the

---

[*] In the second edition of the seventh part, under the inspection of Mr. Ord, this bird is described as new, by the name of *T. glareolus.* Ord thought it identical with the *T. glareolus* of Europe, and named it as such; his synonymes are, therefore, all wrong. The Prince of Musignano thus points out the differences: " *T. chloropigius* differs from *T. glareola,* not only as regards the characters of the tail-feathers, but also in being more minutely speckled, the white spots being smaller; by its longer tarsus; by the lineation of all the tail-feathers, but especially the lateral ones, the bands being broader, purer, and much more regular, whilst the latter tail-feathers of the European species are almost pure white on the inner webs;

42

mossy margins of the mountain springs, brooks, and pools, occasionally stopping, looking at you, and perpetually nodding the head. It is so unsuspicious, or so little acquainted with man, as to permit one to approach within a few yards of it, without appearing to take any notice, or to be the least alarmed. At the approach of cold weather, it descends to the muddy shores of our large rivers, where it is occasionally met with, singly, on its way to the south. I have made many long and close searches for the nest of this bird without success. They regularly breed on Pocano Mountain, between Easton and Wilkesbarre, in Pennsylvania, arriving there early in May, and departing in September. It is usually silent, unless when suddenly flushed, when it utters a sharp whistle.

This species has considerable resemblance, both in manners and markings, to the Green Sandpiper of Europe (*Tringa ochropus ;*) but differs from that bird in being nearly one third less, and in wanting the white rump and tail-coverts of that species ; it is also destitute of its silky, olive green plumage. How far north its migrations extend I am unable to say.

The Solitary Sandpiper is eight inches and a half long, and fifteen inches in extent ; the bill is one inch and a quarter in length, and dusky ; nostrils, pervious ; bill, fluted above and below ; line over the eye, chin, belly, and vent, pure white ; breast, white, spotted with pale olive brown ; crown and neck above, dark olive, streaked with white ; back, scapulars, and rump, dark brown olive, each feather marked along the edges with small, round spots of white ; wings, plain, and of a darker tint ; under tail-covert, spotted with black ; tail, slightly rounded, the five exterior feathers on each side, white, broadly barred with black ; the two middle ones, as well as their coverts, plain olive ; legs, long, slender, and of a dusky green. Male and female alike in color.

YELLOW-SHANKS SNIPE. — SCOLOPAX FLAVIPES. —
Fig. 231.

Arct. Zool. p. 463, No. 878. — *Turt. Syst.* 395. — *Peale's Museum*, No. 3938.

TOTANUS FLAVIPES. — Vieillot.*

Totanus flavipes, *Ord's Edit.* p. 59. — *Bonap. Cat.* p. 26.

Of this species I have but little to say. It inhabits our sea-coasts and salt marshes during summer ; frequents the flats at low water, and seems particularly fond of walking among the mud, where it doubtless finds its favorite food in abundance. Having never met with its nest,

by having the shaft of the exterior primary black, whilst that of the *glareolus* is white."

The two specimens which Mr. Ord shot, in which all the tail-feathers were barred, and which corresponded with *T. glareola*, may have been in fact that species. The Prince of Musignano is of opinion that it is also a native of North America. — Ed.

* *T. flavipes* seems exclusively American. — Ed.

nor with any person acquainted with its particular place or manner of breeding, I must reserve these matters for further observation. It is a plentiful species, and great numbers are brought to market in Boston, New York, and Philadelphia, particularly in autumn. Though these birds do not often penetrate far inland, yet, on the 5th of September, I shot several dozens of them in the meadows of Schuylkill, below Philadelphia. There had been a violent north-east storm a day or two previous, and a large flock of these, accompanied by several species of *Tringa*, and vast numbers of the Short-tailed Tern, appeared at once among the meadows. As a bird for the table, the Yellow-Shanks, when fat, is in considerable repute. Its chief residence is in the vicinity of the sea, where there are extensive mud-flats. It has a sharp whistle, of three or four notes, when about to take wing, and when flying. These birds may be shot down with great facility, if the sportsman, after the first discharge, will only lie close, and permit the wounded birds to flutter about without picking them up; the flock will generally make a circuit, and alight repeatedly, until the greater part of them may be shot down.

Length of the Yellow-Shanks, ten inches; extent, twenty; bill, slender, straight, an inch and a half in length, and black; line over the eye, chin, belly, and vent, white; breast and throat, gray; general color of the plumage above, dusky brown olive, inclining to ash, thickly marked with small triangular spots of dull white; tail-coverts, white; tail, also white, handsomely barred with dark olive; wings, plain dusky, the secondaries edged, and all the coverts edged and tipped with white; shafts, black; eye, also black; legs and naked thighs, long and yellow; outer toe, united to the middle one by a slight membrane; claws, a horn color. The female can scarcely be distinguished from the male.

TELL-TALE GODWIT, OR SNIPE. — SCOLOPAX VOCIFERUS. — Fig. 232.

Stone Snipe, *Arct. Zool.* p. 468, No. 376. — *Turt. Syst.* p. 396. — *Peale's Museum*, No. 3940.

TOTANUS MELANOLEUCUS. — Vieillot.*

T. melanoleucus, *Ord's reprint of Wils.* p. 61. — *Bonap. Synop.* p. 324.

THIS species and the preceding are both well known to our Duck gunners along the sea-coast and marshes, by whom they are detested,

* Bonaparte, in his Nomenclature, remarks, " This bird is undoubtedly the *S. melanoleuca* of Gmelin and Latham, first made known by Pennant. Why Wilson, who was aware of this, should have changed the name, we are at a loss to conceive. Mr. Ord was, therefore, right in restoring it."

The species has not been discovered out of North America, and will take the place in that country of the European Greenshank.

Totanus is a genus of Bechstein, now generally acknowledged as the proper place for the Sandpipers of this form. Many of them do not undergo so decided a change during the breeding season, breed more inland, and, during winter, are as frequently

and stigmatized with the names of the Greater and Lesser Tell-Tale, for their faithful vigilance in alarming the Ducks with their loud and shrill whistle, on the first glimpse of the gunner's approach. Of the two, the present species is by far the most watchful; and its whistle, which consists of four notes rapidly repeated, is so loud, shrill, and alarming, as instantly to arouse every Duck within its hearing, and thus disappoints the eager expectations of the marksman. Yet the cunning and experience of the latter are frequently more than a match for all of them; and, before the poor Tell-Tale is aware, his warning voice is hushed forever, and his dead body mingled with those of his associates.

This bird arrives on our coast early in April, breeds in the marshes, and continues until November, about the middle of which month it generally moves off to the south. The nest, I have been informed, is built in a tuft of thick grass, generally on the borders of a bog or morass. The female, it is said, lays four eggs, of a dingy white, irregularly marked with black.

These birds appear to be unknown in Europe. They are simply mentioned by Mr. Pennant as having been observed in autumn, feeding on the sands on the lower part of Chatteaux Bay, continually nodding their heads; and were called there Stone Curlews.*

The Tell-Tale seldom flies in large flocks, at least during summer. It delights in watery bogs, and the muddy margins of creeks and inlets; is either seen searching about for food, or standing in a watchful posture, alternately raising and lowering the head, and, on the least appearance of danger, utters its shrill whistle, and mounts on wing, generally accompanied by all the feathered tribes that are near. It occasionally penetrates inland along the muddy shores of our large rivers, seldom higher than tide water, and then singly and solitary. They sometimes rise to a great height in the air, and can be distinctly heard when beyond the reach of the eye. In the fall, when they are fat, their flesh is highly esteemed, and many of them are brought to our markets. The colors and markings of this bird are so like those of the preceding, that, unless in point of size, and the particular curvature of the bill, the description of one might serve for both.

The Tell-Tale is fourteen inches and a half long, and twenty-five inches in extent; the bill is two inches and a quarter long, of a dark horn color, and slightly bent upwards; the space round the eye, chin, and throat, pure white; lower part of the neck, pale ashy white, speckled with black; general color of the upper parts, an ashy brown, thickly spotted with black and dull white, each feather being bordered and spotted on the edge with black; wing-quills, black; some of the primaries, and all of the secondaries, with their coverts, spotted round the margins with black and white; head and neck above, streaked with black and white; belly and vent, pure white; rump, white, dotted with black; tail, also white, barred with brown; the wings, when closed, reach beyond the tail; thighs, naked nearly two inches above the knees; legs, two inches and three quarters long; feet, four-toed, the

found on the banks of rivers and lakes, or in inland marshes, as upon the shores. They are extremely noisy when first disturbed; a single individual readily gives the note of alarm, and, when their nests are approached, they display more of the habit of the *Plovers*. — Ed.

* *Arctic Zoology*, p. 468.

outer joined by a membrane to the middle, the whole of a rich orange yellow. The female differs little in plumage from the male; sometimes the vent is slightly dotted with black, and the upper parts more brown.

Nature seems to have intended this bird as a kind of spy, or sentinel, for the safety of the rest; and so well acquainted are they with the watchful vigilance of this species, that, while it continues silent among them, the Ducks feed in the bogs and marshes without the least suspicion. The great object of the gunner is to escape the penetrating glance of this guardian, which it is sometimes extremely difficult to effect. On the first whistle of the Tell-Tale, if beyond gunshot, the gunner abandons his design, but not without first bestowing a few left-handed blessings on the author of his disappointment.

----◆----

SPOTTED SANDPIPER. — TRINGA MACULARIA. — Fig. 233.

Arct. Zool. p. 473, No. 385. — La grive d'eau, *Buff.* viii. 140. — *Edw.* 277. — *Peale's Museum,* No. 4056.

TOTANUS MACULARIUS. — Temminck.*

Ord's reprint of Wils. part vii. p. 64. — *Temm. Man. d'Orn.* ii. p. 656. — *Bonap. Synop.* p. 325. — *Flem. Br. Zool.* p. 102. — Spotted Sandpiper, *Mont. Orn. Dict.* ii. and *Supp. Selby's Illust. of Br. Orn.* w. B. pl. 17.

This very common species arrives in Pennsylvania about the 20th of April, making its first appearance along the shores of our large rivers, and, as the season advances, tracing the courses of our creeks and streams towards the interior. Along the Rivers Schuylkill and Delaware, and their tributary waters, they are in great abundance during the summer. This species is as remarkable for perpetually wagging the tail, as some others are for nodding the head; for, whether running on the ground, or on the fences, along the rails, or in the water, this motion seems continual; even the young, as soon as they are freed from the shell, run about, constantly wagging the tail. About the middle of May, they resort to the adjoining corn-fields to breed, where I have frequently found and examined their nests. One of these now before me, and which was built at the root of a hill of Indian corn, on high ground, is composed wholly of short pieces of dry straw. The eggs are four, of a pale clay or cream color, marked with large, irregular spots of black, and more thinly with others of a paler tint. They are large in proportion to the size of the bird, measuring an inch and a quarter in length, very thick at the great end, and tapering suddenly

* This is one of the most beautiful and most delicately marked among the smaller *Totani;* closely allied to our Common Sand-Lark, *T. hypoleucos,* it is at once distinguished by the spotted marking on the under parts, which contrasts finely with their pure white. They frequent the banks of rivers more than the larger species, and have all a peculiar motion of the body and tail while running. The Spotted Sandpiper is common to both continents, and has been once or twice killed in Great Britain. — Ed.

to the other. The young run about with wonderful speed as soon as they leave the shell, and are then covered with down of a dull drab color, marked with a single streak of black down the middle of the back, and with another behind each ear. They have a weak, plaintive note. On the approach of any person, the parents exhibit symptoms of great distress, counterfeiting lameness, and fluttering along the ground with seeming difficulty. On the appearance of a dog, this agitation is greatly increased ; and it is very interesting to observe with what dexterity she will lead him from her young, by throwing herself repeatedly before him, fluttering off, and keeping just without his reach, on a contrary direction from her helpless brood. My venerable friend, Mr. William Bertram, informs me, that he saw one of these birds defend her young for a considerable time from the repeated attacks of a ground squirrel. The scene of action was on the river shore. The parent had thrown herself, with her two young behind her, between them and the land ; and at every attempt of the squirrel to seize them by a circuitous sweep, raised both her wings in an almost perpendicular position, assuming the most formidable appearance she was capable of, and rushed forwards on the squirrel, who, intimidated by her boldness and manner, instantly retreated ; but presently returning, was met, as before, in front and on flank by the daring and affectionate bird, who, with her wings and whole plumage bristling up, seemed swelled to twice her usual size. The young crowded together behind her, apparently sensible of their perilous situation, moving backwards and forwards as she advanced or retreated. This interesting scene lasted for at least ten minutes ; the strength of the poor parent began evidently to flag, and the attacks of the squirrel became more daring and frequent, when my good friend, like one of those celestial agents, who, in Homer's time, so often decided the palm of victory, stepped forward from his retreat, drove the assailant back to his hole, and rescued the innocent from destruction.

The flight of this bird is usually low, skimming along the surface of the water, its long wings making a considerable angle downwards from the body, while it utters a rapid cry of *weet, weet, weet,* as it flutters along, seldom steering in a direct line up or down the river, but making a long, circuitous sweep, stretching a great way out, and gradually bending in again to the shore.

These birds are found occasionally along the sea marshes, as well as in the interior; and also breed in the corn-fields there, frequenting the shore in search of food; but rarely associating with the other *Tringæ.* About the middle of October, they leave us, on their way to the south, and do not, to my knowledge, winter in any of the Atlantic States.

Mr. Pennant is of opinion, that this same species is found in Britain; but neither his description, nor that of Mr. Bewick, will apply correctly to this. The following particulars, with Fig. 233, will enable Europeans to determine this matter to their satisfaction : —

Length of the Spotted Sandpiper, seven inches and a half; extent, thirteen inches ; bill, an inch long, straight, the tip and upper mandible, dusky, lower, orange ; stripe over the eye, and lower eyelid, pure white ; whole upper parts, a glossy olive, with greenish reflections, each feather marked with waving spots of dark brown ; wing-quills,

deep dusky; bastard wing, bordered and tipped with white; a spot of
white on the middle of the inner vane of each quill-feather except the
first; secondaries, tipped with white; tail, rounded, the six middle
feathers, greenish olive, the other three on each side white, barred
with black; whole lower parts, white, beautifully marked with roundish spots of black, small and thick on the throat and breast, larger and
thinner as they descend to the tail; legs, a yellow clay color; claws,
black.

The female is as thickly spotted below as the male; but the young
birds of both sexes are pure white below, without any spots; they also
want the orange on the bill. Those circumstances I have verified on
numerous individuals.

BARTRAM'S SANDPIPER. — TRINGA BARTRAMIA. — Fig. 234.

Peale's Museum, No. 4040.

TOTANUS BARTRAMIUS. — Temminck.*

Totanus Bartramius, *Ord's reprint of Wils.* vol. vii. p. 67. — Chevalier à longue
queue, *Temm. Man. d'Orn.* ii. p. 650. — Totanus Bartramius, *Bonap. Synop.*
p. 325.

This bird being, as far as I can discover, a new species, undescribed
by any former author, I have honored it with the name of my very worthy
friend, near whose botanic gardens, on the banks of the River Schuylkill, I first found it. On the same meadows, I have since shot several
other individuals of the species, and have thereby had an opportunity
of taking an accurate drawing as well as description of it.

Unlike most of their tribe, these birds appear to prefer running
about among the grass, feeding on beetles and other winged insects.
There were three or four in company; they seemed extremely watchful, silent, and shy, so that it was always with extreme difficulty I
could approach them.

These birds are occasionally seen there during the months of August and September, but whether they breed near I have not been
able to discover. Having never met with them on the sea-shore, I am
persuaded that their principal residence is in the interior, in meadows
and such like places. They run with great rapidity, sometimes spreading their tail and dropping their wings, as birds do who wish to decoy
you from their nest; when they alight, they remain fixed, stand very
erect, and have two or three sharp, whistling notes, as they mount to fly.

---

* The discovery of this species, I believe, is due to our author, who dedicated it
to his venerable friend Bartram. It is admitted by Temminck as an occasional
straggler upon the Dutch and German coasts, and is mentioned as having been only
once met with by himself. Bonaparte asserts, on the authority of Say, that it is
very common in some districts of the extensive Missouri prairies; thus confirming
the opinion of Wilson, that its residence is in the interior, and not on the sea-coast,
like most of its congeners. The lengthened form, more conspicuous in the wedge
shape of the tail, is at variance with the greater part of the *Totani*, and reminds us
of the Kildeer Plover. — Ed.

They are remarkably plump birds, weighing upwards of three quarters of a pound; their flesh is superior, in point of delicacy, tenderness, and flavor, to any other of the tribe with which I am acquainted.

This species is twelve inches long, and twenty-one in extent; the bill is an inch and a half long, slightly bent downwards, and wrinkled at the base, the upper mandible, black on its ridge, the lower, as well as the edge of the upper, of a fine yellow; front, stripe over the eye, neck and breast, pale ferruginous, marked with small streaks of black, which, on the lower part of the breast, assume the form of arrow-heads; crown, black, the plumage slightly skirted with whitish; chin, orbit of the eye, whole belly and vent, pure white; hind head and neck above, ferruginous, minutely streaked with black; back and scapulars, black, the former slightly skirted with ferruginous, the latter with white; tertials, black, bordered with white; primaries, plain black; shaft of the exterior quill, snowy, its inner vane elegantly pectinated with white; secondaries, pale brown, spotted on their outer vanes with black, and tipped with white; greater coverts, dusky, edged with pale ferruginous, and spotted with black; lesser coverts, pale ferruginous, each feather broadly bordered with white, within which is a concentric semicircle of black; rump and tail-coverts, deep brown black, slightly bordered with white; tail, tapering of a pale brown orange color, beautifully spotted with black, the middle feathers centred with dusky; legs, yellow, tinged with green, the outer toe joined to the middle by a membrane; lining of the wings, elegantly barred with black and white; iris of the eye, dark or blue black, eye, very large. The male and female are nearly alike.

RING PLOVER. — TRINGA HIATICULA. — Fig. 235.

Arct. Zool. ii. p. 485, No. 401. — Le petit pluvier à collier, *Buff.* viii. 90. — *Bewick*, i. 326. — *Peale's Museum*, No. 4150.

CHARADRIUS SEMIPALMATUS. — Bonaparte.*

Charadrius semipalmatus, *Bonap. Synop.* p. 296. — American Ring Plover, *North. Zool.* ii. p. 367. — Charadrius semipalmatus ? *Wagl. Syst. Av.* No. 23.

In a preceding part of this work, (Fig. 160,) a bird by this name has been figured and described, under the supposition that it was the Ring

* The smaller *Charadriadæ* of America have been much confused, owing to their close alliance to each other, and to those of Europe, with some of which they were thought to be identical. The Prince of Musignano has clearly pointed out the differences which exist between this and the species figured in No. 160, and which bears a more close resemblance to the little African *C. pecuarius* than either the present species or the *hiaticula* of Europe, (see also our note on that species;) and, although he has not been able to point out such distinctive characters between the latter species and that now under discussion, I have no doubt whatever of their being eventually found quite distinct; and it will be found, by those persons who are inclined to allow so much for the influence of climate in rendering form, color, and plumage distinct, that it is comparatively of no importance, and

Plover, then in its summer dress; but which, notwithstanding its great resemblance to the present, I now suspect to be a different species. Fearful of perpetuating error, and anxious to retract, where this may inadvertently have been the case, I shall submit to the consideration of the reader the reasons on which my present suspicions are founded.

The present species, or true Ring Plover, and also the former, or light colored bird, both arrive on the sea-coast of New Jersey late in April. The present kind continues to be seen in flocks until late in May, when they disappear on their way farther north; the light colored bird remains during the summer, forms its nest in the sand, and generally produces two broods in the season. Early in September the present species returns in flocks as before; soon after this, the light colored kind go off to the south, but the other remain a full month later. European writers inform us, that the Ring Plover has a sharp, twittering note; and this account agrees exactly with that of the present: the light colored species, on the contrary, has a peculiarly soft and musical note, similar to the tone of a German flute, which it utters while running along the sand, with expanded tail and hanging wings, endeavoring to decoy you from its nest. The present species is never seen to breed here; and, though I have opened great numbers of them as late as the 20th of May, the eggs which the females contained were never larger than small bird-shot; while, at the same time, the light colored kind had every where begun to lay in the little cavities which they had dug in the sand on the beach. These facts being considered, it seems difficult to reconcile such difference of habit in one and the same bird. The Ring Plover is common in England, and agrees exactly with the one now before us; but the light colored species, as far as I can learn, is not found in Britain; specimens of it have indeed been taken to that country, where the most judicious of their ornithologists have concluded it to be still the Ring Plover, but to have changed

that identical species, running through a great variety of latitude, will in fact differ little or nothing from each other. I have transcribed the observations of Bonaparte from his Nomenclature of Wilson, which will show his opinion.

He thus observes, — "The remark made by Mr. Ord, relative to the difference between the union of the toes in American and European specimens, is no less extraordinary than correct; I have verified it on the specimens in my collection. This character would seem to show, in the most positive manner, that they are distinct but allied species, differing from each other as *Tringa semipalmata* of Wilson differs from his *Tringa pusilla.*"

The synonymes of Mr. Ord, who noticed one of the principal distinctions in the palmation of the feet, are consequently wrong, and they should stand as above. I have added a synonyme of Wagler, *C. semipalmatus*, which he takes, without any acknowledgment, from Cont. Isis, 1825, and which seems to be this species. He also refers to the *C. hiaticula* of Wilson, (No. 160 of this edition,) under the name of *C. Okenii.* The true *C. hiaticula* has not yet, I believe, been found in North America.

"I have been endeavoring," again writes Bonaparte, "to discover some other markings on my stuffed specimens, that might enable me to establish the species on a more solid basis; but though certain small differences are discernible, such as the somewhat smaller size, and the black, narrow collar of the American, &c., yet we are aware that such trifling differences occur between individuals of the same species; we shall, therefore, not rely on them until our observations shall have been repeated on numerous recent or living specimens. In the mean time, should the species prove to be distinct, it may be distinguished by the appropriate name of *C. semipalmatus.*" —ED.

from the effect of climate. Mr. Pennant, in speaking of the true Ring Plover, makes the following remarks: " Almost all which I have seen from the northern parts of North America, have had the black marks extremely faint, and almost lost. The climate had almost destroyed the specific marks; yet in the bill and habit preserved sufficient to make the kind very easily ascertained." These traits agree exactly with the light colored species, described in our fifth volume.* But this excellent naturalist was perhaps not aware that we have the true Ring Plover here in spring and autumn, agreeing in every respect with that of Britain, and at least in equal numbers; why, therefore, has not the climate equally affected the present and the former sort, if both are the same species? These inconsistencies cannot be reconciled but by supposing each to be a distinct species, which, though approaching extremely near to each other in external appearance, have each their peculiar notes, color and places of breeding.†

The Ring Plover is seven inches long, and fourteen inches in extent; bill, short, orange colored, tipped with black; front and chin, white, encircling the neck; upper part of the breast, black; rest of the lower parts, pure white; fore part of the crown, black; band from the upper mandible covering the auriculars, also black; back, scapulars, and wing-coverts, of a brownish ash color; wing-quills, dusky black, marked with an oval spot of white about the middle of each; tail, olive, deepening into black, and tipped with white; legs, dull yellow; eye, dark hazel; eyelids yellow.

This bird is said to make no nest, but to lay four eggs of a pale ash color, spotted with black, which she deposits on the ground.‡ The eggs of the light colored species, formerly described, are of a pale cream color, marked with small, round dots of black, as if done with a pen.

The Ring Plover, according to Pennant, inhabits America down to Jamaica and the Brazils; is found in summer in Greenland; migrates from thence in autumn; is common in every part of Russia and Siberia; was found by the navigators as low as Owyhee, one of the Sandwich Islands, and as light colored as those of the highest latitudes.§

* Page 345 of this edition.

† It is mentioned as abundant in all " arctic America," by the authors of the *Northern Zoology,* " where it breeds in similar situations to the Golden Plover. Mr. Hutchins reports, that the eggs, generally four, are dark colored, spotted with black. The natives say, that, on the approach of stormy weather, this Plover makes a cheruping noise, and claps its wings." — ED.

‡ BEWICK. § *Arct. Zool.* p. 485.

SANDERLING PLOVER. — CHARADRIUS CALIDRIS. —
Fig. 236.

Linn. Syst. 255. — *Arct. Zool.* p. 486, No. 403. — Le Sanderling, *Buff.* vii. 532. — *Bewick*, ii. 19. — *Peale's Museum*, No. 4204.

CALIDRIS ARENARIA. — Illiger.*

Charadrius calidris, *Wils.* 1st edit. vii. p. 68; and Ch. rubidus, *Wils.* 1st edit. vii. p. 129. — Calidris, *Illig. Prod. Mam. et Av.* p. 249. — Ruddy Plover, *Penn. Arct. Zool.* ii. p. 486; summer plumage. — Sanderling variable, (Calidris arenaria,) *Temm. Man. d'Orn.* ii. 524. — Tringa (Calidris) arenaria, *Bonap. Synop.* — Calidris arenaria, *Flem. Br. Zool.* p. 112. — *North. Zool.* ii. p. 366.

In this well-known bird, we have another proof of the imperfection of systematic arrangement, where no attention is paid to the general habits, but where one single circumstance is sometimes considered sufficient to determine the species. The genus Plover is characterized by several strong family traits, one of which is that of wanting the hind toe. The Sandpipers have also their peculiar external characters of bill, general form, &c., by which they are easily distinguished from the former. The present species, (Fig. 236,) though possessing the bill, general figure, manners, and voice of the Sandpipers, feeding in the same way, and associating with these in particular, yet wanting the hind toe, has been classed with the Plovers, with whom, this single circumstance excepted, it has no one characteristic in common. Though we have not, in the present instance, presumed to alter this arrangement, yet it appears both reasonable and natural that, where the specific characters in any bird seem to waver between two species, the figure, voice, and habits of the equivocal one should always be taken into consideration, and be allowed finally to determine the class to which it belongs. Had this rule been followed in the present instance, the bird we are now about to describe would have undoubtedly been classed with the Sandpipers.

The history of this species has little in it to excite our interest or attention. It makes its appearance on our sea-coasts early in September, continues during the greater part of winter, and, on the approach of spring, returns to the northern regions to breed. While here, it seems perpetually busy, running along the wave-worn strand, following the flux and reflux of the surf, eagerly picking up its food from

* *Calidris* was established for this single species, common over the world, and of form intermediate between the Plovers and Sandpipers. Their make is thicker; they are less slender than the Sandpipers; the bill stronger, but, as in that group, the feet similar to those of the *Charadrii;* and with their manner of running and walking, they possess that peculiar crouch of the head upon the back seen in the Common Ring Plover and its allies. In its summer plumage, it more resembles the changes exhibited in the Knot and Pygmy Curlew than those of the Dunlins. On the shores of Britain, it is generally met with in winter in small flocks, or in spring and autumn, when going to or returning from their breeding quarters.

By Mr. Hutchins it is said to make its nest rudely of grass in the marshes, and lays four dusky colored eggs, spotted with black. — Ed.

the sand amid the roar of the ocean. It flies in numerous flocks, keeping a low, meandering course along the ridges of the tumbling surf. On alighting, the whole scatter about after the receding wave, busily picking up those minute bivalves already described. As the succeeding wave returns, it bears the whole of them before it in one crowded line; then is the moment seized by the experienced gunner to sweep them in flank with his destructive shot. The flying survivors, after a few aërial meanders, again alight, and pursue their usual avocation as busily and unconcernedly as before. These birds are most numerous on extensive sandy beaches in front of the ocean. Among rocks, marshes, or stones covered with sea-weed, they seldom make their appearance.

The Sanderling is eight inches long, and fourteen inches in extent; the bill is black, an inch and a quarter in length, slender, straight, fluted along the upper mandible, and exactly formed like that of the Sandpiper; the head, neck above, back, scapulars, and tertials, are gray white; the shafts, blackish, and the webs, tinged with brownish ash; shoulder of the wing, black; greater coverts, broadly tipped with wh.te; quills, black, crossed with a transverse band of white; the tail extends a little beyond the wings, and is of a grayish ash color, edged with white, the two middle feathers being about half an inch longer than the others; eye, dark hazel; whole lower parts of the plumage, pure white; legs and naked part of the thighs, black; feet, three-toed, each divided to its origin, and bordered with a narrow membrane.

Such are the most common markings of this bird, both of males and females, particularly during the winter; but many others occur among them, early in the autumn, thickly marked or spotted with black on the crown, back, scapulars, and tertials, so as to appear much mottled, having as much black as white on those parts. In many of these, I have observed the plain gray plumage coming out about the middle of October; so that, perhaps, the gray may be their winter, and the spotted their summer dress.

I have also met with many specimens of this bird, not only thickly speckled with white, and black above, but also on the neck, and strongly tinged on both with ferruginous; in which dress it has been mistaken by Mr. Pennant, and others, for a new species; the description of his "Ruddy Plover" agreeing exactly with this.* A figure of the Sanderling in this state of plumage will be introduced in some part of the present work.

* See *Arct. Zool.* p. 486, No. 404.

GOLDEN PLOVER. — CHARADRIUS PLUVIALIS. — Fig. 237.

Arct. Zool. p. 493, No. 399. — *Bewick*, i. 322. — Le pluvier doré, *Buff.* viii. 81.
Pl. enl. 904. — *Peale's Museum*, No. 4198.

CHARADRIUS VIRGINIANUS. — Bonaparte.*

Charadrius pluvialis, *Bonap. Synop.* p. 297. — *North. Zool.* ii. p. 369. — Charadrius Virginianus, *Bonap. Osser. Sulla*, 2d edit. *del Regn. Anim. Cuv.* p. 93. — Charadrius marmoratus, *Wagl. Syst. Av. Char.* No. 42.

THIS beautiful species visits the sea-coast of New York and New Jersey in spring and autumn; but does not, as far as I can discover, breed in any part of the United States. They are most frequently met

---

* The Prince of Musignano, after the publication of his Synopsis of North American Birds, and Observations on Wilson's Nomenclature, pointed out the distinction of the North American and European birds. The plate of Wilson also shows every character of the northern birds. The lengthened bill and legs, the more distinct dorsal spotting, and clearer color of the forehead, the dusky hue of the under parts, and the mention by Ord of the brown axillaries, all point out this bird, which can never be mistaken. The following are the principal distinctions which appear between skins of *C. Virginianus* from India and New Holland, and specimens of *C. pluvialis*, shot this forenoon : —

C. Pluvialis.	C. Virginianus.
1. Total length, 10½ inches.	1. The skins are about 10 inches in length, but are much stretched; 9½, or 8, as mentioned by Wagler, nearly the true length.
2. Length of bill to extremity of gape, 1 inch.	2. Length of bill to extremity of gape, 1½ inch.
3. Length of wing, from joining of bastard pinion to fore arm, and tip of first or longest quill, 8 inches.	3. Length of wing, from joining of bastard pinion to fore arm, and tip of first or longest quill, 6½ inches.
4. Length of unfeathered tibia, ⅜ inch.	4. Length of unfeathered tibia, ¾ inch.
5. Length of tarsus, 1⅝ inch.	5. Length of tarsus, nearly 1⅞ inch.
6. Throat, lower part of the breast, belly, vent, and crissum, pure white.	6. Throat, and all under parts, dull yellowish gray, with darker tips to the feathers.
7. Pale markings on the upper parts, dull gamboge yellow ; spotting, more in oblong spots ; and, on the wing and tail-coverts, take the form of bars.	7. Pale markings on the upper parts, larger, and inclining more to clear white ; above, more in spots on the sides of the feathers.
8. Light markings on the tail, dull and undecided, with a decided dark barring.	8. Light markings on the tail, decided, nearly white ; no dark bar through it.
9. Outer tail-feathers, with pale margins, the distinct and frequent barring through the whole length.	9. Outer tail-feathers, with white tip and outer margin, which shoot down the rachis.
10. Under wing-coverts, and axillaries, pure white.	10. Under wing-coverts, and axillaries, wood brown gray.
11. Lesser wing-coverts, tipped with white, but otherwise of a uniform color.	11. Lesser wing-coverts, tipped and rather broadly edged with white.

C. pluvialis is introduced into the *Northern Zoology*, but I strongly suspect these excellent ornithologists have overlooked the other species. Both may be natives

with in the months of September and October; soon after which they disappear. The young birds of the Great Black-bellied Plover are sometimes mistaken for this species. Hence the reason why Mr. Pennant remarks his having seen a variety of the Golden Plover, with black breasts, which he supposed to be the young.*

The Golden Plover is common in the northern parts of Europe. It breeds on high and heathy mountains. The female lays four eggs, of a pale olive color, variegated with blackish spots. They usually fly in small flocks, and have a shrill, whistling note. They are very frequent in Siberia, where they likewise breed; extend also to Kamtschatka, and as far south as the Sandwich Isles. In this latter place, Mr. Pennant remarks, " they are very small."

Although these birds are occasionally found along our sea-coast, from Georgia to Maine, yet they are no where numerous; and I have never met with them in the interior. Our mountains being generally covered with forest, and no species of heath having, as yet, been discovered within the boundaries of the United States, these birds are probably induced to seek the more remote arctic regions of the continent, to breed and rear their young in, where the country is more open, and unencumbered with woods.

The Golden Plover is ten inches and a half long, and twenty-one inches in extent; bill, short, of a dusky slate color; eye, very large, blue black; nostrils, placed in a deep furrow, and half covered with a prominent membrane; whole upper parts, black, thickly marked with roundish spots of various tints of golden yellow; wing-coverts, and hind part of the neck, pale brown, the latter streaked with yellowish; front, broad line over the eye, chin, and sides, of the same, yellowish white, streaked with small, pointed spots of brown olive; breast, gray, with olive and white; sides, under the wings, marked thinly with transverse bars of pale olive; belly and vent, white; wing-quills, black, the middle of the shafts marked with white; greater coverts, black, tipped with white; tail, rounded, black, barred with triangular spots of golden yellow; legs, dark dusky slate; feet, three-toed, with generally the slight rudiments of a heel, the outer toe connected, as far as the first joint, with the middle one. The male and female differ very little in color.

---

of North America; I have never, however, seen or received extra European specimens of the Golden Plover. I possess *C. Virginianus* from India, Arctic America, and New Holland, which seems, in all those countries, very and exclusively abundant, and has always been confounded with its ally.

In plate 85 of *Ornithological Illustrations*, this bird has, most unaccountably, been described under the title of *C. xanthochielus*, Wagler. It is undoubtedly this species, and figured from New Holland specimens. — Ed.

Arctic Zoology, p. 484.

KILDEER PLOVER. — CHARADRIUS VOCIFERUS. — Fig. 238.

Arct. Zool. No. 400. — *Catesby*, i. 71. — Le Kildir, *Buff.* viii. 96. — *Peale's Museum*, No. 4174.

CHARADRIUS VOCIFERUS. — Linnæus.*

Charadrius vociferus, *Bonap. Synop. North. Zool.* ii. p. 368.

This restless and noisy bird is known to almost every inhabitant of the United States, being a common and pretty constant resident. During the severity of winter, when snow covers the ground, it retreats to the sea-shore, where it is found at all seasons; but no sooner have the rivers broke up, than its shrill note is again heard, either roaming about high in air, tracing the shore of the river, or running amidst the watery flats and meadows. As spring advances, it resorts to the newly-ploughed fields, or level plains bare of grass, interspersed with shallow pools; or, in the vicinity of the sea, dry, bare, sandy fields. In some such situation it generally chooses to breed, about the beginning of May. The nest is usually slight, a mere hollow, with such materials drawn in around it as happen to be near, such as bits of sticks, straw, pebbles, or earth. In one instance, I found the nest of this bird paved with fragments of clam and oyster shells, and very neatly surrounded with a mound, or border of the same, placed in a very close and curious manner. In some cases there is no vestige whatever of a nest. The eggs are usually four, of a bright rich cream or yellowish clay color, thickly marked with blotches of black. They are large for the size of the bird, measuring more than an inch and a half in length, and a full inch in width, tapering to a narrow point at the great end.

Nothing can exceed the alarm and anxiety of these birds, during the breeding season. Their cries of *kildeer, kildeer,* as they winnow the air overhead, dive, and course around you, or run along the ground counterfeiting lameness, are shrill and incessant. The moment they see a person approach, they fly or run to attack him with their harassing clamor, continuing it over so wide an extent of ground, that they puzzle the pursuer as to the particular spot where the nest or young are concealed; very much resembling, in this respect, the Lapwing of Europe. During the evening, and long after dusk, particularly in moonlight, their cries are frequently heard with equal violence, both in the spring and fall. From this circumstance, and their flying about both after dusk and before dawn, it appears probable that they see better at such times than most of their tribe. They are known to feed much on worms, and many of these rise to the surface during the night. The prowling of Owls may also alarm their fears for their young at those hours; but, whatever may be the cause, the facts are so.

* An abundant and well-known species, and peculiar to both continents of America, with some of the West Indian islands. According to the *Northern Zoology,* it arrives on the plains of the Saskatchewan about the 20th of April, and, at that season, frequents the gardens and cultivated fields of the trading post with the utmost familiarity. — Ed.

The Kildeer is more abundant in the Southern States in winter than in summer. Among the rice-fields, and even around the planters' yards, in South Carolina, I observed them very numerous in the months of February and March. There the negro boys frequently practise the barbarous mode of catching them with a line, at the extremity of which is a crooked pin, with a worm on it. Their flight is something like that of the Tern, but more vigorous; and they sometimes rise to a great height in the air. They are fond of wading in pools of water, and frequently bathe themselves during the summer. They usually stand erect on their legs, and run or walk with the body in a stiff, horizontal position; they run with great swiftness, and are also strong and vigorous in the wings. Their flesh is eaten by some, but is not in general esteem; though others say, that, in the fall, when they become very fat, it is excellent.

During the extreme droughts of summer, these birds resort to the gravelly channel of brooks and shallow streams, where they can wade about in search of aquatic insects: at the close of summer, they generally descend to the sea-shore, in small flocks, seldom more than ten or twelve being seen together. They are then more serene and silent, as well as difficult to be approached.

The Kildeer is ten inches long, and twenty inches in extent; the bill is black; frontlet, chin, and ring round the neck, white; fore part of the crown and auriculars, from the bill backwards, blackish olive; eyelids, bright scarlet; eye, very large and of a full black; from the centre of the eye backwards, a strip of white; round the lower part of the neck is a broad band of black; below that, a band of white, succeeded by another rounding band or crescent of black; rest of the lower parts, pure white; crown and hind head, light olive brown; back, scapulars, and wing-coverts, olive brown, skirted with brownish yellow; primary quills, black, streaked across the middle with white; bastard wing, tipped with white; greater coverts, broadly tipped with white; rump and tail-coverts, orange; tail, tapering, dull orange, crossed near the end with a broad bar of black, and tipped with orange, the two middle feathers near an inch longer than the adjoining ones; legs and feet, a pale light clay color. The tertials, as usual in this tribe, are very long, reaching nearly to the tips of the primaries; exterior toe, joined by a membrane to the middle one, as far as the first joint.

GREAT TERN. — STERNA HIRUNDO. — Fɪɢ. 239.

Arct. Zool. p. 524, No. 448. — Le Pierre garin, ou grande Hirondelle de mer, *Buff* viii. 331, *Pl. enl.* 987. — *Bewick*, ii. 181. — *Peale's Museum*, No. 3485.

STERNA WILSONII. — Bonaparte.*

Sterna hirundo, *Bonap. Synop.* p. 354. — St. Wilsonii, *Bonap. Osserv. Sulla,* 2d edit. *Del Regn. Anim. Cuv.* p. 135.

Tʜɪs bird belongs to a tribe very generally dispersed over the shores of the ocean. Their generic characters are these: — Bill, straight, sharp-pointed, a little compressed, and strong; nostrils, linear; tongue, slender, pointed; legs, short; feet, webbed; hind toe and its nail, straight; wings, long; tail, generally forked. Turton enumerates twenty-five species of this genus, scattered over various quarters of the world; six of which, at least, are natives of the United States. From their long, pointed wings, they are generally known to seafaring people, and others residing near the sea-shore, by the name of *Sea Swallows;* though some few, from their near resemblance, are confounded with the Gulls.

The present species, or Great Tern, (Fig. 239,) is common to the shores of Europe, Asia, and America. It arrives on the coast of New Jersey about the middle or 20th of April, led, no doubt, by the multitudes of fish which at that season visit our shallow bays and inlets. By many it is called the Sheep's Head Gull, from arriving about the same time with the fish of that name.

About the middle or 20th of May, this bird commences laying. The preparation of a nest, which costs most other birds so much time and ingenuity, is here altogether dispensed with. The eggs, generally three in number, are placed on the surface of the dry drift grass, on the beach or salt marsh, and covered by the female only during the night, or in wet, raw, or stormy weather. At all other times, the hatching of them is left to the heat of the sun. These eggs measure an inch and three quarters in length, by about an inch and two tenths in width, and are of a yellowish dun color, sprinkled with dark brown and pale Indian ink. Notwithstanding they seem thus negligently abandoned during the day, it is very different in reality. One or both of the parents are generally fishing within view of the place, and, on the near approach of any person, instantly make their appearance overhead; uttering a hoarse, jarring kind of cry, and flying about with evident symptoms of great anxiety and consternation. The young are generally produced at intervals of a day or so from each other, and are regularly and abundantly fed for several weeks, before their wings are sufficiently grown to enable them to fly. At first the parents alight

* Mr. Ord, in his reprint, and C. L. Bonaparte, when writing his Synopsis and Observations on the Nomenclature of Wilson, considered this bird as identical with the *St. hirundo* of Europe. Later comparisons by the Prince have induced him to consider it distinct, and peculiar to America, and he has dedicated it to Wilson. That gentleman mentions, as North American, in addition to the list by Wilson, *St. cyanea*, Lath.; *St. arctica*, Temm.; *St. stolida*, Linn. — Eᴅ.

with the fish, which they have brought in their mouth or in their bill, and, tearing it in pieces, distribute it in such portions as their young are able to swallow. Afterwards they frequently feed them without alighting, as they skim over the spot; and, as the young become nearly ready to fly, they drop the fish among them, where the strongest and most active has the best chance to gobble it up. In the mean time, the young themselves frequently search about the marshes, generally not far apart, for insects of various kinds; but so well acquainted are they with the peculiar language of their parents, that warn them of the approach of an enemy, that, on hearing their cries, they instantly squat, and remain motionless until the danger be over.

The flight of the Great Tern, and, indeed, of the whole tribe, is not in the sweeping, shooting manner of the land Swallows, notwithstanding their name; the motions of their long wings are slower, and more in the manner of the Gull. They have, however, great powers of wing, and strength in the muscles of the neck, which enable them to make such sudden and violent plunges, and that from a considerable height too, headlong on their prey, which they never seize but with their bills. In the evening, I have remarked, as they retired from the upper parts of the bays, rivers, and inlets, to the beach for repose, about breeding time, that each generally carried a small fish in his bill.

As soon as the young are able to fly, they lead them to the sandy shoals and ripples where fish are abundant; and, while they occasionally feed them, teach them by their example to provide for themselves. They sometimes penetrate a great way inland, along the courses of rivers; and are occasionally seen about all our numerous ponds, lakes, and rivers, most usually near the close of the summer.

This species inhabits Europe as high as Spitzbergen; is found on the arctic coasts of Siberia and Kamtschatka, and also on our own continent as far north as Hudson's Bay. In New England it is called by some the Mackerel Gull. It retires from all these places, at the approach of winter, to more congenial seas and seasons.

The Great Tern is fifteen inches long, and thirty inches in extent; bill, reddish yellow, sometimes brilliant crimson, slightly angular on the lower mandible, and tipped with black; whole upper part of the head, black, extending to a point half way down the neck behind, and including the eyes; sides of the neck, and whole lower parts, pure white; wing-quills, hoary, as if bleached by the weather, long and pointed; whole back, scapulars, and wing, bluish white, or very pale lead color; rump and tail-coverts, white; tail, long, and greatly forked, the exterior feathers being three inches longer than the adjoining ones, the rest shortening gradually for an inch and a half to the middle ones, the whole of a pale lead color; the outer edge of the exterior ones, black; legs and webbed feet, brilliant red lead; membranes of the feet. deeply scalloped; claws, large and black, middle one the largest. The primary quill-feathers are generally dark on their inner edges. The female differs in having the two exterior feathers of the tail considerably shorter. The voice of these birds is like the harsh jarring of an opening door, rusted on its hinges. The bone of the skull is remarkably thick and strong, as also the membrane that surrounds the brain; in this respect resembling the Woodpecker's. In both, this provision

is doubtless intended to enable the birds to support, without injury,
the violent concussions caused by the plunging of the one, and the
chiselling of the other

LESSER TERN.—STERNA MINUTA.—Fig. 240.

Arct. Zool. No. 449.—La petite Hirondelle de mer, *Buff.* viii. 337. *Pl. enl.* 996.—
Bewick, ii. 183.—*Peale's Museum,* No. 3505.

STERNA MINUTA.—Linnæus.*

Sterna minuta, *Bonap. Synop.*—*Flem. Br. Zool.* p. 144.—*Temm. Man. d'Orn.*
ii. p. 75.

THIS beautiful little species (Fig. 240) looks like the preceding in
miniature, but surpasses it far in the rich, glossy, satin-like, white plumage with which its throat, breast, and whole lower parts are covered.
Like the former, it is also a bird of passage, but is said not to extend
its migrations to so high a northern latitude, being more delicate and
susceptible of cold. It arrives on the coast somewhat later than the
other, but in equal and perhaps greater numbers; coasts along the
shores, and also over the pools in the salt marshes, in search of prawns,
of which it is particularly fond; hovers, suspended in the air, for a
few moments above its prey, exactly in the manner of some of our
small Hawks, and dashes headlong down into the water after it, generally seizing it with its bill; mounts instantly again to the same
height, and moves slowly along as before, eagerly examining the surface below. About the 25th of May, or beginning of June, the female begins to lay. The eggs are dropped on the dry and warm sand,
the heat of which, during the day, is fully sufficient for the purpose of
incubation. This heat is sometimes so great, that one can scarcely
bear the hand in it for a few moments without inconvenience. The
wonder would, therefore, be the greater should the bird sit on her
eggs during the day, when her warmth is altogether unnecessary, and
perhaps injurious, than that she should cover them only during the
damps of night, and in wet and stormy weather; and furnishes another
proof that the actions of birds are not the effect of mere blind impulse, but of volition, regulated by reason, depending on various inci-
dental circumstances to which their parental cares are ever awake. I

* This species is common to Europe and the northern continent of America.
Bonaparte mentions another closely allied species, which appears to take its place
in South America, and has been confounded with it.

The breeding places of this Tern are somewhat different from many of those
British species with which we are acquainted. Most of the latter breed on rocky
coasts and solitary islands, while the Little Tern prefers flat, shingly beaches,
where the eggs are deposited in the manner described by Wilson,—in some little
hollow or footstep. They become clamorous on approaching the nest, but seem
hardly so familiar or bold as most of the others. The young soon leave the hollow
where they were hatched, and move about as far as their limited powers will allow.—ED.

lately visited those parts of the beach on Cape May, where this little
bird breeds. The eggs, generally four in number, were placed on the
flat sands, safe beyond the reach of the highest summer tide. They
were of a yellowish brown color, blotched with rufous, and measured
nearly an inch and three quarters in length. During my whole stay,
these birds flew in crowds around me, and often within a few yards of
my head, squeaking like so many young pigs, which their voice striking
resembles. A Humming Bird, that had accidentally strayed to the
place, appeared suddenly among this outrageous group, several of
whom darted angrily at him; but he shot like an arrow from them, directing his flight straight towards the ocean. I have no doubt but the
distressing cries of the Terns had drawn this little creature to the
scene, having frequently witnessed his anxious curiosity on similar occasions in the woods.

The Lesser Tern feeds on beetles, crickets, spiders, and other insects, which it picks up from the marshes, as well as on small fish, on
which it plunges at sea. Like the former, it also makes extensive in-
cursions inland along the river courses, and has frequently been shot
several hundred miles from the sea. It sometimes sits for hours together on the sands, as if resting after the fatigues of flight to which
it is exposed.

The Lesser Tern is extremely tame and unsuspicious, often passing
you on its flight, and within a few yards, as it traces the windings
and indentations of the shore in search of its favorite prawns and
skippers. Indeed, at such times it appears altogether heedless of
man, or its eagerness for food overcomes its apprehensions for its own
safety. We read in ancient authors, that the fishermen used to float
a cross of wood, in the middle of which was fastened a small fish for
a bait, with limed twigs stuck to the four corners, on which the bird
darting, was entangled by the wings. But this must have been for
mere sport, or for its feathers, the value of the bird being scarcely
worth the trouble, as they are generally lean, and the flesh savoring
strongly of fish.

The Lesser Tern is met with in the south of Russia, and about the
Black and Caspian Sea; also in Siberia about the Irtish.* With
the former, it inhabits the shores of England during the summer,
where it breeds, and migrates, as it does here, to the south, as the cold
of autumn approaches.

This species is nine and a half inches long, and twenty inches in
extent; bill, bright reddish yellow; nostril, pervious; lower mandible,
angular; front, white, reaching in two narrow points over the eye;
crown, band through the eye, and hind head, black, tapering to a
point as it descends; cheeks, sides of the neck, and whole lower
parts, of the most rich and glossy white, like the brightest satin; upper parts of the back and wings, a pale glossy ash, or light lead color;
the outer edges of the three exterior primaries, black, their inner
edges white; tail, pale ash, but darker than the back, and forked, the
two outer feathers an inch longer, tapering to a point; legs and feet,
reddish yellow; webbed feet, claws, and hind toe exactly formed like
those of the preceding. The female nearly resembles the male, with
the exception of having the two exterior tail-feathers shorter.

* PENNANT.

SHORT-TAILED TERN. — STERNA PLUMBEA. — Fig. 241.

Peale's Museum, No. 3519.

STERNA NIGRA. — Linnæus.*

Sterna plumbea, *Bonap. Nomencl.* No. 244. — Sterna nigra, *Bonap. Synop.* p. 355.

A SPECIMEN of this bird was first sent me by Mr. Beasley of Cape May; but being in an imperfect state, I could form no correct notion of the species, sometimes supposing it might be a young bird of the preceding Tern. Since that time, however, I have had an opportunity of procuring a considerable number of this same kind, corresponding almost exactly with each other. I have ventured to introduce it in this place as a new species; and have taken pains to render Fig. 241 a correct likeness of the original.

On the 6th of September, 1812, after a violent north-east storm, which inundated the meadows of Schuylkill in many places, numerous flocks of this Tern all at once made their appearance, flying over those watery spaces, picking up grasshoppers, beetles, spiders, and other insects, that were floating on the surface. Some hundreds of them might be seen at the same time, and all seemingly of one sort. They were busy, silent, and unsuspicious, darting down after their prey without hesitation, though perpetually harassed by gunners, whom the novelty of their appearance had drawn to the place. Several flocks of the Yellow-Shanks Snipe, and a few Purres, appeared also in the meadows at the same time, driven thither doubtless by the violence of the storm.

I examined upwards of thirty individuals of this species by dissection, and found both sexes alike in color. Their stomachs contained grasshoppers, crickets, spiders, &c., but no fish. The people on the sea-coast have since informed me that this bird comes to them only in the fall, or towards the end of summer, and is more frequently seen about the mill-ponds and fresh water marshes than in the bays; and add, that it feeds on grasshoppers and other insects which it finds on the meadows and marshes, picking them from the grass, as well as from the surface of the water. They have never known it to associate with the Lesser Tern, and consider it altogether a different bird. This opinion seems confirmed by the above circumstances, and by the fact of its greater extent of wing, being full three inches wider than the Lesser Tern; and also making its appearance after the others have gone off.

The Short-Tailed Tern measures eight inches and a half from the point of the bill to the tip of the tail, and twenty-three inches in ex-

* C. L. Bonaparte remarks, — "*S. plumbea* is evidently, even judging only by Wilson's figure and description, no other than the young of the European *S. nigra*, of which so many nominal species had already been made. Indeed, so evident did the matter appear to us, even before we compared the species, that we cannot conceive why this hypothesis did not strike every naturalist, particularly as the *S. nigra* is well known to inhabit these states, though not noticed by Wilson in its adult dress. It is a singular fact, that we hardly observed one adult among twenty young, which were common in the latter part of summer at Long Beach, New York." — ED.

tent; the bill is an inch and a quarter in length, sharp-pointed, and of a deep black color; a patch of black covers the crown, auriculars, spot before the eye and hind head; the forehead, eyelids, sides of the neck, passing quite round below the hind head, and whole lower parts are pure white; the back is dark ash, each feather broadly tipped with brown; the wings, a dark lead color, extending an inch and a half beyond the tail, which is also of the same tint, and slightly forked; shoulders of the wing, brownish ash; legs and webbed feet, tawny. It had a sharp, shrill cry when wounded and taken.

This is probably the *Brown Tern* mentioned by Willoughby, of which so many imperfect accounts have already been given.

BLACK SKIMMER, OR SHEERWATER. — RHYNCHOPS NI-GRA. — Fig. 242.

Arct. Zool. No. 445. — *Catesby,* i. 90. — Le bec-en-ciseaux, *Buff.* viii. 454, *Tab* 36. — *Peale's Museum,* No. 3530.

RHYNCHOPS NIGRA. — Linnæus.*

Rhynchops nigra, *Steph. Cont. Sh. Zool.* vol. xiii. p. 136. — *Cuv. Reg. Anim.* i. 522. — *Bonap. Synop.* — *Less. Man. d'Orn.* ii. p. 385.

This truly singular fowl is the only species of its tribe hitherto discovered. Like many others, it is a bird of passage in the United States; and makes its first appearance on the shores of New Jersey early in May. It resides there, as well as along the whole Atlantic coast during the summer; and retires early in September. Its favorite

---

* This very curious genus is composed, according to ornithologists, of two species, — that of our author and the *R. flavirostris,* Vieillot; though I suspect that another is involved in the birds which I have seen from the southern ocean. In form and plumage they bear a strong resemblance to the Terns, but are at once distinguished by the bill, which will show the greatest instance of the lateral development of that member. The manners of these birds, in adaptation to the structure of the bill and mouth, are noted by our author; and it seems generally thought, that their practice of skimming and cutting the water, as it were in search of food, is their only mode of procuring subsistence. The immense flocks of this species, mingled with Gulls and Terns, with their peculiar mode of feeding on some bivalve shells, is thus described by Lesson, and shows that sometimes a more substantial food is required, for the procuring of which the form of their bill is no less beautifully adapted, and that the opinion of Wilson is at variance with reality : — " Il formait avec les mouettes et quelque autres oiseaux de mer, des bandes tellement épaisses, qu'il resemblait à des longues écharpes noires et mobiles qui obscurcissaient le ciel depuis les rives de Penco jusqu'à l'île de Quiriquine, dans un espace de douze milles. Quoique le bec-en-ciseaux semble défavorisé par la forme de son bec, nous aquîmes la preuve qu'il savait s'en servir avec avantage et avec le plus grande adresse. Les plages sablonneuses de Penco sont en effet remplies de *Mactres,* coquilles bivalves, que la marée descendente laisse presque à sec dans des petites mares ; le bec-en-ciseaux tres au fait de ce phénomène, se place auprès de ces mollusques, attend que leur valve sent ouvre un peu, et profite aussitôt de ce mouvement en enforçant la lame inférieure, et tranchante de son bec entre le valves qui se referment. L'oiseaux enlève alors la coquille, la frappe sur la grève, coupe le ligament du molusque, et peut ensuite avaler celui-ci sans obstacle. Plusieurs fois nous avons été témoins de cet instinct très perfectionné." — Ed.

haunts are low sand bars, raised above the reach of the summer tides; and also dry, flat sands on the beach in front of the ocean. On such places it usually breeds along the shores of Cape May, in New Jersey. On account of the general coldness of the spring there, the Sheerwater does not begin to lay until early in June, at which time these birds form themselves into small societies, fifteen or twenty pair frequently breeding within a few yards of each other. The nest is a mere hollow, formed in the sand, without any other materials. The female lays three eggs, almost exactly oval, of a clear white, marked with large, round spots of brownish black, and intermixed with others of pale Indian ink. These eggs measure one inch and three quarters, by one inch and a quarter. Half a bushel and more of eggs has sometimes been collected from one sand bar, within the compass of half an acre. These eggs have something of a fishy taste, but are eaten by many people on the coast. The female sits on them only during the night, or in wet and stormy weather. The young remain for several weeks before they are able to fly; are fed with great assiduity by both parents; and seem to delight in lying with loosened wings, flat on the sand, enjoying its invigorating warmth. They breed but once in the season.

The singular conformation of the bill of this bird has excited much surprise; and some writers, measuring the divine proportions of nature by their own contracted standards of conception, in the plenitude of their vanity have pronounced it to be "a lame and defective weapon." Such ignorant presumption, or rather impiety, ought to hide its head in the dust, on a calm display of the peculiar construction of this singular bird, and the wisdom by which it is so admirably adapted to the purposes or mode of existence for which it was intended. The Sheerwater is formed for skimming, while on the wing, the surface of the sea for its food, which consists of small fish, shrimps, young fry, &c., whose usual haunts are near the shore, and towards the surface. That the lower mandible, when dipped into and cleaving the water, might not retard the bird's way, it is thinned and sharpened like the blade of a knife; the upper mandible, being, at such times, elevated above water, is curtailed in its length, as being less necessary, but tapering gradually to a point, that, on shutting, it may offer less opposition. To prevent inconvenience from the rushing of the water, the mouth is confined to the mere opening of the gullet, which, indeed, prevents mastication taking place there; but the stomach, or gizzard, to which this business is solely allotted, is of uncommon hardness, strength, and muscularity, far surpassing, in these respects, any other water-bird with which I am acquainted. To all these is added a vast expansion of wing, to enable the bird to sail with sufficient celerity, while dipping in the water. The general proportion of the length of our swiftest Hawks and Swallows, to their breadth, is as one to two; but, in the present case, as there is not only the resistance of the air, but also that of the water, to overcome, a still greater volume of wing is given, the Sheerwater measuring nineteen inches in length, and upwards of forty-four in extent. In short, whoever has attentively examined this curious apparatus, and observed the possessor, with his ample wings, long, tending neck, and lower mandible, occasionally dipped into and ploughing the surface, and the facility with which he procures his food, cannot but consider it a mere playful amusement, when compared with the dashing immersions of the Tern, the Gull, or the Fish-Hawk, who, to the superficial observer, appear so superiorly accommodated.

The Sheerwater is most frequently seen skimming close along shore about the first of the flood, at which time the young fry, shrimp, &c., are most abundant in such places. There are also numerous inlets among the low islands between the sea-beach and mainland of Cape May, where I have observed the Sheerwaters, eight or ten in company, passing and repassing, at high water, particular estuaries of those creeks that run up into the salt marshes, dipping, with extended neck, their open bills into the water, with as much apparent ease as Swallows glean up flies from the surface. On examining the stomachs of several of these, shot at the time, they contained numbers of a small fish, usually called *silver-sides*, from a broad line of a glossy silver color that runs from the gills to the tail. The mouths of these inlets abound with this fry, or fish, probably feeding on the various matters washed down from the marshes.

The voice of the Sheerwater is harsh and screaming, resembling that of the Tern, but stronger. It flies with a slowly flapping flight, dipping, occasionally, with steady, expanded wings and bended neck, its lower mandible into the sea, and with open mouth receiving its food as it ploughs along the surface. It is rarely seen swimming on the water; but frequently rests in large parties on the sand bars at low water. One of these birds, which I wounded in the wing, and kept in the room beside me for several days, soon became tame, and even familiar. It generally stood with its legs erect, its body horizontal, and its neck rather extended. It frequently reposed on its belly, and stretching its neck, rested its long bill on the floor. It spent most of its time in this way, or in dressing and arranging its plumage with its long, scissors-like bill, which it seemed to perform with great ease and dexterity. It refused every kind of food offered it, and I am persuaded never feeds but when on the wing. As to the reports of its frequenting oyster beds, and feeding on these fish, they are contradicted by all those persons with whom I have conversed, whose long residence on the coast where these birds are common, has given them the best opportunities of knowing.

The Sheerwater is nineteen inches in length, from the point of the bill to the extremity of the tail; the tips of the wings, when shut, extend full four inches farther; breadth, three feet eight inches; length of the lower mandible, four inches and a half; of the upper, three inches and a half; both of a scarlet red, tinged with orange, and ending in black; the lower extremely thin; the upper grooved, so as to receive the edge of the lower; the nostril is large and pervious, placed in a hollow near the base and edge of the upper mandible, where it projects greatly over the lower; upper part of the head, neck, back, and scapulars, deep black; wings, the same, except the secondaries, which are white on the inner vanes, and also tipped with white; tail, forked, consisting of twelve feathers, the two middle ones about an inch and a half shorter than the exterior ones, all black, broadly edged on both sides with white; tail-coverts, white on the outer sides, black in the middle; front, passing down the neck below the eye, throat, breast, and whole lower parts, pure white; legs and webbed feet, bright scarlet, formed almost exactly like those of the Tern. Weight, twelve ounces avoirdupois. The female weighed nine ounces, and measured only sixteen inches in length, and three feet three inches in extent; the colors and markings were the same as those of the male, with the exception of the tail, which was white, shafted, and broadly centred with black.

The birds from which these descriptions were taken, were shot on the 25th of May, before they had begun to breed. The female contained a great number of eggs, the largest of which were about the size of duck-shot; the stomach, in both, was an oblong pouch, ending in a remarkably hard gizzard, curiously puckered or plaited, containing the half-dissolved fragments of the small silver-sides, pieces of shrimps, small crabs, and skippers, or sand fleas.

On some particular parts of the coast of Virginia, these birds are seen, on low sand bars, in flocks of several hundreds together. There more than twenty nests have been found within the space of a square rod. The young are at first so exactly of a color with the sand on which they sit, as to be with difficulty discovered, unless after a close search.

The Sheerwater leaves our shores soon after his young are fit for the journey. He is found on various coasts of Asia, as well as America, residing principally near the tropics; and migrating into the temperate regions of the globe only for the purpose of rearing his young. He is rarely or never seen far out at sea; and must not be mistaken for another bird of the same name, a species of Petrel,* which is met with on every part of the ocean, skimming, with bended wings, along the summits, declivities, and hollows of the waves.

STORMY PETREL. — PROCELLARIA PELAGICA. — Fig. 243.

Arct. Zool. No. 464. — Le petrol, ou l'oiseaux tempête, *Pl. enl.* 993. — *Bewick*, ii. 223. — *Peale's Museum*, No. 3034.

THALASIDROMA WILSONII. — BONAPARTE.†

Thalasidroma Wilsonii, *Bonap. Synop.* p. 367. — Procellaria Wilsonii, *Steph. Cont. Sh. Zool.* xiii. p. 224. — Procellaria Wilsonii, *Orn's reprint of Wils.* p. 94. — *Journ. of the Acad. of N. S. of Philad.* iii. p. 231, pl. ix.

THERE are few persons who have crossed the Atlantic, or traversed much of the ocean, who have not observed these solitary wanderers of

* *Procellaria Puffinus*, the Sheerwater Petrel.
† This species, confounded (and with little wonder, from its near alliance,) by Wilson, with the *P. pelasgica*, has been named as above by the Prince of Musignano, another tribute to the memory of our American ornithologist, and he has added the following differences and distinctive characters. Bonaparte has also added the *T. Bullockii* to the American list.

The smaller Petrels of other countries are much allied to these; they amount to a considerable number, many of which are yet undetermined, and are confused with each other, in the want of proper distinguishing characters being assigned to each. It is from this that the *P. pelasgica* has been assigned a distribution so extensive. Some species are found in most latitudes; and from their similarity most observers seem to be unaware when they have passed the boundary of one, and entered the opposite limits of another form.

They resemble each other in another propensity, — that of following the course of vessels, attracted by the shelter afforded in the wake, or retained by the small marine insects and seeds which are sucked into it, and the subsistence they may obtain

44

the deep, skimming along the surface of the wild and wasteful ocean; flitting past the vessel like Swallows, or following in her wake, gleaning their scanty pittance of food from the rough and whirling surges. Habited in mourning, and making their appearance generally in greater numbers previous to or during a storm, they have long been fearfully regarded by the ignorant and superstitious, not only as the foreboding messengers of tempests and dangers to the hapless mariner, but as wicked agents, connected, some how or other, in creating them. " Nobody," say they, " can tell any thing of where they come from, or how they breed, though (as sailors sometimes say) it is supposed that they hatch their eggs under their wings as they sit on the water." This mysterious uncertainty of their origin, and the circumstances above recited, have doubtless given rise to the opinion so prevalent among this class of men, that they are in some way or other connected with that personage, who has been styled the Prince of the Power of the Air. In every country where they are known, their names have borne some affinity to this belief. They have been called *Witches*,[*] *Stormy Petrels*, the *Devil's Birds*, *Mother Carey's Chickens*,[†] probably from some celebrated ideal hag of that name ; and their unexpected and numerous appearance has frequently thrown a momentary damp over the mind of the hardiest seaman.

It is the business of the naturalist, and the glory of philosophy, to examine into the reality of these things ; to dissipate the clouds of error and superstition, wherever they begin to darken and bewilder the human understanding, and to illustrate nature with the radiance of truth. With these objects in view, we shall now proceed, as far as the few facts we possess will permit, in our examination into the history of this celebrated species.

from the refuse thrown overboard. Being most commonly seen when all is gloomy above, the view bounded by the horizon alone, or by a thick atmosphere and boisterous waves, and when they are the only beings visible, running on the " trough of the sea,"

> As though they were the shadows of themselves,
> Reflected from a loftier flight through space,

it can hardly be wondered at, that associations with the spirits have arisen in the minds of men naturally prone, and sometimes wrought up, to superstition, and that they have begotten for themselves such names as are quoted by our author. These ideas are universal. Several small species about the Madeiras bear the name of Anhiga, — conveying the idea of their affinity to imps.

Procellaria Bullockii has been described by Bonaparte, in the Journal of the Academy of Natural Sciences of Philadelphia, as an addition to the birds of America. It is stated to be but rare throughout the Atlantic Ocean, and to be found on the banks of Newfoundland. It is also European, and was first discovered by Mr. Bullock, breeding at St. Kilda, and ought now to stand under the name of its discoverer, *Thalasidroma Bullockii*. They also sometimes occur on the mainland of Britain, and it is remarkable, that all those procured there, have been found in a dead or dying state, in some frequented place — often on the public road. It is expressly mentioned by M. Frecynet, in his voyage *Autour du Monde*, that the small Petrels cannot rise from a flat surface, — such as the deck of a ship. It is possible that the specimens discovered in this state of exhaustion, may have been unable again to resume their flight, and thus perished. Two specimens occurred in Dumfries-shire during the last year, — both found on the public road, — the one dead, the other nearly so. — ED.

[*] *Arctic Zoology*, p. 464.

[†] This name seems to have been originally given them by Captain Carteret's sailors, who met with these birds on the coast of Chili. See HAWKESWORTH'S *Voyages*, vol. i. p. 203.

The *Stormy Petrel*, the least of the whole twenty-four species of its tribe enumerated by ornithologists, and the smallest of all palmated fowls, is found over the whole Atlantic Ocean, from Europe to North America, at all distances from land, and in all weathers, but is particularly numerous near vessels, immediately preceding and during a gale, when flocks of them crowd in her wake, seeming then more than usually active in picking up various matters from the surface of the water. This presentiment of a change of weather is not peculiar to the Petrel alone, but is noted in many others, and common to all, even to those long domesticated. The Woodpeckers, the Snow-Birds, the Swallows, are all observed to be uncommonly busy before a storm, searching for food with great eagerness, as if anxious to provide for the privations of the coming tempest. The Common Ducks and the Geese are infallibly noisy and tumultuous before falling weather; and though, with these, the attention of man renders any extra exertions for food at such times unnecessary, yet they wash, oil, dress and arrange their plumage with uncommon diligence and activity. The intelligent and observing farmer remarks this bustle, and wisely prepares for the issue; but he is not so ridiculously absurd as to suppose that the storm which follows is produced by the agency of these feeble creatures, who are themselves equal sufferers by its effects with man. He looks on them rather as useful monitors, who, from the delicacy of their organs, and a perception superior to his own, point out the change in the atmosphere before it has become sensible to his grosser feelings, and thus, in a certain degree, contribute to his security. And why should not those who navigate the ocean contemplate the appearance of this unoffending little bird in like manner, instead of eyeing it with hatred and execration? As well might they curse the midnight lighthouse, that, star-like, guides them on their watery way, or the buoy, that warns them of the sunken rocks below, as this harmless wanderer, whose manner informs them of the approach of the storm, and thereby enables them to prepare for it.

The Stormy Petrels, or Mother Carey's Chickens, breed in great numbers on the rocky shores of the Bahama and the Bermuda Islands, and in some places on the coast of East Florida and Cuba. They breed in communities, like the Bank Swallows, making their nests in the holes and cavities of the rocks above the sea, returning to feed their young only during the night, with the superabundant oily food from their stomachs. At these times they may be heard making a continued cluttering sound, like frogs, during the whole night. In the day they are silent, and wander widely over the ocean. This easily accounts for the vast distance they are sometimes seen from land, even in the breeding season. The rapidity of their flight is at least equal to the fleetness of our Swallows. Calculating this at the rate of one mile per minute, twelve hours would be sufficient to waft them a distance of seven hundred and twenty miles; but it is probable that the far greater part confine themselves much nearer land during that interesting period.

In the month of July, while on a voyage from New Orleans to New York, I saw few or none of these birds in the Gulf of Mexico, although our ship was detained there by calms for twenty days, and carried by currents as far south as Cape Antonio, the westernmost extremity of Cuba. On entering the Gulf Stream, and passing along the coasts of Florida and the Carolinas, these birds made their appearance in great numbers, and in all weathers, contributing much by their sprightly evolutions of wing to enliven the scene, and affording me every day several hours of amusement. It is indeed an interesting sight to observe these little birds in a gale, coursing over the waves, down the declivities, up the ascents of the foaming surf that threatens to burst over their heads, sweeping along the hollow troughs of the sea as in a sheltered valley, and again mounting with the rising billow, and just above its surface occasionally dropping its feet, which, striking the water, throws it up again with additional force; sometimes leaping, with both legs parallel, on the surface of the roughest waves for several yards at a time. Meanwhile it continues coursing from side to side of the ship's wake, making excursions far and wide, to the right and to the left, now a great way ahead, and now shooting astern for several hundred yards, returning again to the ship as if she were all the while stationary, though perhaps running at the rate of ten knots an hour! But the most singular peculiarity of this bird is its faculty of standing, and even running, on the surface of the water, which it performs with apparent facility. When any greasy matter is thrown overboard, these birds instantly collect around it, and facing to windward, with their long wings expanded, and their webbed feet patting the water, the lightness of their bodies and the action of the wind on their wings enable them to do this with ease. In calm weather they perform the same manœuvre, by keeping their wings just so much in action as to prevent their feet from sinking below the surface. According to Buffon,* it is from this singular habit that the whole genus have obtained the name Petrel, from the apostle Peter, who, as Scripture informs us, also walked on the water.

As these birds often come up immediately under the stern, one can examine their form and plumage with nearly as much accuracy as if they were in the hand. They fly with the wings forming an almost straight, horizontal line with the body, the legs extended behind, and the feet partly seen stretching beyond the tail. Their common note of "*weet, weet,*" is scarcely louder than that of a young Duck of a week old, and much resembling it. During the whole of a dark, wet, and boisterous night which I spent on deck, they flew about the after rigging, making a singular hoarse chattering, which in sound resembled the syllables *patrèt tu cuk cuk tu tu,* laying the accent strongly on the second syllable *tret.* Now and then I conjectured that they alighted on the rigging, making then a lower, curring noise.

Notwithstanding the superstitious fears of the seamen, who dreaded the vengeance of the survivors, I shot fourteen of these birds one calm day, in lat. 33°, eighty or ninety miles off the coast of Carolina, and had the boat lowered to pick them up. These I examined with considerable attention, and found the most perfect specimens as follow:—

Length, six inches and three quarters; extent, thirteen inches and a half; bill, black; nostrils, united in a tubular projection, the upper mandible grooved from thence, and overhanging the lower like that of a bird of prey; head, back, and lower parts, brown sooty black; greater wing-coverts, pale brown, minutely tipped with white; sides of the vent, and whole tail-coverts, pure white; wings and tail, deep black, the latter nearly even at the tip, or very slightly forked; in some specimens, two or three of the exterior tail-feathers were white for an

* BUFFON, tome xxiii. p. 299.

inch or so at the root; legs and naked part of the thighs, black; feet, webbed, with the slight rudiments of a hind toe; the membrane of the foot is marked with a spot of straw yellow, and finely serrated along the edges; eyes, black. Male and female differing nothing in color.

On opening these, I found the first stomach large, containing numerous round, semi-transparent substances of an amber-color, which I at first suspected to be the spawn of some fish; but on a more close and careful inspection, they proved to be a vegetable substance, evidently the seeds of some marine plant, and about as large as mustard seed. The stomach of one contained a fish, half digested, so large that I should have supposed it too bulky for the bird to swallow; another was filled with the tallow which I had thrown overboard; and all had quantities of the seeds already mentioned both in their stomachs and gizzards; in the latter were also numerous minute pieces of barnacle shells. On a comparison of the seeds above mentioned with those of the *gulf-weed*, so common and abundant in this part of the ocean, they were found to be the same. Thus it appears that these seeds, floating, perhaps, a little below the surface, and the barnacles with which ships' bottoms usually abound, being both occasionally thrown up to the surface by the action of the vessel through the water in blowing weather, entice these birds to follow in the ship's wake at such times, and not, as some have imagined, merely to seek shelter from the storm, the greatest violence of which they seem to disregard. There is also the greasy dish-washings, and other oily substances, thrown over by the cook, on which they feed with avidity, but with great good nature, their manners being so gentle, that I never observed the slightest appearance of quarrelling or dispute among them.

One circumstance is worthy of being noticed, and shows the vast range they take over the ocean. In firing at these birds, a quill-feather was broken in each wing of an individual, and hung fluttering in the wind, which rendered it so conspicuous among the rest as to be known to all on board. This bird, notwithstanding its inconvenience, continued with us for nearly a week, during which we sailed a distance of more than four hundred miles to the north. Flocks continued to follow us until near Sandy Hook.

The length of time these birds remain on wing is no less surprising. As soon as it was light enough in the morning to perceive them, they were found roaming about as usual; and I have often sat in the evening, in the boat which was suspended at the ship's stern, watching their movements, until it was so dark that the eye could no longer follow them, though I could still hear their low note of *weet, weet*, as they approached near to the vessel below me.

These birds are sometimes driven by violent storms to a considerable distance inland. One was shot some years ago on the River Schuylkill, near Philadelphia; and Bewick mentions their being found in various quarters of the interior of England. From the nature of their food, their flesh is rank and disagreeable; though they sometimes become so fat, that, as Mr. Pennant, on the authority of Brunnich, asserts, "The inhabitants of the Feroe Isles make them serve the purposes of a candle, by drawing a wick through the mouth and rump, which, being lighted, the flame is fed by the fat and oil of the body." [*]

* *British Zoology*, vol. ii. p. 434.

44 *

GREEN HERON. — ARDEA VIRESCENS. — Fɪɢ. 244.

Arct. Zool. No. 349, 350. — *Catesby*, i. p. 80. — Le Crabier vert, *Buff.* vii. p. 404. — *Lath. Syn.* iii. p. 68. — *Peale's Museum*, No. 3797.

ARDEA VIRESCENS. — Lɪɴɴæᴜs.*

Ardea virescens, *Bonap. Synop.* p..307. — *Wagl. Syst. Av.* No. 36.

Tʜɪs common and familiar species owes little to the liberality of public opinion, whose prejudices have stigmatized it with a very vulgar and indelicate nickname, and treat it on all occasions as worthless and contemptible. Yet few birds are more independent of man than this ; for it fares best, and is always most numerous, where cultivation is least known or attended to ; its favorite residence being the watery solitudes of swamps, pools, and morasses, where millions of frogs and lizards " tune their nocturnal notes " in full chorus, undisturbed by the lords of creation.

The Green Bittern makes its first appearance in Pennsylvania early in April, soon after the marshes are completely thawed. There, among the stagnant ditches with which they are intersected, and amidst the bogs and quagmires, he hunts with great cunning and dexterity. Frogs and small fish are his principal game, whose caution and facility of escape require nice address and rapidity of attack. When on the look-out for small fish, he stands in the water, by the side of the ditch, silent and motionless as a statue ; his neck drawn in over his breast, ready for action. The instant a fry or minnow comes within the range of his bill, by a stroke, quick and sure as that of the rattlesnake, he seizes his prey, and swallows it in an instant. He searches for small crabs, and for the various worms and larvæ, particularly those of the dragon-fly, which lurk in the mud, with equal adroitness. But the capturing of frogs requires much nicer management. These wary reptiles shrink into the mire on the least alarm, and do not raise up their heads again to the surface without the most cautious circumspection. The Bittern, fixing his penetrating eye on the spot where they disappeared, approaches with slow, stealing step, laying his feet so gently and silently on the ground, as not to be

* There are two or three beautiful little Herons confounded under this species, in the same manner from their near alliance, as the Little Bittern of Europe has been with *A. exilis* and *pusilla*. They are all, however, to be distinguished when compared together, or when attention is given to the markings. The nearest ally to *A. virescens* is the East Indian *A. scapularis ;* the upper parts of both are nearly similar, but the neck and under parts differ in being of a deep vinous chestnut in the one, and rich ash gray in the other. In Wilson's Plate, the chestnut color is not represented of a deep enough tint, and too much white is shown on the fore part.

In a specimen which I have lately received from South Carolina, the color of the neck is very deep and rich, almost approaching to that of port wine ; the lengthened feathers of the back are remarkably long, and show well the white shafts which ought to be so conspicuous in both species. The confusion in the greater part of the synonymes must have arisen by the specimens from both countries being indiscriminately compared and described. — Eᴅ.

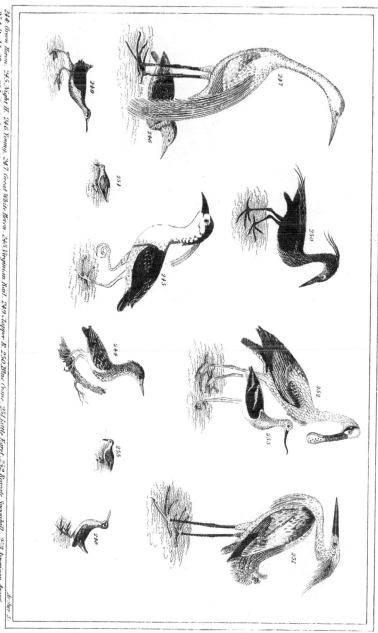

heard or felt; and, when arrived within reach, stands fixed, and bending forwards, until the first glimpse of the frog's head makes its appearance, when, with a stroke instantaneous as lightning, he seizes it in his bill, beats it to death, and feasts on it at his leisure.

This mode of life, requiring little fatigue where game is so plenty, as is generally the case in all our marshes, must be particularly pleasing to the bird, and also very interesting, from the continual exercise of cunning and ingenuity necessary to circumvent its prey. Some of the naturalists of Europe, however, in their superior wisdom, think very differently; and one can scarcely refrain from smiling at the absurdity of those writers, who declare that the lives of this whole class of birds are rendered miserable by toil and hunger; their very appearance, according to Buffon, presenting the image of suffering, anxiety, and indigence.*

When alarmed, the Green Bittern rises with a hollow, guttural scream; does not fly far, but usually alights on some old stump, tree, or fence adjoining, and looks about with extended neck; though, sometimes, this is drawn in so, that his head seems to rest on his breast. As he walks along the fence, or stands gazing at you with out-stretched neck, he has the frequent habit of jetting the tail. He sometimes flies high, with doubled neck, and legs extended behind, flapping the wings smartly, and travelling with great expedition. He is the least shy of all our Herons; and, perhaps, the most numerous and generally dispersed, being found far in the interior, as well as along our salt marshes, and every where about the muddy shores of our mill-ponds, creeks, and large rivers.

The Green Bittern begins to build about the 20th of April; sometimes in single pairs, in swampy woods; often in companies; and not unfrequently in a kind of association with the Qua-Birds, or Night Herons. The nest is fixed among the branches of the trees; is constructed wholly of small sticks, lined with finer twigs, and is of considerable size, though loosely put together. The female lays four eggs, of the common oblong form, and of a pale, light blue color. The young do not leave the nest until able to fly; and, for the first season at least, are destitute of the long-pointed plumage on the back; the lower parts are also lighter, and the white on the throat broader. During the whole summer, and until late in autumn, these birds are seen in our meadows and marshes, but never remain during winter in any part of the United States.

The Green Bittern is eighteen inches long, and twenty-five inches in extent; bill, black, lighter below, and yellow at the base; chin, and narrow streak down the throat, yellowish white; neck, dark vinaceous red; back, covered with very long, tapering, pointed feathers, of a hoary green, shafted with white, on a dark green ground; the hind part of the neck is destitute of plumage, that it may be the more conveniently drawn in over the breast, but is covered with the long feathers of the throat and sides of the neck, that enclose it behind; wings and tail, dark glossy green, tipped and bordered with yellowish white; legs and feet, yellow, tinged before with green, the skin of these thick and movable; belly, ashy brown; irides, bright orange;

* Histoire Naturelle des Oiseaux, tome xxii. p. 343.

crested head, very dark glossy green. The female, as I have particularly observed, in numerous instances, differs in nothing, as to color, from the male ; neither of them receive the long feathers on the back during the first season.

There is one circumstance attending this bird, which, I recollect, at first surprised me. On shooting and wounding one, I carried it some distance by the legs, which were at first yellow ; but on reaching home, I perceived, to my surprise, that they were red. On letting the bird remain some time undisturbed, they again became yellow, and I then discovered that the action of the hand had brought a flow of blood into them, and produced the change of color. I have remarked the same in those of the Night Heron.

NIGHT HERON, OR QUA-BIRD. — ARDEA NYCTICORAX. —
Figs. 245, 246.

Arct. Zool. No. 356. — Le Bichoreau, *Buff.* vii. 435, 439, rol. 22. *Pl. enl.* 758, 759, 899. — *Lath. Syn.* iii. p. 52, No. 13 ; p. 53, young, called there the female. — *Peale's Museum,* No. 3723 ; young, No. 3729.

*NYCTICORAX GARDENII.**

Ardea nycticorax, *Temm. Man.* ii. p. 577. — Gardenian Heron, *Mont. Orn. Dict.* i. — *Bonap. Synop.* p. 306. — *Wagl. Syst. Av.* Ardea, No. 31.

This species, though common to both continents, and known in Europe for many centuries, has been so erroneously described by all the European naturalists whose works I have examined, as to require more than common notice in this place. For this purpose, an accurate figure of the male is given, and also another of what has, till now, been universally considered the female, with a detail of so much of their history as I am personally acquainted with.

* *Nycticorax,* or Night Raven, has been adopted to designate this from among the *ardeadœ,* from the circumstance of their feeding by night, and remaining in a state of comparative rest and inactivity during the day. New Holland and Africa each possess a species. Europe and North America have one in common to both countries ; in the former abundantly distributed, while in the latter it is of rare occurrence, even towards the south ; and, in the northern parts of Great Britain, only a few instances have occurred of its capture.

In form, they are intermediate between the Bitterns and true Herons ; the bill is short, and stronger in proportion than in either ; the feathers on the sides of the neck are lengthened, and cover the hinder part, which is bare to a certain extent ; and, in all the species, the hind head is adorned with (generally three) narrow feathers, in the form of a crest. They feed by twilight, or in clear nights, and take their prey by watching, in the manner of the Herons. They are gregarious ; build on trees ; and, during the season of incubation, are noisy and restless.

The colors, in the adults of the true species, are ash-gray, or pale fawn ; the crown and hind head, and the back, or that part called by the French *manteau,* in the ash-gray species, dark, glossy green ; in the fawn colored, deep chestnut. The young are always of a duskier tinge, and have the centre and tips of each feather white, giving the plumage a spotted appearance. — Ed.

The Night Heron arrives in Pennsylvania early in April, and immediately takes possession of his former breeding-place, which is usually
the most solitary and deeply-shaded part of a cedar-swamp. Groves
of swamp oak, in retired and inundated places, are also sometimes
chosen, and the malou not unfrequently select tall woods, on the banks
of the river, to roost in during the day. These last regularly direct
their course, about the beginning of evening twilight, towards the
marshes, uttering, in a hoarse and hollow tone, the sound *qua*, which
by some has been compared to that produced by the retchings of a
person attempting to vomit. At this hour, also, all the nurseries in
the swamps are emptied of their inhabitants, who disperse about the
marshes, and along the ditches and river-shore, in quest of food. Some
of these breeding-places have been occupied, every spring and summer, for time immemorial, by from eighty to one hundred pairs of Qua-
Birds. In places where the cedars have been cut down for sale, the
birds have merely removed to another quarter of the swamp; but,
when personally attacked, long teased, and plundered, they have been
known to remove from an ancient breeding-place, in a body, no one
knew where. Such was the case with one on the Delaware, near
Thompson's Point, ten or twelve miles below Philadelphia; which
having been repeatedly attacked and plundered by a body of Crows,
after many severe rencounters, the Herons finally abandoned the place.
Several of these breeding-places occur among the red cedars on the
sea-beach of Cape May, intermixed with those of the Little Egret,
Green Bittern, and Blue Heron. The nests are built entirely of sticks,
in considerable quantities, with frequently three and four nests on
the same tree. The eggs are generally four in number, measuring
two inches and a quarter in length, by one and three quarters in
thickness, and of a very pale, light blue color. The ground or
marsh below is bespattered with their excrements, lying all around
like whitewash, with feathers, broken egg-shells, old nests, and frequently small fish, which they have dropped by accident, and neglected
to pick up.

On entering the swamp, in the neighborhood of one of these breeding-places, the noise of the old and the young would almost induce
one to suppose that two or three hundred Indians were choking or
throttling each other. The instant an intruder is discovered, the
whole rise in the air in silence, and remove to the tops of the trees in
another part of the woods, while parties of from eight to ten make occasional circuits over the spot, to see what is going on. When the
young are able, they climb to the highest part of the trees, but, knowing their inability, do not attempt to fly. Though it is probable that
these nocturnal birds do not see well during the day, yet their faculty
of hearing must be exquisite, as it is almost impossible, with all the
precautions one can use, to penetrate near their residence without
being discovered. Several species of Hawks hover around, making an
occasional sweep among the young; and the Bald Eagle himself
has been seen reconnoitring near the spot, probably with the same
design.

Contrary to the generally-received opinion, the males and females
of these birds are so alike in color as scarcely to be distinguished from
each other; both have, also, the long, slender plumes that flow from

the head. These facts I have exhibited, by dissection on several subjects, to different literary gentlemen of my acquaintance, particularly to my venerable friend, Mr. William Bartram, to whom I have also often shown the young, (Fig. 246.) One of these last, which was kept for some time in the botanic garden of that gentleman, by its voice instantly betrayed its origin, to the satisfaction of all who examined it. These young certainly receive their full, colored plumage before the succeeding spring, as, on their first arrival, no birds are to be seen in the dress of Fig. 246; but, soon after they have bred, these become more numerous than the others. Early in October, they migrate to the south. According to Buffon, these birds also inhabit Cayenne, and are found widely dispersed over Europe, Asia, and America. The European species, however, is certainly much smaller than the American, though in other respects corresponding exactly to it. Among a great number which I examined with attention, the following description was carefully taken from a common-sized, full-grown male: —

Length of the Night Heron, two feet four inches; extent, four feet; bill, black, four inches and a quarter long from the corners of the mouth to the tip; lores, or space between the eye and bill, a bare, bluish white skin; eyelids, also large and bare, of a deep purple blue; eye, three quarters of an inch in diameter; the iris of a brilliant blood red; pupil, black; crested crown, and hind head deep, dark blue, glossed with green; front, and line over the eye, white; from the hind head proceed three very narrow, white, tapering feathers, between eight and nine inches in length; the vanes of these are concave below, the upper one enclosing the next, and that again the lower; though separated by the hand, if the plumage be again shook several times, these long, flowing plumes gradually enclose each other, appearing as one; these the bird has the habit of erecting when angry or alarmed; the cheeks, neck, and whole lower parts are white, tinctured with yellowish cream, and under the wings with very pale ash; back and scapulars, of the same deep, dark blue, glossed with green, as that of the crown; rump and tail-coverts, as well as the whole wings and tail, very pale ash; legs and feet, a pale yellow cream color; inside of the middle claw, serrated.

The female differed in nothing, as to plumage, from the male, but in the wings being of rather a deeper ash, having not only the dark, deep green blue crown and back, but also the long, pendent, white plumes from the hind head. Each of the females contained a large cluster of eggs, of various sizes.

The young (Fig. 246) was shot soon after it had left the nest, and differed very little from those which had been taken from the trees, except in being somewhat larger. This measured twenty-one inches in length, and three feet in extent; the general color above, a very deep brown, streaked with reddish white; the spots of white on the back and wings being triangular from the centre of the feather to the tip; quills, deep dusky, marked on the tips with a spot of white; eye, vivid orange; belly, white, streaked with dusky, the feathers being pale dusky, streaked down their centres with white; legs and feet, light green; inside of the middle claw, slightly pectinated; body and wings, exceedingly thin and limber; the down still stuck, in slight tufts, to the tips of some of the feathers.

The birds also breed, in great numbers, in the neighborhood of New Orleans; for, being in that city in the month of June, I frequently observed the Indians sitting in market with the dead and living young birds for sale; also numbers·of Gray Owls (*strix nebulosa*) and the White Ibis, (*tantalus albus*,) for which nice dainties I observed they generally found purchasers.

The food of the Night Heron, or Qua-Bird, is chiefly composed of small fish, which it takes by night. Those that I opened had a large expansion of the gullet, immediately under the bill, that narrowed from thence to the stomach, which is a large, oblong pouch, and was filled with fish. The teeth of the pectinated claw were thirty-five or forty in number, and, as they contained particles of the down of the bird, showed evidently, from this circumstance, that they act the part of a comb to rid the bird of vermin in those parts which it cannot reach with its bill.

GREAT WHITE HERON.— ARDEA EGRETTA.— Fig. 247.

Peale's Museum, No. 3754; Young, No. 3755.

EGRETTA LEUCE. —Jardine.[*]

Ardea leuce, *Illig.* — Ardea alba, *Bonap. Synop.* p. 304. — Ardea egretta, *Wagl. Syst. Av.* No. 7. — *Bonap.* monog. del gruppo Egretta, osserv. sulla, *2d edit.* del reg. anim. Cuv.

This tall and elegant bird, though often seen, during the summer, in our low marshes and inundated meadows, yet, on account of its extreme vigilance and watchful timidity, is very difficult to be procured. Its principal residence is in the regions of the south, being found from Guiana, and probably beyond the line, to New York. It enters the territories of the United States late in February: this I conjecture

---

[*] Among no birds has there occurred so much confusion as among the White Herons, or those more particularly forming the division *Egretts*. They are distributed over every country of the world; are not very different in size; the young are chiefly distinguished by the want of the crest, and are, in many instances, of a plumage similar to the full winter dress; most of the species, when mature, are clothed in a garb of the purest white.

The bird with which our present species is more immediately connected is the *Ardea alba, Gmel.*, a European bird, confounded with the young of *A. egretta*, and not yet, I believe, found in North America. The chief differences are presence of the crest, and much longer proportion of the legs. *A. egretta* seems to range extensively over the continents of America, and some of the islands; I am not aware of its being found elsewhere; and the African, Asiatic, and New Holland allied species will, I suspect, turn out distinct, and most probably belong to their respective countries.

To the North American *egretta* must be added the *Ardea Pealii*, discovered by Bonaparte. It is distinguished from its allies by the flesh color of the bill; is much smaller than *A. alba;* differs from *A. garzetta* by its large, compound crest, and from *A. candissima* by the quality and texture of the ornamental feathers. — Ed.

from having first met with it in the southern parts of Georgia about that time. The high inland parts of the country it rarely or never visits; its favorite haunts are vast, inundated swamps, rice-fields, the low, marshy shores of rivers, and such like places, where, from its size and color, it is very conspicuous, even at a great distance.

The appearance of this bird during the first season, when it is entirely destitute of the long, flowing plumes of the back, is so different from the same bird in its perfect plumage; which it obtains in the third year, that naturalists and others very generally consider them as two distinct species. The opportunities which I have fortunately had of observing them with the train, in various stages of its progress, from its first appearance to its full growth, satisfy me that the Great White Heron with, and that without the long plumes, are one and the same species in different periods of age. In the museum of my friend, Mr. Peale, there is a specimen of this bird, in which the train is wanting; but, on a closer examination, its rudiments are plainly to be perceived, extending several inches beyond the common plumage.

The Great White Heron breeds in several of the extensive cedar swamps in the lower parts of New Jersey. Their nests are built on the trees, in societies; the structure and materials exactly similar to those of the Snowy Heron, but larger. The eggs are usually four, of a pale-blue color. In the months of July and August, the young make their first appearance in the meadows and marshes, in parties of twenty or thirty together. The large ditches with which the extensive meadows below Philadelphia are intersected, are regularly, about that season, visited by flocks of those birds; these are frequently shot, but the old ones are too sagacious to be easily approached. Their food consists of frogs, lizards, small fish, insects, seeds of the splatterdock, (a species of nymphæ,) and small water-snakes. They will also devour mice and moles, the remains of such having been at different times found in their stomachs.

The long plumes of these birds have at various periods been in great request on the continent of Europe, particularly in France and Italy, for the purpose of ornamenting the female head-dress. When dyed of various colors, and tastefully fashioned, they form a light and elegant duster and musquito brush. The Indians prize them for ornamenting their hair, or top-knot; and I have occasionally observed these people wandering through the market-place of New Orleans, with bunches of those feathers for sale.

The Great White Heron measures five feet from the extremities of the wings, and three feet six inches from the tip of the bill to the end of the tail; the train extends seven or eight inches farther. This train is composed of a great number of long, thick, tapering shafts, rising from the lower part of the shoulders, and thinly furnished on each side with fine, flowing, hair-like threads, of several inches in length, covering the lower part of the back, and falling gracefully over the tail, which it entirely conceals. The whole plumage is of a snowy whiteness, except the train, which is slightly tinged with yellow. The bill is nearly six inches in length, of a rich orange yellow, tipped with black; irides, a paler orange; pupil, small, giving the bird a sharp and piercing aspect; the legs are long, stout, and of a black color, as is the bare space of four inches above the knee; the span of the foot measures upwards of six inches; the inner edge of the middle claw is pectinated; the exterior and middle toes are united at the base, for about half an inch, by a membrane.

The articulations of the vertebræ are remarkably long; the intestines measure upwards of eight feet, and are very narrow. The male and female are alike in plumage; both, when of full age, having the train equally long.

VIRGINIAN RAIL.—RALLUS VIRGINIANUS.—Fig. 248.

Arct. Zool. No. 408. — *Edw.* 279. — *Lath. Syn.* iii. p. 228, No. 1, var. A.—
Peale's Museum, No. 4426.

RALLUS VIRGINIANUS. — Linnæus.*

Rallus Virginianus, *Bonap. Synop.* p. 331.

This species very much resembles the European Water Rail, (*Rallus aquaticus,*) but is smaller, and has none of the slate or lead color on the breast, which marks that of the old continent; its toes are also more than proportionably shorter, which, with a few other peculiarities, distinguish the species. It is far less numerous in this part of the United States than our Common Rail, and, as I apprehend, inhabits more remote northern regions. It is frequently seen along the borders of our salt marshes, which the other rarely visits; and also breeds there, as well as among the meadows that border our large rivers. It spreads over the interior as far west as the Ohio, having myself shot it in the Barrens of Kentucky early in May. The people there observe

* In my note upon the genus *Crex,* I mentioned the distinctions existing between that genus *Gallinula* and *Rallus.* The Virginian Rail, and that following, show good examples of the latter form. In their habits they closely agree with the aquatic species of *Crex,* are distributed over all countries of the world, and in general perform partial migrations.

When pursued or *roaded* by a dog, they may be raised once, but the second time will be a task of more difficulty; if the ground is an extensive meadow, they may be followed for an hour without success; but if there are holes or ditches, they will generally seek for one of these, where they conceal themselves beneath some sod, or brow, or thicket of bushes, and may then be easily taken by the hand. I have frequently taken our Common Water Rail in this manner, and sometimes with the head only concealed. They are easily tamed. The structure of the feathers on the forehead and crown of the rails is peculiar, and may be intended as a defence to that part from the friction of the strong grass and reeds among which they are so constantly running. The rachis of each feather is lengthened, and broadened into a flat and sharp point, having the appearance of lengthened scales; in one or two species, the feathers consist of the rachis alone, presenting a horny appearance over the whole forehead. The bastard pinion is furnished with a spur, concealed, however, by the plumage.

The form of the Crakes and Gallinules is well adapted for their peculiar manner of life, but in this group is most conspicuous. The legs are placed far behind; the body is long, much flattened, and remarkably pliable; and the ease and agility with which they run and thread through the long vegetation of the marshes, is almost inconceivable to a person who has not witnessed it.—Ed.

them in wet places, in the groves, only in spring. It feeds less on vegetable, and more on animal, food than the Common Rail. During the months of September and October, when the reeds and wild oats swarm with the latter species, feeding on their nutritious seeds, a few of the present kind are occasionally found; but not one for five hundred of the others. The food of the present species consists of small snail shells, worms, and the larvæ of insects, which it extracts from the mud; hence the cause of its greater length of bill, to enable it the more readily to reach its food. On this account, also, its flesh is much inferior to that of the other. In most of its habits, its thin, compressed form of body, its aversion to take wing, and the dexterity with which it runs or conceals itself among the grass and sedge, are exactly similar to those of the Common Rail, from which genus, notwithstanding the difference of its bill, it ought not to be separated.

This bird is known to some of the inhabitants along the sea-coast of New Jersey, by the name of the Fresh-Water Mud Hen, this last being the common appellation of the Clapper Rail, which the present species resembles in every thing but size. The epithet Fresh-Water is given it, because of its frequenting those parts of the marsh only where fresh-water springs rise through the bogs into the salt marshes. In these places it usually constructs its nest, one of which, through the active exertions of my friend, Mr. Ord, while traversing with me the salt marshes of Cape May, we had the good fortune to discover. It was built in the bottom of a tuft of grass, in the midst of an almost impenetrable quagmire, and was composed altogether of old, wet grass and rushes. The eggs had been floated out of the nest by the extraordinary rise of the tide in a violent north-east storm, and lay scattered about among the drift weed. The female, however, still lingered near the spot, to which she was so attached, as to suffer herself to be taken by hand. She doubtless intended to repair her nest, and commence laying anew; as, during the few hours that she was in our possession, she laid one egg, corresponding in all respects with the others. On examining those floated out of the nest, they contained young, perfectly formed, but dead. The usual number of eggs is from six to ten. They are shaped like those of the domestic Hen, measuring one inch and two tenths long, by very nearly half an inch in width, and are of a dirty white, or pale cream color, sprinkled with specks of reddish and pale purple, most numerous near the great end. They commence laying early in May, and probably raise two brood in the season. I suspect this from the circumstance of Mr. Ord having, late in the month of July, brought me several young ones of only a few days old, which were caught among the grass near the border of the Delaware. The parent Rail showed great solicitude for their safety. They were wholly black, except a white spot on the bill; were covered with a fine down, and had a soft, piping note. In the month of June of the same year, another pair of these birds began to breed amidst a boggy spring in one of Mr. Bartram's meadows, but were unfortunately destroyed.

The Virginian Rail is migratory, never wintering in the Northern or Middle States. It makes its first appearance in Pennsylvania early in May, and leaves the country on the first smart frosts, generally in

November. I have no doubt but many of them linger in the low woods and marshes of the Southern States during winter.

This species is ten inches long, and fourteen inches in extent; bill, dusky red; cheeks and stripe over the eye, ash, over the lores and at the lower eyelid, white; iris of the eye, red; crown and whole upper parts, black, streaked with brown, the centre of each feather being black; wing-coverts, hazel brown, inclining to chestnut; quills, plain deep dusky; chin, white; throat, breast, and belly, orange brown; sides and vent, black, tipped with white; legs and feet, dull red brown; edge of the bend of the wing, white.

The female is about half an inch shorter, and differs from the male, in having the breast much paler; not of so bright a reddish brown; there is also more white on the chin and throat.

When seen, which is very rarely, these birds stand or run with the tail erect, which they frequently jerk upwards. They fly with the legs hanging, generally but a short distance; and the moment they alight, run off with great speed.

———————◆———————

CLAPPER RAIL.—RALLUS CREPITANS.—Fig. 249.

Arct. Zool. No. 407. — *Turt. Syst.* p. 430. — *Lath. Syn.* iii. p. 229, No. 2. — *Ind. Orn.* p. 756, No. 2. — *Peale's Museum*, No. 4400.

RALLUS CREPITANS. — Gmelin.

Rallus crepitans, *Bonap. Synop.* p. 333.

This is a very numerous and well-known species, inhabiting our whole Atlantic coast from New England to Florida. It is designated by different names, such as the Mud Hen, Clapper Rail, Meadow Clapper, Big Rail, &c. &c. Though occasionally found along the swampy shores and tide waters of our large rivers, its principal residence is in the salt marshes. It is a bird of passage, arriving on the coast of New Jersey about the 20th of April, and retiring again late in September. I suspect that many of them winter in the marshes of Georgia and Florida, having heard them very numerous at the mouth of Savannah River in the month of February. Coasters and fishermen often hear them while on their migrations, in spring, generally a little before daybreak. The shores of New Jersey, within the beach, consisting of an immense extent of flat marsh, covered with a coarse reedy grass, and occasionally overflowed by the sea, by which it is also cut up into innumerable islands by narrow inlets, seem to be the favorite breeding-place for these birds, as they are there acknowledged to be more than double in number to all other marsh fowl.

The Clapper Rail, or, as it is generally called, the Mud Hen, soon announces its arrival in the salt marshes, by its loud, harsh, and incessant cackling, which very much resembles that of a Guinea fowl. This noise is most general during the night, and is said to be always greatest before a storm. About the 20th of May, they generally commence laying and building at the same time; the first egg being usually dropped in a slight cavity, lined with a little dry grass pulled for the purpose, which, as the number of the eggs increase to their usual complement, ten, is gradually added to, until it rises to the height of twelve inches or more, — doubtless to secure it from the rising of the tides. Over this the long salt grass is artfully arched, and knit at top, to conceal it from the view above; but this very circumstance enables the experienced egg-hunter to distinguish the spot at a distance of thirty or forty yards, though imperceptible to a common eye. The eggs are of a pale clay color, sprinkled with small spots of dark red, and measure somewhat more than an inch and a half in length, by one inch in breadth, being rather obtuse at the small end. These eggs are exquisite eating, far surpassing those of the domestic Hen. The height of laying is about the 1st of June, when the people of the neighborhood go off to the marshes *an egging*, as it is called. So abundant are the nests of this species, and so dexterous some persons at finding them, that one hundred dozen of eggs have been collected by one man in a day. At this time, the crows, the minx, and the foxes, come in for their share; but, not content with the eggs, those last often seize and devour the parents also. The bones, feathers, wings, &c., of the poor Mud Hen lie in heaps near the hole of the minx; by which circumstance, however, he himself is often detected and destroyed.

These birds are also subject to another calamity of a more extensive kind: After the greater part of the eggs are laid, there sometimes happen violent north-east tempests, that drive a great sea into the bay, covering the whole marshes; so that at such times the Rail may be seen in hundreds, floating over the marsh in great distress; many escape to the main land; and vast numbers perish. On an occasion of this kind, I have seen, at one view, thousands in a single meadow, walking about exposed and bewildered, while the dead bodies of the females, who had perished on or near their nests, were strewed along the shore. This last circumstance proves how strong the ties of maternal affection are in these birds; for of the great numbers which I picked up and opened, not one male was to be found among them; all were females! Such as had not yet begun to sit probably escaped. These disasters do not prevent the survivors from recommencing the work of laying and building anew; and instances have occurred where their eggs have been twice destroyed by the sea; and yet in two weeks the eggs and nests seemed as numerous as ever.

The young of the Clapper Rail very much resemble those of the Virginian Rail, except in being larger. On the 10th of August, I examined one of these young Clapper Rails, caught among the reeds in the Delaware, and apparently about three weeks old; it was covered with black down, with the exception of a spot of white on the auriculars, and a streak of the same along the side of the breast, belly, and fore part of the thigh; the legs were of a blackish slate color; and the bill was marked with a spot of white near the point, and round the nostril. These run with great facility among the grass and reeds, and are taken with extreme difficulty.

The whole defence of this species seems to be in the nervous vigor of its limbs, and thin, compressed form of its body, by which it is enabled to pass between the stalks of grass and reeds with great rapidity. There are also every where among the salt marshes covered ways, under the flat and matted grass, through which the Rail makes its way like a rat, without a possibility of being seen. There is generally one or more of these from its nest to the water edge, by which it may escape unseen; and sometimes, if closely pressed, it will dive to the other side of the pond, gut, or inlet, rising and disappearing again with the silence and celerity of thought. In smooth water it swims tolerably well, but not fast; sitting high in the water, with its neck erect, and striking with great rapidity. When on shore, it runs with the neck extended, the tail erect, and frequently flirted up. On fair ground they run nearly as fast as a man; having myself, with great difficulty, caught some that were wing-broken. They have also the faculty of remaining under water for several minutes, clinging close, head downwards, by the roots of the grass. In a long stretch, they fly with great velocity, very much in the manner of a Duck, with extended neck, and generally low; but such is their aversion to take wing, that you may traverse the marshes where there are hundreds of these birds, without seeing one of them; nor will they flush until they have led the dog through numerous labyrinths, and he is on the very point of seizing them.

The food of the Clapper Rail consists of small shell-fish, particularly those of the snail form, so abundant in the marshes; they also eat small crabs. Their flesh is dry, tastes sedgy, and will bear no comparison with that of the Common Rail. Early in October, they move off to the south; and though, even in winter, a solitary instance of one may sometimes be seen, yet these are generally such as have been weak or wounded, and unable to perform the journey.

The Clapper Rail measures fourteen inches in length, and eighteen in extent; the bill is two inches and a quarter long, slightly bent, pointed, grooved, and of a reddish brown color; iris of the eye, dark red; nostril, oblong, pervious; crown, neck, and back, black, streaked with dingy brown; chin and line over the eye, brownish white; auriculars, dusky; neck before, and whole breast, of the same red brown as that of the preceding species; wing-coverts, dark chestnut; quill-feathers, plain dusky; legs, reddish brown; flanks and vent, black, tipped, or barred with white. The males and females are nearly alike.

The young birds of the first year have the upper parts of an olive brown, streaked with pale slate; wings, pale brown olive; chin and part of the throat, white; breast, ash color, tinged with brown; legs and feet, a pale horn color. Mr. Pennant, and several other naturalists, appear to have taken their descriptions from these imperfect specimens, the Clapper Rail being altogether unknown in Europe.

I have never met with any of these birds in the interior, at a distance from lakes or rivers. I have also made diligent inquiry for them along the shores of Lakes Champlain and Ontario, but without success.

45 *

BLUE CRANE. — ARDEA CÆRULEA. — Fig. 250.

Arct. Zool. No. 351. — *Catesby,* i. 76. — Le Crabier bleu, *Buff.* vii. 398. — *Sloan, Jam.* ii. 315. — *Lath. Syn.* iii. p. 78. No. 45 ; p. 79, var. A. — A. cœrulescens, *Turt. Syst.* D. 379. — *Planch. Enl.* 349. — *Peale's Museum,* No. 6782.

EGRETTA CÆRULEA. — Jardine.

Ardea cærulea, *Linn. Syst.* — *Bonap. Synop.* p. 300. — Ardea cærulescens,
Wagl. Syst. Av. No. 15.

In mentioning this species in his translation of the *Systema Naturæ,* Turton has introduced what he calls two varieties, one from New Zealand, the other from Brazil; both of which, if we may judge by their size and color, appear to be entirely different and distinct species ; the first being green, with yellow legs, the last nearly one half less than the present.* By this loose mode of discrimination, the precision of science being altogether dispensed with, the whole tribe of Cranes, Herons, and Bitterns, may be styled mere varieties of the genus *Ardea.* The same writer has still further increased this confusion, by designating as a different species his Bluish Heron, (*A. cœrulescens,*) which agrees almost exactly with the present. Some of these mistakes may probably have originated from the figure of this bird given by Catesby, which appears to have been drawn and colored, not from nature, but from the glimmering recollections of memory, and is extremely erroneous. These remarks are due to truth, and necessary to the elucidation of the history of this species, which seems to be but imperfectly known in Europe.

The Blue Heron is properly a native of the warmer climates of the United States, migrating from thence, at the approach of winter, to the tropical regions, being found in Cayenne, Jamaica, and Mexico. On the muddy shores of the Mississippi, from Baton Rouge downwards to New Orleans, these birds are frequently met with. In spring they extend their migrations as far north as New England, chiefly in the vicinity of the sea, becoming more rare as they advance to the north. On the sea-beach of Cape May I found a few of them breeding among the cedars, in company with the Snowy Heron, Night Heron, and Green Bittern. The Fig. 250 and description were taken from

---

* I have never traced this species in any Australian collection, and have little doubt that the authors of the assertion *" that it is found there,"* will turn out incorrect. This bird has all the characters of *Egretta* except the color, and will certainly belong to that division, though it has been generally restricted to those of pure plumage. Bonaparte, in his *Nomenclature of Wilson,* says, " The young birds of the year, before their first moult, are altogether pure white, and are therefore apt to be confounded with the young of *A. candidissima."* Wagler, in his excellent Systema, confirms this, and mentions that, in their further change, the upper parts are pale cinereous, tinged with purple, beneath white, the quills partly black, partly white, the tail cinereous. It is curious that in a species clothed with such rich and dark plumage the young should be pure white, the color of the true *Egretta,* while in some of those of snowy covering, the young are a dusky grayish brown. If it can be mistaken in any state for *Egretta candidissima,* it will at once show where it ought to be placed. — Ed.

two of these, shot in the month of May, while in complete plumage. Their nests were composed of small sticks, built in the tops of the red cedars, and contained five eggs, of a light blue color, and of somewhat a deeper tint than those of the Night Heron. Little or no difference could be perceived between the colors and markings of the male and female. This remark is applicable to almost the whole genus; though, from the circumstance of many of the yearling birds differing in plumage, they have been mistaken for females.

The Blue Heron, though in the Northern States it be found chiefly in the neighborhood of the ocean, probably on account of the greater temperature of the climate, is yet particularly fond of fresh-water bogs, on the edges of the salt marsh. These it often frequents, wading about in search of tadpoles, lizards, various larvæ of winged insects, and mud worms. It moves actively about in search of these, sometimes making a run at its prey; and is often seen in company with the Snowy Heron, figured in the same plate. Like this last, it is also very silent, intent, and watchful.

The genus *Ardea* is the most numerous of all the wading tribes, there being no less than ninety-six different species enumerated by late writers. These are again subdivided into particular families, each distinguished by a certain peculiarity — the Cranes, by having the head bald; the Storks, with the orbits naked; and the Herons, with the middle claw pectinated. To this last belong the Bitterns. Several of these are nocturnal birds, feeding only as the evening twilight commences, and reposing either among the long grass and reeds, or on tall trees, in sequestered places, during the day. What is very remarkable, these night wanderers often associate, during the breeding season, with the others, building their nests on the branches of the same tree; and, though differing so little in external form, feeding on nearly the same food, living and lodging in the same place, yet preserve their race, language, and manners, as perfectly distinct from those of their neighbors, as if each inhabited a separate quarter of the globe.

The Blue Heron is twenty-three inches in length, and three feet in extent; the bill is black, but from the nostril to the eye, in both mandibles, is of a rich, light purplish blue; iris of the eye, gray; pupil, black, surrounded by a narrow silvery ring; eyelid, light blue; the whole head, and greater part of the neck, is of a deep purplish brown; from the crested hind head shoot three narrow-pointed feathers, that reach nearly six inches beyond the eye; lower part of the neck, breast, belly, and whole body, a deep slate color, with lighter reflections; the back is covered with long, flat, and narrow feathers, some of which are ten inches long, and extend four inches beyond the tail; the breast is also ornamented with a number of these long, slender feathers; legs, blackish green; inner side of the middle claw, pectinated. The breast and sides of the rump, under the plumage, are clothed with a mass of yellowish white, unelastic, cottony down, similar to that in most of the tribe, the uses of which are not altogether understood. Male and female alike in color.

The young birds of the first year are destitute of the purple plumage on the head and neck.

SNOWY HERON.— ARDEA CANDIDISSIMA.— Fig. 251.

Lath. Sup. i. p. 230. — No. 3748.

EGRETTA CANDIDISSIMA.— Bonaparte.*

Ardea candidissima, *Bonap. Synop.* p. 305. — Monog. del gruppo Egretta. Osserv. Sulla. 2d edit. del Reg. Anim. *Cuv.* p. 101. — *Wagl. Syst. Av.* i. No. 11.

This elegant species inhabits the sea-coast of North America, from the Isthmus of Darien to the Gulf of St. Lawrence, and is, in the United States, a bird of passage; arriving from the south early in April, and leaving the Middle States again in October. Its general appearance, resembling so much that of the Little Egret of Europe, has, I doubt not, imposed on some of the naturalists of that country, as I confess it did on me.† From a more careful comparison, however, of both birds, I am satisfied that they are two entirely different and distinct species. These differences consist in the large, flowing crest, yellow feet, and singularly curled plumes of the back of the present; it is also nearly double the size of the European species.

The Snowy Heron seems particularly fond of the salt marshes during summer, seldom penetrating far inland. Its white plumage renders it a very conspicuous object, either while on wing, or while wading the meadows or marshes. Its food consists of those small crabs usually called *fiddlers*, mud worms, snails, frogs, and lizards. It also feeds on the seeds of some species of nymphæ, and of several other aquatic plants.

On the 19th of May I visited an extensive breeding-place of the Snowy Heron, among the red cedars of Summers's Beach, on the coast of Cape May. The situation was very sequestered, bounded on the land side by a fresh-water marsh or pond, and sheltered from the Atlantic by ranges of sand hills. The cedars, though not high, were so closely crowded together as to render it difficult to penetrate through among them. Some trees contained three, others four nests, built wholly of sticks. Each had in it three eggs, of a pale greenish blue color, and measuring an inch and three quarters in length, by an inch and a quarter in thickness. Forty or fifty of these eggs were cooked,

---

* This species has, like the others, been also confounded with a near ally; Wagler has unravelled the confusion in his *Systema*, and the Prince of Musignano in his Monograph on this group, as quoted above. To make the matter still clearer, I transcribe the Prince's observations on the *Nomenclature of Wilson*. "Two closely-allied species of small White-crested Herons have much puzzled naturalists, who seem to have rivalled each other in confounding them, some by considering them as identical, others by making several nominal species, thus rendering their synonymy almost inextricable. The species are the *A. garzetta* of Europe, and the subject of the present remarks. The latter does not inhabit Europe, but is said to be found in Asia (which we are inclined to doubt) as frequently as on this continent, where it is widely extended. Wilson is free from all the above-mentioned errors, having, as usual, admirably established the species. He was, moreover, judicious in his selection of the English and Latin names; and it was, doubtless, after a careful investigation, that he selected the name of *candidissima*, which Mr. Ord has changed to *A. Carolinensis.*" — Ed.

† "On the American continent the Little Egret is met with at New York and Long Island." — Latham, vol. iii. p. 90.

and found to be well tasted; the white was of a bluish tint, and almost transparent, though boiled for a considerable time; the yolk very small in quantity. The birds rose in vast numbers, but without clamor, alighting on the tops of the trees around, and watching the result in silent anxiety. Among them were numbers of the Night Heron, and two or three Purple-headed Herons. Great quantities of egg shells lay scattered under the trees, occasioned by the depredations of the Crows, who were continually hovering about the place. On one of the nests I found the dead body of the bird itself, half devoured by the Hawks, Crows, or Gulls. She had probably perished in defence of her eggs.

The Snowy Heron is seen at all times during summer among the salt marshes, watching and searching for food, or passing, sometimes in flocks, from one part of the bay to the other. They often make excursions up the rivers and inlets, but return regularly in the evening to the red cedars on the beach to roost. I found these birds on the Mississippi, early in June, as far up as Fort Adams, roaming about among the creeks and inundated woods.

The length of this species is two feet one inch; extent, three feet two inches; the bill is four inches and a quarter long, and grooved; the space from the nostril to the eye, orange yellow, the rest of the bill black; irides, vivid orange; the whole plumage is of a snowy whiteness; the head is largely crested with loose, unwebbed feathers, nearly four inches in length; another tuft of the same covers the breast; but the most distinguished ornament of this bird is a bunch of long, silky plumes, proceeding from the shoulders, covering the whole back, and extending beyond the tail; the shafts of these are six or seven inches long, extremely elastic, tapering to the extremities, and thinly set with long, slender, bending threads or fibres, easily agitated by the slightest motion of the air; these shafts curl upwards at the ends. When the bird is irritated, and erects those airy plumes, they have a very elegant appearance: the legs and naked part of the thighs are black; the feet, bright yellow; claws, black, the middle one pectinated.

The female can scarcely be distinguished by her plumage, having not only the crest, but all the ornaments of the male, though not quite so long and flowing.

The young birds of the first season are entirely destitute of the long plumes of the breast and back; but, as all those that have been examined in spring are found crested and ornamented as above, they doubtless receive their full dress on the first moulting. Those shot in October measured twenty-two inches in length, by thirty-four in extent; the crest was beginning to form; the legs, yellowish green, daubed with black; the feet, greenish yellow; the lower mandible white at the base; the wings, when shut, nearly of a length with the tail, which is even at the end.

The Little Egret, or European species, is said by Latham and Turton to be nearly a foot in length; Bewick observes, that it rarely exceeds a foot and a half; has a much shorter crest, with two long feathers; the feet are black; and the long plumage of the back, instead of turning up at the extremity, falls over the rump.

The young of both these birds are generally very fat, and esteemed by some people as excellent eating.

ROSEATE SPOON-BILL.— PLATALEA AJAJA. — Fig. 252.

Arct. Zool. No. 338.— *Lath. Syn.* iii. p. 16, No. 2.— La Spatule coleur de rose.
Briss. Orn. v. p. 3562, pl. 30.— *Buff.* vii. 456, *Pl. enl.* 116.— *Peale's Museum,*
No. 3553.

PLATALEA AJAJA. — Linnæus.*

Platalea ajaja, *Bonap. Synop.* p. 346.

This stately and elegant bird inhabits the sea-shores of America,
from Brazil to Georgia.   It also appears to wander up the Mississippi
sometimes in summer, the specimen from which Fig. 252 was drawn
having been sent me from the neighborhood of Natchez, in excellent
order; for which favor I am indebted to the family of my late benevolent and scientific friend, William Dunbar, Esq., of that Territory.   It
is now deposited in Mr. Peale's Museum.   This species, however, is
rarely seen to the northward of the Alatamaha River; and even along
the Peninsula of Florida is a scarce bird.   In Jamaica, several other
of the West India Islands, Mexico, and Guiana, it is more common,
but confines itself chiefly to the sea-shore and the mouths of rivers.
Captain Henderson says, it is frequently seen at Honduras.   It wades
about in quest of shell fish, marine insects, small crabs, and fish.   In
pursuit of these, it occasionally swims and dives.

There are few facts on record relative to this very singular bird.
It is said that the young are of a blackish chestnut the first year; of
the roseate color of the present the second year; and of a deep scarlet the third.†   Having never been so fortunate as to meet with them
in their native wilds, I regret my present inability to throw any further
light on their history and manners.   These, it is probable, may resemble, in many respects, those of the European species, the White Spoon-
Bill, once so common in Holland.‡   To atone for this deficiency, I

* This group, remarkable for the curious development of the bill, join a number of characters in common with the Herons and Tantali.   They live during the
breeding season in communities, and feed in twilight; the food is fish and aquatic
animals, and they are said to search in the mud with their bills in the manner of
Ducks, where the soft and closely nervous substance enables them to detect the
smaller insects.   To look at the bill in a stuffed or preserved state, it is hard and
horny, but when living it is remarkably tender, and has rather a fleshy and soft
look and feel   The common British species is easily tamed, and, like most of its
nearer allies, eats voraciously; fish will support them, and even porridge, with a
little raw meat; the gape is very wide, and substances are swallowed in immediate
succession, taken always crosswise, and then tossed over.   The trachea in the
male performs a single convolution in the sternum.   The genus contains three or
four species — that of Europe, found also in India; a species from Africa very near
P. ajaja, peculiar to America; and the *Spatule huppée* of Sonnerat, which Mons.
Temminck thinks distinct.   In all, the young do not attain full plumage till after
the first moult. — Ed.

† Latham.

‡ The European species breeds on trees by the sea side; lays three or four
white eggs, powdered with a few pale red spots, and about the size of those of a
Hen; are very noisy during breeding-time; feed on fish, muscles, &c., which, like
the Bald Eagle, they frequently take from other birds, frightening them by clatter-
ing their bill: they are also said to eat grass, weeds, and roots of reeds: they are

have endeavored faithfully to delineate the figure of this American species, and may, perhaps, resume the subject in some future part of the present work.

The Roseate Spoon-Bill, now before us, measured two feet six inches in length, and near four feet in extent; the bill was six inches and a half long from the corner of the mouth, seven from its upper base, two inches over at its greatest width, and three quarters of an inch where narrowest; of a black color for half its length, and covered with hard, scaly protuberances, like the edges of oyster shells; these are of a whitish tint, stained with red; the nostrils are oblong, and placed in the centre of the upper mandible; from the lower end of each there runs a deep groove along each side of the mandible, and about a quarter of an inch from its edge; whole crown and chin, bare of plumage, and covered with a greenish skin; that below the under mandible, dilatable like those of the genus *Pelicanus*; space round the eye, orange; irides, blood red; cheeks and hind head, a bare, black skin; neck, long, covered with short, white feathers, some of which, on the upper part of the neck, are tipped with crimson; breast, white, the sides of which are tinged with a brown, burnt color; from the upper part of the breast proceeds a long tuft of fine, hair-like plumage, of a pale rose color; back, white, slightly tinged with brownish; wings, a pale wild rose color, the shafts lake; the shoulders of the wings are covered with long, hairy plumage, of a deep and splendid carmine; upper and lower tail-coverts, the same rich red; belly, rosy; rump, paler; tail, equal at the end, consisting of twelve feathers of a bright brownish orange, the shafts reddish; legs and naked part of the thighs, dark dirty red; foot, half webbed; toes, very long, particularly the hind one. The upper part of the neck had the plumage partly worn away, as if occasioned by resting it on the back, in the manner of the Ibis. The skin on the crown is a little wrinkled; the inside of the wing a much richer red than the outer.

AMERICAN AVOSET.— RECURVIROSTRA AMERICANA.—
Fig. 253.

Arct. Zool. No. 421. — *Lath. Syn.* iii. p. 295, No. 2. — *Peale's Museum*, No. 4250.

RECURVIROSTRA AMERICANA.—Linnæus.[*]

Avocette isabelle, Recurvirostra Americana, *Temm. Man. d'Orn.* ii. p. 594. —
Recurvirostra Americana, *Bonap. Synop.* p. 345.

This species, from its perpetual clamor and flippancy of tongue, is called, by the inhabitants of Cape May, the Lawyer; the comparison, however, reaches no farther; for our Lawyer is simple, timid, and perfectly inoffensive.

migratory; their flesh reported to savor of that of a Goose; the young are reckoned good food.

[*] This curious genus contains four known species; perhaps, ere long, another may be made out. They nearly resemble each other, and all possess the turned-

In describing the Long-legged Avoset, in a former part of this work, the similarity between that and the present was taken notice of. This resemblance extends to every thing but their color. I found both these birds associated together on the salt marshes of New Jersey, on the 20th of May. They were then breeding. Individuals of the present species were few in respect to the other. They flew around the shallow pools exactly in the manner of the Long-Legs, uttering the like sharp note of *click*, *click*, *click*, alighting on the marsh or in the water indiscriminately, fluttering their loose wings, and shaking their half-bent legs, as if ready to tumble over, keeping up a continual yelping note. They were, however, rather more shy, and kept at a greater distance. One which I wounded attempted repeatedly to dive; but the water was too shallow to permit him to do this with facility. The nest was built among the thick tufts of grass, at a small distance from one of these pools. It was composed of small twigs of a sea-side shrub, dry grass, sea weed, &c., raised to the height of several inches. The eggs were four, of a dull olive color, marked with large, irregular blotches of black, and with others of a fainter tint.

This species arrives on the coast of Cape May late in April; rears its young, and departs again to the south early in October. While here, it almost constantly frequents the shallow pools in the salt marshes; wading about, often to the belly, in search of food, viz., marine worms, snails, and various insects that abound among the soft, muddy bottoms of the pools.

The male of this species is eighteen inches and a half long, and two feet and a half in extent; the bill is black, four inches in length, flat above, the general curvature upwards, except at the extremity, where it bends slightly down, ending in an extremely fine point; irides, reddish hazel; whole head, neck, and breast, a light sorel color; round the eye, and on the chin, nearly white; upper part of the back and wings, black; scapulars, and almost the whole back, white, though generally concealed by the black of the upper parts; belly, vent, and thighs, pure white; tail, equal at the end, white, very slightly tinged with cinereous; tertials, dusky brown; greater coverts, tipped with white; secondaries, white on their outer edges, and whole inner vanes; rest of the wing, deep black; naked part of the thighs, two and a half inches; legs, four inches, both of a very pale light blue, exactly formed, thinned, and netted, like those of the Long-Legs; feet, half webbed; the outer membrane somewhat the broadest; there is a very slight hind toe, which, claw and all, does not exceed a quarter of an inch in length. In these two latter circumstances alone it differs from the Long-Legs, but is in every other strikingly alike.

The female was two inches shorter, and three less in extent; the head and neck a much paler rufous, fading almost to white on the breast, and separated from the black of the back by a broader band of white; the bill was three inches and a half long; the leg half an inch shorter; in every other respect marked as the male. She contained a great number of eggs, some of them nearly ready for exclusion. The

up bill. In their manners, they assimilate generally with the Totani, feed like them, and are very clamorous when their nest is approached. Like them, also, though possessed of partially webbed feet, they do not swim or take the water freely, except when wading, or by compulsion. — Ed.

stomach was filled with small snails, periwinkle shell fish, some kind of mossy, vegetable food, and a number of aquatic insects. The intestines were infested with tape-worms, and a number of smaller, bot-like worms, some of which wallowed in the cavity of the abdomen.

In Mr. Peale's collection, there is one of this same species, said to have been brought from New Holland, differing little in the markings of its plumage from our own. The red brown on the neck does not descend so far, scarcely occupying any of the breast; it is also somewhat less.

In every stuffed and dried specimen of these birds which I have examined, the true form and flexure of the bill is altogether deranged, being naturally of a very tender and delicate substance.

RUDDY PLOVER. — CHARADRIUS RUBIDUS. — Fig. 254.

Arct. Zool. No. 404. — *Lath. Syn.* iii. p. 195, No. 2. — *Turt. Syst.* p. 415.

CALIDRIS ARENARIA. — Illiger.

Tringa arenaria, *Bonap. Synop.* p. 320.

THIS bird is frequently found in company with the Sanderling, which, except in color, it very much resembles. It is generally seen on the sea-coast of New Jersey in May and October, on its way to and from its breeding-place in the north. It runs with great activity along the edge of the flowing or retreating waves on the sands, picking up the small bivalve shell fish, which supplies so many multitudes of the Plover and Sandpiper tribes.

I should not be surprised if the present species turn out hereafter to be the Sanderling itself, in a different dress. Of many scores which I examined, scarce two were alike; in some the plumage of the back was almost plain; in others the black plumage was just shooting out. This was in the month of October. Naturalists, however, have considered it as a separate species; but have given us no further particulars than that, "in Hudson's Bay, it is known by the name of Mistchaychekiskaweshish," * — a piece of information certainly very instructive.

The Ruddy Plover is eight inches long, and fifteen in extent; the bill is black, an inch long, and straight; sides of the neck and whole upper parts, speckled largely with white, black, and ferruginous; the feathers being centred with black, tipped with white, and edged with ferruginous, giving the bird a very motley appearance; belly and vent, pure white; wing-quills, black, crossed with a band of white; lesser coverts, whitish, centred with pale olive, the first two or three rows black; two middle tail-feathers, black; the rest, pale cinereous, edged with white; legs and feet, black; toes, bordered with a very narrow membrane. On dissection, both males and females varied in their colors and markings.

* LATHAM.

SEMIPALMATED SANDPIPER. — TRINGA SEMIPALMATA. —
Fig. 255.

Peale's Museum, No. 4023.

TRINGA SEMIPALMATA. — Wilson.

Tringa semipalmata, *Bonap. Synop.* p. 316.

This is one of the smallest of its tribe, and seems to have been entirely overlooked, or confounded with another which it much resembles, (*Tringa pusilla*,) and with whom it is often found associated. Its half-webbed feet, however, are sufficient marks of distinction between the two. It arrives and departs with the preceding species; flies in flocks with the Stints, Purres, and a few others; and is sometimes seen at a considerable distance from the sea, on the sandy shores of our fresh-water lakes. On the 23d of September, I met with a small flock of these birds in Burlington Bay, on Lake Champlain. They are numerous along the sea-shores of New Jersey, but retire to the south on the approach of cold weather.

This species is six inches long, and twelve in extent; the bill is black, an inch long, and very slightly bent; crown and body above, dusky brown, the plumage edged with ferruginous, and tipped with white; tail and wings, nearly of a length; sides of the rump, white; rump and tail-coverts, black; wing-quills, dusky black, shafted, and banded with white, much in the manner of the Least Snipe; over the eye a line of white; lesser coverts, tipped with white; legs and feet, blackish ash, the latter half webbed. Males and females alike in color.

These birds varied greatly in their size, some being scarcely five inches and a half in length, and the bill not more than three quarters; others measured nearly seven inches in the whole length, and the bill upwards of an inch. In their general appearance, they greatly resemble the Stints or Least Snipe; but unless we allow that the same species may sometimes have the toes half webbed, and sometimes divided to the origin, — and this not in one or two solitary instances, but in whole flocks, which would be extraordinary indeed, — we cannot avoid classing this as a new and distinct species.

LOUISIANA HERON. — ARDEA LUDOVICIANA. — Fig. 256.

Peale's Museum, No. 3750.

ARDEA LUDOVICIANA. — Wilson.

Ardea leucogaster, *Ord's Reprint*, Part viii. p. 1. — Ardea Ludoviciana, *Bonap. Synop.* p. 304.

This is a rare and delicately-formed species; occasionally found on the swampy river shores of South Carolina, but more frequently along

256. Louisiana Heron. 257. Red Oyster catcher. 258. Hooping Crane. 259. Long billed Curlew. 260. Yellow crowned Heron. 261. Great Heron. 262. American Bittern. 263. Least T. 264. Wood Ibis. 265. Scarlet I. 266. White I. 267. Flamingo.

Archer. Sc.

the borders of the Mississippi, particularly below New Orleans. In each of these places it is migratory ; and in the latter, as I have been informed, builds its nest on trees, amidst the inundated woods. Its manners correspond very much with those of the Blue Heron. It is quick in all its motions, darting about after its prey with surprising agility. Small fish, frogs, lizards, tadpoles, and various aquatic insects, constitute its principal food.

There is a bird described by Latham in his General Synopsis, vol. iii. p. 88, called the *Demi Egret*,[*] which, from the account there given, seems to approach near to the present species. It is said to inhabit Cayenne.

Length of the Louisiana Heron, from the point of the bill to the extremity of the tail, twenty-three inches ; the long, hair-like plumage of the rump and lower part of the back extends several inches farther ; the bill is remarkably long, measuring full five inches, of a yellowish green at the base, black towards the point, and very sharp ; irides, yellow ; chin and throat, white, dotted with ferruginous and some blue ; the rest of the neck is of a light, vinous purple, intermixed on the lower part next the breast with dark slate colored plumage ; the whole feathers of the neck are long, narrow, and pointed ; head, crested, consisting first of a number of long, narrow, purple feathers, and under these seven or eight pendent ones, of a pure white, and twice the length of the former ; upper part of the back and wings, light slate ; lower part of the back and rump, white, but concealed by a mass of long, unwebbed, hair-like plumage, that falls over the tail and tips of the wings, extending three inches beyond them ; these plumes are of a dirty purplish brown at the base, and lighten towards the extremities to a pale cream color ; the tail is even at the tip, rather longer than the wings, and of a fine slate ; the legs and naked thighs, greenish yellow ; middle claw, pectinated ; whole lower parts, pure white. Male and female alike in plumage, both being crested.

PIED OYSTER–CATCHER. — HÆMATOPUS OSTRALEGUS. —
Fig. 257.

Arct. Zool. No. 406. — *Catesby,* i. 85. — *Bewick,* ii. 23. — *Peale's Museum,* No. 4250.

HÆMATOPUS PALLIATUS? — TEMMINCK.[†]

Hæmatopus ostralegus, *Bonap. Synop.* p. 300. — Hæmatopus palliatus ? *Jard. and Selby, Illust. Ornith.* Vol. iii. Plate 125.

THIS singular species, although nowhere numerous, inhabits almost every sea-shore, both on the new and old continent, but is never found

------

[*] See also Buffon, vol. vii. p. 378.

[†] The Oyster-Catchers of Europe and America are said, by Temminck and Bonaparte, to be identical. Such also was the opinion of most ornithologists, and my own, until a closer comparison of American specimens with British showed a dis-

inland. It is the only one of its genus hitherto discovered, and, from the conformation of some of its parts, one might almost be led by fancy

tinction. There is another, however, with which the American bird may be confounded, and I cannot decidedly say that it is distinct — the *H. palliatus*, Temm. I have not seen that species; but from the description of the upper parts being grayish brown, it must either be distinct, or the young state of the North American bird. My specimens of the latter are of the purest black and white.

Bonaparte, in his *Nomenclature*, says, the species is common to both continents; and mentions that he has specimens before him, from each country, decidedly alike. From this circumstance, I should be inclined to give two species to North America, as the distinctions between them are so great as it would be impossible to overlook, on an examination such as he was likely to give.

The following are the distinctive marks of the species in my possession: — The bill appears generally to be more slender; the quills want the white band running in a slanting direction across, being in the American specimen entirely black; the secondaries in the American, except the first, are pure white; in the British specimen, each, except the three or four last, have a black mark near the tips, which decrease in size as they proceed. The whole interior surface of the wing is pure white; in the other it is black, except where the white secondaries appear. In the British bird, the tail-coverts and rump are pure white, the latter running upon the back, until it is hid by the scapulary and back feathers. In the American, the tail-coverts only are white, forming, as it were, a band of that color, interrupted by the black tip of the tail; the whole rump and lower part of the back, black.

If that before us prove distinct, this genus will contain five species, distributed over the whole world, and allied so closely, that every member is alike, with a different distribution only of black and white to distinguish them. They are, the common European bird, perhaps also American, *H. ostralegus;* the Black Oyster-Catcher, *H. niger,* found in Australia and Africa; *H. palliatus,* Temm., South American, and which may turn out to be the immature state of the species we have mentioned; and the *Ostralega leucopus* of Lesson, found on the Malowine Isles, and remarkable in having white legs and feet. The species in my possession may stand as the fifth, under the name of *H. articus.**

As they are allied in form, so they are in habit. They frequent low, sandy beaches, feeding on the shell fish during the recess of the tide, and resting while it flows. The Oyster-Catcher of Europe is to be found on all the sandy British coasts in immense abundance. All those which I have observed breeding, have chosen low, rocky coasts, and deposit their eggs on some shelve, or ledge, merely baring the surface from any moss or other substance covering the rock. When approached, the parents fly round, uttering with great vehemence their clamorous note. I have never found them breeding on a sandy beach, though I have observed these birds for the last ten years, in a situation fitted in every way for that kind of incubation, and have known them retire regularly to a distance of about six or seven miles, (a more populous quarter,) where they had the advantage of a ledge of insulated rocks bounding the coast. A great many, both old and young birds, perhaps among the latter those of a late brood, are always to be found on these coasts, and enliven the monotony of an extensive sand beach, with their clean and lively appearance, and their shrill notes. As the young begin to assemble, the flocks increase; by the month of August, they consist of many thousands; and at full tide, they may be seen like an extensive black line, at the distance of miles. They remain at rest until about half tide, when a general motion is made, and the line may be seen broken, as the different parties advance close to the water edge. After this they keep pace with the reflux, until the feeding banks begin to be uncovered, of which they seem to have an instinctive knowledge, when they leave their resting-

* When this note was written, I had not seen the elaborate review of Cuvier's *Regne Animale* by the Prince of Musignano. He is aware that the North American and European species are distinct, and mentions that the more northern regions produce an additional one; I believe the bird figured by Wilson, and the skins in my possession, will prove to be this, and may stand as I have named it above. That ornithologist also gives as a principal character to *H. palliatus,* that the upper parts are " *di un color fosco invece di nero,*" at variance with the pure black and white of our specimens. — ED.

to suppose, that it had borrowed the eye of the Pheasant, the legs and feet of the Bustard, and the bill of the Woodpecker.

The Oyster-Catcher frequents the sandy sea-beach of New Jersey, and other parts of our Atlantic coast, in summer, in small parties of two or three pairs together. They are extremely shy, and, except about the season of breeding, will seldom permit a person to approach within gunshot. They walk along the shore in a watchful, stately manner, at times probing it with their long, wedge-like bills, in search of small shell fish. This appears evident, on examining the hard sands where they usually resort, which are found thickly perforated with oblong holes, two or three inches in depth. The small crabs called fiddlers, that burrow in the mud at the bottom of inlets, are frequently the prey of the Oyster-Catcher; as are muscles, spout fish, and a variety of other shell fish and sea insects with which those shores abound.

The principal food, however, of this bird, according to European writers, and that from which it derives its name, is the oyster, which it is said to watch for, and snatch suddenly from the shells, whenever it surprises them sufficiently open. In search of these, it is reported that it often frequents the oyster beds, looking out for the slightest opening through which it may attack its unwary prey. For this purpose the form of its bill seems very fitly calculated. Yet the truth of these accounts is doubted by the inhabitants of Egg Harbor, and other parts of our coast, who positively assert, that it never haunts such places, but confines itself almost solely to the sands; and this opinion I am inclined to believe correct, having myself uniformly found these birds on the smooth beach bordering the ocean, and on the higher, dry, and level sands, just beyond the reach of the summer tides. On this last situation, where the dry flats are thickly interspersed with drifted shells, I have repeatedly found their nests, between the middle and 25th of May. The nest itself is a slight hollow in the sand, containing three eggs, somewhat less than those of a Hen, and nearly of the same shape, of a bluish cream color, marked with large, roundish spots of black, and others of a fainter tint. In some, the ground cream color is destitute of the bluish tint, the blotches larger, and of a deep brown. The young are hatched about the 25th of May, and sometimes earlier, having myself caught them running along the beach about that period. They are at first covered with down of a grayish color, very much resembling that of the sand, and marked with a streak of brownish black on the back, rump, and neck, the breast being dusky, where, in the old ones, it is black. The bill is at that age slightly bent downwards at the tip, where, like most other young birds, it has a hard protuberance that assists them in breaking the shell; but in a few days afterwards this falls off.* These run along the shore with great ease and swiftness.

place in small troops, taking day after day the same course. They are difficult to approach, but when one is shot, the flock will hover over it for some time, without heeding the intruder. During flight they assume the ⟩ wedge shape, like Ducks. They feed at night, when the tide is suitable, and are often very noisy. Muscles, and smaller shell fish, crabs, &c. &c., are their most common food. — ED.

* Latham observes, that the young are said to be hatched in about three weeks;

46 *

The female sits on her eggs only during the night, or in remarkably cold and rainy weather ; at other times the heat of the sun and of the sand, which is sometimes great, renders incubation unnecessary. But although this is the case, she is not deficient in care or affection. She watches the spot with an attachment, anxiety, and perseverance, that are really surprising, till the time arrives when her little offspring burst their prisons, and follow the guiding voice of their mother. When there is appearance of danger, they squat on the sand, from which they are with difficulty distinguished, while the parents make large circuits around the intruder, alighting sometimes on this hand, sometimes on that, uttering repeated cries, and practising the common affectionate stratagem of counterfeited lameness, to allure him from their young.

These birds run and fly with great vigor and velocity. Their note is a loud and shrill whistling *wheep-wheep-wheo*, smartly uttered. A flock will often rise, descend, and wheel in air with remarkable regularity, as if drilled to the business, the glittering white of their wings at such times being very conspicuous. They are more remarkable for this on their first arrival in the spring. Some time ago, I received a stuffed specimen of the Oyster-Catcher, from a gentleman of Boston, an experienced sportsman, who, nevertheless, was unacquainted with this bird. He informed me, that two very old men to whom it was shown, called it a *Hagdel*. He adds, "It was shot from a flock, which was first discovered on the beach near the entrance of Boston Harbor. On the approach of the gunner, they rose, and instantly formed in line, like a corps of troops, and advanced in perfect order, keeping well dressed. They made a number of circuits in the air previous to being shot at, but wheeled in line ; and the man who fired into the flock, observed that all their evolutions were like a regularly-organized military company."

The Oyster-Catcher will not only take to the water when wounded, but can also swim and dive well. This fact I can assert from my own observation, the exploits of one of them in this way having nearly cost me my life. On the sea-beach of Cape May, not far from a deep and rapid inlet, I broke the wing of one of these birds, and being without a dog, instantly pursued it towards the inlet, which it made for with great rapidity. We both plunged in nearly at the same instant ; but the bird eluded my grasp, and I sunk beyond my depth ; it was not until this moment that I recollected having carried in my gun along with me. On rising to the surface, I found the bird had dived, and a strong ebb current was carrying me fast towards the ocean, encumbered with a gun and all my shooting apparatus ; I was compelled to relinquish my bird, and to make for the shore, with considerable mortification, and the total destruction of the contents of my powder-horn. The wounded bird afterwards rose, and swam with great buoyancy out among the breakers.

and though they are wild when in flocks, yet are easily brought up tame, if taken young. "I have known them," says he, "to be thus kept for a long time, frequenting the ponds and ditches during the day, attending the Ducks and other poultry to shelter of nights, and not unfrequently to come up of themselves as evening approaches." — *General Synopsis*, vol. iii. p. 220.

On the same day, I shot and examined three individuals of this species, two of which measured each eighteen inches in length, and thirty-five inches in extent; the other was somewhat less. The bills varied in length, measuring three inches and three quarters, three and a half, and three and a quarter, thinly compressed at the point, very much like that of the Woodpecker tribe, but remarkably narrowed near the base where the nostrils are placed, probably that it may work with more freedom in the sand. This instrument, for two thirds of its length towards the point, was evidently much worn by digging; its color, a rich orange scarlet, somewhat yellowish near the tip; eye, large; orbits, of the same bright scarlet as the bill; irides, brilliant yellow; pupil, small, bluish black; under the eye is a small spot of white, and a large bed of the same on the wing-coverts; head, neck, scapulars, rump, wing-quills, and tail, black; several of the primaries are marked on the outer vanes with a slanting band of white; secondaries, white, part of them tipped with black; the whole lower parts of the body, sides of the rump, tail-coverts, and that portion of the tail which they cover, are pure white; the wings, when shut, cover the whole white plumage of the back and rump; legs and naked part of the thighs, pale red; feet, three-toed, the outer joined to the middle by a broad and strong membrane, and each bordered with a rough, warty edge; the soles of the feet are defended from the hard sand and shells by a remarkably thick and callous, warty skin.

On opening these birds, the smallest of the three was found to be a male; the gullet widened into a kind of crop; the stomach, or gizzard, contained fragments of shell fish, pieces of crabs, and of the great king-crab, with some dark brown marine insects. The flesh was remarkably firm and muscular; the skull, thick and strong, intended, no doubt, as in the Woodpecker tribe, for the security of the brain from the violent concussions it might receive while the bird was engaged in digging. The female and young birds have the back and scapulars of a sooty brownish olive.

This species is found as far south as Cayenne and Surinam. Dampier met with it on the coast of New Holland; the British circumnavigators also saw it on Van Diemen's Land, Terra del Fuego, and New Zealand.

WHOOPING CRANE. — ARDEA AMERICANA. — Fig 258. — Male.

Arct. Zool. No. 339. — *Catesby*, i. 75. — *Lath.* iii. p. 42. — La Grue d'Amerique,
Pl. enl. 889. — *Peale's Museum*, No. 3704.

GRUS AMERICANA. — Temminck.*

Grus Americana, *Bonap. Synop.* p. 302. — *North. Zool.* ii. p. 372.

This is the tallest and most stately species of all the feathered tribes
of the United States; the watchful inhabitant of extensive salt marshes,
desolate swamps, and open morasses in the neighborhood of the sea.
Its migrations are regular, and of the most extensive kind, reaching
from the shores and inundated tracts of South America to the arctic
circle. In these immense periodical journeys, they pass at such a
prodigious height in the air as to be seldom observed. They have,
however, their resting-stages on the route to and from their usual
breeding places, the regions of the north. A few sometimes make
their appearance in the marshes of Cape May, in December, particularly on and near Egg Island, where they are known by the name of

* This Crane has also suffered under the too general confusion of names, so
that it becomes somewhat difficult to determine with precision that which should by
priority be allotted to it. It is an extra European species, and seems to be the
Asiatic bird generally known under the name of *G. gigantea*, Pall. Temminck,
however, says that Gmelin changed this name from the original one of *G. leucoge-
ranos*, Pall., and has figured and described it as such in the *Planches Colorées*.
It appears to extend over Asia to China, and specimens have been brought from
Japan. Are they all one species?
America will also possess another majestic Crane, *Grus Canadensis*, Temm.,
inhabiting the northern parts, but not commonly found in the Middle States; it is
met with in summer in all parts of the fur countries, to the shores of the Arctic Sea.
The birds of this genus were formerly arranged among the Herons, to which they
bear a certain alliance, but were, by Pallas, with propriety separated, and form a
very natural division in a great class. They are at once distinguished from *Ardea*
by the bald head, and the broad, waving, and pendulous form of the greater coverts.
Some extend over every part of the world, but the group is, notwithstanding, limited to only a few species. They are majestic in appearance, and possess a strong
and powerful flight, performing very long migrations, preparatory to which they
assemble, and, as it were, exercise themselves before starting. They are social,
and feed and migrate in troops. Major Long, speaking of the migrations of the
second American species, *G. Canadensis*, says, "They afford one of the most
beautiful instances of animal motion we can any where meet with. They fly at a
great height, and wheeling in circles, appear to rest without effort on the surface of
an aerial current, by whose eddies they are borne about in an endless series of rev-
olutions; each individual describes a large circle in the air, independently of his
associates, and uttering loud, distinct, and repeated cries. They continue thus to
wing their flight upwards, gradually receding from the earth, until they become
mere specks upon the sight, and finally altogether disappear, leaving only the discordant music of their concert to fall faintly on the ear, exploring

'Heavens not its own, and worlds unknown before.'"

The *Grus Canadensis*, or Sand-Hill Crane, will be figured and described by the
Prince of Musignano in the remaining volumes of his Continuation, which we hope
erelong to receive. — Ed.

Storks. The younger birds are easily distinguished from the rest by the brownness of their plumage. Some linger in these marshes the whole winter, setting out north about the time the ice breaks up. During their stay, they wander along the marsh and muddy flats of the sea-shore in search of marine worms, sailing occasionally from place to place, with a low and heavy flight, a little above the surface; and have at such times a very formidable appearance. At times they utter a loud, clear, and piercing cry, which may be heard at the distance of two miles. They have also various modulations of this singular note, from the peculiarity of which they derive their name. When wounded, they attack the gunner, or his dog, with great resolution; and have been known to drive their sharp and formidable bill, at one stroke, through a man's hand.

During winter, they are frequently seen in the low grounds and rice plantations of the Southern States, in search of grain and insects. On the 10th of February, I met with several near the Waccamau River, in South Carolina; I also saw a flock at the ponds near Louisville, Kentucky, on the 20th of March. They are extremely shy and vigilant, so that it is with the greatest difficulty they can be shot. They sometimes rise in the air spirally to a great height, the mingled noise of their screaming, even when they are almost beyond the reach of sight, resembling that of a pack of hounds in full cry. On these occasions, they fly around in large circles, as if reconnoitring the country to a vast extent for a fresh quarter to feed in. Their flesh is said to be well tasted, nowise savoring of fish. They swallow mice, moles, rats, &c., with great avidity. They build their nests on the ground, in tussocks of long grass, amidst solitary swamps, raise it to more than a foot in height, and lay two pale blue eggs, spotted with brown. These are much larger, and of a more lengthened form than those of the Common Hen.

The Cranes are distinguished from the other families of their genus by the comparative baldness of their heads, the broad flag of plumage projecting over the tail, and in general by their superior size. They also differ in their internal organization from all the rest of the Heron tribe, particularly in the conformation of the windpipe, which enters the breast-bone in a cavity fitted to receive it, and after several turns goes out again at the same place, and thence descends to the lungs. Unlike the Herons, they have not the inner side of the middle claw pectinated, and, in this species at least, the hind toe is short, scarcely reaching the ground.

The vast marshy flats of Siberia are inhabited by a Crane very much resembling the present, with the exception of the bill and legs being red; like those of the present, the year-old birds are said also to be tawny.

It is highly probable that the species described by naturalists as the Brown Crane (*Ardea Canadensis*) is nothing more than the young of the Whooping Crane, their descriptions exactly corresponding with the latter. In a flock of six or eight, three or four are usually of that tawny or reddish brown tint on the back, scapulars, and wing-coverts; but are evidently yearlings of the Whooping Crane, and differ in nothing but in that and size from the others. They are generally five or six inches shorter, and the primaries are of a brownish cast.

The Whooping Crane is four feet six inches in length, from the
point of the bill to the end of the tail, and, when standing erect, measures nearly five feet; the bill is six inches long, and an inch and a
half in thickness, straight, extremely sharp, and of a yellowish brown
color; the irides are yellow; the forehead, whole crown, and cheeks,
are covered with a warty skin, thinly interspersed with black hairs;
these become more thickly set towards the base of the bill; the hind
head is of an ash color; the rest of the plumage, pure white, the primaries excepted, which are black; from the root of each wing rise numerous large, flowing feathers, projecting over the tail and tips of the
wings; the uppermost of these are broad, drooping, and pointed at
the extremities; some of them are also loosely webbed, their silky
fibres curling inwards, like those of the Ostrich.   They seem to occupy
the place of the tertials.   The legs and naked part of the thighs are
black, very thick and strong; the hind toe seems rarely or never to
reach the hard ground, though it may probably assist in preventing
the bird from sinking too deep in the mire.

LONG-BILLED CURLEW. — NUMENIUS LONGIROSTRIS. —
Fig. 259.

Peale's Museum, No. 3910.

NUMENIUS LONGIROSTRIS. — Wilson.*

Numenius longirostris, *Bonap. Synop.* p. 314. — *North. Zool.* ii. p. 376.

This American species has been considered by the naturalists of Europe to be a mere variety of their own, notwithstanding its difference of
color, and superior length of bill.   These differences not being acci-

* Wilson had the merit of distinguishing and separating this species from the
Common Curlew of Europe, and giving it the appropriate name of *longirostris*, from
the extraordinary length of the bill.   It will fill in America the place of the Common Curlew in this country, and appears to have the same manners, frequenting
the sea-shores in winter, and the rich, dry prairies during the breeding season.   *Numenius arquata*, the British prototype of *N. longirostris*, during the breeding season, is entirely an inhabitant of the upland moors and sheep pastures, and in the
soft and dewy mornings of May and June forms an object in their early solitude,
which adds to their wildness.   At first dawn, when nothing can be seen but rounded
hills of rich and green pasture, rising one beyond another, with perhaps an extensive meadow between, looking more boundless by the mists and shadows of morn,
a long string of sheep marching off at a sleepy pace on their well-beaten track to
some more favorite feeding ground, the shrill, tremulous call of the Curlew to his
mate has something in it wild and melancholy, yet always pleasing to the associations.   In such situations do they build, making almost no nest, and, during the
commencement of their amours, run skulkingly among the long grass and rushes,
the male rising and sailing round, or descending with the wings closed above his
back, and uttering his peculiar, quavering whistle.   The approach of an intruder
requires more demonstration of his powers, and he approaches near, buffeting and
whauping with all his might.   When the young are hatched, they remain near the

dental, or found in a few individuals, but common to all, and none being found in America corresponding with that of Europe, we do not hesitate to consider the present as a distinct species, peculiar to this country.

Like the preceding, this bird is an inhabitant of marshes in the vicinity of the sea. It is also found in the interior, where, from its long bill, and loud, whistling note, it is generally known.

The Curlews appear in the salt marshes of New Jersey about the middle of May, on their way to the north, and in September, on their return from their breeding places. Their food consists chiefly of small crabs, which they are very dexterous at probing for, and pulling out of the holes with their long bills; they also feed on those small sea-snails so abundant in the marshes, and on various worms and insects. They are likewise fond of bramble-berries, frequenting the fields and uplands in search of this fruit, on which they get very fat, and are then tender and good eating, altogether free from the sedgy taste with which their flesh is usually tainted while they feed in the salt marshes.

The Curlews fly high, generally in a wedge-like form, somewhat resembling certain Ducks, occasionally uttering their loud, whistling note, by a dexterous imitation of which a whole flock may sometimes be enticed within gun-shot, while the cries of the wounded are sure to detain them until the gunner has made repeated shots and great havock among them.

This species is said to breed in Labrador, and in the neighborhood of Hudson's Bay. A few instances have been known of one or two pairs remaining in the salt marshes of Cape May all summer. A person of respectability informed me, that he once started a Curlew from her nest, which was composed of a little dry grass, and contained four eggs, very much resembling, in size and color, those of the Mud Hen, or Clapper Rail. This was in the month of July. Cases of this kind are so rare, that the northern regions must be considered as the general breeding place of this species.

spot, and are for a long time difficult to raise; a pointer will stand and road them, and at this time they are tender and well flavored. By autumn, they are nearly all dispersed to the sea-coasts, and have now lost their clear whistle. They remain here until the next spring, feeding at low tide on the shore, and retiring for a few miles to inland fields at high water; on their return again at the ebb, they show a remarkable instance of the instinctive knowledge implanted in, and most conspicuous in the migratory sea and water-fowl. During my occasional residence on the Solway, for some years past, in the month of August, these birds, with many others, were the objects of observation. They retired regularly inland after their favorite feeding places were covered. A long and narrow ledge of rocks runs into the Frith, behind which we used to lie concealed, for the purpose of getting shots at various sea-fowl returning at ebb. None were so regular as the Curlew. The more aquatic were near the sea, and could perceive the gradual reflux; the Curlews were far inland, but as soon as we could perceive the top of a sharp rock standing above water, we were sure to perceive the first flocks leave the land, thus keeping pace regularly with the change of the tides. They fly in a direct line to their feeding grounds, and often in a wedge shape; on alarm, a simultaneous cry is uttered, and the next coming flock turns from its course, uttering in repetition the same alarm note. In a few days they become so wary, as not to fly over the concealed station. They are one of the most difficult birds to approach, except during spring, but may be enticed by imitating their whistle. — ED.

The Long-billed Curlew is twenty-five inches in length, and three feet three inches in extent; and, when in good order, weighs about thirty ounces, but individuals differ greatly in this respect; the bill is eight inches long, nearly straight for half its length, thence curving considerably downwards to its extremity, where it ends in an obtuse knob that overhangs the lower mandible; the color, black, except towards the base of the lower, where it is of a pale flesh color; tongue, extremely short, differing in this from the snipe; eye, dark; the general color of the plumage above is black, spotted and barred along the edge of each feather with pale brown; chin, line over the eye and round the same, pale brownish white; neck, reddish brown, streaked with black; spots on the breast more sparingly dispersed; belly, thighs, and vent, pale, plain rufous, without any spots; primaries, black on the outer edges, pale brown on the inner, and barred with black; shaft of the outer one, snowy; rest of the wing, pale reddish brown, elegantly barred with undulating lines of black; tail, slightly rounded, of an ashy brown, beautifully marked with herringbones of black; legs and naked thighs, very pale light blue, or lead color; the middle toe connected with the two outer ones as far as the first joint by a membrane, and bordered along the sides with a thick, warty edge; lining of the wing, dark rufous, approaching a chestnut, and thinly spotted with black. The male and female alike in plumage. The bill continues to grow in length until the second season, when the bird receives its perfect plumage. The stomach of this species is lined with an extremely thick skin, feeling to the touch like the rough, hardened palm of a sailor or blacksmith. The intestines are very tender, measuring usually about three feet in length, and as thick as a swan's quill. On the front, under the skin, there are two thick callosities, which border the upper side of the eye, lying close to the skull. These are common, I believe, to most of the tringa and scolopax tribes, and are probably designed to protect the skull from injury while the bird is probing and searching in the sand and mud.

YELLOW–CROWNED HERON. — ARDEA VIOLACEA. —
Fig. 260.

Le Crabier de Bahama, *Briss.* v. pp. 481, 41. — Crested Bittern, *Catesby*, i. p. 79. — Le Crabier Gris de fer, *Buff.* vii. p. 399. — *Arct. Zool.* No. 352. — *Peale's Museum*, No. 3738.

NYCTICORAX VIOLACEA — Bonaparte.*

Ardea violacea, *Bonap. Synop.* p. 306

This is one of the nocturnal species of the Heron tribe, whose manners, place, and mode of building its nest, resemble greatly those of the Common Night Heron, (*Ardea nycticorax ;*) the form of its bill is

* This curious species is an instance of one of those connecting links which intervene constantly among what have been defined *fixed groups.* The general form

also similar. The very imperfect figure and description of this species by Catesby, seem to have led the greater part of European ornithologists astray, who appear to have copied their accounts from that erroneous source; otherwise it is difficult to conceive why they should either have given it the name of Yellow-crowned, or have described it as being only fifteen inches in length; since the crown of the perfect bird is pure white, and the whole length very near two feet. The name, however, erroneous as it is, has been retained in the present account, for the purpose of more particularly pointing out its absurdity, and designating the species.

This bird inhabits the lower parts of South Carolina, Georgia, and Louisiana, in the summer season; reposing during the day among low, swampy woods, and feeding only in the night. It builds in societies, making its nest with sticks, among the branches of low trees, and lays four pale blue eggs. This species is not numerous in Carolina, which, with its solitary mode of life, makes this bird but little known there. It abounds on the Bahama Islands, where it also breeds; and great numbers of the young, as we are told, are yearly taken for the table, being accounted in that quarter excellent eating. This bird also extends its migrations into Virginia, and even farther north; one of them having been shot, a few years ago, on the borders of the Schuylkill, below Philadelphia.

The food of this species consists of small fish, crabs, and lizards, particularly the former; it also appears to have a strong attachment to the neighborhood of the ocean.

The Yellow-crowned Heron is twenty-two inches in length, from the point of the bill to the end of the tail; the long, flowing plumes of the back extend four inches farther; breadth, from tip to tip of the expanded wings, thirty-four inches; bill, black, stout, and about four inches in length, the upper mandible grooved exactly like that of the Common Night Heron; lores, pale green; irides, fiery red; head, and part of the neck, black, marked on each cheek with an oblong spot of white; crested crown and upper part of the head, white, ending in two long, narrow, tapering plumes, of pure white, more than seven inches long; under these are a few others, of a blackish color; rest of the neck, and whole lower parts, fine ash, somewhat whitish on that part of the neck where it joins the black; upper parts, a dark ash, each feather streaked broadly down the centre with black, and bordered with white; wing-quills, deep slate, edged finely with white; tail, even at the end, and of the same ash color; wing-coverts, deep slate, broadly edged with pale cream; from each shoulder proceed a number of long, loosely-webbed, tapering feathers, of an ash color, streaked broadly down the middle with black, and extending four inches or more beyond the tips of the wings; legs and feet, yellow; middle claw, pectinated. Male and female, as in the Common Night Heron, alike in plumage.

and appearance is decidedly a *Nycticorax*, and at the extremity of that form we should place it. Its manners, and social manner of breeding, are exactly those of the Qua-Bird, but it possesses the crest and long dorsal plumes of the Egrets. As far as we at present see, it will form the passage from the last-mentioned form to the Night Herons, which will again reach the Bitterns by those confused under the name of *Tiger Bitterns*. — ED.

47

I strongly suspect that the species called by naturalists the Cayenne Night Heron (*Ardea Cayanensis*) is nothing more than the present, with which, according to their descriptions, it seems to agree almost exactly.

GREAT HERON. — ARDEA HERODIAS. — Fig. 261.

Le Heron hupé de Virginie, *Briss.* v. p. 416, 10; Grand Heron, *Buff.* vii. p. 355; *Id.* p. 386. — Largest Crested Heron, *Catesby, App.* pl. 10, fig. 1. — *Lath. Syn.* iii. p. 85, No. 51. — *Arct. Zool.* No. 341, 342. — *Peale's Museum*, No. 3629; *Young*, 3631.

ARDEA HERODIAS. — LINNÆUS.*

Ardea Herodias, *Bonap. Synop.* p. 304. — *North. Zool.* ii. p. 373.

THE history of this large and elegant bird having been long involved in error and obscurity, † I have taken more than common pains to present a faithful portrait of it in this place; and to add to that every fact and authentic particular relative to its manners, which may be necessary to the elucidation of the subject.

* This may be called the representative of the European Heron; it is considerably larger, but in the general colors bears a strong resemblance, and is, moreover, the only North American bird that can rank with the genus *Ardea* in its restricted sense. In manners they are similar, feed in the evening, or early in the morning, when their prey is most active in search of its own victims; but roost at night, except during very clear moonlight. They are extremely shy and watchful, and the height they are able to overlook, with the advantage of their long legs and neck, renders them difficult of approach, unless under extensive cover. When watching their prey, they may be said to resemble a cat, prying anxiously about the sides of the ditches, lake, or stream; but as soon as the least motion or indication of a living creature is seen, they are fixed and ready to make a dart, almost always unerring. Mouse, frog, or fish, even rails, and the young of the larger water fowl, are transfixed, and being carried to the nearest bank or dry ground, are immediately swallowed, always with the head downwards. Their prey appears to be often, if not always, transfixed, — a mode of capture not generally known, but admirably fitted to secure one as vigilant as the aggressor. One or two of the wild and beautiful islets on Lock Awe are occupied as breeding places by the Herons, where I have climbed to many of their nests, all well supplied with trout and eels, invariably pierced or stuck through. None of the species breed on the ground, and it is a curious and rather anomalous circumstance, that the Ardeadæ, the Ibis, and some allied birds, which are decidedly Waders, and formed for walking, should build and roost on trees, where their motions are all awkward, and where they seem as if constantly placed in a situation contrary to their habits or abilities. A heronry, during the breeding season, is a curious and interesting, as well as picturesque object. — ED.

† Latham says of this species, that " all the upper parts of the body, the belly, tail, and legs, are brown; " and this description has been repeated by every subsequent compiler. Buffon, with his usual eloquent absurdity, describes the Heron as " exhibiting the picture of wretchedness, anxiety, and indigence; condemned to struggle perpetually with misery and want; sickened with the restless cravings of a famished appetite; " a description so ridiculously untrue, that, were it possible for these birds to comprehend it, it would excite the risibility of the whole tribe.

The Great Heron is a constant inhabitant of the Atlantic coast, from New York to Florida; in deep snows and severe weather seeking the open springs of the cedar and cypress swamps, and the muddy inlets occasionally covered by the tides. On the higher inland parts of the country, beyond the mountains, they are less numerous; and one which was shot in the upper parts of New Hampshire, was described to me as a great curiosity. Many of their breeding places occur in both Carolinas, chiefly in the vicinity of the sea. In the lower parts of New Jersey, they have also their favorite places for building, and rearing their young. These are generally in the gloomy solitudes of the tallest cedar swamps, where, if unmolested, they continue annually to breed for many years. These swamps are from half a mile to a mile in breadth, and sometimes five or six in length, and appear as if they occupied the former channel of some choked up river, stream, lake, or arm of the sea. The appearance they present to a stranger is singular — a front of tall and perfectly straight trunks, rising to the height of fifty or sixty feet, without a limb, and crowded in every direction, their tops so closely woven together as to shut out the day, spreading the gloom of a perpetual twilight below. On a nearer approach, they are found to rise out of the water, which, from the impregnation of the fallen leaves and roots of the cedars, is of the color of brandy. Amidst this bottom of congregated springs, the ruins of the former forest lie piled in every state of confusion. The roots, prostrate logs, and, in many places, the water, are covered with green, mantling moss, while an undergrowth of laurel, fifteen or twenty feet high, intersects every opening so completely, as to render a passage through laborious and harassing beyond description; at every step, you either sink to the knees, clamber over fallen timber, squeeze yourself through between the stubborn laurels, or plunge to the middle in ponds made by the uprooting of large trees, which the green moss concealed from observation. In calm weather, the silence of death reigns in these dreary regions; a few interrupted rays of light shoot across the gloom; and unless for the occasional hollow screams of the Herons, and the melancholy chirping of one or two species of small birds, all is silence, solitude, and desolation. When a breeze rises, at first it sighs mournfully through the tops; but as the gale increases, the tall mast-like cedars wave like fishing-poles, and rubbing against each other, produce a variety of singular noises, that, with the help of a little imagination, resemble shrieks, groans, growling of bears, wolves, and such like comfortable music.

On the tops of the tallest of these cedars the Herons construct their nests, ten or fifteen pair sometimes occupying a particular part of the swamp. The nests are large, formed of sticks, and lined with smaller twigs; each occupies the top of a single tree. The eggs are generally four, of an oblong, pointed form, larger than those of a Hen, and of a light greenish blue, without any spots. The young are produced about the middle of May, and remain on the trees until they are full as heavy as the old ones, being extremely fat, before they are able to fly. They breed but once in the season. If disturbed in their breeding place, the old birds fly occasionally over the spot, sometimes honking like a goose, sometimes uttering a coarse, hollow, grunting noise, like that of a hog, but much louder.

The Great Heron is said to be fat at the full moon, and lean at its decrease; this might be accounted for by the fact of their fishing regularly by moonlight through the greater part of the night, as well as during the day; but the observation is not universal, for at such times I have found some lean, as well as others fat. The young are said to be excellent for the table, and even the old birds, when in good order, and properly cooked, are esteemed by many.

The principal food of the Great Heron is fish, for which he watches with the most unwearied patience, and seizes them with surprising dexterity. At the edge of the river, pond, or sea-shore, he stands fixed and motionless, sometimes for hours together. But his stroke is quick as thought, and sure as fate, to the first luckless fish that approaches within his reach; these he sometimes beats to death, and always swallows head foremost, such being their uniform position in the stomach. He is also an excellent mouser, and of great service to our meadows, in destroying the short-tailed or meadow mouse, so injurious to the banks. He also feeds eagerly on grasshoppers, various winged insects, particularly dragon flies, which he is very expert at striking, and also eats the seeds of that species of nymphæ usually called spatterdocks, so abundant along our fresh-water ponds and rivers.

The Heron has great powers of wing, flying sometimes very high, and to a great distance; his neck doubled, his head drawn in, and his long legs stretched out in a right line behind him, appearing like a tail, and, probably, serving the same rudder-like office. When he leaves the sea-coast, and traces, on wing, the courses of the creeks or rivers upwards, he is said to prognosticate rain; when downwards, dry weather. He is most jealously vigilant and watchful of man, so that those who wish to succeed in shooting the Heron, must approach him entirely unseen, and by stratagem. The same inducements, however, for his destruction, do not prevail here as in Europe. Our sea-shores and rivers are free to all for the amusement of fishing. Luxury has not yet constructed her thousands of fish ponds, and surrounded them with steel traps, spring guns, and Heron snares.* In our vast fens, meadows, and sea-marshes, this stately bird roams at pleasure, feasting on the never-failing magazines of frogs, fish, seeds, and insects, with which they abound, and of which he, probably, considers himself

---

* " The Heron," says an English writer, " is a very great devourer of fish, and does more mischief in a pond than an otter. People who have kept Herons, have had the curiosity to number the fish they feed them with into a tub of water, and counting them again afterwards, it has been found that they will eat up fifty moderate dace and roaches in a day. It has been found, that in carp ponds visited by this bird, one Heron will eat up a thousand store carp in a year; and will hunt them so close, as to let very few escape. The readiest method of destroying this mischievous bird, is by fishing for him in the manner of pike, with a baited hook. When the haunt of the Heron is found out, three or four small roach, or dace, are to be procured, and each of them is be baited on a wire, with a strong hook at the end, entering the wire just at the gills, and letting it run just under the skin to the tail; the fish will live in this manner for five or six days, which is a very essential thing; for if it be dead, the Heron will not touch it. A strong line is then to be prepared of silk and wire twisted together, and is to be about two yards long; tie this to the wire that holds the hook, and to the other end of it there is to be tied a stone of about a pound weight; let three or four of these baits be sunk in different shallow parts of the pond, and, in a night or two's time, the Heron will not fail to be taken with one or other of them."

the sole lord and proprietor. I have several times seen the Bald Eagle attack and tease the Great Heron; but whether for sport, or to make him disgorge his fish, I am uncertain.

The Common Heron of Europe (*Ardea major*) very much resembles the present, which might, as usual, have probably been ranked as the original stock, of which the present was a mere degenerated species, were it not that the American is greatly superior, in size and weight, to the European species; the former measuring four feet four inches, and weighing upwards of seven pounds; the latter, three feet three inches, and rarely weighing more than four pounds. Yet, with the exception of size, and the rust-colored thighs of the present, they are extremely alike. The Common Heron of Europe, however, is not an inhabitant of the United States.

The Great Heron does not receive his full plumage during the first season, nor until the summer of the second. In the first season, the young birds are entirely destitute of the white plumage of the crown, and the long, pointed feathers of the back, shoulders, and breast. In this dress I have frequently shot them in autumn; but in the third year, both males and females have assumed their complete dress, and, contrary to all the European accounts which I have met with, both are then so nearly alike in color and markings, as scarcely to be distinguished from each other, both having the long, flowing crest, and all the ornamental, white, pointed plumage of the back and breast. Indeed, this sameness in the plumage of the males and females, when arrived at their perfect state, is a characteristic of the whole of the genus with which I am acquainted. Whether it be different with those of Europe, or that the young and imperfect birds have been hitherto mistaken for females, I will not pretend to say, though I think the latter conjecture highly probable, as the Night Raven (*Ardea nycticorax*) has been known in Europe for several centuries, and yet, in all their accounts, the sameness of the colors and plumage of the male and female of that bird is nowhere mentioned; on the contrary, the young, or yearling bird, has been universally described as the female.

On the 18th of May, I examined, both externally and by dissection, five specimens of the Great Heron, all in complete plumage, killed in a cedar swamp near the head of Tuckahoe River, in Cape May county, New Jersey. In this case, the females could not be mistaken, as some of the eggs were nearly ready for exclusion.

Length of the Great Heron, four feet four inches from the point of the bill to the end of the tail; and to the bottom of the feet, five feet four inches; extent, six feet; bill, eight inches long, and one inch and a quarter in width, of a yellow color, in some, blackish on the ridge, extremely sharp at the point, the edges also sharp, and slightly serrated near the extremity; space round the eye, from the nostril, a light purplish blue; irides, orange, brightening into yellow where they join the pupil; forehead and middle of the crown, white, passing over the eye; sides of the crown and hind head, deep slate, or bluish black, and elegantly crested, the two long, tapering black feathers being full eight inches in length; chin, cheeks, and sides of the head, white for several inches; throat, white, thickly streaked with double rows of black; rest of the neck, brownish ash, from the lower part of which shoot a great number of long, narrow-pointed, white feathers, that

47*

spread over the breast, and reach nearly to the thighs; under these long plumes the breast itself, and middle of the belly, are of a deep blackish slate, the latter streaked with white; sides, blue ash; vent, white; thighs, and ridges of the wings, a dark purplish rust color; whole upper part of the wings, tail, and body, a fine light ash, the latter ornamented with a profusion of long, narrow, white, tapering feathers, originating on the shoulders, or upper part of the back, and falling gracefully over the wings; primaries, very dark slate, nearly black; naked thighs, brownish yellow; legs, brownish black, tinctured with yellow, and netted with seams of whitish; in some, the legs are nearly black. Little difference could be perceived between the plumage of the males and females; the latter were rather less, and the long, pointed plumes of the back were not quite so abundant.

The young birds of the first year have the whole upper part of the head of a dark slate; want the long plumes of the breast and back; and have the body, neck, and lesser coverts of the wings, considerably tinged with ferruginous.

On dissection, the gullet was found of great width, from the mouth to the stomach, which has not the two strong muscular coats that form the gizzard of some birds; it was more loose, of considerable and uniform thickness throughout, and capable of containing nearly a pint. It was entirely filled with fish, among which were some small eels, all placed head downwards; the intestines measured nine feet in length, were scarcely as thick as a goose-quill, and incapable of being distended; so that the vulgar story of the Heron swallowing eels, which, passing suddenly through him, are repeatedly swallowed, is absurd and impossible. On the external coat of the stomach of one of these birds, opened soon after being shot, something like a blood-vessel lay in several meandering folds, enveloped in a membrane, and closely adhering to the surface. On carefully opening this membrane, it was found to contain a large, round, living worm, eight inches in length; another, of like length, was found coiled, in the same manner, on another part of the external coat. It may also be worthy of notice, that the intestines of the young birds of the first season, killed in the month of October, when they were nearly as large as the others, measured only six feet four or five inches; those of the full-grown ones, from eight to nine feet in length.

AMERICAN BITTERN. — ARDEA MINOR. — Fig. 262.

Le Butor de la Baye de Hudson, *Briss.* v. p. 449, 25. — *Buff.* vii. p. 430. — *Edw.* 136. — *Lath. Syn.* iii. p. 58. — *Peale's Museum,* No. 3727.

BOTAURUS MINOR. — Bonaparte.

Ardea minor, *Bonap. Synop.* p. 307. — Ardea Mokoho. — *Wagl. Syst. Av.* No. 29.

This is another noctural species, common to all our sea and river marshes, though nowhere numerous. It rests all day among the reeds and rushes, and, unless disturbed, flies and feeds only during the night.

In some places it is called the Indian Hen; on the sea-coast of New Jersey it is known by the name of *dunkadoo*, a word probably imitative of its common note. They are also found in the interior, having myself killed one at the inlet of the Seneca Lake, in October. It utters, at times, a hollow, guttural note among the reeds, but has nothing of that loud, booming sound for which the European Bittern is so remarkable. This circumstance, with its great inferiority of size, and difference of marking, sufficiently prove them to be two distinct species, although, hitherto, the present has been classed as a mere variety of the European Bittern. These birds, we are informed, visit Severn River, at Hudson's Bay, about the beginning of June; make their nests in swamps, laying four cinereous green eggs among the long grass. The young are said to be, at first, black.

These birds, when disturbed, rise with a hollow *kwa*, and are then easily shot down, as they fly heavily. Like other night birds, their sight is most acute during the evening twilight; but their hearing is, at all times, exquisite.

The American Bittern is twenty-seven inches long, and three feet four inches in extent; from the point of the bill to the extremity of the toes, it measures three feet; the bill is four inches long; the upper mandible black; the lower, greenish yellow; lores and eyelids, yellow; irides, bright yellow; upper part of the head, flat, and remarkably depressed; the plumage there is of a deep blackish brown, long behind and on the neck, the general color of which is a yellowish brown, shaded with darker; this long plumage of the neck the bird can throw forward at will, when irritated, so as to give him a more formidable appearance; throat, whitish, streaked with deep brown: from the posterior and lower part of the auriculars, a broad patch of deep black passes diagonally across the neck, a distinguished characteristic of this species; the back in deep brown, barred, and mottled with innumerable specks and streaks of brownish yellow; quills, black, with a leaden gloss, and tipped with yellowish brown; legs and feet, yellow, tinged with pale green; middle claw, pectinated; belly, light yellowish brown, streaked with darker; vent, plain; thighs, sprinkled on the outside with grains of dark brown; male and female, nearly alike, the latter somewhat less. According to Bewick, the tail of the European Bittern contains only ten feathers; the American species has, invariably, twelve. The intestines measured five feet six inches in length, and were very little thicker than a common knitting needle; the stomach is usually filled with fish or frogs.*

This bird, when fat, is considered by many to be excellent eating.

* I have taken an entire Water-Rail from the stomach of the European Bittern. — ED.

LEAST BITTERN. — ARDEA EXILIS. — Fig. 263. — MALE.

Lath. Syn. iii. p. 26, No. 28. — *Peale's Museum,* No. 3814; female, 3815.

ARDEOLA EXILIS. — Bonaparte.*

Ardeola exilis, *Bonap. Synop.* p. 309. — Ardea exilis, *Wagl. Syst. Av.* No. 43. —
Le Heron rouge et noir, *Azar. Voy.* 360. — Descript. opt. auct. *Wagl.*

This is the smallest known species of the whole tribe. It is commonly found in fresh-water meadows, and rarely visits the salt marshes. One, shot near Great Egg Harbor, was presented to me as a very uncommon bird. In the meadows of Schuylkill and Delaware, below Philadelphia, a few of these birds breed every year; making their nests in the thick tussocks of grass, in swampy places. When alarmed, they seldom fly far, but take shelter among the reeds, or long grass. They are scarcely ever seen exposed, but skulk during the day; and, like the preceding species, feed chiefly in the night.

This little creature measures twelve inches in length, and sixteen in extent; the bill is more than two inches and a quarter long, yellow, ridged with black, and very sharp pointed; space round the eye, pale yellow; irides, bright yellow; whole upper part of the crested head, the back, scapulars, and tail, very deep slate, reflecting slight tints of green; throat, white, here and there tinged with buff; hind part of the neck, dark chestnut bay; sides of the neck, cheeks, and line over the eye, brown buff; lesser wing-coverts, the same; greater wing-coverts, chestnut, with a spot of the same at the bend of the wing; the primary coverts are also tipped with the same; wing-quills, dark slate; breast, white, tinged with ochre, under which lie a number of blackish feathers; belly and vent, white; sides, pale ochre; legs, greenish on the shins, hind part and feet, yellow; thighs, feathered to within a quarter of an inch of the knees; middle claw, pectinated; toes, tinged with pale green; feet, large, the span of the foot measuring two inches and three quarters. Male and female, nearly alike in color. The young birds are brown on the crown and back. The stomach was filled with small fish; and the intestines, which were extremely slender, measured, in length, about four feet.

The Least Bittern is also found in Jamaica, and several of the West India islands.

---

* Bonaparte proposes the title of *Ardeola,* as a sub-genus for this species and the *A. minuta* of Britain. They differ from the other (*A. rirescens.* &c.) Small Herons, in having the space above the knees plumed, and in the scapularies taking the broad form of those of the Bitterns and Night Herons, instead of beautifully lengthened plumes.

Three species will constitute this group, that of America, *A. exilis; A. minuta,* of Europe; and *A. pusilla,* Wagl. of New Holland. They are all very similar; the latter has been confounded hitherto with the others. — Ed.

WOOD IBIS. — TANTALUS LOCULATOR. — Fig. 264.

Gmel. Syst. p. 647. — Le Grand Courly d'Amérique, *Briss.* v. p. 335, 3. — Couri-caca, *Buff.* vii. p. 276. *Pl. enl.* 868. — *Catesby*, i. 81. — *Arct. Zool.* No. 360. — *Lath. Syn.* iii. p. 104. — *Peale's Museum*, No. 3832.

TANTALUS LOCULATOR. — Linnæus.*

Tantalus loculator, *Bonap. Synop.* p. 310. — *Wagl. Syst. Av.* No. 1.

THE Wood Ibis inhabits the lower parts of Louisiana, Carolina, and Georgia; is very common in Florida, and extends as far south as Cayenne, Brazil, and various parts of South America. In the United States it is migratory; but has never, to my knowledge, been found to the north of Virginia. Its favorite haunts are watery savannas and

* This species, I believe peculiar to the New World, is extensively dispersed over it, but migratory towards the north. The bird stated by Latham, as identical with this, from New Holland, will most probably turn out the *T. lacteus*, or *leuco-cephalus;* at all events, distinct. The genera *Tantalus* and *Ibis* run into each other in one of those gradual marches where it is nearly impossible to mark the distinction, yet, taking the extremes, the difference is very great. *Tantalus loculator* is the only American species of the former group, principally distinguished by the base of the bill being equal in breadth with the forehead, which, with the face, cheeks, and throat, are bare. In their general manner, they are more sluggish than the Ibis, and possess more of the inactivity of the Heron when gorged, or the sedate gait of the Stork and Adjutants. The known species have been limited to about five in number, natives of America, Africa, and India. The genus *Ibis* is more extensive; they are spread over all the world, and among themselves present very considerable modifications of form. Those of North America are three. The two now figured, and the *I. Falcinellus* of Europe, first noticed by Mr. Ord as a native of that country, in the Journal of the Academy, under the name of *Tantalus Mexicanus*, and afterwards recognized by the Prince of Musignano as the bird of Europe. By Wagler, in his *Systema Avium*, they are put into three divisions, distinguished by the scutellation of the tarsi, and the proportion of the toes. The face is often bare; in one or two the crown is developed into a shield, as in *I. calva;* in a few the head and neck are unplumed, *I. sacra* and *melanocephalus;* and in some, as that of Europe, the face and head are nearly wholly clothed, and bear close resemblance to the Curlews. They are all partly gregarious, feed in small groups, and breed on trees in most extensive communities. They include birds well known for many curious particulars connected with the history and superstitions of nations, and gorgeous from the pureness and decided contrast or dazzling richness of their plumage. To the former will belong the sacred Ibis of antiquity, whose bodies, *in the words of a versatile and pleasing writer*, — "from the perfection of an unknown process, have almost defied the ravages of time; and, through its interventions, the self-same individuals exist in a tangible form, which wandered along the banks of the mysterious Nile in the earliest ages of the world, or, 'in dim seclusion veiled,' inhabited the sanctuary of temples, which, though themselves of most magnificent proportions, are now scarcely discernible amid the desert dust of an unpeopled wilderness." To the others will belong the brilliant species next described, no less remarkable for its unassuming garb in the dress of the first year, and the richly-plumaged, glossy Ibis. The last-mentioned bird is more worthy of notice, holding a prominent part in the mythology of the Egyptians, and occasionally honored by embalment; it is also of extensive geographical distribution, being found in India, Africa, America, Europe, and an occasional stray individual finding a devious course to the shores of Great Britain. A specimen has occurred on the Northumbrian coast within this month. — ED.

inland swamps, where it feeds on fish and reptiles. The French inhabitants of Louisiana esteem it good eating.

With the particular manners of this species I am not personally acquainted; but the following characteristic traits are given of it by Mr. William Bartram, who had the best opportunities of noting them : —

" This solitary bird," he observes, " does not associate in flocks, but is generally seen alone, commonly near the banks of great rivers, in vast marshes or meadows, especially such as are covered by inundations, and also in the vast, deserted rice plantations; he stands alone on the topmost limb of tall, dead cypress-trees, his neck contracted or drawn in upon his shoulders, and his beak resting, like a long scythe, upon his breast; in this pensive posture, and solitary situation, they look extremely grave, sorrowful, and melancholy, as if in the deepest thought. They are never seen on the sea-coast, and yet are never found at a great distance from it. They feed on serpents, young alligators, frogs, and other reptiles." *

The figure of this bird (No. 264) was drawn from a very fine specimen, sent to me from Georgia by Stephen Elliot, Esq., of Beaufort, South Carolina; its size and markings were as follow : —

Length, three feet two inches; bill, nearly nine inches long, straight for half its length, thence curving downwards to the extremity, and full two inches thick at the base, where it rises high in the head, the whole of a brownish horn color; the under mandible fits into the upper in its whole length, and both are very sharp edged; face, and naked head, and part of the neck, dull greenish blue, wrinkled; eye, large, seated high in the head; irides, dark red; under the lower jaw is a loose, corrugated skin, or pouch, capable of containing about half a pint; whole body, neck, and lower parts, white; quills, dark glossy green and purple; tail, about two inches shorter than the wings, even at the end, and of a deep and rich violet; legs and naked thighs, dusky green; feet and toes, yellowish, sprinkled with black; feet, almost semipalmated, and bordered to the claws with a narrow membrane; some of the greater wing-coverts are black at the root, and shafted with black; plumage on the upper ridge of the neck, generally worn, as in the presented specimen, with rubbing on the back, while in its common position, of resting its bill on its breast, in the manner of the White Ibis.

The female has only the head and chin naked; both are subject to considerable changes of color when young, the body being found sometimes blackish above, the belly cinereous, and spots of black on the wing-coverts; all of which, as the birds advance in age, gradually disappear, and leave the plumage of the body, &c., as has been described.

* *Travels,* &c., p. 150.

SCARLET IBIS. — TANTALUS RUBER. — Fig. 265.

Le Courly rouge du Bresil, *Briss*. v. p. 344, pl. 29, fig. 2. — Red Curlew, *Catesby*, i. 84. — *Arct. Zool.* No. 366, 382. — *Peale's Museum*, No. 3864; female, 3868.

IBIS RUBRA. — Vieillot.

Ibis rubra, *Vieill*. — *Bonap. Synop*. p. 311. — *Wagl. Syst. Av*. No. 4. — Ibis ruber, *Wils. Ill. of Zool*. i. pls. 7 and 36, in the plumage of second and first years. — Ibis rouge, *Less. Man. d'Ornith*. ii. p. 254.

This beautiful bird is found in the most southern parts of Carolina, also in Georgia and Florida, chiefly about the sea-shore and its vicinity. In most parts of America within the tropics, and in almost all the West India islands, it is said to be common; also in the Bahamas. Of its manners, little more has been collected, than that it frequents the borders of the sea, and shores of the neighboring rivers, feeding on small fry, shell fish, sea worms, and small crabs. It is said frequently to perch on trees, sometimes in large flocks; but to lay its eggs on the ground, on a bed of leaves. The eggs are described as being of a greenish color; the young, when hatched, black; soon after, gray; and, before they are able to fly, white; continuing gradually to assume their red color until the third year, when the scarlet plumage is complete. It is also said that they usually keep in flocks, the young and old birds separately. They have frequently been domesticated.

One of them, which lived for some time in the Museum of this city, was dexterous at catching flies, and most usually walked about, on that pursuit, in the position in which it is represented in Fig. 265.

The Scarlet Ibis measures twenty-three inches in length, and thirty-seven in extent; the bill is five inches long, thick, and somewhat of a square form at the base, gradually bent downwards, and sharply ridged, of a black color, except near the base, where it inclines to red; irides, dark hazel; the naked face is finely wrinkled, and of a pale red; chin, also bare, and wrinkled for about an inch; whole plumage, a rich, glowing scarlet, except about three inches of the extremities of the four outer quill-feathers, which are of a deep steel blue; legs, and naked part of the thighs, pale red, the three anterior toes united by a membrane as far as the first joint.

Whether the female differs, in the color of her plumage, from the male, or what changes both undergo during the first and second years, I am unable to say from personal observation. Being a scarce species with us, and only found on our most remote southern shores, a sufficient number of specimens have not been procured to enable me to settle this matter with sufficient certainty.

WHITE IBIS. — TANTALUS ALBUS. — Fig. 266.

Le Courly blanc du Bresil, *Briss.* v. p. 339, 10. — *Buff.* viii. p. 41. — White Curlew, *Catesby*, i. pl. 82. — *Lath. Syn.* iii. p. 111, No. 9. — *Arct. Zool.* No. 363.

IBIS ALBA. — Vieillot.

Ibis alba, *Wagl. Syst. Av.* No. 5. — *Bonap. Synop.* p. 312.

This species bears, in every respect except that of color, so strong a resemblance to the preceding, that I have been almost induced to believe it the same, in its white or imperfect stage of color. The length and form of the bill; the size, conformation, as well as color of the legs; the general length and breadth, and even the steel blue on the four outer quill-feathers, are exactly alike in both. These suggestions, however, are not made with any certainty of its being the same, but as circumstances which may lead to a more precise examination of the subject hereafter.

I found this species pretty numerous on the borders of Lake Pontchartrain, near New Orleans, in the month of June, and also observed the Indians sitting in market with strings of them for sale. I met with them again on the low keys, or islands, off the Peninsula of Florida. Mr. Bartram observes that "they fly in large flocks, or squadrons, evening and morning, to and from their feeding places or roosts, and are usually called Spanish Curlews. They feed chiefly on cray fish, whose cells they probe, and with their strong, pinching bills, drag them out." The low islands above mentioned abound with these creatures, and small crabs, the ground in some places seeming alive with them, so that the rattling of their shells against one another was incessant. My venerable friend, in his observations on these birds, adds, "It is a pleasing sight, at times of high winds, and heavy thunder storms, to observe the numerous squadrons of these Spanish Curlews, driving to and fro, turning and tacking about, high up in the air, when, by their various evolutions in the different and opposite currents of the wind, high in the clouds, their silvery white plumage gleams and sparkles like the brightest crystal, reflecting the sunbeams that dart upon them between the dark clouds."

The White Ibis is twenty-three inches long, and thirty-seven inches in extent; bill, formed exactly like that of the Scarlet species, of a pale red, blackish towards the point; face, a reddish flesh color, and finely wrinkled; irides, whitish; whole plumage, pure white, except about four inches of the tips of the four outer quill-feathers, which are of a deep and glossy steel blue; legs and feet, pale red, webbed to the first joint.

These birds I frequently observed standing on the dead limbs of trees, and on the shore, resting on one leg, their body in an almost perpendicular position, as represented in the figure, the head and bill resting on the breast. This appears to be its most common mode of resting, and perhaps sleeping; as, in all those which I examined, the plumage on the upper ridge of the neck, and upper part of the back, was evidently worn by this habit. The same is equally observable on the neck and back of the Wood Ibis.

The present species rarely extends its visits north of Carolina, and, even in that state, is only seen for a few weeks towards the end of summer. In Florida, they are common, but seldom remove to any great distance from the sea.

RED FLAMINGO. — PHŒNICOPTERUS RUBER. — Fig. 267.

Le Flamant, *Briss.* vi. p. 532, pl. 47, fig. 1. — *Buff.* viii. p. 475, pl. 39. *Pl. enl.* 63. — *Lath. Syn.* iii. p. 299, pl. 93. — *Arct. Zool.* No. 422. — *Catesby,* i. pl. 73, 74. — *Peale's Museum,* No. 3545, bird of the first year; No. 3546, bird of the second year.

PHŒNICOPTERUS RUBER. — Linnæus.

Phœnicopterus ruber, *Bonap. Synop.* p. 348.

This very singular species, being occasionally seen on the southern frontiers of the United States, and on the Peninsula of East Florida, where it is more common, has a claim to a niche in our Ornithological Museum, although the author regrets that, from personal observation, he can add nothing to the particulars of its history, already fully detailed in various European works. From the most respectable of these, the *Synopsis* of Dr. Latham, he has collected such particulars as appear authentic and interesting.

"This remarkable bird has the neck and legs in a greater disproportion than any other bird; the length, from the end of the bill to that of the tail, is four feet two or three inches; but to the end of the claws, measures sometimes more than six feet. The bill is four inches and a quarter long, and of a construction different from that of any other bird; the upper mandible, very thin and flat, and somewhat movable; the under, thick; both of them bending downwards from the middle; the nostrils are linear, and placed in a blackish membrane; the end of the bill, as far as the bend, is black; from thence to the base, reddish yellow; round the base, quite to the eye, covered with a flesh colored cere; the neck is slender, and of a great length; the tongue, large, fleshy, filling the cavity of the bill, furnished with twelve or more hooked papillæ on each side, turning backwards; the tip, a sharp, cartilaginous substance. The bird, when in full plumage, is wholly of a most deep scarlet, (those of Africa said to be the deepest,) except the quills, which are black; from the base of the thigh to the claws, measures thirty-two inches, of which the feathered part takes up no more than three inches; the bare part above the knee, thirteen inches; and from thence to the claws, sixteen; the color of the bare parts is red; and the toes are furnished with a web, as in the Duck genus, but is deeply indented. The legs are not straight, but slightly bent, the shin rather projecting.

48

" These birds do not gain their full plumage till the third year. In the first, they are of a grayish white for the most part ; the second, of a clearer white, tinged with red, or rather rose color ; but the wings and scapulars are red ; in the third year, a general glowing scarlet manifests itself throughout ; the bill and legs also keep pace with the gradation of color in the plumage, these parts changing to their colors by degrees, as the bird approaches to an adult state.

" Flamingoes prefer a warm climate ; in the old continent not often met with beyond forty degrees north or south ; every where seen on the African coast, and adjacent isles, quite to the Cape of Good Hope ;[*] and now and then on the coasts of Spain,[†] Italy, and those of France lying in the Mediterranean Sea ; being, at times, met with at Marseilles, and for some way up the Rhone ; in some seasons frequents Aleppo,[‡] and parts adjacent ; seen also on the Persian side of the Caspian Sea ; and from thence, along the western coast, as far as the Wolga ; though this at uncertain times, and chiefly in considerable flocks, coming from the north coast mostly in October and No vember ; but so soon as the wind changes, they totally disappear.[§] They breed in the Cape Verd Isles, particularly in that of Sal.[||] The nest is of a singular construction, made of mud, in shape of a hillock, with a cavity at top ; in this the female lays generally two white eggs,[¶] of the size of those of a Goose, but more elongated. The hillock is of such a height as to admit of the bird's sitting on it conveniently, or rather standing, as the legs are placed one on each side at full length.[**] The young cannot fly till full grown, but run very fast.

" Flamingoes, for the most part, keep together in flocks, and now and then are seen in great numbers together, except in breeding time. Dampier mentions having, with two more in company, killed fourteen at once ; but this was effected by secreting themselves, for they are very shy birds, and will by no means suffer any one to approach, openly, near enough to shoot them.[††] Kolben observes, that they are very numerous at the Cape, keeping in the day on the borders of the lakes and rivers, and lodging themselves of nights in the long grass on the hills. They are also common to various places in the warmer parts of America, frequenting the same latitudes as in any other quarters of the world ; being met with in Peru, Chili, Cayenne,[‡‡] and the coast of Brazil, as well as the various islands of the West Indies. Sloane found them in Jamaica, but particularly at the Bahama Islands, and that of Cuba, where they breed. When seen at a distance, they

[*] In Zee Coow River. — *Philosophical Transactions.* Once plenty in the Isle of France. — *Voyage to Mauritius,* p. 66.
[†] About Valencia, in the Lake Albufere. — DILLON's *Travels,* p. 374.
[‡] RUSSEL's *Aleppo,* p. 69.
[§] *Decouv. Russ.* ii. p. 24.
[||] DAMPIER's *Voy.* i. p. 70.
[¶] They never lay more than three, and seldom fewer. — *Phil. Trans.*
[**] Sometimes will lay the eggs on a projecting part of a low rock, if it be placed sufficiently convenient, so as to admit of the legs being placed one on each side. — LINNÆUS.
[††] Davies talks of the gunner disguising himself in an ox hide, and, by this means, getting within gunshot. — *Hist. of Barbadoes,* p. 88.
[‡‡] Called there by the name of Tococo.

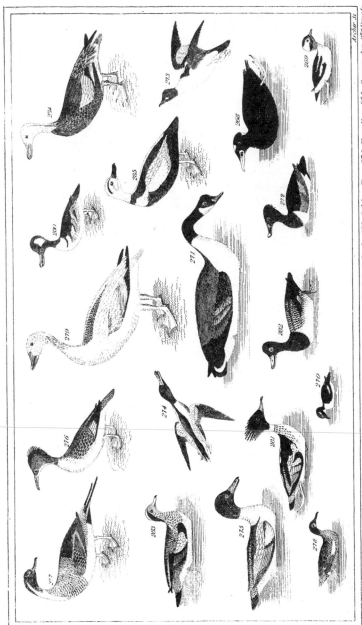

Archer Sc

268. Black or Surf Duck. 269. Buffel headed D. 270. Female. 271. Canada Goose. 272. Tufted Duck. 273. Golden Eye. 274. Shoveler. 275. Goosander. 276.Female. 277.Pin tail Duck. 278. Blue wing Teal. 279. Snew Goose. 280. Hooded or Crested Merganser. 281. Red breasted M. 282. Blue Bill or Scaup Duck. 283.Swer Widgeon.Male. 284. Female Snew Goose. 285. Pied Duck.

appear as a regiment of soldiers, being arranged alongside of one another, on the borders of the rivers, searching for food, which chiefly consists of small fish,* or the eggs of them, and of water insects, which they search after by plunging in the bill and part of the head ; from time to time trampling with their feet to muddy the water, that their prey may be raised from the bottom. In feeding, are said to twist the neck in such a manner, that the upper part of the bill is applied to the ground ;† during this, one of them is said to stand sentinel, and the moment he sounds the alarm, the whole flock take wing. This bird, when at rest, stands on one leg, the other being drawn up close to the body, with the head placed under the wing on that side of the body it stands on.

"The flesh of these birds is esteemed pretty good meat, and the young thought, by some, equal to that of a partridge ;‡ but the greatest dainty is the tongue, which was esteemed by the ancients an exquisite morsel.§ Are sometimes caught young, and brought up tame ; but are ever impatient of cold, and in this state will seldom live a great while, gradually losing their color, flesh, and appetite ; and dying for want of that food, which, in a state of nature at large, they were abundantly supplied with."

BLACK, OR SURF DUCK.— ANAS PERSPICILLATA.—
Fig. 268. — Male.

La grande Macreuse de la Baye de Hudson, *Briss.* vi. 425, 30. — La Macreuse à large bec, *Buff.* ix. p. 244. *Pl. enl.* 995. — *Edw.* pl. 155. — *Lath. Syn.* iii. p. 479. — *Phil. Trans.* lxii. p. 417. — *Peale's Museum,* No. 2788 ; female, 2789.

OIDEMIA PERSPICILLATA. — Stephens.

Oidemia perspicillata, *Steph. Cont. Sh. Gen. Zool.* xii. p. 219. — Oidemia, subgen. Fuligula perspicillata, *Bonap. Synop.* p. 389. — Oidemia perspicillata, *North. Zool.* ii. p. 449. — *Jard. and Selby, Illust. of Ornith.* pl. 138.

THIS Duck is peculiar to America,|| and altogether confined to the shores and bays of the sea, particularly where the waves roll over the sandy beach. Their food consists principally of those small bivalve shell fish already described, spout fish, and others that lie in the sand

---

* Small shell-fish. — GESNER.
† LINNÆUS, BRISSON.
‡ Commonly fat, and accounted delicate. — DAVIES's *Hist. of Barbadoes,* p. 88. The inhabitants of Provence always throw away the flesh, as it tastes fishy, and only make use of the feathers as ornaments to other birds at particular entertainments. — DILLON's *Travels,* p. 374.
§ See PLIN. ix. cap. 48.
|| One or two instances of this bird being killed on the shores of Great Britain have occurred ; and, as an occasional visitant, it will be figured in the concluding Number of Mr. Selby's *Illustrations of British Ornithology.* It is also occasionally met with on the continent of Europe, but generally in high latitudes, and, though unfrequent elsewhere, it is not entirely confined to America. — ED.

near its surface. For these they dive almost constantly, both in the sandy bays and amidst the tumbling surf. They seldom or never visit the salt marshes. They continue on our shores during the winter, and leave us early in May, for their breeding places in the north. Their skins are remarkably strong, and their flesh coarse, tasting of fish. They are shy birds, not easily approached, and are common in winter along the whole coast, from the River St. Lawrence to Florida.

The length of this species is twenty inches; extent, thirty-two inches; the bill is yellowish red, elevated at the base, and marked on the side of the upper mandible with a large, square patch of black, preceded by another space of a pearl color; the part of the bill thus marked swells, or projects, considerably from the common surface; the nostrils are large and pervious; the sides of the bill, broadly serrated, or toothed; both mandibles are furnished with a nail at the extremity; irides, white, or very pale cream; whole plumage, a shining black, marked on the crown and hind head with two triangular spaces of pure white; the plumage on both these spots is shorter and thinner than the rest; legs and feet, blood red; membrane of the webbed feet, black; the primary quills are of a deep dusky brown.

On dissection, the gullet was found to be gradually enlarged to the gizzard, which was altogether filled with broken shell fish. There was a singular hard expansion at the commencement of the windpipe, and another much larger, about three quarters of an inch above where it separates into the two lobes of the lungs; this last was larger than a Spanish hazel nut, flat on one side, and convex on the other. The protuberance on each side of the bill communicated with the nostril, and was hollow. All these were probably intended to contain supplies of air for the bird's support while under water; the last may also protect the head from the sharp edges of the shells.

The female is altogether of a sooty brown, lightest about the neck; the prominences on the bill are scarcely observable, and its color dusky.

This species was also found by Captain Cook, at Nootka Sound, on the north-west coast of America.

BUFFEL–HEADED DUCK. — ANAS ALBEOLA. — Fig. 269, Male; Fig. 270, Female.

Le Sarselle de Louisiane, *Briss.* vi. p. 461, pl. 41, fig. 1. — Le petit Canard à grosse tête, *Buff.* ix. p. 249. — *Edwards*, ii. p. 100. — *Catesby*, i. 95. — *Lath. Syn.* iii. p. 533. — A. bucephala, *id.* p. 121, No. 21; A. rustica, *id.* p. 524, No. 24. — *Peale's Museum*, No. 2730; female, 2731.

CLANGULA ALBEOLA. — Boie.

Fuligula albeola, *Bonap. Synop.* p. 394. — Clangula albeola, *North. Zool.* ii. p. 458.

THIS pretty little species, usually known by the name of the Butter-Box, or Butter-Ball, is common to the sea-shores, rivers, and lakes of the United States, in every quarter of the country, during autumn and winter. About the middle of April, or early in May, they retire to the north to breed. They are dexterous divers, and fly with extraordinary velocity. So early as the latter part of February, the males are observed to have violent disputes for the females. At this time they are more commonly seen in flocks, but, during the preceding part of winter, they usually fly in pairs. Their note is a short *quak*. They feed much on shell fish, shrimps, &c. They are sometimes exceedingly fat, though their flesh is inferior to many others for the table. The male exceeds the female in size, and greatly in beauty of plumage.

The Buffel-headed Duck, or rather, as it has originally been, the Buffalo-headed Duck, from the disproportionate size of its head, is fourteen inches long, and twenty-three inches in extent; the bill is short, and of a light blue, or leaden color; the plumage of the head and half of the neck is thick, long, and velvety, projecting greatly over the lower part of the neck; this plumage on the forehead and nape is rich glossy green, changing into a shining purple on the crown and sides of the neck; from the eyes backward passes a broad band of pure white; iris of the eye, dark; back, wings, and part of the scapulars, black; rest of the scapulars, lateral band along the wing, and whole breast, snowy white; belly, vent, and tail-coverts, dusky white; tail, pointed, and of a hoary color.

The female is considerably less than the male, and entirely destitute of the tumid plumage of the head; the head, neck, and upper parts of the body, and wings, are sooty black, darkest on the crown; side of the head, marked with a small, oblong spot of white; bill, dusky; lower part of the neck, ash, tipped with white; belly, dull white; vent, cinereous; outer edges of six of the secondaries and their incumbent coverts, white, except the tips of the latter, which are black; legs and feet, a livid blue; tail, hoary brown; length of the intestines, three feet six inches; stomach, filled with small shell fish. This is the Spirit Duck of Pennant, so called from its dexterity in diving, (*Arctic Zoology*, No. 487;) likewise the Little Brown Duck of Catesby, (*Natural History of Carolina*, pl. 98.)

This species is said to come into Hudson's Bay, about Severn River, in June, and make their nests in trees in the woods near ponds.* The young males, during the first year, are almost exactly like the females in color.

* LATHAM.

48 *

CANADA GOOSE. — ANAS CANADENSIS. — Fɪɢ. 271.

L'Oye savage de Canada, *Briss.* vi. p. 272, 4. pl. 26. — L'Oie à cravatte, *Buff.* ix. p. 82. — *Edw.* pl. 151. — *Arct. Zool.* No. 471. — *Catesby*, i. pl. 92. — *Lath. Syn.* iii. p. 450. — *Peale's Museum*, No. 2704.

ANSER CANADENSIS. — Vɪᴇɪʟʟᴏᴛ.*

Bernicla Canadensis, *Boie.* — Anser Canadensis, *Bonap. Synop.* p. 377. — *North. Zool.* ii. p. 468. — L. Outarde, *French Canadians.* — Bustard, *Hudson's Bay Settlers.*

Tʜɪs is the Common Wild Goose of the United States, universally known over the whole country ; whose regular periodical migrations are the sure signals of returning spring, or approaching winter. The tracts of their vast migratory journeys are not confined to the sea-coast or its vicinity. In their aërial voyages to and from the north, these winged pilgrims pass over the interior, on both sides of the mountains, as far west, at least, as the Osage River ; and I have never yet visited any quarter of the country where the inhabitants are not familiarly acquainted with the regular passing and repassing of the Wild Geese. The general opinion here is, that they are on their way to the lakes to breed ; but the inhabitants on the confines of the great lakes that separate us from Canada, are equally ignorant with ourselves of the particular breeding places of those birds. There, their journey north is but commencing ; and how far it extends it is impossible for us, at present, to ascertain, from our little acquaintance with these frozen regions. They were seen by Hearne, in large flocks, within the arctic circle, and were then pursuing their way still farther north. Captain Phipps speaks of seeing Wild Geese feeding at the water's edge on the dreary coast of Spitzbergen, in lat. 80° 27′. It is highly probable that they extend their migrations under the very pole itself, amid the silent desolation of unknown countries, shut out since creation from the prying eye of man by everlasting and insuperable barriers of ice.

---

* The appellation *"Geese"* will mark, in a general way, the birds and form to which *Anser* should be generically applied. They are all of large size, possess in part the gait of a gallinaceous bird, are gregarious, except during the breeding season, mostly migratory, and are formed more for extensive flight than for the life of a truly aquatic feeding and diving bird. Most of them, during winter, at times, leave the sea or lakes, and feed on the pastures, or, when to be had, on the newly-sprung grains, while some feed entirely on aquatic plants and animals. The Canada Goose is easily domesticated, and it is probable that most of the specimens killed in Great Britain have escaped from preserves ; it is found, however, on the Continent of Europe, and stragglers may occasionally occur.

On the beautiful piece of water at Gosford House, the seat of the Earl of Wemyss, Haddingtonshire, this and many other water birds rear their young freely. I have never seen any artificial piece of water so beautifully adapted for the domestication and introduction of every kind of water fowl which will bear the climate of Great Britain. Of very large extent, it is embossed in beautiful shrubbery, perfectly recluse, and, even in the nearly constant observance of a resident family, several exotic species seem to look on it as their own. The Canada and Egyptian Geese both had young when I visited it, and the lovely *Anas (Dendronessa) sponsa* seemed as healthy as if in her native waters. — Eᴅ.

That such places abound with their suitable food, we cannot for a moment doubt, while the absence of their great destroyer, man, and the splendors of a perpetual day, may render such regions the most suitable for their purpose.

Having fulfilled the great law of nature, the approaching rigors of that dreary climate oblige these vast, congregated flocks to steer for the more genial regions of the south. And no sooner do they arrive at those countries of the earth inhabited by man than carnage and slaughter is commenced on their ranks. The English at Hudson's Bay, says Pennant, depend greatly on Geese, and, in favorable years, kill three or four thousand, and barrel them up for use. They send out their servants, as well as Indians, to shoot these birds on their passage. It is in vain to pursue them; they therefore form a row of huts, made of boughs, at musket-shot distance from each other, and place them in a line across the vast marshes of the country. Each stand, or hovel, as it is called, is occupied by only a single person. These attend the flight of the birds, and, on their approach, mimic their cackle so well that the Geese will answer, and wheel, and come nearer the stand. The sportsman keeps motionless, and on his knees, with his gun cocked the whole time, and never fires till he has seen the eyes of the Geese. He fires as they are going from him; then picks up another gun that lies by him, and discharges that. The Geese which he has killed he sets upon sticks, as if alive, to decoy others; he also makes artificial birds for the same purpose. In a good day, — for they fly in very uncertain and unequal numbers, — a single Indian will kill two hundred. Notwithstanding every species of Goose has a different call, yet the Indians are admirable in their imitations of every one. The autumnal flight lasts from the middle of August to the middle of October; those which are taken in this season, when the frosts begin, are preserved in their feathers, and left to be frozen for the fresh provisions of the winter stock. The feathers constitute an article of commerce, and are sent to England.

The vernal flight of the Geese lasts from the middle of April until the middle of May. Their first appearance coincides with the thawing of the swamps, when they are very lean. Their arrival from the south is impatiently attended; it is the harbinger of the spring, and the month named by the Indians the Goose moon. They appear usually at their settlements about St. George's day, O. S., and fly northward, to nestle in security. They prefer islands to the continent, as farther from the haunts of man.*

After such prodigious havock as thus appears to be made among these birds, and their running the gantlet, if I may so speak, for many hundreds of miles through such destructive fires, no wonder they should have become more scarce, as well as shy, by the time they reach the shores of the United States.

Their first arrival on the coast of New Jersey is early in October, and their first numerous appearance is the sure prognostic of severe weather. Those which continue all winter frequent the shallow bays and marsh islands; their principal food being the broad, tender, green leaves of a marine plant which grows on stones and shells, and is

---

* *Arctic Zoology.*

usually called sea cabbage; and also the roots of the sedge, which they are frequently observed in the act of tearing up. Every few days, they make an excursion to the inlets on the beach for gravel. They cross, indiscriminately, over land or water, generally taking the nearest course to their object; differing, in this respect, from the Brant, which will often go a great way round by water, rather than cross over the land. They swim well; and, if wing-broken, dive, and go a long way under water, causing the sportsman a great deal of fatigue before he can kill them. Except in very calm weather, they rarely sleep on the water, but roost all night in the marshes. When the shallow bays are frozen, they seek the mouths of inlets near the sea, occasionally visiting the air-holes in the ice; but these bays are seldom so completely frozen as to prevent them from feeding on the bars.

The flight of the Wild Geese is heavy and laborious, generally in a straight line, or in two lines approximating to a point, thus, ▷; in both cases, the van is led by an old gander, who, every now and then, pipes his well-known *honk*, as if to ask how they come on, and the honk of " All's well " is generally returned by some of the party. Their course is in a straight line, with the exception of the undulations of their flight. When bewildered in foggy weather, they appear sometimes to be in great distress, flying about in an irregular manner, and for a considerable time over the same quarter, making a great clamor. On these occasions, should they approach the earth and alight, which they sometimes do, to rest and recollect themselves, the only hospitality they meet with is death and destruction from a whole neighborhood already in arms for their ruin.

Wounded Geese have, in numerous instances, been completely domesticated, and readily pair with the tame Gray Geese. The offspring are said to be larger than either; but the characteristic marks of the Wild Goose still predominate. The gunners on the sea-shore have long been in the practice of taming the wounded of both sexes, and have sometimes succeeded in getting them to pair and produce. The female always seeks out the most solitary place for her nest, not far from the water. On the approach of every spring, however, these birds discover symptoms of great uneasiness, frequently looking up into the air, and attempting to go off. Some, whose wings have been closely cut, have travelled on foot in a northern direction, and have been found at the distance of several miles from home. They hail every flock that passes overhead, and the salute is sure to be returned by the voyagers, who are only prevented from alighting among them by the presence and habitations of man. The gunners take one or two of these domesticated Geese with them to those parts of the marshes over which the wild ones are accustomed to fly; and, concealing themselves within gunshot, wait for a flight, which is no sooner perceived by the decoy Geese, than they begin calling aloud, until the whole flock approaches so near as to give them an opportunity of discharging two, and sometimes three, loaded muskets among it, by which great havock is made.

The Wild Goose, when in good order, weighs from ten to twelve, and sometimes fourteen pounds. They are sold in the Philadelphia markets at from seventy-five cents to one dollar each; and are estimated to yield half a pound of feathers apiece, which produces twenty-five or thirty cents more.

The Canada Goose is now domesticated in numerous quarters of the country, and is remarked for being extremely watchful, and more sensible of approaching changes in the atmosphere than the Common Gray Goose. In England, France, and Germany, they have also been long ago domesticated. Buffon, in his account of this bird, observes, " Within these few years, many hundreds inhabited the great canal at Versailles, where they breed familiarly with the Swans; they were oftener on the grassy margins than in the water;" and adds, " There is at present a great number of them on the magnificent pools that decorate the charming gardens of Chantilly." Thus has America already added to the stock of domestic fowls two species, the Turkey and the Canada Goose, superior to most in size, and inferior to none in usefulness; for it is acknowledged by an English naturalist, of good observation, that this last species " is as familiar, breeds as freely, and is in every respect as valuable as the Common Goose." *

The strong disposition of the wounded Wild Geese to migrate to the north in spring, has been already taken notice of. Instances have occurred where, their wounds having healed, they have actually succeeded in mounting into the higher regions of the air, and joined a passing party to the north; and, extraordinary as it may appear, I am well assured by the testimony of several respectable persons, who have been eye-witnesses to the fact, that they have been also known to return again in the succeeding autumn to their former habitation. These accounts are strongly corroborated by a letter which I some time ago received from an obliging correspondent at New York; which I shall here give at large, permitting him to tell his story in his own way, and conclude my history of this species : —

" Mr. Platt, a respectable farmer on Long Island, being out shooting in one of the bays, which, in that part of the country, abound with water-fowl, wounded a Wild Goose. Being wing-tipped, and unable to fly, he caught it, and brought it home alive. It proved to be a female ; and, turning it into his yard, with a flock of tame Geese, it soon became quite tame and familiar, and in a little time its wounded wing entirely healed. In the following spring, when the Wild Geese migrate to the northward, a flock passed over Mr. Platt's barn-yard; and, just at that moment, their leader happening to sound his bugle note, our Goose, in whom its new habits and enjoyments had not quite extinguished the love of liberty, and remembering the well-known sound, spread its wings, mounted into the air, joined the travellers, and soon disappeared. In the succeeding autumn, the Wild Geese, as was usual, returned from the northward in great numbers, to pass the winter in our bays and rivers. Mr. Platt happened to be standing in his yard when a flock passed directly over his barn. At that instant, he observed three Geese detach themselves from the rest, and, after wheeling round several times, alight in the middle of the yard. Imagine his surprise and pleasure, when, by certain well-remembered signs, he recognized in one of the three his long-lost fugitive. It was she indeed ! She had travelled many hundred miles to

* BEWICK, vol. ii. p. 255.

the lakes; had there hatched and reared her offspring; and had now returned with her little family, to share with them the sweets of civilized life.

" The truth of the foregoing relation can be attested by many respectable people, to whom Mr. Platt has related the circumstances as above detailed. The birds were all living, and in his possession, about a year ago, and had shown no disposition whatever to leave him."

The length of this species is three feet; extent, five feet two inches; the bill is black; irides, dark hazel; upper half of the neck, black, marked on the chin and lower part of the head with a large patch of white, its distinguishing character; lower part of the neck before, white; back and wing-coverts, brown, each feather tipped with whitish; rump and tail, black; tail-coverts and vent, white; primaries, black, reaching to the extremity of the tail; sides, pale ashy brown; legs and feet, blackish ash.

The male and female are exactly alike in plumage.

TUFTED DUCK. — ANAS FULIGULA. — Fig. 272. — Male.

FULIGULA RUFITORQUES. — Bonaparte.

Fuligula rufitorques, *Bonap. Journ. Acad. Nat. Sc. Phil.* — *Synop.* p. 393. — *North. Zool.* ii. p. 453.

This is an inhabitant of both continents; it frequents fresh-water rivers, and seldom visits the sea-shore. It is a plump, short-bodied Duck; its flesh generally tender and well tasted. They are much rarer than most of our other species, and are seldom seen in market. They are most common about the beginning of winter, and early in the spring. Being birds of passage, they leave us entirely during the summer.

The Tufted Duck is seventeen inches long, and two feet two inches in extent; the bill is broad, and of a dusky color, sometimes marked round the nostrils and sides with light blue; head, crested, or tufted, as its name expresses, and of a black color, with reflections of purple; neck, marked near its middle by a band of deep chestnut; lower part of the neck, black, which spreads quite round to the back; back and scapulars, black, minutely powdered with particles of white, not to be observed but on a near inspection; rump and vent, also black; wings, ashy brown; secondaries, pale ash, or bluish white; tertials, black, reflecting green; lower part of the breast and whole belly, white; flanks crossed with fine zigzag lines of dusky; tail, short, rounded, and of a dull brownish black; legs and feet, greenish ash; webs, black; irides, rich orange; stomach filled with gravel and some vegetable food.

In young birds, the head and upper part of the neck are purplish brown; in some, the chestnut ring on the fore part of the middle of the neck is obscure, in others very rich and glossy, and in one or two specimens which I have seen, it is altogether wanting. The back is in some instances destitute of the fine powdered particles of white, while in others these markings are large, and thickly interspersed.

The specimen from which Fig. 272 was taken, was shot on the Delaware, on the 10th of March, and presented to me by Dr. S. B. Smith of this city. On dissection it proved to be a male, and was exceeding fat and tender. Almost every specimen I have since met with has been in nearly the same state; so that I cannot avoid thinking this species equal to most others for the table, and greatly superior to many.

GOLDEN-EYE. — ANAS CLANGULA. — Fig. 273. — Male.

Le Garrot, *Briss.* vi. p. 416, pl. 37. fig. 2. — *Buff.* ix. p. 222. — *Arct. Zool.* No. 486. — *Lath. Syn.* iii. p. 535.

CLANGULA VULGARIS. — Fleming.*

Clangula vulgaris, *Flem. Br. Anim.* p. 120. — *North. Zool.* ii. p. 454. — Fuligula clangula, *Bonap. Synop.* p. 393. — Sub-gen. Clangula.

This Duck is well known in Europe, and in various regions of the United States, both along the sea-coast and about the lakes and rivers of the interior. It associates in small parties, and may easily be known by the vigorous whistling of its wings as it passes through the

* The Golden-Eye is found on both continents, and in the northern parts of Europe during winter, is one of the most common migratory Ducks. The Garrots are distinguished by a short, stout, and compact body; the neck, short; the head, large, and apparently more so from its thick plumage; the bill, short, but thick, and raised at the base; the feet, placed far behind, and formed for swimming. The flight is short and rapid. In habit, they delight more in lakes and rivers than the sea; are generally found in small flocks; are very clamorous during the breeding season, and feed on fish, aquatic insects, molluscæ, &c. Richardson says, *Clangula vulgaris* and *albeola* frequent the rivers and fresh-water lakes throughout the Fur Countries, in great numbers. They are by no means shy, allowing the sportsman to approach sufficiently near; but dive so dexterously at the flash of the gun, or the twanging of a bow, and are consequently so difficult to kill, that the natives say they are endowed with some supernatural power. Hence their appellation of "conjuring," or "spirit Ducks."

In Britain, they are winter visitants, assembling in small parties on the lakes and rivers. On the latter they may be generally found near the head or foot of the stream, diving incessantly for the spawn of salmon, with which I have often found their stomach filled. The party generally consists of from four to ten, and they dive together. At this time, it is not very difficult to approach them, by running forward while they are under water, and squatting when they rise. I have often, in this way, come to the very edge of the river, and awaited the arising of the flock. When taken by surprise, they dive on the instant of the first shot, but rise and fly immediately after.

The young of the first year has been made a nominal species, and is somewhat like the adult females, but always distinguished by larger size, darker color of the plumage of the head, and the greater proportion of white on the wings. The males have the white spot on the cheek perceptible about the first spring, and the other parts of the plumage proportionally distinct. Among most of the flocks which visit our rivers in winter, it is rare to find more than one full-plumaged male in each;

air. It swims and dives well, but seldom walks on shore, and then in a waddling, awkward manner. Feeding chiefly on shell fish, small fry, &c., their flesh is less esteemed than that of the preceding. In the United States they are only winter visitors, leaving us again in the month of April, being then on their passage to the north to breed. They are said to build, like the Wood Duck, in hollow trees.

The Golden-Eye is nineteen inches long, and twenty-nine in extent, and weighs on an average about two pounds; the bill is black, short, rising considerably up in the forehead; the plumage of the head and part of the neck is somewhat tumid, and of a dark green, with violet reflections, marked near the corner of the mouth with an oval spot of white; the irides are golden yellow; rest of the neck, breast, and whole lower parts, white, except the flanks, which are dusky; back and wings, black; over the latter a broad bed of white extends from the middle of the lesser coverts to the extremity of the secondaries; the exterior scapulars are also white; tail, hoary brown; rump and tail-coverts, black; legs and toes, reddish orange; webs, very large, and of a dark purplish brown; hind toe and exterior edge of the inner one, broadly finned; sides of the bill, obliquely dentated; tongue, covered above with a fine, thick, velvety down, of a whitish color.

The full-plumaged female is seventeen inches in length, and twenty-seven inches in extent; bill, brown, orange near the tip; head and part of the neck, brown, or very dark drab, bounded below by a ring of white; below that the neck is ash, tipped with white; rest of the lower parts, white; wings dusky, six of the secondaries and their greater coverts, pure white, except the tips of the last, which are touched with dusky spots; rest of the wing-coverts, cinereous, mixed with whitish; back and scapulars, dusky, tipped with brown; feet, dull orange; across the vent, a band of cinerous; tongue, covered with the same velvety down as the male.

The young birds of the first season very much resemble the females, but may generally be distinguished by the white spot, or at least its rudiments, which marks the corner of the mouth. Yet, in some cases, even this is variable, both old and young male birds occasionally wanting the spot.

From an examination of many individuals of this species of both sexes, I have very little doubt that the Morillon of English writers

---

sometimes not more than two or three are seen during the winter among fifty or sixty immature birds.

The American Ducks belonging to this group are *C. vulgaris albeola* and *C. Barrovii*, or Rocky Mountain Garrot, a new species, discovered by the overland Arctic expedition, and described and figured in the *Northern Zoology*. The following is the description; it has only yet been found in the valleys of the Rocky Mountains.

" Notwithstanding the general similarity in the form and markings of this bird, and the Common Golden-Eye, the difference in their bills evidently points them out to be a distinct species. The Rocky Mountain Garrot is distinguished by the pure color of its dorsal plumage, and the smaller portion of white on its wings and scapulars; its long flank feathers are also much more broadly bordered all round with black. The bases of the greater coverts in the Golden-Eye are black; but they are concealed, and do not form the black band so conspicuous in this species." The total length of a male brought home by the expedition was twenty-two inches in length. — ED.

(*Anas glaucion*) is nothing more than the young male of the Golden-Eye.

The conformation of the trachea, or windpipe, of the male of this species, is singular: Nearly about its middle it swells out to at least five times its common diameter, the concentric hoops or rings, of which this part is formed, falling obliquely into one another when the windpipe is relaxed; but when stretched, this part swells out to its full size, the rings being then drawn apart; this expansion extends for about three inches; three more below this, it again forms itself into a hard, cartilaginous shell, of an irregular figure, and nearly as large as a walnut; from the bottom of this labyrinth, as it has been called, the trachea branches off to the two lobes of the lungs; that branch which goes to the left lobe being three times the diameter of the right. The female has nothing of all this. The intestines measure five feet in length, and are large and thick.

I have examined many individuals of this species, of both sexes and in various stages of color, and can therefore affirm, with certainty, that the foregoing descriptions are correct. Europeans have differed greatly in their accounts of this bird, from finding males in the same garb as the females, and other full-plumaged males destitute of the spot of white on the cheek; but all these individuals bear such evident marks of belonging to one peculiar species, that no judicious naturalist, with all these varieties before him, can long hesitate to pronounce them the same.

SHOVELLER.—ANAS CLYPEATA.—Fig. 274.—Male.

Le Souchet, *Briss.* vi. p. 329, 6, pl. 32, fig. 1.—*Buff.* ix. 191.—*Pl. enl.* 971. — *Arct. Zool.* No. 485.—*Catesby,* i. pl. 96; female. — *Lath. Syn* .iii. p. 509.— *Peale's Museum,* No. 2734.

ANAS CLYPEATA.—Linnæus.*

Anas platyrhynchas, *Raii Synop.* p. 144.—Rynchaspis clypeata, *Leach.* — *Shaw's Zool.* — *Steph. Cont.* xii. 115, pl. 48.—Spathulea clypeata, *Flem. Brit. Anim.* i. 123.—Anas clypeata, *Lath. Ind. Ornith.* ii. p. 856.—Shoveller, *Mont. Ornith. Dict.* and *Sup.* — *Bew.* ii. 345.—*Selby, m. and f. Illust.* pl. 48.—Canard souchet, *Tem. Man.* ii. p. 842. — Anas clypeata, *Bonap. Synop.* p. 382. — *North. Zool.* ii. p. 439.

IF we except the singularly-formed and disproportionate size of the bill, there are few Ducks more beautiful or more elegantly marked

---

* Mr. Swainson, according to his views that the typical group should hold the typical name of the family, has restricted *Anas* (in that sense) to the Shovellers. In fixing upon the typical representation of any large family, that gentleman goes upon the principle of taking the organ most peculiarly important to the whole, and selects that subordinate, or rather primary group, wherein that organ is most fully developed. Thus, in the Ducks, he remarks there is nothing peculiar in diving, or living, both on land and water, or endowments for rapid flight, for many others possess like powers; but when we examine the dilated and softly-textured bill, and more particularly the fine laminæ on the edges, we are struck with a formation at variance with our accustomed ideas of that member, and at once think that it must be applied to something equally peculiar in their economy. We shall thus be war-

than this. The excellence of its flesh, which is uniformly juicy, tender, and well tasted, is another recommendation to which it is equally entitled. It occasionally visits the sea-coast, but is more commonly found on our lakes and rivers, particularly along their muddy shores, where it spends great part of its time in searching for small worms, and the larvæ of insects, sifting the watery mud through the long and finely-set teeth of its curious bill, which is admirably constructed for the purpose, being large, to receive a considerable quantity of matter, each mandible bordered with close-set, pectinated rows, exactly resembling those of a weaver's reed, which, fitting into each other, form a kind of sieve, capable of retaining very minute worms, seeds, or insects, which constitute the principal food of the bird.

The Shoveller visits us only in the winter, and is not known to breed in any part of the United States. It is a common bird of Europe, and, according to M. Baillon, the correspondent of Buffon, breeds yearly in the marshes in France. The female is said to make her nest on the ground, with withered grass, in the midst of the largest tufts of rushes or coarse herbage, in the most inaccessible part of the slaky marsh, and lays ten or twelve pale rust colored eggs; the young, as soon as hatched, are conducted to the water by the parent birds. They are said to be at first very shapeless and ugly, for the bill is then as broad as the body, and seems too great a weight for the little bird to carry. Their plumage does not acquire its full colors until after the second moult.

The Blue-winged Shoveller is twenty inches long, and two feet six inches in extent; the bill is brownish black, three inches in length, greatly widened near the extremity, closely pectinated on the sides, and furnished with a nail on the tip of each mandible; irides, bright orange; tongue, large and fleshy; the inside of the upper and outside of the lower mandible are grooved, so as to receive distinctly the long, separated, reedlike teeth; there is also a gibbosity in the two mandibles, which do not meet at the sides, and this vacuity is occupied by the sifters just mentioned; head and upper half of the neck, glossy, changeable green; rest of the neck and breast, white, passing round and nearly meeting above; whole belly, dark reddish chestnut; flanks, a brownish yellow, pencilled traversely with black, between which and the vent, which is black, is a band of white; back, blackish brown; exterior edges of the scapulars, white; lesser wing-coverts, and some of the tertials, a fine light sky blue; beauty spot on the wing, a

ranted in taking the bill as our criterion, and those birds where we find its structure most fully developed for the type. These are most decidedly to be seen in the Shovellers, a group containing, as yet, only three or four known species; in them we have the utmost dilatation of the bill towards its apex, and the laminæ upon its edges, and long and remarkably delicate. The bird itself possesses a powerful flight, and is a most expert diver and swimmer, but seems to prefer inland lakes or fens to the more open seas and rivers.

To this group will belong the curious Pink-eared Shoveller, from New Holland, remarkable from the tooth-like membrane projecting from the angles of the bill, and differing somewhat from the others in its brown and dusky plumage. Mr. Swainson has formed on account of this membrane a sub-genus, *malacorhynchus*, but in which I am hardly yet prepared to coincide.

It may be mentioned here, that the only birds which possess the lamellated structure of the upper mandible is *pachyptila*, a genus coming near to the Peterels, and *phœnicopterus* of Flamingo. — ED.

changeable, resplendent bronze green, bordered above by a band of white, and below with another of velvety black; rest of the wing, dusky, some of the tertials streaked down their middles with white; tail, dusky, pointed, broadly edged with white; legs and feet, reddish orange, hind toe not finned.

With the above another was shot, which differed in having the breast spotted with dusky, and the back with white; the green plumage of the head intermixed with gray, and the belly with circular touches of white, evidently a young male in its imperfect plumage.

The female has the crown of a dusky brown; rest of the head and neck, yellowish white, thickly spotted with dark brown; these spots on the breast become larger, and crescent shaped; back and scapulars, dark brown, edged and centred with yellow ochre; belly, slightly rufous, mixed with white; wing, nearly as in the male.

On dissection, the labyrinth in the windpipe of the male was found to be small; the trachea itself, seven inches long; the intestines, nine feet nine inches in length, and about the thickness of a crow quill.

GOOSANDER. — MERGUS MERGANSER. — Fig. 275. — Male.

L'Harle, *Briss.* vi. p. 231, 1, pl. 22. — *Buff.* viii. p. 267, pl. 23. — *Arct. Zool.* 465. — *Lath. Syn.* iii. p. 418. — *Peale's Museum*, No. 2932.

MERGUS MERGANSER. — Linnæus.*

Goosander, or Merganser, *Mont. Ornith. Dict. and Supp.* — *Bew. Br. Birds*, ii. p. 254. — *Selby's Illust.* pl. 57. — Mergus merganser, *Bonap. Synop.* p. 397. — *Flem. Br. Anim.* p. 123. — Grande harle, *Temm. Man. d'Ornith.* ii. 881.

This large and handsomely-marked bird belongs to a genus different from that of the Duck, on account of the particular form and serra-

* The genus *Mergus* has been universally allowed. It contains nine or ten species, allied in their general form, but easily distinguished by their plumage. They are truly aquatic, and never quit the sea or lakes except for a partial repose or pluming, or during the time of incubation. Their food is entirely fish, and they are necessarily expert divers; the bill is lengthened and narrow, its edges regularly serrated with recurved points. The breeding places of many of them are yet unknown, but I believe that the greater proportion at that season retire inland to the more sequestered lakes. I am also of opinion that the male forsakes his mate so soon as she begins to sit, about which time he also loses the beautiful crest and plumage in which he is clothed during winter and spring, and assumes a duller garb. The males are remarkable for their difference from the other sex, whence the long-disputed point, now satisfactorily proved, of this and the following bird being different. That of the male is generally black, or glossy green, contrasted with the purest white, or rich shades of tawny yellow; that of the females, the chaster grays and browns. Both are furnished with crests, composed of loose, hackled feathers.

The distribution of the group seems to be European, and both continents of America. I have seen none from India or New Holland, though from the former country they might be expected.

The Goosander is a native of both continents, and is said to breed in the northern parts of Scotland. This I have had no opportunity of verifying. It is frequent during winter on the larger rivers, in flocks of seven or eight, in which there is

tures of its bill. The genus is characterized as follows: — "Bill, toothed, slender, cylindrical, hooked at the point; nostrils, small, oval, placed in the middle of the bill; feet, four-toed, the outer toe longest." Naturalists have denominated it *Merganser.* In this country, the birds composing this genus are generally known by the name of Fisherman, or Fisher Ducks. The whole number of known species amount to only nine or ten, dispersed through various quarters of the world; of these, four species, of which the present is the largest, are known to inhabit the United States.

From the common habit of these birds in feeding almost entirely on fin and shell fish, their flesh is held in little estimation, being often lean and rancid, both smelling and tasting strongly of fish; but such are the various peculiarities of tastes, that persons are not wanting who pretend to consider them capital meat.

The Goosander, called by some the Water Pheasant, and by others the Sheldrake, Fisherman, Diver, &c., is a winter inhabitant only of the sea-shores, fresh-water lakes, and rivers of the United States. They usually associate in small parties of six or eight, and are almost continually diving in search of food. In the month of April they disappear, and return again early in November. Of their particular place, and manner of breeding, we have no account. Mr. Pennant observes, that they continue the whole year in the Orkneys; and have been shot in the Hebrides, or Western Islands of Scotland, in summer. They are also found in Iceland and Greenland, and are said to breed there; some asserting that they build on trees; others, that they make their nests among the rocks.

The male of this species is twenty-six inches in length, and three feet three inches in extent; the bill, three inches long, and nearly one inch thick at the base, serrated on both mandibles; the upper overhanging at the tip, where each is furnished with a large nail; the ridge of the bill is black; the sides, crimson red; irides, red; head, crested, tumid, and of a black color, glossed with green, which extends nearly half way down the neck, the rest of which, with the breast and belly, are white, tinged with a delicate yellowish cream; back, and adjoining scapulars, black; primaries, and shoulder of the wing, brownish black; exterior part of the scapulars, lesser coverts, and tertials, white; secondaries, neatly edged with black; greater coverts, white; their upper halves, black, forming a bar on the wing; rest of the upper parts, and tail, brownish ash; legs and feet, the color of red sealing-wax; flanks, marked with fine, semicircular, dotted lines of deep brown; the tail extends about three inches beyond the wings.

This description was taken from a full-plumaged male. The young males, which are generally much more numerous than the old ones, so exactly resemble the females in their plumage for at least the first, and part of the second year, as scarcely to be distinguished from

generally only one, or, at most, two adult males — the others being in immature dress, or females; thus the latter is said to be the most common. They fish about the bottoms of the streams and pools, and, I believe, destroy many fish. I have taken seven trout, about four or five inches in length, from the stomach of a female.

In Hudson's Bay (according to Hearne) they are called Sheldrakes; the name by which they are also distinguished by the common people in all the rivers in the south of Scotland. — Ed.

them; and, what is somewhat singular, the crests of these and of the females are actually longer than those of the full-grown male, though thinner towards its extremities. These circumstances have induced some late ornithologists to consider them as two different species, the young, or female, having been called the Dun Diver. By this arrangement, they have entirely deprived the Goosander of his female; for, in the whole of my examinations and dissections of the present species, I have never yet found the female in his dress. What I consider as undoubtedly the true female of this species, is figured in No. 276. They were both shot in the month of April, in the same creek, unaccompanied by any other; and, on examination, the sexual parts of each were strongly and prominently marked. The windpipe of the female had nothing remarkable in it; that of the male had two very large expansions, which have been briefly described by Willoughby, who says — "It hath a large, bony labyrinth on the windpipe, just above the divarications; and the windpipe hath, besides, two swellings out, one above another, each resembling a powder puff." These labyrinths are the distinguishing characters of the males; and are always found, even in young males who have not yet thrown off the plumage of the female, as well as in the old ones. If we admit these Dun Divers to be a distinct species, we can find no difference between their pretended females and those of the Goosander, only one kind of female of this sort being known; and this is contrary to the usual analogy of the other three species, viz., the Red-breasted Merganser, the Hooded, and the Smew, all of whose females are well known, and bear the same comparative resemblance in color to their respective males, the length of crest excepted, as the female Goosander (Fig. 276) bears to him.

Having thought thus much necessary on this disputed point, I leave each to form his own opinion on the facts and reasoning produced.

FEMALE GOOSANDER. — Fig. 276.

Peale's Museum, No. 2933. — Dun Diver, *Lath. Syn.* iii. p. 240. — *Arct. Zool.* No. 465. — *Bewick's Brit. Birds*, ii. p. 23. — *Turt. Syst.* p. 335. — L'Harle femelle, *Briss.* vi. p. 236. — *Buff.* viii. p. 272. *Pl. enl.* 953.

MERGUS MERGANSER. — Linnæus.

Syn. of. Fem. or Young. Mergus castor, *Linn. Syst.* i. 209. — Merganser cinereus, *Briss. Orn.* vi. 254. — Dun Diver, or Sparling Fowl, *Mont. Bew.* &c. — Goosander Female, *Selby's Illust.* pl. LVII.

THIS generally measures an inch or two shorter than the male; the length of the present specimen was twenty-five inches; extent, thirty-five inches; bill, crimson on the sides, black above; irides, reddish; crested head and part of the neck, dark brown, lightest on the sides of the neck, where it inclines to a sorel color; chin and throat, white; the crest shoots out in long, radiating, flexible stripes;

49 *

upper part of the body, tail, and flanks, an ashy slate, tinged with brown; primaries, black; middle secondaries, white, forming a large speculum on the wing; greater coverts, black, tipped for half an inch with white; sides of the breast, from the sorel colored part of the neck downwards, very pale ash, with broad semicircular touches of white; belly and lower part of the breast, a fine yellowish cream color — a distinguishing trait also in the male; legs and feet, orange red.

PINTAIL DUCK. — ANAS ACUTA. — Fig. 277.

Le Canard à longue queue, *Briss.* vi. p. 369, 16, pl. 34, fig. 1, 2. — *Buff.* ix. p. 199, pl. 13. *Pl. enl.* 954. — *Arct. Zool.* No. 500. — *Lath. Syn.* iii. p. 526. — *Peale's Museum*, No. 2806.

DAFILA ACUTA. — Leach.*

Dafila caudacuta, *Shaw's Zool.* — *Steph. Cont.* xii. p. 127. — Canard à longue queue au pillet, *Temm. Man. d'Ornith.* ii. 838. — Pintail, *Mont.* — *Bew.* — *Selby's Illust.* pl. 42, m. — Anas acuta, *Cracker.* — *Flem. Br. Anim.* p. 124. — *Bonap. Synop.* p. 383. — Anas (dafila) caudacuta, *North. Zool.* ii. p. 441.

THE Pintail, or, as it is sometimes called, the Sprigtail, is a common and well-known Duck in our markets, much esteemed for the excellence of its flesh, and is generally in good order. It is a shy and cautious bird, feeds in the mud flats, and shallow fresh-water marshes; but rarely resides on the sea-coast. It seldom dives, is very noisy, and has a kind of chattering note. When wounded, they will sometimes dive, and, coming up, conceal themselves under the bow of the boat, moving round as it moves. Are vigilant in giving the alarm on the approach of the gunner, who often curses the watchfulness of the Sprigtail. Some Ducks, when aroused, disperse in different directions; but the Sprigtails, when alarmed, cluster confusedly together as they mount, and thereby afford the sportsman a fair opportunity of raking them with advantage. They generally leave the Delaware about the middle of March, on the way to their native regions, the north, where they are most numerous. They inhabit the whole northern parts of Europe and Asia, and, doubtless, the corresponding latitudes of America; are said, likewise, to be found in Italy. Great flocks of them are sometimes spread along the isles and shores of Scotland and Ireland, and on the interior lakes of both these countries.

* In this beautiful species we have the type of the sub-genus *Dafila*. In it the marginal laminæ begin to disappear, and the bill to assume what may be called a more regular outline, approaching to that of *A. boschas*, our wild and domestic breed. Another peculiarity is the development of the tail, which becomes much lengthened, whence the name of *Sea Pheasant*. In this country they are not very common, which may arise from their being more difficult to procure, by their frequenting the sea rather than any inland water; they are frequently taken, however, in decoys, and I once shot two feeding in the evening on a wet stubble field in company with the Common Wild Duck. — ED.

On the marshy shores of some of the bays of Lake Ontario, they are often plenty in the months of October and November. I have also met with them at Louisville, on the Ohio.

The Pintail Duck is twenty-six inches in length, and two feet ten inches in extent; the bill is a dusky lead color; irides, dark hazel; head and half of the neck, pale brown, each side of the neck marked with a band of purple violet, bordering the white; hind part of the upper half of the neck, black, bordered on each side by a stripe of white, which spreads over the lower part of the neck before; sides of the breast and upper part of the back, white, thickly and elegantly marked with transverse, undulating lines of black, here and there tinged with pale buff; throat and middle of the belly, white, tinged with cream; flanks, finely pencilled with waving lines; vent, white; under tail-coverts, black; lesser wing-coverts, brown ash; greater, the same, tipped with orange; below which is the speculum, or beauty spot, of rich, golden green, bordered below with a band of black, and another of white; primaries, dusky brown; tertials, long, black, edged with white, and tinged with rust; rump and tail-coverts, pale ash, centred with dark brown; tail, greatly pointed, the two middle tapering feathers being full five inches longer than the others, and black, the rest, brown ash, edged with white; legs, a pale lead color.

The female has the crown of a dark brown color; neck, of a dull brownish white, thickly speckled with dark brown; breast and belly, pale brownish white, interspersed with white; back, and root of the neck above, black, each feather elegantly waved with broad lines of brownish white — these wavings become rufous on the scapulars; vent, white, spotted with dark brown; tail, dark brown, spotted with white; the two middle tail-feathers half an inch longer than the others.

The Sprigtail is an elegantly formed, long bodied Duck, the neck longer and more slender than most others.

BLUE–WINGED TEAL. — ANAS DISCORS. — Fig. 278.

Le Sarcelle d'Amerique, *Briss.* vi. p. 452, 35. — *Buff.* ix. p. 279. *Pl. enl.* 966. — *Catesby*, i. pl. 100. — White-faced Duck, *Lath. Syn.* iii. p. 502. — *Arct. Zool.* No. 503. — *Peale's Museum*, No. 2846.

BOSCHAS? DISCORS. — Swainson.

Anas discors, *Cuv. Regn. Anim.* i. p. 539. — *Bonap. Synop.* p. 385. — Anas (boschas) discors. *Swain. Journ. Royal Inst.* No. iv. p. 22. — *North. Zool.* ii. p. 444

The Blue-winged Teal is the first of its tribe that returns to us in the autumn from its breeding place in the north. They are usually seen early in September, along the shores of the Delaware, where they sit on the mud close to the edge of the water, so crowded together that the gunners often kill great numbers at a single discharge. When a flock is discovered thus sitting and sunning themselves, the experienced gunner runs his batteau ashore at some distance below or above them, and, getting out, pushes her before him over the slippery mud, concealing himself all the while behind her: by this method he can sometimes approach within twenty yards of the flock, among which he generally makes great slaughter. They fly rapidly, and, when they alight, drop down suddenly, like the Snipe or Woodcock, among the reeds or on the mud. They feed chiefly on vegetable food, and are eagerly fond of the seeds of the reeds or wild oats. Their flesh is excellent, and, after their residence for a short time among the reeds, becomes very fat. As the first frosts come on, they proceed to the south, being a delicate bird, very susceptible of cold. They abound in the inundated rice-fields, in the Southern States, where vast numbers are taken in traps placed on small, dry eminences, that here and there rise above the water. These places are strowed with rice, and by the common contrivance called a *figure four*, they are caught alive in hollow traps. In the month of April they pass through Pennsylvania for the north, but make little stay at that season. I have observed them numerous on the Hudson opposite to the Katskill Mountains. They rarely visit the sea-shore.

This species measures about fourteen inches in length, and twenty-two inches in extent; the bill is long in proportion, and of a dark dusky slate; the front and upper part of the head are black; from the eye to the chin is a large crescent of white; the rest of the head and half the neck are of a dark slate, richly glossed with green and violet; remainder of the neck and breast is black or dusky, thickly marked with semicircles of brownish white, elegantly intersected with each other; belly, pale brown, barred with dusky, in narrow lines; sides and vent, the same tint, spotted with oval marks of dusky; flanks elegantly waved with large semicircles of pale brown; sides of the vent, pure white; under the tail-coverts, black; back, deep brownish black, each feather waved with large semi-ovals of brownish white; lesser wing-coverts, a bright light blue; primaries, dusky brown; secondaries, black; speculum, or beauty spot, rich green; tertials, edged with black or light blue, and streaked down their middle with white; the tail, which is pointed, extends two inches beyond the wings; legs and feet, yellow, the latter very small; the two crescents of white, before the eyes, meet on the throat.

The female differs in having the head and neck of a dull dusky slate, instead of the rich violet of the male; the hind head is also whitish; the wavings on the back and lower parts, more indistinct; wing, nearly the same in both.

SNOW GOOSE. — ANAS HYPERBOREA. — Fig. 279. — Male.

L'oye de Neige, *Briss.* vi. p. 288, 10. — White Brant, *Lawson's Carolina,* p. 157. — *Arct. Zool.* No. 477. — *Phil. Trans.* 62, p. 413. — *Lath. Syn.* iii. p. 445. — *Peale's Museum,* No. 2635.

ANSER HYPERBOREUS. — Bonaparte.

Anser hyperboreus, *Bonap. Synop.* p. 376. — *North Zool.* ii. p. 467.

This bird is particularly deserving of the further investigation of naturalists; for, if I do not greatly mistake, English writers have, from the various appearances which this species assumes in its progress to perfect plumage, formed no less than four different kinds, which they describe as so many distinct species, viz., the *Snow Goose,* the *White-fronted,* or *Laughing Goose,* the *Bean Goose,* and the *Blue-winged Goose,* all of which, I have little doubt, will hereafter be found to be nothing more than perfect and imperfect individuals, male and female, of the Snow Goose, now before us.

This species, called on the sea-coast the Red Goose, arrives in the River Delaware, from the north, early in November, sometimes in considerable flocks, and is extremely noisy, their notes being shriller and more squeaking than those of the Canada, or Common Wild Goose. On their first arrival they make but a short stay, proceeding, as the depth of winter approaches, farther to the south; but from the middle of February, until the breaking up of the ice in March, they are frequently numerous along both shores of the Delaware, about and below Reedy Island, particularly near Old Duck Creek, in the state of Delaware. They feed on the roots of the reeds there, tearing them up from the marshes like hogs. Their flesh, like most others of their tribe, that feed on vegetables, is excellent.

The Snow Goose is two feet eight inches in length, and five feet in extent; the bill is three inches in length, remarkably thick at the base, and rising high in the forehead, but becomes small and compressed at the extremity, where each mandible is furnished with a whitish rounding nail; the color of the bill is a purplish carmine; the edges of the two mandibles separate from each other, in a singular manner, for their whole length, and this gibbosity is occupied by dentated rows, resembling teeth, these, and the parts adjoining, being of a blackish color; the whole plumage is of a snowy whiteness, with the exception, first, of the fore part of the head all round as far as the eyes, which is of a yellowish rust color, intermixed with white; and, second, the nine exterior quill-feathers, which are black, shafted with white, and white at the root; the coverts of these last, and also the bastard wing, are sometimes of a pale ash color; the legs and feet, of the same purplish carmine as the bill; iris, dark hazel; the tail is rounded, and consists of sixteen feathers; that, and the wings, when shut, nearly of a length.

The bill of this bird is singularly curious; the edges of the upper and lower gibbosities have each twenty-three indentations, or strong teeth, on each side; the inside, or concavity of the upper mandible, has also seven lateral rows of strong, projecting teeth; and the tongue, which is horny at the extremity, is armed on each side with thirteen long and sharp, bony teeth, placed like those of a saw, with their points directed backwards; the tongue turned up, and, viewed on its lower side, looks very much like a human finger with its nail. This conformation of the mandibles, exposing two rows of strong teeth, has, probably, given rise to the epithet Laughing, bestowed on one of its varieties, though it might, with as much propriety, have been named the Grinning Goose.

The specimen from which the above figure and description was taken, was shot on the Delaware, below Philadelphia, on the 15th of February, and on dissection proved to be a male; the windpipe had no labyrinth, but, for an inch or two before its divarication into the lungs, was inflexible, not extensile, like the rest, and rather wider in diameter. The gullet had an expansion before entering the stomach, which last was remarkably strong, the two great, grinding muscles being nearly five inches in diameter. The stomach was filled with fragments of the roots of reeds, and fine sand. The intestines measured eight feet in length, and were not remarkably thick. The liver was small. For the young and female of this species, see Fig. 284.

Latham observes that this species is very numerous at Hudson's Bay, that they visit Severn River in May, and stay a fortnight, but go farther north to breed; they return to Severn Fort the beginning of September, and stay till the middle of October, when they depart for the south, and are observed to be attended by their young, in flocks innumerable. They seem to occupy also the western side of America, as they were seen at Aoonalashka,* as well as Kamtschatka.† White Brant, with black tips to their wings, were also shot by Captains Lewis and Clark's exploring party, near the mouth of the Columbia River, which were probably the same as the present species.‡ Mr. Pennant says, "They are taken by the Siberians in nets, under which they are decoyed by a person covered with a white skin, and crawling on all fours; when, others driving them, these stupid birds, mistaking him for their leader, follow him, when they are entangled in the nets, or led into a kind of pond made for the purpose!" We might here, with propriety, add — *This wants confirmation.*

HOODED MERGANSER. — MERGUS CUCULLATUS. — Fig. 280.

L'Harle huppé de Virginie, *Briss.* vii. p. 258, 8. *Pl. enl.* 935. — L'Harle couronné, *Buff.* viii. p. 280. — Round-crested Duck, *Edw.* pl. 360. — *Catesby,* i. pl. 94. — *Arct. Zool.* No. 467. — *Lath. Syn.* 10, p. 426. — *Peale's Museum,* No. 2930.

MERGUS CUCULLATUS. — Linnæus

Mergus cucullatus, *Cuv. Regn. Anim.* i. p. 540. — *Bonap. Synop.* p. 397. — *Selby, Illust. Brit. Ornith.* pl. 58.

THIS species, on the sea-coast, is usually called the Hairy Head. They are more common, however, along our lakes and fresh-water

* ELLIS's *Narrative.*   † *History of Kamtschatka.*
‡ GASS's *Journal,* p. 161.

rivers, than near the sea; tracing up creeks, and visiting mill ponds, diving perpetually for their food. In the creeks and rivers of the Southern States, they are very frequently seen during the winter. Like the Red-breasted, they are migratory, the manners, food, and places of resort of both being very much alike.

The Hooded Merganser is eighteen inches in length, and two feet in extent; bill, blackish red, narrow, thickly toothed, and furnished with a projecting nail at the extremity; the head is ornamented with a large, circular crest, which the bird has the faculty of raising or depressing at pleasure; the fore part of this, as far as the eye, is black, thence to the hind head, white, and elegantly tipped with black; it is composed of two separate rows of feathers, radiating from each side of the head, and which may be easily divided by the hand; irides, golden; eye, very small; neck, black, which spreads to and over the back; part of the lesser wing-coverts, very pale ash, under which the greater coverts and secondaries form four alternate bars of black and white; tertials, long, black, and streaked down the middle with white; the black on the back curves handsomely round in two points on the breast, which, with the whole lower parts, are pure white; sides, under the wings and flanks, reddish brown, beautifully crossed with parallel lines of black; tail, pointed, consisting of twenty feathers of a sooty brown; legs and feet, flesh-colored; claws, large and stout. The windpipe has a small labyrinth.

The female is rather less, the crest smaller, and of a light rust or dull ferruginous color, entirely destitute of the white; the upper half of the neck, a dull drab, with semicircles of lighter; the white on the wings is the same as in the male, but the tertials are shorter and have less white; the back is blackish brown; the rest of the plumage corresponds very nearly with the male.

This species is peculiar to America; * is said to arrive at Hudson's Bay about the end of May; builds close to the lakes; the nest is composed of grass, lined with feathers from the breast; is said to lay six white eggs. The young are yellow, and fit to fly in July.†

---

* The female, or a young male of this bird, has lately been killed in England, and is figured in the last part of Mr. Selby's Illustrations. This, I believe, is the first instance of its occurrence in Europe. — ED.

† HUTCHINS, as quoted by Latham.

RED–BREASTED MERGANSER. — MERGUS SERRATOR. —
Fig. 281.

L'Harle huppé, *Briss.* vi. p. 237, 2, pl. 23. — *Buff.* viii. p. 273. *Pl. enl.* 207. —
  Bewick, ii. p. 235. — *Edw.* pl. 95. — *Lath. Syn.* iii. p. 432. — *Peale's Museum,*
  No. 2936.

MERGUS SERRATOR. — Linnæus.*

Mergus serrator. *Linn. Syst.* i. 208. — *Bonap. Synop.* p. 397. — L'Harle huppé,
  Temm. Man. ii. p. 884. — Red-breasted Merganser, *Mont. Ornith. Dict.* ii. and
  Supp. Flemm. Brit. Anim. p. 129. — *Selby, Illust. Br. Ornith.* pl. 58.

This is much more common in our fresh waters than either of the
preceding, and is frequently brought to the Philadelphia market from
the shores of the Delaware. It is an inhabitant of both continents.
In the United States it is generally migratory ; though a few are occasionally seen in autumn, but none of their nests have as yet come
under my notice. They also frequent the sea-shore, keeping within
the bays and estuaries of rivers. They swim low in the water, and,
when wounded in the wing, very dexterously contrive to elude the
sportsman or his dog, by diving and coming up at a great distance,
raising the bill only above water, and dipping down again with the
greatest silence. The young males of a year old are often found in
the plumage of the female ; their food consists of small fry, and various
kinds of shell fish.

The Red-breasted Merganser is said, by Pennant, to breed on Loch
Mari, in the county of Ross, in North Britain, and also in the Isle of
Islay. Latham informs us, that it inhabits most parts of the north of
Europe on the continent, and as high as Iceland ; also in the Russian
dominions about the great rivers of Siberia, and the Lake Baikal. Is
said to be frequent in Greenland, where it breeds on the shores. The
inhabitants often take it by darts thrown at it, especially in August,
being then in moult. At Hudson's Bay, according to Hutchins, they
come in pairs about the beginning of June, as soon as the ice breaks
up, and build soon after their arrival, chiefly on dry spots of ground
in the islands ; lay from eight to thirteen white eggs, the size of those
of a Duck ; the nest is made of withered grass, and lined with the

---

* This beautiful species is also a native of both continents, and has similar manners with its congeners. In this country during winter they frequent the sea, but
even in severe weather do not so frequently ascend the rivers. They breed throughout the whole of the north of Scotland, by the edges, or on the small islets of fresh-
water lakes, both sexes being seen in company only so long as the female continues
to lay. The nest is placed in some thicket of brushwood or rank herbage, and is
composed of the same materials which Wilson has mentioned. The eggs are a
rich yellowish fawn color. Both Wilson and some of our British writers mention
them as white, or bluish white. When they have been sat upon for some time, and
approach to maturity, they receive the latter tint from the transparency of the
shell.

The female sits very close, and will allow an intruder to approach within the distance of a yard. All the nests which I have seen had two runs in opposite directions, leading out of the cover, and when disturbed, she followed one of these for a
few yards before taking flight. — Ed.

down of the breast. The young are of a dirty brown, like young Goslings. In October they all depart southward to the lakes, where they may have open water.

This species is twenty-two inches in length, and thirty-two in extent; the bill is two inches and three quarters in length, of the color of bright sealing-wax, ridged above with dusky; the nail at the tip, large, blackish, and overhanging; both mandibles are thickly serrated; irides, red; head, furnished with a long, hairy crest, which is often pendent, but occasionally erected, as represented in the plate; this, and part of the neck, is black, glossed with green; the neck under this, for two or three inches, is pure white, ending in a broad space of reddish ochre spotted with black, which spreads over the lower part of the neck and sides of the breast; shoulders, back, and tertials, deep velvety black, the first marked with a number of singular roundish spots of white; scapulars, white; wing-coverts mostly white, crossed by two narrow bands of black; primaries, black; secondaries, white; several of the latter edged with black; lower part of the back, the rump, and tail-coverts, gray, speckled with black; sides, under the wings, elegantly crossed with numerous waving lines of black; belly and vent, white; legs and feet, red; the tail, dusky ash; the black of the back passes up the hind neck in a narrow band to the head.

The female is twenty-one inches in length, and thirty in extent; the crested head and part of the neck are of a dull sorel color; irides, yellow; legs and bill, red, upper parts, dusky slate; wings, black; greater coverts, largely tipped with white; secondaries, nearly all white; sides of the breast, slightly dusky; whole lower parts, pure white; the tail is of a lighter slate than the back. The crest is much shorter than in the male, and sometimes there is a slight tinge of ferruginous on the breast.

The windpipe of the male of this species is very curious, and differs something from that of the Goosander. About two inches from the mouth, it swells out to four times its common diameter, continuing of that size for about an inch and a half. This swelling is capable of being shortened or extended; it then continues of its first diameter for two inches or more, when it becomes flattish, and almost transparent for other two inches; it then swells into a bony labyrinth of more than two inches in length by one and a half in width, over the hollow sides of which is spread a yellowish skin-like parchment. The left side of this, fronting the back of the bird, is a hard bone. The divarications come out very regularly from this at the lower end, and enter the lungs.

The intention of Nature in this extraordinary structure is probably to enable the bird to take down a supply of air to support respiration while diving; yet why should the female, who takes the same submarine excursions as the male, be entirely destitute of this apparatus?

50

SCAUP DUCK.—ANAS MARILLA.—Fig. 282.

Le petit Morillon rayé, *Briss.* vi. p. 416, 26, A.—*Arct. Zool.* No. 498.—*Lath. Syn.* iii. p. 500.—*Peale's Museum,* No. 2668.

FULIGULA MARILLA.—Stephens.*

Fuligula marilla, *Steph. Cont. Sh. Zool.* xii. p. 108.—*Bonap. Syn.* p. 392.—*North. Zool.* ii. p. 457.—Anas marilla, *Linn.* i. p. 19.—Scaup Duck. *Mont. Ornith. Dict.* i. and *Supp.*—*Bew.* ii. p. 339.—Canard milouinan, *Temm. Man.* ii. p. 865.—Nyroca marilla, *Flem. Br. Anim.* p. 122.—Common Scaup Pochard, *Selby, Illust. Br. Ornit.* pl. 66.

This Duck is better known among us by the name of the Blue Bill. It is an excellent diver, and, according to Willoughby, feeds on a certain small kind of shell fish called scaup, whence it has derived its name. It is common both to our fresh-water rivers and sea-shores in winter. Those that frequent the latter are generally much the fattest, on account of the greater abundance of food along the coast. It is sometimes abundant in the Delaware, particularly in those places where small snails, its favorite shell fish, abound, feeding also, like most of its tribe, by moonlight. They generally leave us in April, though I have met with individuals of this species so late as the middle of May, among the salt marshes of New Jersey. Their flesh is not of the most delicate kind, yet some persons esteem it. That of the young birds is generally the tenderest and most palatable.

The length of the Blue Bill is nineteen inches; extent, twenty-nine inches; bill, broad, generally of a light blue, sometimes of a dusky lead color; irides, reddish; head, tumid, covered with plumage of a dark, glossy green, extending half way down the neck; rest of the neck and breast, black, spreading round to the back; back and scapulars, white, thickly crossed with waving lines of black; lesser coverts, dusky, powdered with veins of whitish; primaries and tertials, brownish black; secondaries, white, tipped with black, forming the speculum; rump and tail-coverts, black; tail, short, rounded, and of a dusky brown; belly, white, crossed near the vent with waving lines of ash; vent, black; legs and feet, dark slate.

Such is the color of the bird in its perfect state. Young birds vary considerably, some having the head black, mixed with gray and pur-

---

* Common also to both continents, and in Britain a most abundant Sea Duck. Though generally to be found in the poultry markets during winter, it is strong and ill-flavored, or what is called *fishy,* and of little estimation for the table. In the Northern Zoology, the American specimens are said to be smaller, but no other distinctions could be perceived; a single northern specimen which I possess, agrees nearly with the dimensions given of the smaller kind, and I can see no other important difference; but there are also larger-sized birds, known to the natives by the addition of "*Keetchee,*" to the name, and I think it probable that two birds may be here confused, which future observations will allow us to separate.

The young of both this bird and the Tufted Pochard have a white band circling the base of the bill, which has caused them to be described as distinct species.—Ed.

ple, others the back dusky, with little or no white, and that irregularly dispersed.

The female has the front and sides of the same white; head and half of the neck, blackish brown; breast, spreading round to the back, a dark sooty brown, broadly skirted with whitish; back, black, thinly sprinkled with grains of white; vent, whitish; wings, the same as in the male.

The windpipe of the male of this species is of large diameter; the labyrinth, similar to some others, though not of the largest kind; it has something of the shape of a single cockle-shell; its open side, or circular rim, covered with a thin, transparent skin. Just before the windpipe enters this, it lessens its diameter at least two thirds, and assumes a flattish form.

The Scaup Duck is well known in England. It inhabits Iceland and the more northern parts of the continent of Europe, Lapland, Sweden, Norway, and Russia. It is also common on the northern shores of Siberia. It is very frequent on the River Ob. Breeds in the north, and migrates southward in winter. It inhabits America as high as Hudson's Bay, and retires from this place in October.*

AMERICAN WIDGEON. — ANAS AMERICANA. — Fig. 283.

Le Canard Jenson, *Pl. enl.* 955. — *Buff.* ix. p. 174. — *Arct. Zool.* No. 502. — *Lath.* iii. p. 520. — *Peale's Museum*, No. 2798.

MARECA AMERICANA. — Stephens.†

Mareca Americana, *Steph. Cont. Sh. Zool.* xii. p. 135. — *North. Zool.* ii. p. 445. — Anas Americana, *Bonap. Synop.* p. 384.

THIS is a handsomely-marked and sprightly species, very common in winter along our whole coast, from Florida to Rhode Island, but

---

* LATHAM.

† This species is closely allied to the European Widgeon, and may be taken as the American analogue. They seem to meet each other about the Arctic circle; that of America extending beyond it, and that of Europe reaching to the European verge. They will form the types of Stephens's genus *Mareca*, which will probably stand in the rank of a more subordinate group only. The form is one of considerable interest, possessing many combinations, which may be found to connect some parts of the natural system. The bird of Europe, except in the breeding season, is mostly an inhabitant of the sea-shore; during a severe winter, a few stray inland to the larger lakes and rivers, but as soon as a recurrence of moderate weather takes place, they return to their more favorite feeding grounds. In Britain they are mostly migratory, and at the first commencement of our harder weather, are found in vast flocks on the flatter coasts, particularly where there are beds of muscles, and other shell fish. During day, they rest and plume themselves on the higher shelves, or doze buoyant on the waves, and only commence their activity with the approach of twilight. At this time they become clamorous, and rising in dense flocks from their day's resort, proceed to the feeding grounds, generally according to the wind in the same tract. At the commencement of winter, they are fat and delicate, much sought after by the sea sportsmen, and are killed in numbers by per-

most abundant in Carolina, where it frequents the rice plantations. In Martinico, great flocks take short flights from one rice-field to another, during the rainy season, and are much complained of by the planters. The Widgeon is the constant attendant of the celebrated Canvass-Back Duck, so abundant in various parts of the Chesapeake Bay, by the aid of whose labor he has ingenuity enough to contrive to make a good subsistence. The Widgeon is extremely fond of the tender roots of that particular species of aquatic plant on which the Canvass-Back feeds, and for which that Duck is in the constant habit of diving. The Widgeon, who never dives, watches the moment of the Canvass-Back's rising, and, before he has his eyes well opened, snatches the delicious morsel from his mouth and makes off. On this account the Canvass-Backs and Widgeons, or, as they are called round the bay, Bald-Pates, live in a state of perpetual contention; the only chance the latter have is to retreat, and make their approaches at convenient opportunities. They are said to be in great plenty at St. Domingo and Cayenne, where they are called Vingeon, or Gingeon. Are said sometimes to perch on trees; feed in company, and have a sentinel on the watch, like some other birds. They feed little during the day, but in the evenings come out from their hiding-places, and are then easily traced by their particular whistle, or *whew-whew*. This soft note, or whistle, is frequently imitated with success, to entice them within gunshot. They are not known to breed in any part of the United States; are common, in the winter months, along the bays of Egg Harbor and Cape May, and also those of the Delaware. They leave these places in April, and appear upon the coasts of Hudson's Bay in May, as soon as the thaws come on, chiefly in pairs; lay there only from six to eight eggs, and feed on flies and worms in the swamps; depart in flocks in autumn.*

These birds are frequently brought to the market of Baltimore, and generally bring a good price, their flesh being excellent. They are of a lively, frolicsome disposition, and, with proper attention, might easily be domesticated.

The Widgeon, or Bald-Pate, measures twenty-two inches in length, and thirty inches in extent; the bill is of a slate color; the nail, black; the front and crown, cream colored, sometimes nearly white, the feathers inflated; from the eye, backwards, to the middle of the neck behind, extends a band of deep glossy green, gold, and purple; throat, chin, and sides of the neck before, as far as the green extends, dull yellowish white, thickly speckled with black; breast, and hind part of the neck, hoary bay, running in under the wings, where it is crossed with fine, waving lines of black; whole belly, white; vent, black; back and

---

sons lying in watch in the track of the known flight, or what, in some parts, is called *slaking*. The most propitious night for this sport is about half moon, and strong wind; the birds then fly low, and their approach is easily known by the whistling of their wings, and their own shrill cry; whence their coast name of *Hew*. They are subject to an annual change of plumage. Mr. Ord mentions, that a few of these birds breed annually in the marshes in the neighborhood of Duck Creek, in the state of Delaware. An acquaintance of the Editor's brought him thence, in the month of June, an egg, which had been taken from a nest situated in a cluster of alders. — ED.

* HUTCHINS.

scapulars, black, thickly and beautifully crossed with undulating lines of vinous bay; lower part of the back, more dusky; tail-coverts, long, pointed, whitish, crossed as the back; tail, pointed, brownish ash; the two middle feathers an inch longer than the rest, and tapering; shoulder of the wing, brownish ash; wing-coverts, immediately below, white, forming a large spot; primaries, brownish ash; middle secondaries, black, glossed with green, forming the speculum; tertials, black, edged with white, between which, and the beauty spot, several of the secondaries are white.

The female has the whole head and neck yellowish white, thickly speckled with black, very little rufous on the breast; the back is dark brown. The young males, as usual, very much like the females during the first season, and do not receive their full plumage until the second year. They are also subject to a regular change every spring and autumn.

YOUNG OF THE SNOW GOOSE. — ANAS HYPERBOREA.—
Fig. 284.

Bean Goose, *Lath. Syn.* iii. p. 464. — White-fronted Goose, *Ibid.* iii. p. 463; *Arct. Zool.* No. 476. — Blue-winged Goose, *Lath. Syn.* iii. p. 469. — *Peale's Museum,* No. 2636.

ANSER HYPERBOREAS. — Bonaparte.

The full-plumaged, perfect male bird of this species has already been figured in No. 270, and I now hazard a conjecture, founded on the best examination I could make of the young bird here figured, comparing it with the descriptions of the different accounts above referred to, that the whole of them have been taken from the various individuals of the present, in a greater or lesser degree of approach to its true and perfect colors.

These birds pass along our coasts, and settle in our rivers, every autumn; among thirty or forty, there are seldom more than six or eight pure white, or old birds. The rest vary so much, that no two are exactly alike; yet all bear the most evident marks, in the particular structure of their bills, &c., of being the same identical species. A gradual change so great, as from a bird of this color to one of pure white, must necessarily produce a number of varieties, or differences in the appearance of the plumage; but the form of the bill and legs remains the same, and any peculiarity in either is the surest mean we have to detect a species under all its various appearances. It is therefore to be regretted, that the authors above referred to in the synonymes, have paid so little attention to the singular conformation of the bill; for even in the description of the Snow Goose, neither that nor the internal peculiarities are at all mentioned.

The length of the bird, represented in Fig. 284, was twenty-eight inches; extent, four feet eight inches; bill, gibbous at the sides, both above and below, exposing the teeth of the upper and lower mandibles, and furnished with a nail at the tip on both; the whole being of

50 *

a light reddish purple, or pale lake, except the gibbosity, which is black, and the two nails, which are of a pale light blue ; nostril, pervious, an oblong slit, placed nearly in the middle of the upper mandible ; irides, dark brown; whole head, and half of the neck, white; rest of the neck and breast, as well as upper part of the back, of a purplish brown, darkest where it joins the white ; all the feathers being finely tipped with pale brown ; whole wing-coverts, very pale ash, or light lead color ; primaries and secondaries, black ; tertials, long, tapering, centred with black, edged with light blue, and usually fall over the wing ; scapulars, cinereous brown ; lower parts of the back and rump, of the same light ash as the wing-coverts ; tail, rounded, blackish, consisting of sixteen feathers, edged and tipped broadly with white ; tail-coverts, white ; belly and vent, whitish, intermixed with cinereous ; feet and legs, of the same lake color as the bill.

This specimen was a female ; the tongue was thick and fleshy, armed on each side with thirteen strong, bony teeth, exactly similar in appearance, as well as in number, to those on the tongue of the Snow Goose ; the inner concavity of the upper mandible was also studded with rows of teeth. The stomach was extremely muscular, filled with some vegetable matter, and clear gravel.

With this, another was shot, differing considerably in its markings, having little or no white on the head, and being smaller ; its general color, dark brown, intermixed with pale ash, and darker below, but evidently of the same species with the other.

PIED DUCK.—ANAS LABRADORA.—Fig. 285.

Arct. Zool. No. 488. — *Lath. Syn.* iii. p. 497. — *Peale's Museum,* No. 2858.

FULIGULA LABRADORA. — Bonaparte.*

Fuligula Labradora, *Bonap. Synop.* p. 391.

This is rather a scarce species on our coasts, and is never met with on fresh-water lakes or rivers. It is called by some gunners the Sand Shoal Duck, from its habit of frequenting sand bars. Its principal food appears to be shell fish, which it procures by diving. The flesh is dry, and partakes considerably of the nature of its food. It is only seen here during winter ; most commonly early in the month of March, a few are observed in our market. Of their principal manners, place, or mode of breeding, nothing more is known. Latham observes, that a pair in the possession of Sir Joseph Banks were brought from Labrador. Having myself had frequent opportunities of examining both sexes of these birds, I find that, like most others, they are subject, when young, to a progressive change of color. The full-plumaged

* The Prince of Musignano places this bird among the *Fuligulæ.* I have had no opportunity of seeing the bird itself, and cannot therefore speak, from examination, as to its station. It seems a true Sea Duck, and agrees in general habits with the Scaups and Pochards. — Ed.

male is as follows: Length, twenty inches; extent, twenty-nine inches; the base of the bill, and edges of both mandibles for two thirds of their length, are of a pale orange color; the rest, black; towards the extremity, it widens a little in the manner of the Shovellers, the sides there having the singularity of being only a soft, loose, pendulous skin; irides, dark hazel; head, and half of the neck, white, marked along the crown to the hind head with a stripe of black; the plumage of the cheeks is of a peculiar bristly nature at the points, and round the neck passes a collar of black, which spreads over the back, rump, and tail-coverts; below this collar, the upper part of the breast is white, extending itself over the whole scapulars, wing-coverts, and secondaries; the primaries, lower part of the breast, whole belly, and vent, are black; tail, pointed, and of a blackish hoary color; the fore part of the legs and ridges of the toes, pale whitish ash; hind part, the same, bespattered with blackish; webs, black; the edges of both mandibles are largely pectinated. In young birds, the whole of the white plumage is generally strongly tinged with a yellowish cream color; in old males, these parts are pure white, with the exception sometimes of the bristly, pointed plumage of the cheeks, which retains its cream tint the longest, and, with the skinny part of the bill, form two strong peculiarities of this species.

The female measures nineteen inches in length, and twenty-seven in extent; bill, exactly as in the male; sides of the front, white; head, chin, and neck, ashy gray; upper parts of the back and wings, brownish slate; secondaries only, white; tertials, hoary; the white secondaries form a spot on the wing, bounded by the black primaries, and four hoary tertials edged with black; whole lower parts, a dull ash, skirted with brownish white, or clay color; legs and feet, as in the male; the bill in both is marked from the nostrils backwards by a singular, heart-shaped outline.

The windpipe of the male measures ten inches in length, and has four enlargements, viz., one immediately below the mouth, and another at the interval of an inch; it then bends largely down to the breast-bone, to which it adheres by two strong muscles, and has at that place a third expansion. It then becomes flattened, and, before it separates into the lungs, has a fourth enlargement, much greater than any of the former, which is bony, and round, puffing out from the left side. The intestines measured six feet; the stomach contained small clams, and some glutinous matter; the liver was remarkably large.

LONG-TAILED DUCK. — ANAS GLACIALIS. — Fig. 286. —
Male.

Le Canard à longue queue de Terre Neuve, *Briss.* vi. p. 382, 18. — *Buff.* ix. p. 202.   *Pl. enl.* 1008. — *Edw.* pl. 280. — *Arct. Zool.* No. 501. — *Lath. Syn,* iii. p. 528. — *Peale's Museum,* No. 2310.

HARELDA GLACIALIS. — Leach.*

Anas glacialis, and Anas hyemalis, *Linn. Syst.* i. p. 202, and 203. — *Lath. Ind.* ii. p. 864. — Fuligula glacialis, *Bonap. Synop.* p. 395. — Long-tailed Duck, *Mont. Ornith. Dict.* i. and *Supp.* — *Bew. Br. Birds,* ii. 363. — Long-tailed Hareld, *Selby's Illust. Br. Ornith.* pl. 61, *m. and f.* — Harelda glacialis, *North. Zool.* ii. p. 460.

THIS Duck is very generally known along the shores of the Chesapeake Bay, by the name of South-Southerly, from the singularity of its cry, something imitative of the sound of those words, and also, that, when very clamorous, they are supposed to betoken a southerly wind; on the coast of New Jersey, they are usually called Old Wives. They are chiefly salt-water Ducks, and seldom ramble far from the sea. They inhabit our bays and coasts during the winter only; are rarely found in the marshes, but keep in the channel, diving for small shell fish, which are their principal food. In passing to and from the bays, sometimes in vast flocks, particularly towards evening, their loud and confused noise may be heard, in calm weather, at the distance of several miles. They fly very swiftly, take short excursions, and are lively, restless birds. Their native regions are in the north, where great numbers of them remain during the whole year; part only of the vast family migrating south, to avoid the severest rigors of that climate. They are common to the whole northern hemisphere. In the Orkneys, they are met with in considerable flocks, from October to April; frequent in Sweden, Lapland, and Russia; are often found about St. Petersburg, and also in Kamtschatka. Are said to breed at Hudson's Bay, making their nest among the grass near the sea, like the Eider Duck, and about the middle of June lay from ten to fourteen bluish white eggs, the size of those of a Pullet. When the young are hatched, the mother carries them to the water in her bill. The nest is lined

* This bird forms the type of Dr. Leach's genus *Harelda.* It is remarkable for the decided change between the plumage of the breeding season and that of the winter, bearing analogy, in many particulars, to the Tringæ and their allies, for the prolongation of the scapulary feathers, and for the narrow, lengthened tail. It is a native of both continents, but in Britain is only met with during winter, in the dress of that season, or in the plumage of the first year. It keeps to the open sea, and seldom ventures inland to rivers or lakes. The following is a description of a specimen killed on the first May, from the *Northern Zoology,* and which agrees nearly with skins in my possession. "The whole upper plumage, the central pairs of tail-feathers, and the under plumage to the fore part of the belly, brownish black; the lesser quills, paler. A triangular patch of feathers, between the shoulders and the scapulars, broadly bordered with orange brown." (In the winter plumage, the long scapulars are pure white, and form a beautiful contrast, hanging over the dark quills.) "Sides of head from the bill to the ears, ash gray; eye stripe, and posterior under plumage, pure white; flanks, sides of the rump, and lateral tail-feathers, white, stained with brown; axillaries and inner wing-coverts, clove brown; bill, black, with an orange belt (*bright vermilion*) before the nostrils." — ED.

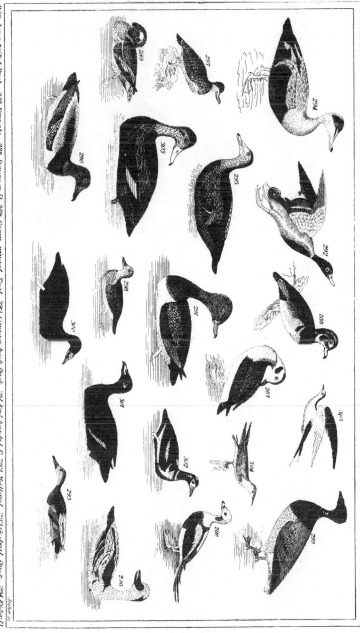

286. Long tailed Duck. 287. Female. 288. Summer D. 289. Green winged Teal. 290. Canvas back Duck. 291. Red headed F. 292. Mallard. 293. Gadwal Duc.ᵗ 294. Eider D. 295. Female. 296. Shovel. 297. Ruddy Duck. 298. Female. 299. Brant. 300. Eider Duck. 301. Tdᵗ 302. Ring neck. 303. Harlequin Duck. 304. Marsh Hen. 305. Lark F.

Trebt. sc

with the down of her breast, which is accounted equally valuable with that of the Eider Duck, were it to be had in the same quantity.* They are hardy birds, and excellent divers. Are not very common in England, coming there only in very severe winters; and then but in small, straggling parties; yet are found on the coast of America, as far south at least as Charleston, in Carolina, during the winter. Their flesh is held in no great estimation, having a fishy taste. The down and plumage, particularly on the breast and lower parts of the body, are very abundant, and appear to be of the best quality.

The length of this species is twenty-two inches; extent, thirty inches; bill, black, crossed near the extremity by a band of orange; tongue, downy; iris, dark red; cheeks and frontlet, dull dusky drab, passing over the eye, and joining a large patch of black on the side of the neck, which ends in dark brown; throat and rest of the neck, white; crown, tufted, and of a pale cream color; lower part of the neck, breast, back, and wings, black; scapulars and tertials, pale bluish white, long, and pointed, and falling gracefully over the wings; the white of the lower part of the neck spreads over the back an inch or two; the white of the belly spreads over the sides, and nearly meets at the rump; secondaries, chestnut, forming a bar across the wing; primaries, rump, and tail-coverts, black; the tail consists of fourteen feathers, all remarkably pointed, the two middle ones nearly four inches longer than the others; these, with the two adjoining ones, are black; the rest, white; legs and feet, dusky slate.

On dissection, the intestines were found to measure five feet six inches. The windpipe was very curiously formed; besides the labyrinth, which is nearly as large as the end of the thumb, it has an expansion, immediately above that, of double its usual diameter, which continues for an inch and a half; this is flattened on the side next the breast, with an oblong, window-like vacancy in it, crossed with five narrow bars, and covered with a thin, transparent skin, like the panes of a window; another thin skin of the same kind is spread over the external side of the labyrinth, which is partly of a circular form. This singular conformation is, as usual, peculiar to the male, the female having the windpipe of nearly an uniform thickness throughout. She differs also so much in the colors and markings of her plumage, as to render a figure of her necessary; for a description of which see the following article

---

FEMALE LONG-TAILED DUCK. — Fig. 287.

Anas hyemalis, *Linn. Syst.* 202, 29. — *Lath. Syn.* iii. p. 529. — *Peale's Museum*, No. 2811.

HARELDA GLACIALIS. — Leach.

THE female is distinguished from the male by wanting the lengthened tertials, and the two long, pointed feathers of the tail, and also by her size, and the rest of her plumage, which is as follows: length,

* LATHAM.

sixteen inches; extent, twenty-eight inches; bill, dusky; middle of the crown, and spot on the side of the neck, blackish; a narrow dusky line runs along the throat for two inches; rest of the head, and upper half of the neck, white, lower half, pale vinaceous bay, blended with white; all the rest of the lower parts of the body, pure white; back, scapulars, and lesser wing-coverts, bright ferruginous, centred with black, and interspersed with whitish; shoulders of the wing, and quills, black; lower part of the back, the same, tinged with brown; tail, pale brown ash; inner vanes of all but the two middle feathers, white; legs and feet, dusky slate. The legs are placed far behind, which circumstance points out the species to be great divers. In some females, the upper parts are less ferruginous.

Some writers suppose the singular voice, or call, of this species, to be occasioned by the remarkable construction of its windpipe; but the fact, that the females are uniformly the most noisy, and yet are entirely destitute of the singularities of this conformation, overthrows the probability of this supposition.

SUMMER DUCK, OR WOOD DUCK. — ANAS SPONSA. —
FIG. 288.

Le Canard d'Eté, *Briss.* vi. p. 351, 11, pl. 32, fig. 2. — Le beau Canard huppé, *Buff.* ix. p. 245. *Pl. enl.* 980, 981. — Summer Duck, *Catesby,* i. pl. 97. — *Edw.* pl. 101. — *Arct. Zool.* No. 943. — *Lath. Syn.* iii. p. 546. — *Peale's Museum,* No. 2872.

DENDRONESSA SPONSA. — RICHARDSON, SWAINSON.*

Anas sponsa, *Bonap. Synop.* p. 385. — Dendronessa sponsa, *North. Zool.* ii. 446.

THIS most beautiful of all our Ducks has probably no superior among its whole tribe for richness and variety of colors. It is called

---

* These lovely Ducks may be said to represent an incessorial form among the *anatidæ;* they build and perch on trees, and spend as much time on land as upon the waters; Dr. Richardson has given this group, containing few members, the title of *dendronessa* from their arboreal habits. Our present species is the only one belonging to America, where it ranges rather to the south than north; the others, I believe, are all confined to India. They are remarkable for the beauty and splendor of their plumage, its glossy, silky texture, and for the singular form of the scapulars, which, instead of an extreme development in length, receive it in the contrary proportion of breadth; and instead of lying flat, in some stand perpendicular to the back. They are all adorned with an ample crest, pendulous, and running down the back of the neck. They are easily domesticated, but I do not know that they have been yet of much utility in this state, being more kept on account of their beauty, and few have been introduced except to our menageries; with a little trouble at first, they might form a much more common ornament about our artificial pieces of water. It is the only form of a *Tree Duck* common to this continent; in other countries there are, however, two or three others of very great importance in the natural system, whose structure and habits have yet been almost entirely overlooked or lost sight of. These seem to range principally over India, and more sparingly in Africa; and the Summer Duck is the solitary instance, the United States the nearly extreme limit, of its own peculiarities in this division of the world. — ED.

the Wood Duck, from the circumstance of its breeding in hollow trees ; and the Summer Duck, from remaining with us chiefly during the summer. It is familiarly known in every quarter of the United States, from Florida to Lake Ontario, in the neighborhood of which latter place I have myself met with it in October. It rarely visits the sea-shore, or salt marshes, its favorite haunts being the solitary, deep, and muddy creeks, ponds, and mill-dams of the interior, making its nest frequently in old, hollow trees that overhang the water.

The Summer Duck is equally well known in Mexico and many of the West India islands. During the whole of our winters, they are occasionally seen in the states south of the Potomac. On the 10th of January, I met with two on a creek near Petersburgh, in Virginia. In the more northern districts, however, they are migratory. In Pennsylvania, the female usually begins to lay late in April or early in May. Instances have been known where the nest was constructed of a few sticks laid in a fork of the branches ; usually, however, the inside of a hollow tree is selected for this purpose. On the 18th of May I visited a tree containing the nest of a Summer Duck, on the banks of Tuckahoe River, New Jersey. It was an old, grotesque white oak, whose top had been torn off by a storm. It stood on the declivity of the bank, about twenty yards from the water. In this hollow and broken top, and about six feet down, on the soft, decayed wood, lay thirteen eggs, snugly covered with down, doubtless taken from the breast of the bird. These eggs were of an exact oval shape, less than those of a Hen, the surface exceedingly fine grained, and of the highest polish, and slightly yellowish, greatly resembling old, polished ivory. The egg measured two inches and an eighth by one inch and a half. On breaking one of them, the young bird was found to be nearly hatched, but dead, as neither of the parents had been observed about the tree during the three or four days preceding, and were conjectured to have been shot.

This tree had been occupied, probably by the same pair, for four successive years, in breeding time ; the person who gave me the information, and whose house was within twenty or thirty yards of the tree, said that he had seen the female, the spring preceding, carry down thirteen young, one by one, in less than ten minutes. She caught them in her bill by the wing or back of the neck, and landed them safely at the foot of the tree, whence she afterwards led them to the water. Under this same tree, at the time I visited it, a large sloop lay on the stocks, nearly finished ; the deck was not more than twelve feet distant from the nest, yet notwithstanding the presence and noise of the workmen, the Ducks would not abandon their old breeding place, but continued to pass out and in, as if no person had been near. The male usually perched on an adjoining limb, and kept watch while the female was laying, and also often while she was sitting. A tame Goose had chosen a hollow space at the root of the same tree, to lay and hatch her young in.

The Summer Duck seldom flies in flocks of more than three or four individuals together, and most commonly in pairs, or singly. The common note of the drake is *peet, peet* ; but when, standing sentinel, he sees danger, he makes a noise not unlike the crowing of a young cock, *oe eek! oe eek!* Their food consists principally of acorns, seeds of the wild oats, and insects. Their flesh is inferior to that of the Blue-winged Teal. They are frequent in the markets of Philadelphia.

Among other gaudy feathers with which the Indians ornament the calumet or pipe of peace, the skin of the head and neck of the Summer Duck is frequently seen covering the stem.

This beautiful bird has often been tamed, and soon becomes so familiar as to permit one to stroke its back with the hand. I have seen individuals so tamed, in various parts of the Union. Captain Boyer, collector of the port of Havre-de-Grace, informs me, that, about forty years ago, a Mr. Nathan Nicols, who lived on the west side of Gunpowder Creek, had a whole yard swarming with Summer Ducks, which he had tamed and completely domesticated, so that they bred and were as familiar as any other tame fowls; that he (Captain Boyer) himself saw them in that state, but does not know what became of them. Latham says, that they are often kept in European menageries, and will breed there.*

The Wood Duck is nineteen inches in length, and two feet four inches in extent; bill, red, margined with black; a spot of black lies between the nostrils, reaching nearly to the tip, which is also of the same color, and furnished with a large, hooked nail; irides, orange red; front, crown, and pendent crest, rich glossy bronze green, ending in violet, elegantly marked with a line of pure white running from the upper mandible over the eye, and with another band of white proceeding from behind the eye, both mingling their long, pendent plumes with the green and violet ones, producing a rich effect; cheeks and sides of the upper neck, violet; chin, throat, and collar round the neck, pure white, curving up in the form of a crescent, nearly to the posterior part of the eye; the white collar is bounded below with black; breast, dark violet brown, marked on the fore part with minute triangular spots of white, increasing in size until they spread into the white of the belly; each side of the breast is bounded by a large crescent of white, and that again by a broader one of deep black; sides, under the wings, thickly and beautifully marked with fine, undulating, parallel lines of black, on a ground of yellowish drab; the flanks are ornamented with broad, alternate, semicircular bands of black and white; sides of the vent, rich light violet; tail-coverts, long, of a hair-like texture at the sides, over which they descend, and of a deep black, glossed with green; back, dusky bronze, reflecting green; scapulars, black; tail, tapering, dark glossy green above; below, dusky; primaries, dusky, silvery hoary without, tipped with violet blue; secondaries, greenish blue, tipped with white; wing-coverts, violet blue, tipped with black; vent, dusky; legs and feet, yellowish red; claws, strong and hooked.

The above is as accurate a description as I can give of a very perfect specimen now before me, from which Fig. 288 was faithfully copied.

The female has the head slightly crested; crown, dark purple; behind the eye, a bar of white; chin and throat, for two inches, also white; head and neck, dark drab; breast, dusky brown, marked with large, triangular spots of white; back, dark glossy bronze brown, with

---

* *General Synopsis*, iii. 547.

some gold and greenish reflections; speculum of the wings, nearly the same as in the male, but the fine pencilling of the sides, and the long, hair-like tail-coverts are wanting; the tail is also shorter.

GREEN-WINGED TEAL. — ANAS CRECCA. — Fig. 289.

Lath. Syn. iii. p. 554. — *Bewick's Br. Birds,* v. ii. p. 338. — *Peale's Museum,* No. 2832.

BOSCHAS CAROLINENSIS. — Jardine.*

Anas Carolinensis, *Lath. Ind. Ornith.* ii. p. 874. — Anas migratoria, Least Green-winged Teal, *Bart. Trav.* p. 293. — Anas crecca, varietas, *Forst. Phil. Trans.* lxii. p. 347. — American Teal, *Lath. Gen. Hist.* x. p. 371. — Anas crecca, *Bonap. Synop.* p. 386. — Anas (boschas) crecca, var. *North. Zool.* ii. p. 443.

THE naturalists of Europe have designated this little Duck by the name of the American Teal, as being a species different from their own. On an examination, however, of the figure and description of the European Teal by the ingenious and accurate Bewick, and comparing them with the present, no difference whatever appears in the length, extent, color, or markings of either, but what commonly occurs among individuals of any other tribe; both undoubtedly belong to one and the same species.

This, like the preceding, is a fresh-water Duck, common in our markets in autumn and winter, but rarely seen here in summer. It frequents ponds, marshes, and the reedy shores of creeks and rivers; is very abundant among the rice plantations of the Southern States;

* Most writers on the ornithology of America have considered this bird as a variety of the European Teal. All, however, agree in their regarding the difference in the variety, and of its being constant in the northern specimens. Thus Dr. Latham mentions the white pectoral band. Forster says, " This is a variety of the Teal, for it wants the two white streaks above and below the eyes; the lower one indeed is faintly expressed in the male, which has also a lunated bar of white over each shoulder; this is not to be found in the European Teal." Pennant, " that it wants the white line which the European one has above each eye, having only one below; has over each shoulder a lunated bar." The authors of the *Northern Zoology* observe, " The only permanent difference that we have been able to detect, after comparing a number of specimens, is, that the English Teal has a white longitudinal band on the scapulars, which the other wants. All the specimens brought home by the Expedition have a broad, transverse bar on the shoulder, which does not exist in the English one." And our author, in his plate, has most distinctly marked the differences. From the testimony of all its describers marking the variety as permanent and similar, I am certainly inclined to consider this bird, though nearly allied, to be distinct; and, as far as we yet know, peculiar to the northern parts of America. I have not been able to procure a specimen for immediate comparison, and only once had an opportunity of slightly examining a northern bird: in it the distinctions were at once perceptible. From their great similarity, no observers have yet particularly attended to the manners of the American bird, or to the marking of the females. If the above observations are the means of directing further attention to these points, they will have performed their intended end. I by no means consider the point decided. — Ed.

51

flies in small parties, and feeds at night; associates often with the Duck and Mallard, feeding on the seeds of various kinds of grasses and water-plants, and also on the tender leaves of vegetables. Its flesh is accounted excellent.

The Green-winged Teal is fifteen inches in length, and twenty-four inches in extent; bill, black; irides, pale brown; lower eyelid, whitish; head, glossy reddish chestnut; from the eye backwards to the nape runs a broad band of rich silky green, edged above and below by a fine line of brownish white; the plumage of the nape ends in a kind of pendent crest; chin, blackish; below the chestnut, the neck, for three quarters of an inch, is white, beautifully crossed with circular, undulating lines of black; back, scapulars, and sides of the breast, white, thickly crossed in the same manner; breast, elegantly marked with roundish or heart-shaped spots of black, on a pale vinaceous ground, variegated with lighter tints; belly, white; sides, waved with undulating lines; lower part of the vent-feathers, black; sides of the same, brownish white, or pale reddish cream; lesser wing-coverts, brown ash; greater, tipped with reddish cream; the first five secondaries, deep velvety black, the next five resplendent green, forming the speculum or beauty spot, which is bounded above by pale buff, below by white, and on each side by deep black; primaries, ashy brown; tail, pointed, eighteen feathers, dark drab; legs and feet, flesh colored. In some, a few circular touches of white appear on the breast near the shoulder of the wing. The windpipe has a small, bony labyrinth where it separates into the lungs; the intestines measure three feet six inches, and are very small and tender.

The female wants the chestnut bay on the head, and the band of rich green through the eye, these parts being dusky white, speckled with black; the breast is gray brown, thickly sprinkled with blackish, or dark brown; the back, dark brown, waved with broad lines of brownish white; wing, nearly the same as in the male.

This species is said to breed at Hudson's Bay, and to have from five to seven young at a time.* In France, it remains throughout the year, and builds in April, among the rushes on the edges of the ponds. It has been lately discovered to breed, also, in England, in the mosses about Carlisle.† It is not known to breed in any part of the United States. The Teal is found in the north of Europe as far as Iceland, and also inhabits the Caspian Sea to the south; extends likewise to China, having been recognized by Latham among some fine drawings of the birds of that country.

* Latham.   † Bewick.

CANVASS-BACK DUCK.   ANAS VALISINERIA. — Fig. 290.

Peale's Museum, No. 2816.

FULIGULA VALISNERIANA. — Stephens.*

Fuligula valisneriana, *Bonap. Synop.* p. 392. — *North. Zool.* iv. p. 450. — Anas valisneriana, *Wilson.*

This celebrated American species, as far as can be judged from the best figures and descriptions of foreign birds, is altogether unknown in Europe. It approaches nearest to the Pochard of England, (*Anas ferina,*) but differs from that bird in being superior in size and weight, in the greater magnitude of its bill, and the general whiteness of its plumage. A short comparison of the two will elucidate this point : The Canvass-Back measures two feet in length by three feet in extent, and, when in the best order, weighs three pounds and upwards. The Pochard, according to Latham and Bewick, measures nineteen inches in length, and thirty in extent, and weighs one pound twelve or thirteen ounces. The latter writer says of the Pochard, "The plumage, above and below, is wholly covered with prettily-freckled, slender, dusky threads, disposed transversely in close-set, zigzag lines, on a pale ground, more or less shaded off with ash," — a description much more applicable to the bird figured beside it, the Red-Head, and which, very probably, is the species meant. In the figure of the Pochard given by Mr. Bewick, who is generally correct, the bill agrees very well with that of our Red-Head ; but is scarcely half the size and thickness of that of the Canvass-Back ; and the figure in the *Planches Enluminées* corresponds, in that respect, with Bewick's. In short, either these writers are egregiously erroneous in their figures and descriptions, or the present Duck was altogether unknown to them. Considering the latter supposition the more probable

* This species is now well established, and can never be mistaken. I am not aware that any thing can be added to Wilson's accurate description, unless it be his description, in poetry, of his first capture of the *Canvass-Back.* — Ed.

> " Slow round an opening point we softly steal,
> Where four large Ducks in playful circles wheel.
> The far-famed *Canvass-Backs* at once we know,
> Their broad, flat bodies wrapped in pencilled snow ;
> The burnished chestnut o'er their necks that shone,
> Spread deep'ning round each breast a sable zone.
> Wary they gaze — our boat in silence glides ;
> The slow-moved paddles steal along the sides ;
> Quick-flashing thunders roar along the flood,
> And three lie prostrate, vomiting their blood !
> The fourth aloft on whistling pinions soared ;
> One fatal glance the fiery thunders poured ;
> Prone drops the bird amid the dashing waves,
> And the clear stream his glossy plumage laves."

Foresters, p. 39.

of the two, I have designated this as a new species, and shall proceed to detail some particulars of its history.

The Canvass-Back Duck arrives in the United States from the north about the middle of October; a few descend to the Hudson and Delaware, but the great body of these birds resort to the numerous rivers belonging to and in the neighborhood of the Chesapeake Bay, particularly the Susquehannah, the Patapsco, Potomac, and James Rivers, which appear to be their general winter rendezvous. Beyond this, to the south, I can find no certain accounts of them. At the Susquehannah, they are called Canvass-Backs; on the Potomac, White-Backs; and on James River, Sheldrakes. They are seldom found at a great distance up any of these rivers, or even in the salt-water bay; but in that particular part of tide water where a certain grass-like plant grows, on the roots of which they feed. This plant, which is said to be a species of *valisineria*, grows on fresh-water shoals of from seven to nine feet, (but never where these are occasionally dry,) in long, narrow, grass-like blades, of four or five feet in length; the root is white, and has some resemblance to small celery. This grass is in many places so thick that a boat can with difficulty be rowed through it, it so impedes the oars. The shores are lined with large quantities of it, torn up by the Ducks, and drifted up by the winds, lying, like hay, in windrows. Wherever this plant grows in abundance, the Canvass-Backs may be expected, either to pay occasional visits, or to make it their regular residence during the winter. It occurs in some parts of the Hudson; in the Delaware, near Gloucester, a few miles below Philadelphia; and in most of the rivers that fall into the Chesapeake, to each of which particular places these Ducks resort; while, in waters unprovided with this nutritive plant, they are altogether unknown.

On the first arrival of these birds in the Susquehannah, near Havrede-Grace, they are generally lean; but such is the abundance of their favorite food that, towards the beginning of November, they are in pretty good order. They are excellent divers, and swim with great speed and agility. They sometimes assemble in such multitudes as to cover several acres of the river, and, when they rise suddenly, produce a noise resembling thunder. They float about these shoals, diving, and tearing up the grass by the roots, which is the only part they eat. They are extremely shy, and can rarely be approached, unless by stratagem. When wounded in the wing, they dive to such prodigious distances, and with such rapidity, continuing it so perseveringly, and with such cunning and active vigor, as almost always to render the pursuit hopeless. From the great demand for these Ducks, and the high price they uniformly bring in market, various modes are practised to get within gunshot of them. The most successful way is said to be decoying them to the shore by means of a dog, while the gunner lies closely concealed in a proper situation. The dog, if properly trained, plays backwards and forwards along the margin of the water; and the Ducks, observing his manœuvres, enticed perhaps by curiosity, gradually approach the shore, until they are sometimes within twenty or thirty yards of the spot where the gunner lies concealed, and from which he rakes them, first on the water, and then as they rise. This method is called *tolling them in.* If the Ducks seem difficult to decoy, any glaring object, such as a red handkerchief, is fixed round the dog's middle, or to his tail; and this rarely fails to attract them. Sometimes, by moonlight, the sportsman directs his skiff towards a flock whose position he had previously ascertained, keeping within the projecting shadow of some wood, bank, or head-land, and paddles along so silently and imperceptibly as often to ap-proach within fifteen or twenty yards of a flock of many thousands, among whom he generally makes great slaughter.

Many other stratagems are practised, and, indeed, every plan that the ingenuity of the experienced sportsman can suggest, to approach within gunshot of these birds; but, of all the modes pursued, none in-timidate them so much as shooting them by night; and they soon abandon the place where they have been thus repeatedly shot at. During the day, they are dispersed about; but towards evening, collect in large flocks, and come into the mouths of creeks, where they often ride as at anchor, with their head under their wing, asleep, there being always sentinels awake, ready to raise an alarm on the least appear-ance of danger. Even when feeding and diving in small parties, the whole never go down at one time, but some are still left above on the look-out.

When the winter sets in severely, and the river is frozen, the Can-vass-Backs retreat to its confluence with the bay, occasionally fre-quenting air-holes in the ice, which are sometimes made for the pur-pose, immediately above their favorite grass, to entice them within gunshot of the hut or bush which is usually fixed at a proper distance, and where the gunner lies concealed, ready to take advantage of their distress. A Mr. Hill, who lives near James River, at a place called Herring Creek, informs me, that, one severe winter, he and another person broke a hole in the ice, about twenty by forty feet, immediately over a shoal of grass, and took their stand on the shore in a hut of brush, each having three guns well loaded with large shot. The Ducks, which were flying up and down the river, in great extremity, soon crowded to this place, so that the whole open space was not only covered with them, but vast numbers stood on the ice around it. They had three rounds, firing both at once, and picked up eighty-eight Can-vass-Backs, and might have collected more, had they been able to get to the extremity of the ice after the wounded ones. In the severe winter of 1779-80, the grass, on the roots of which these birds feed, was almost wholly destroyed in James River. In the month of Janu-ary, the wind continued to blow from W. N. W. for twenty-one days, which caused such low tides in the river, that the grass froze to the ice every where; and, a thaw coming on suddenly, the whole was raised by the roots, and carried off by the fresh. The next winter, a few of these Ducks were seen, but they soon went away again; and, for many years after, they continued to be scarce; and, even to the present day, in the opinion of my informant, have never been so plenty as before.

The Canvass-Back, in the rich, juicy tenderness of its flesh, and its delicacy of flavor, stands unrivalled by the whole of its tribe in this or perhaps any other quarter of the world. Those killed in the waters of the Chesapeake are generally esteemed superior to all others, doubtless from the great abundance of their favorite food which these

51 *

rivers produce. At our public dinners, hotels, and particular entertainments, the Canvass-Backs are universal favorites. They not only
grace but dignify the table, and their very name conveys to the imagination of the eager epicure the most comfortable and exhilarating
ideas. Hence, on such occasions, it has not been uncommon to pay
from one to three dollars a pair for these Ducks; and, indeed, at
such times, if they can, they must be had, whatever may be the price.

The Canvass-Back will feed readily on grain, especially wheat, and
may be decoyed to particular places by baiting them with that grain
for several successive days. Some few years since, a vessel loaded
with wheat was wrecked near the entrance of Great Egg Harbor, in
the autumn, and went to pieces. The wheat floated out in vast quantities, and the whole surface of the bay was in a few days covered
with Ducks of a kind altogether unknown to the people of that
quarter. The gunners of the neighborhood collected in boats, in
every direction, shooting them; and so successful were they, that, as
Mr. Beasley informs me, two hundred and forty were killed in one
day, and sold among the neighbors, at twelve and a half cents apiece,
without the feathers. The wounded ones were generally abandoned,
as being too difficult to be come up with. They continued about for
three weeks, and during the greater part of that time a continual can-
nonading was heard from every quarter. The gunners called them
Sea Ducks. They were all Canvass-Backs, at that time on their way
from the north, when this floating feast attracted their attention, and
for a while arrested them in their course. A pair of these very Ducks
I myself bought in Philadelphia market at the time, from an Egg
Harbor gunner, and never met with their superior, either in weight or
excellence of flesh. When it was known among those people the loss
they had sustained in selling for twenty-five cents what would have
brought them from a dollar to a dollar and a half per pair, universal
surprise and regret were naturally enough excited.

The Canvass-Back is two feet long, and three feet in extent, and,
when in good order, weighs three pounds; the bill is large, rising
high in the head, three inches in length, and one inch and three
eighths thick at the base, of a glossy black; eye, very small; irides,
dark red; cheeks and fore part of the head, blackish brown; rest of
the head and greater part of the neck, bright glossy reddish chestnut,
ending in a broad space of black that covers the upper part of the
breast, and spreads round to the back; back, scapulars, and tertials,
white, faintly marked with an infinite number of transverse, waving
lines or points, as if done with a pencil; whole lower parts of the
breast, also the belly, white, slightly pencilled in the same manner,
scarcely perceptible on the breast, pretty thick towards the vent;
wing-coverts, gray, with numerous specks of blackish; primaries and
secondaries, pale slate, two or three of the latter of which nearest the
body are finely edged with deep velvety black, the former dusky at
the tips; tail, very short, pointed, consisting of fourteen feathers of a
hoary brown; vent and tail-coverts, black; lining of the wing, white;
legs and feet, very pale ash, the latter three inches in width — a circumstance which partly accounts for its great powers of swimming.

The female is somewhat less than the male, and weighs two pounds
and three quarters; the crown is blackish brown; cheeks and throat,

of a pale drab; neck, dull brown; breast, as far as the black extends on the male, dull brown, skirted in places with pale drab; back, dusky white, crossed with fine, waving lines; belly, of the same dull white, pencilled like the back; wings, feet, and bill, as in the male; tail-coverts, dusky; vent, white, waved with brown.

The windpipe of the male has a large, flattish, concave labyrinth, the ridge of which is covered with a thin, transparent membrane; where the trachea enters this, it is very narrow, but immediately above swells to three times that diameter. The intestines are wide, and measure five feet in length.

RED-HEADED DUCK. — ANAS FERINA ? — Fig. 291.

Peale's Museum, No. 2710.

FULIGULA FERINA. — Stephens.*

Steph. Cont. Sh. Zool. p. 193. — Fuligula ferina, *Bonap. Synop.* p. 392. — *North. Zool.* ii. p. 451. — Nyroca ferina, *Flem. Br. Anim.* p. 108. — Le Canard miloun, *Temm. Man.* ii. 868. — Pochard, or Red-headed Widgeon, *Mont. Ornith. Dict.* ii. and *Supp. Bew. Br. Birds*, ii. p. 356. — Red-headed Widgeon, *Selby's Illust. Br. Ornith.* pl. 63, fig. 1.

This is a common associate of the Canvass-Back, frequenting the same places, and feeding on the stems of the same grass, the latter eating only the roots; its flesh is very little inferior, and is often sold in our markets for the Canvass Back to those unacquainted with the characteristic marks of each. Anxious as I am to determine precisely whether this species be the Red-headed Widgeon, Pochard, or Dun Bird † of England, I have not been able to ascertain the point to my own satisfaction, though I think it very probably the same, the size, extent, and general description of the Pochard, agreeing pretty nearly with this.

The Red-Head is twenty inches in length, and two feet six inches in extent; bill, dark slate, sometimes black, two inches long, and seven eighths of an inch thick at the base, furnished with a large, broad nail at the extremity; irides, flame colored; plumage of the head, long, velvety, and inflated, running high above the base of the bill; head and about two inches of the neck, deep glossy reddish chestnut; rest of the neck and upper part of the breast, black, spreading round to the back; belly, white, becoming dusky towards the vent by closely-marked, undulating lines of black; back and scapulars, bluish white, rendered gray by numerous transverse, waving lines of black; lesser wing-coverts, brownish ash; wing-quills, very pale slate, dusky at the tips; lower part of the back and sides under the wings,

* A well-known Duck, common to both continents, keeping to the sea or large lakes, and only in very severe winters wandering to any extent inland. Sometimes seen in the decoys; but very seldom taken, from their expertness in diving under the tunnel. — Ed.

† Local names given to one and the same Duck. It is also called the Poker.

brownish black, crossed with regular zigzag lines of whitish; vent, rump, tail, and tail-coverts, black; legs and feet, dark ash.

The female has the upper part of the head dusky brown, rest of the head and part of the neck, a light sooty brown; upper part of the breast, ashy brown, broadly skirted with whitish; back, dark ash, with little or no appearance of white pencilling; wings, bill, and feet, nearly alike in both sexes.

This Duck is sometimes met with in the rivers of North and South Carolina, and also in those of Jersey and New York, but always in fresh water, and usually at no great distance from the sea; is most numerous in the waters of the Chesapeake; and, with the connoisseurs in good eating, ranks next in excellence to the Canvass-Back. Its usual weight is about a pound and three quarters avoirdupois.

The Red-Head leaves the bay and its tributary streams in March, and is not seen till late in October.

The male of this species has a large, flat, bony labyrinth on the bottom of the windpipe, very much like that of the Canvass-Back, but smaller; over one of its concave sides is spread an exceeding thin, transparent skin, or membrane. The intestines are of great width, and measure six feet in length.

THE MALLARD. — ANAS BOSCHAS. — FIG. 292.

Lath. Syn. iii. p. 489. — *Bewick,* ii. p. 291. — Le Canard sauvage, *Briss.* vi. p. 318, 4. — *Buff.* ix. p. 415, pl. 7, 8. — *Peale's Museum,* No. 2864.

BOSCHAS MAJOR. — WILLOUGHBY.*

Anas boschas, *Linn. Syst.* — *Gmel.* i. p. 538. — *Bonap. Synop.* p. 382. — *Flem. Br. Anim.* p. 123. — Le canard sauvage, *Temm. Man.* p. 385. — Wild Duck, *Mont. Orinth. Dict.* ii. and *Supp.* — Common Wild Duck, *Selby Illust. Br. Ornith.* pl. 5. Anas (boschas) domestica, *North. Zool.* ii. p. 442.

THE Mallard, or Common Wild-Drake, is so universally known as scarcely to require a description. It measures twenty-four inches in length, by three feet in extent, and weighs upwards of two pounds

---

* This well-known species becomes interesting when considered as the stock whence the most flourishing duckeries of the poultry-yard have sprung; it is most amply spread over Europe and America, and I have received it from India. Universally known, it is esteemed for the table, and will fetch a higher price in the markets than most of the others in this country, and in America seems only surpassed by the Canvass-Back. In structure and general economy, it presents a most interesting form, combining the peculiarities of the pelagic and more terrestrial. It will live and find a sustenance in the sea and its coasts, by lakes and rivers, and in the midst of extensive moors and fens; it possesses a powerful frame, and its wings are adapted to strong flight; it can derive its sustenance either from the waters or the more inland pastures and cultivated fields; it is an expert diver when necessity calls it; and its breeding places are chosen by the sides of lakes and marshes, on the stumps of aged trees, like the Summer Duck, and on precipitous cliffs. In the latter situation, I once took the nest of a Wild Duck within ten yards' distance from that of a Peregrine Falcon. It was situated on a project-

and a half; the bill is greenish yellow; irides, hazel; head, and part of the neck, deep glossy changeable green, ending in a narrow collar of white; the rest of the neck and breast are of a dark purplish chestnut; lesser wing-coverts, brown ash; greater, crossed near the extremities with a band of white, and tipped with another of deep velvety black; below this lies the speculum, or beauty spot, of a rich and splendid light purple, with green and violet reflections, bounded on every side with black; quills, pale brownish ash; back, brown, skirted with paler; scapulars, whitish, crossed with fine, undulating lines of black; rump and tail-coverts, black, glossed with green; tertials, very broad, and pointed at the ends; tail, consisting of eighteen feathers, whitish, centred with brown ash, the four middle ones excepted, which are narrow, black, glossed with violet, remarkably concave, and curled upwards to a complete circle; belly and sides, a fine gray, crossed by an infinite number of fine, waving lines, stronger and more deeply marked as they approach the vent; legs and feet, orange red.

The female has the plumage of the upper parts dark brown, broadly bordered with brownish yellow; and the lower parts yellow ochre, spotted and streaked with deep brown; the chin and throat, for about two inches, plain yellowish white; wings, bill, and legs, nearly as in the male.

The windpipe of the male has a bony labyrinth, or bladder-like knob, puffing out from the left side. The intestines measure six feet, and are as wide as those of the Canvass-Back. The windpipe is of uniform diameter, until it enters the labyrinth.

This is the original stock of the common domesticated Duck, reclaimed, time immemorial, from a state of nature, and now become so serviceable to man. In many individuals, the general garb of the tame drake seems to have undergone little or no alteration; but the stamp of slavery is strongly imprinted in his dull, indifferent eye and grovelling gait, while the lofty look, long, tapering neck, and sprightly action of the former bespeak his native spirit and independence.

The Common Wild Duck is found in every fresh-water lake and river of the United States in winter, but seldom frequents the sea-shores or salt marshes. Their summer residence is the north, the great nursery of this numerous genus. Instances have been known of some solitary pairs breeding here in autumn. In England these instances are more common. The nest is usually placed in the most solitary recesses of the marsh, or bog, amidst coarse grass, reeds, and rushes, and generally contains from twelve to sixteen eggs, of a dull greenish white. The young are led about by the mother in the same manner as those of the Tame Duck, but with a superior caution, a cunning and watchful vigilance peculiar to her situation. The male attaches himself to one female, as among other birds in their native state, and is the guardian and protector of her and her feeble brood. The Mallard is numerous in the rice-fields of the Southern States during winter, many of the fields being covered with a few inches of water; and, the

---

ing knoll of heather, jutting from an ivied cliff, and the tenants must often have seen each other in their passage to and from their precious deposits. In this species we have the type of the genus *Boschas*. The centre feathers of the tail are lengthened, but assume a different form, in being regularly rolled or curled up. Some specimens want the white ring round the neck, and in some parts this variety is so common, as to be distinguished by the herds and country people. — ED.

scattered grains of the former harvest lying in abundance, the Ducks swim about, and feed at pleasure.

The flesh of the Common Wild Duck is in general and high estimation; and the ingenuity of man, in every country where it frequents, has been employed in inventing stratagems to overreach these wary birds, and procure a delicacy for the table. To enumerate all these various contrivances would far exceed our limits; a few, however, of the most simple and effective may be mentioned.

In some ponds frequented by these birds, five or six wooden figures, cut and painted so as to represent Ducks, and sunk, by pieces of lead nailed on their bottoms, so as to float at the usual depth on the surface, are anchored in a favorable position for being raked from a concealment of brush, &c., on shore. The appearance of these usually attracts passing flocks, which alight, and are shot down. Sometimes eight or ten of these painted wooden Ducks are fixed on a frame in various swimming postures, and secured to the bow of the gunner's skiff, projecting before it in such a manner that the weight of the frame sinks the figures to their proper depth; the skiff is then dressed with sedge or coarse grass in an artful manner, as low as the water's edge; and under cover of this, which appears like a party of Ducks swimming by a small island, the gunner floats down sometimes to the very skirts of a whole congregated multitude, and pours in a destructive and repeated fire of shot among them. In winter, when detached pieces of ice are occasionally floating in the river, some of the gunners on the Delaware paint their whole skiff or canoe white, and, laying themselves flat at the bottom, with their hand over the side, silently managing a small paddle, direct it imperceptibly into or near a flock, before the Ducks have distinguished it from a floating mass of ice, and generally do great execution among them. A whole flock has sometimes been thus surprised asleep, with their heads under their wings. On land another stratagem is sometimes practised with great success. A large, tight hogshead is sunk in the flat marsh, or mud, near the place where Ducks are accustomed to feed at low water, and where otherwise there is no shelter; the edges and top are artfully concealed with tufts of long, coarse grass, and reeds or sedge. From within this the gunner, unseen and unsuspected, watches his collecting prey, and, when a sufficient number offers, sweeps them down with great effect. The mode of catching Wild Ducks, as practised in India,* China,† the Island of Ceylon, and some parts of South America,‡ has been often described, and seems, if reliance may be placed on those accounts, only practicable in water of a certain depth. The sportsman, covering his head with a hollow wooden vessel, or calabash, pierced with holes to see through, wades into the water, keeping his head only above, and, thus disguised, moves in among the flock, which take the appearance to be a mere floating calabash, while, suddenly pulling them under by the legs, he fastens them to his girdle, and thus takes as many as he can conveniently stow away, without in the least alarming the rest. They are also taken with snares made of horse hair, or with hooks baited with small pieces of sheep's lights,

---

* *Naval Chronicle*, vol. ii. p. 473.
† Du Halde, *History of China*, vol. ii. p. 142.
‡ Ulloa's *Voyage*, i. p. 53.

which, floating on the surface, are swallowed by the Ducks, and with them the hooks. They are also approached under cover of a stalking horse, or a figure formed of thin boards, or other proper materials, and painted so as to represent a horse or ox. But all these methods require much watching, toil, and fatigue, and their success is but trifling when compared with that of the decoy now used both in France and England,* which, from its superiority over every other mode, is well deserving the attention of persons of this country residing in the neighborhood of extensive marshes frequented by Wild Ducks, as, by this method, Mallard and other kinds may be taken by thousands at a time. The following circumstantial account of these decoys, and the manner of taking Wild Ducks in them in England, is extracted from Bewick's *History of British Birds*, vol. ii. p. 294 : —

"In the lakes where they resort," says the correspondent of that ingenious author, "the most favorite haunts of the fowl are observed: then, in the most sequestered part of this haunt, they cut a ditch about four yards across at the entrance, and about fifty or sixty yards in length, decreasing gradually in width from the entrance to the farther end, which is not more than two feet wide. It is of a circular form, but not bending much for the first ten yards. The banks of the lake, for about ten yards on each side of this ditch, (or pipe, as it is called,) are kept clear from reeds, coarse herbage, &c., in order that the fowl may get on them to sit and dress themselves. Across this ditch, poles on each side, close to the edge of the ditch, are driven into the ground, and the tops bent to each other and tied fast. These poles at the entrance form an arch, from the top of which to the water is about ten feet. This arch is made to decrease in height, as the ditch decreases in width, till the farther end is not more than eighteen inches in height. The poles are placed about six foot from each other, and connected together by poles laid lengthwise across the arch, and tied together. Over them a net, with meshes sufficiently small to prevent the fowl getting through, is thrown across, and made fast to a reed fence at the entrance, and nine or ten yards up the ditch, and afterwards strongly pegged to the ground. At the farther end of the pipe, a tunnel net, as it is called, is fixed, about four yards in length, of a round form, and kept open by a number of hoops about eighteen inches in diameter, placed at a small distance from each other, to keep it distended. Supposing the circular bend of the pipe to be to the right, when you stand with your back to the lake, on the left hand side a number of reed fences are constructed, called shootings, for the purpose of screening from sight the decoy-man, and in such a manner, that the fowl in the decoy may not be alarmed while he is driving those in the pipe : these shootings are about four yards in length, and about six feet high, and are ten in number. They are placed in the following manner : —

---

* Particularly in Picardy, in the former country, and Lincolnshire in the latter.

From the end of the last shooting, a person cannot see the lake,
owing to the bend of the pipe: there is then no further occasion for
shelter. Were it not for those shootings, the fowl that remain about
the mouth of the pipe would be alarmed, if the person driving the fowl
already under the net should be exposed, and would become so shy as
to forsake the place entirely. The first thing the decoy-man does when
he approaches the pipe, is to take a piece of lighted turf or peat, and
hold it near his mouth, to prevent the fowl smelling him. He is attended by a dog taught for the purpose of assisting him; he walks
very silently about half-way up the shootings, where a small piece of
wood is thrust through the reed fence, which makes an aperture just
sufficient to see if any fowl are in; if not, he walks forward to see if
any are about the mouth of the pipe. If there are, he stops and makes
a motion to his dog, and gives him a piece of cheese or something to
eat; upon receiving it he goes directly to a hole through the reed
fence, (No. 1,) and the fowl immediately fly off the bank into the
water; the dog returns along the bank, between the reed fences and
the pipe, and comes out to his master at the hole, (No. 2.) The man
now gives him another reward, and he repeats his round again, till the
fowl are attracted by the motions of the dog, and follow him into the
mouth of the pipe. This operation is called working them. The man
now retreats farther back, working the dog at different holes till the
fowl are sufficiently under the net; he now commands his dog to lie
down still behind the fence, and goes forward to the end of the pipe
next the lake, where he takes off his hat and gives it a wave between
the shooting; all the fowl under the net can see him, but none that are
in the lake can. The fowl that are in sight fly forward; and the man
runs forward to the next shooting, and waves his hat, and so on, driving them along till they come to the tunnel net, where they creep in:
when they are all in, he gives the net a twist, so as to prevent their
getting back: he then takes the net off from the end of the pipe, with
what fowl he may have caught, and takes them out, one at a time, and
dislocates their necks, and hangs the net on again; and all is ready
for working again.

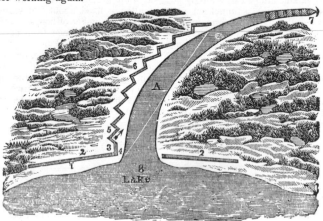

REFERENCES TO THE CUT.

No. 1. Dog's hole, where he goes to unbank the fowl.
    2. Reed fences on each side of the mouth of the pipe.
    3. Where the decoy-man shows himself to the fowl first, and afterwards at the end of every shooting.
    4. Small reed fence to prevent the fowl seeing the dog when he goes to unbank them.
    5. The shootings.
    6. Dog's holes between the shootings, used when working.
    7. Tunnel net at the end of the pipe.
    8. Mouth of the pipe.

"In this manner, five or six dozen have been taken at one drift. When the wind blows directly in or out of the pipe, the fowl seldom work well, especially when it blows in. If many pipes are made in a lake, they should be so constructed as to suit different winds.

"Duck and Mallard are taken from August to June; Teal or Widgeon from October to March; Becks, Smee, Golden Eyes, Arps, Cricks, and Pintails or Sea Pheasants, in March and April.

"Poker Ducks are seldom taken, on account of their diving and getting back in the pipe.

"It may be proper to observe here, that the Ducks feed during the night, and that all is ready prepared for this sport in the evening. The better to entice the Ducks into the pipe, hemp seed is strowed occasionally on the water. The season allowed, by act of Parliament, for catching these birds in this way, is from the latter end of October till February.

"Particular spots, or decoys, in the fen countries, are let to the fowlers at a rent of from five to thirty pounds per annum; and Pennant instances a season in which thirty-one thousand two hundred Ducks, including Teals and Widgeons, were sold in London only, from ten of these decoys near Wainfleet, in Lincolnshire. Formerly, according to Willoughby, the Ducks while in moult, and unable to fly, were driven by men in boats, furnished with long poles, with which they splashed the water between long nets, stretched vertically across the pools, in the shape of two sides of a triangle, into lesser nets placed at the point; and, in this way, he says, four thousand were taken at one driving in Deeping-Fen; and Latham has quoted an instance of two thousand six hundred and forty-six being taken in two days, near Spalding, in Lincolnshire; but this manner of catching them, while in moult, is now prohibited."

52

THE GADWALL. — ANAS STREPERA. — Fig. 293.

Le Chipeau, *Briss.* vi. p. 339, 8, pl. 33, fig. 1. — *Buff.* ix. 187. *Pl. enl.* 958. — *Arct. Zool.* p. 575. — *Lath. Syn.* iii. p. 515. — *Peale's Museum,* No. 2750.

CHAULIODUS STREPERA. — Swainson. *

Anas strepera, *Linn. Syst.* i. p. 200. — *Lath. Ind. Ornith.* ii. p. 859. — *Bonap. Synop.* p. 383. — Canard chipeau, ou ridenne, *Temm. Man.* ii. p. 837. — Gadwall or Gray, *Mont. Ornith. Dict.* i. and *Supp.* — *Bew. Br. Birds,* ii. 350. — Gadwall, *Selby's Illust. Brit. Ornith.* pl. 51. — Anas (chauliodus) strepera, *North. Zool.* ii. p. 440. — Genus Chauliodus, *Swain. Journ. Royal Instit.* No. iv. p. 19.

This beautiful Duck I have met with in the very distant parts of the United States, viz., on the Seneca Lake, in New York, about the 20th of October, and at Louisville, on the Ohio, in February. I also shot it near Big Bone Lick, in Kentucky. With its particular manners or breeding place, I am altogether unacquainted.

The length of this species is twenty inches; extent, thirty-one inches; bill, two inches long, formed very much like that of the Mallard, and of a brownish black; crown, dusky brown; rest of the upper half of the neck, brownish white, both thickly speckled with black; lower part of the neck and breast, dusky black, elegantly ornamented with large, concentric semicircles of white; scapulars waved with lines of white on a dusky ground, but narrower than that of the breast; primaries, ash; greater wing-coverts, black, and several of the lesser coverts, immediately above, chestnut red; speculum, white, bordered below with black, forming three broad bands on the wing, of chestnut, black, and white; belly, dull white; rump and tail-coverts, black, glossed with green; tail, tapering, pointed, of a pale brown ash, edged with white; flanks, dull white, elegantly waved; tertials, long, and of a pale brown; legs, orange red.

The female I have never seen. Latham describes it as follows: — " Differs in having the colors on the wings duller, though marked the same as the male; the breast, reddish brown, spotted with black; the feathers on the neck and back, edged with pale red; rump, the same, instead of black; and those elegant semicircular lines on the neck and breast wholly wanting."

The flesh of this Duck is excellent, and the windpipe of the male is furnished with a large labyrinth.

The Gadwall is very rare in the northern parts of the United States; is said to inhabit England in winter, and various parts of France and Italy; migrates to Sweden, and is found throughout Russia and Siberia.†

* This beautiful Duck is remarkable in presenting, next to the Shovellers, the greatest development of lateral laminæ of the bill; it is also an expert diver.
In Britain they are rare, but appear more common in the lower countries of Europe and towards the north. They seem very abundant in Holland; in the months of September and October they were the most common Duck in the market, and were often seen in abundance on the lakes. It will show Mr. Swainson's genus *Chauliodus.* — Ed.
† Latham.

It is a very quick diver, so as to make it difficult to be shot; flies also with great rapidity, and utters a note not unlike that of the Mallard, but louder; is fond of salines and ponds overgrown with reeds and rushes; feeds during the day, as well as in the morning and evening.

EIDER DUCK.— ANAS MOLLISSIMA.— Fig. 294.— Male.

L'Oye à duvet, ou l'Eider, *Briss.* vi. p. 294, pl. 29, 3. — *Buff.* ix. p. 103, pl. 6. *Pl. enl.* 209. — Great Black and White Duck, *Edw.* pl. 98. — *Bewick,* ii. p. 279. *Arct. Zool.* No. 480.— *Lath. Syn.* iii. p. 470. — *Peale's Museum,* No. 2706.

SOMATERIA MOLLISSIMA. — Leach.*

Anas mollissima, *Linn. Syst.* i. p. 198. — Canard eider, *Temm. Man. d'Ornith.* ii. p. 848. — Eider, or Cuthbert's Duck, *Mont. Ornith. Dict.* i. and *Supp.* — Eider, *Selby, Illust. Br. Ornith.* p. 70. — Fuligula, (sub-gen. somateria) mollissima, *Bonap. Synop.* p. 388. — Somateria mollissima, *North. Zool.* ii. p. 448.

THE Eider Duck has been long celebrated in Europe, for the abundance and excellence of its down, which, for softness, warmth, lightness, and elasticity, surpasses that of all other Ducks. The quantity found in one nest more than filled the crown of a hat, yet weighed no more than three quarters of an ounce;† and it is asserted, that three pounds of this down may be compressed into a space scarce bigger

---

* This other form among the *Anatidæ* was proposed by Dr. Leach, and will contain only two species, the Eider and King Ducks, both common to Europe and America. It is very well marked, and possesses some peculiarities. The birds are truly Sea Ducks, keep entirely to that element, and breed on its shores or islands, and are never, as Dr. Richardson remarks, seen on fresh water. The form is thick, rather flat and heavy; the plumage of the males possesses decided contrasting colors of black and white; the females, reddish brown; the plumage of the head projects far upon the base of the bill, and is of a thick, silky texture, which can be raised or swelled at pleasure, so as to increase the apparent size of the head and neck, and in both species exhibits remarkable colors, not often seen among birds, and very difficult for colorists to represent — pistachia green, and a pleasing dull shade of blue verditer. In the scapulars of the *Anatidæ*, we have already seen a variable structure; they are here of considerable breadth, rigid texture, and curve over the quills, as if curled with an iron. The feet are placed far back, and show great powers for diving. The males undergo a change of plumage, and leave the females as soon as they have commenced sitting, when they may be seen in large flocks by themselves; they commence their migrations much sooner than the females. It is to this bird, that we are principally indebted for the valuable Eider down, though many others of the northern aquatic fowl produce one equally fine, which is often mixed with it. Lemmius remarks, that the Eiders are in immense profusion on the coasts of Norway and Lapland; when hatching, the eggs are often the prey of the Crows and of *Larus marinus*, who drag the female from her nest, and destroy them or the young. The male, however, if he perceives the assault, makes furious attacks, and sometimes succeeds in beating them off. They are very familiar, building close to the houses of the fishermen; the female will even allow herself to be lifted from the eggs and set down again; and sometimes a countryman will carry the young in his hat from the nest to the sea, the Duck running by his side, moaning gently with anxiety. — ED.

† PENNANT.

than a man's fist, yet is afterwards so dilatable as to fill a quilt five feet square.*

The native regions of the Eider Duck extend from 45° N. to the highest latitudes yet discovered, both in Europe and America. Solitary rocky shores and islands are their favorite haunts. Some wandering pairs have been known to breed on the rocky islands beyond Portland, in the district of Maine, which is perhaps the most southern extent of their breeding place. In England, the Fern Isles, on the coast of Northumberland, are annually visited by a few of these birds, being the only place in South Britain where they are known to breed. They occur again in some of the Western Isles of Scotland. Greenland and Iceland abound with them, and here, in particular places, their nests are crowded so close together, that a person can scarcely walk without treading on them. The natives of these countries know the value of the down, and carry on a regular system of plunder, both of it and also of the eggs. The nest is generally formed outwardly of drift-grass, dry sea-weed, and such like materials ; the inside composed of a large quantity of down, plucked from the breast of the female. In this soft, elastic bed she deposits five eggs, extremely smooth and glossy, of a pale olive color ; they are also warmly covered with the same kind of down. When the whole number is laid, they are taken away by the natives, and also the down with which the nest is lined, together with that which covers the eggs. The female once more strips her breast of the remaining down, and lays a second time ; even this, with the eggs, is generally taken away ; and it is said that the male, in this extremity, furnishes the third quantity of down from his own breast ; but if the cruel robbery be a third time repeated, they abandon the place altogether. One female, during the whole time of laying, generally gives half a pound of down ; and we are told, that, in the year 1750, the Iceland Company sold as much of this article, as amounted to three thousand seven hundred and forty-five banco dollars, besides what was directly sent to Gluckstadt.† The down from dead birds is little esteemed, having lost its elasticity.

These birds associate together in flocks, generally in deep water, diving for shell fish, which constitute their principal food. They frequently retire to the rocky shores to rest, particularly on the appearance of an approaching storm. They are numerous on the coast of Labrador, and are occasionally seen in winter as far south as the Capes of Delaware. Their flesh is esteemed by the inhabitants of Greenland, but tastes strongly of fish.

The length of this species is two feet three inches ; extent, three feet ; weight, between six and seven pounds ; the head is large, and the bill of singular structure, being three inches in length, forked in a remarkable manner, running high up in the forehead, between which the plumage descends nearly to the nostril ; the whole of the bill is of a dull yellowish horn color, somewhat dusky in the middle ; upper part of the head, deep velvet black, divided laterally on the hind head by a whitish band ; cheeks, white ; sides of the head, pale pea-green, marked with a narrow line of white, dropped from the ear-feathers ; the

---

* *Salern. Ornith.* p. 416.
† *Letters on Iceland*, by UNO VAN TROIL, p. 146.

plumage of this part of the head, to the throat, is tumid, and looks as if cut off at the end, for immediately below the neck it suddenly narrows, somewhat in the manner of the Buffel-Head, enlarging again greatly as it descends, and has a singular hollow between the shoulders behind; the upper part of the neck, the back, scapulars, lesser wing-coverts, and sides of the rump, are pure white; lower part of the breast, belly, and vent, black; tail, primaries, and secondaries, brownish black; the tertials curiously curved, falling over the wing; legs, short, yellow; webs of the feet, dusky.

Latham has given us the following sketch of the gradual progress of the young males to their perfect colors: — "In the first year the back is white, and the usual parts, except the crown, black; but the rest of the body is variegated with black and white. In the second year, the neck and breast are spotted black and white, and the crown black. In the third, the colors are nearly as when in full plumage, but less vivid, and a few spots of black still remaining on the neck; the crown, black, and bifid at the back part.

"The young of both sexes are the same, being covered with a kind of hairy down; throat, and breast, whitish; and a cinereous line from the bill through the eyes to the hind head."*

FEMALE EIDER DUCK. — Fig. 295.

Peale's Museum, No. 2707.

SOMATERIA MOLLISSIMA. — Leach.

The difference of color in these two birds is singularly great. The female is considerably less than the male, and the bill does not rise so high in the forehead; the general color is a dark reddish drab, mingled with lighter touches, and every where spotted with black; wings, dusky, edged with reddish; the greater coverts, and some of the secondaries, are tipped with white; tail, brownish black, lighter than in the male; the plumage in general is centred with bars of black, and broadly bordered with rufous drab; checks, and space over the eye, light drab; belly, dusky, obscurely mottled with black; legs, and feet, as in the male.

Van Troil, in his *Letters on Iceland,* observes, respecting this Duck, that "the young ones quit the nest soon after they are hatched, and follow the female, who leads them to the water, where, having taken them on her back, she swims with them a few yards, and then dives, and leaves them floating on the water! In this situation they soon learn to take care of themselves, and are seldom afterwards seen on the land, but live among the rocks, and feed on insects and sea-weed."

Some attempts have been made to domesticate these birds, but hitherto without success.

* *Synopsis,* iii. 471.

52 *

THE SMEW OR WHITE NUN.—MERGUS ALBELLUS.—
Fig. 296.

Le petit harle huppé, ou la piette, *Briss.* vi. p. 243, 3, pl. 24, fig. 1.— *Buff.* viii. p. 275, pl. 24. *Pl. enl.* 449.— *Bewick*, ii. p. 238.— *Lath. Syn.* iii. p. 428.— *Arct. Zool.* No. 468.

MERGUS ALBELLUS. — Linnæus.*

Mergus albellus, *Linn. Syst.* i. p. 209. — *Bonap. Synop.* p. 397. — Harle piette, *Temm. Man. d'Ornith.* ii. p. 887. — Minute Merganser, *Mont. Ornith. Dict.* i. and *Supp.* — Lough Diver, and Red-headed Smew, *Penn.* for young and female. — Smew, *Selby, Illust. Br. Ornith.* pl. 69.

THIS is another of those Mergansers commonly known in this country by the appellation of Fishermen, Fisher Ducks, or Divers. The present species is much more common on the coast of New England than farther to the south. On the shores of New Jersey, it is very seldom met with. It is an admirable diver, and can continue for a long time under water. Its food is small fry, shell fish, shrimps, &c. In England, as with us, the Smew is seen only during winter; it is also found in France, in some parts of which it is called *la Piette*, as in parts of England it is named the Magpie Driver. Its breeding place is doubtless in the Arctic regions, as it frequents Iceland; and has been observed to migrate with other Mergansers, and several kinds of Ducks, up the River Wolga in February.†

The Smew, or White Nun, is nineteen inches in length, and two feet three inches in extent; bill, black, formed very much like that of the Red-breasted Merganser, but not so strongly toothed; irides, dark; head, crested; crown, white; hind head, black; round the area of the eye, a large, oval space of black; whole neck, breast, and belly, white, marked on the upper and lower part of the breast with a curving line of black; back, black; scapulars, white, crossed with several faint dusky bars; shoulder of the wing, and primaries, black; secondaries, and greater coverts, black, broadly tipped with white; across the lesser coverts, a large band of white; sides and flanks, crossed with waving lines; tail, dark ash; legs and feet, pale bluish slate.

The female is considerably less than the male; the bill, a dark lead color; crest, of the same peculiar form as that of the male, but less, and of a reddish brown; marked round the area of the eyes with dusky; cheeks, fore part of the neck, and belly, white; round the middle of the neck, a collar of pale brown; breast and shoulders, dull brown and whitish intermixed; wings and back, marked, like those of the male, but of a deep brownish ash in those parts which in him are

---

* The male of this Merganser is one of the cleanest and most delicate looking of the genus, the colors being entirely of the purest black and white. The bill presents a shorter and more dilated form than its congeners, approaching almost to some of the more aberrant Ducks. It is very rare in this country, and appears only in winter. The propagation and extent of the breeding migrations are only surmised, and we possess no very authentic authority upon the subject; they are said, however, to resemble the others. — ED.

† *Dec. Russ.* ii. p. 145.

black; legs and feet, pale blue. The young birds, as in the other three species, strongly resemble the female during the first and part of the second year. As these changes of color, from the garb of the female to that of the male, take place in the remote regions of the north, we have not the opportunity of detecting them in their gradual progress to full plumage. Hence, as both males and females have been found in the same dress, some writers have considered them as a separate species from the Smew, and have given to them the title of the Red-headed Smew.

In the ponds of New England, and some of the lakes in the state of New York, where the Smew is frequently observed, these Red-headed kind are often found in company, and more numerous than the other, for very obvious reasons, and bear, in the markings, though not in the colors of their plumage, evident proof of their being the same species, but younger birds, or females. The male, like the Muscovy Drake and many others, when arrived at his full size, is nearly one third heavier than the female; and this disproportion of weight, and difference of color, in the full-grown males and females, are characteristic of the whole genus.

RUDDY DUCK. — ANAS RUBIDUS. — Fig. 297. — Male.

Peale's Museum, No. 2808.

FULIGULA RUBIDA. — Bonaparte:*

Fuligula (oxyura) rubida, *Bonap. Synop.* p. 391. — Fuligula rubida, *North. Zool.* ii. p. 455. — Anas Jamaicensis, *Ord's edit.* p. 133.

This very rare Duck was shot, some years ago, on the River Delaware, and appears to be an entire new species. The specimen here figured, with the female that accompanies it, and which was killed in the same river, are the only individuals of their kind I have met with. They are both preserved in the superb museum of my much respected friend, Mr. Peale, of this city.

On comparing this Duck with the description given by Latham of the Jamaica Shoveller, I was at first inclined to believe I had found out the species; but a more careful examination of both satisfied me that they cannot be the same, as the present differs considerably in color; and, besides, has some peculiarities which the eye of that acute ornithologist could not possibly have overlooked, in his examination

---

* Bonaparte has proposed this form as the type of a sub-genus, under the name of *Oxyura,* from the form of the tail. And Mr. Swainson observes, "We suspect that this bird, and one or two others of similar form, found by us in tropical Brazil, will constitute a sub-genus." There are many modifications from the *Fuligulæ* in this bird, which would, with additional species, entitle a sub-genus; and, in that case, *Oxyura* may be adopted. They seem very rare, and Wilson has the merit of first distinguishing them; the bill becomes much broader at the tip, and the lamellæ are more prominent than in *Fuligula;* the feet are placed very far back; and the hind toe is furnished with a much narrower membrane. — Ed.

of the species said to have been received by him from Jamaica. Wherever the general residence of this species may be, in this part of the world, at least, it is extremely rare, since, among the many thousands of Ducks brought to our markets during winter, I have never heard of a single individual of the present kind having been found among them.

The Ruddy Duck is fifteen inches and a half in length, and twenty-two inches in extent; the bill is broad at the tip, the under mandible much narrower, and both of a rich, light blue; nostrils, small, placed in the middle of the bill; cheeks, and chin, white; front, crown, and back part of the neck, down nearly to the back, black; rest of the neck, whole back, scapulars, flanks, and tail-coverts, deep reddish brown, the color of bright mahogany; wings, plain pale drab, darkest at the points; tail, black, greatly tapering, containing eighteen narrow-pointed feathers; the plumage of the breast and upper part of the neck is of a remarkable kind, being dusky olive at bottom, ending in hard, bristly points, of a silvery gray, very much resembling the hair of some kinds of seal-skins; all these are thickly marked with transverse, curving lines of deep brown; belly and vent, silver gray, thickly crossed with dusky olive; under tail-coverts, white; legs and feet, ash colored.

FEMALE RUDDY DUCK. — Fig. 298.

Peale's Museum, No. 2809.

FULIGULA RUBIDA. — Bonaparte, Young.

THIS is nearly of the same size as the male; the front, lores, and crown, deep blackish brown; bill, as in the male, very broad at the extremity, and largely toothed on the sides, of the same rich blue; cheeks, a dull cream; neck, plain dull drab, sprinkled about the auriculars with blackish; lower part of the neck and breast, variegated with gray, ash, and reddish brown; the reddish dies off towards the belly, leaving this last of a dull white, shaded with dusky ash; wings, as in the male; tail, brown; scapulars, dusky brown, thickly sprinkled with whitish, giving them a gray appearance; legs, ash.

A particular character of this species is its tapering, sharp-pointed tail, the feathers of which are very narrow; the body is short; the bill, very nearly as broad as some of those called Shovellers; the lower mandible much narrower than the upper.

THE BRANT. — ANAS BERNICLA. — Fig. 290.

Le cravant, *Briss.* vi p. 304, 16, pl. 91. — *Buff.* ix. p. 87. — *Bew.* ii. p. 277. — *Lath. Syn.* iii. p. 467. — *Arct. Zool.* No. 478. — *Peale's Museum*, No. 2704.

BERNICLA BRENTA. — Stephens.*

Bernicla brenta, *Steph. Cont. Sh. Zool.* xii. p. 46. — Oie cravant, *Temm. Man.* ii. p. 824. — Ansa brenta, *Flem. Br. Anim.* p. 127. — Anser bernicla, *North. Zool.* ii. p. 469. — Brent, or Boord Goose, *Mont. Orn. Dict.* and *Supp.* — *Bew. Br. Birds,* ii. p. 311. — Brent bernicle, *Selby, Illust. Br. Orn.* pl. 65.

THE Brant, or, as it is usually written, *Brent*, is a bird well known on both continents, and celebrated in former times throughout Europe for the singularity of its origin, and the strange transformations it was supposed to undergo previous to its complete organization. Its first appearance was said to be in the form of a barnacle shell adhering to old water-soaked logs, trees, or other pieces of wood taken from the sea. Of this Goose-bearing tree, Gerard, in his *Herbal*, published in 1597, has given a formal account; and seems to have reserved it for the conclusion of his work, as being the most wonderful of all he had to describe. The honest naturalist, however, though his belief was fixed, acknowledges that his own personal information was derived from certain shells which adhered to a rotten tree that he dragged out of the sea between Dover and Romney, in England; in some of which he found "living things without forme or shape; in others which were nearer come to ripeness, living things that were very naked, in shape like a birde; in others, the birds covered with soft downe, the shell half open, and the birde readio to fall out, which no doubt were the foules called Barnakles."[†] Ridiculous and chimerical as this notion was, it had many advocates, and was at that time as generally believed, and with about as much reason too, as the present opinion of the annual submersion of Swallows, so tenaciously insisted on by some of our philosophers, and which, like the former absurdity, will in its turn disappear before the penetrating radiance and calm investigation of truth.

The Brant and Barnacle Goose, though generally reckoned two different species, I consider to be the same. Among those large flocks that arrive on our coasts about the beginning of October, individuals frequently occur corresponding in their markings with that called the Bernacle of Europe; that is, in having the upper parts lighter, and the front, cheeks, and chin whitish. These appear evidently a variety of the Brant, probably young birds: what strengthens this last opinion is

---

* Stephens first applied this title, as a generic one, to a considerable number of birds, and gives, as their characters, "distinguished from the Geese by their shorter and slenderer beak, the edges of which are reflected over the lamellæ, and obstruct the view of them." We shall consider the form to which that title should be restricted to be that of the present — the *B. erythropus*, and *B. ruficollis*. Many of those admitted by Stephens show very different characters, and will range elsewhere. — ED.

† See GERARD'S *Herbal*, Art. Goose-bearing Tree.

the fact that none of them are found so marked on their return northward in the spring.

The Brant is expected at Egg Harbor, on the coast of New Jersey,
about the first of October, and has been sometimes seen as early as
the 20th of September. The first flocks generally remain in the bay
a few days, and then pass on to the south. On recommencing their
journey, they collect in one large body, and, making an extensive spiral course, some miles in diameter, rise to a great height in the air,
and then steer for the sea, over which they uniformly travel; often
making wide circuits to avoid passing over a projecting point of land.
In these aërial routes, they have been met with many leagues from
shore, travelling the whole night. Their line of march very much resembles that of the Canada Goose, with this exception, that frequently
three or four are crowded together in the front, as if striving for prece-
dency. Flocks continue to arrive from the north, and many remain in
the bay till December, or until the weather becomes very severe, when
these also move off southwardly. During their stay, they feed on the
bars at low water, seldom or never in the marshes; their principal food
being a remarkably long and broad-leaved marine plant, of a bright
green color, which adheres to stones, and is called by the country people sea cabbage; the leaves of this are sometimes eight or ten inches
broad, by two or three feet in length: they also eat small shell fish.
They never dive, but wade about, feeding at low water. During the
time of high water, they float in the bay in long lines, particularly in
calm weather. Their voice is hoarse and honking, and, when some
hundreds are screaming together, reminds one of a pack of hounds in
full cry. They often quarrel among themselves, and with the Ducks,
driving the latter off their feeding ground. Though it never dives in
search of food, yet, when wing-broken, the Brant will go one hundred
yards at a stretch under water; and is considered, in such circumstances, one of the most difficult birds to kill. About the 15th or 20th
of May, they reappear on their way north; but seldom stop long, unless driven in by tempestuous weather.

The breeding place of the Brant is supposed to be very far to the
north. They are common at Hudson's Bay, very numerous in winter
on the coasts of Holland and Ireland; are called in Shetland Harra
Geese, from their frequenting the sand of that name; they also visit
the coast of England. Buffon relates that, in the severe winters of
1740 and 1765, during the prevalence of a strong north wind, the Brant
visited the coast of Picardy, in France, in prodigious multitudes, and
committed great depredations on the corn, tearing it up by the roots,
trampling, and devouring it; and, notwithstanding the exertions of the
inhabitants, who were constantly employed in destroying them, they
continued in great force until a change of weather carried them off.

The Brant generally weighs about four pounds avoirdupois, and
measures two feet in length, and three feet six inches in extent; the
bill is about an inch and a half long, and black; the nostril large,
placed nearly in its middle; head, neck, and breast, black, the neck
marked with a spot of white, about two inches below the eye; belly,
pale ash, edged with white; from the thighs backwards, white; back
and wing-coverts, dusky brownish black, the plumage lightest at the
tips; rump, and middle of the tail-coverts, black; the rest of the tail-

coverts, pure white, reaching nearly to the tip of the tail, the whole of which is black, but usually concealed by the white coverts; primaries and secondaries, deep black; legs, also black; irides, dark hazel.

The only material difference observable between the plumage of the male and female, is, that in the latter the white spot on the neck is less, and more mottled with dusky. In young birds it is sometimes wanting, or occurs on the front, cheeks, and chin; and sometimes the upper part of the neck only is black;* but in full-plumaged birds of both sexes, the markings are very much alike.

The Brant is often seen in our markets for sale. Its flesh, though esteemed by many, tastes somewhat sedgy, or fishy.

SCOTER DUCK. — ANAS NIGRA. — Fig. 300.

Le macreuse, *Briss.* vi. p. 420, pl. 38, fig. 2. — *Buff.* ix. p. 234, pl. 16. *Pl. enl.* 978. — *Bewick,* ii. p. 288. — *Arct. Zool.* No. 484. — *Lath. Syn.* iii. p. 480. — *Peale's Museum,* No. 2658.

OIDEMIA NIGRA. — Fleming.†

Oidemia nigra, *Flem. Br. Anim.* p. 119. — *North. Zool.* ii. p. 450. — *Bonap. Synop.* p. 390. — Carnard macreuse, *Temm. Man.* ii. p. 856. — Scoter, or Black Diver, *Mont. Ornith. Dict.* ii. and *Supp.* — *Bew. Br. Birds,* ii. p. 325. — Black Scoter, *Selby, Illust. Br. Orn.* pl. 68.

This Duck is but little known along our sea-coast, being more usually met with in the northern than southern districts, and only during the winter. Its food is shell fish, for which it is almost perpetually diving. That small bivalve so often mentioned, small muscles, spout fish, called on the coast, razor handles, young clams, &c., furnish it with abundant fare; and wherever these are plenty, the Scoter is an occasional visitor. They swim, seemingly at ease, amidst the very roughest of the surf, but fly heavily along the surface, and to no great distance. They rarely penetrate far up our rivers, but seem to prefer the neighborhood of the ocean, differing in this respect from the Cormorant, which often makes extensive visits to the interior.

The Scoters are said to appear on the coast of France in great numbers, to which they are attracted by a certain kind of small bivalve shell fish, called *vaimeaux,* probably differing little from those already mentioned. Over the beds of these shell fish the fishermen spread their nets, supporting them, horizontally, at the height of two or three feet from the bottom. At the flowing of the tide the Scoters approach in great numbers, diving after their favorite food, and soon get entangled in the nets. Twenty or thirty dozen have sometimes been taken in a single tide. These are sold to the Roman Catholics, who eat them on those days on which they are forbidden by their religion the use of animal food, fish excepted; these birds, and a few others of

---

* The figure of this bird, given by Bewick, is in that state.
† The plumage on the head and neck of this bird is remarkable for its rigid texture, and the narrow, hackled shape of the feathers. — Ed.

the same fishy flavor, having been exempted from the interdict, on the supposition of their being cold-blooded, and partaking of the nature of fish.*

The Scoter abounds in Lapland, Norway, Sweden, Russia, and Siberia. It was also found by Osbeck between the islands of Java and St. Paul, lat. 30 and 34, in the month of June.†

This species is twenty-one inches in length, and thirty-four in extent, and is easily distinguished from all other Ducks by the peculiar form of its bill, which has at the base a large, elevated knob, of a red color, divided by a narrow line of yellow, which spreads over the middle of the upper mandible, reaching nearly to its extremity; the edges and lower mandible are black; the eyelid is yellow; irides, dark hazel; the whole plumage is black, inclining to purple on the head and neck; legs and feet, reddish.

The female has little or nothing of the knob on the bill; her plumage, above, a sooty brown, and below of a grayish white.

VELVET DUCK. — ANAS FUSCA. — Fig. 301.

Le grande macreuse, *Briss.* vi. p. 423, 29. — *Buff.* ix. p. 242. *Pl. enl.* 956. — *Arct. Zool.* No. 482. — *Bewick*, ii. p. 286. — *Lath. Syn.* iii. p. 482. — *Peale's Museum*, No. 2658; female.

OIDEMIA FUSCA. — Fleming.‡

Oidemia fusca, *Flem. Br. Anim.* p. 119. — *Bonap. Synop.* p. 390. — *North. Zool.* ii. p. 450. — Canard double macreuse, *Temm. Man.* ii. p. 854. — Velvet Duck, *Mont. Ornith. Dict.* — *Bew. Br. Birds*, ii. 322. — Velvet Scoter, *Selby, Illust. Br. Ornith.* pl. 67.

THIS and the preceding are frequently confounded together as one and the same species, by our gunners on the sea-coast. The former, however, differs in being of greater size; in having a broad band of white across the wing; a spot of the same under the eye; and in the structure of its bill. The habits of both are very much alike; they visit us only during the winter; feed entirely on shell fish, which they procure by diving; and return to the northern regions early in spring to breed. They often associate with the Scoters, and are taken frequently in the same nets with them. Owing to the rank, fishy flavor

-----

* BEWICK. † *Voyage*, i. p. 120.

‡ This, with the preceding, and the *O. perspicillata*, constitute the American species of Fleming's genus *Oidemia*. They are all visitants also of the European Continent during winter, and, with the exception of the last, are of rather common occurrence. They are truly Sea Ducks, and never almost leave that element except during the season of incubation. They are expert divers, and feed on fish and marine molluscæ; we find, therefore, the foot expanded, the hallux furnished with a broad membrane, and the legs placed far back. The bill is expanded, and generally swollen at the base; the plumage, thick and compact, and of glossy smoothness; the wings, short, but firm, and sharp-pointed, capable, apparently, of a strong flight for a short while, but unfitted for any prolonged exertion. — ED.

of its flesh, it is seldom sought after by our sportsmen, or gunners, and is very little esteemed.

The Velvet Duck measures twenty-three inches in length, and two feet nine inches in extent, and weighs about three pounds; the bill is broad, a little elevated at the base, where it is black, the rest red, except the lower mandible, which is of a pale yellowish white; both are edged with black, and deeply toothed; irides, pale cream; under the eye is a small spot of white; general color of the plumage brownish black, the secondaries excepted, which are white, forming a broad band across the wing; there are a few reflections of purple on the upper plumage; the legs are red on the outside, and deep yellow, sprinkled with blackish, on the inner sides; tail, short and pointed.

The female is very little less than the male; but differs considerably in its markings. The bill is dusky; forehead and cheeks, white; under the eye, dull brownish; behind that, a large oval spot of white; whole upper parts and neck, dark brownish drab; tips of the plumage, lighter; secondaries, white; wing-quills, deep brown; belly, brownish white; tail, hoary brown; the throat is white, marked with dusky specks; legs and feet, yellow.

Latham informs us, that this species is sometimes seen on the coast of England, but is not common there; that it inhabits Denmark and Russia, and in some parts of Siberia, is very common. It is also found at Kamtschatka, where it is said to breed, going far inland to lay; the eggs are eight or ten, and white; the males depart, and leave the females to remain with the young until they are able to fly. In the River Ochotska they are so numerous that a party of natives, consisting of fifty or more, go off in boats, and drive these Ducks up the river before them, and, when the tide ebbs, fall on them at once, and knock them on the head with clubs, killing such numbers that each man has twenty or thirty for his share.[*]

HARLEQUIN DUCK. — ANAS HISTRIONICA. — Fig. 302.

Le canard à collier de Terre Neuve, *Briss.* vi. p. 362, 14. — *Buff.* ix. p. 250. *Pl. enl.* 798. — *Arct. Zool.* No. 490. — *Lath. Syn.* iii. p. 484.

CLANGULA HISTRIONICA. — Leach.[†]

Clangula histrionica, *Bonap. Synop.* p. 394. — *North. Zool.* ii. p. 459. — Canard à collier, ou histrion, *Temm. Man.* ii. p. 878.

THIS species is very rare on the coasts of the Middle and Southern States, though not unfrequently found off those of New England, where it is known by the dignified title of the *Lord*, probably from the elegant crescents and circles of white which ornament its neck and

---

[*] *History of Kamtschatka*, p. 160.

[†] Dr. Richardson observes of this Duck — " *C. histrionica* haunts eddies under cascades and rapid streams. It takes wing at once, when disturbed, and is very vigilant. We never saw it associating with any other Duck, and it is a rare bird." — ED.

breast. Though an inhabitant of both continents, little else is known of its particular manners than that it swims and dives well; flies swift, and to a great height; and has a whistling note. Is said to frequent the small rivulets inland from Hudson's Bay, where it breeds. The female lays ten white eggs on the grass; the young are prettily speckled. It is found on the eastern continent as far south as Lake Baikal, and thence to Kamtschatka, particularly up the River Ochotska; and was also met with at Aoonalashka and Iceland.* At Hudson's Bay, it is called the Painted Duck; at Newfoundland, and along the coast of New England, the Lord; it is an active, vigorous diver, and often seen in deep water, considerably out at sea.

The Harlequin Duck, so called from the singularity of its markings, is seventeen inches in length, and twenty-eight inches in extent; the bill is of moderate length, of a lead color, tipped with red; irides, dark; upper part of the head, black; between the eye and bill, a broad space of white, extending over the eye, and ending in reddish; behind the ear, a similar spot; neck, black, ending below in a circle of white; breast, deep slate; shoulders, or sides of the breast, marked with a semicircle of white; belly, black; sides, chestnut; body above, black, or deep slate; some of the scapulars, white; greater wing-coverts, tipped with the same; legs and feet, deep ash; vent and pointed tail, black.

The female is described as being less, "the forehead, and between the bill and eye, white, with a spot of the same behind the ear; head, neck, and back, brown, palest on the fore part of the neck; upper part of the breast, and rump, red brown; lower breast and belly, barred, pale rufous and white; behind the thighs, rufous and brown; scapulars and wing-coverts, rufous brown; outer greater ones, blackish; quills and tail, dusky, the last inclining to rufous; legs, dusky." †

The few specimens of this Duck which I have met with, were all males; and from the variation in their colors it appears evident that the young birds undergo a considerable change of plumage before they arrive at their full colors. In some, the white spot behind the eye was large, extending irregularly half way down the neck; in others confined to a roundish spot.

The flesh of this species is said to be excellent.

DUSKY DUCK. — ANAS OBSCURA. — Fig. 303.

Arct. Zool. No. 469. — *Lath. Syn.* iii. p. 545. — *Peale's Museum,* No. 2880.

BOSCHAS? OBSCURA. — Jardine.‡

Anas obscura, *Bonap. Synop.* p. 384.

This species is generally known along the sea-coast of New Jersey, and the neighboring country, by the name of the Black Duck, being

---

* Latham.   † *Ibid.*
‡ Having now arrived at the conclusion of a group which holds a very prominent rank in the ornithology of Northern America, a few general observations

the most common and most numerous of all those of its tribe that frequent the salt marshes. It is only partially migratory. Numbers

regarding their economy, with an enumeration of those species omitted by Wilson, which have been since discovered, may not be deemed improper.

The *Anatidæ*, or those birds generally known under the denominations of Ducks, Geese, and Swans, taken as a family, will range with groups of great extent and varied form, as the Falcons, the Parrots, or Pigeons, and will present similar modifications. The characters of the greater part of the groups which inhabit the northern and temperate regions of the world, have been already drawn by Dr. Leach and Dr. Fleming, and one sub-family has been more lately analyzed by Mr. Swainson, as far as our knowledge of them extends, apparently with tolerable accuracy. They, however, want comparison with the tropical forms, which depart so much in their manners from those we are accustomed to see, and by which our opinions have hitherto been led. The Wood Ducks constituting Mr. Swainson's genus *Dendronessa* — the Long-legged, Whistling Ducks of India — those birds allied to the little Gambia Goose, and those approaching in their form to the *Grallatores*, all want our close examination.

In distribution the *Anatidæ* extend over the world, from the warmest tropics to the extreme Arctic cold, but exist in greatest abundance near the confines of temperate regions, and in northern latitudes. Their habits may be called truly aquatic, as the presence of water is necessary, even in the most aberrant forms, for their healthy support. Some groups are exclusively aquatic, and never quit the sea or large inland lakes, except during the season when the duties of incubation for a while call them to the shore. These may be termed Pelagic or Sea Ducks, and feed on fish and molluscæ; others delight in lakes and rivers as well as the sea, resort more frequently to the land, seek the same nourishment, and both are expert divers. Some hold a middle way, are as much on land as on water, and, in addition to the food of the truly sea species, live on the spawn of fresh-water fish, insects peculiar to muddy banks and slimy pools, with vegetables, such as the tender shoots of the grasses or newly-sown grains, or, while on the shores, upon the *Zostera marina*; while one or two forms resemble the grallatorial birds, and are more independent of water and aquatic nourishment. In their breeding places, they show a like variety, choosing the reedy banks of lakes and rivers, the treacherous morass, the cliffs and desert sands of the sea shore, the burrows of various animals, the hollows of decaying trees in the stupendous forests of America, or in India the welcome shade of the sacred bannian.

Their uses are various and extensive, either as food, or their skins, feathers, and down, for commerce, and articles of wearing apparel, or household comfort. Many species are also domesticated, and in a way less precarious, lend their aid to the wants and luxuries of their owners. In the northern parts of America, this extensive family is most bountifully supplied, and her seay lakes and majestic rivers are suitable nurseries for the innumerable multitudes that annually resort to, and reassemble to perform the duties of incubation. In the warmer parts, many remain at all seasons; but it is in what is called Arctic America, and the Fur Countries, that the prodigious concourse annually arrive, and are so much hunted, both for food and a profitable emolument. Several of the spring months have received appellations from the birds which are most plentiful during them. The expected visitants arrive with remarkable precision, nearly at the same period of the month. They extend over a large space in breadth, and continue flying, without intermission, for many days. The native tribes are prepared by experience, and the signals of their watches, for their appearance; and the first bird — for there are generally a scattered few before — gives notice that the havock should commence.

"They are," says Dr. Richardson, "of great importance in the Fur Countries, as they furnish at certain seasons in the year, in many extensive districts, almost the only article of food that can be procured. The arrival of the water-fowl marks the commencement of spring, and diffuses as much joy among the wandering hunters of the Arctic regions, as the harvest or vintage excites in more genial climes. The period of their migration southwards again, in large flocks, at the close of summer, is another season of plenty, bountifully granted to the natives, and fitting them for encountering the rigours and privations of a northern winter."

To the species of *Anatidæ* which were known to Wilson as inhabitants of Northern America, with which his eighth volume has been almost wholly occupied, the

of them remain during the summer, and breed in sequestered places in the marsh, or on the sea-islands of the beach. The eggs are eight or ten in number, very nearly resembling those of the Domestic Duck. Vast numbers, however, regularly migrate farther north on the

researches of later ornithologists and travellers have added considerably, and the following enumeration of them will serve to fill up the list to last discoveries : —

Somateria, Leach.

1. *S. spectabilis*, Leach. — King, Eider. — Common to both continents, and has much of habits of the Common Eider. One or two specimens have been killed on the northern shores of Great Britain.

Clangula, Leach.

2. *C. Barrovii*, Swain. and Richard. — Rocky Mountain Garrot. See note to p. 575

Cygnus, Steph.

Wilson, in his list of birds, mentions the "Swan;" but from three species at least being natives of the Arctic countries, it is impossible to say whether or not he was aware of any distinctions.

3. *C. musicus*, Bechst., or Wild Swan. — Inhabits the Arctic circle, whence it migrates to both continents.

4. *C. buccinator*, Richardson. — Trumpeter Swan. — Discovered to be unde- scribed by Dr. Richardson during the last overland expedition ; distin- guished by the bill being entirely black, longer and more depressed than in the Common Wild Swan, the tail containing twenty-four feathers, and by a difference in the folding of the windpipe. The Doctor remarks, it is the most common Swan in the interior of 'he Fur Countries. It breeds as far south as lat. 61 deg., but principally within the Arctic circle, and in its mi- grations generally precedes the Geese a few days. It is to the Trumpeter the bulk of the Swan skins imported by the Hudson's Bay Company belong.

5. *C. Bewickii*, Yarrel. — Bewick's Swan. — This bird has lately been dis- covered as a migratory visitant to Britain. Dr. Richardson met with it during the last expedition, and remarks — "This Swan breeds on the sea- coast, within the Arctic circle, and is seen in the interior of the Fur Coun- tries, in its passage only. It makes its appearance among the latest of the migratory birds in the spring, while the Trumpeter Swans are, with the exception of the Eagles, the earliest."

Lewis and Clark, Lawson and Hearne, were all aware of the difference among the American Swans, but they have never, till lately, been really distinguished and characterized.

Anser, Bechst.

6. *A. albifrons*, Bechst. — White-fronted Goose. — Is mentioned by Bona- parte, and is introduced in the *Northern Zoology*. Its breeding places are the woody districts skirting the Mackenzie, to the north of the sixty-seventh parallel, and also the islands of the Arctic Sea.

7. *A. segetum*, Meyer. — Common Bean Goose. — Inhabiting the more Arctic regions. Bonaparte mentions also four additional species as probably ac- cidental inhabitants of the United States and the Arctic countries — *A. cinereus*, Meyer. — *A. rufescens*, Brehm. — *A. medius*, Temm., and *A. ci- neraceus*, Brehm.

Bernicla, Steph.

8. *B. leucopsis*, (*Anas erythropus*, Linn. — *A. leucopsis*, Temm.) — Inhabit-

approach of spring. During their residence here in winter, they frequent the marshes, and the various creeks and inlets with which those extensive flats are intersected. Their principal food consists of those minute snail shells so abundant in the marshes. They occasionally visit the sandy beach in search of small bivalves, and, on these occasions, sometimes cover whole acres with their numbers. They roost at night in the shallow ponds, in the middle of the salt marsh, particularly on islands, where many are caught by the foxes. They are extremely shy during the day; and, on the most distant report of a musket, rise from every quarter of the marsh in prodigious numbers, dispersing in every direction. In calm weather they fly high, beyond the reach of shot; but when the wind blows hard, and the gunner conceals himself among the salt grass, in a place over which they usually fly, they are shot down in great numbers; their flight being then low. Geese, Brant, and Black Duck, are the common game of all our gunners along this part of the coast during winter; but there are at least ten Black Ducks for one Goose or Brant, and probably many more. Their voice resembles that of the Duck and Mallard; but their flesh is greatly inferior, owing to the nature of their food. They are, however, large, heavy-bodied Ducks, and generally esteemed.

I cannot discover that this species is found in any of the remote northern parts of our continent; and this is probably the cause why it is altogether unknown in Europe. It is abundant from Florida to New England; but is not enumerated among the birds of Hudson's Bay, or Greenland. Its chief residence is on the sea-coast, though it also makes extensive excursions up the tide waters of our rivers. Like the Mallard, they rarely dive for food, but swim and fly with great velocity.

The Dusky or Black Duck is two feet in length, and three feet two inches in extent; the bill is of a dark greenish ash, formed very much like the Mallard, and nearly of the same length; irides, dark; upper part of the head, deep dusky brown, intermixed on the fore part with some small streaks of drab; rest of the head and greater part of the neck, pale yellow ochre, thickly marked with small streaks of blackish brown; lower part of the neck, and whole lower parts, deep dusky, each feather edged with brownish white, and with fine seams of rusty white; upper parts the same, but rather deeper; the outer vanes of nine of the secondaries, bright violet blue, forming the beauty spot, which is bounded on all sides by black; wings and tail, sooty brown; tail-feathers, sharp-pointed; legs and feet, dusky yellow; lining of the wings, pure white.

The female has more brown on her plumage; but in other respects differs little from the male, both having the beauty spot on the wing.

ing the Arctic circle, migrating during winter to more temperate regions, and very rare and accidental in the United States.

9. B, *Hutchinsii,* (*Anser Hutchinsii,* Richard. — *Hutchin's Bernacle, North. Zool.* ii. p. 470.) — Described by Dr. Richardson as a variety of the Brant, in the Appendix to Captain Parry's second volume, and distinguished from it during the last Arctic expedition. — ED.

MARSH TERN. — STERNA ARANEA. — Fig. 304.

Peale's Museum, No. 3521.

STERNA ARANEA. — Wilson.*

Sterna aranea, *Bonap. Synop.* p. 354.

This new species I first met with on the shores of Cape May, particularly over the salt marshes, and darting down after a kind of large

* The Prince of Musignano writes the following observations in his *Nomenclature :* —

"A new species of Wilson, referred by Temminck to a bird which he calls *Sterna Anglica,* thinking that it is no other than *S. Anglica* of Montagu. But, as Brehm proves, in his late work, the *S. Anglica* of Temminck is not the *S. Anglica* of Montagu. To the latter he gives the name of *S. risoria,* (which cannot be adopted,) and he calls the former *S. meridionalis.* He does not decide to which of the two species the American *S. aranea* belongs, and expresses the possibility of its being an independent species ; but seems inclined to believe it identical with his *S. meridionalis.* Whether this bird is the *S. Anglica,* Mont., the *S. meridionalis,* Brehm, *Anglica,* Temm., or a distinct species peculiar to the north and south of this continent, it shall be the object of these observations to determine. The specimen deposited by Wilson in the Philadelphia Museum (a single glance at which would have enabled us to decide the question) being unfortunately destroyed, and Wilson's figure and description being too unessential to justify any conclusion, we should have been obliged to have left the matter unsettled, had it not been for the successful zeal of Mr. Titian Peale, whose practical knowledge (the most important) of North American birds is equalled by none. Their favorite haunts, their note, their flight, are perfectly familiar to him. He succeeded in procuring a fine specimen at Long Beach, N. J., just as we were in want of one, and thus enabled us to give with more security the following opinion, which we had previously formed : —

"*S. aranea,* Wils., was a nondescript, different from *S. Anglica,* Mont., but the same with *S. Anglica,* Temm., and *S. meridionalis,* Brehm, and therefore common to both continents. Wilson's name, having the priority, must be exclusively retained, and Brehm's name of *meridionalis* must be rejected. Thus has our author here also first named and described a European bird.

"Mr. Ord was therefore right in not finding himself authorized to change the name. He was right in believing Montagu's bird distinct ; but wrong in thinking Temminck's bird different, though Temminck had positively stated the specimens he had received from the United States and Brazil differed in nothing from his south Europeans. Even as respects the discrepance of *S. Anglica,* Mont., his reasons resting upon the slight difference of an unpublished drawing of Wilson respecting measurements of parts, to which Wilson did not attach great importance, were by no means conclusive. In fact, these measurements are incorrect, with the exception of the tarsus, which corresponds within a trifle of the bird. The bill is two and one eighth inches to the corners of the mouth, and about one and one half inches to the feathers of the forehead ; thus bearing more in favor of Mr. Ord's argument, that it is not the *Anglica,* Mont., than he himself supposed ; but proving that it is no other than *S. Anglica,* Temm., (*meridionalis,* Brehm,) to which, as above stated, Wilson's name of *aranea* must be exclusively applied.

"The principal character we should assign for a ready distinction between these two closely-related species, (in addition to the shorter, thicker, less compressed, and straighter bill, with its edges turned inwards in *Anglica,*) consists in the tarsus, which in *aranea* (owing to its shortness, and the extraordinary length of the nail) is of the same length as the middle toe, including the nail, whilst in *Anglica* it is nearly twice the length, (owing to its superior length, and the shortness of the nail.) The membranes of our bird are also much more scalloped. The habits of the two species are very different. The *S. Anglica,* confined to the sea-shores, feeds alblack spider, plenty in such places. This spider can travel under water, as well as above, and, during summer at least, seems to constitute the principal food of the present Tern. In several which I opened, the stomach was crammed with a mass of these spiders alone; these they frequently pick up from the pools, as well as from the grass, dashing down on them in the manner of their tribe. Their voice is sharper and stronger than that of the Common Tern; the bill is differently formed, being shorter, more rounded above, and thicker; the tail is also much shorter, and less forked. They do not associate with others, but keep in small parties by themselves.

The Marsh Tern is fourteen inches in length, and thirty-four in extent; bill, thick, much rounded above, and of a glossy blackness; whole upper part of the head and hind neck, black; whole upper part of the body, hoary white; shafts of the quill and tail-feathers, pure white; line from the nostril under the eye, and whole lower parts, pure white; tail, forked, the outer feathers about an inch and three quarters longer than the middle ones; the wings extend upwards of two inches beyond the tail; legs and feet, black; hind toe, small, straight, and pointed.

The female, as to plumage, differs in nothing from the male. The yearling birds, several of which I met with, have the plumage of the crown white at the surface, but dusky below; so that the boundaries of the black, as it will be in the perfect bird, are clearly defined; through the eye a line of black passes down the neck for about an inch, reaching about a quarter of an inch before it; the bill is not so black as in the others; the legs and feet, dull orange, smutted with brown or dusky; tips and edges of the primaries, blackish; shafts, white.

This species breeds in the salt marshes; the female drops her eggs, generally three or four in number, on the dry drift grass, without the slightest appearance of a nest; they are of a greenish olive, spotted with brown.

A specimen of this Tern has been deposited in the Museum of this city, [Philadelphia.]

most exclusively on strand birds,* and their eggs, sometimes on fishes; whilst the S. aranea, generally found on marshes, feeds exclusively on insects."

Bonaparte, and the authors of the *Northern Zoology,* have mentioned the following species as also found in North America:—

1. *S. cyana,* Lath.—Inhabiting the tropical seas of America; common on the coasts of the Southern States.

2. *S. Arctica,* Temm.—(*North. Zool.* p. 114.) Bonaparte expresses a doubt that this is the true *Arctica* of Temm.; and the description in the *Northern Zoology* points out some discrepancies.

3. *S. stolida.* Migrates to the North American coasts.

Phaeton, Linn.

These birds, from general appearance, approach near to the Terns, (*S. Caspia;*) but from the want of specimens, I am unable to enter into the proper situation of the form, except from the authority of others. Bonaparte places it between *sula* and *plotus.* The only American species is,

1. *P. æthereus,* Linn., Tropic Bird of Wilson's list. Common during summer on the coasts of the Southern States.—ED.

* Is this correct? Does this Tern kill other sea-fowl, and plunder their nests?—ED.

SOOTY TERN. — STERNA FULIGINOSA. — Fig. 305.

La hirondelle de mer à grande enverguer, *Buff.* viii. p. 345. — Egg-Bird, *Forst. Voy.* p. 113. — Noddy, *Damp. Voy.* iii. p. 142. — *Arct. Zool.* No. 447. — *Lath. Syn.* iii. p. 352. — *Peale's Museum*, No. 3459.

STERNA FULIGINOSA. — Latham.

S. fuliginosa, *Bonap. Synop.* p. 355.

This bird has been long known to navigators, as its appearance at sea usually indicates the vicinity of land; instances, however, have occurred, in which they have been met with one hundred leagues from shore.* The species is widely dispersed over the various shores of the ocean. They were seen by Dampier in New Holland; are in prodigious numbers in the Island of Ascension and in Christmas Island; are said to lay, in December, one egg on the ground; the egg is yellowish, with brown and violet spots.† In passing along the northern shores of Cuba, and the coast of Florida and Georgia, in the month of July, I observed this species very numerous and noisy, dashing down headlong after small fish. I shot and dissected several, and found their stomachs uniformly filled with fish. I could perceive little or no difference between the colors of the male and female.

Length of the Sooty Tern, seventeen inches; extent, three feet six inches; bill, an inch and a half long, sharp-pointed and rounded above, the upper mandible serrated slightly near the point; nostril, an oblong slit; color of the bill, glossy black; irides, dusky; forehead, as far as the eyes, white; whole lower parts and sides of the neck, pure white; rest of the plumage, black; wings, very long and pointed, extending, when shut, nearly to the extremity of the tail, which is greatly forked, and consists of twelve feathers, the two exterior ones four inches longer than those of the middle, the whole of a deep black, except the two outer feathers, which are white, but towards the extremities a little blackish on the inner vanes; legs and webbed feet, black; hind toe, short.

The secondary wing feathers are eight inches shorter than the longest primary.

This bird frequently settles on the rigging of ships at sea, and, in common with another species, *S. stolida*, is called by sailors the Noddy.

* Cook, *Voyage*, i. p. 275.   † Turton.

CINEREOUS COOT.—FULICA AMERICANA.—Fig. 306.

Turton, 1, 424.—*Lath. Gen. Syn.* 3, 275.—*Id. Sup.* 259.—*Ind. Orn.* ii. 777.—
Gcrin. Orn. 5, t. 425.—*Faun. Suec.* 193.—*Scop. Ann.* 1, No. 149.—*Brun.*
190.—*Muller,* No. 216.—*Kram. El.* p. 357, 1.—*Frisch.* t. 208.—*George
Reise,* p. 172.—*La Foulque, ou Morelle, Briss. Orn.* 6, p. 23, 1, pl. 2, fig. 2.—
Buff. Ois. 15, p. 327. *Pl. enl.* No. 197.—The Coot, *Raii Syn.* p. 116, A. 1.
—*Will. Orn.* p. 319, pl. 59.—*Albin.* 1, pl. 83.—*Br. Zool.* No. 220, pl. 77.—
Arct. Zool. No. 416.—Coot, or Bald Coot, *Bewick,* 2, 127.—*Sloane, Jam.* 2,
320.—Fulica Floridana, *Bartram,* p. 296.—*Peale's Museum,* No. 4322.

FULICA AMERICANA.—Gmelin.*

Fulica Americana, *Sab. Append. to Capt. Frank. Exp.* p. 690.—*Bonap. Synop.*
p. 338.—Fulica atra, *Wilson's List.*

This species makes its appearance in Pennsylvania about the first
of October. Among the muddy flats and islands of the River Delaware, which are periodically overflowed, and which are overgrown
with the reed, or wild oats, and rushes, the Coots are found. They
are not numerous, and are seldom seen, except their places of resort be
covered with water; in that case they are generally found sitting on
the fallen reed, waiting for the ebbing of the tide, which will enable
them to feed. Their food consists of various aquatic plants, seeds,
insects, and, it is said, small fish. The Coot has an aversion to take
wing, and can seldom be sprung in its retreat at low water; for, although it walks rather awkwardly, yet it contrives to skulk through
the grass and reeds with great speed, the compressed form of its body,
like that of the Rail genus, being well adapted to the purpose. It
swims remarkably well, and, when wounded, will dive like a Duck.
When closely pursued in the water, it generally takes to the shore,
rising with apparent reluctance, like a wounded Duck, and fluttering

---

* This description commences the ninth and supplementary volume of the original, printed by Mr. Ord, after the decease of Wilson, from his notes. The volume
was published in 1814, and a second edition appeared in 1825, correcting several
mistakes which had occurred in the first. Our present bird was there described as
identical with that of Europe, and a detail of the habits of our native species given
as belonging to it; these Mr. Ord has corrected. The distinctions, I believe, were
first pointed out by Mr. Sabine, in the Appendix to Captain Franklin's Narrative,
and I now add them in that gentleman's words :—
   " They are of the same length, though there is a general inferiority in the size of
the body, as well as of the legs, head, and bill of the American; the bill is smaller,
less thick and strong, and shorter by a quarter of an inch; the callus, independent
of the difference in color in the American bird, extends only half an inch over the
head, but in the European, above an inch; the whole head is smaller; the plumage,
generally, is similar in color and character; the outer margin of the first primary
feathers of the wing, is more conspicuously marked with white, and there are a few
white feathers on the upper edge of the wing; the secondaries in both are tipped
with white; the principal difference in the plumage is, that in the American the
feathers at the vent are quite black, and the under tail coverts white; in the European Coot, these correspond with the rest of the plumage; the legs are much more
slender in the American bird; the tarse of the European measures near two inches
and a half, that of the American not quite two inches; the toes are smaller in like
proportion; the middle toe, including the claw, of the European Coot, is three
inches and three quarters long; of the American, three inches and one quarter
only."—Ed.

along the surface, with its feet pattering on the water.* It is known in Pennsylvania by the name of the Mud-Hen.

I have never yet discovered that this species breeds with us; though it is highly probable that some few may occupy the marshes of the interior, in the vicinity of the ponds and lakes, for this purpose; those retired situations being well adapted to the hatching and rearing of their young. In the Southern States, particularly South Carolina, they are well known; but the Floridas appear to be their principal rendezvous for the business of incubation. "The Coot," says William Bartram, "is a native of North America, from Pennsylvania to Florida. They inhabit large rivers, fresh-water inlets or bays, lagoons, &c., where they swim and feed amongst the reeds and grass of the shores; particularly in the River St. Juan, in East Florida; where they are found in immense flocks. They are loquacious and noisy, talking to one another night and day; are constantly on the water, the broad, lobated membranes on their toes enabling them to swim and dive like Ducks." †

The Coot inhabits the shores of Sweden and Norway; appears in the spring, and very rarely visits the lakes or moors. Is found in Russia, China, Persia, Greenland, and Siberia. It is common in France, particularly in Lorraine.

"This species is met with in Great Britain, at all seasons of the year; and it is generally believed, that it does not migrate to other countries, but changes its stations, and removes in the autumn from the lesser pools, or loughs, where the young have been reared, to the larger lakes, where flocks assemble in the winter. The female commonly builds her nest in a bunch of rushes, surrounded by the water;‡ it is composed of a great quantity of coarse dried weeds, well matted together, and lined within with softer and finer grasses; she lays from twelve to fifteen eggs at a time, and commonly hatches twice in a season; her eggs are about the size of those of a Pullet, and are of a pale brownish white color, sprinkled with numerous small, dark spots, which, at the thicker end, seem as if they had run into each other, and formed bigger blotches.

"As soon as the young quit the shell, they plunge into the water, dive, and swim about with great ease; but they still gather together about the mother, and take shelter under her wings, and do not entirely leave her for some time. They are at first covered with sooty colored down, and are of a shapeless appearance; while they are in this state, and before they have learned by experience to shun danger, the Kite, Moor Buzzard, and others of the Hawk tribe, make dreadful havoc among them."§

---

* In Carolina, they are called Flusterers, from the noise they make in flying over the surface of the water. — A Voyage to Carolina, by JOHN LAWSON, p. 149.

† Letter from Mr. Bartram to the author.

‡ A Bald Coot built her nest in Sir William Middleton's lake, at Belsay, Northumberland, among the rushes, which were afterwards loosened by the wind, and, of course, the nest was driven about, and floated upon the surface of the water, in every direction; notwithstanding which, the female continued to sit as usual, and brought out her young upon her movable habitation.

§ "The Pike is also the indiscriminate devourer of the young of all these waterbirds;" and this, notwithstanding the numerous brood, may account for the scarcity of the species.‖

‖ BEWICK's British Birds, vol. ii. p. 129.

The Cinereous Coot is sixteen inches in length, and twenty-eight in extent; bill, one and a half inch long, white, the upper mandible slightly notched near the tip, and marked across with a band of chestnut, the lower mandible marked on each side with a squarish spot of the like color, edged on the lower part with bright yellow, or gamboge, thence to the tip, pale horn color; membrane of the forehead, dark chestnut brown; irides, cornelian red; beneath the eyes, in most specimens, a whitish spot; the head and neck are of a deep shining black, resembling satin; back and scapulars, dirty greenish olive; shoulders, breast, and wing-coverts, slate blue; the under parts are hoary; vent, black; beneath the tail, pure white; primaries and secondaries, slate, the former tipped with black, the latter with white, which does not appear when the wing is closed; outer edges of the wings, white; legs and toes, yellowish green, the scalloped membrane of the latter, lead color; middle toe, including the claw, three inches and three quarters long.

The bird, from which the foregoing description was taken, (Fig. 306,) was shot in the Delaware, below Philadelphia, the 29th of October, 1813. It was an old male, an uncommonly fine specimen, and weighed twenty-three ounces avoirdupois. It is deposited in Peale's Museum.

The young birds differ somewhat in their plumage, that of the head and neck being of a brownish black; that of the breast and shoulders, pale ash; the throat, gray or mottled; the bill, bluish white; and the membrane on the forehead, considerably smaller.

The young females very much resemble the young males; all the difference which I have been enabled to perceive, is as follows: — breast and shoulders, cinereous; markings on the bill, less; upper parts of the head, in some specimens, mottled; and being less in size.

The lower parts of these birds are clothed with a thick down, and, particularly between the thighs, covored with close, fine feathers. The thighs are placed far behind, are fleshy, strong, and bare above the knees. Sloane says, that "the trachea arteria of the Coots is branched into two, just under the base of the heart, and is compressed as that of the *Ardea cœrulea nigra*."

The gizzard resembles a Hen's, and is remarkably large and muscular. That of the bird which has been described, was filled with sand, gravel, shells, and the remains of aquatic plants.

Buffon describes the mode of shooting Coots in France, particularly in Lorraine, on the great pools of Tiaucourt, and of Indre; hence we are led to suppose, that they are esteemed as an article of food. But with us, who are enabled, by the abundance and variety of game, to indulge in greater luxuries in that season when our Coots visit us, they are considered as of no account, and are seldom eaten.

The European ornithologists represent the membrane on the forehead of the Coot as white, except in the breeding season, when it is said to change its color to pale red. This circumstance would induce one to suppose, that our Coot is a different species from the European, which I have never had the satisfaction to behold; and, indeed, I am much of that opinion.

It is a very rare occurrence, that the Coot is seen in the vicinity of Philadelphia in the spring or summer. The 19th of March, 1814, I had the satisfaction of being presented with one, a female, which was shot in the Schuylkill, at Gray's Ferry. I could see no difference in its plumage and markings, from those of the full grown male, except the head and neck not being of so deep a black. The membrane on the forehead was not more than half the size of that of the female specimen, described above, and it was of the same color, viz., dark chestnut. All the birds which I have ever seen, had this appendage of the same color.

In Lewis and Clark's history of their expedition, mention is made of a bird which is common on the Columbia; is said to be very noisy, to have a sharp, shrill whistle, and to associate in large flocks; it is called the Black Duck.* This is doubtless a species of Coot, but whether or not different from ours, cannot be ascertained. How much is it to be regretted, that, in an expedition of discovery, planned and fitted out by an enlightened government, furnished with every means for safety, subsistence, and research, not one naturalist, not one draughtsman, should have been sent, to observe and perpetuate the infinite variety of natural productions, many of which are entirely unknown to the community of science, which that extensive tour must have revealed!

The Coot leaves us in November for the southward.

The foregoing was prepared for the press, when the author, in one of his shooting excursions on the Delaware, had the good fortune to kill a full-plumaged female Coot. This was on the 20th of April. It was swimming at the edge of a *cripple*, or thicket of alder bushes, busily engaged in picking something from the surface of the water, and, while thus employed, it turned frequently. The membrane on its forehead was very small, and edged on the fore part with gamboge. Its eggs were of the size of partridge shot. And, on the 13th of May, another fine female specimen was presented to him, which agreed with the above, with the exception of the membrane on the forehead being nearly as large and prominent as that of the male. From the circumstance of the eggs of all these birds being very small, it is probable that the Coots do not breed until July.

---

* *History of the Expedition*, vol. ii. p. 194. Under date of November 30th, 1805, they say, — "The hunters brought in a few Black Ducks, of a species common in the United States, living in large flocks and feeding on grass; they are distinguished by a sharp white beak, toes separated, and by having no craw."

PURPLE GALLINULE. — GALLINULA. PORPHYRIO. — Fig. 307.

Gallinula porphyrio, *Latham, Ind. Orn.* p. 768. *Idem.* iii. pt. 1. p. 254. *Id.* 2d, *Sup.* 326. — Germ, *Orn.* v. t. 485. — *Fulica porphyrio, Turt. Syst.* 1, 122. — *Scop. Amer.* 1, No. 152. — La poule sultane. *Briss. Orn.* v. p. 522, pl. 42, ng. 1. — *Buff. Ois.* xv. p. 302. *Pl. enl.* No. 810. — *Raii Syn.* p. 116, 13, 14. — *Will. Orn.* p. 318. — Purple Water Hen, *Edw.* 87. — *Albia,* iii. pl..11. — *Peale's Museum,* No. 4294.

GALLINULA? MARTINICA. — Latham.*

Gallinula Martinica, *Bonap. Synop.* p. 336.

This splendid and celebrated bird is a native of the southern parts of the continent of America; and is occasionally found within the limits of the United States. But we have to regret that it is not in our power to furnish any additional particulars to its history, already detailed in the works of the European naturalists. Travellers in our section of the globe have hitherto been too neglectful of that beautiful, interesting, and useful portion of animated nature, the birds. Content with wandering over an extent of country, noting merely the common-place occurrences of life, the voyager returns to his friends, and unfolds to their attentive ears the history of his adventures. His book is published, read, and thrown aside with the ephemeral sheets, the useful, but soon forgotten newspapers. If the natural history of only one single acre were to be accurately recorded by each traveller, mankind would receive more real benefit and satisfaction from such productions, than from cart-loads of itineraries, descriptive of scenes and manners, which, from being long familiar to us, fail to interest, or disgust by the frequency of their repetition. Curiosity is an active principle, and we could sincerely wish every traveller to be possessed of an abundant share of it; not that impertinent desire to pry into the affairs of families or communities, which distinguishes some individuals; but that laudable thirst for knowledge, which leads one over mountains and precipices, through forests, valleys, and thickets, intent on exploring the inexhaustible treasures of nature.

We have been insensibly led into this train of reflections, in consequence of our chagrin in not finding any account of the subject of this article in the pages of the American traveller, historian, or naturalist. To the Europeans, then, we are compelled to resort, happy that, with their assistance, we shall be enabled to throw some light on the history of a stranger, whose native haunts we have never yet had the good fortune to explore.

"This bird," says Latham, "is more or less common in all the warmer parts of the globe. On the coasts of Barbary they abound, as well as in some of the islands of the Mediterranean. In Sicily, they are bred in plenty, and kept for their beauty; but whether indigenuous there, we are not certain. It is frequently met with in various parts of

---

* This species, in form, runs very much into the *Porphyrio* of Brisson; but without specimens, I cannot decide whether it should rank there, or on the confines of *Gallinula*. The characters of the former group are, the much greater strength of the bill, being almost as high as long, the greater proportional length of legs, and the splendid and metallic lustre of the plumage. In their manners, thev are partly granivorous, and live more upon land than the Water Hens. — Ed.

the south of Russia, and western parts of Siberia, among reedy places; and in the neighborhood of the Caspian Sea not uncommon; but in the cultivated rice grounds of Ghilan in Persia, in great plenty, and in high plumage. The female makes her nest among the reeds, in the middle of March; lays three or four eggs,* and sits from three to four weeks. That it is common in China, the paper-hangings thence will every where testify. It is also met with in the East Indies, the islands of Java, Madagascar, and many others. Our late navigators saw them at Tongataboo† in vast numbers, as well as the islands of Tanna, and other parts. It is also common in the southern parts of America.

"In respect to its manners, it is a very docile bird, being easily tamed, and feeding with the poultry, scratching the ground with the foot, as the Cock and Hen. It will feed on many things, such as fruits, roots of plants, and grain; but will eat fish with avidity, dipping them into the water before it swallows them; will frequently stand on one leg, and lift the food to its mouth with the other, like a Parrot. The flesh is said to be exquisite in taste."

"The moderns," says Buffon, "have given the name of Sultana Hen to a bird famous among the ancients, under the name of Porphyrion. We have frequently had occasion to remark the justness of the denominations bestowed by the Greeks, which generally allude to the distinctive characters, and are therefore superior to the terms hastily adopted in our languages, from superficial or inaccurate views. The present is an instance; as this bird seemed to bear some resemblance to the gallinaceous tribe, it got the name of Hen; but as, at the same time, it differed widely, and excelled by its beauty and port, it received the epithet of Sultana. But the term Porphyrion, indicating the red or purple tint of its bill and feet, was more just and characteristic; and should we not rebuild the fine ruins of learned antiquity, and restore to nature those brilliant images, and those faithful portraits from the delicate pencil of the Greeks, ever awake to her beauties and her animation?

"Both the Greeks and Romans, notwithstanding their voracious luxury, abstained from eating the Porphyrion. They brought it from Lybia,‡ from Comagene, and from the Balearic Islands,§ to be fed‖ and to be placed in their palaces and temples, where it was left at liberty as a guest,¶ whose noble aspect, whose gentle disposition, and whose elegant plumage, merited such honors.

"Scarcely any bird has more beautiful colors; the blue of its plumage is soft and glossy, embellished with brilliant reflections; its long feet, and the plate from the top of its head to the root of its bill, are of a fine red; and a tuft of white feathers under the tail heightens the lustre of its charming garb. Except that it is rather smaller, the

---

* "Buffon says that the pair, which the Marquis de Nesle introduced into France, laid six round, white eggs, about the size of a demi-billiard."

† FORST. *Voy.* i. 448; ii. 358. COOK's *Last Voyage*, i. 239. — AM. ED.

‡ "Alexander the Myndian, in Athenæus, reckons the Porphyrion in the number of Lybian birds, and relates that it was sacred to the gods in that country. According to Diodorus Siculus, Porphyrions were brought from the heart of Syria, with other kinds of birds distinguished by their rich colors."

§ PLINY, lib. x. 46, 49.

‖ BELON.

¶ ÆLIAN, lib. iii. 41.

female differs not from the male, which exceeds the Partridge, but is inferior to a domestic Hen. The Marquis de Nesle brought a pair from Sicily, where they are known under the name of Gallofagiani; they are found on the Lake Lentini, above Catana, and are sold for a moderate price in that city, as well as in Syracuse and the adjacent towns. They appear alive in the public places, and plant themselves beside the sellers of vegetables and fruits to pick up the refuse; and this beautiful bird, which the Romans lodged in their temples, now experiences the decline of Italy."

The length of the Purple Gallinule is fourteen inches; its bill is an inch and a quarter long, red, yellow at the tips; nostril, small, oblong, and near the centre of the bill; irides, tawny; the naked front and crown are red; the head, part of the neck, throat, and breast are of a rich violet purple; the back and scapulars, brownish green; rump, tail, and its coverts, of a duller brownish green; the sides of the neck, ultramarine; wings, the same, tinged with green; the inner webs of the quill-feathers and tail, dusky brown; upper lining and side lining of the wings, under the spurious wing, rich light blue; the belly, thighs, and for an inch behind, dull purplish black; the vent pure white; tail, rounded; thighs, legs, and feet, red; span of the foot, five inches; hind toe and claws, long.

It is somewhat remarkable that Turton, in his translation of the Systema Naturæ, should have perpetuated the error of arranging the Gallinules with the Coots, under the generical appellation of Fulica, to which they have but little resemblance in their habits, and none in the conformation of their feet. As he professed to have been assisted by the works of Dr. Latham, one would suppose that the classification of the latter, especially in this instance, would have been adopted.

In Mr. Peale's collection there is a Gallinule which resembles the above in every respect, except its being considerably smaller.

The bird, from which our drawing was taken, came from the state of Georgia, and is deposited in Peale's Museum. It is reduced, as well as the rest of the figures in the same plate, to one half the size of life.

Since writing the above, I have been informed by Mr. Alexander Rider, the painter, who accompanied the late Mr. Enslen in his botanical researches through the United States, that they observed the Purple Gallinule in a thick swamp, a short distance from Savannah, Georgia. It was very vigilant and shy, and was shot with much difficulty. It is very probable that it breeds there, as the nature of the swamp favors concealment, of which this bird appears to be fond.

Mr. Abbot, of Georgia, likewise informs me, that this species frequents the rice-fields and marshes in the lower parts of the state; it is rare, he having met with only three specimens; he has no doubt that it breeds there. He says that when the bird is living, the naked crown is of a *bright blue*, and the legs *yellow ochre*. We were necessitated to take our description, and to color our figure, from the stuffed specimen in Peale's Museum, and it is possible that we may have been in error with respect to those parts. In Mr. Wilson's drawing, they were colored as we have described them.

GRAY PHALAROPE.—PHALAROPUS LOBATA.—Fig. 308.

Phalaropus lobata, *Lath. Ind. Orn.* p. 776. *Id.* iii. pt. 1, p. 272. — Tringa lobata, *Turt. Syst.* i. 406.— *Muller*, No. 195.— *Faun. Suec.* 179.— *Faun. Groenl.* No. 75.— Le Phalarope, *Briss. Orn.* vi. p. 18, 1.— Le Phalarope afestons dentelés, *Buff. Ois.* xv. p. 349. — Gray Coot-footed Tringa, *Edwards*, pl. 308.— *Bewick,* ii. p. 132.— *Bartram*, p. 294. — *Br. Zool.* ii. No. 218.— *Arct. Zool.* ii. No. 412.

LOBIPES WILSONII.— Jardine.*

Phalaropus, (sub-gen. holopodius,) *Bonap. Synop.* p. 342.— Phalaropus Wilsonii, *Sab. App. to Frank. Narrat.* p. 691.—Lobipes incanus, *Jard.* and *Selby, Illust. Ornith.* pl. 25. — Phalaropus Wilsonii, *North. Zool.* ii. pl. 69.

Of this species, only one specimen was ever seen by Wilson, and that was preserved in Trowbridge's Museum, at Albany, in the state of New York. On referring to Wilson's Journal, I found an account of the bird, there called a *Tringa*, written with a lead pencil, but so scrawled and obscured, that parts of the writing were not legible. I wrote to Mr. Trowbridge, soliciting a particular description, but no answer was returned. From the drawing, which is imperfectly colored, and the description, which I have been enabled to decipher, I have concluded that this species is the Gray Phalarope of Turton. It is worthy of remark, that the ornithologists of Europe have differed somewhat in their account of this bird, as well as of that which follows; and we cannot reconcile our descriptions with theirs. This is owing, we presume, to the scarcity of the species, which has operated against their obtaining subjects recently killed, and has compelled them to have recourse to old or imperfect specimens of the museums.

In the grand and wonderful chain of animated nature, the Phalaropes constitute one of the links between the Waders and the Webfooted tribes, having the form of the Sandpiper with the habits of some of the Ducks; the scalloped membranes on their toes enabling them to swim with facility. They do not appear to be fond of the neighborhood of the ocean, and are generally found in the interior, about the lakes,

---

* In the small group known as *Phalaropus* we have two forms, distinguished by the stouter make, the flat-formed bill, and the development of the webs to the toes in the one, and by the slender bill and greater alliance of the other to the *Totani.* The Prince of Musignano has instituted another sub-group from what appears to me to be only the greater development of the latter form. Following the arrangement of Cuvier, I have retained *Lobipes* for those of slender make, and *Phalaropus* for that of this country, and only one yet discovered.

I have little hesitation in considering the *L. incanus* of ornithological illustrations to be this bird in imperfect plumage. Bonaparte is of opinion that the American bird was a new species; Mr. Ord, that it is some undescribed state of *P. hyperboreus :* with the former of these opinions I agree, and have accordingly adopted the specific name which Sabine had previously chosen for it, but have referred it to the genus *Lobipes* of Cuvier. This plate of our author is one of the very few exceptions where an imperfect representation of the bird is given, the figure being much too stout and thick, and not of that more elegant form, one of the *characteristics* of the *Totani.*

Under this division will also range the Little Red-necked Phalarope, *Lobipes hyperboreus* of Temminck, and the present type of the genus. According to Bonaparte, this species is exceedingly rare and accidental in the United States It will appear in the forthcoming volumes of that gentleman's Illustrations. — Ed.

ponds, and streams of fresh water, where they delight to linger, swimming near the margin in search of seeds and insects. They go in pairs, and we cannot learn that they are any where numerous. These circumstances are sufficient to authorize their removal from a tribe to which they have little resemblance, except in their general appearance. Edwards was the first naturalist who introduced them to the world; and although he seems to have been convinced that they ought to constitute a genus of themselves, yet he contented himself with arranging them with the *Tringæ,* a classification certainly neither scientific nor natural. Turton has fallen into the same error, which Latham and Pennant have judiciously avoided; and in their arrangement, so agreeable to our sentiments of the obvious discriminations of nature, we heartily concur.

The bill of this species is black, slender, straight, and one inch and three quarters in length; lores, front, crown, hind head, and thence to the back, very pale ash, nearly white; from the anterior angle of the eye, a curving stripe of black descends along the neck for an inch or more; thence to the shoulders, dark reddish brown, which also tinges the white on the side of the neck next it; under parts, white; above, dark olive; wings and legs, black; the scalloped membranes on the toes finely serrated on their edges; size of the Turnstone.

The above description, I am convinced, is imperfect; but as I have not an opportunity of seeing the bird, no better can be obtained.

Pennant says that the Gray Phalarope inhabits Scandinavia, Iceland and Greenland; in the last, lives on the frozen side, near the great lakes; quits the country before winter; is seen on the full seas in April and September, in the course of its migration. It is frequent in all Siberia, about the lakes and rivers, especially in autumn — probably in its migration from the Arctic flats; it was also met with among the ice between Asia and America.

The editor has been at considerable pains this spring to procure specimens and information of the two Phalaropes, which are figured and described in this volume; but he is sorry to declare that his endeavors have been unsuccessful. Though he explored our ponds and shores many times with his gun, and made frequent inquiries of sportsmen, yet he neither saw these birds nor heard of them; and has reason to believe that they seldom visit this part of the United States.

54 *

RED PHALAROPE. — PHALAROPUS HYPERBOREA. — Fig. 309.

Phalaropus hyperboreus, Latham, Ind. Orn. p. 775. — *Idem,* iii. pt. 1, p. 270. — *Br. Zool.* ii. No. 219. — *Arct. Zool.* No. 413. — Tringa fulicaria, *Faun. Suec.* No. 179. — *Faun. Groenl.* No. 76. — *Brunnich,* No. 172. — *Muller,* No. 196. — Tringa hyperborea, *Turt. Syst.* 1, 407. — Le Phalarope rouge, *Buff. Ois.* xv. p. 348. *Pl. enl.* 766. — Le Phalarope cendre, *Briss. Orn.* vi. p. 15, 2. — *Raii Syn.* p. 132, A. 7. — Small Cloven-footed Gull, *Wil. Orn.* p. 355. — Coot-footed Tringa, *Edw.* 142, 143. — Red Coot-footed Tringa, *Bartram,* 294. — *Bewick,* ii. 131. — *Peale's Museum,* No. 4088.

PHALAROPUS FULICARIUS. — BONAPARTE.

THIS species measures nine inches in length, and fifteen in breadth; the front and crown are black, barred transversely with lines of white; bill, orange, an inch long, broad above, black towards the tip; throat, sides of the neck, and lower parts, white, thickly and irregularly barred with curving dashes of reddish chocolate; the upper parts are of a deep slate color, streaked with brownish yellow and black; the back scapulars, broadly edged with brownish yellow; tail, plain pale olive; middle of the tail-coverts, black; sides, bright brownish yellow; rump, and wings, dark slate; the primaries are nearly black, and crossed with white, as usual, below their coverts; greater wing-coverts, broadly tipped with white, forming a large band; vent, white; those feathers immediately next the tail, reddish chocolate; legs, black on the outside, yellowish within; hind toe, small, and partly pinnate.

The Red Phalarope is a very rare bird in Pennsylvania; and, as far as we can learn, is but seldom met with in any part of the Union. It is said that they come into Hudson's Bay the beginning of June, and lay four eggs, about the middle of that month, on a dry spot; the young fly in August, and they depart to the southward in September. Whether or not they breed within the territory of the United States, we cannot determine; but it is probable they do, as three were seen on a pond below Philadelphia, in the latter part of May, 1812, one of which was shot, and presented to the editor, who transferred it to Mr. Peale. In consequence of its being in a high state of putridity when received, it was preserved with considerable difficulty, and the sex could not be ascertained. Our figure and description were from this specimen. The person who shot this bird had never seen one of the species before, and was particularly struck with its singular manners. He described it as sitting on the water, dipping in its bill very often, as if feeding, and turning frequently round.

Pennant informs us that the Red Phalarope is found in Scandinavia; is common about the Caspian Sea, and the lakes and rivers adjacent, during spring; but does not extend to the farther part of Siberia. It visits Greenland in April, and departs in September.

WILSON'S PLOVER. — CHARADRIUS WILSONIUS. — Fig. 310.

Peale's Museum, No. 4159, male ; 4160, female.

CHARADRIUS WILSONIUS. — Ord.

Charadrius Wilsonius, *Bonap. Synop.* p. 296.— *Nomenclature*, No. 221.

OF this neat and prettily-marked species I can find no account, and have concluded that it has hitherto escaped the eye of the naturalist. The bird from which this description was taken, was shot the 13th of May, 1813, on the shore of Cape Island, New Jersey, by my ever-regretted friend; and I have honored it with his name.[*] It was a male, and was accompanied by another of the same sex, and a female, all of which were fortunately obtained.

This bird very much resembles the Ring Plover, except in the length and color of the bill, its size, and in wanting the yellow eyelids. The males and females of this species differ in their markings, but the Ring Plovers nearly agree. We conversed with some sportsmen of Cape May, who asserted that they were acquainted with these birds, and that they sometimes made their appearance in flocks of considerable numbers ; others had no knowledge of them. That the species is rare we were well convinced, as we had diligently explored the shore of a considerable part of Cape May, in the vicinity of Great Egg Harbor, many times at different seasons, and had never seen them before. How long they remain on our coast, and where they winter, we are unable to say. From the circumstance of the oviduct of the female being greatly enlarged, and containing an egg half grown, apparently within a week of being ready for exclusion, we concluded that they breed there. Their favorite places of resort appear to be the dry sand flats on the sea-shore. They utter an agreeable piping note.

This species is seven inches and three quarters in length, and fifteen and a half in extent; the bill is black, stout, and an inch long, the upper mandible projecting considerably over the lower; front, white, passing on each side to the middle of the eye above, and bounded by a band of black of equal breadth; lores, black; eyelids, white; eye, large and dark; from the middle of the eye backwards, the stripe of white becomes duller, and extends for half an inch; the crown, hind head, and auriculars, are drab olive; the chin, throat, and sides of the neck, for an inch, pure white, passing quite round the neck, and narrowing to a point behind; the upper breast, below, is marked with a broad band of jet black; the rest of the lower parts, pure white; upper parts, pale olive drab; along the edges of the auriculas and hind head, the plumage, where it joins the white, is stained with raw terra sienna; all the plumage is darkest in the centre; the tertials are fully longer than the primaries, the latter brownish black, the shafts and

---

[*] Bonaparte thus observes in his *Nomenclature*, — " A very rare species established by the Editor, (Mr. Ord,) and dedicated to Wilson. It is the first homage of the kind paid to the memory of this great and lamented self-taught naturalist. The descriptions of several species in the works of former authors come more or less near to it, but after a careful investigation we are satisfied that it is new." — ED.

edges of some of the middle ones, white; secondaries, and greater coverts, slightly tipped with white; the legs are of a pale flesh color; toes bordered with a narrow edge; claws, and ends of the toes, black; the tail is even, a very little longer than the wings, and of a blackish olive color, with the exception of the two exterior feathers, which are whitish, but generally the two middle ones only are seen.

The female differs in having no black on the forehead, lores, or breast, those parts being pale olive.

BLACK-BELLIED DARTER, OR SNAKE-BIRD. — PLOTUS MELANOGASTER. — Fig. 311. — Male.

Salerne, *Orn.* p. 375. — *Will. Orn.* p. 250. — *Turt. Syst.* 1, 351. — *Lath. Gen. Syn.* pt. 2, p. 624. — L'Anhinga, *Buff. Ois.* xvi. p. 253. — Anhinga de Cayenne, *Pl. enl.* No. 959. — Anhinga melanogaster, *Zool. Ind.* p. 22, pl. 12. — Colymbus colubrinus, Snake Bird, *Bartram*, p. 132, 295. — *Peale's Museum*, No. 3188, Male.

PLOTUS ANHINGA. — Linnæus.*

Plotus anhinga, *Bonap. Synop.* p. 411. — Plotus melanogaster, *Ord.* 1st. edit. of *Supp.* p. 79.

THE Black-bellied Darter is three feet three inches in length; the bill is three inches and three quarters long, rather slender, very sharp

---

* This very curious genus contains only two known species — that of our author, common to both continents of America, and the *Plotus Vaillantii* of Temminck, a native of India, Africa, and the South Seas. It has been placed among the *Pelicanidæ* by most ornithologists; but how far all the forms, which are at present included in that family, have a right to be there, I am not at present prepared to determine: if they are, that of *Plotus* will hold a very intermediate rank, particularly in habits, which may lead to some discoveries in the relations to each other. The economy is in a considerable measure arboreal, and in their own family, as now constituted, they show the greatest development of the power of diving, and activity in the water. They show also the extreme structure in the power of darting, and suddenly again withdrawing their head. The Cormorants and Herons possess this power to a great extent, and they all possess a peculiar bend of the neck, observed in certain circumstances of the bird's economy, and into which that part at once puts itself when the bird is dead. This is produced chiefly by the action of two muscles; the one inserted within the cavity of the breast, and running up with a long tendon to the vertebræ beneath the bend; the other inserted in the joint above the bend, and running far down with another slender tendon. The action of these two powers, resisted by the muscles on the back part, produce the peculiar angular bend, and enable the head to be thrown forward with great force. The effect may be easily seen, and produced, by a jointed stick having cords affixed, and acted on in this way. We may here introduce the genera *Pelicanus, Phalacrocorax, Tachypetes, Sula,* and *Heliornis,* with a short notice of the species of America, as pointed out by the ornithologists who have described the productions of that country.

Pelicanus, Linn.

1. *P. onocrotalus.* — White Pelican. — According to Bonaparte, rare and accidental on the coasts of the Middle States, and said by Dr. Richardson to be numerous in the interior of the Fur Countries, up to the 61st deg. parallel.

2. *P. fuscus,* Linnæus. — Brown Pelican. — Common in the Southern States, where it breeds.

pointed, and armed with numerous sharp teeth, towards the tip, for the securing of its prey ; it is black above, and yellow below ; no external nostrils are visible ; the bare space around the eye, and the pouch under the chin, are also yellow ; the slit of the mouth extends beyond the eye ; irides, vivid red ; the head, neck, and whole lower parts, are black, glossed with dark green ; the side of the neck, from the eye backwards, for more than half its length, is marked by a strip of brownish white, consisting of long, hair-like tufts of plumage, extending an inch beyond the common surface, resembling the hair of callow young ; there are a few small tufts on the crown ; the whole upper parts are black, marked in a very singular and beautiful manner, with small, oval spots, and long, pointed streaks of a limy white, which has the gloss of silver in some lights ; the middle of the back, primaries, secondaries, rump, and tail-coverts, are plain glossy black ; on the

Phalacrocorax, Briss.

The species of this genus amount to a considerable number, and are distributed over the known world, but there yet exists confusion among them, from the near alliance of many to each other. The Prince of Musignano seems to have taken the authority of Dumont for the species he enumerates. They are as follows : —

1. *P. carbo.* — Cormorant of Wilson's list. — Tail of fourteen feathers ; rare and migratory in the United States.

2. *P. graculus.* — Tail, twelve feathers ; not uncommon in spring and autumn in the Middle States ; very common in Florida, where it breeds ; though very abundant in the Arctic and Antarctic circles.

3. *P. cristatus.* — Rather rare, and found during winter only in the United States

4. *P. pygmæus.* — Inhabiting the north of both continents.

5. *P. Africanus.* — Inhabiting Africa and America ; not found in Europe.

The Prince of Musignano is doubtful whether the two last are entitled to any place in the ornithology of America, the specimens which he has seen of both being only *reported* to have been killed in that country. He mentions also another, inhabiting the United States, which he has not examined, but thinks may turn out *P. Brazilianus.*

The first four species are common to Europe and America ; the three first are also British. In addition to these, Mr. Swainson has described another in the *Northern Zoology,* under the title *dilophus,* or Double-crested Cormorant, which he cannot reconcile to any of these already described. His characters are, " Tail of twelve feathers ; bill, three inches and a half long ; a crested tuft of feathers behind each eye."

Tachypetes, Vieill.

1. *T. aquilus,* Vieill. — Not uncommon during summer on the coasts of the United States, as far south as Carolina.

Sula, Briss.

1. *Sula Bassana,* Briss. — Common during summer over the coasts of the United States, especially the Southern.

2. *L. fusca,* Briss. — Booby. — Common in summer on the coasts of the Southern States.

Heliornis, Bonat.

1. *H. Surinamensis,* Surinam Heliornis. — An accidental visitant in summer in the Middle States.

I have introduced *Heliornis* here, but without at all placing it in this station from my own opinion of its real place ; the form of the birds contained in it (amounting yet to only two species,) is very curious, and though showing the form of the body, and, according to Bonaparte, of the skeleton of *Plotus,* yet the habits are much more that of the *Grebes.* This agrees with the arrangement by the Prince of Musignano in one range, but I do not so easily see its connection in the opposite direction with *Phæton* and *Sula,* the immediately preceding genera. — ED.

upper part of the back, the white is in very small, oval spots, lengthening as they approach the scapulars and tertials; on the latter they
extend the whole length of the feathers, running down the centre;
these are black shafted; the wings are long and pointed; lesser coverts marked, on every feather, with an oval, or spade-shaped spot of
white; greater coverts nearly all of a limy white; the tail is long,
rounding, and exceedingly stiff, consisting of twelve broad feathers,
the exterior vanes of the four middle ones curiously crimped, the whole
black, and broadly tipped with dirty, brownish white; the thighs are
black; legs, scarcely an inch and a half long; feet, webbed, all the
four toes united by the membrane, which is of uncommon breadth, and
must give the bird great velocity when diving or swimming; the exterior toe, which is the longest, is three inches long; claws, horn
color, strong, and crooked; inner side of the middle one, pectinated;
legs, and feet, yellow. The whole plumage is of extraordinary stiff-
ness and elasticity; that of the neck and breast, thick, soft, and shining. The position of these birds, when standing, is like that of the
Gannets.

Of this extraordinary species we can give little more than accurate
descriptions, and tolerably good portraits, which were taken from two
fine specimens, admirably set up and preserved in the Museum of Mr.
Peale. The Snake-Bird is an inhabitant of the Carolinas, Georgia,
and the Floridas; and is common in Brazil, Cayenne, Senegal, Ceylon,
and Java. It seems to have derived its name from the singular form
of its head and neck, which, at a distance, very much resemble some
species of serpents. In those countries where noxious animals
abound, we may readily conceive that the appearance of this bird,
extending its long neck through the foliage of a tree, would tend to
startle the wary traveller, whose imagination had portrayed objects
of danger lurking in every thicket. It is said to build its nest on a
tree; but of its habits during the season of incubation, the number
and color of its eggs, or the rearing of its young, we are ignorant.
Formerly the Darter was considered by voyagers as an anomalous
production; a monster, partaking of the nature of the Snake and
the Duck; and in some ancient charts, which we have seen, it is delineated in all the extravagance of fiction.

My excellent friend, Mr. William Bartram, gives the following account of the subject of our history: —

"Here is, in this river,* and in the waters all over Florida, a very
curious and handsome bird, — the people call them Snake-Birds; I
think I have seen paintings of them on the Chinese screens and other
Indian pictures; they seem to be a species of *Colymbus*, but far more
beautiful and delicately formed than any other that I have ever seen.
They delight to sit in little peaceable communities, on the dry limbs
of trees, hanging over the still waters, with their wings and tails expanded, I suppose to cool and air themselves, when at the same time
they behold their images in the watery mirror. At such times, when
we approach them, they drop off the limbs into the water, as if dead,
and for a minute or two are not to be seen; when on a sudden, at a
great distance, their long, slender head and neck appear, like a snake

---

* The River St. Juan, East Florida.

rising erect out of the water; and no other part of them is to be seen when swimming, except sometimes the tip end of their tail. In the heat of the day, they are seen in great numbers, sailing very high in the air over lakes and rivers.

" I doubt not but if this bird had been an inhabitant of the Tiber in Ovid's days, it would have furnished him with a subject for some beautiful and entertaining metamorphoses. I believe they feed entirely on fish, for their flesh smells and tastes intolerably strong of it: it is scarcely to be eaten, unless one is constrained by insufferable hunger. They inhabit the waters of Cape Fear River, and, southerly, East and West Florida." *

FEMALE BLACK-BELLIED DARTER, OR SNAKE-BIRD. —
Fig. 312.

White-bellied Darter ? *Lath. Gen. Syn.* vi. p. 622, 1. — *Ind. Orn.* p. 895. — *Peale's Museum*, No. 3189, female.

PLOTUS ANHINGA. — Linnæus.

The female Darter measures three feet five inches in length, and differs in having the neck before of a roan color, or iron gray; the breast, the same, but lighter, and tinged with pale chestnut; the belly, as in the male; where the iron gray joins the black on the belly there is a narrow band of chestnut; upper head, and back of the neck, dark sooty brown, streaked with blackish; cheeks and chin, pale yellow ochre; in every other respect, the same as the male, except in having only a few slight tufts of hair along the side of the neck; the tail is twelve inches long to its insertion, generally spread out like a fan, and crimped like the other on the outer vanes of the middle feathers only.

Naturalists describe a bird of this family, which they call the White-bellied Darter, (*P. anhinga.*) We know of but one species of Plotus found within the United States, and suspect that the female above described is the White-bellied Darter of Latham and others. For the purpose of ascertaining the fact, we wrote to an experienced naturalist residing in Georgia; but, through some unfortunate cause, no answer has been received. It is so many years since our venerable friend, Mr. Bartram, travelled in those regions where the Darters are common, that he has lost all recollection of them, except what relates to their general appearance. We must, therefore, content ourselves with our imperfect knowledge of this singular species, until some favorable occurrence shall enable us to form a correct opinion.

Since the above has been written, the editor has had the satisfaction of receiving from Mr. John Abbott, of Georgia, a valuable communication relative to this bird and some others; for which favor he offers his sincere acknowledgment.

* Bartram's *Travels*, p. 132. — MS in the possession of the author, [Mr Ord.]

Mr. Abbot agrees with us in opinion that the *P. anhinga* is the female of this species. He says —

"Both the Darters I esteem as but one species. I have now by me a drawing of the male, or Black-bellied, only, but have had specimens of both at the same time. I remember that the upper parts of the female were similar to those of the male, except that the color and markings were not so pure and distinct; length, thirty-six inches; extent, forty-six. These birds frequent the ponds, rivers, and creeks, during the summer; build in the trees of the swamps, and those of the islands in the ponds; they construct their nests of sticks; eggs, of a sky blue color. I inspected a nest, which was not very large; it contained two eggs, and six young ones, the latter varying much in size; they will occupy the same tree for a series of years. They commonly sit on a stump, which rises out of the water, in the mornings of the spring, and spread their wings to the sun; from which circumstance they have obtained the appellation of Sun-Birds. They are difficult to be shot when swimming, in consequence of only their heads being above the water."

GREAT NORTHERN DIVER, OR LOON. — COLYMBUS GLACIALIS. — Fig. 313.

Pennant, Br. Zool. 237. — *Arct. Zool.* 439. — Le grand Plongeon tacheté, *Briss. Orn.* vi. 120, tab. 2, fig. 1. — L'Imbrim, ou grand Plongeon de la Mer du Nord, *Buff. Ois.* xv. p. 461. *Pl. enl.* No. 952. — *Turt. Syst.* i. 356. — *Lath. Gen. Syn.* iii. pt. 2, p. 337. — Colymbus maximus caudatus, *Raii Syn.* p. 125, A. 4. — Greatest Speckled Diver, or Loon, *Willoughby, Orn.* p. 341. — Great Speckled Diver, *Bartram,* 295. — *Albin,* iii. pl. 93. — *Bewick's Br. Birds,* ii. p. 168. — *Peale's Museum,* No. 3262, male, and young; No. 3263, female.

COLYMBUS GLACIALIS. — Linnæus.†

Colymbus glacialis, *Bonap. Synop.* p. 420. — *Flem. Brit. Anim.* p. 132. — *North. Zool.* ii. p. 474.

THIS bird in Pennsylvania is migratory. In the autumn, it makes its appearance with the various feathered tribes that frequent our waters; and, when the streams are obstructed with ice, it departs for

---

† The genus *Colymbus,* or the Loons, have been restricted to those large Divers, of which our present species will point out a good example. They are all birds of a large size, truly aquatic; are seldom on land except during incubation; and, though endowed with a considerable power, seldom fly, unless very much pressed by necessity. The Great Northern Diver is very frequent in the Frith of Forth, and there I have never been able either to make up with, or cause one to fly from the sea. I have pursued this bird in a Newhaven fishing-boat, with four sturdy rowers; and, notwithstanding it was kept almost constantly under water by firing as soon as it appeared, the boat could not succeed in making one yard upon it. They are sometimes caught in the herring-nets, and at set lines, when diving.

The Loons and Guillemots approach very near in their characters, except in lesser size, and a particular modification of habit, in the one preferring the sea-shores, or the reedy banks of inland lakes, for breeding places, while the others are

the Southern States.* In the months of March and April, it is again seen, and, after lingering a while, it leaves us for the purpose of breeding. The Loons are found along the coast, as well as in the interior; but in the summer, they retire to the fresh-water lakes and ponds. We have never heard that they breed in Pennsylvania, but it is said they do in Missibisci Pond, near Boston, Massachusetts. The female lays two large, brownish eggs. They are commonly seen in pairs; and procure their food, which is fish, in the deepest water of our rivers, diving after it, and continuing under for a length of time. Being a wary bird, it is seldom they are killed, eluding their pursuers by their astonishing faculty of diving. They seem averse from flying, and are but seldom seen on the wing. They are never eaten.

The Loon is restless before a storm; and an experienced master of a coasting-vessel informed me that he always knew when a tempest was approaching by the cry of this bird, which is very shrill, and may be heard at the distance of a mile or more.

gregarious, and choose the most precipitous cliffs on the sea, and deposit their eggs, without the least preparation, on the bare rock. The construction of the feet and tarse at once points out in the large birds their great facility of diving, and rapid progression under water; the proportional expanse of web is much greater, and the form of it runs into that of *Phalacrorax* and *Sula;* the legs are placed very far back, and the muscles possess very great power; the tarsus is flattened laterally, and thus presents a small surface of resistance; and the whole plumage of the bird is close and rigid, presenting a smooth and almost solid resistance in passing through the water. The adults require at least the first season to attain maturity. Dr. Richardson mentions the following method of shooting them during the winter: — "They arrive in that season when the ice of the lakes continues entire, except, perhaps, a small basin of open water where a rivulet happens to flow in, or where the discharge of the lake takes place. When the birds are observed to alight in these places, the hunter runs to the margin of the ice; they instantly dive, but are obliged, after a time, to come to the surface to breathe, when he has an opportunity of shooting them. In this way, upwards of twenty were killed at Fort Enterprise, in the spring of 1821, in a piece of water only a few yards square."

The present species is the only one described in Wilson's volumes as a native of America. Bonaparte mentions two others, which are also described in the *Northern Zoology,* — the Black-throated Diver, (*Columbus arcticus*,) common in Arctic America, but rare, and only found during winter in the Middle States; and *Colymbus septentrionalis,* Red-throated Diver. All are common also to Europe and Great Britain.

The vast lakes and rivers of America, and her interminable swamps, would seem proper nurseries for another family, the Grebes; and their recluse, yet active aquatic manners, must either have yet prevented the discovery of more species, or this form is comparatively wanting to that division of the world. Two species only are mentioned in Wilson's History, and Bonaparte adds other two. They are as follows, from that gentleman's *Synopsis:* —

Podiceps.

1. *P. cristatus,* LATH. — Crested Grebe of Wilson's List; rare in the Middle States, and only during winter common in the interior and on the lakes.

2. *P. rubricollis,* LATH. — Rare, and during winter only in the Middle States; very common in Arctic America.

3. *P. cornutus,* LATH. — Common during winter, the young especially, in the Middle States.

4. *P. Carolinensis,* LATH. — Little Grebe of Wilson's List; inhabits the whole continent of America, not extending far to the north. Common from Canada to Louisiana, migrating in the Middle States. — ED.

* The Loon is said to winter in the Chesapeake Bay.

This species seldom visits the shores of Britain, except in very severe winters; but it is met with in the north of Europe, and spreads
along the Arctic coast as far as the mouth of the River Ob, in the dominions of Russia.   It is found about Spitzbergen, Iceland, and Hudson's Bay.   Makes its nest, in the more northern regions, on the little
isles of fresh-water lakes: every pair keep a lake to themselves.   It
sees well, flies very high, and, darting obliquely, falls secure into its
nest.   Appears in Greenland in April, or the beginning of May, and
goes away in September, or October, on the first fall of snow.*   It is
also found at Nootka Sound,† and Kamtschatka.

The Barabinzians — a nation situated between the River Ob and
the Irtisch, in the Russian dominions — tan the breasts of this and
other water fowl, whose skins they prepare in such a manner as to
preserve the down upon them; and, sewing a number of these together, they sell them to make pelisses, caps, &c.   Garments made of
these are very warm, never imbibing the least moisture, and are more
lasting than could be imagined.‡

The natives of Greenland use the skins for clothing, and the Indians
about Hudson's Bay adorn their heads with circlets of their feathers.§

Lewis and Clark's party, at the mouth of the Columbia, saw robes
made of the skins of Loons,‖ and abundance of these birds, during the
time that they wintered at Fort Clatsop, on that river.¶

The Laplanders, according to Regnard, cover their heads with a
cap made of the skin of a Loom, (Loon,) which word signifies, in their
language, *lame*, because the bird cannot walk well.   They place it on
their head in such a manner that the bird's head falls over their brow,
and its wings cover their ears.

"Northern Divers," says Hearne, though common in Hudson's Bay,
are by no means plentiful; they are seldom found near the coast, but
more frequently in fresh-water lakes, and usually in pairs.   They
build their nests at the edge of small islands, or the margins of lakes
or ponds; they lay only two eggs; and it is very common to find only
one pair and their young in one sheet of water — a great proof of their
aversion to society.   They are known in Hudson's Bay by the name
of Loons." **

The Great Northern Diver measures two feet ten inches from the
tip of the bill to the end of the tail, and four feet six inches in breadth;
the bill is strong, of a glossy black, and four inches and three quarters
long to the corner of the mouth; the edges of the bill do not fit exactly into each other, and are ragged; the lower mandible separates
into two branches, which are united by a thin, elastic membrane, and
are easily movable horizontally, or receding from each other, so as to
form a wider gap to facilitate the swallowing of large fish; tongue,
bifid; irides, dark blood red; the head, and half of the length of the
neck, are of a deep black, with a green gloss, and purple reflections;
this is succeeded by a band consisting of interrupted white and
black lateral stripes, which encompasses the neck, and tapers to a

* PENNANT.   † COOK's *Last Voyage*, ii. p. 237, Am. ed.
‡ LATHAM.   § *Arctic Zoology.*   ‖ GASS's *Journal.*
¶ *History of the Expedition*, vol. ii. p. 189.
** HEARNE's *Journey*, p. 429, quarto.

point on its fore part, without joining,—this band measures about an inch and a half in its widest part, and, to appearance, is not continuous on the back part of the neck, being concealed by some thick, overhanging, black feathers, but, on separating the latter, the band becomes visible: the feathers which form these narrow stripes, are white, streaked down their centre with black, and, what is a remarkable peculiarity, their webs project above the common surface; below this, a broad band of dark glossy green and violet, which is blended behind with the plumage of the back; the lower part of the neck, and the sides of the breast, are ribbed in the same manner as the band above; below the chin, a few stripes of the same; the whole of the upper parts are of a deep black, slightly glossed with green, and thickly spotted with white, in regular transverse or semicircular rows, two spots on the end of each feather—those on the upper part of the back, shoulders, rump, and tail-coverts, small and roundish, those on the centre of the back, square and larger; those on the scapulars are the largest, and of an oblong square shape; the wing-feathers and tail are plain brown black, the latter composed of twenty feathers; the lower parts are pure white, a slight dusky line across the vent; the scapulars descend over the wing when closed, and the belly feathers ascend so as to meet them, by which means every part of the wing is concealed, except towards the tip. This accommodation is to prevent its retarding the bird in diving. The outside of the legs and feet is black, inside pale blue; the leg is four inches in length, and the foot measures, along the exterior toe to the tip of its claw, four inches and three quarters; both legs and feet are marked with five-sided polygons.

The female Diver is somewhat less than the male; the bill is yellowish; crown, back part of the neck, and whole upper parts, pale brown; the plumage of part of the back and scapulars is tipped with pale ash; the throat, lower side of the neck, and whole under parts, are white, but not so pure as that of the male, having a yellowish tinge; the quill-feathers, dark brown. She has no appearance of bands on her neck, or of spots on her body.

The young males do not obtain their perfect plumage until the second or third year. One which we saw, and which was conjectured to be a yearling, had some resemblance to the female, with the exception of its upper parts being of a darker and purer brown, or mouse color, and its under parts of a more delicate white; it had likewise a few spots on the back and scapulars; but none of those markings on the neck which distinguish the full-grown male.

The conformation of the ribs and bones of this species is remarkable, and merits particular examination.

In the account which some of the European ornithologists give of their Northern Diver, we presume there is an inaccuracy. They say it measures three feet six inches in length, and four feet eight in breadth, and weighs sixteen pounds. If this be a correct statement, it would lead to the surmise that our Diver is a different species; for, of several specimens which we examined, the best and largest has been described for this work; the admeasurement of which bird comes considerably short of that of the European mentioned above. The weight we neglected to ascertain. The Common Wild Goose of our country,

(*A. Canadensis*,) when in good condition, will seldom weigh more than twelve pounds. In order to determine this point, we personally exerted ourselves, and commissioned some of our friends, to procure a good specimen of the Loon during the past season, but without success.

BLACK-HEADED GULL. — LARUS RIDIBUNDUS. — Fig. 314.

Linn. Syst. 225. — La Mouette rieuse, *De Buff.* xvi. p. 232. *Pl. enl.* 970. — La Mouette rieuse à pattos rouges, *Briss.* — *Lath. Gen. Syn.* iii. pt. 2, p. 380. — *Br. Zool.* ii. 252. — *Arct. Zool.* No. 454, 455. — Laughing Gull, *Catesby*, 1, 89. — *Will. Orn.* p. 347, pl. 66. — Pewit, Black-Cap, or Sea-Crow, *Raii Syn.* p. 128, A. 5. — *Bewick*, ii. 200. — *Peale's Museum*, No. 3381.

LARUS ATRICILLA. — Linnæus.*

Larus ridibundus, *Ord.* 1 edit. of *Sup.* p. 89. — Larus atricilla, *Bonap. Synop.* p. 359.

LENGTH, seventeen inches ; extent, three feet six inches ; bill, thighs, legs, feet, sides of the mouth, and eyelids, dark blood red ; inside of

* This Gull is the only one figured by Wilson, though several are mentioned in his list, and, no doubt, had he survived to complete his great undertaking, many others would have been both added and figured. I have introduced a short description of those which have been since noticed by writers on Arctic and Northern zoology, but any observations will be confined, for the present, to the form now before us, perhaps more familiar in the Black-headed Gull of Britain.

The Gulls are distributed over the whole world, and present various forms. They are mostly, however, of graceful appearance, and perform their motions with ease and lightness ; their plumage is often of snowy whiteness, or tinged with a pale blush, adding to its delicacy. By the poets they are employed as emblems of purity, when riding buoyantly on the waves, and weaving a sportive dance, or as accessaries to the horrors of a storm, by their shrieks and wild, piercing cries. In their manners they are the vultures of the ocean, feed indiscriminately on fish or on carrion, and frequently attack birds of inferior power. A dead horse, newly cast upon the beach, will present a picture little inferior to that drawn by Audubon of the American Vultures, on the discovery of some putrid carcass.

Our present bird will rank under the genus *Xema* of Boje, which will contain those of swallow-like form, apparently both a natural and well-defined group. They are not so truly pelagic as many of the other forms — ascend the course of rivers in search of food, and breed by the inland lochs or marshes — are extremely clamorous and intrepid in defence of their young, but during winter are one of the most shy and wary. They undergo an annual change of plumage during the breeding season, obtaining the whole or part of the head of a dark and decided color from the rest of the body, generally shades of deep and rich brown, or gray ; in winter this entirely disappears, and is succeeded by pure white, except on the auriculars, which retain a trace of the darker shade. They feed on fish and insects, and some follow the plough in search of what it may turn up. In fishing, they exhibit occasionally the same manner of seizing their prey as the Terns, hovering above, and striking it under water with the wings closed.

The species which are noticed by the Prince of Musignano, and the authors of the *Northern Zoology*, as inhabiting North America, are —

1. *L. Sabinii*, (*Xema Sabinii*, Leach.) — Discovered by Captain Edward Sabine, breeding in company with the Arctic Tern, on the west coast of Greenland ; they seem confined to high latitudes.

2. *Larus minutus*, Pall. — Inhabiting the North, but seldom seen in the United States.

3. *Larus capistratus*, Temm. — Inhabiting the North, and not very rare during autumn

the mouth, vermilion; bill, nearly two inches and a half long; the nostril is placed rather low; the eyes are black; above and below

on the Delaware and Chesapeake, and found as far inland as Trenton. These will all rank in *Xema*, and Swainson and Richardson have described two under the titles of *L. Franklinii*, and *L. Bonapartii*. These gentlemen seem to think that the American *L. atricilla* is confounded with Temminck's *atricilla*, and that they embrace two species. I have added the descriptions from Dr. Richardson and Mr. Swainson's notes, in their own words. I have no means at present of deciding this point.

4. *L. Franklinii*, Swain. and Richard. — Franklin's Rosy Gull, with vermilion bill and feet; mantle, pearl gray; five exterior quills, broadly barred with black, the first one tipped with white for an inch; tarsus, twenty lines long; hood, black in summer.

" This is a very common Gull in the interior of the Fur Countries, where it frequents the shores of the larger lakes. It is generally seen in flocks, and is very noisy. It breeds in marshy places. Ord's description of his Black-headed Gull (Wilson, vol. ix. p. 89 — present edition, p. 652) corresponds with our specimens, except that the conspicuous white end of the first quill is not noticed: the figure 314 differs in the primaries being entirely black.* The Prince of Musignano gives the totally black primaries, and a tarsus nearly two inches long, as part of the specific character of his *L. atricilla*, to which he refers Wilson's bird; though, in his *Observations*, he states, that the adult specimens have the primaries, with the exception of the first and second, tipped with white. *L. Franklinii* cannot be referred either to the *L. atricilla* or *L. melanocephalus* of M. Temminck: the first has a lead colored hood, and deep black quill-feathers, untipped by white; and the black hood of the second does not descend lower on the throat than on the nape; its quill-feathers are also differently marked, and its tarsus is longer. His *L. ridibundus* and *capistratus* have brown heads, and the interior of the wings gray; the latter has also a much smaller bill than our *L. Franklinii*."

5. *L. Bonapartii*, Swain. and Richards. — Bonapartian Gull. — *North. Zool.* ii. p. 425. — "With a black bill; the mouth and feet, carmine red; wings bordered with white anteriorly; posteriorly, together with the back, pearl gray; six exterior quills, black at the end, slightly tipped with white; the first quill entirely black exteriorly; tarsus, scarcely an inch and a half long; head, grayish black in summer.

" This handsome, small Gull is common in all parts of the Fur Countries, where it associates with the Terns, and is distinguished by its peculiar shrill and plaintive cry. The *L. capistratus* of the Prince of Musignano differs, according to his description, in the first quill being white exteriorly, pale ash interiorly, in the light brown color of its head, and in its tail being slightly emarginated, while the tail of *L. Bonapartii* is even inclined to be rounded laterally, than notched in the middle."

6. *L. roseus*, Macgilliv. — A rare species confined to high latitudes, discovered during Sir Ed. Parry's second voyage, when two specimens were obtained; the one is now in the Edinburgh Museum; the other was presented to Mr. Sabine, whose collection has been lately sold to the Andersonian Museum in Glasgow.

7. *L. tridactylus*, Linn. — Kittiewake, Wilson's List. — Inhabiting both continents.

8. *L. canus*, Linn. — Common Gull, Wilson's List. — Inhabiting both continents; and numerous during winter in the Middle States of America.

9. *L. eburneus*, Gmel. — Inhabits the Arctic circle; migrating occasionally to the temperate regions. A few specimens have been killed in Britain.

10. *L. fuscus*, Linn. — Very common during winter near Philadelphia and New York.

11. *L. argentatoides*, Brehm. — This bird is separated from *Larus argentatus* by Bonaparte, who mentions having shot it on the southern coasts of England. At the same time that he separates it from the Herring Gull, he expresses a doubt of its being the *L. argentatoides* of Brehm. This I cannot at present decide, but have appended, without any abridgment, the observations and description of a bird referred to this, from the *Northern Zoology*; it is very closely allied, at all events, to the *L. argentatus*; and it is of importance that the characters of a species said to be killed on our coasts should be properly investigated.

Larus argentatoides. — Arctic Silvery Gull.

" *Larus argentatus*, Richards. *Append. Parry's Second Voy.* p. 358, No. 22. — *Larus argentatoides*, Bonap. Syn. No. 299. — *Novya*, Esquimaux."

" The Prince of Musignano has distinguished this Gull from *Larus argentatus*, with

---

" Four American specimens of L. *atricilla* are now before me. It is a larger and a totally different species. The three outer quills are wholly black; the fourth tipped for about one inch, and the fifth for half an inch, with black; the extreme white spot at the point of the five first quills is very small in some, and not seen in adult specimens, having these feathers worn." — Sw.

55 *

each eye there is a spot of white; the head and part of the neck are black, remainder of the neck, breast, whole lower parts, tail-coverts,

which it had been confounded by most other writers. It is impossible, therefore, to separate its history, or to cite the descriptions of other authors correctly. It was found breeding on Melville Peninsula; and the eggs that were brought home have an oil green color, marked with spots and blotches of blackish brown and subdued purplish gray. It preys much on fish, and is noted at Hudson's Bay for robbing the nets set in the fresh-water lakes. I have seen no specimens from Arctic America which I can unequivocally refer to the *Larus argentatus*, as characterized by the Prince of Musignano."

Description of a Male, in the Edin. Museum, killed on Melville Peninsula, June 29, 1822.

"Color, mantle, pearl gray. Six outer quills crossed by a brownish black band, which takes in nearly the whole of the first one, but becoming rapidly narrower on the others, terminates in a spot near the tip of the sixth. The first quill has a white tip an inch and a half long, marked interiorly with a brown spot; the second has a round white spot on its inner web, and, together with the rest of the quill-feathers, is tipped with white. Head, neck, rump, tail, and all the under plumage pure white. Bill, wine yellow, with an orange colored spot near the tip of the under mandible. Irides, primrose yellow. Legs, flesh colored.

FORM. — Bill, moderately strong, compressed; upper mandible, arched from the nostrils; nostrils, oblong oval; wings, about an inch longer than the tail; thighs, naked for three quarters of an inch; hind toe, articulated rather high.

The young have the upper plumage hair-brown, with reddish brown borders; the head and under plumage, gray, thickly spotted with pale brown; the tail, mostly brown, tipped with white.

DIMENSIONS. — Length, total, 23 inches; of tail, 7 inches, 3 lin.; of wing, 16 inches, 6 lin.; of bill above, 2 inches; of bill to rictus, 3 inches; from nostrils to tip, 11 lin.; of nostrils, 4½ lin.; of tarsus, 2 inches, 4½ lin.; of middle toe, 2 inches, 1 lin.; of middle nail, 5 lin.; of inner toe, 1 inch, 6 lin.; of inner nail, 4 lin.; of hind toe, 3 lin.; length of hind nail, 2½ lines.

Six individuals, killed on Melville Peninsula, in June, July, and September, varied in total length from 23 to 25 inches, and in the length of their tarsi, from 27 to 31 lines.

Bonaparte thus gives the distinctive characters of the two species : —

L. argentatoides. — Back and wings, bluish gray; quills, black at the point, tipped with white, reaching but little beyond the tail; shafts, black; first primary, broadly white at tip; second, with a round white spot besides; tarsus, less than two and a half inches; nostrils, oval; length, twenty inches.

L. argentatus. — Mantle, bluish gray; quills, black at the point, tipped with white, reaching much beyond the tail; shafts, black; first primary only, with a white spot besides the narrow tip; tarsus, nearly three inches; nostrils, linear; length, two feet. They are closely allied, and may at once be distinguished by the size."

12. *L. argentatus*, Brunn. — Herring Gull, Wilson's List. — Common to both continents, and not uncommon near New York and Philadelphia.

13. *L. leucopterus*, Faber. — Inhabiting the Arctic circle, whence it migrates in winter to the Boreal regions of both continents, advancing farther south in America; not rare in the Northern and Middle States.

14. *L. glaucus*, Brunn. — Inhabiting the Arctic regions, and exceedingly rare in the United States.

15. *L. marinus*, Linn. — Black-backed Gull, Wilson's List. — Not uncommon during winter in the Middle States.

16. *L. zonorhynchus*, Richard. — Ring-billed Mew Gull. A new species, described in *Northern Zoology*. — Bill, ringed rather longer than the tarsus, which measures two and a half inches; mantle, pearl gray; ends of the quills and their shafts, blackish; a short white space on the two exterior ones.

17. *L. bachyrhynchus*, Richard. — Short-billed Mew Gull. Another species described as new in the *Northern Zoology*. — From the description of the present bird, copied from that work, it will be seen that the authors themselves are not decided in their opinions as to the absolute distinction of this and the preceding from *L. canus*, and I have placed them here for the same reason that they are admitted into that valuable work. It is not unlikely that they, or at least the same varieties, may be discovered on our own coasts.

"Short-billed Mew Gull, with a short, thickish bill; a tarsus scarcely two inches long; quills, not tipped with white; a short white space on the exterior ones, and blackish shafts."

"Our specimen of this Gull is a female, killed on the 23d of May, 1826, at Great Bear Lake. Some brown markings on the tertiaries, primary coverts, and bastard wing, with an

and tail, pure white; the scapulars, wing-coverts, and whole upper parts, are of a fine blue ash color; the first five primaries are black towards their extremities; the secondaries are tipped largely with white, and almost all the primaries slightly; the bend of the wing is white, and nearly three inches long; the tail is almost even; it consists of twelve feathers, and its coverts reach within an inch and a half of its tip; the wings extend two inches beyond the tail; a delicate blush is perceivable on the breast and belly.

The head of the female is of a dark dusky slate color; in other respects, she resembles the male.

imperfect sub-terminal bar on the tail, point it out as a young bird, most probably commencing its second spring. The rest of its plumage corresponds with that of *L. zonorhynchus*, except that it wants the extreme white tips of the quill feathers, which, on the third and following ones, are very conspicuous in *L. zonorhynchus*. It differs, however, remarkably, in its bill being shorter, though considerably stouter, than that of our *L. canus*; and, like it, it is wax-yellow, with a bright yellow rictus and point. Its tarsus is nearly one third shorter than that of *L. zonorhynchus*. Many may be disposed to consider this and the preceding as merely local varieties of *L. canus*; and it might be urged, in support of this opinion, that there are considerable differences in the length and thickness of the bills of individuals of the common and winter Gulls killed on the English coasts, which are usually referred to *L. canus*. We have judged it advisable, however, to call the attention of ornithologists to these American birds, by giving them specific names, leaving it to future observation to determine whether they ought to retain the rank of species, or be considered as mere varieties." — RICHARD.

In this place must be introduced the genus *Lestris*, or *Skua*, of which only one species was enumerated by Wilson in his list — the *L. cataractes*, Illiger — the common *Skua Gull* of British ornithologists. The Prince of Musignano mentions, in addition, the now well-known European and British species, *L. parasiticus* and *pomarinus*; another somewhat allied, but not yet well distinguished, *L. Buffonii*, Bojè; and a fifth species is described as new in the *Northern Zoology*, and is dedicated to Dr. Richardson — *L. Richardsonii*. It seems closely allied to *L. Buffonii*, but the distinctions yet want clearness and confirmation. It was found breeding in considerable numbers in the barren grounds, at a distance from the coast. The following are Bonaparte's characters of *L. Buffonii*, by which it is alone known.

" *Lestris Buffonii*, Bojè. Bill, one inch and a quarter from the front, straight, notched; middle tail feathers, gradually tapering, narrow for several inches, ending in a point; tarsus, one inch and a half long, almost smooth. — Adult, brown; neck, and beneath, white, the former tinged with yellow. — Young, wholly brownish.

" Arctic bird, Edw. pl. 148; BUFF. *Pl. enl.* 762. *Lestris crepidata*, Brehm." — BONAP. *Syn.* No. 306.

And I add the observations of Mr. Swainson regarding *L. Richarsonii* : —

" Richardson's Jager, whole plumage, brown; two middle tail-feathers, abruptly acuminated; tarsi, black, twenty-two lines long.

" This specimen appears to us to be in full and mature plumage; we cannot, therefore, view it as the young, or even as the female, of the *Lestris Buffonii* of Bojè, which we only know from the characters assigned to it by the Prince of Musignano. According to this account, the *L. Buffonii* has the bill an inch and a quarter long from the front; ours is only an inch: the tarsi are described as almost smooth, whereas in ours they are particularly rough. The adult, as figured in plate 762 of the *Pl. enl.* has the chin, throat, and sides of the neck quite white; but, in our bird, these parts are of the same pure and decided tint as that of the body, except that the ear-feathers, and a few lower down the neck, have a slight tinge of ochre.* The tarsi also, in both the plates cited by the Prince, are colored yellow. These differences, with the more important one exhibited in the feet, will not permit us to join these birds under one name. Another distinction, which must not be overlooked, is in the color of the feet. Edwards expressly says of his ' Arctic Bird,' (pl. 149, which much more resembles ours than that figured on the plate immediately preceding,) that ' the legs and toes are all yellow;' whereas, in our bird, these members are of a deep and shining black; while the hinder parts of the tarsi, toes, and connecting membrane, are particularly rough." — Sw.

This Jager breeds in considerable numbers in the barren grounds, at a distance from the coast. It feeds on shelly mollusca, which are plentiful in the small lakes of the Fur Countries, and it harasses the Gulls in the same way with others of the genus. — ED.

* The pure color or uniform tint of the lower parts will not stand as characters in our native species they vary constantly. — Ed.

We are inclined to the opinion, that the three Gulls of Latham, viz., the Black-headed Gull, the Red-legged Gull, and the Laughing Gull, are one and the same species, the very bird which we have been describing, the difference in their markings arising from their age and sex. We feel imboldened to this declaration from the circumstance of having ourselves shot Gulls which corresponded almost precisely to those of the above author, of the same habits, the same voice, and which were found associating together.

In some individuals, the crown is of a dusky gray; the upper part and sides of the neck, of a lead color; the bill and legs, of a dirty, dark, purplish brown. Others have not the white spots above and below the eyes; these are young birds.

The changes of plumage, to which birds of this genus are subject, have tended not a little to confound the naturalist; and a considerable collision of opinion, arising from an imperfect acquaintance with the living subjects, has been the result. To investigate thoroughly their history, it is obviously necessary that the ornithologist should frequently explore their native haunts; and, to determine the species of periodical or occasional visitors, an accurate comparative examination of many specimens, either alive or recently killed, is indispensable. Less confusion would arise among authors, if they would occasionally abandon their accustomed walks — their studies and their museums, and seek correct knowledge in the only place where it is to be obtained — in the grand temple of nature. As it respects, in particular, the tribe under review, the zealous inquirer would find himself amply compensated for all his toil, by observing these neat and clean birds coursing along the rivers and coast, enlivening the prospect by their airy movements, now skimming closely over the watery element, watching the motions of the surges, and now rising into the higher regions, sporting with the winds, — while he inhaled the invigorating breezes of the ocean, and listened to the soothing murmurs of its billows.

The Black-headed Gull is the most beautiful and most sociable of its genus. They make their appearance on the coast of New Jersey in the latter part of April; and do not fail to give notice of their arrival by their familiarity and loquacity. The inhabitants treat them with the same indifference that they manifest towards all those harmless birds which do not minister either to their appetite or their avarice; and hence the Black-Heads may be seen in companies around the farm-house, coursing along the river shores, gleaning up the refuse of the fishermen, and the animal substances left by the tide; or scattered over the marshes and newly-ploughed fields, regaling on the worms, insects, and their larvæ, which, in the vernal season, the bounty of Nature provides for the sustenance of myriads of the feathered race.

On the Jersey side of the Delaware Bay, in the neighborhood of Fishing Creek, about the middle of May, the Black-headed Gulls assemble in great multitudes, to feed upon the remains of the king crabs which the hogs have left, or upon the spawn which those curious animals deposit in the sand, and which is scattered along the shore by the waves. At such times, if any one approach to disturb them, the Gulls will rise up in clouds, every individual squalling so loud, that the roar may be heard at the distance of two or three miles.

It is an interesting spectacle to behold this species when about recommencing their migrations. If the weather be calm, they will rise up in the air, spirally, chattering all the while to each other in the most sprightly manner, their notes at such times resembling the singing of a Hen, but far louder, changing often into a *haw, ha, ha, ha, haw!* the last syllable lengthened out like the excessive laugh of a negro. When mounting and mingling together, like motes in the sunbeams, their black heads and wing-tips, and snow-white plumage, give them a very beautiful appearance. After gaining an immense height, they all move off, with one consent, in a direct line towards the point of their destination.

This bird breeds in the marshes. The eggs are three in number, of a dun clay color, thinly marked with small, irregular touches of a pale purple, and pale brown; some are of a deeper dun, with larger marks, and less tapering than others; the egg measures two inches and a quarter by one inch and a half.

The Black-Heads frequently penetrate into the interior, especially as far as Philadelphia; but they seem to prefer the neighborhood of the coast for the purpose of breeding. They retire southward early in autumn.

This species is found in every part of Russia and Siberia, and even in Kamtschatka. They are seen throughout the winter at Aleppo, in great numbers, and so tame, that the women are said to call them from the terraces of their houses, throwing up pieces of bread, which these birds catch in the air.* The Black-headed Gull is common in Great Britain. "In former times," says Bewick, "these birds were looked upon as valuable property, by the owners of some of the fens and marshes in this kingdom, who, every autumn, caused the little islets or hafts, in those wastes, to be cleared of the reeds and rushes, in order properly to prepare the spots for the reception of the old birds in the spring, to which places at that season they regularly returned in great flocks to breed. The young ones were then highly esteemed, as excellent eating, and on that account were caught in great numbers, before they were able to fly. Six or seven men, equipped for this business, waded through the pools, and with long staves drove them to the land, against nets placed upon the shores of these hafts, where they were easily caught by the hand, and put into pens ready prepared for their reception. The gentry assembled from all parts to see the sport. Dr. Plot, in his Natural History of Staffordshire, published in 1686, gives the above particulars, and says that in this manner as many have been caught in one morning as, when sold at five shillings per dozen, (the usual price at that time,) produced the sum of twelve pounds ten shillings; and that in the several drifts on the few succeeding days of this sport, they have been taken in some years in such abundance, that their value, according to the above rate, was from thirty to sixty pounds — a great sum in those days. These were the *See Gulles*, of which we read as being so plentifully provided at the great feasts of the ancient nobility and bishops of this realm. Although the flesh of these birds is not now esteemed a dainty, and they are seldom sought after as an article of food, yet in the breeding season, where accommodation and protection are afforded them, they

* Vide Dr. Russel's description of Aleppo.

still regularly resort to the same old haunts, which have been occupied by their kind for a long time past. This is the case with the flocks which now breed at Pallinsburne, in Northumberland, where they are accounted of great use in clearing the surrounding lands of noxious insects, worms, slugs, &c." *

LITTLE AUK. — ALCA ALLE. — Fig. 315.

Lath. Gen. Syn. p. 327. — *Br. Zool.* ii. No. 233, pl. 82. — *Arct. Zool.* No. 429. — *Turt. Syst.* 1, 338. — *Faun. Suec.* No. 142. — *Faun. Groenl.* No. 54. — *Brun. Orn.* No.106. — *Martin's Spitzb.* 85. — Mergulus Melanoleucos rostro acuto brevi, *Raii Syn.* p. 135. A. 5.— Small Black and White Diver, *Will. Orn.* p. 343, pl. 59. — *Edwards*, pl. 91. — Greenland Dove, or Sea Turtle, *Albin*, 1, pl. 85. — Le Petit Guillemot, *Brisson, Orn.* vi. p. 73, 2. — *Buffon, Ois.* xviii. p. 21, *Pl. enl.* No. 917. — *Bewick's British Birds*, ii. p. 158. — *Peale's Museum*, No. 2978.

MERGULUS MELANOLEUCOS. — Ray.†

Mergulus melanoleucos, *Ray, Synop.* p. 125. — *Flem. Brit. Anim.* p. 135. — Uria (sub-gen. mergulus) alle, *Bonap. Synop.* p. 425. — Little Auk, *Mont. Orn. Dict.* and *Supp.* — *Selby, Illust.* pl. 81. — Uria alle, *North. Zool.* ii. p. 479.

Of the history of this little stranger, but few particulars are known. With us it is a very rare bird, and, when seen, it is generally in

---

* Bewick's *British Birds*, part ii. p. 201.

† I have chosen the name of Ray for this species, as both appropriate, and, as far as my inquiries have led me, entitled to the priority — and the difference in form from the *Guillemots* fully entitles it to the rank of a sub-genus. It is the only bird allied in any way to the Auks, Puffins, &c., which has been figured by Wilson, though several forms occur in the northern seas, and have been pointed out by him, which have not been mentioned, but which will be hereafter figured from the remaining volumes of the *Continuation*, by the Prince of Musignano, now in the press. I have therefore only added an enumeration from the *Synopsis* of that ornithologist, commencing with the Guillemots, for which the genus *Uria* has been adopted; by some the Black Guillemot is separated, on account of straightness of the mandibles, whereas in the Common they are both bent at the tip. In our present state of knowledge, I prefer retaining them together.

Uria, Briss.

1. *U. troile.* Foolish Guillemot. — Common to both continents, and found during winter on the coasts of the United States.

2. *U. Brunichii.* — Sab. — Inhabits both continents, and is common in Davis's Straits, Baffin's Bay, &c. It has been said to have occurred once or twice on the British coasts.

3. *U. grylle.* — Black Guillemot. — Common to both continents, and found during winter along the coasts of the United States. A few pairs breed annually on the rocky islands on the Frith of Forth. I have repeatedly found them on the Isle of May.

4. *U. marmorata,* Lath. — Brown, undulated with chestnut; beneath, dusky, spotted with white; feet, orange; bill, black, one inch long. Inhabits the north-western coasts of America, and the opposite shore of Asia.

These are the characters given by Bonaparte to the last bird. Will it not be the immature state of some other species?

Phaleris, Temm.

1. *P. psittacula,* Temm. — Perrequet Auk. —Inhabits the north-western coasts of America, and the opposite ones of Asia. Common in Kamtschatka.

2. *P. christatella,* Temm. — Crested Auk. —The Prince of Musignano is only of opinion that this may be found on the western shores of America; it is known in the Japan

the vicinity of the sea. The specimen described was killed at Great Egg Harbor, in the month of December, 1811, and was sent to Wilson as a great curiosity. It measured nine inches in length, and fourteen in extent; the bill, upper part of the head, back, wings, and tail, were black; the upper part of the breast, and hind head, were gray, or white, mixed with ash; the sides of the neck, whole lower parts, and tips of secondaries, were pure white; feet and legs, black; shins, pale flesh color; above each eye, there was a small spot of white;* the lower scapulars, streaked slightly with the same. This bird has no heel, and the exterior toe is the largest.

The Little Auk is said to be but a rare visitant of the British isles. It is met with in various parts of the north, even as far as Spitzbergen; is common in Greenland, in company with the Black-billed Auk, and feeds upon the same kind of food. The Greenlanders call it the Ice-Bird, from the circumstance of its being the harbinger of ice. It lays two bluish white eggs, larger than those of the Pigeon. It flies quick, and dives well; and is always dipping its bill into the water while swimming, or at rest on that element; walks better on land than others of the genus. It grows fat in the stormy season, from the waves bringing plenty of crabs and small fish within its reach. It is not a very crafty bird, and may be easily taken. It varies to quite white, and sometimes is found with a reddish breast.†

To the anatomist, the internal organization of this species is deserving attention: it is so constructed as to be capable of contracting or dilating itself at pleasure. We know not what Nature intends by this

seas, and the north-eastern coast of Africa. He thinks also that the *alca antiqua* of Latham may prove a third North American species of *Phaleris.*

Another bird, (*Phaleris cerorhinca*,) entering formerly into this genus, has been separated by the Prince of Musignano, and placed in a sub-genus, *Cerorhinca,* to be figured in his fourth volume.

Cerorhinca, Bonap.

1. *C. occidentalis,* Bonap. — Inhabits the western coasts of North America.

Mormon, Illig.

1. *M. cirrhatus,* Temm. Tufted Auk, Lath. — Inhabits the sea between North America and Kamtschatka; often seen on the western coasts of the United States in winter.

2. *M. glacialis,* Leach. — Puffin of Wilson's List. — Inhabits the Arctic parts of both continents; not uncommon in winter on the coasts of the United States.

This species has of late been looked for on the coasts of Britain, but yet, I believe, without success. The chief and easiest detected difference is in the size and form of the bill. Mr. Pennant observed a difference in the bills of several species from different parts, and Dr. Fleming puts the question, " Have we two species ?" I think it more than probable that this bird has been overlooked, from its near alliance, and that, though comparatively rare, it will be yet found to occur on our own coasts.

3. *Mormon arcticus.* — Puffin of Wilson's List. — The Common Puffin of Europe, and migratory to the temperate shores of the United States.

Alca, Linn.

1. *A. torda.* — Razor-Bill of Wilson's List. — Common in winter along the coasts of the United States.

2. *A. impennis.* — Great Auk. — Inhabits the Arctic seas of both continents, where it is almost constantly resident.

* In Peale's Museum, there is an excellent specimen of this species, which has likewise a smaller spot below each eye

† LATHAM; PENNANT.

conformation, unless it be to facilitate diving, for which the compressed form is well adapted; and likewise the body, when expanded, will be rendered more buoyant, and fit for the purpose of swimming upon the surface of the water.

TURKEY VULTURE, OR TURKEY BUZZARD. — VULTUR AURA. — Fig. 316.

Uruba, aura T. zopilott, *Marcgrave, Mexico,* 207, 208. — *Hernandez, Mex.* 331. — Vultur Gallinæ, Africanæ facie, Carrion Crow, *Sloane, Jam.* ii. p. 294, tab. 254. — *Brown, Jam.* 471. — *Damp. Voy.* ii. pt. 2, p. 67. — *Bartram's Travels,* p. 289. — *Catesby's Carolina,* 1, 6. — Corvus sylvaticus, *Barrere,* 129. — *Lawson's Carolina,* 138. — *Bancroft,* 152. — *Du Pratz,* ii. 77. — *Will. Orn.* 68. *Raii Syn.* No. 180. — *Linn. Syst.* 122. — Carrion Vulture, *Lath. Gen. Syn.* 1, 9, No. 5. *Id. Sup.* p. 2. — *Penn. Arct. Zool.* 1, p. 221. — Vautour du Brésil, *De Buff. Ois.* 1, 246. *Pl. enl.* No. 187. — *Brisson,* 1, 468. — Cozcaquauhtli, *Clavigero, Hist. Mex.* 1, 47. — *Peale's Museum,* No. 11, male; 12, female.

CATHARTES AURA. — Illiger.*

Cathartes aura, *Illig. Prod.* — *Bonap. Synop.* p. 33. — *North. Zool.* ii. p. 4.

This species is well known throughout the United States, but is most numerous in the southern section of the Union. In the Northern

---

* The Vultures are comparatively a limited race, and exist is every quarter of the world, New Holland excepted;† but their range is chiefly in the warm latitudes.

Those of the New World seem to be contained in two genera, *Sarcoramphus* of

† I have said "New Holland excepted," because we have yet no well-authenticated instance of any thing approaching this form from that very interesting country. The New Holland Vulture of Latham rests, to a certain extent, on dubious authority, and cannot now be referred to. I have no doubt that some representing group will be ultimately discovered, which may perhaps elucidate the principal forms wanting to the *Raptores,* and I know that Mr. Swainson possesses a New Holland Bird, whose station he has been unable to decide whether it will enter here, or range with the gallinaceous birds. I trust that that gentleman will, ere long, work out its affinities as far as possible, and give it to the public. — Ed.

and Middle States, it is partially migratory, the greater part retiring to the south on the approach of cold weather. But numbers remain all

Dumeril, and *Cathartes* of Illiger; the one containing the Condur and Californian Vultures; the other, the Turkey Buzzards, &c., of Wilson. They are, perhaps, generally, the most unseemly and disgusting of the whole feathered race, of loose and ill-kept plumage, of sluggish habits when not urged on by hunger, feeding on any animal food which they can easily tear to pieces, but often upon the most putrid and loathsome carrion. They have been introduced by the ancients, in their beautiful but wild conceptions and imagery, and have been imbodied in the tales of fiction, and poems of the modern day, as all that is lurid, disgusting, and horrible. They are the largest of the feathered race, if we except the *Struthionidæ*, or that group to which the Ostrich, Cassowary, and Bustards belong, and have long been celebrated on account of their great strength. Many fabulous stories are recorded of the formidable Condur carrying off men, bullocks, and even elephants.

They have been called the scavengers of nature; and in warm climates, where all animal matter so soon decays, they are no doubt useful in clearing off what would soon fill the air with noxious miasmata. In many parts of Spain, and southern Europe, the *Neophron percnopterus*, or Egyptian Vulture of Savigny, and in America, the native species, are allowed to roam unmolested through the towns, and are kept in the market places, as Storks are in Holland, to clear away the refuse and offal; and a high penalty is attached to the destruction of any of them. In this state they become very familiar and independent. Mr. Audubon compares them to a garrisoned half-pay soldier; " to move is for them a hardship; and nothing but extreme hunger will make them fly down from the roof of the kitchen into the yard. At Natchez, the number of these expecting parasites is so great, that all the refuse within their reach is insufficient to maintain them." They appear also to have been used for a most revolting purpose among barbarous nations, or at least, in conjunction with wild animals, were depended upon to assist in destroying and clearing away the dead, which were purposely exposed to their ravages. Some, however, are elegant and graceful in their form and plumage, and vie with the Eagles in strength and activity. Such is the *Vultur barbatus* of Edwards, the Lammergeyer of the European Alps.

Independent of the species mentioned by our author, three others have been described as natives of this continent. *Sarcoramphus gryphus* and *Californianus* of Dumeril, and the *Cathartes papa* of Illiger; the former supposed to be the celebrated *Roc* of Sinbad, the no less noted Condur of moderns. They are found on the north-west chain of the Andes, frequenting, and not indeed generally met with until, near the limits of eternal snow, where they may be seen perched on the summit of a projecting rock, or sweeping round on the approach of an intruder, in expectation of prey, and looking, when opposed to a clear sky, of double magnitude.

" Moving athwart the evening sky,
Seem forms of giant height."

The stories of their destructive propensities are, to a certain extent, unfounded. No instance is recorded, by any late travellers, of children being carried off, and all their inquiries proved the reverse. It is a much-followed occupation by the peasantry at the base of the Andes, to ascend in search of ice for the luxury of the towns, and their children, at a very tender age, carried with them, are frequently left at considerable distances, unprotected; they always remain in security. The *S. Californianus* was first known from a specimen in the British Museum, brought from California. Mr. Douglas found it more lately in the woody districts of that country; and I have transcribed his interesting account of its manners, &c. " These gigantic birds, which represent the Condur in the northern hemisphere, are common along the coast of California, but are never seen beyond the woody parts of the country. I have met with them as far to the north as 49 deg. north lat., in the summer and autumn months, but no where so abundantly as in the Columbian Valley, between the grand rapids and the sea. They build their nests in the most secret and impenetrable parts of the pine forests, invariably selecting the loftiest trees that overhang precipices on the deepest and least accessible parts of the mountain valleys. The nest is large, composed of strong, thorny twigs and grass, in every way similar to that of the Eagle tribe, but more slovenly constructed. The same pair resort for several years to the same nest, bestowing little trouble or attention

the winter in Maryland, Delaware, and New Jersey; particularly in the vicinity of the large rivers and the ocean, which afford a supply of food at all seasons.

In New Jersey,* the Turkey Buzzard hatches in May, the deep recesses of the solitary swamps of that state affording situations well suited to the purpose. The female is at no pains to form a nest with materials; but, having chosen a suitable place, which is either a truncated hollow tree, an excavated stump, or log, she lays on the rotten wood from two to four eggs, of a dull dirty white, or pale cream color, splashed all over with chocolate, mingled with blackish touches, the blotches largest and thickest towards the great end; the form something like the egg of a goose, but blunter at the small end; length, two inches and three quarters; breadth, two inches. The male watches often while the female is sitting; and, if not disturbed, they will occupy the same breeding place for several years. The young are clothed with a whitish down, similar to that which covers young goslings. If any person approach the nest, and attempt to handle them, they will immediately vomit such offensive matter, as to compel the intruder to a precipitate retreat.

The Turkey Buzzards are gregarious, peaceable, and harmless, never offering any violence to a living animal, or, like the plunderers of the *Falco* tribe, depriving the husbandman of his stock. Hence, though, in consequence of their filthy habits, they are not beloved, yet

in repairing it. Eggs, two, nearly spherical, about the size of those of a Goose, jet black. Period of incubation, twenty-nine or thirty-one days. They hatch generally about the first of June. The young are covered with thick, whitish down, and are incapable of leaving the nest until the fifth or sixth week. Their food is carrion, dead fish, or other dead animal substance; in no instance will they attack any living animal, unless it be wounded and unable to walk. Their senses of smelling and seeing are remarkably keen. In searching for prey, they soar to a very great altitude, and when they discover a wounded deer, or other animal, they follow its track, and when it sinks, precipitately descend on their object. Although only one is at first seen occupying the carcass, few minutes elapse before the prey is surrounded by great numbers; and it is then devoured to a skeleton within an hour, even though it be one of the larger animals — *Cervus elaphus*, for instance — or a horse. Their voracity is almost insatiable, and they are extremely ungenerous, suffering no other animal to approach them while feeding. After eating, they become so sluggish and indolent, as to remain in the same place until urged by hunger to go in quest of another repast. At such times they perch on decayed trees, with their heads so much retracted, as to be with difficulty observed through the long, loose, lanceolate feathers of the collar. The wings, at the same time, hang down over the feet. This position they invariably preserve in dewy mornings, or after rains."

The third species, *C. papa*, not mentioned by Wilson, is introduced in the *Synopsis of Birds of the United States*, by the Prince of Musignano, who mentions its occurrence only in the warmer parts of North America; it appears occasionally in Florida during summer. The other two are of much more frequent occurrence, and are of less noble dispositions, more sluggish. very easily intimidated, and dirty in the extreme. Truly clearing away all animal matter, they assemble in vast troops upon the discovery of some dead, or nearly dying animal, and exhibit at their feasts scenes of the utmost gluttony and filth. Their power of scenting their quarry from afar, has been proved erroneous, by the well-managed experiments of Mr. Audubon; and, indeed, I never was inclined to think that any birds were endowed with any remarkable development of this particular sense. — Ed.

* Mr. Ord mentions New Jersey in particular, as in that state he has visited the breeding places of the Turkey Buzzard, and can therefore speak with certainty of the fact. Pennsylvania, it is more than probable, affords situations equally attractive, which are also tenanted by this Vulture, for hatching and rearing its young.

they are respected for their usefulness; and in the Southern States, where they are most needed, they, as well as the Black Vultures, are protected by a law which imposes a fine on those who wilfully deprive them of life. They generally roost in flocks, on the limbs of large trees; and they may be seen on a summer morning, spreading out their wings to the rising sun, and remaining in that posture for a considerable time. Pennant conjectures, that this is "to purify their bodies, which are most offensively fetid." But is it reasonable to suppose, that *that* effluvia can be offensive to them, which arises from food perfectly adapted to their nature, and which is constantly the object of their desires? Many birds, and particularly those of the granivorous kind, have a similar habit, which doubtless is attended with the same exhilarating effects, as an exposure to the pure air of the morning has on the frame of one just risen from repose.

These birds, unless when rising from the earth, seldom flap their wings, but sweep along in ogees, and dipping and rising lines, and move with great rapidity. They are often seen in companies, soaring at an immense height, particularly previous to a thunder-storm. Their wings are not spread horizontally, but form a slight angle with the body upwards, the tips having an upward curve. Their sense of smelling is astonishingly exquisite, and they never fail to discover carrion, even when at the distance of several miles from it. When once they have found a carcass, if not molested, they will not leave the place until the whole is devoured. At such times they eat so immoderately, that frequently they are incapable of rising, and may be caught without much difficulty; but few that are acquainted with them will have the temerity to undertake the task. A man in the state of Delaware, a few years since, observing some Turkey Buzzards regaling themselves upon the carcass of a horse which was in a highly putrid state, conceived the design of making a captive of one, to take home for the amusement of his children. He cautiously approached, and, springing upon the unsuspicious group, grasped a fine, plump fellow in his arms, and was bearing off his prize in triumph, when, lo! the indignant Vulture disgorged such a torrent of filth in the face of our hero, that it produced all the effects of the most powerful emetic, and forever cured him of his inclination for Turkey Buzzards.

On the continent of America, this species inhabits a vast range of territory, being common,* it is said, from Nova Scotia to Terra del Fuego.† How far to the northward of North California‡ they are found, we are not informed; but it is probable that they extend their

---

* In the Northern States of our Union, the Turkey Buzzard is only occasionally seen. It is considered a rare bird by the inhabitants.

† "Great numbers of a species of Vulture, commonly called Carrion Crow by the sailors, (*Vultur aura,*) were seen upon this island, (New-Year's Island, near Cape Horn, lat. 55 S. 67 W.) and probably feed on young seal cubs, which either die in the birth, or which they take an opportunity to seize upon." Cook calls them Turkey Buzzards. —FORSTER's *Voyage,* ii. p. 516, 4to. London, 1777. — We strongly suspect that the sailors were correct, and that these were Black Vultures, or Carrion Crows.

‡ Pérouse saw a bird, which he calls the Black Vulture, probably the *Vultur aura,* at Monteray Bay, North California. — *Voyage,* ii. p. 203.

migrations to the Columbia, allured thither by the quantity of dead salmon which, at certain seasons, line the shores of that river.

They are numerous in the West India islands, where they are said to be " far inferior in size to those of North America." * This leads us to the inquiry, whether or not the present species has been confounded, by all the naturalists of Europe, with the Black Vulture, or Carrion Crow, which is so common in the southern parts of our continent. If not, why has the latter been totally overlooked in the numerous ornithologies and nomenclatures with which the world has been favored, when it is so conspicuous and remarkable, that no stranger visits South Carolina, Georgia, or the Spanish provinces, but is immediately struck with the novelty of its appearance ? We can find no cause for the Turkey Buzzards of the islands† being smaller than ours, and must conclude that the Carrion Crow, which is of less size, has been mistaken for the former. In the history which follows, we shall endeavor to make it evident that the species described by Ulloa, as being so numerous in South America, is no other than the Black Vulture. The ornithologists of Europe, not aware of the existence of a new species, have, without investigation, contented themselves with the opinion that the bird, called by the above-mentioned traveller the Gallinazo, was the *Vultur aura*, the subject of our present history. This is the more inexcusable, as we expect in naturalists a precision of a different character from that which distinguishes vulgar observation. If the Europeans had not the opportunity of comparing living specimens of the two species, they at least had preserved subjects, in their extensive and valuable museums, from which a correct judgment might have been formed. The figure in the *Planches enluminées*, though wretchedly drawn and colored, was evidently taken from a stuffed specimen of the Black Vulture.

Pennant observes, that the Turkey Vultures " are not found in the northern regions of Europe or Asia, at least in those latitudes which might give them a pretence of appearing there. I cannot find them," he continues, " in our quarter of the globe, higher than the Grison Alps,‡ or Silesia,§ or at farthest Kalish, in Great Poland." ||

Kolben, in his account of the Cape of Good Hope, mentions a Vulture, which he represents as very voracious and noxious. " I have seen," says he, " many carcasses of cows, oxen, and other tame creatures, which the Eagles had slain. I say carcasses, but they were rather skeletons, the flesh and entrails being all devoured, and nothing remaining but the skin and bones. But the skin and bones being in

* PENNANT, *Arctic Zoology.*

† The Vulture which Sir Hans Sloane has figured and described, and which he says is common in Jamaica, is undoubtedly the *Vultur aura.* " The head, and an inch in the neck, are bare, and without feathers, of a flesh color, covered with a thin membrane, like that of Turkeys, with which the most part of the bill is covered likewise ; bill, below the membrane, more than an inch long, whitish at the point ; tail, broad, and nine inches long ; legs and feet, three inches long ; it flies exactly like a Kite, and preys on nothing living ; but when dead, it devours their carcasses, whence they are not molested."—Sloane, *Natural History of Jamaica,* vol. ii. p. 294, folio.

‡ WILLOUGHBY, *Ornithology,* p. 67.

§ SCHWENCKFELDT, *Av. Silesia,* 375.

|| RZACZYNSKI, *Hist. Nat. Poland,* 298.

their natural places, the flesh being, as it were, scooped out, and the wound by which the Eagles enter the body being ever in the belly, you would not, till you had come up to the skeleton, have had the least suspicion that any such matter had happened. The Dutch at the Cape frequently call those Eagles, on account of their tearing out the entrails of beasts, *strunt-vogels*, i. e. Dung-Birds. It frequently happens, that an ox that is freed from the plough, and left to find his way home, lies down to rest himself by the way; and if he does so, it is a great chance but the Eagles fall upon him and devour him. They attack an ox or cow in a body consisting of a hundred and upwards." *

Buffon conjectures, that this murderous Vulture is the Turkey Buzzard, and concludes his history of the latter with the following invective against the whole fraternity : — " In every part of the globe they are voracious, slothful, offensive, and hateful, and, like the wolves, are as noxious during their life, as useless after their death."

If Kolben's account of the ferocity of his Eagle,† or Vulture, be just, we do not hesitate to maintain that that Vulture is not the Turkey Buzzard, as, amongst the whole feathered creation, there is none, perhaps, more innoxious than this species ; and that it is beneficial to the inhabitants of our southern continent, even Buffon himself, on the authority of Desmarchais, asserts. But we doubt the truth of Kolben's story ; and, in this place, must express our regret, that enlightened naturalists should so readily lend an ear to the romances of travellers, who, to excite astonishment, freely give currency to every ridiculous tale, which the designing or the credulous impose upon them. We will add farther, that the Turkey Buzzard seldom begins upon a carcass, until invited to the banquet by that odor, which in no ordinary degree renders it an object of delight.

The Turkey Vulture is two feet and a half in length, and six feet two inches in breadth ; the bill from the corner of the mouth is almost two inches and a half long, of a dark horn color for somewhat more than an inch from the tip, the nostril a remarkably wide slit, or opening through it ; the tongue is greatly concave, cartilaginous, and finely serrated on its edges ; ears, inclining to oval ; eyes, dark, in some specimens reddish hazel ; the head and neck, for about an inch and a half below the ears, are furnished with a reddish, wrinkled skin, beset with short, black hairs, which also cover the bill as far as the interior angle of the nostril, the neck not so much caruncled as that of the Black Vulture ; from the hind head to the neck-feathers the space is covered with down of a sooty black color ; the fore part of the neck is bare as far as the breast bone ; the skin on the lower part, or pouch, very much wrinkled ; this naked skin is not discernible without removing the plumage which arches over it ; the whole lower parts, lining of the wings, rump, and tail-coverts, are of a sooty brown, the feathers of the belly and vent, hairy ; the plumage of the neck is large and tumid,

---

* MEDLEY'S *Kolben*, vol. ii. p. 135.
† These bloodthirsty Eagles, we conjecture, are Black Vultures, they being in the habit of mining into the bellies of dead animals, to feast upon the contents. With respect to their attacking those that are living, as the Vultures of America are not so heroic, it is a fair inference that the same species elsewhere is possessed of a similar disposition.

56 *

and, with that of the back and shoulders, black; the scapulars and secondaries are black on their outer webs, skirted with tawny brown, the latter slightly tipped with white; primaries and their coverts, plain brown, the former pointed, third primary the longest; coverts of the secondaries, and lesser coverts, tawny brown, centred with black, some of the feathers at their extremities slightly edged with white; the tail is twelve inches long, rounded, of a brownish black, and composed of twelve feathers, which are broad at their extremities; inside of wings and tail, light ash; the wings reach to the end of the tail; the whole body and neck beneath the plumage are thickly clothed with a white down, which feels like cotton; the shafts of the primaries are yellowish white above, and those of the tail, brown, both pure white below; the plumage of the neck, back, shoulders, scapulars, and secondaries, is glossed with green and bronze, and has purple reflections; the thighs are feathered to the knees; feet, considerably webbed; middle toe, three inches and a half in length, and about an inch and a half longer than the outer one, which is the next longest; the sole of the foot is hard and rough; claws, dark horn color; the legs are of a pale flesh color, and three inches long. The claws are larger, but the feet slenderer than those of the Carrion Crow. The bill of the male is pure white; in some specimens the upper mandible is tipped with black. There is little or no perceptible difference between the sexes.

The bird from which the foregoing description was taken, (Fig. 316,) was shot for this work, at Great Egg Harbor, on the 30th of January. It was a female, in perfect plumage, excessively fat, and weighed five pounds one ounce avoirdupois. On dissection, it emitted a slight musky odor.

The Vulture is included in the catalogue of those fowls declared unclean and an abomination by the Levitical law, and which the Israelites were interdicted eating.* We presume that this prohibition was religiously observed, so far, at least, as it related to the Vulture, from whose flesh there arises such an unsavory odor, that we question if all the sweetening processes ever invented could render it palatable to Jew, Pagan, or Christian.

Since the above has been ready for the press, we have seen the History of the Expedition under the command of Lewis and Clark, and find our conjecture with respect to the migration of the Turkey Buzzard verified, several of this species having been observed at Brant Island, near the Falls of the Columbia.†

* *Leviticus*, xi. 14. — *Deuteronomy*, xiv. 13.
† *History of the Expedition*, vol. ii. p. 233.

BLACK VULTURE, OR CARRION CROW. — VULTUR JOTA. — Fig. 317.

Bartram, p. 289. — *Gallinazo, Ulloa, Voy.* i. p. 52. — *Zopilot, Clangero, Hist. Mex.* i. p. 47. — Vultur Jota, *Molina, Hist. Chili*, i. p. 185. — *Peale's Museum*, No. 13.

VULTUR JOTA. BONAPARTE.*

Vultur jota, *Bonap. Synop.* p. 23. — Cathartes atratus, *North. Zool.* ii. p. 6.

ALTHOUGH an account of this Vulture was published, more than twenty years ago, by Mr. William Bartram, wherein it was distinctly specified as a different species from the preceding, yet it excites our surprise that the ornithologists should have persisted in confounding it with the Turkey Buzzard, — an error which can hardly admit of extenuation, when it is considered what a respectable authority they had for a different opinion.

The habits of this species are singular. In the towns and villages of the Southern States, particularly Charleston and Georgetown, South Carolina, and in Savannah, Georgia, the Carrion Crows may be seen, either sauntering about the streets, sunning themselves on the roofs of the houses and the fences, or, if the weather be cold, cowering around the tops of the chimneys, to enjoy the benefit of the heat, which to them is a peculiar gratification. They are protected by law, or usage;

---

* Mr. Swainson, in a note to the description of this bird in the *Northern Zoology*, remarks, as a reason for changing the name given by Bonaparte, "We have not considered it expedient to apply to this bird the scientific name of *Jota*, given by Molina to a Black Vulture of Chili, because there is no evidence to prove that it is the Turkey Buzzard of North America." Neither is there present proof that it is not; therefore, we retain Bonaparte's name. — ED.

and may be said to be completely domesticated, being as common as the domestic poultry, and equally familiar. The inhabitants generally are disgusted with their filthy, voracious habits; but, notwithstanding, being viewed as contributive to the removal of the dead animal matter, which, if permitted to putrefy during the hot season, would render the atmosphere impure, they have a respect paid them as scavengers, whose labors are subservient to the public good. It sometimes happens that, after having gorged themselves, these birds vomit down the chimneys, which must be intolerably disgusting, and must provoke the ill will of those whose hospitality is thus requited.

The Black Vultures are indolent, and may be observed in companies, loitering for hours together in one place. They do not associate with the Turkey Buzzards; and are much darker in their plumage than the latter. Their mode of flight also varies from that of the Turkey Buzzard: the Black Vulture flaps its wings five or six times rapidly, then sails with them extended nearly horizontally; the Turkey Buzzard seldom flaps its wings, and, when sailing, they form an angle with the body upwards. The latter, though found in the vicinity of towns, rarely ventures within them, and then always appearing cautious of the near approach of any one. It is not so impatient of cold as the former, and is likewise less lazy. The Black Vulture, on the ground, hops along very awkwardly; the Turkey Buzzard, though seemingly inactive, moves with an even gait. The latter, unless pressed by hunger, will not eat of a carcass until it becomes putrid; the former is not so fastidious, but devours animal food without distinction.

It is said that the Black Vultures sometimes attack young pigs, and eat off their ears and tails, and we have even heard stories of their assaulting feeble calves, and picking out their eyes. But these instances are rare: if otherwise, they would not receive that countenance or protection which is so universally extended to them in the states of South Carolina and Georgia, where they abound.

"This undescribed species," says Mr. Bartram, "is a native of the maritime parts of Georgia and of the Floridas, where they are called Carrion Crows. They flock together, and feed upon carrion, but do not mix with the Turkey Buzzard, (*Vultur aura.*) Their wings are broad, and round at their extremities; their tail, which they spread like a fan when on the wing, is remarkably short. They have a heavy, laborious flight, flapping their wings, and sailing alternately. The whole plumage is of a sable or mourning color." *

In one of Mr. Wilson's journals, I find an interesting detail of the greedy and disgusting habits of this species; and shall give the passage entire, in the same unadorned manner in which it is written:—

"*February* 21, 1809. — Went out to Hampstead † this forenoon. A horse had dropped down in the street, in convulsions; and dying, it was dragged out to Hampstead, and skinned. The ground, for a hundred yards around it, was black with Carrion Crows; many sat on the tops of sheds, fences, and houses within sight; sixty or eighty on the opposite side of a small run. I counted, at one time, two hundred and

* MS. in the possession of Mr. Ord.
† Near Charleston, South Carolina.

thirty-seven, but I believe there were more, besides several in the air over my head, and at a distance. I ventured cautiously within thirty yards of the carcass, where three or four dogs, and twenty or thirty Vultures, were busily tearing and devouring. Seeing them take no notice, I ventured nearer, till I was within ten yards, and sat down on the bank. Still they paid little attention to me. The dogs, being sometimes accidentally flapped with the wings of the Vultures, would growl and snap at them, which would occasion them to spring up for a moment, but they immediately gathered in again. I remarked the Vultures frequently attack each other, fighting with their claws or heels, striking like a cock, with open wings, and fixing their claws in each other's head. The females, and, I believe, the males likewise, made a hissing sound, with open mouth, exactly resembling that produced by thrusting a red hot poker into water; and frequently a snuffling, like a dog clearing his nostrils, as I suppose they were theirs. On observing that they did not heed me, I stole so close that my feet were within one yard of the horse's legs, and again sat down. They all slid aloof a few feet; but, seeing me quiet, they soon returned as before. As they were often disturbed by the dogs, I ordered the latter home: my voice gave no alarm to the Vultures. As soon as the dogs departed, the Vultures crowded in such numbers, that I counted at one time thirty-seven on and around the carcass, with several within; so that scarcely an inch of it was visible. Sometimes one would come out with a large piece of the entrails, which in a moment was surrounded by several others, who tore it in fragments, and it soon disappeared. They kept up the hissing occasionally. Some of them, having their whole legs and heads covered with blood, presented a most savage aspect. Still as the dogs advanced, I would order them away, which seemed to gratify the Vultures; and one would pursue another to within a foot or two of the spot where I was sitting. Sometimes I observed them stretching their necks along the ground, as if to press the food downwards."

The Carrion Crow is seldom found on the Atlantic to the northward of Newbern, North Carolina,* but inhabits the whole continent to the southward, as far as Cape Horn. Don Ulloa, in noticing the birds of Carthagena, gives an account of a Vulture, which we shall quote, in order to establish the opinion, advanced in the preceding history, that it is the present species. We shall afterwards subjoin other testimony in confirmation of this opinion. With respect to the marvellous tale of their attacking the cattle in the pastures, it is too improbable to merit a serious refutation.

"It would be too great an undertaking to describe all the extraordinary birds that inhabit this country; but I cannot refrain from noticing that to which they give the name of *Gallinazo*, from the resemblance it has to the Turkey Hen. This bird is of the size of a Pea Hen, but its head and neck are something larger. From the crop to the base of the bill, it has no feathers: this space is surrounded with a wrinkled, glandulous, and rough skin, which forms numerous warts, and other similar inequalities. This skin is black, as is the plumage

---

* Since writing the above, I have been informed by a gentleman who resides at Detroit, on Lake Erie, that the Carrion Crow is common at that place.

of the bird, but usually of a brownish black. The bill is well proportioned, strong, and a little hooked. These birds are familiar in Carthagena; the tops of the houses are covered with them; it is they which cleanse the city of all its animal impurities. There are few animals killed whereof they do not obtain the offals; and when this food is wanting, they have recourse to other filth. Their sense of smelling is so acute, that it enables them to trace carrion at the distance of three or four leagues, which they do not abandon until there remains nothing but the skeleton.

" The great number of these birds found in such hot climates is an excellent provision of nature; as, otherwise, the putrefaction caused by the constant and excessive heat would render the air insupportable to human life. When first they take wing, they fly heavily; but afterwards, they rise so high as to be entirely invisible. On the ground, they walk sluggishly. Their legs are well proportioned; they have three toes forward, turning inwards, and one on the inside, inclining a little backwards, so that, the feet interfering, they cannot walk with any agility, but are obliged to hop: each toe is furnished with a long and stout claw.

" When the Gallinazos are deprived of carrion, or food in the city, they are driven by hunger among the cattle of the pastures. If they see a beast with a sore on the back, they alight on it, and attack the part affected; and it avails not that the poor animal *throws itself upon the ground,* and endeavors to intimidate them by its bellowing: *they do not quit their hold!* and, by means of their bill, they so soon enlarge the wound, that the animal finally becomes their prey." *

The account, from the same author, of the beneficial effects resulting from the fondness of the Vultures for the eggs of the alligator, merits attention : —

" The Gallinazos are the most inveterate enemies of the alligators, or rather they are extremely fond of their eggs, and employ much stratagem to obtain them. During the summer, these birds make it their business to watch the female alligators; for it is in that season that they deposit their eggs in the sand of the shores of the rivers, which are not then overflowed. The Gallinazo conceals itself among the branches and leaves of a tree, so as to be unperceived by the alligator; and permits the eggs quietly to be laid, not even interrupting the precautions that she takes to conceal them. But she is no sooner under the water, than the Gallinazo darts upon the nest; and, with its bill, claws, and wings, uncovers the eggs, and gobbles them down, leaving nothing but the shells. This banquet would, indeed, richly reward its patience, did not a multitude of Gallinazos join the fortunate discoverer, and share in the spoil.

" How admirable the wisdom of that Providence, which hath given to the male alligator an inclination to devour its own offspring, and to the Gallinazo a taste for the eggs of the female! Indeed, neither the rivers, nor the neighboring fields, would otherwise be sufficient to contain the multitudes that are hatched; for, notwithstanding the rav-

* *Voyage Historique de L'Amerique Meridionale,* par Don George Juan et Don Antoine de Ulloa, liv. i. chap. viii. p. 52. A Amsterdam et à Leipzig, 1752, 4to.

ages of both these insatiable enemies, one can hardly imagine the numbers that remain." *

The Abbé Clavigero, in his *History of Mexico*, has clearly indicated the present species, as distinguished from the Turkey Buzzard : —

" The business of clearing the fields of Mexico, is reserved principally for the *Zopilots*, known in South America by the name of *Gallinazzi* ; in other places, by that of *Aure* ; and in some places, though very improperly, by that of *Ravens*. There are two very different species of these birds — the one, the Zopilot, properly so called ; the other, called the Cozcaquauhtli ; they are both bigger than the Raven. These two species resemble each other in their hooked bill and crooked claws, and by having upon their head, instead of feathers, a wrinkled membrane with some curling hairs. They fly so high, that, although they are pretty large, they are lost to the sight ; and especially before a hail storm they will be seen wheeling, in vast numbers, under the loftiest clouds, till they entirely disappear. They feed upon carrion, which they discover, by the acuteness of their sight and smell, from the greatest height, and descend upon it with a majestic flight, in a great spiral course. They are both almost mute. The two species are distinguished, however, by their size, their color, their numbers, and some other peculiarities. The Zopilots, properly so called, have black feathers, with a brown head, bill, and feet ; they go often in flocks, and roost together upon trees. This species is very numerous, and is to be found in all the different climates ; while, on the contrary, the Cozcaquauhtli is far from numerous, and is peculiar to the warmer climates alone.† The latter bird is larger than the Zopilot, has a red head and feet, with a beak of a deep red color, except towards its extremity, which is white. Its feathers are brown, except upon the neck and parts about the breast, which are of a reddish black. The wings are of an ash color upon the inside, and, upon the outside, are variegated with black and tawny.

" The Cozcaquauhtli is called by the Mexicans *King of the Zopilots* ; ‡ and they say, that, when these two species happen to meet together about the same carrion, the Zopilot never begins to eat till the Cozcaquauhtli has tasted it. The Zopilot is a most useful bird to that country, for it not only clears the fields, but attends the crocodiles, and destroys the eggs which the females of those dreadful amphibious animals leave in the sand to be hatched by the heat of the sun. The destruction of such a bird ought to be prohibited under severe penalties." §

We are almost afraid of trespassing upon the patience of the reader by the length of our quotations ; but as we are very anxious that the subject of this article should enjoy that right to which it is fairly entitled, of being ranked as an independent species, we are tempted to add one testimony more, which we find in the *History of Chili*, by the Abbé Molina.

* *Voyage Historique*, &c., liv. iv. chap. ix. p. 172.
† This is a mistake.
‡ This is the *Vultur aura*. The bird which now goes by the name of *King of the Zopilots*, in New Spain, is the *Vultur papa* of Linnæus.
§ CLAVIGERO's *Mexico*, translated by Cullen, vol. i. p. 47. London.

"The *Jota* (*Vultur jota*) resembles much the *aura*, a species of Vulture, of which there is, perhaps, but one variety. It is distinguished, however, by the beak, which is gray, with a black point. Notwithstanding the size of this bird, which is nearly that of the Turkey, and its strong and crooked talons, it attacks no other, but feeds principally upon carcasses and reptiles. It is extremely indolent, and will frequently remain, for a long time, almost motionless, with its wings extended, sunning itself upon the rocks, or the roofs of the houses. When in pain, which is the only time that it is known to make any noise, it utters a sharp cry like that of a rat; and usually disgorges what it has eaten. The flesh of this bird emits a fetid smell that is highly offensive. The manner in which it builds its nest, is perfectly correspondent to its natural indolence; it carelessly places between rocks, or even upon the ground, a few dry leaves or feathers, upon which it lays two eggs of a dirty white." *

The Black Vulture is twenty-six inches in length, and four feet four inches in extent; the bill is two inches and a half long, of a dark horn color as far as near an inch; the remainder, the head, and a part of the neck, are covered with a black, wrinkled, caruncled skin, beset with short black hairs, and downy behind; nostril, an oblong slit; irides, reddish hazel; the throat is dashed with yellow ochre; the general color of the plumage is of a dull black, except the primaries, which are whitish on the inside, and have four of their broadened edges below of a drab, or dark cream color, extending two inches, which is seen only when the wing is unfolded; the shafts of the feathers white on both sides; the rest of the wing-feathers, dark on both sides; the wings, when folded, are about the length of the tail, the fifth feather being the longest; the secondaries are two inches shorter than the tail, which is slightly forked; the exterior feathers, three quarters of an inch longer than the rest; the legs are limy, three inches and a half in length, and, with the feet, are thick and strong; the middle toe is four inches long, side toes, two inches, and considerably webbed, inner toe, rather the shortest; claws, strong, but not sharp, like those of the *Falco* genus; middle claw, three quarters of an inch long; the stomach is not lined with hair, as reported. When opened, this bird smells strongly of musk.

Mr. Abbott informs me, that the Carrion Crow builds its nest in the large trees of the low, wet swamps, to which places they retire every evening to roost. "They frequent," says he, "that part of the town of Savannah where the hog-butchers reside, and walk about the streets, in great numbers, like domestic fowls. It is diverting to see, when the entrails and offals of the hogs are thrown to them, with what greediness they scramble for the food, seizing upon it, and pulling one against another, until the strongest prevails. The Turkey Buzzard is accused of killing young lambs and pigs, by picking out their eyes; but I believe that the Carrion Crow is not guilty of the like practices. The two species do not associate."

* *Hist. Chili,* Am. Trans. i. p. 185.

RAVEN.—CORVUS CORAX.—Fig. 318.

Turt. Syst. 1, 213.—Korp. Faun. *Suec.* No. 85.—Faun. *Groenl.* p. 62.—*Leems,* 240.—Le Corbeau, *De Buff.* v. 16. *Pl. enl.* No. 495.—*Briss.* ii. 8.—*Penn. Br. Zool.* 1, No. 74.—*Arct. Zool.* No. 134.—*Lath.* 1, 367.—*Bewick,* 1, 100.—*Raii Syn.* p. 39.—*Will. Orn.* p. 121, pl. 18.—*Albin,* ii. pl. 20.—Corvus carnivorus, *Bartram,* p. 290.—*Peale's Museum,* No. 175.

CORVUS CORAX.—Linnæus.

Corvus corax, *Bonap. Synop.* p. 56.—*Flom. Br. Anim.* p. 87.—Raven, *Mont. Orn. Dict.* and *Supp.* p. 67.—*Selby, Illust. Br. Orn.* pl. 27.

A KNOWLEDGE of this celebrated bird has been handed down to us from the earliest ages; and its history is almost coeval with that of man. In the best and most ancient of all books, we learn, that at the end of forty days, after the great flood had covered the earth, Noah, wishing to ascertain whether or no the waters had abated, sent forth a Raven, which did not return into the Ark.* This is the first notice that is taken of this species. Though the Raven was declared unclean by the law of Moses, yet we are informed, that, when the prophet Elijah provoked the enmity of Ahab, by prophesying against him, and hid himself by the Brook Cherith, the Ravens were appointed by Heaven to bring him his daily food.† The color of the Raven has given rise to a similitude, in one of the most beautiful of eclogues, which has been perpetuated in all subsequent ages, and which is not less pleasing for being trite or proverbial. The favorite of the royal lover of Jerusalem, in the enthusiasm of affection, thus describes the object of her adoration, in reply to the following question:—

" What is thy beloved more than another beloved,
O thou fairest among women ? "
" My beloved is white and ruddy, the chiefest among
Ten thousand. His head is as the most fine gold ;
His locks are bushy, and black as a Raven ! " ‡

* Genesis, viii. 7.   † 1 Kings, xvii. 5, 6.
          ‡ Song of Solomon, v. 9, 10, 11.
57

The above-mentioned circumstances taken into consideration, one would suppose that the lot of the subject of this chapter would have been of a different complexion from what history and tradition inform us is the fact. But in every country, we are told, the Raven is considered an ominous bird, whose croakings foretell approaching evil; and many a crooked beldam has given interpretation to these oracles, of a nature to infuse terror into a whole community. Hence this ill-fated bird, from time immemorial, has been the innocent subject of vulgar obloquy and detestation.

Augury, or the art of foretelling future events by the flight, cries, or motions of birds, descended from the Chaldeans to the Greeks, thence to the Etrurians, and from them it was transmitted to the Romans.* The crafty legislators of those celebrated nations, from a deep knowledge of human nature, made superstition a principal feature of their religious ceremonies, well knowing that it required a more than ordinary policy to govern a multitude, ever liable to the fatal influences of passion; and who, without some timely restraints, would burst forth like a torrent, whose course is marked by wide-spreading desolation. Hence to the purposes of polity the Raven was made subservient; and the Romans having consecrated it to Apollo, as to the god of divination, its flight was observed with the greatest solemnity; and its tones and inflections of voice were noted with a precision which intimated a belief in its infallible prescience.

But the ancients have not been the only people infected with this species of superstition; the moderns, even though favored with the light of Christianity, have exhibited as much folly, through the impious curiosity of prying into futurity, as the Romans themselves. It is true that modern nations have not instituted their sacred colleges, or sacerdotal orders, for the purposes of divination; but, in all countries, there have been self-constituted augurs, whose interpretations of omens have been received with religious respect by the credulous multitude. Even at this moment, in some parts of the world, if a Raven alight on a village church, the whole fraternity is in an uproar; and Heaven is importuned, in all the ardor of devotion, to avert the impending calamity.

The poets have taken advantage of this weakness of human nature; and, in their hands, the Raven is a fit instrument of terror. Shakspeare puts the following malediction into the mouth of his Caliban: —

> " As wicked dew as e'er my mother brushed
> With Raven's feather from unwholesome fen,
> Drop on you both ! " †

* That the science of augury is very ancient, we learn from the Hebrew lawgiver, who prohibits it, as well as every other kind of divination. Deut. chap. xviii. The Romans derived their knowledge of augury chiefly from the Tuscans or Etrurians, who practised it in the earliest times. This art was known in Italy before the time of Romulus, since that prince did not commence the building of Rome till he had taken the auguries. The successors of Romulus, from a conviction of the usefulness of the science, and at the same time not to render it contemptible by becoming too familiar, employed the most skilful augurs from Etruria to introduce the practice of it into their religious ceremonies. And, by a decree of the senate, some of the youth of the best families in Rome were annually sent into Tuscany to be instructed in this art. — Vide *Ciceron. de Divin.* ; also Calmet and the Abbé Banier.

† *Tempest,* Act i. scene 2.

The ferocious wife of Macbeth, on being advised of the approach of Duncan, whose death she had conspired, thus exclaims : —

> " The Raven himself is hoarse,
> That croaks the fatal entrance of Duncan
> Under my battlements." *

The Moor of Venice says, —

> " It comes o'er my memory,
> As doth the Raven o'er the infected house,
> Boding to all." †

The last quotation alludes to the supposed habit of this bird's flying over those houses which contain the sick, whose dissolution is at hand, and thereby announced. Thus Marlowe, in the *Jew of Malta*, as cited by Malone : —

> —— " The sad presaging Raven tolls
> The sick man's passport in her hollow beak ;
> And, in the shadow of the silent night,
> Doth shake contagion from her sable wing."

But it is the province of philosophy to dispel these illusions, which bewilder the mind, by pointing out the simple truths, which nature has been at no pains to conceal, but which the folly of mankind has shrouded in all the obscurity of mystery.

The Raven is a general inhabitant of the United States, but is more common in the interior. On the lakes, and particularly in the neighborhood of the Falls of the Niagara River, they are numerous ; and it is a remarkable fact, that where they so abound, the Common Crow (*C. corone*) seldom makes its appearance ; being intimidated, it is conjectured, by the superior size and strength of the former, or by an antipathy which the two species manifest towards each other. This I had an opportunity of observing myself, in a journey during the months of August and September, along the lakes Erie and Ontario. The Ravens were seen every day, prowling about in search of the dead fish, which the waves are continually casting ashore, and which afford them an abundance of a favorite food ; but I did not see or hear a single Crow within several miles of the lakes, and but very few through the whole of the Genesee country.

The food of this species is dead animal matter of all kinds, not excepting the most putrid carrion, which it devours in common with the Vultures ; worms, grubs, reptiles, and shell fish, the last of which, in the manner of the Crow, it drops from a considerable height in the air, on the rocks, in order to break the shells ; it is fond of bird's eggs, and is often observed sneaking around the farm-house in search of the eggs of the domestic poultry, which it sucks with eagerness ; it is likewise charged with destroying young Ducks and Chickens, and lambs which have been yeaned in a sickly state. The Raven, it is said, follows the hunters of deer for the purpose of falling heir to the

---

* *Macbeth*, Act i. scene 5.
† *Othello*, Act. iv. scene 1.

offal;* and the huntsmen are obliged to cover their game, when it is left in the woods, with their hunting frocks, to protect it from this thievish connoisseur, who, if he have an opportunity, will attack the region of the kidneys, and mangle the saddle without ceremony.

Buffon says, that "the Raven *plucks out the eyes of buffaloes,* and then *fixing on the back, it tears off the flesh deliberately ;* and what renders the ferocity more detestable, it is not incited by the cravings of hunger, but by the appetite for carnage; for it can subsist on fruits, seeds of all kinds, and indeed may be considered as an omnivorous animal." This is mere fable, and of a piece with many other absurdities of the same romancing author.

This species is found almost all over the habitable globe. We trace it in the north from Norway to Greenland, and hear of it in Kamtschatka. It is common every where in Russia and Siberia, except within the Arctic Circle;† and all through Europe. Kolben enumerates the Raven among the birds of the Cape of Good Hope;‡ De Grandpré represents it as numerous in Bengal, where they are said to be protected for their usefulness;§ and the unfortunate La Pérouse saw them at Baie de Castries, on the east coast of Tartary; likewise at Port des Francois, 58° 37′ north latitude, and 139° 50′ west longitude; and at Monterey Bay, North California.‖ The English circumnavigators met with them at Nootka Sound,¶ and at the Sandwich Islands, two being seen in the village of Kakooa; also at Owhyhee, and supposed to be adored there, as they were called Eatooas.** Our intrepid American travellers, under the command of Lewis and Clark, shortly after they embarked on the Columbia River, saw abundance of Ravens, which were attracted thither by the immense quantity of dead salmon which lined the shores.†† They are found, at all seasons, at Hudson's Bay;‡‡ are frequent in Mexico;§§ and it is more than probable that they inhabit the whole continent of America.

The Raven measures, from the tip of the bill to the end of the tail, twenty-six inches, and is four feet in extent; the bill is large and strong, of a shining black, notched near the tip, and three inches long; the setaceous feathers which cover the nostrils extend half its length; the eyes are black; the general color is a deep glossy black, with steel blue reflections; the lower parts are less glossy; the tail is rounded, and extends about two inches beyond the wings; the legs are two inches and a half in length, and, with the feet, are strong and black; the claws are long.

This bird is said to attain to a great age; and its plumage to be subject to change from the influence of years and of climate. It is found in Iceland and Greenland entirely white.

The Raven was the constant attendant of Lewis and Clark's party

* This is the case in those parts of the United States where the deer are hunted without dogs; where these are employed, they are generally rewarded with the offal.
† Latham. ‡ Medley's *Kolben*, vol. ii. p. 136.
§ *Voyage in the Indian Ocean*, p. 148.
‖ *Voy. par* I. F. G. De La Pérouse, ii. p. 129, 203, 443.
¶ Cook's *Last Voy.* ii. p. 236. Am. ed.
** *Idem*, iii. p. 329. †† Gass's *Journal*, p. 153.
‡‡ Charlevoix. Kalm. Hearne's *Journey*. §§ Fernandez.

in their long and toilsome journey. During the winter, at Fort Mandan, they were observed in immense numbers, notwithstanding the cold was so excessive, that on the 17th December, 1804, the thermometer stood at 45° below 0.

Like the Crow, this species may be easily domesticated, and in that state would afford amusement by its familiarity, frolics, and sagacity. But such noisy and mischievous pets, in common with parrots and monkeys, are not held in high estimation in this quarter of the globe; and are generally overlooked for those universal favorites, which either gratify the eye by the neatness or brilliancy of their plumage, or gladden the ear by the simplicity or variety of their song.

GREAT-FOOTED HAWK. — FALCO PEREGRINUS.* —
Fig. 322. — Female.

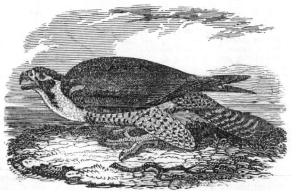

Raii Syn. p. 13, No. 1. — *Turt. Syst.* 1, p. 155. — Belon, *Aves*, 116. — Falco peregrinus niger, *Aldr. Aves*, 1, 239. — Sparviere pellegrino femmina, *Lorenzi, Aves*, tab. 24. — Blue-backed Falcon, Charletoni, *Exercit.* 73. — Peregrine Falcon, *Penn. Br. Zool.* 1, p. 156, No. 48, pl. 20. — *Arct. Zool.* 1, p. 236, No. 97. — *Lath. Syn.* 1, p. 73, No. 52. — Peregrine, or Haggard Falcon, *Will. Orn.* p. 76, tab. 8. — Spotted Hawk, or Falcon, *Edwards*, 1, p. 3. — Black Hawk or Falcon, *Idem*, 1, p. 4. — Le Faucon pelerin, *Briss. Aves*, 1, 341. — *Buff. Ois.* 1, p. 249, pl. 16, et suiv. — *Peale's Museum*, No. 386.

FALCO PEREGRINUS. — Linnæus.†

Falcon peregrinus, *Bonap. Synop.* p. 27. — *North. Zool.* ii. p. 23. — Peregrine Falcon, *Selby, Illust. Br. Orn.* pl. 15, p. 37. — *Flem. Br. Anim.* p. 49. — Falco peregrinus ? Aust. birds in Coll. Linn. Soc. by *Vig.* and *Horsf.* vol. xv. p. 183.

It is with great pleasure that we are now enabled to give a portrait of this celebrated Hawk, drawn of half the size of life, in the best

---

* It is also a European species.

† Among the *Falconidæ* this bird will present that form best adapted for seizing

manner of our deceased friend, and engraved by the accurate and ingenious Lawson.

This noble bird had excited our curiosity for a long time. Every visit which we made to the coast, was rendered doubly interesting by the wonderful stories which we heard of its exploits in fowling, and of its daring enterprise. There was not a gunner along the shore but knew it well; and each could relate something of it which bordered on the marvellous. It was described as darting with the rapidity of an arrow on the Ducks when on the wing, and striking them down with the projecting bone of its breast. Even the Wild Geese were said to be in danger from its attacks, it having been known to sacrifice them to its rapacity.

To behold this hero, the terror of the wild fowl, and the wonder of the sportsmen, was the chief object of our wishes. Day after day did we traverse the salt marshes, and explore the ponds and estuaries which the web-footed tribes frequent in immense multitudes, in the hope of obtaining the imperial depredator; even all the gunners of the district were summoned to our aid, with the assurance of a great reward if

the prey in an open manner by the exercise of their own organs. Noble and bearing in their carriage, the Falcons are as much distinguished from the Vultures by their graceful proportions, "as those of the lion place him in the ranks of creation above the gaunt, ravenous, grisly, yet dastard wolf." Placed, by their strong and powerful frames, far beyond them in all rapacious powers, they feed nearly exclusively on living prey, despising all upon which they have not themselves acted as executioners, and particularly any carrion, which has the least savor of beginning putrescence. For these purposes they are possessed with a compactly-formed body, the neck comparatively short, and supported by muscles of more than ordinary strength; the feet and thighs remarkably powerful, and the wings of that true hirundine form and texture which points out the greater development of their power. The prey is generally struck while upon the wing with a rapid sweep, and is at once borne off, unless completely above the weight of the assailer, when it is struck to the ground, and despatched at more leisure.

The Peregrine Falcon has a considerable geographical range, extending over the whole of temperate Europe, North America, and New Holland. The specimens from the latter country, I may remark, are all smaller in size, but hardly any other distinction can be fixed upon. In Britain, it is abundant on all the rocky coasts towards the north, breeding, and frequenting the precipitous headlands; in many districts inland it is also frequent, but the choice of them is more arbitrary and local. The vale of Moffat, in Dumfries-shire is one of the most favorite stations I am aware of; many pairs breed there, and on the confines of Selkirkshire, choosing their eyries among the precipitous cliffs and streams of that mountainous district; they return to the same rock, year after year, and often fix upon the same nest for their breeding place. When either of the birds are killed, a mate is speedily found by the survivor, and returns with him to the old abode, and some of the eyries there have been known, and handed down to recollection, as far as the annals of the district extend. The Bass Rock, and Isle of May, in the Frith of Forth, each possess a pair, long renowned in deeds of falconry, and the Isle of Man can boast of many a noble bird, whose ancestors have joined in that now nearly-forgotten sport. I am aware of no instance in this country where the Peregrine builds on trees, as mentioned by Ord, in America; nor does it seem its true habit there. Dr. Richardson remarks that it is a rare bird in the wooded districts of the Fur Countries, and the greater part of the specimens which have reached this country have been procured upon the coast.

To the American Falcons may be added the Merlin *F. esalon*, which was met with by Dr. Richardson, who thinks it has been there confounded, from its similarity in some states, with the Pigeon Hawk. We may also mention a bird described by Mr. Audubon as new, under the name of *F. temerarius*, but which appears nothing more than the adult plumage of *F. columbarius*. — Ed.

they procured him, but without success. At length in the month of December, 1812, to the unspeakable joy of Mr. Wilson, he received from Egg Harbor a fine specimen of the far-famed Duck Hawk ; which was discovered, contrary to his expectations, to be of a species which he had never before beheld.

If we were to repeat all the anecdotes which have been related to us of the achievements of the Duck Hawk, they would swell our pages at the expense, probably, of our reputation. Naturalists should be always on their guard when they find themselves compelled to resort to the observations of others, and record nothing as fact which has not been submitted to the temperate deliberations of reason. The reverse of this procedure has been a principal cause why errors and absurdities have so frequently deformed the pages of works of science, which, like a plain mirror, ought to reflect only the genuine images of nature.

From the best sources of information, we learn that this species is uncommonly bold and powerful ; that it darts on its prey with astonishing velocity ; and that it strikes with its formidable feet, permitting the Duck to fall previously to securing it. The circumstance of the Hawk's never carrying the Duck off on striking it, has given rise to the belief of that service being performed by means of the breast, which vulgar opinion has armed with a projecting bone, adapted to the purpose. But this cannot be the fact, as the breast bone of this bird does not differ from that of others of the same tribe, which would not admit of so violent a concussion.

When the water-fowl perceive the approach of their enemy, a universal alarm pervades their ranks ; even man himself, with his engine of destruction, is not more terrible. But the effect is different. When the latter is beheld, the whole atmosphere is enlivened with the whistling of wings ; when the former is recognized, not a Duck is to be seen in the air : they all speed to the water, and there remain until the Hawk has passed them, diving the moment he comes near them. It is worthy of remark, that he will seldom, if ever, strike over the water, unless it be frozen ; well knowing that it will be difficult to secure his quarry. This is something more than instinct.

When the sportsmen perceive the Hawk knock down a Duck, they frequently disappoint him of it, by being first to secure it. And as one evil turn, according to the maxim of the multitude, deserves another, our hero takes ample revenge on them, at every opportunity, by robbing them of their game, the hard-earned fruits of their labor.

The Duck Hawk, it is said, often follows the steps of the gunner, knowing that the Ducks will be aroused on the wing, which will afford it an almost certain chance of success.

We have been informed, that those Ducks which are struck down, have their backs lacerated from the rump to the neck. If this be the fact, it is a proof that the Hawk employs only its talons, which are long and stout, in the operation. One respectable inhabitant of Cape May told us that he has seen the Hawk strike from below.

This species has been long known in Europe ; and in the age of falconry, was greatly valued for those qualifications which rendered it estimable to the lovers and followers of that princely amusement. But we have strong objections to its specific appellation. The epithet *peregrine* is certainly not applicable to our Hawk, which is not migratory, as far as our most diligent inquiries can ascertain ; and, as additional evidence of the fact, we ourselves have seen it prowling near the coast of New Jersey, in the month of May, and heard its screams, which resemble somewhat those of the Bald Eagle, in the swamps wherein it is said to breed. We have therefore taken the liberty of changing its English name for one which will at once express a characteristic designation, or which will indicate the species without the labor of investigation.*

"This species," says Pennant, "breeds on the rocks of Llandidno, in Caernarvonshire, Wales.† That promontory has been long famed for producing a generous kind, as appears by a letter, extant in Gloddaeth Library, from the Lord Treasurer Burleigh, to an ancestor of Sir Roger Mostyn, in which his lordship thanks him for a present of a fine cast of Hawks, taken on those rocks, which belong to the family. They are also very common in the north of Scotland, and are sometimes trained for falconry, by some few gentlemen who still take delight in this amusement, in that part of Great Britain. Their flight is amazingly rapid; one, that was reclaimed by a gentleman in the shire of Angus, a county on the east side of Scotland, eloped from its master with two heavy bells attached to each foot, on the 24th September, 1772, and was killed in the morning of the 26th, near Mostyn, Flintshire." ‡

The same naturalist in another place observes, that "*The American species is larger than the European.*§ They are subject to vary. The Black Falcon, and the Spotted Falcon of Edwards, are of this kind; each preserves a specific mark, in the black stroke which drops from beneath the eyes, down towards the neck.

"Inhabits different parts of North America, from Hudson's Bay as low as Carolina; in Asia, is found on the highest parts of the Uralian and Siberian chain; wanders in summer to the very Arctic Circle; is common in Kamtschatka." ‖

In the breeding season, the Duck Hawk retires to the recesses of the gloomy cedar swamps, on the tall trees of which it constructs its nests, and rears its young secure from all molestation. In those wilds, which present obstacles almost insuperable to the foot of man, the screams of this bird, occasionally mingled with the hoarse tones of the Heron, and the hooting of the Great-horned Owl, echoing through the dreary solitude, arouse in the imagination all the frightful imagery of desolation. Mr. Wilson, and the writer of this article, explored two of these swamps, in the month of May, 1813, in pursuit of the Great Heron, and the subject of this chapter; and although they were successful in obtaining the former, yet the latter eluded their research.

---

* "Specific names, to be perfect, ought to express some peculiarity, common to no other of the genus." — *Am. Orn.* i. p. 65.

† We suspect that Pennant is mistaken; its name denotes that it is not indigenous in Great Britain. Bewick says, "The peregrine, or passenger Falcon, is *rarely* met with in Britain, and consequently is but little known with us." — *British Birds*, part i.

‡ *British Zoology.*

§ If we were to adopt the mode of philosophizing of the *sapient* Count de Buffon, we should infer that the European species is *a variety of our more generous race, degenerated by the influence of food and climate!*

‖ *Arctic Zoology.*

The Great-footed Hawk is twenty inches in length, and three feet eight inches in extent; the bill is inflated, short and strong, of a light blue color, ending in black, the upper mandible with a tooth-like process, the lower, with a corresponding notch, and truncate; nostrils, round, with a central point like the pistil of a flower; the eye is large and dark, surrounded with a broad, bare, yellowish skin, the cartilage over it yellow and prominent; frontlet, whitish; the head above, cheeks running off like mustaches, and back, are black; the wings and scapulars are brownish black, each feather edged with paler, the former long and pointed, reaching almost to the end of the tail; the primaries and secondaries are marked transversely on the inner vanes, with large oblong spots of ferruginous white, the exterior edge of the tip of the secondaries curiously scalloped, as if a piece had been cut out; the tertials incline to ash color; the lining of the wings is beautifully barred with black and white, and tinged with ferruginous; on a close examination, the scapulars and tertials are found to be barred with faint ash; all the shafts are black; the rump and tail-coverts are light ash, marked with large dusky bars; the tail is rounding, black, tipped with reddish white, and crossed with eight narrow bars of very faint ash; the chin and breast, encircling the black mustaches, are of a pale buff color; breast below and lower parts reddish buff, or pale cinnamon, handsomely marked with roundish or heart-shaped spots of black; sides, broadly barred with black; the femorals are elegantly ornamented with herring-bones of black, on a buff ground; the vent is pale buff, marked as the femorals, though with less numerous spots; the feet and legs are of corn yellow, the latter short and stout, feathered a little below the knees, the bare part one inch in length; span of the foot, five inches, with a large protuberant sole; the claws are large and black, hind claw the largest. Whether the cere is yellow or flesh colored, we were uncertain, as the bird had been some time killed when received; supposed the former.

The most striking characters of this species are the broad patch of black dropping below the eye, and the uncommonly large feet. It is stout, heavy, and firmly put together.

The bird from which the above description was taken, was shot in a cedar swamp in Cape May county, New Jersey. It was a female, and contained the remains of small birds, among which were discovered the legs of the Sanderling Plover.

SYNOPSIS

OF THE

BIRDS OF NORTH AMERICA.

LAND BIRDS.

ORDER I. — RAPACES, *Temm.* — BIRDS OF PREY.

FAMILY I. — VULTURINÆ. — VULTURES.

GENUS CATHARTES, *Illiger.* — TURKEY-VULTURES.

1. Cathartes Californianus, *Lath.* — Californian Vulture.

Head, bare, and yellowish red; plumage, brownish black; secondaries, gray, and, together with their coverts, tipped with white. Head of young, dusky, and their plumage edged with light brown; secondary coverts, tipped with brownish white. Nests in the loftiest trees. Eggs, two, nearly spherical, *jet black.* Length of *female*, 55 inches; of *male*, 50. Habitat, California.

Cathartes Californianus, *Bonap. Syn.* p. 22. *Nuttall*, i. 39. *Aud.* v. 240; *Syn.* p. 2, plate 426.

2. Cathartes Aura, *Linn.* — Turkey-Buzzard, *Wilson*, p. 660.

Habitat, from New Jersey, south and west throughout North America.

Cathartes aura, *Bonap. Syn.* p. 22. *Rich. & Swains.* F. Bor. Amer. ii. 4. *Nuttall*, i. 43. *Aud.* plate 151, ii. 296; v. 339; *Syn.* p. 3.

3. Cathartes atratus. — Black Vulture, *Wilson*, p. 667.

Cathartes iota, *Bonap. Syn.* p. 23. *Nutt.* i. 46. *Aud.* ii. 33; v. 345; plate 106. — Cathartes atratus, *Rich. & Swain.* ii. 6. *Aud. Syn.* p. 3.

FAMILY II. — FALCONIDÆ.

GENUS FALCO, *Linn.* — HAWKS.

SUBGENUS AQUILA, *Briss.*

4. Falco Chrysaëtos, *Linn.* — Golden Eagle, *Wilson*, p. 467.

Habitat, from lat. 40° to the north.

Falco fulvus, *Bonap. Sym.* p. 25. *Nuttall*, i. 62. — Falco Chrysaetos, *Aud.* ii. 464. — Aquila Chrysaetos, *Rich. & Swain.* F. B. A. ii. 12. *Aud. Syn.* p. 9; plate 181.

SUBGENUS POLYBORUS, *Vieill.*

5. Falco Brazilienais, *Gmel.* — Brazilian Caracara Eagle.

Upper part of head and nape, brownish black; throat, yellowish white; upper parts, barred with brown and dull white; lower parts, with brown and reddish white. *Male*, 23½, 48. Habitat, Texas and Florida. Nests in tall trees; eggs, two.

Polyborus vulgaris, *Aud.* ii. 350; v. 351; plate 161. — Polyborus Braziliensis, *Aud. Syn.* p. 4.

SUBGENUS HALIÆTUS, *Savigny.*

6. Falco Washingtoni, *Aud.* — Bird of Washington.

Bill, bluish black; cere, yellowish brown; feet, orange yellow; general color of plumage, blackish brown, with a coppery tint. *Male*, 43, 122. Nests in inaccessible cliffs. Habitat, throughout the Union.

Falco Washingtoni, *Aud.* i. 58. *Nutt.* i. 67. — Haliætus Washingtoni, *Aud. Syn.* p. 10; plate 11.

7. Falco leucocephalus, *Linn.* — White-headed Eagle, *Wilson,* pp. 325 and 469.

Habitat, all North America. Nests in high trees. Eggs, four, dull white.

Falco leucocephalus, *Bonap. Syn.* p. 26. *Nutt.* i. 72. *Aud.* i. 160; ii. 160; v. 354; plates 31 and 126. — Aquila leucocephala, *Swain. & Rich.* B. A. ii. 15. — Haliætus leucocephalus, *Aud. Syn.* p. 10.

SUBGENUS PANDION, *Savigny.*

8. Falco haliætus. — Fish-Hawk, *Wilson,* p. 334.

Habitat, all North America.

Falco haliætus, *Bonap. Syn.* p. 26. *Nutt.* i. 18. *Aud.* i. 415; v. 362. — Pandion haliætus, *Aud. Syn.* p. 12.

SUBGENUS FALCO, *Linn.*

9. Falco Islandicus, *Lath.* — Gyr Falcon.

Plumage, white, with slate gray sagittate spots; bill, pale blue; cere and feet, yellow. Young, brownish gray, with spots and margins of reddish white. Nests on high rocks and cliffs. Habitat, from Canada to the Arctic regions. *Male*, 22½, 49. *Female*, 23½, 51¼.

Falco Islandicus, *Rich. & Swain.* F. B. A. ii. 27. *Nutt.* i. 51. *Aud.* ii. 552; iv. 476; *Syn.* p. 15; plates 196 and 366.

10. Falco Peregrinus, *Gmel.* — Wandering Falcon, *Wilson,* p. 677.

Falco peregrinus, *Bonap. Syn.* p. 27. *Nutt.* i. 53. *Rich. & Swain.* F. B. A. ii. 23. *Aud.* i. 85; v. 365; plate 16; *Syn.* p. 16.

*11. Falco columbarius, *Linn.* — Pigeon Hawk, *Wilson,* p. 166.

Habitat, through the whole of North America. Nests in low fir-trees, twelve feet from the ground. Eggs, three, dull yellowish brown, with dark, reddish brown blotches. *Male*, 10¾, 27. *Female*, 14, 30.

Falco columbarius, *Bonap. Syn.* p. 38. *Nutt.* i. 60. *Swain. & Rich.* F. B. A. ii. 35. *Aud.* i. 466; v. 368; *Syn.* p. 16; plate 92. — Falco temerarius, *Aud.* i. 381; plate 75. — Falco Æsulon, *Swain. & Rich.* F. B. A. ii. 37.

---

* Wilson only described the young of this bird. The adult (*Falco temerarius* of Audubon's Biography) differs principally in the bluish gray color of its plumage, which takes the place of the brownish gray of the young.

12. Falco sparverius, *Linn.* — Sparrow Hawk, *Wilson,* pp. 171 and 300.

Habitat, throughout the Union ; rare near Boston. *Male* and *Female,* 12.

Falco sparverius, *Bonap. Syn.* p. 27. *Nutt.* i. 58. *Rich. & Swain.* F. B. A. ii. 31. *Aud.* ii. 246 ; v. 370 ; *Syn.* p. 17 ; plate 142.

SUBGENUS BUTEO, *Bechst.*

13. Falco vulgaris, *Willoughby.* — Common Buzzard.

General plumage, chocolate brown ; primaries, black ; inner webs, white, barred with brownish black ; tail, with ten dusky bars on a reddish brown ground, the last dark bar broadest ; under parts, yellowish white. Habitat, Fur Countries and Rocky Mountains. *Female,* 23. Nests in trees. Eggs, five, greenish white, with dark brown blotches.

Buteo vulgaris, *Aud. Syn.* p. 5. *Rich. & Swain.* F. B. A. ii. 47. — Falco buteo, *Aud.* iv. 508 ; plate 372.

14. Falco Harrisii, *Aud.* — Harris's Buzzard.

Plumage, chocolate brown ; wing-coverts, reddish brown ; upper tail-coverts, base, and end of tail, white. *Female,* 24. Habitat, Mississippi.

Falco Harrisii, *Aud.* v. 30 ; plate 392. — Buteo Harrisii, *Aud. Syn.* p. 5.

15. Falco Harlani. — Black Warrior.

Plumage, chocolate brown, glossed with bluish gray ; tail, lighter than back, narrowly barred with brownish black, and tipped with brownish red ; lower parts, paler, anteriorly streaked, posteriorly barred with brownish black. *Male,* 21, 45. *Female,* 22. Habitat, Louisiana.

Falco Harlani, *Aud.* i. 441 ; v. 380 ; plate 86. *Nutt.* i. 105. — Buteo Harlani, *Aud. Syn.* p. 7.

16. Falco lineatus, *Gmel.* — Red-shouldered or Winter Hawk, *Wilson,* pp. 314 and 457.

Habitat, Eastern and Middle States. Nests in trees. Eggs, grayish white, blotched with dark brown. *Male,* 16, 38. *Female,* 19.

Falco lineatus, *Aud.* i. 296 ; v. 380 ; plates 56 and 71. — Falco hyemalis, *Bonap. Syn.* p. 33. *Nutt.* i. 106. *Aud.* i. 364 ; *Syn.* p. 7.

17. Falco Pennsylvanicus, *Wilson.* — Broad-winged Hawk, *Wilson,* p. 460.

Habitat, Eastern and Middle States. Nests in trees. Eggs, five, grayish white, blotched with dark brown. *Male,* 16, 38. *Female,* 19.

Falco Pennsylvanicus, *Bonap. Syn.* p. 29. *Nutt.* i. 105. *Aud.* i. 461, and v. 377 ; plate 91. — Buteo Pennsylvanicus, *Aud. Syn.* p. 7.

18. Falco lagopus, *Wilson.* — Rough-legged Hawk, *Wilson,* pp. 302 and 456.

Habitat, northern portion of North America. Nests in low trees. *Male,* 21½, 51½. *Female,* 23.

Falco niger, *Wilson.* — Falco lagopus, *Bonap. Syn.* p. 32. *Rich. & Swain.* F. B. A. ii. 52. *Wilson,* iv. 59, and v. 216. *Aud.* ii. 377, and v. 217. — Falco Sancti Johannis, *Bonap. Syn.* p. 32. — Buteo lagopus, *Aud. Syn.* p. 8 ; plates 166 and 422.

19. Falco borealis, *Gmel.* — Red-tailed Hawk, *Wilson,* pp. 450 and 452.

Habitat, the whole continent. Nests in high trees. Eggs, five, dull white, blotched with brown. *Male*, 20½. *Female*, 24.

Falco borealis, *Rich. & Swain.* F. B. A. ii. 50. *Nutt.* i. 102. *Aud.* i. 265, and v. 378.— Falco leverianus, *Wilson*, vi. 78.— Buteo borealis, *Aud. Syn.* p. 6; plate 51.

SUBGENUS ELANUS, *Sav.*

20. Falco dispar, *Temm.* — Black-shouldered Hawk.

Ash gray above; head, tail, and lower parts, white, with a large bluish black patch on the wing above, and a smaller one beneath; feet, orange yellow. *Male*, 14, 40. *Female*, 16¾, 41½. Habitat, Southern States and Texas.

Falco dispar, *Aud.* iv. 397; plate 352.— Falco melanopterus, *Bonap. Am. Orn.* ii.; *Syn.* p. 31; *App.* p. 435.— Elanus dispar, *Aud. Syn.* p. 13.

SUBGENUS ICTINIA, *Vieillot.*

21. Falco plumbea, *Gmel.* — Mississippi Kite, *Wilson*, p. 241.

Habitat, Southern States. Nests in high trees. Eggs, three, light green, blotched with deep chocolate brown, globular.

Falco Mississippiensis, *Wilson*, iii. 80.— Falco plumbeus, *Bonap. Syn.* p. 90. *Aud.* ii. 108, and v. 374; plate 117.— Ictinia plumbea, *Aud. Syn.* p. 14.

SUBGENUS NAUCLERUS, *Vig.*

22. Falco furcatus, *Linn.* — Swallow-tailed Hawk, *Wilson*, p. 447.

Habitat, Texas and the Southern States. Nests in the high trees. Eggs, greenish white, with brown blotches.

Falco furcatus, *Wilson*, vi. 70. *Bonap. Syn.* p. 31. *Aud.* i. 368, and v. 371; plate 72. Nauclerus furcatus, *Aud. Syn.* p. 14.

SUBGENUS ASTUR, *Cuv.*

23. Falco palumbarius, *Linn.* — Goshawk, *Wilson*, p. 453.

Habitat, northern parts of the continent. Nests in trees. Eggs, three, bluish white and spotted with reddish brown.

Falco palumbarius, *Bonap. Syn.* p. 28. *Aud.* ii. 241; plates 141 and 36.— Falco atricapillus, *Nutt.* i. 85.— Accipiter palumbarius, *Rich. & Swain.* ii. 39.— Astur palumbarius, *Aud. Syn.* p. 18.

24. Falco Cooperi, *Bonap.* — Cooper's Hawk.

Plumage, bluish gray; tail, with broad blackish bands, tipped with white. *Male*, 20, 36. *Female*, 22, 38. Nests in tops of trees. Eggs, three, globular, dull white. Habitat, southern part of United States; Columbia River.

Falco Cooperii, *Bonap. Syn. App.* p. 433.— Falco Stanleii, *Aud.* ii. 245; i. 186; plates 36 and 141.— Astur Cooperi, *Aud. Syn.* p. 18.

25. Falco Fuscus, *Gmel.* — Sharp-shinned Hawk, *Wilson*, pp. 404, 407.

Habitat, the whole continent; migratory.

Falco Pennsylvanicus, *Wilson*, vi. 13.— Falco velox, *Wilson*, vi. 116. *Bonap. Syn.* p. 29. *Nutt.* i. 87.— Falco fuscus, *Bonap. Syn. App.* p. 433. *Aud.* iv. 522; plate 374.— Accipiter Pennsylvanicus, *Rich. & Swain.* ii. 44.— Astur fuscus, *Aud. Syn.* p. 18.

SUBGENUS CIRCUS, *Bechst.*

26. Falco cyaneus, *Linn.* — Common Harrier, *Wilson*, p. 445.

Habitat, Columbia River, Texas, and United States. Nests on the ground. Eggs, four, spherical, bluish white.

Falco uliginosus, *Wilson,* vi. 67. — Falco cyaneus, *Bonap. Orn.* ii. 30. *Nutt.* i. 109. *Aud.* iv. 396; plate 356. — Buteo cyaneus, *Rich. & Swain.* ii. 55. — Circus cyaneus, *Aud. Syn.* p. 19.

FAMILY III. — STRIGINÆ, *Aud.*

GENUS STRIX, *Linn.* — OWLS.

SUBGENUS SURNIA, *Dumeril.*

27. Strix funerea, *Gmel.* — Hawk Owl, *Wilson,* p. 444.

Habitat, to the north of lat. 35°. Nests in trees. Eggs, two, white.

Strix Hudsonica, *Wilson,* vi. 64. — Strix funerea, *Bonap. Syn.* p. 25. *Nutt.* i. 115. *Rich. & Swain.* ii. 92. *Aud.* x. 550; plate 378. — Surina funerea, *Aud. Syn.* p. 21.

28. Strix nyctea, *Linn.* — Snowy Owl, *Wilson,* p. 297.

Habitat, northern part of the continent.

Strix nyctea, *Bonap. Syn.* p. 36. *Nutt.* i. 116. *Rich. & Swain.* ii. 88. *Aud.* ii. 135; v. 382. — Surnia nyctea, *Aud. Syn.* p. 21; plate 121.

29. Strix passerina, *Linn.* — Sparrow Owl.

General color of upper parts, chocolate brown; hind neck, with large white spots; feathers on the back with large roundish spots; tail, with four reddish white bands; lower parts, dull yellowish white. *Female,* 10½. Habitat, Nova Scotia. Egg, in my possession, spherical, dull white.

Strix nyctea, *Aud.* v. 269. — Surnia passerina, *Aud. Syn.* p. 22; plate 432.

30. Strix cunicularia, *Gmel.* — Burrowing Owl.

Bill, grayish yellow; claws, black; upper parts, light yellowish brown, spotted with white; quills and tail, with triangular reddish white spots; throat and ruff, white; under parts, yellowish white, with reddish brown bars. *Male,* 10, 24. *Female,* 11. Habitat, west of the Mississippi.

Strix cunicularia, *Bonap. Orn.* i. 68. *Nutt.* i. 118. *Aud.* v. 264; plate 432. — Surnia cunicularia, *Aud. Syn.* p. 23.

31. Strix passerinoides, *Temm.* — Columbian Day Owl.

Upper parts, olivaceous brown; head, with small yellowish white spots; quills, tail, and facial disk, spotted with white; lower parts white. *Male,* 7. Habitat, Columbia River.

Strix passerinoides, *Aud.* v. 271; plate 432. — Surnia passerinoides, *Aud. Syn.* p. 23.

SUBGENUS ULULA.

32. Strix Tengmalmi, *Gmel.* — Tengmalm's Owl.

Upper parts, grayish brown, tinged with olive; feathers of head and neck, with white spots; scapulars, quills, and tail, also with white spots; ruff and lower parts, yellowish white; throat, white. *Male,* 11. *Female,* 12. Habitat, north of lat. 45°. Nests in trees. Eggs, two, white.

Strix Tengmalmi, *Rich. & Swain.* ii. 94. *Aud.* iv. 559; plate 480. — Ulula Tengmalmi, *Aud. Syn.* p. 24.

33. Strix Acadica, *Gmel.* — Acadian Owl, *Wilson*, p. 309.

Strix passerina, *Wilson*, iv, 61. — Strix Acadica, *Bonap. Syn.* p. 38. *Swain. & Rich.* ii. 97. *Nutt.* i. 137. *Aud.* ii. 567, and v. 307; plate 199 — Ulula Acadica, *Aud. Syn.* p. 24.

SUBGENUS STRIX, *Linn.*

34. Strix Americana, *Aud.* — American Barn Owl, *Wilson*, p. 440.

Habitat, Southern States. Nests on the ground. Eggs, white.

Strix flammea, *Wilson*, vi. 57. *Bonap. Syn.* p. 38. *Nutt.* i. 139. *Aud.* ii. 403; v. 388; plate 171. — Strix Americana, *Aud. Syn.* p. 25.

SUBGENUS SYRNIUM, *Cuv.*

35. Strix cinerea, *Linn.* — Cinereous Owl.

Upper parts, grayish brown, variegated with grayish white; lower parts, variegated with yellowish white. *Female*, 30½, 48. Habitat, north of 42°. Nests in high trees.

Strix cinerea, *Nutt.* i. 128. *Swain & Rich.* ii. 77. *Aud.* i. 364; plate 351. — Syrnium cinereum, *Aud. Syn.* p. 26.

36. Strix nebulosa, *Linn.* — Barred Owl, *Wilson*, p. 304.

Bonap. Syn. p. 38. *Nutt.* i. 133. *Aud.* i. 242; v. 386; plate 46. — Syrnium nebulosum, *Aud. Syn.* p. 27.

SUBGENUS OTUS, *Cuv.*

37. Strix Otus. — Long-eared Owl, *Wilson*, p. 449.

Strix otus, *Bonap. Syn.* p. 37. *Nutt.* i. 130. *Aud.* iv. 573; plate 383. — Otus vulgaris, *Aud. Syn.* p. 28.

38. Strix brachyotus, *Linn.* — Short-eared Owl, *Wilson*, p. 307.

Male, 15, 40. *Female*, 17, 45. Nests in bushes. Eggs, four, bluish white.

Strix brachyotus, *Bonap. Syn.* p. 37. *Nutt.* i. 132. *Aud.* v. 273; plate 432. — Otus brachyotus, *Aud. Syn.* p. 28.

SUBGENUS BUBO, *Cuv.*

39. Strix Virginiana, *Gmel.* — Great-horned Owl, *Wilson*, p. 435.

Strix Virginiana, *Bonap. Syn.* p. 37. *Nutt.* i. 124. *Aud.* i. 313; v. 393. — Bubo Virginianus, *Aud. Syn.* p. 29.

40. Strix asio, *Linn.* — Mottled Owl, *Wilson*, pp. 201 and 383.

Old bird, with brownish red plumage; young, with the upper parts pale brown, spotted with brownish black; quills, light gray, barred with brownish black; throat, yellowish gray.*

Strix asio, *Nutt.* i. 120. *Aud.* i. 486; v. 392. — Bubo asio, *Aud. Syn.* p. 29.

---

* Mr. Audubon reverses this order, making the brown plumage the old birds, and the red, the young. Mr. Samuel Cabot, Jr. exhibited before the Boston Natural History Society an old red bird, which he shot in the act of feeding some young brown ones, which he also exhibited. — See *Journal of the Boston Society*, ii. 126.

ORDER II. — INSESSORES, *Vigors*.

FAMILY I. — CAPRIMULGIDÆ.

GENUS CAPRIMULGUS, *Linn.*

41. Caprimulgus Carolinensis, *Gmel.* — Chuck-Will's-Widow, *Wilson*, p. 462.

Caprimulgus Carolinensis, *Bonap. Syn.* p. 61. *Aud.* i. 273; v. 401; *Syn.* p. 311; plate 52.

42. Caprimulgus vociferus, *Wilson.* — Whip-Poor-Will, *Wilson*, p. 376.

Caprimulgus vociferus, *Bonap. Syn.* p. 62. *Nutt.* i. 614. *Aud.* i. 422; v. 405; plate 82; *Syn.* p. 31.

43. Caprimulgus Virginianus. — Night Hawk, *Wilson*, p. 371.

Caprimulgus Virginianus, *Bonap. Syn.* p. 62. *Rich. & Swain.* ii. 62. *Nutt.* i. 619. *Aud.* ii. 273. — Chordeiles Virginianus, *Aud. Syn.* p. 32.

FAMILY II. — HIRUNDINIDÆ, *Vigors*.

GENUS I. — CYPSELUS, *Linn.*

44. Cypselus pelasgius, *Linn.* — Chimney Swallow, *Wilson*, p. 359.

Cypselus pelasgius, *Bonap. Syn.* p. 63. *Nutt.* i. 609. *Aud.* ii. 329; v. 319; plate 158. — Chaetura pelasgia, *Aud. Syn.* p. 33.

GENUS II. — HIRUNDO, *Linn.*

45. Hirundo purpurea, *Linn.* — Purple Martin, *Wilson*, p. 365.

Hirundo purpurea, *Bonap. Syn.* p. 64. *Nutt.* i. 598. *Aud.* i. 115; v. 408; *Syn.* p. 34; plate 23.

46. Hirundo bicolor, *Vieill.* — White-bellied Swallow, *Wilson*, p. 356.

Hirundo bicolor, *Bonap. Syn.* p. 65. *Nutt.* i. 605. *Aud.* i. 491; v. 417; plate 98; *Syn.* p. 35.

47. Hirundo fulva, *Vieill.* — Republican or Cliff Swallow.

Upper part of head, back, and wing-coverts, black, with bluish green reflections; forehead, white, tinged with red; chin, throat, and neck, brownish red; under parts, grayish white; tail slightly emarginate, not forked like the following. Habitat, north of 40° and Rocky Mountains. Breeds as near Boston as Jaffrey, N. H. Nests under eaves. Eggs, five, white, with reddish brown spots.

Hirundo fulva, *Bonap. Am. Orn.* i. 63; *Syn.* p. 64. *Nutt.* i. 603. *Aud.* i. 353; v. 415; *Syn.* p. 35; plate 78.

48. Hirundo rustica, *Linn.* — Barn Swallow, *Wilson*, p. 348.

Hirundo rustica, *Aud.* ii. 413; v. 411; *Syn.* p. 35; plate 173. — Hirundo Americana, *Swain. & Rich.* ii. 329. — Hirundo rufa, *Bonap. Syn.* p. 64. *Nutt.* i. 601.

49. Hirundo thalassina, *Swain.* — Violet green Swallow.

Upper part of head, deep green, changing gradually into the dark purple of the neck; back, grass green; rump and upper tail-coverts, carmine purple; under parts, white. *Mule*, 4⅟₂. Nests on bluffs. Eggs, four, clay color, with spots of reddish brown. Habitat, California, Rocky Mountains, and Oregon.

Hirundo thalassina, *Aud.* iv. 597; plate 385; *Syn.* p. 36.

50. Hirundo riparia, *Linn.* — Bank Swallow, *Wilson*, p. 358.

Hirundo riparia, *Bonap. Syn.* p. 65. *Rich. & Swain.* ii. 333. *Nutt.* i. 607. *Aud.* iv. 584; plate 385; *Syn.* p. 36.

51. Hirundo serripennis, *Aud.* — Rough-winged Swallow.

Distinguished from the preceding by projecting filaments along the edge of the wing. *Male*, 5¾, 12½. Habitat, Louisiana and South Carolina.

Hirundo serripennis, *Aud.* iv. 593; plate 375; *Syn.* p. 37.

FAMILY III. — HALCYONIDÆ, *Vigors*.

GENUS ALCEDO, *Linn.*

52. Alcedo Alcyon, *Linn.* — Belted King-Fisher, *Wilson*, p. 227.

Alcedo Alcyon, *Bonap. Syn.* p. 48. *Nutt.* i. 594. *Rich. & Swain.* ii. 339. *Aud.* i. 394; v. 540; plate 77; *Syn.* p. 173.

FAMILY IV. — MUSCICAPIDÆ, *Vigors*.

GENUS I. — MUSCICAPA. — FLYCATCHERS.

SUBGENUS MILVULUS, *Swain.*

53. Muscicapa Savana, *Bonap.* — Fork-tailed Flycatcher.

Tail, twice the length of the body; head and cheeks, black; feathers of crown, yellow at base; back, ash gray; rump, bluish black; lower parts, white. *Male*, 14¼, 14. Habitat, Louisiana.

Muscicapa Savana, *Bonap. Orn.* i. 1; *Syn.* p. 67. *Nutt.* i. 274. *Aud.* ii. 387. — Milvulus tyrannus, *Aud. Syn.* p. 39; plate 168.

54. Muscicapa forficata, *Gmel.* — Swallow-tailed Flycatcher.

Head, cheeks, and hind neck, ash gray; back, brownish gray; rump, dusky; anterior wing-coverts, scarlet; tail-feathers, black, three outer, rose colored; under parts, white before, rose colored behind. *Male*, 11. Habitat, Arkansas.

Muscicapa forficata, *Bonap. Orn.* v. 15; *Syn.* p. 67. *Nutt.* i. 275. *Aud.* iv. 426; plate 359. — Milvulus forficatus, *Aud. Syn.* p. 38.

SUBGENUS MUSCICAPA.

55. Muscicapa verticalis, *Say.* — Arkansas Flycatcher.

Upper parts, ash gray; back, tinged with yellow; top of head, bright vermilion; throat, grayish white; neck, ash gray; lower parts, pure yel-

58 *

low. *Male*, 9, 15¼. Habitat, Columbia River, Rocky Mountains, Texas, and Louisiana.

Muscicapa verticalis, *Bonap. Orn.* i. 18; *Syn.* p. 67. *Nutt.* i. 273. *Aud.* iv. 422; plate 359; *Syn.* p. 39.

56. Muscicapa dominicensis, *Brisson.* — Pipiry Flycatcher.

Upper parts, ash gray, shaded with brown, posteriorly; concealed vermilion patch on top of head; lower parts, ash gray in front, yellowish gray behind. *Male*, 8¼, 14¾. Habitat, Florida to South Carolina.

Muscicapa dominicensis, *Aud.* ii. 392; plate 172; *Syn.* p. 39.

57. Muscicapa tyrannus, *Linn.* — Tyrant Flycatcher, *Wilson*, p. 140.

Muscicapa tyrannus, *Bonap. Syn.* p. 66. *Nutt.* i. 205. *Aud.* i. 403; v. 420; plate 79; *Syn.* p. 40.

58. Muscicapa crinita, *Linn.* — Crested Flycatcher, *Wilson*, p. 147.

Muscicapa crinita, *Bonap. Syn.* p. 67. *Nutt.* i. 271. *Aud.* ii. 176; v. 423.

59. Muscicapa Cooperi, *Nutt.* — Cooper's Flycatcher.

Upper parts, grayish olive brown; secondaries, margined with brownish white; rump, white; lower parts, grayish white. Habitat, from Texas to Massachusetts. *Male*, 7½, 12¾. Nests in trees. Eggs, four, yellowish cream white, with reddish brown spots.

Muscicapa Cooperi, *Nutt.* i. 282. *Aud.* ii. 422; v. 422; plate 174; *Syn.* p. 41. — Tyrannus borealis, *Rich. & Swain.* i. 141.

60. Muscicapa acadica, *Gmel.* — Green-crested Flycatcher, *Wilson*, p. 148.

Muscicapa acadica, *Nutt.* i. 288. *Bonap. Syn.* p. 68. *Aud.* ii. 256; v. 427; plate 144; *Syn.* p. 42.

61. Muscicapa fusca, *Gmel.* — Pewit Flycatcher, *Wilson*, p. 149.

Muscicapa fusca, *Bonap. Syn.* p. 68. *Nutt.* i. 278. *Aud.* ii. 122; v. 424; plate 120; *Syn.* p. 43.

62. Muscicapa virens, *Linn.* — Wood Pewee, *Wilson*, p. 151.

Muscicapa virens, *Nutt.* i. 285. *Bonap. Syn.* p. 68. *Aud.* ii. 93; v. 425; plate 115, *Syn.* p. 43.

63. Muscicapa minuta, *Wilson.* — Small-headed Flycatcher, *Wilson*, p. 443.

Muscicapa minuta, *Bonap. Syn.* p. 86. *Nutt.* i. 296. *Aud.* v. 291; plate 434; *Syn* p. 44.

64. Muscicapa Ruticilla, *Linn.* — Redstart, *Wilson*, pp. 68 and 405.

Muscicapa Ruticilla, *Bonap. Syn.* p. 68. *Nutt.* i. 291. *Aud.* i. 202; v. 428; plate 40; *Syn.* p. 44.

65. Muscicapa, Saya, *Bonap.* — Say's Flycatcher.

Upper parts, grayish brown; upper tail-coverts and tail, brownish black; neck, light grayish brown; breast and abdomen, shaded with reddish. *Male*, 7. Habitat, Arkansas, Columbia River, and Fur Countries.

Muscicapa Saya, *Bonap. Orn.* i. 20; *Syn.* p. 67. *Rich. & Swain.* ii. 142. *Nutt.* ii. 277. *Aud.* iv. 428; plate 359; *Syn.* p. 41.

66. Muscicapa nigricans, *Swain.* — Rocky Mountain Flycatcher.

Head, neck, and back, sooty brown; remainder, except middle of breast, abdomen, and lower tail-coverts, which are white, grayish brown *Male*, 7. Habitat, Mexico and California.

Muscicapa nigricans, *Aud.* v. 302; plate 434; *Syn.* p. 42.

67. Muscicapa Phœbe, *Lath.* — Short-legged Pewit.

Upper parts, olivaceous brown; fore part of neck, breast, and sides, light dusky gray, tinged with olive; abdomen, pale dull yellow. *Male*, 6¾. Habitat, Columbia River, Fur Countries, and Labrador. Nests in low bushes. Eggs, seven, light blue, spotted with small brown specks.

Tyrannula Richardsonii, *Swain. & Rich.* ii. 146. — Muscicapa Richardsonii, *Aud.* v. 299; plate 434; *Syn.* p. 42.

68. Muscicapa Traillii, *Aud.* — Traill's Flycatcher.

Upper parts, dusky olive; head, darker; grayish ring round the eye; two bands of grayish white on wing; secondaries, margined with same; throat and breast, ash gray; abdomen, pale yellow. Habitat, Arkansas and Columbia River. *Male*, 5¾, 8½.

Muscicapa Traillii, *Aud.* i. 236; v. 426; plate 45; *Syn.* p. 43

69. Muscicapa pusilla, *Swain.* — Least Pewee.

Upper parts, light greenish brown; wings, olive brown, with two bands of dull white; secondaries, margined with same; tail, olive brown; neck, breast, and sides, ash gray; under parts, pale yellow. *Male*, 5⅙. Habitat, Columbia River, Fur Countries, Labrador, and Newfoundland. Nests in bushes. Eggs, five, white, thinly spotted with red.

Tyrannula pusilla, *Rich. & Swain.* ii. 144. — Muscicapa pusilla, *Aud.* v 288; plate 434; *Syn.* p. 44.

SUBGENUS CULICIVORA, *Swain.*

70. Muscicapa cærulea, *Lath.* — Blue-gray Flycatcher, *Wilson*, p. 199.

Muscicapa cærulea, *Nutt.* i. 297. *Aud.* i. 431; plate 84. — Sylvia cærulea, *Bonap. Syn.* p. 85. — Culicivora cærulea, *Aud. Syn.* p. 46.

GENUS II. — PTILOGONYS, *Swain.*

71. Ptilogonys Townsendi, *Aud.* — Townsend's Ptilogonys.

General color, dull brownish gray; quills and coverts, dusky brown; edge of wing, dull white; secondaries, with a faint patch of light brownish gray on the outer web towards the end; middle tail-feathers, grayish brown, the rest blackish brown; paler underneath. Habitat, Columbia River. *Female*, 8¼. Nest and eggs, unknown.

Ptilogonys Townsendi, *Aud.* v. 206; plate 419; *Syn.* p. 46.

FAMILY V. — LANIADÆ, *Vigors.*

GENUS LANIUS. — SHRIKE.

72. Lanius borealis, *Vieill.* — Great American Shrike, *Wilson*, p. 49.

Lanius borealis, *Rich. & Swain.* ii. 111. *Nutt.* i. 258. — Lanius septentrionalis, *Bonap. Syn.* p. 72. — Lanius excubitor, *Aud.* i. 531; v. 534; plate 192. — Lanius borealis, *Aud. Syn.* p. 157.

73. Lanius Ludovicianus, *Linn.* — Loggerhead Shrike, *Wilson*, p. 225.

Lanius Ludovicianus, *Bonap. Syn.* p. 72. *Nutt.* i. 261. *Aud.* i. 300; v. 300.

FAMILY VI. — MERULIDÆ, *Vigors.*

GENUS I. — TURDUS. — THRUSH.

74. Turdus migratorius, *Linn.* — Robin, *Wilson*, p. 20.

Turdus migratorius, *Bonap. Syn.* p. 75. *Nutt.* i. 338. *Aud.* ii. 190; v. 442; plate 131; *Syn.* p. 89. — Merula migratoria, *Rich. & Swain.* ii. 176.

75. Turdus mustelinus, *Gmel.* — Wood Thrush, *Wilson*, p. 15.

Turdus mustelinus, *Bonap. Syn.* p. 75. *Nutt.* i. 343. *Aud.* i. 372; v. 446; plate 73; *Syn.* p. 90.

76. Turdus nævius, *Gmel.* — Varied Thrush.

Upper parts, deep leaden gray; head, darker; tail, dusky; reddish orange band over eye; two of same on wings; another on primaries; lower parts, reddish orange, paler behind; grayish black band on neck; another crossing lower parts. *Female*, tinged with olive brown; the bands, paler. Habitat, Columbia River, California, and Fur Countries.

Orpheus meruloides, *Rich. & Swain.* ii. 187. — Turdus nævius, *Aud.* iv. 489; v. 284; plates 369 and 433; *Syn.* p. 89.

77. Turdus Wilsonii, *Bonap.* — Wilson's Thrush, *Wilson*, p. 392.

Turdus Wilsonii, *Bonap. Syn.* p. 76. *Nutt.* i. 349. *Aud.* ii. 362; v. 446; plate 166; *Syn.* p. 90.

78. Turdus solitarius, *Wilson.* — Hermit Thrush, *Wilson*, p. 390.

Turdus minor, *Bonap. Syn.* p. 75. *Nutt.* i. 346. *Rich. & Swain.* ii. 184. *Aud.* i. 303; v. 445; plate 58. — Turdus solitarius, *Aud. Syn.* p. 91.

79. Turdus nanus, *Aud.* — Dwarf Thrush.

Upper parts, light olivaceous brown; rump and tail, brownish red; quills, dusky brown, margined with brownish red; lower parts, grayish white; neck and breast, yellowish red, spotted with triangular brown marks. *Male*, 6, 9½. Habitat, Columbia River.

Turdus nanus, *Aud.* v. 201; plate 419; *Syn.* p. 91.

SUBGENUS ORPHEUS, *Swain.*

80. Turdus polyglottus, *Lath.* — Mocking Bird, *Wilson*, p. 107.

Turdus polyglottus, *Bonap. Syn.* p. 74. *Nutt.* i. 320. *Aud.* i. 108; v. 438; plate 21; *Syn.* p. 87.

81. Turdus montanus, *Townsend.* — Mountain Mocking Bird.

Upper parts, grayish brown; wing and tail, grayish black; white spots on end of three lateral tail-feathers; lower parts, whitish; triangular dusky spots forming a line from the base of the bill; throat, middle of breast, abdomen, and lower tail-coverts, unspotted. *Male*, 8. Habitat, Rocky Mountains. Nests in bushes. Eggs, four, emerald green, with olive spots of two shades.

Turdus montanus, *Aud.* iv. 487; plate 369. — Orpheus montanus, *Aud. Syn.* p. 87.

82. Turdus felivox, *Bonap.* — Cat Bird, *Wilson*, p. 157.

Turdus felivox, *Bonap. Syn.* p. 75. *Nutt.* i. 332. *Rich. & Swain.* ii. 192. *Aud.* ii. 171; v. 440; plate 128. — Orpheus Carolinensis, *Aud. Syn.* p. 88.

83. Turdus rufus, *Linn.* — Brown Thrush, *Wilson*, p. 152.

Turdus rufus, *Bonap. Syn.* p. 75. *Nutt.* i. 328. *Aud.* ii. 102; v. 441; plate 116. Orpheus rufus, *Rich. & Swain.* ii. 189. *Aud. Syn.* p. 88.

GENUS II. — SEIURUS, *Swain.* — WAGTAIL THRUSHES.

84. Seiurus aurocapillus. — Golden-crowned Thrush, *Wilson*, p. 155.

Seiurus aurocapillus, *Swain. & Rich.* ii. 227. *Aud. Syn.* p. 93. — Sylvia aurocapilla, *Bonap. Syn.* 77. — Turdus aurocapillus, *Nutt.* i. 355. *Aud.* ii. 253; v. 447; plate 143.

85. Seiurus Novæboracensis, *Gmel.* — Water Thrush, *Wilson*, p. 233.

Turdus aquaticus, *Aud.* v. 284; plates 19 and 433. — Sylvia Novæboracensis, *Bonap. Syn.* p. 77. — Seiurus aquaticus, *Rich. & Swain.* ii. 229. — Turdus Novæboracensis, *Nutt.* i. 353. *Aud.* i. 99.

GENUS III. — CINCLUS, *Bechst.* — DIPPER.

86. Cinclus Americanus, *Swain.* — American Dipper.

Head and neck, chocolate brown; upper parts, very deep bluish gray; lower, lighter, and tinged anteriorly with brown. *Male,* 7½, 10½. Habitat, Rocky Mountains, Oregon, and North California.

Cinclus Pallassii, *Bonap. Orn.* ii. 173. *Nutt.* v. 368. — Cinclus Americanus, *Rich. & Swain.* ii. 173. *Aud.* iv. 493; v. 303; plates 370 and 435; *Syn.* p. 86.

GENUS IV. — ANTHUS, *Bechst.* — PIPIT.

87. Anthus Ludovicianus, *Lichtenstein.* — Brown Lark, *Wilson*, p. 387.

Anthus spinoletta, *Bonap. Syn.* p. 90. *Aud.* i. 49. — Anthus pipiens, *Aud.* i. 408; v. 449; plates 108, 80. — Anthus Ludovicianus, *Aud. Syn.* p. 48.

FAMILY VII. — SYLVIADÆ, *Vigors.*

GENUS I. — SYLVIA, *Linn.* — WARBLERS.

SUBGENUS MYIODIOCTES, *Aud.*

88. Sylvia mitrata, *Bonap.* — Hooded Warbler, *Wilson*, p. 254.

Habitat, from Texas to Virginia. Nests in low bushes. Eggs, four, dull white, spotted with red at larger end.

Sylvia mitrata, *Bonap. Syn.* p. 79. *Aud.* ii. 66; v. 465. — Muscicapa Selbyii, *Aud.* i. 46; plates 9 and 10. — Myiodioctes mitrata, *Aud. Syn.* p. 49.

89. Sylvia pardalina, *Bonap.* — Canada Warbler, *Wilson*, p. 253.

Sylvia pardalina, *Bonap. Syn.* p. 79. — Muscicapa Canadensis, *Aud.* ii. 17; plate 103. — Myiodioctes Canadensis, *Aud. Syn.* p. 49.

90. Sylvia Bonapartii. — Bonaparte's Flycatching Warbler.

Upper parts, light grayish blue; lower parts, and a band on the forehead, ochre yellow; neck, with a few faint dusky spots. *Male*, 5¼. Habitat, Louisiana.

Muscicapa Bonapartii, *Aud.* i. 27. — Myiodioctes Bonapartii, *Aud. Syn.* p. 49; plate 5.

91. Sylvia formosa, *Bonap.* — Kentucky Warbler, *Wilson*, p. 244.

Habitat, Kentucky. Nests in reeds. Eggs, four, white, with red dots.

Sylvia formosa, *Aud.* i. 196. *Bonap. Syn.* p. 34. — Myiodioctes formosa, *Aud. Syn.* p. 50; plate 38.

92. Sylvia Wilsonii, *Bonap.* — Wilson's Black-Cap, *Wilson*, p. 255.

Sylvia Wilsonii, *Bonap. Syn.* p. 86. *Nutt.* 149. — Muscicapa Wilsonii, *Aud.* ii. 148; plate 124. — Myiodioctes Wilsonii, *Aud. Syn.* p. 50.

SUBGENUS SYLVICOLA, *Swain.*

93. Sylvia coronata, *Wilson.* — Yellow-Rump Warbler, *Wilson*, p. 184 and 416.

Nests in low trees. Eggs, of a light rosy tint, spotted with brown. Habitat, from Texas northward.

Sylvia coronata, *Bonap. Syn.* p. 78. *Nutt.* i. 361. *Aud.* ii. 303; plate 153. — Sylvicola coronata, *Aud. Syn.* p. 51.

94. Sylvia Auduboni, *Townsend.* — Audubon's Warbler.

In male, upper parts, bluish ash gray, streaked with black; rump, throat, and patch on sides of body, yellow; white patch on wing; quills and tail, brownish black, margined with grayish white; cheeks, black; lower parts of neck, breast, and sides, black and white; rest, white. *Female*, crown without yellow spots; upper parts, light brownish gray; lower, whitish. *Male*, 5¾. Habitat, Columbia River.

Sylvia Audubonii, *Aud.* v. 52; plate 395. — Sylvicola Auduboni, *Aud. Syn.* p. 52.

95. Sylvia striata, *Lath.* — Black-Poll Warbler, *Wilson*, p. 287 and 466.

Nests in low trees. Eggs, four.

Sylvia striata, *Bonap. Syn.* p. 81. *Nutt.* i. 383. *Aud.* ii. 201; plate 133. — Sylvicola striata, *Aud. Syn.* p. 52. *Rich. & Swain.* ii. 218.

96. Sylvia pensilis, *Lath.* — Yellow-throated Warbler, *Wilson*, p. 139.

Nests in high trees. Eggs, pure white, with purple dots, four.

Sylvia pensilis, *Bonap. Syn.* p. 79. *Aud.* i. 434; plate 85. — Sylvicola pensilis, *Aud. Syn.* p. 53.

97. Sylvia castanea, *Wilson.* — Bay-breasted Warbler, *Wilson*, p. 161.

Sylvia castanea, *Bonap. Syn.* p. 80. *Nutt.* i. 382. *Aud.* i. 358; plate 69. — Sylvicola castanea, *Aud. Syn.* p. 53.

98. Sylvia icterocephala, *Lath.* — Chestnut-sided Warbler, *Wilson*, p. 162.

Nest found in Brookline in a bush. Eggs, three, milk white, with purple blotches.

Sylvia icterocephala, *Bonap. Syn.* p. 80. *Nutt.* i. 380. *Aud.* i. 306. — Sylvicola icterocephala, *Aud. Syn.* p. 54.

99. Sylvia pinus, *Lath.* — Pine-Creeping Warbler, *Wilson*, p. 206.

Sylvia pinus, *Bonap. Syn.* p. 81. *Nutt.* i. 387. *Aud.* ii. 202; plate 111. — Sylvia Vigorsii, 1. 153. — Sylvicola pinus, *Aud. Syn.* p. 54.

100. Sylvia parus, *Wilson.* — Hemlock Warbler, *Wilson*, pp. 232 and 403.

Sylvia parus, *Bonap. Syn.* p. 82. *Aud.* ii. 205. — Sylvia autumnalis, *Bonap. Syn.* p. 74. *Aud.* i. 447. *Nutt.* i. 392. — Sylvicola parus, *Aud. Syn.* p. 55; plates 88 and 134.

101. Sylvia virens, *Lath.* — Black-throated Green Warbler, *Wilson*, p. 183.

Nests on ground. Eggs, five, light flesh color, with purple spots.

Sylvia virens, *Bonap. Syn.* p. 80. *Nutt.* i. 376. *Aud.* v. 70; plate 399. — Sylvicola virens, *Aud. Syn.* p. 55.

102. Sylvia maritima, *Wilson.* — Cape May Warbler, *Wilson*, p. 465.

Sylvia maritima, *Bonap. Syn.* p. 79. *Nutt.* i. 356. *Aud.* v. 156; plate 314. — Sylvicola maritima, *Aud. Syn.* p. 56.

103. Sylvia cærulea, *Wilson.* — Blue-green Warbler, *Wilson*, pp. 185 and 265.

Sylvia azurea, *Bonap. Syn.* p. 85. *Orn.* ii. 27. *Aud.* i. 255; v. 456; plates 48 and 49. — Sylvia rara, *Bonap. Syn.* p. 82. *Aud.* i. 258. — Sylvicola cærulea, *Aud. Syn.* p. 56.

104. Sylvia Blackburniæ, *Lath.* — Blackburnian Warbler, *Wilson*, p. 231.

Sylvia Blackburniæ, *Bonap. Syn.* p. 80. *Nutt.* i. 379. *Aud.* ii. 208; v. 73; plates 135 and 399. — Sylvicola Blackburniæ, *Aud. Syn.* p. 57.

105. Sylvia æstiva, *Gmel.* — Yellow-Poll Warbler, *Wilson*, p. 169.

Sylvia æstiva, *Bonap. Syn.* p. 83. *Nutt.* i. 365. *Aud.* ii. 276. — Sylvia Childsonii, *Aud.* i. 180. — Sylvicola æstiva, *Aud. Syn.* p. 57; plates 35 and 95.

106. Sylvia Rathbonii, *Aud.* — Rathbone's Warbler.

General color of plumage, bright yellow; upper parts, olivaceous; quills and tail, wood brown. Female, similar. Male, 4½. Habitat, Mississippi.

Sylvia Rathbonii, *Aud.* i. 333. — Sylvicola Rathbonii, *Aud. Syn.* p. 58; plate 65.

107. Sylvia petechea, *Lath.* — Red-Poll Warbler, *Wilson*, p. 271.

Sylvia petechea, *Bonap. Syn.* p. 83. *Nutt.* i. 364. *Aud.* ii. 259 and 360; plates 163 and 164. — Sylvicola, *Aud. Syn.* p. 58. — Rich. & Swain. ii. 215. — Sylvia palmarum, *Bonap. Syn.* p. 78.

108. Sylvia Americana, *Lath.* — Yellow-Back Warbler, *Wilson*, p. 270.

Sylvia Americana, *Aud.* i. 78; plate 15. *Bonap. Syn.* p. 33. — Sylvicola Americana, *Aud. Syn.* p. 59.

109. Sylvia Townsendi, *Nutt.* — Townsend's Warbler.

Upper parts, light greenish olive; cheeks and throat, black; band over the eye, one on side of neck, and fore part of breast, yellow; under parts, white; sides, with dusky spots; tail, blackish brown, two outer feathers, nearly wholly white. Male, 4⅝. Habitat, Columbia River.

Sylvia Townsendi, *Aud.* i. 36; plate 393. — Sylvicola Townsendi, *Aud. Syn.* p. 59.

110. Sylvia occidentalis, *Towns.* — Hermit Warbler.

In male, upper parts, bluish gray, spotted with black; head, cheeks, and sides of neck, bright yellow; throat, black; breast and abdomen, white; bands on wings and two outer tail-feathers, white. In female, upper parts, gray; throat, whitish, spotted with dusky. *Male*, $3\frac{5}{12}$. Habitat, Columbia River.

Sylvia occidentalis, *Aud.* v. 55; plate 395. — Sylvicola occidentalis, *Aud. Syn.* p. 60.

111. Sylvia nigrescens, *Towns.* — Black-throated Gray Warbler.

Upper parts, bluish ash gray; middle of back and tail-coverts, streaked with black; head, neck, cheeks, and part of breast, black; band, from nostril to eye, yellow; band over eye, and another from lower mandible along neck, white; breast and abdomen, white, with black lines; two bands on wings and outer tail-feathers, white. *Male*, 5. Habitat, Columbia River.

Sylvia nigrescens, *Aud.* v. 57; plate 395. — Sylvicola nigrescens, *Aud. Syn.* p. 60.

112. Sylvia Canadensis, *Linn.* — Black-throated Blue Warbler, *Wilson*, pp. 170 and 393.

Sylvia Canadensis, *Bonap. Syn.* p. 84. *Nutt.* i. 398. *Aud.* ii. 309; plates 148 and 155. — Sylvia sphagnosa, *Bonap. Syn.* p. 85. *Nutt.* i. 406. *Aud.* ii. 279. — Sylvicola Canadensis, *Aud. Syn.* p. 61.

113. Sylvia maculosa, *Lath.* — Black and Yellow Warbler, *Wilson*, p. 231.

Nests in low trees. Eggs, four, white, with reddish spots.

Sylvia maculosa, *Bonap. Syn.* p. 78. *Rich. & Swain.* ii. 213. *Nutt.* i. 370. *Aud.* ii. 145; i. 260; v. 458; plates 50 and 123. — Sylvicola maculosa, *Aud. Syn.* p. 61.

114. Sylvia discolor, *Vieill.* — Prairie Warbler, *Wilson*, p. 245.

Nests in bushes. Eggs, five, milk white, with lilac blotches and lines.

Sylvia discolor, *Bonap. Syn.* p. 83. *Nutt.* i. 294. *Aud.* i. 76; plate 14. — Sylvicola discolor, *Aud. Syn.* p. 62.

115. Sylvia montana, *Wilson.* — Blue Mountain Warbler, *Wilson*, p. 402.

Sylvia montana, *Aud.* v. 291; plate 434. — Sylvia tigrina, *Bonap. Syn.* p. 83. — Sylvicola montana, *Aud. Syn.* p. 62.

116. Sylvia agilis, *Wilson.* — Connecticut Warbler, *Wilson*, p. 370.

Sylvia agilis, *Bonap. Syn.* p. 84. *Nutt.* i. 399. *Aud.* ii. 227; v. 81; plate 138. — Sylvicola agilis, *Aud. Syn.* p. 63.

SUBGENUS TRICHAS, *Swain.*

117. Sylvia Macgillivrayi, *Aud.* — Macgillivray's Warbler.

Male, olive green, above; head and neck, bluish gray; lower parts, bright yellow; loral band, black. In female, the neck and band, ash gray. *Male*, $5\frac{1}{4}$, $6\frac{1}{2}$. *Female*, 5. Habitat, Columbia River.

Sylvia Macgillivrayi, *Aud.* v. 75; plate 399. — Trichas Macgillivrayi, *Aud. Syn.* p. 64.

118. Sylvia Philadelphia, *Wilson.* — Mourning Warbler, *Wilson*, p. 163.

Sylvia Philadelphia, *Bonap. Syn.* p. 85. *Nutt.* i. 404. *Aud.* v. 79. — Trichas Philadelphia, *Aud. Syn.* p. 64.

119. Sylvia trichas. — Maryland Yellow Throat, *Wilson*, p. 59.

Sylvia trichas, *Aud.* i. 121 ; v. 463 ; plates 92 and 94, *Nutt.* i. 401. — Sylvia Marilandica, *Bonap. Syn.* p. 85. — Sylvia Roscoe, *Aud.* i. 124. — Trichas Marilandica, *Aud. Syn.* p. 65.

120. Sylvia Delafieldii, *Aud.* — Delafield's Warbler.

Male, with a black band across forehead; upper parts of head, light grayish blue, tinged with green ; rest of upper parts, yellowish green ; lower parts, rich yellow; sides, greenish yellow. *Male*, 5¼. Habitat, North California.

Sylvia Delafieldii, *Aud.* v. 307. — Trichas Delafieldii, *Aud. Syn.* p. 65.

SUBGENUS HELINAIA, *Aud.*

121. Sylvia Swainsonii, *Aud.* — Swainson's Warbler.

Upper parts, olive brown ; head, tinged with red ; lower parts and band over eye, yellowish gray; abdomen, whitish. *Male*, 5¼, 8½. Habitat, from South Carolina to Massachusetts.

Sylvia Swainsonii, *Aud.* ii. 563 ; v. 462; plate 198. — Helinaia Swainsonii, *Aud. Syn.* p. 66.

122. Sylvia vermivora, *Lath.* — Worm-eating Warbler, *Wilson*, p. 237.

Sylvia vermivora, *Bonap. Syn.* p. 86. *Aud.* i. 177 ; v. 460 ; plate 34. — Helinaia vermivora, *Aud. Syn.* p. 66.

123. Sylvia Protonotarius, *Lath.* — Prothonotary Warbler, *Wilson*, p. 236.

Sylvia Protonotarius, *Bonap. Syn.* p. 86. *Nutt.* i. 410. *Aud.* i. 22; v. 460 ; plate 3. — Helinaia Protonotarius, *Aud. Syn.* p. 67.

124. Sylvia chrysoptera, *Linn.* — Golden-winged Warbler, *Wilson*, p. 170.

Sylvia chrysoptera, *Bonap. Syn.* p. 87. *Nutt.* i. 411. *Aud.* v. 154. — Helinaia chrysoptera, *Aud. Syn.* p. 67.

125. Sylvia Bachmanii, *Aud.* — Bachman's Warbler.

Male, with upper parts, yellowish green; crown, black; hind neck, gray; forehead, line over eye, cheeks, chin, and breast, yellow ; black patch on fore neck. Female, with tints fainter. *Male*, 4 1/12, 6¼. *Female*, 3⅝. Habitat, South Carolina.

Sylvia Bachmanii, *Aud.* ii. 483 ; plate 185. — Helinaia Bachmanii, *Aud. Syn.* p. 68.

126. Sylvia carbonata, *Aud.* — Carbonated Warbler.

Upper part of head, black; back and sides, dusky green, spotted with black ; line over eye and under parts, yellow. *Male*, 4¾. Habitat, Kentucky.

Sylvia carbonata, *Aud.* i. 308 ; plate 60. — Helinaia carbonata, *Aud. Syn.* p. 68.

127. Sylvia peregrina, *Wilson.* — Tennessee Warbler, *Wilson*, p. 243.

Sylvia peregrina, *Bonap. Syn.* p. 87. *Nutt.* i. 412. *Aud.* ii. 307 ; plate 154. — Helinaia peregrina, *Aud. Syn.* p. 68.

128. Sylvia solitaria, *Wilson.* — Blue winged Yellow Warbler, *Wilson*, p. 167.

Sylvia solitaria, *Bonap. Syn.* p. 87. *Nutt.* i. 410. *Aud.* i. 102. — Helinaia solitaria, *Aud. Syn.* p. 69 ; plate 20.

129. Sylvia celata, *Say.* — Orange-crowned Warbler.

Male, with upper parts, dull green; rump, yellowish green; crown, orange, concealed by the gray tips; lower parts, dull olivaceous yellow. Female, with crown duller. *Male*, 5½, 7$\frac{11}{12}$. Habitat, Texas to Nova Scotia. Eggs, four, green, with black spots.

Sylvia celata, *Bonap. Syn.* p. 88; *Orn.* i. 45. *Nutt.* i. 413. *Aud.* ii. 449; plate 178. — Helinaia celata, *Aud. Syn.* p. 69.

130. Sylvia rubricapilla, *Wilson.* — Nashville Warbler, *Wilson*, p. 266.

Sylvia rubricapilla, *Bonap. Syn.* p. 87. *Nutt.* i. 412. *Aud.* i. 450; plate 89. — Helinaia rubricapilla, *Aud. Syn.* p. 70.

SUBGENUS MNIOTILTA, *Vieill.*

131. Sylvia varia. — Black and White Creeper, *Wilson*, p. 205.

Sylvia varia, *Bonap. Syn.* p. 81. — Certhia varia, *Aud.* i. 452; v. 471. *Nutt.* i. 384. — Mniotilta varia, *Aud. Syn.* p. 71, plate 90.

GENUS II. — TROGLODYTES, *Cuv.* — WREN.

132. Troglodytes obsoletus, *Say.* — Rock Wren.

Upper parts, yellowish brown, and, excepting rump, barred with grayish brown; wings, similarly barred; lower parts, grayish white; sides, yellowish red. *Female*, 6. Habitat, Rocky Mountains and Columbia River.

Troglodytes obsoleta, *Bonap. Orn.* i 6. *Nutt.* i. 435. *Aud.* iv. 443; plate 36; *Syn.* p. 73.

133. Troglodytes Ludovicianus, *Bonap.* — Carolina Wren, *Wilson*, p. 137.

Troglodytes Ludovicianus, *Bonap. Syn.* p. 93. *Nutt.* i. 429. *Aud.* i. 399; v. 466; plate 78; *Syn.* p. 74.

134. Troglodytes ædon, *Vieill.* — House Wren, *Wilson*, p. 87.

Troglodytes ædon, *Bonap. Syn.* p. 92. *Nutt.* i. 422. *Rich. & Swain.* ii. 316. *Aud.* i. 427; v. 470; plate 83; *Syn.* p. 75.

135. Troglodytes palustris, *Wilson.* — Marsh Wren, *Wilson*, p. 135.

Troglodytes palustris, *Bonap. Syn.* p. 93. *Nutt.* i. 439. *Rich. & Swain.* ii. 319. *Aud.* i. 500; v. 467; plate 100; *Syn.* p. 76.

136. Troglodytes hyemalis, *Vieill.* — Winter Wren, *Wilson*, p. 94.

Troglodytes hyemalis, *Rich. & Swain.* ii. 318. *Nutt.* i. 427. *Aud.* iv. 430; plate 360; *Syn.* p. 76. — Troglodytes Europeus, *Bonap. Syn.* p. 93.

137. Troglodytes Bewickii, *Aud.* — Bewick's Wren.

Upper parts, dusky brown, tinged with gray; lower parts, grayish white; sides, tinged with brown; yellowish white band from mandible half way down neck. *Male*, 5, 6½. Habitat, from Pennsylvania to the south-west.

Troglodytes Bewickii, *Aud.* i. 96; v. 467; plate 18; *Syn.* p. 74. *Nutt.* i. 434.

138. Troglodytes Americanus, *Aud.* — Wood Wren.

Upper parts, reddish brown; lower parts, brownish gray; barred on neck, breast, sides, and abdomen. *Male*, 4$\frac{7}{8}$, 6¾. Habitat, Maine and

Vermont. Nests in the ground. Eggs, clay color, with purplish red blotches and lines.

Troglodytes Americana, *Aud.* ii. 452 , v. 469 ; *Syn.* p. 75, plate 179.

139. Troglodytes Parkmanii, *Aud.* — Parkman's Wren.

Upper parts, reddish brown, barred with dusky ; lower parts, dull brownish white. Length, 4⅙. Habitat, Columbia River.

Troglodytes Parkmanii, *Aud.* v. 310 ; *Syn.* p. 76.

140. Troglodytes brevirostris, *Nutt.* — Short-billed Marsh Wren.

Upper parts, brownish black, intermingled with white ; streak over eye, pale yellow ; throat and breast, grayish white ; lower parts, reddish brown. *Male*, 4⅜, 5⅝. Nest, spherical, built in reeds. Eggs, six, pure white. Habitat, from Massachusetts, south.

Troglodytes brevirostris, *Nutt.* i. 436. *Aud.* ii. 427 ; v. 469 ; *Syn.* p. 77 ; plate 175.

GENUS III.—REGULUS.

141. Regulus Cuvieri, *Aud.* — Cuvier's Regulus.

Upper parts, dull grayish olive ; forehead, lore, and line over eye, black ; band across forehead, grayish white ; semilunar band, enclosing a vermilion space, on sides of head, black ; lower parts, grayish white. *Male*, 4¼, 6. Habitat, Pennsylvania.

Regulus Cuvieri, *Aud.* i 228 ; plate 55 ; *Syn.* p. 84. *Nutt.* i. 416.

142. Regulus satrapa, *Licht.* — American Regulus, *Wilson*, p. 84.

Regulus cristatus, *Bonap. Syn.* p. 91. — Regulus tricolor, *Nutt.* i. 420. *Aud.* ii. 456 ; plate 183. — Regulus satrapa, *Aud. Syn.* p. 82.

143. Regulus calendula, *Linn.* — Ruby-crowned Regulus, *Wilson*, p. 55.

Regulus calendula, *Bonap. Syn.* p. 91. *Nutt.* i. 415. *Aud.* ii. 456 ; plate 195 ; *Syn.* p. 83.

GENUS IV.—SIALIA, *Swain.*

144. Sialia Wilsonii, *Swain.* — Blue-Bird, *Wilson*, p. 37.

Sialia Wilsonii, *Aud. Syn.* p. 84. — Saxicola sialis, *Bonap. Syn.* p. 39. — Erythaca Wilsonii, *Rich. & Swain.* ii. 210. — Ampelis sialis, *Nutt.* i. 444. — Sylvia sialis, *Aud.* ii. 84 ; v. 452 ; plate 113.

145. Sialia occidentalis, *Towns.* — Western Blue-Bird.

Male, with upper parts and throat, ultramarine blue ; fore part of back, breast, and sides, chestnut red ; lower parts, light blue : abdomen, whitish. Female, upper parts, dull grayish blue ; back, tinged with brown ; under parts, pale red ; abdomen, light gray. *Male*, 7. *Female*, 6¾. Habitat, North California and Oregon. Nests in holes of trees.

Sialia occidentalis, *Aud.* v. 41 ; plate 393 ; *Syn.* p. 84.

146. Sialia arctica, *Swain.* — Arctic Blue-Bird.

Male, upper parts, ultramarine, with a tinge of green ; head, neck, and part of breast, light greenish blue, fading into white, behind. Female, upper parts, grayish brown ; rump and wing-coverts, blue ; neck and anterior portion of the breast, reddish gray ; lower parts, brownish-gray.

Male, 7¼. *Female*, 6¾. Habitat, Fur Countries, Rocky Mountains, and Columbia River.

Erythaca arctica, *Rich. & Swain.* ii. 209. — Sialia arctica, *Nutt.* ii. 573. *Aud.* v. 38; plate 393; *Syn.* p. 84.

FAMILY VIII. — CERTHIADÆ, *Vigors.* .

GENUS I. — CERTHIA, *Linn.* — CREEPER.

147. Certhia familiaris, *Linn.* — Brown Creeper, *Wilson*, p. 81.

Certhia familiaris, *Bonap. Syn.* p. 95. *Nutt.* i. 585. *Aud.* v. 158; plate 415; *Syn.* p. 72.

GENUS II. — PARUS, *Linn.* — TIT.

148. Parus bicolor, *Linn.* — Tufted Tit, *Wilson*, p. 92.

Parus bicolor, *Bonap. Syn.* p. 100. *Nutt.* i. 236. *Aud.* i. 199; v. 472; plate 39; *Syn.* p. 78.

149. Parus atricapillus, *Linn.* — Black-Cap Tit, *Wilson*, p. 91.

Parus atricapillus, *Bonap. Syn.* p. 100. *Nutt.* i. 241. *Aud.* iv. 374; plate 353; *Syn.* p. 79.

150. Parus Carolinensis, *Aud.* — Carolina Tit.

Differs from the preceding only in size, and in having cheeks and neck white, and under parts grayish white, tinged with yellow. *Male*, 4¼, 6. Habitat, from New Jersey, south. Breeds in hollow stumps. Eggs, pure white.

Parus Carolinensis, *Aud.* ii. 341; v. 414; plate 160; *Syn.* p. 78.

151. Parus Hudsonicus, *Lath.* — Hudson's Bay Tit.

Upper parts, light brown, tinged with gray; fore neck, black; cheeks, sides of neck, breast, and abdomen, white; sides, yellowish brown. *Male*, 5, 7. Habitat, from Massachusetts to Hudson's Bay. Nests in hollow stumps.

Parus Hudsonicus, *Aud.* ii. 543; plate 194; *Syn.* p. 79.

152. Parus Rufescens, *Towns.* — Chestnut-backed Tit.

Head and hind neck, dark brown; fore neck, of a deeper tint; cheeks and sides of neck, white; back, rump, and sides, chestnut; lower parts, grayish white. *Male*, 4½. Habitat, Columbia River.

Parus rufescens, *Aud.* iv. 371; plate 353; *Syn.* p. 80.

153. Parus minimus, *Towns.* — Chestnut-crowned Tit.

Head and hind neck, pale brown; upper parts, brownish gray; lower parts, brownish white; sides, tinged with reddish. *Male*, 4½. Habitat, Columbia River. Nest on bushes, shaped like a long purse, with entrance at top. Eggs, six, pure white.

Parus minimus, iv. 382; plate 353; *Syn.* p. 80.

FAMILY IX. — VIREONINÆ, *Aud.*

GENUS VIREO, *Vieill.*

154. **Vireo flavifrons, *Vieill.* — Yellow-throated Vireo, *Wilson*, p. 77.**
Vireo flavifrons, *Bonap. Syn.* p. 70. *Nutt.* i. 302. *Aud.* ii. 119; v. 428; plate 119; *Syn.* p. 160.

155. **Vireo solitarius, *Vieill.* — Solitary Vireo, *Wilson*, p. 186.**
Vireo solitarius, *Bonap. Syn.* p. 79. *Nutt.* i. 305. *Aud.* i. 147; v. 342; plate 28; *Syn.* p. 160.

156. **Vireo Noveboracensis, *Gmel.* — White-eyed Vireo, *Wilson*, p. 200.**
Vireo Noveboracensis, *Bonap. Syn.* p. 70. *Nutt.* i. 306. *Aud.* i. 328; v. 431 and 483; plate 63; *Syn.* p. 161.

157. **Vireo gilvus, *Vieill.* — Warbling Vireo, *Wilson*, p. 385.**
Vireo gilvus, *Bonap. Syn.* p. 70. *Nutt.* i. 309. *Aud.* ii. 114; v. 433; plate 118; *Syn.* p. 161.

158. **Vireo Bartrami, *Swain.* — Bartram's Vireo.**
Upper parts, light yellowish olive; crown, deep gray, bordered by a blackish line; band, from nostril over eye, yellowish white; lower parts, grayish white; sides, greenish yellow. *Male*, 4½, 7¾. Nest, pensile. Eggs, pure white.
Vireo Bartrami, *Swain. & Rich.* ii. 235. *Aud.* v. 296; plate 435; *Syn.* p. 161.

159. **Vireo olivaceus, *Linn.* — Red-eyed Vireo, *Wilson*, p. 133.**
Vireo olivaceus, *Bonap. Syn.* p. 71. *Rich. & Swain.* ii. 233. *Aud.* ii. 287; v. 430; plate 150; *Syn.* p. 162.

FAMILY X. — PIPRADÆ, *Vigors.*

GENUS I. — ICTERIA, *Vieill.*

160. **Icteria viridis, *Gmel.* — Yellow-breasted Chat, *Wilson*, p. 60.**
Icteria viridis, *Bonap. Syn.* p. 69. *Nutt.* i. 299. *Aud.* ii. 223; v. 433; plate 137; *Syn.* p. 163.

GENUS II. — BOMBYCILLA, *Briss.* — WAX-WING.

161. **Bombycilla garrula, *Vieill.* — Bohemian Wax-Wing.**
Differing from the following species principally in size. *Male*, 9¾, 16¼. Habitat, from Massachusetts to the north.
Bombycilla garrula, *Bonap. Syn.* p. 438; *Orn.* ii. 16. *Rich & Swain.* ii. 237. *Nutt.* ii. 579. *Aud.* iv. 464; plate 363; *Syn.* p. 165.

162. **Bombycilla Carolinensis, *Briss.* — Cedar Bird, *Wilson*, p. 70.**
Bombycilla Carolinensis, *Bonap. Syn.* p. 59. *Nutt.* i. 248. *Aud.* i. 227; v. 494; plate 43; *Syn.* p. 165.

59 *

FAMILY XI. — ALAUDINÆ, *Aud.*

GENUS ALAUDA, *Linn.* — LARK.

163. Alauda alpestris, *Linn.* — Shore Lark, *Wilson*, p. 57.

Nests on the ground. Eggs, five, clay colored, spotted with brown. Habitat, from Texas to Labrador.

Alauda alpestris, *Bonap. Syn.* p. 102. *Rich. & Swain.* ii. 245. *Nutt.* i. 455. *Aud.* ii. 570 ; v. 588 ; plate 200 ; *Syn.* p. 96.

FAMILY XII. — FRINGILLIDÆ. — FINCHES.

GENUS I. — FRINGILLA. — FINCH.

164. Fringilla iliaca, *Bonap.* — Fox-colored Sparrow, *Wilson*, p. 223.

Nests on ground. Eggs, five, light green, blotched and spotted with brown. Habitat, from Labrador south.

Fringilla iliaca, *Bonap. Syn.* p. 112. *Rich. & Swain.* ii. 257. *Nutt.* i. 514. *Aud.* ii. 58 ; v. 512 ; plate 108 ; *Syn.* p. 119.

165. Fringilla Townsendi, *Aud.* — Townsend's Finch.

Upper parts, dark olivaceous brown, with a tinge of red ; sides of neck and body, and feathers of leg, similar ; rest, white, with brown triangular spots. *Female*, 7, 10½. Habitat, Rocky Mountains.

Fringilla Townsendi, *Aud.* v. 236 ; plate 424 ; *Syn.* p. 119.

166. Fringilla cinerea, *Gmel.* — Brown Finch.

Upper parts, brownish gray, tinged with olive and streaked with reddish brown ; three bluish gray bands on head ; on cheek, a white line, and beneath it a dusky brown band ; throat and fore part of neck, white, with reddish brown streaks ; middle of breast, yellowish white ; sides, dark yellowish brown. *Male*, 6, 8. Habitat, North California. Nest and eggs hardly distinguishable from those of the Song Sparrow.

Fringilla cinerea, *Aud.* v. 22 ; plate 390 ; *Syn.* p. 119.

167. Fringilla melodia, *Wilson.* — Song Sparrow, *Wilson*, p. 176.

Fringilla melodia, *Bonap. Syn.* p. 108. *Nutt.* i. 486. *Aud.* i. 126 ; v. 507 ; plate 25 ; *Syn.* p. 120.

168. Fringilla Mortoni, *Aud.* — Morton's Finch.

Head, ash gray ; longitudinal band, on side, black ; externally, one of grayish white ; throat, white, surrounded with a black band ; band round the neck, chestnut ; lower parts, dull brownish white ; sides, grayish brown. *Male*, 5¼. Habitat, North California.

Fringilla Mortoni, *Aud.* v. 314 ; *Syn.* p. 120.

169. Fringilla Pennsylvanica, *Lath.* — White-throated Sparrow, *Wilson*, p. 222.

Nests on the ground. Eggs, four, green, marked with reddish brown.

Fringilla Pennsylvanica, *Bonap. Syn.* p. 108 ; *Rich. & Swain.* ii. 256. *Nutt.* i. 481. *Aud.* i. 42 ; v. 497 ; plate 8 ; *Syn.* p. 121.

170. Fringilla leucophrys, *Gmel.* — White-crowned Finch, *Wilson*, p. 295.

Nests on the ground. Eggs, five, sea green, blotched with brown.

Fringilla leucophrys, *Bonap. Syn.* p. 107. *Nutt.* i. 479. *Rich. & Swain.* ii. 255. *Aud.* ii. 88; v. 515; plate 114; *Syn.* p. 121.

171. Fringilla atricapilla, *Gmel.* — Black and Yellow-crowned Finch.

Upper part of head, black; median, longitudinal band, yellow, changing behind to gray; upper parts, yellowish brown, tinged with gray; two bands across wing, white; throat, neck, and breast, light gray; abdomen, brownish white. *Male*, 8.

Emberiza atricapilla, *Aud.* v. 47; plate 394. — Fringilla atricapilla, *Aud. Syn.* p. 122.

172. Fringilla graminea, *Gmel.* — Bay-winged Finch, *Wilson*, p. 296.

Fringilla graminea, *Bonap. Syn.* p. 108. *Rich. & Swain.* ii. 254. *Nutt.* i. 482. *Aud.* i. 473; v. 502; plate 90. — Emberiza graminea, *Aud. Syn.* p. 102.

173. Fringilla passerina, *Wilson.* — Yellow-winged Sparrow, *Wilson*, p. 239.

Fringilla passerina, *Bonap. Syn.* p. 109. *Nutt.* i. 494. *Aud.* ii. 180; v. 497; plate 130. — Emberiza passerina, *Aud. Syn.* p. 103.

174. Fringilla pusilla, *Wilson.* — Field Sparrow, *Wilson*, p. 174.

Fringilla pusilla, *Bonap. Syn.* p. 110. *Nutt.* i. 499. *Aud.* ii. 229; plate 139. — Emberiza pusilla, *Aud. Syn.* p. 104.

175. Fringilla socialis, *Wilson.* — Chipping Sparrow, *Wilson*, p. 177.

Fringilla socialis, *Bonap. Syn.* p. 109. *Nutt.* i. 497. *Aud.* ii. 21; v. 517; plate 104. — Emberiza socialis, *Aud. Syn.* p. 105.

176. Fringilla Canadensis, *Lath.* — Tree Sparrow, *Wilson*, p. 175.

Fringilla Canadensis, *Bonap. Syn.* p. 109. *Rich. & Swain.* ii. 252. *Nutt.* i. 495 *Aud.* ii. 511; v. 504; plate 188. — Emberiza Canadensis, *Aud. Syn.* p. 105.

SUBGENUS NIPHÆA, *Aud.*

177. Fringilla hyemalis, *Linn.* — Snow Bird, *Wilson*, p. 178.

Nests on the ground. Eggs, four, yellowish white, spotted with red. One nest only as yet known to naturalists.

Fringilla hyemalis, *Bonap. Syn.* p. 109. *Rich. & Swain.* ii. 259. *Nutt.* i. 491. *Aud.* i. 72; v. 505, plate 13. — Niphæa hyemalis, *Aud. Syn.* p. 106.

178. Fringilla Oregona, *Towns.* — Oregon Snow Bird.

Head, neck, and portion of breast, black; lower parts, white; sides, tinged with brown; back, reddish brown; rump, dull gray. Female, with head and neck, blackish gray; back, brownish red. *Male*, 6¼. Habitat, Columbia River.

Fringilla Oregona, *Aud.* v. 68; plate 398. — Niphæa Oregona, *Aud. Syn.* p. 107.

SUBGENUS AMMODRAMUS, *Swain.*

179. Fringilla maritima, *Wilson.* — Sea-Side Finch, *Wilson*, p. 311.

Fringilla maritima, *Bonap. Syn.* p. 110. *Nutt.* i. 505. *Aud.* i. 471; plate 93. — Ammodramus maritimus, *Aud. Syn.* p. 109.

180. **Fringilla Macgillivrayi**, *Aud.* — Macgillivray's Finch.

Upper parts, dull olivaceous gray, streaked with blackish brown; yellowish brown streak over eye; throat and fore neck, grayish white; breast and sides, yellowish gray. marked with brownish black streaks; breast and abdomen, grayish white, tinged with yellowish brown. *Male*, 5½, 7¾ Habitat, Texas and along the Gulf of Mexico.

Fringilla Macgillivrayi, *Aud.* ii. 285; iv. 394; v. 499; plate 355. — Ammodramus Macgillivrayi, *Aud. Syn.* p. 110.

181. **Fringilla caudacuta**, *Lath.* — Sharp-tailed Finch, *Wilson*, p. 312.

Fringilla caudacuta, *Bonap. Syn.* p. 110. *Nutt.* i. 504. *Aud.* ii. 281; v. 499; plate 149. — Ammodramus caudacutus, *Aud. Syn.* p. 111.

182. **Fringilla palustris**, *Wilson.* — Swamp Sparrow, *Wilson*, p. 220.

Fringilla palustris, *Bonap. Syn.* p. 110. *Aud.* i. 331; v. 508. — Fringilla Georgiana, *Nutt.* i. 502. — Ammodramus palustris, *Aud. Syn.* p. 111; plate 64.

SUBGENUS PEUCÆA, *Aud.*

183. **Fringilla Bachmanii**, *Aud.* — Bachman's Finch.

Upper parts, brownish red, tinged with bluish gray; band over eye, ochre yellow; throat, pale yellowish gray, with two short dusky streaks on each side; lower parts, light yellowish gray. *Male*, 6, 7½. Habitat, South Carolina.

Fringilla Bachmanii, *Aud.* ii. 366; plate 165. — Peucæa Bachmanii, *Aud. Syn.* p. 112.

184. **Fringilla Lincolnii**, *Aud.* — Lincoln's Finch.

Upper parts, yellowish, streaked with brownish black; grayish blue band on head; throat, white, streaked, and spotted with dusky; fore part of breast and sides, grayish yellow, streaked with dusky; lower parts, grayish white. *Male*, 5¾, 8⅙. Habitat, Labrador.

Fringilla Lincolnii, *Aud.* ii. 539; plate 193. — Peucæa Lincolnii, *Aud. Syn.* p. 113.

SUBGENUS LINARIA, *Ray.*

185. **Fringilla borealis**, *Temm.* — Mealy Redpoll Linnet.

Male, head, crimson; cheeks, sides, and rump, carmine; band on forehead and throat, black; upper parts, dusky, streaked with brownish white; lower parts, grayish white. *Male*, 5¼, 9. Habitat, Labrador and Columbia River.

Fringilla borealis, *Aud.* v. 87; plate 375. — Linaria borealis, *Aud. Syn.* p. 114.

186. **Fringilla linaria**, *Wilson.* — Lesser Redpoll, *Wilson*, p. 288.

Fringilla linaria, *Bonap. Syn.* p. 112. *Rich. & Swain.* i. 267. *Nutt.* i. 512. *Aud.* iv. 533; plate 375. — Linaria minor, *Aud. Syn.* p. 114.

187. **Fringilla pinus**, *Wilson.* — Pine Finch, *Wilson*, p. 180.

Fringilla pinus, *Bonap. Syn.* p. 111. *Nutt.* i. 511. *Aud.* ii. 455; v. 509; plate 180. — Linaria pinus, *Aud. Syn.* p. 115.

SUBGENUS ERYTHROSPIZA, *Bonap.*

188. **Fringilla purpurea**, *Gmel.* — Purple Finch, *Wilson*, pp. 79 and 386.

Nest, found in Roxbury, on a low tree. Eggs, four, green, spotted with black, elongated.

Fringilla purpurea, *Bonap. Syn.* p. 114. *Rich. & Swain.* ii. 264. *Aud.* i. 24; v. 200; plate 4. — Erythrospiza purpurea, *Aud. Syn.* p. 125.

189. Fringilla frontalis, *Say.* — Crimson-fronted Finch.

Forehead, and band over eye, crimson ; throat, breast, sides, and rump, carmine ; upper parts, grayish brown, tinged with crimson ; lower parts, yellowish white. *Male*, 6¼. Habitat, Rocky Mountains.

Pyrrhula frontalis, *Bonap. Orn.* i. 1. *Nutt.* i. 534. — Fringilla frontalis, *Aud.* v. 230; plate 424. — Erythrospiza frontalis, *Aud. Syn.* p. 125.

190. Fringilla tephrocotis, *Swain.* — Gray-crowned Finch.

Plumage, umber brown ; head, ash gray, spotted with black ; wing-coverts, rump, and sides, tinged with rose red. *Male*, 6. Habitat, Saskatchewan River.

Fringilla tephrocotis, *Aud.* v. 232; plate 424. — Erythrospiza tephrocotis, *Aud. Syn.* p. 126.

GENUS II. — EMBERIZA, *Linn.* — BUNTING.

191. Emberiza Americana, *Gmel.* — Black-throated Bunting, *Wilson*, p. 36.

Emberiza Americana, *Aud.* iv. 599; plate 384; *Syn.* p. 101. — Fringilla Americana, *Bonap. Syn.* p. 107. *Nutt.* i. 461

192. Emberiza Townsendii, *Aud.* — Townsend's Bunting.

Head, cheeks, neck, breast, and sides, deep bluish gray ; head, streaked with black ; back, yellowish brown, streaked with dusky ; rump, yellowish gray ; line over eye, white ; throat, white, with two black bands ; abdomen, grayish white. *Male*, 5¾, 9. Habitat, Pennsylvania ; only one ever found.

Emberiza Townsendii, *Aud.* ii. 183; v. 90; plate 400; *Syn.* p. 101.

193. Emberiza grammaca, *Say.* — Lark Bunting.

Male, three bands of white on head, with two of chestnut between ; upper parts, light grayish brown, streaked with dusky except on back and rump ; two yellowish white bands on wings ; tail, except middle feather, tipped with white ; white streak beneath eye ; cheeks, chestnut, with anterior black spot, under them a broad white band ; lower parts, white. Female, head, like back ; sides, streaked with brown. *Male*, 6½, 8¼. Habitat, Upper Missouri.

Fringilla grammaca, *Bonap. Orn.* i. 47. *Nutt.* i. 480. *Aud.* v. 17; plate 390. Emberiza grammaca, *Aud. Syn.* p. 101.

194. Emberiza Savanna, *Bonap.* — Savannah Sparrow, *Wilson*, pp. 224 and 313.

Fringilla Savanna, *Bonap. Syn.* p. 109. *Nutt.* i. 489. *Aud.* ii. 63; v. 516; plate 109. — Emberiza Savanna, *Aud. Syn.* p. 103.

195. Emberiza pallida, *Swain.* — Clay-colored Bunting.

Upper parts, light yellowish brown, streaked with brownish black ; brownish white band over eye ; cheeks, pale brown ; sides of neck, very light buff ; lower parts, grayish white. *Male*, 5⅙. Habitat, Missouri Plains and Fur Countries.

Emberiza pallida, *Rich. & Swain.* ii. 251. *Aud.* v. 66; plate 398; *Syn.* p. 103.

196. Emberiza Henslowii, *Aud.* — Henslow's Bunting.

Upper parts, light yellowish brown, streaked with brownish black; back and scapulars, tinged with red; lower parts, light brownish yellow; sides, streaked with black. *Male,* 5. Habitat, from New York south.

Emberiza Henslowii, *Aud.* i. 360; v. 498; plate 70; *Syn.* p. 104.

SUBGENUS PLECTROPHANES, *Meyer.*

197. Emberiza Lapponica, *Linn.* — Lapland Lark Bunting.

Head and neck, black; white band over eye; brownish red crescent on hind neck; feathers on rest of upper parts, black, margined with yellowish red; lower parts, white; sides, streaked with black; plumage varies some in winter. Habitat, Fur Countries. Nests on the ground. Eggs, seven, ochre yellow, with brown spots.

Emberiza Lapponica, *Bonap. Orn.* i. 53. *Syn.* p. 440. *Rich. & Swain.* ii. 248. *Nutt.* i. 463. *Aud.* iv. 472; plate 365; *Syn.* p. 98.

198. Emberiza picta, *Swain.* — Painted Lark Bunting.

Head, deep black, with three bands of white on each side; upper parts, brownish yellow, spotted with black; band of white on smaller wing-coverts; lower parts and band across back, buffy orange. *Male,* $6\frac{1}{6}$.

Emberiza picta, *Rich. & Swain.* ii. 250. *Nutt.* ii. 589. *Aud.* v. 91; plate 400; *Syn.* p. 99.

199. Emberiza ornata, *Towns.* — Chestnut-collared Lark Bunting.

Top of head, streak, and spots behind ear, and breast, black; band over eye, throat, sides of neck, abdomen, lower tail-coverts, and three lateral tail-feathers, white; belt of yellowish red on hind neck; upper parts, gray, spotted with dusky, *Male,* 5¼. Habitat, Rocky Mountains.

Emberiza ornata, *Aud.* v. 44; plate 394. — Plectrophanes ornatus, *Aud. Syn.* p. 99.

200. Emberiza nivalis, *Linn.* — Snow Bunting, *Wilson,* p. 212.

Emberiza nivalis, *Bonap. Syn.* p. 103. *Rich. & Swain.* ii. 247. *Nutt.* i. 458. *Aud.* ii. 515; v. 496; *Syn.* p. 99; plate 189.

GENUS III. — SPIZA, *Bonap.* — PAINTED BUNTING.

201. Spiza Ciris, *Wilson.* — Blue-headed Bunting, *Wilson,* p. 234.

Fringilla Ciris, *Bonap. Syn.* p. 107. *Nutt.* i. 477 *Aud.* i. 279; v. 517; plate 53. — Spiza Ciris, *Aud. Syn.* p. 108.

202. Spiza cyanea, *Wilson.* — Indigo Bird, *Wilson,* p. 66.

Eggs, five, pure white.

Fringilla cyanea, *Bonap. Syn.* p. 107. *Nutt.* i. 473. *Aud.* i. 377; v. 503; plate 74. — Spiza cyanea, *Aud. Syn.* p. 108.

203. Spiza amœna, *Say.* — Lazuli Painted Bunting.

Male, upper parts, light greenish blue; loral space, black; two white bands on wing; broad yellowish red band on breast; lower parts, white. *Female,* upper parts, light yellowish brown; rump, greenish blue; fore parts, pale yellowish red, fading into white behind. *Male,* 5¼. Habitat, from Arkansas to Columbia River.

Fringilla amœna, *Bonap. Orn.* i. 61. *Syn.* p. 106. *Nutt.* i. 478. *Aud.* v. 64 and 230; plate 393. — Spiza amœna, *Aud. Syn.* p. 109.

GENUS IV.— CARDUELIS, *Cuv.*—GOLDFINCH.

204. Carduelis tristis. American Goldfinch, *Wilson,* p. 7.

Nests in trees. Eggs, five, pure milk white. Wilson's description is wholly wrong.

Fringilla tristis, *Bonap. Syn.* p. 111. *Nutt.* i. 507. *Aud.* i. 172; v. 510; plate 33. — Carduelis Americana, *Rich. & Swain.* ii. 268. — Carduelis tristis, *Aud. Syn.* p. 116.

205. Carduelis Magellanicus, *Vieill.* — Black-headed Goldfinch.

Head and throat, black; back, rump, and lower parts, yellowish green; wings, black, with two bands of yellowish green. *Male,* 4¾. Habitat, Kentucky.

Fringilla Magellanica, *Aud.* v. 46; plate 394. — Carduelis Magellanicus, *Aud. Syn.* p. 116

206. Carduelis psaltria, *Say.* — Arkansas Goldfinch.

Head, black; neck, back, and scapulars, yellowish green, spotted with brown; pale yellow band on secondary coverts. Female, without black on head. *Male,* 4½, 8. Habitat, Rocky Mountains.

Fringilla psaltria, *Bonap. Syn.* p. 111. *Nutt.* i. 510. *Aud.* v. 85; plate 400. — Carduelis psaltria, *Aud. Syn.* p. 117.

207. Carduelis Yarrellii, *Aud.* — Yarrell's Goldfinch.

Upper part of head, black; upper parts, yellowish green and yellow; two bands on wings; lower parts, bright yellow. *Male,* 4. Habitat, Upper California.

Fringilla Mexicana, *Aud.* v. 282; plate 433. — Carduelis Yarrellii, *Aud. Syn.* p. 117.

208. Carduelis Stanleyi, *Aud.* — Stanley's Goldfinch.

Head, black; upper parts, yellowish green, streaked with dusky; wings with two bands; lower parts, greenish yellow, fading into white. *Male,* 4¾. Habitat, Upper California. Not figured.

Aud. Syn. p. 118.

GENUS V. — PIPILO, *Vieill.* — GROUND FINCH.

209. Pipilo arcticus, *Swain.* — Arctic Ground Finch.

Head, neck, breast, and upper parts, black; sides, and lower tail-coverts, orange red; lower parts, white. Female, brown, where male is black. *Male,* 8½. *Female,* 8. Habitat, Columbia River and Fur Countries.

Pyrgita arctica, *Rich. & Swain.* ii. 260. *Nutt.* ii. 589. — Fringilla arctica, *Aud.* v. 49; plate 394. — Pipilo arcticus, *Aud. Syn.* p. 123.

210. Pipilo erythrophthalmus. — Ground Robin, *Wilson,* pp. 121 and 159.

Fringilla erythrophthalma, *Bonap. Syn.* p. 112. *Nutt.* i. 515. *Aud.* i. 151; v. 511; plate 29. — Pipilo erythrophthalmus, *Aud. Syn.* p. 124.

GENUS VI. — CORYTHUS, *Cuv.* — PINE FINCH.

211. Corythus Enucleator. — Pine Grosbeak, *Wilson*, p. 53.

Pyrrhula enucleator, *Bonap. Syn.* p. 119. *Rich. & Swain.* ii. 262. *Nutt.* i. 535. *Aud.* iv. 414; plate 358. — Corythus enucleator, *Aud. Syn.* p. 127.

GENUS VII. — LOXIA, *Linn.* — CROSSBILL.

212. Loxia curvirostra, *Linn.* — Common Crossbill, *Wilson,* p. 291.

Loxia curvirostra, *Bonap. Syn.* p. 117. *Nutt.* i. 583. *Aud.* ii. 559; v. 511; plate 197; *Syn.* p. 128.

213. Loxia leucoptera, *Gmel.* — White-winged Crossbill, *Wilson,* p. 294.

Loxia leucoptera, *Bonap. Syn.* p. 117; *Orn.* ii. *Rich. & Swain.* ii. 263. *Nutt.* i. 540. *Aud.* iv. 467; plate 364; *Syn.* p. 129.

GENUS VIII. — CORYDALINA, *Aud.* — LARK FINCH.

214. Corydalina bicolor, *Towns.* — Prairie Lark Finch.

Male, black, tinged with gray; patch on wing, white. Female, smaller; upper parts, grayish brown; lower parts, white. *Male,* 7. Habitat, Platte River.

Fringilla bicolor, *Aud.* v 19; plate 390. — Corydalina bicolor, *Aud. Syn.* p. 130.

GENUS IX. — COCCOTHRAUSTES, *Brisson.* — BULLFINCH.

SUBGENUS PITYLUS, *Cuv.*

215. Coccothraustes cardinalis, *Linn.* — Cardinal Grosbeak, *Wilson,* p. 123.

Fringilla cardinalis, *Bonap. Syn.* p. 113. *Nutt.* i. 519. *Aud.* ii. 336; v. 514; plate 159. — Pitylus cardinalis, *Aud. Syn.* p. 131.

SUBGENUS COCCOBORUS, *Swain.*

216. Coccothraustes cœrulea. — Blue Grosbeak, *Wilson,* p. 240.

Fringilla cœrulea, *Bonap. Syn.* p. 114. *Nutt.* i. 529. *Aud.* ii. 140; v. 508; plate 127. — Coccoborus cœruleus, *Aud. Syn.* p. 132.

217. Coccothraustes Ludoviciana. — Rose-breasted Grosbeak, *Wilson,* p. 182.

Tanagra Ludoviciana, *Bonap. Syn.* p. 105. *Nutt.* i. p. 471. *Aud.* ii. 385; v. 90; plate 354. — Coccoborus Ludovicianus, *Aud. Syn.* p. 137.

218. Coccothraustes melanocephalus, *Swain.* — Black-headed Grosbeak.

Head, throat, wings, and tail, black; band on hind neck, fore parts and sides of neck, breast, and sides, dull reddish orange; middle of breast, axillars, and lower wing-coverts, light yellow; back, black, streaked with yellowish red; two white bands on wing. *Male,* 8½. Habitat, Rocky Mountains.

Fringilla melanocephala, *Aud.* iv. 519; plate 373. — Coccoborus melanocephalus, *Aud. Syn.* p. 133.

219. Coccothraustes vespertina, *Cooper.* — Evening Grosbeak.

Head and neck, black ; band over eyes, rump, axillars, abdomen, and lower tail-coverts, yellow ; line, margining base of bill, black ; cheeks, lower part of hind neck and throat, dark yellowish olive. Female, upper parts, brownish gray ; lower parts, pale gray. *Male,* 8. *Female,* 7½. Habitat, Columbia River.

> Fringilla vespertina, *Bonap. Orn.* ii. plate 14. *Syn.* p. 113. *Aud.* iv. 515 ; v. 235. — Coccothraustes vespertina, *Rich. & Swain.* ii. 269. *Nutt.* i. 594. *Aud. Syn.* p. 134.

GENUS X.—PYRANGA, *Vieill.*

220. Pyranga æstiva, *Gmel.* — Summer Red-Bird, *Wilson,* p. 63.

Nests in trees. Eggs, five, light blue.

> Tanagra æstiva, *Bonap. Syn.* p. 105. *Nutt.* i. 469. *Aud.* i. 232 ; v. 518 ; plate 44. — Pyranga æstiva, *Aud. Syn.* p. 136.

221. Pyranga rubra. — Scarlet Red-Bird, *Wilson,* p. 125.

> Pyranga rubra, *Bonap. Syn.* p. 105. *Rich. & Swain.* ii. 273. *Nutt.* i. 465. *Aud.* iv. 388 ; plate 354. — Pyranga rubra, *Aud. Syn.* p. 136.

222. Pyranga Ludoviciana, *Wilson.* — Louisiana Tanager, *Wilson,* p. 207.

> Tanagra Ludoviciana, *Bonap. Syn.* p. 105. *Nutt.* i. 471. *Aud.* iv. 385 ; v. 90 ; plates 354 and 400. — Pyranga Ludoviciana, *Aud. Syn.* p. 137.

FAMILY XIII.—STURNIDÆ, *Vigors.*

GENUS I.—ICTERUS.—TROOPIAL.

223. Icterus Baltimore, *Linn.* — Baltimore Oriole, *Wilson,* pp. 10 and 458.

> Icterus Baltimore, *Bonap. Syn.* p. 51. *Nutt.* i. 152. *Aud.* i. 66 ; v. 278 ; plates 12 and 423 ; *Syn.* p. 143.

224. Icterus Bullockii, *Swain.* — Bullock's Hangnest.

Head, hind neck, anterior portion of back and band on fore neck, deep black ; forehead, band over eye, cheek, sides of neck and breast, rich orange yellow ; lower parts, paler ; rump, yellow, tinged with green ; large white patch on wing. *Male,* 7¼. Habitat, Rocky Mountains, Columbia River, and California.

> Icterus Bullockii, *Aud.* v. 9 and 278 ; plates 388 and 433 ; *Syn.* p. 143.

225. Icterus spurius, *Gmel.* — Orchard Oriole, *Wilson,* p. 43.

> Icterus spurius, *Bonap. Syn.* p. 51. *Nutt.* i. 165. *Aud.* i. 221 ; v. 485 ; plate 42 ; *Syn.* p. 144.

SUBGENUS DOLICHONYX, *Swain.*

226. Icterus agripennis, *Bonap.* — Bob-o'Link, *Wilson,* p. 129.

> Icterus agripennis, *Bonap. Syn.* p. 53. *Nutt.* i. 185. *Aud.* i. 283 ; v. 286 ; plate 54. — Doliconyx oryzivora, *Aud. Syn.* p. 138. *Rich. & Swain.* ii. 278.

SUBGENUS MOLOTHRUS, *Swain.*

227. Icterus pecoris. — Cow Blackbird, *Wilson*, p. 187.

Icterus pecoris, *Bonap. Syn.* p. 53. *Nutt.* i. 178. *Aud.* i. 493 ; v. 233 and 490 ; plates 99 and 424. — Molothrus pecoris, *Aud. Syn.* p. 139. *Rich. & Swain.* ii. 277.

SUBGENUS AGELAIUS, *Swain.*

228. Icterus xanthocephalus, *Bonap.* — Saffron-headed Blackbird.

Head, neck, and breast, orange yellow ; two black bands over eye ; rest of plumage, glossy black, except two white bands on wings. Female, principally of a chocolate brown color. *Male*, 9. Habitat, California and Fur Countries.

Icterus icterocephalus, *Bonap. Orn.* i. 27. — Icterus xanthocephalus, *Bonap. Syn.* p. 52. *Rich. & Swain.* ii. 281. *Nutt.* i. 176. *Aud.* v. 6. *Syn.* p. 140 ; plate 388.

229. Icterus tricolor, *Aud.* — Red and White shouldered Blackbird.

Plumage, glossy, bluish black ; smaller wing-coverts, deep carmine ; their first row, white. *Male*, 9. Habitat, North California.

Icterus tricolor, *Aud.* i. ; plate 388 ; *Syn.* p. 141.

230. Icterus gubernator, *Aud.* — Red and Black shouldered Blackbird.

Plumage, glossy bluish black ; smaller wing-coverts, scarlet, their first row tinged with yellow, and broadly tipped with black. Female, principally of a brown color. *Male*, 9. Habitat, California.

Icterus gubernator, *Aud.* v. 211 ; plate 420 ; *Syn.* p. 141.

231. Icterus phœniceus, *Linn.* — Red-winged Blackbird, *Wilson*, p. 281.

Icterus phœniceus, *Bonap. Syn.* p. 62. *Rich. & Swain.* ii. 280. *Nutt.* i. 169. *Aud.* i. 348 ; v. 487 ; plate 67. — Agelaius phœniceus, *Aud. Syn.* p. 141.

GENUS II. — QUISCALUS, *Vieill.* — CROW BLACKBIRD.

232. Quiscalus major, *Vieill.* — Boat-tailed Crow Blackbird.

Resembling the following species to a great degree, differing from it principally in size and in its concave tail. *Male*, 15¾, 23¾. *Female*, 12⅝, 18. Nest and eggs also resemble those of the versicolor, but are larger.

Quiscalus major, *Bonap. Syn.* p. 54 ; *Orn.* i. 35. *Nutt.* i. 192. *Aud.* ii. 504 ; v. 480.

233. Quiscalus versicolor, *Vieill.* — Common Crow Blackbird, *Wilson*, p. 217.

Quiscalus versicolor, *Bonap. Syn.* p. 54 ; *Orn.* i. 42. *Nutt.* i. 194. *Aud.* i. 35 ; v. 481 ; *Syn.* p. 146.

234. Quiscalus ferrugineus, *Lath.* — Rusty Grakle, *Wilson*, p. 216.

Quiscalus ferrugineus, *Bonap. Syn.* p. 55. *Nutt.* i. 199. *Aud.* ii. 325 ; v. 483 ; plate 147 ; *Syn.* p. 146. — Scolecophagus ferrugineus, *Rich. & Swain.* ii. 286.

GENUS III. — STURNELLA, *Vieill.* — MEADOW STARLING.

235. Sturnella Ludoviciana, *Linn.* — Meadow Lark, *Wilson*, p. 203.

Sturnella Ludoviciana, *Rich. & Swain.* ii. 282. *Aud. Syn.* p. 148. — Sturnus Ludovicianus, *Bonap. Syn.* p. 50. *Nutt.* i. 147. *Aud.* ii. 216 ; v. 492 ; plate 136.

FAMILY XIV. — CORVIDÆ, *Vigors*.

GENUS I. — CORVUS, *Linn.* — CROWS.

236. Corvus Corax, *Linn.* — Raven, *Wilson*, p. 673.

Corvus Corax, *Bonap. Syn.* p. 56. *Rich. & Swain.* ii. 290. *Nutt.* i. 202. *Aud.* ii. 1; v. 476; plate 101; *Syn.* p. 150.

237. *Corvus Americanus, *Aud.* — American Crow, *Wilson*, p. 318.

Corvus Americanus, *Aud.* ii. 317; v. 477; plate 161; *Syn.* p. 150. — Corvus Corone, *Bonap. Syn.* p. 56. *Rich. & Swain.* ii. 291. *Nutt.* i. 209.

238. Corvus ossifragus, *Wilson.* — Fish Crow, *Wilson*, p. 343.

Corvus ossifragus, *Bonap. Syn.* p. 57. *Nutt.* i. 216. *Aud.* ii. 268; v. 479; plate 146; *Syn.* p. 151.

SUBGENUS PICA, *Briss.*

239. Corvus pica, *Linn.* — Common Magpie, *Wilson*, p. 316.

Corvus pica, *Bonap. Syn.* p. 57. *Nutt.* i. 219. *Aud.* iv. 408; plate 357. — Pica melanoleuca, *Aud. Syn.* p. 152.

240. Corvus Nuttallii, *Aud.* — Yellow-billed Magpie.

Similar to the above, except in the green of its head, the brown of its back, and its yellow bill. *Male*, 18. Habitat, Texas to Rocky Mountains.

Pica Nuttallii, *Aud. Syn.* p. 152. — Corvus Nuttallii, *Aud.* iv. 450; plate 362.

241. Corvus Bullockii, *Wagler.* — Columbian Magpie.

General color, blue; cheeks, fore neck, and anterior part of breast, black; lower parts and tips of outer tail-feathers, white. *Male*, 21, 36. Habitat, North California.

Corvus Bullockii, *Nutt.* i. 220. *Aud.* i. 283; plate 96. — Pica Bullockii, *Aud. Syn.* p. 152.

GENUS II. — GARRULUS, *Briss.* — JAY.

242. Garrulus Stelleri, *Gmel.* — Steller's Jay.

Head, neck, and back, brownish black; forehead, rump, and wings, blue; wing-coverts, ultramarine, barred with black; tail, blue, with dusky bars. *Male*, 13. Habitat, Rocky Mountains and Columbia River. Nests in trees. Eggs, four, pale green, with olive brown specks.

Corvus Stelleri, *Bonap. Orn.* ii. 44; *Syn.* p. 438. *Nutt.* i. 229. *Aud.* iv. 453; plate 362. — Garrulus Stelleri, *Rich. & Swain.* ii. 294. *Aud. Syn.* p. 153.

243. Garrulus cristatus, *Linn.* — Blue Jay, *Wilson*, p. 1.

Garrulus cristatus, *Rich. & Swain.* ii. 295. *Aud. Syn.* p. 154. — Corvus cristatus, *Nutt.* i. 224. *Bonap. Syn.* p. 58. *Aud.* ii. 11; v. 475; plate 102.

244. Garrulus ultramarinus, *Bonap.* — Ultramarine Jay.

Head, neck, sides, wing, and tail, light blue; back, light grayish brown;

---

* It seems unaccountable, that Wilson, familiar as he may be supposed to have been with the habits of the European species, should have confounded it with our Common Crow. They are quite distinct species.

lower parts, gray, passing into white. *Male*, 12. Habitat, Columbia River and Upper California.

Corvus ultramarinus, *Aud.* iv. 456 ; plate 362. — Garrulus ultramarinus, *Aud. Syn.* p. 154.

245. Garrulus Floridanus, *Bartram.* — Florida Jay.

Head, sides, and neck, light blue ; back, very light grayish brown ; band over forehead and eyes, bluish white ; fore neck, grayish white, bordered by a light blue band ; lower parts, purplish gray. *Male*, 11¼, 14. Habitat, Florida. Nests in trees. Eggs, four to six, olive, marked with black.

Corvus Floridanus, *Bonap.* p. 58. *Nutt.* i. 230. *Aud.* i. 444 ; plate 87. — Garrulus Floridanus, *Aud. Syn.* p. 154.

246. Garrulus Canadensis, *Linn.* — Canada Jay, *Wilson*, p. 211.

Garrulus Canadensis, *Rich. & Swain.* ii. 295 and 296. *Nutt.* i. 232 ; v. 599. *Aud. Syn.* p. 155. — Corvus Canadensis, *Bonap. Syn.* p. 58. *Aud.* ii. 53 ; v. 208.

GENUS III. — NUCIFRAGA, *Brisson.*

247. Nucifraga Columbiana. — Columbian Nutcracker, *Wilson*, p. 209.

Nucifraga Columbiana, *Aud.* iv. 459. *Syn.* p. 156 ; plate 362. — Corvus Columbianus, *Bonap. Syn.* p. 57. *Nutt.* i. 218.

FAMILY XV. — SITTINÆ, *Aud.*

GENUS SITTA. — NUTHATCH.

248. Sitta Carolinensis, *Linn.* — White-breasted Nuthatch, *Wilson*, p. 24.

Sitta Carolinensis, *Bonap. Syn.* p. 96. *Nutt.* i. 581. *Aud.* ii. 299 ; v. 473 ; plate 152 ; *Syn.* p. 167.

249. Sitta Canadensis, *Linn.* — Red-bellied Nuthatch, *Wilson*, p. 27.

Sitta Canadensis, *Bonap. Syn.* p. 96. *Nutt.* i. 583. *Aud.* ii. 84 ; v. 474 ; plate 125 ; *Syn.* p. 167.

250. Sitta pusilla, *Lath.* — Brown-headed Nuthatch, *Wilson*, p. 165.

Sitta pusilla, *Bonap. Syn.* p. 97. *Nutt.* i. 584. *Aud.* ii. 151 ; plate 125 ; *Syn.* p. 168.

251. Sitta pygmæa, *Vigors.* — Californian Nuthatch.

Head and neck, dull grayish brown ; back, dull leaden gray ; lower parts, brownish white. *Male*, 3⅚. Habitat, California. Habits and mode of breeding, unknown.

Sitta pygmæa, *Aud.* v. 163 ; plate 415 ; *Syn.* p. 168.

FAMILY XVI. — TROCHILIDÆ, *Vigors.*

GENUS TROCHILUS, *Linn.* — HUMMING BIRD.

252. Trochilus Mango, *Linn.* — Mango Humming Bird.

Head, neck, and back, green, with bronze and golden reflections ; tail, of mingled black, green, blue, steel blue, and purple ; neck and breast, black, margined with green ; lower parts, dark purple. *Male,* 4¾, 8. Habitat, Florida Keys.

Trochilus Mango, *Aud.* ii. 480 ; plate 184 ; *Syn.* p. 170.

253. Trochilus Anna, *Linn.* — Anna Humming Bird.

Head and throat, blood red, changing to gold and blue ; upper parts of golden green ; lower parts, brownish white. *Male,* 3⅚. Habitat, Rocky Mountains towards California. Nests in bushes. Eggs, two, pure white.

Trochilus Anna, *Aud.* v. 238 ; plate 425 ; *Syn.* p. 170.

254. Trochilus colubris, *Linn.* — Common Humming Bird, *Wilson,* p. 115.

Trochilus colubris, *Bonap. Syn.* p. 98. *Rich. & Swain.* p. 323. *Nutt.* i. 588. *Aud.* i. 248 ; v. 544 ; plate 47 ; *Syn.* p. 70.

SUBGENUS CELASPHORUS, *Swain.*

255. Trochilus rufus, *Gmel.* — Rufous Ruffed Humming Bird.

Upper parts, cinnamon orange, glossed with green and purple ; orange red bands above and below eye ; throat fire-red, changing to purple, yellow, &c. ; reddish white band on fore neck ; lower parts like upper ; abdomen, whitish. *Male,* 3 7/12. Habitat, from California to Nootka Sound. Nests in bushes. Eggs two, white.

Trochilus rufus, *Rich. & Swain.* ii. 324. *Aud.* iv. 555 ; plate 379. — Selasphorus rufus, *Aud. Syn.* p. 171.

FAMILY XVII. — PICIDÆ, *Vigors.*

GENUS PICUS, *Linn.* — WOODPECKER.

256. Picus imperialis, *Gould.* — Imperial Woodpecker.
Picus imperialis, *Bonap. Syn.* p. 44. *Nutt.* i. 564. *Aud.* i. 341 ; v. 525 ; plate 66 ; *Syn.* p. 175.

257. Picus principalis, *Linn.* — Ivory-billed Woodpecker, *Wilson,* p. 272.
Picus principalis, *Bonap. Syn.* p. 44. *Nutt.* i. 564. *Aud.* i. 341 ; v. 525 ; plate 66 ; *Syn.* p. 175.

258. Picus pileatus, *Linn.* — Pileated Woodpecker, *Wilson,* p. 279.
Picus pileatus, *Bonap. Syn.* p. 44. *Rich. & Swain.* ii. 304. *Nutt.* i. 567. *Aud.* ii. 74 ; v. 533 ; *Syn.* p. 176 ; plate 13.

259. Picus lineatus, *Linn.* — Lineated Woodpecker.

Head, carmine, dusky line from nostril to eye ; patch over ear, leaden gray ; line down neck, enlarging towards the tail, deep black ; band on side of head ; patch on wing, white ; crimson patch at base of lower jaw ; breast, black ; chin, yellowish white ; lower parts, brownish white, barred with black. *Male,* 15. Habitat, Columbia River.

Picus lineatus, *Aud.* v. 315 ; *Syn.* p. 176. Not figured.

260. Picus Canadensis, *Gmel.* — Canadian Woodpecker.

Head and neck, glossy black ; band over eye ; one from mouth, back-

60 *

wards, and lower parts, white; band on occiput, scarlet; band from bill to eye; narrow band from base of bill to shoulders; shoulders and four middle tail-feathers, black; outer one, partially white. *Male*, 10½, 17¾. Habitat, Fur Countries.

Picus Canadensis, *Aud.* v. 188; plate 417; *Syn.* p. 177. — Picus villosus, *Rich. & Swain.* ii. 305.

261. Picus Phillipsii, *Aud.* — Phillips's Woodpecker.

Head, orange yellow; hind neck, glossy black; white band over eye; black band joining another white one from mouth to eye; upper parts, black, tinged with brown; tail, as in preceding species; lower parts, white. *Male*, 10½. Habitat, Massachusetts, one specimen only found.

Picus Phillipsii, *Aud.* v. 186; plate 417; *Syn.* p. 177.

262. Picus Martinæ, *Aud.* — Martin's Woodpecker.

Head, scarlet; forehead and occiput, black; several black and white bands over eye, and from base of bill toward eye and neck; upper parts, black, in some places tipped and spotted with white; lower parts, white, tinged with gray and red. *Male*, 9⅙. Habitat, Canada.

Picus Martinæ, *Aud.* v. 181; plate 417; *Syn.* p. 178.

263. Picus Harrissii, *Aud.* — Harris's Woodpecker.

Head and hind neck, glossy black; bands of scarlet, black and white on occiput, and from bill toward eye and hind neck; upper parts, black; feathers along middle, tipped with white; lower parts, brownish white; has no white spots on wing-coverts. *Male*, 9. Habitat, Columbia River.

Picus Harrissii, *Aud.* v. 191; plate 417; *Syn.* p. 178.

264. Picus villosus, *Linn.* — Hairy Woodpecker, *Wilson*, p. 102.

Picus villosus, *Bonap. Syn.* p. 46. *Nutt* i. 575. *Aud.* v. 164; plate 416; *Syn.* p. 179.

265. Picus pubescens, *Linn.* — Downy Woodpecker, *Wilson*, p. 104.

Picus pubescens, *Bonap. Syn.* p. 46. *Rich. & Swain.* ii. 307. *Nutt.* i. 576. *Aud.* ii. 81; v. 539; plate 112; *Syn.* p. 180.

266. Picus Gairdneri, *Aud.* — Gairdner's Woodpecker.

Black above, with scarlet occipital band, brownish white beneath; spotted with white; spots smaller than in preceding. Length, 6¾. Habitat, Columbia River.

Picus Gairdneri, *Aud.* v. 317; *Syn.* p. 180. Not figured.

267. Picus querulus, *Wilson.* — Red-cockaded Woodpecker, *Wilson*, p. 164.

Nests in holes in trees. Eggs, four, white.

Picus querulus, *Bonap. Syn.* p. 46. *Nutt.* i. 577. *Aud.* v. 12; plate 389; *Syn.* p. 180.

268. Picus Auduboni, *Trudeau.* — Audubon's Woodpecker.

Upper parts, black; lower, white, with a tinge of brown; the sides very faintly barred with dusky; tufts covering the nostrils, white; head, yellowish; white band over eye, black one behind it; back tipped with white. *Adult*, 7, 13½. Habitat, Louisiana.

Picus Auduboni, *Aud.* v. 194; plate 417; *Syn.* p. 181.

269. Picus ruber, *Gmel.* — Red-breasted Woodpecker.

Head, neck, and breast, deep carmine; upper parts, black, variegated with white ; lower parts, yellow ; sides, undulated with dusky. *Male,* 8, 14. *Female,* 8. Habitat, Upper California. Nests in holes of trees. Eggs, four, pure white.

> Picus ruber, *Aud.* v. 179 ; plate 416 ; *Syn.* p. 181.

270. Picus varius, *Linn.* — Yellow-bellied Woodpecker, *Wilson,* p. 100.

> Picus varius, *Bonap. Syn.* p. 45. *Rich. & Swain.* ii. 309. *Nutt.* i. 574. *Aud.* i. 519 ; v. 537 ; plate 190 ; *Syn.* p. 182.

271. Picus Carolinus, *Linn.* — Red-bellied Woodpecker, *Wilson,* p. 75.

> Picus Carolinus, *Bonap. Syn.* p. 45. *Nutt.* i. 572. *Aud.* v. 469 ; plate 415 ; *Syn.* p. 183.

272. Picus erythrocephalus. — Red-headed Woodpecker, *Wilson,* p. 96.

> Picus erythrocephalus, *Bonap. Syn.* p. 45. *Rich. & Swain.* ii. 316. *Nutt.* i. 569. *Aud.* i. 141 ; v. 536 ; *Syn.* p. 184.

273. Picus torquatus, *Wilson.* — Lewis's Woodpecker, *Wilson,* p. 210.

> Picus torquatus, *Bonap. Syn.* p. 46. *Nutt.* i. 577. *Aud.* v. 176 ; plate 416 ; *Syn.* p. 184.

SUBGENUS APTERNUS, *Swain.*

274. Picus arcticus, *Swain.* — Arctic Three-toed Woodpecker.

Three-toed ; upper parts, glossy bluish black ; lower, white ; sides and wing-coverts, transversely barred with black ; crown, saffron yellow ; white line behind eye ; another succeeded by a black one from upper mandible to ear-coverts. Female, without yellow on head. *Male,* 10½, 16. Habitat, Massachusetts to Fur Countries.

> Picus tridactylus, *Bonap. Orn.* ii. 14. *Syn.* p. 46. *Nutt.* i. 578. *Rich. & Swain.* ii. 313. *Aud. Syn.* p. 182. — Picus tridactylus, *Aud.* ii. 198 ; plate 132.

275. Picus hirsutus, *Vieill.* — Banded Three-toed Woodpecker.

Three-toed ; upper parts, glossy black ; head, with blue reflections ; back and wings, tinged with brown ; anterior of head, yellow, spotted with white ; white band from bill to occiput ; back, banded with white. *Male,* 9. Habitat, Fur Countries.

> Picus tridactylus, *Rich. & Swain.* ii. 311. — Picus hirsutus, *Aud.* v. 184 ; plate 417 , *Syn.* p. 183.

SUBGENUS COLAPTES, *Swain.*

276. Picus auratus, *Linn* — Golden-winged Woodpecker, *Wilson,* p. 29.

> Picus auratus, *Bonap. Syn.* p. 44. *Nutt.* i. 561. *Aud.* i. 191 ; v. 550 ; plate 37 ; *Syn.* p. 184. — Colaptes auratus, *Rich. & Swain.* ii. 314.

277. Picus Mexicanus, *Swain.* — Red-shafted Woodpecker.

Head and neck, grayish brown ; forehead and band over eye, dull red ; carmine patch on each side of throat ; back, reddish brown, spotted with black ; rump, white ; tail-coverts, black, barred with white ; lower parts, reddish white ; black spots forming a semilunar patch on the forepart of breast. *Male,* 13½. *Female,* 13. Habitat, Rocky Mountains to the Saskatchawan.

> Picus Mexicanus, *Aud.* v. 174 ; plate 416. *Syn.* p. 184. — Colaptes Mexicanus, *Rich. & Swain.* ii. 315.

FAMILY XVIII. — CUCULIDÆ, *Vigors.*

GENUS COCCYZUS, *Vieill.* — AMERICAN CUCKOO.

278. Coccyzus Americanus, *Linn.* — Yellow-billed Cuckoo, *Wilson,* p. 267.

Coccyzus Americanus, *Bonap. Syn.* p. 42. *Nutt.* i. 551. *Aud.* i. 18; v. 520; plate 2; *Syn.* p. 187.

279. Coccyzus erythrophthalmus, *Wilson.* — Black-billed Cuckoo, *Wilson,* p. 269.

Coccyzus erythrophthalmus, *Bonap. Syn.* p. 42. *Nutt.* i. 556. *Aud.* i. 570; v. 523; plate 32; *Syn.* p. 187.

280. Coccyzus seniculus, *Lath.* — Mangrove Cuckoo.

Upper parts, greenish brown; head with a gray tinge; lower parts, brownish orange; outer tail-feathers tipped with white. *Male,* 12, 15. Habitat, Florida Keys. Nests in trees. Eggs, two, light green.

Coccyzus seniculus, *Nutt.* i. 558. *Aud.* ii. 390; plate 169; *Syn.* p. 188.

FAMILY XIX. — PSITTACIDÆ.

GENUS CENTURUS, *Ruhl.* — PARRAKEET.

281. Centurus Carolinensis. — Carolina Parrakeet, *Wilson,* p. 246.

Psittacus Carolinensis, *Bonap. Syn.* p. 41. *Nutt.* i. 545. *Aud.* i. 135; plate 26. — Centurus Carolinensis, *Aud. Syn.* p. 189.

ORDER III. — RASORES, *Vigors.*

FAMILY I. — COLUMBIDÆ.

GENUS COLUMBA, *Linn.* — DOVE.

282. Columba fasciata, *Say.* — Band-tailed Pigeon.

Head, fore neck, and breast, reddish purple, whitish towards abdomen; hind neck, greenish brown, with a white ring; upper parts, grayish blue; rump and sides, blue; tail, grayish blue, with a black band. *Male,* 16. *Female,* 15½. Habitat, Rocky Mountains to Columbia River. Eggs, two, placed on the ground without any nest, yellowish white with minute spots.

Columba fasciata, *Bonap. Syn.* p. 119; *Orn.* i. 77 *Nutt.* i. 624. *Aud.* iv. 479; *Syn.* p. 191; plate 367.

283. Columba leucocephala, *Linn.* — White-headed Pigeon.

Upper parts, grayish blue; lower, paler; head, white; hind neck, dark purplish brown; lower parts and sides, green, changing to gold, mixed with black. *Male,* 14¼, 23½. *Female,* 14. Habitat, Florida Keys. Nests in trees. Eggs, two, white.

Columba leucocephala, *Bonap. Syn.* p. 119; *Orn.* ii. 15. *Nutt.* i. 625. *Aud.* ii. 443; v. 557; plate 177; *Syn.* p. 191.

284. Columba Zenaida, *Bonap.* — Zenaida Dove.

Upper parts, light yellowish brown; middle tail-feathers, like back; the rest, grayish blue, with broad black band towards the end; extremity, bluish white; lower parts, light brownish red, paler on the throat, and passing into a grayish blue on the sides; lower wing-coverts, light blue: deep blue spot behind eye; another large, below, on neck. *Male*, 11½, 18½. *Female*, 10½. Habitat, Florida Keys. Nests on the ground. Eggs, two, pure white.

Columba Zenaida, *Bonap. Syn.* p. 119. *Nutt.* i. 625. *Aud.* ii. 354; v. 558; plate 162; *Syn.* p. 191.

285. Columba montana, *Linn.* — Key West Pigeon.

Upper parts, brownish red; head and hind neck, with purplish and green reflections; sides of neck, cream color, with lilac, green, blue, and purple tints; back, purplish red; broad band beneath eye and throat, white; neck and breast, purple; rest, cream colored. *Male*, 11¾, 17½. Habitat, Key West. Nests in trees. Eggs, two, pure white.

Columba montana, *Aud.* ii. 382; plate 167; *Syn.* p. 192.

286. Columba passerina, *Linn.* — Ground Dove, *Wilson*, p. 409.

Nests in bushes. Eggs, two, white.

Columba passerina, *Bonap. Syn.* p. 120. *Nutt.* i. 635. *Aud.* ii. 471; v. 558; plate 182; *Syn.* p. 192.

GENUS II. — GEOPHILUS, *Selby.* — GROUND PIGEON.

287. Geophilus cyanocephalus, *Selby.* — Blue-headed Ground Pigeon.

Upper parts, chocolate, tinged with olive; lower parts, brownish red; upper part of head, bright blue, encircled by a black band; band of white under eye; broad black patch on fore neck, margined with white beneath; on sides, a patch of light blue. *Male*, 12¼, 17½. Habitat, Florida Keys.

Columba cyanocephala, *Aud.* ii. 411; plate 172. — Starnœnas cyanocephala, *Aud. Syn.* p. 193.

GENUS III. — ECTOPISTES, *Swain.* — LONG-TAILED PIGEON.

288. Ectopistes migratoria, *Linn.* — Passenger Pigeon, *Wilson*, p. 394.

Columba migratoria, *Bonap. Syn.* p. 120. *Rich. & Swain.* ii. 363. *Nutt.* i. 629. *Aud.* i. 319; v. 561; plate 62. — Ectopistes migratoria, *Aud. Syn.* p. 194.

289. Ectopistes Carolinensis, *Linn.* — Carolina Turtle Dove, *Wilson*, p. 388.

Columba Carolinensis, *Bonap. Syn.* p. 119. *Nutt.* i. 426. *Aud.* i. 91; v. 555; plate 7. — Ectopistes Carolinensis, *Aud. Syn.* p. 195.

FAMILY II. — PAVONIDÆ, *Vigors.*

GENUS MELEAGRIS, *Linn.* — TURKEY.

290. Meleagris gallopavo. — Wild Turkey.

Breeds, from Texas to Vermont; in the interior, to Missouri, and thence to Michigan. Nests on the ground. Eggs, from ten to fifteen, of a yellowish cream color, sprinkled with reddish dots.

Meleagris gallopavo, *Bonap. Orn.* i. 79; *Syn.* p. 122. *Nutt.* i. 630. *Aud.* i. 1 and 33; v. 559; *Syn.* p. 197.

FAMILY III. — TETRAONIDÆ, *Vigors.*

GENUS I. — ORTYX, *Steph.* — AMERICAN PARTRIDGE.

291. Ortyx Virginiana. — Common Quail, *Wilson*, p. 413.

Perdix Virginiana, *Bonap. Syn.* p. 124. *Nutt.* i. 647. *Aud.* i. 388; v. 564; plate 76.
— Ortyx Virginiana, *Aud. Syn.* p. 199.

292. Ortyx Californica, *Lath.* — Californian Quail.

Head, crested; forehead, yellow; crest, black; head, brown, margined
with white; throat, white, margined with a white semilunar band; neck,
ash gray, marked with black; breast, grayish blue above, yellowish below; centre, chestnut; lower parts, yellowish brown. *Male*, 9¼. *Female*, 9.
Habitat, Upper California.

Perdix Californica, *Aud.* v. 152; plate 413. — Ortyx Californica, *Aud. Syn.* p. 199.

293. Ortyx plumifera, *Gould.* — Plumed Partridge.

Head, plumed; head, neck, breast, and back, bluish gray; bands on
neck, white; plume, black; throat, chestnut; rump, reddish brown;
breast, chestnut, with black and white band. *Male*, 1. *Female*, 10. Habitat, Columbia River and California.

Perdix plumifera, *Aud.* v. 226; plate 422. — Ortyx plumifera, *Aud. Syn.* p. 200.

294. Ortyx neoxenus, *Vigors.* — Welcome Partridge.

Upper parts, olive brown; rufous streak behind eye; lower parts, dark
brown, marked with numerous roundish white spots. Length, 7½. Habitat, California.

Perdix neoxenus, *Aud.* v. 228; plate 423. — Ortyx neoxenus, *Aud. Syn.* p. 200.

GENUS II. — TETRAO, *Linn.* — GROUSE.

295. Tetrao umbellus, *Linn.* — Common Ruffed Grouse, *Wilson,* p. 430.

Tetrao umbellus, *Bonap. Syn.* p. 126. *Rich. & Swain.* ii. 342. *Nutt.* i. 657. *Aud.*
i. 211; v. 560; plate 41; *Syn.* p. 202.

296. Tetrao cupido, *Linn.* — Pinnated Grouse, *Wilson,* p. 256.

Tetrao cupido, *Bonap. Syn.* p. 126. *Nutt.* i. 662. *Aud.* ii. 490; v. 559; plate 186;
Syn. p. 204

297. Tetrao Canadensis, *Linn.* — Canada Grouse.

Upper parts, banded with brownish black and light gray; tail, brownish
black, tipped with a band of reddish yellow; lower parts, black; throat,
with a white spot on end; band of white spots behind eye. *Male*, 15¾,
21¾. *Female*, 15½, 21. Habitat, from New York to Labrador.

Tetrao Canadensis, *Bonap. Orn.* iii. plate 20; *Syn.* p. 127. *Rich. & Swain.* ii. 346.
Nutt. i. 667. *Aud.* ii. 437; v. 563; plate 176; *Syn.* p. 203.

298. Tetrao obscurus, *Linn.* — Dusky Grouse.

Upper parts, blackish brown; crest, grayish brown; hind neck, undulated with bluish gray; rump, yellowish gray; tail, black; neck and
breast, grayish black; throat, barred with white; lower parts, blackish
gray. *Male*, 22. *Female*, 19½.

Tetrao obscurus, *Bonap. Orn.* iii. plate 18; *Syn.* p. 127. *Rich. & Swain.* ii. 344.
Nutt. i. 666. *Aud.* iv. 646; plate 361; *Syn.* p. 203.

299. Tetrao Urophasianus, *Bonap.*--- Cock of the Plains.

Upper parts, light yellowish brown, marked with brownish black ; tail, with ten bands of yellowish white ; throat, whitish, with brown spots ; white band across throat ; sides of neck, white ; breast and abdomen, black. *Male,* 30, 36. *Female,* 22. Habitat, Rocky Mountains, and Columbia River. Nests on the ground. Eggs, seventeen, wood brown, with chocolate blotches.

Tetrao Urophasianus, *Bonap.* iii. 21. *Rich. & Swain.* ii. 358. *Nutt.* i. 666. *Aud.* iv. 503 ; plate 371 ; *Syn.* p. 205.

300. Tetrao Phasianellus, *Linn.* — Sharp-tailed Grouse.

Upper parts, variegated with yellowish red, brownish black, and white ; tail, white, at base, variegated ; yellowish white band beneath eye ; throat, reddish white, with dusky spots ; breast and sides, with dusky spots ; abdomen, white. *Male,* 17½, 23. Habitat, Rocky Mountains. Nests on the ground. Eggs, thirteen, white.

Tetrao Phasianellus, *Bonap. Orn.* iii. 57. *Syn.* p. 127. *Rich. & Swain.* ii. 361. *Nutt.* i. 669. *Aud.* iv. 469 ; plate 382 ; *Syn.* p. 205.

301. Tetrao saliceti, *Swain.* — Willow Grouse.

Plumage in winter, nearly white ; tail, black. In summer, head and neck, bright chestnut ; upper parts, brownish black, barred with yellow ; lower parts, white. *Male,* 17, 26½. *Female,* 16, 26. Habitat, from Maine north. Nests on the ground. Eggs, fourteen, fawn color, spotted with reddish brown.

Tetrao saliceti, *Rich. & Swain.* ii. 351. *Nutt.* l. 674. *Aud.* ii. 528; plate 191. — Lagopus albus, *Aud. Syn.* p. 207.

302. Tetrao mutus, *Aud.* — American Ptarmigan.

In winter, nearly white. In summer, loral black band beyond eyes ; upper parts, fore neck, and sides, reddish yellow, undulated with brown and grayish white ; little white on under parts and only in patches. *Male,* 14¾. Habitat, Melville Island and Churchill River.

Tetrao mutus, *Rich. & Swain.* ii. 350. *Aud.* v. 196. — Lagopus Americanus, *Aud. Syn.* p. 207.

303. Tetrao rupestris, *Gmel.* — Rock Ptarmigan.

Nearly white in winter. In summer, variegated with black, reddish yellow, and white ; lower parts, barred with brownish black and reddish yellow. *Male,* 13½. Habitat, from Labrador to the Arctic Seas. Eggs, reddish brown, spotted with darker brown.

Tetrao rupestris, *Rich. & Swain.* ii. 354. *Nutt.* i. 610. *Aud.* iv. 483 ; plate 368. — Lagopus rupestris, *Aud. Syn.* p. 208.

304. Tetrao leucurus, *Swain.* — White-tailed Ptarmigan.

In winter, wholly white. In summer, head and neck barred with blackish brown and brownish white ; upper parts, blackish brown, barred with reddish yellow ; breast, abdomen, and sides, pale reddish yellow, broadly barred with blackish brown ; tail, white. Length, 12. Habitat, Rocky Mountains.

Tetrao leucurus, *Rich. & Swain.* ii. 356. *Nutt.* ii. 612. *Aud.* v. 200 ; plate 418. — Lagopus leucurus, *Aud. Syn.* p. 208.

WATER BIRDS.

ORDER I. — GRALLATORES, *Temm.*

FAMILY I. — RALLIDÆ, *Vigors.*

GENUS I. — GALLINULA, *Briss.* — GALLINULE.

305. Gallinula Martinica, *Linn.* — Purple Gallinule, *Wilson*, p. 637.
Gallinula Martinica, *Bonap. Syn.* p. 336. *Nutt.* ii. 221. *Aud.* iv. 37 ; plate 305 ; *Syn.* p. 210.

306. Gallinula chloropus, *Linn.* — Florida Gallinule.
Frontal plate and bill, carmine ; latter, tipped with yellow ; head, neck, and lower parts, grayish black ; abdomen, with yellowish tinge ; white streaks on sides. *Male*, 14, 22. Habitat, from South Carolina south and west. Nests among reeds near the water. Eggs, nine, dull cream color, spotted with brown and amber.
Gallinula galeata, *Bonap. Orn.* iv. 128. *Nutt.* ii. 223 — Gallinula Chloropus, *Aud.* iii. 330 ; plate 244 ; *Syn.* p. 210.

GENUS II. — FULICA, *Linn.* — COOT.

307. Fulica Americana, *Gmel.* — American Coot, *Wilson*, p. 633.
Fulica Americana, *Bonap. Syn.* p. 338. *Nutt* ii. 229. *Aud* iii. 291 ; v. 568 ; plates 239, 212.

GENUS III. — RALLUS, *Linn.* — RAIL.

308. Rallus Virginianus, *Linn.* — Virginia Rail, *Wilson*, p. 529.
Rallus Virginianus, *Bonap. Syn.* p. 334. *Nutt.* ii. 205. *Aud.* iii. 41 ; v. 573 ; plate 205 ; *Syn.* 216.

309. Rallus crepitans, *Gmel.* — Clapper Rail, *Wilson*, p. 531.
Rallus crepitans, *Nutt.* ii. 201. *Aud.* iii. 33 ; v. 570 ; plate 204 ; *Syn.* p. 215.

310. Rallus elegans, *Aud.* — Fresh Water Marsh Hen.
Upper part of head and hind neck, dull brown ; line over eye, orange ; upper parts streaked with brownish black and olive ; wing-coverts, chestnut ; sides of body, undulated with brown and grayish white. *Male*, 19, 25. Habitat, south of New Jersey. Nests on ground. Eggs, ten, dirty white, with brown blotches.
Rallus elegans, *Aud.* iii. 27 ; plate 303 ; *Syn.* p. 215.

SUBGENUS ORTYGOMETRA, *Leach.*

311. Rallus Carolinus, *Linn.* — Common Sora Rail, *Wilson*, p. 193.
Rallus Carolinus, *Bonap. Syn.* p. 334. *Nutt.* ii. 208. *Aud.* iii. 251 ; v. 572. — Ortygometra Carolinus, *Aud. Syn.* p. 213 ; plate 233.

312. Rallus Noveboracensis, *Lath.* — Yellow-breasted Rail.
Upper parts and sides, brownish black, longitudinally streaked with

yellow, and transversely barred with white; band over eye, reddish yellow; one behind eye, blackish brown; fore part of neck and breast, light reddish yellow; abdomen, white. *Male*, 7¾, 12¼. Habitat, Louisiana and Florida. Nests on the ground. Eggs, ten, pure white.

Rallus Noveboracensis, *Bonap. Orn.* iv. 136; *Syn.* p. 335. *Rich. & Swain.* ii. 402. *Nutt.* ii. 402. *Aud.* iv. 251; plate 329. — Ortygometra Noveboracensis, *Aud. Syn.* p. 213.

313. **Rallus Jamaicensis**, *Briss.* — Least Water Rail.

Head and lower parts, purplish gray; sides, wing-coverts, and abdomen, barred with grayish white; hind neck and fore part of back, dark chestnut; rest of upper parts, grayish black, tinged with brown and barred with white. *Male*, 6. Habitat, from Louisiana to New Jersey.

Rallus Jamaicensis, *Aud.* iv. 359; plate 349. — Ortygometra Jamaicensis, *Aud. Syn.* p. 214.

GENUS IV. — ARAMUS, *Vieill.* — COURLAN.

314. **Aramus scolopaceus**, *Vieill.* — Scolopaceous Courlan.

Plumage, chocolate brown, with purple and brown reflections; throat, whitish; elliptical white spots on hind neck; lanceolate white spots on breast. *Male*, 25¾, 41. *Female*, 25, 42. Habitat, Florida. Nests in tufts of grass. Eggs, six.

Aramus scolopaceus, *Bonap. Orn.* iv. 111; *Syn.* p. 39. *Nutt.* ii. 68. *Aud.* iv. 543; *Syn.* p. 217; plate 377.

FAMILY II. — GRUIDÆ, *Vigors.*

GENUS I. — GRUS, *Briss.* — CRANES.

315. **Grus Americana**, *Foster.* — Whooping Crane, *Wilson*, p. 548.

Grus Americana, *Bonap. Syn.* p. 302. *Rich. & Swain.* ii. 372. — *Aud.* iii. 202 and 441. *Nutt.* ii. 34. *Aud. Syn.* p. 219; plates 225 and 261. — Grus Canadensis, *Rich. & Swain.* ii. 273. *Nutt.* ii. 38.

GENUS II. — IBIS, *Cuv.*

316. **Ibis falcinellus**, *Linn.* — Glossy Ibis.

Bill, black; base part of head, grayish blue; feet, grayish black; head, glossy green, with purplish reflections; neck, back, breast, and abdomen, dark chestnut; part of breast shaded with green; sides, dusky, tinged with green, as well as lower wing and tail-coverts; edge of wing and anterior scapulars, brownish red; upper parts, dark green, glossed with purple; primaries, black, shaded with green; tail, glossy, with purple reflections. *Male*, 25, 42. Habitat, from the Middle Atlantic States to Texas. Place and manner of breeding, unknown.

Ibis falcinellus, *Bonap. Syn.* p. 312. *Nutt.* ii. 88. *Aud.* iv. 608; *Syn.* p. 257; plate 387.

317. **Ibis rubra**, *Linn.* — Scarlet Ibis, *Wilson*, p. 563.

Habitat, southern part of the Union, rare.

Ibis rubra, *Bonap. Syn.* p. 311. *Nutt.* ii. 84. *Aud.* v. 62; *Syn.* p. 257; plate 397.

318. **Ibis alba**, *Linn.* — White Ibis, *Wilson*, p. 564.

61

Nests on bushes or trees. Eggs, three, dull white, blotched with pale yellow, and irregularly spotted with deep reddish brown.

Ibis alba, *Bonap. Syn.* p. 312. *Nutt.* ii. 86. *Aud.* iii. 173; v. 593; plate 222; *Syn.* p. 257.

GENUS III.— TANTALUS, *Linn.*— WOOD IBIS.

319. **Tantalus loculator,** *Linn.*— Wood Ibis, *Wilson*, p. 561.

Tantalus loculator, *Bonap. Syn.* p. 310. *Nutt.* ii. 82. *Aud.* iii. 128; plate 216; *Syn.* p. 258.

GENUS IV.— PLATALEA, *Linn.*— SPOONBILL.

320. **Platalea Ajaja,** *Linn.*— Roseate Spoonbill, *Wilson*, p. 538.
Nests on tops of mangroves. Eggs, three, granulated, pure white.

Platalea Ajaja, *Bonap. Syn.* p. 346. *Nutt.* ii. 79. *Aud.* iv. 188; plate 321; *Syn.* p. 280.

GENUS V.— ARDEA, *Linn.*— HERON.

321. **Ardea nycticorax,** *Linn.* — Night Heron, *Wilson*, p. 524.

Ardea nycticorax, *Bonap. Syn.* p. 306. *Aud.* iii. 275; v. 600; *Syn.* p. 261; plate 236.— Ardea discors, *Nutt.* ii. 54.

322. **Ardea violacea,** *Linn.* — Yellow-crowned Heron, *Wilson*, p. 552.

Ardea violacea, *Bonap. Syn.* p. 306. *Nutt.* ii. 52. *Aud.* iv. 290; *Syn.* p. 262; plate 336.

323. **Ardea lentiginosa,** *Swain.* — American Bittern, *Wilson*, p. 558.
Eggs, of a uniform dull olivaceous color.

Ardea minor, *Bonap. Syn.* p. 307. *Nutt.* ii. 60. *Aud.* iv. 296; plate 337.— Ardea lentiginosa, *Rich. & Swain.* ii. 374. *Aud. Syn.* p. 263.

324. **Ardea exilis,** *Wilson.*— Least Bittern, *Wilson*, p. 560.

Ardea exilis, *Bonap. Syn.* p. 308. *Nutt.* ii. 266. *Aud.* ii. 77; v. 606; plate 210; *Syn.* 263.

325. **Ardea virescens,** *Linn.* — Green Heron, *Wilson*, p. 522.

Ardea virescens, *Bonap. Syn.* p. 307. *Nutt.* ii. 63. *Aud.* iv. 274; plate 333; *Syn.* p. 264.

326. **Ardea occidentalis,** *Aud.* — Great White Heron.
Bill, tibiæ, and hind part of tarsi, yellow; anterior part of latter, dull green; plumage, entirely white; feathers of the head, elongated and lanceolate. *Male*, 54, 83. *Female*, 50, 75. Habitat, Southern Florida Keys and Texas. Nests in low trees, a few feet above high-water mark. Eggs, three, 2¾ inches in length, 1⅜ in breadth, of an uniform plain light bluish green color.

Ardea occidentalis, *Aud.* iii. 542; v. 596; plate 264; *Syn.* p. 264.

327. **Ardea herodias,** *Linn.* — Great Blue Heron, *Wilson*, p. 554.

Ardea herodias, *Bonap. Syn.* p. 304. *Nutt.* ii. 42. *Aud.* iii. 87; v. 569; plate 211; *Syn.* p. 265.

328. **Ardea Ludoviciana,** *Wilson.* — Louisiana Heron, *Wilson*, p. 542.

Nests in trees. Eggs, three, pale blue, inclining to green.

Ardea Ludoviciana, *Bonap. Syn.* p. 305. *Nutt.* ii. 49. *Aud.* iii. 317; v. 606; *Syn.* p. 266; plate 217.

329. **Ardea candidissima,** *Gmel.* — Snowy Heron, *Wilson,* p. 536.

Ardea candidissima, *Bonap. Syn.* p. 305. *Nutt.* ii. 49. *Aud.* iii. 317; plate 242; *Syn.* p. 267.

330. **Ardea cœrulea,** *Linn.* — Blue Heron, *Wilson,* p. 534.

Ardea cœrulea, *Bonap. Syn.* p. 300. *Nutt.* ii. 58. *Aud.* iv. 58; plate 307; *Syn.* p. 266.

331. **Ardea egretta,** *Gmel.* — Great American Egret, *Wilson,* p. 527.

Ardea alba, *Bonap. Syn.* p. 304. *Nutt.* ii. 47. — Ardea egretta, *Aud.* iv. 600; plate 386; *Syn.* p. 266.

332. **Ardea rufescens,** *Gmel.* — Reddish Egret.

Feathers of the head and neck, elongated, very narrow, loose, and with linear-acuminate tips; those of the back, very long, recurved, and with loose filaments; bill, pale flesh color, its base, black; feet, ultramarine blue; plumage of head and neck, light reddish brown; back and wings, grayish blue; long train feathers, yellowish towards extremity; lower parts, grayish blue, paler than upper; in the young, the plumage is white; feet, dusky green. *Male,* 31, 46. Habitat, Florida Keys and Texas. Nests in trees, usually mangroves. Eggs, three, pale sea green.

Ardea Pealii, *Bonap. Orn.* iv. 96. *Nutt.* ii. 49. — Ardea rufescens, *Aud.* iii. 411; v. 624; plate 256; *Syn.* p. 266.

FAMILY III. — CHARADRIADÆ, *Vigors.*

GENUS I. — CHARADRIUS, *Linn.* — PLOVER.

333. **Charadrius melodus,** *Ord.* — Piping Plover, *Wilson,* p. 345.

Charadrius melodus, *Aud.* iii. 154; v. 578. *Nutt.* ii. 18. *Bonap Syn.* p 296. *Aud. Syn.* p. 224; plate 322.

334. **Charadrius Helveticus,** *Linn.* — Black-bellied Plover, *Wilson,* p. 486.

Charadrius Helveticus, *Bonap. Syn.* 298. *Nutt.* ll. 26. *Aud.* iv. 280; plate 334; *Syn.* p. 221. — Vanellus melanogaster, *Rich. & Swain.* ii. 370.

*335. **Charadrius marmoratus,** *Wagler.* — Golden Plover, *Wilson,* p. 345.

Charadrius, *Bonap. Syn.* p. 287. *Rich. & Swain.* ii. 623. *Nutt.* ii. 16. *Aud.* ii. 623. — Charadrius marmoratus, *Aud.* v. 585; plate 300; *Syn.* p. 222.

336. **Charadrius vociferus,** *Linn.* — Kildeer Plover, *Wilson,* p. 507.

Charadrius vociferus, *Bonap. Syn.* p. 297. *Rich. & Swain.* ii. 368. *Nutt.* ii. 22. *Aud.* iii. 191; v, 577; *Syn.* p. 223; plate 350.

---

* The Golden Plover, of America, has been regarded by authors as the same as the European bird. Mr. Audubon has, however, in his Synopsis, pronounced it a distinct species. He says, "This species, which closely resembles Charadrius pluvialis, is distinguishable by having the tarsus slightly longer, the toes somewhat shorter, and the axillar feathers always light gray, they being white in that species, which very probably exists in North America, although I am not at present in possession of specimens and cannot with certainty describe it as belonging to that country."

337. **Charadrius Wilsonius,** *Ord.* — Wilson's Plover, *Wilson,* p. 643.

Charadrius Wilsonius, *Bonap. Syn.* p. 296. *Nutt.* ii. 21. *Aud.* iii. 73; v. 577; plates 284 and 209; *Syn.* p. 223.

338. **Charadrius semipalmatus,** *Bonap.* — American Ring Plover, *Wilson,* p. 500.

Charadrius semipalmatus, *Bonap. Syn.* p. 296. *Rich. & Swain.* ii. 367. *Nutt.* ii. 21. *Aud.* iv. 256; v. 579; plate 330; *Syn.* p. 224.

339. **Charadrius montanus,** *Towns.* — Rocky Mountain Plover.

Bill, black; feet, dull yellow. Forehead, a band over the eye; fore part of neck, and lower parts, white; crown of head and nape, dark yellowish brown; sides, hind part of neck, and upper parts, ochre yellow; central portion of the feathers, grayish brown; wing coverts, lighter; primary coverts and quills, dusky; their shafts and margins, white; tail, yellowish brown, tipped with yellowish white. *Female,* 8¼. Habitat, Rocky Mountains.

Charadrius montanus, *Aud.* iv. 362, plate 350; *Syn.* p. 223.

GENUS II. — APHRIZA, *Aud.* — SURF BIRD.

340. **Aphriza Townsendii,** *Aud.* — Townsend's Surf Bird.

Bill, dusky, orange at base; feet, bluish green; upper parts, blackish gray; quills, grayish black; a broad band of white on wing; ends of secondary coverts, bases, and more or less of the margins and tips of the quills, having a streak of dusky on inner web; shafts of quills, upper tail-coverts, and base of tail, white; rest of tail, black; throat, grayish white; cheeks, neck, and breast, dull gray; lower parts, white, with gray streaks. *Female,* 11. Habitat, Columbia River.

Aphriza Townsendii, *Aud.* v. 249; plate 428; *Syn.* p. 226.

GENUS III. — STREPSILAS, *Illiger.* — TURNSTONE.

341. **Strepsilas interpres,** *Linn.* — Turnstone, *Wilson,* p. 480.

Eggs, four, pale yellowish green, marked with irregular patches and streaks of brownish red, and a few lines of black.

Strepsilas interpres, *Bonap. Syn.* p. 299. *Rich. & Swain.* ii. 371. *Nutt.* ii. 30. *Aud.* iv. 31; plate 304; *Syn.* p. 227.

GENUS IV. — HÆMATOPUS.

*342. **Hæmatopus palliatus,** *Temm.* — American Oyster-Catcher, *Wilson,* p. 543.

Hæmatopus palliatus, *Nutt.* ii. 15. *Aud.* iii. 181; v. 580; plate 223; *Syn.* p. 228.

343. **Hæmatopus Backmanii,** *Aud.* — Bachman's Oyster-Catcher.

Bill, vermilion, fading to yellow towards the end; feet, white, tinged

---

* The bird described and figured by Wilson as Hæmatopus ostralegus was probably H. palliatus. It has never yet been ascertained with certainty that the former was ever seen in this country; we have therefore followed the example of Audubon in omitting it. In his description of the female and young, as well as in his whole history of their habits, Wilson undoubtedly had the latter bird in view, and we have very little doubt that he was wholly mistaken in supposing H. ostralegus to be a bird of America.

with flesh color; plumage, chocolate brown, darker on the head, tinged with bluish gray, quills, lighter on the under surface. *Male*, 17½. Habitat, North-West Coast and Mouth of Columbia River.

Hæmatopus Bachmanii, *Aud.* v. 245, plate 427; *Syn.* p. 229.

344. Hæmatopus Townsendii, *Aud.* — Townsend's Oyster-Catcher.

Bill, vermilion, paler at end; feet, blood red; plumage, chocolate brown; on the head, neck, and breast, darker, and tinged with bluish gray; shafts of quills, whitish, their under surface, light brownish gray; wing-coverts, narrowly tipped with brownish white. *Female*, 20. Habitat, coast of California and along the shores of the Pacific Ocean.

Hæmatopus Townsendii, *Aud.* v. 247; plate 427; *Syn.* p. 229.

FAMILY IV. — SCOLOPACIDÆ, *Vigors.*

GENUS I.—TRINGA, *Linn.*—SANDPIPER.

345. Tringa cinerea, *Wilson.* — Ash-colored Sandpiper, *Wilson*, p. 482.

Tringa Islandica, *Bonap. Syn.* p. 350. *Nutt.* ii. 125. *Aud.* iv. 130; plate 315; *Syn.* p. 231. — Tringa cinerea, *Rich. & Swain.* ii. 387.

346. Tringa alpina, *Linn.* — Red-backed Sandpiper, *Wilson*, p. 475.

Eggs, four, light greenish yellow, irregularly spotted with deep brown.

Tringa alpina, *Bonap. Syn.* p. 317. *Rich. & Swain.* ii. 383. *Nutt.* ii. 186. *Aud.* iii. 580; plate 290; *Syn.* p. 301.

347. Tringa semipalmata, *Wilson.* — Semipalmated Sandpiper, *Wilson*, p. 542.

Tringa semipalmata, *Bonap. Syn.* p. 316. *Nutt.* ii. 136. *Aud.* v. 111; plate 405; *Syn.* p. 336.

348. Tringa pusilla, *Wilson.* — Little Sandpiper or Peep, *Wilson*, p. 347.

Nests on the ground in Labrador. Eggs, four, large for the bird, cream yellow, blotched and dotted with dark amber.

Tringa pusilla, *Bonap. Syn.* p. 319. *Nutt.* ii. 120. *Aud.* iv. 180; *Syn.* p. 237; plate 320.

349. Tringa pectoralis, *Bonap.* — Pectoral Sandpiper.

Bill, olive green; feet, yellowish green; upper part of head, reddish brown, the central part of each feather, brownish black; faint whitish line from bill to beyond the eye; sides of head, front and sides of neck and breast, light brownish gray, with longitudinal dark brown lines; chin, breast, and abdomen, white: feathers of upper parts, brownish black, edged with reddish brown, those on wings, lighter; outer secondaries tinged with gray and tipped with white; tail, light brownish gray, margined and tipped with white. *Male*, 9¼, 18. Habitat, from Nova Scotia to Maryland.

Tringa pectoralis, *Bonap. Orn.* iv. 44; *Syn.* p. 318. *Nutt.* ii. 111. *Aud.* iii. 601; v. 582; plate 294; *Syn.* p. 232.

350. Tringa maritima, *Brunnich.* — Purple Sandpiper.

Bill, deep orange; feet, light orange, head, grayish brown, tinged with purple; sides and neck, deep purple; back and wings, brownish black with purple gloss; middle tail-feathers, brownish black, tinged with

61 *

purple; lateral, shaded with ash gray; breast, sides, and abdomen, white. In winter, lower parts, pale gray; upper parts with their purple tints much fainter. *Male*, 19½, 14¾. Habitat, from Hudson's Bay to New York. Eggs, pyriform, yellowish gray, spotted with pale brown.

Tringa maritima, *Bonap. Syn.* p. 318. *Rich. & Swain.* ii. 382. *Aud.* iii. 558; plate 284; *Syn.* p. 233.

351. Tringa rufescens, *Vieill.* — Buff-breasted Sandpiper.

Bill, olive green; feet, yellowish green; upper parts, grayish yellow, each feather, blackish brown in the centre; quills and coverts, grayish brown, greenish black at the end, with the tip, whitish; inner webs, whitish, and dotted with black in undulating lines; two middle tail-feathers, grayish brown; at end, dark brown, glossed with green and tipped with white; head, neck, and sides, yellowish red, the throat paler; sides, spotted with brownish black; lower parts, paler and unspotted. *Male*, 8, 18. Habitat, from Labrador to Pennsylvania.

Tringa rufescens, *Nutt.* ii. 113. *Aud.* iii. 451; plate 265; *Syn.* p. 233.

352. Tringa subarquata, *Temm.* — Curlew Sandpiper.

Bill, dark olive; feet, light olive green; head, neck, and breast, light yellowish red; sides, whitish; lower tail-coverts, white, with a brownish black spot towards the end; on upper part of head, central parts of feathers, dark brown; hind neck and sides, streaked with same; upper parts mottled with brownish black and light red; rump, pale brownish gray; upper tail-coverts, white, spotted with brown and red; tail, brownish gray, glossed with green. Habitat, from Florida along the coast to high latitudes.

Tringa subarquata, *Bonap. Syn.* p. 317. *Nutt.* ii. 104. *Aud.* iii 444; plate 263; *Syn.* p. 234.

353. Tringa himantopus, *Bonap.* — Long-legged Sandpiper.

Bill, greenish black; legs, yellowish green. In summer, upper parts, brownish black, tinged with reddish white; rump, and upper tail-coverts, white, transversely barred with dusky; tail, light gray; primary coverts, brownish black; secondaries, brownish gray, margined with reddish white; broad whitish line over eye; forepart and sides of neck, grayish white, tinged with red and streaked with dusky; lower parts, pale reddish, barred with dusky. In winter, the colors have a lighter shade. *Male*, 7½ — 8¾, 15½ — 17. *Female*, 8½ — 10½, 16½ — 18. Habitat, from Texas to Fur Countries.

Tringa himantopus, *Bonap. Syn.* p. 316. *Rich. & Swain.* ii. 380. *Nutt.* ii. pp. 138, 140, 141. *Aud.* iv. 332; plate 344; *Syn.* p. 235. — Tringa Douglasii, *Rich. & Swain.* ii. 235.

354. Tringa Schinzii, *Brehm.* — Schinz's Sandpiper.

Bill and feet, dusky green; upper parts, brownish black, tinged with yellowish gray; the scapulars, with light red; wing-coverts, grayish brown, tipped with white; tail-feathers, white, with a dusky spot, except the central two, which are blackish, with grayish white markings; sides of head, fore neck, front of breast, grayish white, with small black spots; rest of lower parts, white. *Male*, 7½, 14¾. Habitat, from Florida to Labrador.

Tringa Schinzii, *Bonap. Syn.* p. 249. *Rich. & Swain.* ii. 384. *Nutt.* ii. 109. *Aud.* iii. 529; plate 278; *Syn.* p. 236.

355. Tringa arenaria. — Sanderling Sandpiper, *Wilson*, p. 503.

Calidris arenaria, *Rich. & Swain.* ii. 366. *Nutt.* ii. 4. — Tringa arenaria, *Bonap. Syn.* p. 320. *Aud.* iii. 231; v. 582; plates 230 and 285; *Syn.* p. 237.

GENUS II. — TOTANUS, *Bechst.* — TATLERS.

356. Totanus Bartramius, *Wilson.* — Upland Plover, *Wilson,* p. 499.

Nests on the ground. Eggs, four, yellowish white, spotted with purplish brown.

Totanus Bartramius, *Bonap. Syn.* p. 262. *Rich. & Swain.* ii. 391. *Nutt.* ii. 169. *Aud.* iv. 24; plate 303. — Tringa Bartramia, *Aud. Syn.* 231.

357. Totanus semipalmatus, *Lath.* — Semipalmated Snipe or Willet, *Wilson,* p. 477.

Totanus semiphalmatus, *Rich. & Swain.* ii. 388. *Nutt.* ii. 144. *Aud.* iii. 510; v. 585; *Syn.* p. 245; plate 274.

358. Totanus macularius, *Wilson.* — Spotted Tatler, *Wilson,* p. 497.

Totanus macularius, *Bonap. Syn.* p. 325. *Nutt.* ii. 162. *Aud.* iv. 81; plate 310; *Syn.* p. 242.

359. Totanus solitarius, *Wilson.* — Solitary Tatler, *Wilson,* p. 493.

Nests in the grass or on the bare sand. Eggs, greenish yellow, with spots and patches of umber.

Totanus chloropygius, *Bonap. Syn.* p. 325. *Rich. & Swain.* ii. 393. *Nutt.* ii. 159 *Aud.* iii. 576; v. 583; plate 200. — Totanus solitarius, *Aud. Syn.* p. 242.

360. Totanus flavipes, *Lath.* — Yellow Shanks Tatler, *Wilson,* p. 494.

Totanus flavipes, *Bonap. Syn.* p. 324. *Rich. & Swain.* ii. 390. *Nutt.* ii. 152. *Aud.* iii. 573; v. 586; plate 288; *Syn.* p. 243.

361. Totanus vociferus, *Wilson.* — Telltale Tatler, *Wilson,* p. 495.

Eggs, four, pyriform, two and a quarter inches long, and one and a half broad, pale greenish yellow, blotched with purplish gray.

Totanus vociferus, *Rich. & Swain.* ii. 389. *Nutt.* ii. 148. *Aud. Syn.* p. 244. — Totanus melanoleucus, *Bonap. Syn.* p. 324. *Aud.* iv. 68; plate 308.

362. Totanus glottis. — Green Shank Tatler.

Bill, dusky green; legs, grayish green; lower parts and back, excepting anterior portion, head and cheeks, pure white; loral band, with small oblong spots of grayish brown; sides of lower part of fore neck and a portion of the breast, faintly undulated with gray; neck, grayish white, lineated with grayish brown; tail, grayish white, undulated with light brown; spots on four outside feathers. Habitat, Florida. *Male,* 11.

Totanus glottis, *Nutt.* ii. 68. *Aud.* iii. 483; plate 269; *Syn.* p. 244.

GENUS III. — LIMOSA, *Briss.* — GODWIT.

363. Limosa Fedoa, *Linn.* — Great Marbled Godwit, *Wilson,* p. 479.

Limosa Fedoa, *Bonap. Syn.* p. 328. *Rich. & Swain* ii. 395. *Nutt.* ii. 173. *Aud.* iii. 287; v. 590; plate 238; *Syn.* p. 246.

364. Limosa Hudsonica, *Lath.* — Hudsonian Godwit.

Bill, grayish yellow, blackish at tip; feet, bluish gray; head and neck, brownish gray, with darker lines; a band from the bill over the eye, and the throat, grayish white; back, deep gray; scapulars, brownish black, with white markings on edge of feathers; tips of primary coverts, bases of quills, broad band over rump, white; tail-feathers and upper tail-coverts, brownish black, their bases, white; lower parts, bright yellowish red; sides, mottled with dark brown; abdomen and lower tail-coverts, paler and variegated with dusky; lower wing-coverts, blackish brown, edged with whitish. Habitat, throughout the Union. *Male*, 15¾, 28. *Female*, 16¼, 29.

> Limosa Hudsonica, *Rich. & Swain.* ii. 396. *Nutt.* ii. 175. *Aud.* iii. 426; v. 592; plate 258; *Syn.* p. 247.

GENUS IV. — SCOLOPAX, *Linn.* — SNIPE.

365. Scolopax Wilsonii, *Temm.* — Common Snipe, *Wilson*, p. 411.

Nests in the moss of swamps. Eggs, four, yellowish olive, blotched with umber.

> Scolopax Wilsonii, *Bonap. Syn.* p. 330. *Rich. & Swain.* ii. 401. *Nutt.* ii. 185. *Aud.* iii. 332; v. 583; plate 243; *Syn.* p. 248.

366. Scolopax Drummondii, *Swain.* — Drummond's Snipe.

Dorsal plumage and wings, mostly brownish black; head and scapulars reflecting green, and barred with yellowish brown; stripes of this color from forehead to nape; middle dorsal plumage, fringed with white; rump and tail-coverts, greenish black, with ferruginous ends, crossed by a blackish line and tipped with white; under plumage, wood brown, with spots of umber; flanks and under tail-coverts, barred with black and white; belly, white. Length, 11½. Habitat, Fur Countries, Rocky Mountains.

> Scolopax Drummondii, *Rich. & Swain.* ii. 400. *Aud.* v. 319; *Syn.* p. 249; not figured.

367. Scolopax Noveboracensis. — Red-breasted Snipe, *Wilson*, p. 488.

> Scolopax Noveboracensis, *Rich. & Swain.* ii. 398. *Nutt.* ii. 181. *Aud.* iv. 285; plate 335; *Syn.* p. 249. — Scolopax grisea, *Bonap. Syn.* p. 330.

GENUS V. — MICROPTERA. — WOODCOCK.

368. Microptera Americana. — American Woodcock, *Wilson*, p. 426.

> Scolopax minor, *Bonap. Syn.* p. 331. *Aud.* iii. 474. — Rusticola minor, *Nutt.* ii. 194. — Microptera Americana, *Aud. Syn.* p. 250; plate 268.

GENUS VI. — RECURVIROSTRA, *Linn.* — AVOSET.

369. Recurvirostra Americana, *Linn.* — American Avoset, *Wilson*, p. 539.

Nests in high grass. Eggs, four, of a dull olive color, marked with irregular blotches of black, and with others of a fainter tint.

> Recurvirostra Americana, *Bonap. Syn.* p. 394. *Rich. & Swain.* ii. 375. *Nutt.* ii. 74. *Aud.* iv. 168; plate 318; *Syn.* p. 252

GENUS VII. — HIMANTOPUS, *Briss.* — STILT.

370. Himantopus nigricollis, *Vieill.* — Black-necked Stilt, *Wilson*, p. 490.

Nests near margins of ponds. Eggs, four, pyriform, pale yellowish clay color, plentifully marked with large, irregular blotches and lines of brownish black.

Himantopus nigricollis, *Bonap. Syn.* p. 322. *Nutt.* ii. 8. *Aud.* iv. 247; plate 327; *Syn.* p. 253.

GENUS VIII. — NUMENIUS, *Briss.* — CURLEW.

371. Numenius borealis, *Lath.* — Esquimaux Curlew, *Wilson,* p. 473.

Nests on the shore. Eggs, four, pyriform, green, with spots of umber brown.

Numenius borealis, *Bonap. Syn.* p. 314. *Rich. & Swain.* ii. 378. *Nutt.* ii. 101. *Aud.* iii. 69; v. 590; *Syn.* p. 255; plate 208.

372. Numenius longirostris, *Wilson.* — Long-billed Curlew, *Wilson,* p. 550.

Numenius longirostris, *Bonap. Syn.* p. 314. *Rich. & Swain.* ii. 376. *Nutt.* ii. 94. *Aud.* iii. 240; v. 587; plate 231; *Syn.* p. 254.

373. Numenius borealis, *Lath.* — Esquimaux Curlew.

Bill, brownish black ; lower mandible, flesh colored at the base ; upper part of head, brownish black, streaked with pale yellowish brown, having an indistinct central, and two lateral, lines of whitish ; upper parts, brownish black, spotted with light brownish yellow ; wing-coverts and secondaries, of a lighter tint, similarly spotted ; tail, barred with light grayish brown and dark brown ; breast and sides, grayish yellow, with transverse and longitudinal dark markings ; head and neck, yellowish gray, striped with dark brown ; lower wing and tail-coverts, similarly barred ; axillars, of a rufous buffy tint, regularly banded. Male 14½, 27⅜. Habitat, from Texas to the Fur Countries.

Numenius borealis, *Bonap. Syn.* p. 314. *Rich. & Swain.* ii. 378. *Nutt.* ii. 101. *Aud.* iii. 69; v. 590; plate 208; *Syn.* p. 255.

ORDER II. — NATATORES, *Temm.*

FAMILY I. — PINNATIPEDES, *Temm.* — LOBE-FOOTED SWIMMING BIRDS.

GENUS I. — PHALAROPUS, *Briss.*

374. Phalaropus fulicarius, *Bonap.* — Red Phalarope, *Wilson,* p. 642.

Breeds very far to the north. Eggs, 1¼ by ⅞, dull greenish yellow, irregularly blotched and dotted with reddish brown.

Phalaropus fulicarius, *Bonap. Syn.* p. 301. *Rich. & Swain.* ii. 407. *Nutt.* ii. 236. *Aud.* iii. 404; plate 255; *Syn.* p. 239.

SUBGENUS LOBIPES, *Cuv.*

375. Phalaropus hyperboreus, *Lath.* — Hyperborean Phalarope.

Upper parts, grayish black ; head, lighter and more tinged with gray ; scapulars and some of the feathers of the back, edged with yellowish red ; head and neck of same color ; throat and sides of upper part of the neck, white ; wing-coverts and quills, brownish black, tinged with gray ; shafts of quills, tips of secondaries, and broad bar on secondary coverts, white; tail, light gray; the feathers margined with white, the two middle, light brownish gray; upper tail-coverts, white, barred with dusky; breast and abdomen, white. *Male*, 6, 13½. Habitat, from Labrador to New York. Nests on the ground, in the vicinity of small fresh-water lakes. Eggs, four, deep buff, marked with blotches of reddish brown.

> Phalaropus hyperboreus, *Bonap. Syn.* p. 342. *Nutt.* ii. 239. *Aud.* iii. 118; v. 595; plate 215. — Lobipes hyperboreus, *Aud. Syn.* p. 240.

376. **Phalaropus Wilsonii,** *Sabine.* — Wilson's Phalarope, *Wilson,* p. 640.

Eggs, three, cream yellow, spotted and blotched with umber brown.

> Phalaropus Wilsonii, *Bonap. Syn.* p. 342; *Orn.* iv. 59. *Rich. & Swain.* ii. 405. *Nutt.* ii. 245. *Aud.* iii. 400; plate 254. — Lobipes Wilsonii, *Aud. Syn.* p. 241.

FAMILY II. — ANATIDÆ, *Vigors.*

GENUS I. — PHŒNICOPTERUS, *Linn.* — FLAMINGO.

377. **Phœnicopterus ruber,** *Linn.* — American Flamingo, *Wilson,* p. 565.

Nests on the ground. Eggs, two, dirty white.

> Phœnicopterus ruber, *Bonap. Syn.* p. 348. *Nutt.* ii. 71. *Aud.* v. 255; plate 431; *Syn.* p. 269.

GENUS II. — ANSER, *Briss.* — GOOSE.

378. **Anser Canadensis,** *Linn.* — Canada Goose, *Wilson,* p. 570.

> Anser Canadensis, *Bonap. Syn.* p. 377. *Nutt.* ii. 349. *Rich. & Swain.* ii. 468. *Aud.* iii. 1; v. 607; plate 201; *Syn.* p. 270.

379. **Anser Hutchinsii,** *Rich.* — Hutchins's Goose.

Bill, feet, and claws, black; head and neck, glossy black; large triangular patch of white on each side of head and neck; upper parts, brownish gray, margined with yellowish gray; abdomen and lower tail-coverts, white; hind part of back, brownish black; primary quills and tail-feathers, deep brown. Adult, 25, 50. Habitat, from Maine to Arctic Regions, and Columbia River. Eggs, four, pure white.

> Anser Hutchinsii, *Rich. & Swain.* ii. 470. *Aud.* iii. 526; plate 277; *Syn.* p. 271.

380. **Anser leucopsis,** *Bechst.* — Barnacle Goose.

Bill, feet, and claws, black; anterior part of head, broad space above eye, sides of head, and throat, white; feathers, margining the bill, and line from bill to eye, brownish black; neck, bluish black; rump and tail-feathers, deep black; upper and lower tail-coverts, and sides of rump, pure white. *Male*, 27, 56. *Female*, 23½, 52. Habitat, northern parts, accidental.

> Anser leucopsis, *Bonap. Syn.* 377. *Nutt.* ii. 355. *Aud.* iii. 609; plate 296; *Syn.* p. 271.

381. **Anser Bernicla,** *Linn.* — Brent Goose, *Wilson,* p. 621.

> Anser Bernicla, *Bonap. Syn.* p. 378. *Rich. & Swain.* ii. 469. *Nutt.* ii. 358. *Aud.* v. 24, 610; plate 391; *Syn.* p. 272.

382. Anser albifrons, *Bechst.* — White-fronted Goose.

Bill, carmine red; feet, orange; claws, white; head and nock, grayish brown; a white band, margined with blackish brown on the forehead, back, gray, tinged in fore part with brown, the rest with white; breast, abdomen, lower tail-coverts, sides of rump, and upper tail-coverts, white; breast and sides, patched with brownish black. *Male,* 27¼, 60. Eggs, dull yellowish green, with indistinct patches of a darker tint, 2¾ inches in length by 1¾. Habitat, Southern States in winter, Arctic Regions in summer.

Anser albifrons, *Bonap. Syn.* p. 376. *Rich. & Swain.* ii. 456. *Nutt* ii. 346. *Aud.* iii. 568; plate 286; *Syn.* p. 272.

383. Anser hyperboreus, *Gmel.* — Snow Goose, *Wilson,* p. 585, 593.

Eggs, yellowish white, three inches by two.

Anser hyperboreus, *Bonap. Syn.* p. 376. *Nutt.* ii. 344. *Rich. & Swain.* ii. 467. *Aud.* iv. 562; plate 371; *Syn.* p. 273.

GENUS III. — CYGNUS, *Meyer.* — SWAN.

384. Cygnus Buccinator, *Rich.* — Trumpeter Swan.

Bill and feet, black; plumage, pure white; upper part of head, often brownish red. In young, bill, flesh color; feet, yellowish brown; upper parts of head and cheeks, reddish brown; throat, nearly white; other parts, grayish white, tinged with yellow. *Adult,* 68. *Young,* 52½, 91. Breeding places unknown. Habitat, North California to Fur Countries.

385. Cygnus Americanus, *Sharpless.* — American Swan.

Bill and feet, black; orange spot on each side of base of former; plumage, pure white. Young, gray. *Male,* 53, 84.

Cygnus Americanus, *Aud.* v. 133; plate 411; *Syn.* p. 275.

GENUS IV. — ANAS, *Linn.* — DUCK.

386. Anas Boschas, *Linn.* — Mallard Duck, *Wilson,* p. 608.

Anas Boschas, *Bonap. Syn.* p. 383. *Rich. & Swain.* ii. 442. *Nutt.* ii. 378. *Aud.* iii. 164; plate 221; *Syn.* p. 276.

387. Anas obscura, *Gmel.* — Dusky Duck, *Wilson,* p. 626.

Anas obscura, *Bonap. Syn.* p. 384. *Nutt.* ii. 392. *Aud.* iv. 15; *Syn.* p. 276; plate 202.

388. Anas strepera, *Linn.* — Gadwall Duck, *Wilson,* p. 614.

Anas strepera, *Bonap. Syn.* p. 383. *Rich. & Swain.* ii. 440. *Nutt.* ii. 383. *Aud.* iv. 353; plate 348; *Syn.* p. 278.

389. Anas Breweri, *Aud.* — Brewer's Duck.

Bill and feet, dull yellow; head and upper part of neck, deep glossy green; patch of pale reddish yellow from base of bill, over cheeks, down the neck; space over and behind the eye, dull purple; ring of pale yellowish red on middle of neck; lower parts, dull brownish red, with a transverse band of dusky; upper parts, dull grayish brown, undulated with dusky; rump and upper tail-coverts, black; tail-feathers, light brownish gray, edged with whitish; lower parts, grayish white, edged with yellow. Habitat, Louisiana. *Male,* 23, 39.

Anas Breweri, *Aud.* iv. 302; plate 338; *Syn.* p. 277.

390. Anas Americana, *Gmel.* — American Widgeon, *Wilson*, p. 591.

Anas Americana, *Bonap. Syn.* p. 384. *Nutt.* ii. 389. *Aud.* iv. 337; plate 345; *Syn.* p. 279. — Mareca Americana, *Rich. & Swain.* ii. 445.

391. Anas acuta, *Linn.* — Pintail Duck, *Wilson*, p. 582.

Anas acuta, *Bonap. Syn.* p. 383. *Nutt.* ii. 386. *Aud.* iii. 214; v. 615; *Syn.* p. 279; plate 227. — Anas caudacuta, *Rich. & Swain.* ii. 441.

392. Anas sponsa, *Linn.* — Wood Duck, *Wilson*, p. 598.

Dendronessa sponsa, *Rich. & Swain.* ii. 446. — Anas sponsa, *Bonap. Syn.* p 385. *Nutt.* ii. 394. *Aud.* iii. 52; v. 618; plate 206; *Syn.* p. 280.

393. Anas Carolinensis, *Steph.* — American Green-winged Teal, *Wilson*, p. 601.

Anas crecca, *Bonap. Syn.* p. 386. *Nutt.* ii. 400. *Aud.* iii. 218; v. 616; plate 228. Anas Carolinensis, *Aud. Syn.* p. 281.

394. Anas discors, *Linn.* — Blue-winged Teal, *Wilson*, p. 583.

Anas discors, *Bonap. Syn.* p. 385. *Rich. & Swain.* ii. 444. *Nutt.* ii. 397. *Aud.* iv. 111; plate 313; *Syn.* p. 282.

395. Anas clypeata, *Linn.* — Shoveller Duck, *Wilson*, p. 577.

Anas clypeata, *Bonap. Syn.* p. 382. *Rich. & Swain.* ii. 439. *Nutt.* ii. 383. *Aud.* iv. 241; plate 327; *Syn.* p. 284.

GENUS V. — FULIGULA. — SEA DUCK.

396. Fuligula Valisneria, *Wilson.* — Canvass-Back Duck, *Wilson*, p. 603.

Fuligula Valisneria, *Bonap. Syn.* p. 392. *Rich. & Swain.* ii. 450. *Nutt.* ii. 430. *Aud.* iv. 1; plate 301; *Syn.* p. 285.

397. Fuligula ferina, *Linn.* — Red-headed Duck, *Wilson*, p. 607.

Fuligula ferina, *Bonap. Syn.* p. 392. *Rich. & Swain.* ii. 452. *Nutt.* ii. 434. *Aud.* iv. 198; plate 322; *Syn.* p. 286.

398. Fuligula marilla, *Linn.* — Scaup Duck, *Wilson*, p. 590.

Fuligula marilla, *Bonap. Syn.* p. 392. *Rich. & Swain.* ii. 456. *Nutt.* ii. 437. *Aud.* iii. 226; v. 614; plate 229; *Syn.* p. 286.

399. Fuligula rufitorques, *Bonap.* — Ring-necked Duck, *Wilson*, p. 574.

Fuligula rufitorques, *Bonap. Syn.* p. 393. *Rich. & Swain.* ii. 453. *Nutt.* ii. 439. *Aud.* iii. 259; plate 234; *Syn.* p. 287.

400. Fuligula rubida, *Wilson.* — Ruddy Duck, *Wilson*, pp. 619 and 620.

Fuligula rubida, *Bonap. Syn.* p. 390. *Rich. & Swain.* ii. 455. *Nutt.* ii. 426. *Aud.* iv. 326; plate 343; *Syn.* p. 288.

401. Fuligula Labradora, *Lath.* — Pied Duck, *Wilson*, p. 594.

Fuligula Labradora, *Bonap. Syn.* p. 391. *Nutt.* ii. 428. *Aud.* iv. 471; plate 332; *Syn.* p. 288.

402. Fuligula fusca, *Linn.* — Velvet Duck, *Wilson*, p. 624.

Fuligula fusca, *Bonap. Syn.* p. 390. *Rich. & Swain.* ii. 449. *Nutt.* ii. 419. *Aud.* iii. 354; plate 247; *Syn.* p. 289.

403. Fuligula perspicillata, *Linn.* — Surf Duck, *Wilson*, p. 567.

Fuligula perspicillata, *Bonap. Syn.* p. 389. *Rich. & Swain.* ii. 449. *Nutt.* ii, 416. *Aud.* iv. 161; plate 317; *Syn.* p. 289.

404. Fuligula Americana, *Swain.* — American Scoter, *Wilson*, p. 623.

Fuligula Americana, *Bonap. Syn.* p. 390. *Nutt.* ii. 422. *Rich. & Swain.* ii. 450. *Aud.* v. 117; plate 408; *Syn.* p. 290.

405. Fuligula mollissima, *Linn.* — Eider Duck, *Wilson*, pp. 615 and 617.

Fuligula mollissima, *Bonap. Syn.* p. 389. *Nutt.* ii. 406. *Aud.* iii. 344; v. 611; plate 246; *Syn.* p. 291. — Somateria mollissima, *Rich. & Swain.* ii. 448.

406. Fuligula clangula, *Linn.* — Golden-Eye Duck, *Wilson*, p. 575.

Fuligula clangula, *Bonap. Syn.* p. 393. *Nutt.* ii. 441. *Aud.* iv. 318; v. 105; plates 303 and 342; *Syn.* p. 292. — Clangula vulgaris, *Rich. & Swain.* ii. 456. — Clangula Barrovii, *Rich. & Swain.* ii. 453.

407. Fuligula albeola, *Linn.* — Buffel-headed Duck, *Wilson*, p. 568.

Fuligula albeola, *Bonap. Syn.* p. 394. *Rich. & Swain.* ii. 458. *Nutt.* ii. 445. *Aud.* iv. 217; *Syn.* p. 293; plate 325.

408. Fuligula histrionica, *Linn.* — Harlequin Duck, *Wilson*, p. 625.

Fuligula histrionica, *Bonap. Syn.* p. 394. *Rich. & Swain.* ii. 459. *Nutt.* ii. 448. *Aud.* iii. 612; v. 614; plate 297; *Syn.* p. 294.

409. Fuligula glacialis, *Linn.* — Long-tailed Duck, *Wilson*, pp. 596 and 597.

Fuligula glacialis, *Bonap. Syn.* p. 395. *Rich. & Swain.* ii. 460. *Nutt.* ii. 453. *Aud.* iv. 103; plate 312; *Syn.* p. 295.

410. Fuligula spectabilis, *Linn.* — King Duck.

Bill, flesh colored; sides of upper mandible and lobes over bill, bright orange; band separating lobes, and patch on throat, black; upper part of head, ash gray; sides of head, pale bluish green; fore neck, cream colored; sides and hind part of neck, patch on wings and on each side of rump, white; hind part of back, scapulars, large wing-coverts, and secondary quills and tail, brownish black, latter glossed with green; primary quills, tail, breast, and abdomen, blackish brown; lower wing-coverts, white; outer, brown. *Male*, 25. *Female*, 20. Habitat, from Massachusetts north. Eggs 2⅝ inches by 1¾, of a uniform dull greenish color.

Fuligula spectabilis, *Bonap. Syn.* p. 389. *Nutt.* ii. 414. *Aud.* iii. 523; plate 276; *Syn.* p. 290. — Somateria spectabilis, *Rich. & Swain.* ii. 447.

411. Fuligula dispar, *Gmel.* — Western Duck.

Bill, grayish blue; upper part of head and broad band surrounding the neck, white; throat and feathers round the eye, black; green patch on nape, margined with black; broad band on neck, and whole of back, velvet black, with green reflections; smaller wing-coverts, white; secondary, bluish black, terminating in a white band; tail, lower tail-coverts, and abdomen, black; breast and sides, reddish buff, fading into white towards neck and shoulders; bluish black spot on each side of lower part of neck. *Male*, 16.

Fuligula stelleri, *Bonap. Syn.* p. 394. — Fuligula dispar, *Aud.* v. 253; plate 430; *Syn.* p. 293.

GENUS VI. — MERGUS. — MERGANSER.

412. Mergus merganser, *Linn.* — Goosander, *Wilson,* pp. 579 and 581.

Mergus merganser, *Bonap. Syn.* p. 397. *Rich. & Swain.* ii. 461. *Nutt.* ii. 460. *Aud.* iv. 461; plate 331; *Syn.* p. 297.

413. Mergus serrator, *Linn.* — Red-breasted Merganser, *Wilson,* p. 588.

Mergus serrator, *Bonap. Syn.* p. 397. *Rich. & Swain.* ii. 462. *Nutt.* ii. 463. *Aud.* v. 92; plate 401; *Syn.* p. 298.

414. Mergus cucullatus, *Linn.* — Hooded Merganser, *Wilson,* p. 586.

Mergus cucullatus, *Bonap. Syn.* p. 397. *Rich. & Swain.* ii. 463. *Nutt.* ii. 465. *Aud.* iii. 246; v. 616; plate 233; *Syn.* p. 299.

*415. Mergus Albellus, *Linn.* — Smew, or White Merganser, *Wilson,* p. 618.

Mergus Albellus, *Bonap. Syn.* p. 398. *Nutt.* ii. 467. *Aud.* iv. 350; plate 347; *Syn.* p. 299.

FAMILY III. — PELECANIDÆ, *Vigors.*

GENUS I. — PHALACROCORAX, *Briss.* — CORMORANT.

416. Phalacrocorax carbo. — Common Cormorant.

Bill, dusky; lower mandible, whitish at base; gular sac, yellow; plumage, black, glossed with deep greenish blue; white patch at base of gular sac and on side over thigh; wings and part of back, gray, glossed with bronze, their margin, greenish black; tail, grayish black. In summer, with a small black occipital crest. *Male,* 37, 62. Habitat, from New York to the north. Nests on precipitous rocks. Eggs, four, 2⅝ inches by 1¾, pale bluish green.

Phalacrocorax carbo, *Bonap. Syn.* p. 402. *Nutt.* ii. 479. *Aud.* iii. 458; plate 266; *Syn.* p. 302.

417. Phalacrocorax dilophus, *Swain.* — Double-crested Cormorant.

In summer, with an elongated tuft from behind each eye; bare space on head, and gular sac, rich orange; plumage, greenish black, strongly glossed with green; tail, black. *Male,* 33, 51. Habitat, from Maryland to Labrador. Eggs, 2½ inches by 1½; four.

Pelecanus dilophus, *Rich. & Swain.* ii. 473. — Phalacrocorax dilophus, *Nutt.* ii. 483. *Aud.* iii. 420; v. 629; plate 257; *Syn.* p. 302.

---

* It is with no small degree of hesitation that I venture to retain the Smew among the birds of North America. But one specimen has ever been actually known to have been obtained here. This was by Mr. Audubon, in Louisiana, and, undoubtedly, was but a chance visitor. Wilson was deceived in supposing it "common in New England." It is utterly unknown here, nor has it ever yet been discovered in the Arctic Regions. The conclusion, therefore, seems unavoidable that an individual of this species may very rarely wander from the eastern continent to America, but that it cannot be rightly regarded as one of our birds.

418. Phalacrocorax Floridanus, *Aud.* — Florida Cormorant.

In summer, with elongated plumage behind each eye; bare space on head and gular sac, rich orange; plumage, greenish black, glossed with green; tail, brownish black. *Male*, 29¼, 46½. Habitat, Florida. Nests in mangrove trees. Eggs, four, 2¼ inches by 1⅜, of a light bluish green color, concealed by a coating of calcareous matter.

Phalacrocorax Floridanus, *Aud.* iii. 387; v. 632; *Syn.* p. 303; plate 251.

419. Phalacrocorax Townsendi, *Aud.* — Townsend's Cormorant.

Plumage of neck and sides interspersed with linear white feathers; gular sac and bare skin on forehead, bright orange; upper part of head and hind neck, dusky, tinged with green; hind part of back, greenish black; rest of upper parts, brownish gray; feathers, edged with black; outer primaries and tail-feathers, black; sides of head, fore part of neck and breast, light yellowish brown; middle of neck, darker; sides, abdomen, and tibial feathers, shaded into brownish black, tinged with green. *Male*, 35. Habitat, Columbia River.

Phalacrocorax Townsendi, *Aud.* v. 149; plate 412; *Syn.* p. 304.

420. Phalacrocorax resplendens, *Aud.* — Violet-green Cormorant.

Gular sac and bare skin on head, bright orange; plumage, deep green, changing, according to the light, into black and purple; white piliform feathers, terminated by filaments along the sides of neck and body; quills and tail-feathers, brownish black and less glossy. *Female*, 27. Habitat, Columbia River.

Phalacrocorax resplendens, *Aud.* v. 148; plate 422, *Syn.* p. 304.

GENUS II. — PLOTUS, *Linn.* — ANHINGA.

421. Plotus Anhinga, *Linn.* — American Anhinga, *Wilson*, pp. 644 and 647.

Nests in bushes and trees. Eggs, four, 2⅜ inches by 1¼, of a uniform whitish color.

Plotus Anhinga, *Bonap. Syn.* p. 411. *Nutt.* ii. 507. *Aud.* iv. 136; plate 316; *Syn.* p. 306.

GENUS III. — TACHYPETES, *Vieill.* — FRIGATE PELICAN.

422. Tachypetes Aquilus, *Linn.* — Frigate Bird.

Bill, purplish blue, white in the middle; gular sac, orange; bare skin round eye, blue; feet, carmine above, orange beneath; plumage, brownish black; head, neck, back, breast, and sides, with green and purple reflections; wings, tinged with green. Adult, 41, 86. Habitat, throughout the Gulf of Mexico. Nests in trees. Eggs, three, 2⅞ inches by 2, greenish white.

GENUS IV. — PELECANUS, *Linn.* — PELICAN.

423. Pelecanus Americanus. — American White Pelican.

Plumage, white; elongated feathers on breast, pale yellow; alula, primary, and outer secondaries, black, with white shafts; inner ten secondaries white. *Male*, 61¾, 103; bill, 13¾. Habitat, from Texas to South Carolina.

Pelecanus Americanus, *Aud.* iv. 88; plate 311; *Syn.* p. 305.

424. Pelecanus fuscus, *Linn.* — Brown Pelican.

Bill, grayish white, with carmine spots; bare space between bill and eye, blue; gular sac, greenish black; feet, black; fore part of head, light yellow; rest of head, white; white stripe margining sac; anterior space between back and sides of neck, dark chestnut brown; back and wings, dusky; central parts of feathers, grayish white; primaries, brownish black; tail, light gray; lower parts, brownish gray; sides of neck and body with narrow, longitudinal white lines. Adult, 52, 80. Habitat, from Texas to North Carolina. Nests in trees. Eggs, three, whitish.

Pelecanus fuscus, *Bonap. Syn.* p. 401. *Nutt.* ii. 476. *Aud.* iii. 376; v. 212; plates 251 and 421; *Syn.* p. 309.

GENUS V. — SULA, *Briss.* — GANNET.

425. Sula fusca, *Linn.* — Booby Gannet.

Bill and naked parts, at its base, bright yellow; dusky spot before eye; feet, yellow; claws, white; head, neck, upper parts, and lower surface of wings, dusky brown, tinged with gray; breast, abdomen, and lower tail-coverts, pure white. *Male*, 31, 49¼. Habitat, Florida and Gulf of Mexico. Nests in bushes.

Sula fusca, *Bonap. Syn.* p. 408. *Nutt.* ii. 500. *Aud.* iii. 63; *Syn.* p. 311; plate 207

426. Sula Bassana, *Linn.* — Common Gannet.

Bill, bluish gray, tinged with green at base; bare space about eye; lines on bill and gular membrane, blackish blue; feet, brownish black; claws, grayish white; upper part of head and hind neck, buff colored. *Adult*, 40½, 75. Habitat, along the whole coast. Nest on rocky cliffs. Egg, single, pure white.

Sula Bassana, *Bonap. Syn.* p. 408. *Nutt.* ii. 495. *Aud.* iv. 222; plate 326; *Syn.* p. 311.

GENUS VI. — PHAËTON, *Linn.* — TROPIC BIRD.

427. Phaëton æthereus, *Linn.* — Common Tropic Bird.

Bill, tarsi, and hind toes, yellow; rest of foot, black; plumage, pale pink; two middle tail-feathers, deeper curved; spot before eye, and band behind it, black; black band across wing; spot of same color on primary coverts. *Male*, 29½, 38. *Female*, 26, 34. Habitat, Florida. Rare.

Phaëton æthereus, *Bonap. Syn.* p. 409. *Nutt.* ii. 503. *Aud.* iii. 442; plate 262; *Syn.* p. 312.

FAMILY IV. — LARIDÆ, *Vigors.*

GENUS I. — RHYNCHOPS, *Linn.* — SKIMMER.

428. Rhynchops nigra. — Black Skimmer, *Wilson*, p. 514.

Rhynchops nigra, *Bonap. Syn.* p. 352. *Nutt.* ii. 264. *Aud.* iv. 203; plate 323; *Syn.* p. 314.

GENUS II. — STERNA, *Linn.* — TERN.

429. Sterna Cayana, *Lath.* — Cayenne Tern.

Bill, carmine; feet, black; upper part of head and occiput, greenish black; sides of head, fore neck, and lower parts, white; upper parts, grayish blue; edges of wings, whitish; tail, of paler tint than back; outer feathers nearly white. *Male*, 14, 34. Cosmopolite. Eggs, two, 2⅝ inches by 1⅞, pale yellowish green, spotted with umber and purple.

> Sterna Cayana, *Bonap. Syn.* p. 353. *Nutt.* ii. 208. *Aud.* iii. 505; v. 639; plate 273; *Syn.* p. 316.

430. Sterna Anglica, *Montague.* — Marsh Tern, *Wilson*, p. 630.

> Sterna aranea, *Bonap. Syn.* p. 354. — Sterna Anglica, *Nutt.* ii. 269. *Aud.* v. 127; plate 410; *Syn.* p. 316.

431. Sterna Cantiaca, *Gmel.* — Sandwich Tern.

Bill, black; its tip, yellow; feet, black; head and hind neck, bluish black; sides of head, neck, and lower parts, white; sides and breast, tinged with pink; fore part of back, scapulars, and upper surface of wings, grayish blue; rump and tail, white. *Adult*, 15¾, 33¾. Habitat, from Texas to the Floridas. Eggs, three, yellowish gray, blotched with umber, pale blue, and reddish.

> Sterna Cantiaca, *Aud.* iii. 531; plate 279; *Syn.* p. 317. *Nutt.* ii. 276.

432. Sterna fuliginosa, *Lath.* — Sooty Tern, *Wilson*, p. 632.

> Sterna fuliginosa, *Bonap. Syn.* p. 355. *Nutt.* ii. 284. *Aud.* iii. 263; v. 641; plate 235; *Syn.* p. 317.

433. Sterna hirundo, *Linn.* — Common Tern, *Wilson*, p. 509.

> Sterna hirundo, *Bonap. Syn.* p. 354. *Rich. & Swain.* ii. 412. *Nutt.* ii. 271. *Aud.* iv. 74; plate 309; *Syn.* p. 318.

434. Sterna Havellii, *Aud.* — Havell's Tern.

Bill, black; base, brown; tip, yellow; feet, orange; broad band of black surrounding the eye; fore part of head, cheeks, and lower parts, pure white; hind head and nape, dusky gray, mixed with white; upper parts, light bluish gray; rump, white. *Adult*, 15½. Habitat, from Texas to South Carolina.

> Sterna Havellii, *Aud.* v. 122; plate 409; *Syn.* p. 318.

435. Sterna Trudeaui, *Aud.* — Trudeau's Tern.

Bill, black; base of lower mandible, tips, and edge of both, yellow; feet, orange; claws, brown; black grayish band surrounding eye, and extending towards nape; fore part of head, cheeks, and throat, white; rest of plumage, except axillar feathers, lower wing-coverts, and rump, which are white, grayish blue. *Adult*, 16. Habitat, Great Egg Harbor and Long Island. Rare.

> Sterna Trudeaui, *Aud.* v. 125; plate 409; *Syn.* p. 319.

436. Sterna arctica, *Temm.* — Arctic Tern.

Bill and feet, vermilion, tinged with carmine; upper part of head and occiput, greenish black; sides of head and chin, white; upper parts, pale grayish blue, rump, bluish white; tail and its coverts, white; outer web of two lateral feathers, dusky gray; neck, breast, and sides, pale grayish blue; abdomen, lower tail-coverts, and lower surfaces of wings and tail, white. *Male*, 15½, 32. Eggs, three, laid on the bare rock, 1¼ by ⅞ of an inch, light umber, blotched with umber. Habitat, along the Atlantic coast, from New Jersey to Labrador.

> Sterna arctica, *Bonap. Syn.* p. 354. *Rich. & Swain.* II. 414. *Nutt.* ii. 275. *Aud.* iii. 366; plate 250; *Syn.* p. 319.

437. Sterna Dongallii, *Mont.* — Roseate Tern.

62 *

Bill, brownish black, orange at base; feet, vermilion; upper part of head and occiput, bluish black; hind neck, white; rest of upper parts, pale bluish gray; edges of wings, white; lower parts, roseate; under surface of wings and tail, white. *Male*, 14⅚, 30. Habitat, Florida Keys. Eggs, laid on the bare ground, three, 1¾ inches by 1⅛, clay color, spotted with umber and purple.

Sterna Dongallii, *Aud.* iii. 296; plate 240; *Syn.* p. 320. *Nutt.* ii. 278.

438. Sterna nigra, *Linn*, — Black Tern.

Bill, brownish black; feet, reddish brown; head, neck, breast, sides, and abdomen, grayish black; lower tail-coverts, white; lower wing-coverts, bluish gray; upper parts, dark bluish gray. *Adult*, 9, 24. Habitat, Mississippi River and its tributaries. Nests in tussocks of grass. Eggs, four, greenish buff, spotted with umber and black.

Sterna nigra, *Bonap. Syn.* p. 355. *Rich. & Swain.* ii. 415. *Nutt.* ii. 282. *Aud.* iii. 535; v. 642; plate 270; *Syn.* p. 321.

439. Sterna minuta, *Linn*. — Least Tern, *Wilson*, p. 511.

Sterna minuta, *Bonap. Syn.* p. 355. *Nutt.* ii. 280. *Aud.* iv. 175; plate 319; *Syn.* p. 321.

440. Sterna stolida, *Linn*. — Noddy Tern.

Plumage, sooty brown; primaries and tail-feathers, brownish black; upper part of head, grayish white; black spot over eye. *Male*, 16⅛, 32. Habitat, Gulf of Mexico. Nests in bushes. Eggs, three, 2 by 1⅜, reddish yellow, spotted with dull red and faint purple.

Sterna stolida, *Bonap. Syn.* p. 356. *Nutt.* ii. 285. *Aud.* iii. 516; v. 642; plate 275; *Syn.* p. 322.

GENUS III. — LARUS, *Linn*. — GULL.

441. Larus Sabini, *Sabine*. — Fork-tailed Gull.

Bill, black; tip, yellow; feet, black; head and upper part of neck, blackish gray, terminated by a collar of pure black; lower neck, lower parts, tail, and tail-coverts, white; back and wings, bluish gray, except terminal portion of secondaries and tips of primaries, which are white; primaries, black. *Male*, 13, 33. Habitat, from Maine to the Arctic Seas. Eggs, two, olive, with brown blotches.

Larus Sabini, *Rich. & Swain.* ii. 428. *Nutt.* ii. 295. *Aud.* iii. 561; plate 275; *Syn.* p. 323.

442. Larus Rossii, *Rich*. — Ross's Gull.

Bill, black; feet, vermilion; head, neck, lower parts, rump, and tail, white; tinge of pink in lower parts; narrow collar of black; back, scapulars, and both surfaces of wings, grayish blue; tips of scapulars and secondaries, white. *Adult*, 14. Habitat, Arctic Seas.

Larus Rossii, *Rich. & Swain.* ii. 427. *Aud.* v. 324; *Syn.* p. 323.

443. Larus Bonapartii, *Rich*. — Bonaparte's Gull.

Bill, black; feet, orange, tinged with vermilion; head and upper part of neck, grayish black; a white band divided by a narrow white line margining the eyes behind; lower part of neck, edge of wing, rump, tail, and lower parts, white; back, scapulars, and wings, light grayish blue. *Adult*, 14⅛, 32¼. Habitat, throughout the Atlantic coast.

Larus capistratus, *Bonap. Orn.* iv; *Syn.* 358. — Larus Bonapartii, *Rich. & Swain.* ii. 425. *Nutt.* ii. 294. *Aud.* iv. 212; *Syn.* p. 324; plate 323.

444. Larus atricilla, *Linn.*— Black-headed Gull, *Wilson*, p. 652.

Larus atricilla, *Bonap. Syn.* p. 359. *Nutt.* ii. 201. *Aud.* iv. 118; plate 314; *Syn.* p. 324.

445. Larus Franklinii, *Rich.* — Franklin's Rosy Gull.

Bill and feet, vermilion; neck, rump, tail, and under plumage, white; latter, tinged with red; black hood on nape; upper parts, bluish gray; quills, terminated with white. *Male*, 17. Habitat, Fur Countries.

Larus Franklinii, *Rich. & Swain.* ii. 424. *Aud.* v. 323; *Syn.* p. 325.

446. Larus tridactylus, *Linn.* — Kittiwake Gull.

Bill, greenish yellow; feet, black; head, neck, rump, and lower parts, white; back and upper surface of wings, grayish blue; tips of first five quills, black; fifth, with a small white tip; tips of the others, white. *Adult*, 18, 36½. Nests on ledges of rocks. Eggs, three, olive green, spotted with brown, 2¼ by 1⅞.

Larus tridactylus, *Bonap. Syn.* p. 359. *Rich. & Swain.* ii. 423. *Nutt.* ii. 298. *Aud.* iii. 186; plate 224; *Syn.* p. 326.

447. Larus eburneus, *Gmel.* — Ivory Gull.

Bill, yellow; feet, black; plumage, white. *Adult*, 14, 91. Habitat, accidental on the American coast.

Larus eburneus, *Bonap. Syn.* p. 360. *Rich. & Swain.* ii. 419. *Nutt.* ii. 301. *Aud.* iii. 571; plate 287; *Syn.* p. 326.

448. Larus zonorhynchus, *Rich.* — Common American Gull.

Bill, greenish yellow, with broad band of black; feet, greenish yellow; plumage, white, excepting wings and back, which are light grayish blue. *Adult*, 20, 48. Habitat, throughout North America. Eggs, four, 2¾ by 1⅞, dark cream color, blotched with different shades of purple, umber, and black.

Larus canus, *Rich. & Swain.* ii. 420. *Nutt.* ii. 300. — Larus brachyrhynchus, *Rich. & Swain.* ii. 422. — Larus zonorhynchus, *Rich. & Swain.* ii. 421. *Aud.* iii. 98; v. 638; plate 212; *Syn.* p. 327.

449. Larus leucopterus, *Fabr.* — White-winged Silvery Gull.

Bill, gamboge yellow, orange spot near end of lower mandible; feet, flesh color; plumage, white, except back and wings, which are light grayish blue. *Adult*, 26, 50. Habitat, from New York to the Arctic Seas.

Larus leucopterus, *Bonap. Syn.* p. 361. *Rich. & Swain.* ii. 418. *Nutt.* ii. 305. *Aud.* iii. 553; plate 272; *Syn.* p. 327.

450. Larus occidentalis, *Aud.* — Western Gull.

Bill, yellow, with orange red patch on lower mandible; feet, flesh color; head, neck, lower parts, rump, and tail, white; back and wings, grayish blue. *Male*, 27.

Larus occidentalis, *Aud.* v. 320; *Syn.* p. 328.

451. Larus argentatus, *Brunnich.* — Herring Gull.

Bill, gamboge yellow, with orange red patch on lower mandible; feet, flesh color; head, neck, lower parts, rump, and tail, white; back and wings, grayish blue; tips of quills, white, or with white spots. *Male*, 23, 53. Habitat, along the whole coast. Nests on trees or on the ground. Eggs, three; 3 by 2; dull yellowish, blotched with umber.

Larus argentatus, *Bonap. Syn.* p. 360. *Nutt.* ii. 304. *Aud.* iii. 580; v. 638; plate 291; *Syn.* p. 328.

452. Larus glaucus, *Brunn.* — Glaucous Gull.

Bill, gamboge yellow, with carmine spot on lower mandible; feet, flesh color; head, neck, lower parts, rump, and tail, white; back and wings, light grayish blue. *Adult*, 30. Habitat, Arctic Regions.

Larus glaucus, *Bonap. Syn.* p. 361. *Rich. & Swain.* ii. 416. *Nutt.* ii. 306. *Aud.* v. 59; plate 396; *Syn.* p. 329.

453. Larus marinus, *Linn.* — Saddle-Back Gull.

Differs from preceding principally in having back and wings of a dark slate color. *Male*, 29½, 67. Habitat, the whole coast. Nests on the ground. Eggs, three, 2⅞ by 2⅓, greenish gray, spotted with umber, purple, and brownish black.

Larus marinus, *Nutt.* ii. 308. *Aud.* iii. 305; v. 636; plate 249; *Syn.* p. 329.

GENUS IV. — LESTRIS, *Illiger.* — JAGER.

454. Lestris pomarinus, *Temm.* — Arctic Jager.

Bill, dull green; upper parts and sides of head, anteriorly, brownish black; upper part of neck, yellowish white; rest, white, barred with brownish black; breast, white; sides, abdomen, and lower tail-coverts, white, barred with brownish black; back and wings, brownish black; lower surface of wings, barred with white and dusky. *Female*, 20¼, 48. Habitat, from Massachusetts northward. Nests near the edges of lakes. Eggs, two, or three, grayish olive, marked with blackish spots.

Lestris pomarina, *Bonap. Syn.* p. 364. *Rich. & Swain.* ii. 429. *Nutt.* ii. 315. *Aud.* iii. 396; v. 643; plate 253; *Syn.* p. 332.

455. Lestris Richardsonii, *Swain.* — Richardson's Jager.

Bill, grayish black, tinged with blue above; feet, black; plumage, sooty brown, darker on head, primary quills, and tail; cheeks, and sides of neck, dull yellow; fore part of neck, and breast, white. *Male*, 18½, 40. Habitat, from Massachusetts to the north. Eggs, 2⅜ by 1⅝, dull grayish yellow, patched with umber and faint purple.

Lestris Richardsonii, *Rich. & Swain.* ii. 433. *Nutt.* ii. 319. *Aud.* iii. 503; plate 272; *Syn.* p. 332.

456. Lestris parasiticus, *Linn.* — Arctic Jager.

Bill, grayish black, tinged with blue above; feet, black; tarsus, yellow; neck and lower parts, white; former, tinged with yellow; upper and fore part of head, blackish brown; upper parts, blackish gray; primary quills and tail-feathers, brownish black; the shafts of the former, white. *Male*, 23, 45. Habitat, the whole Atlantic coast. Nests on the ground. Eggs, two, dark oil green, with blotches of liver brown, 2⅓ by 1½.

Lestris Buffonii, *Bonap. Syn.* p. 364. *Rich. & Swain.* ii. 430. *Nutt.* ii. 317. *Aud.* iii. 470; *Syn.* p. 333; plate 267.

GENUS V. — DIOMEDEA, *Linn.* — ALBATROSS.

457. Diomedea chlororhynchos, *Gmel.* — Yellow-nosed Albatross.

Bill, black, except ridge, tip of upper mandible, and crura of lower, which are yellow; feet, yellow; head and neck, ash gray; fore part of back, shaded into ash gray; wings, brownish black; hind part of back, rump, and upper tail-coverts, white; tail, deep gray; anterior lower part of neck, breast, sides, abdomen, lower tail-coverts, some of axillaries, and larger wing-coverts, white; the others, brownish black. Length, 37. Habitat, mouth of Columbia River and Pacific Ocean.

Diomedea chlororhynchos, *Aud.* v. 326; *Syn.* p. 334; not figured.

458. Diomedea nigripes, *Aud.* — Black-footed Albatross.

Bill, brownish black; feet, black; fore part of head, cheeks, and throat, dusky gray; rest of upper parts, sooty brown, tinged with gray; lower parts, dull gray, deeper in front. Length, 36. Habitat, coast of California.

Diomedea nigripes, *Aud.* v. 327; *Syn.* p. 334; not figured.

459. Diomedea fusca, *Aud.* — Dusky Albatross.

Bill, black; feet, yellow; head and upper part of neck, grayish black, tinged with brown; rest of neck, all the lower parts, back, and rump, light brownish gray; wings, brownish black; primary quills and tail-feathers, grayish black. *Adult*, 34. Habitat, coast about the mouth of Columbia River.

Diomedea fusca, *Aud.* v. 116; *Syn.* p. 335; plate 407.

GENUS VI. — PROCELLARIA, *Linn.* — FULMAR PETREL.

460. Procellaria gigantea, *Linn.* — Gigantic Fulmar.

Bill and feet, yellow; plumage, deep brown, tinged with gray, lighter on lower parts, and especially on the lower surface of the wings. Length, 36. Habitat, off Columbia River.

Procellaria gigantea, *Aud.* v. 330; *Syn.* p. 336; not figured.

461. Procellaria glacialis, *Linn.* — Common Fulmar.

Bill, feet, and claws, yellow; head, neck, and lower parts, pure white; back and wings, light grayish blue; rump, paler; tail, bluish white; primary quills and coverts, blackish brown. *Male*, 8, 18. Habitat, Atlantic coast, from New York north. Nests in holes of rocks. Egg, single, white, 2⅞ by 2.

Porcellaria glacialis, *Bonap. Syn.* p. 369. *Nutt.* ii. 330. *Aud.* iii. 416; plate 264; *Syn.* p. 336.

462. Procellaria Pacifica, *Aud.* — Pacific Fulmar.

Bill and feet, yellow; head, neck, and lower parts, pure white; back and wings, light grayish blue; feathers, becoming dark gray towards the end; primary quills and coverts, blackish brown, tinged with gray. *Adult*, 18; bill, 1¾. Habitat, North-West coast.

Procellaria Pacifica, *Aud.* v. 331; *Syn.* p. 336; not figured.

463. Procellaria tenuirostris, *Aud.* — Slender-billed Fulmar.

Bill, yellow, except nasal plate, half of the ungus of upper mandible, and tip of the lower, which are black; feet, yellow; claws, brownish black, plumage, grayish blue, paler on lower parts, head, and neck; primary quills and coverts, blackish gray. Length, 18½. Habitat, off Columbia River.

Procellaria tenuirostris, *Aud.* v. 333; *Syn.* p. 337; not figured.

GENUS VII. — PUFFINUS, *Briss.* — SHEARWATER.

464. Puffinus cinereus, *Lath.* — Wandering Shearwater.

Bill, yellowish green; tip, brownish black; feet, light greenish gray; webs and claws, yellowish flesh color; upper parts, deep brown; hind neck, paler, tinged with gray; primary quills and tail, brownish black; lower parts, grayish white; lower wing-coverts, white, grayish brown towards the end; lower tail-coverts, similar. *Male*, 20, 45. Habitat, the Atlantic coast and ocean.

Puffinus cinereus, *Bonap. Syn.* p. 370. *Nutt.* ii. 334. *Aud.* iii. 555; plate 283; *Syn.* p. 338.

465. Puffinus Anglorum, *Ray.* — Manks Shearwater.

Bill, deep greenish black; inner and middle of outer side of tibia, dull orange; rest, greenish black; upper parts, brownish black; lower, white. *Adult*, 15, 32. Habitat, from Maine north. Breeds in burrows. Egg, single, white.

Puffinus Anglorum, *Bonap. Syn.* p. 371. *Nutt.* ii. 336. *Aud.* iii. 604; plate 295; *Syn.* p. 338.

466. Puffinus obscurus, *Lath.* — Dusky Shearwater.

Bill, light blue; tips, black; outside of tarsus and toes, indigo black; inside and webs, pale yellowish flesh color; upper parts, sooty black; lower, white. *Male*, 11, 26. Habitat, along the Atlantic coast and Gulf of Mexico.

Puffinus obscurus, *Bonap. Syn.* p. 371. *Nutt.* ii. 337. *Aud.* iii. 620; plate 299; *Syn.* p. 339.

GENUS VIII. — THALASIDROMA, *Vigors.* — PETREL.

467. Thalasidroma Leachii, *Temm.* — Leach's Petrel.

Bill and feet, black; plumage, dark grayish brown; quills and tail, brownish black; smaller wing-coverts and inner secondaries, light grayish brown; rump, sides of abdomen, and outer lower tail-coverts, white; upper tail-coverts also white, but with a black terminal band. *Male*, 8, 18½. Habitat, from Massachusetts to Newfoundland. Nests in holes in rocks. Egg, single, white.

Thalasidroma Leachii, *Bonap. Syn.* p. 367. *Nutt.* ii. 326. *Aud.* iii. 434; plate 260; *Syn.* p. 340.

468. Thalasidroma Wilsonii, *Bonap.* — Mother Carey's Chicken, *Wilson*, p. 517.

Thalasidroma Wilsonii, *Bonap. Syn.* p. 367. *Nutt.* ii. 322. *Aud.* iii. 486; v. 645; plate 270; *Syn.* p. 340.

469. Thalasidroma pelagica, *Linn.* — Least Petrel.

Bill and feet, black; general color of upper parts, grayish black, with a tinge of brown; lower parts, sooty brown; secondary coverts, margined externally with dull grayish white; feathers of rump and upper tail-coverts, white; latter, tipped with black. *Male*, 5¾, 13½. Habitat, Banks of Newfoundland.

FAMILY V. — ALCIDÆ, *Vigors*.

GENUS I. — MORMON, *Illiger*. — PUFFIN.

470. Mormon cirrhatus, *Lath.* — Tufted Puffin.

Bill, yellowish red; ridge, bright red; feet, bright red; two tufts of loose feathers on sides of head behind the eye; face, white; upper parts, brownish black, glossed with blue; lower, sooty brown, tinged with gray on the abdomen; part of the sides and under wing-coverts, grayish brown. *Male*, 15, 22½. Habitat, Arctic Seas.

Mormon cirrhatus, *Bonap. Syn.* p. 429. *Nutt.* ii. 539. *Aud.* iii. 364; plate 249; *Syn.* p. 342.

471. Mormon glacialis, *Leach.* — Large-billed Puffin.

Bill and feet, orange yellow; sides of head and lower parts, white; upper part of head, light brownish gray, tinged with lilac; a broad collar extending to the lower mandible, of a dark grayish brown tint below, gradually passing into brownish black, glossed with blue; primary quills and their coverts, brownish black; part of sides and under wing-coverts, grayish brown. *Male*, 13, 24½. Habitat, Bay of Fundy. Rare.

Mormon glacialis, *Bonap. Syn.* p. 430. *Nutt.* ii. 541. *Aud.* iii. 599; plate 293; *Syn.* p. 343.

472. Mormon arcticus, *Linn.* — Common Puffin.

Basal rim and first ridge of both mandibles, dull yellow; intervening space, grayish blue; the rest, bright red; feet, vermilion; throat and sides of head, grayish white; upper parts, grayish black, tinged with blue; middle of neck and upper parts, deep black, glossed with blue; under parts white; sides, dusky. *Male*, 11¾, 23. Habitat, from Georgia to Labrador. Nests in holes in the ground. Eggs, white, 2½ by 1¾.

Mormon arcticus, *Bonap. Syn.* p. 430. *Nutt.* ii. 542. *Aud.* iii. 105; plate 213; *Syn.* p. 342.

GENUS II. — ALCA, *Linn.* — AUK.

473. Alca impennis, *Linn.* — Great Auk.

Feet and bill, black; grooves in latter, white; head, neck, and upper parts, black; throat and sides of the neck, tinged with chocolate brown, the wings with grayish brown; head, hind neck, and back, glossed with olive green; fore part of neck below and all lower parts, white, as are a large oblong patch before the eye, and the tips of the secondary quills. *Adult*, 29, 27¼. Habitat, Newfoundland.

Alca impennis, *Nutt.* ii. 553. *Aud.* iv. 316; plate 341; *Syn.* p. 344.

474. Alca Torda, *Linn.* — Razor-billed Auk.

Bill, black, with a white band across each mandible; feet, head, neck, and upper parts, black; head, hind neck, and back, glossed with olive green; throat and sides of neck, tinged with chocolate; lower parts, white; white line from eye to the bill. *Male*, 17, 29½. Habitat, from Maine north. Eggs laid on bare ground, two, 3⅛ by 2⅛, white, blotched with reddish brown.

Alca Torda, *Bonap. Syn.* p. 431. *Nutt.* ii. 547. *Aud.* iii. 112; v. 628; plate 214; *Syn.* p. 345.

GENUS III. — PHALERIS, *Temm.* — PHALERIS.

475. Phaleris cristatella, *Gmel.* — Curled-crested Phaleris.

Bill, scarlet; tips, yellow; tuft of recurved feathers on anterior of fore-head; upper parts, brownish gray; lower, purplish gray; line of elongate white feathers from eye to side of neck. *Adult*, 10. Habitat, North-West coast of America.

Phaleris cristatella, *Aud.* v. 102; plate 402; *Syn.* p. 347.

476. Phaleris nodirostris, *Bonap.* — Knob-billed Phaleris.

Bill, deep red; knob, blue; feet, dusky gray; upper parts, brownish black; fore parts and sides of head, streaked with white feathers; lower parts, white, mottled with dusky. *Adult*, 6. Habitat, North-West coast.

Phaleris nodirostris, *Aud.* v. 101; plate 402; *Syn.* p. 346.

GENUS IV. — MERGULUS, *Ray.* — SEA-DOVE.

477. Mergulus Alle, *Linn.* — Common Sea Dove, *Wilson*, p. 658.

Uria Alle, *Bonap. Syn.* p. 425. *Rich. & Swain.* ii. 479. *Nutt.* ii. 531. *Aud.* iv. 304; plate 339; *Syn.* p. 347.

GENUS V. — URIA, *Lath.* — GUILLEMOT.

478. Uria antiqua, *Gmel.* — Black-throated Guillemot.

Bill and feet, yellow; head and upper part of neck, black, excepting a band of elongated feathers beginning over the eye, and extending down the hind part of the neck, and a broad band of white commencing behind the ear, and curving forward to join the white, which is the general color of the lower parts except the flanks, which are black; back, wings, and tail, grayish black. *Adult*, 10½. Habitat, North-West coast.

Uria antiqua, *Aud.* v. 100; *Syn.* p. 349; plate 402.

479. Uria occidentalis, *Bonap.* — Horn-billed Guillemot.

Bill, orange yellow; feet, grayish yellow; upper parts, black; lower parts, white; two bands of white feathers on each side of head. *Adult*, 15½. Habitat, North-West coast.

Cerorhyncha occidentalis, *Bonap. Syn.* p. 428. *Nutt.* ii. 538. — Ceratorhyncha occidentalis, *Aud.* v. 104. — Uria occidentalis, *Syn.* p. 349.

480. Uria Brunswickii, *Sabine.* — Large-billed Guillemot.

Bill, black; feet, dusky, tinged with red; plumage, grayish black on upper parts; sides of head and throat, tinged with brown; lower fore part of neck, breast, abdomen, edges of wings, and tips of secondaries, white; sides, streaked with grayish black. *Male*, 18½, 30. Habitat, from Maine north. Egg, 3½ by 2⅛, bluish green, streaked and spotted with black.

Uria Brunswickii, *Bonap. Syn.* p. 424. *Rich. & Swain.* ii. 427. *Nutt.* ii. 529. *Aud.* iii. 336; *Syn.* p. 349; plate 345.

481. Uria Troile, *Linn.* — Foolish Guillemot. — Murre.

Bill and feet, black; upper parts, grayish black; sides of head and throat, tinged with brown; fore neck, breast, abdomen, edges of wings, and tips of secondaries, white; sides streaked with grayish black. *Male*, 17½, 30. Habitat, from Maine north. Eggs, three, laid on the bare ground, with variously colored ground, spotted and streaked with umber, brown, &c., 3⅜ by 2.

Uria Troile, *Bonap. Syn.* p. 424. *Rich. & Swain.* ii 477. *Nutt.* ii. 526. *Aud.* iii. 142; plate 218; *Syn.* p. 350.

482. Uria Grylle, *Linn.* — Black Guillemot.

Bill, black; feet, vermilion; upper parts, black, tinged with green; lower parts, brown; patch on each wing, white. Plumage, white in winter. *Adult*, 13⅞, 21½. Habitat, from New York north. Eggs, three, 2⅜ by 1⅝, white, blotched with dark purple.

Uria Grylle, *Bonap. Syn.* p. 423. *Nutt.* ii. 523. *Aud.* iii. 148; v. 627; plate 219; *Syn.* p. 350. *Rich. & Swain.* ii. 478.

483. Uria Townsendii, *Aud.* — Slender-billed Guillemot.

Bill and claws, black; feet, yellow; upper parts, brownish black; feathers of back margined with light gray; lower parts, band on nape and lower wing-coverts, grayish brown. *Adult*, .10. Habitat, coast near Columbia River.

FAMILY VI. — COLYMBIDÆ, *Vigors.*

GENUS I. — COLYMBUS, *Linn.* — DIVER, OR LOON.

484. Colymbus glacialis, *Linn.* — Common Loon, *Wilson,* p. 648.

Colymbus glacialis, *Bonap. Syn.* p. 420. *Rich. & Swain.* ii. 474 *Nutt.* ii. 513 *Aud.* iv. 43; plate 306; *Syn.* p. 353.

485. Colymbus arcticus, *Linn.* — Black-throated Diver.

Bill, black; feet, grayish blue; edge of tarsus, and part of webs, livid flesh color; fore part and sides of head, throat, and sides of neck, light bluish gray; fore part and sides of head, darker; upper parts, glossy bluish black, tinged with green anteriorly, and brown posteriorly; two longitudinal bands of white bar; scapulars, marked with square white spots; wing-coverts, with roundish spots of same; tail, blackish brown; fore neck, purplish black, ending with a transverse band of linear white spots; beyond the sides of neck, blackish brown, with longitudinal white streaks; lower part of neck streaked with dusky and white; lower parts, pure white except a dusky band on sides. *Male*, 29, 39½. Habitat, interior and along the coast. Eggs, three, 3 by 2, chocolate, tinged with olive and spotted with dark umber and black.

Colymbus arcticus, *Bonap. Syn.* p. 420. *Rich. & Swain.* ii. 475. *Nutt.* ii. 517. *Aud.* iv. 345; plate 346; *Syn.* p. 354.

486. Colymbus septentrionalis, *Linn.* — Red-throated Diver.

Bill, bluish black; feet, brownish black; anterior of tarsus and webs, flesh color; fore part and sides of head, throat, and sides of neck, bluish gray; fore part of neck, rich brownish red; hind part of head and neck, longitudinally streaked with greenish black and pure white; upper parts, brownish black, tinged with green, mottled with white; lower parts, white, excepting sides, where grayish brown is intermingled. *Male*, 19, 25. *Female*, 18, 24. Habitat, from Maryland north. Nests near edges of fresh water. Eggs, three, 3 by 1¾, deep olive brown, marked with darker dull brown.

Colymbus septentrionalis, *Bonap. Syn.* p. 421. *Rich. & Swain.* ii. 476. *Nutt.* ii 519. *Aud.* iii. 20; v. 625; plate 202; *Syn.* p. 354.

GENUS II. — PODICEPS, *Lath.* — GREBE.

487. Podiceps cristatus, *Lath.* — Crested Grebe.

Bill, blackish brown, tinged with carmine; feet, greenish black, tinged with grayish blue; upper part of head and tufts, grayish black, tinged with green; sides of head and throat, white; fore neck, white, tinged with brown; breast, silvery white; sides, reddish brown, with dusky streaks; upper parts, brownish black; sides of neck, and the rump, tinged with reddish; wing-coverts, grayish brown. *Male*, 24, 33. Habitat, throughout the whole country. Eggs, four, 2¼ by 1½, yellowish white.

Podiceps cristatus, *Bonap. Syn.* p. 417. *Rich. & Swain.* ii. 410. *Nutt.* ii. 250. *Aud.* iii. 595; plate 292; *Syn.* p. 357.

488. Podiceps rubricollis, *Lath.* — Red-necked Grebe.

Bill, brownish black, yellow at base; tarsi and toes, greenish black externally, yellow on the inner side; upper part of head, grayish black; lower part, ash gray, with a white line from base of lower mandible to beyond the eye; hind part of neck, and upper parts, grayish black; fore part and sides of neck, brownish red; breast and sides, silvery white, tinged with gray. *Male*, 18¾, 32. Habitat, from New York to Fur Countries. Eggs, four, 2 by 1¼, greenish white.

Podiceps rubricollis, *Bonap. Syn.* p. 417. *Rich. & Swain.* ii. 411. *Nutt.* ii. 253. *Aud.* iii. 617; v. 620; *Syn.* p. 357; plate 298.

489. Podiceps cornutus, *Linn.* — Horned Grebe.

Bill, bluish black, yellow at tip; feet, dusky externally, dull yellow internally; forehead, grayish brown; upper part of head, bluish black, as are the sides, fore neck, and ruff feathers; broad band over eye, and elongated tufts behind, yellowish brown; fore neck, brownish red; lower parts, white; sides, reddish brown; abdomen, dull gray; upper parts, brownish black, tinged with gray. *Male*, 14¾, 25½. Habitat, throughout North America. Nests near the edge of fresh water. Eggs, five to seven, 1¼ by 1⅝, yellowish cream color.

Podiceps cornutus, *Bonap. Syn.* p. 417. *Rich. & Swain.* ii. 411. *Nutt.* ii. 254. *Aud.* iii. 429; v. 423; *Syn.* p. 557; plate 259.

490. Podiceps auritus, *Lath.* — Eared Grebe.

Bill, bluish black; feet, dusky gray externally, greenish gray internally; tuft on each side of head, orange; head and neck, deep black; upper parts, brownish black; wings, grayish brown, with a broad patch of white; lower parts, silvery white, except sides, which are light red. *Adult*, 13. Habitat, rare, if ever, in America.

Podiceps auritus, *Nutt.* ii. 256. *Aud.* v. 108; plate 404; *Syn.* p. 358.

491. Podiceps Carolinensis. *Lath.* — Pied-billed Dobchick.

Bill, pale blue; feet, grayish black; upper part of head and throat, black; neck and sides of head, light grayish brown; lower parts of neck, grayish yellow; back, brownish black; breast, silvery white; abdomen, brownish gray; sides, mottled with grayish brown. *Male*, 14, 23. Habitat, throughout North America. Nests near edge of fresh water. Eggs, five, 1¼ by ⅞, light greenish white.

Podiceps Carolinensis, *Bonap. Syn.* p. 418. *Rich. & Swain.* ii. 412. *Nutt.* ii. 259. *Aud.* iii. 359; v. 624; plate 248; *Syn.* p. 359.

THE END.

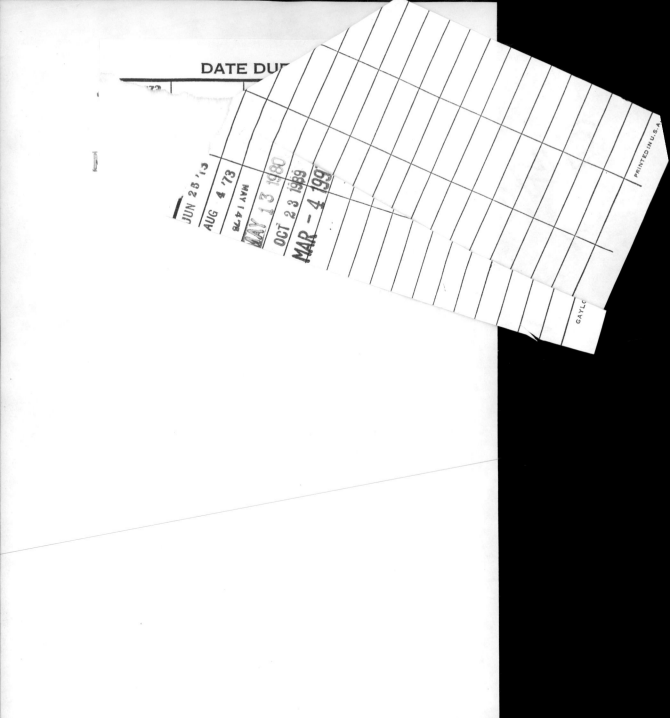